D1605955

A History of
African Higher Education
from Antiquity to the Present

Recent Titles in
Studies in Higher Education

Internationalization of Higher Education in the United States of
America and Europe: A Historical, Comparative, and Conceptual Analysis
Hans de Wit

Academic Staff in Europe: Changing Contexts and Conditions
Jürgen Enders, editor

Higher Education in the Developing World: Changing Contexts and
Institutional Responses
David Chapman and Ann Austin, editors

Academic Pathfinders: Knowledge Creation and Feminist Scholarship
Patricia J. Gumport

Globalizing Practices and University Responses: European and
Anglo-American Differences
*Jan Currie, Richard DeAngelis, Harry de Boer,
Jeroen Huisman, and Claude Lacotte*

Changing Course: Making the Hard Decisions to Eliminate
Academic Programs
Peter D. Eckel

A History of
African Higher Education
from Antiquity to the Present

A CRITICAL SYNTHESIS

Y. G-M. Lulat

Studies in Higher Education
Philip G. Altbach, Series Editor

Westport, Connecticut
London

Library of Congress Cataloging-in-Publication Data

Lulat, Y. G. -M.
  A history of African higher education from antiquity to the pres-
ent : a critical synthesis / Y. G-M. Lulat.
    p. cm.—(Studies in higher education)
  Includes bibliographical references and index.
  ISBN 0–313–32061–6 (alk. paper)
    1. Education, Higher—Africa—History.   2. Africa—Colonial influ-
ence—History.   I. Title.   II. Series.
  LA1503.L85   2005
  378.6′09—dc22   2004028717

British Library Cataloguing in Publication Data is available.

Library of Congress Catalog Card Number: 2004028717
ISBN: 0–313–32061–6

First published in 2005

Praeger Publishers, 88 Post Road West, Westport, CT 06881
An imprint of Greenwood Publishing Group, Inc.
www.praeger.com

Printed in the United States of America

The paper used in this book complies with the
Permanent Paper Standard issued by the National
Information Standards Organization (Z39.48–1984).

10 9 8 7 6 5 4 3 2 1

Copyright Acknowledgment

The author and publisher gratefully acknowledge permission to quote from the following:

Verses from *Inferno* in Allen Mandelbaum's translation of *The Divine Comedy of Dante Alighieri*. Permission granted free of charge by BANTAM BOOKS, a division of Random House, Inc.

With deepest gratitude,
to
Philip G. Altbach,
educator and comparativist par excellence, and a mentor
to many—who probes, questions, complains, persuades,
but above all, encourages and supports.

Contents

Preface   ix

1   Introduction: Setting the Parameters   1
2   Premodern Africa   41
3   Afro-Arab Islamic Africa   107
4   Anglophone Africa—I   207
5   Anglophone Africa—II: Ethiopia, Liberia, and South Africa   265
6   Europhone Africa   331
7   Thematic Perspective: The Role of Foreign Aid   379
8   Conclusion: The Colonial Legacy and Beyond   429

Appendix I: An Exploration into the Provenance of the
                  Modern African University   447
Appendix II: The Historical Antecedents of the Disjuncture Between
                  Premodern and Modern African Higher Education   479

Appendix III: European Colonial Empires in Africa
                  on the Eve of Political Independence   535
Glossary   541
Bibliography   545
Index   603

Preface

In the four main fields to which this multidisciplinary work belongs, African studies, comparative and international black studies (studies of the African diaspora), comparative and international education, and higher education, the number of books that deal exclusively with a unified continent-wide historical survey of African higher education amount to, amazingly (such have been the sorry fortunes of that continent even in the academic arena—see, for instance, Martin and West 1999), just one. That one book of course is Ashby (1966). Given this circumstance, then, any new work on the subject should be considered a welcome addition (however self-serving this may appear), regardless of the scope of its terrain—further justifications for its publication being superfluous.

Still, it would be of some service to the reader to know how this work differs from Ashby: it differs from it in three essential ways: temporally, geographically and analytically. That is, this work covers a much longer historical timeline (from antiquity to the present) than Ashby does; it brings almost the entire continent in its purview (Ashby's geographic focus is India and sub-Saharan Africa, but even in the case of the latter he excludes many countries); and analytically it is written from a critical perspective (by and large Ashby is an apologia for British colonial higher education policies—compare, for instance, Nwauwa [1997]). However, despite these differences, on its own terms, Ashby remains an important work; consequently this book seeks to add to Ashby, rather than to replace it.

This work differs from Ashby in another significant way: an effort has been made to situate the history of universities in Africa in a global context. Specifically, in Appendix 1 and 2 the story of the provenance of the university at the generic level and Africa's place in that story is examined. By structurally placing this particular topic at the end of the book should not, however, be taken to imply marginality of relevance in terms of the main body of the work; rather it speaks simply to the desire to lessen the burden on the lay reader who may only have passing interest in this specific aspect of African history, given the complexity and range of issues one must perforce consider when tackling this topic—for instance: the ideological formation of Europe, the Westernization of an Eastern religion (Christianity), the emergence of the Afro-Islamic civilization and empire, the East to West diffusion of knowledge in the Afro-Eurasian ecumene and the origins of the so-called scientific revolution, the global consequences of the "Columbian error" (Christopher Columbus's inadvertent arrival on the shores of Hispaniola), the rise of the Atlantic slave trade, the geographic specificity of modes of production, and so on. In other words, if the reader with an avid interest in African history generally, and African higher education specifically, were to seek guidance in reading this work then the recommended itinerary would take this sequential form: Chapters 1 and 2, and then turning to Appendix 1, 2, and 3, followed by Chapters 3 through 8. (As for all others, they may do well to simply adhere to the run of the contents listing.)

Even though history was not intended to be their primary focus, this work is also an effort to supplement the useful but brief continent-wide surveys produced on behalf of the Association of African Universities, Yesufu (1973) and Ajayi, Goma, and Johnson (1996); and the much, much longer and detailed geographically comprehensive multiauthored volume edited by Teferra and Altbach (2003). Of the three, the last requires special emphasis; for it is absolutely in a class of its own (and one wishes there were similar works available for other regions of the world). Even though, as just noted, history is not its primary focus, the analytical depth (thirteen thematic chapters on all the major topics of relevance to higher education in Africa, ranging from finance through language issues to student activism), the scope of geographic coverage (fifty-two detailed chapters covering every country on the continent) and contemporaneity is such that it is indispensable to anyone who desires a grounding (the choice of this word here is deliberate) in the current circumstances of African higher education. The reader would be well advised to have that book handy while going through this work. In fact, omissions in this work imposed by constraints of space can be addressed to some degree of usefulness by consulting that densely printed tome.[1]

As one would expect with a project that has been many years in the making (to the deep chagrin of the editors—sorry!), one is bound to accumulate heavy debts. However, there is a common tendency among scholars, while momentarily in the grip of ecstatic relief at completing (such is the nature of the scholarly enterprise) what is usually nothing less than an embodiment of blood, sweat, and tears, to profusely thank all and sundry, including those only tendentiously connected with the project—such as the family dog, Toto! I will resist this temptation by making a distinction between those whose help was graciously welcome, yet without it this project would still have gone on to completion *and those without whose assistance this project would not have seen the light of day* and/or *were instrumental in improving its quality*; it is the latter whom I must publicly thank.

At the very top of the list is Professor Philip G. Altbach (who first suggested I write this book and patiently stayed with the project);[2] and next in line is my departmental chair, L. S. Williams; followed by the late L. Stewart (in Capen); and those in the dean's office, most especially M. Malamud, who together made it all possible. Very special thanks to T. M. Jennings for her assiduity and patience in taking care of the final prepress stages of production. The rest I will mention alphabetically: R. Clarke; G. Johnson-Cooper; R. V. Desforges; P. P. Ekeh; J. Heidemann; K. Henry; D. Hewett-Elson; A. M. McGoldrick; J. G. Pappas; K. L. Reid *and her extremely helpful crew at the circulation desk*; P. Stevens, Jr.; D. Teferra; the folks in the interlibary loan department (Ann, Fran, and Sandy); the staff at the publishers, most especially E. A. Potenza; and my physicians. A million thanks guys!

I must also thank the U. B. College of Arts and Sciences for financially assisting with the preparation of the index; and the permissions and copyright department of Bantam, a division of Random House, Inc. for allowing me to reproduce a few verses of Dante's *Inferno* from Allen Mandelbaum's translation of *The Divine Comedy of Dante Alighieri*. Of course, it goes without saying, that profound thanks are also due to the numerous scholars, past and present, whose works I have drawn upon, or occasionally railed against, listed in the bibliographic section at the end of this work. Yes, absolutely, I take full responsibility for any errors, fallacies and misinterpretations that may still remain.[3]

NOTES

1. Remembering that the present is always tomorrow's history, mention should also be made here of the recent launch (in 2003) of the *Journal of Higher Education in Africa* (edited by Damtew Teferra), jointly by the Boston College Center for International Higher Education in United States and the Council for the Development of Social Science Research in Africa (CODESRIA) in Senegal, that promises to be—judging by the several issues that have already been published—an important source of research, information, and hopefully serious *debate* on African higher education, in years to come. Note that the journal also maintains a companion website. See the website for International Network for Higher Education in Africa, an initiative of the Boston College Cen-

ter for International Higher Education, at www.bc.edu/inhea. The center also issues a quarterly scholarly newsletter titled *International Higher Education* (accessible for free through their website at www.bc.edu/cihe) that should be de rigueur reading for any one interested in issues of comparative and international higher education. Consider, for instance, one of its latest issues (summer 2005) which has two sections that are of relevance to the issues raised at the end of Chapter 8—one section is titled "Globalization, Trade, and Accreditation" and the other is titled "Private Higher Education." Updates on the current status of national higher education systems are also available through the International Bureau of Education website (accessible by a link at the UNESCO website).

2. It is impossible to identify all teachers who have had a hand in one's intellectual development over the course of a lifetime; however, there are some whose contribution is such that they occupy a permanent seat in that place of gratitude in one's mind reserved for one's greatest teachers. One such person is my teacher and mentor, Professor Philip G. Altbach. (Does he share all the conclusions reached in this work? No, of course not.)

3. One more thing: A pet peeve that I cannot resist articulating: teachers who underline personal books (and who encourage their students to do the same) ought to be put away—the habit invariably migrates to books that belong to others: such as library books! Obviously they never learned that books are sacred.

1

Introduction:
Setting the Parameters

It is a truism that any survey of a much neglected subject, in this case a history of the development of higher education in Africa, carries the weight of its importance entirely by itself. Not much need be said further; even an introduction may be an exercise in superfluity. However, because this is a work of history it carries with it a special obligation (the accomplishment of which is one of the twin objectives of this introduction—the other is the indication of aspects of method); it is one that stems from this fact: all history is inherently a selective chronicle (at the very least for reasons of limited time and space—memory/ book pages—if for no other), the composition of which, whether one likes it or not, is the prerogative of the historian. In other words, "historical truth" is always relative (though not, one must emphasize, and as will be explained later, in the nihilistic sense)—it is in the nature of the enterprise; therefore, the best that one can ask of a historian under the circumstances is to render transparent his/ her historiographical intent. It is obligatory, then, to begin this work by enumerating briefly the broad historiographical parameters that will dictate the choice of the historical record that will be highlighted in the chapters to follow.[1]

HISTORIOGRAPHICAL PARAMETERS

(1) The short interregnum occupied by colonialism (astounding as it may sound to many, lasting no more than a mere seventy to eighty years for much of

Africa) in the long history of a continent that spans millennia, does not embody the sum total of all there is to know about African higher education. That is, such a vast continent as Africa has had a sufficient level of cultural diversity for parts of it to boast the existence of institutionalized forms of higher education long before its Westernized form was introduced to it during the era of European colonialism. This belies the still-persistent notion (albeit no longer subscribed to by most Western academics, except sotto voce) best captured not so long ago—in fact in historical terms only yesterday (1965)—by that well-known British historian Hugh Trevor-Roper in his what one can only describe as a gaumless response to calls for the teaching of African history: "Perhaps, in the future, there will be some African history to teach. But at present there is none, or very little; there is only the history of the Europeans in Africa. The rest is largely darkness, like the history of pre-European, pre-Columbian America. And darkness is not a subject for history...[other than a means to] amuse ourselves with the unrewarding gyrations of barbarous tribes in picturesque but irrelevant corners of the globe; tribes whose chief function in history, in my opinion, is to show to the present an image of the past from which, by history, it has escaped" (p. 9). [2]

(2) The mode of Africa's insertion into the post–1492 trajectory of global history (see Appendix II), of which the colonization of the continent by Europe was simply an expression of its final phase, left an imprint on the development of its higher education, as on much else, that has not always been advantageous to the overall healthy development of the continent. Specifically focusing on colonialism and its impact on the development of African higher education, consider the Janus-faced character of colonial education policies (encouraging the liberatory potential of the colonially mediated introduction of education in general, even while simultaneously undermining it with educational policies ensuing from the exigencies of maintaining the colonial subjugation of the continent), Africa's colonial education inheritance was not only quantitatively paltry, but ill-suited to the demands of escaping the straightjacket of an externally defined neoclassical economic notion of Africa's "comparative advantage."

(3) Buffeted by the twin scourges of proauthoritarian regimes (in part nurtured by the massively disastrous Cold War policies of the principal dyadic protagonists), and a neoliberal vision of the role of the African state vis-à-vis development held by those in the West controlling the purse strings of foreign development assistance, the postindependence history of African higher education in much of the continent highlights a continuing saga of trials and tribulations of survival and relevance. Even in the case of societies at the extremities of the continent (North Africa and South Africa), with comparatively different historical traditions from the rest, one can observe disquieting symptoms of disequilibrium, albeit for different reasons, that undermine one's optimism for the future. In other words, the promise of a prominent role for higher education in the national development effort trumpeted so loudly in those heady days of

the first glow of the postindependence era would soon founder in the sands of the Western neoliberal obsession with the unbridling of the forces of global markets where capital has been allowed a completely free hand to dominate, exploit, distort, and destroy national economies across the length and breadth of the continent.

(4) There is an aura of unrealism in much of the literature on the history of education in Africa (and probably elsewhere for that matter) in which there is a failure to acknowledge that however much modern African elites came to demand Western secular education, it arrived in Africa as part of the colonial cultural package and to that extent it was "tainted." In other words, colonial education, at all levels, was always a political enterprise too. As an instrument of colonial hegemony, at the very least there were efforts to use it to neutralize resistance to the colonial project, but most certainly not to encourage it. Consequently, how much of it, at what levels, in what forms, and for who among the colonized it was to be provided was ultimately a function of a deliberate political calculus (this was true at the beginning of the colonial project, as well as at the end). This is not to suggest by any means that the colonial subjects were merely passive targets of colonial educational strategies, but rather that it is impossible to view any history of colonial education (at any level) separately from the political and economic contexts in which it was situated.[3] One should also point out here that because it was a handmaiden of the colonial project, the institution of higher education would acquire roles that were inimical to the long-term interest of African countries: elitism, curricular irrelevance, and so on.

(5) Historically, long before the arrival of European colonialism, those parts of Africa that possessed institutions of higher learning could boast of a tradition of higher education that included the belief that the pursuit of knowledge for its own sake was a worthy endeavor that any society would want to encourage. In time, however, following the arrival of colonialism, this approach to higher education was, by and large, jettisoned in favor of an exclusively utilitarian view of higher learning. Consequently, while to the planners of higher education during the colonial era its task was primarily political (social control), whereas during the postindependence era it has been economic (human capital), the truth is that higher education (like all education) is not so easily targeted. For it is an inherently unwieldy "weapon" that any state employing it will discover sooner or later. The reason is obvious, but somehow, time and again, it escapes the social engineers—education's stock in trade is the human mind, which is inherently unpredictable (so unpredictable that we have a whole field specializing in it called *psychology*). During the colonial era, education in general, and higher education specifically, far from serving as a means of social control, turned out to be a source of subversion of the colonial order. In the postindependence era, even in once highly authoritarian dirigiste societies, such as that of Nasserite Egypt at one end of the continent and former apart-

heid South Africa at the other, there were limits to the use of higher education for state-engineered ends. Related to this point: no matter how logical, elegant, scientific, and efficient a particular plan may be for a higher education system or institution, at the end of the day it is politics that determine what kind of a plan will be implemented. It is not "experts" but politicians who decide what is best for society, for good or ill.

(6) Following from the preceding point, for all its ubiquity today, *formal* education (the key word here is formal) still belongs to that sector of society that in the greater scheme of things is not particularly important *in and of itself.* Educators will of course take considerable umbrage at this statement, but one has history to turn to for support. Major human transformations (empire building, economic revolutions, political revolutions, and so on) were a product of on-the-job training, not formal education. In the great pantheon of achievers, regardless of their spatial and temporal domicile, scholars are rarely to be found (and even less so in their role as scholars). This point immediately brings up the matter of the role of higher education in a national development effort (a burning issue in Africa today as different panaceas are brought out to attempt to jumpstart what is now by all accounts a failed postindependence development trajectory). The question that is often raised is in the context of scarce resources and mass illiteracy: What comes first, the provision of higher education or general national development? The truth is that neither one nor the other comes first, they are *dialectically* intertwined—meaning that while higher education can be harnessed in the national development effort, its own development is contingent upon the very same effort (but which in turn brings to the fore for consideration that entire panoply of internal and external variables that may be subsumed under the term "the political economy of development," which range from internal political stability to global trade and financial regimes). Support for this position—which neither the detractors nor the promoters of African higher education will find to their liking—comes from considering, for instance, the cases of the following seemingly disparate countries: Egypt, Ethiopia, Liberia, Libya, and apartheid South Africa.

The first four countries permit us to render moot these traditionally highlighted impediments to development: the absence of capital (Libya has plenty of it); the colonial legacy (neither Ethiopia nor Liberia was colonized in the same manner as much of the rest of the continent); and the curricular and structural imbalance in which there is an inordinate emphasis on the humanities at the expense of science and technology (Egypt has managed to correct this imbalance, in fact some may argue that it has gone in the opposite direction). The failure, so far, of countries such as Libya and Egypt to leverage (to borrow a much beloved term of U.S. businesses today) their higher educational systems in the service of growth and development—and in the case of the former amidst a plentiful supply of capital—points to the immense difficulties of prying open the international economic order purely on the back of higher education. Tinkering with higher educational systems in themselves—as Egypt's Muhammed Ali found out more than a 100 years ago—is but only one side of the equation (domestic and international political economy broadly understood is the other). As for former apartheid South Africa, its experience provides us with the conclusive case: Its relative economic success, compared to the rest of the continent, depended on a unique combination of political and economic circumstances that were rooted in the period when it was colonized (in the seventeenth-century, that is prior to the "Scramble for Africa," when Europe was still relatively weak) in which higher education was not the most important variable. Yet apartheid South Africa came to boast the most developed higher education system on the entire continent—even though it was highly inegalitarian. On the other hand, going outside the continent for a moment, consider the current experiences of China and India. Their relative explosive national development effort is taking place amidst circumstances where each of them accounts for high rates of illiteracy among their populations—perhaps as much as 30% in the case of India. This fact, however, has not dissuaded them from placing great stress on higher education, including in the form of overseas study (the majority of the foreign student population studying in the United States today come from these two countries alone).

(7) The late Professor Edward Said, in subjecting an important cultural artifact, the European literary discourse on the imperium, to his ruthlessly incisive razor-sharp analytical scalpel, came away with the conclusion: "What are striking in these discourses are the rhetorical figures one keeps encountering in their descriptions of the 'mysterious East,' as well as stereotypes about 'the African [or Indian or Irish or Jamaican or Chinese] mind,' the notions about bringing civilization to primitive or barbaric peoples" (1993: xi; parenthetical material in the original). To turn to a different source, to the horse's mouth as it were: In his advocacy of a Western (British) form of education for India, that nineteenth-century British Parliamentarian Lord Thomas Babington Macaulay (already a legend in his day for his oratory) would comment: "I am quite ready to take the Oriental learning at the valuation of the Orientalists themselves. I have never found one among them who could deny that a single shelf of a good European library was worth the whole native literature of India and Arabia.... It is I believe, no exaggeration to say, that all the historical information which has been collected from all the books written in the Sanskrit language is less valuable than what may be found in the most paltry abridgements used at preparatory schools in England" (1935 [1854]: 349).

And the point of these two references? From men like Macaulay, Rudyard Kipling, and on to the present, apologists of European imperialism have often pointed to education (in its institutionalized sense) as among the many gifts of "civilization" it bequeathed to the barbaric and "benighted" masses of the Afro-Asian, Australasian, and American ecumenes. Their detractors, on the other hand, have legitimately pointed out that the education that was brought by imperialism was not in its genuine liberatory form, but rather it was a tainted form of education, aimed simply to serve as yet one more device in the arsenal of *cultural imperialism*—the effort to dominate the human mind through cultural artifacts in the service of subjugation and empire building.[4] This argument has been best and most explicitly advanced by Carnoy: "Western formal education came to most countries as part of imperialist domination. It was consistent with the goals of imperialism: the economic and political control of the people in one country by the dominant class in another. The imperial powers attempted through schooling, to train the colonized for roles that suited the colonizer" (1974: 3). Be that as it may; the truth, however, is that the biggest indictment of the education that the imperial powers brought to Africa was not so much that it was tainted (which it was), but rather that *even in its tainted form it was not enough!* That is, there should have been more of it. To the postcolonialist crowd, this may indeed be a startling statement. To explain, in the context of Africa at any rate (this argument, perhaps, may not be applicable to other parts of the European colonial empire—Asia, for instance), the colonial powers did not make a sufficient concerted effort (except at the very end) to cultivate a vibrant *indigenous* capitalist class—an effort in which higher education of course would have loomed large. Imperialism was not about egalitarianism and social justice; it was certainly not about socialism; it was about capitalism. However, the tragedy is that even on these (its own) terms, it came up very short. The helter-skelter effort made toward the end, on the eve of independence, to develop universities merely left the excolonies with a "castrated" elite incapable of masterminding the development of their countries; for in the one most important area it was powerless: the economic sphere. The outcome of this circumstance was anticipated long ago by Fanon; in describing the characteristics of the postindependence African elite, he observed: "Seen through its eyes, its mission has nothing to do with transforming the nation; it consists, prosaically, of being the transmission line between the nation and a capitalism rampant though camouflaged, which today puts on the mask of neocolonialism." He continues, "In its beginnings, the national bourgeoisie of the colonial countries identifies itself with the decadence of the bourgeoisie of the West. We need not think that it is jumping ahead; it is in fact beginning at the end. It is already senile before it has come to know the petulance, the fearlessness, or the will to succeed of youth" (1978 [1961]: 152–53). The legacy today, of course, of this belated birth of what Fanon labels as the "national bourgeoisie" is all too evident: an elite consumed with what he called decadence, *but without the means to sustain it* because of its lack of ownership of capital—especially in its productive sense (after all some of the petroleum-producing countries in the north of the continent do own considerable amounts of capital), the outcome of which has been circumstances ranging from rampant self-destructive rent-seeking and kleptomania to political disintegration.[5]

On European Colonialism and Education

(8) The subject of colonialism and its legacy raises a broader problem of historiography (as it has been unfolded in the pages of this work), which can be described this way: Although the duration of the time period occupied by European colonialism in the history of the continent, is, as already indicated, a short one, it has to be conceded that its legacy (a topic of discussion in the concluding chapter) has proven to be anything but short; in fact, it endures to the present day. Consequently, it is necessary to consider the following key features of the *generic* Western colonial enterprise that shaped everything else that ensued, *including the development of colonial higher education.*

(a) We can begin by observing that at the heart of every colonial enterprise, and modern Western colonialism was especially marked in this regard, is the commandeering of the actual or potential resources of the colony—whatever form they may be in: human, land, flora, fauna, and so on—for the development of the colonizing (metropolitan) entity.[6] Further, that this objective must be met, at least over the long-run, without provoking permanent debilitative resistance from the colonized, but on the contrary must elicit their cooperation (even if only grudging), and to this end the following two are essential prerequisites: the exploitation should not be so severe as to jeopardize the colonial enterprise itself (the goose must not be killed), and yet, at the same time, the exploitation of resources should provide a sufficient largesse such as to permit the inclusion of a significant enough part of the colonial population in its expropriation—specifically the part destined to play a compradorial role.

(b) Although some of the literature on colonialism in the latter half of the twentieth-century (up to the present) has correctly pointed to the enormous human and other costs to the victims of the colonial project in the colonies, one should not forget that European colonization also exacted a heavy price from the rank-and-file citizenry (the masses) in the metropole, as well. For, given that the Western colonialist project took place during the era of capitalist imperialism (as distinct from the "imperialisms" of the precapitalist era—such as that of the Egyptians, the Greeks, the Persians, the Romans, etc.), the principal beneficiaries of that project in the metropole, in relative terms, were primarily the transnational capitalist enterprises (such as the British South Africa Company, or the Compagnie Francaise de l'Afrique Occidentale) and their ruling class allies, and not the majority of the citizenry as a whole (the working classes and the peasantry). Under these circumstances—and especially against the backdrop of an era when Western countries were beginning to be buffeted by the winds of democracy, thereby bringing to the fore the matter of accountability of actions undertaken by the state—the cooperation of the citizenry in both the financing of the project (taxation) as well as the donation of their bodies in those instances where resistance in the colonies needed to be overcome by military means (soldiers), required the deployment of what may be termed as a "persuasion packet" comprising three basic components: coercion (e.g., mandatory conscription), economic incentives, and ideology. The last two were generally fused together in the promise of upward mobility *while engaged in undertaking moral good,* which was expressed, in turn, through five avouchments: the colonial project would enhance economic growth at home, which consequently would create jobs (employment) and overall prosperity for all; it would provide opportunities for a better and a richer life through emigration to the colonies (colonial settlement); it would enhance the status of the nation in an increasingly competitive world—economically and politically—(nationalism); it would permit the work of God to be carried out (Christian proselytism); and it was a morally desirable undertaking because it would allow the backward and the primitive to become civilized ("white man's burden"—Christian charity).

The last requires further elaboration; for, the ideology of the "white man's burden"—which on the surface may appear to be riddled with the naivete of do-gooder innocence but yet at its core rests on a potent combination of racism and self-aggrandizement—has in fact proven to be particularly enduring in various guises, and has never really been jettisoned completely by the West, to this day.[7] Among the earliest manifestations of this component of the Western colonial ideology in Africa arose with the Western colonial projects in Islamic North Africa (beginning with the Napoleonic invasion of Egypt). The West would argue (vide: Napoleon's proclamation mentioned in Chapter 2) that the European colonization of the Islamic countries was an act of altruism aimed at freeing the populace from, on one hand, the tyranny and oppression of the traditional Muslim rulers (e.g., the Ottoman Mamluks), and on the other, the economic backwardness that these rulers had imposed on their countries. In other words, colonialism was not only an altruistic response to oriental despotism (read Islamic despotism), they argued, but that it was a response that was *invited* by such despotism.[8] What is more, the truth of this reasoning, they felt, was self-evident in the inability of these countries to militarily resist the West. (In this twisted reasoning so characteristic of the architects and champions of the Western imperialist project, the inability to resist imperialist aggression was itself presented as a justification for the very aggression.) Now, while objectively it may have been true that these were the conditions prevailing in Islamic Africa, *they were significant only in the context of the post–1492 transformations that Western Europe was undergoing and which were propelling it toward global hegemony* (see Appendix II). Despotism or no despotism, the source of Western imperialism lay within the West; it had nothing to do with the conditions prevailing in Islamic Africa (or the rest of Africa for that matter). There is also, of course, the small matter of these same post–1492 Western transformations underwriting the relative economic backwardness of the Islamic countries in the first place on the eve of European colonization![9] Anyhow, the veracity of the foregoing (regarding ideological justifications) was demonstrated by the refusal of the colonial powers (such as the French) to permit the further development of the preexisting *madrasah* system (with one or two exceptions—as in Tunisia), not because they were educationally inefficient (which they had now become as a result of colonially mediated changes in society at large), but for fear that it would be an incubator of oppositional movements.[10] Moreover, even when the French did begin to develop an alternative secular education sector, it was a half-hearted endeavor at best.

Of the several forms that colonialism took (colonies, protectorates, spheres of influence, trust territories, etc.), the protectorate and the trust territory were considered by the West as the truest embodiment of Western altruism as represented by the concept of the "white man's burden." Western colonial powers promised to assist the protectorate to modernize and thereby facilitate, in due course after an appropriate dose of tutelage, its elevation to a level *almost* commensurate with other "civilized" (read Western) nations; in other words, unlike in the case of a "true" colony, the stated objective was not permanent occupation and emasculation of the target.[11] It was always made clear to all interested parties, from the very beginning, that the colonial presence would be transient. While such a belief may have been genuinely present among some of the ideologues of the colonial project, the truth, however, lay elsewhere. For one thing, the unrealism of such declarations was evidenced even on the ideological terrain alone by the inability to indicate the fount of this newly discovered altruism—recall that in the case of Islamic North Africa specifically, it was a region that once (and some may argue that this continues to be the case today) hosted societies that were implacable enemies of the West.

However, it is when considered from the perspective of the national purse (which, except in the rarest circumstances, has little patience for altruism) that the truth readily surfaces. A protectorate was acquired for the same fundamental reason as a colony, to enhance the economic wellbeing of the colonizer directly (if the protectorate happened to have known actual or potential natural and human resources) or indirectly for geopolitical benefits.[12] Ergo, the difference between a colony and a protectorate was in essence simply a matter of difference in approach at realizing this same objective. In the case of the French this difference was captured in the concepts of *assimilation* and *association*. Now, one of the elements of the concept of association was the principle of *indirect rule* where the indigenous rulers were not swept aside, as the logic of a colonization project would have dictated, but were permitted to continue governing, but under the watchful eye of the colonial power and on terms set by its agenda (the authorship of which was the exclusive preserve of the colonial power). There were two obvious benefits of this approach: it was, in relative terms, highly cost effective; and it was easier, again in relative terms, to command acquiescence from the target. It is against this backdrop that we must evaluate the objectives of, for example, the French in seeking to preserve the traditional madrasah system (even if they may have attempted to tinker with it here and there in the interest of structural efficiency) for the masses, but while

also encouraging, simultaneously, some modicum of alternative secular education for a tiny elite that they hoped would play the necessary compradorial role
in the colonial (protectorate) project.

(c) While keeping the foregoing in mind, when one examines, for example,
the colonial histories of South Africa, Zimbabwe, and Algeria on one hand, and
Nigeria, Guinea, and Benin on the other, following on Thomas (1994), a significant historical fact that is too often forgotten when surveying European colonial practices in Africa (and elsewhere for that matter) becomes readily clear:
that colonialism was not a unitary totality. That is, whether or not one buys
Thomas's central thesis that "colonialism is not best understood primarily as a
political or economic relationship that is legitimized or justified through ideologies of racism or progress[; r]ather, colonialism has always, equally importantly and deeply, been a cultural process; its discoveries and trespasses are
imagined and energized through signs, metaphors and narratives; even what
would seem its purest moments of profit and violence have been mediated and
enframed by structures of meaning" (p. 2), it is true that even when considering
the colonial practices of a single colonial power there were meaningful differences among competing models of colonialism that grew out of a dialectic between the nature of the *temporally specific* forces in the metropole that believed in and demanded the implementation of the colonial project, and how
those who were to be colonized reacted to the project. From the perspective of
higher education, specifically, these differences translated into, for example,
how the different colonies experienced the presence (or absence) of colonially
mediated higher education—immaterial of sharing the common denominator of
a single colonizing power.[13]

(d) Inherent in the logic of colonialism was expansion; that is, colonies
were a precursor to the expansion of the metropole—geographically, economically, politically, and culturally. Therefore, directly ruled colonies were a transient stage on the path toward their eventual economic and cultural absorption
by the metropole—which even if not envisaged at the beginning, in the end
that is the strategy that was pursued by most Western colonial powers in the
face of nationalist struggles for independence.[14] Now, if possession of colonies
was to be a transient phase then everything was to be done to ensure continued
political, legal, economic, and cultural linkages (both institutional and ideological) between the colonies and the metropole, so as not to disrupt the actual
and potential avenues of advantage established during the colonial phase that
the metropolitan transnational capitalist enterprises enjoyed vis-à-vis emergent
indigenous, postindependence enterprises (as well as enterprises from other rival metropoles); and, further, where there were colonial settler populations,
their interests too be preserved. In other words, and most especially in the context of the spiraling Cold War that emerged at the very time that the winds of
political independence were about to blow across the continent, it was of absolute importance to the ruling classes of the West that their former colonies in-

herit ideologically like-minded compradorial ruling elites—one need not be a rocket scientist to deduce the importance of a metropolitan inspired higher education in this regard—who would develop their newly independent countries along the path of stable compradorial capitalist democracies, and not along some radical alternative path, such as that represented by the totalitarian bureaucratic socialism of the then USSR (or China or even Cuba). (Some have termed the relationship that such connections embodied as one of modern imperialism or *neocolonialism*.) Notice also that even the Cold War was couched in terms of the "white man's burden": the Africans (as well as others in the PQD world) needed to be saved from the scourge of evil atheistic communism.

(e) While this work hews to the theory of the primacy of the economic in explaining the modern Western imperialist project—acting as both a motivator *and* a facilitator (the latter in terms of the necessary resources without which no such project could have ever taken off the ground; something that those who overly emphasize the ideational aspect of the project tend to forget)—it is still necessary to also draw attention to the ideational dimension of the project since it is that dimension that helped to grease the wheels of imperialism, so to speak, both at home and in the colonies.[15] To elaborate, colonialism also required, on one hand, the cultural domination of the colonized in order to obtain voluntary compliance with their political and economic subjugation (that is once they had been militarily brought to heel—a brutal and bloody process termed euphemistically as pacification), and on the other, an ideological justification for the project at home, as just mentioned above, so as to elicit the acquiescence of the citizenry to the massive expenditures (of both public monies and the lives of the working class soldiery) necessary for implementing the project. Concentrating now on the first aspect (cultural domination), it made sense that one of the most important instruments to effect it was colonial education. By means of colonial education, the ideologues of the colonial project often argued, the colonized could be molded into compliant colonial subjects; yet there was an inherent contradiction buried within this strategy: too much of it could lead to recalcitrance, not compliance, because of the very nature of education—its potential to liberate the mind, especially with the acquisition of its core instrument, literacy.[16] There was also, however, a more mundane consequence: The demand for jobs by graduates commensurate with their educational certification. To take care of the potential for both these deleterious outcomes (which in practice would have taken the form of rebellious nationalism on one hand, and on the other, competition for the colonizer's jobs), colonialists adopted two basic strategies with varying levels of success: truncate and constrict the metropolitan curriculum upon its transplantation to the colony and at the same time place artificial barriers on the educational ladder by providing minimal or no access to postsecondary or sometimes even postprimary education. As Gosnell (2002: 46) puts it with respect to French colonial education policy in Algeria: "Encouraging the intellectual development of Africans would be like giving sweets to a child: they might taste good but would ruin his digestion."

In Islamic Africa, however, it should be further noted, the colonialists were faced with a third problem: how to neutralize the oppositional potential of an existing education system, the madrasah system. The solution to this problem was sought in one or more of these strategies: starve it off resources by confiscating the *waqfs*; enforce a new curriculum in the system; abolish some of the institutions altogether; freeze it in a precolonial timeframe by preventing its further evolution in terms of content; develop alternative colonially controlled institutions (complete with ulama on the payroll of the colonial state); and, perhaps the most effective, refuse to recognize madrasah education as legitimate for all secular sector employment.[17] The French (and to some extent the other colonial powers as well, British, Italians, and so on.) pursued one or more of all these strategies in Afro-Arab Islamic Africa. In the end, of course, they, like all authoritarian regimes, discovered much to their consternation, that education, counterintuitive as it may seem, was a clumsy instrument of social control. No matter how tightly they may have managed educational provision in terms of content and quantity, somehow, sooner or later, some of its products rose up to bite the hand that fed them.[18] For, it is the products of the colonial education institutions who eventually rose to challenge the very colonial system itself and provided the leadership for its overthrow, sometimes violently and sometimes peacefully.

(f) Given the simultaneity of the following two of the many necessities of the colonial project: political and cultural domination on one hand, and on the other the conquest of its inescapable dyadic logic, resistance (since no society will voluntarily accede to any form of colonial subjugation), acquiescence by the colonized to their domination (their pacification) required the brutalization of their cultures (in the same way that their political subjugation had required the brutalization of their bodies by way of military defeat).[19] In practice this entailed the construction of the racist ideological edifice of social Darwinism—the fallacious application of Charles Darwin's theory of natural selection to human societies to justify the equally fallacious biologically deterministic division of humanity into hierarchic categories of race, class, gender, and so on, and whose policy consequences would in time include such horrors as the eugenics movement in the United States and the final solution of the Nazis—to underwrite the policies necessary to secure this brutalization.[20] To construct this edifice the ideologues of the colonial project turned for help to two principal sources to provide them with the requisite arsenal of racist stereotypes: the discipline of anthropology (which even at the best of times, like psychology, is a suspect discipline considering that its stock in trade is human difference, actual and manufactured—recall that, as a discipline, it began its life in the nineteenth-century on the back of *scientific racism*); and the phantasmagorial tales of the world outside Europe found in travelogues of those European travelers with unusually fertile, and may we add, sexually repressed minds.[21] Now, from the perspective of education per se, social Darwinism provided the justification for the tainted form of education that was exported to the colonies in the first phases of the colonial project, which was usually referred to as adapting Western education to local conditions.

Now although the term adapt (and adaptation) occurs fairly frequently in colonial education literature generally, it is very important to distinguish between the two senses of the word in which it occurs historically (for one was far from benign compared to the other). In one sense it was used neutrally to mean the same as that defined by any dictionary, which in relation to education referred to the modification of some features of a transplanted education system (pedagogy, texts, language of instruction, and so on.) to suit the specific circumstances of the recipient of the transplantation on purely legitimate pedagogic grounds. In another sense, which is of particular relevance here, its use implied that the system was to be adapted to suit, on one hand, the mental capabilities of an entire people—judged to be an intellectually inferior people (namely blacks and other colonized peoples)—and on the other, the subservient political and economic status of the same people relative to their colonial masters. In other words, adaptation meant subpar educational provision of Western education to blacks and others on both racist and political grounds. The study by Reilly (1995) provides an excellent example of what this meant at the policy-level in anglophone Africa where he traces the linkages in the first decades of the twentieth-century among the racist ideas of three contemporaries: Thomas Jesse Jones, J. H. Oldham (a British missionary official with great influence on matters of colonial education in British government and missionary circles) and Charles T. Loram (a white South African educator and one time government official whose influence on educational policy in South Africa vis-à-vis black South Africans was just as profound), which were the basis of educational policy for blacks in the U.S. South and in British colonial Africa in the early part of the twentieth-century. Reilly explores in his study how the social Darwinist beliefs of these three came to influence educational provision for Africans in the British colonial Africa generally and in South Africa specifically. That is, all three were firm believers in the *Hampton/Tuskegee model* of education where the primary objective was to increase the productive value of black labor through vocational education, but at the same time deny them access to academic education available to whites so as to keep them subservient to white overlordship (constituting the same recurring theme that has marked the entire history of black/white relations in the post–1492 era: racism as the handmaiden of capitalism and white privilege).

The Hampton/Tuskegee model, as King (1971) who did a seminal study on the subject, explains, rested on what was once euphemistically called industrial education. The ideological underpinnings of this form of education is summarized by him as the "disavowal of all political ambition on the part of the Negroes, and a readiness to stay in the South as a steady labor supply" (p. 8).[22] Among the clearest statements of what this model meant, however, is to be found in a massive two-volume study of the status of African American education that was done by Thomas Jesse Jones for the Phelps-Stokes Fund and which was published by the U.S. government's Bureau of Education division of the Department of the Interior a year after its completion in 1916 (U.S. Government 1969 [1917]).[23] In that study Jones laid out, though not in so many words, the problem: unenlightened whites (especially in the U.S. south) did not seem to see any value in the education of African Americans; on the other hand African Americans hungered for education, but of the type (literary academic education) unsuited to their political and economic circumstances: against the backdrop of a rural agrarian economy in which most African Americans were mired as cheap labor, one that was shorn of their civil rights in the context of a rapidly evolving Jim Crow driven neofascist political order (though that is not exactly how he described these circumstances).[24] A policy for African American education needed to address two problems; that whites needed to be persuaded in the value of educational provision for African Americans, and the latter needed to be persuaded in the value of an education (industrial education) that did not encourage them to challenge their political and economic circumstance. (Note the uncanny similarity to the education problem in British colonial Africa during the same period.)

(g) Looking back at the rapidity with which most of Africa became independent of colonial rule in the late 1950s and early 1960s (replicating, interestingly, roughly the same speed with which it had been dismembered and colonized at an earlier time), there is a tendency to assume that the colonial powers had all along intended it to be so. The fact that the colonial powers were just as surprised as their subjects at this development. Yes, it is true that they had stated that they did not wish to rule the colonies forever (with the exception, perhaps, of the settler colonies), but neither did they plan to vacate Africa so early and so quickly. After all, the war that had been fought against fascism in Europe (1939–45) by Britain, the United States, and other Allied countries, and in which many colonized peoples (including Africans) participated on the side of the European colonial powers, was, despite the propaganda of the Allies, a war fought for the freedom of only the European nations—not the colonized elsewhere. Hence, hopes of liberation from European colonialism that the colonized had begun to entertain as a result of participating in World War II on the side of the Allied forces and lending credibility to documents such as the *Atlantic Charter*, were to quickly founder on the rocks of post–World War II reality in which a new war was about to emerge between the United States and its allies on one hand, and the Soviet Union and its allies on the other: the *Cold War*.[25]

Initially, then, the commencement of the Cold War, as the 1940's came to a close, would be accompanied by a renewed effort on the part of the European powers to cling to their colonial possessions, even as they began the long and arduous task of rebuilding their own war-torn countries, and even after having saved themselves from the same fate that they were now so keen to continue foisting on other peoples. In this ignoble task, however, they would have behind them the unexpected, tacit, and sometimes overt support of the United States. From the point of view of the United States, the struggle for freedom and democracy in the colonies, it was felt, could only lead to expansionary opportunities for its Cold War opponent, the Soviet Union; therefore such struggles had to be opposed. Consequently, many colonies in Africa and Asia discovered that contrary to wartime promises made, or expectations falsely engendered, freedom from colonization would entail their own mini-world wars. Colonies ranging from Vietnam through India to Algeria all found themselves involved in various types of bitter, anticolonial struggles in which thousands among the colonized would perish.

Yet within a decade of the beginning of the Cold War (1947–48), most of the colonies in the Afro-Asian ecumene had been granted independence (with the exception of a few, such as the Portuguese colonies in Africa). Why? They had underestimated the resolve of the colonial subjects to end their subjugation; that is in the face of an increasingly intransigent nationalism in Algeria, India, Vietnam, and other places a war-weary, self-weakened Europe found it prudent to release their colonies from formal bondage—and in this task, as an additional motivator, they had the constant pressure of the Soviet Union who had begun to emerge as the champion of the colonized elsewhere even as it hypocritically built its own imperial empire in Eastern Europe. *However, in retrospect, one may boldly venture that perhaps both the nationalists and the European powers were in error in committing so quickly to decolonization.* Independence was not accompanied by a sufficiently gelled political and economic institutional framework such as to give it the kind of stability that would be necessary to undertake the arduous task of development. Higher education is a case in point. It is only when it became clear that independence was just around the corner that the colonial powers began to hastily develop and implement plans for a proper higher education system closely patterned on theirs. All notions of the supposed inferiority of the black intellect suddenly evaporated—nothing but the best would now do. It is against this backdrop that one must view the accelerated development of higher education on the eve of independence.

(h) It is in the context of these principal characteristics of the Western colonial enterprise that one must examine the development of higher education in all of colonial Africa—*not just British colonial Africa.* Now, while the ground-level details of its path of development, as will be shown in the chapters ahead, varied on the basis of place, time, and the colonial power in question, the basic underlying determinants of this path were fairly uniform throughout the continent.[26] The most salient of which were these (listed in no particular order; plus some, be forewarned, are contradictory given the specifics of the historical trajectory that unfolded in both the colonies and the metropole over the approximately 150 years of colonial rule in Africa):

- The subjugation and domination of the African people, both physically and mentally, that constituted the colonial project was facilitated at the *ideological* level by the colonial belief that the Africans were an intellectually inferior people, forever destined to be "drawers of water and hewers of wood"; therefore, while educational provision was necessary, it did not need to be elevated beyond the basic (elementary schooling).
- The logical desire by Christian missionaries, who in many cases were the first to enter the arena of formal education in the colonies, to control the agenda of education for the purposes of facilitating their own missionary objectives meant, in practice, opposition to secularization of higher education—in fact they advocated a very attenuated form of higher education—one primarily targeted at the provision of rudimentary ecclesiastical (priests) and primary school teacher training.
- In colonial settler Africa, the lopsided class competition between the colonial settlers (who, in the colonial context, as a group constituted an elite) and the emerging but dominated African nationalist elites, manifest through racially bounded struggles over the means for upward mobility, resulted in pressures to deny Africans opportunities for access to higher education—an important avenue for upward mobility even during the colonial period.
- The need to reduce the administrative expense of the colonial project required the training of some Africans (especially in areas without colonial settler populations) for administrative and teaching positions, even if low-level; which therefore necessitated the provision of some form of higher education.
- There was a metropolitan reluctance to encourage the full development of higher education given its view, at the policy-level (for both racist and economic reasons), that African colonies were economically destined to, on one hand, serve as markets for mass consumer goods cheaply produced by the metropole, and on the other, as contributors of natural resources and agricultural inputs to the metropolitan economy. (In other words, economic development among the African colonies was not envisaged, even in the long-run, in terms of industrialization—regardless of economic sector: manufacturing, agriculture, science, and technology, and so on.; with the exception, to a limited extent, of the mineral extractive sector.)
- Regardless of which approach was used in implementing the colonial project, *indirect rule* (British colonial Africa) or *assimilation/association* (in the rest of colonial Africa) the logic of these approaches demanded provision of higher education for the Africans; however in the face of such realities as settler pressures, racism, incipient nationalism, etc., this logic was often resisted.
- The combination, on one hand, of Christian missionary proselytism (which provided Africans access to a common language and literacy in places where it did not exist—with the ensuing desire for more secular knowledge, etc.), and on the other, colonialist activities (which helped to erode traditional agrarian economies, and to some degree, particularistic ethnic/linguistic boundaries) in time led to the emergence of a new African elite, a nationalist elite, that in the face of blocked economic and political opportunities came to demand modern higher education as a means for

advancing their economic, nationalist, and trans-nationalist (Pan-Africanism) agendas.

* The realization in the metropole that the probability of granting formal independence to the colonies sooner then expected under the twin pressures of the political-economic fallout from World War II and rising African nationalism—required putting into place cultural strings that would continue to bind the former colonies to the metropole (e.g., development of higher education with institutional linkages to metropolitan higher education institutions), especially against the backdrop of the growing Cold War international rivalry among the post–World War II emergent powers (e.g., China, United States, the Soviet Union).

* In their demand for higher education that was qualitatively no different from that available in the metropole—given the triple pressures of pragmatism (job hunting), modernization (the desire to acquire authentic symbols of modernity), and racism (as a response to centuries of racist propaganda and innuendos regarding their intellect), the Africans insisted that they did *not* wish to be shielded from what others of a later generation would label as "cultural imperialism."

* The rational desire by the metropole to institute *regional* higher education institutions for reasons of optimum allocation of resources (economies of scale) floundered in the face of intra-regional competition among the colonies during the colonial period, as well as in the postcolonial period (notwithstanding the Pan-Africanist grandstanding of many African nationalists).

* The demand by Africans, which was supported by the metropole as logical, that in the absence of *graduate*-level education in the foreseeable future in the newly independent former colonies required overseas study in the metropole for those wishing to pursue studies at that level, in turn meant that academic standards and structures within the former colonies had to be closely patterned on those of metropolitan institutions to ensure the smooth academic transition of the student.

ISSUES OF METHOD

In identifying the foregoing themes, it should quickly become clear that it is an exercise that highlights a fact about history that historians are generally loath to admit to: that perhaps more than any other discipline, history can never aspire to be neutral; it is by its nature always a contested terrain (however one wishes it to be otherwise). As already noted, the truth is that truth in history is relative. That is, there is no such thing as historical truth because all histories are a form of myths, not in the sense that historical facts are manufactured in the minds of historians (which sometimes does happen of course), but in the sense that histories by definition carry with them the inherent biases of the historians who produced them—emanating at the minimum from such factors as the historian's ideological world view; the impossibility of considering every known historical fact; the interpretive significance one adduces to a given historical event; the fact that history is always tentative, that is a permanent work in progress given the constant potential for new facts to come to light as new documents are discovered, new archaeological findings emerge, and so on.[27]

Now, if all histories are myths then the real task is to determine which of the competing myths is the most analytically cogent.[28] In other words, it does not imply a nihilistic relativism—a symptom of which, as the late Maxine Rodinson (2002: 116) wryly commented, is the mistaken assumption that one has a license to "surrender to [one's] favorite ideology since subjectivity will permeate [one's] scholarship anyway." After all, as he further reminds us: "If I say there is no truth, how could I argue that this very statement is true?" It ought to be pointed out here that this work has not relied on a single theoretical approach (from the perspective of method). Whether it is the Marxism of E. P. Thompson, or the postmodernism of Jean Baudrillard and Raymond Williams, or the *annales* approach of Fernand Braudel and Marshall Hodgson, or the structuralism of Ferdinand de Saussure, Claude Levi-Strauss and Michel Foucault, or the poststructuralism of Jacques Derrida and Robert Berkhofer, or even the empiricist positivist approach of conventional historians, the stance adopted has been that they all have something to contribute toward the inherently multifaceted task of historical knowing. None of these methodological approaches alone possesses the golden key to the strong room of correct or authentic historiography. What is more, in the case of those like the poststrucuralists one must be especially wary of their ideas of what constitutes correct historiography considering that their true vocation, as intellectual eunuchs, is not history per se but the study of the fictitious outpourings of others.[29]

Consequently, it is necessary to render transparent the methodological signposts that have guided the writing of this work. (1) Writing nearly 700 years ago, the celebrated Afro-Arab historian, Ibn Khaldun, observed in his *Muqaddimah*: "History is a discipline widely cultivated among nations and races....Both the learned and the ignorant are able to understand it. For on the surface history is no more than information about political events, dynasties and occurrences of the remote past....The inner meaning of history, on the other hand, involves speculation and an attempt to get at the truth, subtle explanation of the causes and origins of existing things, and deep knowledge of the how and why of events" (Khaldun 1967, Vol. 1: 6). It is this latter trait, in addition to the obvious trait of a careful examination of sources, that encompass the concept of critical history in this work. In other words, the critical part in the book title is not an attempt at making the title a little jazzy. Rather, it speaks to two basic elements of method in this work: an iconoclastic approach to cherished shibboleths and a critique of power relations (understood in their broadest sense), in terms of both the sociology of the production of knowledge (here one means, for example, examining the ideological underpinnings of questions asked, conclusions reached, etc., and the historical data itself—for instance the actual course of development on the ground of higher education at a given moment).

(2) Although the conventional nation-state approach to history has been retained in this work, it is tempered by a global approach as well. That is, taking

a leaf from Ibn Khaldun's historiographical method (which, notice, long predated that of the French *Annales* school), this work assumes that a history of an institution written from the perspective of so broad a canvas as an entire continent (which in its geographic expanse can gobble up Argentina, China, Europe, India, and the United States, all at once) and traversing across a huge swath of time measured in millennia, requires exploding all boundaries of time and space. To advance a thesis it may be necessary to go as far east as China or as far West as the Americas, even while Africa remains the focus of this work.

(3) Although the geographic (country-by-country) approach constitutes the principal format of this work, a special effort has been made to lend it an explicit comparative dimension in the analyses that accompany it. There is good reason for this: it is forced on us by the very project itself; for a history that traverses huge temporal and geographic boundaries willy-nilly precipitates questions of a comparative nature. Yes, it is true that every society is unique unto itself, rendering comparisons a foolhardy exercise; still one can carefully negotiate the minefield of generalizations to emerge with useful conclusions. What is more, it is by means of the comparative method that, quite ironically, one can nullify glib generalizations. Consider, for instance, the problem of student political activism. The failure to date to emerge with a coherent unified theory to explain it, despite its ubiquity in Africa (and to a lesser extent elsewhere—in Asia and Latin America), must be credited to the analytical obstacles thrown up by the comparative method. The suggestion, for instance, that student political activism is likely in the context of weak political institutions is negated by the experiences of apartheid South Africa. Or alternatively: that a society with deep grievances and contradictions will attract student activism is belied by the experience of the former Soviet Union, which did not experience a Tiananmen as a prelude to its disintegration. Or the suggestion that weak political states are susceptible to student activism is nullified by the experiences of Egypt. To give another example: no continent-wide survey (and the emphasis here must be on continent-wide) of any topic, including higher education, can fail to throw up the mind-numbing realization that regardless of colonial heritage (British, French, etc.) and regardless of geography (north, south, east, and west), Africa continues to bear the marks of the mode of its absorption into the post–Columbian European-dominated global economic system (see Appendix II); symptomatic of which is the current circumstances of the continent where peace and prosperity are rare far-flung isolated islands amidst an ocean of interminable chaos and misery—highlighted by this sobering fact: the majority of the world's most war-torn and poverty-stricken countries are congregated in Africa. One can go on.

(4) It is a truism that history is written by conquerors. Historical works that examine Africa's history covered by the colonial interregnum (which in strictly temporal terms is no more than a mere blip in the continent's long history) can cover acres, to exaggerate somewhat; but works for other periods while grow-

ing are much, much fewer in number. While there are good logistical reasons for this (accessibility of written records for one), it would be also true to say that it has a lot to do with what is considered as worthy history. In this work there is a conscious effort to go beyond the colonial period. Since this is a history of higher education that falls primarily within what one may call *mac-ro*educational history (one that explores the historical evolution of the nexus between education and society—in contrast to *micro*educational history that studies the history of the content of education), this has meant exploring the historical antecedents of the current state of higher education in a continent that once hosted vibrant institutions of higher education *long before Europe became the West as we know it today.*

(5) There is something deeply schizophrenic about most writings (past and present) on African history: the failure to bridge the gap, as a consequence of the enduring legacy of Eurocentric historical perspectives, between the pre-colonial and the colonial—not in terms of pointing to its existence, but *explaining* why there is this gap. That is, the identification of the processes that permitted the rise of Europe and the simultaneous subjugation of the continent, symbolic of which was the arrival of Jan Anthoniszoon van Riebeeck and his party in the lands of the Khoikhoi (1652), followed later by Napoleon's invasion of Egypt (1798), and still later (1880s onward), the infamous "Scramble for Africa." This failure to explain rather than describe is symptomatic of the Eurocentric assumption of the naturalness of this cataclysmic historical process.[30] In other words, it is not enough, to take the specific example of this work, to show that Africa was not as backward as signified by the phrase the "dark continent" by describing the existence of precolonial higher education institutions and then simply jumping from there onto to a description of the development of higher education under European colonialism. True scholarship demands historiographical *analysis* not simply historical description. That is, the demonstration of African historicity carries with it the exegetical obligation to explain the gap between the premodern and the modern in the historical trajectory of a continent that would be host to two of the most advanced civilizations in the world for their time: the Egyptian and the Islamic. However, in the effort to meet this obligation one is forced to undertake considerable digression into exploration of a number of complex variables that all hinge on the basic thesis that the rise of Europe and the demise of the Afro-Asian ecumene were two sides of the same historical coin. Consequently, this task has been reserved for Appendix II. Therein, dear reader, you will find an exploration of the logical consequences for African historiography that all historians ought to confront upon establishing the historicity of the continent (the mandate of Chapter 1).

(6) A proper account of the origin and development of so important an institution as a university cannot be abstracted from the history of the society of which it is a part. Consider, for example, this truism: Institutions of higher

learning always exist at the sufferance of the ruling (or protoruling) classes for it is their progeny who are the first and (usually) the last customers. Consequently, Is it possible at all to explore the history of a given institution of higher learning without also paying heed to the social structural configuration of the day? Not really.

(7) This work is less about the history of the inner details of higher education: the specifics of curricula, calendrical structures, finance, governance, and so on, than the external society/ higher education nexus. This is not because the former is unimportant, but because one must begin by first considering the founding of higher education institutions before one can even proceed to look at their internal workings. Now, with adequate time, space (book pages), and availability of resources, perhaps both could have been treated equally.

(8) In light of the particular historical approach adopted by this work (described earlier), it is true that this can only be a work of a generalist, but certainly not a specialist. In bringing this fact to the fore, the objective is to also question that relentless movement in history departments toward ever greater specialization and where in the academic pecking order the generalist historian is increasingly looked at askance by the specialist. This is an unfortunate development, for the field needs both, neither is more important than the other. The generalist gives meaning to the work of the specialist by rescuing it from the domain of academic navel-gazing; which also implies, conversely, that without the contributions of the specialist the generalist is left with nothing but conjectural story-telling. (This tension is akin to the one between basic research versus applied research in the sciences.) Moreover, there are dangers in over specialization; vide the warning by Rodinson (2002: 117–18) to the Orientalists, which is just as applicable to other specialists:

The demands of specialization and the desire for career advancement—both all-pervasive elements—have contributed to the Orientalists's self-satisfied acceptance of their academic ghetto. While specialization is obligatory to the conducting of serious and profound scientific work, *it tends at the same time to promote a narrow and restricted vision.* Concentrating on an academic career and on the interests of the profession is replete with attractions and dangers: the gratification obtained from recognition, the prestige of earning honor and degrees (not without personal material advantages), the excitement of struggles for power—power the scope of which is wretchedly limited but the possession of which arouses passions worthy of a Caesar or a Napoleon! It is probably inevitable that self-interested career advancement increases the distortions already caused by specialization" (emphasis added).

This problem of course also touches on another sort of generalist versus specialist tension: the disciplinary versus the interdisciplinary approach. Again, given the objectives of this work, it cannot be but interdisciplinary. Anything less would be to emerge with a highly simplistic historical picture.

(9) The historiography in this work has a penchant for multicausal explanations of major historical events. However, this approach may render one open to the complaint that all one is doing is generating a laundry list of factors (everything, including the kitchen sink!) without really explaining any thing; In other words, it is symptomatic of an unsophisticated view of history. This matter brings up a problem historians face all the time. Cain and Hopkins (1993: 51) in defense of their monocausal thesis in their magnum opus that seeks to explain the origins of British imperialism identify it this way:

We can all agree that complex events are likely to have complex causes. By drawing up an impressive list of candidates, historians can readily display their scholarship, and by including everything they can protect themselves from hungry critics on the prowl for omissions. The trouble with this procedure is that it can easily redefine the problem instead of solving it. To accept the infinite complexity of historical events is not to acquire immunity from the obligation to select some segments of evidence rather than others and to judge their relative importance. The appeal to multicausality can easily degenerate into an attempt to duck this challenge by referring to the need to avoid the errors of monocausality and determinism.

In this work, the multicausal explanations offered attempt to circumvent this problem in this way: to include only that set of variables that is of sufficient significance to render the explanation hollow with the omission of any one of them. That is, by assembling all the variables together and then by a process of subtracting/adding them it is possible to emerge with only the ones that are worthy of constituting the multicausal explanation. Obviously, others will have to judge the degree of success achieved in the effort. The truth is that, whether historians like it or not, history does not unfold neatly (except, perhaps, in their books). It is almost impossible to emerge with monocausal explanations for major historical events that transcend huge temporal and geographic boundaries. Consider for example the problem of explaining the abolition of the Atlantic slave trade, which was an important precursor to the "Scramble for Africa." Are we to simply subscribe to the explanation advanced by Eric Williams (1994 [1944]) with his emphasis on the economic (and mind you his explanation is highly persuasive) or should we go with Drescher's multicausal explanation in which the movement of the abolitionists and their allies (e.g., the working class) is also an important constituent part (see Drescher 1999). About the significance of the latter: recall that at the time when the antislavery Brussels Conference of 1889–90 took place, at which all the major powers of the day (the United States and Turkey included) were gathered, the slave trade was still a highly lucrative enterprise—especially, by that point, within Africa itself.[31]

Does it not make sense, instead, to argue that both philanthropy and politics on one hand, and economics on the other, had a part to play? That is, whereas the first abolitionist was that first unfortunate soul grabbed off the shores of

Africa, the dream of abolition would not come to pass for at least another 300 or more years in which while the antislavery philanthropic spirit was also never absent, it is only after major economic transformations had transpired (as a result of which slave labor was not only increasingly unnecessary but inimical to Western economic interests) that leant concrete political meaning to the philanthropic movement of the abolitionists. In short, demands that were once considered unreasonable became reasonable not because the moral and philosophical reasoning behind them had changed, but the social context had changed—in this case the mode of production. To give another example, Can one seriously produce a monocausal explanation for the rise of the civil rights movement in the United States (after all, *Brown v. Board of Education* had already been won by the NAACP lawyers by time the movement began)? Which historian, today, would deny that the successes (or failures) of large-scale social movements are always a function of the dialectical interplay between *agency* and *structure*—the latter expressed by the conjuncture of fortuitously propitious historical factors. One other point on this issue: on a different plane, the problem of multicausal versus monocausal explanations is often (though not always) an expression of the specialist versus generalist problematic explained earlier.

(10) Of what use is a book on a history of higher education? In an age of fragmented knowledge where history is just but one discipline among many how easy it is, sadly, to think that it is irrelevant to our lives (even though events that contradict this assumption are always before us).[32] Still, one cannot dismiss the question. After all, this book has been written for a number of audiences, among whom are also policymakers. So how can history (or in this case a history of higher education) help them? While history has many uses, the least of them is that it has lessons to teach us (in the vein of that *mythical* saying, those who do not learn the lessons of history are doomed to repeat it). Human beings are incapable of learning lessons from history (otherwise we would not, for example, have wars today) for the simple reason that each so-called lesson is contingent upon the specifics of the historical circumstances in which it occurred. History can be useful in a different way, however—in a way that is analogous to the medical history that doctors require us to give them. History permits us to understand how the present came to be the way it is, and on the basis of that knowledge we may, perhaps, attempt to forge an alternative future. The present is always a product of history, but as humans we have the capacity not to be imprisoned by that history. To point to another analogy—the logic behind the appointment of *truth and reconciliation* commissions. Whatever else their limitations may be, through catharsis and forgiveness they help to write, *on the basis of history,* a new future. However, Kallaway (who explicitly deals with this question as well) suggests a possible alternative use, with which I have no disagreement: "At best historical research can reveal the complex, contradictory reality that policymakers have to somehow accommodate

and transform. A historical perspective should provide a warning to those who are inclined to resort to narrow, dictatorial strategies that emerge from 'neat, internally consistent models' by 'indicating deep-seated trajectories of change and it helps to suggest which policy frameworks have a chance of succeeding and which are completely inappropriate'" (2002: 6).

However, there is something else to which Kallaway also alludes: While it may be self-evident to historians, it is much less so to educators that the ubiquity of institutions of higher learning today must not blind us to the fact that they represent among the highest achievements of civilization. And it is precisely for that reason their history cannot be abstracted from the history of the very civilizations they are a part. To delve into the history of institutions of higher learning is to confront the story of civilization itself in all its complexity. Those of us who are privileged to be a part of them today owe it to both our students and ourselves to know something of that rich and complex history—which includes an appreciation of the blood, sweat, and tears that accompanied the sacrifices of our progenitors. From this perspective, the study of a history of higher education does not require any justification (for it is part of who we are as educators and as beneficiaries of the learning that comes out of them).

(11) At some points in this work, some readers may deem the language as too emotive for a scholarly treatise. There are occasions in history when an effort at an *aseptic* account of events does not necessarily translate into desirable critical scholarly objectivity, but on the contrary, a barely concealed subjectivity. One such occasion from recent memory are the killings in Rwanda; another are the killings in Bosnia; and another of course is the holocaust in Nazi Germany. Have we forgotten so soon the *killing fields* of Cambodia? Is an aseptic account of these *horrendous atrocities* possible without demeaning the memory of those who perished? The same applies to the colonization of the Afro-Asian and American ecumenes by Western Europe over the course of some 400 years (from around 1500 to around 1900). That the events took place a long time ago should not in any way lessen the magnitude of the revulsion that any civilized person should feel toward these events; we owe it to the millions who died over the centuries, and who, recall, had never done anything to merit the brutality that was unleashed on them, *to describe it as it really happened* (sugar coating the events with aseptic language constitutes gross injustice—it leaves one siding with the perpetrators of these crimes against humanity). Even in more recent times the killings did not end: Is it possible to describe aseptically the unleashing of poison gas on the Ethiopians by the Italians in the course of their invasion of that country in 1935? Or the experiences of blacks under apartheid in South Africa? Is it possible at all to describe aseptically the torture, murder and imprisonment of hundreds of school children (some as young as eight or nine) by the apartheid regime at its height of madness? That the loudest cries for an aseptic rendition of this history comes from the very people whose forbears were at the heart of these events should alert one to the possi-

bility that there is something more going on here: the refusal to confront the truth and thereby grapple with its moral and philosophic consequences. The usage of labels such as pacification (compare with today's favorite term of the U.S. military—whose stated policy, incidentally, is not to keep a count of the enemy dead—collateral damage) by historians does not constitute critical objectivity. On the contrary, it is not only a shorthand way of writing off human beings as mere thrash that had to be swept aside in the interest of an imperial agenda (and to add insult to injury, justified by the hypocritical ideology of the "white man's burden"—we must slaughter you in order to civilize you!), but a shameless exercise in prostituting one's intellect.[33]

Jargon

While still on method, a word or two about jargon. Higher education as a term in this work refers primarily to that part of an educational system comprising universities and degree-granting colleges. However, when one goes back into history, in the absence of all other forms of higher education in a given society, higher education may also mean any postprimary level education (e.g., secondary-level education, teacher-training). Very often higher education institutions proper developed out of rudimentary lower-level institutions—as was the case historically in medieval Europe, for instance. To take another example, the once much-celebrated University of Makerere in Uganda began life as a vocational school, with a total of enrollment of fourteen day (in contrast to residential) students—all young males—in the founding year of 1922, that offered courses in just three subjects: carpentry, building arts, and mechanics.[34]

Following upon the excellent work of Lewis and Wigen in their *Myth of Continents* (1997), an effort has been made in this work to dispense with two egregious terms: the "third world" and "developing countries."[35] The normative hierarchy implicit in the term third world is simply unwarranted in this day and age. Moreover, it is an erroneous term now given the dissolution of the Soviet bloc and the rapid erosion of communism in China (the so-called second world). As for developing countries it simply does not make sense today (if it ever did). New categories are needed to designate the different levels of economic development.[36] While any categorization will, to some degree, be arbitrary, it must do the best it can to come as close to reality as possible without, however, becoming so unwieldy that it loses its user-friendly value; but certainly any thing is probably better than the current scheme that lumps, for example, Burkina Faso and Djibouti in the same category with Brazil and India or Ireland and Hungary with Germany and United States. Toward this end, five categories appear to strike a proper balance: predeveloping (e.g., Burkina Faso, Jamaica, Zambia); quasi-developing (e.g., Egypt, Nigeria, Pakistan, South Africa); developing (e.g., Brazil, India, Poland, Russia, South Korea); developed (e.g., Australia, Canada, Denmark); and over-developed (e.g., Britain, Germany, United States). Sometimes, where necessary, in the text these five categories will be collapsed into two primary divisions expressed as: pre/quasi/developing (PQD) countries, and over/developed (OD) countries.[37]

From the perspective of Afro-Arab Islamic Africa specifically (and the argument applies to Ethiopia as well), given its intellectual and religious heritage (described in Chapter 1 and in Appendix I), the concept of modernity must be disentangled from the two other factors associated with this concept: secularism and Westernism. That is, one must make a distinction between *modernization* (the possession of a scientistic rationality in the political/ economic/ technological domains—Hodgson's technicalism—see Appendix II), *Westernization* (signifying the influence of a Western Christian-inspired European culture: language, cuisine, clothing, holidays, entertainment, etc.); and *secularization* (the absence of an overarching religious value system). On the basis of these distinctions, to underline the foregoing, one may conjecture the following illustrative permutations: Secularization is possible without modernization or Westernization (as is evident in Turkey for example) where the key distinguishing factor is the jettisoning of Islamic religious values. Westernization may involve only the acquisition of superficial Western cultural accoutrements but not necessarily modernity (such a development is usually manifest by acquisition of Western materialist culture at the consumption-level but not the production level); and modernization does not have to involve wholesale Westernization (as has been the case in some of the Asian countries) or the abandonment of Islamic religious values.[38] Anyhow, the relevance of this fact stems from the observation that local elites (then, as today) in Islamic Africa failed to see this distinction in their demand for secular education for their progeny, which in reality turned out to be a quest for status that they hoped would not only be commensurate with that of the colonial elites, but would also distinguish them from the rest of the masses. Yet, even if we may concede that their motivations in this regard were not so calculating; and therefore the source lay elsewhere—namely, their belief that the relative backwardness of their countries was surely a function of religion, specifically Islam, they were even in this regard as much in grievous error as those who take a similar stance today, both in the East and in the West.[39] The condition of underdevelopment and all the attendant ills are surely a misfortune of not simply Afro-Arab Islamic Africa, but non-Islamic Africa too. In fact, one may broaden this observation to a global-level and point out that both Islamic countries and Christian countries—for example, those in Latin America and the Caribbean—and even Buddhist countries are plagued by this misfortune; the fundamental source of which will be explored in Appendix II.

Of the many concepts used in this work, there is one that is of such importance that it deserves special mention at this early point: the concept of *dialectic*. It is a concept that is not uncommon in philosophy, but it is not that philosophical meaning of the word that is of direct relevance here. Rather, its use in this book is more generic in the sense that it denotes the process where two seemingly unrelated factors impinge on one another *cyclically* such as to permanently render the fate of each, to be in the hands of the other. For example: factor A impinges on factor B such as to change factor B and thereby enable B to impinge on factor A, which in turn is altered, enhancing its capacity to continue impinging on factor B. Now, B is further altered, enhancing its capacity to continue impinging on factor A—and so the cycle continues. Still on jargon: for specialized terms appearing in the section dealing with higher education in Afro-Arab Islamic Africa, a glossary has been provided at the back.

STRUCTURE AND SUMMARY

Now, having laid out the broad parameters of historiographical intent and method, there remain two other matters to attend to: an outline of the structure of the book and a succinct summary of this work (if such a thing is possible considering the vast terrain that the book has been required to cover by the subject matter). The structure of this work is governed by both geographic and thematic perspectives. The geographic focus is to be found in chapters 3 through 6 in consonance with the division of the continent, for purposes of this work, into three broad regions: Afro-Arab Islamic Africa (Chapter 3), anglophone Africa (Chapter 4), and europhone Africa (Chapter 6). Anglophone Africa has merited an extra chapter because of the special historical circumstances of Ethiopia, Liberia, Namibia and South Africa (Chapter 5).

The thematic dimension of the work is handled by Chapters 1, 2, 7, and 8—in addition to Appendix 1 and 2 (already discussed in the preface). In Chapter 1, substantive comments on the central historiographical and methodological parameters of this work are indicated, while Chapter 2 explores the development of African higher education beginning in antiquity and extending into the premodern period. Chapter 7 addresses the matter of the history of foreign aid in the development of African universities over the past half a century or so, that is, in the postindependence era. Of special interest in that chapter is the now generally accepted view among scholars with more than a tangential interest in African higher education that the dominant role played by that multilateral financial institution, the World Bank, in the formation and implementation of higher education policy in Africa has been, historically, far from benign.[40] The conclusion (Chapter 8) has been assigned the task of taking stock of the legacy of European colonialism in Africa from the perspective of higher education, as well as briefly indicating what possible future may be in store for the generic public African university at a time when the relentless push toward commodification of all knowledge by the bean counters (aided and abetted by their allies, the pseudointellectual representatives of the ignorantsia), at the behest of the omnipresent globalized capital, is threatening the very concept of a university (as traditionally understood as a hallowed institution of higher learn-ing with a lineage that goes back centuries *engaged in the public good*).

Turning now to summation: The history of the development of African higher education cannot be separated from, on one hand, at the generic level, its provenance as among the embodiments of a civilization's pinnacle of achievements in which its evolution has truly been a function of global civili-zational influences, and on the other, at the specific (African) level, the given configuration of the historical matrix of political, economic, and social factors in which such an institution is perforce embedded. Consequently, it is an insti-tution that has been burdened, under the aegis of various political imperatives, by a variety of roles that go beyond the educational; and the successes and fail-ures in meeting these roles have rested on a *dialectic* between the course of its development and the configuration of the given historical matrix in a specific instance. In sum, civilizations shape institutions of higher learning in as much as institutions of higher learning shape civilizations; the inability to compre-hend this truism may be considered as among the root causes of the current aw-ful predicament of most African universities across the length and breadth of the continent.[41]

NOTES

1. The lay person, understandably, is often confused by the term historiography; it has two meanings: one denotes the study of the writing of history (that is, as a sociology of knowledge enterprise) and the other is the explanation of history by means of theo-retical analysis. In this sense, then, juxtaposing historiography against history, the latter simply denotes a description of historical events (akin to news stories); in other words, it is the datum of historiography.

2. Or consider this: in his recent published introductory text on African civilizations, Ehret (2002) is constrained to make this observation:

Africa lies at the heart of human history. It is the continent from which the distant ancestors of every one of us, no matter who we are today, originally came. Its peoples participated integrally in the great transformations of world history, from the first rise of agricultural ways of life to the vari-ous inventions of metalworking to the growth and spread of global networks of commerce....Yet traditional history books, ironically, have long treated Africa as if it were the exemplar of isolation and difference—all because of a few very recent centuries marked by the terrible events of the slave trade....That sad heritage continues to shape the envisioning of Africa today, not just in the West, but all across the non-African world and sometimes in Africa as well... .Even historians them-selves, involved these days in crafting courses and writing books on world history, find it pro-foundly difficult to integrate Africa into their global story (pp. 3–4).

There is another related matter that ought to be raised here; it concerns a form of in-tellectual arrogance that underlies the assumption that a single book, and one of modest length at that, can do justice to the history of higher education of an entire continent as huge and complex as Africa. Clearly, this is an arrogance that flows from the marginality of Africa in Western historical scholarship. Consider these facts: if one were to fit the landmass of Europe (excluding the former Soviet Union) and China altogether into Africa, there would be space left over for the whole of United States (excluding Alaska) and still enough to accommodate the whole of India! The small amount of space remaining would hold Argentina and New Zealand. Therefore, Africa, it bears repeating, is a huge continent (approximately 11,700,000 square miles, or 30,303,000 square kilometers)! However, the continent is not simply geographically enormous, but it also has a huge diversity of races, ethnicities and cultures. Through the complex historical processes of climatically influenced evolution, breeding, and immigration, Africa today has races, languages, and religions representative of almost the entire planet. Hence blacks, whites, browns and yellows are all represented in Africa. Moreover, no other continent has as many countries within it as does Africa—over fifty (comprising a quarter of the entire U.N. membership). Yet, this is not all; as just noted above, African history— recorded African history for that matter—spans millennia (rendering the celebration of the year 2000 a few years ago as nothing more than merely a celebration of the Eurocentric imprint on world calendars.) Consequently, the assumption that a single book can meaningfully accomplish a survey of the entire history of the development of higher education throughout the continent, from antiquity to the present—something that would be best entrusted to a multivolume work—is, to put it mildly, not only foolhardy, but smacks of, to repeat, arrogance! More importantly, it calls into question the usefulness of such an exercise. Given the exigencies of the scholarly publishing business, however, one is left with little choice other than the consolation that one has to begin the struggle somewhere. This book, therefore, dear reader, constitutes no more than the broadest of sketches of the development of higher education in Africa.

3. In fact, one can go so far as to say that all formal education in all societies at all times is also a political enterprise, intimately tied up with the extant power relations, regardless of from what perspective one views these relations: class, gender, race, and so on. Education is never neutral, however much one may wish it otherwise (see Carnoy 1974).

4. See Ballantyne (2002) for examples of other cultural artifacts in the service of the imperial project.

5. This is a problem that, on a much smaller scale of course, is not unlike one experienced by African American mayors of U.S. cities. After a long struggle for civil rights, African Americans managed to record significant successes among which their election to mayoral positions of large cities has been emblematic. Yet, no sooner had they taken hold of the reigns of political power they discovered that the resources that they needed to manage and develop their cities were not there because the gravity of economic power (always in the hands of Euro-Americans) had shifted from the cities to the Euro-American dominated suburbs and beyond. The outcome has been predictable: decaying inner cities with all their attendant ills—from homelessness to rampant crime to dysfunctional educational systems (see, for example, Massey and Denton 1993).

6. Yes, of course, it is true that not all colonial projects begin with economic objectives in the forefront—it is quite possible that initially other considerations may be paramount (security issues, rivalry with other powers, internal politics, etc.)—but at the end of the day, a colony must help pay its way (so to speak) in some manner. One is often stunned by the necessity to point out to Westerners (especially Eurocentrists), even

in this day and age, that Western colonialism at heart was always a project about exploitation at the economic-level and oppression at the political level; it was most certainly not a philanthropic project, nor was it about democracy and human rights. In fact, about the latter: it will do well to forcefully remind Westerners that colonialism was just as much a totalitarian political system as the other more well-known ones that would later emerge out of the ideological crucibles of fascism (Nazi Germany and Italy) and Leninist-Stalinism (China and the former Soviet Union).

7. Witness the U.S.-led democracy projects in Iraq and Afghanistan—formerly havens of oriental despots. Perhaps the most boldly articulated embodiment of the "*white man's burden*" was the mission civilisatrice of the French, which one French colonial governor, Raphael Sallers, described it thusly as late as 1944, at the Brazzaville Conference:

> Evidently, the purpose of our civilization is to bring civilization to others. So we civilize, that is to say, we are not content to provide merely a surplus of material wellbeing, but we also impose moral rules and intellectual development. And by what methods and according to whose example should we do this, if not by our own methods and according to the example of our own civilization, in the name of which alone we may speak? For what authority would we have to speak in the name of the civilization whose people we are trying to improve? (from Shipway 1999: 142).

Note: The phrase "white man's burden" comes from an 1899 poem of the same title by Rudyard Kipling, which was the notion that Europeans had a divinely mandated duty to free Africans (and other colonial peoples) from the prison of heathen darkness and savagery by bringing them into the light of Christian civilization and modernity. (In the U.S. context, this "responsibility" with respect to Africa, from the perspective of African Americans, took the form of the project for "African redemption.")

8. Compare with the subsequent arguments made by the United States and the British to justify their invasion of Iraq in 2003 once it became clear that the Iraqis did not possess weapons of mass destruction after all (the original justification for the invasion).

9. As Cherif (1989: 448, 476), for instance, observes: "it would be futile to look for the causes of the problems of nineteenth-century North Africa in purely local circumstances and to attribute these difficulties, as has been done in the past, to one-sided considerations such as the archaic nature of society, secular backwardness and the defects peculiar to the civilizations of North Africa—and not to those of Europe—in general." In other words, Cherif argues further: "Sooner or later, and with varying degrees of violence, each of the countries of the Maghreb was subjected to the same process, one which led from autonomy to dependence. It is therefore useless to seek the reason for this collapse at the local level in the errors committed by a particular ruler or in the unscrupulous behavior of a particular European agent. A single external factor, namely the expansion of Western capitalism, sealed the fate of the Maghreb, just as it sealed the fate of the rest of the non-European world."

10. In the end, as it turned out, their fears were not entirely unjustified. For, although the decolonization literature usually provides centrality to the role of the comprador elite (the nationalists) in anticolonialist struggles, if we take the example of Afro-Arab Islamic Africa, we notice that sections of the traditional Islamic elite (the ulama) played a role in this struggle too (just as sections of it, like the nationalists, played an

opposite role—cooperating with the colonialists). Take the instance of Algeria, the French attempt to completely emasculate Algeria culturally (and of course even spatially) ran into the wall of Islam. A religion that had such a pervasive role in the lives of their societies, and given the backdrop of the Crusades in their collective memory, could not be simply dismissed out of hand by a relatively brief interregnum the colonial period constituted. In other words, among the traditional institutions, the madrasah system—the haunt of the ulama— also played a role in fomenting anticolonial sentiments and inspiration.

11. Racism dictated the presence of the qualifier "almost."

12. It ought to be noted here that in ascribing motivations to the colonial project (what ever forms it took: outright colonization, imposition of protectorates, declarations of spheres of influence, etc.) what is most important at the time decisions were made was perceptions more than actual facts on the ground. That is to say that even if later it was proven that the colonial project in respect of a specific acquisition turned out to be economically unsound (in terms of hard numbers: the value of surplus extraction minus the cost of acquiring and maintaining the colony averaged annually over the life of the colony) that fact was irrelevant in terms of the original decision; belonging as it is in the category of hindsight. To be sure, economics alone, at first glance, was not the only motivator in the case of specific acquisitions; however, in the final analysis it was (even if it turned on simply strategic interests, like protecting an economically important route to some other part of the world).

13. What is also being suggested here, at the methodological level, is that the study of colonialism can elicit the most fruitful insights when it is approached by a tripartite comparative method: temporal (e.g., pre and postindustrial capitalism); competing models (e.g., settler colonialism versus trusteeship colonialism); and contrasting national styles (e.g., French versus English, or *indirect rule* versus direct rule).

14. The absorption was only in a hierarchic sense—the colonies, even in the postindependence period when nominal political control by the metropole had been terminated, would always remain the metropole's hinterland.

15. Who can doubt, for example, that the jingoistic rise of French nationalism within Europe (shaped to some extent by the traumatic psychological fallout emanating from such misadventures as the Franco-Prussian War (July 19, 1870–May 10, 1871) and the subsequent loss of Alsace-Lorraine—not to mention the earlier Napoleonic debacles at the Battles of Trafalgar (October 21, 1805) and Waterloo (June 18, 1815)—had a major ideological impact on the political calculus of the architects of the French colonial project as visions of a grand French empire continued to dance in their heads (even if this time it meant going outside Europe altogether). In fact, Lucas (1964: 26), among others, is explicit on this: "In 1875, French pride was still deeply wounded by the loss of Alsace-Lorraine [it was regained permanently only after World War II] in the Franco-Prussian War.... Then a group of politicians led by Jules Ferry saw a way to divert French attention from Alsace-Lorraine, and at the same time to demonstrate French vitality to the world: France would regain prestige and grandeur by conquering a new colonial empire. Discreetly encouraged by Bismarck, France set out to acquire her largest empire in history: Indo-China, North, West and Equatorial Africa."

16. Take the example of British colonial Africa, the educational policy—which was forged, as Reilly (1995) has shown, in the colonial education laboratories, of Ireland,

Jamaica, the southern U.S. and British colonial India—that would be pursued in that part of Africa was a dual pronged policy where on one hand education would be aimed at increasing the productive capacity of the servile masses without encouraging among them notions of upward mobility, and on the other a small cadre of Fanonian compradorial elite would be nurtured to assist with maintaining the colonial order (but in the case of neither group would education be permitted to encourage demands for freedom). The task regarding the latter was best described by Thomas Macaulay of colonial India's Supreme Council and head of the Committee of Public Instruction in 1835: "We must at present do our best to form a class who may be interpreters between us and the millions whom we govern; a class of persons, Indian in blood and color, but English in taste, in opinions, in morals, and in intellect" (Macaulay 1935 [1835]: 349). Yet there was a contradiction in such a policy that did not entirely escape the colonialists themselves; as one of them would astutely observe: "If well directed, the progress of education would undoubtedly increase our moral hold over India, but, by leading the Natives to a consciousness of their own strength, it will as surely weaken our physical means of keeping them in subjection" (from Carnoy 1974: 92). One may also note here parenthetically that even after independence had been achieved, the essential principle underlying the original colonial education policy—increasing the exploitive value of labor without encouraging revolt—would never be completely abandoned and in fact remains the unarticulated part of the mission of African higher education to this day (this time at the behest of globalization, which, in truth, is nothing more than a pseudonym for old-fashioned postindependence Western imperialism).

17. See Ruedy's discussion of these strategies in relation to the Algerian experience for example to see how these strategies were implemented (Ruedy 1992). Note: A glossary of key Islamic terms has been provided at the back of the book.

18. Examples of this phenomenon are legion even in noncolonial contexts: Communist China, the Communist Eastern Europe, Occupied Palestine, apartheid South Africa, and so on. Take China, for instance, in the context of its highly regimented education system, it would appear that on the face of it Tiananmen should have been an impossibility.

19. Colonialism was rarely a peaceful affair. While it is impossible to know precisely how many throughout the Afro-Eurasian and American ecumene were murdered in the course of implementing the Western colonial project, in the nineteenth-century alone, a combined figure of a half a million per year average would not be far fetched (see Ahmed 1992).

20. The functions of racism were complex; on one hand, it was used directly to justify colonialism (the colonized were an inferior peoples—their inferiority was attested to by their cultural and physiognomic difference as well as their failure to resist their colonial subjugation in the first place—hence not only they did not deserve the natural resources they possessed, but they were destined to be hewers of wood and drawers of water for Europeans), and on the other, it was used to underwrite policies (e.g., in the area of education) that were instrumental in justifying and maintaining colonialism ("white man's burden"). Generally speaking, the former function held sway where permanent colonial settlement was the desired end, while the latter was relevant to those situations (such as in the case of protectorates) where permanent settlement was not an immediate objective.

21. Two basic approaches by Western anthropologists had proven particularly fruitful on this matter: the study of the behavior of the oppressed (but, tellingly, minus its structural determinants); and the biological determinist-driven study of physiognomy. Taking Britain as an example, they studied the urban poor (who were classified a separate race by the upper classes), and the Irish (arguably the first colonial subjects of the British) and concluded that the ills that plagued them (including poverty, unemployment and homelessness) was attributable to their racial inferiority! On the basis of their spurious findings they emerged with their racial hierarchies where the wealthy Anglo-Saxon male was placed at the pinnacle, and subject peoples in the colonies in North America, and later elsewhere, at the very bottom (and their own poor, the Irish, Jews and other Europeans, in between). A similar line of thinking also developed in France, well described by Cohen (1980). By the middle of the nineteenth-century, to turn to the second approach, they came up with the "science" of *phrenology* and *craniometry* (also well described by Cohen). Specifically, they argued that the supposed lack of cultural, economic and political achievements among blacks when contrasted with that of the Europeans spoke to their status as inferior beings—which was proven by the fact that they differed physically from whites in their skin color, facial and skeletal structure, and above all the size of their crania. The last was considered particularly important because it was suggested, falsely, that cranium size determined brain size (and hence intellect) and a comparative study of the crania of blacks and whites, they again falsely argued, showed that the latter's was bigger than the former's. Not surprisingly, the collection and measurement of skulls became an important activity of European anthropologists, with the European skull serving as the benchmark for the norm. Statistical measurement of skulls as a way of indicating everything from a propensity for crime to class origins to gender roles and above all racial hierarchy soon gave rise to the fields of craniometry and phrenology. European physical anthropologists came to believe that through such measurements they could scientifically prove the existence of a racial hierarchy among humans. In an age when scientism was all the rage who could fail to accept these scientific findings. With the coincidence of this age with the age of Western imperialism (scientism was in fact nurtured by this imperialism), it is little wonder that racism among European intellectuals (let alone the European masses) became firmly entrenched (and continues to this day, in various guises, to shape their thinking on almost all matters of relevance to peoples outside Western Europe—vide Eurocentrism, see Appendix II). As for relevant names, those familiar with the literature on the subject will recognize the following as among the many dramatis personae of social Darwinism and racist anthropology: Louis Agassiz, Charles Davenport, William Edwards, Franz Joseph Gall, Francis Galton, Comte de Joseph-Arthur Gobineau, Samuel Morton, Herbert Spencer, and William Graham Sumner. Considering that the issue of race often tends to be neglected in discussions of the ideological provenance of colonial thinking and policy by Western historians in general (by both, those on the left and the right), especially when writing about colonial education, the reader may wish to pursue the subject further by consulting the following sources: Asad (1991); Cohen (1980); Curtis (1968); Himmelfarb (1983); Lorimer (1978); Mangan (1993); Pieterse (1992); Reilly (1995); Said (1993); Smedley (1993); Shipman (1994); Stocking (1982 1988). (See also the discussion of the Hamitic theory in Chapter 2.)

22. There is a profoundly sad irony in the origins of this model; as will be evident in

a moment, an African American came to play a pivotal role in its genesis, a man by the name of Booker T. Washington. The Tuskegee Institute (to be also called Tuskegee College, and today continues on as Tuskegee University) began its life as a teacher training college in a place from which it took its name; it was established in 1881 by the state of Alabama. The Euro-American trustees of the college appointed Booker T. Washington to head the new institution upon advice from his mentor Samuel Chapman Armstrong—the Euro-American brigadier general who had been in charge of African American troops during the U.S. Civil War and who, with philanthropic help, had founded in 1868 Tuskegee's precursor, Hampton Institute, to train recently emancipated African Americans in the industrial arts. Taking Armstrong's educational philosophy (known as the Hampton idea) of combining training in practical vocational skills with Christian morality, a strong work ethic, and a deep sense of gratitude toward and humility before one's (white) benefactors, Washington developed it further almost to the level of a religion. Faced with the reality of an unrelenting, brutal and ever-spiraling terrorism unleashed on African Americans by Euro-Americans under the aegis of the protofascist Jim Crow laws that came to govern the South in the postreconstruction era—among the hallmarks of which was the routine gruesome murders (lynching) every year of innocent African Americans by the score all over the South, as well as anyone else who dared to oppose these laws, by Euro-American mobs dressed in their Sunday best (so as to obliterate the recently won civil and human rights of African Americans in the service, at the core, of that age-old problem of Southern agrocapitalists, access to a plentiful supply of cheap labor)—Washington took to heart the Hampton idea and publicized it with even greater fervor by politicizing it. Note: for a visual history and the historical significance of lynching see Allen, Als, Lewis, and Litwack (2000); Apel (2004); Dray (2002); Tolnay and Beck (1995); and Wells-Barnett (1997). Arguing that the road to the recapture of civil rights by African Americans did not lie in political agitation, but exemplary hard work and Christian morality, Washington would immortalize himself by that oft quoted line in a speech he delivered on the occasion of the Cotton States and International Exposition in Atlanta in 1895 (to which he had been invited to speak by its Euro-American organizers), that came to be known as the Atlanta Compromise:

To those of the white race who look to the incoming of those of foreign birth and strange tongue and habits for the prosperity of the South, were I permitted I would repeat what I say to my own race, "Cast down your bucket where you are." Cast it down among the 8,000,000 Negroes whose habits you know.... [For],...you can be sure in the future, as in the past, that you and your families will be surrounded by the most patient, faithful, law-abiding, and unresentful people that the world has seen....In all things that are purely social we can be as separate as the fingers, yet one has the hand in all things essential in mutual progress. (Washington 1985 [1895]: 151–52)

Earlier in the same speech Washington had told his mainly Euro-American audience that because of ignorance and inexperience, African Americans had been in error, following emancipation, in pursuing the very top instead of beginning at the bottom: "that a seat in Congress or the State Legislature was more sought than real estate or industrial skill; that the political convention or stump speaking had more attractions than starting a dairy farm or truck garden" (p. 150). It is not clear whether Washington sincerely believed in what he preached as he went around the country; or, like a politician, he was merely grandstanding and telling his (usually Euro-American audience) what they wanted to hear (surely, a man as astute as Washington must have known that the economic salvation of African Americans he was championing was dialectically intertwined with their political salvation; that is, in the contradictory world of a capitalist racist democracy, one was not possible without the other). What is clear, however, is that against the backdrop of Jim Crow, the Euro-American establishment heard what they wanted to hear; they would reward him accordingly through gifts to "his" Institute—as well as personally to himself (materially and otherwise). To put the matter differently: his—perhaps understandable—pragmatic response to Jim Crow terror was fortified by the dialectic between the growth of Tuskegee, together with his personal stature, and his advocacy of uncle tommery. In other words, then, until the civil rights movement came into being in the late 1950s, Tuskegee became the educational beacon of the hat in hand, "yes Masah!" uncle tom strategy of grappling with the always potentially volatile black/white race-relations in the United States, and in colonial Africa. Little wonder then, that patronizing white liberals like Thomas Jesse Jones and Charles T. Loram (who mistook their racism, like so many white liberals of today, for wholesome liberalism—recall that neither had ever publicly championed opposition to Jim Crow or apartheid), together with those blacks like James E. Kwegyir Aggrey who aspired to fill Washington's (uncle tom) shoes, became fervent advocates of the Hampton/Tuskegee model and philosophy. Yes, of course, there was a touch of hypocrisy in all this; for none of the fervent advocates of industrial education would have risen to the commanding heights of the world of black education (which had given them the opportunity to prescribe industrial education for others) on a diet of that same education; on the contrary, they had received (and/or self-taught) the same liberal classical education that they did not wish others to have!

It goes without saying that even in its day, the Hampton/Tuskegee model was not received with equanimity by everyone; it drew considerable criticism from some sections of the black community on both sides of the Atlantic. In the United States, men such as W.E.B. DuBois saw the model for what it was—an attempt to create an obedient conservative black underclass unwilling to challenge the Jim Crow status quo. Writing some decades after the founding of Tuskegee, he would comment:

The system of learning which bases itself upon the actual condition of certain classes and groups of human beings is tempted to suppress a minor premise of fatal menace. It proposes that the knowledge given and the methods pursued in such institutions of learning shall be for the definite object of perpetuating present conditions or of leaving their amelioration in the hands of and at the initiative of other forces and other folk. This was the great criticism that those of us who fought for higher education of Negroes thirty years ago brought against the industrial school (DuBois 1996: 417).

In Africa, harsh criticism by some was also reserved for people like Aggrey. For example, when the Phelps-Stokes Education Commission visited South Africa, James S. Thaele, a leading pro-Garvey African National Congress official in Cape Town, who himself had studied in the United States, described Aggrey as "that theologian whom, in the American terminology, we simply dismiss as 'a me-too-boss-hat-in-hand nigger'." Many black South Africans were especially incensed at statements such as the following by Aggrey: "In this year of 1921, the spirit of the union, of British justice, is in this land; it is being felt now as never before because of the War and because of the restlessness. What we need is some great messiah of the Anglo-Saxon race to rise up and give fair play and reciprocity. I have dedicated my life to see that we work for cooperation. I pray that before long South Africa will be the best place on earth for white and black; so that Great Britain may lead the whole world; that the lion and the lamb shall lie down together, and a little child may lead them" (Hill and Pirio 1987: 229). Reilly (1995) has suggested that Aggrey's role in British colonial Africa was the same as that of Booker T. Washington's in the U.S. South—as an antidote to black nationalism. (For a biography of Aggrey, who would later become the principal of Achimota College, which was commissioned by the Phelps-Stokes Fund, see Smith 1971 [1929].) At the end of the day, as King (1971: 258) points out, the very notion that "the Negro could by education be immunized against politics," was foolhardy indeed. It did not work in the United States and neither did it work in Africa; for education by its very nature is always subversive.

23. The Phelps-Stokes Fund was founded in 1911 through the generosity of the granddaughter of Daniel Lindley (a U.S. missionary who had worked in South Africa), Caroline Phelps-Stokes, following her death two years earlier. The Phelps family, as the name suggests, was closely linked to the transnational corporation, Phelps-Dodge Corporation. In her will, she had specified that the income from the endowment that was the fund was to be expended for a number of social welfare purposes as well as "for the education of Negroes, both in Africa and the United States....through industrial schools" (from United States 1916 [vol. 1]: xi). See King (1971) for more on the education-related work of the Fund in the United States and in Africa.

24. Jim Crow refers to the racial segregation that had existed de facto in the United States prior to the Civil War (primarily brought about as a result of the massive immigration of the European working class and peasantry to the United States in the early 1800s) that became de jure following the abolition of slavery with the return of the former confederate governments to power in the post–Reconstruction era (effected through the use of terror—see Nieman 1991) in spite of the 13th, 14th and 15th Amendments to the U.S. constitution that had firmly established the civil and human rights of African Americans. The power of an alliance of white agrarian and urban capitalist classes in the U.S. South bent on restoring as many features of the old slave order as possible, operating through such terrorist groups as the Ku Klux Klan, was such that not only did they systematically and brutally disenfranchise African Americans (and other blacks), but managed to create a political and legal environment in which the U.S. Supreme Court reversed the legislative intent of the amendments—by means of a ruling in an infamous case called *Plessey v. Ferguson* (1896) that came up with the bogus concept of separate but equal. (The concept would not be overturned until its ruling in another case, *Brown v. Board of Education* [1954]). However, like its counterpart, apartheid (in South Africa), Jim Crow evolved to be more than simply racial segregation; it was a neofascist political order, a protototalitarian system in which the civil and human rights of those whites who opposed racial segregation (albeit a tiny minority) were also wiped out. The term Jim Crow itself is said to originate from a song sung by an enslaved African American owned by a Mr. Crow and overheard and later popularized (beginning in 1828 in Louisville) by Daddy Rice (Thomas Dartmouth Rice) through the medium of

black minstrel shows—comedic song and dance routines performed by whites in black-face based on highly demeaning negative stereotypes of African Americans. The song's refrain went:

Wheel about and turn about
And do jis so,
Ebry time I wheel about
I jump Jim Crow

For more on Jim Crow the following sources considered together should suffice: Allen (1994), Nieman (1991), Patterson (2001), Pfeifer (2004), Watkins (1994). (See also the resources at the website www.jimcrowhistory.org.)

25. The Atlantic Charter was a press release issued on August 14, 1941 (following a secret meeting on a ship off the coast of New Foundland between U.S. president Franklin Roosevelt and British prime minister Winston Churchill), had made reference in Article III to the right of all peoples to self-determination of government, and freedom. Even though the charter was formulated with the European peoples in mind, elites in the colonies, in bouts of grandiose optimism, looked upon the document as the death knell for imperialism everywhere. The United States was perceived by many Asian and African leaders as the harbinger of their freedom. This was an illusion; for, as Noer (1985: 17) has correctly observed, the United States did not really include the European colonies in its rhetoric on self-determination, freedom, and human-rights. (Of course, in a very different sense, both Britain and the United States were indirectly responsible for the present freedom of these former European colonies. One only has to surmise with horror what their fate would have been had the Germans and their fascist ally, Italy, won the Second World War.)

26. Those that were specific to a region (as in the case of say Afro-Arab Islamic Africa) are covered in the appropriate chapters below.

27. To highlight the biases that plague Western history, consider Glubb's comment on Islam (which in the pages that follow will consume some of our attention):

I have referred on several past occasions to the extraordinarily narrow prejudices which, for many centuries, have governed the teaching of history in the West. One of the deepest of these prejudices has been the omission of the history of the Muslim nations from the syllabuses of schools and universities. This omission was doubtless based on the hatreds bred in the long wars between the Muslims and the Christian West, from the rise of Islam in the seventh-century to the dominance of Europe in the seventeenth—a 1,000 years of struggle for power. Today, perhaps, some people are ready to admit that true history is the history of the human race and that the great Muslim nations of the past contributed generously to the culture of the West today. But prejudices imbibed for so many centuries die hard. Historical works on Greece, Rome and Europe continue to increase on our bookshelves, but works on the past history of the Muslim nations are few and far between (Glubb 1973: 7).

28. In fact, the difficulties that plague the historian's craft are highlighted by considering a problem that is rarely addressed by historians, if ever: that life is full of most amazing coincidences. Consequently, what a historian may ascribe to a set of events as a product of deliberative human agency may simply have been an outcome of a coinci-

dence and no more!

29. For accessible summaries of these and other approaches to historiography see Berger, Feldner, and Passmore (2003); Cohen and Roth (1995); Green and Troup (1999); and Stuchtey and Fuchs (2003).

30. The forcefulness of this point is brought up every time I ask my students the question: Why is it that it was Africans (and not some other people) who were enslaved in the Americas? The usual answer I get is because they were black. Of course, this problem is part of a wider one: the continuing marginality (with a few exceptions) of Africa in Western-authored world histories (see the summative discussion, for instance, by Eckert 2003.)

31. See Miers 1975 for a fascinating account of the conference, its antecedents and the consequences of the Brussels Act (General Act for the Repression of African Slave Trade)—signed on July 2, 1890. (The text of the Act is reproduced in Miers as Appendix 1, pp. 346–63.) In addition to the sources mentioned, see also Carrington (1988); Solow and Engerman (1987); and Solow (1991) for more on the debate concerning the abolition of the Atlantic slave trade.

32. Compare the ongoing spirited effort to rewrite the history of a U.S. presidency (Reagan) even before its principal architect's dead body has turned cold. In fact, just the other day, a student exasperatedly blurted out, "you can't change history, so why do we have to learn it?" A birthday marks a historical event. Why do you celebrate your birthday? (Gifts... Ahhh gifts).

33. How powerfully enduring the ideology of the "*white man's burden*" is can be assessed by even a cursory examination of the rhetoric in the West (especially in the United States) surrounding the recent U.S. invasions of Afghanistan and Iraq in which countless thousands of innocent civilians, many of them children, have perished.

34. It is from such inauspicious beginnings that the university would eventually emerge. For more on the institution see Chapter 4.

35. They, of course, systematically expose the ridiculousness and the inherent political nature (Eurocentric) of other terms as well, such as the Middle East. Consider, Morocco lies west of England; How then can Morocco be viewed as part of the so-called Middle East'? In any case, Where does the East begin and the Middle East end, or where does the West end and the Middle East begin—especially on a spherical planet? The term Middle East, it may be noted, arose to solve two ideological problems facing Latin Europe: how to marginalize, on one hand, Communist Europe (considered part of the East), and on the other, Islamic Mediterranean/ Red Sea region (also considered part of the East). "The most popular solution has been," they state, "to designate a new entity, the Middle East, and to give it quasi-continental status as an interstitial area linking Europe, Asia and Africa" (p. 63). However, to take on all of the current meta-geographic misusage in this work would place undue burdens on the reader. One has to leave part of the struggle, then, for another time.

36. Leys (1971: 32), writing more than three decades ago pointed out the problem: "The very expression developing countries has come to sound embarrassing precisely because it so obviously rests on the linear conception [of development] and sometimes refers to countries which are in fact stagnating or even regressing." (For more on the concept of linearity, exemplified by the Rostowian take-off trajectory, see Chapter 7.)

37. Of course, no one ever dares to admit, be it academics or politicians, the inher-

ent dissemblance that undergirds such terminology—that in order for all to achieve the much sought after status of developed we would need the resources of three or more planet earths combined since the present status of the over developed is being maintained on the basis of their consumption of more than two-thirds of the world's resources (even though they constitute a mere one third of the world's population).

38. The phenomenon of the resurgence of the so-called Islamism today in most of Afro-Arab Islamic Africa (and elsewhere) is but a symptom of this definitional difference which the West has missed in its myopic analysis of the situation, positing it as a phenomenon of incomprehensible religion-inspired "civilizational luddism" that harks back to a medieval era.

39. However, the temptation to pursue such an erroneous line of thinking is so strong that it continues to be publicly articulated. Witness the remarks of the former head of the Anglican church in England, Lord Carey, at a talk in Rome on March 25th, 2004, in which he linked Islam with inherent backwardness. (News story available at www.bbc.com.)

40. Those who choose to read only Chapter 7 but not the rest of the work, and even then only cursorily, may come away somewhat confused. See endnote 110 in Chapter 3, as to why.

41. One other matter, which appropriately belongs to notes: This work is replete with numerous and sometimes lengthy explanatory notes. The point of raising this readily observable fact? As an expression of the anti-intellectual and anti-scholarly tradition that runs through the entire 350-year history of our plebian dominated intellectual culture in this country (itself an expression of the station in life that most of our immigrant forebears sprang from) we often have an exasperated impatience with notes. But if the text of (especially) a work of history can be likened to a tree, then the notes are the leaves without which the text is reduced to a limp, simplistic and less than vibrant rendition of the subject matter. For, the nuances of the complexity of a subject such as history (especially one with a topic that attempts to cover, at a considerable risk of pretentiousness, an entire continent, and not only that, but with a timeline that ranges from antiquity to the present!) simply cannot be captured entirely in the text without seriously damaging its organizational coherence. With this justification, then, dear reader, you are urged to read the notes too.

2

Premodern Africa

History without historiography is meaningless. This chapter, therefore, has two objectives: one is to establish the precolonial historical record; the other is to confront the more contentious task of examining the larger theoretical implications of this record. Ultimately any historical record is of value only to the extent that it is the subject of a historiographical exegesis. (Upon further reflection, it appears that the historical record is equally contentious, as will be evident shortly.) First, however, a necessary point of prolegomena: The conventional dichotomous periodization by historians of African history into, principally, the precolonial and colonial periods may give pause to those seeking an anti-Eurocentric perspective on African history (see Appendix II). The matter raises not only the issue of a foreign (in this case European) temporal standard as a marker of African historical chronology (How often does one come across, for example, a periodization of European history labeled "Europe during the pre-imperialist period" or "Europe during the imperialist period?"), but as if that is not enough, there is the underlying implication of not only a general failure among historians to provide an equitable historical treatment of both sides of the dichotomous divide—hence suggestive of the relative unimportance of a strictly African history versus the hybridized Euro-African history, especially when viewed against the unequal weights of time involved (temporally, the colonial period is merely an infinitesimal blip when compared to the precolonial period, which stretches back in time to the very birth of humankind several million years ago)—but also a dyadic evaluational dimension to the dichotomy, usually manifest at the subterranean level of "ideology": savagery versus civilization, darkness versus light, evil versus good, stasis versus progress, primitive versus modern, and so on.

Now, if one is cognizant of this problem as pervading much of African history, why then repeat this convention in this work? What is more, as if to add insult to injury, only one chapter is devoted to the precolonial era, while the rest of the book, in essence, covers the colonial period on, up to the present. There are three principal reasons that may be adduced in defense, but strictly from the perspective of this particular work. It is a matter of incontrovertible historical fact that there were simply far fewer institutions of higher education during the precolonial period than during the colonial period; in terms of human history (not prehistory), the precolonial period was never simply a purely African period, any more than say a European historical period was purely European, or an Asian historical period was purely Asian. The colonial period, whether one likes it or not, marked a permanent rupture from all that had gone on before of such level and magnitude as to force on any historian of Africa the perspective of a dichotomous periodization—though not necessarily with the ideological baggage it has come to acquire (see Appendix II).

THE HISTORICAL RECORD

In consideration of the enormous weight given in history books to that period of African history that commences with the arrival of Europeans in Africa under the aegis of the European voyages of "exploitation" and later, imperialism (see Appendix II), it is necessary to begin with the following question: Did higher education exist in precolonial Africa at all? If there is one person who can be credited with producing one of the earliest works on the history of higher education in Africa, then it is Eric Ashby. His response to this question is, therefore, of interest. His answer is, yes, higher education "is not new to the continent of Africa, but the modern universities in Africa," he continues, "*owe nothing to this ancient tradition of scholarship*" (emphasis added). He states further, "[t]he modern universities of Africa have their roots not in any indigenous system of education, but in a system brought from the West" (1966: 147). In other words, according to Ashby, the existence of premodern higher education is of no relevance to considerations of modern higher education in Africa today. Why? Because there is no continuity between precolonial higher education and modern African higher education, which he asserts is an entirely Western invention.

Of course, Ashby neglects to explain why there is no continuity: the deflection of the African historical trajectory by the intrusion of European imperialism. Be that as it may, Ashby is, by and large correct about the matter of continuity, but he is absolutely mistaken about the second assertion (see Appendix I). In any case, whether or not precolonial higher education institutions in Africa have any relevance to the development of modern higher education in Africa today, it is still necessary to consider them, if for no other reason than to firmly register the point, that African history does not begin only with the arrival of European colonialism. In other words, for the sake of historical accuracy, any survey of the historical development of higher education in Africa must consider its entire history. Yet, there is more to this matter than just the issue of historical accuracy, as will be indicated in the conclusion to this chapter.

In the effort to identify the existence of precolonial higher education institutions in Africa, it would help by first noting that higher education cannot exist in any society without the presence of books, which in turn requires the availability of the written word. Historically, the origins of writing and books have generally been associated with the emergence of an organized state and/ or organized religion (usually the two have gone hand in hand in a theocratic alliance). In other words, writing and books emerged as a response to the bureaucratic needs of the state and/ or the requirements of religious practice and education. (This certainly was the case in that most ancient of known civilizations, the Sumerian; see Kramer 1981.) In time, once the written language was invented, it also became available for scholarly pursuits of a more secular nature to eventually effect the displacement of the oral tradition by the written one. In other words, writing marginalized the bard and the orator and the writer and the scholar took their place. "Civilization has few miracles," as Parsons (1952: 106) sagely observes, "to compare with the transmission of ancient learning on frail papyrus or tougher parchment." Not surprisingly, then, in the case of precolonial Africa all instances of higher education that are known of so far are associated with religions and their religious books—which, needless to say, presuppose the existence of written languages; there are principally three: that of the ancient Egyptians, that of the Ethiopian Christians, and that of the Muslims. Therefore, the account that follows structurally corresponds to the geographic domains of these three.[1] Also note that in the absence of a separate secular educational system, as was the case with most premodern societies with rare exception, religious higher education institutions did double duty: they provided training for both religious and secular (state) purposes.

HIGHER EDUCATION IN ANCIENT EGYPT

Pharaonic Egypt's Per-ankh

The transition of human societies from rudimentary forms of social existence, rooted in a hunting-and-gathering mode of production, to more complex forms marked by such features as settled agriculture, urbanization, literacy, social differentiation, a redistributive economy, state formation with well-defined political structures (that is, all those features that speak to only one fundamental factor: the existence of surplus)—and that may legitimately be termed as civilization in its nonjudgmental sense—does not appear to have a definitive causal factor, other than the presence of one critical variable: agriculturally easy access to a constant and plentiful food supply. This itself, it must be stressed, is an arbitrary function of climate and geography. (The succinctly summarized comparative study by Bard and Fattovich (2001) of early state formation in the Egypt and Ethiopia of antiquity, with their vastly differing climatic and geographic environments, is highly illustrative.)

It is not surprising then that the chance discovery by the Neolithic peoples of Northeast Africa of the existence of rich alluvial soils in the Nile valley in Egypt amidst an ocean of slowly but relentlessly desiccating Sahara, would unknowingly propel them toward the creation of one of Africa's and the world's early great civilizations: the Egyptian civilization. Along the way, in this cultural journey, they were probably assisted by their geographic proximity to other peoples—especially those of the Near East (Mesopotamia, for example), from whom they would receive via direct and indirect economic interactions periodic infusions of critical genetic and cultural material (in the form of immigrants, foods, agricultural practices, artistic and architectural traditions, etc.) that would become the basis for some of their own innovations to give rise to an African civilization that was unique to itself—the key word here is unique. The chronological zone of transition within which this process occurred was probably around 5000 to around 3000 B.C.E., by which time the known dynastic period of Egyptian history would commence and the capstone in the march toward civilization, the invention of writing (in this case the Egyptian hieroglyphic writing), would be firmly in place. Defensively insulated by the Sahara, the Africans of Egypt would have the luxury, for almost 2,000 years, to devote most of their energy toward unprecedented cultural, artistic, and architectural achievements.[2]

It follows, then, that the quest for the first instance of higher education institutions in Africa must perforce begin in ancient Egypt. Logic would suggest that any civilization that was as accomplished and sophisticated as the Egyptian civilization, and that was of such considerable longevity, must have had some type of formal educational system to impart the high arts, religious education, medical education, and so on, to the younger generation. In other words, individualized (usually familial-based) apprenticeship alone may not have been a sufficient vehicle for this purpose. After all, it is now well-known that from around c. 3000 B.C.E. there existed, as Bernal (2001) points out, specialized professions (e.g., astronomy, medicine, magic, scribal arts). To be sure, the Egyptians may not have had exact replicas of the modern university or college, but it is certainly true that they did possess an institution that, from their perspective, fulfilled some of the roles of a higher education institution. One such institution dating from around c. 2000 B.C.E. was the *per-ankh* (or the House of Life). It was located within the Egyptian temples, which usually took the form of huge campuses, with many buildings, and thousands of employees.[3]

Now, some have referred to the *per-ankh* as a library or a "scriptorium," where scribes wrote and kept their papyri. This indeed it was, but it should be emphasized that the *per-ankh* was no ordinary library. The *per-ankh* was in essence an institution of multiple roles. Yes, it was a repository for the sacred texts, but it also housed the administrative records of the kingdom, as well as the temple itself. Yet, it appears that it did more than that: it was also the place where texts on all the various branches of Egyptian religious, philosophical, medical, and scientific knowledge were produced and stored. However, it has been suggested that there also existed separate institutions that served as libraries in the usual sense (see Clagett 1989). Ghalioungui (1973: 30) reminds us that even as early as the sixth dynasty (2345 B.C.E.) there is reference to a high civil servant as the Governor of the House of Books, pointing to the presence of important collections of papyri. (Later, perhaps, it may be conjectured, these Houses of Books would become part of the *per-ankh*s.)

Moreover, it should be pointed out here that the term scribe describes someone who was more than just simply a manuscript-copying clerk; rather, the scribe was a learned person who combined within him (evidence so far suggests that they were all males) the "training of a calligrapher, a philosopher, a scholar, and a scientist" (Ghalioungui 1973: 28; see also Clagett 1989).[4] Consider, for instance, how the scribe who was nominated by the priests to accompany the pharaoh Psammetik II on his journey to Syria was addressed in explaining his nomination: "None other than you in this town can leave for Syria; look, you are a Scribe of the House of Life, there is nothing on which you would be questioned to which you would not find an answer" (from Ghalioungui,1973: 66). From this perspective, then, the *per-ankh* was also a research institute of a kind where new knowledge was brought forth out of the old. In fact, it is thought that even Greek physicians visited the *per-ankh* at Memphis to study the medical texts housed there (Wilkinson 2000: 74). Ghalioungui (1973: 63–64) goes a step further on this point: he discusses the very high probability that such Greek luminaries as Plato, no less, made scholarly visits to ancient Egypt. He, interestingly, points out that from at least the Eighteenth Dynasty there were Greek interpreters present at the royal palace.

At the same time, the *per-ankh* was also a higher educational institution of sorts that like other higher educational institutions that were to emerge in other parts of the world thousands of years on, combined religious education with secular education. For the Egyptians, as would be the case for many other peoples in millennia to come, knowledge did not neatly divide into the religious and the secular; to them each flowed seamlessly into the other—as is so clearly indicated in that masterly synthesis of evidence from a host of papyri (Edwin Smith, Chester Beatty, Carlsberg, Kahoun, Ramesseum, Leyden, London, Berlin, etc.), and a variety of archeological sources, that Paul Ghalioungui's riveting study of medical science in ancient Egypt, *The House of Life, Per-ankh: Magic and Medical Science in Ancient Egypt* (1973), represents. Therefore, those destined for the professions (scribes, doctors, lawyers, architects, astronomers, etc.) received their education alongside those who were to join the priesthood in the *per-ankh*. In this regard, compare with the early medieval European and Islamic universities. Clearly, as Wilkinson (2000: 74) observes, the genealogical roots of the very concept of a university as it was to be developed hundreds of years later by the Islamic and Christian societies—as, in its most elemental sense, a gathering of religious and secular scholars for the purpose of research and study—can be traced to the *per-ankh*.[5] Moreover, the *per-ankh* was not only restricted to the teaching of theoretical knowledge, it was also a place for the teaching of the practical arts such as sculpture and other crafts. It is also thought that the pharaohs themselves sometimes studied in these institutions; this certainly appears to have been the case with Ramses IV, a literary person of considerable knowledge (Ghalioungui 1973: 67).

The eventual demise of the Egyptian civilization also, of course, spelled the demise of the *per-ankh*. To account for the end of this uniquely African civilization is a task that lies well outside the subject matter of this book. Ergo, it will suffice to simply note that the civilization began its downward spiral starting roughly with the Twenty-Third Dynasty in 1070 B.C.E. as a result of a combination of factors, such as internal corruption, imperialistic ambitions, foreign invasions, and so on, so that by the time Alexander the Conqueror arrived in Egypt some 700 years later, in 332 B.C.E., the civilization of ancient Egypt was well into its twilight (see Mysliwiec 2000 for a fascinating account of this late period of ancient Egyptian history).

Now, interestingly, the next instance of higher education in ancient Africa that is known of, so far, is still to be found in ancient Egypt, but it emerges during the period of the Ptolemaic dynasty in the form of the *Bibliotheca Alexandrina* complex. Before proceeding further, however, two additional points need to be made: (1) Had the *per-ankh*s of ancient Egypt undertaken systematic credentialing of bodies of students—there is, however, no evidence yet unearthed that points to this—then their designation as universities in the true sense of the word would not be farfetched. Nevertheless, it is necessary to stress this point: as Ghalioungui (1973) and Canfora (1990), for example, observe, the Alexandrina complex was heir to the legacy of the *per-ankh* as a religio-secular institution that gathered together in a single place of study concentrations of the most outstanding scholars and masters of the day, from near and far. In other words, the modern university, college, research institute, think-tank, research library, and so on of today, has a lineage that spans millennia and can be traced back to the Alexandrina complex and thence to ancient Egypt's *per-ankh*.

(2) There emerges from the foregoing an important matter that cannot be sidestepped. It can be articulated thusly: Having established the existence of a prototype version of higher education institutions in ancient Egypt, which of course constitutes one of the major institutional expressions of a vibrant intellectual life of any society in any time period, it invariably raises the further

question of whether ancient Egyptian knowledge and learning had any significance for other contemporaneous—at the very minimum—societies outside Africa. Greece, perhaps? Now, what appears to be an innocent and ordinary scholarly question has in recent years acquired an unseemly, racially inspired, ideological baggage as expressed by the intense and vitriolic disagreements between *Eurocentrists* such as Mary Lefkowitz and *Afrocentrists* such as Maulana Karenga and Molefe Asante over the broader question of the significance of the Egyptian (read: black) civilization vis-à-vis the genesis of the Western (read: white) civilization. The former say that Western civilization owes nothing of determinative substance to Africa (ancient Egyptian or otherwise), while the latter say they owe a lot and in fact they "stole" most of their ideas from ancient Egyptians.[6]

Then there is Martin Bernal, of the *Black Athena* fame; he too may be categorized here as an Afrocentrist of a sort (however, given the moderation in his claims and a more convincing attempt at marshalling evidence in support of his positions, perhaps a better label for him would be neo-Afrocentrist.[7] Anyhow, he has almost single-handedly resurrected—based on a remarkable and Herculean scholarship—a more moderate Afrocentric point of view (relative to that of the Afrocentrists proper), which he describes as the "Ancient model" (in contrast to the prevalent "Aryan model" that places the origins of the Greek civilization entirely within Europe—and northern for that matter), that if we accept that Western civilization has its roots in ancient Greece, then ancient Greece had some of its roots in, primarily, Phoenicia and ancient Egypt through the process of colonization by the latter of the former. One would be seriously remiss not to quickly mention in the same breath that many critics (not all by any means Eurocentrists—see the excellent overview and synthesis by Howe 1998 and Berlinerblau 1999; plus van Binsbergen 1997 and Wigen and Lewis 1997 are also of relevance here) have pointed out what appear to be significant flaws in his work so far. Leaving aside the fact that it is highly unlikely that any scholarship undertaken on as grand a scale as Bernal's *Black Athena* project can be entirely flawless, the truth probably lies somewhere in between the Ancient and Aryan models—as it so often does in disagreements of this type where incontrovertible evidence is not always available and whatever evidence is accessible is subject to conflicting, but legitimate interpretations.[8]

Hellenistic Egypt's Bibliotheca Alexandrina

If our knowledge of higher education in the Egyptian civilization remains woefully sketchy, then one is on a slightly more surer ground as one turns to another important instance of higher education in African antiquity: the museum/ library complex at Alexandria (the Bibliotheca Alexandrina complex), which has once again risen like the legendary phoenix from the ashes, more than 1,000 years following its destruction.[9] The Alexandrian museum/library complex was established in that period of the Egyptian civilization known as the Hellenic period that would be ushered in by the arrival in Egypt, in December 332 B.C.E., of that infamous and ruthless Macedonian, Alexander the Conqueror (often referred to in history books as Alexander the Great), whose imperialistic ambitions would spawn an empire stretching from Macedonia to as far as India. Although the slaughter of the defeated was one of the hallmarks of many of his military expeditions, the Egyptians were spared this fate because they saw him not as an invader, but as a liberator. The warm welcome by the Egyptian populace accorded to Alexander enabled him to easily obtain the peaceful (and wise) surrender of the Persian satrap Mazaces. He thereby conquered Egypt without doing battle, while at the same time liberating the Egyptians from the much-disliked Persians who had become the rulers of Egypt from 664 B.C.E. under the Achaemenid dynasty.

Enticed by the hospitable geography of the ancient Mediterranean village seaport of Rakotis (established around 1500 B.C.E.) located on the western edge of the Nile River delta between the sea and the fresh water Lake of Mareotis, Alexander commanded it to be the site of his new Egyptian capital and a naval base for his fleet. As was his practice, in his typical ego flattering flourish, he named the capital after himself. It is with this beginning that the Greco-Egyptian city of Alexandria would become, in time, one of the world's greatest cities of antiquity and a major center of scientific and philosophical research. The task of placing the new capital on to this illustrious path, however, fell to his viceroys: first, Cleomenes, and later, after Alexander's death on June 13, 323 B.C.E. in Babylon, Ptolemy I Soter.

The Alexandrian empire did not survive the death of its creator, having been held together by the dint of his personality. The wealthiest and most prestigious province in the empire that was Egypt fell to the lot of Ptolemy I Soter who, in time, would proclaim himself the new Egyptian king, thereby launching a new dynasty. That the Egyptians accepted the new rulers was a testimony to the diplomatic and political acumen of the Ptolemys, as well as their respect for the culture of pharaonic Egypt. For instance, they generously dispensed patronage to the Egyptian nobility, they established a new religion that brought together Greek and Egyptian beliefs through the worship of the sun god Serapis (a reinvented Egyptian god of the underworld from Memphis); they restored some of the Egyptian temples that the Persians had destroyed; and so on.

Now, just before his death in 283 B.C.E., it is said, Ptolemy I Soter, who was also a man of letters, ordered the construction of a museum/library complex near the royal palace in the Greek section of the city known as the *Brucheion*. In this effort, it is thought, he was implementing an idea that was not originally his; for it had been the wish of Alexander to have a library built in the new city that would bear his name. It was to be dedicated to the worship of the Muses—a group of sister goddesses in the Greco-Roman religion who each were patrons of different artistic and intellectual endeavors. Ptolemy I Soter did not live long enough to see the entire project completed; it was left to his son, Ptolemy II Philadelphus, to see it through. The complex was both a religious and a secular institution and as such it would enjoy patronage throughout the reign of the Ptolemies, including the appointment for life of full time, salaried staff headed by a librarian who also served as royal tutor to the king. The religious component of the complex, the place of worship of the Muses (the *mouseion*), was headed by the priest of the Muses. (It may be noted here that the modern term museum has its etymological origins in that Greek word *mouseion*.)

The complex comprised living quarters for the community of poets, philosophers and scholars that ran it, lecture rooms, a botanical garden, a zoological park, astronomical observatory, and the great library. In time, the complex would become a truly great monument to human knowledge and learning, built to gather together—either through purchase, systematic copying, or even forcible acquisition—every available work known to the librarians. The library's collection even included what was then and even today the priceless works of Aristotle; though how the library came to acquire these works remains a mystery to this day (see Tanner 2000 for one conjectural thesis). The zeal of the librarians in acquiring works is attested to by the naming of sections of the library's holdings as ship libraries because they were constituted from works confiscated from passing ships by customs officials. The supposed practice was that all books aboard a ship were copied and then returned to their owners, while the copies (catalogued as "from the ships") became part of the ship libraries. However, one may legitimately surmise, as MacLeod (2000a: 5) does, that many a traveler left Alexandria without their originals (or perhaps even without any copies at all). At one point, the library is thought to have amassed over a half a million works on rolls of papyri in an age when, it must be remembered, there was no paper and no printing press. Clearly, in terms of its acquisitions policy, the Bibliotheca Alexandrina complex was a multicultural institution that, over time (it would be in operation for almost 600 years), would attempt to bring together in one place the contributions of the Asian, Egyptian, Hellenic, Judaic, Mesopotamian, and Roman worlds.

The fact that the person entrusted by Ptolemy I Soter with the establishment of the complex was the Athenian Demetrius Phalereus speaks volumes for what the complex became. Why? Because Demetrius, who besides being a Greek orator, statesman, and philosopher, was also an ex-pupil of Plato's famous ex-pupil, none other than Aristotle himself. One can, therefore, confidently assume that from the very beginning the complex, in terms of its mission (and possibly its physical design) bore the hallmarks of Aristotle's Lyceum, an academy that he founded for the purposes of scholarly endeavors in a variety of scientific and philosophical fields of inquiry.

The ultimate practical objective of the Ptolemys, it would appear, was twofold: the complex would serve as a symbol of prestige that spoke for the cultured or civilized status of their dynasty, and it would be a vehicle for cultural and intellectual domination of other cultures through appropriation of all written knowledge where ever and when ever it was available. This was not an unusual practice as MacLeod (2000a) reminds us. Empire builders of antiquity had long grasped the importance of acquiring and translating works from other cultures as a means of gaining valuable insights into intellectual and other accomplishments of these cultures that could facilitate their domination. (Note that the present-day practice of national libraries in metropolitan countries, such the Library of Congress, systematically acquiring foreign produced materials, one may legitimately argue, is a continuation of this tradition. See also Casson 2001 for an excellent account of other libraries in the ancient world.)

The true significance of the complex, however, was not that it was simply a unique repository of knowledge for the time period, but like the proverbial moths being drawn to a candlelight, it attracted scholars from near and far. For, unlike today, libraries of the past were also important seats of learning where the librarians themselves too were, one and at the same time, scholars in residence. Hence, over time, the Bibliotheca Alexandrina became the source of prodigious and remarkable intellectual scholarship which, many centuries later, through the agency of the Muslims, would help to ignite the European Renaissance.[10]

Until new evidence comes to light, it is safe to say that the library complex was not a university in the modern sense in that it probably did not undertake *systematic teaching* and *credentialing* of bodies of students, even though research, teaching, and learning took place there. However, this much is certain: on its own terms, it did clearly function as a university and an international research institute, and a very important one at that. This is further underlined by the fact that dinners and symposia featuring philosophical, scientific, and literary disputations were regularly sponsored by the complex (often present among the invited guests were the Ptolemys themselves). Moreover, its staff were called upon, from time to time, to offer lessons to members of the royal family.

The Bibliotheca Alexandrina was undoubtedly an institution of higher education, in fact one can go so far as to say that it was among the world's earliest known prototype universities.[11] At the same time, the library's presence, it is especially worth noting, helped to sustain a thriving publishing industry, thereby assisting in the dissemination of the knowledge that the library acquired, and produced, to all the four corners of the ancient world. From this perspective, the library was also indirectly responsible for helping to permanently preserve works that would have been lost forever when it underwent periodic and later final destruction. About this last point, the demise of the museum/ library complex was a cataclysmic scholarly disaster of massive proportions, the consequences of which can hardly be even imagined.

The Destruction of the Bibliotheca Alexandrina

So, exactly how then did this magnificent institution of higher learning eventually meet its end? The short answer is that no one really knows with absolute certainty because of a couple of problems: the lack of information regarding the exact layout of the complex internally, as well as externally with respect to the palace, and the fact that the complex included a smaller daughter library (created around 235 B.C.E. by Ptolemy III in the Serapeum [Temple of Sarapis]) and warehouses where acquisitions were initially stored while they were awaiting cataloguing. This yields four major architectural units that could have fallen victim to destruction by fire at different times or at one and the same time: the museum, the main library, the daughter library, and the warehouses—thereby generating much confusion as to when the complex was destroyed and by whom among the following four main probable culprits: the Roman general Julius Ceasar in 48/47 B.C.E. who set off an accidental fire provoked by a civil war among the last of the Ptolemaic dynasty (between Cleopatra VII and her brother Ptolemy XIII) in which Ceasar had become embroiled; the Roman emperor Aurelian in 272 C.E., who in the course of putting down a rebellion razed most of the Brucheion to the ground; the virulently antipagan Christian patriarch of Alexandria, Theophilus, who in 391 C.E. ordered the destruction of all pagan temples in Alexandria; and Amr ibn al-'As, the leader of the conquering Muslims, who supposedly burned the library upon the orders of the Caliph Omar ibn Khattab in 642 C.E.

What is the stand on this matter of the various authorities on whose work this part of the chapter is primarily based? Casson (2001) and Barnes (2000) side with Edward Gibbon (1910 [originally written 1776–88]) and Alfred J. Butler (1998 [1902]), who both conclude that by the time the Muslim Army arrived in Egypt under the command of Amr ibn al-'As, the Bibliotheca Alexandrina complex had long passed into memory (El-Abbadi 1992 and Canfora 1989 are also of the same opinion); therefore, the Muslims could not have destroyed the complex—a viewpoint that, however, is not favored by Parsons (1952) and Zeydan (1952), for example, who insist that the Muslims were definitely the culprits. The preponderance of evidence—albeit much of it circumstantial—is in favor of Gibbon's and Butler's position. Both Gibbon (1962 [1910]: 345–47), and Butler (1998 [1902]: 401–26)—who interestingly labels the complex as a university in its own right and who feels compelled to deny that he is simply defending the Muslims in this matter, rather he only wants "to establish the truth"—draw attention to a number of disquieting facts; such as: the story that the Muslims burned the library makes its appearance for the first time more than five centuries after the event is supposed to have taken place!; the story is fraught with "absurdities" (e.g., the books being used to heat 4,000 bath houses over a period of six months, instead of being burned in a large bonfire on the spot; in the seventh-century most of the books in Egypt were made of vellum—not papyri—which does not burn as fuel, etc.); the principal protagonist in the story, John Philoponus, was long dead before the arrival of the Muslims; the existence of the library is nowhere alluded to in the literature of fifth, sixth and early seventh centuries; the contemporary and erudite chronicler at the time, the Coptic bishop, John of Nikiou, would not have passed over the event in silence; the treaty signed between the Muslims and the Alexandrians on the surrender of the city to the Muslims had a clause in it allowing the Romans to remove all valuables as they pleased during a seven-month period that preceded the actual arrival of the Muslims in the city; and so on.

In conclusion, Butler, echoing Gibbon, also makes this telling observation: that had it been necessary to defend the Muslims from this charge, then "it would not be difficult to find something in the nature of an apology." Why? Because, the Muslims, he says, "in later times certainly set great store by all the classical and other books which fell into their hands, and had them carefully preserved and in many cases translated. Indeed they set an example, which modern conquerors might well have followed." Recall too, that, in the words of Cohen (1994: 398): the "Islamic civilization was the first in world history to consider the acquisition of knowledge a thing necessary for every person; hence the Islamic origins of such institutions as the public library and the school for higher learning, or *madrasah*."[12] Now, it is up to you, esteemed reader, to arrive at your own conclusion regarding this awful tragedy of the intellect; and in this regard it is worth while remembering that, in the words of Hedon (1963: vii): "[i]n the last resort the historian, like any humble member of a trial jury, is compelled to let his instinct and his experience of human affairs supplement the contradictory assertions put before him, or else he is a fool."

HIGHER EDUCATION IN PREMODERN ETHIOPIA

Ethiopia, sometimes also referred to as Abyssinia in history books and identified as the fabled land of Prester John in the fertile imagination of medieval Europe, is one of the oldest countries on the planet. There is archeological evidence to show that human presence in Ethiopia can be traced as far back as some four million years; that is, to the time when *Australopithecus afarensis*, the ape-like (but bipedal) ancestor of the modern human, roamed the Ethiopian landscape. However, coming much, much closer to the present, it is the founding of the indigenous and powerful trading kingdom of Aksum, the process probably commencing in the second-century B.C.E., in northern Ethiopia that is of interest because the seeds for the emergence of premodern higher education in Ethiopia were sown in that kingdom with the conversion of its kings to Christianity, beginning with Emperor Ella Amida—the father of King Ezana I—in fourth-century C.E. when the Axumite empire was at its apogee. (Some 300 years later, a new religion would come on the scene and it too, in time, would contribute to the development of higher education in precolonial Ethiopia, namely Islam.)

There is a common myth among the lay public that Christianity first arrived in Africa through the agency of Western European missionaries beginning in the fifteenth-century, but both the Egyptian and Ethiopian experiences prove that this is certainly not so. Focusing on Ethiopia, the precise events that led to the official adoption of Christianity (Monophysite version) by the Aksumite crown has to do with the chance arrival at the royal court in the city of Aksum, around 340 C.E., of two enslaved young brothers and students of philosophy, Frumentius and Aedesius, from the ancient Mediterranean port of Tyre. They had been kidnapped while they were returning home from India; they had gone there on a scholarly visit with a relative (the philosopher Meropius of Tyre). It was Frumentius, the more learned of the two, who was responsible for the formal introduction of Christianity to Ethiopia around the same time (fourth-century) as Christianity arrived in Western Europe through the missionary efforts of men such as Ulfilas (Germany), Martin of Tours (France) and St. Patrick (Ireland). Frumentius, who later upon his manumission would be consecrated as Bishop Frumentius in about 347 C.E. by the Alexandrian Coptic bishop, Athanasius the Great, was greatly helped in his self-appointed task of proselytizing by the fact that while in the service of the Crown he had delivered of himself well, winning the hearts and minds of those who would be among the first converts to the new faith, the royal family itself.

At a broader level, the factors that appear to have facilitated the adoption of Christianity by the Axumites were these two: a preexisting philosophical disposition rooted in a vague monotheism—derived probably from contacts with Christian traders in the preceding centuries—and the perception that it was a religion that could bring benefits given that it was associated with such powerful rulers as the Roman emperor (Constantius II). Of course, as is normal with any new faith, the adoption of Christianity as a nation-wide religion would take many more years; moreover, its close association with the state would also ensure that its fortunes would trace the ebb and flow of the power of the various dynasties to come.[13]

In mentioning southern Arabia a moment ago, reference ought to be made here, too, of its influence in the emergence of writing in Aksum—a necessary precondition for higher education, as noted earlier—in the form of the Ethiopic alphabet in which Ge'ez is written. Ge'ez was one of the main languages of Aksum, which, while no longer spoken today, still remains the liturgical language of the Ethiopian church. The alphabet in all likelihood was borrowed from the Sabaens, but it was given a local twist: according to legend, says Wagaw (1991), King Ezana decreed that the writing should go from left to right and not retain its original right to left orientation so as to imbue it with the tradition of Christian writing (in other words, Greek and Latin). In addition, new marks were integrated into the borrowed alphabet to allow an easier rendering of vowels in a syllabary that was entirely made up of consonants (the user supplied the vowels).

The Axumite kingdom, in time, passed into history and a new line of Ethiopian kings emerged out of a crucible of rebellious violence from among the Agew people of the Ethiopian interior, known as the Zagwe dynasty. Now, it is not necessary here to go into the whys and wherefores of the demise of the Axumite kingdom; it will suffice to simply note that, as has been the case with every civilization, empire and kingdom of the past that continue to enthrall us to this day, its eclipse, which commenced some time in the seventh-century, was underwritten by both internal and external factors (and among the latter the rise of Islam was particularly important as Muslim shipping eroded Axum's monopoly over international trade in the Red Sea-Indian Ocean region) working dialectically over a long period of time.[14] The Zagwe dynasty would claim direct descent from the line of Axumite kings; but evidence so far suggests that the claim was fabricated for the purposes of underwriting their legitimacy. The church, however, it appears, went along with this claim in an implicitly understood exchange for a state financed, concerted campaign of church development by way of endowments and monuments. For example, the famous rock-hewn churches, numbering no less than eleven, built at the behest of Emperor Lalibela (ruled between 1185 and 1225) at their capital, Roha (present-day Lalibela), are a testimony to this effort. As the decades wore on, more violence facilitated the replacement of the Zagwe dynasty by another one in 1270: the present-day self-styled Solomonid dynasty that claims a line of descent from King Solomon himself—yet another legitimacy driven mythological concoction, but this time lacking in the slightest pretense of even a modicum of credibility, so outlandish is the myth (see Marcus 1994: 17–18 for details). The Ethiopian church, however, once again, rose to the occasion by putting its imprimatur on the myth and immortalizing it in an early fourteenth-century work called *Kebra Negast* ("Glory of Kings")—a hodgepodge of historical, allegorical, and apocalyptic mythology authored by a group of Tigrayan scribes, which in time would acquire the status of a sacred work for Ethiopian Christians.

It will be clear from the foregoing, then, that the institutionalization of Christianity in Ethiopia occurred primarily on the basis of a church-state symbiosis.[15] One other point, the significance of which will be clear in a moment: monasticism, according to legend, says Richard Pankhurst in his introduction in Kalewold (1970), arrived in Ethiopia during the reign of Emperor Ella Amida through the agency of nine Syrian monks. Now, not too long after Christianity had become the official state religion, with the king henceforth as its protector, the church began to establish a decentralized, *monastic dominated* educational "system" that would include higher education to meet the specialized needs of both the state and itself—commencing, of course, with that most basic of all administrative needs: literacy. In fact, up until the beginning of the twentieth-century when Western-style secular higher education was introduced, the state's administrative personnel (general administrators, judges, governors, etc.) received their training in this system (or on occasions toward the end of the nineteenth-century they were sent to institutions abroad).

The emergence of premodern higher education in Ethiopia, therefore, occurred from the very beginning within the context of a mutually reinforcing alliance—developed over the centuries against a backdrop of a feudal order—between the church and the state. Note too that the existence of a syllabary fostered from time to time a vibrant intellectual climate marked by such expressions of intellectual life as the production of manuscripts, the development of Ge'ez literature, philosophical disputations, establishment of libraries, artistic and architectural accomplishments, etc. (see Wagaw 1990 for details) that—even if restricted only to the clergy and the nobility—could have had nothing but a positive impact on the birth and growth of higher education in premodern Ethiopia.

The pinnacle of the monastic educational system, which usually took twenty-eight years to reach (starting from the elementary school level), according to Wagaw (1979), was occupied by a higher education institution known as *Metsahift Bet* (or the "School of Holy Books") located in such traditional centers of learning as those found in the provinces of Begemder and Gojam. Wagaw states that the *Metsahift Bet* was "in essence a university where the whole approach to learning, including the qualifications of the professors, methods of teaching and learning, and the popular attitude toward the leadership of the community of scholars, reflected maturity of mind and the ideal of democracy in action" (1979: 21). Those who managed to reach this stage undertook specialized studies in such theological areas as canonical laws, the computation of time and calendar, religious philosophy, religious literature, church history, and so on.

Below the *Metsahift Bet* were two other higher educational levels: the *Qine Bet* (School of Poetry) and below it the *Zema Bet* (School of Hymns).[16] Education at these levels was more restricted in terms of subject matter as may be inferred from their names. In the *Qine Bet*, for example, the primary focus was on religious Ge'ez poetry and literature with the aim of graduating poets of exemplary creativity and skill.[17] However, even when considering the *Metsahift Bet* it must be conceded that the curricular focus was considerably narrow.[18] The characterization of this institution as a "university" by Wagaw (1979) must therefore be seen as an exaggeration (an institution of higher education? Yes, that it is). Science and astronomy, for example, had almost no place in the curriculum. In fact, on the contrary the feeling was that scientific investigations were an intrusion into what was God's exclusive domain and therefore to be shunned.

There were some other serious failings too of the system. Considering the close connection between the church and the state in the context of a feudal political and social order, the higher education system, for the most part, was the preserve of the ruling elites—its graduates (all male) it must be pointed out, were destined for either secular or religious leadership (or both) depending upon their lineage. Moreover, the health of the system was greatly affected by the degree of interest of the ruling monarch in intellectual and ecclesiastical pursuits. For example, relative to others, monarchs such as Zera-Yakob (reigned 1434–1468), Yohannes I (reigned 1667–1682), Iyasu I (reigned 1682–1706) and Iyasu II (reigned 1730–1755), who were all men with extensive intellectual, artistic, and ecclesiastical interests, played significant roles directly and indirectly in the development of the monastic educational system. The problem, however, is that such monarchs were few and far between, thus rendering the positive impact of the state on higher education episodic, which did not make for a healthy educational system at any level over the long-term. In fact, on this matter the prevailing tradition was for the ruling classes to avoid literacy. For, as Milkias (1976) observes, "[i]lliteracy among the ruling classes was neither exceptional nor reprehensible." "As a matter of fact," he continues, "traditionally, reading and writing were not only looked down upon as the Amhara proverb 'the worst of beasts is the scorpion, the worst of men is the debtera' attests to, but were also associated with occult powers."[19]

Incidentally, since this proverb mentions the debtera (plural debtrawoch) and given their important place among the premodern Ethiopian intelligentsia, a word or two about the debtrawoch is in order here. In Ethiopian society the debtrawoch were both loved and feared; they were loved because of their scribal skills ("copying texts from the sacred books, writing letters and petitions for a fee, running ecclesiastical affairs, or serving as chroniclers in the courts of kings and nobles" [Milkias, p. 82]), but they were also feared because of the general perception that they dealt in the occult. The latter perception, however, was a further source of bread and butter for the debtrawoch: for a fee they could be approached for charms, amulets and so on. How did one become a debtera? There were three necessary qualities: an inordinate thirst for knowledge (if there is one overriding quality of the debtrawoch it was that they were highly learned persons); an opportunity to go through the more than two decades long higher education ladder just described; and (for obvious reasons), dogged perseverance. In sociological terms the importance of the debtera lay not only in his possession of scribal skills, but it is through the person of the debtera that one can locate the interface between the church and the feudal order, as Milkias explains:

As the institution of education, the church supplied the secular power with its pen, ideas, ideologies, and the interpreters and justifiers of its legitimacy. To this extent, the linkage of the educated was two-sided. On the one hand, they hinged on the ecclesiastical hierarchy as a conduit to the secular powers, and, on the other, they aspired to win the favors of the secular powers who were the sources of their income. This dual dependence was not, by any means, a fragile one. Both secular and spiritual powers needed the educated: the former for administrative and ideological reasons, the latter for the very existence of the church as a religious and educational institution (p. 85).[20]

Given this powerful role played by the church through the products of its higher educational system, it is understandable that it did everything it could to retain its monopoly over education in Ethiopia even after Ethiopians were exposed to the existence of other forms of education, notably secular Western education. For, as Milkias points out, "[c]ontrary to popular belief...the influence of the church on Ethiopian people was not so much due to the religious fervor of the populace, but due to the monopoly the church enjoyed over education, thereby being not only the main agent of political socialization, but also the only custodian of the discourse of legitimation" (p. 86). Not surprisingly, despite the fact that Ethiopia had a free hand in developing its own educational policies (unlike colonial Africa), even with the onset of modernity (that for purposes of convenience one may date with the Battle of Adwa, in 1896, when the Ethiopians defeated the Italians), Western secular education would take a long time to come to Ethiopia. The resistance put up by the church was only overcome, initially, by a surreptitious approach: the first Western-type school established in Ethiopia by the government (Mennelik II school founded in 1908) specialized primarily in language training and was staffed by Egyptian Coptic clergy. (As noted elsewhere, 1908 was the same year that Egypt was founding its first secular *university*.) But the die was cast; with the founding of each new secular educational institution the church's monopoly grip on education was loosened; in the end it had no control over the development of this form of education that the vast majority of Ethiopians, in time, would aspire toward—as in rest of Africa. The church-run schools of course would continue; but that is not where the ruling classes would send their children, or for that matter most of the rest of the Ethiopian populace (compare here with the fate of the madrasahs in the Islamic empire, discussed later.) In other words, one must agree with Milkias that given that the power of the Ethiopian church was intimately linked with its monopoly over education, once that monopoly was broken it marked for the church the beginning of its slide toward political marginality in the affairs of the state; the coup de grace, however, would not come until the rise of the Derg following the 1974 revolution. The troubling question, however, is, Why didn't this whole process begin much earlier? Thereby placing Ethiopia on a completely different historical trajectory with profoundly positive consequences for the Ethiopian people. The answer is to be found in what may be termed as the "Ethiopia/ Japan anomaly" to be discussed later in this work.

Islamic Education

Among the most successful global propaganda achievements of an African state in modern history clearly has to be that of Ethiopia; it has managed to

convince the world that Ethiopia is and has always been a Christian country.[21]
Yet Ethiopia, with its close geographic proximity to the original homeland of
Islam and surrounded by Muslim neighbors, has always been, both a Christian
and a Muslim country (that is, after the birth of Islam). In fact, Christians have
always been a minority in Ethiopia throughout its history, that is, relative to the
rest of the population as a whole. Yes, it is true that because of the strong alliance of Christianity with the Ethiopian state, Muslims (and others, such as
Ethiopian Jews [*falashas*]) from time to time have been victims of horrendous
persecutions (for example, during the reigns of King Amde-Siyon [1314–44],
and Emperors Yishak [1413–30], Zera-Yakob [1434–68], and Yohannes I
[1667–82]), including forcible conversions to Christianity (for example during
the reigns of Emperors Tewodros II [1855–1868], Yohannis IV [1872–1889],
and Menelik of Shewa [1889–1913]) in a replay of what the Muslims did to the
Christians during the former's successful but brief onslaught on the Ethiopian
state some centuries before. In fact, it is only with the revolution of 1974 that
the status of the Muslims began to improve in relation to that of the Christians—until the new dictators (the military junta known as the *Dergue,* an Am-
haric word for council or committee) turned against both in their drive to create
a secular state. Nonetheless, Muslim Ethiopians, far from being a small minority in Ethiopia, have accounted for a considerable proportion of the population.
At present they make up 45–50% of the total and if one takes into consideration the 12–18% of animists and others, they form a slight majority relative to
the Christians who constitute 35–40%. Moreover, as will be noted in a moment, had it not been for the assistance of the Portuguese, it is quite possible
that Ethiopia today would be a Muslim country.

Ironically, Islamic presence in Ethiopia began in 615 C.E. with Aksum
hosting, as an act of mercy, a small contingent of Muslim refugees from Arabia
during the time of Prophet Muhammed when Islam in its early days of inception was still under persecution. However, its significant presence, achieved on
the back of long distance trade and commerce, would not come about until
some centuries later when, by the middle of the thirteenth-century, Islamic
principalities and sultanates (e.g., the sultanates of Dahlak, Dawaro, Ifat, and
Shoa) had emerged to become a firm part of the Ethiopian political landscape
with the waning of the kingdom of Aksum. However, with the emergence of
the new Solomonid dynasty with its imperial ambitions it was inevitable that
the uneasy modus vivendi reached by the Christian state with the Ethiopian
Muslims, especially in the central highlands, would, as its power waxed over
the subsequent centuries, progressively deteriorate; to be replaced by endemic
and bloody conflicts. Finally, it would all come to a head in the sixteenth-
century during the reign of Emperor Lebna Dengel (1508–40) with the rise of
the charismatic Muslim leader of Harar, Imam Ahmed ibn Ibrahim al-Ghazi
(nicknamed by the Ethiopian Christians, Ahmed the *Gran*). Uniting a variety of

ethnic groups under the banner of Islam he would launch a holy war (*jihad*) against the Christian state, almost annihilating it.

Beginning with the decisive battle of Sembure Kure in 1529 (a tail-end battle in an ongoing war that started in 1526 and provoked by the Christians against the sultanate of Adal in the east) and going on until 1543 when a Portuguese soldier's bullet felled al-Ghazi, the Muslims would bring the Ethiopian state to its knees. Along the way the Muslims wreaked unimaginable barbaric havoc on the Ethiopian church, looting and laying waste its churches and monasteries and, in flagrant violation of Qur'anic injunctions, putting to the sword any one who refused to convert to Islam. It is only in 1543, by which time two-thirds of the Ethiopian empire was now under the sway of the Muslims, that providence would at long last take the side of the Ethiopian state. In a coincidence of coincidences, it had just so happened that two years before, a Portuguese fleet had arrived at the Eritrean port of Massawa on the Red Sea from its base in the Portuguese Indian colony of Goa to counter the growing influence of the Ottomans in the region. The Ethiopian Christians beseeched them for assistance, and the Portuguese were only too happy to oblige and do battle with the Muslims, their sworn enemies (see Appendix II). Al-Ghazi and his forces, however, were not to be stopped; they soundly defeated the Ethiopians and their Portuguese allies. But two years later, it would be a different story. The tide would turn against al-Ghazi. His death on the battlefield in February of that fateful year of 1543, at a place east of Lake Tana, so demoralized his army that they were decisively routed. Thereafter, the Solomonid dynasty reconquered the territories lost to the Muslims, eventually reducing al-Ghazi's meteoric *jihad* to a whirlwind that had come and gone. Though that is not to say that the Islamic presence in Ethiopia would be extinguished. It would continue to survive; its fortunes, however, would ebb and flow as before, down the centuries, with each political gyration of the Solomonid dynasty.

It is against this backdrop one must consider the development of Islamic higher education in Ethiopia, in the form of *madrasahs*. Since these institutions will be the subject of discussion at some length in a moment and in Appendix I, it will suffice now to simply note that it is during the long interstitial periods of peace and prosperity over the centuries that the Ethiopian Muslims, like all Muslim communities elsewhere in the Islamic empire (and like their Ethiopian Christian counterparts too), developed vibrant centers of higher learning. However, given the vicissitudes of Muslim fortunes none would survive to the present, except for one: the town of Harrar. The disappearance of most centers of learning over the course of Ethiopian history should not be taken to imply, however, that the Ethiopian Muslims did not and have not retained their madrasahs in their individual communities.[22]

While the monastic educational system and the madrasahs may have been adequate for the needs of the Ethiopians when viewed narrowly in terms of transmission of ecclesiastical knowledge—coupled with the production of religious and administrative personnel for a premodern feudal era—from the perspective of the task of modernization that the state would eventually feel compelled to embark upon, especially following the attempted takeover of the country by foreigners (the Italians) in the 1890s, the problem becomes self-evident. An entirely new higher educational system had to be imported almost wholesale from abroad. This will be the subject of the section on modern Ethiopia in Chapter 5.

HIGHER EDUCATION IN PRECOLONIAL ISLAMIC AFRICA

If it is true (and the jury of history, as pointed out earlier, has yet to render an *incontrovertible* verdict on this), that the great Alexandrian library complex, that is whatever had remained of it as the fortunes of the Roman Empire waned, was destroyed in a pyrotechnical fit of incalculable ignorance by the Muslims following their arrival in 639 C.E. in Egypt, then this great tragedy constitutes among the supreme ironies of history. Why? There are two reasons: First, it is they who, in time, would become the custodians of the knowledge that came out of that complex when the lights of learning were reduced to a flicker all over Europe by the depredations of the barbarians that poured out of the European forests, plunging it into the so-called Dark Ages (see Appendix I). Second, the only known precolonial higher education institutions in Africa, besides those established by the ancient Egyptians and the Ethiopians, were those founded by the Muslims. However, this is moving the discussion somewhat far ahead of itself; one must pause here because there are one or two relevant matters of context that must be dispensed with right away; albeit briefly. First, a short exegesis into the emergence of the Islamic empire and civilization is in order, and then there is the very important matter of clarification regarding nomenclature: Muslim in place of Arab.[23]

One will probably never know why the three monotheistic religions of Judaism, Christianity, and Islam, which together geographically hold sway over most of the globe today, all originated in the sands of the Middle Eastern desert. Be that as it may, the last to emerge among them, and hence the youngest, is Islam. From a theological point of view, this position in the chronological hierarchy was not a good omen; for much in the same way that Judaism, centuries earlier, had come to see the newly emergent religion of Christianity as an upstart and a usurper, so too did both of them together now regard Islam thusly. Islam's recognition of the other two as its forebears appeared to have merely intensified their animosity (see Lewis 1993, for more on the theological and chronological differences, and their consequences for relations between the three religions). Consequently, the nascent religion felt vulnerable; and all the more so given the nature of its birth: in the womb of armed conflict as its immediate enemies, the pagan Arabs in the city of Mecca (where Islam was first proclaimed by its messenger, Prophet Muhammed), attempted to vanquish it. It is perhaps not surprising then, that Islam—which means "to submit to the will of *God*" (that is, the monotheistic God of Moses and Jesus and referred to in Arabic as *Al'lah*)—would begin a march of conquest soon after it had managed to become the dominant religion in Saudi Arabia (by 632 C.E.) to subdue its enemies: the Christian Byzantines to their West and the polytheistic Persians to their east. Unbeknownst to them, and to anyone else for that matter, it would be a march that would eventually culminate in the creation of an empire that in geographic magnitude would be excelled by only one other empire in the entire history of humankind: that of the British more than 1,000 years later.[24]

Consider the nature of this feat, as that great doyen of African history, Basil Davidson (1995: 126–127), reminds us: on July 16, 622 C.E., Islam is effectively born with the arrival in Medina from Mecca of four exhausted and penniless fugitives, Prophet Muhammed and his three companions; yet within only a mere twenty-two years of this highly inauspicious beginning, by 644, the Muslims had taken over Saudi Arabia, Syria, Egypt, and conquered Alexandria; by 670 they were ruling most of North Africa; by 711 they were in Spain, two years later they had arrived in Portugal, and a year later again, in 714, they were in France, to be eventually stopped in their westward expansion, it would be appear, some years on, in 733, by Charles Martel at the Battle of Poitiers (sometimes also referred to as the Battle of Tours) near the Loire River.[25] In the East, by 651, the Muslims had absorbed the Persian empire that had lasted more than 1,000 years, and in time they would go into India, and beyond (see also Watt 1972). What is even more remarkable—the magnitude of which, tragically, is further reinforced when viewed from the vantage point of today's widespread political, economic, and social disarray (often wrapped in a cocoon of unmitigated absolutist tyranny for good measure) that characterizes much of the Islamic world; vide: Afghanistan, Algeria, Egypt, Iran, Iraq, Pakistan, Saudi Arabia, Somalia, Sudan, and so on)—is that in those lands where the Muslims achieved some degree of permanence, their invasions did not reproduce the large-scale chaos and mindless destruction characteristic of the invasions of, say, the European barbarians of two centuries earlier: the Vandals, Goths, Visigoths, or, say, the Mongols of the Golden Horde of five centuries later. Instead, as Davidson (1995: 126–127) points out: "In Africa, Spain and Asia these victories laid the groundwork for a civilization that could and did unite men of religion, learning and philosophy from the Mediterranean to Arabia, from the plains of the western Sudan to the hills of China, and bore a light of tolerance and social progress through centuries when Europe, impoverished, provincialized and almost illiterate, lay in distant battle and confusion." And even after the widespread devastation that the Muslims suffered at the hands of the Mongol invaders in the thirteenth-century, they would rise up again in the following century to produce the Ottoman Empire that would last into the twentieth-century. It would be a process that would, in yet another one of those strange ironies of history, involve the conversion of the Mongols themselves to

Islam and their enlistment into rebuilding the empire, which at its apogee would now stretch from Central Asia in the East to southeastern Europe in the West, incorporating countries as diverse as the Ukraine and Egypt; Syria and Greece; Israel and Hungary; Iraq and Bosnia; Saudi Arabia and Romania; and so on. Yet, despite the enormous magnitude of the diversity of peoples and cultures that the empire incorporated, it would work for nearly another 600 years, held together by structures and institutions rooted in the religion of Islam. A key question that emerges here is this: Given the magnitude, the speed and the longevity, how were the Muslims able to achieve so much? An interplay—repeat, interplay—of at least eight factors, albeit in various permutations and, it must be stressed, *at various levels of adherence in practice*, were probably critical in ensuring their success. The following is a quick rundown of them in no particular order on the basis of various sources (e.g., Ahmed 1975; Butler 1998 [1902], Courbage and Fargues 1997; Esposito 2000; Hillenbrand 1999; Hodgson 1974; Hourani 2002; Stanton 1990; and Watt 1965.

First, was the deep military discipline of the Islamic forces, which was an outcome of a combination of two factors: the belief that they were engaged in holy wars (*jihad*) and a powerful zeal to go the extra mile—characteristic of converts to a new religion. Second, was the weakness of the conquered in terms of disarray within the governing regimes on one hand, and on the other, the resentment of the populace against the regimes that ruled them because of oppression (it was not unusual for the Muslims to be welcomed as liberators *or to be simply indifferent to their arrival*—instead of putting up resistance). Third, was the philosophy of tolerance following conquest—for example, by virtue of a covenant (the *dhimma*) promulgated by the Islamic state, the conquered received protection; in return they were only required to pay a poll tax (the *jizya*), they were not required to convert, neither were they enslaved, and nor were their cultural and religious institutions destroyed—compare, for example, with the orderly arrival of the Muslims in Jerusalem in 638 C.E. with the mind-numbing horrifying carnage inflicted by the Crusaders when they stormed its walls on July 15, 1099.[26] (Conquest, in other words, did not necessarily mean conversion, since conversion by force is prohibited by the Qur'an. This was in marked contrast, for example, to how the Christian states treated other religious groups—witness the Spanish Inquisition—in their realm. See Mastnak 2002, for more on this.) Fourth, was the absolute unity of the temporal and the eternal in Islamic theology, which meant that the mechanics of statecraft—including taxation, economics and law—were among the elements of conquest that the Muslims brought with them, it did not have to be invented on an ad hoc basis (the surest door to anarchy and confusion). Fifth, was the concept of the global community (*ummah*), which preached the absolute unity of all Muslims regardless of their class status or race or ethnicity or nationality (one result of this view was that the subjugated could achieve parity with their rulers through conversion, while another was the universality of Islamic citizenship where all Muslims enjoyed virtually the same rights where ever they traveled in the empire). Sixth, was the ritualistic simplicity of worship (those who converted to Islam found that it was a very unpretentious and austere religion in terms of rituals and lifestyle, including the absence of a priestly class (which always has the potential to degenerate into a parasitically oppressive class—as had occurred in some of the societies that the Muslims came across). Seventh, was the multicultural unity of the Islamic world—which found its religious expression in the *hajj* (the annual pilgrimage to Mecca, which is mandatory on all Muslims at least once in their lifetime if they can afford it)—an outcome of which was that Islam did not recognize nationalistic and ethnic boundaries: all cultures and all nations were welcome into the faith on an equal footing; in this sense it was a truly multicultural religion. Eighth, was the urban commercial character of Islam (given that it was born in an urban commercial environment. One outcome of this was that economic prosperity, derived from commerce and trade across the length and breadth of the empire, was an integral part of the package that the Muslims brought with them. (Regarding this last factor, it is instructive to note here that, as Curtin (1984: 107), reminds one, it is commerce and not arms that accounts for the presence of Muslims in China and Indonesia—countries that each host the largest population of Muslims in the world.) Nineth, was the practice of the Muslim generals to provide a peaceful alternative to armed battle to those they were about to confront. To explain, an important innovation that the Muslims introduced (for the time period) was that before formal hostilities commenced, they would offer three choices to their enemies: either to convert to Islam, or surrender peacefully and be allowed to retain life, religion, property and general way of life (except that a poll tax would be levied, as noted earlier), or do battle. Many would choose the second alternative.

A second matter that must be dealt with is the use of the term Arab by Western historians whenever they refer to Muslims. This is erroneous for two reasons: First, then (as today) not all Arabs were Muslims and equally certainly, not all Muslims were Arabs. In fact, from the very beginning of the founding of Islam, for example, there were African converts to Islam residing in Saudi Arabia. (See, for example, Talib [1988] for a fascinating account of the African diaspora in Asia.) Second, given the relatively (the key word here is relatively) inclusive nature of Islam, the Islamic military forces had many other nationalities among them besides Arabs, but many of whom were Muslims too. (It should be remembered that the Arab population simply did not have the numbers to create the huge armies that arose in the course of the Islamic conquests.) From a strictly theological point of view Islam does not recognize the concept of the chosen race; in fact, such socially divisive markers as racism and nationalism (contrary to current practice in Islamic countries) are forbidden.[27] However, it does recognize the supremacy of Muslims over others, but even here there is a qualifier: it recognizes Christianity and Judaism as legitimate religions (their adherents are referred to in Islam as the "People of the Book").

Now, to move on with the discussion: It is a truism, as noted earlier, that any religion that possesses the written word, in the form of a holy book(s), will make provisions for some form of religious education, beginning with literacy, and going on to higher education. The Islamic injunction was that every Muslim community had to provide for the education of its young in, at the minimum, basic religious matters (which included of course the learning of Arabic, the memorization of the Qur'an, and some acquaintance with the *Shari'ah* (Islamic laws) and the *hadith* (authenticated utterances and injunctions of the Prophet Muhammed). This educational system would evolve beyond elementary levels of education to include higher education institutions, such as prototype universities. This is attributable of course to another truism: that you need to train the teachers, and then the teachers of the teachers.

There were, however, other powerful conducive factors in this regard specific to Islam; going by Stanton (1990), Totah (1926), and others, they include the following (listed in no order of importance): (1) In the absence of a clergy, there emerged a scholarly class (the *ulama*) whose legitimacy could only rest on erudition and piety—unlike in the case of Christianity where legitimacy (at the immediate level) derived from an ecclesiastical bureaucracy. The absence of a clergy, one ought to explain, stemmed from the specifics of Islamic theology in which there is a deliberate absence of provision for transcendental intercession between the faithful and their Creator through the agency of other human beings—no matter how holy and pious.[28] (2) Islam's need for an ulama arose, in the first place, because Islam is a juridical-based religion, which itself was an outcome of two principal factors: first, its theology rested on the unity of the temporal and the divine so that pursuit of one's faith did not end at the mosque door, but extended into every corner of one's life, ranging from the private to the public, and second, the Qur'an did not provide details for all aspects of religious practice; it had to be supplemented with *hadith* and in the matter of the minutiae of every day life, the *sunnah* (the Prophet's behavioral precedents as verified by *hadith*).[29] (3) The high value placed by Islam on learning in general for its own sake, which included the view that the study of the natural worlds (biological, physical, etc.) was an aid to one's faith because it was a form of pietistic contemplation of the attributes of God. The Islamic civilization required, as already noted earlier, all of its adherents, male and female, young and old, rich and poor, to acquire knowledge (something that no other civilization had ever mandated before). (4) The use of Arabic as the liturgical language of Islam, which created a need to provide instruction in the use of this language to the vast numbers of non-Arab converts. (5) The role of Arabic (which was a language that already had within it the potential to articulate, as and when the need arose, "philosophical, theological, and scientific abstractions" [Stanton 1990: 9]) as the lingua franca of the elites, including the intellectual elites, in the Islamic empire facilitated intellectual discourse across a wide expanse of space and time, thereby enhancing the potential for the development of higher education within the empire.[30] (6) The requirement of the annual mandatory pilgrimage to Mecca that further enhanced intellectual discourse as Islamic scholars from all across the Islamic world gathered annually in a single place for worship and spiritual rejuvenation. (From this perspective, Mecca served and continues to serve, as a worldwide annual "conference," albeit a highly informal one, of Muslim scholars of every ethnicity and nationality.) (7) The necessity to provide some educational training for government officials as their numbers multiplied with each successive wave of expansion of the empire. (8) The injunction that one learn the basic regulations pertaining to one's occupation or profession to ensure that one remained within the boundaries of Islamic law *even as one engaged in the pursuit of material interests*. (9) Like all major religions that aspired to global universality, Islam was not spared the development of fractional tendencies arising out of controversies, heresies, and so on; one outcome of this was attempts to use educational institutions to either counter or encourage these tendencies.

"From the beginning, then," to quote Berkey (1992: 6), "Islam was a religion of the book and of learning, a society that esteemed knowledge and education above almost every other human activity." Ergo: "Islam's high estimation of the value of knowledge translated naturally into broad-based social and cultural support for education" (p. 3).[31] Now, the Islamic higher education institutions that the Muslims established for themselves all over the Islamic world, including in Africa, usually took the form of schools and proto-universities or colleges (called madrasahs) that were attached to mosques or run independently from them out of other public (and private) premises.[32]

A model Islamic higher education system—the key word here is model, for in a sense the system (this term is not being used here in an organizational sense because Islamic higher education institutions were usually independent and self-financed; they were only linked together by the commonality of features and the informal interchange of teachers, scholars, and students) was always a work in progress—found in various permutations throughout Islamic Africa (and elsewhere in the Islamic world) looked like this: At the apex was the madrasah, which was established by means of an endowed charitable trust called *waqf*.[33] It was usually, but not always, attached to a major urban mosque where Friday congregational prayers took place (Friday being the holiest day of the week for Muslims) and included a residential component for its poor and out-of-town students.[34] The curriculum of the madrasahs was typically made up of three categories: the first dealt with the fundamental Islamic sciences: Qur'anic exegesis (*tafsir*); the traditions of Prophet Muhammed, namely behavioral precedents (*sunnah*) and public utterances (*hadith*); and Islamic law (*Shari'ah*), which itself was made up of two components: Islamic law proper (*al-fiqh*) and the sources of this law (jurisprudence—termed *usul al-fiqh*). The second comprised elements of language, namely: the Qur'anic language (*al-lughah*)—which in this case of course it was classical Arabic; grammar (*al-nahw wa'l-sarf*); literary style and rhetoric (*al-balaghah*); literature (*al-adab*); and the art of Qur'anic recitation (*al-qira'at*). The third category, which was usually considered to be of slightly lower level of importance included subjects such as astronomy, history, medicine, and mathematics. Below the madrasahs came the *halqahs* or the study circles located in congregational mosques (*jami-al-masjid*)—the principal mosques in a city or district where the Friday sermons and prayers took place.

The subjects taught in *halqahs* were varied, but always included some basic Islamic jurisprudence, Arabic grammar, hadith, and so on. Below the *halqahs* were the *majlis* found in all types of mosques (*masjids*), other than the congregational mosque; they were, in essence, an informal variety of the *halqahs*. The person who usually taught in the majlis was the prayer leader of the mosque (the *imam*). Under these two masjid connected institutions were the elementary schools known as the *kuttab* (also known as the *maktab*; the names are interchangeable), which taught the most elementary aspects of religious observance together with some Qur'anic recitation in Arabic (regardless of the children's native tongue).[35] It should be pointed out here that at some major *jami-al-masjids* (as at *al-Azhar* and at *al-Zaitouna*—see later in this chapter). All these institutions could be found under one roof. In other words, it was not uncommon for such major institutions to have within its precincts, at one and the same time, children starting their first lessons in literacy and adults pursuing what may be considered as the equivalent of graduate-level studies. Other characteristics of this education system worthy of note, include these:

How well the system functioned *in practice* was dependent a great deal on distance from the major towns and cities. That is, the quality of the system (in terms of resources, instructional effectiveness, repute, etc.) tended to degrade as one got further away from major population centers.[36]

It was a mass-based, relatively democratic education system—which was highly unusual for any civilization up to that point—hence ability to pay was not usually an issue because education was, for the most part, free.[37] (Even where it was not free, especially at the higher, specialized levels of the system, provisions were generally made for talented students without means to be awarded scholarships.) This development spoke to the fact that Islam, on one hand, enjoined on all parents the compulsory education of their children, at least up to the first rung of the system (the *kuttab* level), and on the other, mandated all communities to educate a select few, the very talented, to the highest educational-level in order to meet the staffing needs of the system as a whole, as well as ensure the availability of a cadre of ulama for juridical duties. The reason for this was that the ability to recite the Qur'an *in Arabic*, together with the acquisition of knowledge of basic foundational aspects of the religion, was obligatory on all Muslims (male and female) at the individual level; and at the level of society as a whole, it was obligatory to have persons well versed in community-level religious matters; ranging from presiding over legal disputes to execution of inheritance laws to taking care of funerary matters.[38] As to who was allowed to progress up the educational ladder; in keeping with the democratic nature of the system, merit more than financial circumstances was the determining factor (for the most part, though not always—students of ability from poor family backgrounds were sometimes unable to go forward because their parents needed their labor). Note: that there could be no deviation from this principle was guaranteed by the fact that further progression depended on a solid memorization of the Qur'an *in its entirety*—not an easy feat to accomplish—and that ability as all societies know instinctively is more a function of genetics and dedication rather than financial or social standing.

Regarding the financial basis of the system: it rested primarily on charitable contributions (from all who could afford it to the best of their ability), especially in the form of trust funds (*waqf qhayri*) mentioned earlier. Such contributions in Islam held a special pride of place among those many voluntary meritorious deeds encouraged on the faithful. It may be noted that for the wealthy, including the rulers, there were two immediate benefits that accrued from this: legitimacy and enhanced standing in the community, and for some a personal religious fulfillment that comes out of executing a religious duty.[39]

Regardless of what level one is concerned with, the educational system of the Islamic empire, for the most part, was based on an institutional context of organizational decentralization and considerable structural informality in that some of the basic structural elements that one associates with modern educational institutions were largely absent.[40] Teaching, learning, and scholarship to a great extent relied on word-of-mouth repute of teachers (not institutions per se as will be pointed out in a moment), and of course, self-dedication of the student.

Pedagogy at the higher education-level relied mainly on the scholastic method where, by means of lectures in front of a radially seated study circle (the most senior students being closest to the teacher), a select body of venerated and often unchanging texts (this was a world where despite the existence of paper and awareness of the invention of the printing press, printing never really took hold because of a misguided notion that the mechanical printing of religious texts was sacrilegious) would be pored over to raise contrarian arguments and then proceeding to vanquish them with quotes from the same text (see Appendix I).[41]

An important dimension of instruction in the madrasahs was an even more informal (but hardly any less important) device: *peer learning*. Peer learning provided the necessary pedagogical intimacy between the teacher and learner that was usually lacking in the formal study circles. This is where acquisition of basic concepts, memorization, engagement with the texts, discussions, and so on, took place (a modern equivalent of the role of peer learning is that provided by the tutorial or recitation in universities in the United States). In fact, without peer learning it is unlikely that the system could have functioned at all.

Despite the ubiquity of the educational system, given its decentralization and informality coupled with its religious functions, the role of the state, if it was present at all, tended to be restricted for the most part to the financing of the system (which even then was episodic at best, depending on the philanthropic proclivities of a given ruler), and not its control. Therefore, the *ulama* (in their atomized entity—since Islam does not have ecclesiastical bureaucracies) had almost total control of all the components that made up the system (with all that it implied for relevance to the changing needs of their societies).

The role of the *ulama* in the education system went beyond simply staffing the madrasahs; it is they and not the madrasahs themselves that were the repository of educational excellence, fame, reputation, and so on. In other words, one or two teachers of great repute, in terms of learning *and* piety, could easily make or break a madrasah with their ability to attract (or the reverse) both a large following of students from near and far, and *waqf* contributions. In the Islamic educational system, education was always, in the last instance, personal, not institutional.[42] This is nowhere more clearly attested to than in the artifact of the *ijaza* (discussed later). Ergo, peripatetism was always an intrinsic part of Islamic education. Both, teachers and students traveled great distances, including going abroad, to learn and teach. In other words, the foreign student or scholar is not as modern a person as one may think. Such institutions of higher learning as al-Azhar, al-Zaitouna, al-Qarawiyyin, as well as the madrasahs of major Islamic centers of learning like Cordoba, Baghdad, Damascus, and Timbuktu, always had a significant component of its population comprising foreign students and scholars (including at times non-Muslim foreign students as well).

Madrasahs almost always were also centers of worship, therefore Islamic higher education institutions tended to have multifaceted roles. It would have been rare for a *waqf* of a madrasah not to make provisions for worship by providing stipends for the imam (prayer leader), the *muezzin* (caller to prayers), Qur'anic reciters, and so on. Learning in Islam always had an explicit spiritual dimension to it.[43]

Above the madrasahs there existed in an even more informal outlet for higher education, but it was of no less significance: the *hajj* (the mandatory pilgrimage to Mecca/ Medina) The *hajj* permitted the congregation of Islamic scholars from across the length and breadth of the Islamic world creating in a sense opportunities for scholarly interchange that can generously be described as a "world university" without walls.

From about thirteenth to fourteenth-century onward, as a result of external forces buffeting the Islamic empire (discussed in Appendix II), the madrasah system began to enter a period of slow but steady decline in terms of the general quality of the education that it imparted so that by the time we arrive at the end of the eighteenth-century the system, with rare exception, was incapable of *efficiently* serving the religious needs of the community; and equally importantly, could not meet the new human capital and other allied educational needs that the forces of modernization threw up through out the empire. One consequence of this was that the state had to either overhaul the madrasah system all together or to simply go outside it and create an alternative secular educational system.

Side by side with the madrasah system, there was also another one, but which was even more informal and it was primarily restricted to large wealthy cities that had acquired a reputation as centers of learning. This system specialized in what was known as the foreign sciences (*awail*)—secular subjects such as medicine, astronomy, mathematics, philosophy, and so on. The institutions that made up this system included private and public libraries, research institutes (known as *Bait al Hikmah* or House of Wisdom), hospitals (known as *bimaristan* to which there was almost always a teaching unit attached), and even bookstores. Additionally, there existed guilds for the teaching and learning of vocational subjects (iron smithing, jewelry-making, clerical studies, etc.) and military academies to teach martial arts to a select few.[44]

In Africa, while some form of Islamic higher education on the basis of the foregoing institutions existed in every locality where there was a sizeable Muslim population, places that came to be regarded as centers of learning with an extensive higher education system teaching both Islamic and foreign sciences were of course few; they included: Cairo (which boasts the famous al-Azhar University that was founded as a madrasah in 969 C.E.); Fez in Morocco (the modern-day Qarawiyyin University in Fez began its life as a madrasah in 859 C.E.); Timbuktu in Mali (which, with its various madrasahs—such as the Sankore madrasah—became Islamic West Africa's premier center of learning); Al-Qayrawan (Kairouan) in Tunisia (founded in 674 by the commander of the Muslim Army that conquered Tunisia (in 670), Uqbah ibn Nafi, and which would in time become one of the most important centers of learning in the Maghreb).[45] Tunisia would also come to host another important Maghrebi institution, to be discussed in a moment: the madrasah attached to the *al-Zitouna* mosque, which has survived through the centuries to become the modern al-Zaitouna (Ezzitouna) University of today (not surprisingly, it proclaims itself as the oldest university in the Islamic world).

Al-Zaitouna

No firm date is possible to discern, so far, from the historical record as to specifically when the al-Zaitouna mosque, which in time would become the basis of an important mosque-college, was first built: one view has it that it was constructed at the time of the capture of Tunis in 698–99 C.E. by Hassan Ibn al-Numan, while another states that the mosque began its life in 732–33 under Ubayd-allah Ibn Habhab.[46] However, we do know that the Aghlabids carried out major renovations of the mosque sometime in the middle of the ninth-century and, as one would logically expect in the case of institutions as old as al-Zaitouna, further improvements took place periodically at various times through out its history (e.g., around 990–95 under the Zirids; 1250, 1277, 1316, 1438–39 under the Hafsids; 1894 during the time of the French protec-torate).[47]

At the same time, one cannot say with certainty that the mosque was an im-portant scholarly institution from its very inception; in fact, on the contrary, it is more likely that for most of the early part of the history of the mosque there were other madrasahs that were of greater importance within Tunis itself and even more so at al-Kayrawan, which was an important center of learning (no doubt an associative development of the fact that it was the capital of the entire Maghreb at one point), where madrasahs at mosques such as that of Ukba bin Nafi had achieved considerable preeminence.[48] The importance of al-Zaitouna madrasah probably began to wax from around the time of the Hafsids as Tunis itself acquired significance as the capital of Ifriqiya (as Tunisia was then called).

By the time of the Spanish invasion of Tunis and their desecration of the mosque (together with the destruction of its library) following their occupation of La Goletta on July 14, 1534, al-Zaitouna boasted scores of halqahs (number-ing as many as 70 or more) within its precincts. In time, the madrasah would recover and its fortunes would improve considerably as its waqf income was supplemented by funding provided by the Husaynid dynasty (c. 1715–1957). As for the nature of its curriculum, it was typical of other major madrasahs such as al-Azhar and al-Qarawiyyin, though many of the texts used at the insti-tution came from Muslim Spain. The influence of Muslim Spain (which came about as a result of Spanish ulama seeking refuge in the Maghreb from the Re-conquista) was also present in the pedagogy in that there was a greater empha-sis on memorization than was the case at madrasahs in Egypt and elsewhere in the East.[49] Among the illustrious sons of the institution have included the thir-teenth-century encylopedist, Ahmed Tifachi, the geographer Abdallah Tijani; and the brilliant historian and sociologist, Abderrahman Ibn Khaldoun (Ibn Khaldun). (For more on the institution in the modern era, see Chapter 3).

Al-Qarawiyyin

Al-Qarawiyyin began its life as a small mosque constructed in 859 C.E. by means of an endowment bequeathed by a wealthy woman of much piety, Fatima bint Muhammed al-Fahri. She was originally from Kayrawan in Tunisia and she had migrated with her family to Fez (also known as Fas). The ruler in her time, whose permission would have been most likely sought for such a pro-ject, was Amir Yahya Ibn Idris, the grandson of Idris II. Subsequent architec-tural additions (alcoves, expansion of prayer halls, minarets, cupolas, madrasahs, fountains, library, etc.) to the building to reach its present Hispano-Arab form and compass would include the contributions of: Amir Dawoud, a grandson of Idrisi I (in 877); Amir Ahmed bin Abil-Said, a Zanata Amir and vassal of the Umayyad caliph of Cordoba in Muslim Spain who provided the funding (in 956); al-Muzaffar, the son of the famous Muhammed Ibn Abu Amir al-Mansur (c. 938–1002) of Cordoba who ruled Muslim Spain from 978 until his death (a cupola, among other additions, in 998); Ibn Muisha al-Kinani, a qadi under Amir Ali bin Yousuf (beginning in 1134 and not completed until 1144); Abu Inan Faris, a Marinid sultan (in 1349—founded the library, which was later significantly expanded by Ahmed al-Mansur, a Saadi sultan); and the present Alawite dynasty, who through the designation of the inner city (called *madina*) of Fez, where the mosque is located, as a World Heritage Site by UNESCO, continues to contribute to its survival.

While instruction at the mosque must have begun almost from the beginning, it is only when it had become a Friday congregational prayer mosque (*jami masjid*) by the end of tenth-century that its reputation as a center of learning in both religious and secular sciences (philosophy, astronomy, mathematics, etc.) must have begun to wax. By the twelfth-century it had firmly established its reputation, attracting scholars from all over Islamic North Africa (including as far south as Timbuktu) and Muslim Spain. After the decline of Muslim Spain, especially from the thirteenth-century onward brought on by the *Reconquista*, coupled with the transfer of the Moroccan capital by the Saadis from Fez to Marrakash its star would slowly but inexorably begin to wane.

It would appear then that the institution reached its apogee probably sometime between the fourteenth and fifteenth centuries; thereafter stasis and later a slow but steady decline would set in. The curriculum would become narrow, focusing almost exclusively on the religious sciences and even here certain fields were taught less and less, such as Qur'anic exegesis (tafsir). The institution still remained the university equivalent for Morocco itself, but its significance abroad certainly waned. Some effort was made to introduce curricular and pedagogic reforms (for example in 1788 by Sultan Muhammed bin Abd Allah; and in 1845 by Mawlay Abd al-Rahman) to the institution, but over the long-term their impact must have been marginal.

As is usually the case with any institution that relied on informal administrative structures, there are no reliable statistics available on student enrollment, number of faculty, and so on. It is possible to guess that it may have once enrolled up to 3,000 students; by the time we arrive in the twentieth-century, however, there were less than a 1,000. As for faculty it is that thought there were 425 scholars teaching there in 1830, but by 1906 their number had dropped to 266, and of them only 101 were still teaching, the rest were officials in the Sultan's administration (referred to as the *Makhzen*) (Porter 2002: 131).

Among the highlights of learning in the history of the institution that we know of include these: At one time Maimonides (Moses Ben Maimon), the distinguished Jewish philosopher and physician to Sultan Saladin (of Crusade fame), had studied there (1159–65); many celebrated scholars from Muslim Spain who sought refuge from the unfolding Reconquista made it their institutional home (especially from the thirteenth-century onward following the Battle of Al-Uqab [also known as Battle of Las Navas de Tolosa] on July 16, 1212, when the combined forces of Aragon, Castile, Leon, Navarre, and Portugal, under the banner of a pope-sanctioned crusade, permanently broke the back of Muslim rule in Spain by defeating the Almohad Army led by caliph Muhammed an-Nasir); and Ibn Khaldun had studied and taught there.[50] (Note, like Timbuktu [described later], the Medina in Fez where al-Qarawiyyin is located was declared a World Heritage site by UNESCO in 1981. The institution's history for the period following the arrival of French colonial rule in 1912, up to the present, is covered in Chapter 3.)[51]

The Madrasahs of Timbuktu: Jewels of Islamic West Africa

The city of Timbuktu began its life sometime in the late eleventh-century C.E. as a trading encampment of the Tuareg community (a Berber-speaking Islamized pastoralists) in the Sahelian desert at a point where the River Niger, Africa's third largest river, produces a huge internal delta at a section on the river known as the Niger Bend, in what is present-day Mali. From this beginning, it would eventually grow into a major city and acquire considerable international fame in the process; albeit some of it undeserved given the exaggerations—especially in Europe. Even though no one in Europe knew exactly where Timbuktu was, many, for centuries, according to Gardner (1968), had come to believe in such myths as that that it was the greatest city of culture and architectural achievements in Africa where houses, even had roofs made of gold!

Of course, by the time the first European adventurers had made their way to the city, inevitably drawn to it like moths to a candle, 700 years or so later in the nineteenth-century, it had long entered the stage of decay—their disappointment is palpable (see their accounts in Gardner 1968). Anyhow, while in its heyday it may not have had roofs of gold, it certainly did have gold of a different type: that currency of the mind: scholarship and learning. Writing in 1896, the French traveler Felix Dubois, makes this point this way following his visit to the city: to be sure the city was wanting in architectural achievements (understandably, he suggests, considering the lack of readily available time-insured building materials such as stone, given the city's geographic location); nevertheless, "[u]nable, therefore, to develop the sensuous arts, Timbuctoo [sic] reserved all her strength for the intellectual, and here her dominion was supreme." He goes on to quote a West African proverb: "Salt comes from the north, gold from the south, and silver from the country of the white men, but the word of God and the treasures of wisdom are only to be found in Timbuctoo" (Dubois 1969 [1896]: 275–76).

Located as it was on the synaptic intersection of great land and water routes of the Sahel, the Sahara and the Savannah of West Africa, it is perhaps not surprising that along with the ensuing commerce-driven prosperity there emerged scholarly communities attached to the various mosques in the city, quite possibly patterned, Hiskett (1984) surmises, on the al-Azhar mosque university (discussed later); though al-Qarawiyyin may have also had significant influence because of its relative proximity. For, there is no doubt that at the apogee of its existence Timbuktu was involved in a vibrant scholarly traffic of persons and ideas between itself and other centers of learning in the Islamic empire (Cairo, Damascus, etc.) as a consequence of three interrelated factors: the excellence of its learning; the mandatory annual pilgrimage to Mecca; and the use of Arabic as the medium of scholarly instruction and discourse. Moreover, for most of its history, it remained an autonomous city—a prototype city state—because of its Islamic heritage. (In other words, for the surrounding state of the day, from an administrative point of view, but not taxation of course, the city was usually perceived as a foreign implant to be left alone.)

Interestingly, even though Timbuktu was a Muslim city, it was not an Arab or Berber city, but an indigenous West African city in which were to be found many different racial/ ethnic groups living together (a sine qua non of any large settlement worthy of being characterized a city) and who participated in its governance through the agency of a multiethnic Islamic scholarly patriciate. According to Saad (1983: 110), in the long history of Timbuktu there is no record of racially/ ethnically-based societal conflict. This should not be surprising for two reasons, one that racism/ ethnicism is, at the theological-level at least, prohibited in Islam (see, however, the discussion on this matter later), and two, in a religious community where erudition and piety, as already noted earlier, was a major avenue of achieving high status, anyone of any ethnicity could achieve these. Consequently, he explains, in Timbuktu there was seemingly little tolerance for racial/ ethnic prejudices.

That a scholarly patriciate governed Timbuktu, explains Saad (1983) in his detailed and well documented social history of that city, stemmed from the specific circumstances of the introduction of Islam into West Africa: diffusion. To elaborate, unlike in the case of North Africa, the engine for the spread of Islam into other regions of Africa was not wars of conquest; rather, in most of West Africa, certainly (and in East Africa too), for example, Islam arrived primarily through trade and commerce. The process, which was greatly facilitated by the rapid development of the trans-Saharan trade following the arrival of that Saharan ship of the desert, the camel (introduced probably in the second-century C.E., but most definitely well established by the time the Muslim traders made their first appearance) is succinctly summarized by Hiskett (1984: 30) in his detailed survey of the development of Islam in West Africa: "It is a common human characteristic that people who think alike and follow the same way of life are inclined to assist each others trading activities more readily. Moreover, where credit is based very largely on personal reputations and contracts[, which] have to be fulfilled to unknown or distant persons, men are more likely to trust those who share their religion. This was especially so in the case of Muslims. The *Shari'ah* included strict regulations for the conduct of trade. As the trade expanded, so conversion to Islam grew." This, however, is to establish need; there is the matter of the agency of conversion. In the special circumstances of West Africa, the agency was Islamic higher education, which took two forms: that of the traditional place-established (settled) institutions—like those in Timbuktu—and a peripatetic system resting on itinerant scholars (see also Levtzion and Pouwels 2000).

Now, one outcome of this diffusionary mode of transmission was that as the Islamic communities began to emerge in West Africa, they felt compelled to exert their Islamic identities in order to retain their Islamic image. Within this circumstance, the right to govern came to be strongly rooted in an Islamic concept of legitimacy, which is, as just noted, based on erudition and piety (at least in principle, though not always in practice). Concomitantly, as Saad (1983) points out, dynastic changes based on politico-military factors found elsewhere in the Islamic world, were, in the context of Islamic West Africa, of much lesser importance.

Against this backdrop, it is not surprising that Timbuktu would come to boast Muslim scholars—both indigenous and foreign—of wide repute within the Islamic world. Yet, viewed only in these terms, from the perspective of Islamic West Africa, it was not unique; there were other towns and cities that had similar traditions of Islamic higher education (Hiskett 1984). The uniqueness of Timbuktu stemmed from its autonomy, size, and the magnitude of its commercial prosperity—which was a factor primarily of geography—where it came to play the role of a capital city for the pastoralists of the Sahel and the Sahara and which in turn allowed it to be the emporium of the indigenous peoples of all ethnicities and beliefs across much of West Africa.

Moving on, it should be pointed out here first, that even though the name Sankore is often associated with higher education in Timbuktu, hence the name Sankore University (as in one of the chapter headings in Dubois 1969 [1896]), Sankore was by no means the only mosque or even always the most important mosque in Timbuktu that imparted higher education. There were others in different parts of the city, though only two have survived to the present day, besides Sankore (examples include *Jingerebir, Sidi Yahya* and market *(jami al-suq)* mosques).

At all these mosques, however, the general model of higher education appears to have been the same. Going by Saad (1983), the existence of an erudite savant of wide repute who would attract a number of students to pursue the study of Qur'anic interpretation (tafsir), grammar, law, theology, and so on. From among the students a smaller number, the most advanced, would specialize in the indepth study of a theological or a legal work as the last stage of the curriculum or as a separate but concurrent curricular activity. Note that these classes were not held only at mosques, they were also offered in teachers homes. Further, students did not always restrict themselves to classes at a single mosque; they were free to attend classes at other mosques too, especially if they wished to study a subject not offered at their's. Did the students have to pay for their studies? The simple answer is yes and no. While there was no set tuition, explains Hiskett (1984), students paid their teachers either in cash or in kind on the basis of affordability.

Running parallel with this system was what Saad calls a system of tututorialships that involved a very personalized study relationship between the master and a few of his most promising students who would be well into their adulthood upon entry into the system. Upon completion of the tututorialship the student would be conferred with a certificate that specified the subjects mastered and at what level of depth. This certificate (a licencia docendi called *ijaza*) was in essence a teaching certificate and a certificate of academic pedigree, where the teacher specified the line of descent of the teaching—which often spanned several generations of teachers—that the student had received (see Hiskett 1984: 57–58 for details). Needless to say, the value of the *ijaza* was directly proportional to the scholarly repute of the master. Ergo, it was not unusual for students to study under several masters.

It is the tutorial system that was the means for entry into the scholarly patriciate—at the apex of which was the jurisconsult *(mufti)* who alone had the authority to offer legal opinions (fatwa) on matters that required clarification. Given the political importance of the tutorial system, it ought to be noted here that it was not accessible to all and sundry on the basis of pure academic merit. Political, familial, economic, and other such connections of the student also had a part to play, in addition to academic merit. As for the curriculum, it was typical of most madrasahs of their day in the Islamic empire.

If the Timbuktu madrasahs were the jewels of the West African Islamic world, then surely al-Azhar was the jewel of possibly the entire Islamic world during some phases of its history. Al-Azhar, however, continues to thrive to this day, though it has had to undergo considerable secular modernization along the way; yet, in contrast, the mosque universities of Timbuktu did not survive. They slowly withered away as the fortunes of the city waned in the period immediately leading up to the arrival of French colonialism in West Africa in the nineteenth-century (1894), and thereafter. Why did the city not retain its glory and continue to prosper? The answer is a simple one: its raison d'etre disappeared with the advent of modern transportation and colonial boundaries: trans-Sahelian and trans-Saharan trade. (Also, an invasion by Morocco in 1590 did not help matters.) Today Timbuktu is a lowly provincial capital, though in 1988 it was placed by UNESCO on its list of World Heritage Sites (see their website). Now, on to al-Azhar, which today ranks as among the oldest higher education institutions in the world.

Al-Azhar: The Jewel of North Africa

It is ironic that one of the most prestigious higher education institutions in the Islamic world today is not to be found in the land of the birth of Islam, but in what used to be one of the African provinces of the empire: Egypt—but then, such is the roll of the dice of history. Al-Azhar began its life as a *halqah* in a newly constructed congregational mosque *(jami al-masjid)* that was built in 972 C.E. by the Fatimid dynasty, which had conquered Egypt in 969 from their base in Tunisia.[52] The new mosque was part of a larger project of the conquerors who, under the leadership of their general, named Jawhar (a Greek convert to Islam, from Sicily), sought to establish a new capital near the old administrative center of al-Fustat and which they would name Al-Qahirah; hence the Europeanized derivation: Cairo.[53] The name al-Azhar, it may be noted, originates from the name of Prophet Muhammed's daughter, Fatimah al-Azhar-Zahra, whose lineal descendents were the Fatimids, or at least so they claimed. -

As a *halqah*, al-Azhar would be one of many that Cairo would come to boast as it eventually developed into a major center of learning in the Islamic empire. However, what would distinguish this particular *halqah* from the others from almost the very beginning is not only the fact that it was part of a *jami al-masjid* established by the Fatimids, but also the presence of two well-known Sh'ite scholars of Islamic jurisprudence, *Ibn Killis* (Abu al-Faraj Yakub ibn-Yusuf ibn-Killis, a convert from Judaism to Islam) and Ali ibn al-Numan, at the *jami al-masjid*. Their scholarly forensics would soon set al-Azhar on to the path of prestige and renown as Sh'ite students from near and far, including Sh'ite foreign students, journeyed to study there. In their desire to promote their particular version of Islamic theology, the Fatimids became enthusiastic benefactors of al-Azhar (exemplified, for instance, by the appointment of salaried resident teachers; the construction of the institution's first, it is thought, student dormitory in 988; the founding of an important research library in 1005; the establishment of permanent endowments for the mosque itself; periodic remodeling and the building of additions; etc.).[54]

The close ties to the ruling dynasty, however, was a double-edged sword as the institution would find out in time: a well endowed patronage could disappear overnight should the dynasty collapse or be replaced by a hostile one; which indeed happened around the middle of the twelfth-century as a combination of factors (dissension, corruption, unpopularity, external pressures, etc.) led to the dynasty's eventual demise. The formal end came with the death of the last Fatimid caliph in 1171. The new ruler of Egypt, *Salah Ad-din Yusuf ibn Ayyub* (Saladin—the Kurdish founder of the Ayyubid dynasty and of the great anti-Crusader fame who recaptured Jerusalem from the Frankish Christians on October 2, 1187), allowed al-Azhar to almost wither away on the vine so to speak. His hostility to it was no doubt underwritten by the fact that he was a Sun'ni Muslim with no interest in supporting a Sh'ite institution. Instead, the

Ayyubids established a number of rival madrasahs (as a means for curtailing or even eliminating what they considered as the Sh'ite heresy) within the Islamic empire; among the more well-known ones in Cairo included *al-Madrasah al-Kamiliyah* and *al-Madrasah al-Salihiyah.* (See Leiser 1976, for more on this development.)

Since it is the Ayyubids, however, who would be the first to introduce the institution of the madrasah to Egypt, the al-Azhar halqahs would, in time, become inadvertent beneficiaries of Ayyubid dynastic rule as a result of this educational innovation by undergoing two major changes: al-Azhar itself would be transformed into a madrasah, and its curriculum would be expanded to represent the typical madrasah curriculum. This institutional change would be formalized in 1340 with the building of a separate college next to the mosque during the reign of the Mamluks—the dynasty that replaced the Ayyubids in 1250.[55] This is not to say, however, that the change would spell the end of kuttab-level instruction at the institution. One of the hallmarks of al-Azhar was that even as it progressed toward its status as an institution of higher learning, it still retained (and continues to retain) its connections with elementary education. Al-Azhar was also a mosque and therefore young Cairene children were entitled to come and learn their basics there much in the same way that other children did at mosques all over Egypt and the rest of the Islamic world. (It was not unusual to find on one side of the same mosque premises young children receiving their first instructions in the recitation of the Qur'an, while on the other side old men with beards engaged in advanced studies [see Dodge 1961: 103].[56])

The Mamluks (who began ruling Egypt after deposing the Ayyubid dynasty in 1250 during the course of a succession dispute within the dynasty) were positively disposed toward al-Azhar, which was, by now, no longer a Sh'ite institution; consequently, al-Azhar would once again find its place in the sun. This development was no doubt helped by the fact that during this period, al-Azhar and other places of learning in Cairo came to assume considerable importance for the Islamic world as a whole because of the Mongol devastation (see Appendix II) that led Cairo to replace cities like Baghdad as a major center of Islamic learning. It is under the reign of the Mamluk sultan al-Malik al-Zahir (1260–77) (known in history books as Baybars) that the process of restoring al-Azhar to its former glory was begun with some seriousness. Whatever their failings, and there were many, from the perspective of education specifically the Mamluks must be credited with greatly contributing to the development of the higher education infrastructure in Egypt. Certainly, the infrastructure that the French had found upon their arrival in 1798 was to a large extent the handy work of the Mamluks (Berkey 1992).

Why did the Mamluks display such great interest in the development of this infrastructure? After all, one would assume that given that they were (as already noted) a militaristic foreign elite of slave origins, the development of cultural institutions (religious, educational, or otherwise) would have been at the very bottom of their list of concerns. One answer is provided by Behrens-Abouseif (1994: 271): "The control of the rulers over religious institutions has always been a fact in the history of Muslim societies." Therefore, she continues, "[b]y acting as patrons of religious foundations, rulers sought to gain the support of the population and the opinion-making religious establishment, thus surmounting ethnic and cultural barriers, which often existed between rulers and subjects." However, this was not the only reason; the Mamluks were also Muslims. Therefore, besides the matter of cultural endowments as a means of political legitimation, we must also add motivations that derived (at least for some if not all) from a genuine desire to fulfill their duties as Muslims for reasons of piety (as well as expiation of sins).[57]

Some 300 years or so later, in 1517, it would be the turn of the Mamluk dynasty to be marginalized; it would be replaced by the Ottoman Turks as Egypt became a province in the Ottoman Empire (their marginalization was only in dynastic terms, for, in time, a residuum of the dynasty would manage to win back considerable autonomy for itself from the Ottomans—hence in Chapter 3 they are referred to as the Ottoman Mamluks). Fortunately for al-Azhar, the change in regime did not prove to be adverse to its interests; the Ottomans too followed in the tradition of the Mamluk dynasty by continuing its support of the institution. By this point al-Azhar had acquired a status of distinction within the Islamic empire as the madrasah par excellence—one that was without peer. The ulama who taught there were held in high esteem, not only in Egypt, but in other parts of the empire as well, including Saudi Arabia, the birthplace of Islam. Not surprisingly, it would attract students from all over the Islamic world in large numbers—though exactly how many students were studying at al-Azhar at any given time in the pre-Napoleon era will probably never be known since no statistical records appear to have been kept.

It ought to be noted that in addition to its religious and educational functions, al-Azhar had two other equally important roles: as a legal institution given that it was the home of the Grand Shaykh of Egypt (the Mufti) who was the arbiter of the last instance in a society that was governed, at least for the most part, by Islamic law (the *Shari'ah*), and as a social institution where the populace gathered during times of distress for refuge and guidance (as when Egypt was invaded by the French under Napoleon Bonaparte).[58]

The increasing student population in turn led to the development, most probably during the Ottoman period, of an administrative structure that divided the students into units on the basis of either nationality, or region, or the four schools of thought (known as *madhab*s) in Islamic law and jurisprudence. These units, which were also residential for out-of-town students, were called *riwaq*s and they were headed by members of the faculty. Examples of the *riwaq*s include *Riwaq al-Sa'aidah* (for students from upper Egypt); *Riwaq al-Shawaam* (for foreign students from Syria); *Riwaq al-Jawah* (for foreign students from Indonesia); *Riwaq al-Sulaymaniyah* (for foreign students from Afghanistan and Khurasan); *Riwaq al-Jabartiyah* (for foreign students from Djibouti, Ethiopia, and Somaliland); and so on.

Another innovation during the period of Ottoman rule, was that sometime in the seventeenth-century, the madrasah began to be administered by a rector *(Shaikh al-Azhar)* chosen by the ulama from among themselves. The first rector was Muhammed Abdullah al-Khurashi who held his position until 1690.[59] Later, under the Khedives, beginning with Muhammed Ali, appointment to this position would forever become the prerogative of the state, but with some advisory input from the ulama.

"Admission" (quotes are appropriate as will be evident in a moment) to study at al-Azhar, especially in the case of students who came from outside Cairo, depended on two primary factors: possession of some level of literacy and competence in reciting the Qur'an and access to funds from parents and relatives for lodging and board, or for the very indigent, from al-Azhar itself—which usually took the form of lodging space and food rations.[60] However, since there was no entrance exam or even a formal admission process, it is quite likely that those students who came from the more remote parts of Egypt and elsewhere in the Islamic empire where the *kuttab*s were not well developed, their level of learning would not have included literacy (notwithstanding their rote memorization of the Qur'an.) Upon arrival at the institution the new student, after having secured access to the essential matters of board and lodge (usually with the assistance of relatives or friends), simply assigned himself to whatever study circle he found appropriate to his education level.[61] The normal period of study for most students, who usually arrived in their early teens, was about eight years, whereupon the student would emerge as a school teacher or a legal assistant or a junior administrative official or an *imam* (a prayer leader at a mosque). A select few, the very dedicated, would continue in their studies to eventually become a *qadi* (a judge). (The Islamic empire, regardless of who the dynastic rulers were, was administered on the basis of the *Shari'ah*; and it is higher education institutions such as al-Azhar that trained the personnel required to implement the *Shari'ah*.) Prior to 1872, formal diplomas attesting to the completion of studies were not available; instead the practice was for individual teachers to issue an *ijaza*.

The finances of al-Azhar, in terms of both capital and recurrent expenditure, as with all large madrasahs in the Islamic world, were based on two principle sources: the *waqf* endowments (which usually took two main forms, agricultural/ commercial property and rentable buildings) and gifts from the state (either in cash or in kind or both and often given on an annual basis at the beginning of the holy month of Ramadan). As with modern higher education endowments, benefits from a *waqf* accrued either to the whole institution or to parts of it (e.g., a given *riwaq* or even a specific ulama chair), depending upon the instructions of the donor, which under Islamic law were, in essence, written in stone.[62] Considering the prestige and status of al-Azhar at one time in its history, it was often the philanthropic target of private wealthy patrons. At the same time, however, only the rarest of rulers would have failed to want to ingratiate himself with the institution through both *waqfs* and annual gifts. Ergo, through a process of historical accumulation, al-Azhar amassed over the centuries a considerable amount of *waqf* property (until it lost a large part of it to the depredations of Muhammed Ali, see Chapter 3).

In addition to institutionally mediated support, both faculty and students also supplemented their salaries and stipends with services to the community (e.g., undertaking Qur'anic recitations during the month of Ramadan at other mosques in the city that possessed waqfs assigned for that purpose, or presiding at weddings and other similar social functions, or offering individualized tuition to the children of the wealthy, or in the case of the ulama serving as judges). [63] Note that while employment at al-Azhar for members of the ulama was more or less permanent (barring some major egregious behavior on their part), it is intriguing that a similar circumstance was also extended to the student; to explain, once a student became a recipient of institutional support (usually in his second or third year), the student had access to it for the rest of his life so long as he remained a student at the institution. (One is familiar with the concept of tenured faculty, but tenured students? That is novel.) It is known in fact that some students, from time to time, did remain at al-Azhar for most if not all of their lives, for religious or other personal reasons.

As for the curriculum, it remained typical of a large madrasah, so that even as late as the eighteenth-century when the French under Napoleon conquered Egypt (in July of 1798), thereby ending nearly 300 years of Ottoman rule, the curriculum of al-Azhar still did not countenance the foreign sciences. But, by the time the French had departed a mere three years later, in 1801, following their defeat by the British forces, al-Azhar in this respect would never be the same again. The ulama there had been taught a lesson: even 1,000 years of Muslim rule could be brought to an end; something had to change in the education of the Muslims so that they would be better equipped to confront the emerging foreign threats that Western imperialism represented. While understandably the immediate reaction was to turn toward even greater conservatism, with the arrival of Khedival rule the ulama were slowly coerced by secular forces to embark on a tortuous journey of curricular reform (and accompanied by physical expansion) so that by the time Egypt had gained full independence from British domination in 1952, al-Azhar was no longer a madrasah, but a full-fledged university in its modern sense—the foreign sciences were no longer foreign in al-Azhar. In 1961, al-Azhar would formally become part of the Egyptian national higher educational system as its further secularization, under pressure of the Egyptian government, continued. This change, however, did not imply that the ulama no longer taught there; they still do—but their curricular and administrative hold on it would be progressively weakened (see Chapter 3). From a purely religious point of view, al-Azhar no longer holds the pride of place that it once did in the Islamic empire as a whole; though within the narrower geographic confines of the Islamic Middle East and North Africa, its prestige remains unrivaled to this day.[64]

HISTORIOGRAPHICAL IMPLICATIONS

Having established the precolonial historical record, now comes the equally important task of pointing out the significance of this record in *historiographical* terms. There are at least three central issues that emerge from this record that must be dealt with: the importance of establishing African *historicity*; the need to expunge Eurocentrism from accounts of the origins of the modern university; and the importance of, again, expunging Eurocentrism from explanations of how Europe was able to "hijack" the trajectory of African history and thereby engineer the marginalization of precolonial higher education institutions in favor of colonially imported models. Because of the depth, complexity, and contentiousness of the subject matter, often requiring exegetical forays into corners of history whose relevance may not be readily apparent at first glance, Appendixes I and II have been assigned the task of addressing the second and third issues, while this chapter will concentrate on the first.

On African Historicity

The preceding account of precolonial higher education in Africa, needless to say, helps to highlight the fallacy that without European colonialism no progress would have come about in Africa. There are some who may consider this dimension of the raison d'etre of this chapter as somewhat irrelevant in this day and age. But is this really so? For, the bizarre idea first popularized by the likes of such Western intellectuals as Georg Hegel that prior to the arrival of Europeans, Africa was a dark continent immobilized in time and peopled by child-like savages who could not have possibly made any history may no longer be openly articulated today, but if the continuation of the racist discourse in Western countries (the continuing rancorous debate over the merits of affirmative action for black Americans in higher education in the United States, for instance, is just one infinitesimal example) is any indication, such sentiments continue to plague the Western psyche, even if only at subterranean levels among the majority of the populace. Ergo, those, like Cooper (1993) and Howe (1998), who believe that in this day and age the continuing emphasis on African historicity is nothing less than plaintive overinsistence are on this score naive—extremely naive. Consider that even as late as the mid–1990s "respectable" Euro-American academics could not resist dressing the following Hegelian view of Africans in the "modern" garb of pseudoscientific research on intelligence (a good example of which was the work of Richard J. Hernstein and

Charles Murray 1994): "Negroes are to be regarded as a race of children who remain immersed in their state of uninterested naïveté. Good-natured and harmless when at peace, they can become suddenly enraged and then commit the most frightful cruelties." Hegel then continues that while "[t]hey cannot be denied a capacity for education," the fact still remains that "they do not show an inherent striving for culture." He goes on: "In their native country the most shocking despotism prevails. There they do not attain to the feeling of human personality, their mentality is quite dormant, remaining sunk within itself and making no progress, and thus corresponding to the compact, differenceless mass of the African continent" (Hegel 1971 [1845]: 42–43). Surely, the existence of complex civilizations and kingdoms in Africa prior to the arrival of Europeans ought to have long ago put to rest such preposterous notions—though, perhaps not quite: to explain these achievements they came out with their specious theory of Hamites (Robertshaw 1990). Before going on to consider this theory, one should also be reminded here of the fact that the Eurocentric model, in various guises, continues to hold sway in the writing of world history generally (see Appendix II).

When Europeans first stumbled across the architectural and artistic expressions of the wondrous achievements of Africans of antiquity (e.g., the Pyramids, the Zimbabwe Ruins, etc.) a dominant view that emerged among them to explain their origins was that they were the handiwork of a race of people from outside Africa.[65] As Edith Sanders (1969) explains, while tracing the origins of this particular Western myth: "[t]he Hamitic hypothesis is well-known to students of Africa. It states that everything of value ever found in Africa was brought there by the Hamites, allegedly a branch of the Caucasian race." However, she further explains, "[o]n closer examination of the history of the idea, there emerges a previous elaborate Hamitic theory, in which the Hamites are believed to be Negroes." In other words, as she observes, "[I]t becomes clear then that the hypothesis is symptomatic of the nature of race relations, that it has changed its content if not its nomenclature through time, and that it has become a problem of epistemology" (p. 521). Not surprisingly, her carefully reasoned exegesis unveils a wicked tale of the lengths to which Westerners have gone to deny an entire continent part of its history; all for the purpose of constructing a racist ideology that could permit the rape of a continent without causing so much as a twinge in the consciences of even the most ardent of Christians. In fact, with great convenience, the myth actually begins in the Christian cosmological realm. The necessity to describe the origins and role of this myth here (albeit briefly) stems, of course, from its pervasive influence on Western attitudes toward the darker peoples of the world ever since the rise of Christianity in the West, generally, and more specifically, its subterranean influence on how Western colonial policies on education (as well as in other areas of human endeavor) in Africa were shaped and implemented—as will be shown in the pages to come. Furthermore, there is also the fact of its continuing lingering presence even to this day, in various permutations at the subconscious and conscious levels, in the psyche of most Westerners when they confront Africa—symptomatic of which, to give just one example, is the virulent attack on Bernal by the Eurocentrists (mentioned earlier).

Now, as just noted and bizarre though this may appear, the Hamites make their entry into the Western racist discourse initially as a degenerate and accursed race, not as an exemplary, high achieving race (relative to black people) that they were eventually transformed into. Those familiar with the Bible will recall that in it there are two versions of Noah, the righteous and blameless patriarch who is saved from the Great Flood by a prior warning from God that involves the construction of an ark by Noah (Genesis 6: 11–9: 19); and the drunken Noah of Genesis 9: 20–9: 27 who inflicts a curse on one of his three sons, Ham. It is the latter version that is of relevance here. Here is how the story goes in the King James version of the Bible:

20. And Noah began to be an husbandman, and he planted a vineyard: 21. And he drank of the wine, and was drunken; and he was uncovered within his tent. 22. And Ham, the father of Canaan, saw the nakedness of his father, and told his two brethren without. 23. And Shem and Japheth took a garment, and laid it upon both their shoulders, and went backward, and covered the nakedness of their father; and their faces were backward, and they saw not their father's nakedness. 24. And Noah awoke from his wine, and knew what his younger son had done unto him. 25. And he said, Cursed be Canaan; a servant of servants shall he be unto his brethren. 26. And he said, Blessed be the LORD God of Shem; and Canaan shall be his servant. 27. God shall enlarge Japheth, and he shall dwell in the tents of Shem; and Canaan shall be his servant.

Thus was born the Biblical curse of Ham (which in reality was a curse on his son Canaan).[66] Initially, in the period of Latin Christianity of the Middle Ages, the curse of Ham was used as a justification for the existence of slavery in a generic sense, that is without reference to skin color. Considering that slavery during this period encompassed all manner of European ethnicities and was not restricted to people of African descent alone, this is not surprising. However, by the time one arrives in the seventeenth-century when the enslavement of Africans is now well underway in the Americas, the curse of Ham becomes the justification for this enslavement; that is Ham and his progeny have been transformed into an accursed black people ordained by God to be slaves of white people (the progeny of Japheth) in perpetuity. (Aside: placed hierarchically in between these two groups were the progeny of Shem, namely, Jews and Asians.) Before reaching this point, however, first there had to be a connection made between the color black and the curse of Ham. The problem is best described by Goldenberg (2003: 195):

To biblical Israel, Kush was the land at the furthest southern reach of the earth, whose inhabitants were militarily powerful, tall, and good-looking. These are the dominant images of the black African in the Bible, and they correspond to similar images in Greco-

Roman culture. I found no indications of a negative sentiment toward Blacks in the Bible. Aside from its use in a proverb (found also among the Egyptians and the Greeks), skin color is never mentioned in descriptions of biblical Kushites. That is the most significant perception, or lack of perception, in the biblical image of the black African. Color did not matter.

So, the question is how did color enter into the curse? Here, there is some disagreement. Goldenberg suggests that the linkage takes place through two principal exegetical changes: the erroneous etymological understanding of the word Ham as referring, in root, to the color black (which also spawns another serious exegetical error, the replacement of Canaan with Ham in the curse); and the exegetical seepage of blackness into the story of the curse (which originally, he observes, was colorless) as it was retold, beginning, perhaps, in the third or fourth-century C.E. with Syriac Christians via a work titled the *Cave of Treasures*, and then further taken up by the Arab Muslims in the seventh-century following their conquest of North Africa (and the two, in turn, later influencing the Jewish exegetical treatment of the story). Goldenberg further observes that the *Cave of Treasures* in its various recensions down the centuries extends the curse to not just Kushites, but all blacks defined to include, for example, the Egyptian Copts, East Indians and Ethiopians (that is they are all descendents, according to the *Cave of Treasures*, of Ham). Hence, Goldenberg quotes one version as reading "When Noah awoke...he cursed him and said: 'Cursed be Ham and may he be slave to his brothers'...and he became a slave, he and his lineage, namely the Egyptians, the Abyssinians, and the Indians. Indeed, Ham lost all sense of shame and he became black and was called shameless all the days of his life forever" (p. 173).

On the other hand, taking the lead from Graves and Patai (1966)—as for example Sanders (1969) does—the connection, it is suggested, occurs via the agency of Jewish oral traditions (*midrashim*), specifically those contained in one of the two Talmuds, the Babylonian Talmud (*Talmud Bavli*)—the other Talmud is the Palestinian Talmud (*Talmud Yerushalmi*). The Talmuds were a compilation of *midrashim*, which for centuries had been transmitted orally, put together by Jewish scholars in their academies in Palestine and in Babylonia. Although the *Talmud Bavli* was compiled in fifth-century C.E., it did not make its appearance in Europe until probably sixth-century C.E. Now, the *midrash* relevant here was concocted, according to the gloss by Graves and Patai (1966: 122), in order to justify the enslavement of the Canaanites by the Israelites; and here is how it goes (reproduced from the version compiled by Graves and Patai 1966: 121):

(d) Some say that at the height of his drunkenness he uncovered himself, whereupon Canaan, Ham's little son, entered the tent, mischievously looped a stout cord about his grandfather's genitals, drew it tight, and [enfeebled] him.... (e) Others say that Ham himself [enfeebled] Noah who, awakening from his drunken sleep and understanding what had been done to him, cried: "Now I cannot beget the fourth son whose children I would have ordered to serve you and your brothers! Therefore it must be Canaan, your first-born whom they enslave....Canaan's children shall be born ugly and black! Moreover, because you twisted your head around to see my nakedness, your grandchildren's hair shall be twisted into kinks, and their eyes red; again because your lips jested at my misfortune, theirs shall swell; and because you neglected my nakedness, they shall go naked, and their male members shall be shamefully elongated." Men of their race are called Negroes, their forefather Canaan commanded them to love theft and fornication, to be banded together in hatred of their masters and never to tell the truth.

Anyhow, regardless of whether it was early Eastern Christians, or Jews or Muslims who were responsible for corrupting the biblical story along two axes, replacing Canaan with Ham and rendering Ham black, this much is incontrovertible: Medieval Christians in the West would in time adopt it as their very own because it would allow them to develop an ideology of exploitation and oppression of black peoples, especially beginning in the fifteenth-century onward, without violating their religious sensibilities.

Notice then that through this mythological trickery two basic elements of Christian cosmology are retained: that one, all human beings are descended from a common ancestor (Adam whose line of descent includes Noah) and that, two, not all human beings are equal. Hence, the peoples of the European peninsula (the conventional use of the term continent in relation to Europe is an ideologically driven misnomer as a quick glance at a world atlas will confirm) on one hand, and the peoples of the African and Asian continents on the other, stand in a racial hierarchical relationship of master/ servant/ slave. Since this was a Biblical determined order, it followed then that no Christian need lose sleep over the morality of exploiting and enslaving other human beings.

Now the question that one must ask here is, When do the descendants of Ham, while still residing in Africa, rejoin the family of Europeans as a subgroup of Caucasians? It occurs during the period of the beginnings of the colonization of Africa. There are two factors that account for this development: the emergence of scientific explanations of race during the era of the Enlightenment when theological explanations began to give way to scientific explanations of the natural world; and the arrival of Napoleon's Army in Egypt in 1798, accompanied by French scientists who would go on to establish the new discipline of Egyptology. The former factor established the possibility of polygenesis as an alternative to the biblical theory of monogenesis (all human beings were descendents of Adam); that is not all human beings have a common ancestor, but that some had emerged separately as a subspecies of humankind. The latter factor's role turns on the startling discovery by the French scientists that the Egyptian civilization, that is the civilization of black people, was the precursor of the Western civilization. Now, this finding met with considerable opposition in the West since for some it flew in the face of the prevalent racist notions that dialectically justified and drew succor from the ongoing Atlantic slave trade, while for others it stood in opposition to the biblical notion of black people as accursed descendents of Ham. The resolution of the problem of determining who were the ancient Egyptians, therefore, was resolved by turning to a polygenetic explanation. Specifically, following a rereading of the Bible the notion emerged that the Egyptians were the descendents of that other son of Ham, Mizraim, who it was argued had not been cursed as Canaan had been. By isolating Canaan from his brothers, Mizraim and Cush, it was possible to suggest that only the descendents of Canaan had been cursed, and not those of Mizraim and Cush.

The ancient Egyptians therefore were not a black people, it was argued, but a Caucasian subgroup, the Hamites. To provide scientific support for this view, Western scientists in the nineteenth-century, especially those working in the United States (perhaps spurred on by the need to justify slavery in the face of rising abolitionist sentiments), emerged with the bogus "science of craniometry," that purported to prove on the basis of the measurement of human skulls a hierarchy of intelligence among different groups of people (blacks with supposedly the smallest crania, and hence the smallest brain, falling to the very bottom).[67] On the basis of this bogus science it was quickly established that the ancient Egyptians were not black Africans, but Hamites. However, it is important to point out here that the Hamites were not completely shorn off of their early inferior status as descendants of the accursed Ham. Rather they were considered to be an inferior subgroup of the Caucasian group, but superior to black peoples. (In other words, a new internal hierarchy was established among the descendants of Jephet where the Tuetonic Anglo-Saxons were at the very top and the Hamites at the very bottom and eastern and southern Europeans— Slavs, Italians, Portuguese, Greeks, etc.—somewhere in the middle.) Thus was born the infamous Hamitic theory that was used to explain any expression of the grandeur of African history that Europeans came across. Hamites were Africans, but they were Caucasian in origin—they came from outside Africa.[68]

NOTES

1. There is a tendency in much of Western writing on Africa to divide the continent into North Africa and Sub-Saharan (or Black) Africa, even in the absence of a geographic division, and then proceed to deny that North Africa can be legitimately considered as part of the African continent; rather they insist that it is part of the Arab world of the "Middle East" (the latter term itself is of course a misnomer, although for the sake of convenience it is retained in this book). The most obvious example of this approach has been, until very recently, the highly unwarranted excision of the Egyptian civilization from African history. However at the level of popular culture it continues to be evident through the common use of the phrase Sub-Saharan Africa in the media. A good example of this is evidenced by such publications as the annual tomes put out by Europa Publications titled Africa South of the Sahara and the Middle East and North Africa as part of its otherwise useful references series called "Regional Surveys of the

World." Furthermore, such are the times we live in that there are those within Africa itself (both north of the Sahara and south of the Sahara) who would concur with this artificial bifurcation of the continent. The truth is that just as Eastern Europe is part of Asia and part of Europe at one and the same time, North Africa belongs to both sides, the African side and the Middle Eastern side. It is not simply that geography dictates that North Africa be seen as part of Africa, but culture and history as well. At the most basic level consider the fact that British colonial Africa, as in the cases of French, Italian and Spanish colonial Africa, also included parts of North Africa. To put the matter in another way: If modern African culture is a fusion of Western and African cultures, then the only differentiating factor that separates modern North African culture from modern Sub-Saharan African culture is that modern North African culture incorporates a third culture: Arabic Islamic culture. Yes, it is true that Arabic is not an indigenous African language any more than English, French or Portuguese is, even though its arrival in Africa precedes others by some 1,000 years—a long enough period to shed its tramontane status. (On the other hand, one could challenge this statement by suggesting, as Mazrui (1986) does, that from a geographic point of view the Arabic peninsula ought to be considered part of Africa; and therefore Arabic is not a foreign language. The fact that this is not how the peninsula is usually seen today, is a function of Western engineering—the Suez Canal—and Western domination of world cartography.) At the heart of the definitional problem is the matter of race, not geography; that is, the racism of the West (which has always sought to create racial hierarchies—positing peoples defined as black at the bottom and those defined as white at the top and the rest in between); combined with the racism of the North Africans and Africans themselves, is the root of this problem. Since this issue will be discussed further in its different manifestations, it will suffice for the moment to simply state that this work will not succumb to any racist project (whoever may be its past and present architects). Instead, the insisted position is that North Africa is as much part of Africa as it is part of the Middle East. In fact, we will go even one step further and insist that there is a geographic and cultural unity that brings together Africa, Asia and Europe in the form of that great Afro-Eurasian ecumene a la Hodgson (1974; 1993). (See also Wigen and Lewis [1997] who discuss this matter at some length.)

2. For recent literature that provides an accessible general introduction to ancient Egyptian history see Mysliewiec (2000); Shaw (2000); and Wilkinson (2000).

3. There appears to be some confusion, as Richard Wilkinson (2000) in his lavishly and beautifully illustrated gold mine of a book, The Complete Temples of Ancient Egypt, points out, about the nature and purposes of temples in the Egyptian civilization that stems from a failure to see that they did not perform the same role as temples in many other cultures—that is, as, simply, places of religious worship. To be specific, the Egyptian temples were at once secular and religious institutions. The immense size of many of the temple campuses speak to the fact that they did not all exist purely for religious purposes; they often performed many other wider functions. Wilkinson (2000: 7) describes the scenario well: "Within the walls of most of these monuments, sanctuaries and treasuries, offices and palaces, slaughterhouses and schools might be found. Not only were many of the religious complexes centers of government, economy and commerce, but also within these temples ancient science and scholarship thrived and the nature of existence itself was pondered by generations of learned priests." There is a very

good reason why the temples had a multiplicity of functions: in the Egyptian world the divine and the secular were inseparable.

4. Compare here with the description that Kramer (1981: 4) provides of the earliest known scribes, those of Sumeria. The Sumerian scribe was "the scholar scientist, the man who studied whatever theological, botanical, zoological, mineralogical, geographical, mathematical, grammatical, and linguistic knowledge was current in his day, and who in some cases added to this knowledge." In other words, it would not be too far fetched to conjecture that the role of the Egyptian scribe may have been modeled on that of the Sumerian scribe.

5. In consonance with the concept of civilizational cross-fertilization, or more simply civilizational borrowings, it is possible that in tracing the genealogy of the *per-ankh* itself, one may be taken to an earlier time to a place outside Egypt: to Sumeria, where it appears that the functions of the Sumerian scribal schools were not unlike those of the *per-ankh*. See Kramer (1981) for an interesting description of the Sumerian schools.

6. The fact is that these are people with a political agenda: one that has nothing to do with scholarly truth, but which has everything to do with racist politics peculiar to the United States—perhaps, not surprisingly, given the deeply entrenched racist culture that pervades that society. Only those who are products of a racist society would be obsessed with, for example, asking the question: Were the ancient Egyptians black? Not only is the premise of the question absolutely asinine (for, what is black if nothing more than an ideologically driven historically rooted social construction, the applicability of which to a different society in a different age and place is an absolutely meaningless exercise), but as Howe (1998) correctly points out, it has nothing to do with advancing our knowledge of the Egyptian civilization by even one iota. The best that one can say if one must insist on an answer, if only to appease the demands of a racist society, is that the skin palette of ancient Egyptians was the same as the one today: one of a dark to light continuum—with the darkest hue to be found in the south and the lightest in the north. More importantly, there is no evidence, so far, that in ancient Egyptian society this gradation was accorded any political or social significance—even though it was a highly stratified society in many other ways. For more on this subject see Berlinerblau (1999); Keita (1993); and the various contributions to the section titled "Race," in Lefkowitz and Rogers (1996: 103–166). Note that Bernal (1987) does not say much on the subject directly; rather his entire project is relevant indirectly. See also Lewis and Wigen (1997) for a critique of Afrocentrists, as well as their Eurocentrist detractors.

For some of the ideas espoused by the Afrocentrists see, for example, Asante (1992), Asante and Mazama (2002); Diop (1983); James (1992 [1954]); and Karenga and Carruthers (1986). To be fair to the Afrocentrists, it must be emphatically stated that they did not invent the racialization of history; that contemptible honor must go to the Eurocentrists of yesteryear, who with their mythologically rooted Semitic/ Hamitic theories, sought to denigrate Africans and their achievement. See Appendix II for more on these theories and their influence on Western perceptions of Africa.

7. It ought to be noted here that Bernal himself has never claimed that he is an Afrocentrist, and neither do Afrocentrists proper view him as such.

8. Moreover, it is necessary to point out here that the question of the origins of the Western civilization, as framed by the debate between the Afro and Eurocentrists, needless to say, betrays, fundamentally, a deep asininity (rooted, of course, in a barely con-

cealed racist project). How? Because there is, from the perspective of truth, a perverse refusal to recognize that among the incontrovertible lessons of history is the common-sensical fact that no civilization can ever develop in isolation from contemporaneous and/ or historical influences—whatever their agency: war, conquest, colonization, commerce, travel, etc.—emanating from other cultures and civilizations that are in spatial and/ or temporal proximity. Moreover, this is a hugely amorphous process that is not only devoid of solid boundaries of time and magnitude—consequently, it is virtually impossible to draw clear demarcations between originality and imitation, especially in the realm of ideas—but, more often than not, involves a creative domestication of borrowings and influences as opposed to wholesale mechanistic transplantations. The observations of Bard and Fattovich (2001: 277–278), for example, on the genesis of a unitarian state—without which there would have been no Egyptian civilization—in early dynastic Egypt (and in Axum too), captures this point admirably; as they put it: "Both the Early Dynastic Egyptian state and the Aksumite state did not evolve in isolation, but were (specific) sociopolitical adaptations to processes and interactions occurring on a much larger scale in the ancient Near East, Northeast Africa, and (for Aksum) the Mediterranean and south Asia." They continue, "there is evidence of fairly complex economic interaction and long-distance trade with other hierarchical polities, and concomitant with this was the probable spread of ideas/ models of hierarchical control and organization." In light of the foregoing, then, it will suffice to say that the learning of the ancient Egyptians probably did find its way to the Greeks and helped to shape their civilization in some way; however, exactly what kinds and levels of influence and what type of mechanisms were involved are questions that will, in terms of exactitude, probably remain chimerical for a long time to come, if not forever. No civilization that had traversed the expanse of time for as long as the Egyptian civilization did—some 3000 years—and that was in such close geographic proximity to what was probably one of the busiest highways of cross-cultural interchanges in the history of the world up to that point, the Mediterranean and the Red Sea, could have remained outside that process; both, as a donor and as a recipient. (See also van Binsbergen (1997a), who raises a similar point in his masterly summary and review of Bernal's work.) Yet, having said all this, one must confront this fundamental political question that arises from the debate surrounding Bernal's work (especially in North America): What does it matter who influenced who, or who borrowed from who? Only the narrow minded and the bigot is unable to celebrate the fact that the foundation of all human progress is cultural diversity because only such diversity generates influences and borrowings in the first place—no matter what the source: black, brown, red, white, or yellow culture.

9. In its latest incarnation—officially opened on October 16, 2002—it is a massive 69,000 square meters, 3500 seat, state-of-the-art library built to house 4 million volumes and preserves that ancient tradition of duality of functions: a repository of knowledge and a seat of higher learning.

10. The museum/ library complex came to boast among its patrons a number of very famous scholars indeed, including:

Archimedes (c. 290–212 B.C.E.): the preeminent mathematician who, among his many intellectual gifts, bequeathed the law of hydrostatics or the "Archimedes Principle" (the true weight of an immersed body in fluid is its weight minus the weight of the fluid it displaces), and the hydraulic screw to raise water which is still in use in some parts of the world.

Aristarchus of Samos (c. 310–230 B.C.E.): an astronomer who taught that the solar system was heliocentric almost 2000 years before Copernicus.

Erasistratus of Ceos (lived during the period that included the year 250 B.C.E.): an anatomist and physician who is considered by some as the founder of physiology.

Eratosthenes of Cyrene (c. 276–194 B.C.E.): one of those who served as heads of the library, and who, as a geographer, among his many accomplishments, accurately measured the circumference of the earth—he was off by only 15%—by astronomically measuring latitudinal differences; he also taught that one could reach the east by sailing west, and so on.

Euclid (lived during the period that included the year 300 B.C.E.): among the most famous mathematicians who not only founded a school of mathematics in Alexandria, but also authored the multivolume magnum opus on geometry titled Elements.

Herophilus (c. 335–280 B.C.E.): a physician in Alexandria who studied the human body by means of dissections—hence his status as the founder of scientific anatomy.

Manetho (lived during the period that included the year 300 B.C.E.): an Egyptian priest, who as a scholar of the history of ancient Egypt wrote in Greek the famous Aegyptiaca, the surviving fragments of which are still of use to Egyptologists of today.

Philitas of Cos (c. 330–270 B.C.E.): poet and grammarian who is credited with establishing the Hellenistic school of poetry in Alexandria.

Strabo (c. 64 B.C.E.–23 C.E.): geographer and historian whose many writings included Geography, perhaps the only comprehensive treatise on all the peoples and countries known to the Greeks and Romans of his period.

Theophrastus (c. 372–287 B.C.E.): one the famous pupils of Aristotle who inherited the directorship of Aristotle's Lyceum and who, as a philosopher and botanist, among other writings, authored such influential works as History of Plants, Etiology of Plants, History of Physics, and so on.

Zenodotus of Ephesus (lived in the third-century B.C.E.): one of those who served as heads of the library, and who, as a grammarian, produced what is thought to be the first critical edition of Homer.

Hypatia (c. 370–March 415 C.E.): a renowned philosopher, astronomer and mathematician of her day was considered an authority on Neoplatonism (a la Plotinus and Lamblichus). Sadly, she was brutally murdered by an overzealous mob of Christians as they set about destroying everything deemed pagan, which it is said included, possibly, the looting and burning of the Alexandrian library complex—as well as Jewish synagogues, culminating in the illegal expulsion of the Alexandrian Jews—during the dominion of Cyril, who in 412 had succeeded his uncle Theophilus as the patriarch of Alexandria (it was the latter who had first initiated the reign of antipagan terror, beginning in 391, with the encouragement of the Roman emperor Theodosius I).

11. The Associated Press reported recently (May 2004) the discovery, by a Polish-Egyptian archeological team (the Polish team was headed by Grzegory Majderek), of a group of thirteen auditoria (lecture halls) in the Late Antique section of modern Alexandria that were part of the Bibliotheca Alexandrina complex. It is estimated that together the auditoria could have catered to a population of as many as 5,000 lecture attendees (students?). What this finding suggests is that one can legitimately argue that on its own terms—that is for its time period—the Bibliotheca was also a university and not just a library or research institute. For more on the discovery, see, for example the story in the Los Angeles Times (Home Edition), dated May 9th, 2004 on p. A3 by Thomas H. Maugh II, titled "Archeologists Find Fabled Center of Learning in Egypt; The University of Alexandria Drew Some of the Ancient World's Most Famous Scholars." Interestingly, in

the story the head of the Egyptian Supreme Council for Antiquities, the renowned Egyptologist, Zahi Hawass, is quoted as saying that the artifacts found at the discovery were "typical of a classroom," adding "When I stood in front if it recently, it looked like I was in front of an old university."

12. Though the orgy of looting and burning in April 2003 by Iraqis of museums and libraries of unfathomable scholarly value in Iraq—the birthplace of what is thought to be the world's first civilization, the Mesopotamian civilization—following the illegal invasion of that country in March of 2003 by U.S. and British armed forces (who by all accounts in a fit of incalculable ignorance of history were more concerned with preserving oil pumping installations than protecting these institutions, despite the pleas of their own experts of antiquity)—lends a slightly different color to the matter. Mention ought to be made here also of the barbaric behavior of the Turkish Muslims who invaded northern India (toward the end of the twelfth-century) to give rise to Islamic rule there (the Sultanate of Delhi). In the early phases of their invasion, because they viewed both the Buddhist and Hindu religions as unworthy of even a modicum of respect given their polytheistic character, they subjected their religious centers (which were also their centers of learning) to a vandalism of incalculable magnitude. One consequence of this, as Pacey (1996: 23) for example points out, is that it probably dealt Indian science a permanent setback.

13. For more on the arrival of Christianity in Ethiopia, as well as on the Kingdom of Aksum in general, see Bard and Fattovich (2001); Burstein (1998); Kobischanov (1979 [1966]); Mekouria (1981); and Munro-Hay (1991). For a general introduction to the history of Ethiopia see Henze (2000); Marcus (1994); Zegeye and Pausang (1994); and Zewde (2001).

14. See, for example, Mekouria 1988 and Marcus 1994 for details. While on this subject, one can legitimately argue that the beginnings of the eventual collapse of the kingdom could be traced to its loss of political control over South Arabia in the latter half of the sixth-century (around 570 C.E.) at the hands of an expeditionary force sent by the Sassanids to destroy the Ethiopian vassalic hold over the country. Axum proved incapable of responding to the Sassanids.

15. This development, as Tamarat 1984 reminds us, would serve as a double-edged sword for the Ethiopian church: on one hand it would have the resources necessary to expand and thrive, yet on the other its effort to universalize itself throughout Ethiopia would always remain a chimeric objective given the association by the non-Christian populace with state (feudal) oppression. Consequently, it is not surprising that with the overthrow of the feudal order in 1974, the church's fortunes took a turn for the worse from which it has never fully recovered.

16. At this first level, there were three further branches of specialization: first came the study of Dugua (liturgical music composed by a sixth-century Ethiopian scholar, Yared); followed by Zamare (Eucharist songs) and Mewaset (commemoration and funeral songs), and the third branch involved the study of Kedasse (general liturgy). Any one wishing to specialize in all three would have had to allocate at least six years of his life to the task, two for each (see Milkias 1976 for more).

17. Milkias (1976) states that philosophy was also taught at this level, but only at the most prestigious institutions (such as those located in the monasteries in Gojam Province: Woshara, Wadela, and Gonj). Among the principal texts taught were these two: the

philosophical critiques of Judaism, Christianity and Islam authored by Zera Yakob; and Metsahafe-Falasfa Tabiban (the Book of Wise Philosophers).

18. The main syllabus at this level, depending upon the size and prestige of the institution, comprised the study of, first, Kedusan Metsaheft (comprising the sacred books of Old and New Testaments); followed by Awaledt (literature of fiction) and Gedle (books on monasticism). After these first three subjects came subjects such as Tarike Negest (monarchic history), Kebra Negast (Glory of the Kings), Zena-Ayehud (History of the Jews), Lessane-Tarik (historical tales), and so on (see Milkias 1976).

19. The association of magic with literacy in societies where only a tiny minority had it is perhaps to be expected. To the vast majority, the nonliterate, the drawing of meaning out of incomprehensible symbols must have appeared as an exercise in magic; especially when this feat was associated with individuals who performed the role of a shaman or a witchdoctor. While in Ethiopia, at one time, literacy may have been viewed as demonic (going by Milkias), in some other parts of Africa it was the obverse in the sense that precisely because of the perception that it had magical properties literacy had to be sought after; this appears to have been the case in some non-Islamic societies that were nonliterate and which were just beginning to be exposed to literacy through the agency of European colonialism. That is, long after the collective memory of military defeat at the hands of Europe because of its possession of superior weapons (guns) had faded, a belief slowly emerged that it was literacy (and formal education) that accounted for the superiority of Europe—hence its ability to subjugate Africa. The outcome of this substitution of objective facts with subjective perceptions was an insatiable thirst for formal Western education (especially in a context—as during the early phase of the colonial era—where such education was deliberately made inaccessible to the general populace, and where it was available, it was accessible only through the agency of the missionary—the modern witchdoctor). The foregoing is all conjectural, but it is suggestive; and, perhaps, explains the obsession to this day among Africans, Asians and others outside Europe for formal educational qualifications. From a different perspective, it may also explain the obsession among the three religions of the desert (Judaism, Christianity and Islam) with the word. This line of reasoning, it should be pointed out in the interest of scholarly integrity, is not entirely original on the part of this author. Besides Milkias, it was also suggested by a mentor, Professor Philips Stevens, Jr., in an e-mail missive dated July 20, 2004, to the author that is brief enough to be quoted in full:

I'd like to suggest [an angle] of education in Africa that I have long thought about—since my Peace Corps days as a teacher in Nigeria, 1963–66: the magical power of literacy, hence its tremendous appeal. I think I [have] mentioned the magical power of words, and how that power is enhanced with writing—making the word permanent, and anonymous—in two articles currently in print: in my entry, "Magic," in David Levinson and Melvin Ember (eds.), Encyclopedia of Cultural Anthropology, Holt 1996; and "Magic, Sorcery and Witchcraft," in Philip M. Peek and Kwesi Yankah (eds.) African Folklore: An Encyclopedia, Routledge 2004; also in Henry Louis Gates and Anthony Appiah (eds.), Africana, 2nd. ed., Oxford 2005 (in press). But these are only brief mentions, no details. You'll have to interview me for more!

20. In describing this role of the debtrawoch, you may do well dear reader, by also comparing it with the role of the ulama in Islamic societies, described later. For more on

the debtrawoch see also Wagaw (1990).

21. Consider, for instance, one of the few works specifically on the development of higher education in Ethiopia from antiquity to the present, Wagaw (1990); there is no mention in it of Islamic education (let alone the existence of Muslim Ethiopians). In fact, the hegemony of the Christian Ethiopians has been such that for centuries the legitimacy of the citizenship of Muslim Ethiopians was never acknowledged; they were simply referred to as "Muslims in Ethiopia."

22. This section on Islam in Ethiopia draws upon the following sources: Ahmad (1997), Ahmed (2001), Braukämper (2003), Ehrlich (1994), Gibb (1997), Haberland (1992), Hassen (1990), Kapteijns (2000), Tamrat (1984), Trimingham (1965), and the section titled "Education and Human Resources" in volume III of the massive multiauthor three-volume work on Ethiopian studies edited by Fukui, Kurimoto, and Shigeta (1997).

23. Another matter of nomenclature must also be dealt with here: the term "Islamic empire" is used through out this work interchangeably between the formal Islamic empire that existed under a single ruler (the Caliph) in the early years of Islam, as well as in the later years (in the form of the Ottoman Empire), and the informal Islamic empire that was present at other times in Islamic history and which encompassed several Muslim empires but with no ties to each other, other than those of civilization (religion, trade, commerce, etc.)

24. For an introductory overview—repeat, introductory overview—of the history of Islam in general, these two sources should suffice: Esposito (2000), and Savory (1976).

25. It ought to be pointed out here that Western historians have tended to exaggerate the significance of this battle. As Mastnak (2002: 99–100) observes in his extensively researched book, it was just one battle among many fought between the Muslims and the Franks in southern France around the middle of the eighth-century; plus, he argues, it was just one of a series that various Frankish princes, the Carolingians, undertook against others (such as the Saxons, as well as other Christian princes), for the sake of "booty, power and territory." See also Cardini (2001).

26. Consider, for instance, the quote below from a farewell address by the first Caliph of Islam, Syeddina Abu Bakr, delivered before the first Muslim expeditionary force to depart Saudi Arabia (on its way to do battle with the much feared army of one of the superpowers of its day, the Byzantine Empire) following the death of Prophet Muhammed. As Salahi (2004:5) points out, the rules of engagement—which long predated the Geneva Conventions—that the Muslim armies of that period were assigned paid great heed to human rights (and this in an age when "war meant what it means to all humanity today: a wave of senseless, careless, indiscriminate destruction").

Learn the following ten points and always bear them in mind: Do not do any act of treason to your community or to yourselves; and never betray anyone. Do not disfigure a dead body. Never kill a child, an elderly person, or a woman. Do not destroy or burn any date farm, and never cut down a fruit tree. Do not slaughter a sheep, cow or camel except for your food. You will come across some people who devote themselves to worship in hermitages, so leave them alone to do what they please. (from Salahi 2004: 5).

27. Though in practice this has not always been adhered to at all times in all places. While all forms of racism and ethnocentrism are highly objectionable, what is espe-

cially disquieting is when it is expressed against fellow coreligionists in a theological context where all are supposed to be equal before God. Hence, even though the only two references to skin color (one tangential and the other specific) in the entire Qur'an has to do with affirming God as the architect of all things, including diversity in human pigmentation, and the admonition that piety supersedes all distinctions in the eyes of God—as Lewis (1990: 54) explains: "[t]he Qur'an gives no countenance to the idea that there are superior and inferior races and that the latter are foredoomed to a subordinate status; the overwhelming majority of Muslim jurists and theologians share this rejection." Muslim Arabs, however, contrary to Islamic teachings, quite often (which is not to say always) appear to have favored those who most closely approximated their own skin color; which they mistakenly perceived as "white." Certainly the current arrogance, vis-à-vis other Muslim peoples of color, but who happen not to be "Arabs," expressed some times openly and sometimes sotto voce, that one finds among many Muslim Arabs—who usually and hypocritically consider themselves as the true inheritors and custodians of the religion of Islam regardless of their level of practical commitment to it—appears to have always been part of the Arab Islamic tradition. Here, for example, is what the Arab Muslim Ibn Khaldun—arguably one of the foremost philosophers of history of the medieval era—had to say about black Africans: "Their qualities of character are close to those of dumb animals. It has even been reported that most of the Negroes of the first zone dwell in caves and thickets, eat herbs, live in savage isolation and do not congregate, and eat each other." (Though in fairness to him he did not think much of Europeans either for in the next sentence he writes: "The same applies to the Slavs." His explanation for this supposed inferiority of blacks and whites was that it had to do with climate. (Khaldun 1967, Vol. 1: 168–69)

What is particularly disturbing is that such prejudice has at times been expressed in extremely virulent forms, with horrendous consequences for their victims. Two examples in support of this point; one from the past, and the other from the present: during the era of the slave trade, Muslim Arab slave traders were not entirely above enslaving their fellow Muslims and selling them into bondage—simply because the latter were not, in the eyes of the former, racial co-equals. (Here, the matter of the theological position of Islam on slavery is of relevance: it was akin to that of Christianity and Judaism, and is well summarized by Diouf (1998: 10): "Islam neither condemned nor forbade slavery but stated that enslavement was lawful under only two conditions: if the slave was born of slave parents or if he or she had been a pagan prisoner of war. Captives could legally be made slaves if the prisoner was a kafir (pagan) who had first refused to convert and then declined to accept the protection of the Muslims. In theory, a freeborn Muslim could never become a slave.") One ought to also point out, however, that the corrupting influence of the slave trade did not spare black African Muslim slave traders from succumbing to the same temptation; they too at times sold their fellow black African Muslims into slavery. The enslaved Muslims who became part of the humanity dragged across the oceans (see Diouf) were more than likely sold, mainly, by non-Muslim black African enslavers, but it is not beyond the realm of the possibility that a few were also sold by both black African and Arab Muslim enslavers. All this was in the past, but what about today? The short answer is that things have not changed much for the better. Consider, for instance, what is going on today in the Sudanese Muslim province of Darfur where government supported "Arab" militias are embarked on a mass slaughter of, this time, fellow Muslims (unlike in Sudan's south where the target of Khartoum's genocidal tendencies for the past several decades have been Christians/ animists) who they consider as black and therefore inferior. The irony of this horror is that the so-called Arabs involved in the conflict are Arabized black Africans, phenotypically indistinguishable from their fellow Sudanese (whether Muslims, Christians or animists) they are slaughtering. (For more on this conflict visit the www.bbc.com website and search their archives of news stories.)

In raising this entire matter of Arab racism one risks being accused of abandoning historical objectivity; in defense, dear reader, you are asked to consult sources by others who have looked at this issue with some diligence; such as Bernard Lewis. In his book Race and Slavery in the Middle East: An Historical Enquiry (1990), he meticulously documents the history of the nefarious attitudes of Muslim Arabs on the race question. He begins by noting that the arrival of Islam in the Afro-Eurasian ecumene introduced a new equation in the matter of race relations: the potential to associate skin pigmentation with "otherness" (something that was rare up to that point in the ancient world where otherness was more a matter of ethnicity [such as linguistic or religious differences] and/ or nationality [e.g., Greeks versus Persians] rather than race). This potential emerged out of the fact that for the first time in human history Islam created "a truly universal civilization" where "[b]y conquest and by conversion, the Muslims brought within the bounds of a single imperial system and a common religious culture peoples as diverse as the Chinese, the Indians, the peoples of the Middle East and North Africa, black Africans, and white Europeans," and not only that, but the obligatory requirements of the Hajj (pilgrimage to Mecca enjoined on all Muslim adults, if they can afford it, at least once in their lifetime) placed members of all these groups into direct and close contact with each other (p. 18). Against this background, the transformation of the potential to the actual (theological prohibitions notwithstanding), for a variety of reasons (including holdovers from pre-Islamic times of Arab prejudices), was a matter of time; thereby leaving us with a circumstance that he summarizes thusly: "The cause of racial equality is sustained by the almost unanimous voice of Islamic religion—both the exhortations of piety and the injunctions of the law. And yet, at the same time, the picture of inequality and injustice is vividly reflected in the literature, the arts, and the folklore of the Muslim peoples. In this, as in so much else, there is a sharp contrast between what Islam says and what Muslims—or at least some Muslims—do" (p. 20). Consequently, even among subordinate populations, such as slaves, according to Lewis, hierarchic distinctions were often imposed: white slaves tended to fare better than black slaves in almost all respects. What is worse was that as the African slave trade (both the trans-Saharan and the Atlantic) became ever more lucrative, there was a corresponding rise in the putrescence of Muslim Arab attitudes on this matter—exemplified, as already noted a moment ago, in the enslavement of black Muslims too.

The amazing irony in all this, to complicate matters, is that today there are, in truth, very few Muslim Arabs who can claim a pure Arab ancestry. Regardless of how racist Arabs think of other peoples of color, or how their equally racist detractors from among the people of color think of them, Arabs (especially those in Afro-Arab Islamic Africa), like that segment of the population categorized as "black" in the United States, range from the whitest white to the blackest black! In other words, the category Arab is less a category of skin-color and phenotype, than it is a linguistic and cultural category. That this should be so is not surprising considering that as the Islamic empire came to encompass a heterogeneity of colors, Muslim Arabs came to genetically intermingle with ethnicities from across the entire Afro-Eurasian ecumene over the millennia.

There is one other matter that ought to be noted here in the interest of scholarly integrity: while it is true that Lewis's detractors have accused him of "orientalist" bias (a variant of Eurocentrism as indicated in Appendix II) in his work—and they may well be correct, especially in the case of his earlier works—as with all Eurocentrists, it would be wrong to assume that everything he has written is ipso facto false. In fact, in this instance, his 1990 work, one finds, is well researched and documented, even if his earlier work (Lewis 1971) on the same subject may have been less so. More importantly, on this particular issue, Lewis does not stand alone. For instance, see Davis 2001; Fisher 2001; Goldenberg 2003; Gordon 1989; Hunwick and Powell 2002; Marmon 1999; Segal 2001; and Willis 1985. (A defensive view from the other side is available via Kamil 1970.) For a trenchant critique of Lewis, see Nyang and Abed-Rabbo (1984); Halliday (1993), is also relevant here.

28. In other words, Islam does not require a priestly class to perform rites (no matter how profound the event, as in the case, for example, of weddings or funerals or even in the matter of conversion to the faith) as a means to bind the faithful to their religion; nor is there any provision for that class of people found in some religions who lay claim to special magical/ spiritual powers emanating from the Creator to be used in the service of the faithful (shamans for example). From this perspective, religion for Muslims is a personal undertaking—a matter solely between the believer and the Creator with no intermediary in between (not even Prophet Muhammed). Moreover, the lack of a need for a priestly and/ or theurgical class has been further assured by, on one hand, the utter simplicity of executing religious rites and on the other the devolution of responsibility for those rites that require community participation, such as weddings and funerals, on to the entire community (instead of a select category of people, priests and/ or shamans). The consequence of one of these fundamental characteristics of Islam is well described by Eccel (1984: 335): "With priesthood ruled out, and the saintly repositories of mystical secrets and sacred power disfavored, the ulama have elaborated a cogent set of disciplines by which, having mastered them, they may establish themselves as a professional religious elite qua jurists, as well as teachers and preachers." Eccel further observes, "[I]n this they were aided by an epistemology that is oriented to rationality, their hallmark." It is little wonder, then, that piety in Islam has meant more than faithful adherence to ritualistic requirements; it has also included the acquisition of knowledge. Having said all this there is one qualifying observation that must be made: in practice in some Islamic countries (such as those in the Maghrebi North Africa), the masses—who are less conversant with the tenets of Islam—have often fallen prey to the sacrilegious practice of saint worship, which to all intents and purposes borders on superstition and magic harking back to a pre-Islamic era.

29. Consider the variety of subjects that fall under the purview of Islamic law: inheritance law; family law; principles of trade, commerce, and banking; dietary regulations; principles of environmental protection; principles of state governance; principles of taxation; the laws of war; principles of personal conduct (including dress); principles of foreign policy; principles of crime and punishment (murder, theft, etc.); principles of hygiene; and so on.

30. Interestingly, even today, the Muslim ulama of every nationality—African, Chinese, European, East Indian, etc.—still uses Arabic as its lingua franca. One may also note here that at a certain time in the history of East-West relations (see next chapter) Arabic was also used by Western intellectuals because it was the language of science.

31. For more on the importance of knowledge in Islam see Rosenthal (1970).

32. In some places, as in Morocco for example, the madrasah may refer exclusively to either a mosque university's student dormitories, or to places of learning that do not have dormitories attached to them (found usually in the countryside) (Porter 2002: 10).

33. It may be noted here that the first madrasah, known as al-madrasah al-Nizamiyah, was founded in Baghdad in 1067 by the powerful Seljuk Turk governor, Nizam-al-Mulk. It is this madrasah that became the model for nearly all madrasahs that were established throughout the Islamic empire in subsequent years. About waqfs: there are in practice two types of waqfs, the public or charitable trust (referred to as waqf *qhayri*) and the private family trust (known as waqf *ahli*). It is the former and not the latter that was among the mainstays of the madrasah system. (For more on the role of waqfs in the madrasah system in general see Makdisi 1981; as for, specifically, waqfs in Egypt see Behrens-Abouseif 1994; Berkey 1992; and Eccel 1984). Note also that elsewhere in North Africa waqf may go by the name *hubus* (or *habous*).

34. See Eickelman (1985) and Eccel (1984) for an idea of what student dormitories looked like and how room space was allocated.

35. Other names for the kuttab-level institutions include Qur'anic schools (usually in French literature); msid (in Morocco—the name is a corruption of masjid); and khalwah (in Sudan). It may also be noted that in parts of Afro-Arab Islamic Africa where Sufism holds considerable sway, as in the Maghreb, madrasah-level institutions are also called zawiyahs—which in reality, are more than just madrasahs; they are religious centers with diverse functions run by Sufi orders. (For an excellent example of a Sufi order and its zawiyah see the study by Clancy-Smith 1994.) (A Sufi is a practitioner of Sufism, a form of ascetic ecstatic mysticism, practiced and venerated in some parts of the Islamic world, but which while in other parts is considered an embodiment of deep profanation; that is, a heretical innovation (referred to in Islam as bid'aa).

36. This tragic phenomenon, incidentally, is characteristic of this day and age as well; no country any where in the world, no matter how wealthy, advanced, etc., it may be, has been able to fully and effectively grapple with this iniquity in their educational systems.

37. In stating that the system was relatively democratic, one is acknowledging here that in practice female students were generally excluded from the upper levels of the system, but not at the ground level.

38. Although Islamic theology in itself places no barriers to the acquisition of knowledge by women (on the contrary encourages women to participate in this endeavor too), in practice, as a result of local customs, the madrasah system tended to be male dominated as one went up the educational ladder beyond the kuttab level. Recall that in the pre-Islamic era, most societies throughout the region that came to be encompassed by the Islamic empire did not give equal emphasis to the education (formal) of boys and girls, whatever form such education took. This was true of the Greeks as it was of the Chinese; it was true of the Egyptians as it was of the Persians; it was true of the Romans and the Byzantines as it was true of the Indians; and it was true of the

Christians as it was true of Jews. Yet, as Berkey (1992) shows, there were individual Muslim women of exceptional character who did persevere with their education in the face of severe obstacles to achieve comparable status with their male peers. (See also Dunbar (2000) who examines the place of Muslim women in African history; and Clancy-Smith 1994 who provides us with a study of a Muslim woman notable of considerable learning and influence in the period of French colonial rule in Algeria.)

39. An aside of current interest: Westerners today fail to understand this basic fact when they puzzle over why the Saudis, for example, took to financing madrasahs in Islamic communities around the world. It should also be pointed out that the support of madrasahs did not depend entirely on the wealthy; the day to day expenses of less well to do students, for example, were often supplemented by donations in kind (food, clothing, etc.) from ordinary people who by means of these donations wished to secure the same religious blessings as those sought by the wealthy patrons. In Islam, as in most other religions, the religious value of an act of charity is not tied to the magnitude of the charity itself, but in relation to one's ability to undertake it.

40. Such as a formal curricula; universally recognized formal admission qualifications, procedures, and programs of study; formal completion of study examinations; teacher certification; formal vertical and horizontal institutional linkages; inspectorates and accreditation mechanisms; distinct diurnal and calendrical time structures (e.g., class periods and semesters—other than that imposed by the timetable of the mandatory five daily prayers, and the month of fasting); detailed written regulations; classrooms with desks and chairs; an elaborate hierarchic bureaucracy; and so on. One may also note here that in general there was no concept of failure in madrasahs. Withdrawal from a madrasah could occur at any time for whatever reasons that were specific to the student without incurring a mantle of failure from society at large—only personal regret was usually the main negative outcome of not completing one's studies as originally intended. In Islam (as in Judaism and Buddhism, to give other examples) the pursuit of higher learning was less motivated by instrumentalist concerns (employment), than by the desire for pietistic self-betterment.

41. Even though the basic elements of the madrasah system were roughly the same, there were some pedagogical differences between madrasah systems in different parts of the Islamic empire. The scholastic method was therefore not universal, but it appears to have been the dominant teaching method in many parts of the Islamic empire. See Eickelman's comment on this matter (1985: 95–96).

42. Yet paradoxically, despite this highly personal nature of Islamic higher education, major centers of learning (such as Cairo), came to boast a large number of public buildings (with the requisite waqfs for their upkeep) for the sole purpose of encouraging teaching and learning.

43. What also follows from this multidimensional role of the madrasah is that there was considerable fluidity in not only the use of space, but also of relations between the madrasah and the community in which it was located; exemplified, for instance, by the welcome accorded to worshippers, whatever their profession, to join study or lesson circles of their choice for how often and however long they wished—though out of deference to regular students such "transient students" would sit at the outer edge of the circle. (In a sense one may liken this practice to the modern concept of course auditing.)

44. Some cities (such as Cairo during the Mamluk dynastic period) also came to

have other unique institutions of higher learning such as convents for the sufis (Muslim ascetics)—see Berkey (1992). For more on the Islamic educational system prior to the advent of Western imperialism in Africa (and in the Islamic empire generally), see: Berkey (1992); Dodge (1961, and 1962); Eccel (1984); Eickelman (1985); Heyworth-Dunne (1939); Iqbal (2002); Leiser (1976); Makdisi (1981); Nakosteen (1964); Reichmuth (2000); Saad (1983); Tibawi (1972); and Totah (1926).

45. Maghreb is the shortened form of the Arabic term that the conquering Muslims applied to all of North Africa west of Egypt: Bilad al-Maghreb (meaning Lands of Sunset). The Maghreb as a province of the Islamic empire was known as Ifriqiyah.

46. Official literature issued by the present-day incarnation of the madrasah, the University of Ezzitouna, in proclaiming that it is the oldest Islamic university states that the mosque was built by Ubayd-allah Ibn Habhab in 734 and its madrasah functions began in 737. (Note: al-Zaitouna is also spelled Ezzitouna and al-Zaytuna.)

47. About the various dynasties: The Aghlabids reigned from 800 to 909 C.E. from the capital city they founded, al-Kayrawan; the dynasty was begun by Ibrahim ibn al-Aghlab (ruled from 800 to 812) who was the governor appointed to be in charge of Ifriqiyah by the Abbasid caliph, Harun ar-Rashid. The Zirid dynasty was begun by the Kabylie Berber governor (appointed by the Fatimids) of al-Kayrawan, Yousuf Buluggin I ibn Ziri (ruled from 972 to 995). The dynasty reigned from 972 to 1152 in Ifriqiyah and from 1012 to 1090 in Granada in Muslim Spain (the Granadian branch was begun by Zawa ibn Ziri). The Hafsid dynasty was also a Berber dynasty; it was founded around 1229 by Abu Zakariyya Yahya and they ruled until the Ottoman takeover of Tunisia in 1574. (For more on these dynasties see Abun-Nasr 1987).

48. Green (1978: 29–30) suggests that the madrasah does not really come into its own until the nineteenth-century when the Husaynids congregated ulama recruited from other madrasahs at this particular institution.

49. The differences in Muslim educational practices in Islamic North Africa are discussed by Ibn Khaldun; see volume three of the Rosenthal translation of his fourteenth-century work, the Muqaddimah (Khaldun 1967).

50. See Porter (2002); and the entry under al-Karawiyyin in the Encyclopedia of Islam for more on this institution.

51. It ought to be mentioned in passing that the al-Qarawiyyin (also spelled al-Karawiyyin) was not the only major mosque-college in Morocco during the precolonial era; there were others too (albeit of slightly lesser importance, such the Ibn Youssef Mosque-college in Rabat, and the Yusufiya Mosque-college in Marrakesh (see Eickelman 1985, for more).

52. In devoting almost exclusive attention to al-Azhar as the premier madrasah of North Africa two points need to be stressed: one, that it achieved this status only in the later phases of its history (otherwise in its early years it was just one madrasah among many); and two, that this was not the only madrasah in Cairo; there were many other madrasahs besides al-Azhar even at the time of the French invasion. Al-Azhar's eventual preeminence was an outcome of fortuitous circumstances (see Berkey 1992).

53. The Fatimids belonged to the Ismailiah wing of the Sh'ite half of the great schism (the other half being Sun'nite) that engulfed Islam immediately following the murder of the third caliph of the Muslims, Omar ibn Khattab, in 656. For more on the Fatimids see Brett (2001), and Halm (1997).

54. Commenting on the origins of al-Azhar, Eccel (1984) makes this interesting observation: "These then we may number among the paradoxes of Egyptian history: the al-Azhar, the most renowned center of Sun'ni orthodoxy, was established by a general of Christian origins (Jawahar the Sicilian) and a minister of Jewish origins (Ibn Killis of Baghdad) to be a Shi'ite madrasah-mosque; and even though it became a center of Egyptian nationalism against Napoleon, and later against the British, it was founded by one foreign conqueror, a Sicilian, and made Sun'ni by another, a Kurd" (p. 115–116). Such then is the spice of history; and yet the unwashed still lament that history is bland intellectual discourse.

55. Given the critically important role played by this very unique dynasty (1250–1517), together with its residuum (1517–1798), in the cultural and educational life of Egypt for close to 600 years, down to the beginning of modern Egyptian history, demands a digression on exactly who these people were. The name mamluk is an Arabic word that stands for owned and in the Arabs color-conscious terminology it came to refer to "white" slaves, in this case military slaves from Central Asia. (Black slaves were called abd, which today has come to signify any black person, slave or not—see Lewis 1990.) From around nineth-century onward, Muslim rulers, from time to time, had used soldiers of slave origins (military slaves) in their armies. While the use of slaves by a state for purposes other than domestic labor or economic production was not unique to the Muslims (vide the presence of government slaves [servi Caesaris] in the Roman empire and among other European entities [e.g., the Burgundian Kingdom, medieval Germany, Muscovy], or consider the use of slaves in U.S. armies during the Civil War), there was one distinct difference, explains Pipes (1981): these were slaves systematically acquired and formally trained for only one purpose: to serve as professional soldiers in the armies of the state. From this perspective they were not slaves in the ordinary sense of the word because they were part and parcel of the praetorian state apparatus, for by the time they were ready to assume their duties the nature of their bondage had transmuted from one based on coercion to one relying on allegiance. (The slaves, for the most part, did not acquire their freedom by means of formal process of manumission, but by means of a self-conscious decision to usurp power under certain extraordinary circumstances—Pipes calls it "ipsimission" though perhaps a better word would be "automanumission"—if and until that point was reached they were still fundamentally slaves, but only in the sense that they had a master whose jurisdiction over their lives was not optional.) Pipes suggests that military slaves were ubiquitous throughout the Islamic empire where four-fifths of the various Muslim dynasties regularly employed them in their armies. He states further that among them those in Sub-Saharan Africa were most especially dependent on military slaves (p. 52).

Turning specifically to the military slaves in North Africa (the mamluks) who in time gave rise to their own dynasties: first, we may enquire into how they were acquired (and from where) by the Islamic state? The general procedure involved their procurement at a young age (around twelve) from non-Muslim sources on the periphery of the Islamic empire (mainly from the Central Asian steppes from among the various Turkish nomadic tribes, though sometimes, as under the Fatimids, they also came from some parts of Africa such as the Sudan) and then providing them with training in the martial arts and the rudiments of Islamic beliefs and practices—in general mamluks were Muslims, though, as with the ordinary populace, the depth of their piety varied from person to person. Irwin (1986) comments that the criticism by some historians that they were not good Muslims is not true of all Mamluks; in fact there were times when some had "a stronger commitment to Islam and better knowledge of its tenets than the majority of their subjects." He further observes that "[o]n the whole the mamluks are best understood as being public servants, so long as one also understands that they were the servants of God, not of their subjects" (p. 153). On the matter of their provenance, one would assume that the acquisition of young children for military enslavement in far off lands must have been a brutal and cruel process for them and their parents, and at the level of individual families this most certainly must have been so; however, it appears that the matter is a little more complex than that. To be sure, such mechanisms of acquisition as capture in warfare and extraction as human tribute did exist; but consider further Irwin's description of other avenues: "On the steppes warfare—the raiding of other tribes herds of livestock and the taking into captivity of the defeated—formed a crucial part of the nomad economy. The slavers who sold the [young non-Muslim] Turks to the Islamic regimes were for the most part themselves Turks. At times of hardship, particularly of drought, families might sell their own children into captivity. Then again it occasionally happened, particularly in later centuries, that a man inspired by ambition might sell himself into captivity" (Irwin 1986: 4).

How did the Mamluks end up becoming rulers of Egypt (and Syria)? It has to do with the nature of military slavery: The use of such slaves was always a double-edged sword: the rulers could also become their targets, which is what happened in Egypt when Turkish Mamluks rebelled and overthrew the Abbasid dynasty in 1250 and established their own instead—but interestingly it was based on a dynastic lineage that was secured by means of nonhereditary succession where each generation of rulers came out of fresh purchases from their original homeland of young new mamluks. The Mamluk dynasty lasted until 1517 when it was defeated by another group of Turks, the Ottomans (Muslim nomadic Turkmen who under their leader Uthman—hence the derivation Ottoman—founded an empire that lasted for more than 600 years, from around 1400 to 1922, and encompassed a vast and highly diverse terrain that at one time included, besides Turkey: the Arabian peninsula, Bosnia, Egypt (and almost all of North Africa), Greece, Hungary, Iraq, Israel, Romania, Serbia, Syria, and the Ukraine).

Compared to the Ottoman period in Egypt, the period of Mamluk dynasty, especially the early part (about first 100 years or so—up to 1382), appears generally to have been one of significant cultural enlightenment and prosperity (though with regard to the latter probably much less so for the Egyptian peasantry). As Behrens-Abouseif (1994: 271) has observed: "The Mamluk sultans [rulers] had been great sponsors of religious institutions," so much so she continues that "[t]heir foundations in Cairo can be considered in their totality to be the greatest achievement of its kind in the Muslim medieval world." It is also true that a major contribution of the Mamluks was to save Egypt from the Mongol devastation with their defeat of them in Palestine and Syria; they were responsible too for getting rid of the last remnants of the Crusaders from the Levant. In a global sense, then, the pre-Ottoman Mamluk dynasty did a great service to the Arabic Islamic civilization by playing a critical role in its preservation. It may be noted here that even after the dynasty's overthrow, remnants of it continued to rule Egypt and in time, as the Ottoman state weakened, they were able to win back much of their power; though they still remained nominally beholden to the state through tribute payments.

They ruled until around 1800 (see Chapter 3). This latter group of mamluks are described in this work as the Ottoman Mamluks. Considered from this perspective, Mamluk rule lasted for nearly 600 years; however Behrens-Abouseif's point is well taken: the continuity between the dynasty and its residuum was "in form only" in that while they continued to be recruited mainly from the Caucasus, Ottoman rule introduced a new element: the residuum became a hereditary aristocracy (1994: 270). From the perspective of their role in maintaining the cultural and educational institutions through waqf endowments, the tradition, however, was continued. For more on the Mamluks (besides Irwin, Pipes, and Behrens-Abouseif), see Berkey (1992); Glubb (1973); and Petry (1994).

56. Interestingly, this unity of student age levels in the provision of education has been retained by al-Azhar to this day; that is, in the al-Azhar university system one can commence education in the first grade and not leave the system until after completing the doctorate.

57. Yet again a material interest of a different order can not be ruled out either from the constellation of motivations: the waqfs were also a means for shielding wealth from expropriation by the state, thereby enabling the individual Mamluk rulers to pass on their wealth to their descendents by entrusting to them the management of the waqfs (a legitimate device that carried with it remuneration).

58. For more on these other functions of al-Azhar, which increased in importance during the period of Ottoman Mamluk rule, see Behrens-Abouseif (1994) who suggests that this development is attributable to the fact that during the Ottoman period, the al-Azhar ulama served for the Ottoman government in Istanbul as a form of a counterweight to the local Mamluk governors.

59. Behrens-Abouseif (1994: 94) suggests that it is possible that this post emerged earlier, probably in the sixteenth-century when it was held by one Shaykh Muhyi al-Din Abd al-Qadir al-Ghazzi. However, even if this is so, it is from the seventeenth-century she states that the post began to acquire considerable political importance, especially since the Shaykh al-Azhar was also the Mufti. (In 1961 the two offices would be separated so that the state could have greater control over the institution through the office of the rector.)

60. The literature indicates that the quality of life of a student at al-Azhar was greatly determined by whether one relied exclusively on the institution for board and lodging or whether one also had access to family resources. Those who were most dependent on al-Azhar could look forward to a life of very few creature comforts, with undernourishment, inadequate clothes, primitive bedding and so on as constant companions. What is more, merely showing up for studies at al-Azhar did not automatically entitle one to food rations since demand often exceeded supply; one had to survive on one's own resources for up to two years or more before one was eligible for rations. Clearly, to survive at al-Azhar one had to be extremely dedicated if one's family was not well-off. There was, however, one very important fringe benefit enjoyed by all students that must have helped considerably in this regard: exemption from military service and corvee labor. See Dodge (1961) for more on student life at al-Azhar.

61. The very informality of the entire operation of al-Azhar, it must be noted, was both its strongest and weakest points: on one hand, from the perspective of class and ethnicity (though not sex) it was a democratic institution where higher learning was

within the grasp of anyone willing to apply himself; yet it also permitted considerable academic laxity and behavioral indiscipline— even to the point of falling prey to the temptations of the worst attributes of urban street life (crime, solicitation of prostitutes, etc.) (Eccel 1984: 149). Moreover, periodic violent confrontations between students and teachers, or among each of the two groups themselves, over allocation of waqf and other benefits were not unknown. There was also operational indiscipline in areas such as lodging where it appears that as student numbers grew, the living quarters of the students correspondingly grew worse—squalid is the term that comes to mind and it's the term Eccel uses (p. 172).

62. Eccel (1984: 125), draws attention to an intriguing practice regarding waqfs established for specific ulama: the benefits were sometimes inheritable by their descendants!

63. In later years, of course, with the advent of the Khedives in the nineteenth-century, the ulama received monthly salaries from the government from a fund established for that purpose and which in part was based on the waqfs of al-Azhar (and whose administration was now handled by the government—see Chapter 3).

64. For more on al-Azhar see Behrens-Abouseif (1994); Berkey (1992); Dodge (1961); Crecelius (1968); Eccel (1984); and Heyworth-Dunne (1939). Note: each of these sources emphasize different periods in the evolution of al-Azhar, therefore it is advisable to consult all of them together to obtain a comprehensive picture of the institution.

While going through the foregoing examination of madrasahs in the Afro-Arab Islamic world, many will not help but be reminded that madrasahs have in recent years acquired an unsavory reputation in the Western media. They are being blamed for fomenting "Islamized" terrorism. One or two words on this issue, therefore, would not out of place here. To begin with, it is ironic that we in the West (especially in the United States) with all of our sophisticated information gathering and knowledge producing resources (from spy satellites to think-tanks) have an inordinate thirst for silliest explanations for complex issues of global importance, especially those rooted in pre/ quasi/ developing countries. (The source of this phenomenon is not too difficult to discern: it is a combination of two factors: the realization that to delve deeper into causes is to risk unearthing the complicitous role of the West; and good old-fashioned racism where the West has never shaken off a notion that it developed in the heyday of Western imperialism that peoples of color are, on one hand, child-like and easily misled; and on the other, prone to violence and savagery.) Yes, madrasahs may have a role to play, but it's a minor one. We refuse to consider the possibility that the existence of such madrasahs in the first place is a symptom of a much larger problem: the specific political and economic configurations that exist in the Islamic countries and regions and in which the West has had a determinative role. There are three essential elements to these configurations: the lack of economic development (hence mass unemployment, widespread poverty and an unconscionable elite-mass gap in living standards), lack of democracy (hence the persistent massive violations of the human rights of the citizenry, ranging from vote-rigging to arbitrary imprisonment, torture and murder), and the perceived Western assault on the dignity of the Muslim ummah (exemplified by the refusal to resolve the Israeli/ Palestinian conflict and the related occupation of Islam's second holiest city, Jerusalem, by Israel.) The last factor is particularly important considering that the other two factors are also present in other parts of the world—such as much of Africa, the Caribbean and Latin America—and yet they do not produce anti-Western suicide bombers. Yes, it is true that sometimes the organizers (and even the perpetrators) of the terrorist acts may not necessarily be from hopeless poverty-stricken backgrounds (Osama Bin Laden is supposed to come from a wealthy family), but the fact that these people continue to emerge time after time (9/11—a date that will be etched forever in the annals of U.S. history—is just one of a series of terrorist acts spanning decades) and are supported by countless misguided foot soldiers who most often do the actual dying (the terrorist planners who dispatch the young men and women on suicidal bombing missions do not usually send their own children) speaks to the existence of this matrix. Consequently, no amount of braying into the wind that "they are jealous of our democracy"; "they do not like freedom"; etc. (serving essentially as a cover to further ramp up an already bloated military-industrial complex and to undermine the very democracy that is supposed to distinguish us from the rest of the world), or putting pressures on other countries to disband their madrasahs is in itself going to address the root causes of this phenomenon. One is always perplexed as to why it is so difficult for the denizens of executive mansions in the capitals of the West to understand that the best security stems from converting the foe to a friend, and that any other approach dooms us all to a constant potential of being blown to smithereens as we go about our daily business. Note: For more on the topic of the provenance of Islamized terrorism (there is no such thing as Islamic terrorism) see, for example, Hershberg and Moore (2002); Munjee (2001); Murden (2002); and Sonbol (2000)—to get a proper handle on the topic you are advised dear reader to consult these sources together. For a Eurocentric populist view on the subject see the 1998 work by that arch Eurocentrist, Samuel P. Huntington, titled (tellingly) *The Clash of Civilizations and the Remaking of World Order*. Thanks to the efforts of his publisher, Simon & Schuster, it generated much commotion at the time of its publication, but of course little enlightenment. That the best one can say about that work is that it is pure cant masquerading as academic scholarship—attested to by his basic thesis which he prefaces with what he calls an old truth that he quotes from a character in Michael Dibdin's novel, *Dead Lagoon*: "There can be no true friends without true enemies. Unless we hate what we are not, we cannot love what we are." Ergo the premise of Huntington's entire work: "For peoples seeking identity and reinventing ethnicity, enemies are essential, and the potentially most dangerous enmities occur across fault lines between the world's major civilizations" (p. 20).

65. For a discussion of the politics behind the anthropological explanations of the origins of the Zimbabwe Ruins (Great Zimbabwe) see Kuklick (1991) who describes the depth of ridiculousness to which they had sunk—exemplified by a decree by the white minority government of Ian Smith that government employees who publicly disseminated the now long established fact (e.g., through carbon dating) that the Zimbabwe Ruins were of indigenous (African) provenance and not some mythical foreign race would lose their jobs.

66. It may be noted here that it is the ancestors of Canaan, the Canaanites, who are conquered by the Israelites giving rise to that well-known passage in the Bible (Joshua 9:21) "And the princes said unto them, Let them live; but let them be hewers of wood and drawers of water unto all the congregation; as the princes had promised them" (emphasis added). The Canaanites living in the city of Gibeon saved themselves from the

possibility of being massacred by Joshua (for no other reason beyond the fact that their land had now been promised by God to the Israelites) by pretending to be foreigners from outside the Land of Canaan and entering into a peace truce with Joshua. However, upon discovering this deception, Joshua cursed the Gibeonites relegating them forever to become "hewers of wood and drawers of water" in the service of the Israelites.

67. The literature on the historical origins of the ideology of racism in the West is fairly extensive. As an entry-point into this literature the following select sources will prove to be, for present purposes, more than adequate: Bieder (1986); Davies, Nandy, and Sardar (1993); Drescher (1992); Frederickson (2002); Gould (1971); Hannaford (1996); Huemer (1998); Jackson and Weidman (2004); Jordan (1968); Kovel (1988); Libby, Spickard, and Ditto (2005); Niro (2003); Pieterse (1992); Reilly, Kaufman, and Bodino (2003); Shipman (1994); Smedley (1993); Stanton (1960); and Wolpoff and Caspari (1997). Note that although Jordan, and Libby, Spickard, and Ditto are very specific to the U.S. context, they are included here because of their treatment of an important element in the formation of Western racist ideologies not given as much attention in the literature as it deserves: the role of sexuality.

68. For more on the Christian cosmological and "scientific" roots of Western racist discourse, see also the sources mentioned in the preceding note.

3

Afro-Arab Islamic Africa

INTRODUCTION

There is a tendency in much of Western writing on Africa to divide the continent into North Africa and sub-Saharan (or black) Africa, even in the absence
of a geographic division, and then proceed to deny that North Africa can be legitimately considered as part of the African continent; rather they assert that it
is part of the Middle East (which itself, of course, as already noted, is a misnomer—although for the sake of convenience this term is retained in this
work). The most obvious example of this approach has been, until very recently, the highly unwarranted excision of the Egyptian civilization from African history (see Chapter 2). Such are the times we live in that there are those
within Africa itself (both north of the Sahara and south of the Sahara) who
would concur with this artificial bifurcation of the continent.[1] The truth is that
just as Eastern Europe is both part of Asia and part of Europe, North Africa too
belongs to both sides, the African side and the Middle Eastern Side. It is not
simply that geography dictates that North Africa be considered part of Africa,
but culture and history as well. For if *modern* African culture is a fusion of
Western and African cultures, then the only differentiating factor that separates
modern North African culture from modern sub-Saharan African culture is that
modern North African culture incorporates a third culture: Arabic Islamic culture. Yes, it is true that Arabic is not an indigenous African language, any more
than English, French, or Portuguese is, even though its arrival in Africa pre-

cedes the others by over 1,000 years—a long enough period to shed its tramontane status. On the other hand, one could challenge this statement by suggesting, as Mazrui (1986) does, that from a geographic point of view the Arabic
peninsula ought to be considered part of Africa; and therefore from this perspective Arabic is not a foreign language. However, the fact that this is not how
the peninsula is usually seen today is a function of Western engineering (the
Suez Canal) and Western domination of world cartography.

Anyhow, as this chapter proceeds to consider those countries that together
constitute that part of Africa that we may legitimately label today as Afro-Arab
Islamic Africa because of a common linguistic (Arabic—with the exception of
one or two countries) and religious (Islamic) heritage, it is necessary to begin
by delineating a number of points of prolegomenous significance that are applicable, to varying degrees of course, to the history of higher education across
this entire region. But first we need to dispense with three issues of methodological import: (a) While for the purposes of this work, Afro-Arab Islamic Africa refers to that part of Africa comprising these countries: Algeria, Djibouti,
Libya, Mauritania, Morocco, Sahrawi (Western Sahara), Sudan, Tunisia, and
United Arab Republic (Egypt), not all of them will receive individualized
treatment here for reasons of space—see Teferra and Altbach (2003) for those
countries that are left out of this work.[2]

(b) Any suggestion of unrelenting cultural homogeneity throughout the region is unintentional; for, as Abun-Nasr (1987: 5), for example, reminds us: the
general linguistic and religious unity of Afro-Arab Islamic Africa should not
be allowed to obscure the fact that it is a region with highly diverse ethnic
populations given not only the presence of ethnicities from much further south
of the coastal hinterland (Berbers, Sudanese, Somalis, etc.), but also the infu-
sion/assimilation of ethnicities and/or long-lasting cultural imprints from across
the Mediterranean and the Red Sea (north, east, and west); represented by, in
addition to the Arabs, the British, Byzantines, French, Greeks, Italians, Jews,
Persians, Phoenicians, Romans, Spanish, Turks, and so on. Furthermore, there
continues to exist to this day sizeable minority populations in this region who
adhere to non-Islamic faiths, principally: animism, Christianity, and Judaism.
Yet on the other hand, notwithstanding this fact, from the perspective of a history of higher education in the region, one can still acknowledge that these
countries are in possession of a common cultural heritage that while in relative
terms is recent, it extends well over one 1,000 years; ergo, giving it a level of
durability that has helped to significantly *reduce* (not necessarily eliminate)
those *differences* among the countries of the region that have ensued from even
more recent and continuing but disparate influences of the variegated European
colonial mantle thrown over them during the course of the nineteenth and
twentieth centuries by the British, the French, the Italians, and the Spanish.

(c) Given that these are countries that were once part of the vast global Islamic empire, they all possessed some form of the *madrasah* system, but to

varying degrees of development obviously. Some, such as Egypt, Morocco, and Tunisia had institutions of higher learning that at one time were of sufficient international repute as to attract students from all across the Islamic empire; while others, such as Djibouti, had a more rudimentary system. Since the madrasah system has already been discussed at some length in Chapter 1, attention in this chapter is directed principally to higher education during the European colonial and postcolonial eras.

On the basis of the foregoing methodological backdrop, among the factors that have had a significant impact on the history of higher education in Afro-Arab Islamic Africa there are a number that emerge as being of sufficient universality—in terms of the region—to deserve their delineation here as part of this prolegomena (before we go on to look at the region from a geographic country-by-country perspective, beginning with Egypt). There are at least five factors that are worthy of mention.

The first concerns the specific elite configurations that have marked this region throughout its recent history. The development of higher education and the quantitative/qualitative forms it took was, as one would expect, primarily the handiwork of the elites *(linked together in various permutations)* at a given moment in time. During the precolonial period the principal elites comprised (1) a praetorian foreign, but Muslim, ruling elite (e.g., Ottomans, Mamluks, sultans, amirs), (2) the landed aristocracy, (3) the indigenous and foreign mercantilist class, and (4) the traditional religious elite (the *ulama*). In the colonial period the same configuration existed except for three major changes: the ruling elites lost their position, with one or two exceptions, to an externally imposed non-Muslim elite, the foreign Western colonial elite; a new subordinate comprador administrative elite recruited from among the traditional elites (as well as non-elites) was created by the colonialists to staff the colonial bureaucracies at the ground level; and all the indigenous elites, new or old, were rendered subordinate to the foreign colonial elite.[3] With the end of colonialism and the exit of the colonial administrative elite, a new elite emerged to take its place. This new postindependence elite was made up entirely of either an emergent nationalist elite (which itself grew out of the colonial comprador administrative elite), or it was a combination of remnants of the precolonial ruling elite and the colonial comprador elite. In some cases (as in Egypt, Libya, or Sudan, for example), after some time had elapsed following political independence, yet another new elite arrived on the scene, the praetorian bureaucratic elite, to which all other elites became subordinate (at least in political terms).[4] Now, several related points flow from the foregoing: (a) the role of the ulama as the principal architects of higher education began to erode with the arrival of, first, colonialism and thereafter the secular postindependence era (though it never was and has never been completely obliterated). (b) With the arrival of European colonialism all the indigenous elites (with the exception, for the most part, of the ulama) soon bought into the colonialist approach to Islam in general and the madrasah system, specifically: that it was irrelevant to a "modern-izing" society. *(One must never forget that ultimately the success of the colonial project depended on the collaboration of existing and emerging elites with the colonial elite in the administration of the colonies.)* [5] This was expressed in three principal ways: demanding that the colonial regime provide secular higher education for their children; sending their children abroad to obtain Western higher education; and working toward the establishment of secular higher education institutions within the country—with or without the cooperation of the colonialist regimes (see also the next item.) (c) It would not be far-fetched to view the struggle for independence from colonial rule as essentially a struggle between a foreign and the indigenous elites over the resources (human and natural) of a given country; rather than a struggle between colonialism and authentic and democratic independence. In other words, for the masses political independence simply entailed, in the most fundamental sense, exchanging one set of oppressors with another (to describe the countries that make up Afro-Arab Islamic Africa, with one or two possible exceptions, as essentially police states would not be far from the mark); and higher education, *at the level of practice*, was enlisted to help legitimate this circumstance. (d) Where the new praetorian bureaucratic elite is dominant, the central avenue of elite reproduction is access to elite private or overseas education; one function of which is to enable a bilingual facility among the elite that is not generally available to the masses. ("Arabization" has almost always been reserved primarily for the masses, notwithstanding the nationalist rhetoric of the elites.)

The second is about the ulama. Any inference from the account that follows below that the ulama were (and are) a homogenous group is invalid; for, as with all *intellectual elites* (those of the present-day West included) they were often riven by a variety of considerations, depending upon time and place: political, economic, doctrinal, personal ambition, and, yes, even petty jealousies of the most mundane variety. Not surprisingly, their response to the colonial presence was often contradictory; in some instances they collaborated with the colonial power (e.g., some of the *shaykhs* and *sufi* leaders in Morocco and Algeria), while in others they carried out oppositional activities, primarily on the ideological plane.[6] In this regard they were, of course, continuing an ancient tradition where some sections of the ulama had found it in their own personal interest to cooperate with the ruling authorities of the day irrespective of the openly abysmal record of the authorities regarding civil and human rights, not to mention the matter of adherence to the *Shari'ah*; while others took on the more difficult and dangerous task of fomenting opposition to such authorities. (The former, to justify their stance, usually took cover behind the Islamic injunction to Muslims to obey authority—by omitting the qualifier "just and God-fearing.")

The third concerns the concept of "Western" higher education. Whatever the Islamic roots of *Western* higher education (see Appendix I), by the time of

European imperialism it had (like so much else, economy, society, military, state, etc.), diverged from Islamic higher education far beyond any immediately recognizable presence of common origins, so that the term *Western* higher education does have some limited significance for our present purposes. Leaving aside such matters as organizational forms, calendrical and diurnal structures of programs of study, pedagogy, course content, and so on, the most important difference was that Western education was by and large secular in orientation—even that provided by missionary education (in relative terms). For the nationalist-oriented elites that emerged this divergence was seen in evaluative terms: Western education was superior and Islamic education was inferior—it had to be jettisoned.[7] Yet, had colonialism not intervened, it is not at all clear that the madrasah system would still have been marginalized in favor of a secular/Westernist education that the indigenous elites (leaving aside the ulama) quickly took to, like ducks to water, under the aegis of the colonial mantle, rather than the alternative: *the system eventually evolving to meet new challenges.* (Reminder: no society will retain for long an educational system that is completely irrelevant to its needs.) The structural informality of the system and its apparent "disorder" (itself a problematic concept since disorder is only manifest against an externally mediated juxtaposition of externally rooted, hence foreign, "order") does not mean that the madrasah system did not serve the needs of their communities; it is only as a consequence of foreign threats and invasions in the post–1492 world that their relevance for the sudden changed circumstances of their societies became moot. A related issue that emerges here is that given their stated objective to "civilize" the Muslims, Why didn't the colonial powers, such as the French with their explicitly articulated ideology of *mission civilisatrice,* simply abolish the madrasah system altogether? There are several reasons why they (to turn to the French again) refrained from doing this: (a) It would have gone against their assurance to the Muslims that they would not interfere with their religion—an assurance designed to buy their acquiescence (even though in practice it was a promise not fully kept). (b) The French felt that the madrasah system could be useful for ideological purposes if they could staff if with vetted ulama who would help in legitimating French rule—an approach that did have some success in the early years of colonial rule. (c) Maintaining the madrasah system was in keeping with their actual (if not stated) aim of keeping the masses of the Muslims from becoming too educated to pose a potential threat to the French presence in terms of both colonial rule as well as competition for jobs. (d) It would have been simply too expensive to provide secular education to all the Muslims; the French were not willing to release the necessary resources for such an endeavor. (e) In the specific case of Algeria, there was the issue of racist settler resistance to any effort at improving the lot of the Muslim Algerians from any perspective to ensure their own settler supremacy within the social order. (This last point speaks to the conflict that often emerged throughout colonial Africa wherever there were settler colonies (Algeria, Kenya, South Africa, Zimbabwe, and so on) between the metropole and the settlers regarding how best to govern a settler colony—a conflict that more often than not went in the favor of the settlers until the indigenous, following the growth of nationalism, took matters into their own hands.)

The fourth is about the colonial educational policies. Colonialism was not implemented on the basis of a one-size-fits-all template by a colonial power; there were always adjustments made in terms of strategy depending on what forces were encountered in a given context. Hence, if one compares the educational policies of the French with respect to Algeria, Tunisia, and Morocco, for instance, this fact becomes self-evident as will be shown in a moment. First, however, this preliminary observation: unlike in Algeria where a foreign colonial elite was brought in to supplant the traditional elite (the Ottoman Mamluks), in the case of Morocco and Tunisia, the French chose to deliberately develop an indigenous compradorial elite. However, here again there was some difference between Morocco and Tunisia for the reason that Tunisia, unlike Morocco, had a "foreign" traditional elite, the Ottoman Mamluks. Consequently, and especially with an eye toward the future, in the case of Morocco the objective was to cultivate a compradorial elite from among the preexisting traditional elite (the urban Arab elite) whose legitimacy would not be an issue compared to that of an Ottoman Mamluk elite (had one existed) in the eyes of the masses; whereas in the case of Tunisia, a new secular/Westernist elite was created/emerged out of the Arabs and Berbers drawn from the urban as well as the rural populations; the Ottoman Mamluks, were for the most part, sidelined (after all, in the eyes of the masses, they had forfeited their right to rule in a future independent Tunisia for failing to prevent the arrival of European colonialism). What then did this imply for colonial educational practice in these countries? In Algeria, educational provision for all Algerians (elites or the masses) was not of a primary concern to the colonial authorities, at least not in practice and definitely not to the same extent as was the case in Tunisia and Morocco. In the latter two, the French accepted their responsibility to attend to the education of the Tunisians and the Moroccans by, on one hand, strengthening rather than weakening the existing madrasah system; and on the other, ensuring that educational provision for the elites and the masses was not identical since the former were to be groomed for positions of some authority, even if compradorial. Yet, even here there was some difference: unlike in the case of Morocco, in Tunisia, the French chose to support local initiatives for alternative secular/Westernist education for the elites—especially in the face of ulama intransigence to reform the al-Zaitouna mosque-college; whereas in Morocco they chose to use the existing mosque-college, the al-Qarawiyyin, to continue training the elite, until it was no longer practical. This was possible since the existing Moroccan elite was not to be transformed or substituted; it would be allowed to continue to draw on traditional avenues of legitimacy. Therefore, to the French the *preservation* (which implied no reforms) of the existing avenue for elite training and recruitment, al-Qarawiyyin, was considered desirable (the ulama would cooperate because they were not being threatened with any kind of major reforms that would undermine their power).[8] In other words, then, French educational policy was not absolutely uniform throughout its colonial empire in Africa. There was some difference that flowed from the so-called "assimilationist" (e.g., Algeria) versus the "associationist" (e.g., Morocco) colonial policies. However, any effort to identify and delve into all the nuances of difference would simply extend the scope of this work beyond the space permitted. Moreover, for our purposes, it is not even clear if this approach is necessary considering our interest in broad strokes rather than fine lines. Still, those interested in this line of inquiry may wish to look at, for example, Porter (2002), and Segalla (2003).

The fifth relates to the general history of the part of Islamic North Africa west of Egypt—referred to as the Maghreb. Any consideration of the history of the nations that make up the Maghreb forces one to confront the observation that in the phantasmagoric twists and turns of human history is to be found this twist: When the French colonized Algeria one of the myths they attempted to foist on the Algerian people (to be repeated on others all across Africa, and not only by them, but by the other colonial powers as well) is that they did not have a history until the French arrived on the scene (Naylor 2000). For the Algerians this utterly ridiculous fallacy must have been a bitter irony. The French were obviously patently ignorant of their own history; for, many centuries before (as noted in Chapter 1) the French in their barbaric state had encountered within their own borders, in southern France, the ancestors of the very people whose history they now wished to obliterate. A few centuries later, following that confrontation, they would have occasion to meet them again, by way of the Crusades. Yet, at the time of both these encounters, by almost any measure, the Muslims, compared to the French, were agents of an advanced civilization. Now, in 1830 the French had the audacity to proclaim themselves as the "Greeks of the world" who had come to bring civilization to the benighted! (p. 16). In fact, contrary to French essentialist propaganda, Algerian and other Maghrebi peoples had a history that went back not hundreds, but thousands of years! There is evidence of hominid presence (c. 200000 B.C.E.) and Neanderthal presence (c. 43000 B.C.E.) in North Africa, and the beautiful cave paintings found at a number of locations in that region (e.g., at Tassili-n-Ajjer in southern Algeria) speak to a Neolithic hunting people who lived from around 8000 B.C.E. to 4000 B.C.E. in a pre-desiccated (hence pre-Sahara) environment of the savannah—complete with lakes, rivers and a variety of animals from giraffes to elephants to hippopotami. From around 3000 B.C.E. onward the region became the domain of a single human-type but fragmented across the vast North African terrain into a number of ethnicities; these in turn fused to become, over time, the Berber peoples. By the time the Canaanites (or more commonly the Phoenicians) arrived from the region that we now call Lebanon to settle on the Maghrebi coast (approximately 900 B.C.E.)—to establish a century or so later (814 B.C.E.) a settlement at a place occupied by today's Tunis that they appropriately named Carthage (meaning new town)—the Berbers were now a well established linguistically and culturally unique African people organized into tribes and states. In 146 B.C.E. the Romans destroyed the city of Carthage as a terminus in a series of wars (beginning from 264 B.C.E. to 241 B.C.E.—which we know as the First Punic War) they had fought with the Carthaginians who had over time expanded to give rise to the Carthaginian state (with armies that included Berber soldiers and at times vacillating Berber allies, Numidians).

The French were simply one more group of invaders of the Maghreb in a long history of invaders that included the Romans too (approximately 24–429 C.E.); the Vandals, led by their king, Gaiseric (429–533 C.E.); the Byzantines (533–642 C.E.); and the Arab Muslims (from 642 C.E. onward) with their various dynasties: Umayyads (661–750); Abbasids (750–909); and the Fatimids (909–72). After the Fatimids withdrew eastward to Egypt, Berber dynasties would now takeover, such as the Zirids (972–1148); the Hammadids (1011–1151); Almoravids (1106–47); and the Almohads (1125–1271).[9] Then would come a number of lesser dynasties ruling different parts of the Maghreb (the Merinids, Zayanids, and Hafsids), to be followed finally by the Ottomans in 1516.

In outlining this highly condensed history of the Maghreb on the eve of the arrival of European imperialism three additional points may be noted: (1) When Islam arrived in the Maghreb the Berbers especially those living on or near the coast, were Christians (conversion to Christianity had begun in the second-century C.E. and would continue over the next 200 years). However, by the end of the eighth-century, most of them had converted to Islam while continuing to retain much of their language and culture. (Today all Berber communities are Muslims, though vestiges of pre-Islamic beliefs and practices may still be found among some of them and despite efforts to Arabize them, most still speak their own languages.) (2) The invasion of Europe in the eighth-century by Muslims and the subsequent colonization of parts of southern Europe (see Appendix I) was a combined Afro-Arab-Berber affair, and both the Almoravid and Almohad dynasties ruled Muslim Spain (from the eleventh to thirteenth centuries) when it was their turn to occupy the stage of Maghrebi history (the import of this fact can be assessed by reading Appendix I). (3) Initially, Islamic North Africa as a whole was a single Islamic polity; however, with the rise of various autonomous dynasties (e.g., the Hafsids in Tunisia), this polity fragmented to eventually become the basis for the independent countries that we recognize today.[10]

EGYPT

When Napoleon and his army disembarked in the small Egyptian fishing village of Marabou (located a short distance west of Alexandria) on July 1, 1798, his primary motivation for this Egyptian adventure was the circumscription of the growing British commercial interests in the Mediterranean/Red Sea region as part of his ongoing efforts to cripple Britain. However, this small framed man, whom women had nicknamed Puss-in-Boots on account of his hat and boots appearing to overwhelm his frame, had other megalomaniacal ambitions as well. Harking back to the exploits of other conquerors of Egypt centuries before him (Cambyses, Alexander the Conqueror, Gaius Octavius, etc.), he believed that under French colonial tutelage Egypt had the economic potential to become one of the crown jewels of his empire.[11] What was required was for the French to extricate Egypt from the grip of the Ottoman Mamluks and commence the process of restoring it to its former glory (and, quite remarkably, to this end he had actually brought along with him a large 167-person contingent of top French scientists, artists, engineers, and scholars to study the Egyptian past and present, as a first step in the project).[12] Unquestionably, the Ottomans (specifically in the guise of the resurgent Ottoman Mamluk rulers—the rather lackluster descendants of the original Mamluk dynasty that had ruled Egypt from 1250 until its defeat by the Ottomans in 1517, but who by the 1600s had managed to win back from their Ottoman overlords considerable, though not complete, autonomy), were presiding over an Egypt that was no longer as vibrant as it used to be.[13] The very fact that Napoleon had met so little *credible* resistance from the Ottoman Mamluks (who, recall, were in a sense heirs to the Abbasid dynasty, whose founder, Salah Ad-din Yusuf ibn Ayyub, Saladin, had once been the scourge of Crusader Europe) was in itself telling: Egypt, on the cusp of the nineteenth-century, as most of the rest of the Ottoman Empire, now lagged far behind Europe, from almost any perspective one cared to consider—economically, politically, and militarily.[14] Ergo, the arrogance of the French notwithstanding, there was some truth to Napoleon's view that Ottoman Mamluk rule had not bode well for the fortunes of Egypt—of course this was not entirely of their own making, for (as indicated in the preceding chapter), some of the same post–1492 forces that had been propelling Europe toward global hegemony were also responsible for taking the wind out of Ottoman sails all across its empire, including its North African provinces.[15]

As the French team looked around, the educational landscape they beheld was one that was characteristic of most of Islamic Africa at that particular moment in history: namely, *in view of the times*, a medieval moribund madrasah-based educational system (see Chapter 1 for details of this system) that through years of neglect had been rendered quite incapable of fully meeting the challenges of a rapidly changing and modernizing world—albeit in this regard, Egypt was still slightly better off compared to the other parts of Islamic Africa (for Cairo had managed to retain vestiges of its former role as among the major

centers of learning in the Islamic empire). The fact that the Ottomans were custodians of a civilization that at one time in its history had been at the forefront
of intellectual and scientific achievement and at whose feet a medieval Europe
had once learned much (as was shown in Appendix I), appears not to have de-
tracted them from imposing an intellectual insularity in their empire that was
quite unbecoming of those who had been enjoined by their religion to seek
knowledge to the ends of the earth (Massialas and Jarrar 1983: 8–9). The problem, perhaps, was misplaced arrogance that ensues from military might; or may
be it was the lack of a pre-Islamic tradition among the Ottomans of venerating
the written and the spoken word (that the Arabs, for example, had possessed in
their pre-Islamic days); or possibly it was the idea that anything coming out of
the lands of their Christian enemies was not only unworthy of emulation, but
its incorporation into a culture that saw no separation between the spiritual and
the material spheres of life, would smack of heresy; or it was a combination of
all three.

Or then again, perhaps, Bernard Lewis (1982) has a point. He begins by
stating the problem: "It may well seem strange that classical Islamic civilization which, in its earlier days, was so much affected by Greek and Asian influences should so decisively have rejected the West." Why? A possible answer he
says is that "[w]hile Islam was still expanding and receptive, Western Europe
had little or nothing to offer but rather flattered Muslim pride with the spectacle of a culture that was visibly and palpably inferior. What is more, the very
fact that it was Christian discredited it in advance." This view, he argues, had in
time become ossified to eventually produce this result: "Walled off by the military might of the Ottoman Empire, still a formidable barrier even in its decline,
the peoples of Islam continued until the dawn of the modern age to cherish—as
some of us in the West still do—the conviction of the immeasurable and immu-
table superiority of their own civilization to all others. For the medieval Muslim, from Andalusia to Persia, Christian Europe was a backward land of ignorant infidels." However, he continues: "It was a point of view which might
have been justified at one time; by the end of the Middle Ages it was becoming
dangerously obsolete." Whatever the reason, what is certainly true is that the
Ottoman Muslims never felt compelled, at any time up to this point, to *consciously and systematically* send missions to the land of the infidels to seek
new knowledge in a manner that earlier Muslim rulers had done (recall the effort of the Abbasids to import Greek works from Byzantium as part of their
translation projects), or in a manner that the infidels had undertaken centuries
before at the time of the Reconquista (see Appendix I)—or what one Muslim
ruler of Egypt was about to do now (see below).

Although the French presence proved to be, thanks in part to the British, of
extremely short duration, a mere blip in the 5,000-year history of the country
(Napoleon fled back to Europe the following year, leaving his troops ma-
rooned; though they would hang on to the country until their defeat on June 27,

1801, by a combined British and Ottoman expeditionary forces). For the Egyptians, and the rest of Islamic Africa, however, it was pregnant with implications: for it was a wake-up call to the fact that the invasion marked the inauguration of a completely new type of imperialism—a type that the Muslims (or any other peoples on the planet for that matter) had never experienced before— it was one that was powered by the relentless economic, political, and technological forces unleashed by the post–1492 emergent industrial capitalism in Western Europe (described in the preceding chapter). In other words, these were not your typical European Crusaders of yesteryear who had ravaged the Levant from time to time and against whom the Muslims had been more than an equal match. The Napoleonic invasion represented nothing less than the thin end of the wedge of modern Western European imperialism on the African continent; and it would not be long before, under its aegis, the fabric of Islamic cultural unity, and even Ottoman-inspired political cohesion, of Islamic Africa would be torn asunder forever, leaving in its wake distinct new national entities in the form of Algeria, Djibouti, Libya, Mauritania, Morocco, Sahrawi (Western Sahara), Sudan, and Tunisia, which have survived to the present day.[16] (Note: while the account that follows begins by considering Egypt first, being the largest and oldest nation among this group, the rest of it has been structured around these national entities in the alphabetical order just indicated.)

Now, if there was one person who quickly understood what the Muslims were facing in these changed times then it was the highly ambitious Muslim Albanian military officer in the employ of the Ottoman expeditionary force sent to deal with the French, Muhammed Ali (1769–1849). When the Ottomans withdrew their force, they left behind the Albanian contingent that Ali had headed as second in command; and Ali, who until his arrival in Egypt was a person of nonentity, found himself in some position of influence as one of the officers in charge of it. Perhaps drawing upon his background as the son of a commander of irregulars in the employ of the Ottoman governor (of the port city of Kavalla in Macedonia), and who beginning from childhood had become involved in his father's (Ibrahim Agha) moonlighting enterprise (trading in tobacco), he quickly became enmeshed in the political intrigues that arose with the sudden exit of the French.[17] Following a revolt against the Ottoman viceroy in 1805, Mohammed Ali got the Ottomans, who in practical terms had little choice in the matter, to install him (with the blessing of the Egyptian ulama—a decision that they would soon come to regret) as governor of Egypt.[18] He would quickly commence a program of placing Egypt on the long road to modernity (but it would be a modernity in the North African-style: one that comprises an unstable fusion of Islam, secular Westernization and praetorian absolutism).

Though not an Egyptian by birth, he would earn himself the appellation of a patriot more than a century and a half later from those modern Egyptian historians with less than an eye for accuracy of historical facts. For while he did much to prepare the groundwork for the secular Western transformations to come, they were largely by default—his primary objectives were always those of personal ambition and self-aggrandizement.[19] Consider this, for instance: he embarked on a massive program of expropriating the landed aristocracy and thereby effectively converted Egypt into a single, gigantic "plantation," producing cotton (the highly profitable long-staple variety) and sugarcane, complete with near slave-like conditions for the peasantry, that he and his progeny would henceforth own. Although he was aware of the need to industrialize as a means of accumulating more wealth, as well as facilitate the modernization of his new conscript army (unlike the Mamluks, his armies did not depend entirely on military slaves), a project that was very dear to his heart having seen at first hand what a modern army could do on the battlefield, his efforts at industrialization foundered on the rocks of lack of adequate human and financial capital, mismanagement of national resources (he embarked on a number of military adventures abroad, including the conquest of Sudan), and spirited opposition from Western powers (principally Britain—see, for example, Marsot 1984).[20]

The dynasty that he gave rise to, called the *Khedive*, lasted until its overthrow in 1952—though from 1822 to 1922 it was in power only nominally and at the pleasure of a Western occupying power, the British.[21] The higher education legacy of this dynasty and its British overlords was characterized by these principal developments: the marginalization of the madrasah system; the dispatch of foreign student missions to the West; establishment of modern military schools; and the creation of the first secular university (albeit, initially, a privately-funded institution), the University of Cairo.

As part of his program of monopolizing the country's resources, Ali also practically abolished the *waqfs* (the educational trusts) of the madrasahs, including those of al-Azhar, by looting their resources. Ali was fully cognizant of the fact that if he was going to effect the modernization of his army (the first priority) and develop the country's resources generally to finance it, he needed personnel trained in what he felt were modern Western ways. He, however, chose to pursue this project by going outside the madrasah system. (This was a strategy that would also be emulated by the colonial powers whenever they came across madrasahs elsewhere in Africa.) Several factors lay within this approach: lack of a coherent educational policy (since all policy was determined on ad hoc basis, as is typical of autocracies); lack of resources to modernize the madrasah system (which, recall, regardless of its numerous defaults, was still a mass, relatively democratic, educational system that would have required enormous resources for its modernization); his disdain of education for the masses (Ali was no populist); his narrowly conceived education goals (to be explained in a moment); and an astute perception that forcing change on the system (which invariably implied significant secularization) ran the risk of so completely alienating the ulama that they would be tempted to mobilize mass opposition to his regime. Clearly, then, whatever modernization that Ali felt was necessary required alternative secular higher education institutions. To this end, Ali embarked on a two-pronged approach: a program of sending foreign students to study abroad while simultaneously importing Western expatriate intellectual labor; and the construction of an ad hoc inverse secular educational pyramid—beginning with single-school "militarized" colleges and then, as an afterthought, to overcome unforeseen bottlenecks in student recruitment, lower-level institutions (hence the term "inverse pyramid").

As far as records show, the first foreign student to be sent abroad, according to Heyworth-Dunne (1939) was Uthman Nuraddin, who left for Italy in 1809 and after five years there went on to study for two more years in France; he returned in 1817. Another of the earliest foreign students whose name has not been erased from history (most of the relevant student records were destroyed, it is thought, by a chance fire in the Citadel in 1820) was Nikula Musabiki. He was sent to study printing in Italy. By the time of the first much-celebrated *major* foreign student mission (sent in July of 1826, comprising initially 42 students, with 2 joining the group later), a total of some 28 students had been sent out sporadically to various parts of Europe (e.g., England, France, Germany, and Italy) to study the technical and military arts and sciences (engineering, shipbuilding, printing, and so on). The historical fame of the 1826 mission, however, is not entirely undeserving: it was distinct from earlier efforts in that it involved not only the dispatch abroad of a fairly large contingent at a single moment (with all the attendant national publicity), but it was sent to just one European country; in this case, France—one must hasten to add here that as far as Ali was concerned, this choice was determined on purely pragmatic grounds. It was certainly not for the purposes of building cultural ties with Egypt's former enemy, but for reasons of convenience in that the French appeared to have been more than enthusiastic (for obvious reasons) about hosting this large contingent of foreign students.[22]

Typically, Ali took a personal interest in the education of these students, so much so that he would regularly send them letters of exhortation, enjoining on them discipline and diligence. Heyworth-Dunne observes that Ali even took to demanding monthly reports of progress, including an indication from them of all the books they had read; and he would reprimand them in no uncertain terms if their progress was not up to his standards. Once, a group of students returned with their medical qualifications, but due to an administrative error, without having pursued doctoral-level studies. Ali promptly sent them back to Paris the same year (1836) to complete their doctorates, while at the same time imposed on each of them the responsibility of translating into Arabic all the textbooks they covered in their studies (his aim here was to create a supply of textbooks for domestic educational needs). Rarely in the history of higher education had a nation's leader followed the education of the country's foreign students with such diligent advertence—but perhaps this was to be expected of an autocrat like Ali who was not only a man in a hurry, but was ever mindful of returns on investment, especially given the large financial outlays involved in the foreign student project.

In subsequent years, the flow of Egyptian foreign students at the behest of Ali (and his successors) continued apace both individually as well as in small and large groups, so that by the time of Ali's passing (in 1849) Heyworth-Dunne calculates, a total of 349 students had been sent to Western countries to study. The clock had gone full circle; it had taken 1,000 years: those who were once producers and transmitters of knowledge were now its recipients; and those who were once the recipients were now the producers and transmitters; such are the ways of history. Since these foreign student missions to the West were the first ever sponsored by an African state (and possibly even in the entire Islamic world), they bear further scrutiny along several axes:

Student background: The selection process was, as one would expect, generally arbitrary, where academic merit was certainly not paramount, if at all. Instead, they were chosen from within the upper echelon of the country's social structure (hence with Turko-Egyptians predominating). In terms of sex they were (it would appear) all male; and regarding age they tended to be older (early to mid-twenties), falling outside the normal age range for those pursuing undergraduate studies. Contrary to what many have thought (see for example Vatikiotis 1991: 97) the majority of the students were not from the madrasah system, as is indicated by the fact that very few of them were graduates of al-Azhar (Eccel 1984). Upon reflection this should not be surprising: to be sent to study abroad was in itself a prestigious assignment, hence the sons of the elite were most likely to receive preference over others.

Fields and subjects of study: Their specialties were primarily aimed at assisting Ali with the development of a praetorian industrial state; the following sample listing of what the 1826 mission studied is telling: agriculture; arms-making; chemistry; civil administration; diplomacy; hydraulics; mechanics; medicine; military administration; military engineering; mining; naval administration; naval-engineering.[23] In later years the list would be expanded to include such vocational subjects as: calico-printing; candle-making; cloth-dyeing; furniture and carpet-making; gun-making; jewelry-making; pottery-making; silk-weaving; shoe-making; and watch-making.

Educational success: To what extent were these first wave of foreign students successful in achieving their academic goals? It appears that on balance not very much— for several reasons: lack of adequate prior academic preparation because they were generally not selected on the basis of academic merit; the fact that the secular part of the educational system within Egypt was not yet developed enough to permit sufficient preparatory training; and the students had to first learn a foreign language upon arrival in the host country, which interfered with the overall efficiency of their education (and their age in this regard did not help matters). However, one can surmise that in later years, by learning through hindsight, the success rate must have improved.

Efficiency of employment: Upon their return the students were not always placed in occupations commensurate with their qualifications. Heyworth-Dunne gives examples: a naval graduate found himself in the finance department; a student who had studied diplomacy was assigned to a job completely unrelated to diplomacy; a hydraulics engineering graduate was asked to teach chemistry; some who had studied military administration were placed in the civil administration; and so on. Misemployment (or *under-employment* to use a better term) appears to have been the order of the day.

Overall impact on society: Regardless of whether or not they had completed their studies with thunderous success, or whether they were employed with due regard to their specialties upon their return, this much is incontrovertible: the fact that this was the first generation of Egyptians who had been sent out to obtain secular Western education their impact on Egyptian society would, in time, prove to be profound; and this was nowhere more so than through their employment in the various educational institutions that Ali set up with the assistance of not only the returned foreign students, but also imported Western expatriates (see later). However, their impact can not be measured simply in terms of the overall goals of Ali's limited military dictated modernization program, but also in terms of the unintended consequences (which are intrinsic to any large-scale educational effort of this kind), of which these two stand out for mention: (1) It led to the development of a deeply bifurcated elite social structure: a new elite (transmuted out of the old Turko-Egyptian aristocracy, which would be combined later with an emergent Arabized Egyptian elite) comprising a Westernized, militarized, and *secular* stratum (wherein all power resided) sitting atop a religious establishment of the ulama. In the context of a country with an Islamic tradition on one hand, and on the other an economy that may be labeled as a *dependent economy*, this development would have serious repercussions for the course of Egyptian history in the decades to come.[24] (2) Besides the matter of birth, there would henceforth be a new coin of the realm in terms of elite membership and legitimacy; and it would be two-sided: on one side, possession of a secular higher education qualification and, on the other, the requirement that the qualification be of Western provenance—ergo: for the elite, "study abroad" would become forever a fixture of Egyptian higher education (and for that matter in the rest of Africa and in many other parts of the PQD world as well) without any rational regard to national human capital needs.

In addition to the immediate human capital needs of the agricultural and military-industrial enterprises that Ali hoped to satisfy by dispatching the foreign student missions, he was also aware of the necessity, for cost-effective reasons, of providing similar education and training within Egypt itself for the same purpose. However, what this also meant is that the education agenda he conceived was an extremely narrow one, where, as Heyworth-Dunne (1939: 152) explains, "[n]ot a single institution was set up philanthropically or for the sole purpose of improving the intellectual outlook of the people." Therefore, in keeping with his strictly utilitarian approach to the educational effort and given that Ali's educational goals were overwhelming dictated by his military and entrepreneurial needs, the first secular higher education institutions to be set up were of the single specialty vocational-type, usually modeled on Italian or French institutions, and which were attached to the military in one way or another. The following list of schools (which were usually named "School of... followed by the name of the specialty—as in *Madrasat at-Tubjiya,* School of Artillery, or *Madrasat al-Jihadiya,* School of War), with an indication of the year in which they were established, is illustrative: 1816: military training;

1820: mathematical sciences; 1821: surveying; 1819–23: military training (schools or more correctly camps established in Aswan, Cairo, Farsut, and An-Nakila); 1825: two schools, school of war, and school of navy; 1827: three schools, martial music, medicine, and veterinary medicine; 1829: two schools, civil service, and pharmacy; 1830: signaling; 1831: five schools, artillery, cavalry, chemistry, industrial arts, and irrigation; 1831–32: maternity; 1832: infantry; 1833: establishment of ten schools of war munitions in upper Egypt. The list goes on (see Heyworth-Dunne (1939) and Eccel (1984) for more examples going up to 1911. Anyhow, one gets the picture of the new secular but narrowly circumscribed higher education landscape that Ali created.

A mere listing such as this one does not, however, tell us in any way what the establishment of these institutions entailed and what were their general characteristics; therefore a few observations in this regard are in order. In the early years, ideas for the establishment of the various institutions often came from expatriates that Ali had hired, though later some of the foreign-student returnees would also take the initiative in this respect. The teaching staff for the schools were initially recruited from abroad (principally France and Italy, and after 1882, England). However, with the return of foreign student missions some of their members were also recruited for this purpose. The language of instruction varied from institution to institution depending on the nationality of the instructors, but the predominant languages were Turkish, Arabic, and French; later of course English would be added.[25] The students came from within the ruling elite stratum, but in circumstances where there was a shortage of students, recruitment was broadened to coerce capable students from the lower strata of society to go to these schools.[26] Since these were state schools, students did not pay any tuition and in many instances free board, lodging, clothing, and stipends were also provided. Upon graduation students were for the most part immediately taken into the employ of the armed forces or government administration.

While the development of these institutions experienced the usual teething problems that one would expect in any circumstance where educational enterprises modeled on alien teaching and learning practices were being established, there were some problems that were specific to the extant Egyptian culture; of which the following five stand out for mention: One, the Islamic culture in Egypt (and perhaps this was true throughout the Islamic world) had seen so much intellectual retrogression that there was resistance to the study of some subjects. For instance: a special edict (fatwa) had to be sought from the ulama to permit the study of anatomy when the school of medicine was founded. Or consider this: in 1831–32, when the school of maternity was first established (as a division within the school of medicine), it failed to attract any students at all because Egyptian parents would not permit their daughters to attend it. The school then resorted to a novel solution with Ali's encouragement: it recruited its first students forcibly by purchasing Ethiopian and Sudanese slave girls in the Cairo slave market! Later, it would augment its student body by turning to a group of orphan girls who had been under treatment at the Cairo hospital (and who upon discharge would have come under government care) as well as purchasing more slave girls. (See Heyworth-Dunne (1939: 132); he also notes that upon graduation—which in itself was a commendable achievement since the first step in their education had entailed teaching them literacy—the midwives were given the same rank as the male graduates of the medical school.)

Two, there was the problem of language. That is, the importation of learning from non-Arabic sources always involved grappling with the linguistic barrier. Whether it was expatriate instructors (who for the most part did not speak Arabic) or textbooks written in foreign languages, the end result was always that much greater educational inefficiency. The problem is highlighted by Heyworth-Dunne, for instance, in his description of the effort to establish the first veterinary school in Egypt: the instructor, a Frenchman, was assigned an interpreter who could speak Arabic, Italian, and Turkish but not French, thereby spawning "the usual intrigues between teachers, interpreters, students, and officials" (p. 133). [27] Now, it is true that in the matter of expatriate instructors it was a temporary problem because in time trained Egyptians were hired to replace them; however, the problem of books in a foreign language was never fully resolved and in fact in successive decades as modernization progressed with dizzying speed in the West (especially after the Second World War) and the flow of books there became a torrent, it simply got worse and worse—this circumstance was of course not unique to Egypt only, other Arabic-speaking Islamic countries were also equally affected. The difficulty initially was lack of resources, coupled with the absence of an imaginative leadership, to permit a *systematic* (the key word here is systematic) translation of books. Years later, with the oil boom the resource constraint was eased considerably, but the leadership issue did not disappear and has not disappeared. The result is that to this day the Islamic world in Africa and the Middle East remains starved of books published in the Arabic language commensurate with its higher and general education needs. At the same time, as if the books problem is not enough, in most Egyptian universities, as in almost all universities throughout North Africa, the languages of instruction tend to be dual: Arabic in some faculties, while in others usually either English or French or even both. One can only surmise the educational inefficiencies involved as a result, especially when the rest of the educational system at the lower levels is, for the most part, monolingual (mainly Arabic).

Three, Ali's new higher education institutions created resistance to them among Egyptian parents (until long after he had passed from the scene). The reason is that parents rightly associated these institutions with service in his armed forces, which they dreaded (even to the point, on occasions, of acquiring self-inflicted injuries). The conditions of service were such that parents did every thing they could to shield their children from being recruited into the armed forces either directly, or indirectly—through Ali's education institutions. (There was also, however, the "small" matter of the near certainty of having to participate in Ali's military adventures abroad.)

Four, in the absence of a secular general education system, the new higher education institutions were initially accompanied by instructional facilities befitting primary and secondary school levels (where, as already noted, sometimes illiteracy itself had to be dealt with as the first order of business). It wasn't just the lack of secular institutions, however, that created additional hurdles for these new institutions to overcome. There was also the problem of the rapid decay of the only extant education system in the country to which Ali was forced to turn for his students: the traditional madrasah system. Yet it was a decay accelerated by Ali's own policies. To explain: unless parents were severely destitute, their general inclination was to avoid sending their children to the madrasahs (already on their knees because of the waqf expropriations) for fear that their children would be available for recruitment into the new higher education institutions *and thence into Ali's armed forces* (Heyworth-Dunne 1939: 153).[28]

Five, given the state ownership of all the major means of production and considering the militaristic ambitions of Ali, the employment of the graduates of the secular higher education institutions (including those who had been sent to study abroad), was not only primarily in the government sector, but such employment was almost guaranteed. In consequence, it set a bad precedent for generations to come where Egyptian graduates would come to regard employment in government bureaucracies virtually a birthright unless a better remunerative private sector employment was available.

At the age of eighty Muhammed Ali relinquished his grip on the ship of state (and a year later, on August 2, 1849, he died as a result of natural causes). It is doubtful if any of his enemies had ever thought that the old lion would last that long as the ruler of Egypt. Anyhow, What can one say then of the educational legacy that Ali left to the Egyptians? It was, in a nutshell, a mixed one: on one hand he had helped to open the door to secular/Western education, yet on the other the opening was merely a crack given the autocrat's highly circumscribed vision of the future of the country that he had inadvertently come to rule, coupled with the constraints placed on him by Europe in terms of his ambitions for the autonomous industrialization of Egypt. The fact that his rise to power was itself a consequence of a European invasion was perhaps a portent of the future that Egypt was destined to pursue: never independent enough to build on past glories. Within a mere three decades or so of his passing, the infidels would takeover Egypt once more (this time it would be the British). He would have been apoplectically outraged beyond words. He may not have been a good practicing Muslim; but he was a Muslim never the less (no, he was not a nationalist; the rise of Egyptian nationalism was yet to come).

In 1882, a variety of factors emanating from within Egypt (coalescing around one word, misrule) and in Europe (which could be boiled down to one word as well, imperialism) conspired together to bring about the loss of Egyptian independence, marked by the arrival of British protectorate rule. In the period up to that point, commencing with the death of Muhammed Ali in 1849, Egypt, which had seen the reigns of successor Khedives in the persons of Abbas I (1849–54), Sa'id Pasha (1854–63), Ismail Pasha (1863–79), and Taufik Pasha (1879–83), was more or less adrift rudderless in a sea of ever mounting political and economic machinations of European powers as they relentlessly jockeyed with each other to chip away at the shrinking Ottoman Empire. Only a Muhammed Ali incarnate could have, probably, saved Egypt from the fate of 1882, but none would arise from among his Khedival progeny— such was the cost of hereditary rule that befell one of the crown jewels in the House of Islam.[29]

Anyhow, from the perspective of higher education during this period (1849–82), the following were the principal developments: (1) Initially, there was a basic retrenchment of the system that Ali had left; many schools were closed for financial, political, myopic, and other reasons (for example: school of languages and accounting closed in 1851; schools of accounting, architecture, civil engineering and war closed in 1861)—even the *Diwan al Madaris* was abolished in 1854, though it would be reestablished some years later in 1863. (2) The practice of sending foreign student missions to Europe, however, continued—though on a limited scale. (3) A few schools were reorganized and some new schools were started (for example, the school of medicine was closed in 1855 and reopened the following year after its reorganization; the school of military engineering was opened in 1858 and in 1866 its curriculum would be expanded to include irrigation and architecture; in 1880 the Khedival Teachers College was set up to produce secular oriented secondary school teachers; in 1868 the schools of administration and languages, surveying, and accountancy, and egyptology were established). (4) The principle of providing free education, which included the provision of clothing, food, lodging, and stipends, continued—albeit at varying levels of adherence as one moved away from the cities. (5) The fortunes of the madrasah system improved considerably, relative to what they had been during Ali's rule, as a modest but credible effort was made at expanding and rationalizing the system for the first time in its history. All in all, the fate of higher education by the end of this period of Egyptian history, considering the initial retrenchment, could be characterized as one of some, but still very limited, developmental progress—when viewed purely in quantitative terms. Qualitatively? Well, that was another matter. For as a state-of-the-art report on the entire education sector submitted on December 19, 1880, by an education commission set up for that purpose (under the leadership of Ali Pasha Ibrahim) clearly indicated, it left a great deal to be desired.[30]

The British remained in Egypt until 1956, but their formal protectorate rule ended in 1922. During the protectorate phase of their presence the development of higher education (in quantitative terms came almost to a standstill), for the uppermost guiding principle in Egyptian affairs under the English was financial austerity. However, there were two major developments that occurred during this period that were of considerable significance to the higher education sector, though they did not arise out of specific British initiatives, but from initiatives of the Egyptians themselves. First, was the initiative by the Egyptians to set up a secular university, the University of Cairo. Second, was an unforeseen consequence of the British presence in Egypt: it created, on one hand, a tripartite power struggle between the Khedives, the British, and the emerging secular government elite over control of the wakfs, with resultant implications for the finances of al-Azhar; and on the other a duopolistic political struggle between the Khedives and the government elite for influence in the country, as a consequence of which al-Azhar became a focus of their attention. The long-term outcome of both these factors was that al-Azhar was propelled in the direction of two major sets of much needed reforms: one dealing with the internal efficiency of the institution and the other relating to the broader relevance of the institution within the changing Egyptian socioeconomic landscape (there is more later about these changes).

Cairo University was inaugurated in 1908, though it began its life as the Egyptian University, a private university. As this was the first secular university in Egypt, the circumstances of its birth deserves attention. Among the earliest proponents of the idea of a university in Egypt were, as would be expected, among the foremost persons of influence of the day outside the ulama. They included the brothers Ahmad Zaghlul (judge) and Saad Zaghlul (judge and later education minister); J. E. Marshall (the British Judge on the Court of Appeals); Yaqub Artin (an Armenian civil servant who first proposed the idea in 1894); Qasim Amin (judge on the Court of Appeals); Jurji Zaydan (the Syrian editor of the magazine *al-Hilal*); Mustafa Kamil (the founder of the Watani Party and a staunch anti-imperialist); Ahmed Manshawi (a wealthy landlord); and Muhammed Abduh (the religious reformer and later Mufti). While each may have had different motivations, they were all united in their belief that a country desirous of Western modernity needed a secular institution of higher learning to train the modernizing elite. Sending students to study abroad was not, they felt, the most efficient way of achieving this goal. It wasn't simply the utilitarian factor at work, however; there was the nationalist factor too, that is, the perception among some that a country as large and prosperous as Egypt deserved a *secular* university as a symbol of its march toward modernity. As for al-Azhar, some consciously, and others unconsciously, had written it off as not a viable basis for the creation of the kind of university they had in mind; unwieldy, recalcitrant, traditional, and too democratic in its enrollment base, they felt that it was better to continue with the practice begun almost a century earlier by Muhammed Ali—simply bypass the institution (at least for the time being) by creating alternative institutions, of which the *Dar-ul-Uum* (teacher training college), the School of Law *(Madrasat al-Qaada al-Shari'ah)* and the Egyptian Military Academy were the latest examples.

At a fund-raising meeting (catalyzed by a pledge a few months earlier of some 500 Egyptian pounds by a Mustafa Kamil al-Ghamrawi), called on October 12, 1906, at the house of Saad Zaghlul, a group of twenty-six Western-oriented Egyptian persons of consequence collected over 4,000 Egyptian pounds in pledges, formed a steering committee and launched the university project. It would take another two years before it actually saw fruition. At this point one would be remiss not to mention the fact that the project was born without the blessing of the British. In fact, with the exception of one or two individuals (e.g., Marshall), it was staunchly opposed by them through the person of their first Consul-General (1883–1907), the all but in name khedive and autocratically arrogant Orientalist, Lord Cromer (peeraged in 1892, therefore his real name until then was Sir Evelyn Baring), who not only felt that it would be a drain on the education budget, but feared creating potential nationalist malcontents, as had occurred, he felt, in India where he had served for a while.[31]

Anyhow, the British notwithstanding, under the patronage of the Khedive Abbas Hilmi II (his control of the waqf department allowed him to allocate an annual grant out of waqf funds to the university project), and the energetic leadership of Prince Ahmed Fuad I (who was always on the look out for opportunities to enhance his influence), the project got to a promising start by raising respectable amounts of donations from members of the royal family and other members of the Egyptian elite. It became a reality in a rented mansion owned by a Greek tobacco merchant on December 21, 1908.

Initially, the university only had part-time hires who taught such subjects as literature, history, and philosophy. Later, while the university awaited the return of students it had sent abroad for training (on staff development fellowships), it recruited its teachers from the only two acceptable institutions in town: the *Dar-ul-Ulum* and the School of Law; they did not come from al-Azhar (which the new university, perhaps understandably, looked at askance).[32] Other hires, mainly Orientalists, came from Europe, principally France, Germany, and Italy. Incidentally, the United States was not represented (since at the time the Middle East was not yet one of its stomping grounds) either in the founding of the university or in teaching.[33] Depending on the courses, the university engaged in multiple languages of instruction, primarily Arabic, French, and English (which must have produced considerable difficulties for the students one may surmise here). Its students, as long as they could pay the tuition fee (which had the effect, even if unintentional, of essentially rendering the institution a preserve of the elites), were recruited without regard to ethnicity, nationality, religious affiliation or even sex. About the last, the thirty-one female students enrolled in the first year of the university's operation spoke to the fact that for the first time in the history of modern Egypt, women had access to what may be called a regular secular university education within the country.[34] As for enrollment numbers, in its second year of operation (1909–10) the university had a total of 415 students enrolled in a program comprising all of eight courses taught by eight professors (Reid 1990: 45). On the curricular side, the university was deliberately conceived to be a corrective to what was perceived by Egyptian intellectuals as a tradition (established by Muhammed Ali) within the secular education sector that placed too much emphasis on education of a utilitarian value (economics, law, engineering, etc.) The university wished to be an arts and humanities institution where the watch word in the university's mission was, according to its architects, "knowledge for the sake of knowledge." From the perspective of general student life, this was not a full university in the sense we understand it today. For one thing, there was no campus with student residences (which reinforced its orientation toward students from elite backgrounds—for a student from rural Egypt student campus accommodation, then as today, was an absolute necessity); institutionalized extracurricular activities (like sport) were absent; and such student support services as guidance and counseling did not exist.[35]

Although the creation of the Egyptian University represented a cherished dream come true for the Western-oriented Egyptian elite, its early years were not easy ones notwithstanding the depth of goodwill that the institution commanded from most of the elite; the main problem was financial, which got worse with the onset of World War I and thereafter. At one point there was even talk of canceling classes altogether so dire had the situation become. Fortunately for the institution, history had a rosier future planned; it began with one event: the playboy prince had become king. That is, the university found a lifeline in the shape of its first rector (1909–13), Prince Fuad I, who was crowned king in 1922 (and ruled until his death in 1936). Within three years, with his help, the Egyptian University would cease to be a private university; it was reincarnated as a state university. Three years later still, it would move to a new campus with Western (and many can legitimately argue, ugly) utilitarian architecture so as to make, as Reid (1990: 79) observes, "a clean symbolic break with the Islamic past." The "new" university began with four faculties: arts (based on the absorption of the old university), science, medicine, and law. Ten years later, in 1935, engineering, commerce, and agriculture would be added. A year later, it would incorporate the venerable *Dar-ul-Ulum*. (As if to emphasize the transformations, a few years after the death of the king it was renamed Fuad I University.) Expansion would continue in succeeding years to include more faculties, as well as institutes (oceanography, African studies, research, cancer, etc.), and thereby becoming a full-fledged modern secular university. However, another historical event would be instrumental in pushing the transformation along: the abolition of the monarchy in 1952. (Symbolically, the university would experience yet another name change as a result to become what it is today: the University of Cairo.) In 1955, the university would expand abroad by being among the earliest institutions in the world to inaugurate a practice that is beginning to be commonplace today: a branch university *in another country*: specifically the establishment of three faculties in Khartoum: arts, law, and commerce.

While the University of Cairo is the oldest secular university in Egypt, at about the time when the university was being conceived, there was talk in some circles (mainly by non-Egyptians) of creating another private university. Few, perhaps, among the Egyptian elite would have been interested in the idea, given the source of the plans. Still, within only about a decade of the establishment of Cairo University, this other private university came into being too—and what is more, history would contrive a historical linkage, albeit tenuous, between the two. In other words, the next oldest secular university founded in the modern period in Egypt is the private American University in Cairo (AUC). Its creation had been suggested as early as 1899 by its U.S. founders, the United Presbyterian missionaries, but the idea was shelved because of British opposition, as well as the intervention of World War I.[36] However, even in the face of such discouragement, in 1919 an opportunity arose that the AUC board of trustees felt compelled not to pass up: a dramatic drop in Cairo's real estate prices presented them with an opening they were astute enough to grab. It permitted them to purchase a home for their new institution at a fire-sale price; it was none other (such are the ways of history) than the very building owned by the wealthy Greek tobacco merchant, Nestor Gianaclis, that had been the first home of Cairo University; and which it had had to vacate in 1914 because it could no longer afford the rent (Reid 1990).[37]

The American University in Cairo began operations in 1920 (opened for classes on October 5), but in its first years it was essentially a secondary school (as noted below); only later it would enlarge to become a university.[38] There were two curricular tracks that a student could choose from at this level: the arts course, where instruction was offered in English (aimed at those who wanted to study at universities abroad or at AUC itself as university-level courses were added) and a "government" course that was comparable to the regular government secondary school education with instruction in Arabic. By 1927 the AUC was offering eight years of instruction that included four years of college-level education similar to that available in U.S. universities—which meant that unlike the British-modeled Egyptian University, where students specialized in a single subject, students at AUC pursued a four-year undergraduate liberal arts curriculum where specialization was not permitted (other than having a major and a minor), but instead students were exposed to a variety of courses in the arts, humanities, social sciences, and the natural sciences. The AUC would also begin offering special English language instruction classes for not only its own prospective students but, through its adult education program, to others who were not AUC students. The university continued to offer preuniversity-level education for another twenty-five years or so when it became a university in the traditional sense, complete with various curricular divisions (e.g., college of arts and sciences, school of oriental studies, etc.), and unique to Egyptian higher education landscape, a program of campus-based extracurricular activities—including athletics—for its students where a student was expected to be a member of at least one club for purposes of out of class cultural enlightenment.

The expulsion of the British en masse from Egypt on the eve of the eventful 1952 military coup proved to be a boon for the university in later years as the Egyptians (especially the Westernized secular elites) increasingly became enamored with the United States.[39] Even after official relations with the United States soured and Egypt turned to the Soviet Union for assistance, the AUC, adapt at walking the tightrope of Egyptian cultural and political realities, retained sufficient goodwill in Egypt to assure its continued existence.[40] In time, despite its small size, and considering that it was a private fee-paying university of Christian missionary origins, the university came to play an important role in Egypt as a university of choice for the children of the elite, especially women, and those desirous of emigrating. What is remarkable is that even a person like Nasser felt compelled to secure elite status for his progeny by sending his daughter to AUC. The wife of Husni Mubarak also studied there.[41]

From the perspective of Egyptian higher education as a whole, the significance of the presence of the AUC can be traced along four major avenues: exposure to principles and methods of high-quality U.S. university education, at both graduate and undergraduate levels; access to excellent (in relative terms) library research facilities—in fact to say that the AUC library is a regional resource would not be an exaggeration; and access to first-class English-language training developed over many years through trial and error; and exposure to top U.S. and other scholars invited by the AUC from time to time to give lectures. As for the AUC and its U.S. backers, the AUC presence in Egypt has been a source of goodwill for U.S. higher education, not just in Egypt but in neighboring countries too. The AUC would also acquire importance for the U.S. government as well (to be especially emphasized after the *infitah*—see below) for such purposes as providing Arabic-language training for U.S. government officials (such as its embassy staff) on one hand, and on the other, English-language training for Egyptians working on either U.S.-funded assistance projects or for those awarded scholarships to study at U.S. universities.[42] In a sense, then, the AUC has served and continues to serve as an educational equivalent of a U.S. embassy in Egypt and its environs.[43]

Besides these first two secular universities, Egypt would see the founding of two others before that fateful year of 1952 (to be explained in a moment): the Faruq I University in Alexandria (later renamed University of Alexandria), which opened in 1942 by incorporating the University of Egypt's branch faculties of law and arts that had been established in that city in 1938; and Ibrahim Pasha University in Cairo (later renamed Heliopolis University after the suburb in which the campus came to be located, though today it is known by the Arabic version of the name as the University of Ain Shams) a few years on, in 1950. The driving force behind the birth of these new institutional scions of the University of Egypt was student overcrowding at the mother university, as well as a desire to open opportunities for university education elsewhere in the country.

Any periodization of *modern* Egyptian history, for any purpose, does not allow circumvention of 1952. Why? For in that year, on July 23, a group of young junior officers calling themselves the "Free Officers" executed a military coup (thankfully for the Egyptians a relatively peaceful one) against the constitutional monarchy, ushering in what may be called a populist praetorian oligarchy. Without going into the whys and wherefores of this event, it marked for Egypt an important break (*disjuncture,* perhaps, would be a better word since one of the fundamental lessons of history is that it is impossible for a society to engineer a complete break with its past) with its recent history in a number of ways: the overthrow of formal rule by two groups of foreigners, the Ottomans and their nominal affiliates, the Turko-Circassian-Albanian aristocracy, and more recently the British (still the power behind the throne even after 1922), and their replacement with Egyptian Arabs; the overthrow of the fledgling constitutional democracy with the return to the age-old practice of rule by a praetorian few; and an attempt (the key word here is attempt) at change in ideological direction from the capitalist West to the communist East, bringing in its wake a moderation of elitism with a significant dose of populism in national development policies. The period we have in mind here then is 1952 to the present, or to be accurate from 1954 to the present (1954 being the year when, in April, one of the officers, Jamal Abdel Nasser, engineered a coup within the military coup with the deposition of General Muhammed Naguib from the presidency). For higher education in Egypt these past fifty or so years have been a very important period for several reasons:

In keeping with Nasser's new ideology of "Arab Socialism," coupled with yet another stab at industrialization from above, there was a greater push toward a larger state involvement in higher education in terms of sector planning than had ever occurred before as the country moved toward a centralized management of the economy—a process that also featured an unusual emphasis on the cooptation of professionals (engineers, scientists, doctors, etc.) into the administrative bureaucracy (see discussion later).[44] From tuition-free education to mandates of what a student could study (in keeping with projections of human capital needs) to educational expansion, to guaranteed state employment of all university graduates, higher education in Egypt would never be the same again. In nearly all these respects, it is instructive to note, Nasser was not doing something that had not been tried before, though of course the rhetoric was different. In other words, much of what Nasser tried to do was reminiscent of Muhammed Ali's efforts.

The state also moved to exert political control over internal administrative and day to day operations of institutions by means of various legal decrees (e.g., law no. 504 of 1954, law no. 49 of 1972, etc.) where university autonomy was virtually obliterated. Reid (1990: 169) provides us with a portentous example of what Nasserism would mean in practice, as he graphically puts it with reference to Cairo University: "Few dropouts ever get the chance later in life to overhaul their alma maters. [Jamal] Abdel Nasser and his minister of education, Kamal al-Din Husayn, did. Both attended Cairo's Faculty of Law for a few restless months before being admitted to the military academy and—as it turned out—a new road to power. By 1954 they were in a position to reform the university, which they believed had failed them and Egypt." The university (and the higher education sector as a whole) was given a taste of the flavor of Nasser's understanding of the concept of university autonomy on September 21, 1954, when he forced the dismissal from the university of a motley group (in terms of political sympathies) of some sixty to seventy faculty—ranging from full professors to graduate teaching assistants—without any explanation (p. 170). Obviously, military men, especially those of lower ranks, are hardly expected to understand, let alone respect, a concept such as "academic freedom." Even the curriculum was not out of bounds: Nasser insisted that all universities include in their curricula a national curriculum with mandatory courses in Arab socialism and allied subjects (see Reid for more on this).

Yet, at the same time, in terms of educational provision, the post–1952 period would witness nothing less than an explosion of unparalleled growth for the higher education sector with the establishment of many new universities (together with numerous branch faculties and other higher education institutions) on one hand, and on the other a simultaneous increase in enrollments at existing institutions, as well as the number of students dispatched for study abroad.[45] Here is a list of universities (minus branch faculties) that were created, beginning with those in the state sector: University of Assiut (1954); University of Tanta (1972); University of El-Mansoura (1972); University of El-Zagazig (1974); University of Helwan (1975); University of El-Minia (1976); University of El-Menoufia (1976); University of Suez Canal (1976); University of South Valley (1994). The private sector saw the founding of these universities: University of Sixth of October (1996); University of Misr for Science and Arts (1996); University of October for Science and Technology (1996); University of Misr International (1996). Such a large-scale expansion of the higher education sector (and the ensuing difficulties that have arisen) requires an explanation. A *combination* of four explanatory factors immediately come to mind: populism, the former Soviet Union, parents, and human capital theory.

Whatever the faults of the praetorian oligarchic "dynasty" (and there are many, not least among them high-level corruption, authoritarianism, and the massive violations of the human rights of the citizenry) that Nasser helped to create and which now rules Egypt, it has been one of a decidedly populist bent; that is, possessing in relative terms (the key word here is *relative*) a genuine desire to do more for the Egyptian masses than the previous dynasties had ever done in probably the entire history of the country.[46] In their quest to narrow the elite/mass economic gap, therefore, they saw mass access to education as a principal avenue of upward mobility for the children of the fellahin and the working classes. Hence, even as they clamped down on the universities, purging them of any potential political malcontents, they simultaneously abolished university tuition fees in state institutions (on July 26, 1962).[47] Twelve years on, looking back on their accomplishments, they explained their rationale for expanding access in one of their government reports thusly: "Higher education before the revolution...placed impediments in the way of the poorer classes, narrowed the circle of higher education, and subjected the enrollment of students to class considerations in which the position of the family concerned, favoritism and financial standing played a prominent part. The picture has been totally reversed in the revolutionary age where higher education has taken a successful leap forward with the collapse of the class rule, the establishment of social justice, and of equal opportunity.... The big development, started with the reduction of tuition fees, culminated in the introduction of free education in all stages up to higher education" (Reid 1990: 174). [48]

As the United States first, and later, Britain, moved to isolate Egypt as being too radical (provoking Nasser in turn to nationalize the Suez Canal that led to an international crisis, 1956–57, from which Nasser emerged, in relative terms, victorious), and especially following Egypt's defeat a decade on by the U.S.-backed state of Israel in the 1967 Arab-Israeli Six-Day War, Nasser turned to the only other country outside the West that he deemed capable of assisting Egypt—following in the footsteps of Muhammed Ali to seek help from whoever was competent to deliver it—with that age-old goal that Ali had espoused: modernization of the armed forces, and industrial autonomy. That country, of course, was the former Soviet Union.[49] Against the backdrop of the Cold War, it was only too glad to oblige. Now, one of the influences that emanated from that quarter (in addition to a reinforcement, for obvious reasons, of the populism of the Nasserite autocracy) was an emphasis on the expansion of higher education to generate scientific and technological human capital. (The emphasis on science and technology in higher education was now pursued with the same level of vigor as in the days of Ali.)

By the 1950s, it had become clear to all parents in Egypt that those with a secular state education stood the best chance of securing a well paying job; ergo they and their children began to demand greater access to such education, most especially at the lower levels initially (in view of the less than adequate development of this sector). Later, however, as the economic value of secondary education began to wane as a result of the law of supply and demand, they turned their sights on to higher education. In this sense the policies pursued during the era of Nasser (1952–70) of greatly expanding the provision of primary and secondary education were coming home to roost. Seeking a secondary education alone, by the 1970s, simply did not suffice with the result that pressure mounted for higher education expansion as a whole, and for the establishment of universities in the provinces and not just in places like Cairo and Alexandria—as well as increases in enrollments at existing universities (the elite University of Cairo, for instance, would soon be transformed into a mass university).

Adding to the foregoing mix of factors, was the support derived from the theory of human capital that international development agencies had come to champion where education was viewed as an *investment* item and not as a *consumption* item in national budgets. This theory posited that what PQD countries were missing in their effort to boost economic growth was trained person power (or human capital). In time the theory would degenerate into a simplistic and crass policy prescription for massive increases in educational expenditures irrespective of wider socioeconomic contexts, sweeping country after country into its ambit (see Chapter 7 for more on this theory and its limitations).

On September 20, 1970, Jamal Abdel Nasser died of a heart attack; by the time of his premature death (he was only 54) he had achieved a larger than life stature on the African continent and in the Middle East; and those who succeeded him remain, in the eyes of the Egyptian masses, mere shadows of him in terms of charisma and vision.[50] Be that as it may, his successor, Muhammed Anwar el-Sadat (one of the original members of the Free Officers) did not wait long to jettison Nasser's Arab Socialism; consequently, Egypt experienced yet another ideological sea change with the announcement by Sadat a year after the culmination of the 1973 Arab-Israeli October war of his pro-Western so-called "Open Door" policy (known as *infitah*). Egypt would reorient away from the former Soviet Union to eventually become, practically, after the Camp David Accords (September 17, 1978), and, ironically, like Israel, a client state of the United States (or an "informal ward" as Moore (1994: 212) puts it; both countries are on the U.S. dole)—the move would cost him his life as Egyptian extremists would gun him down at a military parade on October 6, 1981.[51] His vice-president, also a military man, Muhammed Hosni Said Mubarak, would inherit the presidency.

Now, from the perspective of the core elements of higher education policy, this changing of the guards, did not and has not marked a major change; rather the policies adopted during Nasser's time have for the most part continued, most especially in terms of access (as just indicated). Higher education policy is, as they say, the "third rail" of Egyptian politics, no one dares touch it, except with the greatest circumspection. This is not to say, however, that the sector has not experienced any policy changes at all. In two areas, for example, one observes some important changes: the economic structural adjustment policies pursued at the behest of the United States and the West has also had some moderating influence, in favor of the universities, on the issue of the state versus university autonomy; and the debate that had occurred on the heels of the *infitah* on the desirability of allowing (beyond the American University in Cairo) the establishment of private—therefore feepaying—universities as one way of dealing with overcrowding in the public institutions (as well as lessening the cost of training the children of the elite—by obviating their need to go abroad in the early part of their university careers) went in favor of the proponents; hence the creation of four new private universities in 1996 as already indicated.

Following the inauguration of the *infitah* there were two other significant (but nonpolicy related) changes that the higher education sector would experience that are worthy of noting: first, the increasing cooperation between the United States and Egypt with the flow of U.S. dollars in the wake of the accords began to have some impact on the academic culture (textbooks, U.S.-inspired research agendas, scholarly exchanges, student culture, etc.) of Egyptian universities.[52] At the same time, while this change was underway, Egyptian universities began to face a new kind of student political activism (which, as in the case of most universities throughout Africa, had always been part of their landscape, except for a short time when it had abated under Nasser's authoritarian rule). This new form of activism would be part of the rise of Islamism in Egypt that had been engendered, initially, during Sadat's era when he had turned to the Islamists to serve as a bulwark against the Egyptian Left—as one would expect, the university campuses were drawn into this struggle.[53] However, in later years, especially in the period following his peace treaty with Israel (arranged a year after the accords, on March 26), the chickens would come home to roost. At the same time, the fact that the massive expansion of the higher education sector had taken place without regard to Egypt's ability to finance this expansion has not helped matters. Student activism, secular or religious, is probably guaranteed under circumstances such as these: "If a student desires to attend classes, sometimes as large as 5,000 in a lecture, he must fight for space. If he does not want to attend classes, he can buy the professor's lecture notes, the text, and only appear for the end-of-year exams, which are constructed and graded by groups of professors and therefore must come from the text. Obviously there is not enough space for all the students to attend classes. When exams are given, tents are constructed in open campus areas in order to accommodate students" Cochran (1986: 71–72). She further observes: "Because their salaries are low, some professors teach at two or three different universities, commuting on unreliable trains, poor roads or through congested traffic. They may not arrive for their classes, making the printing and selling of lecture notes an economic and educational necessity." If this was the circumstance at the time she was writing nearly two decades ago, today it has gotten infinitely worse (except, of course, for the children of the wealthy).

We have now arrived in the present. From the hesitant, strictly utilitarian, beginnings during Muhammed Ali's rule to the present, secular higher education in Egypt has experienced tremendous growth, greatly expanding access to huge segments of the population that had been hitherto left out. It is no longer the preserve of the elites, new or old. This is a phenomenal achievement that even Egypt's detractors would have to concede. Yet, on the other hand, as the Egyptians themselves would admit, masking this immense positive achievements are serious imbalances, though by no means all unique to Egypt as will be shown later. From geographic inequality of access to elitist access through private education, from massive overcrowding in classrooms to stultifying end-of-year exams dominated pedagogy (as just noted), from rising budgetary constraints to inadequate logistical supplies for research and learning, the higher education sector in Egypt is facing what must appear at this juncture as insurmountable challenges. Even the rising influence of U.S. presence in Egypt has not been an unmitigated blessing—ranging from the further complication of the university system as U.S. influence has been added to the traditional British/French mix that had guided the system in the past, to confusion in research priorities, to aggravation of the brain drain.

Then there is the matter of graduate unemployment and underemployment as the economy staggers under the burden of a relentless ever-expanding supply of job-seekers chasing fewer and fewer jobs. Even the escape route afforded some university graduates to seek employment in other countries in the region is now beginning to erode with the maturity of the higher education sector in these countries, bringing on tap their own human capital resources. Regarding this issue is an intriguing matter that has been raised by Moore (1994) and in which there are lessons for other countries in Africa (and indeed elsewhere in the developing world). It concerns the consequences for economic development in a country, as in the case of Egypt, with not only a glut of highly educated professionals *but where many of whom (as noted earlier) have become part of the administrative bureaucracy of the state.* Using the example of engineers in Egypt he shows that even though engineers are among the desirable group of professionals to have in any society that has industrialization as one of its major goals, in the absence of mechanisms that can allow engineers to flourish *as engineers* their talent is essentially wasted. As he observes: "Though trained to play the most strategic roles of industrial society, they contributed little to the development syndrome [*a la* "modernization theory"]— social differentiation, equality, administrative capacity—even though these corresponded respectively to the Nasserist formulas of corporatism, socialism, and statism. The engineers were joined in a professional corporation but could not develop a more rational division of labor, differentiating themselves in keeping with their society's technical needs, keeping up with the latest technological developments, and adapting such developments to the local industrial infrastructure." At the same time, he further observes: "Formally, in terms of numbers, degrees, and status, the profession was flourishing, but in reality engineering education and research were deteriorating, and the engineers were emigrating" (p. 205). What is more, in a context where even at the highest levels of the state bureaucracy engineers and other professionals pervade one would assume that at the very least, if nothing else, rationalism and professionalism would be the order of the day at the administrative levels of society. Yet, here again this has not been the experience of Egypt, so far. So, what gives?

The answer, explains Moore, is to be found in a combination of two principal factors: "diminishing economic resources and an impoverished political system"(p. 206). In other words, the failure to date of the professional classes (such as those represented by the engineers) to make a meaningful contribution to the development of Egypt, even when they have become a visible part of the higher echelons of the state bureaucracy—suggesting, ostensibly, access to decision-making power—is rooted in the prevalence of authoritarianism (termed by Moore as Sultanism) and political-economic corruption on one hand, and on the other, the general poverty of the state and society as a whole in terms of access to adequate supplies of capital coupled with *sophisticated* technological know-how (itself a function of Egypt's place within the international economic system). Authoritarianism has led to politicization of even matters that are fundamentally of a technical nature; corruption has meant wastage, misuse, and inefficient allocation of scarce resources (including, through nepotism, human capital itself), not to mention the diversion of talent toward rent-seeking enterprises; and lack of access to sufficient amounts of capital of course implies projects simply cannot be planned or executed (regardless of whether they are undertaken on the initiative of the state or on the basis of private entrepreneurship). The fact that Egyptian engineers, as Moore astutely points out, do just as well as or even better than other engineers in the right circumstances—such as when they emigrate to the West—lends credence to this explanation.

Yet, even after the *infitah*, things have not improved much for the professional classes *in terms of their potential to contribute to the development of Egypt*; for in reality the *infitah* has not meant desirable and real structural changes at the political-level (the enactment of superficial multiparty national elections are a case in point), nor has it opened up access to the amounts of capital Egypt really needs. In fact on the contrary, regarding the latter, the massive invasion of foreign-owned transnational monopolies has merely served to exacerbate this situation with their tendency to concentrate in the distribution/service realm of the economy (exemplified by the building and operation of luxury oriented facilities for the elites, such as chain stores, hotels, international banks, fast-food chains, etc., that only serve to emphasize the wretchedness of the poverty of the masses), rather than the production realm. Yet, even when they have gone into the production realm it has not been at the substantive manufacturing and industrial levels, but ephemeral (production of processed foods, for example, or manufacture of consumer goods based on assembly of almost wholly imported components). Moreover, their increasing presence has been a source of a net drainage of investable capital. One important exception in the production realm is of course the petroleum sector where foreign capital is clearly present, but here again their presence takes on a perverse form: their monopoly of technology, which has rendered the Egyptian engineers, to use Moore's words, "marginal appendages of an international technology, mere translators of foreign technical instructors" (p. 209). (Compare this situation with that of China where foreign capital has become intimately involved with manufacturing and industrial production at all levels, albeit even there distortions are not entirely absent.) Under these circumstances, the true role of engineering and other professions in Egypt, remains in the main, simply one of serving as an avenue for the *legitimation* of a compradorial elite status. Clearly then, production of human capital in itself, does not ipso facto translate into a potential for development. Egypt demonstrates to us that there are severe limits to development against a backdrop of politically "defanged" professional classes (no matter how well trained and professional they may be) amidst a general poverty of resources. While this fact should perhaps be obvious to any one with even a modicum of intelligence, it appears that it has escaped the proponents of human capital theory (see discussion in Chapter 7).

al-Azhar

We can not leave Egypt before taking another look at al-Azhar (see Chapter 1). Although, today, in the Egypt of the twenty-first-century, the institution may appear to some to be irrelevant and anachronistic; an institution from a bygone era, given its primary role in the past as a religious institution and which it continues to perform, albeit on a more muted scale, to this day. The fact is that even as secular forces, especially in the shape of the Westernized Egyptian elite, persist in their effort to push Egypt toward what many among this elite would probably prefer, the execution of an Egyptian version of the 1924 Turkish solution, al-Azhar's place in the Egyptian higher education system and in Egyptian society as a whole continues to remain one of singular importance.[54] More importantly: whatever its detractors among the Westernized elite may think of the institution, the fact is that al-Azhar has managed to change sufficiently over the years to secure its continued relevance to the Egypt of today.

The institution, however, would have to concede that this change had to be foisted on to it by outsiders as they dragged the institution's ulama kicking and screaming into the modern age.[55] In other words: in the modern era, the beginning of which in Egypt we may trace to the demise of the Ottoman Mamluk rule, the impetus for the reforms that the institution has had to succumb to (eventually) have rarely come from autonomous (internal) initiatives. Instead, they have come from Egypt's successively diverse ruling regimes: the French, the Khedives, the British, and finally the praetorian Nationalists—each, however, motivated primarily by the same ultimate agenda, whatever the ideological patina of the day: how to use al-Azhar as an ally (given the institution's historical centrality and sociopolitical legitimating role within Egyptian society, patiently secured through its monopoly of Islamic higher learning over the centuries), in the perpetual struggle to dominate and exploit the seemingly long-suffering Egyptian peasantry, the *fellahin*, as a means to the larger objective of harnessing the fecundity of the Nile valley for self-aggrandizement; or failing that, how best to neutralize and marginalize the institution. (It may be noted here that such has been the importance of al-Azhar in the life of Egypt that none of these regimes ever thought it wise to simply abolish and replace it with an institution closer to their hearts.[56]) The irony in all this, from the perspective of the institution's original mission as one of the premier places of Islamic higher learning in North Africa and the Middle East, is that it forced the ulama toward some acceptance of that basic (Islamic) principle it had long forgotten: that not only must knowledge and learning go beyond the immediate confines of the religious sciences, that is the secular also has a place in the institution's curricula, but that its quest must not brook self-defeating administrative and curricular morass.[57]

When the French arrived in Egypt they found al-Azhar in the state described in Chapter 1. While Napoleon did initially attempt to elicit the support of the ulama for his designs on the country, the atrocious French behavior (which, in the eyes of the Egyptian Muslims, went well beyond the usual military effort to quell resistance into the domain of cultural arrogance, sacrilegious conduct, and wanton brutality—the last exemplified, for instance, by the murder of hundreds of Cairene women, after labeling them as prostitutes, and discarding their decapitated bodies in sacks into the Nile river [Herold 1963: 161]) put to rest any possibility of amicable Franco-Egyptian relations. Instead, such behavior brought out the full force of the ire of the ulama; al-Azhar became actively involved in fomenting Egyptian resistance to the infidels. The French did not hesitate to respond with even harsher measures; they executed some of the ulama and temporarily occupied al-Azhar. (Later, the ulama themselves would close the institution for about a year, from June 1, 1800 to June 2, 1801, as they waited for the political situation to stabilize.)[58]

Yet, if the ulama had thought that in their support of an Albanian cavalry officer, in the ensuing power struggles in the Cairo Citadel following the French departure from Egypt, they would find a friend and a worthy patron, they were sadly mistaken. Muhammed Ali may have been a Muslim, but the fortunes of Islam were not his primary focus of attention; he had far more narrower and earthly ambitions, as already noted. Ali was not against al-Azhar per se, but his policy of looting the wakfs put a large negative dent in the financial circumstances of the institution. Such was the power of this autocrat that while this action constituted, from the perspective of Islam, among sacrileges of the highest order, the ulama were unable to put up any effective resistance to this move. Further, while it was he who would start the process of making inroads into the governance of the institution by assigning the responsibility of select-ing the rector *(Shaykh al-Azhar)* to the state, rather than leaving it exclusively in the hands of the ulama as had been the practice hitherto, he refrained from imposing any major institutional change on al-Azhar or on the madrasah sys-tem as a whole. The fact is that for Ali the institution, by being allowed to con-tinue to play its age-old role of providing human capital for administrative and educational purposes, had its uses for his projects. In time, however, the mod-ernizing changes that Ali had set in motion would no longer permit the isola-tion of al-Azhar from the impact of these changes long after the old lion had passed on.

Before proceeding to describe the highlights of the educational reforms that were imposed on al-Azhar, slowly but surely, from 1805 onward (but most es-pecially after 1849) by the various governing regimes that came to occupy the seat of power in Cairo, it would be helpful to summarize the context out of which these reforms grew by describing the interests of the various competing parties and constituencies that eyed the fate of the institution, as all manner of socioeconomic and political change swirled around it, over the course of some one and a half centuries. *(This summary will necessarily imply, it must be cau-tioned, considerable oversimplification of the complex landscapes of the edu-cation-society nexus that developed in Egypt over a period of some 150 years.)*

The ulama (1801 to the present): Their interest was to resist any reforms that upset the status quo; after all they were hardly in a position to champion the basic spiritual source of these reforms: the trend toward secularism and Westernization (read Christianization) that would not only greatly reduce their own societal influence, but which they felt would undermine Islam itself in Egypt. Moreover, they perceived the reforms as constituting nothing less than advancing the cause of imperialist infidels, which had to be resisted at all cost. (For them salvation from Western imperialism lay in resisting Westernization itself at all levels, a position that was completely the reverse of the one adopted by the Egyptian Westernizing elite.) Later, when they realized that the reforms were inevitable, their interest was then to see that not only were their own posi-tions within the institution preserved, but the role of the institution within the education sector and in society at large was not completely marginalized. This entailed in their view demands for control over those competing institutions that they felt were making encroachments into their curricular territory (such as the *Dar-ul-Ulum* and the School of Law, *Madrasat al-Qaada*), and control over feeder institutions (primary and secondary schools) that provided it with its students.[59]

The students and their parents. (1801 to the present): Initially, their inter-ests coincided with those of the ulama. Recall that the primary purpose of al-Azhar at its founding was not the production of graduates for secular oriented employment or even religious employment. The fact that the institution attracted large numbers of students even in the face of certain unemployment upon graduation was a testimony to the fact that attendance at the institution was considered a religious duty. Witness, then, for instance, the student strikes at the instigation of the ulama in 1908 and 1909 that led to the temporary closure of the university. However, later, all this was to change as the modernization efforts of Egypt moved apace because now two distinct categories of people began to emerge: those, who through their employment with the state and other entities on the basis of secular qualifications obtained from state schools in the newly emerging political and economic sectors enjoyed a materially prosperous life (enhanced by goods of the machine age); and those doomed to a life of poverty. In other words, the introduction of formal credentialing for purposes of state employment in Egypt (a process begun by Ali), in time, had a devastating effect on the fortunes of later generations of al-Azhar graduates (and graduates from other similar institutions). Therefore, student interests began to diverge from those of the ulama, but only to the extent that reforms would secure for them acceptance of al-Azhar qualifications by the state for purposes of employment. That the students did not demand a complete overhaul of the institution in the direction of a secular institution was due to two factors: First, the students and their parents still valued a religious component to their education; and second, admission to al-Azhar was easier (relative to state schools) for children of the rural poor (given that their academic preparation for higher-level studies was generally less than adequate, not to mention financial considerations). One should note here that in the modern era, speaking to the second factor, class origins became ever more significant in Egypt's educational system, where increasingly the madrasah system became the preserve of the poor, while the state schools (to be joined later by private schools) became the educational homes of the children of the new and old elites. In other words, as in the case of all societies progressing toward the secular and the modern, education became the avenue of both class *formation* and class *reproduction*.

The Khedives (1805–1922): As traditional rulers they greatly valued the sociopolitical legitimating role of al-Azhar, but they were also conscious of the need to reform the institution even if, initially, only for the limited purpose of getting it to function more efficiently in terms of its own self-described mission as an Islamic institution of higher learning.[60] The first reforms they imposed on al-Azhar attempted to address matters such as the curricula, teaching expertise, entrance qualification of the students, and so on. Later, they began to demand even more changes as they became conscious of the fact that al-Azhar, with its medievally rooted anarchic laissez faire administrative traditions (see Chapter 1), was an administrative embarrassment as an institution of higher learning. By the beginning of the twentieth-century, as the political value of al-Azhar increased for the Khedival dynasty (in the face of erosion of their powers in other areas of society at the behest of British colonialism) they had come to realize that the modernizing transformations underway in the broader society were accelerating at such a pace that the earlier hesitant steps taken to introduce reforms in al-Azhar had to be undertaken with greater firmness, with or without the cooperation of the ulama, if al-Azhar was to survive.

The British (1882–1922): While they regarded al-Azhar as an anachronistic institution, they recognized its legitimating value, the benefit of which they felt would accrue to them by not interfering with it. (Later, however, as they became involved in a three way power struggle [between the Khedive, the secular-oriented government elite, and themselves] over the control of waqf property, they did have an indirect impact on the circumstances of al-Azhar.)

The constitutional monarchs (1922–52): The interests of the Monarchs was to accumulate as much power and influence as the constitutional arrangement permitted; this implied siding with the ulama when it suited the Monarchs as they enmeshed themselves in power struggles with the government.

The constitutional government and the prerevolution secularizing Egyptian elite (1922–52): Their interests were the opposite of the monarchs in that they would have preferred to completely secularize al-Azhar and convert it into a Western-style university. As members of a newly emerging Western secular elite, some of them even went so far as to openly advocate the elimination of Islam from all public life (as in post–1924 Turkey). For them, while the West embodied everything that was worthy of emulation (they felt the Islamic civilization had no longer anything to offer Egypt), complete Westernization was the only key to freedom from Western imperialism.

The praetorian oligarchic dynasty (1952 to present): While the dynasty was also firmly wedded to the secular Westernization project, like all other rulers before them, it recognized the legitimating role of al-Azhar. However, without wishing to abolish it, they still insisted on reforms—drastic reforms. They had no time for any form of resistance from the ulama (or any one else for that matter) to their agenda of creating a new Egypt—an Egypt that was Western, but independent from the West, and secular, but mindful of the cost of taking the Ataturk route—both, internally (in terms of political stability) and externally (in terms of the new leadership role they envisaged for their country within the Islamic world of North Africa and the Middle East). From a foreign policy perspective, they also quickly became conscious of the potential al-Azhar presented through its ability to attract foreign students from all over the Islamic world (see Eccel's [1984] consideration of this issue at some length). At the same time, they rightly saw education as the vehicle for creating the necessary human capital needed to execute the modernization of Egypt. Therefore, to them al-Azhar had its uses; however, it needed secularizing reforms; and they would be carried out—through the barrel of a gun if necessary.

It is against the background of the tug of these often contradictory forces that al-Azhar was brought to the present form that it now assumes—namely, still a religious institution but much (though not all) of it operating in a secular

Western mode like other Egyptian universities. The journey of reform would take more than a 150 years, propelled ultimately by a combination of the 'stick' of political pressure and the 'carrot' of the struggle to compete for "funds, students and jobs" (Reid 1990: 140). The highlights of this journey include the following:

The first major reform came by means of a Khedival decree issued on February 3, 1872 (supplemented by laws in 1885, 1888, and 1895), which introduced an examination system for the ulama to determine their competence to teach at the university, and placed a limit on the total number of subjects offered. In 1885, attention would now turn to the students: an order was issued to begin formal registration of students and the rationalization of the circumstances of their accommodations.

The next major reform was the creation within the institution of the al-Azhar Administrative Council, in 1894, a permanent policy body (but with the state having veto powers over it) headed by al-Azhar's rector to look into every aspect of al-Azhar's operation and propose changes. Government control over the institution was further initiated by introducing government-paid salaries for the ulama the following year. (This was an important innovation because it made reforms that much easier; it could be used both as a carrot and a stick.) In the same year too, the formal appendance of other madrasahs to al-Azhar would begin with the *Ahmadi* madrasah. Other accretions in later years would include, in 1925, the *Dar-al-Ulum* (the teacher training college), set up in 1872 to train Arabic-language teachers, initially, because of the correct perception that al-Azhar had deteriorated to such an extent that it could not carry out even this very basic function well; and the School of Law *(Madrasat al-Qaada al-Shari'ah)*, originally established in 1907 to bypass al-Azhar resistance to curricular reform in legal studies.[61]

Two years later, in 1896, with the decree of the first al-Azhar Organization Law on July 1, the process of reform would acquire a greater degree of resolve on the part of the state—even as opposition to the reforms grew among the ulama and the students. In the following year, such matters as delineation of a program of study, class attendance, student behavior, teacher performance, the school calendar, and so on, would become the object of regulations. In the same year an order would be issued for the institution of a student admissions committee and the establishment of examinations (oral) for the two principal qualifications one could obtain from the institution: the *ahliya* diploma (requiring a minimum of eight years of study) and the *alimiya* degree (based on a minimum of twelve years of study).

A year later, in 1897, the first seeds were sown of a proper library with the purchase of bookcases; it would begin to grow until by 1936 the library holdings had been centralized and a number of full time employees were in charge of their maintenance. The creation of a central library at al-Azhar was not only important in terms of immediate learning needs, but in terms of the preservation of rare books and manuscripts as well.

In 1911 another al-Azhar Organization Law would be promulgated, followed in the same year by the al-Azhar Internal Organization Law. The aim of these laws was to bring further rationality to the administration of al-Azhar (matters ranging from procedures for hiring, firing and promotion of faculty to allocation of teaching loads to student admission requirements to establishment of new madrasahs (in the form of institutes [ma'hads]). During that year written exams for students were also introduced to the institution.

The year 1930 would witness the expansion of al-Azhar by means of the Reorganization Law (issued on November 15) with the addition of three new colleges: the College of Islamic Jurisprudence, the College of Theology, and the College of Arabic. In that year al-Azhar also came to be regarded officially as a university, for by this point many of the principal features (including such mundane matters as the use of desks and chairs) characteristic of a secular university were now integral to the institution. The following year the Internal Law of Personnel would tackle matters such as faculty disciplinary measures and procedures. The 1930 law would be supplemented by another law passed in 1933 and these two laws would then be folded into the March 26, 1936, law, the regulations of which in essence established the university's constitution. At the same time the law specified a comprehensive program of study for the entire al-Azhar system.

On June 22, 1961, the rubber-stamping national assembly enacted the al-Azhar reforms legislation that Nasser had been demanding. Its purpose? To "nationalize" the university by forcing on to it far-reaching secular oriented reforms that no ruler before had dared undertake. This effort entailed building a new campus at some distance from al-Azhar to house the new secular colleges by which the oligarchs hoped to make al-Azhar more relevant to Egypt's human capital needs. These colleges would include ones for communications, engineering, languages and translation, medicine, and science. For the first time, a girls college would be appended to the institution: the al-Azhar Girls College, which would offer programs of study to women in a variety of disciplines. New faculty were brought into these colleges without regard to their religious credentials and by separating the offices of the university rector and Egypt's supreme religious leader, the Grand Shaykh (or *Mufti*—he is elected by a body of prominent ulama, of whom many teach at the university), the oligarchs introduced a new equation into the governance of the institution: the rector need no longer be one of the ulamas.

The long struggle waged by outsiders to modernize al-Azhar was now complete.[62] While the reforms forced on to it by the oligarchs must have been the most excruciatingly painful of all the reforms ever imposed on it, they did not completely destroy al-Azhar. Consequently, Al-Azhar remains today among those few universities in Africa and elsewhere that can boast its own unified cradle-to-grave education system (that is, from first grade to a doctorate—comprising schools at the primary, preparatory, general secondary, and technical secondary-levels followed by its own institutes and colleges, all outside a parallel secular education system), yet its original role as an Islamic center of higher learning for domestic *and* foreign Muslim students has been preserved. (In an ideal world, for the majority of Egyptians one would surmise, there would be a single unified educational system for Egypt preserving the best of both systems—however, the die was cast almost 200 years ago by Muhammed Ali, it is unlikely to change any time soon, if ever.) At the same time, al-Azhar continues to be the home of the ulama and the Mufti.[63]

As for its other historic role, however, as an avenue for upward mobility for the children of the lower classes, it has been bypassed by the secular state education system; the proportion of Egyptian primary school children who enter the al-Azhar education system is now less than 2% of the national total (Reid 1990), the clearest indication that to gain entry into the upper classes, al-Azhar is not the most efficacious way to go. At the same time, this statistic also speaks to the fact that al-Azhar is not critically important to Egypt, relative to other universities, *when viewed strictly in terms of secular human capital needs.* Rather, the relevance of al-Azhar for Egyptians stems from that broader societal role it has always played: the source of legitimation for the ruling classes; except the source of this legitimation is now primarily circuitous (the ulama have lost their legitimating role): in supporting the continued existence of al-Azhar, the ruling elite assures the Egyptian majority that it acknowledges the view of the majority that Egypt is both an Arab and an Islamic country—even though the elite itself may have completely different ideas. This legitimating role it should be added, has become of even greater importance of late as a result of a resurgence of Islam among the masses in Egypt and elsewhere in Islamic Africa.

ALGERIA

Less than a mere forty years after Napoleon's ill fated foray into Egypt, the French takeover of Algeria (which was marked by more than the usual level of brutality and slaughter) began with the capture of Algiers in 1830 and, later, annexation of the country in July 1834; bringing to an end almost three centuries of Ottoman Mamluk rule.[64] Despite, this time, strong initial armed resistance in some parts of the country, the French triumphed—at least momentarily (they would still be forced to leave, eventually, as will be indicated shortly, but that day of reckoning would be postponed for another 130 years or so). In the mean time, almost from the beginning, the French encouraged European colons (settlers) from France and elsewhere in Europe to settle in Algeria in large numbers so that by 1930 there were almost a million of them crawling all over Algeria. As has been the case in almost all colonial territories established by

European settlers throughout the world in modern history, and despite the treaties and agreements rammed down their throats, the indigenous Algerians were subjected to all kinds of racist humiliations and socioeconomic and political injuries—thereby rendering whatever legal protections they had attendant upon the incorporation of the country into a Greater France a complete sham.[65] In a replay of a number of similar scenarios of European settler colonization, from the United States to Brazil to South Africa to Australia, millions of acres of land was looted from the Algerians and turned over to the colons; and to add insult to injury a onerous tax system was imposed on them to help finance their own subjugation and depredation at the hands of not just any colonizers, but ones who, as Christians, had been enemies of Islam for over 1,000 years. Living under the umbrella of a monumental lie (a particular forte of human beings) the colons, feigning ignorance of the "natural law of prior claim," convinced themselves that not only Algeria belonged to them by right, but that it is the indigenous who were the foreigners in this bit of overseas France. Under the circumstances, it is perhaps not surprising that both the colons and the Algerians would, in time, take to the gun with considerable fervor as the looters and the owners fought to settle the question of rightful domicile. In other words, independence would come to Algeria through massive violence and bloodshed as a guerrilla war (characterized by remorseless savagery on both sides) was unleashed by the Algerians under the oftquoted, though fallacious, slogan "Islam is my religion, Arabic is my language, Algeria is my country," in the same year, in 1954, that France was dealt a humiliating defeat by barefoot and illiterate peasants in another part of its colonial empire (at Dien Bien Phu in Vietnam).[66] The Algerian uprising under the FLN *(Front de Liberation Nationale)* would end with French capitulation in 1962 and the simultaneous exodus of thousands of French settlers, together with some of their Algerian collaborators—but not before they had inflicted on the country widescale vandalism prompted by spiteful rage (millions of dollars worth of state property would be looted and destroyed by these representatives of the "Greeks of the world," the self-appointed harbingers of an enlightened civilization). The project of *mission civilisatrice* ('civilizing mission') had collapsed under its own weight of unmitigated hypocrisy and lies.[67]

Against this backdrop, in surveying the development of higher education in Algeria following the arrival of the French, it is possible to extract six main motifs: First, was the French colonial effort at dominating the existing madrasah system by means of such measures as the wholesale looting of their waqfs (which invariably led to the demise of many of them and as if this was not enough, even a number of major mosques were taken over and converted into churches—the resultant deep humiliation of the religious sensibilities of the Muslim Algerians at a time when religion was an important force in their lives can only be surmised; it is certainly beyond description); the sponsorship of alternative French-controlled madrasahs out of a few existing and some new ones in which the teaching of French, among other humiliations, became mandatory; the prohibition of the founding of any others that were not under French supervision.[68]

Second, was the creation of secular institutions targeted primarily at the settlers (though children of a small Algerian Muslim minority, the compradorial elite, were admitted to these institutions too). The earliest of these began as separate institutes (first medicine and pharmacy in 1859, and then ten years later law, arts and letters, and science), which eventually coalesced to form in 1909 the University of Algiers with a student population of 1,605 (though only a tiny fraction of whom were Algerians [Tibawi 1972: 166]). By 1950–51 the student population at the university had reached 5,000, but of them only 213 were Algerians.[69] In 1961 the university spawned two university centers with faculties of law, letters, medicine, and science at Oran and Constantine (though here again the Algerian presence in the student population was miniscule).[70]

Third, by the time of the eve of the Second World War, under the twin pressures of supply far outstripping demand for education among Algerians, and at the same time an inability on the part of the French to fully control a surgent nationalist effort to create madrasahs outside the French-dominated system, the Association of Muslim Algerian Ulama, founded in 1931 by Abd al-Hamid Ibn Badis, began developing what came to be known as the Free Madrasah system; the most prominent of which was the Al-Madrasah al Badisiyya (Ben Badis Institute) in Constantine (begun in 1936), which by 1950 had some 720 students.[71] (Graduates of these madrasahs, as in the precolonial era, who wanted to pursue further studies went on to either al-Azhar or al-Zaitouna in Tunis or al-Qarawiyyin in Morocco.)

Fourth, following independence, by which time the articulation (not abolition) of the precolonial mode of production with the new colonially mediated capitalist mode of production was now complete, the need to generate human capital resources under these changed circumstances led to a progressive marginalization of the madrasahs by default as the expansion of secular higher education under the aegis of the praetorian nationalist controlled state rapidly moved apace. The fruit of this development would be the creation of a host of new secular institutions: University of Constantine (founded in 1961 at Constantine as a university center attached to University of Algiers, but reconstituted as an independent university in 1969); University of Annaba (founded in 1971 at Annaba as Institute of Mining and Metallurgy but reconstituted as a university in 1975); Houari Boumediene University of Science and Technology (founded in 1974 in Algiers); University of Oran (founded in 1961 at Oran as a university center attached to the University of Algiers, but reconstituted as an independent university in 1966); University of Science and Technology of Oran (founded in 1975); and Ferhat Abbas University (founded as a university center in Setif in 1978, but later transformed into its present form in 1985). Other higher education institutions created after independence included university centers at Mostaganem, Sidi-bel-Abbes, Tiaret, Tizi-Ouzou, and Tlemcen. One interesting development was the opening in 1984, in response to the increasing strength of the Islamist tendencies within the country, of a university devoted exclusively to the Islamic sciences: Emir Abdel Kader University for Islamic Sciences. The dizzying scale of expansion of the higher education sector in the postindependence period is best described by Bennoune (1988): "The number of students registered in the national universities increased from 3,718 in 1962–63 to 55,148 in 1978–79. In fifteen years (1962–77)," he observes, "the number of university students multiplied by a factor of 14.6. The annual average growth of students of higher education was 10% during the three-year plan (1967–9), 25.7% during the first four-year plan (1970–3), and 14.7% during the second four-year plan (1974–7)." He continues: "[t]he total number of students...increased from 61,610 in 1979–80 to 166,600 in 1986–7" (pp. 229, 289).

Fifth, while in terms of organization and pedagogy, most of the new Algerian universities, like their precursor, the University of Algiers, were patterned on the French universities (though at the curricular-level an important difference, as would be expected, was the teaching of certain arts and social science subjects, including law, in Arabic—one of the priorities established by the new government was the Arabization of the education system and to this end it would open in 1967 several Arabic training colleges)—following 1971, a number of educational reforms were instituted, which, like those in other parts of Afro-Arab Islamic Africa, included moving higher education toward a much greater emphasis on science and technology than ever before; widening access to women, and students from rural and lower class backgrounds (democratization); indigenization of university faculty together with some parts of the curriculum; and an increasing effort at the bureaucratic management of human capital formation (in contrast to leaving it to the dictates of the labor market) through such measures as curricular reforms, targeted production of graduates, assignment of state-funded scholarships, and so on.

However, as has been the case in most of Africa, the promises held out by the higher education sector have, in general, failed to *fully* materialize. As Bennoune, to quote him once more, puts it: "If the mission assigned to the universities is to raise society's consciousness and understanding of itself, of its culture and experience as well as of other people's cultures and experiences and also to teach the students how to master modern science and technology in order to increase the production of goods and services, they have failed, for political reasons, to fulfill it" (p. 291). His suggestion, however, that it was politics that accounted for this outcome does not tell the full story: economics also had a major part to play in the sense of the externally mediated obstacles to development imposed by the Western-dominated global economic system.

Sixth, is the impact on higher education of the development of an Islamist tendency in Algerian national politics in the 1980s and its subsequent, probably unforeseen, consequence as a transformed military wing of the praetorian oligarchy moved to crush it: a brutal military campaign notorious for its headline grabbing atrocities waged over a period *of more than a decade* against the civilian population in the name of defeating the Islamists.[72] The outcome of this horrendous Algerian nightmare for higher education has been nothing less than catastrophic: One, it politicized the academy to an unprecedented level as it was forced by circumstances to take sides (for neither the praetorians nor their Islamist adversaries would brook any protestations of neutrality); two, confrontations between the praetorian state and the students became endemic; three, members of all segments of the academy (students, teachers, administrators, etc.) *in their hundreds* were harassed, intimidated, raped, jailed without cause *or simply murdered* irrespective of their beliefs and opinions; four, the universities have been infiltrated with agents of the security apparatus (whose stock in trade includes blackmailing female students for sex and to get them to inform on their peers) thereby creating a permanent culture of fear and intimidation even as the more visible forms of repression have in recent years lessened; and five, thousands of talented Algerian faculty left the country for employment abroad to escape the violent chaos in the country. The net effect of all this, on top of the severe financial straits that the education sector as a whole has been experiencing since the mid–1980s, has been to drastically (to put it mildly) erode its quality and vibrancy.

One may also note here that, at the same time, the net effect of the direct imposition of the military will on the polity (of which the long blood-soaked nightmare has been symptomatic), for the effort toward cultural authenticity that the call for Arabization had represented, has suffered a major setback. In fact, the new faction, being staunch secular, anti-Islamic Francophiles, have little time for any of the traditional *integrative* cultural mechanisms: Islamization, Arabization, and even anticolonial nationalism (given the faction's treacherous pro-French role during the war of liberation). One implication for higher education of this circumstance is that the those supporting the increased use of French (or English) are now receiving greater support from the state.

LIBYA

Before the arrival of the Arabs in 643 with their capture of Tripoli from the Byzantines, Libya essentially constituted three different entities: Cyrenaica in the east, Tripolitania in the west, and Fezzan in the southwest; and like the rest of North Africa it had seen in its long variegated history many invaders, going all the way back to the Phoenicians who were the founders of Tripoli. The roots of its present shape lie in the arrival of both Ottoman rule in 1551 when Sinan Pasha retook Tripoli from the Knights Hospitallers of St. John of Malta, and some centuries later, European colonial rule, which, by the time of Libya's colonization by the Italians, had managed to surround it with no less than six countries: Egypt and Sudan in the east, Chad and Niger in the south, and Algeria and Tunisia in the west.[73] Ottoman rule would last until 1912, with one major hiccup: in 1711, we see the emergence of the characteristic independent Ottoman Mamluk dynasty nominally beholden to the Ottomans in Istanbul: the dynasty established by Ahmed Qaramanlis. The Qaramanlis dynasty would survive until 1835 when the Ottoman Turks reestablished direct rule from Istanbul in order to save Libya from the same fate, European (French) colonization, that had befallen its other adjacent province on Libya's Western frontier: Algeria. As it turned out, it was a futile mission. Libya managed to retain its independence from European colonialism under the Ottoman's only for a short time, and even that mainly because of a political stalemate among the European powers on the matter of its colonization, which was only broken on September 29, 1911—not by the bigger imperial powers, but by the Italians (who, impelled, like the other powers, by the same heady imperialist cocktail of economics and grandeur, coupled with calculated opportunism, declared an unprovoked war on the Turks and mounted an invasion on October 3). While the invasion proved to be no easy walk to victory, precipitating as it did a spirited guerilla resistance from the Libyans and the Ottomans, about a year later, on October 18, Italian fortunes improved considerably with the decision of the Ottoman's to withdraw from Libya.[74] However, it was a pyrrhic victory; for, Italian colonial rule would not survive for long; thanks to the Second World War—and which in any case, as a consequence of Libyan resistance, had never managed to go beyond the major coastal towns until the emergence of fascism under Benito Mussolini in Italy inaugurated a renewed and an exceptionally brutal Libyan campaign (in which thousands of Libyans were massacred) that saw the final defeat in 1930 of the lone Sanussi holdout, Said Omar al-Mukhtar.[75]

Colonial rule, from the perspective of education in general and higher education specifically, was characterized by an unremitting saga of *relative* neglect for a number of reasons. As in Algeria, the violence that accompanied the process of colonization led to considerable destruction of indigenous institutions including many madrasahs (*zawiyahs*) and there was little effort to rebuild them. The Italians (again like the French in Algeria), aimed to convert Libya into virtually an Italian province through a program of massive settler colonization (by 1940 there were 110,000 settlers), which entailed a dual-track segregationist education policy where some educational provision would be made for the settlers but not for the Libyan masses. Then there was the Second World War, which not only led to massive destruction of almost everything, material and institutional, that the Italians had introduced as the country passed from Italian hands into British and then into German and finally back into British and French hands, but the British and French military administrations that took over control of Libya were concerned less with socioeconomic and political development of any kind than simply maintaining an imperial presence in the country (with the least amount of financial expenditure necessary) while a decision was made on Libya's political fate. The sum total of the outcome of these circumstances is captured best by Elbadri (1984: 24): "In 1952, ninety percent of the population was illiterate and there were about fourteen university graduates in the whole country."

On December 24, 1951, as a result of a United Nations decree, Libya became the first colonial country to gain independence on the African continent.[76] This development, it is thought, was largely because of a promise made by the British to the Sanussiya, in exchange for the cooperation of the Sanussiya during the ferocious 1940–42 military campaigns in Libya, that they would not allow the Italians to return. The truth, however, probably lies elsewhere: most likely it has to do with the emerging postwar geopolitics of the region. Bearman (1986) suggests that there was a collusive attempt by the British and the Italians to get the United Nations to declare Libya a U.N. trust territory under Italian mandate, but the United States would have none of it (as a U.N. trust territory, its emerging arch Cold War enemy, the Soviet Union, would have meddled in U.S. plans to continue to retain its World War II military base, Wheelus Field Airbase, on the outskirts of Tripoli). Another factor that may have helped to persuade the British and the Italians to capitulate to U.S. demands was, probably, the fact that petroleum, which would eventually transform Libya from one of the poorest countries on the continent (and possibly the world) to the richest—in terms of per capita GNP—would not be discovered until 1959.[77] Independence brought a constitutional monarchy with the head of the Sanussiya, Amir Muhammed Idris, being proclaimed king over a tripartite federal state.[78] His close alliance with the West, specifically the British, coupled with grievances provoked by his misrule, however, would in time cost him his crown; for, he was overthrown in a bloodless coup on September 1, 1969, by a group of radical young nationalist-minded, pan-Arabist military officers led by a 27-year-old lieutenant: the son of a nomadic Bedouin peasant who would evolve to become on the international scene a quixotic and mercurial gadfly, and on the home front a populist, but an equally temperamental, leader—in other words, a mini but erratic version of Nasser—by the name of Muammar al-Qhaddafi.[79]

On the domestic front, Qhaddafi (under his particular variant of praetorian state capitalism—enunciated as *Libyan socialism* or *Third Universal Theory* in two successive editions of his manifesto, the so-called *Green Book*) would embark on a massive populist program of social expenditures that would include the funding of an explosive expansion of educational provision for Libyans at all educational levels under the slogan "knowledge is a right of all citizens." [80] Perhaps more than most PQD countries, Libya's populist praetorian autocracy saw in its education policies a panacea for not only the country's economic backwardness, but also a means for the modeling of a new Libyan citizen loyally in tune with the autocracy's evolving ideology of an international anti-West radicalism on one hand and for the Libyan variant of pan-Arabism on the other. Under a regime of virtually unlimited financial resources following the long overdue OPEC oil price hikes of 1973 that would more than quadruple the price per barrel of oil within a year, coupled with the nationalization of all foreign-owned petroleum corporations, the country's oldest secular university, University of Libya (founded in 1955 in Benghazi beginning with the College of Arts, Letters and Sciences), over the next several decades would cease to be the only university in the country. In 1974 the university would split into two separate institutions with the creation of University of Garyunis, also in Benghazi. Then would come other institutions, including, Sebha University (established in 1983 at Sebha); Al-Arab Medical University (founded in 1984 in Benghazi); the Bright Star University of Technology (set up in 1981 at Adjabia); and the long distance university, appropriately named The Open University (created in 1987 in Tripoli). There are a number of other lesser higher education institutions as well, but all sporting university appellations; they include Al-Fatheh University of Medical Sciences in Tripoli, Al-tabal-Gharbi University in Zintan, Al-Tahadi University in Sirt, Derna University in Derna, Nasser University in Al-Khoms, Omar-Al-Mukhtar University in Al-Bayda, and the Seventh of April University in Zawia. (It may be noted that the predominant language of instruction at most higher education institutions in Libya, besides Arabic, is English, rather than Italian or French.)[81]

It is instructive to note that despite the enormous wealth Libya has enjoyed (relative to most other countries in Africa) over the past three decades, and the enormous effort put into expanding all levels of the education sector, the country remains essentially a one-horse town in strictly economic terms—dependent primarily on petroleum. Even in agricultural terms it has failed to develop the sector to keep pace with population expansion; the result is that whereas once it was relatively self-sufficient in food production, today it imports three-quarters of its food needs. Clearly, large amounts of investable surplus, together with a concerted effort at human capital production, still does not ipso facto translate into meaningful development. While economic mismanagement does have some explanatory role here, compared to many other African countries, it is of negligible significance. The real issue is the same that has bedeviled almost all PQD countries, especially those in Africa: the nature of their relations with the international economic system that is deeply biased toward maintaining their role as primary commodity producers.

MOROCCO

From the perspective of history, Morocco, as part of the Maghreb, saw its fair share of outsiders contribute to its annals: Phoenicians, Carthaginians, Romans, Vandals, Byzantines, Arab Muslims, Portuguese, Spanish, and the French. The most enduring legacy, of course, has been that of the Muslims (they arrived in 682) because the original inhabitants, the Berbers, in time converted to Islam; followed by that of the French who established colonial rule of a much different order—one characteristic of the modern post–1492 period. Skipping about 1,000 years of history of Muslim rule under a variety of Arab and Berber dynasties (such as the Idrisids, Almoravids, Almohads, Merinids) to come closer to the modern era, we witness the arrival of the Portuguese in Morocco beginning with the capture of Ceuta in 1415; however, they were not able to hold on to the country long enough to reach modern times because 1492 and the benefits of the post–1492 developments that ensued were yet to materialize (see Appendix II). For, a century and a half or so later, the Moroccans were able to throw out the Portuguese by dealing them a severe defeat in 1578. However, in the transformed circumstances of the Afro-Eurasian ecumene two and a half centuries on, by which time no North African state could effectively hold a candle to the economic and military might of any European power, it would be a different matter. Morocco's effort to get rid of the Spanish from Moroccan soil in 1859/1860 proved to be a disaster.[82] In fact, it would be one of several factors (which would include economic disarray within the country) that would lead, a few decades later, in 1912, to the imposition of a French protectorate with the blessing of other European powers—in itself telling—notably Britain. When the French arrived the Sharifian Alawite dynasty was in power; and it continues to be so to this day (their luck in this regard no doubt secured by the ability of the Moroccans to resist Ottoman rule in the sixteenth-century—Morocco has the distinction of being the only North African country that did not succumb to the Ottomans to become part of their empire, even nominally).[83] Between 1912 and 1956 when independence came to Morocco and the sultanate would be transformed into a monarchy, France ruled most of the country; but it allowed Spain to continue its presence in parts of the north, and south of the country. The end of French rule also led to the withdrawal of the Spanish in 1960 from most of the zones they had occupied (Ifni would be vacated in 1969), except for a few northern coastal enclaves they continue to hold to this day.[84]

Given the differing economic strengths of the French and the Spanish, together with their unequal zones of control, during the colonial period the predominant influence in the education sector in Morocco was that of the French. Their policy in its essence was similar to the one they adopted with respect to Tunisia: not to disrupt the traditional madrasah system, but on the contrary work toward its preservation.[85] As in Tunisia, the long-term objective of this strategy had a threefold dimension to it: first, continue to provide a modicum of education to the masses (a strategy that at the same time obviated the incurrence of major financial costs—which would have surely attended the introduction of an alternative—secular/Western—education system); second, be perceived to be not in opposition to Islam by supporting its existing institutions; and three obtain the acquiescence of the ulama to French hegemony by not threatening the ulama's institutional base. At the same time, the French also made some provision for the education of a compradorial elite. In the case of Morocco, interestingly, this also entailed the support of the al-Qarawiyyin mosque-college along an opposite line of approach to the one they adopted with respect to al-Zaitouna, as will be indicated in a moment.

When the French imposed their protectorate on Morocco the circumstance of al-Qarawiyyin was, as mentioned in Chapter 1, not as it had been in its heyday, centuries before. However, that is not to say that the institution had become completely irrelevant to the needs of Moroccan society; for, one of the functions it had acquired over the preceding several centuries was to serve as a higher educational outlet for the sons of notables who would join the sultan's administration (referred to as the *mekhzen,* short for *rijaal al-mekhzen*). What this implied was that the student body was fragmented along four *coterminous* avenues: ethnicity (Arab versus Berber), geographic origin (rural versus urban), status (notable versus commoner), and income (rich versus poor) with almost no movement across these social fissures. The students in effect were segregated both residentially (the poor rural Berber commoners, referred to as the Sousi, were housed in the madrasahs while their opposite counterparts, the Fassi, lived with their families in the city), and at the places of instruction *within* the institution. What the French chose to do was to exploit this dual role of al-Qarawiyyin: as an Islamic higher education institution for all, and as an educational institution for the sons of the nobility. While they did encourage some reforms in terms of mainly *structural* rationalization (as opposed to *content* rationalization)—covering matters such as calendars, appointment of teachers, salaries, schedules, general administration, the replacement of the *ijaza* with the *shahada alamiyah* certificate, and so on—through various decrees, for example, in 1914, 1918, 1927, 1931, 1933, and 1947, their main approach was to insist that the institution not deviate from its traditional educational curricula *as defined by them* (see Porter 2002). In practice what this meant was to unnaturally freeze education at al-Qarawiyyin from further evolution lest it evolve in a direction that would produce graduates who would challenge the legitimacy of not only the French colonial presence, but also the compliant sultanate itself for cooperating with the infidel.[86] In addition, the French instituted ranks among the ulama and kept control of hiring and promotion; hence further ensuring the development of a body of compliant ulama. In other words, the French sought to mold the existing ulama and future ulama graduates into a worldview that was stuck in the fifteenth century (use of texts written after the fifteenth century were, for instance, discouraged, and unlike the colonial practice in Algeria's madrasahs, French was not permitted at the institution) thereby hopefully prevent any possibility of a radical type of Islam from emerging—such as the one that arose in Algeria—that could challenge French hegemony (Porter 2002). The spirit of this policy was captured best by the first French governor (1912–25), Marshall Hubert Lyautey, arguably among the enlightened French colonial governors, that is as far as French colonial governors go, when he stated: "We must never forget that the native does not like to 'change the face of things,' if I may be permitted the expression; but that provided that the 'face' to which he has become accustomed remains the same, he is indifferent to which regime keeps it that way" (from Rabinow 1989: 164–65).[87] The Moroccans themselves, however, did not support this approach (except perhaps some of the ulama); they wanted an overhaul of the curriculum to not only include newer (secular) subjects like math and geography, but they also wanted to upgrade the religious subjects. The French, however, would have none of it. (Instead, to provide secular education to another group of select few, they created for them secular institutions, as will be noted in a moment.) To deflect complaints from some Moroccans that the French were relegating them to stagnation the French argued that their policies were driven by the desire to "respect" Islam and Moroccan customs and tradition.

Although in 1947 it became part of the state-sponsored educational system, undergoing further reforms, in both structure and content, it is only with independence, in 1956, that the government moved to completely reorganize al-Qarawiyyin (by means of a royal decree of February 6, 1963), which included shutting down the program at the mosque in 1957 by moving it to new premises, an old French Army barracks. Further, the new organizational structure that would emerge of what was now officially called the University of Qarawiyyin (beginning in 1965) included the establishment of geographically dispersed faculties and institutes—such as a faculty of Islamic law in Fez; a faculty of Arabic Studies in Marrakech (which incorporated the Yusufiyya Madrasah founded in the precolonial era), a faculty of theology at Tatwan (which absorbed the Institute of Higher Religious Studies established after 1944 by the Spanish), and an institute specializing in the traditions of the Prophet in Rabat. Clearly, the Moroccans felt that the ossified education of al-Qarawiyyin bequeathed to them by the French was not what they felt was relevant for a new Morocco. In the newly organized and newly located University of Qarawiyyin, Morocco could train students in the Islamic sciences that could meet the challenges of a postindependent Morocco based on new texts, new curricula, professionally trained teachers, and so on. By turning their back on the Mosque and its madrasahs, it appeared the Moroccans had closed a Chapter in Moroccan higher education, which even though centuries in the making was in the end found wanting, thanks to the French. Yet, some thirty years later, the Moroccans decided to reopen classes at the Mosque. In 1988 King Hassan II would preside over the reinauguration of Islamic education in the al-Qarawiyyin Mosque. The question is, Why?

In part, this move, after an almost thirty-year absence of organized learning at the Mosque, was motivated by the continuing effort to recreate an authentic tradition in the life and activities of Fez's madina (where al-Qarawiyyin is located), which had been declared a World Heritage Site by UNESCO in 1981 as a result of a Moroccan petition (tourist dollars no doubt having something to do with it); and in part it was a desire by the Monarchy (the sultanate became a monarchy in 1957) to counter the subversive potential of the newer curricular tendencies of the existing modern faculties of the University of al-Qarawiyyin. Feeling increasingly insecure in a world where few monarchies with executive powers continue to rule, the decision to resuscitate teaching and learning at the Mosque was a direct attempt to recreate a compliant body of ulama that would acquire legitimacy by going through a traditional Islamic system complete with its medieval trappings of both curriculum and physical space (e.g., modern conveniences are not permitted in the madrasahs or at the mosque), ostensibly motivated by pure motives: to seek knowledge for its own sake. Such a traditionally educated cadre of ulama, it was felt, would be a more reliable source of legitimacy for the current dynasty. By making the memorization of the entire Qur'an as among the major qualifications for admission to the Mosque program, true Islamic knowledge would issue forth from this institution untainted by modern perspectives available in the existing faculties and at other Islamic institutions in the country. The irony of ironies in this whole exercise is that the traditional (also referred to as original) Islamic education that was to be imparted was a replica of the one that the French had devised on the basis of their colonially determined definition of traditional, and which was the same education that had been rejected by urban and rural students alike and abandoned in 1957, as not suited to the needs of a modern Morocco. Not surprisingly, those involved with modern Islamic studies look askance at this revival of traditional education, deeming it as primitive and irrelevant; plus the fact that those who attend the Mosque-based program of the university are in the main poor rural students (the sons of the rich) does not help matters. The student numbers are also telling: in the year 2000, of the 8,000 students at al-Qarawiyyin University's four Islamic faculties, only 200 were attending the traditional education program at the Mosque. In truth, the rich, with rare exception, had never found the concept of the pursuit of knowledge for the sake of knowledge very appealing anywhere at any time in the Islamic empire. (For more on the foregoing see Porter 2002.)

Moving beyond al-Qarawiyyin, as noted, the French were not completely averse to secular/Westernist education for some of the Moroccan elite (after all they needed a cadre that could mediate administratively between themselves and the rest of the Moroccan population); they therefore established the College Moulay Idriss in Fez, the College Moulay Yousef in Rabat, and the Institute of Higher Moroccan Studies (Institut des Hautes Etudes Musulman, opened in 1920) to educate a compradorial elite. Education at the these institutions, which were similar to the Sadiki College in Tunisia, combined Islamic and French subjects and languages (the language of instruction, as was now the practice throughout Islamic Africa, depending upon the subject matter: Arabic for the Islamic subjects and French for the secular subjects). The creation of these institutions, however, would bring about a slow but steady demise of al-

Qarawiyyin as more and more of the Moroccan elite, together with others, began to send their children to the secular Westernist institutions where they received bilingual education. By 1922, the student population at Qarawiyyin had dwindled to just about 300 total (Porter 2002: 411), and as just mentioned, following independence classes at the Mosque would be abandoned.

By means of a royal decree in 1957, the University of Rabat was established (to be later renamed Muhammed V University in 1975) with faculties of letters, Islamic law, law, medicine, and science. In 1962 the university had established branches at Fez and Casablanca; the total enrollment of the university was about 4,000 students of whom 600 were women (Tibawi 1972: 175) In keeping with other secular higher education institutions in former French African colonies, it used French as the principal medium of instruction and was patterned on French universities. Soon more universities would be established: the Averroes School of Applied Medicine, founded in Casablanca in 1959; these three created in 1975: Hassan II University (at Casablanca); Sidi Mohammed Ben Abdellah University (at Fez); and Cadi Ayyad University (at Marrakech); and following a major decentralization of the higher education system in 1989, these: Ibn Zohr University (at Agadir); Chouaib Doukkali University (at El Jadida); Ibn Tofail University (at Kenitra); and Abdelmalek Es-Saadi University (at Tetouan). Other postindependence institutions include: Mohammed I University (founded in 1978 at Oujda); Moulay Ismail University (founded in 1981 at Meknes); Hassan II University (founded in 1992 at Mohammedia); Mohammed V Souissi University (founded in 1992 at Rabat).

SUDAN

To those with some familiarity with Africa, any mention of Sudan immediately conjures up in one's mind three simultaneous mental constructs of this country, each jostling for prominence, relating to size and topography, ancient African history, and ethnically-driven civil wars marked by much savagery and brutality against civilian populations. One may as well, then, consider an overview of the country along these axes.

Sudan is the largest country on the planet's second largest continent. Stretching some 1,400 miles from Egypt in the north, to Uganda at its southernmost reaches, it covers an area of nearly a million square miles (exact area is 2,505,800 sq km) encompassing, as one would expect, a huge diversity of flora, fauna and people, and bordering on no less than seven countries, besides the two just mentioned. To the east there is Eritrea, and Ethiopia; in the south, Kenya and the Democratic Republic of the Congo; and to the west are the countries of Libya, Chad and the Central African Republic. Topographically, it is marked by two salient features: it shares the Red Sea coast with Egypt and others in the northeast, and it is home to the Nile River as it journeys its way north to Egypt—but not only that, the country is also host to the Nile's dual headwaters, the Blue Nile (which originates in the Ethiopian highlands) and the White Nile that meanders across the southern part of the country from the Ugandan border (to eventually join the Blue Nile in the vicinity of the country's capital, Khartoum). To round out this highly abbreviated geography, mention can be made of its climatic terrain; it is characterized by three major natural divisions: desert in the north, rain forest in the south, and a north to south blend of savannah and swampland (known as the *As Sudd*) in between.

Given this geography, it is not difficult to surmise that the country's history stretches back thousands of years into antiquity. There is evidence of human habitation going back 60,000 years into the Paleolithic period, and by the time one comes into the Neolithic period (around eighth to third millennia B.C.E.) a sedentary agricultural way of life among a people characterized by a genetic fusion of Mediterranean peoples and African peoples—facilitated by the Nile River—was now well established. In other words, an important portion of ancient Sudanese history is inseparable from that of Egypt's (and thence the Mediterranean's). Egyptian sources going as far back as to the Old Kingdom (c. 2650–2130 B.C.E.) refer to the central Nile region, the southern portion of Nubia—in antiquity a region encompassing northern Sudan from Khartoum to Egypt and from the Libyan desert to the Red Sea—as the land of the Cush (or the "wretched") with whom the Egyptians had vibrant commercial and other transactions. Hundreds of years later, during the era of the New Kingdom (c. 1575–1105 B.C.E.), they would administratively incorporate Cush as one of its provinces. As the fortunes of pharaonic Egypt waxed and waned, a time would come when the Cushites would become rulers of Egypt—with the last Cushite pharaoh being Taharqa (690–664 B.C.E.—the fourth king of the 25th Egyptian dynasty, which is also sometimes known as the "Ethiopian" dynasty because the Greeks referred to Cush as Ethiopia).

As ancient Egypt fell into disorder, coming under the control of various foreigners—first the Achaeminid Persians (525–332 B.C.E.), followed by the Macedonian Greeks (332–30 B.C.E.), and culminating with the Romans (30 B.C.E.–642 C.E.)—the Cushites, under the leadership of Taharqa, who it is thought came to settle among them sometime after 650 B.C.E., asserted their independence, establishing their headquarters further southward at Meroe, to eventually give rise to the Meroetic kingdom (comprising an area stretching from the sixth cataract to present-day Khartoum). This Egypto-Cushite kingdom would last for almost a 1,000 years and come to enjoy much prosperity, accompanied by impressive cultural efflorescence. The demise of the Meroetic kingdom would be the handiwork of the emergent Axumite kingdom of Ethiopia, whose army would attack and destroy Meroe city (c. 350 C.E.).

The successor to the Meroetic kingdom would be various smaller states, of which not much is known, but which by the sixth century would come to comprise Christian Nubia practicing Monophysite Christianity, which arrived through the agency of Egyptian Coptic missionaries. The sunset of the Christian Nubian kingdoms (who would mark their apogee in the period encompassing the nineth to tenth centuries) would come about at the hands of yet another source from without, through the rise of Islam in Saudi Arabia. Although Nubian-Arab relations were of long standing as part of Nubia's commercial contacts stretching through Egypt into the Red Sea and Mediterranean basins and beyond, the arrival of Muslim Arabs in Egypt in the seventh century would set in motion a completely different historical trajectory for Nubia and the rest of Sudan (as would be the case for the rest of North Africa as well).[88]

Over yet another period of more than 1,000 years, primarily (though not entirely) through the peaceful agency of immigration, trade and commerce, almost all of Nubia (that is, northern Sudan) would undergo Islamic Arabization at all levels: linguistic, cultural and genetic. Now, the key developments in this historical process of relevance to the emergence of present-day Sudan are these three: at the level of ethnicity, the genetic merger between Arabs and locals; at the cultural level the supplanting of local languages with Arabic on one hand, and the demise of Christianity and its replacement with Islam as the religion of choice on the other; and at the political level the emergence of various Muslim sultanates and fiefdoms (such as that of the Kashifs, the Funj, the Fur, and the Sannar). The relevant time period is parenthesized by these chronological markers: the arrival of Amr ibn al-'As in Egypt in 639 C.E. and the imposition of colonial rule through military force by Egypt's Muhammed Ali, primarily in the interest of slave-raiding, on Sudan in 1821—which would inaugurate the period of Sudanese history referred to as the Turkiyah (lasting until 1885).

Sudan has the dubious honor of being embroiled in what is perhaps the longest running civil war on the African continent. It began about a year before Sudan became independent of British colonial rule in 1956 when a group of southern Sudanese (the Anya Nya) launched a guerilla war with the objective of secession. Over the period of the next *fifty* years, almost *up to the present* (except for a short interregnum from 1972 to 1983) the ensuing civil war would be characterized in the south by: huge civilian population displacements; the use of food as a weapon of war by the government in times of famine and the resultant civilian deaths running into the thousands; massive human rights violations on both sides, including horrendous atrocities ranging from rape, torture, and murder to destruction of homes and livelihoods; the revival of the practice of enslavement of the southern Sudanese by some among the northerners with almost no opposition from the government; the wanton air-bombardment of civilians by government planes; the almost total absence of economic development, in relative terms, in the southern regions; and of course the failure by either side to achieve their objectives (which speaks to the remarkable perseverance of the southerners, led by the Sudanese People's Liberation Army—formed in 1983 under the command of the U.S.-educated John Garang—in the face of overwhelming military odds). What is more, as if this particular conflagration has not been enough, yet another one has emerged in the western province of Darfur that, in terms of violence and suffering, is an almost exact replay of the conflict in the south and perhaps even worse (in the period of just two years, while the United Nations wrangles over the definition of the conflict as "genocide," as suggested by the United States, hundreds of thousands have died and nearly two million have been displaced).

As of this writing (2005), the situation is that after nearly three years of ne-gotiations, hosted by the Kenyan government, there is a real promise of peace in the south with the signing of a peace agreement between the Sudanese Peo-ple's Liberation Army and the government on January 9, 2005, in Nairobi, which among its other provisions includes the sharing of Sudan's oil wealth (currently at more than 300,000 barrels a day) on a fifty-fifty basis with the south, and even more importantly, one that will give the southern Sudanese an opportunity to have a referendum on autonomy after six years. The conflict in Darfur, sadly, continues (and there is talk of rebellions breaking out in some other parts of the country as well).[89]

A burning question that emerges from the foregoing is, of course, Why? Was it necessary for nearly two million people to die in order for those in Khartoum to arrive at a peace deal with the south, and how many more will have to die before peace arrives in Darfur and the rest of the country? The popular media in the West has generally portrayed the conflicts in Sudan as ra-cial and religious; and there is some truth to this, but the picture is much more complex as Lesch (1999) demonstrates:

The 27 million Sudanese...vary significantly by language and religion. More than 50 ethnic groups can be identified, which subdivide into at least 570 distinct peoples. Forty percent of the population comprises Arabized peoples living in the north, and 26 percent are African peoples who also live in the north; the remaining 34 percent are African peoples in the south, who speak more than a hundred indigenous languages. About 70 percent of the population is Muslim; 25 percent adheres to indigenous religions, and 5 percent is Christian, consisting of Africans in the south, who converted to Christianity during the twentieth; and a small Coptic and Syrian Arab communities in the north. Linguistic and religious differences overlap; nearly all the Arabized peoples and most of the African peoples indigenous to the north are Muslim (p. 218).

Clearly, then, to suggest, for instance, that the conflict in Darfur is religious would be nonsense because the people of Darfur are Muslim as are those at-tacking them: the government-organized militias called the Janjaweed, com-prising essentially Arabized pastoralists—who more often than not are indis-tinguishable phenotypically from the people they are attacking. In other words, Sudan is an example par excellence of a society in which race is patently a so-cial construction. For political reasons, the Sudanese ruling elites over the cen-turies have found it in their interest to emphasize their "Arab" roots, *both real and imagined*, in their effort to monopolize the resources of the country. The irony is that the "real" Arabs in Saudi Arabia and elsewhere, do not consider the Sudanese (whatever their claims on Arab heritage) as Arab at all. In fact, the name "Sudan," from their perspective, captures their view admirably; it is the shortened form of the Arabic designation *bilad al-sudan*, the "lands of the blacks." As has already been noted, Islam does not recognize racial or any other divisions in the *ummah*, yet the tragedy is that this has not prevented the Arabized Sudanese Muslims (Arabo-Sudanese) from carrying out their nationally divisive and exploitative projects, thereby fomenting the conditions that have led to horrendous civil wars. Note that what is also being suggested here is that even if the Arabized northerners had succeeded in converting the south to Islam, a project that was consciously pursued by various Sudanese regimes, it would not have guaranteed the absence of a civil war. Hence, for instance, the conflict in Darfur between Muslims and Muslims suggests that perhaps a better handle on that conflict comes from viewing it as one between pastoralists (the Arabized element) and a sedentary people for water and grazing rights against a backdrop of an ever-expanding Sahel. Moreover, Sudan, also presents us with a compelling case of the failure of "political Islam." The move toward the imposition of the Shari'ah on the country, begun under the dictatorship of General Gaafer Nimeiry (came to power by means of a military coup in 1969) for political reasons rather than those of piety, and continued by various regimes that have followed him, did not create even a remote possibility for the emergence of a democracy that would respect the human and civil rights of all Sudanese; given, as indicated elsewhere in this chapter, the absence, historically, of an interest among the ulama in the Islamic empire to work toward the development of a constitutionally relevant body of law within the Shari'ah *with the potential to meet the challenges of a post-Columbian world* when it arose— expressed, for instance, in the continuing mind-boggling incongruence between, on one hand, an obsession among them with such minutia of daily life as how to take a bath, and on the other, the almost total lack of a concern with such matters as how to elect a democratic government, or manage economic development, and so on. Even the extensive body of Islamic law on the conduct of war, or respect for the rights of the *dhimmi*, has been conveniently dispensed with by Sudanese regimes, even as they have hypocritically professed adherence to the Shari'ah.

In sum, then, at the root of the conflicts in Sudan, as in much of the rest of post-colonial Africa (Algeria, Congo, Ethiopia, Liberia, Nigeria, Sierra Leone, etc.), has not been race or religion per se, *but ethnicity manipulated for political ends*. Note that in such a context there is a dialectic that emerges between the political uses of ethnicity and the preservation of ethnic boundaries, and it is a dialectic that is always, by definition, inimical to any project for democracy. (Compare here, for instance, the political/economic functions of racism in the United States today.[90]) In the case of Sudan, specifically, the ability to effect such uses of ethnicity has historically involved higher education itself against the backdrop of well-intentioned policies of a British colonial order.

That is, historically, the narrowly conceived ethnicity-circumscribed nationalism of the Arabo-Sudanese elites which never envisioned, even in their wildest dreams, full political participation of *all* Sudanese, drew succor from higher education, against a background of British colonial policies aimed at protecting the south from northern encroachment in the interest of opposing slavery and Islam—which in a sense were intertwined since the business of slave trading, following the arrival of Islam in Nubia, would eventually pass into the hands of the Muslims. (It should be emphasized that the commerce of slavery long predated the arrival of Islam in North Africa, or elsewhere for that matter.)

British colonial rule arrived in Sudan, it is possible to assert, at the instigation of the French at the time when Egypt was under British overlordship.[91] The arrival of the French explorer Jean-Baptiste Marchand by an overland route from the west coast on July 10, 1898, at Fashoda on the White Nile (about 400 miles south of Khartoum), so that the French could boast to the world they had "pissed into the Nile upstream from Khartoum" (Andrew and Kanya-Forstner 1974: 70) and thereby lay colonial claims on a vast transcontinental region stretching from the west to the east coast of Africa, momentous as it was from his perspective—constituting the realization of a dream that he had first outlined some three years earlier and doggedly pursued—proved in the end to be nothing more than a French expeditionary farce. For the British had their own colonial ambitions of a north-south transcontinental possession and with the threat of war between the two colonial powers over Fashoda, the French backed down—on September 19, General Horatio Herbert Kitchener (Lord Kitchener) had hurriedly arrived in Fashoda upon learning of the French presence there to press for British claims, but in the name of Egypt, after having routed the Mahdist Army at Omdurman a week earlier on September 2. (In other words, Marchand's small expeditionary force would have been no match for Kitchener's large well-equipped army.)

By means, on one hand, of an addendum to the Anglo-French Convention on West Africa signed June 14, 1898, and on the other, the ratification of a treaty between Britain and Egypt on January 19, 1899, Sudan in all but name became a British colony, known as the Anglo-Egyptian condominium. Nominally, of course, the Kitchener Anglo-Egyptian expeditionary force had been sent to restore Sudan to Egyptian suzerainty after the Egyptian Turkiyyah administration had lost control over Sudan following a successful Arabo-Sudanese rebellion in 1885—led by Muhammad Ahmad ibn Abd Allah (who had proclaimed himself as the *Mahdi*, a long awaited messianic redeemer who would bring about a just and corrupt-free Islamic state)—and which saw the death of the British general Charles George Gordon when the Mahdist forces razed Khartoum, an event for which the British never forgave the Mahdists.

Now, two salient points of relevance emerge here: first, is that the British, upon taking charge of Sudan following the collapse of the Mahdist state, came to adopt a dual pronged colonial policy of, on one hand, appeasing the former

Mahdists by encouraging their rehabilitation by absorbing them into the colonial administration, and on the other making sure in every way possible that Arabo-Sudanese influence and activities would be restricted to their northern home-base; the south, for all intents and purposes, was declared out of bounds—not even Arabic was permitted to be taught there. Consequently, by the time independence came to Sudan, it was in almost all respects (geographically, culturally, linguistically, economically, etc.) a deeply bifurcated nation along a north-south axis. In other words, British colonial rule, far from uniting the country, merely reinforced the preexisting north-south divisions. Second, perhaps in an effort to appease his conscience—word had eventually leaked out that behind the grim statistics of nearly 27,000 killed or wounded among the Mahdists (against less than 500 dead among Kitchener's men), thanks to superior weapons, lay a picture of massive atrocities against the Sudanese— Kitchener embarked on a fund-raising campaign in England to raise capital for the construction of a college for the Sudanese, in memory of Gordon. Shortly after his return to England, in a letter addressed to the British press dated November, 30, 1898, Kitchener appealed:

I call your attention to an issue of very grave importance arising immediately out of the recent campaign in the Sudan. The region now lies in the pathway of our Empire, and a numerous population has become practically dependent on our race. A responsible task is laid upon us, and those who have conquered are called upon to civilize....I accordingly propose that at Khartoum there should be founded and maintained with British money a college bearing the name of Gordon Memorial College....Certain questions will naturally arise as to whom exactly we should educate....We should begin by teaching the sons of the leading men, the heads of villages, the heads of districts. They belong to a race very capable of learning, and ready to learn....The fund required for the establishment of such a college is one hundred thousand pounds....It is for the provision of this sum....that I now desire to appeal, on behalf of a race dependent upon our mercy, in the name of Gordon, and in the cause of that civilization which is the life of the Empire of Britain (from his letter reproduced as an appendix in Beshir 1969).

The response of the British public was overwhelming (for both Gordon and Kitchener were viewed as heroes) and within two months the sum needed was not only raised but surpassed, with contributions coming from as far away places as Australia, New Zealand, India and even the United States. Thus was born Gordon Memorial College, but as Sharkey (2003) has demonstrated in her extensive study of the origins of Sudanese nationalism during the colonial period, this college became almost exclusively the haunt of the Arabo-Sudanese elite. It is they who would develop the Sudanese nationalism that would propel Sudan to eventual independence, but it would be one that would be narrowly circumscribed, resting on values derived from the Arabic language and culture, and the Islamic faith. More importantly, however, this nationalism would emerge *against a backdrop of an ethnically determined hierarchic social structure* in which membership of either the formerly enslaved (Afro-Sudanese) or the former enslavers (Arabo-Sudanese) determined one's status—not necessarily religious affiliation. By restricting admission to the college almost exclusively to Arabo-Sudanese elite males, which in turn meant access for them to positions in the colonial administration (albeit at lower levels), primarily in order to gain support from the elite for the British colonial presence in Sudan, the British became unwitting accomplices to the development of this attenuated form of nationalism.

Gordon Memorial College

Gordon Memorial College opened its doors in 1902, with Kitchener himself officiating, on a campus built on the bank of the Blue Nile. Only handpicked sons of the Arabo-Sudanese elite would be the first enrollees. Sharkey (2003) points out that British officials from the education department literally went door-to-door visiting prominent Arabo-Sudanese families looking for student recruits. Although there was some initial reluctance to allow their sons to enroll for fear that the college was a Trojan horse for Christian evangelization, their fears were soon put to rest once they realized that the teachers included Muslim alims and the curriculum included the Islamic sciences. The college did not as a rule admit Christian students from the south, instead the few from there who qualified for higher education, in later years, were sent to Makerere College in Uganda. To ensure a steady stream of students the college also opened a number of primary schools in Khartoum and in Omdurman. Whether it was the primary schools or the college itself, the chief admission criteria (observes Sharkey) was social status even it meant lowering standards or providing financial assistance.

In the history of the development of higher education in Sudan, Gordon Memorial College holds pride of place. Therefore a closer look at this institution is in order. To begin with, it ought to be noted that while it had the appellation of college attached to its name, in reality it was not a college in the true sense of the word. Even after a period of some thirty years of existence, it would remain essentially a secondary-vocational school (in fact, initially it was a little more than an upper-level primary school.). That said, given the context of an absence of any other institution at or above its level capable of providing Western-style education, it was considered by all concerned as an institution of higher learning. Among the college's other characteristics, of general interest, included an annual student population of some 300–400; a curricular program that included both literary academic education and pre-professional training for teachers, surveyors, engineers, and later, after the opening of the Kitchener School of Medicine, medical personnel (biology, physics, chemistry, etc.); vocational instruction; and programs in athletic and other extra-curricular activities. As the college expanded it acquired such other non-teaching units as a research laboratory for tropical disease (the Wellcome Tropical Research Laboratories) donated by pharmaceutical magnate, Sir Henry Wellcome, the Antiquities Service, the Natural History Museum, and the Ethnological Museum. The large student dormitories included a common dining hall, and students were expected to assist with the cleaning and maintenance under a strict disciplinary regime. The college even had a Boy Scouts program, begun in 1917—that is less than years after the original founding of the movement (in Britain by Robert Baden-Powell in 1908).

In 1937, the college would undergo an important development: an inspection of the college by the De La Warr Commission (see Chapter 4). The commission did not have many positive things to say about the college. In a letter to the governor-general, Lord De La Warr would observe: "The Gordon College, which should have achieved a continuously rising standard throughout the thirty years of its existence, has failed not only to attain the complete university standard which its founders envisaged, but even to reach the stage of university entrance" (from Beshir 1969: 117). Against the backdrop of such criticism, it was decided to reorganize the college and accordingly in 1945 a new Gordon Memorial College was reconstituted that among other changes incorporated the various schools that had emerged in the 1930s and supervised by different government departments—namely, the schools of law, agriculture and veterinary science, engineering and science, and arts. From this time on, the College would make steady progress toward university status. At the same time, the college was freed from direct government control and supervision and placed under a governing council with an independent constitution. Two years later, in 1947, the new college would enter into the special relationship with the University of London that the Asquith Commission (see chapter 4) had recommended as a means of upgrading higher education institutions throughout the British colonial empire. In fact, the college was the first institution in British colonial Africa to be transformed into what came to be known as the "Asquith college." In 1951 the college absorbed the hitherto independent Kitchener School of Medicine to create a faculty of medicine against a backdrop of further transformation of the entire college as it became the University College of Khartoum. Following independence in 1956, the college would be transformed again to become the University of Khartoum. In that year it had a population of slightly over 100 full time teaching staff and some 600 students.

The oldest Sudanese university, therefore, is the University of Khartoum. The second oldest is the Sudan University for Science and Technology; it was originally founded in 1950 as Khartoum Technical Institute. Later the institute would become a polytechnic in 1967 and achieve university status in 1975. In 1990 it would be reconstituted to become the institution it is today. Omdurman Islamic University, in terms of age, comes third. Its history dates back to around the time when Gordon Memorial College was first opened. The Sudanese ulama, perhaps not wishing to be left out of the new education game in town, opened a madrasah with the support of the colonial administration called ma'had al-ilmi in 1912, patterned on al-Azhar, at the Omdurman mosque. While its staff salaries came from a government subsidy, the madrasah itself could not qualify for government funds because it was not under the supervision of the education department. The rationale behind the government's support of the ma'had is that the governor-general (Sir Francis Reginald Wingate) believed that it was better to encourage students to remain in the country instead of going to al-Azhar for further study, so as to shield them from possible anti-British influence while in Cairo. In time, the ma'had developed to become a national institution under government supervision. Its graduates were destined primarily for teaching posts in primary-level schools (the kuttabs and khalwas), although some did find jobs in local Shari'ah courts. Later, in 1924, it would become a college and then in 1965 acquire university status. In 1975 it would be reconstituted into its present incarnation. (See Beshir 1969 for more on the ma'had.)

Other Sudanese higher education institutions include: Red Sea University (created in 1994); University of Juba (established in 1977); University of Gezira (founded in 1975); and Shandi University (set up in 1990). There are also a number of lesser institutions at the college level, but referred to in their titles as universities; they include: Sinar University, Atbara University, Bahr-Elghazal, Dongola University, El-Azhari University, El-Dalang University, El-Gadarif University, El-Mahadi University, El-Nielien University, El-Obied University, University of Qur'an and Islamic Studies, and Upper Nile University.

By way of concluding this section, we may make these further observations: The account so far has been about higher education in the north, but what about in the south? The studies by both Beshir (1969) and Sanderson and Sanderson (1981) allows one to come away with the conclusion that the conscious decision of the British to leave the task of educational provision in the south in missionary hands, meant that the south experienced virtually no development at the higher education level (or even at the secondary school level). When independence came, the northern-dominated government saw little reason to change the status quo in this regard. The eruption of civil war ensured that the pre-independence circumstance of the south would remain, more or less, its permanent fate, until now (with the exception of the founding of University of Juba). Should peace hold, this, however, will now change. The question one may ask here then is this: When higher educational provision in the south begins to accelerate, will it have an integrative influence or a disintegrative one from the perspective of national unity? If the history of the north is any guide, one may legitimately surmise that it will be the latter.

The 1989 coup that brought the current regime to power, inaugurated a new and, from the perspective of some, a more ominous era for higher education in Sudan: a fundamental realignment of higher education toward support for the regime's Islamist influenced ideological agenda on one hand, and on the other a shift away from state subsidies for student finance.

The relationship between the University of Khartoum and the government has always been a thorny one from the perspective of students. During the colonial period the bone of contention was of course nationalism; in the postindependence period it has been the nature of the Sudanese state as it has moved back and forth across the dictatorship-democracy divide. In other words, as in almost all other countries in Africa, student political activism at the university has been an integral part of its history.[92]

TUNISIA

Prior to the arrival of the French colonial rule, as we have already noted, Tunisia, as part of North Africa, had a rich history that went back thousands of years. A brief note then on the modern period is in order: At the Congress of Berlin in 1878, the European powers agreed to France's claims over Tunisia as part of its sphere of influence; it would be a matter of time before France proceeded to make good on this claim by invading Tunisia from Algeria in 1881.[93] The desperate diplomatic and other maneuvers of the Tunisian Ottoman Mamluks had, in the end, worked to save Tunisia only from the exact fate of the Algerians: direct colonization; instead, Tunisia was declared a protectorate—notwithstanding the demands of the Algerian colons that Tunisia be thrown open to full colonial settlement as a colony. In practice, whether a colony or a protectorate, Tunisia was no longer free to chart its own destiny (though it was spared the brutal excesses of French colonization that the Algerians were forced to endure). Although, the Tunisians did offer some resistance to the French invasion, it was nowhere near that put up by the Algerians; ergo, within two years Tunisia was completely under French control. Nominally, the Husaynids were still in charge, but France pulled the strings. In 1955, after widespread but relatively peaceful nationalist agitation, Tunisia was granted limited self-rule, to be followed a year later by complete independence. Independence meant not only the end of French tutelage, but also the end of the Husaynid dynasty; the new rulers (whose political baptism of fire had involved imprisonment in Vichy France, only to be freed by the Nazis in 1942 and handed over to Mussolini's Fascist Italy, who then a year later allowed them to return to Tunisia) were not from the traditional aristocracy—though despite the modernist trappings of an independent Tunisia, in practice, as in most of Islamic Africa, they would soon recreate the autocracy of the Ottoman Mamluk dynasties, albeit infused with secularism and Westernism, under the leadership of the officially proclaimed president-for-life, Habib ibn Ali Borguiba (reigned from the time of independence until just three years before his death in 2000).[94]

Al-Zaitouna

It will be recalled that in Chapter 1 there was occasion to describe the oldest higher education institution in Tunisia, or even the entire Islamic Africa and the Middle East, the al-Zaitouna mosque-college or madrasah. Now, in the modern era, the evolution of al-Zaitouna in terms of its functioning and teaching would continue when it received some fillip with reforms introduced by the Ottoman Mamluks; specifically, Ahmed Bey in December 1842, and Khayr al-Din (ruled from 1873–77) in 1875.[95] The 1842 decree gave the madrasah a charter that formalized its educational functions as well as making it the center of higher education in Tunisia (the non mosque-based madrasahs in the city were as a consequence converted into residential quarters for students of al-Zaitouna); while the 1875 decree, among other things, sought to introduce governmental supervision of the institution, inject some professionalism in ulama conduct, as well as expand its curricular provisions. As may be surmised these reforms were only partially successful.[96] Following the arrival of the French (Tunisia was declared a protectorate in 1881) the institution over time underwent two contradictory developments: student agitation (marked by vigorous periods of unrest, as in 1910–12, 1928–30, 1947–50) for educational reform in consonance with the secularizing tendencies introduced by the French in Tunisia and championed by secularist Tunisians that, not surprisingly, were generally resisted by the ulama; and growing enrollments (both, in its Tunis and provincial locations where it had established branches)—the numbers speak for themselves: in 1881: 600; in 1927: 9,818; and in 1956: 20,000 (see the entry "Zaytuna" in *Encyclopedia of Islam* (1986).[97] It may be noted here that French policy toward the institution was, for the most part, to leave it alone; for, like in Morocco (but unlike in Algeria), they felt that their aims would be better facilitated by co-opting the madrasah system rather than grievously weakening it.[98] There was one key exception, however, to this approach: in 1898 a commission was created to introduce curricular and pedagogical reforms at the institution. The rationale behind it, apparently, was a French desire (supported by secularist minded Tunisian bureaucrats) to elevate the al-Zaitouna in importance to a level beyond that enjoyed by al-Azhar in the Islamic world; as one of the French principals involved in the appointment of the commission, Louis Machuel, privately stated: "I dreamed of having in Africa Minor, which was now entirely under French domination, an Arab intellectual center of which the rays of influence would beam to all the other Islamic countries—a sort of vast and genuine Muslim university in which Arabic studies would be reformed and improved according to new methods and to which scientific notions (modest at first then later more extensive) would bring a new strengthening" (from Green 1978: 178).[99] Although the commission had a number of ulama from al-Zaitouna, in addition to the French and secularist oriented Tunisians, on it and despite what appeared to the French and the secularists as worthy proposals to bring modern rationality to educational practices at the institution, the ulama, perhaps predictably, made sure that the reforms remained a pipe dream; they steadfastly opposed them, fearing that the reforms would turn out to be a Trojan horse for not only fundamentally altering the mission of the institution, but also peripheralizing their own role within it.[100] Following Tunisian independence in 1956, however, and with the autocratic secularists fully in charge, the ulama could do nothing but acquiesce: the madrasah was forced to undergo major changes when it lost its primary and secondary-level educational functions and instead it was converted into a modern university specializing in the Islamic sciences—plus in keeping with these reforms it was moved to new premises. The formal appellation of university to the institution however would have to await the arrival of the once reformist president Ben Ali; it would become the University of Ezzitouna in 1988. In comparison to al-Azhar, the institution, although it continues to function (it has a population of about 1200 students), is of relatively low importance, both in educational terms as well as in social terms—thanks to the trenchant secularism of the Tunisian autocracy.

Besides al-Zaitouna, there were two other institutions worthy of note that existed prior to the arrival of French colonial rule, but they were of much more recent vintage and, significantly, were not part of the madrasah system: Bardo Military Academy and Sadiki College. Bardo was founded in 1840 for the same reasons that Muhammed Ali had established his military academies in Egypt: to provide training for a new cadre of military officers who could help modernize the army. The school enrolled between forty and sixty students from the Tunisian elite and offered instruction in military related and technical subjects (mathematics, engineering, fortifications, etc.); as well as Islamic and Arabic oriented subjects. The school was bilingual: French was the language of instruction for the former set of subjects (taught by French and other European instructors) and Arabic for the latter. Hawkins (2003) states that in terms of its original mission the school was a failure: it had a negligible impact on the modernization effort; however, at another level the school achieved, he points out, considerable significance: as in Egypt, its graduates went on to become the new secularist- and Westernist- oriented elite who championed the development of Western-style education outside the madrasah system. The fruit of this effort was manifest thirty-five years after Bardo had opened its doors: the founding in 1875 of Sadiki College by the reformist prime minister, Khayr al-Din (came to office in 1873)—a building that was once part of an army barracks was requisitioned for the purpose. Its curriculum was centered around the objective of producing civil servants and offered instruction in French and Italian, in addition to Arabic. A strong emphasis was placed on mathematics and sciences, though the Islamic sciences were not entirely neglected. In 1911 it began granting diplomas and in 1930 its curriculum was changed to conform to a typical French lycee curriculum. Many of the graduates of this college would go on to become Nationalist leaders of Tunisia—even Tunisia's president-for-life dictator, Habib Borguiba, had gone there for a short time before an illness forced him to withdraw from the school.

To provide additional openings to Tunisians who wanted to pursue secularist-oriented education, the alumni of Sadiki, following in the footsteps of the alumni of Bardo, and with the full cooperation and support of the French, established the al-Jamiya al-Khalduniyya Institute in 1896 (it was named after Ibn Khaldun) The ostensible rationale for its founding was that it would be a complement to Zaytouna by allowing that institution's students to obtain training in subjects that Zaytouna did not wish to include in its curriculum (such as the French language, geometry and surveying, medicine, accounting, etc.). In practice, al-Khaldunniyya (together with Sadiki), served to undermine the hitherto central position occupied by Zaytouna within the Tunisian higher education landscape. However, the significance of these institutions, in terms of the future of Tunisia, went beyond that of education. They would in time become the incubators of a new class of Tunisians: a secularist/Westernist nationalist elite with minimal connections with the old precolonial elite and who, through a political party they would establish, the Neo-Destour (New Constitution), would lead Tunisia to independence.[101] On the eve of Tunisian independence in 1956, a relatively peaceful event in comparison to neighboring Algeria, an Institute of Higher Studies *(Institut des Hautes Etudes)* was created In 1945 with sections covering law, economics, and administration; science and premedicine, and preengineering studies; sociology and history; Arabic studies; and archeology. Initial enrollment of Tunisians in the new institution was modest; for instance, in 1950 out of a population of 702 students only, 176 were Tunisians; the rest were French and others. (The total higher education enrollment for all Tunisians in the same year was 604 students at secular institutions [Tabawi 1972: 160–161]). Independence, however, would change everything: like almost all nationalists in nearly all former European colonies, the Tunisian nationalists decided to stake the entire future of their country on the provision of secular/Westernist education (education would receive in 1972 almost a third of the nation's budgetary allocation; compare with the 14% in 1950 when still under the French [Hawkins 2003: 106]). In 1960, the institute would become the basis of the establishment of the University of Tunis. Initially the new university had four constituent colleges: arts and science; law; politics and economics; and Islamic law and religious studies—made possible by converting Zaitunah into a constituent college of the university. Other institutions were also appended to the university, such as a teacher's training college. Later, the university was reorganized into four separate institutions: Tunis I (University of Letters, Arts and Human Sciences); Tunis II (University of Sciences, Techniques and Medicine—established in 1988); Tunis III (University of Law, Economics and Management—created in 1987); and Ezzitouna (Zaytouna) University Tunis. Other higher education institutions in Tunisia today include: University of the Center, Sousse (set up in 1986) and University of Sfax, South (also founded in 1986). Tunisian universities, as would be expected, are patterned on French universities (with the exception of Zaytouna), but with both French and Arabic as languages of instruction (as at almost all universities in Islamic Africa, French is used in the sciences primarily, and Arabic in the arts and letters courses).[102]

CONCLUSION

By way of conclusion, we will delineate on the basis of the foregoing record, themes that are of specific relevance to the postindependence period. The first theme that forcefully stands out is that almost the entire region has been guided by these central objectives in its development of the higher education sector in the postindependence period: marginalization (sometimes de jure, sometimes de facto) of the traditional madrasah system; a massive expansion of enrollments to allow greater access to sections of society that had hitherto limited access to secular Westernist higher education; an appreciable effort at increasing female enrollments throughout the education sector as a whole; some attempts, though not always successful, at linkage of higher education growth with explicitly stated socioeconomic development goals; Arabization; indigenization of personnel. (Some of these objectives will be discussed later.)

Second, termination of direct colonial rule did not lead to a demand by the masses (let alone the elites) for a return to status-quo ante in the education sector. In other words, however much there may have been opposition to European colonialism, the vast majority of the formerly colonized populations were now hooked on to the colonially bequeathed education almost as if it were a drug. For the Muslim masses the madrasah system, *as traditionally constituted*, was no longer a viable option in an independent Islamic Africa (as, of course, elsewhere on the continent). Only the education of the infidel would now do. The question is, Why? It has to do with the difference between the old and new colonialisms: unlike the previous or classical forms of colonialism (those of the Greek, Roman, and Islamic eras, for example), modern European colonialism was a completely different kind of colonial animal never witnessed by human beings before: it involved the importation of an entirely new mode of production, industrial capitalism—but without however fully destroying the old, instead hijacking it to become an appendage of the new.[103] In practice this meant two things: one, that this was, for all intents and purposes, an irreversible transformation, in that it not only entailed the transmutation of old social structures, but extrication from a Western-dominated international economic system was now an impossibility; and two, material success in this new order required access to secular higher education introduced by colonialism. In time, therefore, even the masses began to clamor for this type of education with a vengeance. However, insofar as the promises held out for such education have failed to materialize for many, disillusionment has set in for some—such as the Islamists (more on them in a moment).

Third, where traditional Islamic education has been allowed to exist, government strategy, as one would expect, has been to co-opt it into non-oppositional forms of education; the historic role of the ulama to legitimate the reign of a ruler only on the basis of their adherence to that fundamental precept of Islam to "enjoin good and forbid evil" has been compromised in the service of an autocratic police state (much as it often had in the past as well). Therefore, true adherence to Islam has meant the belief among significant sections of the population of the necessity to go, paradoxically, outside the officially supported traditional Islamic institutions. In a sense this a replay of what occurred during the colonial period in some parts of the region. Ergo, it is important to stress that the current rise of Islamism in much of Afro-Arab Islamic Africa that often poses a threat to the ruling autocracies is not a product of the traditional madrasah system.[104] In other words, the political influence of the madrasah system on the current secular higher education sector has been marginal, if any. In fact, whether traditional or secular, the rise of Islamism has had little to do with higher education per se (even though it may have manifestations in that sector—as in the demand for Arabization, increased focus on Islamic studies, etc.), rather, its source lies elsewhere: alienation among the masses from the status quo engendered by such factors as these: (a) Whereas secularism in Western Europe had nurtured economic, political, and social progress, in the Islamic world the reverse has been true where it has been associated with economic and political chaos resting on a bedrock of massive and persistent violations of the human rights of the citizenry characteristic of police states (vide: Iran during the reign of the Shah, which was a staunch secularist ally of the West, or Iraq during the rule of Saddam Hussein—until his invasion of Kuwait on August 2, 1990, once also a secularist ally of the West—or today's Algeria with its pro-West secular military despots.) Note this circumstance is not unique to the Islamic world, but is endemic throughout the PQD world, especially in the poorest regions, such as much of Africa, should inure us from subscribing to the notion that this is a modern instance of Oriental despotism. (b) The ongoing Israeli/Palestinian conflict, which many Westerners tend to forget not only highlights current Islamic impotency vis-à-vis the West, especially when viewed against a background of memories that run deep (witness the continuing ideological relevance of the Crusades—see Appendix I), but it is a conflict that includes a struggle between Muslims and non-Muslims over the second holiest city for all Muslims throughout the world: Jerusalem.[105] (c) The association of the internal repression perpetrated by local autocracies with their treasonous links (in the eyes of the masses) with the traditional enemies of Islam: Christian West—including the United States (often dubbed the *Great Satan*).[106]

Fourth, the type of economy that was created in the postindependence era in much of the region has tended to be state-capitalist.[107] However, the consequence of the dominant role played by the state within the economy from the perspective of higher education has included: micromanagement of career choices of students; employment of large numbers of graduates in bloated state bureaucracies; an emphasis on science and technology training but without the concomitant expansion of appropriate training facilities, not to mention the inability to develop the requisite economic sectors to provide employment for graduates; and the discouragement of private sector education.

Fifth, historically, from the very beginning of the appearance of formal education in the Islamic empire (that is long before the arrival of the West), educational access had not depended on the ability to pay; it was almost always tuition free. During the colonial era this practice was continued (with a few exceptions), but for a different reason: as a way to entice students into the new secular/Westernist educational institutions at the time of their first appearance. Given this history, and adding to it the socialist rhetoric of the postindependence period, higher education in the public sector throughout the region has remained essentially tuition-free. The repercussions for state budgets is self-evident; and at the same time, user-fees as a politically volatile subject is also self-evident.

Sixth, as with tuition-free education, the concept of foreign study had been intrinsic to Islamic higher education long before the arrival of colonialism. However, with colonialism this concept underwent some change: foreign study did not mean going abroad to study at Islamic institutions, but rather Western institutions. In other words, during the colonial era, and even more so during the postindependence period, students from Afro-Arab Islamic Africa (as from the rest of Africa) went to study in the West (and continue to do so) in droves—both on state and privately funded sponsorship. For Islamic Africa, the outcome of this global intellectual transhumance has been a multiedged sword: (a) it has helped to enhance the stock of human capital within Islamic Africa; (b) it has helped to reinforce the power of the compradorial elites (since it is mainly their children who have had the opportunity to study abroad, historically) by allowing them to develop a unique bilingual secularist/Westernist *in-culture* (in contrast to the *out-culture* of the masses); and (c) it has helped to subsidize the human-capital resources of the West through the phenomenon of *braindrain*, where some foreign students, usually the brightest, fail to return after completion of their studies for a variety of reasons.

Seventh, almost all the Islamic Afro-Arab countries have made considerable strides in emphasizing science and technology in their development of higher education—a situation that is the obverse of much of the rest of Africa. However, as just noted, this emphasis has not been matched by a breakthrough toward self-sustained economic development. In fact, on the contrary, it appears that the function of qualifications in science and technology have been to simply imbue their holders with an extra edge of prestige (relative to arts and social science degree holders) in their quest for employment in all sectors, including mundane non science-related government bureaucratic jobs (while for a minority, the very talented, it has garnered them a ticket on the braindrain gravy train). In other words, *underemployment* appears now to be the order of the day. How does one explain this phenomenon? It would seem that almost the same imperialist forces that had stopped Muhammed Ali of Egypt over a century ago dead in his tracks as he tried to industrialize Egypt, continue to plague North Africa (and the rest of Africa for that matter): a combination of political and economic muscle of the West ensuring that Africa continues to remain, by and large, an economic basket case. The following description of the fate of the Algerian precolonial urban economy, for instance, as a result of colonial intrusion is as much valid today as it was then: "[T]he opening of the Algerian market to the French speculators and the thrusting of the entire economy, without any tariff protection, first into the 'metropolitan' and then into the international market, undermined the local market for Algerian handicrafts.... In sum, all the Algerian traditional craft manufacturers were ousted by French industrial products. Thus the integration of the Algerian economy into the 'world system' also provoked the disintegration of the precolonial urban activities" (Bennoune 1988: 67). Today the role played by colonialism is now performed by the Western-dominated international regime of the World Trade Organization, but the effects remain the same: the inability of PQD countries to move into industrial manufacture on a sustained scale (unless their postindependence histories have included a period of relative withdrawal from the world economy, combined with an economically astute and politically stable governmental regimes). In other words, higher education *by itself* is powerless to move countries economically. However, in the specific case of Afro-Arab Islamic Africa one may concede a unique problem specific to higher education that is detrimental to economic development: an overemphasis on science and technology, which has resulted in at least three hindrances: inadequate *qualitatively appropriate* training because of a dearth of resources (competent teachers, laboratories, supplies, books, equipment, optimum teacher/student ratios, etc.) in the face of demand for student places running far ahead of supply; inadequate economic opportunities (in terms of capital and economic know-how) to create science- and technology- based businesses; and three, quite paradoxically, an insufficient number of highly trained arts/social science graduates who alone (relatively speaking) have the capacity for imaginative socioeconomic planning and entrepreneurial creativity that can permit the exploitation of scientific and technological human capital. (This last problem is highlighted by the truism that, for the most part, scientists rarely make good politicians, managers or even business persons. The latest evidence on this, albeit anecdotal, comes from the experience in the 1990s in the United States of many newly created computer technology firms foundering for lack of good business/management skills on the part of their technologically creative founders—this is not to suggest by any means that this was the only problem they faced.) It appears that the competence to solve technical/scientistic problems does not necessarily equip one to possess what one may call visionary imagination that can facilitate the resolution of macrolevel social and economic problems for one very obvious reason: human beings are simply too complex and unpredictable to be amenable to the kind of problem-solving that can be undertaken with inanimate or nonhuman objects/subjects.

Eighth, almost all the postindependence nationalist leaders of Afro-Arab Islamic Africa (as in much of the rest of Africa) were, to varying degrees, committed to some reduction of social and economic inequality in their countries—their autocratic rule notwithstanding—especially in the immediate afterglow of achieving political independence. After all, populism was a sine qua non of nationalist struggles for independence. In this effort they turned to higher education as a means of reducing the elite/mass socioeconomic gap.[108] However, as experience has proven, they, like countless social engineers throughout the world, including in the former communist East and in the West, have been naive (no matter how well intentioned) on this score. The key problem has been addressing the thorny issue of equality of higher educational opportunity. As elites have shown time and again across the planet and throughout modern history, democratization of access merely calls forth greater ingenuity on their part to secure the intergenerational continuity of their status—for example by means of private schooling, education friendly child-rearing practices (which often only wealthy parents can afford), private tutorials to prepare for national gate-keeping exams, moving residences to exclusive neighborhoods to facilitate easier access to superior schools, access to nepotism, elite biases of educational foreign aid, their capacity to shoulder the burdens of income foregone, and so on. In other words, while the expansion of the higher education provision on the basis of more student places, coupled with such measures as tuition-free education, a strategy that has characterized the development of higher education in Afro-Arab Islamic Africa (and the rest of the continent too) in the postcolonial era did, initially, have some ameliorative effect on the inequality of educational opportunities across different strata, in general it has been a transient phenomenon. In fact, on the contrary, as Lewis and Dundar's (2002) pithy summary of the pertinent literature on the subject indicates, the obverse has been the outcome over the long-term (not just in Africa, but almost throughout the world) of democratization of access through traditional measures: the historically privileged elite groups have increased their share of participation rates, while at the same time being subsidized by the rest of the population who are denied access to higher education because of factors just noted, coupled with other, historically determined, impediments, such as: cultural biases against the education of women; the urban bias of institutional location that adds additional financial burdens on the children of the rural poor (often the majority in almost all countries in Africa) who can ill afford it; the poor quality of lower-level educational institutions for the less privileged (which includes the absence of a rigorous college preparatory secondary school curriculum and inadequate or nonexistent career guidance opportunities at the secondary-level); the lack of adequate institutional supports in higher education institutions for children from lower socioeconomic status backgrounds that would help to match their admission rates with their *completion* rates; and so on.[109] Clearly, as this author noted more than two decades ago (Lulat 1982), in the absence of other social policies aimed at addressing the imbalance in power relations in a society, there is a severe limit to how much higher education can accomplish in reducing socioeconomic inequality. In fact, evidence in this regard is so strong across all societies throughout the world that one can be even more emphatic and simply state (depressing though this conclusion may be to the champions of social justice) that the vitiation of the class-reproduction function of higher education, against a backdrop of unequal power relations across classes, is a chimeral endeavor.

Ninth, from the purely technical point of human capital production the experiences of countries like China, Korea, Taiwan, and to some degree even the former Eastern bloc countries, there is little incompatibility between an authoritarian police state and higher education. The problem for higher education comes from the disruptive tendencies that ensue as a result of opposition to the authoritarianism that may take sometimes positive forms and at other times highly destructive forms (as has occurred in Algeria, for instance).

Tenth, it should be clear from the foregoing that a university has many uses beyond the instrumental (knowledge production and human capital formation) with which we are so enamored today. There was a time when a university (broadly defined) also existed as an expression of a society's piety where acquisition of knowledge for its own sake was considered a worthy goal to which a person could devote his/her entire life without social reprobation. However, there were other uses too, but of a political variety; such as serving as a potential source of legitimacy for ruling dynasties (or conversely as a seat of opposition to the state—for example, during the period of European colonial rule). The university was also at times a recruiting ground for new elites or a means of transformation of old elites into new (especially in the colonial and postindependence periods). Yet, in our penchant for viewing higher education in a strictly instrumentalist fashion (measured in terms of returns on investment—see Chapter 7) we often fail to recognize that even today, some of these same functions continue to be performed.[110] Given these multiplicity of roles, it should not be surprising that universities have the potential to be sites of much contention; consequently, universities are "political" institutions as well—especially, given their enormous appetite for financial resources, when they are state-funded. Those who are concerned with educational efficiency and educational reforms tend to overlook this basic fundamental fact. In the same vein:

the foregoing historical survey also highlights an important fact about knowledge: it is not neutral. Knowledge has a sociological dimension to it in the sense that not all knowledge has equal social value; that is, some kinds of knowledge have greater social significance than others *independent of content.* For instance, secular knowledge obtained from Western institutions today has greater value than knowledge from a local institution throughout Islamic Africa (as well as the rest of the continent) because access to this knowledge implies access to symbols of elite status. Or take the example of the current conflict between three principal categories of knowledge in Islamic Africa: secular/Western knowledge, postindependence modernist-savvy Islamic knowledge (which does not, for example, depend on mnemonics), and traditional or classical mnemonic-oriented, knowledge-pursued-for-its-own-sake, Islamic knowledge. (In an ideal world, for the Muslim, the boundaries between these categories would be diffuse, but given the matrix of existing power relations this is not the case.)[111]

Eleventh, the great strides that Islamic Africa has made in the direction of expanding higher educational access has often occurred at the expense of quality (as already indicated). This is a problem that afflicts the rest of the continent as well and it will be discussed in greater detail later.

Finally, again, as with the rest of the continent, an important feature of the higher education sector in Islamic Africa has been student political activism from the very beginning of the arrival of colonially mediated higher education institutions. This activism continues to the present day, both in Islamic Africa and elsewhere on the continent.

NOTES

1. At the heart of the definitional problem is the matter of race, not geography; that is, the racism of the West—which has always sought to create racial hierarchies (positing peoples defined as black at the bottom and those defined as white at the top and the rest in between)—combined with the racism of the North Africans and Africans themselves, is the root of this problem. To elaborate, racism in any society creates hierarchies within which there is a struggle among the subordinates to identify with the dominant (even though they are all victimized, albeit to varying degrees, by the racism of the dominant group); moreover, it is a struggle that is encouraged by the dominant group—representing a divide-and-rule strategy. Classic examples of this phenomenon at work can be found in the United States; consider, for instance, that in that country North African Arabs are classified "white," or the fact that lighter complexioned blacks have, historically, tended to fare (relatively) better than their darker-skinned brethren. However, what is true of individual societies is also true at the global level. See, for instance, the discussion by Hawkins (2003) on how Tunisians see themselves, relative to Sub-Saharan Africa (which can be summarized in one sentence: they are in Africa but they are not of Africa), and one suspects that the Tunisian perspective is replicated all over Afro-Arab Islamic Africa, including, ironically, Sudan—a country where more than anywhere else in Afro-Arab Islamic Africa most of its

Arab population had long merged genetically with the indigenous African population (notwithstanding the insistence by the ruling classes in Khartoum that they are Arabs and not Africans). In fact, with reference to the Sudan, the situation there has become so bizarre, that "peoples who have virtually no Arab 'blood' call themselves Arab by virtue of an adopted lineage that they trace symbolically to the family of the Prophet or to important Arab dynasties and tribes" in order to gain a higher social status (Lesch 1998: 211). There is probably no Afro-Arab leader today, with the exception, perhaps, of Libya's Muammar al-Qaddhafi, who shares Nasser's vision of being both Pan-Arab and Pan-African at one and the same time. To complicate matters even further, in Afro-Arab Islamic Africa, the more than thousand year presence of Arabs in that region has led to considerable intermingling with original populations (e.g., Berbers and black Africans). Consequently, from a purely phenotypical perspective, Arabs (like African Americans in the United States, for instance) range across a diverse hue, so much so that in some parts, they are completely indistinguishable from either black Africans or Berbers.

2. Those living in certain parts of East and West Africa where Islam is the dominant religion (e.g., in Somalia and in some parts of Kenya, Malawi, Nigeria, Senegal, Tanzania [Zanzibar], etc.) may raise objections to their exclusion from this particular chapter. Are they not eligible to be considered part of Afro-Arab Islamic Africa as well? Strictly from the perspective of this chapter, the answer is, yes and no. Yes, they are part of Afro-Arab Islamic Africa if the focus of this chapter was exclusively religion, but that is not the case; further, they are excluded from this chapter because of two other reasons: their heritage does not have a strong enough Arabic cultural input to merit their consideration along side such Afro-Arab countries of North Africa as, for instance, Egypt or Morocco. This view draws succor from a comparative examination of two general histories, one focusing on Arab peoples (Hourani 2002) and the other on Islamic peoples elsewhere on the continent (Levtzion and Pouwels 2000). Even more importantly, however, since they do not have a separate political existence as national entities in their own right (though Somalia in this regard is an exception), the trajectory of higher education development in their areas has not been independent of the rest of the countries of which they are constituent parts.

3. The compradorial character of the colonially created new indigenous elite is exemplified by the one in Algeria; there they were pejoratively called *beni-ouis-ouis* (meaning "sons of yes-men") by the Algerian masses. It is from among this very elite, as Entelis (1986: 32) points out, that the future Algerian nationalists would be recruited.

4. The nature of this new elite is captured well by Entelis (1986: 209) in his description of the Algerian elite: "Contemporary Algeria has evolved into a bureaucratic polity—a political system in which power and national decision making are shaped almost exclusively by the employees of the state, and especially by the topmost levels of the officer corps, single-party organization, and civilian bureaucracy, including the significant socioeconomic class of managers and technicians." In other words: this elite does not really represent a particular class, rather it is a class in itself—especially when considered in the context of state capitalism (which is the economic system that is dominant almost throughout Afro-Arab Islamic Africa). In fact, the state is the elite. However, with recent moves toward limiting state capitalism under policies of structural adjustment (e.g., in Egypt), one is beginning to witness a fusion of this praetorian ruling elite with members of the other more traditional elites, such as the mercantilist elite.

5. This does not mean that they accepted colonialism per se insofar as it signified an external overlordship. The local elites did, in time, recover their political composure suffi-

ciently to espouse nationalist aspirations of self-rule, but these aspirations had usually little to do with ambitions of working for a new egalitarian society in which the inherent inequalities created by colonialism would be the focus of ameliorative attention in a postcolonial order. Considering the postcolonial historical trajectory of Afro-Arab Islamic Africa on one hand, and on the other the prevailing circumstances of all the countries of the region regarding this matter, the truth of the following restatement of this issue is self-evident: the nationalist elites were merely competing with the foreign colonial elite for the same objective—how to exploit the masses for their own gain—something that, writing nearly a half a century ago, that psychiatrist and political observer from the Caribbean, Frantz Fanon (1968 [1961]), so astutely foresaw: "In its narcissism, the [nationalist elite] is easily convinced that it can advantageously replace the [colonial elite]." He continues, "[I]n an underdeveloped country an authentic [nationalist elite] ought to…put at the people's disposal the intellectual and technical capital that it has snatched when going through the colonial universities. But unhappily we shall see that very often the [nationalist elite] does not follow this heroic, positive, fruitful, and just path; rather, it disappears with its soul set at peace into the shocking ways—shocking because anti-national—of a traditional bourgeoisie, of a bourgeoisie which is stupidly, contemptibly, cynically bourgeois" (p. 150). But what does he mean by "cynically bourgeois?" He is referring to the incapacity of the nationalist elite to rise up above its own petty interests in the service of the true interests of the entire nation in whose name it had fought for independence in the first place— exemplified by its championing of all those ills that we have come to associate with underdevelopment today: sectarianism, economic and political corruption, administrative inaptitude, looting of national resources, massive and sustained violations of the human rights of the citizenry, pursuit of compradorial economic projects, and so on. (See his chapter, "Pitfalls of National Consciousness," for more.) A corollary of the foregoing is this central feature of compradorial ideology: their wholesale acceptance of the general mantra and belief propagated by many Westerners at all levels of society (from the media to think-tanks to academia) that if the developing world could be remade in the present likeness of the West (the most graphic instance of which is the current U.S. project to "bring democracy" to Iraq) than all their problems of poverty, etc., would disappear. Some sections of the compradorial elite, reacting with self-hate at the comparative technological and economic backwardness of their societies had even "proclaimed Western civilization as the highest stage of man's spiritual and material development; declared Islamic civilization and culture dead and useless; and advocated the adoption of Western civilization and culture without reservations as the only way for the advancement of their country" (Vatikiotis 1991: 308). Yet, such a view consistently fails to notice the most basic error of this Eurocentric line of reasoning: the present did not emerge ex nihilio; that is, the present of the West is constructed out of a past; that is a post–1492 past (see Appendix II). And it is a past in which these very same countries were victims of Western imperialist predations that underwrote Western economic progress on one hand, and on the other its obverse: their underdevelopment (see Appendix II). In other words, to remake in the image of the present, then one must also remake in the image of the past (an impossible project); or alternatively, failing that, we must emerge with other ideas than the simplistic notions of remaking oneself in the likeness of others.

6. It should be noted here that, as Eickelman (1985) points out in relation to Morocco for instance, once members of the ulama who taught in the major madrasahs like al-Qarawiyyin and the Yusufiya were put on government payroll (regardless of how paltry the

salary was) by the French colonial authority, their standing in the community, with rare exceptions, dropped precipitously. They were no longer held in high esteem by the community because now they were almost no different from other paid colonial civil servants.

7. In reality, there was a seeming ambivalence (once colonialism was a fact) among the local elites (excluding the ulama) toward Western secular education introduced by the colonial powers: on one hand they accused it of undermining indigenous culture and education; yet on the other they complained that they were not being given access to the genuine thing, but rather to a watered down version. How does one explain this ambivalence? The first argument was for the consumption of the masses (necessary to obtain their support for the anti-imperialist struggle), while the second was their perception that without access to such education they could not effectively compete with the colonial elite on its own terms. This fact allows us understand why, once independence came to these countries the indigenous elites (both the old and the new) opted for a secular Western education system and not an Islamic oriented modern education system.

8. The irony, in the case of Morocco, was that even when the ulama and students did desire some reforms the French resisted them for fear that a noncompliant elite would emerge from al-Qarawiyyin.

9. The French invasion (like the other modern European invasions) was, of course, unique in all of Maghrebi history, as has been pointed out earlier.

10. See the relevant chapters of volumes 1 through 4 of the monumental, multiauthored, 8 volume *General History of Africa* sponsored by UNESCO (1981–93) for a useable survey of the precolonial history of North Africa.

11. Many years later, Napoleon would characteristically muse about his ambitions in Egypt: "I was full of dreams. I saw myself founding a religion, marching into Asia, riding an elephant, a turban on my head, and in my hand a new Koran that I would have composed to suit my need" (Herold 1963: 5). Egypt in his mind was a staging post for an even larger goal: the conquest of India. Napoleon, however, was also at heart a practical man. In Egypt he saw the possibility of much economic wealth for France.

12. A concrete legacy of their brief stay in Egypt, besides the discovery of the famous Rosetta Stone in a village called Rashid (hence the derivation Rosetta) not too far from Alexandria, included the team's preparation of a prodigious serially published work (in Paris, 1809–28) titled *Description de l'Égypte*. (For a recent edited English extract of this work see Russell [2001], which not only has textual excerpts from it, but also includes reproductions of the impressive folios of engravings of Egyptian monuments prepared by the French team).

13. Remember, the distinction here between *Ottoman Mamluks* and the Mamluk dynasty proper rests on periodization as well as the politically transformed character of the Mamluk rule of Egypt under the Ottomans (see Chapter 2).

14. For a usable descriptive summary of the principle military encounters between Napoleonic and Ottoman Mamluk forces see Volume 1 of Russell (2001). For a more detailed examination of Napoleon's sojourn in Egypt see Herold (1963).

15. One must be extremely wary here of not giving in to the temptation of positing an orientalist spin on the source of Egypt's (or the Ottoman Empire's) relative "backwardness." To be sure, Ottoman Mamluk rule had been marked by considerable oppression of the populace, coupled with anarchy-inducing internecine struggles, but to seek an explanation for the waning fortunes of Egypt exclusively in the nature of Ottoman Mamluk rule alone is to discount the very real adversities that had now beset the rest of the entire Afro-

Eurasian ecumene (outside Europe) with the emergence of Europe's global hegemonic ambitions in the twilight years of the eighteenth-century (see Appendix II). Moreover, even with regard to the specific character of Ottoman Mamluk rule one must be cautious in condemning it completely out of hand; for what Petry (1994: 3) observes about their forbears (the original Mamluk dynasty) was applicable, albeit to a considerably lesser degree one must concede, to them too: "Yet despite their excesses, the Mamluks hardly disdained matters of state security, mass prosperity, public welfare, or spiritual piety. On occasion, they showed genuine compassion for suffering endured by even the meanest of their subjects. In the prospect of their own destitution, they sustained a rich program of cultural endowment."

16. The French invasion would also prompt the commencement in the same year of the formal colonial takeover of India by the British. Therefore, while quite often the immediate motivations for European colonialism may have been political, the underlying rationale was always long-term economic gain of the type dictated by the needs of industrial capitalism as its transmutation from mesocapitalism moved apace in Europe around the turn of the century.

17. See Marsot (1984), for a well researched biography of Ali.

18. To ensure that there would be no possibility of any future opposition to him from the old rulers, the Ottoman Mamluks, in a modus operandi that had become characteristic of political affairs in the "peace-loving" and "brotherly" House of Islam, Ali had their leaders massacred en masse when the opportune moment presented itself—at a military investiture ceremony for his son in the Cairo Citadel (in March 1811).

19. What is more, Ali never trusted the Egyptians; like the Mamluks and others before them, he, as Marsot (1984) puts it, "despised the Egyptians and looked upon them as an inferior race of dirty peasants (*pis fallah*) created to work for the benefit of their masters, the rulers" (p. 109). Marsot further notes: "To him Egypt was a piece of property he had acquired by guile and ability. The Egyptians were there to do his bidding; they could become cannon fodder, workers and fellahin, or even minor administrators, but no more. The very ethnicity of the Turks made them fit for government" (p. 131). Not surprisingly, he would concentrate all power within the hands of his family and himself. That is, as Hunter (1984) has shown, his administration was not only Turkish in terms of ethnicity and language, but he allocated key offices of responsibility to his kith and kin (they were brought over later from his hometown after he took power). The question then that has been raised by historians, states Hunter, is whether Ali was just another Mamluk ruler or the true founder of modern Egypt; the answer, Hunter replies, was that he was both.

20. In addition to the encounter with the French, he would have another opportunity to observe closely the might of the European armed forces: when his navy, together with that of the Ottomans, would be dealt a humiliating defeat by a combined naval force of the British and other European imperial powers at the Battle of Navarino (on October 20, 1827), which was forced on him for successfully squelching a Greek rebellion against the Ottomans in Morea (Peloponnisos peninsula of modern Greece)—a project he had undertaken at the behest of the Ottoman sultan—needless to say they had to abandon the reconquest and two years later all of Greece would be independent of Ottoman Turkish rule (see Fahmy 1997, regarding the battle and its effect on Ali). For more on Muhammed Ali and his autocracy see Batou (1991); Cuno (1992); Fahmy (1997); Hunter (1984); Marsot (1984); and Rivlin (1961); and for a general history of post–1798 Egypt, see Sonbol (2000) and Vatikiotis (1991). Note: it is important to read Sonbol first before any of the other

sources because she provides a corrective to the orientalist bias in some of them.

21. Even after 1922 when Britain formally ended the protectorate status of Egypt, Britain continued to dominate Egyptian affairs by interfering in its internal politics—motivated by the desire to secure its communications (the Suez Canal), commercial and security interests (in fact, British armed forces did not vacate Egypt until 1956).

22. Regarding the issue of culture, accompanying this group was also a chaplain (an imam) to take care of the group's religious needs; his name Shaykh Rifa'ah. He, as it turned out (perhaps not unexpectedly since he was a graduate of al-Azhar and therefore inured to the rigors of study), used his leisure time in France productively to return as "[t]he most successful of the batch from an Egyptian point of view," according to Heyworth-Dunne; he also makes this additional comment about him: "It was sheer accident that gave to Egypt a revivalist, a reformer and the father of modern Arabic literature" (p. 167).

23. The term *praetorian* is being used in this work loosely to denote an authoritarian polity that is led by the military and derives its legitimacy from the use of military force—military dictatorships are examples par excellence of such a polity.

24. This "new" ruling class—new only in the sense that, on one hand, the old Turkish mamluk aristocracy, together with the Egyptian notables and merchant class, took on a secularist Westernist ideological framework to legitimate their elite positions, and on the other it was joined by an emerging Western-trained Egyptian nationalist bureaucratic elite (which later would also incorporate a military elite following the overthrow of the monarchy)—came to consider, like their Western orientalist mentors and supporters, that the ills of Egypt (and the Islamic world generally) were rooted in Islam itself. Overawed by the material progress of the West, they fell into the trap of confusing secularism and Westernism with modernity. In other words, secularism and Westernism became both the readily visible mark of social structural differentiation and a source of ruling-class self-legitimacy—the latter function was captured in the following formula: secularism/Westernism = modernity = "progress" = fitness to rule in a modern world—regardless that such rule was autocratic (and hence anti-democratic) in form. For more on the genesis of the current Egyptian ruling class, aptly described by Sonbol as the "new Mamluks," see Eccel (1984), and Sonbol (2000). (Both sources, however, should be considered together.)

25. By 1858, when it was decreed that all government correspondence was to be in the Arabic language, Arabic had supplanted the Turkish language in higher educational institutions as well. The linguistic barrier between the old Ottoman Mamluk aristocracy and the emergent Egyptian administrative elite was now in tatters as the two elites began their long journey toward a marriage of convenience.

26. See below for an explanation of why coercion was often necessary.

27. To give another example, consider the problem faced by the medical school when it was first established. Let us allow Heyworth-Dunne again to describe the difficulty: "It was a most curious situation; a hundred Egyptian students from al-Azhar who knew only Arabic and who had never received any training but in Arabic grammar, *Qur'an*ic Exegesis, Fikh, etc., gathered together in order to be trained in medical and scientific subjects of which they had not the slightest idea by a number of European teachers who did not know the language of their students and who themselves were not even homogenous, Clot, Bernard, Barthelemy, Duvigneau being French, Gaetani, Spanish, Celesia, Alessandri and Figari, Italian, Ucellli, a Piedmontese and Pruner, a Bavarian" (p. 127). The solution, which of course was far from satisfactory, Heyworth-Dunne goes on to explain, was the use of a cumbersome instructional method involving interpreters. Notice also that he brings out

here the problem of recruiting qualified students in the absence of adequate secular educational facilities at the secondary/primary school levels.

28. Later, Ali did become cognizant of the problems he had created for the madrasah system and in response to which he directed the establishment of several new madrasahs in upper Egypt in 1833 (however, it appears that possibly only the poorest students attended them—to avail themselves of the rations, clothing and allowances that became the hallmark of all education institutions that were set up by Ali). Some years later still, in 1837, a department of education (Diwan al-Madaris) was created to begin the process of reorganizing the provision of secular education in Egypt, and it involved the establishment on a modest scale of three types of hierarchically related educational institutions: primary schools, preparatory schools and special schools (these were the vocational-type schools looked at above). Yet, on the other hand many of these schools (at all levels) did not survive much longer beyond Ali's reign for reasons of Khedival misrule, politics, and finances. It is only with the passage of the Law of 10th Rajab, 1284 (November 7, 1867) during the reign of the Khedive Ismail Pasha that a serious attempt was made to breathe new life into a crippled madrasah system. Under this law some of the waqfs were restored to the madrasahs to the extent possible (though the effort had begun earlier with the passage of the Land Law of 1858) and the establishment of new ones were encouraged (though there was one fundamental change in the status of waqfs, henceforth the state would play a major role in their supervision); a greater effort was made to standardize instruction in the system; part of the system was brought under government control; examinations were introduced; and so on. See Heyworth-Dunne (1939) for details.

29. It is highly doubtful, for example, that one as astute as Ali would have acceded to the kinds of terms that Sa'id Pasha accepted in the Suez Canal Concession of 1858.

30. For more on all these developments during the period under discussion see Heyworth-Dunne (1939), and Eccel (1984).

31. Cromer, it may be noted here, like many other Westerners at the time and since then, also believed that countries that had huge rates of illiteracy (as in the case of Egypt) had no business attempting to develop higher education. Obviously he was patently ignorant of the history of universities in Europe: the first ones had emerged there in the twelfth-century (see Appendix I) as islands amidst a sea of illiteracy and ignorance.

32. About the staff development recruits, Reid (1990) tells us that the institution sent out a total of twenty-four students for foreign study in the period 1908–25. Unfortunately, for the institution, it turned out to be money not well spent: only five returned with doctorates to teach at the university (and of these only three stayed on to teach for a meaningful period of time). The problem with the staff development program was the same that all foreign student missions had experienced from Muhammed Ali's days to the present (a problem that is not even unique to Egypt but appears to be universal): a high wastage rate, for a multiplicity of reasons: ranging from the financial to student indiscipline to the brain drain (where students refuse to return upon completion of their studies).

33. There was, however, one small tenuous connection, of sorts, with the United States that the university dearly wished it had not brought about: a conferment of an honorary degree on ex-President Theodore Roosevelt in March 1910; wantonly oblivious to the smoldering Egyptian nationalism, his address to the institution echoed the British position that Egyptians were not mentally or institutionally ready yet to forsake British colonial tutelage. The university and the country were livid; Roosevelt, in the typical arrogant and racist fashion characteristic of much of the history of Western relations with the rest of the

Afro-Eurasian ecumene, dismissed the Egyptian reaction with the words: "That speech of mine at Cairo was a crackery jack. You should have seen the Fuzzy Wuzzie's faces as I told them off. They expected candy, but I gave them the big stick. And they squirmed, Sir; they squirmed" (from Reid 1990: 43).

34. A year later a special women's section was opened under the leadership of a French female professor, A. Couvreur—the latter fact in itself, as Reid (1990) reminds us, represented a milestone for women's education in Egypt and elsewhere; and even from the perspective of the West, it was an important achievement because female professors there too were rare. It ought to be noted here that from the perspective of higher education in general, that is going beyond university education per se, whether secular or religious, women did have access to such education prior to 1908 (recall the training in the School of Midwifery in Ali's time, or to give another example: according to Reid [1990: 108], the establishment of the Sanieh Training College permitted, from 1900 onward, women to train as primary school teachers in the state system), but it was always either on an ad hoc or a highly limited basis. True institutionalized access to full university education commenced with the Egyptian university and thereafter continued to accelerate to the point where even al-Azhar would end up admitting female students.

35. The university opened its first student dormitory (for males) in 1949, while female students had access to university rented housing. In 1957, however, they too would have their own regular dormitory.

36. The United Presbyterian mission in Egypt (which came to be known simply as the American Mission) was already involved in the educational enterprise in Egypt; by 1899 it was operating some 171 primary/secondary-level schools with some 15,000 students. The one place where it did not have a secondary-level school however, was Cairo; consequently it made sense that some of its missionaries [such as Andrew Watson, the father of Charles R. Watson who would become the first president of AUC (1919–45]) would broach the idea for such an institution for Cairo—to be modeled on two other institutions it was operating elsewhere in the region, but outside Egypt, Robert College in Istanbul and Syrian Protest College in Beirut (would evolve to become the American University in Beirut). The two decades that would elapse before the dream expressed in 1899 became a reality spoke to the mountains that had to be moved as funding was secured and administrative and political hurdles were overcome. Among the many dramatis personae involved in this endeavor (see the account by Murphy 1987) included the indefatigable Charles Watson, who beginning in 1902 had been heading the activities of the United Presbyterian Board of Foreign Missions in India and the Middle East, the principal of the American Mission-run secondary school in Asiut in upper Egypt, Assiut College, Robert S. McClenahan; and Elise Weyerhaeuser and her husband William Bancroft Hill—as the name indicates, Elise came from the Weyerhaeuser family who owned the largest timber enterprise in the United States and this connection became a financial lifeline for the AUC project over the years. In the genesis and implementation of the project there are several markers that are worthy of mention here: (a) Although the term "university" was used from the very beginning, it initially implied a hope rather than reality in that when the AUC would first open its doors it would offer only secondary-level education. (b) Although it is the Presbyterians who must be credited with the original idea for the institution, by the time of its implementation it had become a project that attempted to involve other Protestant groups in the United States as well (albeit with limited success). (c) While the university was to be a Christian Protestant institution operated by U.S. Americans, the objective was not overt proselytiza-

tion, because of an awareness that Muslims rarely converted; instead the underlying rationale for the project was to have a Protestant Christian presence in Egypt's educational landscape that could serve as a beacon of U.S. American "secular" enlightenment for higher education students of any religion. However, very early on, at least from around 1923, the university's connections with the churches began to move toward the nominal until the institution would become what it is today, a primarily secular institution. (Without this change over the course of the institution's history, it is doubtful that it could have survived some of the more turbulent anti-foreigner, and at times anti-American, phases of modern Egyptian nationalist history.) (d) The legal basis for the university as a U.S.-domiciled institution of higher learning required a charter from a U.S. agency; the board of education of the District of Columbia was the source for the charter (on July 11, 1919). However, it would not receive accreditation until 1982 (from the prestigious Middle States Commission on Higher Education—a nongovernmental, voluntary, peer-based organization.) (e) Given the financial difficulties of the churches, the primary source of funding for the project was from inception based on private, usually religious inspired, philanthropic contributions (from people such as the Weyerhaeusers).

37. Originally, the AUC wanted to establish its campus near the Pyramids of Giza, but as a result of opposition from Egyptians and the British that idea was scuttled. Interestingly, such are the ways of history, that today, located as it is in downtown Cairo, the main AUC campus has the distinction of occupying among the most expensive real estates (7.3 acres) in the world. More recently (1997), it purchased a 260-acre property some thirty-five kilometers east of its present location in New Cairo where it intends to relocate some time in the future (as of this writing, early-2005, the new AUC campus is still in the architectural planning stage).

38. Initial enrollment during its first 1920/21 academic year was 142 students; while its first college level students—admitted in 1925/26—would number 51. Total enrollments for the institution (based on Murphy 1987) show the following progression over a fifty year period: 1920/21 academic year: 142; 1930/31: 355; 1940/41: 433; 1950/51: 689; 1960/61: 383 (by this time it was no longer offering secondary-level education); 1970/71: 1378. (Current—2005—student population is approximately 5,000.) Note: these figures do not include enrollments in its adult education programs.

39. An indication of this fact is Egyptian foreign study missions. As Reid points out, for example, that whereas the tradition of sending foreign students abroad had meant sending them to Europe (chiefly Britain by the 1940s), by the early 1960s the United States and Canada would begin to surpass European countries in this regard (p. 165).

40. Consider the revised mission statement of the AUC issued in 1958; it reflected the considerable acumen and flexibility of the AUC to adapt to changing political circumstances: "The American University at Cairo seeks to be an excellent small experimental university, coming out of the American cultural and educational tradition, stressing the liberal arts in its undergraduate program and choosing especially needed and timely areas for development of its graduate program, and working toward the end of producing educated and responsible citizens of Egypt, the Middle East, and the world at large, and encouraging by its existence, as well as by its programs, both the West (especially America) and the Middle East, a common effort to understand, appreciate and work with each other" (from Murphy 1987: 140). There was one other reason, according to Murphy, why Nasser did not nationalize the AUC as he had all other foreign educational institutions under Law No. 160: his perception that the AUC would be an avenue for maintaining cultural ties with the

United States that he did not wish to sever.

41. For more on the AUC, see Murphy 1987, which is the only source that provides a comprehensive history of the institution.

42. The U.S. government over the years would also become involved in directly providing funding for university activities, including its capital program. As with any privately-funded higher education institution, finances have always been a difficult part of the AUC's checkered history, and the saga of these difficulties is well captured by Murphy.

43. However, one would be remiss if it is not pointed out that not all Egyptians view the institution with equanimity; some Islamists view it as a subversive institution given its association with the United States on one hand and the Egyptian Westernized secular elite on the other.

44. Nasser's "Arab socialism" was one of the various "socialisms" embraced in the 1960s and the 1970s by some of those countries in the developing world that sought to steer a middle course in the global Cold War rivalries between the United States and the former Soviet Union—these countries also came to be known as the nonaligned nations. (In the African context other examples include the "socialisms" of Kwame Nkrumah's Ghana, Sekou Toure's Guinea, Julius Nyerere's Tanzania, Muammar al-Qaddhafi's Libya, and Kenneth Kaunda's Zambia). While the ignorantsia in the West took the self-proclaimed "socialist" notions by the leaders of these countries as indicative of a communist takeover, nothing could have been further from the truth. They were socialist only in name, for they remained essentially capitalist in orientation with the exception of two main differences: the nationalization of the major means of production, and the institution of centralized economic planning (and even that was usually a charade)—in other words, these "socialisms" were variants of state capitalism embedded in populist-tempered authoritarian political systems. Moreover, their hallmark included articulation and imposition of their tenets on skeptical societies by charismatic leaders such that with their passage their socialisms also went with them. It is rare, therefore, to find today any leader on the African continent propounding any kind of socialism, Arab, African, or anything else. In Egypt, Sadat's infitah was, not surprisingly, a rejection of Nasser's Arab Socialism.

45. Consider, for instance, the case of Cairo University: whereas at the time of the coup it had just under 19,000 students, within a mere two decades, by 1970, the student population had climbed to 50,000 (Reid 1990: 175–176). In 1970, to give another example, some 700 students in that single year—compare with the estimated total figure of 349 for the entire period of Muhammed Ali's rule already mentioned—were sent to study abroad in a variety of countries, both in the former Soviet bloc countries and in the West (Hyde 1978: 140).

46. The original coup took place on July 23, 1952, with General Muhammed Naguib as president and prime minister and Nasser as the deputy prime minister and minister of the interior. The use of the term "dynasty" is appropriate (even if in this case bloodline is not the unifying factor in leadership successions) given the as yet unbroken continuity of the oligarchy (see also Sonbol 2000).

47. Up until 1978, even the large contingent of foreign students, numbering in the thousands, studying in Egypt were exempt from tuition fees.

48. Regarding the elite/mass gap, while there is no doubt, as, for instance, Williamson (1987) has noted, that increased higher educational access for children of the lower classes did, initially, have considerable impact on income inequality in Egypt, it was a short-lived outcome. In fact, on the contrary, with the passage of time, there was even a reversal of this

particular intended function of higher education as remnants of the old and newer middle and upper classes moved to consolidate their position by a variety of mechanisms (private schooling, nepotism, etc.) to ensure access for their children to the best and most prestigious institutions. See for example Moore's (1994) discussion of this phenomenon with respect to engineering education in Egypt. For more on education in general and higher education in particular during the Nasserite period, besides Williamson and Moore, see also Abu Izzeddin (1981); Cochran (1986); and Hyde (1978).

49. Sonbol (2000: 124) reminds us that until the United States expressed its hostility to Nasser's regime, Nasser had defined the West as not including the United States. In other words, his hostility toward the West did not include a rejection of the United States. (Compare with the initial stances of Ho Chi Minh and Fidel Castro toward the United States, they too had seen it as a potential ally at one point in their political careers before the United States moved to disabuse them of that notion.) Clearly, the Cold War imperatives of foreign policy, in themselves artificially manufactured, had completely warped the U.S. view of the world, much in the same way as the current struggle against "terrorism" has distorted its perceptions of global realities—characterized by such infantile drivel as "they don't like freedom that is why they are engaged in terrorism" passing for intelligent analysis (thereby demonstrating the truism that brawn and brain do not always go together).

50. See Abu Izzedin (1981) for a historical survey of the Nasserite period.

51. See Hinnebusch (1988) for a historical survey of the Sadat years.

52. One change that followed on the heels of the *infitah* (but had little to do with it directly) was the coincidence of the oil price boom of the early 1970s. Its effect was to encourage the Egyptian professoriate to pour out on to the international labor market—specifically the Middle Eastern, where a rapidly escalating supply of petrodollars fueled the desire of the oil-rich countries to seek large-scale development of their infrastructures, including educational systems. The consequences of this braindrain on the Egyptian universities, as one may surmise, was far from salutary (Reid 1990). On the matter of foreign (U.S.) influences on Egyptian higher education see Cochran (1986) who, for instance, observes among its deleterious consequences the widening of the elite/mass gap brought on by U.S. aid assistance to the higher education and other sectors: "It is evident to the Egyptian people that the United States is supplying aid to Egypt, some Egyptians are getting richer and going to the States and Americans are becoming more visible in Egypt." "Moreover," she continues, "rampant corruption only further frustrates the effective use of incoming capital. Innumerable Egyptian professionals and bureaucrats have climbed aboard the USAID gravy train and are riding it for all they're worth, which, in an increasing number of cases, is quite a lot. Enjoying high disposable incomes, they of course are in search of purchases and pleasures, further discrediting themselves, their government, and American assistance in the process" (1986: 113).

53. This is not to imply by any means that Sadat was responsible for the rise of Islamism in Egypt, for it is a development that to varying degrees has swept across most of Islamic Africa (if not the Islamic world in general) in recent decades—and to that extent it is indicative of complex but related causes going well beyond Sadat's policy. In other words, even without Sadat Egypt would have still experienced this phenomenon, but perhaps not to the extent that it has had Sadat not coddled up to the Islamists (until they forced his hand, but by then it was too late).

54. About the Turkish solution: reference here is to the effort of that Westernizing secular autocratic zealot by the name of Mustafa Kemal Ataturk who, beginning in 1924 (as the

West looked on approvingly—though absolutely clueless as to what kind of Turkey the autocrat was really creating, certainly not modern and not democratic), sought to forcibly expunge Islam from Turkish society, lock, stock and barrel, leaving in its wake the secular Western praetorian Turkey of today with its ridiculous schizophrenic mask—believing that this Anatolian peninsula is a European country at the illusory level, but yet firmly Asian in terms of geographic and cultural reality. For a history of secularism in Turkey see Berkes (1964) and Macfie (1994).

55. See the account in Eccel (1984) for details of the resistance the ulama put up to the reforms imposed on al-Azhar.

56. There may be another reason why this has been the case: at the end of the day, the ulama has nearly always found it expedient to cooperate with whoever held the reigns of power in the country. In other words, the ulama has never, except on the rarest of occasions, posed a serious and credible threat to any of the rulers who have ambled through the corridors of Egyptian Islamic history. As Lazarus-Yafeh (1995: 175) has astutely observed about the ulama in general (not simply in Egypt): "[a]lmost everywhere they supported any Muslim authority uncritically, thereby safeguarding not only the continuity of the Islamic system but their own political and economic security as well."

57. A cautionary note is in order here: The effort to reform al-Azhar was ultimately motivated by instrumentalism. Whereas in the past education was merely the transmission of knowledge, skills and values from one generation to the next, with the advent of colonialism it acquired a new baggage: the task of remaking an entire society anew (Coleman 1965: 3). Consequently, education became "vocationalized" (instrumentalized). But education is more than that because it leads to the adoption of "civilized" attitudes, which, ironically, includes the principle of the acquisition of knowledge for its own sake. To the ulama who resisted reforms, the matter was not simply a refusal to change in order to protect their perceived interests; it was also a question of the fundamental mission of their enterprise highlighted by this hypothetical scenario: Suppose one knew that there would never be an opportunity to use one's literacy to make a living; would one therefore forego literacy altogether (in the absence of any other obstacle (Hawkins 2003, also discusses this issue). In Islam the pursuit of religious knowledge, as explained in Chapter 1, is in itself an aspect of piety.

58. Napoleon was stunned by the seeming ungratefulness of the population because he had tried to present himself to the Egyptians as their liberator from the oppressive Ottoman Mamluks. As his proclamation to the Egyptians had read in part: "People of Egypt, you will be told that I have come to destroy your religion. This is an obvious lie; do not believe it! Answer back to those imposters that I have come to restore to you your rights and to punish the usurpers.... Henceforth, with [God's] help, no Egyptian shall be excluded from high office, and all shall be able to reach the highest positions.... Once you had great cities, large canals, a prosperous trade. What has destroyed all this, if not greed, the iniquity, and the tyranny of the Mamluks?" (To access the entire proclamation, see Herold 1963: 69–70.) One may note here, with an eye to the present, how history has a ceaseless penchant for uncannily repeating itself: compare the goings on in Iraq today (2004) with the West thrown into the abyss of incomprehension at the seeming ingratitude of the Iraqis.

59. One should also mention here that sometimes reforms were imposed on al-Azhar because of the misdeeds of the ulama themselves that stemmed from internal conflicts over sources and amount of remuneration, leadership positions, and so on. Moreover, the historically rooted self-destructive penchant of the various factions among the ulama to turn to

external actors for support during moments of internal crisis, created further opportunities for outsiders, as they pursued heir own agendas, to foist reforms on al-Azhar. It appears that for the ulama autonomy was sacrosanct only during times of unity against a common foe.

60. Consider this: In 1872 a teacher training college called the *Dar-ul-Ulum* would be established to take care of the perpetual problem of shortages of competent Arabic language teachers. Now, even though the college was staffed by Azhari graduates and concentrated on producing language teachers (though in later years other subjects, secular, were slowly added), as Eccel (1984) reminds us, the very fact that it was felt necessary to establish a separate college for subject matter that rightfully belonged to al-Azhar, spoke volumes for the abysmal state of education at that institution.

61. Later, with the transformation of the Egyptian University into a state institution, the *Dar-ul-Ulum* would be transferred out of Al-Azhar to the new state university.

62. Since all major long-lasting changes in society occur as a result of the dialectic between the ideational and material, one ought to indicate here the key dramatis personae of the al-Azhar reform effort; they include (besides the ulama whose main role appears to have been more of reacting to, rather than initiating, change): Muhammed Abduh, 1849-1905 (a religious scholar, social reformer and ardent admirer of the West in the latter part of his life, who despite his blindness went to study at Al-Azhar [graduating from there as an alim in 1877, and where he would also later lecturer]; in time, with British help, he was elected as Egypt's mufti in 1899); Jamal ad-Din al-Afghani, 1838–97 (an Iranian anti-imperialist Sh'ite, itinerant agitator and scholar-journalist and one time mentor of Muhammed Abduh); Khedive Ismail Pasha, 1830–95 (Khedive from 1863–79); Taha Hussein, 1889–1973 (graduate of al-Azhar and the Egyptian University [Cairo University] and who also taught at the same university Arabic literature); Sa'ad Zaghlul Pasha ibn Ibrahim, 1857–1927 (a graduate of al-Azhar and the School of Law, he was the leader of the nationalist Wafd Party that helped engineer Egyptian independence in 1922; from 1906 to 1910 he was the minister of education; and Jamal Abdel Nasser 1918–70 (ruled Egypt from 1954 until his death).

63. For more on the reforms at al-Azhar and the history of Egyptian secular higher education generally see Crecelius (1968); Dodge (1961); Eccel (1984); Heyworth-Dunne (1939); Radwan (1951); Reid (1990); and Vatikiotis (1991).

64. The complete conquest of Algeria would allude them until after more than 100,000 French troops had laid waste to large parts of the country in their pursuit of the rebel guerilla forces of Abd al-Qadir ibn Muhyi al-Din (popularly known as Amir Abdel-Qadir) from 1839–47. Though even here a more vigorous adherence to historical facts would extend the period of the French conquest for another 100 years to the French takeover of the Anti-Atlas in 1934; up to that point it had had to contend with a number of other wars of resistance in the hinterland, including the celebrated Berber uprising under the leadership of Muhammed al-Muqrani that was only put down in 1871.

65. Consider, for example, the *Indigenous Code* (applicable only to Algerians—not the settlers); among its "forty-one unconscionable provisions," to quote Entelis (1986: 32), included these: Algerian Muslims were not allowed to utter anything against France and the French state; they were not allowed to move freely within the country without a permit; they could not become teachers in any educational establishment (private or state) without French authorization.

66. The slogan was fallacious because one part of it was not applicable to all Algeri-

ans: the part about Arabic since Arabic is not the language of an important minority in the country, the Kabyles (a Berber group); they have their own languages and culture. In fact, this issue has been an important bone of contention between the Arab-dominated government and the Kabyles. Note: Dien Bien Phu is a famous village in North Vietnam. During the Franco-Vietnamese War it was chosen as the site where the French colonial army (heavily infused with U.S. supplied weaponry), under the leadership of General Henri Navarre, was to break the back of the Vietnamese guerrilla army, commonly known as the Viet Minh, which was leading the Vietnamese struggle for independence from French colonial rule—reimposed with the support of the United States following the Second World War. (During the war the French had been expelled from Vietnam by the Japanese.) The French had announced this objective to the world and they assured all concerned that no rag tag army of PQD peasants would be able to resist their trained men and modern armor. As it turned out, the Viet Minh under the leadership of the brilliant military strategist, General Vo Nguyen Giap, proved to be more than an equal match for the French. The Viet Minh, on May 7, 1954, forced the final and permanent capitulation of the French in Vietnam—albeit at great cost to the Vietnamese, in terms of lives lost. Nevertheless, the victory proved to be not only a military one for the Vietnamese, but also a psychological one that reverberated positively far beyond Vietnam among other PQD peoples. It proved that PQD peasants could defeat a modern industrial power—a lesson that later would have to be taught time and again: to the Portuguese in Africa; the French (again) in Algeria; the United States in South Vietnam; and not too long ago, the Russians in Afghanistan.

67. The process of French decolonization, however, would prove to be somewhat more intractable, not only because of the almost total domination of all facets of Algerian society during more than 100 years of French colonial rule, but because the new praetorian secular bureaucratic elite that took over the reigns of power did not wish to sever all connections with France. For more on Algerian past and recent history see Abun-Nasr (1987); Bennoune (1988); Ciment (1997a); Entelis (1986); Gosnell (2002); Naylor (2000); the pseudonymous Martinez (2000); Roberts (2003); and Ruedy (1992). Note: for balance it is important that if Naylor and Martinez are consulted, then Roberts should be read as well.

68. About the weakening of the madrasah system: the damage the French inflicted on it was such that even a zealous proponent (and contemporary observer) of the French imperialist project like Alexis de Tocqueville (of the *Democracy in America* fame), following his trip to Algiers in 1841, was moved to lament: "Muslim society in Africa was not uncivilized; it was merely a backward and imperfect civilization [sic]. There existed within it a large number of pious foundations, whose object was to provide for the needs of charity or for public instruction. We laid our hands on these revenues everywhere, partly diverting them from their former uses; we reduced the charitable establishments and let the schools decay [kuttabs], we disbanded the seminaries [madrasahs]. Around us knowledge has been extinguished, and recruitment of men of religion and men of law has ceased; that is to say we have made Muslim society much more miserable, more disordered, more ignorant, and more barbarous than it had been before knowing us" (from his writings on empire and slavery [Tocqueville 2001: 140–41]). It may also be noted here that the legendary penchant of the French for the separation of church and state appears to have had minimal impact on their desire, for obvious reasons, to fully dominate the madrasah system to the point where they even helped fund mosques and pay the stipends of the ulama in charge of them.

69. In 1954 the total number of Algerians receiving secular higher education throughout the country was a paltry 685, however, eight years later at independence in 1962 it had

climbed to 3,000, and thereafter the growth was simply exponential: within about two decades, by 1984, the total number had exploded to reach 107,000! (Tibawi 1972: 168; Entelis 1986: 91)

70. In 1967 the university had a total enrollment of some 10,000 students of whom a majority (80%) were Algerians (and of these 20% were women). (Tibawi 1972: 170).

71. Ibn Badis (Ben Badis—in Gallicized Arabic "Ibn" is usually spelled "Ben") was the scion of a prominent Muslim Berber family (who ironically had good cooperative relations with the French), and interestingly, was a graduate of al-Zaitouna and al-Azhar. For more on him see Alghailani (2002), whose work shows how this particular section of the Algerian ulama represented by Ibn Badis and his colleagues and the Association they helped found played a critical role in the evolution of Algerian nationalist struggle for independence. (Needless to say, by the time Ibn Badis arrived on the scene, much of the rest of the Algerian ulama had been either cowed or co-opted by the French.)

72. While this is not the place to delve into a detailed account of the course of events that led the military junta to plunge Algeria into an abyss of remorseless and widespread violence and terror that would consume tens of thousands of lives of innocent children, women and men and out of which it is just beginning to emerge, it will suffice to note this much: As the praetorian, FLN (*Front de Liberation Nationale*) dominated, nationalist elite proceeded over the course of some three decades following independence to constitute itself into a secular, and ironically, a Francophile oligarchy (socialist in rhetoric but pragmatic in practice), it produced along the way a deep economic, political, and cultural alienation in the rest of the population as the elite-mass gap widened, from almost all perspectives, to a chasm. With the collapse of oil prices in the mid–1980s (over 90% of Algeria's foreign-exchange earnings, which pays for almost everything Algerians consume, including food, come from the sale of oil and gas) this alienation reached boiling point as the country experienced unprecedented turbulent mass agitation during the month of October 1988, forcing the oligarchy to loosen its political stranglehold on the country while it simultaneously continued with the highly unpopular (understandably) program of structural adjustment that the West—by manipulating the instruments of international credit—was forcing it to implement. Consequently, it moved to permit for the first time the formation of other political parties and the holding of general elections with the hope that the carrot of a modicum of democracy would obviate the need for the stick of even greater repression of an economically beleaguered populace. At the same time, this strategy was welcomed and encouraged by France—the Western country with the closest connections with Algeria— not so much for reasons of the new dawn of "democracy" in Algeria (after all democracy and human rights have never been among the top items on the agenda of Western relations with the nations of the Afro-Asian and the Caribbean-Latin American ecumene at any time in the history of these relations, notwithstanding the current pious rhetoric of Western politicians), but because it held out the promise of the marginalization of their old nemesis against whom they had fought bitterly during the Algerian revolutionary war of independence and who they have never forgiven for the loss of "our *l'Algerie francaise*" (French Algeria) and who, in the postindependence period, to add insult to injury, had, through their pursuit of the objectives of "socialism" (namely state capitalism), long placed obstacles in the path of the French in their quest to dominate the strategic and lucrative Algerian petroleum sector. The first elections held were municipal and regional elections which took place in 1990, and a year later came the first round of elections for a parliament that was to be entrusted with the task of authoring a new constitution for Algeria. However, to the hor-

ror of the praetorian oligarchs (most especially the military wing and their Western allies), the municipal as well as the parliamentary elections were won by an unlikely alliance of mass-based groups with Islamist leanings, the FIS (Front Islamique du Salut—Islamic Salvation Front), and it appeared to most that the scheduled second round of parliamentary elections (for January 1992) would also be won by the FIS, but most certainly not by the FLN, hitherto the sole political party in Algeria.

Clearly, decades of indulgence in a potent combination (for an Islamic country) of ostentatious materialist, secularist and Westernist excesses by the praetorian oligarchy, coupled with its penchant for severe political repression and flagrantly rampant corruption against a backdrop of widespread nationwide economic disarray replete with mass poverty and unemployment, had finally come home to roost (see, for instance, Tessler 1997). However, rather than speaking to these specific causal factors explaining the rise of the Islamist tendency in Algeria (Islamism proper has been the preserve of a very small minority), the military wing of the praetorian oligarchy—aided and abetted by the West, principally France—characteristically, and spurred on no doubt by exaggerated apocalyptic visions of a Maghrebi version of post–Shah Iran, nullified the first round of parliamentary elections of December 1991, cancelled the second round and instituted a military coup on January 11, 1992. They (and their French allies) could not, however, have foreseen the result of this patently retrogressive action; it would precipitate violent opposition which in turn would elicit nothing less than cataclysmic blood-soaked military repression—as savage in its brutality as that which characterized French repression during the war of independence itself (complete with state-sponsored El Salvadoran-type right-wing death squads engaging in unspeakable barbarity; even the GIA [Armed Islamic Group] to which some of the atrocities have been credited appears to be in the pockets of the Algerian security apparatus). Baldly stated thus, this foray into the provenance of the Algerian blood-soaked political nightmare necessitates several further observations: First, in apportioning blame for the horrendous atrocities, assassinations, etc., the most important question (as in the case of so many other similar circumstances all over the world; vide: the Palestinian conflict, the Chechnyan conflict, the current so-called "war on terror") is not who is responsible for specific acts of violence and barbarity, but rather, who is responsible for creating the conditions that have led to, what is always the case, a pattern of such acts in the first place. For without raising the latter question, the former question not only becomes one of simple criminal wrong-doing requiring the attention of the security apparatus, but closes off any possibility of coming up with solutions (requiring political attention) to prevent the recurrence of such acts. In the Algerian case, the answer to the latter question is self-evident to any one who has studied the Algerian blood-soaked nightmare with some diligence. Second, in circumstances where analysis of seemingly inexplicable events leaves one hopelessly nonplussed, the doorway to enlightenment is sometimes to be found in a more nuanced analysis, such as sub macro-level explorations of the key actors. In this particular instance this certainly is the most fruitful approach. Hence, any proper understanding of the recent blood-soaked Algerian history and the role of the military in shaping it necessitates one to go beyond considering the military wing of the Algerian praetorian oligarchy as a monolithic entity. The fact is that it comprises factions and the faction that is of interest here is the one that has been ominously (for the Algerian masses) on the ascendance in recent years—in a sense signifying a creeping coup within the broader 1992 military coup—the watershed year being 1988 when highly consequential changes began taking place in the military high command and continuing until 2000 (Roberts 2003). This faction consists primarily of France's old allies from the days of the Algerian war of liberation; namely, those Algerian collaborators (or to be blunt, traitors), who had served under the French, but who, after seeing the writing on the wall on the eve of Algerian independence, had quickly switched sides to become Algerian *pseudonationalists*. It is in the main these ex-French Army officers (who had learned their *dirty war* tricks from the French), more than any one else within the Algerian military wing, who were behind the dirty war campaign—with its massive stomach churning and mind-numbing human rights abuses (the barbaric torture of suspects, the massacres of civilians, the use of napalm, the false propaganda, etc., etc.) and which has left those in the outside world unfamiliar with the nuances of recent Algerian history hopelessly at sea in finding reasonable explanations for this particular turn of events in a country that had once held out, for many in Algeria and in the rest of the Third World, so much promise upon the conclusion of the war of liberation; other than falling back on hoary essentialist (meaning in this case Orientalist) explanations a la Oriental despotism. Third, the role of the French (and by proxy the West) in aiding and abetting the violent Algerian nightmare—albeit inadvertently it must be stressed emphatically, to repeat: inadvertently—demands elaboration; taking the lead from Roberts 2003: it is not that they had wished Algeria to descend into the hellhole of nightmarish violence and bloodshed (after all such conditions can hardly be conducive to any form of advantageous relations, economic or political, for any country; unless the objective is outright looting of resources—as has been the case in some other countries in Africa, such as the Democratic Republic of the Congo, Liberia, and Sierra Leone), but rather, in quietly championing the demise of the traditional nationalist populist state capitalism—which the FLN nationalists had long pursued (under Ahmed Ben Bella and Houari Boumediene regimes)—through coercive encouragement of the adoption of structural adjustment policies so as to permit French capital to resubordinate the Algerian petroleum dominated economy, they discovered their natural allies in this endeavor, at this particular juncture of Algerian history, to be the ex-French Army officers—hence those with Islamist tendencies had to be vanquished (especially when one adds Western stereotypes of Islamists to the equation), together with the FLN. At the practical policy-level the role of the French in the Algerian nightmare is summarized thusly by Roberts (2003: 338): "The withholding of assistance from Boudiaf, the opposition to Abdesselam's strategy, the reckless insistence on rescheduling, the failure to support Zeroual's dialogue in 1994, the sly manipulation of the Rome Platform, the negative reaction to Zeroual's election in 1995, the refusal to support the UN's mission to observe the June 1997 elections, the calculated patronizing of Algiers since 1998; the list is long and could be lengthened" (see Roberts to make sense of these individual acts and their consequences). Fourth, from the perspective of the masses not all oppressors are the same. For all the tyranny of the FLN dominated praetorian oligarchy of yesteryear, the current military junta that forms the dominant part of the Algerian praetorian oligarchy is infinitely worse. Sadly, one cannot rule out more violent conflict in years to come for it lacks legitimacy on five counts: they have not achieved their power through the ballot box; they were not the architects of Algeria's independence, as the true FLN elite are; as secularists they are virulently anti-Muslims (not just anti-Islamists); they are unpatriotic in their economic policies as they systematically, under the structural adjustment regime, abandon state capitalism (it is worth remembering that for all its faults, from the perspective of the masses, it has at least two positive features: a built-in bias toward national economic sovereignty, and state-sponsored welfare patronage); and they are developing a close alliance with the West, especially the United States (In a nutshell: they are not in the least bit the custodians of Algerian national sovereignty without which there can be, in reality, no coherent Algerian state.) Fifth, the holding of recent legislative (2002) and presidential elections (2004), coupled with the fact that they have been on the whole unmarred by violence, does not necessarily speak to the emergence of democracy in Algeria; for, so long as the military junta continues to remain the actual power behind the throne—even in the mechanics of the election process itself (proscribing parties, banning candidates, encouraging ballot-tempering, etc.)—Algerian democracy will remain a sham. The French (and by proxy other Western governments) in placing their stamp of approval on them are of course not in the least bit bothered by this "minor" fact. The French drive to convert Algeria into yet another Western client-state in Afro-Arab Islamic Africa (compare Egypt) will brook no nonsense from those who insist on the "genuine thing." At the same time, the propaganda moves by the Algerian military junta to take advantage of the September 11, 2001, terrorist attacks on the United States by positing opposition to its brutal repression as solely an expression of Islamist terrorism has paid of dividends; the United States has firmly aligned itself behind the junta. (September 11, 2001, proved a godsend to a variety of dictatorships all across the planet seeking to entrench their rule as they lined up to be blessed as allies in the so-called "war on terror," by the United States. This development in turn, has been a godsend for Western capital in its relentless effort to expand its domination of the planet (supported by most current dictatorships—the lone holdouts, perhaps, being those of Cuba and north Korea). Under these circumstances, the global future promises to be even more turbulent.) For sources on this postindependence nightmare inflicted on Algeria by the pseudonationalist military faction over the course of the past thirteen to fourteen years, see Ciment (1997a); Human Rights Watch (2003); Naylor (2000); the pseudonymous Martinez (2000); and Roberts (2003). (Note: among these sources Roberts is mandatory for his analysis appears to be the most cogent).

73. About the presence of the Hospitallers: Tripoli had been conquered some years earlier, in 1510, by Christian Spain during the reign of Ferdinand the Catholic; the city (together with Malta) was bestowed on the Hospitallers by Charles V—King of Spain and Holy Roman emperor.

74. The Turks were forced to give up Libya mainly because of their military defeat elsewhere: in the Balkans (at the hands of a Russian sponsored alliance of Turkey's rebellious Eastern European provinces, known as the Balkan League).

75. Al-Mukhtar was the head of the Sanussiya, a Sufi missionary brotherhood which was founded by an Algerian Sufi, Sidi Muhammed ibn Ali-as-Sannusi, in Yemen in 1837 as a puritanical revivalist movement that, like other Sufi orders, sought to purge Islam from what it saw as accretions of heretical innovations (bidaa). The Sannusi would establish their first religious complex (zawiyah) in Cyrenaica in 1843 and from there they would soon come to dominate much of the Libyan countryside, eventually coming to play the role of, to exaggerate slightly, a state within a state until their defeat by the Italians in 1930. One may also point out here that it is the Sanussi who would bring forth the first constitutional monarch of an independent Libya.

76. Recall that the one other country vying for this distinction, Egypt, did not gain its "real" independence until after the Nasserite coup that finally terminated the behind-the-throne British presence in the country (plus, in any case, some may semantically argue, Egypt was never a formal colony of any European power).

77. In other words, it is quite unlikely that independence would have come to Libya so soon and so easily, one can safely conjecture, had the petroleum discoveries occurred be-

fore 1951 (regardless of U.S. diplomatic pressures or any wartime promises made by the British to the Sanussiya).

78. In 1963 Libya would become a unitary state when the three autonomous provinces of Cyrenaica, Tripolitania and Fezzan would be merged by royal decree on April 27.

79. The latest manifestation of his mercurialism is his decision to cozy up to the West despite decades of being in the cross hairs of Western assassination attempts and being branded variously as "mad dog of the Middle East," "the most dangerous man in the world," etc., by the United States for waging a proxy war against the West, principally Britain and the United States. Consider this: the beneficiaries of the Libyan petroleum largesse, as part of its proxy war, would range from the Irish Republican Army to the Palestinians, from rebels in Chad to the Black Panthers in the United States, and from Uganda's brutal dictator Idi Amin to the Iranians. To the majority of the population in the West, however, his name would become synonymous with PanAm Flight 103: a dastardly in flight destruction on December 21, 1988, of a Pan American Boeing 747 passenger plane by means of an explosive device over Lockerbie, Scotland, in which all those aboard (259) perished (as well as eleven on the ground killed by falling debris) and which some have thought was a response, at the behest of the Iranians, to an equally horrendous event: the shooting down of an Iranian Air-Bus on July 3, 1988, by the U.S. guided-missile ship, the U.S.S. Vincennes (supposedly by mistake, but whose commanders never the less would later be awarded medals of honor by the U.S. Congress) where all 290 passengers and crew aboard died. For more on Qaddhafi's personal imprint on Libya and Libyan foreign policy see Bearman (1986) and Vanderwalle (1995).

80. Considering that Qaddhafi has played such a dominant role in shaping the course of post–1969 Libya, including needless to say, its educational development, it is necessary to consider for a moment his most cherished publication in which he lays out his ideas of how a society should be governed and the path it should pursue. To begin with the perspective from which the book is written can be accessed by considering such comments by Qaddhafi as these two:

The great rich nations spend large sums of money to invent bombs and to create new nuclear weapons, and to nourish the projects of space invasion. Also these nations pay large sums of money on false advertisement and propaganda, and spend on projects of psychological warfare; instead of helping the people and other nations of the world who are suffering from diseases, hunger, malnutrition, and the crazy rise of prices. Such careless nations are no doubt led by the devil itself. They follow the Theory of Malthus and not the message of the Bible.

By the grace of God we have left communism far behind us. We are much more progressive than communism, which in our opinion transformed itself into a reactionary system. The works of Lenin, Marx and Engels, are meaningless now; history has passed them by.

So what then can one honestly say (without giving in to the sport of either Qaddhafi-bashing or its opposite), about Qaddhafi's much-maligned and derided (especially in the West) *Green Book* which he has published in three parts: (1) *The Solution of the Problem of Democracy: "The Authority of the People"*; (2) *The Solution of the Economic Problem*; and (3) *"Socialism": The Social Basis of the Third Universal Theory*. Upon reading this publication (the text of which is available at various sites, such as www.mathaba.net, on the Internet) there are three points that immediately come to the fore: First, there is considerable justification for the derision that most intellectuals in the West and elsewhere have exhibited toward the publication; for it is nothing more than an inchoate simplistic mishmash of a dab of this and a dab of that from what appears to be the author's under-standing of a number of sources: the Western capitalist democratic tradition, Marxism, Is-lam, anarchism and possibly his own nomadic Berber tradition. Second, that one is forced to take this publication seriously only because its author has the dictatorial powers to im-pose (or at least he has tried to impose) some if not all the ideas propounded in the book on a country of some strategic importance to the West (and therefore by implication the rest of the world). Third, that perhaps the best that can be said about the *Green Book* regards not so much its content, but what it tells us about the author: that for a man of such humble economic and educational background, and even more importantly when compared with the preoccupations of other dictators on the continent and elsewhere (essentially, self-aggrandizement), it demonstrates a praiseworthy effort at grappling with the most difficult issues of modern societies, ranging from governance to matters of existence. Of course, the most damning aspect of the *Green Book* is that it is authored by someone who thinks he has all the answers (and in fact within the confines of his own country has the necessary powers of a dictator to act like he does) and therefore no one should dare question it, ex-cept on the pain of imprisonment, torture and even death (as some Libyans have discov-ered).

What about education? Does the *Green Book* have anything to say directly about edu-cation? Part three does, it has a section titled "Education". Here is a small sample of his thoughts on the subject:

Education, or learning, is not necessarily that routinized curriculum and those classified subjects in textbooks which youths are forced to learn during specified hours while sitting in rows of desks. This type of education now prevailing all over the world is directed against human freedom. State-controlled education, which governments boast of whenever they are able to force it on their youths, is a method of suppressing freedom.

This does not mean that schools are to be closed and that people should turn their backs on education, as it may seem to superficial readers. On the contrary, it means that society should pro-vide all types of education, giving people the chance to choose freely any subjects they wish to learn.

Ignorance will come to an end when everything is presented as it actually is and when knowl-edge about everything is available to each person in the manner that suits him or her.

That the book is a collection of little more than inchoate ramblings is not difficult to conclude.

81. For more on education in Libya see Elbadri (1984); Monastiri (1995); and Teferra and Altbach (2003).

82. In reality, the Moroccans were maneuvered by the Spanish into armed conflict (by means of unreasonable demands for territory and money as compensation for real and imagined injuries of centuries past) because the new Spanish government of Leopoldo O'Donnell needed a war to distract the populace from the political chaos that had engulfed Spain by 1858, and in the words of Pennel (2000: 64–65), "the only enemy that the Span-ish Army could conceivably beat was Morocco." Even though the Spanish Army proved to be more incompetent than usual, the Moroccans were even more so.

83. The founder of the Alawi dynasty was Mawlay ar-Rashid, whose occupation of Fez in 1666 gave birth to the dynasty. It is under his iron rule that much of Morocco was brought together under one titular roof—the disparate warring tribes were no match for his forces. (He ruled until his death in 1672.)

84. Notwithstanding the much-vaunted Arab/Islamic nationalism of North Africa, Spain continues to rule the port of Ceuta (together with Melilla, Alhucemas, Chafarinas Islands, and Penon de Valez de la Gomera); constituting part of its five-link chain of Spanish North African enclaves which by rights belong to Morocco. Originally, it had been conquered by the Portuguese in 1415; however a little over a 100 years later, in 1580, the Spanish took it over—though Spanish suzerainty over the port was formally confirmed by the Portuguese only after another 100 years had gone by, with the 1688 Treaty of Lisbon. Morocco's periodic efforts to gain control of the port (the latest being the 1859/1860 effort) came too late as just indicated. What is more, to add insult to injury: Morocco had to cede even more territory (enabling Ceuta to enlarge its borders) and pay onerous compensation to the Spanish following the 1859/1860 debacle—the latter injury that the Moroccans found difficult to handle was among the factors that helped to propel Morocco into the arms of the French. That the Spanish continue to occupy Moroccan soil is an affront that the autocratic Monarchy considers well worth the economic aid and other benefits it derives from Spain (though what some sections of the masses, especially the Islamists, think abut the issue is another matter). From the perspective of higher education, this semi autonomous city-state, like Melilla too, possesses a number of institutions (e.g., a teacher-training college, a school of nursing) that are affiliated with a Spanish university, the University of Granada.

85. The quotation marks around madrasah is to draw attention to what was already indicated in Chapter 1: that in the Maghreb the term had a different meaning: it referred to the dormitories of the students attending a mosque-college, not the mosque-college itself; however, this applied only to the urban areas, in the rural areas the original meaning was retained.

86. In fact their insistence on "tradition" went so far as to also include the forced preservation in amber (so to speak) of even the physical space and amenities; In other words, they even resisted things like electric lighting, the use of blackboards, modernization of toilets, and so on.

87. Lyautey's insistence on tradition (which Rabinow explains was not a result of reaction on the part of Lyautey, but conservatism) had a dual pronged objective: First, was to save Morocco from the predations of the colons for whom he had little sympathy: in his words: "[d]epraved and blind to the true meaning of the Protectorate, to the legitimate rights of the natives, the colonists claim for themselves all the rights of Frenchmen, behaving as conquerors in a conquered land, disdaining the laws and institutions of a people which exists, owns, keeps accounts, which wants to live and which does not intend to let itself be despoiled or enslaved" (from Rabinow 1989: 285). The second was to harness the existing traditional social structure for his vision of the colonial mission in Morocco (which Rabinow describes as the introduction of *technical modernity*—in contrast to modernity in general which includes *social modernity*); again, to quote Lyautey: "Vex not tradition, leave custom be. Never forget that in every society there is a class to be governed, and a natural-born ruling class upon whom all depends. Link their interests to ours" (from Rabinow 1985: 285).

88. For sources on Sudan in antiquity see Adams (1977), Arkell (1973), Crawford (1951), Edwards (2004), Hassan (1967), Holt (1975), and Shinnie (1967, 1978).

89. One ought to mention here that the response of the international community to the massive suffering unleashed by the Sudanese government on portions of its population over the past decades, and which continues in Darfur, has been, to all intents and

purposes, one of relative shameful neglect—How else can one explain its magnitude and longevity? For sources on terror and war in Sudan, as well as general political developments in that country in the postindependence era, see: Amnesty International (2004a, 2004b), Anderson (1999), Beswick (2004), Burr and Collins (2003), Evans (2002), Garang and Khalid (1987), Glazer (2004), Harir, Tvedt, and Badal (1994), International Crisis Group (2002), Jok (2001), Khalid (2003), Layish and Warburg (2002), Lefkow (2004), Lesch (1998), Niblock (1987), Oduho and Deng (1963), Patterson (2003), Scott (1985, 2000), Sidahmed (1996), Warburg (2003), Woodward (1990). See also the news archives on Sudan available at the www.BBC.com website. Another useful source is the historical dictionary on Sudan by Loban, Kramer, and Fluehr-Lobban (2002).

90. The following sources, considered together, provide an adequate entry point into this topic: Bell (1988, 1990), Omi and Winant (1994), Orfield and Eaton (1996), and Rothenberg (2005).

91. The following sources, taken together, provide an ample survey of the arrival of British colonial rule in Sudan, as well as its origins and aftermath: Abdel-Rahim (1969), Bates (1984), Collins (1983), Daly (1991, 2002), Lewis (1987), Nicoll (2004), Powell (2003), Sanderson and Sanderson (1981), and Sharkey (2003). For a brief overview of the history of Sudan beginning in the seventh century up to the present, only Holt and Daly (2000) will do.

92 For sources on higher education in Sudan see Beshir (1969), Carr-Saunders (1961), El Gizouli (1999), El-Tayeb (1971), El Tom (2003), Kitchen (1962), Lobban, Kramer and Fluehr-Lobban (2002), Maxwell (1980), Sanderson and Sanderson (1981), and Sharkey (2003).

93. The 1878 Congress of Berlin was in a sense equivalent to the infamous 1885 Berlin West Africa Conference that finalized the European dismemberment of the African continent, except it applied to Europe in relation to the domains of the Ottoman Empire.

94. A word of caution: autocracy in present-day Islamic Africa may tempt one into believing that it is a feature intrinsic to the religion of Islam; however, even a cursory glance at the rest of Africa should help put to rest such a notion.

95. Ahmed Bey (Ahmed ibn Mustafa—*bey* is the shortened version of the Turkish word for governor *beylerbey*), who ruled from 1837 to 1855, was the tenth ruler in the Husaynid dynasty (reigned from 1705 to 1957 and started by an Ottoman Mamluk, al-Husayn ibn Ali); he was involved in a number of reform efforts aimed at modernizing Tunisia. Khayr ad-Din, also a zealous reformer, was prime minister from 1873 to 1877.

96. See Green (1978) and Hawkins (2003) on the specifics of the reforms and their fate at the hands of the al-Zaitouna ulama.

97. Green (1978: 214–20) has a fairly lengthy discussion of the 1910 student strike at al-Zaitouna (aided and abetted by secularist Tunisians, including students from Sadiki College) which, in essence, arose out of student grievances regarding some of the very matters that the 1898 reform effort had tried to address, but was also a reflection, he suggests, of a class division between the children of the urban elite and those of rural (and therefore less well-off) backgrounds—the strike had been dominated by the latter group. (Needless to say, the strike also enlarged the wedge between the ulama and the secularists to the detriment of the former in a future postindependent Tunisia. In other words, the characteristic anticolonial alliance between the ulama and the nationalists that emerged in Algeria and Morocco, Green states, did not materialize in Tunisia.)

98. See Green (1978), for more on the French education policies in Tunisia.

99. On the face of it, to a Westerner, this may have appeared to be a laudable goal: traditional Islamic education would be preserved and even expanded; but in reality it represented an approach that was quintessentially representative of Orientalism: the Westerner would define what constituted tradition and would supervise its evolution (yet always against a backdrop of an understanding that however much respect an Eastern culture deserved, it was still inferior to Western culture).

100. Concerning the French attitude toward the madrasah system in general and al-Zaitouna specifically, one may note this irony of history: their conciliatory approach helped to make al-Zaitouna an important refuge for scholars and students from Algeria escaping from the depredations inflicted on the madrasahs of Algeria by the very same people, the French.

101. Almost all the early leaders of the Neo-Destour, states Hawkins (2003), were graduates of Sadiki College.

102. It ought to be pointed out here that unlike countries such as Algeria, Egypt, and Morocco, independent Tunisia has never felt uncomfortable with French in their educational system; In other words, Arabization of the educational system has never been their goal, stated or otherwise. In fact given the obsession of the Tunisians with everything French, it is almost as if French neocolonialism has been a badge of honor for the Tunisians. (As Tunisia's historians never tire to point out: the first wife of the Tunisian dictator Habib Borguiba was a white French woman.)

103. This particular configuration where there was an interpenetration of the new and old modes of production, but yet each retaining some level of autonomy (even within a context of domination by one of the other) sufficient to guarantee identifiability of each, is sometimes referred to as the *articulation of modes of production*. Note, mode of production is being used here to mean not simply the mechanics of the means of production, but also the social relations of production (the relations of power that exist between producers and the nonproducers in terms of control of the means of production).

104. The concept of *Islamism* requires definition at this point. To begin with it is important to stress that, as Roberts (2003) reminds us, Islamism should not be conflated with so-called "Islamic fundamentalism." In fact the latter does not really exist because all Muslims who practice their religion are in a sense "fundamentalists." Why? Because the Qur'an is unlike the Bible (hence the fallacy of the analogy between Christian fundamentalism and so-called Islamic fundamentalism) in that the Qur'an is primarily a constitutional document prescriptive in intent—whereas in contrast the Bible is essentially a historical document. In other words, to be a fundamentalist in Islam is to adhere to the true tenets of Islam, it does not imply a form of "anti-scientific eccentricity appropriate to fundamentalist Christianity," as Roberts puts it (p. 4), where the objective of the Christian fundamentalist is essentially the advocacy of the literal truth of creationism as it appears in the Book of Genesis. So, what then is Islamism? It refers to the belief among some sections of Muslims that it is possible and necessary to dissolve the division between church and state (or more correctly between mosque and state) that currently exists almost throughout the Islamic world—with the exception of one or two instances (such as Iran). While in theory that may be so, in practice it has amounted to merely a call to replace the current secular authoritarianism of the praetorian oligarchies that dominate (what are virtually) police states that make up a large part of the Islamic world with an equally virulent brutal authoritarianism of a theocracy with a matching horrendous anti-Islamic human rights record

(vide the experiences of Islamist rule in Afghanistan, Iran and perhaps one may also add to the list, Sudan). The problem is not just a question of good intentions gone awry, but a fundamental theoretical weakness emanating from the refusal by the ulama to grapple with what Islam has to say on such critical questions as representative government, human rights, checks and balances, social inequality, economic exploitation, the nation-state, the modern world economy, science and technology, and so on—not in terms of airy-fairy nostalgic references to the caliphates of the past (capped with the usual escapist lines like "God knows best" or "God will take care of it"), but in terms of real, practical, day to day program of action. No Islamist has yet come up with a single example of what a concretely viable Islamic constitution, one that can be implemented in the modern world of today, would look like. The problem is highlighted by Lazarus-Yafeh (1995: 175) when he accurately observes about the ulama "It is a puzzling historical fact that although Islam produced some of the greatest empires the world has ever known, the ulama eschewed for centuries the issues of the political and constitutional structure of the state and preferred, much like the sages of the small, dispersed Jewish people, to deal in great detail with such problems of the divine law as prayers and fasting or purity and impurity." There are two related conjectural explanations one may hazard to offer here for this circumstance: One, is that in Islam a political tradition arose where the executive and the legislative branches of government were considered to be subordinate—at least nominally if not always in practice—to the judiciary (since the latter drew its legitimacy from the scriptures). Yet, as we all know, in the context of the complexity of the modern world of today the judiciary, by itself, lacks the wherewithal to be able to fully confront the complex daily tasks of modern governance. Two, is that in its early caliphal history, Islam was perceived to have been ruled by God-fearing and just rulers (even if autocratic) who obeyed Islamic law, the effect of which was to obviate the thorny task of grappling with the issue of devising a political system with the potential to neutralize an unjust and oppressive ruler should one emerge in the future (that is a democratic political system). At the same time, there arose a tradition of almost blind obedience to those in charge of the state. In other words, on the issue of political authority, while Islamic doctrine evolved to include injunctions for obeying authority, it had little to say in practical terms on what to do if that authority was unjust or non-Islamic because the issue of democracy simply did not enter the equation, especially in a context where Islam did not recognize the separation of church and state. However, even when in later times it became absolutely necessary to confront these thorny issues, especially following the arrival of Western imperialism, the ulama were still found wanting. The reason this time was a peculiar dialectic that had emerged where the traditional refusal by the ulama to accord importance to *awail* (the foreign sciences) in the curricula of madrasahs as they insisted on hewing to the traditional categories of mnemonic knowledge as a response, ironically, to the increasing irrelevance of Islam in matters of a modern economy and state in a post–1492 Western-dominated global arena, in turn, continued and continues to reinforce this irrelevance. The frustration presented by this dialectic has surfaced among some—repeat, *some*—sections of Islamists in the form of terrorism (which is tragically ironic given that, supposedly, an important element of Islamism, by definition, is self-righteousness and piety, and Islamic piety—unlike Christian piety of the Crusader era—does not brook terrorism, however the terrorism may be defined.) The political failure of Islamism in the context of a modern world stems from the fact that it has emerged as a political enterprise of an essentially flag-waving anarchic identity politics bereft of concrete Islamic proposals to address the very problems that are at the root of the rise of Islamism (and this failure one must stress is not because Islam is wholly incapable of supplying these proposals, but for lack of intelligent philosophic analysis of how Islam can provide the answers to the problems of governance in a modern world). Perhaps, Moore (1994) comes closest to the mark when he defines Islamism as "a political ideology akin to nationalism and should be viewed primarily as an abstract assertion of collective identity. Like nationalism, it may harbor a variety of contents or purposes. Consequently it may take many forms, depending on the social and political contexts in which it is expressed. Like nationalism in a colonial situation, however, it becomes a vehicle for collective action when alternative channels are suppressed or lose their legitimacy" (Moore 1994: 213). For a discussion of Islamism, especially with reference to Afro-Arab Islamic Africa, see the following: Beinin and Stork (1997), Ciment (1997a), Entelis (1997), Naylor (2000), Sonbol (2000), and Wickham (2002).

105. On the other hand, Jerusalem is extremely important to the Jews as well, it is their holiest city—something that the Jordanians conveniently overlooked when they were in charge of East Jerusalem from 1948 to 1967, preventing Jews (in complete violation of Islamic law) from visiting the most sacred of their holy shrines, *Ha-kotel Ha-ma'aravi*, or the Western Wall, or sometimes referred to by others as the "Wailing Wall". Two wrongs do not make a right, however: the present Israeli refusal to recognize that for Muslims too (and to some extent the Christians as well) the city is of great religious significance, second in importance to Mecca itself, has been one of the gigantic flies in the ointment bedeviling the effort to peacefully resolve the Israeli/Palestinian conflict. In other words: until the Israelis and their Western allies recognize the fact that Jerusalem (at least the part that hosts Qubbat as-Sakhrah [Dome of the Rock] and the al-Aqsa Mosque) is not for the Palestinians to bargain over as if it is their exclusive patrimony, the resolution of the conflict—and all that it entails for global peace—is that much further away. Yet the tragedy is that the resolution of this particular part of the conflict does not require the assistance of a rocket scientist: Jerusalem can easily be governed by a triumvirate of representatives of the three religions guaranteeing equal access to the three faiths to their holy shrines without any hindrance; but the Israelis (whose numbers total no more than a mere 6.5 million), no doubt emboldened by the carte blanche support of the United States for whatever policies that have taken their fancy in recent decades vis-à-vis the Palestinians—especially against the backdrop of a weak, demoralized and an ineffectual Islamic world—have yet to consider this option. The outcome of this state of affairs is that we must all pay the price: be potential victims of, seemingly mindless, "Islamic" terror. To credit such terrorism to radical imams in madrasahs is to miss the point by a mile!

106. In other words: It would be wrong to think that the roots of Islamism lie entirely in the political economic realm, there are also cultural and social factors involved too. For some segments of the Muslim intelligentsia their affinity with Islamism is a result of their frustration with what they perceive as the humiliation of a civilization that was once the better of the present Western civilization; emblematic for them is the oppression of Muslims (aided and abetted by the West) in as far-flung places as Bosnia, Iraq, Kosovo, Chechnya, China, and Palestine. For the masses, in addition to their economic woes, the appeal of Islamism includes not only the matter of Islamic dignity, but also their disgust with the secularist Westernism and crass materialism of their autocratic rulers (the latter only serving to further highlight their economic degradation).

107. Westerners, including academics, often mistakenly label state capitalism as "socialism" on the basis of the rhetoric of governments of relevant countries, as well as be-

cause the state usually owns the major units of the means of production. So, What then is the difference between ordinary "private" capitalism and state capitalism? Simply put, in a state-capitalist system surplus is appropriated at the individual level even while the means of production is collectively owned; in almost every other key aspects (production for profit, etc.) it is similar to an ordinary capitalist system. One may further note here that from the perspective of PQD countries, such as those in Africa, the state-capitalist route proved irresistible for many following independence on several counts; such as: it allowed the possibility of dispensing state patronage for populist projects and programs; it answered the demand for national economic sovereignty against a backdrop of colonially determined domination of the local economy by foreign (Western) capital; and it has been an avenue for the personal enrichment of the ruling autocracies. From a purely economic point of view, state capitalism (compared to ordinary capitalism) is simply too inefficient, for it is a truism that bureaucracies lack the will and the wherewithal to engage in efficient entrepreneurial activities. In recent years, state capitalism, has been of course the target of a concerted effort on the part of the West to obliterate it: that is, PQD countries, such as those in Africa, have been forced to implement (primarily by means of manipulation of avenues and mechanisms of international credit and legitimated through the rubrics of neoclassical economics) the policy of what is euphemistically dubbed as *structural adjustment* by the chief architect of the policy, the World Bank. The net effect of these policies has been a "recolonization" of the most lucrative sectors of the economy by foreign (primarily Western) capital, destruction of nascent industries through cheaply produced imports and increased pauperization of the masses—the latter, in turn, provoking political instability (as in the case of Algeria). In a sense, this is a replay of what occurred in the immediate aftermath of 1492 (see Appendix II).

108. That education in general, but higher education specifically, should be burdened with this task is testimony to the power of the belief in one of the central and most enduring tenets of modern capitalist democracy: meritocracy. Such is the depth of the belief in this concept that its proponents are completely blind to its inherent fallacy. To explain: meritocracy is a concept that sees the allocation of material rewards in society as resting on merit, which itself is assumed to be based on such qualities of an individual as intelligence, effort and ambition and not on membership of preordained social groups—whatever their definitional criteria: class, sex, race, ethnicity, and so on. In other words: from the meritocratic point of view, one's class status in society is based on social achievement, not social ascription. One of the most widely used and accepted measurement of social achievement in modern societies today is educational qualifications or academic achievement. Now, in a meritocratic society academic achievement is presumed to rest on equality of educational opportunity. However, equality of educational opportunity itself is supposedly governed by the principle of meritocracy: namely that academic achievement is a function of one's individual qualities of intelligence, effort and ambition in school, and not on one's social background, be it in terms of class, race, sex, ethnicity, and so on. It follows from all this that if there is a slippage in academic achievement then explanation for it must be sought in flaws in the individual's qualities (perhaps there is limited intelligence, perhaps there is insufficient effort, perhaps ambition is lacking, etc). And if this slippage is consistent among some social groups then these flaws must also be universal within these groups. (A corollary of this view is that since these groups (leaving class aside) are presumed to be biological constructs, regardless of what science states, the flaws are biologically determined and hence society is powerless in the face of their immutability.) However, the meri-

tocratic logic rests on the assumption that we do *not* live in a society that is social structurally riven for historically determined reasons (rather than biological reasons), and where social groups exist in unequal power relations. But is this assumption correct? Is the social structure biologically determined? More to the point, Does academic achievement rest solely on individual qualities? Is it not possible that it may also depend on where one is within the social structure because one's location in that structure allows one access to specific educational advantages (manifest in such ways as access to resource-rich schools, qualified teachers, safe neighborhoods, etc.) In fact, research in support of this point is so extensive and ubiquitous in the field of education that it even renders reference citations to it redundant.

109. It is sobering to note that even in countries of the former Soviet bloc with explicit authoritarian agendas of eliminating socioeconomic class differences, the higher education sector continued to be biased in favor of the children of the elites—old and new. (Lewis and Dundar 2002). (One suspects that the same probably held true for China and Cuba.) For more on issues of equity in higher education see also Ziderman and Albrecht (1995).

110. A word of caution here about reading Chapter 7. What exactly is being suggested in that chapter? That, since it is impossible to measure the true economic significance of education generally and the generic university specifically—one of the central theses being advanced in the chapter—(or that since they help to reinforce inequality in society by serving as vehicles of class-reproduction), one may as well dispense with the university altogether as a luxury most of the countries in Africa can ill afford? (After all, this is exactly the line that has been taken hitherto by institutions such as the World Bank, but from the other side of the argument: yes, you can measure the economic worth of all education—vide, human capital theory and rates-of-return studies—and universities have come up short relative to other levels.) Such a conclusion would be a complete misreading of the thrust of the chapter. In fact, a reviewer, with some chagrin, did raise this issue—after reading only Chapter 7, but not the other chapters (because of time constraints)—albeit in a slightly different way:

I was sitting on the edge of my chair, as if [I was watching] a Hitchcock thriller, wondering when on earth [the author was] going to challenge, rather than merely deride, the World Bank's argument that universities [in Africa] are a poor investment, given the low rate[s] of social return…. When we finally [come] to the rebuttal, right at the end of the chapter, I find the [author goes] through the [same] hoary…arguments, long since established and well known, of the inadequacies in human capital theory. Well, alright, but just because the World Bank is relying on inadequate theory to support their unwillingness to fund universities, this does not in itself make universities a good investment. Universities might be a poor investment for other reasons, or might even be economically and socially damaging. Where is [the author's] alternative theory to show that universities deserve international funding, either because they actually are a good economic investment, or for other reasons?

In fairness, the reviewer, however, also goes on to note in the same breadth, "Maybe there is a proper justification for (the present scale of [development]) of universities in Africa somewhere else in the book, and [the author] can escape from this dilemma by some suitable cross reference. Otherwise, [the author is] asking the reader to make the assumption that a university is necessarily a good thing until somebody can conclusively prove otherwise. (Why not the converse proposition?)"

When Chapter 7 is placed in the context of this entire work then the thesis being put forward is that history shows us that all advanced civilizations have possessed institutions of higher learning in some form, but not purely for their directly measurable economic significance as understood by practitioners of the so-called "economics of education" (see critique in Chapter 7)—compare here the raison d'etre for the creation of the Bibliotheca Alexandrina in ancient Egypt (see the preceding chapter). Institutions of higher learning (that is the generic universities) serve many diverse functions and this is especially true of the modern university (which in most of Africa is the public university). Yes, of course, important parts of them (such as the professional schools and the science and technology research centers) do contribute directly to the economy by providing trained personpower and critical scientific/technological knowledge, but universities at the end of the day are not glorified vocational schools. It is not without reason after all, that even where institutions are created primarily for their vocational functions (broadly understood), such as "institutes of technology," they soon acquire the curricular mantle of a generic university. Universities, in other words, also have a number of non-economic functions, but which are critical to the health of a modern society, such as: training leaders; raising the level of education (broadly understood) within a society generally—thereby raising the potential for greater enlightened thinking, creativity, etc. Moreover, where they enjoy academic freedom they serve as beacons of democracy. A succinct description of this multi-faceted role of the modern university is perhaps best captured by Article 1 of the UNESCO sponsored "World Declaration on Higher Education for the Twenty First Century: Vision and Action" (UNESCO 1998):

We... participants in the World Conference on Higher Education, assembled at UNESCO Headquarters in Paris, from 5 to 9 October, 1998... affirm that the core missions and values of higher education, in particular the mission to contribute to the sustainable development and improvement of society as a whole, should be preserved, reinforced and further expanded, namely, to: (a) educate highly qualified graduates and responsible citizens able to meet the needs of all sectors of human activity, by offering relevant qualifications, including professional training, which combine high-level knowledge and skills, using courses and content continually tailored to the present and future needs of society; (b) provide opportunities *(espace ouvert)* for higher learning and for learning throughout life, giving to learners an optimal range of choice and a flexibility of entry and exit points within the system, as well as an opportunity for individual development and social mobility in order to educate for citizenship and for active participation in society, with a worldwide vision, for endogenous capacity-building, and for the consolidation of human rights, sustainable development, democracy and peace, in a context of justice; (c) advance, create and disseminate knowledge through research and provide, as part of its service to the community, relevant expertise to assist societies in cultural, social and economic development, promoting and developing scientific and technological research as well as research in the social sciences, the humanities and the creative arts; (d) help understand, interpret, preserve, enhance, promote and disseminate national and regional, international and historic cultures, in a context of cultural pluralism and diversity; (e) help protect and enhance societal values by training young people in the values which form the basis of democratic citizenship and by providing critical and detached perspectives to assist in the discussion of strategic options and the reinforcement of humanistic perspectives; (f) contribute to the development and improvement of education at all levels, including through the training of teachers.

It is instructive to compare here also the "Accra Declaration on GATS and the Internationalization of Higher Education in Africa" issued at a conference organized by the Association of African Universities, UNESCO, and the South African Council on Higher Education (reproduced in no. 36, summer 2004, issue of *International Higher Education,* pp. 5-7 [a quarterly newsletter of the Boston College Center for International Higher Education]):

We participants, in this workshop on the Implications of WTO/GATS for Higher Education in Africa assembled in Accra, Ghana from 27–29 April 2004:

Recalling: the Universal Declaration of Human Rights (1948), Article 26, paragraph 1, which affirms that "Everyone has the right to education" and that "higher education shall be equally accessible to all on the basis of merit...."

Noting: The negative impact of decades of structural adjustment policies and inadequate financing on the viability of higher education institutions as teaching and research institutions in Africa.... the lack of transparency in GATS [General Agreement on Trades in Service sponsored by the World Trade Organization] deliberations, and insufficient knowledge and understanding of the full implications of GATS for higher education, especially in developing country contexts.

Declare· A renewed commitment to the development of higher education in Africa as a "public mandate" whose mission and objectives must serve the social, economic and intellectual needs and priorities of the peoples of the African continent while contributing to the "global creation, exchange and application of knowledge" (AAU Declaration on the African University in the Third Millennium)....

No society that aspires toward political, economic and social modernity can do without a university even in a context of, yes, poverty and mass illiteracy (compare, for instance, the socio-economic and political contexts within which the medieval universities of Europe existed). We must champion the development of flagship public universities, most especially in the face of the current subtle and not so subtle onslaught against them from forces of reaction sponsored by globalized corporate capital—is it any wonder that in response to this ominous onslaught there is now talk among some universities to patent the word "university" in order to protect its historically-rooted structural and mission agenda of viewing education as *a common good* (Halvorsen and Skauge 2004—see also endnote 21 in Chapter 8). In doing so, however, *the effort must not rest simply on grounds of their economic worth as generators of capitalist accumulation.* (But what about the issue of ever-mounting national budgetary constraints? One possible answer is, against the backdrop of equally ever-mounting global corporate profits and average per capita GDP growth rates in the OD countries, for the lords of globalized corporate capital and their pseudointellectual allies to advocate a global program of beating swords into ploughshares; the other is to call for the democratization [from each according to his/her/its ability] of national and corporate tax-structures, which almost throughout the world, albeit to varying degrees, are skewed in favor of the corporate rich and the powerful.) To justify the existence of universities purely on grounds of economic theory not only creates the problem of the cogency of the theory in the first place, but it also runs up against the counter lessons of historical experience. For example, consider the matter of the universities vis-à-vis the so called scientific revolution in Europe (see the discussion in Appendix 1), or consider the matter of the role of universities in the genesis of the so-called "East Asian Miracle." Regarding the latter, as Carnoy, for example, has convincingly demonstrated:

The role of universities in bringing countries into a competitive position in the new world economy is inextricably tied to the broader policies in which their governments engage to achieve economic and social development. There is very little evidence in any of the countries studied that high quality science and engineering or technical research in universities created the basis for technological development in the economy. Rather, the success of the Korean and Singapore cases depended on an overall set of "developmental state" strategies that pushed export-driven economic growth and technological upgrading into science-based industrial production (Carnoy 1994: 90).

One other point: The foregoing discussion should not detract in the least bit from the fact that universities as they presently exist in Africa are in need of dire reform, especially in terms of finances, curricula and the matter of social structural inequality of access. (See, for example, Doss, Evenson and Ruther [2004].)

111. See also Gorman (2003) for an excellent study of the politics of knowledge; in this instance the politics behind Egyptian historiography, where he demonstrates that "historical interpretation is empowered by political forces as a means of defining, reinforcing, justifying and above all contesting what is politically legitimate and feasible" (p. 197).

4

Anglophone Africa-I

In one of those tragic ironies of history, it is the official Anglo-American effort to eradicate the Atlantic slave trade—necessitated by the industrial transformations of Western Europe and North America and legitimated by the antislavery movement of the abolitionists—that would propel the European powers toward the direct colonization of Africa.[1] For, henceforth, the actual and *perceived* potential economic significance of Africa (as a supplier of natural resources and as a market for Europe's manufactures), to an industrializing Europe had become of even greater importance in Europe's view than the continent's role hitherto as a supplier of servile labor, which for some 300 years or so the nascent European powers had been content to leave in the hands of private European entrepreneurs and the Africans themselves.[2] That the fate of the Africans at the hands of an expanding Europe would be no different from that of the Asians was simply a matter of time; the growing internal rivalry among the militarily and industrially advancing European powers would see to that.

While there is considerable disagreement among historians over who fired, *and for what immediate reason*, the opening salvo in what historians came to dub as the *Scramble for Africa* involving the rapid dismembering of the African continent from around the 1870s to 1900 (most especially following the infamous Berlin West Africa Conference, November 1884–February 1885—also known as simply the Berlin Conference), in reality that particular question is of less importance than the fact that 1492 had preordained Africa's historical trajectory to be politically and economically intertwined with that of Europe's to a much greater degree than had ever been the case before (see Appendix II).[3] Discounting the colonial intrusions on the extremities of the continent (North Africa and South Africa), the timespan within which almost the entire continent was gobbled up by Europe was amazingly short indeed, less than thirty years or so. After the dust of colonization had settled, those among the European countries who emerged with some piece of Africa were Belgium, Britain, France, Germany (before World War I), Italy, Portugal, and Spain.[4] (Even the Dutch had a piece for a short time, but that was before the scramble.) In terms of percentage of the continent that the different powers came to rule (under various administrative guises—colony, trust territory, protectorate, etc.) Britain led the pack.[5] After Britain, the next major European colonial power on the continent was France, followed by Portugal, Italy, and Spain, in that order.[6]

Soon after British colonialism had become entrenched in Africa (excluding southern Africa—see below), it emerged with the colonial policy of *indirect rule* (and later to be followed by the policy of eventual *self-rule*). Immaterial of which policy one considers, both required the training of an indigenous political elite for the purposes of governance; though not in competition with the colonial elite it must be emphasized, but subservient to it.[7] One would assume, therefore, that from the very beginning the British government should have been busy setting up a comprehensive educational system in its African colonies. In reality, this was not the case for reasons that will become clear as the chapter proceeds. Under the circumstances, the survey of the historical landscape of higher education in British colonial Africa immediately generates a periodization made up of three principal periods: the era of benign neglect (about early 1800s to 1920s) where the British were not opposed to higher education for Africans in principle, but at the same time were not willing to do much about it in practice; the era of partial neglect (about 1920s to 1945), where a few institutions were established at the subuniversity level on an ad hoc basis; and the era of Asquith colleges (about 1945 to early 1960s) that saw the implementation of a coherent and forceful, but belated, British policy on developing higher education in the colonies. (The postcolonial period, following independence, would inaugurate the era of national universities— approximately early 1960s to the present; that period will occupy the second section of this chapter.)

BRITISH COLONIAL POLICY, 1800s–1920s

Among the first institutions of higher education to be established in the nineteenth-century were Fourah Bay College in Freetown (1826); Gordon Memorial College in Khartoum (1898); Lovedale Institution in South Africa (1841); the South African College at Cape Town (1829); the University of the Cape of Good Hope (1873); and Victoria College at Stellenbosch (1829). Given the unique historical circumstances of South Africa among all the British

African colonies, a separate section has been reserved for its institutions in the next chapter. Before proceeding further a qualifier: the definition of what constituted *higher education* during this early period is being stretched here somewhat because most of these institutions began (like most of the early institutions of higher learning throughout the world) by initially providing secondary school-level education so as to create the appropriately certified student cohort they would later need for their college-level classes when these were slowly brought on line. In other words, in their life histories there were three distinct stages: they began by providing secondary-level education (and in some cases even primary-level education), then they added university-level classes and therefore functioned as hybrid institutions providing both preuniversity-level and university-level education, and, finally, as alternative secondary school-level institutions emerged, they shed their preuniversity-level classes to evolve fully into institutions of higher learning.

Fourah Bay College

Fourah Bay College was the first and only higher education institution in all of anglophone Africa (outside South Africa). Consequently, in historical terms, Fourah Bay is an important institution, not only for chronological reasons, but also because it came to play a significant role in the genesis of a West African nationalist elite. Like most other higher education institutions in British colonial Africa in the early years, Fourah Bay was founded for the purposes of theological training through the initiatives of Christian missionaries. The particular group involved here was the Church Missionary Society (for a time the Wesleyans were also associated with the college) based in England. Their motives for establishing Fourah Bay were similar to those of other missionaries working elsewhere in colonial Africa in that they saw it as a logical extension of their ongoing involvement in formal education. Western Christian missionaries had become involved with formal education almost from the moment they arrived in Africa for a number of critical reasons specific to their proselytizing mission: the need to stamp out the slave trade and substitute it with other morally acceptable and peace- and stability-inducing economic activities; propagate literacy to facilitate religious instruction; and develop a cadre of local teachers and pastors to accelerate evangelization (see Berman 1975 and Sivonen 1995 for an extended look at the missionary role in African education).

Initially, during the first two decades or so, Fourah Bay did not have as much success as anticipated in attracting students for theological training and a decision was made to close the institution in 1859. The college was reopened in 1863 with renewed hope that recruits would be forthcoming. However, it was not until May 1876 when the college would be affiliated to Durham University (the first university to be established in England in more than 200 years [opened in 1832] since the founding of the medieval universities of Oxford and Cambridge), for degree granting purposes as well as curricular direction that its future would be assured. This development was a direct outcome of the involvement of two other parties to the debate over the matter of higher education in Sierra Leone that ensued following the temporary closure of the institution: African nationalists like James Africanus Beale Horton (a medical doctor and a graduate of Fourah Bay), James Johnson (an Anglican pastor and also a graduate of Fourah Bay), and Edward Blyden (a Caribbean Pan-African essentialist and professor of classical languages at Liberia College), and the local colonial administration in the person of the acting governor of Sierra Leone, John Pope Hennessy.

Now, there is some historical irony in the fact that graduates of Christian missionary educational institutions would, in time, emerge to severely criticize, perhaps ungratefully, the very education that they had received from the missionaries. The missionaries, of course, never anticipated the size of the Pandora's box that they helped open through their evangelically determined educational efforts. Thus, some among these early members of the African educated elite argued that what was really needed was a secular West African university that would go beyond the confines of missionary-oriented education, which they felt was narrow, intellectually stifling, and dogmatic. They called for, instead, a government-funded, world-class, secular higher education that was at once celebratory, in curricular terms, of the intrinsic superiority of African culture (as some of them would suggest) and be directly responsive to the dictates of the political, economic, and social development of West Africa.

Underlying this call, there were two concurrent but contradictory views at work in their motivations: one view was that, yes, Western civilization was superior to that of others, including that of the Africans, and therefore worthy of emulation, but that this superiority was not, however, attributable to race as Westerners were want to argue; rather, it was asserted, educational opportunity (this was the classic nurture-versus-nature argument). In this view (Horton was among its advocates), then, Africans could be considered in cultural terms as "Europeans in waiting." In contrast, people such as Blyden were adamant that not only there was nothing wrong with African culture, per se, but also European culture was in many ways an inferior culture. Not surprisingly, he detested the educated African of his day for being too eager to emulate Europeans. Consider, for example, the views of Edward Blyden on this matter, which he expressed in the course of an exchange of letters in December 1872 with Hennessy. He wrote in one of his letters to the acting governor:

All educated Negroes suffer from a kind of slavery in many ways far more subversive of the real welfare of the race than the ancient physical fetters. The slavery of the mind is far more destructive than that of the body. But such is the weakness and imperfection of human nature that many even of those who bravely fought to remove the shackles from the body of the Negro transfer them to his mind with as little compunction as ever

Hawkins or Da Souza prosecuted the slave trade; and do not feel themselves called upon to give the slightest attention to questions like these (quoted from his letter reproduced in the documents section of Ashby 1966: 444–45).

Blyden was not an indigenous African, and perhaps this had a bearing on his advocacy of race pride (in the tradition of the Afrocentrists of today). Therefore, for him an African university would have been an excellent vehicle for instilling race pride in the African who was being led astray by European education.

To the deep chagrin of the missionaries, the acting governor would respond sympathetically. In the spirit of the slowly evolving position of the British that their ultimate goal was to prepare British West Africa for eventual self-government (a position articulated in the *Report of the Parliamentary Committee* of 1865), Hennessy adopted the view that a West African university would not only provide higher education opportunities for both the children of the rich and the talented poor in West Africa, but would also help to shield West Africans from what he felt was the morally corrupting influences inherent in overseas study (Ashby 1966).[8]

The missionaries were, of course, extremely unhappy with both the nationalists and the acting governor. They not only perceived ingratitude for all that the missionaries had done in the field of formal education, but they also felt directly threatened by the secular direction that was being proposed for higher education in West Africa. For the missionaries, retention of monopoly control over formal education was absolutely critical because experience had shown that formal education was the best avenue for spreading the Gospel in Africa. Plus to add insult to injury, as Ashby (1966) points out, the fact was not lost on the missionaries that it is they themselves (but unbeknown to those outside their circle) who had, a few years earlier, first begun discussing the possibility of upgrading Fourah Bay to a higher-level institution. Not surprisingly, feelings would run high among them. (See, for example, the correspondence reproduced in the documents section of Ashby 1966.)

In the end, a compromise of sorts was reached where the Church Missionary Society agreed to expand the college by opening it up to fee-paying (lay) students, as well as affiliating it to Durham University as noted earlier; and the curriculum was also broadened, though it still remained primarily theological. To the great disappointment of Horton, Blyden, and others who shared their views, the newly reformed Fourah Bay did not even remotely approach their cherished dream of a secular and prestigious but "Africanized" West African university. Take, for instance, the curriculum: it did not include any of the fields of study that the nationalists had proposed—neither African studies, nor agriculture, nor architecture; neither economics, nor engineering, nor for that matter law, medicine, and science. The nationalists, consequently, turned their energies toward the idea of private sponsorship of higher education, but nothing much would come of that strategy for a long time either.[9]

Note that however legitimate the demands for a local university may have been from perspectives other than the issue of race pride (which was nothing more than the mirror image of Eurocentrist racism), and notwithstanding the fact that they were indirectly instrumental in the reopening of Fourah Bay, one must caution here in ascribing too great a significance to the role of this small articulate group of Africans on this matter; for, there is reason to believe that in this regard their views may not have been entirely representative of those of other Africans. This is because for a very long time, coming all the way into the early postindependence era, there was a strong opinion among Africans that no local higher education institution could provide educational qualifications that in terms of status and prestige could compete with those obtained from metropolitan institutions abroad. Plus, given the absence (or in some cases nascence) of graduate-level education, they feared, rightly or wrongly, that a local degree could stand in the way of gaining admission to graduate-level study in the metropole because metropolitan institutions would perhaps not recognize the degree. (Many were also probably conscious of the irony that the advocates of indigenous higher education were themselves in possession of foreign credentials—though they would have argued, perhaps, that this was so through no fault of their own.) [10]

By the time the Elliot Commission (see below) visited the Fourah Bay some seventy years later in 1944, the college had managed to acquire, going by the commission's report, the following fairly respectable profile (especially when compared to the very limited profile of its earlier incarnation): its full-time faculty, including the principal, numbered six and almost all had degrees (from British universities, though one also had a degree from a U.S. university in addition to his British degree). Racially—yes... a relevant issue given the colonial context—they were evenly divided between black and white, though the principal was white. Interestingly, the white members of staff were not paid a regular salary, but instead received stipends or grants because they were missionaries (however, in reality the stipend for an unmarried missionary [nearly double for the married] amounted to more than the salary of the African faculty member—300 pounds sterling versus an average of 210 pounds). The all-inclusive tuition fee for all students was 60 pounds sterling per academic year; however, it was reduced for those studying for the ministry. There were two concurrent programs of study at the college, university education (undergraduate students could choose from a general arts degree, or specialization in a group of divinity subjects, while graduate students had the choice of a diploma in either education or theology); and primary school teacher training (a three-year course, of which the last year was set aside for an internship). The academic year was of course the same as that of Durham's, it was divided into three terms. Admission to the university program depended on successfully completing a competitive school matriculation exam administered from Durham, while those applying for the teacher training component had to have the senior school certificate (in practice, however, the junior school certificate was also accepted owing to a dearth of applicants). Those studying to be clergy were only required to have been nominated by the missions, they did not have to sit for any entrance exams. The total student population of the college in 1943 was twenty-five, of whom twenty were in the university program; and roughly half (thirteen—the majority of whom were in the university program), came from outside Sierra Leone. (Compare these numbers with those studying abroad: there were in 1945, sixty-two students from Sierra Leone studying in Britain and Ireland.)

The fact that the first educational institutions at any level were founded by missionaries indicates that in the early years of British colonialism, direct governmental involvement in the provision of formal education in general and higher education in specific was minimal—restricted by and large to providing subventions to educational institutions founded and run by the missionaries. In fact, as Ashby (1966) observes, in the period preceding the First World War there was no formal British educational policy for the colonies in Africa to speak of. A partial explanation for this situation lies in the general view held in the nineteenth-century by Europeans, including the British, of the ineducability of Africans because they were considered intellectually inferior— notwithstanding the protestations of the missionaries to the contrary (Lyons 1970). At the same time, going by Nwauwa (1996), there were a number of other factors at work as well, such as, there was resistance from colonial officials in the colonies (especially the settler dominated ones) because they did not wish to lose their jobs to educated Africans; the British, in the pre-1884 Berlin Conference era, were still in two minds about retaining their colonial possessions in West Africa (which they dubbed the "white man's grave" because of such deadly tropical diseases as malaria); and they were extremely wary of increasing administrative expenditures in the colonies.

Formation of Early Colonial Policy

Perhaps more than any other Western democracy, for good or ill, Britain appears to have always had a penchant for appointing advisory bodies (fact-finding, usually transient, committees and commissions comprising prominent captains of government, industry and civil society) to advise it through their plenary reports on major macrolevel policy issues, especially of a social nature (such as education). It is not surprising, therefore, that when the British government did begin to move toward the development of a formal policy on African higher education, it did so through these bodies. Consequently, if one is to come up with even a modicum of understanding of the historical antecedents of the eventual establishment of higher education institutions in British colonial Africa, then one has no other recourse but to take a look at the various committees and commissions—in terms of the reports they issued—that the British government appointed from time to time in response to pressures emanating from both the force of historical events (e.g., the Second World War), economic growth, and interested parties (e.g., the colonial subjects themselves, the missionaries, the administrations in the colonies, etc.).

Moreover, in taking a look at some of the findings discussed in these reports, one can also extract issues that are still of considerable relevance today, in terms of sound policy and best practice. Now, among these advisory bodies, those worthy of consideration here are: the Madden Commission (1841); the Advisory Committee on Education in the Colonies (set up in 1923); the Phelps-Stokes Commission to East Africa (1925—while not a strictly British government body, the British had a hand in its set up; hence it included among its members Hanns Vischer, the permanent secretary who headed of the Advisory Committee, who would represent both the colonial office and the committee); the Currie Subcommittee (1933); De La Warr Commission (1937); the Channon Subcommittee (1943); the Elliot Commission (June 1945); and the Asquith Commission (July 1945).[11]

The first official effort, of a kind, to investigate the state of educational provision in the colonies took place, according to Lyons (1970), through the agency of Dr. Richard R. Madden, M.D., who was sent to West Africa as the Royal Commissioner broadly charged with a survey of the political, economic, and other conditions in the settlements of Gambia, Sierra Leone, and the Gold Coast. In the consequent report he submitted in 1841, he would preposterously indicate, on the basis of flimsiest evidence, that while the African, in his childhood, exhibited a learning capability comparable to that of the European, by the time he reached adulthood this capability had atrophied significantly to the point where he was now an intellectual inferior. (He blamed this development, in consonance with the pseudoscientific thinking of his day, on tropical climate.) His recommendation, then, was that the schooling of the African should be aimed at teaching nonintellectual pursuits, specifically vocational training; anything else he said would be a waste of time.[12]

Madden's basic message, that Western education should be adapted to the special circumstances of the African, would be reiterated in different guises as years went by, and would eventually become part of official educational policy for a time—but for different reasons: political and economic, rather than intellectual. The process by which this happened is that by the time one arrives in the early 1920s, not only had Britain committed itself to the colonial project in the post–1884 Berlin Conference era, but the missionary presence in the education field in the African colonies had grown to a point where they were able to exert meaningful pressure on the British government to play a greater role in the provision of education in the colonies. The specific mechanism involved was the publication of the findings of a U.S.-missionary-instigated commission, the Phelps-Stokes Commission to West Africa, in 1922, on the state of education in British colonial Africa. This report, coupled with perennial demands for education from a number of Africans themselves (in the 1920s the call would be taken up by nationalists like J. E. Casely Hayford, the founder of the National Congress of British West Africa) and the increasingly clearer recognition in the corridors of Whitehall that colonial overlordship should gradually be replaced with colonial "trusteeship"—a concept that had emerged out of the peace negotiations covering the colonies of the World War I vanquished European power, Germany—prompted the government to set up a permanent advisory committee in 1923: the *Advisory Committee on Education in the Colonies*. The precise words of the undersecretary of state for the colonies, Major Olmsby-Gore, in making the announcement in parliament were: "we were led to this largely as the result of a most extraordinarily interesting report issued by Dr. Jesse Jones, who has traveled, not only through the British Colonies, but through French Africa and the Belgian Congo and the Portuguese Colonies" (Jones 1925: xx). The British were, in fact, so impressed with the commission's report, published in 1922 (Jones 1922), that they invited the commission to visit South, Central, and East Africa—resulting in the issue by the commission of a second report in 1925. During the interwar period British educational policy in Africa was guided primarily by the educational recommendations of the commission, which, as indicated earlier, rested on the principle that what Africans needed was vocational training, lots of it, and not liberal academic education. (For an analysis of the commission's work see King 1971.)

With the help of this body, the British government became formally and actively involved with the development of policy on education in colonial Africa.[13] The committee, through its advice to the Colonial Secretary, set the tone for British colonial policy on education in general in the African colonies, which can be summarized thus: first, to supplement, and not to compete with the existing missionary educational effort; second, to extend the benefits of basic literacy to as many people as resources would permit; third, to provide training for the development of a cadre of low-level government officials (such as office clerks, interpreters, messengers, etc.); fourth, to provide vocational educational opportunities; and fifth, to permit the development of some level of higher education, especially in such areas as teacher, agricultural, veterinary, and paramedical training (see Brown 1964). In sum, the first formally adopted policy on education by the British, was, by and large, determined by the educational philosophy advocated by the Phelps-Stokes Commission (and which itself had evolved out of efforts to educate the fairly recently emancipated African Americans), namely, adapt Western education to the political and economic *colonial* circumstance of the African by emphasizing industrial and vocational training at the expense of literary and academic education—the key word here is *adapt*, a code word for the nonacademic, vocational education, much beloved by the commission's chair, Thomas Jesse Jones.[14]

Initially, official educational policy, in line with the thinking represented by the missionaries on one hand and private groups such as the Phelps-Stokes

Commission on the other, would pay insufficient attention to the provision of higher education in Africa—at least from the perspective of the Africans. It is not that they were opposed to any form of higher education per se, it should be noted, but rather they did not see it as a priority and certainly they expected any development of higher education in British colonial Africa to be restricted to the Tuskegee-type of higher education, considered to be well adapted to the mind and circumstance of black peoples everywhere.

However, within roughly a decade, this situation would change. Why? With the ever-increasing nationalist agitation for independence in India, coupled with the economic and political advancement of Britain that no longer necessitated direct colonial rule to the extent that it did in the preceding centuries, it had begun to dawn on many within British ruling circles that British colonial rule everywhere, including in Africa, would have to come to an end *in not-too-distant future.* In other words, the inherent promise of trusteeship, self-government, would have to be implemented. (Though it may be noted that on the eve of World War II, however, very few if any within Britain—or even in the colonies for that matter—would have surmised how soon the not-too-distant future would arrive as a result of the War.) Consequently, they began to adopt a more realistic view toward the deepening thirst for university-level higher education among Africans. Higher education was essential for the development of a cadre of indigenous leadership that when the time was ripe could takeover the reigns of government in the various British colonies—but while still maintaining ties to Britain.[15] Moreover, the British were also very concerned about the fact that Africans on their own had been going overseas for higher education (to Europe and North America) with the very real danger of coming back "contaminated" with inappropriate radical intellectual ideas, such as Pan-Africanism and Bolshevism (Furley and Watson 1978). In fact, the Phelps-Stokes Commission itself had already begun to sound warning bells in this regard; thus it would note in its second report on education in Africa:

The demand for [higher] education cannot long be delayed. Already a few Native pupils requiring special training for technical, agricultural or teaching service, as well as those who desire to enter the professions, have gone to Europe or America to continue their education. The necessity to do this is a serious handicap to Native Africans who have the capacity for advancement. The cost is almost prohibitive, the break from all African surroundings is unfortunate, *and the entrance into the perplexing and conflicting tides of European or American life is fraught with danger to mind and morals.* (Emphasis added. Jones 1925: 44)

BRITISH COLONIAL POLICY, 1920s–1945

For a number of reasons specific to the circumstances of a particular colony that could range anywhere from the need for clerical personnel, to African demands, to the presence of an enlightened colonial administration, a number of higher educational institutions were established in anglophone Africa in the 1920s and 1930s. They include, for instance, the Achimota College in Ghana (1924), the Kitchener Memorial School of Medicine in Sudan (1924), Government College at Ibadan in Nigeria (1929), and Higher College at Yaba, again, in Nigeria (1934).

Now, in order to get a feel for what such institutions were like in British colonial Africa on the eve of the implementation of Asquith, what follows are brief profiles of Yaba and Achimota constructed on the basis of the Elliott Commission report. Of course, no two higher education institutions, it is true, can be identical even in the same country, let alone those scattered across different countries. However, given the uniformity of (1) time period (early 1940s); (2) overall objectives of the institutions (production of intermediate-level human capital); and (3) *political* culture (British colonialism), there is merit in adducing reasonable typicality to these profiles (taken together) for British colonial Africa as a whole (excluding the settler colonies).

Higher College at Yaba

Commencing then, with the Higher College at Yaba, one may trace its profile along the following lines:

Origins. The college began its life in 1932 in temporary buildings, but its formal opening took place in 1934 with its move to permanent quarters. The principal purpose behind its establishment was to provide subdegree level training (though government officials had voiced expectations that some time in the future it would develop toward granting degree-level qualifications in association with a British university) for those who would be employed by various government departments.

Plant. The campus consisted of six newly constructed separate blocks of buildings parceled out to the following functions: three for teaching/ learning (one each, with appropriate laboratories, for engineering, physics, chemistry, and biology); one for the administration and the library; one consisting of a set of multipurpose lecture halls; and the sixth constituted four student dormitories (each with the capacity to house twenty-two students) with their own separate dining halls and kitchens. The library held roughly 3,600 books, mainly textbooks and reference works on science and it had an annual budget of 60 pounds sterling for acquisitions.

Programs. The curricula rested on courses in science targeted at students who would spend roughly half of their time at the college and then complete their education during the other half as interns at professional training facilities elsewhere in the country. So, for example, a student wishing to become an assistant agricultural officer would spend two years at Yaba and then two more years as an intern at the training facilities at the Moor Plantation at Ibadan some 100 or so miles away. Upon completion of this training the student will have graduated with a diploma in agriculture. The only student group that received its entire training at Yaba were the engineering students (their program lasted five years). Other fields of study at Yaba were forestry (2/2, that is two years at Yaba and two years as interns elsewhere), medicine (1.5/5), surveying (2/2), veterinary science (1.5/5.5) and secondary school teacher training (3/1).

Finance. Yaba, in terms of its recurrent expenditures, was funded entirely by the Nigerian colonial government; though fees did supplement the budget, but to a very insignificant extent. Nominally, the all-inclusive fee (tuition, room and board) was 50 pounds sterling annually for instate (Nigerian) students, but then only for the first three years of a program. (For out-of-state students the cost was 75 pounds sterling annually for the duration of the entire program.) Now, in practice, up to a third of the students did not pay fees at all (as a reward, it appears) for superior performance on entrance examinations; while the remainder had their fees reduced to just 15 pounds annually on grounds of economic hardship (moreover, payable in installments after graduation and, incredibly, refundable if the student failed to complete the program of study). On top of this highly liberal approach to fees, education students agreeing to teach in mission schools for five years following graduation, had their fees waived.

Admission. Usually about 150 students in any given year from government secondary schools were eligible to sit for the college-administered competitive entrance exams in the required subjects (English, geography, history, chemistry, physics, biology, and mathematics) for the thirty-five to forty slots available at the college. (These exams were in addition to the traditional secondary school graduation exam—known as the Cambridge School Leaving Certificate Examination administered by the University of Cambridge) that all secondary school students were required to sit for in Nigeria, and in the rest of British colonial Africa for that matter.) Students at missionary-run secondary schools were generally excluded by default from eligibility to participate in these exams because of their school curriculum; for, as a rule, science subjects (with the exception of one or two) were not taught in these schools. Note, however, that even after qualifying, admission into a specific program of study, was not entirely a matter of one's choice; it was also dictated by the vacancy needs of the government—much to the deep chagrin of the students.

Students. The student population in 1939 stood at about ninety-five (interestingly, compare this figure with other Nigerian students studying in Britain and Ireland at that time, about twice as many, 193—usually, with the exception of a handful, self-sponsored). Up to that point, through out the six-year history of the college, only two of the students were women. As for nationality, very few students had come from outside Nigeria (mainly from Dahomey, Ghana, and Sierra Leone); the reason is not difficult to surmise given the college's orientation toward employment in the Nigerian government civil service; as well as the fact that qualifications obtained from the college did not have much currency in West Africa, outside of Nigeria. The Elliott Commission report provides no information on the social background of the students.

Administration. The principal of the college was the sole decision maker in the sense that there was no internal governing structure. Moreover, he held the post not through recruitment, but by appointment by the government's director of education. There was an external advisory body made up of representatives from various sectors of society, but in practice it was inactive.

Faculty. The college had a teaching staff of nine made up of those who were recruited from civil service personnel in appropriate government departments (agriculture, forestry, etc.) and those who were recruited directly from the teaching profession. In terms of ethnicity, three of the nine were blacks and the remainder were whites; all served as full-time instructors and almost all possessed a bachelor's degree or a higher qualification.

Achimota College

Origins. Like Yaba, Achimota was also conceived, when it was opened in 1924, as an institution that *over the long-run* would progress toward the status of a university college. However, unlike Yaba, it did not simply provide teacher training and higher education, but it also offered kindergarten, primary-level, and secondary-level education—all from within one site. In 1944, however, the kindergarten and primary school were abolished (as part of the plan to move Achimota along toward the provision of higher education exclusively). Achimota was then left with three divisions: a secondary school, the teacher training component, and what it called the university department (the higher education wing of the college).

Plant. The spacious campus located some six miles inland from Accra had within it two groups of buildings separated by a quarter of a mile. One group, the smaller, housed the secondary school and the larger served the university department and the teacher training component. The campus also had some social amenities such as a hospital that provided free medical care, as well as a small museum specializing in African anthropology and natural history. As for the library, it was the largest in all of West Africa with a collection of some 16,000 books on various subjects in the social sciences, and an annual budget of 300 pounds sterling for collection development. (The needs of the science students were met by a smaller separate science library located in the science building.) The library also made its services available, on the basis of a refundable deposit, to those outside the college community.

Programs. The university curriculum rested on the preparation of students for the external exams of the University of London at the both the intermediate-level (roughly equivalent to junior-level studies in U.S. universities) and at the degree-level. Specifically, they had a choice of intermediate arts, intermediate science, intermediate engineering, B.Sc. engineering, intermediate science (economics). The intermediate level usually lasted two years. As for the subjects studied, here is an example: students pursuing the intermediate arts had to choose four subjects from among the following (but one of which had to be Latin): English, Latin, geography, history, economics, and pure mathematics; while students studying for the intermediate science exam chose four subjects from among these: applied mathematics, pure mathematics, physics, chemistry, botany, and zoology. Those working for an engineering degree spent two additional years with each year constituting a separate stage (part I exam taken in the first year, and part II in the second). Interestingly, the Elliot Commission's report waxes lyrical about the presence of a music teacher at Achimota to enhance the extracurricular activities of the students in the areas of music, dance, and drama because it helped to make Achimota what it referred to as "a multilateral institution." "The net result," the report continued, "is well-developed individuals with an all-round interest in every side of education and with some appreciation of the value of contributions to knowledge than the purely academic" (p. 41).

Finance. The overall budget of the college in 1944 was 54,000 pounds sterling and its expenditure was entirely the prerogative of the Council. In other words, the money was made available to the college as an annual government grant. Now, a little over half of the 15,000 pounds sterling annual budget of the *university department*, came from the grant, the rest was made up from the all-inclusive tuition fees (72 pounds per year for engineering students, while the rest paid 48 pounds per year).

Admission. Students should have passed successfully either the school leaving certificate exam, or the University of London school matriculation exam or the competitive entrance exam administered by the college. Those with the Cambridge school leaving certificate and wishing to study science or engineering had to have credit in one science subject and/ or in additional mathematics. Despite these requirements, the number of qualified applicants usually exceeded the number of places available. For example, in 1943, of the ninety-nine students who had applied for admission, sixty were deemed eligible for admission, but only fifty-two were eventually admitted. In the preceding year the ratio had been considerably worse: about only half of the eligible applicants found places.

Students. Slightly over half of the university department students were on scholarships of one type or another, with the bulk coming from the colonial government of Ghana. All students lived on campus and their total population was 102 (by way of comparison, the number of students from Ghana studying in Britain were eighty-nine, in 1945). Although Achimota from the very beginning of its founding had insisted on female enrolment at the kindergarten and primary-levels, it appears that female representation did not commensurately progress up the educational ladder as one would logically assume—probably for reasons that will be discussed elsewhere in this book below. Consequently, in the university department, female students were only slightly better represented than at Yaba: in 1939 there were none, but in subsequent years through 1942 one per year, while two in 1943 (out of an average annual total enrollment of sixty-three for the period). As for social class origins, the Elliott Commission report makes the general comment that "students are drawn from all sections of the community" (p. 43). There were also a number of out-of-state students, notably from Nigeria and a few from Sierra Leone, and fewer still from Gambia.

Administration. Unlike Yaba, Achimota had an independent governing body, the Achimota Council, in charge of overall college policies and control of property. The council had sixteen members, representing a number of different constituencies: the college administration, government, faculty, staff, the missionaries, students and alumni. The principal of the college was appointed by the Governor of Ghana, usually on the basis of recommendations from the council.

Faculty. The college had a total of twenty-two members of faculty who divided their time between the university program and the secondary school on campus— nineteen of them held degrees from British universities, while one each from universities in Canada and Italy, and the remaining faculty member was a qualified engineer. Of the twenty-two, five were blacks and three of them had undertaken graduate studies in England. The pay of the African faculty was only a fraction less (one-sixth) than that of their white counterparts, which was unusual for the time period. The report also noted that relations between the black and the white faculty were good on both professional and social levels. "This relationship," the report further commented, "was considered by the [faculty] to be enhanced by the strong Christian influence which had pervaded the life of the college" (p. 43).

Currie Report

It is against this backdrop, that a subcommittee was appointed by the Advisory Committee, under the leadership of Sir James Currie, to look into the matter of higher education provision in British colonial Africa. The subcommittee issued its report in December 1933 (though it was not published, at the time). As for specific recommendations on the development of higher education in the colonies, the Currie Report did not mince any words:

II. The present position, as we see it, is that, while the colleges at Achimota, Makerere, Yaba, and Khartoum do not yet as a whole approach a real university standard, inevitably and of their own momentum they tend toward this final point. At the same time the African thirst for higher education remains unabated; if this is not satisfied at home it can only lead to an increasing efflux of undergraduate African students toward the Universities of Europe and America. The social and intellectual undesirability of this procedure in the African's own interest needs no laboring here.... IV. There is a grave danger, as we see it, of the Africans' zeal for education being neglected and ignored by the Government to whom they ought to be able to look for its reasonable satisfaction.... V. Our conclusion upon these considerations is that the only right policy for the Government is to think out ahead a scheme of developing selected institutions in Africa up to a real university standard, and that this policy, as soon as decided upon, should be publicly announced as officially adopted. We are of the opinion that such a university must almost necessarily proceed through the same stages by which the university colleges in England (e.g., Birmingham, Leeds, Manchester, Liverpool, Reading) have gained university rank (quoted from the Currie Report, reproduced in the documents section appended to Ashby 1966).

It should be stressed that in the matter of higher education, the subcommittee fully endorsed the extant policy first propounded by the Phelps-Stokes Commission, namely that it should be oriented toward technical and vocational training and not liberal academic education of the type that African essentialists like James Africanus Beale Horton had called for. Endorsing this type of curricula, the Currie Report would state "we do not ignore the importance of more purely academic studies. But we feel that, having regard to the situation in Africa as it exists today, the first essential is to attempt to secure for the country that reasonable degree of social and economic security, without which there can be no solid or lasting basis for any cultural life" (quoted from the Currie Report reproduced in the documents section appended to Ashby 1966).

If the Currie Report had seen the light of day, it would have turned out to be a seminal document. However, this was not to be. Not only was the report not published, but in fact it was forgotten, observes Ashby (1966: 197). The report's recommendations had run afoul of the colonial governments among whom the colonial office had circulated the report for comments—most especially in West Africa where they did not perceive any urgent necessity for higher education. One can only surmise here their reasons for this negative attitude (it would cut into their budgets; create competition for jobs, etc.), which however was not shared by the officials in Uganda. The positive attitude expressed in Uganda prompted the appointment of, yes, another commission.

Hence, a year after the Currie Report was submitted, a report was issued by a yet more influential body, chaired by Earl De La Warr (then parliamentary under-secretary for the colonial office). Unlike the Currie subcommittee, the De La Warr Commission was concerned specifically with the issue of upgrading the institutional status of just one institution, Makerere College in Uganda, to a university college and, in time, a full university. However, the significance of the commission stems from the fact that its report, unlike the Currie Report, was published (in 1937), thereby making it (as Ashby 1966, points out) the first public articulation of British colonial policy on higher education in Africa. At the same time, the report is important because it suggested a significant change in policy. The commission's wholehearted recommendation that Makerere College be raised to the level of a university college with institutional affiliation to the University of London was a public indication, for the first time, of the direction in which the winds of British colonial higher education policy were now blowing.[16] That is, the British government no longer saw the development of higher education in the African colonies purely from the narrow and highly utilitarian perspective of the educational policy suggestions of the Phelps-Stokes Foundation. It was now publicly acknowledged that the aspirations of Africans for a secular university-level education would be foundational to policy. Moreover, the commission's advocacy of some degree of Africanization of university curricula, especially the arts, suggested considerable enlightened sensitivity to the local environment.

Advocacy of this new line of thinking was further indicated by acceptance of the Channon Report by the colonial office. This report (published in 1943) was prepared by the subcommittee that Sir James Currie had once chaired, with the guidance of Professor H. J. Channon. Professor Channon had steadily taken over the important role of serving as a fount of ideas performed by Sir James Currie, following the latter's death in 1937. The report clearly called for an approach to higher education in the colonies that was genuinely university-oriented and not oriented primarily toward vocational training. Moreover, the report suggested that dependence on externally awarded degrees was not in the best (long-term) interests of the colonies because it stunted efforts toward indigenization of higher education. "Each of these Universities," it stated, "must therefore be indigenous and must not be subject to some arbitrary pattern introduced from Great Britain. Apart from providing the customary facilities for professional study, these Universities must be designed to fructify native cultural possibilities, and to study problems in their local, rather than in their foreign forms. This seems to us a compelling reason why the curriculum in some subjects should differ from that in use in Great Britain" (quoted from the report reproduced in the documents section of Ashby 1966: 510).

The Channon Report also raised an issue that is still of considerable relevance today in Africa: the matter of research as an integral part of the mission of the university. It would state: "we consider it as highly important that research should come to be regarded as being of no less importance than teaching in the life of the colleges. Unless steps are taken greatly to broaden their life, the colleges will certainly fail to achieve the objective of becoming the intellectual centers of their territories." The report goes on to emphasize the absolute necessity of "ensuring that the present divorce of research from teaching is not perpetuated" (quoted from the report reproduced in the documents section of Ashby 1966: 514).

It had taken more than half a century for the British colonial government to come around to accepting an educational policy on higher education that the West African essentialists had advocated decades earlier. However, the implementation of this change in policy direction would have to await the passage of the Great Depression of the 1930s and the Second World War (1939–45)—two cataclysmic events that would place the implementation of any major new colonial policies by all the colonial powers anywhere on the continent in temporary deep freeze.

BRITISH COLONIAL POLICY, 1945–1960s

As the Second World War ended, the British colonial secretary appointed two higher education commissions in 1943, the Elliot Commission and the Asquith Commission, in response to the now generally accepted view among the British ruling circles that independence in the British colonies was simply a matter of time, and that when independence came to the colonies, the indigenization of the government civil service, the development of primary and secondary education, health services, and so on, would all create a demand for trained leadership and personpower (human capital).

The task of the Elliot Commission—chaired by Walter Elliott and whose members included Channon, as well as, unusually for the time period (but suggestive of the changing thinking on colonial questions in Whitehall), some West Africans, was to produce a report on the state of higher education in West Africa and make recommendations. While the report (published in June 1945 following their three-month study tour of British West Africa (comprising Gambia, Gold Coast (Ghana), Nigeria, and Sierra Leone), undertaken from January, 15 to April, 10 in the preceding year), fully endorsed the development of higher education in British West Africa on the basis of the existing three institutions (Fourah Bay, Yaba, and Achimota), what is interesting about it is that it was not a unanimous report but a divided one.[17] In other words, it comprised two reports, one by the majority and other by a minority of the commission members.[18]

The bone of contention was the question of establishing a single federated West African university college (favored by the minority), or separate national university colleges (see below for what a "university college" is). Given the continuing relevance of this issue today (as will be pointed out in a moment) it is useful to delve further into why a severe disagreement arose among commission members over this matter. Essentially, the majority view was that the state of economic and political development of West Africa was such that it merited the creation of independent university colleges in the three largest of the British West African colonies (Ghana, Nigeria, and Sierra Leone), especially considering that the seedlings for these university colleges were already present in the form of the three colleges, and a number of "technical institutes" (vocationally oriented postsecondary institutions).

The minority view, however, favored a single West African university college, with the three existing colleges evolving toward the status of *Territorial Colleges*—that is, tributary preparatory colleges (a role not unlike that performed by two-year community colleges in the United States) to funnel students to the single regional university college.

So, what was their rationale for this proposal about which they were so adamant that they insisted on a bifurcated report in order that their views be known? Essentially, their argument rested on four factors: only the concentration of resources in a single institution would permit the telescoping of time from decades to years (in terms of developing a world-class research university); there were as yet inadequate numbers of students with appropriate entrance qualifications (in terms of pursuing senior and graduate-level studies) available to fill places at all the three planned university colleges (in light of as yet insufficiently developed secondary education facilities); there were insufficient resources available (in terms of finance, faculty, staff, buildings, libraries, laboratories, equipment, etc.); and the curricula (in terms of fields of study), coupled with research programs, would not be comprehensive enough to meet the development needs of the entire region. About the last point, they criticized, for example, the recommendation by the majority that Fourah Bay College continue to concentrate (under the existing management of the Church Missionary Society) only in the arts and theology, with the sciences being added slowly, and much later on, in the future. In other words, the minority wanted the creation of a truly first class university college as soon as possible that would not only be comprehensive in its curricular offerings and research facilities, but would also address the all important issue of academic *quality*. As they stated:

We encountered in West Africa the almost unanimous desire of representative African opinion that any facilities for higher education provided should be of high quality. It was constantly urged upon us that West Africans must be able to obtain in their own country at the earliest moment both university education and qualifications equivalent to those which they could obtain in Great Britain; status and quality were always to the forefront of discussion. We agree with this view which we regard as of high importance (United Kingdom 1945[b]: 146).

To the minority on the commission, the majority were more concerned with, as they put it, "quantity" (in contrast to "quality," p. 141). In fact, to the minority the institutions that the majority were proposing would *in practice* (even though the majority had clearly warned against the danger of lowering of academic standards, p. 122) be little more than glorified secondary schools for a long time to come, given the resource constraints. Here is how they described the problem that emerges when higher education institutions "are burdened with the task of making good the deficiencies of secondary education...[i]nstead of being free to concentrate on its development as a university institution, it tends to become *a continuation school*; there is always a heavy wastage rate of unsuccessful students; the development of the research and other activities properly associated with a university institution is almost impossible, for under such conditions staff of the quality required are not attracted; lastly, the best students whose presence would contribute so much to the creation of the high standards required, naturally prefer to go elsewhere" (p. 144—emphasis added).

Were the minority on sure ground regarding their criticisms? Given the extant economic conditions of British West Africa in 1945, well described by the commission itself in the first part of its report, the answer is yes; however, in the end, politics (national rivalries among the West Africans—albeit not stated in so many words—the minority had proposed that the new regional university be built in Nigeria) triumphed over the concern for speed, rationality, comprehensiveness, and quality.[19] This was very regrettable for the future development of higher education in Africa. While more will be said about this issue later, had the majority gone along with the minority it is possible that West Africa could have forged a path that other regions on the continent could have later emulated: namely that even under severe resources constraints, it is still possible to develop, by means of rational concentration of resources, a truly comprehensive, relevant, first rate, research university serving the needs of an entire region without regard to national boundaries/ rivalries and, at the same time, able to withstand economic vicissitudes. Such institutions, in most of Africa, even decades after independence, have yet to emerge—whether nationally or regionally (with the exception, *perhaps*—the doubt here speaks to the economic misfortunes that have befallen the African continent in recent decades— of a few countries, such as Egypt, Nigeria, and South Africa). On the contrary, as will be shown below, given the ever-spiraling resource constraints, the vast majority of universities in Africa today either continue to be little more than "continuation schools" or if they were not such before, have most certainly sunk to that level today.

Before proceeding to look at the report of the Asquith Commission whose recommendations, in essence, as it would turn out, would manage to echo those of both the Elliot majority *and* the Elliot minority (in a manner), it would not be out of place here to draw attention to four other indicators of the astuteness of the Elliot commission—in terms of their prescience regarding the kinds of problems that African universities would have to grapple with in years to come: On academic standards they observed: "Academic standards alone do not make a university. A university is a community whose purpose is the advancement and dissemination of knowledge. Insofar as the passing of examinations is the main object of the student so far does the university fail in its purpose; insofar as learning is pursued for learning's sake so far it succeeds. The attainment of this ideal calls for a cooperative effort by both teachers and taught" (p. 122).

As for research, they reiterated the sentiments expressed by Channon: "[W]e have all through our Report stressed the importance of research. We stress it again here in the conviction that the first essential to progress toward full university status is the selection of a first-rate teaching staff who will not only inspire their pupils but will themselves be constantly contributing to the advance of knowledge" (p. 122). On the role of community service they would note: "We have repeatedly stated our belief that university institutions in West Africa can and should have an active influence beyond the immediate university circle of staff and students. university education is not and cannot be a thing detached from the community.... We cannot lay down in detail the lines of such development in West Africa: the university institutions will themselves have to find out the ways in which they can best serve their own communities and the communities which lie beyond their borders" (p. 121).

On the contradictions of developing higher education in a nonliterate society (something that organizations such as the World Bank never understood when it became involved with education in Africa—see below): "To suggest that university standards can only be based on universal popular education is to ignore the whole history of universities themselves. The great scholars of earlier centuries were not the product of a universal literacy in every artisan's or peasant's hut. It was the reverse. The education of the many was made possible by the prolonged and intense study of the few. West Africa is in an epoch of its own. Total illiteracy and high standards of learning will exist side by side for many years to come" (p. 17).

One ought to point out here, however, that, as Ashby (1966) reminds us, many of these concerns emerged as a consequence of the British experience with higher education in colonial India and they were particularly concerned about learning lessons from that experience (which had left them with an awfully bad taste in their mouths—chief among them being the proliferation of low quality institutions that in time became hotbeds of nationalist agitation). Other concerns derived from the East Indian experience included, besides standards, the importance of research (as a response to the overemphasis on the arts and humanities); the need for mentor institutions in Britain (because of poor quality control); the importance of well-qualified teachers, which translated into not only the ability to perform in the classroom, but also continuous renewal through scholarship and research; and the necessity for institutional autonomy (because the British colonial government in India had too much political control over the universities).

The Asquith Colleges

The Asquith Commission (which issued its report in June 1945) was headed by Justice Cyril Asquith, and its official mandate was: "To consider the principles which should guide the promotion of higher education, learning and research and the development of universities in the Colonies; and to explore means whereby universities and other appropriate bodies in the United Kingdom may be able to cooperate with institutions of higher education in the Colonies in order to give effect to these principles"[20] (United Kingdom 1945a: 3). The commission would end up proposing the establishment of *university colleges*—that is, institutions with affiliation to universities in Britain in the tradition of the Fourah Bay College—in all the British colonies (not just those in Africa), in line with the ideas that had been formulated principally by Currie, De La Warr, Channon, and Elliot.[21]

A major guiding principal of the Asquith Commission was not to repeat what may be called the "Yaba mistake," which was the provision of university-type education but without it being certified as such. The Nigerian colonial authorities had determined that Nigeria did not yet require a genuine university-level institution at the time when Yaba was founded. However, the Nigerians themselves, needless to say, were of a different mind; as Janus (1980) notes, educated Nigerians resented the institution as a poor substitute for the real thing. In other words, the commission knew that what ever policies it came up with had to speak to the African desire for true *world-class* higher education. The compromise it reached was explained by its report thusly: while the establishment of universities in the colonies was urgent, the first step toward this goal was the founding of university colleges, and not full universities. The reason: it felt that to give degree-granting status to a newly established institution of higher learning was premature, because, in its words: "[a]n institution with the status of a university which does not command the respect of other universities brings no credit to the community which it serves." It then went on to conclude: "We cannot say how long the university college stage will last, because the length of this period depends upon much that cannot be foreseen" (United Kingdom 1945a: 13).

In an impressively short time, on the basis of the commission's report, a number of higher education institutions that were sometimes referred to as the *Asquith Colleges* were established through the agency of a remarkable combination of British government finance (facilitated by the Colonial Development and Welfare Acts of 1940 and 1950), and British university expertise in the form of the Inter-University Council for Higher Education in the Colonies—established in 1946 as an implementation of the recommendations of the commission.[22] These institutions, which for the most part were an upgrade of existing institutions, were to be residential and provide university-level education emphasizing liberal arts and sciences. Their governance involved British universities (principally, the University of London) and the Inter-University Council. Graduates of the Asquith Colleges received their degrees from the University of London on the basis of the affiliation of the colleges to the university.

The basic mechanism of the affiliation was that while the council was responsible for recruiting staff, the university, in cooperation with the faculty of the colleges, set the curricular and examination standards. Examples of the Asquith Colleges include: The University College of Ghana (at Legon, opened in October 1948); University College of Sierra Leone (established by upgrading the existing Fourah Bay College in 1960); The University College at Ibadan (opened in 1947); Khartoum University College (created in 1949 by merging the existing Gordon Memorial College and the Kitchener Medical School); Makerere College (upgraded in 1949); the Royal Technical College at Nairobi (founded in 1951); and the segregated University College of Salisbury (established in 1953, but upgraded two years later to become the University College of Rhodesias and Nyasaland with affiliation to the University of London).[23]

Clearly, then, on the eve of independence, in most of British colonial Africa some form of higher education at the university level was now evident. But not only that, it was university-level education that, in terms of rigor and quality, was comparable to that in the metropole (Ashby 1966: 256). However, establishment of full-fledged university education where institutions would grant their own degrees and no longer be affiliated with the universities in Britain, would have to await independence.

THE ERA OF NATIONAL UNIVERSITIES

The end of colonial rule ushered in a new phase in the history of higher education in Africa: the era of national universities. Country after country, in the wake of independence, founded national universities by either creating completely new institutions or transforming the existing ones. The impetus for the development of this phase grew out of a mixture of both nationalistic ambitions where the national university joined such other symbols of sovereignty as the flag, the national anthem, the international airport, the national bank, the national currency, and so on, and genuinely perceived discontent with the existing university colleges that the colonial powers had bequeathed the new governments.

The British, understandably, had looked to their own universities for models when creating the Asquith colleges. It would have been unusual for a major colonial power to do anything else. Plus, it should also be remembered that at the time when the colleges were being set up, general African opinion in anglophone Africa was that the British university model was the best model and that any modification of it would imply a lowering of standards. In Ashby's words "Over standards and quality of education the debate was overwhelmingly in favor of preserving the British academic heritage" (1966: 236). What is more, initially at least, there was very strong support in most African leadership circles (many of whom had obtained their degrees at universities abroad, principally in Britain) of an externally-awarded degree that the university colleges facilitated. To them, an indigenous degree from the newly created colleges would have spelled inferior degrees. The Asquith Commission was also aware of this issue as one of its members (Fred Clarke of the University of London) had observed, albeit in a different context:

They [the Africans] may well look askance at any modified form of the London degree, adapted to local conditions, even if the point of equivalence were beyond all doubt. They would probably reject altogether any form of degree which left room for doubt and would prefer to take the external degree as it stands, even if that should mean a considerable amount of private study (from Nwauwa 1997: 149).

Nwauwa suggests that there was a race dimension to this issue as well. That is, any suggestion of adaptation was interpreted as acceding to the European stereotype of the African as intellectually inferior—and therefore incapable of handling undiluted western education. In his words: "After almost a century of indoctrination that Africans were inferior either intellectually, creatively or in abstract thinking, it was essential that the curricula of proposed colonial universities should approximate that offered in the United Kingdom." Additionally, he observes, "[i]t was necessary, not only to build self-worth in African students but also to establish in the colonial administrations the principle of equality, for salary and other purposes, of Africans trained locally and expatriates educated overseas" (p. 149). Not surprisingly, even the idea of adapting the curricula was, at the beginning, resisted by Africans for fear that it meant dilution of quality and standards.

However, despite the best intentions of the British, and despite the initial preferences of the modern emergent African elite, the fact was that the British university model was not the most appropriate for the specific circumstances of the African nations. In time, this became clear to all concerned, precipitating dissatisfaction among many of them with the Asquith college model (the institutional face of what Nwauwa has labeled, somewhat unkindly, "British 'university imperialism'"). The discontent rested, according to Ajayi, Goma, and Johnson (1996), on four principal issues: One, the existing enrollment was too small, targeting only an elite; there was need to increase enrollment and broaden recruitment to cover all sections of the population by, among other things, breaking open the cloistered physical environment of the college and admitting a commuter-based college population. Two, the curricular offering was much too limited for the needs of a rapidly developing nation in a hurry to catch up with other advanced nations (they ignored fields of applied science and technology), and at the same time did not even make a pretense of incorporating locally relevant subjects such as African history, African religions, African languages, and so on. Ashby (1966: 244) notes, for example, that ten years after the university college was created in Nigeria, its curriculum was still bereft of such subjects as "engineering, economics, law, geology, anthropology, sociology, public administration, or Arabic and Islamic studies and it had taken eight years to establish a department of education." Three, the degree structure was narrowly conceived, providing insufficient flexibility in the kinds of major and minor specializations that students could undertake. Four, there was insufficient attention given to making the institution a full educational partner of the community in which it was located; therefore, there was need to develop community service programs, adult education classes, long-distance education services, and so on. In making these criticisms, the model of the university that the critics appeared to have in mind was one that incorporated two key features of the land-grant colleges in the United States: democratic student recruitment and democratic degree structures and curricular outlay.[24]

Higher Education Reform: The Land-Grant Model

Perhaps not surprisingly, therefore, the first major higher education commission to advise an independent African country was U.S.-funded and included U.S. educators—reference here is to the Ashby Commission (official title: *The Commission on Post-School-Certificate and Higher Education in Nigeria*) that the Carnegie Corporation financed to look into the education needs of the newly independent (1960) Federal Republic of Nigeria. The commission, which submitted its report to the Nigerians in 1960, was headed by Sir Eric Ashby, Master of Clare College Cambridge and a strong proponent of higher education reform in post–World War II Britain. The commission had operated from the perspective that the insistence on *quality* and *standards* should not be an excuse for not reforming the Asquith model, by noting that there was confusion between what quality meant and what standards meant. As Ashby (1966: 259) points out in his book: "The concept of standards is quite different from the concept of quality. It would be difficult to maintain that the quality of higher education in (say) the University of London is higher than that in Harvard or Gottingen or Melbourne. It would be nonsense to assert that the standards of achievement for admission or for the award of a degree are the same in these universities." The watchword for the commission, therefore, was "reform" and "relevance" and its recommended university model was one that fused elements of the British and U.S. models.

It ought to be pointed out here that the commission was not breaking entirely new ground in turning to the U.S. model (specifically the land-grant university model) as worthy of emulation by an African country. It already had before it the example of the University of Nigeria, established by law in 1955 (though actual classes would not commence until 1960) at Nsukka as a regional university. The institution was the brain child of Dr. Nnamdi Azikiwe, who while studying and teaching in the United States (from 1925 to 1933) had become greatly smitten by the U.S. land-grant model.[25] Although his earlier efforts to found an African university in West Africa following his return from the United States had come to naught, on the eve of Nigerian independence it would be an entirely different circumstance: for by then not only had the British colonial authorities firmly accepted the need for higher education in its African colonies, but Azikiwe, who by now was among Nigeria's foremost nationalist leaders was well placed to bring to fruition his long cherished dream for a West African university modeled on U.S. institutions.[26] During one of his later visits to the United States, he had, for instance, articulated his desire for such a university thusly in a speech he delivered in 1947 in New York:

Surely if we can have "Yale in China," "American University in Turkey," "American University in Beirut" I see no reason why we should not have "Lincoln University [or] Howard University in Africa." I trust that all those who are interested in this project of adjusting human relations will bear in mind this idea of establishing a university in West Africa in order to make the bridgehead in Africa more secure and more intrinsic in its value to the cause of understanding, goodwill and fellowship with the United States (from Howard 1982: 111).

Upon finding himself as the premier of the Eastern Region in 1954 when his party won the regional election, Azikiwe (who would also later become the president of an independent Nigeria in 1963) wasted no time, and within a year he was in the United States, once more knocking on doors for assistance with his pet project. On this occasion, at long last, backed by his status as one of the emerging leaders of a country on the verge of attaining independence and against the backdrop of a spiraling Cold War, he would find ready ears for his project in the one place where it mattered most: in Washington. The U.S. government would soon sign on to the project, with Michigan State University being contracted to serve as the midwife for it. (The British government, not wishing to allow the United States completely free reign, would also become involved.)

When the University of Nigeria opened its doors at Nsukka (with an initial enrollment of some 200 students) it was, in principle, an institutional embodiment of the land-grant influenced U.S. *multiversity* model in which such vocationally oriented subjects as journalism, agriculture, teacher training, general studies, and so on, were part of the university curriculum from the very beginning (unlike, for instance, at the strictly British modeled University of

Ibadan).[27] At the same time, to ensure a wider-class background of students, the entrance qualifications were pegged at a less elitist standard (students did not have to have A-levels, O-levels sufficed) and even more radically, unlike the other Nigerian institutions, it was empowered to award its own degrees from the moment it opened its doors.[28]

Working from the lofty premise that the development of higher education in a PQD country should first and foremost be guided by development and personpower needs, rather than national budgetary dictates, the Ashby Commission recommended that Nigeria establish three new federally controlled universities (at Enugu, Lagos, and Zaria) on the twin principles of diversity and flexibility in degree structures and the curricula (on principles akin to those characteristic of the U.S. land-grant college model). Although the report was accepted by the Nigerian federal government, in the end, for political reasons, the Nigerians decided to build only one federal university (at Lagos) and created three other universities in the regions under local (regional) control. This, however, would only be the beginning. For, in the years ahead higher education expansion in Nigeria, would turn out, to put it succinctly, explosive. Consider the following chronological highlights of the establishment of universities in Nigeria: In 1962, five were created: Ahmadu Bello, Ibadan, Lagos, Nigeria, and Ife (the last would be reconstituted in 1987 as Obafemi Awolowo University); in 1972, one: Benin (a reconstitution of the Institute of Technology of Benin City established in 1970); in 1975, four: Calabar, Jos, Maiduguri, and Sokoto (the last would be reconstituted in 1988 as Usmanu Danfodiyo University Sokoto); in 1977, three: Ilorin, Port Harcourt, and Bayero (the last was a reconstitution of Ahmadu Bello College founded in 1960); in 1979: seven: a Federal University of Agriculture in each of the states of Benue and Ogun and a Federal University of Technology in each of the states of Gongola, Imo, Ondo, Niger, and Bauchi (the last would be reconstituted in 1988 as Abubakar Tafawa Balewa University of Technology); in 1980, three: Bendel State, Federal University of Technology Owerri, and Anambra State (the last would be reconstituted in 1992 as Nnamdi Azikiwe University); in 1981, three: Imo State, Rivers State, and Federal University of Technology Yola; in 1982: two: Ogun State and Ondo State; in 1983, three: Lagos State, Federal University of Technology Minna, and Cross River State (the last to be reconstituted in 1991 as University of Uyo); in 1985, one: Nigerian Defense Academy; in 1988, three: Abuja, University of Agriculture of Makurdi, and University of Agriculture Abeokuta (created out of a merger of the Federal University of Technology—founded in 1983—and University of Lagos); in 1991, one: Federal University of Technology Akure. Of course, impressive as this quantitative development has been by African standards, at the qualitative level there is much that leaves to be desired: to put it bluntly, not all universities are created equal. Staff shortages, overcrowding, grossly inadequate logistical facilities, and so on, have been endemic among the newer institutions. What is worse is that even the older flagship universities have in recent years succumbed to this state of affairs.

The Problem of Autonomy

If the university becomes an important symbol of sovereignty—as has been the case in most parts of Africa—then it is also quite likely that it will become an object of politicization; especially if it is perceived to be an alien institution that monopolizes a disproportionate allocation of financial resources. This was exemplified quite early on (beginning in 1959 and reaching its climax in 1961), in the case of Ghana, where the vociferous and charismatic Ghanaian leader, Nkwame Nkrumah, demanded direct participation in the governance of the University College of Ghana at Legon. The unstated bone of contention was patronage: Nkrumah and his Convention People's Party wanted to commandeer the college as one more avenue for conferring patronage on favored associates through appointments to key positions (including teaching positions). The stated criticism (which by no means was entirely unjustified) by Nkrumah and others in his government, however, was that the college was not adapting to the needs of the country in terms of indigenization of both the curricula, as well as the teaching and administrative staff. Resistance from the academic community to the criticism was perceived as intolerable arrogance; especially on the part of the students and the foreign teaching staff (the expatriate personnel). A partial denouement to the simmering conflict came with the reconstitution of the college into the University of Ghana in 1962 and the concurrent installation of Nkrumah as the chancellor of the university; the firing of vocal critics in 1964; the resignation of the vice-chancellor (Dr. Connor Cruise O'Brien) in 1965; and the military coup in 1966 that deposed Nkrumah and banished him into obscure exile in Egypt. It was a partial denouement because the departure of Nkrumah did not lead to an end to the struggles between the university and the government; rather they became "institutionalized" with the permanent distrust that developed between the university constituency and the government over the motives of each (Ajayi, Goma, and Johnson 1996).

The state-university conflict in Ghana highlighted an evolving trend in Africa that to this day has yet to see a satisfactory culmination: the problem on one hand of universities retaining their autonomy, and the issue of *endemic* student political activism on the other (which has often worked to the detriment of the former imperative).[29] The former has two interrelated parts to it: the freedom of the university to organize its own internal affairs as an independent corporate entity, and the right of the faculty and students to engage in teaching and learning without external interference (academic freedom). While the latter may also be related to university autonomy, in practice it has been more about the self-arrogated responsibility by students to be active participants in civil society—often on matters beyond those of academic concern.

Given that the state has the monopoly over both the purse strings and the coercive apparatus, most African governments have had no qualms in infringing on university autonomy, sometimes brazenly and sometimes quietly; even though all institutions (probably without exception) were established with constitutions that guaranteed their autonomy (including academic freedom). In other words, in almost all instances of state-university conflict in Africa, it is rare that the university has emerged unscathed or triumphant. One may credit this circumstance to the larger issue of "modern" democracy, which, as any student of African politics knows, has had, to put it very mildly, a checkered record in Africa ever since Europe set foot on the continent (that is from the colonial period on to the present).[30] As for the matter of student political activism; the success of African countries in crushing it has been characterized by winning numerous battles but, so far, losing the war.[31]

Two other higher education developments during Nkrumah's reign was the conversion of the Kumasi College of Science and Technology into a successful university: the Kwame Nkrumah University of Science and Technology (later the name reverted back to Kumasi University of Science and Technology after he was deposed); and the founding of a poorly planned, but well motivated science teacher training college in 1962: University College of Science and Education. In later years, two other universities would be created: the University of Cape Coast (a reconstitution in 1971 of the University College of Cape Coast founded in 1962) and University for Development Studies (created in 1992 at Tamale).

Experimenting with Structure

Elsewhere in former British colonial Africa, the early 1960s saw the attempt to implement a bold experiment in East Africa with the creation in 1963 of an autonomous degree granting *federated* university (but still supervised to some extent by the Inter-University Council in London), the University of East Africa, out of three constituent colleges: The Royal University College (formerly a technical college) in Kenya, Makerere University College in Uganda, and the newly established University College of Dar es Salaam in Tanzania. To the architects of the university, the 1958 working party appointed by the colonial office and led by University of London's Sir John Lockwood, it made sense to have a federated university. Among other things, such a university would have served as an important symbol of unification in the new East African Community—a political and economic union that the British created out of the three geographically contiguous former colonies of Kenya, Uganda, and Tanganyika, that not only shared political boundaries but also some elements of colonial and precolonial history.

The basic principles on which the new university valiantly (given the external disintegrative political milieu) tried to operate were these: (a) It was not affiliated to the University of London (though it maintained some relationship with that university for purposes of *quality control*) and hence it acquired the right to issue its own degrees. (b) It formulated a common budget that was based on subscriptions to a common fund. (c) There were budgetary realloca-tions from the most developed of the constituent units (Makerere) to the other two emerging units in order to accelerate their development and thereby bring them on par with Makerere. (d) There was a push toward development of pro-fessional schools and areas of specialization and expertise in each of the three units, but on the basis of nonredundancy. (e) Students were enrolled from across the entire region by each of the units. (f) The three units retained as much administrative autonomy as was feasible from the perspective of a fed-eral structure. (g) Administration of the university itself rested on a council and a senate to which the constituent units elected members.

Sadly, the East African Community did not last; with its collapse, the fed-erated university, too, fragmented into its three constituent units as independent universities: Makerere University, University of Nairobi, and University of Dar es Salaam (having lasted all of seven years—1963–1970). The overriding fac-tor in the demise of both was that bane of postindependence African politics: negative recalcitrant nationalism fueled by ethnically driven sectarianism en-gendered by, in this case, cross-border, intra-elite conflicts—but politely dubbed by Ashby, who foresaw the institution's demise only three years into its life, as "aspirations for political and cultural autonomy" (1966: 317). (See also Furley and Watson 1978, and Maxwell 1980, for the minutiae detailing the birth and collapse of the university, and from which the foregoing observation has been extracted.)[32]

In later years the three countries would see more higher education expan-sion with the creation of the following public institutions, among others: In Kenya: Egerton University (a reconstitution in 1987 of the University of Nai-robi University College, which itself had been reconstituted in 1986 from Eger-ton Agricultural College that had been founded in 1939), Jomo Kenyatta Uni-versity of Agriculture and Technology (a reconstitution in 1993 of a constituent college of Kenyatta University, which itself had been reconstituted in 1988 from an agricultural and technology college that had been founded in 1981), Kenyatta University (created in 1985 out of Kenyatta University College that itself was established in 1972), Maseno University College (founded in 1990 as a constituent college of Moi University), and Moi University (established in 1984); in Uganda: Mbarara University of Science and Technology (created in 1989); and in Tanzania: Muhimbili University College of Health Sciences (a reconstitution in 1991 of the faculty of medicine of the University of Dar Es Salaam), Sokoine University of Agriculture (a reconstitution in 1984 of the faculty of agriculture, forestry and veterinary sciences), and the Open Univer-sity of Tanzania (founded in 1992). In addition to these institutions, a number of private universities would also emerge in two of the three countries.

Sir John Lockwood was also responsible for the creation of a university in a country, Zambia, that was once part of yet another failed experiment in a political and economic union of contiguous British colonies with shared elements of colonial and precolonial history: the partially autonomous Federation of Rhodesias and Nyasaland located in the upper reaches of southern Africa. The federation was created in 1952 out of a union of three countries, but it disintegrated in 1963, leading a year later to the independence of Northern Rhodesia (became Zambia) and Nyasaland (became Malawi).[33] Meanwhile, the remnant of the federation, Southern Rhodesia, which had been a self-governing colony at the time of its entry into the federation, was left with an uncertain political future. Consequently, emboldened by years of policy drift in London regarding the question of independence and black majority rule in Southern Rhodesia, the European settler minority (5% of the population) formally requested independence in March of 1963. Much to their surprise, Britain refused; instead, it proclaimed five principles that it insisted would have to serve as a basis for any form of independence. Among these principles was one that the settlers vehemently opposed: the requirement that concrete progress be made toward black majority rule. Two years later, on November 11, 1965, under the leadership of a dour man by the name of Ian Smith, the European minority decided to take matters into their own hands by proclaiming a unilateral declaration of independence (they renamed the country Rhodesia). It would take a decade and a half and British-led international sanctions, coupled with sporadic armed conflict (in which countless civilian lives would be consumed) between the minority government and a black liberation movement, the Patriotic Front, before the European settlers would succumb to black majority rule in 1980 in the newly named independent country of Zimbabwe.

Southern Rhodesia inherited the university college in Salisbury (Harare), which at its inception had ostensibly been created to serve a multiracial student population. In practice, however, all effort was made to discourage black student enrollment as well as the comingling of black and white students outside the classroom through such measures as the segregation of halls of residence, dining facilities, and so on. During the era of minority rule under Ian Smith, the college would be reconstituted as the University of Rhodesia; however, for symbolic and pragmatic reasons described by Murphree (1977), the university retained its original charter. The consequence of that was this paradox: even as Ian Smith's Rhodesian Front party continued to push racial segregation at almost all levels of society and polity, the university would remain multiracial. But not only that, its black student population continued to increase to the point where at the time of independence in 1980 it was now the majority of the total student population. Financial support for the students came primarily from private sources; for the vast majority it was provided by the World University Service, a nongovernmental organization (Chideya 1991).

Following independence, the governing legal instrument, the Royal Charter, was replaced by the University of Zimbabwe Act of 1982. This development marked a major first step in the effort to "Africanize" the university. Although the University of Zimbabwe remains the country's flagship university to this day, the country ceased to be a single university country upon the recommendation of the 1988 Commission of Inquiry (on the desirability of a second university) with the inauguration in 1990 of a second university: the National University of Science and Technology at Bulawayo. Two years later a third university was founded, but under private sponsorship.

Sir John Lockwood chaired the committee that was instrumental in founding the University of Zambia in 1966—an independent institution that would grant its own degrees. The committee was funded jointly by the Carnegie Corporation and the British Ministry of Overseas Development and it was put together by the British Inter-University Council and the American Council on Education on the basis of membership drawn from both Britain and the United States. A year earlier in Malawi, the University of Malawi had been created on the basis of a report (issued in 1964) produced by a four-member team funded by the U.S. Agency of International Development and selected by the American Council on Education. Unlike the University of Zambia, the university was created out of five, geographically dispersed, constituent colleges, each specializing in different fields: agriculture, education, technology, social sciences, and so on.

What is of importance to note here, as Ashby (1966) with justifiable approval points out, is that the two universities represented the furthest in the development of those anglophone African universities that were based on a significant modification of the colonially inherited British university model—achieved by incorporating principles derived from the U.S. land-grant philosophy. This philosophy had emerged from the establishment in the nineteenth-century of publicly-funded universities in each of the states that made up the United States through the agency of bills introduced by Vermont's representative, Justin Smith Morrill, in the U.S. Congress—and which passed them in 1862 and 1890 to become the Morrill (or Land-Grant) Acts. The purpose of the legislation was to enable states to raise revenue through, initially, federal grants of land to each state and later through direct cash disbursements on an annual basis by Congress for, in the words of the oft-quoted passage from the 1862 Act "the endowment, support, and maintenance of at least one college where the leading object shall be, without excluding other scientific and classical studies, and including military tactics, to teach other branches of learning as are related to agriculture and mechanic arts...in order to promote the liberal and practical education of the industrial classes in the several pursuits and professions in life."

The rationale for the modification of the British university model (a la Asquith) was explained by Lockwood thus:

The special relationship schemes with London and Durham have been extremely successful within the limits of their possibilities. Their weakness is that they have carried over into Africa the highly selective processes and types of degree courses which have grown up in the United Kingdom since the 1939–45 war. In a sense, African university development has been the victim of our own educational history in the last twenty years. Expatriate staff have naturally taken with them habits and ideas current in the United Kingdom but not necessarily relevant to the urgent needs of an African country. What they have done, they have done remarkably well and deserve the highest praise. But a nagging question has become more and more insistent during the last few years whether we and they were right to concentrate as we did on converting the university colleges into academic counterparts of English university institutions with high entrance standards and highly specialized honors courses (from Ashby 1966: 286–87).

So, what did the modification entail? Specifically, the newly created universities represented a move to a university education that was characterized by structural diversity, flexibility and curricular relevance, but that at the same time did not sacrifice high quality and standards. The specific changes that this move entailed, included these: (1) The move away from specialized single subject honors degree in the arts to a general degree in any number of fields, including professional/ vocational fields of study. (2) The broadening of the disciplinary structure to include medicine and applied technology—specifically the various fields of engineering. (3) The expansion of the curricula to include vocational subjects. (4) The move from a three-year degree to a four-year degree in order to eliminate the sixth form A-level General Certificate in Education as a university entrance requirement. (Entrance requirement would be based on the fifth form O-level, thereby broadening the field of student recruitment.) (5) The dedication of the first year to a general program of study with required courses. (6) The postponement of specialization to the graduate level. (7) The broadening of the mission of the university to include community outreach through programs such as agricultural extension services, public health education, extramural evening courses, long-distance correspondence courses, and so on.[34]

For the first decade or so, all the three former territories of the federation remained single university countries. With the exception of Malawi, the other two countries now boast at least two or more universities. The case of Zimbabwe has already been noted; as for Zambia it acquired a new university in 1987, the Copperbelt University (at Kitwe), with the reconstitution of a constituent institution of the University of Zambia, the University of Zambia at Ndola founded in 1978. The curricular focus of the new university from the very beginning has been business and technology.

The idea of interterritorial universities, for obvious reasons of economies of scale, universalization of quality and standards, academic prestige, and so on, has always had some appeal in some political and higher education circles in Britain and in the African colonies, beginning with the proposal for a University of West Africa by Horton as early as 1862. Now, whereas the idea never came to pass in West Africa, it was implemented in the East African Community and in the Federation of Rhodesia and Nyasaland (in the form of the University College of Rhodesia and Nyasaland at Salisbury). However, as noted earlier, for primarily nationalistic reasons, the two implementations did not succeed for long. Incredibly, the same higher education scenario was replayed in yet another part of British colonial Africa with the establishment in 1964 of the University of Basutoland, Bechuanaland Protectorate and Swaziland (to be renamed two years later, with the achievement of political independence by the first two countries, as University of Botswana, Lesotho, and Swaziland).

At inception, the university was federal only in name because only Lesotho had a campus, while the other two countries did not. Lesotho had been fortunate to have a private Catholic institution named University College of Pius XII established in 1945 (initially affiliated to University of South Africa). The college became the first campus of the federal university. Later, the other two countries managed to acquire campus facilities of their own and as their confidence, resources and misplaced nationalistic zeal grew, they were able to engineer a complete dissolution of the university into independent national universities in a two-step process: the first to leave was the Lesotho campus with the founding of the National University of Lesotho in 1975. The remaining two countries were left with the rump, the University of Botswana and Swaziland, until it too disintegrated in 1982 into University of Botswana and University of Swaziland. Given the small size of these countries, all three remain to this day single university countries (though Botswana now also boasts a college, the Botswana College of Agriculture founded in 1991, and a polytechnic, the Botswana Polytechnic).[35]

NOTES

1. Other conjunctural factors would include the ending of the Napoleonic Wars and the European "discovery" of a Native American medicine for the treatment of Malarial fever around the middle of the 1600s in South America: the bark of the cinchona tree—though its medicinal derivative, quinine, would not be available until after 1820. (As we all know from school textbooks malaria was among the major scourges that European colonialists had to struggle against in places like Africa.)

2. This was because of a combination of three main factors: the economics of slave procurement, health-related constraints and the relative military weakness of the European states vis-à-vis themselves as well as the Africans.

3. In other words, the question: Was it Britain or France or Belgium who was responsible for setting off the Scramble for Africa is not as important a question insofar as this work is concerned as, Was Africa destined to be colonized by Europe? (See Appendix II.) Plus, those still interested in the former question are confronted with the intractable problem of picking out a cogent explanation from several equally compelling

ones. For example, Was the trigger the British takeover of Egypt beginning in 1882 and culminating with their confrontation with France at Fashoda on the Nile River? Or was it the treaty with the Makoko in 1882 by the French (through their agent Savorgnan de Brazza) which led to their claims over part of the Congo and their establishment of colonies in West Africa? Or was it the French proclivity toward empire building (which now included Africa as a target) as expressed in the views held by people such as the French minister for colonial affairs, Jean Jaureguiberry; or should one lay the blame on Bismarck's sudden realization that without empire building in Africa, Germany would be disadvantaged vis-à-vis other powers? Or perhaps it was simply the generalized built in drive toward European global expansion. At the end of the day, there is no single explanation that can cover so vast a continent as Africa—all motives to varying degrees had a role to play: strategic (e.g., protecting sea routes); financial and commercial gain (trade and investment); humanitarian (squelching the slave trade within the continent); diplomatic (status, honor, and prestige within Europe); personal ambitions (as those of the Cape-to-Cairo arch-imperialist "I-would-annex-the-planets-if-I-could" Cecil Rhodes in southern Africa). About the last: the part played by Rhodes in the British colonization of southern Africa should not be underestimated (see Magubane 1996, for instance). Employing his enormous ill-gotten wealth (even by the standards of his day) he did everything he could to realize his dream of a British colonial Africa stretching from the Cape to Cairo. In fact, his megalomaniacal dreams went beyond that, consider this musing a la Adolf Hitler: "I contend that we are the first race in the world, and that the more of the world we inhabit the better it is for the human race. I contend that every acre added to our territory means the birth of more of the English race who otherwise would not be brought into existence....The furtherance of the British Empire, for the bringing of the whole uncivilized world under British rule, for the recovery of the United States, for making of the Anglo-Saxon race but one empire. What a dream! But yet it is probable. It is possible" (quoted in Magubane 1996: 102). For more on this subject, the following should suffice as entry points into the literature: Boahen (1985); Cain and Hopkins (1993); Collins, Burns and Ching (1994); Harlow and Carter (1999); Hopkins (1986); Newbury and Kanya-Forstner (1969); Robinson, Gallagher and Demy (1961); Sanderson (1965); Taylor (1967); and Wesseling (1996). Note: the actual legislative instrument that came out of the Berlin Conference, the General Act of the Conference of Berlin, February 26, 1885, is reproduced in Harlow and Carter (a documentary sourcebook on imperialism).

    4. A question not usually posed by historians, but pops up in classrooms from time to time out of those mental recesses so peculiar to the student mind: Why didn't the United States participate in the Scramble for Africa? This is not an illogical question as it may seem at first blush. After all the United States was represented at the Berlin Conference. Plus, it is not as if the United States had never had any inkling of the economic potential of Africa: its relations with at least one part of Africa, the Cape, went as far back as when the Dutch first settled there (see Rosenthal 1968); plus U.S. whalers were a common sight off the coasts of southern Africa in the heyday of whaling and its was not unusual for them to engage in barter with the coastal Africans, such as the Khoikhoi and the Tsonga (see Haywood 1967; see also Booth 1976 on early U.S. relations with southern Africa). The likeliest answer is that the United States was already engaged in its own colonial project: the colonization of the remaining Native American lands to the

west (a process that was identical in almost all respects to the European colonial projects in Africa—so much so that it even had a counterpart to the Battle of Isandhlwana: the Battle of Little Bighorn (Custer's Last Stand), where George Armstrong Custer's 7th Cavalry met defeat in 1876 at the hands of the Sioux on the Little Bighorn River (see Floca 1974 for a comparative study of the two battles). In other words, it did not need new colonial adventures, especially when it would have also meant competing with other colonial powers. Mention ought to be made here too of the U.S. imperial wars of aggression as further draining U.S. imperial energy: the Mexican-American War against Mexico (after forcing a war on it in 1846 that lasted until the signing of the Treaty of Guadalupe Hidalgo on February 2, 1848, the United States absorbed the two territories of New Mexico and California into the U.S. union, and confirmed the earlier forcible annexation of Texas in 1845); and the Spanish-American War against Spain (forced on it by the United States in 1898, as a consequence of which the United States took over the Philippines as its colony, despite Filipino guerrilla resistance (the United States would rule it from 1898 to 1946), absorbed Guam and Puerto Rico, and coerced Spain out Cuba and occupied it until 1934—though it continues to occupy a portion of it to this day: the infamous Guantanamo Bay).

5. Contrary to what the British may have consciously thought once (in the vein of the views of such arch imperialists as Cecil Rhodes, Rudyard Kipling, Thomas Macaulay, etc.), or may still subconsciously think today, their eventual near monopoly of the modern Western colonial enterprise in the wake of Columbus, has to be credited, like so many other things in history, not to some mythical, genetically determined, intellectual prowess, but to that more mundane phenomenon of history described in Appendix II: the conjuncture of fortuitously propitious historical factors (one such factor, for example, was the British defeat of the Spanish Armada in 1588). Thus it was that Africa—at least a very large portion of it—became one of their more prominent possessions in a colonial empire that spanned almost the entire planet (it is said that once upon a time the British empire was so vast that the sun never set in the empire). In Africa, its colonial possessions (if one includes protectorates, trust territories, etc.), numbering more than twenty (making it the largest colonial power on the continent) ranged from Egypt on the Mediterranean to South Africa on the South Atlantic and from Nigeria on the Atlantic to Kenya on the Indian Ocean.

6. See Appendix III for a snapshot of the European colonial empires in Africa at the time of independence.

7. Yes, it is true, as Nwauwa (1997) points out, that during the heyday of the British colonial policy of *indirect rule* there was always fear among British colonial officials of the university educated (uppity) African who would not fit in with the colonial administrative scheme—hence explaining in part their reluctance to provide opportunities for higher education in their African colonies. However, the fact that some institutions were established, even if reluctantly, prior to the change of policy heralded by the Elliott and Asquith Commissions, indicates that the British did in the end see some value in providing education at least to the children of the traditional chiefly rulers (upon whom, that is the rulers, the administrative structure of *indirect rule* rested).

8. One should not underestimate the impact of this policy consideration on the decision to eventually provide a modicum of higher education opportunity during the colonial period. As Roberts has observed "The development of higher education for Africans

both in South Africa and in British colonial Africa was intended to reduce the flow of African students overseas. This subject is still too little known" (Roberts 1990: 229). The British colonial policy of indirect rule, which depended in part on traditional African rulers for governance, did not have much use for educated Africans who were not from the chieftancy establishment. As Roberts points out "By 1900 Africans were debarred from the administrative (or 'political' branches of government." The reason he states was that "both in London and Africa officials were keen to strengthen the powers of chiefs as a way of restricting the influence of educated Africans....African rulers by divine right were judiciously cultivated" (pp. 33–34). Yet, at the same time, the indirect pressure from Africans themselves as they sought higher education overseas in ever-increasing numbers reluctantly led the colonial authorities to conclude that locally provided higher education was better (less potential for subversive activities—at least that is what they hoped) than one available overseas over which they had no control. Of course, by the time it became clear that independence was just around the corner in the decade after the Second World War there was a reversal of policy and the traditional rulers were not only marginalized, but the Western-educated African was now given pride of place in the new dispensation that would lead to political independence.

A question one may ask, however, is how extensive was this (often privately sponsored) flow of African overseas students from anglophone Africa prior to the 1950s? One may respond by first noting that the tradition of Africans going to study in Europe, albeit in ones and twos, even long before the arrival of European colonialism was already established (Northrup [2002(a)] gives examples going back to the seventeenth-century). Consequently, it is not surprising that as European colonialism took root in Africa, Africans would continue the tradition with even greater vigor. Now, while there are no comprehensive statistics available on the subject, understandably, it is accurate to say that from the perspective of British colonialism it was significant enough to cause anguish among British colonial administrators. Roberts provides a sampling of the flow: (a) a conference of African students in London in 1913 attracted some 40 students. (b) Between 1930 and 1937 an annual average of 53 West Africans were studying for degrees in Britain; the figure would increase to 71 from 1938 to 1940. These figures do not include those who were studying for law degrees, who it appears were the trail blazers in the area of overseas study. (c) By 1906 some 150 students from South Africa had gone to study in the United States, the preferred destination (unlike for the West Africans). (d) Students from elsewhere in colonial anglophone Africa (leaving aside Liberia) would also begin to go to the United States so that between 1920 and 1938, for instance, a total of 32 students from Nigeria had gone to the United States.

One ought to also point out here that, in contrast, colonial Europhone Africa was less averse to encouraging African students to go and study in the metropole—in line with its "assimilationist" approach to colonial rule. Though this is not to say that African students from that part of Africa found it any easier to go overseas; especially since postprimary education was even more poorly developed there than in colonial anglophone Africa.

9. See Ashby (1966), Janus (1980), and Nwauwa (1996), for more on this debate. Janus also draws attention to the views of Casely Hayford another of the early West African intellectuals who called for the establishment of a local university, not only for reasons of racial pride, but also for nationalistic reasons—in this sense an improvement

on the views of people like Horton and Blyden.

10. It may also be pointed out here that even to this day an educational qualification obtained from abroad carries with it a cachet that an equivalent local qualification does not—and this attitude applies not only to Africa but perhaps to all countries, to varying degrees of course, around the world outside the West. What reason can one ascribe to this phenomenon? There are primarily two reasons: in many instances (though not always) there is the objective fact that institutions abroad were, and to this day still are, qualitatively better because of their access to resources; and there is the lingering inferiority complex born of centuries of cultural, economic, and politico-military insubordination to the might of Western imperialism. Additionally, in Africa specifically, in the years preceding independence, there was the legitimate feeling that the best way to answer the European notions of racial superiority was to, in a sense, beat them at their own game: to successfully compete in their own institutions in the metropole with their brightest and best! In other words, building a local university with an "Africanized" curriculum would not cut it; it would only invite derision. Under the circumstances, it is not surprising then (see the discussion by Janus 1980: 146 on this matter) that the initial establishment of university-level higher education institutions in anglophone (and even francophone) Africa prior to independence was not always a result of enthusiastic pressure from Africans themselves; rather it was a policy decision that, for the most part, was imposed on them.

11. Years in parentheses indicate when they wrote or published their reports.

12. This view of the intellectual abilities of Africans (and the African Diaspora in general) was, of course, a variant of the more pervasive "scientific" rationalization of racism that had become current in Madden's day based on craniometric and related studies.

13. Reilly (1995) reminds us that prior to the formation of this body, there was the Shuttleworth Report of 1847, which, while of specific reference to the freed slaves of Jamaica, had implications for British colonies elsewhere too. That report, he explains, was a precursor to the kind of thinking that would develop a little later in relation to freed slaves in another English-speaking part of the Americas (the U.S. South): the best education for them was *industrial education* (ala Samuel Chapman Armstrong's Hampton Institute and Booker T. Washington's Tuskegee Institute in the United States and proselytized in the British colonies by the Phelps-Stokes Commission).

14. For more on this issue, see Chapter 5, and Reilly (1995)—as well as Foster (1965), King (1971), Sivonen (1995), and Watkins (1994).

15. As the Asquith Commission (see below) had explained:

His Majesty's Government has entered upon a program of social and economic development for the Colonies which is not merely the outcome of a desire to fulfill our moral obligations as trustees of the welfare of colonial peoples, but is also designed to lead to the exercise of self government by them. In the stage preparatory to self government universities have an important part to play; indeed they may be said to be indispensable. To them we must look for the production of men and women with the standards of public service and capacity for leadership which self-rule requires (United Kingdom 1945a: 10).

16. The following are among the important chronological markers in the historical

development of this once prestigious institution: August 1922, the institution would be renamed Makerere College (from Uganda Technical College, which in initial planning documents had been simply known as Central Technical School); 1923–24, training in rudimentary medicine, surveying, engineering, and agriculture introduced and the first permanent building of the growing institution was opened; 1925, a two-year teacher training course commenced; 1926, the college became a residential institution with enrollment henceforth restricted only to residential students; 1936, enrollment had increased to 153 students with a few coming from neighboring countries of Kenya and Tanzania; 1938, the basic recommendation of the De La Warr commission that Makerere be developed into a university level college was accepted; and in the same year there was a leap in the quality of life at the developing institution marked by the introduction of electricity to campus buildings; 1945, the first female students (numbering all of six) were admitted; in the same year the Asquith Commission Report was published and its recommendations that Makerere be upgraded to a full university college in association with the University of London was accepted; 1947, general education courses in arts and sciences (labeled higher courses) were introduced; 1950, the college would enter into a special relationship with the University of London as one of the Asquith colleges and be renamed the University College of East Africa; 1952, student protest against the quality of food in the dining halls would escalate to the point where the institution would suffer its first student-instigated temporary closure; 1954, the number of teaching staff had risen to 90, and the student population stood at 448 of whom seventeen were women; 1961, the college became a constituent part of a tripartite federal structure (incorporating a college each from Kenya and Tanzania) to become simply Makerere University College; 1963, the college (with its two other partners) became an independent university granting its own degrees as the University of East Africa. For more on the early history of Makerere see Macpherson (1964), Perham (1964), and Sicherman (2005). Sicherman is also good for the recent checkered history of the university.

17. Of the three, Yaba was an exception, in the sense that the commission proposed that instead of upgrading Yaba to a university college, a completely new institution be created at a different location, at Ibadan, for reasons that one need not be concerned with here (but which the report, of course, explains.)

18. The majority report was signed by Walter E. Elliot, J. R. Dickinson, J. F. Duff, B. Mouat Jones, K. A. Korsah, I. O. Ransome Kuti, Eveline C. Martin, E. H. Taylor-Cummings, and A. E. Trueman (both the chair and the West Africans were with the majority). The minority report was signed by H. J. Channon, Geoffrey Evans, Julian Huxley, Creech Jones and Margaret Read.

19. Initially, the colonial office had accepted the one university proposal (albeit primarily for economic reasons), and had issued a dispatch to the colonial administrations in British West Africa stating so. However for a variety of factors both within the colonies and in Britain the majority view eventually prevailed (see Janus [1980] for more). The problem of the status and prestige disjuncture (which of course was also rooted in "economics") could have been resolved, Janus suggests, if links had been established between the technical colleges of arts, science and technology with the British universities. Through such links their prestige could have been enhanced. The minority recommendation, however, was handicapped by another issue: through out their colonial ex-

perience Africans had witnessed the fact that all high-level colonial administrators usually had degrees in the arts and humanities; they did not have vocational/ technological type qualifications.

20. The members of the commission, besides Asquith, were: Donald Cameron, A. M. Carr-Saunders, H. J. Channon, Fred Clarke, J. F. Duff, Lord Hailey, James C. Irvine, Richard W. Livingstone, R. Marrs, L. M. Penson, Margery Perham, R. E. Priestley, J. A. Ryle, R. V. Southwell, J. A. Venn, and A. V. Hill. For more on the commission, see also, besides its own report, Ashby (1966), Carr-Saunders (1961), Janus (1980), Maxwell (1980), and Nwauwa (1997).

21. A parallel body was also set up to advise on the development of "colleges of further education," called the Advisory Committee on Colonial Colleges of Arts, Science and Technology (ACCAST), by the secretary of state for the colonies in 1949. Unfortunately, the committee did not have as much impact on the African colonies as did Asquith for political (opposition by Africans) and other reasons (see Janus 1980, for more).

22. See Maxwell (1980) for more on the work of the Council. A question that emerges here is why did the British begin to feel compelled, especially on the eve of the Second World War, that it was time to move beyond the hitherto traditional approach to its colonies of doing everything possible to make them financially pay their own way, to one that emphasized the British responsibility to assist with their development (of which the passage of the 1929 Colonial Development Act, and even more significantly a decade or so later the Colonial Development and Welfare Act of 1940, was symptomatic). The answer lies in several factors that emerged coincidentally at the same time; however among them two were particularly determinative: one was the increasing incidence of nationalist inspired unrest in some of the British colonies; and the other was to provide some moral justification (for both domestic and international consumption) for maintaining British colonial rule in the face of an emergent Nazi Germany's demands for a return of its former African colonies that it had lost to the trusteeship system (see Appendix III) in the wake of its defeat during the First World War. An internal memo by a government official captured one of the sentiments that underlay the newly emerging British policy on colonial development, beautifully:

At the present time it is a matter of the highest political importance that His Majesty's Government should be able to show unassailable justification for its claim that it acts as a beneficial trustee for its subject peoples, and that there is urgent need for us to undertake an effective forward movement in developing the progress of social services, including the improvements of labor conditions, nutrition, public health, education, housing and so forth, in the Colonial Empire (from Constantine 1984: 233).

Besides Constantine, see also Kent (1992) and Morgan (1980) for more on this subject.

23. A note about Fourah Bay: a few years following independence in 1961, Fourah Bay would be federated with another institution (in 1967) called Njala College. Now what is interesting about Njala is that it grew out of a completely different tradition. Njala College was established as a Land-Grant institution with the advisory assistance of the University of Illinois, on June 22, 1964, by the Sierra Leone government (in actuality it had already opened its doors a year earlier, on June 13, 1963). This new univer-

sity had four faculties: agriculture, basic sciences, arts, and education. Its creation was rooted both in a real need for university training in the area of agriculture that was not available at Fourah Bay, and in the necessity to provide access to university education to those living in the hinterland (primarily the Mendes) who were of a different ethnicity from those who lived on the coast—the Creole. (See Janus 1980 for more on the problems that ensued following the federation.)

24. See also the section titled "American Influence on African Universities" in Ashby (1966) in which he points out other limitations of the British model in comparison to the U.S. model from the perspective of African higher education.

25. One should point out here that Azikiwe, like his self-proclaimed hero, James E. K. Aggrey (and such others as the future president of Ghana, Kwame Nkrumah) were among the many hundreds of African students who were beneficiaries of the African American missionary inspired largesse of African American higher education—via such institutions as Howard, Lincoln, and Tuskegee). In other words, through such U.S.-educated Africans (many of whom would go on to occupy important leadership positions on the continent), African Americans left an indirect imprint on the development of higher education in Africa (or the quest for it). As Howard (1982) has correctly pointed out:

Among the least recognized but most lasting consequences of the black American missionary presence in Africa is the inspiration it provided to generations of young Africans to seek higher education in the United States, very often at predominantly black, church-related institutions. Less chronicled still is the considerable impact on African higher education of American educational models introduced by Africans returning from their North American sojourn (p. 95).

26. It was not without reason that Azikiwe had long felt that the U.S. model (rather than the British civic model with its highly elitist curricular bent) was better suited to the circumstances of an African country, which he said called "for a realistic approach to the problems of higher learning....We must frankly admit," he continued, "that we can no longer afford to flood only white collar jobs at the expense of the basic occupations and productive vocations, which can be so intelligently directed to create wealth, health, and happiness among the greatest number of our people, particularly in the fields of agriculture, engineering, business administration, education and domestic science" (from Ashby 1966: 277). See also Henry (1976) for an exploration of why Africans who studied in the United States found the U.S. higher education system much to their liking. For more on Azikiwe, see Azikiwe (1961, 1970).

27. Strange though it may appear from the vantage point of today, the curriculum (classical liberal arts) that came with the British model was not sympathetic toward applied science and technology (e.g., medicine, agriculture, engineering, pharmacy, etc.); nor of course the vocational/entrepreneurial arts (business, accounting, journalism, etc.) The reason is that this model was designed for education in the arts and humanities primarily, with the social sciences and basic sciences (biology, physics, chemistry) following in tow. Applied science and technology was not considered to be the proper domain of universities; rather, it belonged to lower level higher education institutions: colleges, institutes, medical schools (attached to hospitals), and so on. The explanation for this approach lies in the curricular traditions of the British universities where their develop-

ment had begun in the preindustrial age and hence their association of vocational or me-chanical arts with the working classes (therefore not befitting institutions that served primarily an upper-class clientele).

Bullough (1961), in the course of exploring the social structural force of class at work in the emergence of the medical profession in medieval Europe, makes a very tell-ing point when he observes that in the past technology had been the mother of science (later, of course, the roles would reverse). Now, so long as there was no status conflict between those involved with technology (the practitioners of the mechanical arts—members of the laboring classes) and those who were scientists (practitioners of the speculative arts—members or aspiring members of the upper classes) the development of science and technology would move hand in hand. This certainly was the case prior to the full institutionalization of intellectual labor in universities; and the visible fruits of which were such significant medieval inventions as "the water wheel, windmills, counterweight, artillery, mechanical clocks, gunpowder, and so forth" (p. 204).

To the extent, then, that technology (the applied dimension of science) was associ-ated with manual labor and hence the laboring classes, *the institutionalization of science in the academy* would lead to a neglect of technology in preference for "pure" science. This is precisely what happened after the middle of the fourteenth-century as the devel-opment of the medieval universities moved apace (the first few universities appeared in the twelfth-century). However, the ideological justification for this general liberal edu-cation curricular approach was couched in educational terms: the true mission of a uni-versity was not preparation for professional careers, but the pursuit of knowledge for its own sake (a luxury that only the children of the wealthy could afford was besides the point). (See also Ben-David 1992 on this curricular tradition.)

On the other hand, with the onset of the industrial revolution some 400 years later, one would assume that the disdain for the applied sciences within the academy would have evaporated—especially among the newer universities that emerged during the in-dustrial revolution (such as the civic universities of Britain—Manchester, London, etc.—that in time would become the models for export to Britain's African colonies. This did occur, but only to a very limited extent. Why? The weight of tradition was simply too hard to overcome, especially in the context of an institution such as the uni-versity. Universities, as those familiar with their histories will know, are notoriously (and paradoxically one may add) conservative in their practices.

Notice, however, that in contrast to the path of development taken by the British universities, the universities in the United States, in time, took a different path where the speculative sciences and the mechanical arts were brought under one roof in the guise of the *multiversity* (a term coined, albeit disapprovingly, by Kerr 1966)—the Land-Grant university being the epitome. Clearly, transplantation into a different culture can be a counterweight to tradition—but only when given time! The U.S. multiversity did not come into being until almost two centuries later. (Though note that the old tradition has not been completely eliminated from the landscape of U.S. higher education; it contin-ues to live on in the private four-year liberal arts college, serving roughly the same cli-entele: the children of the wealthy.) Consequently, the establishment of colonial univer-sities in Africa did not take the route that would have led to a greater emphasis in their curriculum on the applied sciences (together with such vocational arts like accounting, business, etc.). As Ashby (1964) explains:

The idea that universities in tropical Africa might recapitulate the phylogeny of universities in Europe, and begin (as universities in Salerno and Bologna began) as societies primarily concerned with vocational training in technologies and professions, was not part of the "Asquith doctrine." If it had been, one might have seen in British West Africa a fresh and totally different pattern of higher education, with agriculture, engineering, economics, medicine, and teacher training at the core of the curriculum and "pure scholarship" in science and the humanities arising as natural consequences of these vocational studies (pp. 57–58).

Ashby further comments: "There was an opportunity to do for Africa in the 1960's what the Morrill Act did for America in the 1860s, namely to make a new contribution to the idea of a university. But the Asquith Commission took no account of American experience" (p. 58). Therefore, institutions, such as the University of Nigeria and the University of Zambia were exceptions.

It ought to be also noted here, that the neglect of the applied sciences (and the vocational arts) in the British civic universities, without much detriment to the development of Britain's scientific and technological capacities, was only possible because of the parallel development of a robust system of non-university, postsecondary educational and research institutions—which include private research institutes of major business corporations. This course of development, however, was not to be easily replicated in the African colonies where higher education of any kind came so late on the scene—practically on the eve of independence. Consequently, it fell to the universities to incorporate these fields of study into their curricula and which they did, but not to the levels required by the needs of their countries.

28. Sadly, within a few years of its founding, the university would suffer grievous destruction during the Nigerian (Biafran) Civil War (1967–70), thereby limiting the impact in Nigeria of the U.S. land-grant experiment (if one may venture to call it that). (For more on the university see also Maxwell 1980 and Okafor 1973.)

Note: *A-levels* refers to the Advanced Level of the General Certificate Examination (G.C.E.) which students took in their sixth year of secondary education (form six). Following on the British tradition, this was the general practice in most universities in former British colonial Africa. *O-levels* refers to the Ordinary Level of the G.C.E. that students sat for in their fifth year of secondary education.

29. See Ashby (1966) and Curle (1962) for a discussion specifically of the Ghanaian incident and its ramifications for university autonomy. Ajayi, Goma, and Johnson (1996) is also relevant here, but from the perspective of the continent as a whole.

30. During the colonial era, for obvious reasons, democracy did not and could not exist. As for the postindependence era, the fate of democracy in Africa can be discerned by considering these stark facts compiled by the African Development Bank: Between 1963 and 2000 there were 180 leadership successions in Africa. Of these over 50% took place through coups, wars or invasions. The rest involved retirement, assassinations or impeachment. Only about 7% occurred because the incumbent lost an election. During this same period, to look at this matter from a different angle, the political life over 200 regimes was terminated by means of coups, civil wars or invasions. The report from which this data comes (African Development Bank 2001), further observes:

Africa is famous for leaders with long tenure. Fourteen present national heads in the region have been in office for between ten and 20 years; nine have served more than 20 years. The mean tenure for all former African leaders is 7.2 years, and about twice that for leaders who died in office or retired.

Of the 101 past leaders who left office due to a coup or similar unauthorized event, roughly two-thirds were killed, imprisoned, or banished to a foreign country. Twenty-seven former rulers died violently, counting five whose deaths appear to have been independent of a coup or coup attempt. The remaining 22 leaders in this category clearly perished as a direct result of coups. Of Africa's overthrown leaders who were not executed or assassinated, 37 were detained and held in jail or placed under house arrest. Twenty-nine other ex-leaders were forced into exile, at least temporarily. That figure does not include nine ex-leaders who experienced periods of both imprisonment and banishment.

31. It would appear that student political activism is a malady (when viewed from the perspective of the authorities of the day) that any society that wishes to have any form of organized higher education must endure, from time to time, in some form. Before proceeding further, however, one ought to define what one means by "student political activism"; it refers primarily to political activism that is either outside sanctioned channels (student unions and associations for example) or is outside what may be considered as normal teaching and learning or extracurricular campus activities. By definition, then, this activism is invariably oppositional to either the authorities within the institution or to the government of the day or both.

As just implied, such activity has been part of the history of institutions of higher education from the very beginning of their inception. For example, the town-and-gown conflicts of the medieval European universities are today enshrined in the histories of those institutions and celebrated as the precursors of the evolution of autonomy and academic freedom in the modern Western university (see, for example DeConde, 1971). Turning specifically to Africa, even the precolonial institutions of al-Azhar, al-Zaitouna, al-Qarawiyyin, etc., were not immune. It is of course with the establishment of colonial higher education institutions that student activism begins to come into its own in Africa. Kerr (1968), for instance, states that as soon as the student body at the first higher education institution for Afro-South Africans had passed the 200 mark (clearly you need some critical mass) in the years 1941 and 1942 there were "successive outbreaks of defiance of authority."

Since the provision of Western secular higher education was still in its infancy during the colonial era, it is only with independence that we see the emergence of widespread activism across the length and breadth of the continent (there is a built in contradiction in this statement that will be made obvious in a moment). Two countries that saw very active student activism of national consequence before much of the rest of the continent are of course Egypt and Algeria. And in both cases students were part of the wider nationalist movements: in Algeria it was the armed struggle against French colonial rule, while in Egypt it was against the British presence in Egyptian politics coupled with opposition to the Egyptian political establishment, considered by them to be weak and ineffective (see Ehrlich 1989). Now while it is true that in both cases students were also responding to their own difficult socioeconomic circumstances, what has intrigued historians and political scientists is that even when students have not faced such circumstances in the years immediately after independence in the rest of Africa, they have not refrained from oppositional activism. In other words: while one does not have to be a rocket scientist to surmise that deeply felt socioeconomic grievances (usually shared with the rest of the masses) arising from oppressive circumstances will trigger large-scale endemic oppositional activity—such as in the cases of French colonial Algeria, or Egypt prior to 1952, or Zimbabwe during white minority rule, or South Africa during apartheid, or Ethiopia under the despotic rule of Emperor Haile Sellaisse—what has been difficult to understand is the persistence of this student oppositional activism in Africa in the postindependence era up to the present. The contradiction has been that just as when one would expect that the students would have sat back and savored the fruits of the nationalist struggles of their elders, ranging from freedom from colonially imposed indignities to national pride to guaranteed elite membership, they still could not resist taking to the streets. What is more, it appears that there was not a single African country that did not experience nationally visible student protests in the first decade of independence. What is even more puzzling is that the students undertook these activities at great risk to their lives and limbs, not to mention their future careers. Consider for example Legum's description of the events of 1971—which he named "The Year of the Students":

Conflicts in a score of countries led to the closing down of 11 universities and the dissolution of students unions during the year and to other drastic action against student militants or against whole batches of students....Faced by student challenges, most African governments showed the same tendency of considering what kind of reforms to introduce only after acting toughly—closing down universities, expelling students, dissolving student unions; and, invariably, giving their strong backing to the university authorities. This kind of response was typical of all governments, irrespective of whether they are of the right (as in Madagascar, Ivory Coast, Zaire and Ethiopia); or of the left (as in the Sudan and the Congo People's Republic) (1972: A3).

However, 1971 was not unique. Coming right down to the present, the continent continues to exhibit an enduring pattern of student political activism. See, for instance, the chronology by Federici and Caffentzis (2000) covering the period 1985–1998 (as well as the chapter on the same subject in Teferra and Altbach 2003). Of course, in more recent years, the students have had to deal with their own bread-and-butter issues emerging out of the structural adjustment initiated retrenchment in African higher education (in addition to their other more traditional concerns with democracy, human rights, good governance and the like.) As they observe: "[t]he hundreds of dead students, the thousands arrested and tortured, the many more who have demonstrated and gone on strike in the face of violent repression between 1985 and 1998, teach us that the struggle for access to knowledge is not passé in Africa" (p. 115). Two things should be clear by this point: as Altbach (1989) has observed that when one compares student political activism in Africa with that in the rest of the world: it has a character of permanence and its sociopolitical consequences tend to be more profound (probably more governments in Africa, for example, have been brought down by students—acting in concert with other groups in society of course—than elsewhere in the world).

The question still remains, Why? All who have looked at this question have come way away shaking their heads completely nonplussed (clearly all the usual measures:

murders, torture, rapes, imprisonment, etc., has done little over the decades to dissuade students from taking to the streets). While it is difficult to explain the longevity of African student oppositional activism across time, it is perhaps less difficult to explain why such activism has often had a greater impact on their societies than has been the case elsewhere in the world. The best explanation that has been offered for the latter circumstance is the one that Burawoy (1976) offered in the course of explaining the student disruptions of 1971 at the University of Zambia. To begin with he noted that past literature on student political activism, as had been characterized by a singular failure to delineate anything that could remotely pass as theory sufficient to allow satisfactory explanation of it. Instead there emerged approaches that depended upon either isolation of such structural variables as the supposed axiomatic disjuncture between universities and societies, the inherently critical role of intellectuals, incipient elite competition since students are supposed to constitute potential elite members, archaic organizational structures within educational institutions, poorly developed political institutions, etc.; or identification of variables pertaining to student consciousness such as class background of students, family background (whether father was liberal or authoritarian), the "stage of youth in the maturation" process, and so on. There was also a third approach that eclectically brought together elements of the first two approaches but failed to weave them together into an organic whole. (Note that in criticizing these past approaches a distinction must be made between those concerned with analyzing student activism at the group-level and student activism at the individual level—that is in terms of which individual within a given student body becomes available for participation in student activism. (This distinction, of course, speaks to issues of *structure* versus *agency*.) Viewed from the latter perspective some of the past approaches were highly relevant.) In response to these failures, Burawoy emerged with his own (structural) approach which he explains thus:

[T]he university performs not just a single function but a multiplicity of functions and it is the relationship among these functions that determines, at the structural level, the propensity to engage in political activity. Second, the political consciousness of the institution's members is determined not merely by their roles within the university but by other roles they held in the past, hold in the present, or anticipate occupying in the future. Third, the outbreak of student protest must therefore be understood as the outcome of the interaction of a specific student consciousness and the structural contradictions which inhere in the functions of the university (p. 78).

Among the multiplicity of functions that the university performs, Burawoy states, there are three that are significant among African nations: the intrinsic function (training indigenous manpower); the symbolic function (the university symbolizing the attainment of the status of nationhood) and the solidary function (the university performing "an integrative role supporting the dominant political organs and abstaining from opposition to government positions.") The significant point about these functions is that they are inherently contradictory, and conflict generating in character especially in the context of political systems characteristic of African nations in general, which tend to be systems with low level of institutionalization and hence are unsuited to the management of potential conflict.

32. To elaborate on why the disintegration of the University of East Africa was not

in the long-term interest of the region (or the rest of the continent for that matter): To begin with, we may note that it is ironic that while African leaders have never tired of blaming colonialism for all their ills, almost all of them have clung tenaciously to the haphazard and often illogical national borders that colonialism imposed on Africa. Driven by the petty and selfish desires of remaining dictators in their fiefdoms (aided and abetted by their former colonial masters), with rare exception none has been courageous enough to work toward a *United States of Africa*: a political and economic union that the continent so desperately needs. What is more, it is doubly ironic that the very Europe that artificially created these African countries, is itself relentlessly forging ahead toward a "borderless" Europe (clearly demonstrating that internal conflagrations, however longstanding, are not insurmountable). That Africa must unite, at the very least in economic terms, is not a question of pandering to romantic notions that have surfaced from time to time among intellectuals in Africa and the Diaspora of a mighty power emerging, at last, to hold its own against other powers on the planet, but it is necessitated by the simple fact that if it is to ever escape the political and economic morass it is in today, then economic unity of some kind is absolutely essential. Such a unity would permit it to acquire four important economic advantages: the development of economic muscle vis-à-vis others in the global arena (witness the sickeningly shameful divide-and-dominate strategies used against the Africans by such wealthy countries as the United States in the recent round of Doha world trade talks in Geneva in July of 2004), the creation of its own internal markets to help fuel growth, the acquisition of productive efficiency through economies of scale, and the judicious husbanding of its natural resources coupled with the protection of its environment. (See the work of Green and Seidman 1968, who were among the earliest proponents of African unity on economic grounds, for more on why unity makes so much sense in terms of economic development.) It is not simply a coincidence that many of the economically successful countries in the world are either large political entities themselves, or are virtually de facto members of these entities (e.g., Japan, China, India, Taiwan, Hong Kong, the United States, Canada, the European Economic Community, etc.).

However, if one may take a page from the recent history of Europe, the initial path to a borderless Africa may lie in the less romantic, but yet meaningful, sectorally diverse, cross-border institution building that rests on the premise of exploiting economies of scale. One such institution that holds out the promise of cross-border cooperation for the mutual benefit of all participants is the university. Universities need not wait for a borderless Africa, they can help toward its realization by engaging in the creation of cross-border consortia where universities can share resources optimally, develop regional centers of research specialization, exploit the educational benefits of the flow of students and faculty across borders, and so on. Cross-border institution building is the quickest way to demonstrate the practical benefits of a borderless Africa as a precursor to its eventual creation. It is for this reason that the politically induced failure of the University of East Africa was not a good omen for the future of East Africa. (Compare also the opposition to the founding of a single university in West Africa mentioned earlier, and the collapse of the tripartite university of Botswana, Lesotho and Swaziland mentioned below). Had the University of East Africa succeeded then it could have served as a model (or at the very least a role model) for similar ventures in other parts of Africa.

Note: the idea of an East African Community was revived recently with its formal launching at Arusha on January 15, 2001. The chief proponent of the revived concept appears to be Tanzania. While its too early to tell how successful the new Community will be, it does signify a step in the right direction. Perhaps the most concrete manifestation of the move toward a common union was the commencement on January 1, 2005, of the first phase of the unification of tariffs among the three countries on imports from each other. Yet even this significant economic move has not been entirely devoid of petty wrangling; Uganda is demanding that some 174 products it produces receive exemption from removal of tariffs in order to protect its emerging industries.

33. The fragmentation of the federation, which ironically (in light of what will be said in a moment) was created by the British as a bulwark against the expanding domination of southern Africa by apartheid South Africa, was, sadly, to be expected; the reason is not far to seek: consider the example of—and for our present purposes, quiet appropriately—the history of the development of education in general, and higher education specifically, in Zambia; which can be best described as one of neglect and sheer irresponsibility; especially during the federation years. That is, compared to many other former British colonies elsewhere in Africa, at the time of independence Zambia had come to inherit a greatly distorted formal education system. While educational provision at the primary-level was fairly well developed (though only in relative terms), the system was marked by a poorly developed postprimary level with only a few secondary schools; and with the exception of an equally few teacher and vocational training colleges, no higher education institutions to speak of. What is more: the fact that copper mining would bring great wealth to the country, especially in the post–World War II era, had—to add insult to injury—only a marginal positive impact on this state of affairs. The question is, Why? The answer boils down to just one word: race.

Addressing this same issue, Lungu (1993), in a fairly informative and well researched article, attempts to prove that the matter was more complex than that; yet, in the end, all the evidence he marshals points to the same direction: racial discrimination. Whether Africans were viewed as inherently inferior in intellectual terms (initially— from 1880s to 1920s), or simply as a threat to the political and economic interests of the European settler minority (later—from 1930s onward to independence), his article unequivocally demonstrates that the relative failure of African demands, Christian missionary-led efforts, and recommendations by various British government appointed commissions on higher education, all turn on various manifestations (perhaps therein lies Lungu's "complexity") of this single factor. Even in the post–phrenological, post– Phelps-Stokes, Asquith Commission era, Zambia's African majority did not see respite from opposition, this time presented by the European settlers, to their quest for higher education. That is, the European settler dominated colonial government—whose hand vis-à-vis the African majority was greatly strengthened when Zambia and Malawi were federated in 1952 (against the wishes of the African majority in the two countries) with the then settler self-governing, racially segregated colony of Southern Rhodesia—did everything to undermine the development of education in general, and secondary and higher education specifically, if it was for the benefit of Africans. The European settlers in the federation shared the same views as their kinsmen elsewhere in southern Africa on the proper place of the African: hewers of wood and drawers of water; consequently, secondary and higher education for the African majority had no place in the political calculations of settler dominated governments of southern Africa. The following extracts from views expressed by settler representatives on the question of educational advancement of Africans, that Lungu himself quotes in his article, provides a window into the official settler mentality in colonial Zambia (as well as in the neighboring countries of Malawi and Zimbabwe):

To subordinate the interests of civilized Britons to the development of alien races, whose capability of substantial further development has not been further demonstrated, appears to be contrary to the natural law (p. 216).

We white people have not come here to raise the native in the scale of civilizations. Our main objective is to survive ourselves, to improve our conditions if we can, and to raise a family and perpetuate our race (p. 217).

Education should be available to the native, but only as far as his economic position warrants. It should not be done in advance of his position as this might tend to develop a class of "Babu" natives—all book learning and no desire to work—dissatisfied with their position and a nuisance to everybody else (p. 217).

With the formation of the Federation of Rhodesia and Nyasaland, there appeared for a moment that, at long last, Zambia would see the creation of at least a university college. And one was eventually established in 1955, but not in Zambia. The University College of Rhodesia and Nyasaland was set up in Southern Rhodesia in Salisbury—again for racist reasons: the largest settler population in the federation resided in Southern Rhodesia. Moreover, even though its charter mandated a multiracial approach to admissions and staff recruitment, in practice this was not always the case. Enrollment of black students was discouraged, as was recruitment of black teaching and administrative staff. The few black students who were admitted faced an officially mandated racially segregated campus. Not surprisingly, nationalist leaders in Zambia (and in Malawi) discouraged their fellow citizens from sending their children to the university college in Salisbury (Lungu 1993).

The fact is that right from the very beginning, the Federation of Rhodesias and Nyasaland had been conceived—at least in the minds of the European settlers—as a Trojan horse to entrench settler political power and to further their own economic interests by siphoning off money from copper-rich Zambia (as well as extracting cheap labor from Malawi) for the benefit of the settlers in Zimbabwe who formed a majority of the federation's settler population. Africans were aware of this fact and they had vehemently opposed its formation, but being powerless it was to no avail. Given these circumstances, once Britain had agreed to independence for Zambia and Malawi following a nationalist-led campaign demanding it, the federation, was practically dead—it was officially disbanded on December 31, 1963. Independence came to Zambia a few months later, in October 1964. A mere two years later, in 1966 (on March 17), the first of the two present universities in the country, the University of Zambia, opened its doors in Lusaka with a student population of a little in excess of 300 students. The other university, Copperbelt University, would not be established until two decades later, in 1987. (For corroborative studies on the history of education in Zambia, see, for example: Kuster 1999, Metzler 1988, Ragsdale 1986, Snelson 1970, and Wilkin 1983).

34. For more on the characteristics of the U.S. academic model from a comparative perspective, see Altbach (1998) and Ashby (1964, 1966). Ben-David (1992 [1977]) is also relevant here. See also Lungu (1980) for more on the African experience with the Land-Grant model.

35. It would be instructive here, dear reader, to look more closely at what a modern post-independence African university looks like in practice in Anglophone Africa today. For this purpose a case-study of sorts will be built of an institution that the author is personally familiar with: the University of Zambia. The case-study rests on the following topics: (1) Governance and University Autonomy, (2) Student Admission and Enrollments, (3) Finance, (4) Programs of Study, (5) Graduate Studies and Research, (6) Faculty Recruitment and Retention, (7) Community Service, and (8) Student Activism and Academic Freedom.

First, however, a brief history of the institution is in order. The idea of creating a Zambian university was first mooted, it is said, secretly in hotel bedrooms (such was the African fear of European settler opposition) at the UNESCO sponsored Conference on the Development of Higher Education in Africa convened in 1962 (September 3-12) in Tananarive (Stabler 1968). After all, the conference itself had gone along with the settler position that the higher education needs of the Federation were to be met by the university college in Salisbury for at least twenty more years—up to 1980 (UNESCO 1963:78). Although two years later, a UNESCO education planning mission to the country would recommend the creation of a university (UNESCO 1964). The recommendation, however, had already been upstaged with the execution of the first concrete steps toward the establishment of a university—symbolized by the secret and informal appointment (that is without the knowledge of the Federal settler government) of the Lockwood Committee in 1963. It was set up with the advice of the American Council on Education and the Inter-University Council for Higher Education Overseas in Britain and funded by the British government and the Carnegie Corporation of New York. The committee was chaired by Sir John Lockwood, master of Birbeck College, University of London, who had by now distinguished himself as an astute visionary and a strong proponent of the U.S. land-grant model in the field of higher education planning. It issued its report in late 1964 and the new government—now barely two months old—accepted its principal recommendations and proceeded to appoint a provisional council.

The Lockwood Committee reported that it was guided in its planning by two key assumptions; in its words: "firstly, that the university must be responsive to the real needs of the country; secondly, that it must be an institution which on merit will win the respect and proper recognition of the university world" (Lockwood Committee 1964). The outcome of this thinking was the creation of a university that departed considerably from the earlier pattern of education planning that had characterized the Asquith university colleges. For example the new university would issue degrees in its own right—it was not a conduit for degrees offered by a foreign university. Moreover, it set the entrance requirements at the logistically less onerous level of form five Ordinary Level Certificate (equivalent to the Scholastic Aptitude Test in the United States), rather than the form six Advanced Level Certificate. To maintain standards, the undergraduate degree program was stretched to four years (as is the case in U.S. institutions) in contrast to the typical three years. Now, on to the case-study.

Governance and University Autonomy. From the perspective of governance, the university comprises (besides the Deans and the heads of departments) the following principal governing offices and bodies: the Chancellor; the Vice Chancellor, the Registrar, the Bursar, the University Council, the Senate, and Boards of Studies. The Chancellor's office is a titular office and until the so called Third Republic came into being, it was occupied by the country's head of state (the president). Now the occupant of the office is appointed by the head of state from among the nation's "distinguished" persons. The vice chancellor is equivalent to the president in U.S. universities, in other words, administratively, he is the chief executive officer. Until recently, the University Council appointed the vice chancellor. Now, his appointment is the responsibility of the Minister of Education. The University Council itself is also appointed by the minister and the composition of its membership is at the minister's sole discretion–usually it comprises the top level administrators of the university, representatives from the senate and the student body, and persons outside the university representing various constituencies: the government itself, industry and the professions. The Registrar and the Bursar are appointed by the University Council and their role is to assist with the administration of the academic and financial aspects of the university, respectively.

The university senate comprises members of the academic teaching staff and its role is almost identical to that of senates in U.S. universities: it is concerned strictly with university wide academic policies dealing with such matters as pedagogy, general degree requirements, enrollments, curriculum, procedures for faculty hiring and promotion, etc. Each school has a board of studies appointed by the Senate comprising the school's academic staff as well as representatives from other schools in the university. It is chaired by the school's dean, and its role is to determine such academic matters as what courses are taught, in what sequence, the degree requirements for the specific school, course syllabi, etc. In other words, matters that would ordinarily be within the purview of departments in U.S. universities is handled at the school level by the boards of studies.

Until the passage of the 1999 University Act, it would be true to say that the university had enjoyed a considerable degree of university autonomy. To be sure, the government on many occasions had moved to close the university and expel students (and at times even members of the teaching staff) when it had felt, rightly or wrongly, that students (primarily) had gone beyond simple criticism of government policies to provocation of opposition that had the potential to undermine its survival. In non-turbulent times, however, when the ruling regime has not felt threatened, the University Council had indeed been the supreme governing body and governmental influence on it was highly restricted—effected primarily through its minority representatives on the Council. The new Act, however, introduced a major sea change: it is the Minister of Education who has effective power over the university, as the Act among other things, provides the minister with sweeping powers—exemplified by the minister's ability to bypass the University Council and/or the University Senate at will. This change was not greeted with equanimity by the university community; they were vehemently opposed to the change, but despite an attempt to derail it, through legal challenges in the courts, they were powerless in the end to block it. (The challenge came from the three of the four unions at the university, representing the students, the academics and non-professional staff, in one of those rare instances of a unified stand.)

Student Admission and Enrollments. It was decided by the Lockwood Committee that admission to the university was no longer going to depend on possession of A-levels (Advanced Level of the General Certificate Examination—G.C.E.) which students completed in their sixth year of secondary education (form six). Following on the British tradition, this was the general practice in most universities in former British colonial Africa. In the case of Zambia, however, the Lockwood Committee was emphatic that in the interests of the rapid development of human resources this was not an effective route to take. It rightly reasoned that given the poor state of secondary education at the time of independence and the concomitant dearth of sixth forms, "an attempt to gear minimum university entrance requirements to the possession of a Higher School Certificate or a corresponding equivalent of A-level at G.C.E. would so narrowly limit academic opportunities as to defeat the national interest" (Lockwood Committee 1964). Instead, it decided that O-levels (Ordinary Level of the G.C.E.) would be acceptable, and not only that, but the sixth form in secondary education would be abolished altogether—in the process freeing up resources for the development of education in general. By adding one more year of study to the undergraduate degree than that current in British universities (thereby making it a four year degree as in U.S. universities) the committee felt that it represented a sufficient academic compensation for the loss of the sixth year of secondary education. Although there was palpable protest in the country from some of the higher education constituencies, in the end the decision to accept and implement the committee's recommendation has stood the test of time (see Tembo [1973] for more on this issue).

Today an applicant requesting admission for an undergraduate degree must, at the minimum, have the following qualifications: passes at credit level in at least five subjects in the Zambian School Certificate (or Cambridge Overseas School Certificate); or (b) passes in at least five subjects in the General Certificate of Education Ordinary Level Examinations. At the same time, the subjects must be selected from a list specified by the university to ensure clear separation of content (in other words related subjects—e.g. biology and zoology—can not be considered as meeting the five subject requirement).

Interestingly, the Lockwood Committee had recommended that the student body should not be composed entirely of Zambian nationals, but it should also admit a small proportion of non-Zambian nationals living within and without the country. In other words, even though there are today far more Zambian applicants than the number of places available for them in the university, the university tradition that originates in antiquity of admitting non-nationals to an institution of higher learning has been retained at the university. The catchment area for foreign students is, as would be expected, the English speaking Southern African region. The percentage of non-nationals as a proportion of the whole student body is roughly 5%.

Finance   At the time of independence, the view of the government was that no qualified citizen should be denied access to education for lack of funds. With a healthy budget, thanks to the high price of copper (the country's economic mainstay, as noted at the beginning of the chapter) the government could afford to hold this expansive view. Consequently, for nearly two decades following independence, there were virtually no fees charged by government financed or supported institutions at any level: primary, secondary or tertiary. However, in the face of severe budgetary constraints in the aftermath of the collapse of the world copper prices, it slowly dawned on the government that free education, while highly desirable, was no longer affordable. It would take roughly another decade following the onset of the economic crisis, however, before it would take hesitant steps, beginning in the mid-1980s, toward implementing a system of modest cost-sharing at all levels of the educational system.

Yet, even today, the proportion of the cost-sharing that students are responsible for is still quite small: at the university level its 25% of the annual tuition that the university receives from the government (approximately 3500.00 U.S. dollars equivalent), on behalf of each student, through a bursary (scholarships) system. (Virtually all university students of Zambian nationality are on bursaries, as are college students at government financed/ supported institutions.) A higher level of cost-sharing by students, while dearly cherished by the present government, is hamstrung by three major constraints: political opposition from students and parents; the inability to come up with a bureaucratically viable means-tested student loan scheme; and the sheer magnitude of poverty within the country. About the poverty constraint: the fact is that those who are potentially able to afford higher tuition fees are most likely not even study-ing at government institutions: they are either in private institutions or they are studying abroad.

On the institutional side, the matter of finance has become a highly problematic issue in the face of the persistent government budgetary difficulties. Moneys are not always made available to the universities on a timely basis. Moreover, inflationary erosions receive scant at-tention—despite their disheartening magnitude in recent years—when budgetary allocations are made by the government. Of course, the universities (as well as some of the technical/business colleges) could reduce their endemic financial difficulties by decreasing their massive dependence on the government by developing independent sources of finance. To date, how-ever, neither alumni dependent, endowment-based financial support, nor entrepreneurial based financial support has been effectively exploited. The reasons are primarily three: tradition (the modern British university tradition to which Zambia is heir does not rely on private sources of financial support for institutions of higher learning—unless run by Christian missions); lack of imagination (to break out of the box of tradition); and mismanagement (where entrepreneurial initiatives have been undertaken).

While alumni dependent endowment-based sources of finance may not be a viable option in the absence of a philanthropic tradition among the Zambian well-to-do, there is an alterna-tive mechanism that remains to be tried to develop an endowment base: raise funds through ex-ternal, governmental bilateral pledges and locate the endowment, for revenue-generating in-vestment purposes, externally (in say the United States or the United Kingdom). To begin to foster a philanthropic tradition among the Zambian elite, including the alumnus of the univer-sity, the bilateral pledges by external government donors could be made on the basis of match-ing grants (e.g. every dollar raised within Zambia could be matched threefold by external do-nors).

As for raising funds through entrepreneurial activities, in the immediate time horizon, this holds a more realistic promise. There are at least seven areas within the university that have the potential to produce entrepreneurial outlets: agriculture, architecture, engineering, computer services, human medicine, printing and publishing, and veterinary medicine. However, a full scale effort in this regard must be accompanied by allocation of seed capital, and above all, the hiring of competent business managers. Some entrepreneurial activities have already been un-dertaken (e.g. operation of a farm and an internet service), but they have not been allowed to reach their full revenue-generating potential for lack of effective business management (as well as alleged misappropriation of funds and resources by university officials).

Programs of Study. Students are admitted in their first year to either the School of Humanities and Social Sciences or to the School of Natural Sciences, depending upon what path their univer-sity career is planned to take. Thereafter, they will proceed in either one of two directions: re-main within the Schools (a minority) to pursue relevant majors or move on (the majority) to the other specialized schools in the university (education, engineering, law, etc.) Depending on where they go, their course of study will last anywhere from four to seven years. For example, the length of the education degree is four years, that of the engineering degree is five years, while that of veterinary medicine is six and that of medicine is seven.

From its inception the university avoided the British tradition of single-subject honors de-grees in liberal studies in favor of less specialized degrees characteristic of U.S. land-grant universities. The thinking was, and correctly so, that students graduating at the undergraduate level) with a major and a minor field specializations, achieved on the basis of a broad array of course offerings, were better placed to help with the development of the country's human capi-tal resources—especially at the administrative and managerial levels—where personnel capa-ble of performing in a variety of jobs are in greater demand than those trained for only one type of work. At the same time, the university curriculum was designed, again for human capital reasons, to be heavily oriented toward professional training: education, engineering, law, medicine, etc. (For an extended discussion on the merits of this U.S. oriented approach to degree structures and curricular planning, see Ashby 1966.) It ought to be pointed out here, however, that the emphasis on professional training has been taken to such an extreme as to deny a rightful place for the performing arts (music, dance, painting, theater, etc.) in the university curriculum. Yet, even in a developing country, there is need at the very minimum, of arts teachers for deployment in schools. In the absence of an arts program, however, it has not been possible to graduate teachers capable of teaching art, music, etc. From the perspective of the development of the creative and intellectual functions of a child's brain, the arts are absolutely crucial. The long term damage to the creative and intellectual development of Zambian children, given the continued absence of arts teachers in schools, is incalculable; but none the less real. (See Akapelwa [1989] for a discussion of problems of music education in Zambia.)

Typically, in a four year degree program, students take a minimum of four, year-long, courses per year that results in a basic 16-course degree. Each course requires a minimum of four contact hours per week, per academic year, and therefore it is equivalent to eight credit hours in terms of U.S. higher education. (The minimum number of credit hours, therefore, a student must successfully complete is 128.) Courses equivalent to four credit hours also exist, but they are termed and considered as "half-courses." Depending on which year of study a student is in, the student is expected to register for the appropriate course series (the 100 series are designed for the first year of study, the 200 series for the second year of study, etc.) Out of the 16 courses, the student will construct a program of study that may follow the path of a traditional single subject specialization or may cross subject boundaries but while still retaining disciplinary coherence. The person responsible for ensuring that students are registered in appropriate courses is the head of the department (without his/her permission a student may not register in any course). For good or ill, there is no separate academic advisement system for students akin to that in U.S. universities.

Graduate Studies and Research. The School of Graduate Studies coordinates the graduate studies program at the university. However, the University of Zambia, like its counterpart (Copperbelt University) is primarily an undergraduate institution. Students who wish to proceed to graduate level studies will find that their choices are somewhat limited in that while a master level degree is now offered by all the schools (but not in all programs), very few offer a doctoral level degree. The master's degree, regardless of the school in which it is being taught, is normally a two year program comprising course work in the first year (concluding with a comprehensive written examination) and research leading to a dissertation in the second year. Under special circumstances the first year may be waived. The minimum duration of the program for full-time students is, under normal circumstances, fifteen months and the maximum is three years.

After more than thirty years of existence, the nascence of graduate level education is an indication of the hard times that the university has fallen upon over the past two decades or so. Graduate education places special demands on an institution: ranging from the hiring of graduate level teaching staff through to provision of research facilities, including a library with extensive and continuously updated holdings. All this however, implies money, which the university sorely lacks. At the same time, the long standing practice, until recently, of sending staff development fellows (graduates recruited for eventual appointment as members of the teaching staff upon successful completion of graduate studies) abroad for their masters degrees did not help matters. In other words, little if any attention was paid to using the staff development program as an incubator for graduate studies.

Under a regime of adequate financial resources, one would have also seen by now a desirable shift in the mission of the university toward greater emphasis on graduate level education. This would have involved the off-loading of undergraduate programs of study onto four-year "university colleges" (colleges in special relationship with the university, offering University of Zambia degrees) established across the country. In years to come these university colleges then would have matured into independent universities in their own right offering their own degrees. However, this is all wishful thinking at this point; for, there is as yet no university college in the country.

As would be expected, in the absence of a well developed doctoral level graduate studies program, the research activities of the university are also at a low level of development. It is not that no research is taking place, but that faculty productivity, for reasons adduced below, is pathetically low. (Evidence of this fact comes not only from personal observations, but can also be determined by searching global bibliographic databases by employing the search criteria of author's institutional affiliation). Moreover, to heighten the absence of a vibrant, coherent and relevant research program across the entire university, much of the research being undertaken today by individual faculty—usually on their own initiative—is at the behest of external development aid agencies, who all have their own specific agendas. The result is that such externally induced research remains uncoordinated, and even worse, findings are often restricted to the archives of the sponsor with almost no benefit for those not connected with the sponsor.

Every country needs a coordinated research program, that in the absence (as is the case in Zambia) of a chain of linked research institutes is, by default, the mandate of the university. There are many factors that have worked against the use of the university as "a creative center of research" (to use the words of the Lockwood Committee report (1964:1)); they include: (a) The persistence to date of a general tradition within, both, the university administration and the government of viewing the university as no more than a human capital resource factory— despite occasional pronouncements to the contrary. (b) The failure to develop a research inducing infrastructure (ranging from funding support through adequate computational and lab facilities to proper library resources—even such basic necessities as photocopying facilities are not easily available to faculty.) (c) The lack of a clearly articulated and systematically enforced policy on the place of research in the spectrum of faculty duties (with the result that the research initiative is left almost entirely to ambitious or academically enthusiastic individuals— especially since tenure is not determined by research output as is usually the case in research universities in the United States). (d) The practice of overloading faculty with teaching and administrative duties, leaving those who are dedicated to their duties with practically little time for anything else, let alone research. (e) The emerging practice of faculty moonlighting at other jobs to augment the ever shrinking salaries (in the face of spiraling inflation and static salary bases) which further depletes the already small time/energy budget for research. (f) The lack of adequately trained and competent administrative and secretarial help that can assist with easing the burden of performing day-to-day chores and thereby create time for research. (g) The absence of a well developed publishing infrastructure, both within and without the university, that can provide additional motivation and an outlet for one's research effort. (h) The slow but sure erosion of general faculty morale (discussed elsewhere in this chapter).

Faculty: Recruitment and Retention. As has already been pointed out, Zambia began at independence with a pool of university graduates that was among the smallest in British colonial Africa. Not surprisingly, then, the establishment of new institutions and the expansion of existing ones required a massive recruitment of expatriate personnel from almost all corners of the world, but principally the Commonwealth countries. In this regard, the university was no exception; its founding required the wholesale importation of teaching staff, as well as the upper administrative staff—even the head cook, at one point, in the university's dining hall was an expatriate, as was the person in charge of maintaining the university grounds! In light of these circumstances, the university launched an aggressive staff development program to facilitate the rapid indigenization of the teaching and administrative staff. The program involved identifying outstanding graduates of the university who wished to pursue a teaching/administrative career in the university and providing them with scholarships to pursue graduate studies (at both masters and doctoral level abroad, coupled with the guarantee of a teaching/ administrative position upon successful completion of their studies. It is a testimony to the success of this program that indigenization of the teaching and administrative staff at the university is now more or less complete. (For more on the program see Kashoki 1994.)

The few expatriate personnel who can still be found at the university are there because some teaching fields (e.g. medicine) still lack sufficient Zambian applicants and because of the university's enlightened policy that at least 10% of teaching positions should be reserved for foreign teachers (to ensure the university's linkage with the international university community). Parenthetically, it ought to be noted that the success of the staff development program is also an indication of the high quality and standards, in academic terms, that the university had maintained until recently. The staff development fellows who went to study abroad could not have been successful in their studies if this was not so. The range of educational institutions at which the current Zambian teaching staff obtained their graduate level qualifications speaks volumes, in this regard; here is a sample: Cambridge, Guelph, Harvard, Helsinki, London, Manchester, Oxford, Sussex, Toronto, Tulane, etc.

In waxing lyrical about the success of the staff develop program, however, one cannot lose sight of a number of serious ongoing and emergent issues concerning faculty personnel that need to be addressed by the university: the problem of low research output; the problem of the underdevelopment of graduate studies; the problem of attrition through brain drain; and the problem of faculty morale. The first two are discussed elsewhere in this note.

Under the circumstances of an existing deep shortfall in indigenous human capital resources at independence and a further exacerbation of this shortfall in the post-independence period created by the massive (though foolhardy) development of the parastatal economic sector, the government unabashedly raided the university's best and brightest to meet its own personnel needs—and the latter unhesitatingly left the university, succumbing to the blandishments of higher pay, richer perks, and elevation of status (compare this situation with that in South Africa today). From the very beginning, then, the university has had to deal with the contradictory circumstances of a concerted program for the rapid indigenization of personnel against a backdrop of a constant hemorrhage of the same personnel into the external labor market. This contradiction, sadly, has not evaporated; it continues, but in a slightly different guise: the blandishments are no longer from the government (which is now not only poverty stricken, but has for quite some time stood over, at the behest of its international creditors, the painful demolition of the parastatal sector), but from universities elsewhere in Africa—especially southern Africa. In other words, any faculty member who can find a position at a university outside the country is most likely going to leave, as many have already done. Countries that have received Zambian university teaching personnel include Botswana, Namibia, South Africa and Swaziland. (This is a replay of the experiences of many West African universities over the past two and a half decades.) It is even rumored that in some institutions, expatriate Zambians staff entire departments! What is worse, this braindrain problem threatens to become even more severe with the passage of time given the deteriorating economic situation in the country and the resultant impoverishment of the university itself (see below) amidst a low faculty morale.

Symptomatic of the low faculty morale is not only the braindrain of course, but the unusual involvement of faculty in industrial action (organized by their union), leading sometimes to the closure of the university (normally its the students behind these closures—see below). There are, as is usually the case, a number of factors behind the erosion of morale among faculty at the university; they include: (a) Faculty salaries have not kept up with inflation. (b) The chronic under-funding of the university has led to a serious deterioration of academic infrastructure and resources: from physical plant to the library. (c) Teaching loads are heavy as class enrollments have ballooned; not to mention the added task of undertaking distance teaching. (d) The recent government attack on university autonomy has not helped matters. There is the feeling (justified) that the university is slowly being turned into a government department with all the negative implications that entails for an institution of higher learning. (e) Administrative inefficiencies and even corruption (where top level administrators have been accused of siphoning off or misspending thousands of dollars) has become yet one more lance piercing the heart of faculty morale.

Community Service. Where there is a crying need to solve so many development related problems urgently, and where the universities are often the sole or primary repositories of cutting-edge research and knowledge (a circumstance shared by most African countries, including Zambia), it stands to reason that, in principle, community service must be considered among the foundational pillars of the university mission. Some may even go further and suggest that community service is integral to the mission of any university anywhere in the world today. But, what precisely does one mean by "community service" from the perspective of higher education? For, there is without doubt a nebulous ring to the concept, given the expansiveness of the terrain that the words conjure up. (One could easily put forth the argument, for instance, that the training and credentialing of students is a community service.) Essentially, community service is the extension of university expertise to the world outside the university, the community, in the service of improving the quality of life of the community and which is effected through a university model in which community service is integral to all aspects of the university: mission, structure and organization, hiring and promotion, curriculum and teaching, research and publications, etc. Now, in Zambia, the vision had always been that the university would be intimately involved with community service. After all, it had been partially modeled on the U.S. land-grant university as indicated earlier in this chapter. (The U.S. land-grant university, in the early days of its development, had community service built centrally into its mission—though today it has deviated far from this original model.)

In practice, however, the university has not lived up to the concept of community service as just defined. In fact, on the contrary, one may argue that with the exception of a few traditional avenues (such as running the teaching hospital, or allowing the public access to the university's library facilities) the university has hitherto followed the path taken by many other universities elsewhere in Africa: as essentially ivory towers, far removed from the problems of society at large. The following indictment, offered nearly two decades ago by Colin Leys, of African universities still, sadly, stands today and the University of Zambia is not exempt from it: "There are relatively few issues among all those raised during the debate—on the development role of universities in developing countries—of the 1960s which appear to have been resolved. There are comparatively few areas of university life and practice where one cay say that a particular way of doing things, or even an accepted set of guiding principles, has been generally established as right or best from the point of view of making the maximum contribution to development" (Leys 1971).

What have been the obstructing factors in the realization of a "developmental university," where community service is at the heart of the University of Zambia's mission? The following stand out for mention (in no order of significance): First, has been the history of the university: while its academic structure (in terms of curricular offerings, degree structures, entrance requirements, etc.) may have been influenced by the land-grant model, its overall mission was still modeled on the traditional British university if not on paper, at least in terms of overall practice. From this perspective, the production of trained personnel who could staff the heavily expatriate dominated bureaucracies and corporations was the dominant guiding principle of the university mission, as noted earlier. Second, the heavy reliance of the university itself on expatriate staff—the vast majority coming from the United Kingdom—dictated by the lack of indigenous academics, simply served to entrench the traditions of universities not oriented toward community service. Third, even when indigenization of the academic and administrative personnel was almost complete by the beginning of the 1990s, the fact that the new indigenous personnel had obtained their higher degrees from Western universities, meant that they were not predisposed toward breaking out of the traditional modus operandi—witness, for example, the principle promotion criteria for faculty at the university: number of publications in refereed academic media (which for obvious reasons implies Western academic media). Fourth, related to the preceding point, the desire to maintain some kind of parity, in terms of international status, with universities world-wide only served to ensure that there was not much deviation from the norm of relegating community service to the position of a distant cousin in terms of actual university practice. Fifth, the government itself, has been averse to turning to the university for research assistance—in part because of the inheritance of a British governmental tradition (where consultation with universities has not been a common historical practice) and in part because the university has always appeared to politicians as an alien institution that they could not fully comprehend (the fact that almost none of them possessed, through no fault of their own to be sure, higher degrees did not help matters). Sixth, the significant role played by external multilateral and bilateral foreign aid agencies in the country's development effort ensured that, until recently, research expertise invariably came from abroad.

However, things are changing—a little, but perceptibly: that is, there is now a greater involvement of the university in community service than has been the case in the past—even if it is still on an ad hoc basis. A number of factors account for this development: First, the severe budgetary problems of the university has pushed it in the direction of looking for ways to diversify its traditional source of funding support, which has implied engaging in entrepreneurial activities based on its expertise (two examples that have already been mentioned: the operation of a commercial farm and a commercial internet service). Second, the continuing downward slide in faculty salaries effected by the ravages of two and three digit inflation has pushed some faculty to engage in the increasingly lucrative (one gets paid in U.S. dollars) cottage industry of "development consultancy." Paradoxically, the very factor that had once been an impediment to the use of the university's expertise for development oriented research, the foreign aid agencies, are responsible for the growth of this cottage industry. What has changed? The general approach of external development agencies toward local research has been slowly changing: many now increasingly feel, and rightly so, that local expertise, where available, is better suited to do the requisite research than imported expertise—plus its cost-effective. Third, the government itself has begun to adopt a more positive view of the university (in so far as assistance with development research is concerned), because many of the high level personnel in government, today, are now university trained—a vast majority of whom got their degrees from the two universities.

Yet, there is no gainsaying this fact: the universities have a long way to go toward evolution into true community service oriented institutions. For this to happen, it will require a complete institutional overhaul. Nothing as yet, suggests that this is in the offing. In fact, one may even venture to say, that unless there is a world-wide movement, especially in the West, for the emergence of the truly genuine community service university, the University of Zambia, like most other universities elsewhere in the developing world, will remain as they are today. Universities may engage in revolutionary cutting-edge knowledge and research at the disciplinary levels, but at the level of institutional operation and organization they are notoriously conservative.

Student Activism and Academic Freedom. Any one familiar in the slightest with the history of the University of Zambia, cannot help but notice the constant theme of student unrest disrupting the academic life of the university—even to the extent of precipitating closures of the campus through government decrees. The number of times the university has been closed—for periods ranging from one month to six months or more—as a result of student activism is indicated by the following sample list of month/year, in descending order, the university was prematurely closed (the primary cause of the student unrest that precipitated the closure is indicated in parenthesis): August, 2000 (boarding fees); January, 2000 (tuition fees); May 1999 (meal allowances); March, 1997 (meal and book allowances); November, 1996 (national politics); April, 1990 (national politics); April, 1989 (tuition fees); May, 1986 (campus politics (dispute over administrative matters)); February, 1984 (campus politics); April, 1981 (national politics); February, 1976 (national politics); July, 1971 (national politics). While these closures may suggest a severe lack of academic freedom at the university, in truth however this is not entirely so. To be sure, at times government reaction to student criticisms regarding government policies have been hasty, harsh, and undemocratic, but at other times it has had no choice but to intervene in the interest of campus safety and security.

Of course, student activism is not unique to Zambia; however, what is remarkable about the student activism at the University of Zambia is its permanence. Even in the face of police/ military brutality (besides the standard obligatory beatings, also involving at times: rapes, imprisonment without charges, and even killings), and frequent expulsion of student leaders, the students have, over the years, remained undaunted. What are the causes of the student unrest, which it must be conceded has greatly raised the unit cost of higher education in Zambia as well as producing other negative academic consequences (disruption of teaching, learning, etc.)? The government's answer, provided through the report of a commission of inquiry (the Bobby Bwalya Commission) appointed in April 1997 to look precisely into this question is that the students are motivated by selfish concerns—they point to unrest over matters such as fees, allowances, etc. in recent years (Zambia 1998). This is a partial answer and it is a simplistic answer because it does not address the student unrest in the period prior to the onset of the endemic fiscal crisis that has plagued the university since the mid-1980s. Consider this fact: student unrest (which would culminate in the expulsion of the president of the students union) began as early as the first year of its operations in 1966. Student activism of such long duration in a context where the actual "personnel" are constantly turning over (as a result of graduation, or resignation, or academic dismissal, or expulsion) suggests a more complex explanation (as already discussed elsewhere in this chapter).

For more information on the university, in addition to the sources already mentioned, see Burawoy (1976), Galabawa (1993), Lulat (1981, 1989), Lungu (1980, 1993), Metzler (1988), Siaciwena (1997), Sikwibele (1989), Stabler (1968), University of Zambia (1977).

5

Anglophone Africa—II: Ethiopia, Liberia, and South Africa

Ethiopia, Liberia, and South Africa (together with Namibia) have merited separate treatment in this work because of their unique historical circumstances: the first two (Ethiopia and Liberia) did not experience, to all intents and purposes, Western colonial rule—discounting the five-year Italian interlude in Ethiopia. As for South Africa, while it was once a colony of Britain, it had long achieved independence from it. However, its uniqueness further stems from the fact that independence did not imply democracy by way of majority rule, but instead minority rule, which in practice led to the development of what may be best called, for lack of a better term, a neofascist political order (one in which all the hallmarks of fascism were present: capitalism, racism, jingoism, militarism, and authoritarianism, but which was tempered by a modicum of democracy for the minority). As for Namibia, until its independence in 1990 it was virtually an apartheid colony of South Africa (much in the same way that Eritrea was a colony of Ethiopia).

ETHIOPIA (MODERN PERIOD)

Any examination of the history of higher education in Ethiopia must invariably begin with a chronological demarcation between the modern and the premodern periods. Since we have already covered the premodern period in Chapter 2 our mandate here is to look at the modern period. However, to bring us up to speed we would do well to briefly recap Ethiopia's premodern history recognizing at the same time that the Ethiopian state has maintained continuity up to the present (except for a brief interregnum, as will be explained in a moment), making it among the oldest surviving states in the world. Chapter 2 indicated that the eventual demise of the Axumite kingdom (a process that had begun some time in the seventh-century with the rise of Islam) had not marked a final sunset in the history of the evolving Ethiopian state; instead new rulers emerged would continue to steer the kingdom as it expanded and contracted over the centuries depending upon their political and military strength (or weakness). Of these rulers we are familiar with those who came to constitute two specific dynasties: the *Zagwe dynasty* (circa eleventh-century to 1270) and the *Solomonid dynasty* (1270–1974). It is during the reign of the Solomonids, a line that began with the murder in 1270 of the legitimate Zagwe ruler Yitbarek by a usurper, Yekuno Amlak (who would later concoct, with the assistance of the Ethiopian church, the King Solomon/ Queen of Sheba myth mentioned in Chapter 2) that the Ethiopian empire would expand through military conquest to roughly its current borders and in the process beat back the covetous invasions of others—the Egyptians, the Italians, and the Mahdists from Sudan—in the latter half of the nineteenth-century; and, remarkably, hold at bay the imperial powers of France and Britain. Neither wanted the other to takeover Ethiopia, thereby reaching a modus vivendi that allowed Ethiopia to retain by default its autonomy even as most of the rest of the continent was gobbled up by Europe. The dramatis personae of the dynasty in these events were Emperors Tewodros II (ruled 1855–68), Yohannes IV (ruled 1872–89), and Menelik II (ruled 1889–1913, prior to that he was the king of the Shewa from 1865–89).

From the perspective of modernization, one may date it as commencing hesitantly under Tewodros II, but later with some seriousness with the first expulsion of the Italians from Ethiopia. Italy had invaded Ethiopia in 1872 with a wink and a nod from the British when it seized Aseb (which in time became part of its Eritrean colony that Italy established in 1890). However, its efforts to colonize the entire country proved futile; the Ethiopians decisively defeated them on March 1, 1896, at the Battle of Adwa under the leadership of Menelik II, marking the first time in modern history that an *African* country had defeated a European power (with all the psychological fallout it entailed for both the vanquished and the victor—compare Dien Bien Phu). Despite this defeat, the Italians did not erase their dreams of colonizing Ethiopia; consequently, about four decades later, in October 1935, they were back to reassert their imperial ambitions, but this time with an ideological overlay of fascism. Initially they were successful—thanks to the liberal use of poison gas by the Italians against the Ethiopian Army—but again only for a short time: their defeat by a combined British (ironically) and Ethiopian force facilitated their exit from Ethiopia once again (in 1941).

The Italian occupation of Ethiopia was marked by the unusual development (in colonial terms) of bringing to a halt all efforts to develop Western-style education already underway from the days of Menelik II and now accelerated under the aegis of Emperor Haile Sellaisse I (born 1892, ruled from 1930 until his deposition in 1974). This, to some extent, was perhaps inevitable given the circumstances in which the Italians arrived in Ethiopia: in the context of a fascist political order under Benito Mussolini back home. In fact, what was even more tragic for the Ethiopians was that the Italians went out of their way to execute as many Ethiopian intellectuals as they could lay their hands on—such was their understanding of the "white-man's-burden." Therefore, further secular educational development in Ethiopia had to await the end of the Second World War.[1]

The original confrontation with the Italians had proved to be a wake-up call for the Ethiopians; they had to begin modernizing their country on a more concerted basis than before. Though as Marcus (1990: 106) reminds us, Mennelik II was not astute enough to consider the possibility of full modernization based on industrialization and social structural transformations as a bulwark against Western imperialism—as in the case of Meiji Japan (and also attempted to some degree by Egypt's Muhammed Ali). Whether such modernization would have succeeded had Mennelik tried it, is of course another matter. Muhammed Ali's experience suggests that it would have probably failed. Anyhow, under Mennelik II's leadership, Ethiopia introduced a modest program of economic and technological modernization that included the beginnings of secular, Western-style schooling. An important date is 1908 in the history of modern education in Ethiopia: in that year the Menelik II school opened with Egyptian Copts serving as teaching staff. (That this was an important milestone for Ethiopia is highlighted by the fact that just as it was opening its first primary school, in that same year Egypt, a country only a hop and a jump away, was opening its first university.) At the same time, the Ethiopians also began sending officially sponsored students for study abroad, mainly to France (which through persistent diplomacy had managed to garner for itself considerable cultural influence in the country, so much so that in the secular schools that were set up prior to 1941 French was the principal medium of instruction).[2] French cultural influence, however, would be replaced by British cultural influence after 1941, which would first arise because of Britain's role in assisting the Ethiopians to bring to an end Italian rule. (Ethiopia's postwar alignment with another important English-speaking country, the United States, would also help in this regard.)[3]

Following the war, efforts to develop modern secular education resumed in Ethiopia and it would now include the provision of higher education. The initiative for this effort came from the secondary schools (Haile Selassie I Secondary School, Tafari Makonnen School, and the British-run General Wingate Secondary School), which all wanted a higher education outlet for their students against the backdrop of an increasingly prohibitive solution, for financial reasons, of sending students abroad. Despite the difficult history of Jesuit relations with the Ethiopian Christians—where the latter not only regard Catholicism as anything but true Christianity, according to Wagaw (1990: 71), but whose presence in Ethiopia since their arrival in the sixteenth-century (with the Portuguese Army that had been invited to help fight the Muslims), over the subsequent 100 years or so, in his words, "led to the death of one king, the abdication of another, and a large measure of civil strife"—it is to the Jesuits that Emperor Selassie turned for help in setting up the college, specifically Jesuits from Canada led by Dr. Lucien Matte who had been principal of the Tafari Makonnen School since 1945. In July 1950, the college was upgraded to become the University College of Addis Ababa.[4] Initially it was a two-year institution, preparing students for either further overseas study or vocational certificate education. Unlike college-level higher education institutions in other parts of colonial Africa, the University College did not have a direct affiliation with any overseas university. This is not to say, however, that for reasons of, primarily, international recognition of degrees and quality control, the Ethiopians had not explored the possibility of affiliating the new college to the University of London (in the same manner as was the case with the Asquith Colleges of British colonial Africa); but in the end they balked at the prospect of losing too much control over the development of their institution, as well as the higher financial price tag that such an association entailed. Hence, despite a positive report prepared by a visiting team invited by the Ethiopians from the University of London, and issued a month later (April 1953) agreeing that affiliation would be in the best interest of the fledgling institution, the Ethiopians informed the university that they had decided against the idea after all (Wagaw 1990).[5]

The first degrees were granted at commencement on July 26, 1954, only two days before the college received its civil charter from the government establishing it as an autonomous institution of higher learning reporting to a board of governors. Over this four-year period, the institution had grown to enroll a student population of some 400 hundred students. Between 1954 and 1961, the college would see even more rapid expansion as more fields of study were incorporated (secondary school teacher training, commerce, economics, public administration, etc.). During the college's first decade other institutions of higher learning were also established, such as the College of Technology (1952) in Addis Ababa; College of Agriculture (founded in 1953 with U.S. assistance at Jimma and later moved to a specially built campus at Alemaya); College of Public Health (established in 1954 with the assistance of the United Nations and the United States at Gondar); Institute of Building Technology (founded in 1954 with Swedish aid), and the Holy Trinity Theological College (1960). Mention should also be made here of the privately-funded Holy Family University Institute established in Asmara by the Camboni Sisters Missionary Congregation to prepare students for further study in Italy.[6]

Given the feudal character of the Ethiopian social order, an important matter that any consideration of the history of higher education in Ethiopia necessarily demands attention is that of student selection; that is, Who among the Ethiopians had access to this emerging secular higher education system? Surprisingly, higher educational provision in Ethiopia initially rested on the principle that need should not stand in the way of the pursuit of a higher education—a principle that would be universally adopted elsewhere in postindependence Africa; therefore all students, immaterial of their family background and gender roles, who qualified for admission were entitled to a full government scholarship that covered almost everything: from tuition to room and board to even some clothing![7] On the other hand, again as elsewhere in Africa, while meritocracy was the watchword, students who came from within areas where the secondary schools were located (Addis Ababa, Shoa, and Harar) stood a better chance than others of gaining admission. In other words, historically determined geographically-based privileges (urban versus rural) did manage to filter through (compare suburban versus inner city schools in the United States) in the student selection process.[8]

In 1961, the University College would reach a significant milestone: it would become the basis of the new Haile Selassie I University, which would also incorporate the other colleges in the country. For assistance with creating the new university, the Ethiopians had turned to the United States, who provided both capital for selected buildings and equipment, as well as management and planning expertise. The last took the form of a U.S. government sponsored team from the University of Utah that arrived in Ethiopia in August 1959 to survey Ethiopia's higher education needs and make appropriate recommendations. The team spent two months in the country and produced a detailed report that became the basis for the establishment of the new university system. A U.S. academic, Dr. Harold Bently, served as the interim president until a qualified Ethiopian could be found to head the institution. Kassa Wolde-Marriam, who served as president of the new university from 1962 to 1969, turned out to be the person to fit the bill (he would be followed by Dr. Aklilu Habte, one of the first graduates of the then University College). With Ethiopian resolve, coupled with external assistance, the university would make rapid progress in its early years as is attested by Maxwell (1990: 409):

Between 1964 and 1970 the university grew to be the largest in English-speaking Africa. In 1964, 1,774 students were enrolled in full-time courses and a further 1,523 on extension programs; in 1969/ 70, the corresponding numbers were 4,636 and 2,261. In 1969, 277 students graduated with degrees and 741 with certificates as against 209 and 98 respectively in 1964.

From the perspective of organization and governance, the university was not modeled on any specific model or tradition; but not surprisingly, United States and British influence was palpable considering that the language of instruction was English.[9] As for personnel, the majority of the teaching and high-level administrative staff, as was the case with almost all African universities elsewhere on the continent in the early years of the postindependence era, came from a variety of countries. Wagaw (1990) points out that fifteen different nationalities were represented at the university; the majority of whom though were British and U.S. Americans in roughly equal proportion. (By the time of the 1974 revolution, however, sufficient strides had been made in indigenizing personnel, so that three-quarters of the staff were now of Ethiopian origin.)

Besides the British, the United States (and later the former Soviet bloc countries and to a lesser extent, a number of others such as Japan and India), one would be remiss in not also mentioning the important role played by the Swedes as well in the development of secular higher education in Ethiopia. After all, relations between the Swedes and the Ethiopians were of long-standing, going all the way back to when the Swedish Evangelical Mission had sent to Ethiopia its first three missionaries (in 1866 in the persons of L. J. Lange, P. E. Kjellberg, and C. J. Carlsson). Within the same year of their arrival they had set up a missionary school in Massawa. Moreover, Ethiopia was one of the first two countries (the other was Pakistan) that the Swedes had selected as targets for their overseas development assistance with the creation by the Swedish government of the Central Committee for Technical Assistance to Less Developed Areas in 1952 to coordinate what would turn out to be an exemplary role by the Swedes in international development assistance. Their first foray into higher education specifically, however, began with the establishment in 1954 of the Ethio-Swedish Institute of Building Technology, which later (in 1973) would become a constituent part of the newly created university as the College of Technology Southern Campus. The institute at its creation was jointly financed on a fifty-fifty basis between the Swedish and the Ethiopian government. Other forms of assistance in the higher education sector also included the financing of scholarships for overseas study by Ethiopian students, undertaken not necessarily only in Sweden, but in other Western countries as well.[10]

Although the absence of a unitary academic tradition as a role model created administrative and other difficulties, one advantage coming out of this circumstance is that there was greater room for innovation; and none exemplified better in this regard than the implementation of a program of community service for students called the Ethiopian University Service. The program was launched on April 17, 1964, and it required all students in their penultimate year to spend twelve months in the countryside teaching in return for a modest stipend. The aim of the university was to provide students with an opportunity to make an immediate contribution to the development of their country while acquainting them with the practical problems of this effort. At the same time, from the perspective of the government, it was a way of resolving, at least partially, the problem of teacher shortages. Although, as perhaps would be expected, there was initially resistance from the students to this forced interruption of their studies, in the end they acquiesced and even came to see much value in it for themselves as well as for the communities they served. As Wagaw has observed: "despite the errors in judgment, misutilization, administrative inefficiency, lack of cooperation from professional workers, financial problems, irrelevant field placements, political and economic hardships, community resistance, and occasional mistakes in the art of teaching and human relations, there was no doubt that the year the students spent away from the university was, in many ways, the most educational aspect of their entire university experience" (1990: 200–201).

On the other hand, it is doubtful if the program would have ever been launched had its unintended consequences (also of an educational nature) had been foreseen. For it is clear that for many students their experiences in the countryside would have a profound galvanizing effect in terms of their political consciousness—embodied, for instance, in the slogan they would soon come to adopt in their emerging opposition to the monarchy and the feudal order: "land to the tiller!"[11] Consider that writing only two years earlier, Kehoe (a U.S. academic who at that time was the dean of women at the university) had characterized the average Ethiopian student thusly: "although educated Ethiopians generally profess a passionate patriotism, they are quite averse to any display of it which requires manual labor." She further comments: "In view of a recent sit-down strike, staged in an attempt to get open library stacks and better food, it seems that these students have little appreciation of the benefits heaped upon them by their indulgent government. Since most of the young men and women now attending the regular session of the university (about 460 in all) have achieved little academic distinction, it is difficult to see what national purpose is served by coddling them" (1962: 475–76).

Amidst the pomp and circumstance and national jubilation that accompanied the opening of the new university by the Emperor at a convocation on December 18, 1961, no one could have foreseen (least of all Haile Selassie himself) that the new institution would become a Trojan horse for the demise of the Solomonid dynasty and its associated feudal order. For, less than a mere two decades later, in 1975, the university would be renamed Addis Ababa University—a name change that was emblematic of a cataclysmic political transformation of Ethiopia: the abolition in the preceding year of the monarchy with the deposition of Haile Selassie by a military-led coup in which the Ethiopian university (and secondary school) students would play a crucial role.[12] The immediate catalytic event behind the coup on September 12, 1974 was Selassie's insensitivity to and mismanagement of the awful famine that had consumed thousands upon thousands of rural lives in the drought-ridden environmentally degraded northern regions of Shewa, Tigray, and Welo in 1973/1974. Yet, hitherto, the more than thousand-year-old monarchy had been able to withstand all manner of tribulations (civil wars, invasions, famines, rebellions, etc.) So, what had changed?

It appears that the famine was the straw that broke the camel's back. That is, the deep contradictions arising from the development of new secular institutions of modernity (such as the university—which to its credit paid, in relative terms, more than lip service to the concept of academic freedom) against the backdrop of an increasingly despotic, tyrannical, and inept monarchy astride over a corrupt autocratic feudal order in which the three historically long-standing principal protagonists of oppression in Ethiopia, the monarchy, the nobility, and the church, continued to keep the peasantry in abject poverty and slave-like servility, found their political expression in an emerging oppositional revolutionary student movement. What is more, it was one that espoused, as one would perhaps logically expect in a twentieth-century feudal context and against the background of the Cold War (where the United States, unlike the Soviet Union, firmly sided with the monarchy), a Marxist-Leninist ideology.[13] That students took on this role is not surprising; as in other parts of Africa, it was the only group among the elite that was not "compromised" with the capacity to articulate grievances against the status quo. As Wagaw, who as an Ethiopian and as the dean of students had the opportunity to observe the evolving student movement at close hand, has commented (but who begins by first noting that the "the national university provided students with a protective umbrella under which they were able to conceive, develop, and eventually act upon their political ideologies"): "From the early 1960s they were, for all practical purposes, the only organized, educated group that was able to challenge the hitherto supposed invincible power of the emperor" (1990: 225–26).

Students on their own, however, as politically and administratively inexperienced youth (not to mention their transient status qua students) are incapable of bringing about a new order regardless of how well versed they may be in articulating grievances; they must have credible allies from society at large (vide the lessons of Tiananmen).[14] In Ethiopia they found their ally in the military, but with disastrous consequences for the country as a whole, including the students themselves. Most of their leadership was eventually slaughtered two years later by the military junta (known as the *Dergue* and led by one Mengistu Haile Mariam who emerged as the strongman) in the context of power struggles, which in part were ideologically-driven as factions within and without the military, in their ignorance—fostered by the corrupting influence of Leninism—of the basic Marxian principle that a credible transition to socialism in a society can only occur on the heels of a fundamental transformation of the forces of production so as to unleash the requisite resources to underwrite distributive justice (as encapsulated in the dictum: from each according to her/ his ability to each according to his/ her need), contested the blueprint for a new "socialist" order.[15] Soon, driven by a virulently potent combination of both greed for power and the effort to messianically implement a well-meaning but ill-conceived ideology, the self-proclaimed Marxist-Leninist government of Mengistu rapidly gave rise to an autocracy inherently incapable, like all such autocracies (compare the Khmer Rouge of Cambodia that came to power only a year after the Dergue) of accepting that ends rarely if ever justify means, and in the process tragically plunged the country into an era of political and economic darkness and chaos where civil war and man-made famines stalked the land on an even greater scale, punctuated by the Dergue's brutality and terror (in fact an officially sponsored 1977 phase of which was actually dubbed the *Red Terror Campaign*)—the destruction of the feudal order proved to be the only silver lining (at least initially for some of the peasantry before brutal Soviet-style collectivization was later imposed on them).[16]

Eventually, by 1991, the country had spun completely out of control; the chaos was too much even for Mengistu and as Eritrean and Tigrayan rebel forces closed in on Addis Ababa, he uncharacteristically turned tail and fled (without informing almost anyone) on May 21 of that year to Zimbabwe, where whose autocratic leader Robert Mugabe, cut roughly from the same political and ideological cloth as Mengistu's, gave him refuge.[17] The new Ethiopia that officially emerged on the ruins of the Dergue dominated Ethiopia on May 28, 1991, was no longer a unitary state but a federation—with a modicum of democracy to underwrite its legitimacy; though full peace and political stability continues to remain elusive (see, for example, Pausewang, Tronvoll, and Aalen 2002).[18] At the same time, the politically and economically much-discredited ideology of Marxist-Leninism was abandoned; the Ethiopian masses, aided and abetted by their religious institutions, had never taken to it kindly. They had found its potent blend of unbending secularism and brutal blood-soaked authoritarianism, against the backdrop of a pattern of disastrous economic policies pursued under its aegis, simply too much to bear, whatever its other merits may have been.

During the years when the Dergue was in power, the fortunes of higher education in Ethiopia had taken a familiar turn (from the perspective of countries hewing the Marxist-Leninist line): as part of a broader educational effort to lower the rates of illiteracy and increase educational opportunities, higher education was greatly expanded by upgrading existing institutions and creating new ones, with a strong emphasis placed on human capital formation in consonance with the dictates of centralized "socialist" economic planning. The new institutions included Awassa College of Agriculture (established in 1976); Wondogenet College of Forestry (1977); Addis Ababa College of Commerce (1979); Ambo College of Agriculture (1979); Jimma College of Agriculture (1979); Jimma Institute of Health Sciences (1982); and Arba Minch Water Technology Institute (1986). In addition, the regime upgraded the College of Agriculture at Alemaya to an autonomous university in 1985 called Alemaya University of Agriculture. While this expansion was a positive achievement, its full impact was considerably diminished by the regime's inability to finance it at appropriate levels as it continued to squander the nation's resources on futile civil wars precipitated by its tyrannical and reckless policies (there was a time when the Dergue was battling more than twelve, primarily ethnic-based, armed uprisings across the country; all going on at once).

At the same time, measures were taken by the Dergue to defang the oppositional potential of the students through curricular changes and by wiping out academic freedom (any form of opposition to government policies by students was deemed treasonous, meriting harsh retribution). Those who did not heed the warning or happened to be at the wrong place at the wrong time paid with their lives—such as during the Red Terror Campaign. There were three other important developments within higher education: as Ethiopia's ties grew with the Soviet bloc countries, expatriate teaching staff from Western capitalist democracies were increasingly replaced by those from the Soviet bloc; again as a consequence of these ties a significant part of the flow of officially sponsored students going to study abroad was diverted from traditional destinations to the Soviet bloc; and the political and economic upheavals thrown up by the Dergue-led revolution created a massive braindrain with the exodus of Ethiopian students, faculty and members of the intelligentsia generally to the United States and other Western capitalist democracies as refugees. While, for obvious reasons, there are no hard figures in terms of how many of Ethiopia's brightest sons and daughters were lost to the country, it is quite likely that they numbered in the thousands (the total number of Ethiopians from all walks of life who left Ethiopia to seek asylum elsewhere are said to have totaled over three million during the Mengistu period).

The Dergue's overthrow did not diminish the pace of higher education expansion; for, in this regard the new federal government remained committed to the policies of its predecessor. Among the new institutions that would be founded in the post–Dergue period include Mekelle Business College (established in 1991); Mekelle University College (1993); Nazareth Technical College (1993); Ethiopian Civil Service College (1994); Dilla College of Teacher Education and Health Sciences (1996); and School of Medicine Laboratory Technology (1997). There was, however, one major policy change that the new federal government implemented: encouraged by institutions such as the World Bank, it has permitted the founding of private higher education institutions (e.g., Awassa Adventist College, People to People College in Harar, and Unity College in Addis Ababa) unlike its predecessor—which, characteristically, had prohibited the establishment of private educational institutions. The federal government has also adopted a policy of systematic upgrading of the college-level institutions to university status through a process of institutional accretion as soon as resources permit. One purpose of this approach is to permit the creation of regionally-based universities (in order to bring balance to the geographically lopsided higher education sector) without requiring large capital outlays that would be attendant upon the establishment of completely new turnkey institutions.[19] To provide a quantitative picture of how far Ethiopians have come in their quest for higher education, consider these two figures: when the University College of Addis Ababa opened in 1950 it had all of twenty-one students (all males), today the country's total university-level enrollment stands at over 40,000 (and of whom about 15% are females). (Needless to say, while quantitative expansion is one thing, qualitative control is quite another; as is the case with most of the rest of Africa, the latter has suffered considerably under a regime of inadequate financial resources.)

This picture of continuing higher education expansion presented here, albeit baldly, may on the surface appear to be suggestive of good things to come for the people of Ethiopia; at long last. However, old habits die hard. As already noted, it was not long before Ethiopia and Eritrea became embroiled in an immensely wasteful and costly war (in terms of both human life and resources). To highlight the utter foolishness of the leadership in both countries with regard to matters of peace and stability (shared of course by the African leadership in other parts of the continent as well)—without which it is impossible to fully reap the benefits of any kind of education—the village of Badme, where the border dispute first erupted, had been so completely obliterated that the U.N.-sponsored Boundary Commission appointed to help resolve the dispute could not locate the village! As of this writing, the problem of stability is not only in relation to neighbors; there continues to remain within the country a seething undercurrent of ethnic-based real and imagined grievances with a constant potential to erupt into yet another cycle of self-destructive fratricidal bloodletting, despite the transition from a unitary to a federal state to take care of precisely this problem.

There is one other matter that must be addressed by way of concluding this section on Ethiopia: it has to do with why the Ethiopians waited for so long before they began their foray into modern secular education, even though they had no constraints emanating from colonial policies to contend with. Yes, it is true that an immediate explanation for this is that there was resistance from the church (as was indicated in Chapter 2). But this does not explain everything; for in the end the church *was* defanged on this matter. The problem of delayed access to modern secular education was in reality a symptom of a wider problem: the delay by the Ethiopians in undertaking, until in a sense it was too late, a spirited modernization effort—thereby giving rise to a problematic that was first introduced to you dear reader in Chapter 2 (albeit in passing) as the Ethiopia/ Japan anomaly. This anomaly emerges in a tantalizing way: Why is it that one of the only two countries on the African continent that did not experience colonialism (Liberia being the other) failed to follow the same course as that pursued by Meiji Japan—using the strategy of modernization (revolution from above) to secure for itself a path to sustained development and prosperity, and above all security from European imperialism? (About the last, one has to wonder how Ethiopia's modern history would have unfolded had Italy, following its second invasion on the eve of the Second World War, not sided with Hitler and instead chosen to be in the camp of the Allied forces.) The question becomes particularly poignant when one considers, as Levine (1997) reminds us, two facts: Ethiopia and Japan are the only two countries in modern history that militarily beat back European imperialism (one with its defeat of the Italians on the first round in 1896, and the other with its defeat of the Russians in 1905, respectively); and second, intellectuals in both countries were long aware of each other's unique positions in history (see, for instance, Aoki and Kurimoto 1997).

Before proceeding further, however, one has to concede that to even mention Japan and Ethiopia in the same breath is to elicit among many an apoplectic consternation at what they perceive as nothing less than a naive comparison of bananas and mangoes, born of a "fevered imagination" to quote Levine (1997—see also Kebede 1997). Yet, to those even vaguely familiar with the history of the two nations, the comparison, however, is not farfetched at all. To begin with, there are a number of characteristics that the two countries, in many ways so far apart geographically and otherwise, share that highlight the anomaly. For example, each was intimately involved in international trade for centuries, that is, long before the advent of Europe on their doorsteps; neither was colonized by Europe (discounting the brief five-year occupation of Ethiopia in 1936–41 by the Italians); both possessed a well-developed feudal political order; both have histories that go back thousands of years; and both sought to build regional empires (in which both succeeded temporarily, though the Ethiopian empire would last much longer, but eventually it too would disintegrate). (See Levine 1997 for a more detailed look at other similarities, and differences, in the historical trajectories of the two countries.)

Yet, from the perspective of the present these similarities pail into stark insignificance. While one is among the wealthiest countries of the world that can, in economic terms, hold its own against any Western country, including the United States, the other is among the poorest, belonging to the category of not developing, nor even quasi-developing, but pre-developing nations. (Compare, for instance, these two basic statistics: per capita GDP in 2003 for Ethiopia was a paltry $700 as against Japan's $27,000; and Ethiopia's life-expectancy at birth was roughly *half* of that of Japan's!)

Anyhow, it should be clear, then, as to what is meant by the Ethiopia/Japan anomaly. Japan's escape from European imperialism was surely an important factor in its eventual rise to economic dominance in Asia, yet the same experience did not have an identical effect on the economic fortunes of the Ethiopians; instead, they have shared the same fate as most of the rest of Africa that was colonized by Europe.[20] What historical factors, then, account for such a chasmic divergence of their historical trajectories? The answer to this question has been reserved for Appendix II, for reasons that will be clear upon reading the appendix in its entirety.

LIBERIA

The origins of modern Liberia lie in the establishment in 1822 of a coastal settlement for free African Americans, the manumitted, and "recaptives" on the west coast of Africa, at Cape Mesurado, at the mouth of St. Paul River.[21] The main force behind this enterprise was a private religious but nondenominational organization: the American Society for the Colonization of Free People of Color (better known as simply American Colonization Society), founded in the United States in 1816 by Presbyterian ministers and supported by other denominations, as well as notables among the Euro-American laity. Its members and supporters included three U.S. presidents: Abraham Lincoln, James Madison, and James Monroe. The society's first president was Bushrod Washington, a U.S. Supreme Court Justice no less. Its founding and work was an outcome of a coincidence of diverse interests, including some African Americans who longed for a territory they could call their own in the hope that it would be the route to salvation from the inequities and injustices of a racist United States; the clergy (both African Americans and Euro-Americans) and like-minded laity who wished to extend the Gospel to the "heathens" in Africa; some Euro-Americans who wanted to see an end to the population of free African Americans because they saw in them a threat to the U.S. slave system; other Euro-Americans (like Abraham Lincoln) who saw in the society's work the solution to their antiblack racism by completely and permanently removing the object of their racism from U.S. shores; and abolitionists (like the Quakers) who viewed the resettlement project as a humanitarian gesture to freed slaves by facilitating their return "home."[22] Whatever the motives, by the time the U.S. Civil War broke out in 1861 the society had managed to settle in Liberia, to varying degrees of success, close to 19,000 African American settlers and "recaptives."[23]

Liberia was initially ruled by the society, with U.S. government support, until 1847 when it became self-governing under the leadership of an Americo-Liberian, by the name of Joseph Jenkins Roberts.[24] In subsequent years the Americo-Liberians would gain recognition for Liberia from other European powers. Extension of Americo-Liberian rule over the indigenous African populations in the hinterland, however, would take many more decades. In 1894, the colony would be christened Liberia (after the Latin word *liber*— meaning free) by a Society's official, Ralph Randolph Gurley, while the settlement at Cape Mesurado would be named Monrovia (after James Monroe).

The first higher education institution to be founded in Liberia was Liberia College in Monrovia. It was sponsored by the Colonization Society with the help of grants from a Boston-based philanthropy, the Trustees of Donations for Education in Liberia; it opened its doors in 1862, although plans for it had already been in the works for more than a decade, to an enrollment of seven (Americo-Liberian) students—though its preparatory section would come to enroll many more. (Among its first presidents would be none other than Edward Blyden—from 1881 to 1885.) The motives for establishing the college, on the part of its U.S. backers, included, interestingly, the desire to prevent Liberians from being sent to study in England, as had already begun to happen. They felt that the Liberians would return from England with less enthusiasm for *republicanism*. As is to be expected, the college operated along the same lines as any other U.S. college of the period; it was administered by a local board of trustees, but with some supervision from the United States. In other words: "The college, from the foundations of the buildings (brick and timber all sent from Boston) to the foundations of the curriculum, was exotic—an American intrusion on the West African coast" (Livingstone 1976: 255). As if to underline its U.S. origins, the college was marred in its development by "racial" conflict among the Americo-Liberian staff—between negroes on one side (represented by men such as Blyden and Alexander Crummell), and mulattoes on the other (represented by its president, J. J. Roberts). An example of the myriad ways in which this conflict surfaced was the efforts by Blyden (both before and after he had managed to become president of the college) to make the curriculum more relevant to Liberia, by, for example, introducing the study of Arabic (so that Liberians could develop better relations with the Afro-Liberian Muslim population of the interior), as well as other African languages.[25] He also tried to diversify the college's enrollment, but with little success, by admitting Afro-Liberian students.[26] The mulattoes (together with other Americo-Liberians, as well as the missionaries) were incensed at such an affront to the status quo. Not surprisingly, under such circumstances of endemic conflict, the college did not receive the unconditional support of the ruling mulatto elite that would have made for a much more vibrant institution than it turned out to be. Consider, for example, that between 1864 and 1903 only eleven students graduated with degrees. Of course, inadequate finances, always a major fly in the ointment, throughout the history of the college did not help matters—plus as their own economic power waned in the face of foreign competition by the early part of the twentieth-century, so did the fortunes of the college worsen.[27] (Even after the college took on a new form—as a modern university—the race question never completely disappeared from its life; for, later it would resurface with horrible vengeance, albeit indirectly and propelled from external political forces, as will be indicated shortly.)

Missionary educational activity in Liberia by the U.S.-based Methodist Episcopal Church lead to the establishment in 1889 of another higher education institution: a vocational college, the Hoffman Institute; a decade or so later, in 1897, it would become the Cuttington College and Divinity School (renamed after the treasurer, R. Fulton Cuttington, of the Board of Missions of the Episcopal Church, the sponsors of the institution). In 1949, Cuttington was upgraded, in part with the assistance of the Ford Foundation, the U.S. government and the Liberian government, to a four-year liberal arts (but still private) college, and relocated some 120 miles away from Monrovia to a rural setting at

Suacoco. Occupying a 1500-acre government-donated site, the new Cuttington University College and Divinity School, as a private four-year liberal arts college, funded from a variety of sources, was a testament to the influence of the United States on Liberian higher education; for elsewhere in former British colonial Africa such an institution (the key concept here is *private*) would have been almost unheard of.[28] The Methodists were also responsible for the founding in 1838 of a seminary; however, it was subsequently chartered as a college in 1898 to become the College of West Africa. Visiting the college in 1926, James Sibley (who had been sent to Liberia to survey the state of higher education there by the American Advisory Committee on Education in Liberia—a body comprising representatives from a number of missionary and other organizations), did not have much praise for the parlous state of the institution due its lack of resources; and caustically observed: "If a college is to be maintained by any American organization, in fact as well as in name, it ought to be run in a manner which will not bring discredit upon missionary institutions as such." He continued: "If the church is not in a position to foster or maintain an institution of this nature, it should retire from this particular field" (pp. 76–77). In one way or another, the college managed to survive into the present.

In 1997, the U.S.-based African Methodist Episcopal Church upgraded Monrovia College, which it had founded in 1892, into a four-year liberal arts college and renamed it A.M.E. University. In other words, African American missionary activity in the educational arena in Liberia has also been of longstanding. Sibley, who visited the college in 1926, described it thusly:

It occupies a beautiful site of thirteen acres on the outskirts of Monrovia. It is the most imposing building in the Republic, being a large three-story structure of concrete, surrounded on three sides by wide verandahs. The building was erected at considerable expense, and contains space for an assembly room, class rooms, dining hall, living quarters for the teachers in charge, and sections set aside for dormitory purposes, for both young men and young women (p. 79).

He goes on to say that the enrollment stood at less than 100 students. He also made this interesting comment: "It is unfortunate that the institutions of higher learning in Monrovia cannot be coordinated in some way, so that, in spite of denominational differences, they may made to serve in an effective manner the interests of higher education in the republic" (p. 80). In other words, in the absence of state involvement in *systematic* educational planning and provision, from the very beginning, higher education in Liberia developed on a haphazard basis.

Not to be outdone, the secular champions—in contrast to the missionaries—of the white man's burden in the United States, represented in this instance by the Phelps-Stokes Fund, helped Liberia to import the Fund's version of secular higher education for blacks (the much celebrated Hampton/Tuskegee model) by assisting with the founding of the Booker T. Washington Industrial and Agricultural Institute (the name said it all).[29] The institute would open with great fanfare before a gathering of some 2,000 people in 1929; and in his dedication address, the U.S. minister to Liberia, W. T. Francis, would explain to the gathering that Miss Olivia Phelps Stokes had provided in her will for the founding of exactly such an institute in the ancestral homeland of Booker T. Washington so that its inhabitants may also benefit from the work he had started (Marable 1982).[30]

After a major fire had burned Liberia College to the ground, it was rebuilt and reopened as the University of Liberia in 1951. The university would also incorporate the Booker T. Washington Institute (which fittingly would become the university's School of Agricultural and Mechanical Arts). A college of medicine, the A. M. Dogliotti College of Medicine, would also come to the university, but much later, in 1970; it would be made possible by a combined effort of the Liberian government, the Vatican, and the University of Turin in Italy. As would be expected, the general pattern of governance, degree structure, curriculum, and so on, was patterned on U.S. educational institutions. Complaining that the first two presidents of the university were from the United States, and that the majority of the teaching staff were foreign even two decades after its founding, a member of the university's administration, writing in 1973 (Seyon 1973), legitimately criticized the university for not being responsive to the needs of Liberia. In fact, the disjuncture between the state and the university was such, he states, that the state in turn rarely, if ever, consulted the university in matters of both national development planning and implementation of development programs. He attributed this lack of institutional relevance to the development needs of the country on the importation of a U.S. higher education culture that saw close institutional linkages between a university and the state as dangerous: it would undermine university autonomy.[31] On the other hand, against the backdrop of recurring budgetary crises this was perhaps the least of the university's problems. Even more tragically, a decade or so later, events would render his criticism meaningless: the university, like other Liberian educational institutions, would be struggling for its very survival—many would not succeed. The reason? It will be clear in a moment. Besides the university and Cuttington, mention may also be made of the founding of a technical college called Harper Technical College in 1971. A few years later, in 1978, it would be renamed the William V. S. Tubman College of Technology and moved to a rural area (a politically mandated relocation, but which deprived the college of the needed linkages with industry).

Americo-Liberians are fond of losing no opportunity to remind with great pride any one willing to listen, that unlike other countries in Africa, including Ethiopia (which they insist was an Italian colony, even if only for a few years), Liberia was not a colony of any country, including the United States. On the other hand, of course, indigenous Liberians (like the Mandinka, Krahn, Gola, etc.) have a completely different take on this, since they never willingly suffered the far from benign internal "colonial" rule of the Americo-Liberians.[32] Consider these two events: in 1931 a League of Nations investigation revealed that Americo-Liberians were involved in the export of indigenous Africans as semi-slave labor (see Sundiata 2003); in May 1980, after decades of despotic rule by William V. S. Tubman (1943 to 1971) and his successor William R. Tolbert, the lower ranked members of the army, dominated by the Krahn, rebelled and under the leadership of a twenty-eight-year old master sergeant by the name of Samuel K. Doe, and overthrew the government.[33] The latter event would in time (especially beginning in 1989 with a cross-border invasion led by a small band of rebels headed by one Charles Taylor, a former procurement clerk in Doe's government), set the stage for an orgy of bloodletting in which thousands upon thousands would die as various newly emergent pseudoliberation fronts led by kleptocratic war lords would vie for control of the country.[34] (Tragically, among the Western patrons of the Doe regime, the United States— for whom Liberia had served as the regional headquarters of the Central Intelligence Agency—simply looked on.) The deadly blood-soaked mayhem, characteristic of the pillaging and destruction of Europe by the Vandals in the fifth-century (or that of the Nazis in the twentieth), would not come to an end until around 1995.[35] In July 1997, in that uniquely African twist of fates, almost full peace was restored with the election of one of the chief villains in the start of the original conflagration, Charles Taylor, to the Liberian presidency.[36] Peace, however, would not last long; within a few years, Taylor's authoritarian and corrupt government was the object of both ire and envy of rebels, and the country would once more descend into the cauldron of a mercilessly brutal fratricidal war. It would only end with international intervention that would see Taylor in exile in Nigeria, and the emergence of a new government in Liberia.

Needless to say, higher education, like all other formal education, as well as other institutions, would suffer a severe setback during the nearly two decades long bloody chaos. Among the first acts, for example, of the Doe regime was to temporarily close the university after physically assaulting the students and faculty (involving murder, rape, etc.). Even before the outbreak of armed conflict, the Liberian economy had been on the verge of bankruptcy—with the obvious attendant consequences for all state-funded educational institutions. The conflict merely helped to flatten the economy and almost everything associated with it. With the massive destruction of physical plant, the looting of resources, the forcible and voluntary recruitment of large numbers of the student population by one side or the other in the raging armed conflict (the horrifying abduction of children, some as young as seven, to be used as child-soldiers and sex-slaves was an important trademark of the conflict), the exodus abroad of many members of the teaching and administrative staff, and starved of funds (even after peace had been temporarily restored after 1997), the entire education sector, including higher education, would see a heart-wrenchingly massive reversal in its development from all perspectives—thereby proving, yet once again, that education, development and peace are dialectically interrelated. What is more, the future, as of this writing, does not look very promising.

Looking back over the history of Liberia, it is quite clear that the heritage of being one of the two countries in Africa that was not a European colony has not (as in the case of its counterpart in this regard, Ethiopia), necessarily stood it in good stead. Bounded on all sides by colonialism from its inception, the Liberians steadily lost their economic autonomy to international forces (the arrival of the transnational corporation Firestone being emblematic); thereby underwriting a trajectory that has not been that much different from that of its colonized neighbors (such as Sierra Leone, for instance). Symptomatic of this circumstance, was that the level of higher education provision in Liberia was not markedly different from that of its colonized neighbors.

However, to blame international forces alone on the country's predicament is to oversimplify matters: one cannot discount the fact that its development has also been hamstrung by the fact that from inception the country was in another sense (but no less significantly) a "colony." That is, the "internal colonialism" of the Americo-Liberians vis-à-vis the indigenous, the Afro-Liberians, led them to divert their developmental energy to retaining power in the face of ever-rising discontent on the part of the subjugated majority, coupled with rent-seeking on a national scale. (For example, the agreement to allow the Firestone Plantation Corporation to establish rubber plantations for a song in 1926, and the flooding of the country by transnational carpetbaggers in the 1990s to essentially loot the country's natural resources by Charles Taylor's kleptocratic government, is symptomatic of the latter behavior.) Not surprisingly, education was never really felt by the Americo-Liberian ruling elite to be a top priority of the country; leaving it for the most part in the hands of foreigners (missionaries, foreign aid donors, and the like) to this day. The following observation made in 1962 has continued to remain valid, for the most part, until the present; that is, even in the absence of the fratricidal war, it is unlikely that the educational circumstances of Liberia would have been that much different under the continuing overlordship of the Americo-Liberians:

While members of the Americo-Liberian ruling class measured their superiority over the [indigenous] people of the hinterland in terms of "modernity" versus the indigenous inhabitants' "primitiveness," they were not very education-minded until recently. Education was at times more formal than substantial, and there has often been a tendency to concentrate on appearances rather than content....Furthermore, as many Liberians are quick to point out, the country has had no experience of colonialism. Whatever else this may have meant, it prevented the Liberians from developing a university of good quality, alert school inspectors, and an educational service trained in modern pedagogical techniques (Kitchen 1962: 348–49). [37]

SOUTH AFRICA

The evolution of South African higher education, as would be logically expected, is intimately intertwined with a political, economic, and social history in which, perhaps more so than in any other part of anglophone Africa, racism was a salient determinative factor.[38] In fact, one may note here that the uniqueness of this historical circumstance on the continent is such that to seek an analogous case *in its totality* one must go outside the continent altogether: to the U.S. South. Ergo, to delve, at least briefly, into that history is to lay the groundwork for a clearer understanding of the specifics of the historical trajectory followed by South African higher education, the hallmark of which has been, until recently, a racially determined chasmic duality both qualitatively and quantitatively.

For the Africans of South Africa, their first *sustained* contact with Europeans that would transform their subsequent history forever began in the context of the post–1492 development of the West–East transoceanic trade discussed in Appendix II. Specifically, it commenced with the arrival of a team of Dutch men employed by the then globally powerful United East India Company (also known as the Dutch East India Company) and led by one, Jan Anthoniszoon van Riebeeck, to establish a fort and a marine way station for their ships plying between Europe and the Far East.[39] The fateful date was April 6, 1652.[40] Colonization of territory, it appears, was not the original intent when van Riebeeck and his men dropped anchor in Table Bay at the southernmost tip of the African continent (named the Cape of Good Hope by the Portuguese explorer Bartolomeu Dias in 1488—but later renamed Cape Town by the British). Their inability to develop a reliable supply of meat and agricultural produce on the basis of barter with the African peoples of the area, who called themselves the Khoikhoi (meaning "men of men" but whom the Dutch referred to as the Hottentots) soon forced them to establish a permanent colonial settlement; setting in motion the typical set of events that would characterize the establishment of permanent European colonial settlements generally elsewhere in the AfroAsian and American ecumene (Algeria, Australia, Brazil, Canada, Hispaniola, New Zealand, United States, etc.): the forcible alienation of lands of the indigenous involving genocidal campaigns against them by means of a combination of superior force of arms and inadvertent, usually, biological warfare (by means of newly introduced diseases), *and justified by a white supremacist ideology.*[41] In other words, it is not at all historically certain that had the Cape of Good Hope not been of strategic importance to the seventeenth-century European merchant marine, South Africa would have still become host to a permanent European settler population two centuries before the Scramble for Africa and in the process driving the African people into that dark nightmarish tunnel of murder, pillage and racist oppression spanning more than 300 years in length, from 1652 to 1994 (and in which apartheid, far from being an aberration of history, would be simply a logical culminating interregnum), that would leave them in the state they are in today—characterized by "high levels of unemployment; the abject poverty of 50 percent of the population; sharp inequalities in the distribution of income, property, and opportunities; and high levels of crime and violence" (Terreblanche 2002: 4).

Although both the French and the British would take possession of it for brief periods of time from the Dutch, in the end it was the British who came to rule Cape Town and its immediate hinterland the Cape Province from 1806 onward (officially passed into their hands in 1814 with the termination of the Napoleonic Wars). The imposition of British colonial rule, the abolition by them of slavery in the colony in 1833, and the quest for new pasturelands for their cattle, would together conspire to provoke a mass exodus inland of the original Dutch, German, and French Huguenot European settlers who, over a period of about a 100 years, had fused to form a white ethnic group calling itself, in one of those cruel jokes of history, "Africans" (or in their language *Afrikaners*)—though they would also be known as the *Boers* (farmers)—with a unique subculture and a distinct language forged out of a mixture of European and African languages, but in which Dutch would remain the dominant strain, called *Afrikaans*. This exodus, called the *Groot Trek* (or Great Trek—took place roughly over a decade from the mid–1830s to mid–1840s) resulted in further loss of lands owned by the indigenous Africans and the formation of three new colonies by the Afrikaners: Natalia (in 1840, but annexed by the British in 1845 to become, later, the province of Natal), Transvaal (in 1852), and Orange River Colony (in 1854—to be known later as Orange Free State). In other words, following the arrival of British colonialism, from the perspective of the indigenous Africans, the same chain of events that had been set in motion by the entry of the Dutch into their lands more than a 100 years earlier would be replayed, but with even greater ferocity, on a nightmarishly recurring basis at various levels of magnitude for almost another 100 years or so all across the region that would eventually become the Republic of South Africa. Central to this pattern of events would be the same theme: European hunger for land ending in dispossession of the Africans, but only after superior weapons had inflicted a devastating military defeat on them; followed by their near enslavement as sources of cheap labor.[42] (Only their vast numerical superiority spared them the fate that befell the Native Americans, for instance, or the Aboriginal peoples in Australia.)

Now on the basis of the forgoing super-telescoped history of South Africa, it is necessary to extricate several historical developments of significance that helped to determine the eventual shape that South African society took and which in turn impacted the evolution of South African higher education. First, in 1899 a war (known as the Boer War) engineered by Cecil Rhodes following, not coincidentally, the discovery of gold in the Witswatersrand broke out between the British and the Transvaal Republic that lasted until 1902, whereafter, together with the Orange Free State, it became a British colony. However, a dream long held by Cecil Rhodes came to pass in August of 1909 (though he did not live to see it, he died in 1902) when the British parliament approved a plan to unify all the four British colonies (which by then had dominion status, that is they were all self-governing); it was duly signed into law by the British crown on December 2, 1909. A few months later, on May 31, 1910—eight years following the conclusion of the Boer War—the government of the new Union of South Africa took office. It was nothing less than a government of a European racist minority; for the unification process had entirely excluded everyone except the whites with the result that the new political framework completely eschewed all political rights, plus many economic and human rights, of blacks (and it must be emphasized that this was not for want of trying on the part of blacks to have their rights included). Moreover, the new government was a minority government of a minority: that is, it was an Anglo-South African dominated government; it would take nearly four more decades before the Afrikaners, who formed a majority of the white population, got their act together to eventually come to power in 1948 when their party (the National Party) won the whites only national elections.

Second, over the course of time spanning a couple of centuries the twin processes of land alienation and the extraction of labor and cattle from the African agricultural system brought their precapitalist self-sufficient subsistence economic system to the brink of collapse in that it ceased to be an *independent viable self-sustaining economic system*. This in turn rendered the conversion of the self-employed independent African farmer into a wage worker; henceforth dependent for his/ her living on "selling" his/ her labor within the emergent capitalist economic system.[43] Now, while this social structural transmutation (albeit initially not in the classic sense of full proletarianization with no links to nonwage, agriculturally derived livelihood) implied that the African was now a participant within the capitalist economic system such that in theory he could, if he so wished, engage in capitalist accumulation activities in his own behalf. In practice, however, a combination of racist laws, *later* codified as part of the *apartheid* system, coupled with the historical loss of his land and the resources under it and on it ensured that this would not be the case. Purely through racist legislation the African was forcibly relegated to the bottom of the socioeconomic ladder in the new South African economy that emerged with one overriding purpose: *to serve as a source of cheap labor for white capital.* Two sectoral examples graphically demonstrate how this occurred. In Kimberley, upon the discovery of first alluvial diamonds and the ensuing diamond rush Africans were, initially, also able to stake their own claims (upon payment of the requisite fee) alongside the white diamond miners. Within a few years, however, in the words of one of the white diggers of the period, "the European digger pointedly declined to recognize Jim Crow's *bona fides*, and would have none of him" (Welsh 1971: 181). In consequence, by 1876 Africans had been reduced to low paid servile labor. To add insult to injury: they were housed in large labor camps (not unlike concentration camps), and forced to work for the white mine owners. Similarly, following the discovery of gold, legislation was enacted to ensure that the Africans did not benefit from this discovery in any way. Hence Africans (as well as others who were not whites) "were barred from the right to acquire mining licenses; from the right to trade in minerals; from the right to reside on proclaimed ground; and from the right to establish shops on such ground" (Johnstone 1976: 23). In fact the Gold Law of the Transvaal bluntly stated that "No colored person may be a license holder, or in any way be connected with the working of the gold mines, except as a working man in the service of whites" (Johnstone 1976: 23).

In the agricultural sector, the tale was also one of a similar gross injustice. In the early 1900s a significant number of Africans still had access to sizable plots of land—either through squatting on land originally owned by them but forcefully expropriated by the settlers, or by renting it from those settlers who could not farm all the land they lay claim to in exchange for 50% of the African peasant's produce (sharecropping), or through domicile rights in the *reserves*. Responding to an exploding market for agricultural produce created by the rapid urbanization that came in the wake of diamond and gold mining, many Africans took to producing for this market. That is they became peasants—small farmers consciously and overtly tied into the capitalist system. But this peasantization of the African subsistence farmer was to prove a short-lived process. The settlers adopted legislative measures to nip the growth of the African peasant class in the bud. Chief among these was the passage of the 1913 *Native Land Act,* which set aside for blacks a measly 7% (to be augmented over time to 13%) of the total land area of the country, much of it agriculturally poor, even though they made up three-quarters of the population (not to mention the fact that originally it had been their land). The act, however, went even further: it not only prohibited African farming on white settled lands, but also forbade Africans from legally purchasing land from whites. Why were the whites against the emergence of an African peasant class?[44] Surely, if "civilizing" the Africans was among the supposed burdens of the white man in Africa (an important line in white ideological drivel) what better method could be found than to convert the precapitalist African into a tax-paying, commodity-consuming capitalist. The answer is that this class, had it been allowed to entrench itself, would have created serious problems for whites, and they are summarized by Wilson and Thompson (1969/ 1971 vol. 2: 127) thus: "By the time of Union [1910] two problems were dominating the thinking of whites with regard to blacks on the farms. First was the perennial problem of labor shortage. Second was fear lest the land gained by conquest should be lost through the market; for, except in the Free State where such a thing had long been forbidden, Africans were buying farms. The Land Act of 1913 was passed in an attempt to resolve both these problems at once."[45]

Third, in 1948 there come to pass what many outsiders had thought was the impossible: the government of Jan Christiaan Smuts was replaced by the National Party-led government of Daniel Malan following the defeat of Smuts' United Party in the national whites only elections of that year. While the world dismissed Malan's plan of *institutionalizing* the hitherto de facto segregation of the races to be the basis for a new political system for a Jim Crow-type South Africa as a crackpot idea, to the vast majority of whites in South Africa the plan appeared to be sound and reassuring—not only did it promise to guarantee continued minority rule and economic domination of the majority (so as to secure its labor), but also racial and cultural "purity" for the whites. The specific guiding agenda of the new apartheid government is summarized best in a sentence or two by Kallaway (2002a: 13): "They were keen to promote the interests of Afrikaner politics against English domination of economic, social and cultural life, against big business and its control by 'alien forces of Anglo-Jewish capitalism,' and against 'black encroachment' on 'white interests.' They were for the promotion of Afrikaner business and culture and the 'salvation of 'poor whites.'"" In other words, and it is important to stress this, apartheid was at once an economic project and a political project—the two were intimately and dialectically related. Apartheid was never meant to wish black people away, on the contrary it needed black people, but only as sources of cheap labor (and to this end it meant dominating and controlling them on the basis of that classic *separate-but-equal* ruse first perfected in the United States) Ergo, to say that apartheid was a modernized form of slavery is not to engage in cheap theatrical polemics, but to describe it as it really was designed (and came) to be. [46]

Building on existing racist legislation (such as the 1907 *Education Act No. 25*, and the 1913 *Natives Land Act*) and centuries old customary Jim Crow practices, various National Party-led governments systematically erected and perfected a highly oppressive, neofascist, racially segregated, super-exploitative, sociopolitical economic order that came to be called *apartheid* (Afrikaans for "separateness").[47] Initially, the system would rest on a base of three socially constructed races: Africans, Coloreds, and whites; but later, a fourth would be added: Indians. A little later, the system would be modified to fragment the African majority into its smaller ethnic components fictively rooted geographically in separate rural *labor* reservations (which would be first called *bantustans* and later dignified with the label "homelands") carved out of the measly 13% of land that had been allocated to Africans by the 1913 Native Land Act. (In other words, apartheid was also a form of colonialism—internal colonialism.) Of the various legislation that underpinned the system, among the more salient were the 1949 *Prohibition of Mixed Marriages Act*; the 1950 *Population Registration Act*; the 1950 *Group Areas Act*; the 1953 *Reservation of Separate Amenities Act*; the various internal security acts that not only proscribed any form of opposition to the apartheid system, but permitted imprisonment without trial; the various *pass laws* that severely curtailed the freedom of movement of Africans by requiring them to carry a *pass*—a form of internal passport—at all times; and the 1959 *Promotion of Bantu Self-Government Act, which* created the pseudosovereign internal African states just mentioned.[48]

From the perspective of higher education, the key legislative landmarks during the apartheid era were these: the 1953 *Bantu Education Act,* which centralized and transferred all responsibility for the education of Africans from local governments, and the missionaries, to the apartheid state;[49] the 1959 *Extension of University Education Act,* which created separate higher education facilities for the three black ethnic groups (Africans, Coloreds, and Indians) and at the same time forbade them from attending predominantly whites-only universities without prior approval from the government;[50] the 1959 *University College of Fort Hare Transfer Act* (made the college an ethnically-based institution serving Xhosa students); and the 1983 *Universities Amendment Act* that handed over responsibility for admission of blacks to the whites-only universities.[51] The essential rationale that underlay the new education system that the apartheid state strove to create for Afro-South Africans shortly following its inception was best articulated by one of its chief architects the one-time professor at the University of Stellenbosch, Dr. Henrik Verwoerd—in 1954, however, the minister for native affairs (and who later would go on to become the prime minister [1958-1966]):

More institutions for advanced education in urban areas [i.e., white areas] are not desired. Deliberate attempts will be made to keep institutions for advanced education away from the urban environment and to establish them as far as possible in the Native reserves....There is no place for the [Native] in the European community above the level of certain forms of labor. Within his own community, however, all doors are open. For that reason it is of no avail for him to receive training which has as its aim absorption in the European community, where he cannot be absorbed. Until now he has been subjected to a school system which drew him away from his own community and misled him by showing him the green pastures of European society in which he was not allowed to graze (from Christie and Collins 1984: 173).

Fourth, although the evolving apartheid police-state had managed to brutally crush the largely nonviolent antiapartheid movement by the time of the arrest and subsequent life imprisonment of Nelson Mandela and his colleagues in 1964 (a strategy of which the 1960 Sharpeville massacre was emblematic) with the proscription of all antiapartheid organizations as well as all antiapartheid activities of any kind, it failed in the end to stem the struggles for a democratic nonracist South Africa waged by politically committed blacks (together with a handful of their courageous white sympathizers—some of whom, as in the case of many of their black compatriots, would pay with their lives for this struggle). No amount of imprisonment without trial, torture, murders, and other less violent strategies of repression mounted by the apartheid state prevented this eventuality to come to pass: the victory of the African National Congress in the first ever multiracial nation-wide elections held in 1994; that is just in time to see an aging but still sprightly Nelson Mandela (freed in 1990) to become South Africa's first black president.[52]

It is against the backdrop of such an awful and tortured history that one must view the development of higher education in South Africa; which, as in most other parts of British colonial Africa, began with missionary initiatives. Missionary societies such as the Paris Evangelical Mission, the London Missionary Society, the Scottish Presbyterian Mission, and so on, all felt the need to establish higher education institutions in the areas of pastoral, teacher, and agricultural training as a logical extension of their evangelical work.

Since de facto racial segregation (and to some degree de jure as well) had always been part of South African history from the first day that Jan van Riebeeck and his party stepped ashore, missionary educational activity was not limited, as some may assume, only to an African clientele.[53] Supported by government subventions, private higher education initiatives led to the establishment, for example, of the South African College in Cape Town in 1829 for the English-speaking Anglo-South Africans and Victoria College for the Afrikaans-speaking Afrikaners in Stellenbosch. The earliest government foray into higher education, however, was initially limited to the creation of an examining body in 1858, the Board of Public Examinations in Literature and Science, that was responsible for administering exams to graduates of various colleges with the aim of standardizing higher education credentials. The functions of the Board were taken over in 1873 by a nonteaching institution, the University of the Cape of Good Hope. By sitting for examinations administered by the university, candidates could obtain nationally accepted degrees. Following independence from Britain and the concomitant formation of the Union of South Africa in 1910, the university was reconstituted to become the University of South Africa (UNISA) in 1916 with six affiliated university colleges—though it itself remained a nonteaching institution—namely: Grey University College in Bloemfontein; Huguenot University College in Wellington; Natal University College in Pietermaritzburg; Rhodes University College at Grahamstown; Transvaal University College in Pretoria; and Witwatersrand University College in Johannesburg. Along the same lines of development, the South African College at Cape Town became the University of Cape Town and Victoria College was transformed into University of Stellenbosch. Except for Stellenbosch and the university colleges in Pretoria and Bloemfontein (which were Afrikaans-speaking), all the institutions were English-speaking. Five years later, in 1921, a balance of sorts was created between English and Afrikaans-speaking institutions among the UNISA UCs with the reconstitution of the Dutch Reformed Church Christian College in Potchesftroom as a University College.

Higher Education for Blacks

The idea of a government-funded college for Africans had begun to be floated as early as 1902 with the ending of the Boer War when Dr. James Stewart, principal of South Africa's famous Lovedale Mission (established by the Presbyterians in 1841 in the Eastern Cape), added his voice to those of African leaders. Of course, Africans themselves hungered after an institution of higher learning; a factor that cannot be discounted, for instance, as Campbell (1989a) has explained, in the alacrity with which the Ethiopian Church folded itself into the American Methodist Episcopal Church shortly after the former's founding. Early efforts to bring reality to their dream in this regard, however, foundered on the rocks of inadequate resources. (See Campbell's account of the fortunes of some these early ventures.) That Lovedale would soon be at the forefront of this initiative was not surprising; it was among the most successful of the missionary enterprises in South Africa serving Africans: by early 1900s this United Free Church of Scotland Mission station had grown into an extensive educational, theological, and vocational complex—complete with a primary school; a middle school; a teacher-training school; a vocational arts department that trained students in carpentry, wagon-making, shoe-making, printing, dressmaking, and so on; a hospital with a nursing school; a printing press; an extensive farm; and a thriving church.[54] In tracing the origins of the idea of a college for blacks, one would be guilty, however, of gross dereliction of duty if one does not also indicate that altruism was but one component in the project; for both, the missionaries and the state (and perhaps one may also add some of the African leaders to the mix as well), it was also a response to the African American factor.

Even though it is among the relatively neglected aspects of South African history, African American presence (both direct and indirect) at critical points in that history has been significant enough to merit our serious attention. African American presence in South Africa, at the turn of the twentieth-century—the period that is of relevance here—would come to assume three important forms: religious, educational, and indirectly, political, with important consequences for South Africa in both educational and political terms.

The Role of African Americans

The earliest *large-scale* presence of African Americans in South Africa, it appears, was a result of happenstance.[55] In 1894, an African jubilee choir group from South Africa calling itself the African Native Choir was on a tour of the United States and Canada under the leadership of two not-so-upright Euro-South African businessmen. Perhaps not surprisingly, during the tour they ran into severe financial difficulties that left them stranded in Cleveland, Ohio (Chirenje 1976: 254). While little is known of what became of others, eight of them were able to obtain assistance from local African American clergy. Among them was a 21-year-old student by the name of Charlotte Manye

Maxeke. Quite serendipitously by all accounts, she was put in contact with Bishop Benjamin Arnett of the African Methodist Episcopal (AME) Church who was known to be a strong supporter of African American mission activity in Africa. Arnett helped Maxeke to enroll in a college run by the denomination, called Wilberforce University, in Ohio. At the same time, he opened his home to her making her part of his family. [56] Now, it so happened that Maxeke's correspondence with her sister in South Africa fortuitously came to the attention of none other than Mangena Mokone, the leader of the newly formed Ethiopian Church. [57] Mokone had been a minister in the English Wesleyan Methodist Church of South Africa and had not long before resigned from it in October, 1892. [58] Upon learning of her good fortune, Mokone immediately set about writing to the AME. In a letter to a Bishop Henry McNeal Turner, he informed him about his own church: "I am the minister of the...[Ethiopian Church] mission and also the originator of the same. I have two ordained ministers or priests and seven deacons. It is entirely managed by us blacks of South Africa" (Chirenje 1976: 258). Mokone then went on to ask for assistance with the sponsorship of Africans to study at U.S. institutions.

In contacting Turner, little did Mokone know that he was dealing with a remarkable man; one who, among other things, not only had the distinction in 1863 of being the first African American chaplain to be appointed to the U.S. Army by Abraham Lincoln (Williams 1982), but who was also consumed by thoughts such as the following: "If all the riff-raff white-men worshippers, aimless, objectless, selfish, little-souled and would-be-white negroes of this country were to go to Africa, I fear it would take a chiliad of years to get them to understand that a black man or woman could be somebody without the dictation of a white man.... There isn't much real manhood in the negro in this country today" (from Chirenje 1976: 258). Bishop Turner was a grand visionary who saw in African American missionary activity in Africa the salvation (economic, political and spiritual) of both Africans and African Americans. Thus Turner shared the sentiments of many of his contemporaries who not only believed in the Christian duty to evangelize, but also saw a moral duty in assisting Africa, the land of their forefathers, to "redeem and regenerate" itself. Plus he was among the staunchest supporters of the back to Africa movement that was fashionable in the late 1800s. [59]

Consequently, given the pro-mission sentiment toward the end of the nineteenth-century among African American clergy in general and those in the AME in particular, engendered in part by Euro-American missionary interest in Africa too, initial inquiries from Mokone quickly led to a strong interest within the AME to extend its existing African missionary activities to South Africa as well. Within a year of commencement of contacts between the AME Church and the Ethiopian Church, plans were initiated to form a union between the two, culminating in the consummation of a triumphant tour of African South Africa in 1898 by Turner. [60] By 1906 the AME had established its presence in

the Cape, the Transvaal, the Orange Free State, Natal, Basutoland, Bechuanaland, Swaziland, Southern Rhodesia, and Barotseland. Its membership had
reached nearly 11,000 and its ministers numbered some 250. By 1914, its
membership would exceed 18,000 (Williams 1982: 57).

The AME Church, as would be expected, also became involved in education: it opened a number of primary and central primary schools, as well as the
three principal institutions of higher education: Bethel Institute (which trained
teachers and evangelists), Chatsworth Institute (which provided industrial
training), and the Lillian Derrick Institute for Boys (later it would be called the
Wilberforce Institute). The last, as Campbell's account shows, had considerable
impact on the education of Afro-South Africans, being responsible for training
"[o]ver the course of a half a century...countless AME ministers, as well as an
entire generation of African schoolteachers in the Transvaal" (1989a: 320). An
AME school at Evaton near Vereeniging, thirty miles south of Johannesburg
became the germ of the Wilberforce Institute. Its rudimentary beginnings are
indicated by the fact that in 1908 its buildings comprised two mud and daub
huts.[61] From such humble origins it would grow into a credible educational institution, though it would never make it to the status of a true postsecondary institution of higher learning; that is a college or a university modeled on its U.S.
namesake as its founders had originally hoped. The problem, at least in the
early years, was always lack of funds. The mother church in the United States,
with extensive commitments of its own and drawing on a flock that itself in
relative terms was not economically well off, was unable to carry through its
yearly commitments to help fund the institution on a regular basis. At the same
time there were pressures from the government to modify its curriculum and
adapt it to the needs of the African (namely a Tuskegee-style curriculum)
popularized in South Africa by people such as Charles T. Loram. Though here,
admittedly, the Institute faculty, who were either African Americans or Afro-
South Africans trained in the United States went along with the notion of an
adapted curriculum. What this meant in practice was a curriculum emphasizing
vocational education or industrial education as it was called then. In the end the
Institute was taken over by the apartheid government in the wake of the 1953
Bantu Education Act; and by closing down or transferring its various sections
reduced it over time to a school whose sole purpose was to train students for
the ministry. (For more on the ebb and flow of the Institute's fortunes, see
Campbell 1989a.)

Ironically, AME Church missionary activity in South Africa was, in a large
measure, facilitated by the fact that Euro-South Africans, in their ignorance,
initially perceived all African Americans as harbingers of the Booker T. Washington ideology. Euro-South Africans, like their white counterparts in the
United States, had welcomed the ideas of Washington. They were particularly
impressed, for example, by the achievements represented by the Hampton and
Tuskegee Institutes. Moreover, any "philosophy" that advocated political qui-

escence on one hand, but hard work on the other, and one propounded by black people themselves, was bound to appear as music to Euro-South Africans ears.[62] In fact, some effort was made via the import of Tuskegee graduates, with the active cooperation of the British colonial office, to establish a "miniature Tuskegee Institute" at the American Zulu Mission in Natal, and develop other similar training programs, such efforts, says Noer (1978: 113), in the end did not amount to much because of a variety of problems; not least among them the reluctance of European employers to replace European workers with African workers.

By the first decade of the 1900s, however, Euro-South Africans had begun to resent the presence of African Americans in general. On one hand there was the matter of the rightful place of the black man (which included the African American) in the general scheme of things, but which the African American was want to challenge. In fact, African Americans had already begun to protest at the social restrictions they were being subjected to—for example, harassment on sidewalks, harassment on trains, being refused to purchase liquor, and so on. In 1904 a group of sixteen African Americans complained to the U.S. representative in Johannesburg, demanding that their rights "as natives and citizens of United States," be protected. If the behavior and complaints of African Americans represented a thorn in the side of Euro-South Africans, what really helped to turn them away from African Americans—eventually precipitating their almost total expulsion from South Africa—was undoubtedly activities of those African Americans who supported Bishop Turner's "radical" views.[63] Euro-South Africans were not entirely blind to the political implications of the Ethiopian movement. Consequently, when the Bambatha rebellion took place in Natal not only was the movement blamed for the rebellion, but so were African Americans in general and those associated with AME Church in particular.[64] Even before the rebellion, Euro-South African denominations and the government authorities had already begun to voice their concern over the influence of African Americans—especially members of the AME Church. In 1898, for example, among the criticisms they leveled against Ethiopianist Africans in the Euro-South African run *South African Congregational Magazine* was this one: "There is not a vestige of spirituality in this [Ethiopian] movement. In connection with it the Ethiopian does not change the skin, nor the leopard his spots, but only his ministerial diet. He is taking black missionary from America instead of white missionary from England. That is all the difference. He turns English Methodism out of the door to bring Negro Methodism down the chimney. He bites the white hand that has ministered for many years...and kneels to kiss the black hand whose opening promises to make him a bishop" (from Chirenje 1976: 267).

Under the circumstances, it is not surprising that there began in 1903 an investigation of the AME Church and Ethiopianism led by the *South African Native Affairs Commission*; it culminated in a five-volume report in 1905 that just stopped short of recommending the outlaw of the AME in South Africa. Testimony presented before the commission by many Euro-South Africans was characterized by themes such as the following, expressed by Reverend James Scott, a Free Church of Scotland missionary from Natal: "I would like to say that there is a danger of a great deal of evil happening through these Blacks from America coming in and mixing with natives of South Africa These men from America for generations suffered oppression and they have naturally something to object to in the white man. These men from America come in and make our natives imagine they have grievances when there are no grievances" (from Chirenje 1976: 272). Bishop L. J. Coppin, the first resident African American Bishop sent out to South Africa by the AME Church in 1901, together with a number of other African Americans, testified however, to the effect that the views of Bishop Turner were not the views of the AME Church.[65] Such testimony proved strong enough to dissuade the commission from proscribing the church. Hence the report concluded that African Americans, through direct and indirect influence and financial support, were responsible for much of the militancy of the Ethiopian churches. It further noted that Ethiopianism was a movement that stood against Euro-South Africans. It called upon African Americans to refrain from "mischievous political propaganda" if they wished to continue their ecclesiastical work in South Africa (Noer 1978: 120).

What is of particular interest here, however, is that in addition to blaming African Americans, the report also laid blame for the militancy of Ethiopianism at the door of U.S.-trained Africans. Here the report was drawing attention to a well-known fact: the role played by U.S. educational institutions, especially African American institutions, in the education of Afro-South Africans. For instance, by 1900 there were ten who had studied or were studying at Lincoln University, while at Wilberforce University there were eleven (Williams 1982: 153; see also Campbell 1989a). By 1907, it was estimated by the South African authorities that 150 Afro-South Africans had studied in the United States and of whom some twenty had participated in the Bambatha rebellion (Noer 1978: 122). The disquiet that this "study-abroad movement" provoked is captured by the lament of a Euro-South African missionary: "Each year an increasing number of young men and women are sent from Africa, at the expense of the American Methodist Episcopalian body, to study in the negro universities of the United States. There they obtain a superficial veneer of knowledge, while breathing the atmosphere of race hatred which pervades these so-called seats of learning" (Campbell 1989a: 261).

By 1910, says Noer, the position of African American clergy in South Africa had deteriorated to a level where all were viewed with suspicion, and efforts were initiated to curtail their movement and work. Later, they would be excluded nearly altogether from any ecclesiastical activity by means of a regulation that required foreign missionaries to obtain a government permit to do their missionary work. To the Euro-South Africans, just as they had once seen all African Americans as harbingers of the Booker T. Washington message, now all African American missionaries came to symbolize Ethiopianism and violence, and hence a threat to their hegemony. Even Theodore Roosevelt would join in the fray by siding with the Euro-South Africans in an address to the AME Church convention in Washington, DC, in January of 1909 (Williams 1982). Resentment against African Americans in general by the beginning of World War I was also spurred, says Noer (1978), by a general perception among the Euro-South Africans that the African American was a clear example of what the African should not be allowed to become.

Under the circumstances, the idea of a Native College in South Africa appeared to all concerned, especially the relevant Euro-South Africans (missionaries, government officials, etc.) as having come at a particularly opportune time. As Campbell (1989a) observes, even the report of the *South African Native Affairs Commission* had recommended that such a college be established in order to stem the flow of Afro-South African students to the United States. [66] Even though, side-by-side with the influence of the AME Church, a significant number among the African elite were also influenced by ideas of Booker T. Washington derived from educational study in the United States (for just as there were two major competing political schools of thought among African Americans in the United States at that time represented by people such as Washington on one hand, and Turner on the other, there were also two political schools of thought among Afro-South Africans, one Ethiopianist and the other Washingtonian), the Euro-South Africans were not astute enough to make the distinctions, blinded as they were by their racism that posited before them an undifferentiated mass of natives being misled by "foreign natives."[67] After the founding of Fort Hare (to which we will return in a moment), the South African government, states Campbell, would move to severely restrict Afro-South African student flow to the United States—using the pretext that an institution of higher education existed for blacks within the country.

Fort Hare

By the time the Union of South Africa was consummated in 1915, the college idea as originally advanced by the likes of Lovedale's principal (who incidentally had also testified before the *South African Native Affairs Commission*) had taken firm root and the originally proposed Inter-State Native College that was to serve African students from all the four provinces (as well-as from the rest of southern Africa) was now about to become reality with the support of African leaders, an annual financial subsidy from the new Union government and the cooperation of all the major Euro-South African missionary churches: The college would open its doors as the South African Native College in 1916 with all of just two faculty members: the newly arrived Scotsman by the name of Alexander Kerr (who was also appointed head of the college) and Davidson

Don Tengo Jabavu, the son of the well-known African educator and publisher of the first African newspaper in South Africa, John Tengo Jabavu.

The college was located adjacent to the Lovedale complex on the site of an old abandoned fort built in 1846 called Fort Hare, but which was now part of the lands owned by the Presbyterians. It was open to both male and female students; it was multidenominational, residential, private (therefore fee-paying) but received a modest government subsidy, and served not only African students, but Coloreds and East Indians as well (15% of seats were reserved for the latter group—in time the college came to serve Africans exclusively as the East Indians acquired their own college, Sastri College, and as a consequence of post–1948 apartheid policies).[68] Initially, the focus of the new college was on providing secondary education but later it would begin adding college-level classes to eventually become a full college by the 1940s. The college did not itself award degrees; instead, following in the footsteps of the white colleges, it prepared students for external degrees granted by the University of South Africa. The college's first undergraduates received their degrees in 1924; there were only two: Z. K. Matthews and E. Ncwana (though to the institution's credit they were not spared a full graduation ceremony).[69] The curriculum, as the college evolved, and given its need to prepare students for the University of South Africa exams, was oriented toward the arts and sciences (botany, chemistry, English literature, history, mathematics, philosophy, zoology, and so on). It also provided teacher training and training for medical assistants and those intending to proceed to study medicine abroad.

It is of interest to note here that even though the example of Lovedale was nearby (with its industrial education approach to schooling), and even though Kerr had visited the Tuskegee Institute—see Kerr (1968) for an account of his visit—(and not to mention C. T. Loram's membership of the college's governing council), the Hampton/Tuskegee influence was not a major presence in the mission of the college.[70] In fact on this score Kerr writes: "Missionaries have been blamed for giving him [the African] an education which is merely bookish, but when they teach him such arts as building and carpentry, they find that their protégés are debarred from employment by the only persons with capital enough for undertaking contracts requiring their services. As long as such a condition of affairs prevails," he goes on, "the education of the African is bound to have a bookish bias, and his field of employment to lie amongst the professions: ministers, teachers, doctors, lawyers, civil servants, journalist" (p. 130).[71] It is instructive to note here, to draw attention to the character of the times, that given the extreme dearth of educational opportunities for blacks at any level in those days, especially postprimary level, against the backdrop of a racially segregated society, the students, in Kerr's words, possessed "an unspoiled enthusiasm for, and a profound faith in, education, an enthusiasm and faith *which sometimes had an element of pathos in it*." Tellingly, he also observes in the same breath: "Any hesitation one might have had in regard to the innate ability or specific capacities of the African, about which various fallacies were current and seemingly deeply ingrained in the minds of ordinary citizens [whites], had become less tenable" (1968: 129, emphasis added). In other words: even when one concedes that the educational potential of blacks were no different from those of whites, a racist society was going to make sure that that potential would be placed in a straight jacket of racist barriers. This point was most graphically expressed in the college's 1937 graduation ceremony by the then Minister for Education, J. H. Hofmeyr: He began by first stating that he "did not like the phrase 'the development of the Native [African] on his own lines.'" Why? He explained: "All too often it is a cloak for sheer hypocrisy. All too often it means either no development at all or as little development as possible; it means keeping the Native 'in his place.' And for all too many of the people of this country, the real thought which underlies that phrase is expressed in Dickens version of the ancient prayer:

> Oh, let us love our occupations,
> Bless the squire and his relations,
> Live upon our daily rations,
> And always know our proper stations.

Yet, further on in his address he does a neat about turn. Arguing that the life circumstances of the African will always be different from those of the European's (at least for the foreseeable future) he concludes: "And that being so, it does seem to me to follow, that the scope and content of education should not in present circumstances be the same for the African as for the European." He continues:

[I]t should be accepted as the aim of Native education to minister to distinctive Native [socioeconomic] development. I accept such development as also the right aim of our general Native policy. There are facts of difference of which account must be taken— there is no absolute equality between European and African. As Dr Oldham [mentioned earlier in this chapter] has pointed out, men are not equal in their capacity to serve the community, nor are they equal in their needs. Of these inequalities our policy of development through education and otherwise must take due account" (from his speech, Hofmeyr 1938: 149, 151.)

Clearly this was a version of the *separate-but-equal* doctrine of the Jim Crow era in the United States, except here it was expressed in terms of *equal-but-separate*. Within about ten years or so the logic of such thinking would find its ultimate expression in the enactment of *apartheid* laws following the election victory of the Afrikaners in 1948. The college would soon loose its private status, as already mentioned, passing into the hands of the apartheid government, despite much resistance by the institution, as it sought to gain total control over all facets of the lives of blacks, including education; with this takeover it was reconstituted as the University College of Fort Hare and affiliated to Rhodes University in Grahamstown—about two decades later, in 1969, Fort Hare would become a university in its own right (but by which point it had become nothing more than an apartheid institution—that is in spirit a mere shadow of its former self). Upon the creation of the homeland political system, the university was placed under the control of the homeland government of the Ciskei in 1986. Today Fort Hare lives on, but it is beset by serious problems of leadership among other things (see below).

Note that the importance of Fort Hare in the history of South African higher education stems not only from the fact that it was the first university college for Africans in South Africa, but that in its early years, as Ajayi, Goma, and Johnson (1996) observe, it played a similar role for the African elite of South Africa (actually the whole of English-speaking southern Africa to be exact) as Fourah Bay did for the West African elite. As they remind us, among the Fort Hare graduates are a number of persons who would achieve considerable preeminence (or perhaps notoriety); such as Mongosuthu Buthelezi (became head of the Transkei Homeland); Sir Seretse Khama (became president of Botswana); Ntsu Mokhele (became prime minister of Lesotho); Robert Mugabe (became president of Zimbabwe); and Robert Sobukwe (became leader of the South African nationalist organization called the Pan-Africanist Congress). Even Nelson Mandela (became president of South Africa) went to Fort Hare, but he did not survive long there; he was expelled by the institution. This roster certainly vindicates Kerr's prescient comment that "[t]he only real test of the value of a [c]ollege is to be found in the careers of its *alumni* as they make their way through life." He continues: "There is already evidence that when the time comes to assess their achievements, many of those who owe part of their education to Fort Hare will be found to have justified their training by their services in public life and in various professions, learned and other" (1968: ix). Of course, the tragic irony is that, as in the case of the historically black universities in the United States, the ending of segregation in South Africa has led to the eclipse of Fort Hare as a premier institution of higher learning for black South Africans.

Following the advent of apartheid, building on the preexisting higher education system, there arose three sets of higher education institutions: one for blacks in the cities; one for blacks in the homelands and one for whites. Consequently, on the eve of "independence" in 1994, the South African higher education landscape looked like this: The black city institutions comprised: University of the Western Cape (created in 1969 out of University College of the Western Cape founded in 1959 as a UNISA affiliate); University of Durban-Westville (created in 1972 out of University College Durban, which was founded in 1961 as an affiliate of UNISA); Medical University of Southern Africa (founded in 1976); and Vista University—with campuses at Bloemfontein,

East Rand, Mamelodi, Port Elizabeth, Sebokong, Soweto, and Welkom (founded in 1981).[72]

In the homelands, besides the University of Fort Hare, were these institutions: University of the North—with main campus at Sovenga and a satellite campus at Qua Qua (reconstitution in 1970 of University College of the North founded in 1959 as a UNISA affiliate); University of the Zululand—with main campus at Empangani and satellite campus at Umlazi (reconstitution in 1969 of University College of the Zululand founded in 1959 as a UNISA affiliate); University of the Transkei—with a satellite campus at Butterworth (created in 1976 out of a branch of Fort Hare); University of North-West (reconstitution in 1994 of University of Bophuthatswana founded in 1979); and University of Venda (reconstitution in 1983 of the Venda campus, founded in 1981, of the University of the North).

As for the white institutions, they included the following: Stellenbosch University (created in 1916 out of Victoria College of Stellenbosch founded in 1879); University of Cape Town (reconstitution in 1916 of South African College founded in 1829); University of the Witwatersrand (reconstitution in 1922 of Transvaal Technical Institute founded in 1904—which itself was a reincarnation of the South African School of Mines and Technology founded in 1896); University of Pretoria (inaugurated in 1930 by reconstituting the University College of Pretoria founded in 1908); University of Natal—with campuses at Durban and Pietermaritzburg (reconstitution in 1949 of Natal University College founded in 1909); University of the Orange Free State (created in 1950 out of Grey University College founded in 1855); Rhodes University—with a campus at East London (reconstitution in 1951 of Rhodes University College founded in 1904); University of Potchefstroom for Christian Higher Education (founded in 1951); University of Port Elizabeth (inaugurated in 1965 by reconstituting a branch of Rhodes University); and Rand Afrikaans University (founded in 1968).

The hallmark of this roster of higher education institutions, that when considered together as a single system, was unmatched in terms of magnitude and institutional diversity anywhere on the continent, except in the case of Egypt, was of course a great chasm of racially determined disparity—overwhelmingly in favor of whites—at almost every level in both quantitative and qualitative terms (not unlike the disparities between the historically black colleges and the historically white universities in the United States): gross enrollment ratios, budgetary allocations, physical plant, services, teachers, students, curricula, governance, and so on. Apartheid, like Jim Crow, may have adhered to the notion of separate but equal in the later stages of its evolution, but it was always in terms of rhetorical hope, never in terms of reality. In any case, even within the confines of its own logic, had it been possible, financially, to achieve some level of parity in terms of enrollment and resources, there would still have been the serious political problem of absorbing the output in a labor market that was highly constricted for blacks. All manner of occupations and position levels within them were barred to blacks to ensure a near 100% employment rate for Euro-South Africans. Though it is also true that given the magnitude of racial disparity in higher education provision, the apartheid state did permit two ameliorative outlets: it allowed a small percentage of blacks with the requisite qualifications to enter the white institutions through permits (until the passage of the *Universities Amendment Act* no. 83 of 1983 the permits were issued by the state, thereafter it was up to the universities to grant admission, if they so wished, but on the basis of "acceptable" black-white ratios).

Here enlightened self-interest was the greater of the motivator than notions of equity: as in the case of colonialism, apartheid required a compradorial cadre of blacks to minister to the needs of other blacks: doctors, teachers, and the like—and of course to staff the bureaucracies in the homelands. (There was another factor too that entered the equation of black higher education expansion: in the 1960s, as Mabokela [2000] reminds us, South Africa was experiencing an economic boom—fueled by massive increases in foreign investment—which created a rising need for skilled labor *even from among blacks*, who hitherto had been designated to be repositories of only unskilled labor). At the same time, insofar as the value and status of the degrees blacks obtained, they were for a while on par with those of Euro-South Africans because the degrees were granted by the University of South Africa to which the black colleges were affiliated—but only until 1969, however.[73] This last factor, at least until 1969, was perhaps the only saving grace of an iniquitous education system in which not only the canons of a civilized higher education system had been completely overturned by the apartheid government, but operating from a mind set of running a police state, the black institutions were subjected to the kind of control that one associates with fascist societies.[74]

In the discussion so far, our focus has been on black higher education, and rightly so, because blacks together constitute over three-quarters of the population. Moreover, this approach is forced on us by the fact that South African higher education (as with almost everything else) has evolved in part as a response to this circumstance: a minority attempting to dictate (and often succeeding) all aspects of society's agenda ever since it stepped foot in the country. However, one would be remiss in not saying a word or two about how the Euro-South African component of higher education has been shaped by the historical forces of external (British) and internal (apartheid) colonialism. The following thoughts come to mind:

First, there are two traditions that have evolved among Euro-South African institutions: one is the British liberal tradition and the other is the Afrikaner tradition. The differences are manifest at many levels, ranging from the most obvious (such as language of instruction) to the less obvious (such as pedagogy) and the general institutional culture. Moreover, following the advent of apartheid, the Anglo-South African institutions took upon themselves to serve as the intellectual bastions of a minority within a minority under siege (compare the situation of English-speaking McGill University in French-speaking Quebec). From the perspective of blacks these two divergent traditions led to a *relatively* greater openness on the part of the Anglo (or English-speaking) institutions than was the case with the Afrikaner institutions. In the postapartheid era, while the Anglo institutions have had less difficulty in increasing black enrollments, the Afrikaner institutions in this regard have fared less well (though Coloreds appear to have done better at these institutions because their mother tongue generally tends to be Afrikaans compared to other blacks who generally speak English as their first or second language). (See Mabokela 2000 and 2001 on the impact of the differences of these two traditions on blacks in the postapartheid era.)

Second, because the Anglo-South Africans had historically dominated both the South African polity (except during the apartheid interregnum) and economy, the Anglo institutions had access to greater resources in relative terms than their Afrikaner counterparts, which had translated into the evolution of more robust institutions—with the concomitant higher levels of prestige in the pecking order of institutions. Further, in this regard, the fact that the language of instruction in these institutions is one of the world's prominent lingua franca, has also been of considerable help. In other words, to have a degree from say the University of Cape Town is not the same as possessing a degree from say University of Stellenbosch; a degree from the former carry's with it a greater cache of marketability and status.

Third, historically, because of their liberal traditions, the English-speaking universities (e.g., Cape Town, Natal, and Witwatersrand) continued to admit black students in small numbers even after the apartheid state took over. However, that is not to say that the black students were admitted on the basis of full equality: depending upon the institution they were subjected to internal segregation in activities ranging from class instruction to dormitory residence to institutionally organized social activities. So, yes these institutions were liberal, but only to a limited extent.[75] Moreover, it does not appear that apartheid regulations alone must be blamed for this circumstance; the institutions themselves accepted the fundamental racist culture of apartheid South Africa, even if they felt uncomfortable with the more egregious manifestations of it. (See, for instance, the experiences of the University of Witwatersrand on this matter as described by King [2001] and Woods [2001].)[76] In fact, on the basis of their account one may legitimately argue that it is highly doubtful that, for instance, the faculty at these institutions were somehow able to shield themselves completely from the prevalent beliefs regarding the ineducability of the black mind—beliefs that as late as the 1930s drew succor from "racial science."[77]

Fourth, to the extent that education budgets have limits, the comparatively resource-rich status of the Euro-South African universities taken together, was acquired historically on the basis of a severe diminution of funding allocated to the black institutions. In other words, against the backdrop of the zero-sum logic of government budgets, the apartheid determined grossly unequal budgetary expenditures, in favor of the former institutions, accounts for a great deal of difference in the quantitative and qualitative circumstances of the two different racially marked groups of institutions. (See Nkomo 1984, and Wolpe 1995 for more on the implications of this issue—e.g., the de facto role specialization of the two groups of institutions in the *teaching* versus *research* institutional missions and its consequences.)

Fifth, related to the preceding point, the hugely unequal funding of lower-level (preuniversity) educational institutions (in favor of the Euro-South African institutions), also meant that the quality of student intake, at the aggregate level, worked in favor of the Euro-South African institutions and against the black institutions.[78] This difference has emerged today in the form of a qualitative difference in the ability of many black students to succeed academically, in comparison to their white counterparts. (See, for instance, Anderson 2002; and compare with the current circumstances of black students in predominantly white U.S. universities where many of whom come from relatively poorly funded racially marked inner city schools.)

Postapartheid South Africa (PASA)

On February 2, 1990, the state president, F. W. de Klerk, during his state-of-the-union speech in South African parliament, would make one of the most important government announcements in South African history: that his government was immediately lifting its thirty-year ban on the oldest and most prominent antiapartheid organization, the African National Congress (ANC). Furthermore, his government would permit the ANC, the South African Communist Party, the Pan Africanist Congress, and others to become openly active again; and that the world's most famous political prisoner who had been in jail for twenty-seven years, Nelson Mandela, would soon be freed to facilitate negotiations between blacks and whites for a new apartheid-free South Africa based on universal franchise.

In 1994, the apartheid system officially came to an end with the election of the ANC to power under the leadership of the new president, Nelson Mandela. This would mark the second independence of South Africa (the first being in 1910 when it was set free from British colonial rule). How, then, has the higher education sector in the postapartheid South Africa (PASA) fared in this new and of course still-evolving, but radically different, political and economic climate? The short answer to this question is that it depends upon one's perspective: Is the glass half full or half empty? There is no question that in the central and most overriding task facing higher education in PASA, democratization, great strides have been made, especially at the level of enrollments. Institution after institution that had historically served an almost all white student population has seen major demographic changes where black African students in some cases now approach a near majority (Vergnani 1998).

On the other hand, it is already clear that the road ahead for higher education in PASA is littered with daunting obstacles that history has shown are endemic to a desegregating society (compare, for example, the case of the United States) and as if that is not enough this particular society is also attempting to *decolonize*—even if the target is an internal form of colonialism. But it does not end here: added to these two onerous tasks there is also the perceived need, felt rightly or wrongly, by South African universities (like perhaps most universities around the world) to also respond to the pressures of globalization. In the effort to meet the challenges of desegregation, decolonization, and globalization, among many obstacles that have emerged, those of a more belligerent bent require cataloguing: at least eight categories can be identified; they are (in no particular order): (1) student finance, (2) embezzlement and mismanagement of funds, (3) the future of former black universities (FBUs), (4) affirmative action and former white universities (FWUs), (5) curricular relevance at FWUs, (6) university brain drain, (7) higher education restructuring, and (8) state finance of higher education.

Space permits only a brief elaboration of each, beginning with the first category: many universities, especially, the FBUs are facing extremely serious budgetary difficulties because of their inability to collect tuition from their chiefly black students—who, quite often, are simply too poor to afford the tuition. The state is attempting to do what it can by increasing funds for student financial aid, but it is not enough (Vergnani 1999b). During the apartheid era the neglect of fiscal control over FBUs in the homelands bordered on the criminal; not surprisingly, the chickens have now come home to roost: many are plagued by high levels of embezzlement and mismanagement of funds. In 1999, for example, at least six were being audited for this problem, including the venerable University of Fort Hare (Vergnani 1999a, b). Budgetary difficulties at the FBUs have been compounded by sharp drops in enrollments, in some cases by as much as 50%, as students have bolted for the more resource-rich and more prestigious FWUs. The result is that their very existence has been threatened, and some have begun to openly speculate that their permanent demise is not very far off. In fact, in October 1999, the United States (through its Agency for International Development) funded a strategy session for them to map their survival—after all the United States is not entirely without experience in this area (Vergnani 1999a, b).

Inevitably, given the different histories and leadership at the FWUs, the response to affirmative action challenges at all three levels of recruitment, student, teaching staff and governance, has varied from hesitantly lukewarm to genuinely positive (echoes of the United States). This in turn has precipitated in some instances a severe (and at times even disruptive) backlash from black students, staff, and politicians (Hugo 1998; Vergnani 1998). Given the nearly

100-year history of most of the FWUs one would assume that curricular relevance would not be an issue; however, apartheid had ensured that in the social sciences especially, subject matter of import to the black experience was hardly ever taught (echoes of the United States). One unfortunate outcome of this circumstance has been a highly polarized, often meaningless, cynical and bordering on the comic, debate between two camps: the so-called Eurocentrists and the Afrocentrists (Hugo 1999b—again, echoes of the United States).

In the new government's effort to redress the racial imbalance in the polity, economy and society as a whole, no effort has been spared to recruit the relatively few black academics to essential and highly remunerative posts, but with potentially crippling consequences for the future of academe and civil society in terms of, at the very least, academic racial harmony and balance as well as the development of an intelligentsia (this brain drain has echoes in independent Africa) (Hugo 1998). Apartheid created artificial duplication of services as well as irrational imbalances in higher education resource allocation. This factor, together with such others as the need to broaden the mission of the university to include extending its teaching/learning services to adults who in their youth had foregone an education in their struggles against apartheid ("liberation before education" was a popular slogan among the black youth once), calls for a radical restructuring of the entire higher education sector (Fourie 1999; Hugo 1998; Vergnani 1999c).

Higher education is among the most voracious sectors of government budgets in PQD countries, and this fact is quickly dawning on the new PASA government: the result is that pressure is mounting on higher education institutions to grapple with what often appears to be the impossible to those entrusted with finance in academe: drawing blood from stone, by doing more with less. It is not just the universities that are a drain on the new government's budget, but the relatively large network of subuniversity-level higher education institutions as well; like the *technikons*. These are vocational colleges that offer subdegree level qualifications (diplomas and certificates) in a variety of applied fields: accounting, computing, secretarial services, commercial arts, and so on. (Note, however, since 1995 they have acquired permission to offer degree-level programs all the way to doctoral-level studies; that is, some are consciously evolving toward university status.) Examples include: Border Technikon, Cape Technikon, Eastern Cape Technikon, Mangosuthu Technikon, M. L. Sultan Technikon, North-West Technikon, Peninsula Technikon, Port Elizabeth Technikon, Setlogelo Technikon, Technikon Natal, Technikon Northern Gauteng, Technikon Free State, Technikon Pretoria, Technikon Southern Africa, Technikon Witwatersrand, Unitra Technikon, and Vaal Triangle Technikon.)[79]

To conclude this section, the irony of South African history is that unlike in the case of the other independent African countries to the north, South Africa has had enough time (almost three centuries), bought, some may legitimately argue, at an unacceptable price (in terms of lives destroyed and blood spilt), to institutionalize the processes of peaceful and meaningful change. If there is any country in Africa best equipped to bring about change in higher education in the service of a new future, then it is surely PASA. (Consider this fact: no matter what antiapartheid propagandists may claim, the dissolution of the apartheid system was relatively peaceful—it did not entail a full-scale civil war that many thought was inevitable.) To what extent, however, the Euro-South African minority population that at the moment still possesses monopoly over the resources of the country is willing to cooperate is, of course, another matter. Already there are serious indications of trouble ahead (reminiscent of the U.S. experience—though while the United States can afford the luxury of proceeding with, relatively speaking, business-as-usual, because those with the monopoly over resources are also the majority, in South Africa the situation is not the same); as Terreblanche (2002) observes regarding a current attitude of Euro-South Africans:

Many whites (especially younger people) are inclined to say that they themselves did nothing wrong, and can therefore not be blamed for the effects of white domination and apartheid....[They] are usually adamant that the large-scale "benefits" (broadly defined) that accumulated in their hands and in those of their parents and grandparents during the extended period of colonialism belong to them and them alone. But what these whites fail to realize is that these "benefits" are "contaminated," because they were largely accumulated by means of systematic exploitation. It is rather hypocritical of whites to claim these benefits with greedy self-righteousness but decline any responsibility (directly or indirectly) for the evil of colonialism and its ugly consequences (p. 5).

NAMIBIA

By way of concluding this chapter, a brief look at Namibia would not be out of place. In many ways the history of Namibia is closely linked to that of South Africa's; for, this former German colony was handed over to Britain following the First World War by the League of Nations to be governed indefinitely, by proxy twice removed: on its behalf by Britain and on *its* behalf by South Africa. Until Namibia achieved independence in March 1990, South Africa had tenaciously and ruthlessly held on to it despite an intensifying nationalist armed resistance struggle in the final decade and near unanimous world condemnation—underlined in 1971 by a ruling by the International Court of Justice at The Hague that South Africa's continued occupation of the country was illegal. By rights Namibia should have become independent decades before when the people of Namibia made petitions for independence to the newly formed United Nations, and later in the face of South African intransigence, gave rise to a more concrete institutional vehicle for their demands with the formation of SWAPO (the South West Africa People's Organization), in 1960. Instead, even after the United Nations assumed its de jure mandate over Na-

mibia in 1967 (U.N. Resolution no. 2248), tragically, with Western conniv-
ance—especially the United States, whose role in the history of Namibia's independence struggle, most specifically in its later stages, mid–1970s onward,
can only be described, to put it in the mildest terms, as shameful and dastardly
(comprising one of its countless blots in the long history of its relations with
Africa)—the Namibian people were forced to continue to endure the same
cruel fate that their forbears had suffered when the Germans had first annexed
it by means of naked deceit and treachery in the 1880s: relentless oppression
marked by virulent racism, wanton brutality and countless massacres.[80] A flavor of the legacy of the South African occupation of Namibia can be had from
the following description from a 1999 report by the Presidential Commission
on Education, Culture and Training:

> Namibia has greater disparities in wealth than any other country in the world. At one
> end of the scale are prosperous people living in fine houses and with all the comforts of
> modern society. At the other end are people living in abject poverty; they are hungry
> and diseased, and lack adequate shelter, food and amenities. The children of the first
> group attend schools which are the equivalent of schools in the capital cities of the most
> advanced countries, while the children of the latter group attend schools which are to-
> tally inadequate for their needs, without toilets, adequate classroom facilities, electric-
> ity, telephone communication, textbooks, and writing materials (from Hopson 2001:
> 123).

Prior to independence, the apartheid system in Namibia had minimal provision for education in general for Afro-Namibians, and until much later, no
higher education facilities at all for any one. Instead, Afro-Namibians were allowed partial access to the black higher education institutions in South Africa,
while Euro-Namibians had full access to the Euro-South African institutions
there. However, those Namibians living outside Namibia had access to a higher
education institution for Namibians founded by the United Nations in 1974 in
Zambia at Lusaka called the *United Nations Institute for Namibia* (disbanded
in 1990). Six years later, in 1980, the apartheid government decided to establish a low-level higher education institution in Windhoek called the Academy
for Tertiary Education to provide training for teachers, secretaries and the like.
Five years later the institution was expanded and reorganized into three units:
the University of Namibia (provided mainly teacher training), the Technikon of
Namibia, and something called College for Out-of-School Training (provided
vocational training).

In keeping with usual practice when a country achieves independence in
anglophone Africa, the new SWAPO-led government appointed a Presidential
Commission on Higher Education in 1991, funded in part by external donors
including the Ford Foundation and the British government, to look into all aspects of developing a comprehensive higher education system for Namibia
headed by a Briton, John Turner (pro-vice chancellor of the University of

Manchester). Other external (non-Namibian) members of the commission came from Ghana, the United States, and Zimbabwe. Interestingly there was not a single person on the commission panel from South Africa—see listing in Coombe (1993)—because, according to Coombe, who was a member of the commission, the Namibian government wished to "break out of the inward-looking isolationism of apartheid and colonial rule" (p. 61) that had characterized much of the latter part of Namibia's history. Most of the recommendations of the report were accepted by the government and a new University of Namibia came into being on September 1, 1992, on the ruins of the academy whose dissolution had been recommended by the commission (because of overwhelming public opposition to this apartheid created institution). Later, in 1994, the surviving remnants of the academy (the technikon and the vocational college) would be combined to form the new Polytechnic of Namibia—a protouniversity.

Before ending this section, there are three interesting points that are worthy of noting about Namibia's effort to develop its higher education system: one concerns the issue of human capital theory in educational planning: the report would note "National 'manpower forecasts' have a deservedly bad name internationally, because most of the variables which affect the demand for personnel are complex and unpredictable" (from Chapter 1 of the report as reproduced in Coombe 1993: 72). Obviously, Namibia, in achieving independence so late, would be a beneficiary of one silver lining: to learn from the experience of others who achieved their independence decades ago. Second, concerns academic freedom: Namibia is among the few nations in the world where the national constitution has an explicit clause in it about respect for academic freedom: "All persons shall have the right to...freedom of thought, conscience and belief, which shall include academic freedom in institutions of higher learning" (Article 21 (1) (b)—from Coombe, p. 69). The third concerns tuition: students would attend the university tuition-free (by means of government scholarships); however in 1997 under pressure of budgetary constraints the government made a decision to scrap the scholarships and instead institute tuition and a student loan scheme.[81]

NOTES

1. See Sbacchi (1985) on Ethiopia's experiences under the Italians.

2. Beginning in the preceding century, unofficially sponsored students were already going to study abroad—through either family support or missionary support (see Zedwe 2001). By 1959, more than a thousand students had been sent abroad to nearly thirty different countries; though the lion's share was hosted by the United States, Canada, Egypt, Germany, Italy, Lebanon, Britain, France, Israel, and India in that order (see Kitchen 1962: 125).

3. For more on modern Ethiopian history the following considered together provide a usable overview: Fukui, Kurimoto and Shigeta (1997); Marcus (1994), Perham (1948), Zewde (2001)

4. Other efforts in this direction had preceded on a lesser scale, for example, the establishment in 1944 of three institutions: Technical School of Addis Ababa, Commercial School of Addis Ababa, and Teacher Training School.

5. For a more detailed account of the British responses to Ethiopia's tentative requests for assistance see Maxwell (1980) who also suggests that the initial offer of assistance was turned down because of resistance from the Jesuits over curricular control (specifically the teaching of philosophy).

6. In 1964, by which time Eritrea had lost its federal autonomy it would be renamed the University of Asmara and over the next decade it would be brought in line with other Ethiopian institutions, marked by the replacement of Italian with English as the language of instruction and the loss of its Italian academic heritage. (In 1990, as the Eritrean war of independence reached a decisive stage, the Dergue moved against the university; closing it and dispersing its faculty, students, staff and university resources to institutions in Ethiopia. This effort to neutralize what it considered as a treasonous institution proved to be a futile endeavor; for the Dergue itself would be out of power within a year.) Today a reconstituted University of Asmara is the lynchpin of an evolving higher education system in independent Eritrea.

7. Why did the African countries insist on providing free university education (in the form of scholarships) that also included student welfare subsidies? Tuition-free university education was in itself a major financial burden on the state treasury; Why then add to it the costs of student welfare subsidies, such as free board and lodge? There are several explanations for this approach. First, there was the issue of equity: it was felt that no qualified student academically eligible to attend a university should have to face the prospect of being denied admission because of penury. In part this was an attempt to redress what was felt as an injustice that colonialism had perpetrated on Africans by denying higher educational opportunities (where these were available) to the academically deserving on grounds of financial constraints—even while recognizing that most of these students came from family backgrounds that simply did not have the requisite financial resources given the iniquitous economic policies of the colonial governments themselves. Second, in the policy context of the human-capital approach to educational planning, governments felt that the dire need to develop human capital resources overrode such impediments as the inability to finance one's university education. Third, even where it became clear that many of the students came from families who were now doing well in the postindependence era and could afford to pay their own way, there lacked a tradition and an administrative mechanism for cost recovery through (for example) student loans. After all, this approach to the financing of universities was not common in the Metropole either. Means-tested, cost-recovery approaches to university finance has historically been the preserve of the one major Western power that did not have any colonies in Africa: the United States.

8. To address this very problem the egalitarian minded Dergue-led government (see below) in its early years had implemented an affirmative action program to redress the geographically determined class imbalance in higher education by introducing new selection criteria more favorable to the disadvantaged rural students, but the program

failed and was discontinued. Wagaw (1990: 241) explains what happened: "For the most part...students admitted on such criteria, who had never seen a laboratory or an organized library, encountered serious language problems and were unable to survive the unfamiliar world of the urban colleges." Consequently, he observes, "[m]any failed, and the experiment was discontinued with the tacit admission that until the quality of the rural schools was improved the problem of unequal access to colleges would remain intractable."

9. The emerging Ethiopian higher education system was a deliberate patchwork of academic traditions cobbled together with a mixture of foreign and Ethiopian finance. Both economic reasons (a dearth of resources prompting requests for foreign aid from whoever was willing to provide it), as well as a desire to retain cultural autonomy, lay behind this approach. Consider the following examples: the predominating influence in the area of buildings technology was that of the Swedes, in medicine it was that of the British, in law and agriculture it was the United States, in engineering it was German, and so on. Clearly, as Maxwell 1980 points out, from the perspective of organizational rationality and efficiency this was not an ideal situation. In fact the problem had already been foreseen years earlier; writing in 1948 Perham had observed about the emerging secular education system:

[T]here is the danger that in this important formative stage the Ethiopians, by using their usual method of turning to many nations at once, may get fragments from the experience and ideals of each without getting the fullest and best influence from any one national tradition.... The Ethiopians may succeed in avoiding cultural confusion, but the perpetual changes of plans, persons, and nationalities have undoubtedly produced something not far off administrative confusion in education and have discouraged many of those who were honestly trying to do good work for Ethiopia (pp. 256–57).

To make matters worse, the new university was geographically dispersed; it operated out of three separate locations within Addis Ababa and two other sites located hundreds of miles away.

10. Even though foreign aid generally, as well as that earmarked specifically for the education sector, from Ethiopia's former traditional allies, the United States and the British, greatly diminished in the postrevolution Mengistu period, other countries (such as the Swedes, the Japanese, the Indians and so on) continued to provide it. For more on the Swedish development aid to Ethiopia see Abraham (1993); Gumbel, Nystrom, and Samuelsson (1983); and Norberg (1977).

11. This principle of community service would also be adopted by the Dergue (see below); they would send students into the countryside to help with the implementation of some of its programs (such as educating the peasantry about the land reforms and the national literacy campaign).

12. This was not the first time a serious effort had been made by the newly emergent secular intelligentsia to overthrow the monarchy: In 1960 an attempted coup, but without military support, had cost its ring leaders their lives. The deep involvement of students in his downfall must have been especially bitter to the aging monarch; for whatever his many other faults, he had worked tirelessly to develop secular education in general and higher education in particular. Like all African leaders of his generation, he viewed the salvation of his country to lie ultimately in modern secular education. (He

could point with satisfaction to the fact that after the military, the education sector commanded pride of place in budgetary allocations of the state, consuming about a fifth of it by the time of the second attempt at his overthrow.) But like the missionaries and the Colonial rulers elsewhere in Africa, Selassie never foresaw the potential for modern education to help undermine the existing political order (compare: students and the political order in present day theocratic Iran).

As for his fate after the coup? He was imprisoned in his own palace for a short time before, it is now thought, he was murdered by strangulation the following year on the orders of the Dergue, which at the time had put out the story that he had died of natural causes. (Recall that the Dergue, led by Mengistu, had already executed some months earlier on November 23, 1974, some sixty people comprising members of the royal household, former high-ranking government officials and a even a few recalcitrants—in Mengistu's eyes—from within its own ranks).

13. That the Ethiopian students and many of the emerging Ethiopian intelligentsia took to Marxist-Leninism like ducks to water (see Balsvik 1985), even though modern Ethiopian higher education was a creature of the Western capitalist democracies and even though the Ethiopians who went to study abroad went, with rare exception, to Western countries, has to be explained by their legitimate perception that ideological support for the overthrow of the Ethiopian feudal order had to be sought outside the Western capitalist democracies (who after all were allies of the Ethiopian monarchy), in places that had undergone—albeit at a much earlier time—their own revolutionary overthrow of the feudal order (e.g., the Soviet Union and China) and who at the same time were not allies of the Ethiopian monarchy. It is instructive to note here the characterization by Kehoe of the average student at the university as "largely anti-U.S., resenting America as a big, bomb-happy, cigar-smoking, materialistic, gadget-run, ranch-type, godless, skyscraper-trimmed, speed and sex mad, liquor-loving plutocracy" (1962: 477). What is more, she observes that this view was held even by those who had returned from study in the United States. However, she does not tell us why the students came to adopt this view.

14. Student political activism continues endemically in Ethiopia even today; that is, replaying what has always been and continues to be a "student tradition" in most of postindependent Africa. For example, in April 2001 students from University of Addis Ababa ignited a conflict with the government over issues of academic freedom on campus that resulted in the usual pattern of political mayhem: riots, deaths, arrests, and a temporary closure of the university by the government. The following year too, there was more conflict between students and the authorities, but this time in the state of Oromia (on this occasion the issue was both academic freedom and curricular reforms). For more on the student role in the 1974 revolution see Asres (1990), Balsvik (1985), Milkias (1982), and Wagaw (1990). Of the sources that deal with the origins and aftermath of the 1974 revolution from a wider perspective, the following have proved helpful: De Waal (1991); Fukui, Kurimoto and Shigeta (1997); Haile-Selassie (1997); Markakis (1987); Ottaway (1990); Tiruneh (1993); and Zegeye and Pausewang (1994).

15. In ignoring this principle they were not alone of course: compare the fate of others who have pursued this path, such as their future Soviet and Cuban allies. The Soviet empire, together with its Marxist-Leninism, is gone and by all accounts Cuba appears to be on its last legs too. One may also draw attention here to what China has had to be-

come: a capitalist, though still authoritarian, state. Note: The Soviets and the Cubans became allies of Ethiopia in 1977 when, on the basis of geopolitical calculations, they decided to side with Ethiopia in its struggle with Somalia (until then a Soviet ally) over Ethiopia's disputed Somali-speaking Ogaden region, and went on to provide massive military assistance to recapture the region from the Somalis who, taking advantage of the internal political chaos in Ethiopia, had invaded it that same year.

16. In "fairness" to the Dergue: As Tekle (1990: 39) observes:

The use of force and terror has always been a vital element in Ethiopian politics and the systematic use of terror is not unique to the [Dergue] regime. While there is no intention to justify his heinous crimes, it must be clear that Mengistu cannot, in all fairness, be given a special place in Ethiopian history for bloodthirstiness, barbarity and sadism. Holocausts have taken place during the reigns of many respected monarchs, including the most-admired Tewodros II and Menelik II....Terror has always been used after great deliberation and calculation to ensure maximum damage and psychological effect....There was no moral limitation to its uses. It is to be recalled that Haile Selassie's favorite method of terrorist intimidation consisted of the indiscriminate, saturation aerial bombing of civilian targets such as crowded marketplaces on traditionally designated market days.

17. On the role of Eritrea in bringing down the Dergue: The forcible dissolution by the Allies of the Italian colonial empire in Africa at the end of the Second World War, had presented a dilemma for the United Nations, as it acquired guardianship of the Italian colonies, with respect to Eritrea. Its people demanded independence, while at the same time Ethiopia laid claim to it. As a compromise, in 1952, the United Nations federated Eritrea to Ethiopia; however, whatever autonomy the Eritreans enjoyed in the federation soon evaporated as Ethiopia annexed it in 1962 and dissolved the federation. The United Nations did nothing about this flagrant aggression, thereby precipitating a highly destructive and long-drawn-out guerrilla war between Eritrea and Ethiopia in which the former emerged triumphant; attested to by its march on Addis Ababa together with its Tigrayan allies. Ethiopia would recognize Eritrean independence in 1993, though a border dispute between the two would soon erupt (in May 1998) leading to massive loss of life on both sides over the course of two years of armed conflict (although an uneasy peace has come to the disputed area, the border conflict remains unresolved). For more on Eritrea and its war of independence see Cliffe and Davidson (1987); and Marcus (1995). See also Young (1997) on the Tigrayan revolution that was also instrumental in the demise of the Dergue.

18. The transformation has also been a geographically traumatic one for the Ethiopians: for the first time in their roughly 3,000-year history they do not have an outlet of their own to the sea; they are landlocked—an awful disadvantage in a strife ridden continent.

19. The material on education in this section draws on the following sources: Abraham (1993); the section titled "Education and Human Resources" in volume 3 of the massive multiauthor three-volume work on Ethiopian studies edited by Fukui, Kurimoto and Shigeta (1997); Kiros (1990); Kitchen (1962); the chapters on Eritrea and Ethiopia in Teferra and Altbach (2003); Saint (2004), Wagaw (1979, 1990); Yohannes (2002); and Wartenberg and Mayrhofer (2001).

20. For a brief overview of the Meiji restoration, the following sources, when considered together, should suffice: Hardacre and Kern (1997), Hirschmeier (1964), Keene

(2002), Kornicki (1998), Lincicome (1995), and Wilson (1992).

21. In actuality, the first attempt at settlement had taken place two years earlier when the ship Elizabeth had left New York on January 31, 1820, amidst much fanfare with 86 African Americans (interestingly, all free African American volunteers; and who also included families with children) bound for what was to become Liberia. This first effort did not succeed; both disease and resistance from the indigenous Africans put paid to that initial attempt. Until the second (this time successful) attempt, the survivors had been forced to seek refuge in nearby British ruled Sierra Leone. Schick 1982 draws attention to another factor that also contributed to the early difficulties that marked the colonization project: intense denominational rivalry among the settlers (not to mention "ethnic" antagonisms).

Note: "Recaptives" were Africans removed from slave ships impounded in the Atlantic after the importation of slaves from abroad into the United States, though not slavery itself, had become an illegal activity under U.S. law in 1808. It is the desire to resettle the recaptives that the U.S. federal government used as an excuse for its involvement in the Liberia project.

22. As Clegg (2004) reminds us, the notion of returning African Americans to Africa (or alternatively removing them to some other place outside the United States) was as old as the hills; that is, even Thomas Jefferson, for example, had suggested as early as 1776 that African Americans should be relocated to some place outside the then U.S. borders (though still within the continent—a few years later, however, he would take up the idea of sending them back to some part of Africa). In his exhaustive study of the various currents that kept this notion alive and eventually brought it into fruition, Clegg suggests that an important minority among Euro-Americans who for long had cherished the dream of a back to Africa movement (for African Americans of course) were the Society of Friends (Quakers); for, among Euro-Americans, they were the first to systematically take up the banner of abolitionism, beginning some time toward the end of the eighteenth-century. It ought to be noted, however, that as with the rest of the pro-abolitionists in the wider Euro-American population, this shift in their sentiment regarding slavery was a long time in the making, taking place over a period of more than a century and moreover one cannot discount the backdrop of a changing economic context that rendered slavery no longer absolutely essential to the personal economic well-being of the Friends. In other words: as is so often the case with social movements of a humanitarian nature, it was the changing dialectic between economic self-interest and religiously driven humanitarian concerns (tempered by the contradiction of an inherent racism) that eventually propelled the Friends toward abolitionism—an offshoot of which was their support for colonization of Africa by African Americans.

As for African Americans themselves, the majority of their leadership (Bishop Henry Mcneal Turner were among the exceptions), came to see the colonization project for what it really was: a racist project and they would have nothing to do with it. To them, the very idea that a people whose blood, sweat and tears had helped to build the country should now be banished from it was the height of injustice. However, it is possible that in later years many among the rank and file in the South, burdened by the weight of post–Reconstruction era Jim Crow, did come to subscribe to the idea of emigration to the motherland; but lack of money and the absence of regular shipping to Africa proved insurmountable barriers. (Moreover, in an ironic twist of events, in this period, there was now resistance to the emigration scheme from whites in the South! Clegg explains why: they, specifically the capitalist class, needed their labor.) The fact that so few African Americans, in the end, went to Africa to settle speaks volumes on this matter. (Besides Clegg, see also Redkey 1969, on the African American response to the colonization project.) One may also note here that the dream of returning to the "motherland" (specifically Liberia) was revived later among many ordinary African Americans, albeit only briefly, in the early 1920s through the agency of Garveyism— but it remained only that, a dream (see Sundiata 2003).

23. To a lesser degree, the society was also assisted in this venture by smaller state-based (though often autonomous) branches; such as the Massachusetts Colonization Society, the Maryland Colonization Society, the New York Colonization Society, the Tennessee Colonization Society, and so on. The plantation aristocracy and its allies in some Southern states (such as Alabama, Georgia, South Carolina) appeared, however, to be against the idea of colonization; hence these states did not see the establishment of colonization societies within their borders. For example, the Georgia legislature had passed a resolution as early as 1827 saying that plans by the American Colonization Society to establish "an African colony, at the distance of 3,000 miles, on a barbarous and pestilential shore" was unconstitutional (Clegg 2004: 150).

24. Descendants of the African American settlers came to be known as Americo-Liberians, while those of the recaptives were called the *Congo(s)'*.

25. As he would state in his inaugural presidential address (delivered on January 5, 1881):

It will be our aim to introduce into our curriculum also the Arabic, and some of the principal native languages, by means of which we may have intelligent intercourse with the millions accessible to us in the interior, and learn more of our country. We have young men who are experts in the geography and customs of foreign countries; who can tell all about the proceedings of foreign statesmen in countries thousands of miles away; we can talk glibly of London, Berlin, Paris, and Washington; know all about Gladstone, Bismarck, Gambetta and Hayes; but who knows anything about Musahdu, Medina, Kankan or Sego, only a few hundred miles from us? Who can tell anything of the policy or doings of Fanti-doreh, Ibrahima Sissi, or Fahqueh-queh, or Simoro of Boporu, only a few steps from us? These are hardly known. Now as Negroes, allied in blood and race to these people, this is disgraceful (Blyden 1967).

26. It should be noted that the sponsors in the United States were always of the opinion that the college should also work toward enrolling Afro-Liberians so that it could become a means of "civilizing" the natives—an objective, motivated by the evangelical spirit, that had always been integral to the Liberia project as a whole for many of the Euro-Americans involved in the colonization project from the time of its inception.

27. For more on the college, besides Livingstone, see also: Hoff (1962, 1987), and Liebenow (1969).

28. The private, four-year liberal arts college is a very uniquely U.S. institutional gloss on the imported traditions of Cambridge and Oxford—especially in terms of the mission of the university and the clientele (see Ben-David 1992).

29. In the U.S. context, this "responsibility" with respect to Africa, from the perspective of African Americans, took the form of the project for "African redemption."

30. The model on which the institute was based was the clearest example of the

considerable influence that the Tuskegee Institute came to have on higher education, albeit only for a short time, in anglophone Africa. Had it not been for the Second World War and the forces that it unleashed that would assist in hastening the dismantling of the European colonial empire, it is possible that the Tuskegee influence would not have been as ephemeral as it really turned out to be—especially in terms of actual institutional implementation of the model. As Marable (1982) demonstrates, the influence of Tuskegee—actively fostered by the Phelps-Stokes Fund (one of the institute's major benefactors)—was effected through a variety of mechanisms: besides those already noted (such as the two Thomas Jesse Jones-led commissions of inquiry to Africa and the hosting of numerous African foreign students at the institute), they included study trips to the institute by policymakers; its representation at relevant conferences and on boards of trustees; and its advisory role on specific projects (as in the case of the Booker T. Washington Institute). The apogee of this influence was undoubtedly reached during the presidency at Tuskegee of Robert Russa Moton (from 1915–1935), the successor to Booker T. Washington. As Marable (1982) observes:

Under Moton's administration, Tuskegee emerged as a model for black educational systems throughout British colonial Africa. Hundreds of missionaries, political administrators, and educators studied Tuskegee Institute's programs, visited the campus, and applauded its president. Tuskegee administrators and former faculty members gave their services to colonial governments in agricultural and educational programs....Through his extensive correspondence, Moton became acquainted with almost every significant intellectual, religious leader or political activist in Africa (pp. 77, 81).

Moton, a graduate of Hampton Institute, was, in a sense, a protégé of both Samuel Chapman Armstrong and Booker T. Washington. Upon the latter's death, Moton inherited Washington's mantle and became the steward of Tuskegee and the country's unofficial consultant on African American affairs. Subscribing to the same philosophy as that of Washington's, he courted Euro-American liberals with as much fervor as his mentor; the proof of which was visible in the endowment of Tuskegee: under his leadership it would more than triple, from about $2 million to $8 million. Moton, however, as just noted, was, like many other African American intellectuals and notables of his generation, also a firm believer in the concept of the white-man's burden (or "African redemption.") Further, believing that the surest path to taking up this burden lay in a combination of Christian evangelism, secular education as conceived at Hampton and Tuskegee, Moton (like such ambassadors of the Tuskegee gospel in Africa as Thomas Jesse Jones, J. E. Kwegyir Aggrey and Charles T. Loram), became an indefatigable champion of the model for all the "benighted" in Africa, and elsewhere. (Marable reminds us, for example, that among the many foreign pilgrims to visit Tuskegee, always received graciously by Moton, was Mahatma Gandhi's representative Charles F. Andrews.) Of course, it goes without saying that his belief in the Tuskegee model, as was the case with his mentor Washington, was buttressed by the twin carrots of helpings from the white liberal largesse, and the headiness that ensued from being accorded prominence, in the context of the extraordinarily virulent Euro-American racism of the day, in "black education affairs" that was of some domestic and international significance.

   31. He gave examples of what this culture meant in practice: an agricultural re-

search center was established independently of the university, even though the university had a school of agriculture; a public administration institute was created (again independently of the university which already had a program in public administration); for a while the government had funded scholarships for overseas study in areas that the university's curricula covered—signifying wastage of scarce foreign exchange; and even more amazingly, the budgetary allocation for scholarships for overseas study exceeded that for the university as a whole (p. 210–211). One ought to point out, however, that perhaps this circumstance was not unique to Liberia. As already noted in the preceding chapter, the issue of relevance (or lack of it) was also brought up in the case of the Asquith Colleges. See also the other contributions in the work in which Seyon appears, that is Yesufu (1973).

32. In fact, the first attempts to establish colonial settlements in Liberia were accompanied—as was the case with colonial projects in many other parts of Africa—by deceit, fraud and the barrel of a gun, such was the resistance to the project by the indigenous Liberians who did not see the African Americans as their long-lost brothers returning home.

33. In other words, right from the very beginning, not much love was lost between the settlers and the indigenous. As Livingstone (1976) reminds us, those early settlers never saw themselves as Africans, but rather as refugees from the United States living in Africa. Even the 1847 Declaration of Independence had no mention in it of Africa as their motherland, and this, he says, despite the fact that some of them were only first- or second- generation African Americans! In fact, to say that they (and their descendants coming all the way to the present) saw themselves as a people of a different race would not be stretching the truth too far; as he further observes: "The race problem of the United States, with significant mutations, was...reproduced in Liberia: near-white replaced white as the badge of a social elite that thought itself superior to the emigrant Blacks and aborigines, and the Blacks of Liberia who smarted under this discrimination generally regarded themselves superior to the native aborigine" (p. 249–50). (See also Clegg 2004 and Sundiata 2003.)

34. Some writers have termed the armed bloody conflagrations that have befallen many African countries during the postindependence era as "civil wars." That is a misnomer, for it suggests armed conflict over ideology on how best to organize society. In a number of African countries war has not been motivated by ideology at all; rather it has been rooted in ethnically-based kleptocracy, pure and simple—examples include: Democratic Republic of the Congo, Liberia, Sierra Leone and Somalia. On the other hand, some wars have been bona fide civil wars; examples would be Algeria, Sudan (in the south), Angola, and Mozambique. If, by means of this categorization, there is the suggestion of an evaluative judgment between the two types of blood-letting then it is not without reason: a civil war has the potential for end, whereas a kleptocratic fratricidal war is potentially endless.

35. The journey by human beings (or those appearing to masquerade as such) into the dark abyss of "*un*civilization," the hallmark of which being unbelievably stomach-turning barbarity, appears to be much easier to make then the converse journey toward civilization in its truest sense—immaterial of the ethnicity involved (vide: the Nazi death camps; the killing fields of Cambodia; the genocide in Rwanda; the atrocities of the apartheid security apparatus in South Africa; the tortures, murders, and disappear-

ances in Pinochet's Chile; the Serb atrocities in Bosnia and Croatia; the tortures and murders in U.S.-run prison camps in Afghanistan and Iraq; and so on). In this particular instance, witness the mind-numbing atrocities of the various Liberian factions, a hint of which (and it can be nothing more than that for words in these circumstances prove hopelessly inadequate) comes through from the following chilling account:

> Some describe the pain of seeing a spouse or child die because of malnutrition or the unavailability of medical care. Others tell of seeing their girlfriends, wives, daughters, or sisters raped and killed. One young man reported being forced to kill his own fiancée. Weeping uncontrollably, he followed orders to execute the person he loved most because he knew the alternative for her would be a much more painful and prolonged death. A common tale from the war is that soldiers would make a wager as to the sex of an unborn child and then cut open the pregnant woman's stomach to settle the bet. Less dramatic, but nevertheless an atrocity of war, men tell of being beaten and then forced to "thank" their torturers for the needed discipline (from Sundiata 2003: 331).

36. Arguing that since he had been primarily responsible for the kleptocratic fratricidal war (in which the use of brain-washed and drugged child soldiers was just one of the many horrors that became the trademark of the senseless conflict) and therefore only he could bring peace, he rode to the victory on a bizarre and repugnant slogan to emerge out of, to quote Sundiata (2003: 332), "the killing fields of Liberia," that went: "He Kill My Ma, He Kill My Pa: I will Vote for Him!" (from Sundiata, p. 332).

37. For more on Liberian higher education, besides the sources already mentioned, see also the chapter on Liberia in Teferra and Altbach 2003; Maxwell 1980; Seyon 1977; and Sibley 1926. To get a sense of the fate of the University of Liberia during the war see the brief article by Seyon 1997 (who, it may be noted, is also the author of the chapter on Liberia in Teferra and Altbach). The opening paragraph of the article chillingly reads:

> I arrived in Monrovia in March 1991—after nearly eight years of exile in the United States—and was shocked by the destruction of the University of Liberia—the country's only national institution of higher learning. In July 1990, the campus became the battlefield for opposing forces of Charles Taylor's National Patriotic Front of Liberia and Liberia's military dictator—Samuel K. Doe—for control of the city. The combatants seemed determined to destroy not just Liberia, but also its mind and soul—as embedded in and symbolized by the university (p. 2).

38. Given this fact, it is necessary to alert the reader to the confusing terminology used by South Africans over the course of their history to identify the different (real and imagined) ethnic groups that make up that country; the following clarification for the purposes of this work should suffice: Africans: the indigenous black people of Africa, including Afro-South Africans (sometimes they are further subdivided into different ethnicities: KhoiKhoi, Tswana, Xhosa, Swazi, Zulu, etc.); Afrikaners: descendants of the original Europeans who settled in South Africa prior to the arrival of British colonialism; Asians (or Afro-Asians): all peoples of Southeast Asian descent (includes East Indians, Pakistanis, etc.) Blacks: all peoples of color (Afro-South Africans, Coloreds, East Asians, etc.); Coloreds: all peoples with "racially" mixed parentage; English (or Anglo-South Africans): descendants of British colonial settlers and immigrants; Europeans (or Euro-South Africans or "Eurosa" for short): all peoples of European descent

(but not including Coloreds); The following are considered either pejorative terms or are used infrequently today: Bantus (Africans), Boers (Afrikaners), Indians (Asians), Kaffirs (Africans—pejoratively equivalent to "niggers" in the United States), Malays (people of Malaysian descent), Natives (Africans).

39. Interestingly, this was the very same company that had hired the English explorer Henry Hudson in 1609 to explore the river named after him, Hudson River (in the state of New York).

40. That is, less than fifty years after the founding of the first permanent British colonial settlement in North America, Jamestown (on May 14, 1607); and less than twenty-five years after the Dutch West India Company through its agent Peter Minuit supposedly "bought" the island of Manhattan (in 1626) from Native Americans (whose cultures, recall, did not recognize the commodification of land) for the munificent sum of just 24 dollars!

41. The Khoikhoi, a peaceful cattle-herding people with a hunting and gathering economy, who until the arrival of Van Riebeeck had had fairly amicable relations with passing European ships that dropped by for fresh water and food with some regularity, were virtually decimated—the few who survived, as with the Native Americans in North America, were over time banished to reservations or absorbed into the rest of the population—genetically amalgamating with both the early Europeans and later other African ethnicities to give rise to, in the South African racial context, a new ethnicity: Coloreds. In addition to the Khoikhoi, the Europeans also encountered at this early stage of colonization the San, who also suffered the same fate as their Khoikhoi brethren, plus a number of Bantu-speaking peoples. The last would take much longer to defeat as they were more numerous and better organized, especially as one went into the hinterland (mention has already been made here, for instance, of the Battle of Isandhlwana).

42. To serve as a brief reminder: a sample of the many battles of aggression fought against the Africans leading to the eventual subjugation of the African peoples in South Africa (belying the myth of settling "empty lands" popular until recently among South African whites), would include the following: 1659, and 1673–77: the defeats of the Khoikhoi by the Dutch East India Company settlers; 1781: Adriaan van Jaarsveld and his men attack the Xhosa and drive them out of the Suurveld East area over the Fish river, in the process stealing their cattle numbering over 5,000 heads; 1834–35: war between the British and the Xhosa in which the Xhosa are defeated and their leader Hintsa killed and mutilated; 1837: the Dutch settlers defeat the Ndebele; 1838: Battle of the Blood River, where the Zulus are defeated by the Afrikaners; 1873: suppression of the rebellion by Hlubi chief Langalibalele in Natal; 1876: the Pedi under Sekhukhune, repel an attack by Afrikaner commandos; 1877–78: suppression of rebellions by Tswana, Khoikhoi, Griqua, and Xhosa; 1879: Zululand is conquered by British forces (despite their initial defeat by the Zulus at the battle of Isandhlwana), and who in the same year also defeat the Pedi and depose Sekhukhune; 1880: the southern Sotho under Letsie stage a rebellion against the British—it is partially successful; and 1898: the Venda are subjugated by the Afrikaners.

43. A specific example of a people that underwent this process are the southern Nguni. This is how Wilson and Thompson (1969/ 1971, Vol. 2: 257) describe their fate: "By the 1870s the southern Nguni, alone among the Bantu-speaking peoples of South

Africa, had had a full century of continuous contact with white people. They had suffered a series of defeats in which, time after time, their huts had been burnt, their cattle captured, their fields devastated. Successive blocks of land had been taken from them and turned into farms. Whole communities had been expelled from their homes and shunted about the country....Poverty was becoming endemic among the southern Nguni and the only way they had to alleviate it was by going out to work for white people."

44. It may be noted that the emerging African peasant class had engaged in agricultural production in the absence of government support (such as price supports, land bank loans, etc.) that the white farmers enjoyed. For example, in the period 1911 to 1936 the percentage share of the total government expenditure on agriculture allocated to African farmers was a little over half of 1%, the rest was spent on white agriculture (Lanning and Mueller 1969: 82). Other factors, besides legislation, that assisted in the destruction of the nascent peasant class included: overcrowding in the reserves, which among other things precipitated ecological destruction and the introduction of the hut tax which forced Africans to seek work on white farms and mines in order to have the requisite cash to pay the tax (see Bundy 1979). In the long-run, over the next three decades or so, the net effect of the act was to wipe out the emerging African peasant class. One other consequence of the destruction of the precapitalist African agrarian economic system and the prevention of the development of a viable African capitalist agriculture was the introduction of hunger as an almost permanent feature of African life. As Wylie (1989: 159) explains: "A century ago South Africa's industrial revolution began to transform the wealth of the region and the health of its inhabitants. On the fringes of the industrial centers, hunger became endemic rather than seasonal. Two processes were at work: law effectively excluded black people from the abundance now available year around; preindustrial strategies for adapting to food shortages no longer worked. The weakest members of rural black society—those whose labor had the least monetary value—began to suffer from unprecedented malnutrition."

45. The repercussions of the act were to be far-reaching and profound; not least among them was the great hardship and misery that immediately befell the peasants in that dark winter of 1913. A hint of the extent of this misery can be found in the graphic and eloquent report of a black South African (Solomon Tshekisho Plaatje) who toured the countryside to observe the effects of the act in behalf of the black activist organization the South African Native National Congress. Beginning with the words: "'[p]ray that your flight be not in winter, said Jesus Christ; but it was only during the winter of 1913 that the full significance of this New Testament passage was revealed to us," Plaatje (1969 [1916]: 58) goes on to describe an encounter with a Dutch policeman in Transvaal, in which the policeman describes the fate of the peasants thus: "Some of the poor creatures I knew to be fairly comfortable, if not rich, and they enjoyed the possession of their stock, living in many instances just like Dutchmen. Many of these are now being forced to leave their homes. Cycling along this road you will meet several of them in search of new homes, and if ever there was a fool's errand, it is that of a Kaffir trying to find a new home for his stock and family just now" (1969: 66).

46. It is important to remind ourselves that apartheid, in time, helped to create political and economic stability (through the massive suppression and oppression of blacks by means of a police-state-type apparatus) that proved highly profitable for both domestic and international capital. Foreign investment would pour in from many Western

countries, including the United States, to participate in the super-exploitation (meaning capital eschewed such normal costs of labor reproduction as adequate nutrition, health care, education, old age pensions, etc.) of African labor. However, over the long-run the stability turned out to be ephemeral.

47. Recall that some of the architects of this order were open admirers of Nazi Germany!

48. This was a deft move on the part of the apartheid architects to further divide the majority, the Afro-South Africans, into their component ethnic groups (always justified of course on grounds of protecting their cultures, way of life, etc.) as part of the classic strategy of divide-and-rule. Notice that with such a division it was possible to create the illusion that the Euro-South African population (which was spared the internal ethnic divisions that it too possessed: Dutch, English, French, Germans, Italians, Jews, etc.) was not a minority population after all. Needless to say, the legacy of enforcing the ethnic divisions among the Afro-South Africans continues to haunt the South African political landscape. (For more on the legislative and institutional structures of apartheid see Omond 1985 and other sources on South African history mentioned below.)

49. The act was preceded by a fact-finding commission of inquiry headed by W.W.M. Eiselen known as the Commission of Enquiry into Native Education 1949–1951. Other similar commissions that would be instrumental in giving shape to higher education in South Africa include: The Tomlinson Commission, 1950–1954 (which would come out with an astounding fifty-one-volume report), chaired by F. R. Tomlinson and whose mandate was to look into every aspect of life in the "homelands" with a view toward making them the geographic basis of apartheid; The Commission of Enquiry on Separate Training Facilities for Non-Europeans at Universities, 1953–1954, chaired by J. E. Holloway; and The Commission on the Separate University Bill, 1957–1958, chaired by M.D.C. de Wet Nel. In 1981 there was the report of the Human Sciences Research Council Provision of Education in the Republic of South Africa (the de Lange Commission Report), but despite the accompanying hoopla it did not lead to any major policy changes. (In the postapartheid era, the most important commission was the National Commission on Higher Education whose findings would lead to the 1997 Higher Education Act that reorganized higher education in South Africa with a view toward its greater democratization.)

50. The enactment of the Extension of University Education Act resulted in the founding of the following university colleges (leaving aside Fort Hare, which was now reserved for Xhosa students): the University College of Zululand (to serve Zulus and Swazi students); University College of the North (to serve North-Sotho, South-Sotho, Tsonga, Tswana, and Venda students); University College of Durban-Westville (to serve East Indian students); University College of Western Cape (to serve colored students). Segregation of higher education, however, was not the only intent: the objective also included a strict supervisory control of all aspects of black higher education—even at the institutional level—by the state; the depth of this control went so far that, as Ashby (1966: 347) observed, it was "more fitting for a reformatory than for an academic community." This micromanagement of higher education, however, did not extend to the Euro-South African institutions. As for the curriculum, it was restricted mainly to the arts and humanities and law; fields such as engineering and medicine were absent. As for quantitative provision, in terms of enrollment: compared to the Euro-South Africans,

to say that blacks had a raw deal would be an understatement (in 1965, for example, and comparing only Afro-South Africans [that is not including Coloreds and East Indians] and Euro-South Africans, the ratio was 1:75 in favor of the latter—Nkomo 1984: 79).

51. Other legislative actions may also be mentioned here: the 1969 University Acts that converted the Afro-South African University Colleges (Fort Hare, North and Zululand) into "autonomous" degree granting institutions—that is they became universities (at least in name); 1971 Extension of University Education Act (aimed to correct what the apartheid state felt were certain abuses to the system of granting permits to black students to pursue certain courses of studies not available at their institutions); and the 1977 Bantu Universities Amendment Act (provided a greater measure of autonomy in terms of governance than before).

52. The conjunctural factors that dialectically produced this momentous outcome in the face of years of brutal repression by the apartheid state (a repression that also had the support of Britain, France, Germany, Israel, Japan, the United States and most other (though not all) of the Western countries until almost the very end are many and varied): among them the more salient are these: (a) The arrival in South Africa of African American missionaries (especially those of the African Methodist Episcopal Church) in the 1890s (to be supported later by Garveyism in the 1920s), who would assist in fomenting nationalist sentiments among the emergent African elite. (b) The 1917 Russian revolution that gave birth to the USSR, a some time idealist and a some time opportunist Cold War ally of countries in the Afro-Asian and South American ecumene battling European/ U.S. colonialism and imperialism. Among the beneficiaries of aid from this Eastern European ally would be the proscribed African National Congress and the South African Communist Party and who because of it would be kept alive internationally, if not domestically; and the liberation movements fighting Portuguese colonialism in Africa. (c) The achievement of political independence in the early 1960s elsewhere in Africa that enabled many South African exiles and their organizations to find refuge (e.g., in countries such as Tanzania and Zambia). (d) The military coup in Portugal in 1974, precipitated by the guerrilla wars of the black liberation movements in the Portuguese colonies, that (together with the fall of the white minority government in Zimbabwe under pressure from the black guerrilla movement a few years later) would lead to the collapse of the cordon sanitaire that had physically and psychologically protected the European racist minority in South Africa (and Zimbabwe) from the radical nationalism of independent Africa; as a consequence of which a rapid change in the political consciousness of the black urban youth within South Africa would be engendered. (e) The launching in the early 1970s of the *Black Consciousness Movement* (based on philosophical inspirations derived from the African American Black Power theorists of the 1960s) by the black South African Students Organization (founded in 1968) and its charismatic leader Steven Biko, which saw as its immediate task the reversal of the psychological capitulation of the black masses. (f) The politicizing effects of the dramatic emergence of black labor unrest in the Durban area in 1972/73 (aided and abetted by, among others, radical white students associated with the white National Union of South African Students) against the backdrop of an economic recession and other economic contradictions that were beginning to come to a head in the early 1970s. (g) The defeat in January/ February 1976 of the invading South African expeditionary force in Angola at the hands of the Angolans and their Cuban allies that forever laid to rest the supposed

invincibility of whites in southern Africa and which in turn spawned an even greater resolve among young blacks to fight the apartheid state. (h) The 1976 Soweto rebellion by
school children, which would not only take the African National Congress and the
apartheid government by surprise but would help to further raise their political consciousness—even in the absence, thanks to the laws of the apartheid state, of any legitimate avenue for political activity by blacks. This heightened consciousness would
set in motion a long series of rebellions, protest marches, demonstrations, boycotts,
strikes, and defiance campaigns that would continue endemically throughout the "law-
and-order" years of P. W. Botha and F. W. De Klerk, thereby creating not only a climate
of political instability in the country but also help to revive the moribund African National Congress and the worldwide antiapartheid movement. (i) The decision by Botha
as part of his reform package—itself originating out of the pressures precipitated in the
aftermath of the Soweto rebellion—to create a bogus tricameral parliament in 1984
which still shut out the African majority from access to political power that led to the
emergence of the antiapartheid United Democratic Front, and a fresh round of even
more widespread and intense protests and rebellions in 1985/ 86. And this resistance
would provoke, in turn, an equally intense Apartheid government repression sufficient
to get the international antiapartheid movement to convince governments and businesses of countries, such as the United States and those in Western Europe, to begin imposing various forms of economic sanctions on South Africa (including divestment and
disinvestment). (j) The birth of the Civil Rights Movement in the United States in the
late 1950s, coupled with the dastardly assassination of John F. Kennedy in 1963 (which
would bring into the White House a person with much legislative savvy, Lyndon Baines
Johnson, who would help to engineer the passage of the stalled Civil Rights legislation),
that set the stage for the emergence of an important antiapartheid U.S. constituency (African Americans) with legislative power and influence sufficient to cause (through the
Free South Africa Movement of the early 1980s) the demise of Reagan's policy of constructive engagement and the legislative enactment of wider economic sanctions against
South Africa in 1986 (including the passage of the 1986 Comprehensive Antiapartheid
Act). (k) The defeat of the apartheid government forces in southern Angola (again) in
1988 at the hands of Angolan/ Cuban/ Namibian forces. (l) The successes of the South
African "economic miracle" of the late 1950s and the 1960s achieved on the backs of
blacks which led to the political ascendance of the city and the political demise of the
countryside in the context of important social structural changes among the two principal protagonists: among the Afrikaners the development of a business class strong
enough to challenge the power of the traditional classes that had depended on a virulent
racist Afrikaner nationalism; and among the blacks the development of a large urbanized working class strong enough to challenge the apartheid state. At the same time, this
apartheid-driven economic miracle would begin to experience internal economic contradictions at two levels: the "crisis of over-production" resulting from the diminishing
internal market within the European population (but yet without any hope of expanding
this market into the black community as long as apartheid curtailed the community's
purchasing power), and the increasing inability to continue shouldering the rising costs
of maintaining the apartheid system in the face of escalating resistance from blacks and
falling profit margins. (It may be noted here, if its not already apparent, that one of the
key threads weaving together this tapestry of seemingly disparate events scattered

across three different continents and through different time periods was the political and economic role of the United States)

For more on South African history (including current history), in addition to the sources already mentioned earlier, see also: Badat (2002 [1999]), Bell and Ntsebeza (2001), Bizos (1998), Campbell (1989), Campbell (1989a), Cock and Nathan (1989), Coleman (1998), Davenport and Saunders (2000), Davis (1987), Hill and Pirio (1987), Hirson (1979), Johnson (1988), Legum (1988), Mermelstein (1987), Murray (1987), Saul and Gelb (1986), Thompson (2001), Walshe (1969), Welsh (1999), Wolfers and Bergerol (1983), and Wylie (2001).

53. As Magubane 1996 demonstrates, the holier-than-thou self-satisfied notion held by some Anglo-South African liberal historians that racial segregation in South Africa was the handiwork of the narrow minded ultra-racist Afrikaners, finding its ultimate expression in their construction of the apartheid state after they took over power in 1948 does not stand up to scrutiny: the truth is that long before the National Party took office the British themselves had already laid the groundwork for the creation of such a state. Magubane in this matter, therefore, also takes care of the illusion among some doctrinaire-plagued South African neo-Marxists that any accounting for the genesis of the apartheid state must reside entirely in the examination of class relations; race being simply irrelevant. Just as in the era of Jim Crow U.S. South, South African capital ultimately benefited from the dialectical relationship between race and class that had evolved over the centuries in which the racism of the white working class was used to divide it from the black working class to the eventual detriment of both. Of course, it is true that in all capitalist societies exploitation resides ultimately in the sphere of production (something that becomes obviously clear when one looks at racially homogenous societies), but it is also true that capital will employ whatever preexisting potential avenues of social fissure (gender, religion, race, political ideology, etc.) that may be available to not only facilitate continuation of this exploitation but to actually intensify it. In other words, focusing on race specifically, the most important function of racism (where it exists) in capitalist societies is its ability to permit the simultaneous subjectification of the objective (exploitation) and the objectification of the subjective (race) at the ideological level in order to permit the exploitation of the entire working class. It is only when one looks at the issue of the race-class nexus in these terms that one can also explain such phenomena as the *super*-exploitation of the racially discriminated population (where wages do not even reflect the basic cost of labor reproduction); the scapegoating of them in order to secure political stability; and the ability of capital to resist with considerable success efforts of the working class to increase the public wage (tax-based resources distributed democratically—e.g., publicly-funded education, health services, environmental protection measures, etc.) even against the backdrop of an accelerating pace of capital accumulation (vide: the persistent budgetary "crises" amidst continuously rising GNP growth rates). An example illustrating the foregoing with even greater clarity emerges when one looks at the U.S. South during the slave era: even though slavery was inimical to the economic interests of the white working class and peasantry, they cooperated with plantation capital to maintain the slave order—so much so that they were willing to die on its behalf during the U.S. Civil War. (For an excellent analysis of the race-class nexus, albeit in the U.S. context—but of relevance, from the perspective of theory, to South Africa too—see Allen's remarkable two-volume magnum

opus: *The Invention of the White Race* [1994].)

54. From the perspective of the historian, the Lovedale complex is of considerable interest from another direction: In one of those ironies of history, it was a model for two institutions of higher education established by the revolutionary African National Congress when it was in exile. However, it was unlikely that it was a conscious model; rather the exigencies of providing educational and other opportunities to a community not considered an organic part of the host country, coupled with a particular philosophic approach to education, forced its architects to unwittingly reproduce this model. The only difference was the absence of the theological component in the analogy, for these were secular institutions, and of course while they shared the same characteristic with Lovedale of possessing overall goals for their institutions that were not strictly educational there was a fundamental difference: one was concerned with Christian proselytization, while the other with secular revolutionary proselytization. Reference here, then, is to the two educational/ vocational complexes that the ANC established in Tanzania during its exile years: one at Mazimbu called the Solomon Mahlangu Freedom College (established in 1978) and the other at Dakawa not too far north of Mazimbu, the Dakawa Development Center (established in 1982). Neither institutions, which were eventually disbanded in 1992, when the ANC returned from exile, were really colleges, but like Lovedale provided primary- and secondary- level education. They were set up in response to the influx of teenage refugees from apartheid South Africa following the Soweto Rebellion; funding and materials came from a variety of sources including the United Nations, some Scandinavian countries and the former Soviet Union. In order to meet their needs, as well as those of other adult exiles, these complexes came to have, besides the educational components (primary/ secondary-level education, adult education classes), such facilities as skills training centers (carpentry, bricklaying, plumbing, etc.), a daycare center, hospitals and clinics, a home for single mothers, a prison, workshops for making furniture, leather goods, clothing, etc., and farms. Now what is of particular interest here is their conscious effort to incorporate into their educational practice the concept of respect for manual labor; the approach was termed "education with production." As at Lovedale the rationale was that both the students and the institution would benefit from the labor/ education connection: the students would gain practical skills and respect for non-elitist labor, while the institution would save on labor costs. Note, however, that while the strategy was not so different from that advocated by Jesse Jones or as practiced in the Jeanes Schools established in the U.S. South and exported to some parts of anglophone Africa during the colonial era—e.g., Kenya, a central difference was the overall purpose. In the case of the ANC the objective was the formation of a new revolutionary and egalitarian society, whereas in the case of the former the objective was the reverse: to support the inegalitarian colonial order. The central question that emerges here then is how far did they succeed in this education with production approach—which recall was also the strategy that Tanzania itself was attempting to pursue under Julius Nyerere's program of *education for self-reliance*. The sad truth, according to Morrow, Maaba, and Pulumani (2002), is that despite the good intentions of the ANC leadership, practice fell far short of the ideal. The principal reason was resistance from both students and teachers who felt that the production component was a distraction and even demeaning. Plus the availability of plentiful cheap labor (provided by Tanzanians) did not help matters. If there is any consolation that the ANC leadership may draw from

their experiment is that they others with even greater resources who have tried the same approach in the end failed; one has in mind here the mission schools during the colonial era, and the experiences of China during the reign of Mao ze Dong and of course Tanzania itself. So long as society rewards labor and education differently (not only in monetary terms but in terms of intangibles like status and prestige) such approaches to education are doomed to failure however well intentioned. (For more on the ANC centers in Tanzania see also McFadden 1990 and Morrow 1998).

55. Sporadic African American contact with South Africa can be dated as far back as the days when U.S. whaling ships visited the coast of South West Africa (Namibia). These ships had among its sailors African Americans too. One may also mention here various African American business people who visited or lived in South Africa from time to time—such as Captain Harry Foster Dean. Interestingly, it appears that among his objectives in visiting South Africa in 1900 was location of land that could be colonized by African Americans to form a black-ruled nation. This one time African American businessperson, quite unusually was also a shipowner: he owned the ship *Pedro Gorino* (which, however, he lost in dubious circumstances to some unscrupulous English business men in South Africa) (see Burger 1976 for more on Dean).

56. According to Hull (1990: 103–04), Charlotte herself graduated from Wilberforce University in 1901 to become the first black South African woman to have a university degree. She returned to South Africa to become an educator; she set up the Wilberforce Institute in the Transvaal which in time would become a leading secondary school. Given her interest in political activism (she had been much enamored with the ideas of W.E.B. DuBois and the Afro-American Niagara Movement [the precursor of the NAACP]), she would also be instrumental in the founding of the African National Congress in 1912.

57. Named after references in the Bible, such as Psalm 68: 31: "Ethiopia shall soon stretch out her hands unto God." Ethiopianist churches were African secessionist churches that broke away from the white-dominated Christian missionary churches for "political" rather than for scriptural reasons. See Campbell (1989a) who describes the racism that permeated Christian missionary activity in South Africa which in time would provoke the characteristic schismatic response of the African clergy (not unlike that witnessed in the U.S. churches).

58. The immediate specific incident that provoked Mokone, and a number of his other colleagues, to found the new church in Pretoria in November of 1893 that they named the Ethiopian Church, was an all-white meeting of Wesleyan ministers from which they had been excluded (Odendaal 1984: 25).The decision by the church in 1886 to segregate its religious and other services, set in motion, it appears, a range of discriminatory practices that Mokone would enumerate in a "Declaration of Independence" he issued upon his resignation (Chirenje 1976: 257).

59. African Americans of the period, like many today too, had a fascination with Africa that was contradictory in the extreme: it was the land of their forefathers, but it was peopled by the primitive and the backward. In other words, as we have already seen with reference to Liberia, for African Americans, Africa was both a source of pride and shame (see Campbell 1989a, Clegg 2004, Jacobs 1982, and Redkey 1969).

60. The AME Church was founded in 1787 by an ex-slave, Richard Allen, as a result of frustration with the racist discrimination that permeated the U.S. Methodist Epis-

copal Church. In terms of causal origins, therefore, both the Ethiopian Church and the AME Church shared a similar background. Contact between the AME Church and the Ethiopian Church via the agency of Turner, therefore, proved to be fortuitously propitious for Africans in South Africa For, had it not been for the AME, it is doubtful that the Ethiopian Church in South Africa would have thrived, given the inexperience of its leaders, lack of resources, and animosity from the white churches and authorities.

61. It may be noted here that this was not the first attempt to found the Wilberforce Institute. Some time earlier, Charlotte Manye with her fiancée and fellow U.S. graduate and recently ordained AME minister Marshall Maxeke, had tried to establish one on land donated to the AME by a chief in the northeast Transvaal. It had failed for lack of funds. They would eventually return to take charge of the school in 1912.

62. Prior to the arrival of the AME in South Africa, whatever influence African Americans had had on Afro-South Africans had been mainly one of relative political passivity (Chirenje 1976: 251). This was clearly represented in the political orientations of such prominent leaders as John Langalibalele Dube who fully shared the ideas of Booker T. Washington. Dube, who received his initial education at the Congregational American Board Mission, was sent by the mission to the United States for further education in 1887. He returned to South Africa in 1892 after having spent two years at Oberlin College in Ohio, and after working at various jobs in the United States. Following four years of preaching to his native Zulu people, Dube went back to the United States to pursue further studies; this time at Union Missionary Training Institute in New York City. Three years later, in 1899, he was ordained as a Congregational minister and returned to South Africa. It was during those years that he struck up friendship with Booker T. Washington. He was even invited to give the commencement address in 1897 at the Tuskegee Institute in Alabama. Dube became very impressed with Washington's ideas on education, and shortly after returning to South Africa he helped to set up the Zulu Christian Industrial School modeled after the Tuskegee Institute. Later, Dube would assist in the founding of the South African Native National Congress (SANNC) in 1912, and of which he became the first president. (In 1925 the name of the organization would be changed to the African National Congress [ANC].) In his presidential acceptance speech before members of the SANNC, Dube would state among other things: "Booker Washington is to be my guiding star (would that he were nigh to give us the help of his wise counsel). I have chosen this great man, firstly because he is perhaps the most famous and the best living example of our Africa's sons; and, secondly because, like him, I, too, have my heart centered mainly in the education of my race. Therein, methinks, lies the shortest and best way to their mental, moral, material and political betterment" (from Walshe 1970: 55). Men like Dube not only viewed the Afro-South African masses with suspicion, and believed in Tuskegee-type self-help programs and Christian education, but saw their salvation as lying in the hands of the British, at least the liberal segment among the British (Marable 1976). The fact that Dube, for example, was able to mount a challenge (albeit an unsuccessful one) to the highly discriminatory South African Natives Land Act between 1912 and 1915 with the help of paternalists and liberals within the British colonial administration was to him and his colleagues proof positive of the advisability of conservative accommodationist political tactics. Discussing Dube, Marable explains that throughout Dube's life he (Dube) sought the advice and company of the same type of white liberal politicians, businessmen and reli-

gious leaders in the United States, Britain, and South Africa that Washington depended upon to maintain his "personal hegemony over Black America," and in the process produced his own version of a conservative accommodationist African nationalism (1976: 333). Walshe describes the essence of the political thinking that produced this type of nationalism thus: "In both countries [United States and South Africa] the white population was seen as permanent and there was the expectation of a constitutional struggle based on moral claims. Those civil liberties already enjoyed by their white fellowmen were to be gradually extended, and equal opportunity within the established practices of society was the goal. Freedom was neither national independence nor a socialist reformation, but freedom for individual achievement and a nonwhite contribution to the wider society" (1970: 54–55).

The arrival of the AME Church missionaries in South Africa, therefore, was fortuitously propitious in that they helped the African Ethiopianists in moving the African masses in the direction of genuine African nationalism; that is one not guided by white liberal paternalism. This is not to suggest that the AME missionaries were radicals in the tradition of the Garveyists; in fact when compared to them the missionaries were very conservative, but rather that unlike such compradorial intellectuals as Booker T. Washington in the United States and Dube in South Africa, they were not overly enamored of white tutelage—at least in the first few decades of their arrival in South Africa (that is while the influence of men such as Bishop Turner was still palpable). Psychologically, this had a major implication for Africans who for many years had been taught by Euro-South Africans that they were incapable of doing anything for themselves. In a sense then the AME introduced the ideology of *Black Consciousness* to Africans by means of the *medium* as well, not just the *message'*; that is through their practice as an independent black church organization the medium also became the message. As Johnson (1978: 219) explains: "The very existence of a large, internationally organized church-run entirely by black people put the lie to the [white] southern African notion that blacks could not run their own affairs. In the midst of a society which prohibited virtually all nontraditional forms of African authority and decision-making this image had a great impact on the rising self-awareness and self-confidence in the African community." Is it surprising then that very shortly after the arrival of the AME in South Africa it became the object of white hatred?

There was, however, another very significant dimension too to the political contribution of the AME Church: it was the first black organization in South Africa that looked at blacks not in terms of ethnically divided groups but as a single national entity; i.e., a South African entity and even a Pan-African entity. As Ngubo (1981: 154) observes, the AME's "work and influence transcended linguistic and territorial boundaries and initiated an organizational pattern that united Zulu, Xhosa, and Sotho groups in a common cause."

63. Even though Ethiopianism was not a political movement per se, it had the effect of complementing the political activities of some among the Afro-South African can elite. It has to be remembered, as Odendaal (1984) points out, that the original source of dissension between the Euro-South African and the Afro-South African clergy was not over matters of biblical interpretation and church tenets but rather over social issues. Therefore, by definition, the Ethiopianist churches carried with them a covert political message: African nationalism. As he explains: "The relationship between the so-called

Ethiopian or separatist church movement and the politically active groups.... was a highly significant factor in inter-African cooperation and in the political activation of Africans at grassroots level. Hitherto, while scholars have recognized the political implications of religious independence, they have had the difficulty in establishing direct connections between the independent church movement and participation in the emergent political organizations. However, the link is emphatic" (p. 82). The most convincing evidence of the political impact of Ethiopianism on the growth of African nationalism comes from many of the leaders of the Ethiopian churches themselves. For besides being church leaders they were also actively involved in activities of organizations such as the South African Native Congress; names include: Pambani Mzimba, James Dwane, Jonas Goduke, Mangane Mokone, I. G. Sishuba, H. R. Ngcayiya, and Edward Tswewu (p. 82).

64. The rebellion probably did receive some ideological nourishment from Ethiopianism but it was not instigated by the Ethiopianists. The immediate source of the rebellion (which would cost the Africans some 4,000 lives in retaliation for the dozen or so whites killed) was a deep and widespread grievance, among other grievances, against the imposition of a poll tax on all adult males in Natal by the government in 1905 (Odendaal 1984: 68).

65. Euro-South Africans had to come know about Bishop Turner and his views as a consequence of a whirlwind five-week visit to South Africa by the latter in 1898 (see Page 1982 for an account of the visit and its consequences).

66. The recognition of this "problem" one may note here, was not unique to South Africa; elsewhere in colonial anglophone Africa the same concern for the supposed pollution of the African mind through overseas study (especially in the United States) was among the factors that impelled the British colonial authorities to move toward providing some form of higher education locally.

67. Among the sources mentioned in the text, the reader will do well to also consult Campbell's detailed and helpful study (1989a) of the AME in South Africa and the U.S./South African education nexus. In addition, see also Davis (1978) and Jacobs (1982)—especially the chapters by Manning Marable and Carol A. Page in the latter.

68. During the period 1916 to 1949 total enrollments for the entire period for the different groups were roughly as follows: Afro-South Africans: 943; Coloreds: 123; and East Indians: 96 (Nkomo 1984: 41).

69. Matthews would go on to have an illustrious career including serving, together with Kerr, on the Carr-Saunders Commission. Eventually he would return to Fort Hare to become one of its faculty members. Matthews was also among the few black witnesses that testified before the Eiselen Commission (Commission of Enquiry into Native Education 1949–1951, chaired by W.W.M. Eiselen), which helped to transition the responsibility for African education that had hitherto laid with others into the hands of the South African apartheid state in the interest of a greater internal efficiency and rationality. (See the discussion about this commission by Fleisch 2002 and Kros 2002.)

70. Regarding the matter of education plus work approach ("industrial education"), Kerr only observes that at the time of his visit in 1922, both Hampton and Tuskegee were, in response to, in his words, "other times, other needs," (p. 99) moving away from it toward a more conventional type of higher educational institution. He does not anywhere indicate that the education-plus-work approach is what he preferred for Fort

Hare.

71. Missionaries in anglophone settler Africa generally played a more progressive role, in relative terms, than missionaries elsewhere in colonial anglophone Africa in that more often they were likely to side with the Africans in opposition to government policies that aimed to impose flagrant racist injustice on blacks. In view of this general stance, it is not surprising that there was at times little love lost between the missionaries and the white minority governments of the day—this was most clearly evident, for example, during the eras of white minority rule in Zimbabawe and South Africa. (See, for instance, Krige 1997, as well as a contemporaneous view by a missionary himself, Shepherd [1955] on the divergent views of the missionaries and the minority governments on the education of Afro-South Africans.) This is not to say by any means that the missionaries were advocates of black majority rule; on the contrary they still favored white minority rule, but one that was liberal enough to not completely vitiate Christian teachings of brotherhood and oneness of humankind (even if it was a qualified oneness). (See also Campbell 1989a on this issue.)

72. In 2004 University of Durban-Westville would merge with University of Natal to form the University of KwaZulu Natal.

73. The existence of this institution of higher education from the earliest part of South African history benefited black South Africans (and whites, too, of course), in another way: for those who were enterprising enough and had access to a modicum of resources, they could obtain a degree from it without having to attend a college—by preparing for its exams privately (such as through commercial correspondence courses).

74. As with the rest of Africa, there is a severe dearth of comprehensive historiographical studies of higher education in South Africa—especially studies that focus on black higher education; however, information from the following sources when cobbled together provide a usable historical picture (as well as, in the case of a few, a doorway into current circumstances): Abdi (2002), Anderson (2002), Ashby (1966), Badat (2002 [1999]), Bunting (1994), Kallaway (1984 and 2002b), Marcum (1982), Teferra and Altbach (2003), Kerr (1968), Loram (1969 [1917]), Malherbe (1925/ 1977), Mabokela (2000), Mabokela and King (2001), and Nkomo (1984, and 1990). For more on Fort Hare see the overview of sources by Morrow and Gxabalashe (2000). For those who would like to pursue comparisons of the United States and South African racial experiences, the following should prove more than adequate entry points into relevant issues: Cell (1982); Frederickson (1981, 1995); Greenberg (1980); Hamilton, Huntley, Alexander, Guimaraes, and James (2001), and Van den Berghe (1967).

75. As black South Africans will often remind one, being liberal in South Africa does not ipso-facto mean being less racist than an Afrikaner, it just means being less open about being a racist. (Compare the racism of the northern whites and southern whites in the United States.)

76. For a counter view, see the two apologias on Wits place in South African higher education history by Murray (1997) and Shear (1996). (Palmer's [1951] contemporaneous description of another liberal university, the University of Natal is also of relevance here, as is Welsh 1979.)

77. On education and racial science in South Africa see Appel (1989); compare also with the racial attitudes of the predominantly white northern universities in the United States during the Jim Crow era and their legacy.

78. See Kallaway 1984 (especially parts one and two), and Poel (1935) for a historical overview of schooling for Afro-South Africans. (Poel is particularly interesting because of the time period in which it was written; compare also with another of his contemporary Hofmeyr 1938.)

79. See d'Almaine, Manhire and Atteh (1997) and Reynolds (2001) for a brief overview of them, as well as the website *Study South Africa* (at www.studysa.co.za), which aims at providing the most current comprehensive overview of the entire South African higher education system for those wishing to study in South Africa.

80. To say that Namibia's nearly 100-year history of colonization by the Germans and the minority governments of South Africa, and the struggles of the Namibian people to resist it, can only be written with tears of blood would be a gross understatement. For more on this history see, for instance, Brittain (1988), Johnson and David (1988), Katjavivi (1988), Leys and Brown (2001), Silvester and Gewald (2003), and Sogott (1986).

81. For more on Namibian higher education see also Amukugo (1993) and Turner (1990).

6

Europhone Africa

This chapter considers the history of higher education during and after the colonial period of those portions of Africa ruled by various European colonial
powers other than the British, but excluding Afro-Arab Islamic Africa. It is
necessary to begin by observing that any survey of policies on higher education
of these other European colonial powers raises the much broader question of
comparing differences and similarities between the two broadly categorized
approaches to colonial practices in general in Africa: the *indirect rule* of the
British and the *direct rule* of the others: the French, the Portuguese, and so on.[1]
In other words, did the so-called *assimilationist/associationist* policies of
France and the *indirect rule* approach of Britain, for example, have any significant differences for those they colonized?

Of course there were differences. In general, the French had less respect for
indigenous traditions than did the British. For instance, a local African poten-
tate in anglophone West Africa was more likely to retain some shreds of his
power and dignity than if he were in francophone Africa. Even the much
vaunted self-proclaimed notion that the French were less racist than the British
toward the Africans—as a French colonial official declared at the 1944 Brazzaville Conference: "[b]y instinct as well as reason Frenchmen shun racial discrimination"—is, as Cohen (1980) demonstrates in a work devoted entirely to
the subject, just that, a notion (from Cohen, p. x). A more useful question to
ask, however, is this: given the difference between the two approaches to colonial rule, Were there any significant differences for the Africans *in terms of the*

final outcomes of their colonial experiences? In the larger scheme of things, did one group emerge better off than the other? That is, at the end of the day, did it really matter if you were colonized by the French or the British? The unequivocal answer is no; it did not really matter.

Generally speaking, the French and the British were on par in terms of their *overall* economic and political impact on their colonies across the continent; the ultimate test of this fact are the *current* circumstances of their former colonies: neither the francophone nor the anglophone colonies have fared worse or better relative to each other. What really did matter was a different variable: whether the colonies were targets of colonial settlement. Regardless of whether the colony was anglophone or francophone, it mattered a great deal to the lives of the colonized if their territory became the object of colonial settlement. The experiences of Africans living in colonial settler Africa (Algeria, Angola, Kenya, Zimbabwe, South Africa, etc.) were infinitely more burdensome—to put it mildly—than those of Africans living in nonsettler colonial Africa (Chad, Nigeria, Morocco, Malawi, etc.). With rare exception, it also meant that the struggle for independence had to be preceded by a violent struggle between the settlers and the Africans, in which, invariably, the poorly armed Africans died in far, far greater numbers than did the settlers—even though in the end the Africans did gain their independence.

If, on the other hand, Portugal is added to the equation then it is a different story. Given the economic weakness of Portugal compared to both Britain and France, *coupled with the presence of a ruthless dictatorship in that country for the better part of the twentieth-century (1926–1974)*, the four lusophone countries in Africa came off far worse as a group than did the anglophone and francophone countries; in fact for some of them it is only now that they are experiencing the kind of a long promised new dawn that others had witnessed decades ago, in the early 1960s. Moreover, in terms of general economic development, during the colonial period, the lusophone countries reflected the economic poverty of Portugal relative to the other two colonial powers. Did it matter, then, if you were colonized by the British or the Portuguese? It absolutely did.

Turning specifically to higher education: Was there any fundamental difference between, say, French and British practices insofar as the Africans were concerned? (The Portuguese would not even feature in this discussion because for the most part they did not establish higher education institutions in their colonies.) At one level, yes, of course. The differences were as real as the current cultural, pedagogic, and institutional differences between universities in Britain and France. France is not Britain; they have different historical traditions. However, what did these differences mean over the long-term? Were francophone universities better equipped than anglophone ones in meeting the needs of their postindependence societies, or was the reverse true? Here the answer is the same as the one above: relative to each other, francophone universities have neither been superior nor inferior to their anglophone counterparts in how they have acquitted themselves in postindependence Africa.

On another level, there was a fundamental difference between europhone Africa and anglophone Africa: when modern higher education was introduced and in what quantity. In general, it is true to say that compared to anglophone Africa, modern higher education came late to much of europhone Africa, and where it was introduced early it was fairly paltry. Ergo, when one thinks about higher education in Africa prior to the Second World War, invariably it is the anglophone institutions (such as Achimota, Fourah Bay, Gordon Memorial, Yaba, Makerere, and so on) that come to mind. The reason for this fact will become clear in a moment.

THE FRANCOPHONE COLONIES OUTSIDE NORTH AFRICA

Unlike the British, the French almost always had a definite policy on education in general (at least on paper) from the very beginning of the African colonial project, which flowed out of its ideology of assimilation. As the governor-general of French West Africa would observe in his policy statement on the tasks of colonial education, in December 1930: "The most cautious of realists, and those least liable to be carried away by the enthusiasms of the apostle or the neophyte, have had to confess how great a part education and its problems play in colonization, and the extent to which every problem in colonial policy is essentially in the nature of an educational problem, but an educational problem raised to the vaster proportions of a problem in racial evolution" (from the documents section of Mumford 1970: 88). The French policy had a two part objective to it: work toward the provision of higher education for a small select elite (those deemed to be come in time the *evolue* or "black Frenchmen") and low-level education for the masses.[2] Turning to the governor-general again: "Up to now we have been concerned only with the training of the individual, the evolution of a native intelligentsia. More and more shall we have to turn our attention to large-scale education, to the training of the multitude." Quoting another official he would go on to remark: "We mean to bring about for the native a greater degree of progress in a few decades than he has achieved in thousands of years" (from Mumford 1970: 92). These, however, were just words; the reality was something else. That is, in the decades leading up to the Second World War, the delusionary (at least in terms of actual practice) colonial policies of assimilation and association pursued by the French that mythically regarded the African colonies as provinces of France, separated from the mother country only by geography, paradoxically ensured that, in comparative terms, the development of any form of modern education, let alone higher education, would be weakly developed or, depending upon the time period, be almost nonexistent in the African colonies—most especially in the case of those that were outside Afro-Arab Islamic Africa.

In other words, while the French had a fully articulated de facto educational policy (relative to the British, for instance), almost from the moment they began to acquire colonies in Africa, that grew out of its colonial ideology of assimilation, by the time independence came to much of Africa in the 1960s, it was clear that educational development in francophone Africa at all levels had lagged far behind that in anglophone Africa. Why this paradox? Because, in practice, the French never applied their educational policy consistently. They (like the other europhone colonial powers who also espoused versions of the ideology of assimilation) ran into the reality of the contradiction inherent in this ideology. Any colonial ideology of assimilation rests on the twin incompatible foundations of racial equality and civilizational superiority (which in practice often translated into racial superiority—most especially in those colonies where there were sizeable numbers of colonial settlers, usually referred to as *colons* in the case of francophone Africa).

The French, like everyone else, were fully aware of the power of formal education as a vehicle for cultural and social change. Therefore, one would have expected to have seen in francophone Africa a well-developed educational system (at all levels), relative to anglophone Africa, yet this was not the case. Hence, while the French may have talked about creating an assimilated elite in theory, in practice they did not endeavor to provide higher education opportunities, especially at the university level, that could have really worked to bring about such an elite. On the contrary, their main concern was to prevent its development lest it threaten the interests of the French colonial administration at the higher levels of the bureaucracy (as well as in other areas of society). Moreover, in much of francophone Africa, because of the poor development of education facilities in general, very few Africans, prior to World War II, had the necessary preparatory opportunities to facilitate study in French universities.

Among the specific factors that worked to contradict the publicly stated policies, these four were salient: First, the French government, unlike the British, did not usually encourage missionaries (without necessarily prohibiting them outright) to establish educational facilities because it felt that the primary purpose of Western education was to universalize French secular culture and not evangelization (Mumford 1970). An outcome of this stance was that the French colonies were denied access to that extraordinary missionary energy and zeal in providing formal schooling—whatever its shortcomings—that was characteristic of missionary presence in much of anglophone Africa.

Consider, for instance, the situation in the federation of French Equatorial Africa: while it is true that initially education in the federation had been principally in the hands of the French Catholic missionaries, and to a lesser extent protestant missionaries (such as the Swedish Protestant Mission), the problem was that they lacked the resources to create postprimary education facilities, let alone provide opportunities for higher education.[3] The only exception was, as one would expect, the provision of mission seminary education—which in one sense did constitute postprimary education, albeit with very targeted objectives. Examples of the seminaries include the following in the federation: Mayoumba Seminary (located near Point-Noire) founded by Bishop Derouet in 1897. M'Bamou Seminary (near Brazzaville) created in 1913 by Bishop Augouard, though originally it was established at Landana, Cabinda in 1879. Around the same time a theological college was founded in Libreville, Gabon to serve all the Catholic missions of the federation.

How successful were these religious establishments in achieving their limited goals? A report prepared in 1939 suggested it had been very limited. The problem, as just noted, was that work of the missionaries in French colonial Africa was hampered by the ambivalence expressed by French officials regarding the missionary role because of an increasing antipathy among French politicians toward any kind of presence in state affairs (including in the matter of the provision of education), of organized religion as France steadily moved toward the concept of strict separation of church and state. (In this regard, it may also be added that the existence in France of a virulently anticlerical government, in the early part of the twentieth-century, did not help matters.) This ambivalence is described in the following quote from an observer of the period: "Any impartial observer must agree that the Catholic missions in Equatorial Africa have made it a rule to work hand in hand with the authorities and to add their efforts to those of the civil servants and of the settlers in order to introduce in this land of ignorance and savagery [sic] the elements of civilization which, in time, will allow our subjects to raise themselves to our level." He is then puzzled at the attitudes of the French colonial officials toward the missionaries: "Hence, one can no longer understand the ostracism which threatens one of the best elements for the propagation of the great and generous ideas of civilizing France" (from Lucas 1964: 81–82). A consequence of this ambivalence, then, was to further retard educational development in francophone Africa.

Second, France staffed the civil service in the colonies almost exclusively with French personnel at nearly all levels, including even the clerical level; as a result, the demand for trained African clerical personnel was considerably dampened. This is not to say that there were no demands whatsoever for low-level African administrative personnel; rather that when compared to anglophone Africa it was minimal. Francophone Africa was an extension of France (in the mind of the French administrators), therefore hiring French civil servant personnel even at the lowest levels of the colonial administration seemed natural. Though following the 1944 Brazzaville Conference (see below), however, this circumstance would soon change: the French came to accept the general principle that Africans were going to be henceforth allowed to take up "positions of greater responsibility" (Lucas 1964: 87) in colonial government bureaucracies.

Third, unlike in the case of its colonies in Indochina (where, as Kelly [1984] points out, the French had developed an extensive formal educational system), the Africans in francophone areas did not possess an autonomous and indigenous formal educational system that would have required replacement in the interest of political stability in the colonial order. Yes, to be sure, in the areas where Islam was dominant there did exist some form of formal schooling (in the form of the Qur'anic schools). The fact here, however, is that the French, according to Kelly (1984), did not see such schooling as an incubator of oppositional culture of a politically threatening nature. Qur'anic schooling was, of course, oppositional, but primarily in terms of retardation of the incipient spread of French secular education; and this the French could live with.

Fourth, as already noted above, the "scientific" theories of racism were also influential in explaining the contradictory polices of the French (as with the other colonial powers). Consider the following sentiment expressed by the French educational theorist, Gustave Le Bon:

One easily makes a school graduate or a lawyer of a Negro or of a Japanese; but one only gives him a simple veneer, altogether superficial, without acting on his mental constitution, and without his knowing how to take any part in it. That which no instruction can give him, because only heredity creates them, are the forms of thought, the logic, and especially the character of Western man. This Negro or this Japanese will accommodate all the diplomas possible without ever arriving at the level of an ordinary European (from Gifford and Weiskel 1971: 676).

Given such sentiments, which soon became widespread in French colonial circles at the end of the nineteenth and the beginning of the twentieth centuries, Gifford and Weiskel suggest that whatever notions of "assimilation" that had been entertained by the French were jettisoned in favor of a more pragmatic approach to educational policies in general in francophone Africa. In other words: by the beginning of the twentieth-century, the realization among the French ruling circles that the project of making the francophone countries truly part of a greater France was simply impractical considering that the overseas territories taken together dwarfed the metropole, they moved toward the concept of *association* (in contrast to assimilation). The idea here was that the colonies would still be part of the empire, but developing at their own pace according to their own cultural agendas. Association, therefore, was assimilation without *gallicization* and the emergent "scientific" theories of racism were pressed into service to legitimate this change in colonial policy. With this policy transition there simultaneously developed the notion of "adapting" French education to the African mentality.

As for the almost total absence of, specifically, college-level higher education opportunities in francophone Africa at the time of independence: it was assured by two other factors: the obvious one of a poorly developed lower-level educational system (which, therefore, rendered it incapable of playing the necessary tributary role vis-à-vis higher education); and the belief that higher education was best provided in France itself for the few elite Africans (the potential *evolue*) who could qualify to go there (so as to ensure that they received an authentically French higher education [Ajayi, Goma, and Johnson 1996]). Ashby (1966: 368) also mentions one more factor that, initially, discouraged the development of higher education in French colonial Africa: the African elite itself. That is, even after the French had become relatively more aggressive in creating a formal educational system at primary and secondary-levels (especially after Brazzaville), the African elite was not yet ready to countenance locally provided higher education opportunities; lest they be inferior, either in perception or in reality or in both, to those available in France.

Plus, there was this allurement as well: France had begun to provide scholarships to all secondary school graduates in its African colonies (still only a few at this time) who could qualify to study at French universities. The availability of this overseas higher education avenue meant that African *evolues* were even less interested in the development of local higher education than in ensuring that Africans would continue receiving higher education in France. Their fear was that locally provided higher education would not be equivalent to higher education in the metropole and hence their ability to compete with the French for jobs, and so on, either in the colonies or in France itself, would be greatly undermined. In fact, some West African leaders like Leopold Sedar Sengor even went so far as to oppose the creation of the *Institut des Hautes Etudee* at Dakar in 1950 as a move that was premature (see also Janus 1980).

Up until the 1950s, therefore, the only higher education institutions in all of French colonial Africa that are worthy of mention are these few: the Tananarive Medical Institute (founded in 1896); a medical college in Dakar created in 1918 (that would later be reconstituted in 1948 as the Medical and Pharmaceutical School); the Insitut Francais d'Afrique Noire (also in Dakar and founded in 1938 for the purpose of research into Arab and African societies); the Ecole Normal William Ponty (established in Goree in 1903 and named after Governor William Ponty) to provide teacher training and rudimentary medical training; the School of Marine Engineering (also in Goree); and a school of veterinary medicine and a polytechnic (both in Bamako).

Of these institutions, Ecole Normal William Ponty would acquire the same significance for the creation of an African-educated elite in French colonial West Africa as did Fourah Bay College with respect to British colonial West Africa. That is, for a whole generation of francophone West African nationalist leaders, Ponty would serve as an incubator for nationalist consciousness and leadership ambitions (Kitchen 1962: 456–57). In other words, the French did in the end establish a few "higher education" institutions in the period before the Second World War, but they were at the sub-university level (glorified secondary schools) and which had four basic advantages: they gave credence, even if nominal, to their ideology of assimilation (in terms of its educational implications); their graduates would not be qualified enough to compete with the local colonial elite at the higher levels of society, economy, and polity; they would help meet the demand for clerical personnel at the lower levels of the colonial governmental hierarchy; and they would assuage whatever demand that may have existed for higher education among the Africans.

However, with the commencement of the 1950s, the French had become more cognizant of their higher education responsibilities in the colonies; prompted in part by the increasing cost of educating Africans at French universities, and in part out of a conscious and unabashed belief that they had to do more, by way of culturally binding the colonies to the metropole, in preparation for the eventuality of some form of political autonomy in the colonies. (The half-hearted attempts at assimilation against a backdrop of racist discriminatory practices ensured that French colonies would not be immune from the development of nationalism and demands for independence.) Consider the following prevailing sentiment in French ruling circles—expressed as early as 1900 by the inspector general of the French educational system (and who was also at the same time the vice-chairman of the consultative committee on education in the French colonies): "If the administrative, economic, and financial autonomy of the colonies appears to me to be very desirable, it is perhaps all the more necessary to attach them to the Metropole by a very solid psychological bond, against the day when their progressive emancipation ends in a form of federation, as is probable...that they be, and they remain, French in language, thought and spirit" (from Ashby 1966: 365).

The crucial turning point, of course, as with the British, was prompted by the Second World War. The war set in motion events that led to a more concerted attempt by the French (as with the British) to implement their macro-colonial policies of assimilation/association. The French were motivated by the desire to compensate for their marginalization and humiliation at the hands of the Nazis by reemphasizing their global position as a major European power by virtue of their possession of a large colonial empire (see Marshall 1971). One outcome of this was the January-February 1944 Brazzaville Conference, where for the first time African aspirations to higher education would receive sympathy.[4] It should also be noted that a year prior to the conference, France had created a fund specifically targeted at large-scale development of its colonies under a ten-year plan (1947–1956) called FIDES (Fonds d'Investissement pour le Developpment Economique et Social); this had never been done before; it would receive budgetary allocation until 1958. However, FIDES directed its attention primarily at the development of lower-level education and technical (vocational education) in francophone Africa; almost nothing was done to develop genuine higher education. (One problem with FIDES was that it was not meant to cover all costs; recurrent costs had to come out of colonial government budgets—consequently, the impact of FIDES on educational development in the French colonies was to that extent stunted.)

Among the tangible fruits of the conference was a French government decree issued on February 20, 1946, that saw Congo-Brazzaville take its first step toward acquisition of higher education in the form of a vocational education institution when a secondary school, the Edouard-Renard School of Brazzaville was upgraded and renamed *Ecole des Cadres Superieurs de Brazzaville*. The new institution offered a three-year course that a student could take in any of the three principal departments: administration (which included subjects such as finance, general administration, posts, radio broadcasting, and telegraphy and telephone); science (which covered architecture, general medicine, mining, pharmacy, public works, and veterinary science); and teacher-training. It was designed to serve not only Congo-Brazzaville but the other three territories in the federation of French Equatorial Africa.

Another benefit that came out of the conference was the award of thousands of scholarships to African veterans of the Second World War by means of the ordinance of August 4, 1945, to study at French universities. As with the veterans in France, these fiver-year scholarships carried with them not only free tuition, but also stipends based on need. It apparently did not occur to the French that a more efficient method would have been to follow the British path of building university colleges in Africa, so enthralled were they by their desire to create a gallicized African elite. Yet, it did not take long before the French were witnesses to the folly of trying to educate thousands of African students in France, rather than in their home countries. They soon began to confront such problems as the increasing strain on their educational budgets imposed by the relatively heavy financial cost of the program; the poor academic preparation of many students—some of whom had acquired scholarships on grounds other than merit—imposing unacceptable academic burdens on the French universities; the failure of many of the students to return home upon graduation (or upon dropping out); and so on. Furthermore, to the consternation of the French, many of the African students exhibited a complete lack of gratitude by organizing a student union (the Federation of Students of Black Africa [FEANF]) that not only had the temerity to associate itself with communists, but began to denounce French colonialism in general and the policy of assimilation in particular.

Consequently, France began to create overseas branches of French universities in the African colonies—in a few instances beginning earlier in the preceding decades—in the form of institutes of higher education that in time became the foundational basis for national universities. Hence in Madagascar (Malagasy Republic), for instance, besides the school of medicine, institutes for law, science, education, and so on, were created by French universities at various times, beginning in 1941. They were eventually gathered together in 1960 to form the University of Tananarive (in 1973 it would be reconstituted as the University of Madagascar comprising a number of regional university centers specializing in different fields).

Similar developments took place elsewhere in francophone Africa. In Senegal, the process of founding the University of Dakar in 1957 began with the establishment of the Dakar Medical School in 1918. In Ivory Coast, the genesis of the University of Abidjan (founded in 1964 after the country withdrew from the ill-fated Federation of French West Africa) was rooted in the founding of the University of Paris-sponsored center for higher education in law, science, and liberal arts, in 1958.[5] The Federal University of Cameroun (reconstituted as the University of Yaounde in 1972 when Cameroon changed from a federal to a unitary state) began its life first in the form of various institutes for law, liberal arts, agriculture, teacher training, and so on, beginning in 1959 and culminating in the establishment of the university in 1962 under the sponsorship of University of Toulouse. In Brazzaville, the University of Bordeaux helped to establish in 1959 the Center of Advanced Administrative and Technical Studies (later to become, in 1971, the Marien Ngouabi University).

It should be pointed out here that the French would have preferred to have had regional universities in francophone Africa rather than national universities (for roughly the same reasons as specified by the minority Elliott report in respect of anglophone West Africa) and to some degree they did succeed to this end with the Institut at Dakar (became a university in 1957). Up until 1968 it admirably served the whole of francophone West Africa; thereafter nationalism took over as the Senegalese expelled many of the foreign African students (who made up a majority of the student body, 53%) following student disturbances. Once independence came, other African countries quickly abandoned their reticence toward acquiring universities of their own because now the universities acquired a political meaning; they joined that panoply of symbols of nationhood (the national anthem, the flag, an international airport, etc.). However, even with the establishment of these national universities it did not imply a radical departure from the past in terms of structure, curricula, and so on. Relevance, at least for the first decade or so, continued to remain of far less importance than "international currency" by way of mimicry.

In developing these universities, the French made absolutely sure that they would not be autonomous institutions—in terms of French control and influence. Given its assimilationist/associationist policy, and considering that the French higher education system is highly bureaucratized this was, perhaps, to be expected. To clarify the latter point: the French government plays a very intrusive role, through administrative decrees, in the day-to-day operations of the university (a concept that, undoubtedly, would be viewed with absolute horror by universities in most of the anglophone world). When France established higher education institutions in the colonies, therefore, they were virtually, in almost every sense, the overseas campuses of French universities. So, for example, when the University of Dakar was established, a decree from the French ministry of education promulgated it as the eighteenth university in the French higher education system. Initially, the Africans themselves too would not have it any other way. Close administrative and curricular alliance with French higher education institutions held the promise (which the Africans greatly cherished, even if not always realized in practice) of fluid transitions, when necessary, between institutions in the former colonies and the metropole of students and staff, as well as the equivalency of educational qualifications in the francophone world irrespective of the geographic location of the awarding institutions.

One should note here that the French idea of independence for its colonies never really paralleled that of the British. In fact, had the French had their own way, they would have probably clung on to their colonial empire to this day—albeit as semiautonomous states within a federation. Hence, whether it was the reforms of "those of the Popular Front in 1936–37, those which emerged from the 1944 Brazzaville Conference..., or even those which resulted from Gaston Defferre's Loi-cadre of 1956," the end goal was always the preservation of the colonial empire (Shipway 1999: 131). See also Panter-Brick (1988) who states that paradoxical it may appear at first sight, even when France reluctantly came to accept the inevitability of some form of political independence for its African colonies "it was axiomatic and explicitly stated, not only in French official circles but also among francophone nationalists, that the counterpart to independence was interdependence and close cooperation, that decolonization should preserve rather than destroy une presence francaise" (p. 73).

Not surprisingly, an important difference between the post–World War II French and British policies on higher education was that whereas the British saw the Asquith colleges as a mechanism for creating internationally recognized African national universities, the French saw their task as creating additional French universities that happened to be located abroad (in this case, francophone Africa). That is, although there was some room for maneuver in terms of rendering the curricula, for instance, relevant to local circumstances that the special relationship with the University of London afforded the Asquith colleges, in francophone Africa the supervisory role of the French universities was in this regard inflexible. The fact is that in the early years, the francophone universities were designed to be simply extensions of the French universities. The matter of adaptation simply did not cross the minds of the French or the Africans. In other words: the mission of gallicization was never completely abandoned by the French. For the Africans, this meant that their degrees from these local institutions were interchangeable with those of the metropolitan institutions. It also meant that a student could interrupt his/her studies midway and proceed to complete it at a university in France with almost no loss of credits. Even in the postindependence era, the Africans couldn't have been happier with this arrangement.

As one may expect then, even after independence, the universities in the former French colonies continued to maintain strong administrative links with French universities where the French ministry of education still retained considerable administrative responsibilities over them—as provided by *concordats* that the independent countries signed with France for this purpose. At least in the immediate postindependence period, then, one could state without any hesitation (as, indeed, Ashby [1966: 371] does) that the university in francophone Africa was a very close copy of the university in France, from whatever perspective one looked at it: administration, curriculum, degree structure, academic culture, and so on. Moreover, France not only took care of staffing the institutions, but it was even responsible for their financing, at least into the early part of the postindependence period (Ajayi, Goma, and Johnson 1996).

It ought to be pointed out here that France's ability to finance the operation of universities in its former colonies, was of course, greatly assisted by the fact that at the time of independence there were very few universities. Of these countries: Burkina Faso (formerly Upper Volta), Cameroon, Central African Republic, Benin (formerly Dahomey), Chad, Congo-Brazzaville, Cote d'Ivoire (formerly Ivory Coast), Djibouti (French Somaliland), Gabon, Guinea, Malagasy Republic (Madagascar), Mali (formerly French Soudan), Niger, Senegal, and Togo, only the following had universities (or colleges that were about to become universities): Cameroon, Congo-Brazzaville, Cote d'Ivoire, Malagasy, and Senegal.

In other words, the British dictum of adapting the metropolitan higher education institution to African needs and circumstances that almost always permeated all policy pronouncements on education in the African colonies (not always put into actual practice, as noted earlier), was not even accorded the status of well-meaning pretense, by either the French or the Africans, in francophone Africa during the period of colonial rule and, with rare exception, during most of the first decade of independence. One of the rare exceptions, was, of course, Guinea. The radicalism of the nationalists in that country had ensured that Guinea would opt out of joining the short-lived French Community, even on the very real pain of suffering immediate and complete pullback of all civil service personnel, financial aid, technical development aid, and so on, puerilely promised by France to the recalcitrant. Consequently, Guinea's ties with France were sufficiently cut to permit an alternative path to higher education development involving aid support from countries such as the former Soviet Union for a very specific type of higher education: one that was very directly and narrowly targeted at clearly identified personpower needs—along the principles of vocational training, in a sense. For example, the Conakry Polytechnic, which was built, equipped, and funded by the Russians to train teachers and engineers at both professional and subprofessional levels, would for a long time remain the principle higher education institution in Guinea.

In the effort toward autonomous economic development (including higher education), Guinea would be joined by another francophone country, Mali (though it did not opt out of membership of the French community). With the support of some former Eastern bloc countries, including the former Soviet

Union, Mali established a number of institutes of higher education in such fields as education, medicine, engineering, public administration, and so on—but, again, in direct consonance with specific personpower needs. (In 1986, these institutes would be grouped together to form the University of Mali).

As the first decade (the 1960s) of political independence drew to a close, and the 1970s began, the close higher education ties that had existed between France and the independent francophone countries started to loosen as France relinquished its financial responsibility over their higher education institutions. This process of indigenization grew out of a number of factors, not least among them, the crisis among the universities in France in that fateful year of 1968. The reverberations of that crisis extended to Africa with the disturbances at Dakar, for example, as students went on strike in protest at cuts in their stipends. It then dawned on the African leadership that they were helping to finance educational institutions that were foreign in all but name; it was time to change that.

The French on their part also accepted this change in view, recognizing too that it was about time that African graduates remained in their own countries, rather than seeking employment in France. Degrees from the African universities were no longer interchangeable with French degrees, they were now simply equivalents and even that only for the purposes of graduate study in France. The issue here for the French was not just the moral problem of encouraging a brain drain from Africa, but also self-interest: to lessen the pressure on their own labor markets, as well as forestall racial tensions. There were other factors at work as well: the growth of self-confidence among the Africans, arising out of experience and maturity, to develop in autonomous directions; an increasing awareness of the obviousness of the necessity for adapting higher education to local needs and circumstances (Africa was not Europe, no matter what mental gymnastics one engaged in); and the development of resurgent nationalism. About the last point, continuation of close relations with the former colonial power began to be viewed with a strongly jaundiced eye by the younger emerging African elite. Among other things, they felt, justifiably, that their employment opportunities were being heavily curtailed by the continued large presence of French personnel in the public sector (Ajayi, Goma, and Johnson 1996).

The 1970s also saw two other important developments regarding higher education in francophone Africa: First, the smaller countries that had not acquired their own universities at independence were now busy setting up university centered national higher education systems—many on the basis of higher education centers created in the preceding decade. For example, Benin created the Universite National du Benin; Central Africa, University of Bangui; Chad, University of Chad; Togo, the Universite du Benin—Lome; Gabon, Omar Bongo University and Masuku University of Science and Technology; and Senegal transformed the University of Dakar to University of Senegal (later to be renamed Cheikh Anta Diop University in 1987). Second, the pace of enrollment in higher education institutions escalated rapidly; student populations virtually exploded multiplying, in some instances by three to four times the original numbers of the preceding decade (Ajayi, Goma, and Johnson 1996).

THE PORTUGUESE COLONIES

The Portuguese educational policy in its African colonies paralleled that of the French in that it too believed in the notion that higher education was to be reserved only for an elite few (the *assimilado*) and that it should be provided in Portugal to ensure authenticity (Kitchen 1962). Of course, such a policy also went well with the circumstances of the relatively resource poor Portuguese colonial government and which, moreover, had a long history of neglecting the education of its own people in Portugal (Samuels 1970). It is not surprising, then, that despite the fact that the Portuguese were in Africa for a far longer period than any other colonial power (from late fifteenth-century onward), their educational record, relative to that of the other colonial powers in Africa, was absolutely abysmal. In fact, it is thought that in Angola and Mozambique, for example, the illiteracy rate among Africans in 1958 was close to 100% (Kitchen 1962; and Azvedo 1980).

On the other side of Africa, in Mozambique, the situation was a little better. But there too, neglect was still the order of the day for many decades. Even the Jones African Education Commission would observe the following about the Portuguese educational policy in Mozambique: "The failure to formulate and execute sound policies for the development of the Native people is evidenced by the almost negligible provision for Native education and by the lack of any substantial encouragement in support of the valuable educational services of the missions" (Jones 1925: 312).

As for any form of higher education, up until the early 1960s it simply did not exist in Portuguese colonial Africa. One can not put it any more plainer. In 1962, however, they set up two higher education institutions which would become, in 1968, the University of Luanda, and the University of Lorenco Marques—but both were established to primarily serve the children of the Portuguese settlers. For example, out of a student population of 540 at the University of Lourenco Marques in 1966, only one student was a Mozambican African (Azvedo 1970: 199).

Independence came to Portuguese colonial Africa through the barrel of a gun. That is, the Portuguese were forced to leave their colonies in 1975 as a result of wars of liberation fought by African nationalists in the three colonies of Angola, Guinea-Bissau, and Mozambique. In Angola and Mozambique, this forcible exit, however, did not really spell peace. Instead, in support of their ideological agendas, apartheid South Africa, the then minority ruled government of Rhodesia, and a host of other external players (including the Central Intelligence Agency and right wing churches from the United States) helped foment in Mozambique, and sustain in Angola, an armed rebellion led by opportunist warlords with a penchant for mind-numbing barbarity.

The two countries would descend into a bloodbath of unimaginable savagery and cruelty, perpetrated mainly by the rebels in their attempts to render the countries ungovernable, in which the chief victims were innocent civilians—thousands, including children, would be maimed, tortured, slaughtered and mutilated. The matter, however, cannot be left here. Given the scale and duration of the bloodbath and infrastructural destruction in the postindependence era, at least a brief account of its antecedents becomes mandatory; for only then can one comprehend the lack of development in the two countries of Angola and Mozambique in all sectors, including higher education. (Moreover, it will provide a glimpse into how seemingly locally rooted conflicts in Africa have sinister international linkages often traceable to the West, most especially the United States—hence pointing to the reasons why the promise of a new dawn heralded by political independence has often remained unfulfilled for millions of Africans across the continent to this day.)

The Revolutionary Struggle against Portuguese Colonialism

In the early 1960s, as the European colonial powers were beginning to gear up to hand over political independence—nominal though it would turn out in the end—to their African colonies, there was one power, the oldest on the African continent, that was bracing itself to do exactly the reverse. That power was Portugal, paradoxically one of the poorest countries in Europe, but characteristically ruled by a fascist government. It had four colonies in Africa: Angola, Mozambique, Guinea-Bissau, and Cape Verde. Over the period of roughly four centuries its rule in these territories had been marked by a level of brutality and exploitation matched only, perhaps, in terms of duration and intensity, by its neighboring country, Spain—when Spain was the colonial ruler in South America. (Perhaps not coincidentally, both countries share similar geographical, political, and economic attributes.)[6]

Given the intensity of the oppression, Africans in the Portuguese colonies were especially hopeful that their turn for freedom would come soon too, as they watched with expectation their neighbors achieve independence, often relatively peacefully. But this was not to be, and instead the Portuguese authorities, in a typical fascist fashion, responded to peaceful nonviolent mass actions for independence with ferocious reprisals aimed at striking permanent terror within the populace with the misguided and illusory aim of banishing from among them all hopes of freedom and independence. Hence the infamous Portuguese massacres at Mueda in Mozambique (in June 1960), at Luanda in Angola (in March 1959), and at Pidgiguiti docks in Guinea-Bissau (in August

1959) were all examples of the Portuguese resolve to hang on to their colonies—and as the Africans in these countries would soon find out, through the agency of NATO, the United States and other Western powers would help the Portuguese in this ignominious endeavor.

The nascent nationalist leadership in these countries were left with no choice but to prepare their own response in kind: armed revolutionary violence. Realizing that nonviolent peaceful protests against colonial rule would simply result in the mass murder of their people by the Portuguese tyrants they launched revolutionary armed struggles in the three colonies, quite independently of each other. In Angola the struggle would begin in 1961, in Guinea-Bissau in 1963, and in Mozambique in 1964.

Initially, declarations of war on the Portuguese colonialists were mainly an act of bravado and publicity hype. Not only were the nationalists totally inexperienced in the art of military warfare, but lacked the necessary military personnel and material resources. Perhaps even more troublesome, they, at the same time, faced the daunting task of convincing their fellow citizens to overcome their fear of the might of the Portuguese security police and army as well as their doubts at their ability to overthrow nearly 400 years of foreign rule, and join them in the revolutionary struggle. The Portuguese, on their part, brought up on centuries of self-fed diet of self-made illusory notions of the inferiority of the black man, coupled with their smug knowledge that they possessed all the modern fire-power (much of it U.S. supplied), were just as equally skeptical as the majority of the black populace, at the nationalists' announcement of the launch of armed revolutionary struggles.

Yet, as other peasantries have demonstrated elsewhere in the world, Algeria, China, Cuba, Eritrea, Nicaragua, Vietnam, and not long ago Afghanistan (when the Russians were there), with patient persuasion and guidance, coupled with a sound theory of revolutionary guerrilla warfare derived from context-specific praxis, and with material support from external friends, even the seemingly invincible foe can eventually be made to drink at the fountain of *Dien Bien Phu.*

In time, the nationalists were able to build their nascent rag-tag guerrilla bands into relatively effective armies in each of the three colonies so that within a little over a decade the Portuguese were engaged in a full-scale war on three fronts in Africa. Despite the massive assistance from the United States and NATO and despite the assassination by Portuguese agents of two of the key founding leaders of the revolutionary struggles—Amilcar Cabral of PAIGC on January 20, 1973, and Eduardo Mondlane of FRELIMO in 1969—the Portuguese would soon face their own Dien Bien Phu in two of the three colonies: in Guinea-Bissau on May 25, 1973, when the guerrilla forces of the PAIGC would capture a strategic fortified enemy base camp at Guiledje; and in Mozambique in the middle of 1970 (May to August) when the Portuguese, mobilizing 35,000 troops under the leadership of General Kaulza de Arriaga, launched their Operation Gordian Knot to break the back of FRELIMO once and for all, but failed to crush the southern front opened by FRELIMO against all odds in Tete province.[7]

The result of the heavy defeats suffered by the Portuguese Army at the close of the 1960s and the beginning of the 1970s was massive demoralization within its rank and file, reaching all the way to the highest officials. Consequently, the decision in 1974 by the Portuguese dictator Marcello Caetano (successor to Antonio Salazar) to pour 10,000 additional troops into Africa to join the beleaguered 160,000 troops already present there, was the straw that broke the camel's back. It set in motion Portugal's famous military coup in April 1974, engineered by a group of soldiers calling themselves Movimento das Forcas Armadas (Armed Forces Movement), culminating in the installment of one of their generals, Antonio de Spinola, as the country's new president. Spinola, by no means a radical having fought under Hitler and on the side of Franco in the Spanish Civil War, had already earned a reputation for opposing the costly war in Africa by suggesting in his book (Spinola 1974) that the military solution was not the whole answer to retaining the colonies, but that a political solution was also necessary in the form of limited autonomy. (Not surprisingly, the book would cost him his job: he would be fired by Caetano.)

Hoping that Portugal would continue to have strong economic links with its colonies if it could effect a slow power-transition to moderates, Spinola announced his willingness to accept a cease-fire and to undertake discussions about limited autonomy; but not independence—a plan that, note, the United States, characteristically, also liked. Fortunately (or perhaps unfortunately) for the Portuguese colonies, Spinola lost the power struggle that ensued in the months immediately following the coup to a radical faction of army officers. Very quickly, the new regime set about cutting loose their formal colonial ties with their colonies. In 1974, Guinea-Bissau and Cape Verde achieved independence; in 1975, Mozambique and Angola achieved theirs. Needless to say, the collapse of the Portuguese colonial empire, deemed by many to be highly improbable only a decade or so before, sent shock waves throughout southern Africa and led to a relatively new balance of power within the region.[8]

Angola

Now, when Portugal was forced by events to grant independence to its African colonies in early 1975, it became clear to the West that while it could not do much (at least immediately) about the accession to power of FRELIMO in Mozambique and PAIGC in Guinea-Bissau (two liberation movements with fresh memories of the imperialist collaboration between Portugal and the United States in efforts to crush their struggle for independence, and who had long established their legitimacy to rule through their success in emerging as the only effective liberation movements in their respective countries), it still had some leeway in dealing with another similar organization: the MPLA of Angola.[9]

Not only was the MPLA undesirable to the West, especially the United States, for the same reasons that the other two movements were undesirable, but there was also a much more heightened fear of losing a country such as Angola to a hostile (albeit for good reason) liberation movement. Why? Angola, unlike Mozambique and Guinea-Bissau, was too important to the West. Its importance was both economic, because of its extensive oil and other mineral reserves, as well as strategic, because of its long Atlantic coastline. Moreover, it was in close geographic proximity to then apartheid South Africa (an important U.S. ally) in one sense, via South African-controlled Namibia, yet in another sense far enough (so it appeared on the map), compared to the situation of Mozambique, to escape South African economic and military hegemony (see Wolfers and Bergerol 1983). The opportunity that presented itself to the West to prevent MPLA from coming to power arose out of the history of the liberation struggle itself in Angola where MPLA was never able to fully achieve complete mastery of the countryside vis-à-vis its two principal rivals: the FNLA and UNITA. To the West the solution was to encourage, through motivational and material support, FNLA and UNITA to launch a war against MPLA.[10]

When it became clear that the Portuguese, following the military coup in Lisbon in April 1974, would be soon withdrawing from Angola, the West (principally the United States) immediately began to assist with efforts to crush the MPLA, even though on January 15, 1975, all three movements had signed the Alvor agreement under the auspices of the Portuguese at a seaside resort in Portugal. The agreement was supposed to lay the basis for a multiparty transitional government to takeover power from the Portuguese (with formal independence scheduled for November 11, 1975). Note here that from the beginning the CIA's Angola program was kept secret from the U.S. public, its architects fully aware that the program would be too controversial. This was clearly spelled out in a July 14, 1975, CIA options paper for consideration by the 40 committee. As Stockwell (1978: 54) summarizes it:

The paper discussed the risks, concluding that the security of our program would be better protected if the Angolans got arms which had belonged to the Zairean Army rather than from the U.S.A.... Broad allegations of "massive" American assistance to Mobuto and Roberto would not hurt us too badly. But a leak from an official American source would be damaging. The U.S. would be held to blame for spreading the civil war in Angola. The major fear was that some American official would leak the program to the American press, the American public.

The CIA's desire to keep the U.S. public ignorant of U.S. involvement in Angola was so intense that it began a campaign of disseminating false news to news agencies abroad, which then relayed the news (in the seemingly normal operation of international news exchange) back to news agencies in the United States. Stockwell explains the technique:

Propaganda experts in the CIA station in Kinshasa busily planted articles in the Kinshasa newspapers, Elimo and Salongo. These were recopied into agency cables and sent on to European, Asian, and South American stations, where they were secretly passed to recruited journalists representing major news services who saw to it that many were replayed in the world press. Similarly, the Lusaka station placed a steady flow of stories in [the ever gullible] Zambian newspapers and then relayed them to major European newspapers. The propaganda output from Lusaka was voluminous and imaginative, if occasionally beyond credibility (p. 194).

Among the examples of false stories planted by the CIA, according to Stockwell, was one that appeared in the *Washington Post* of November 22, 1975, which stated that UNITA had taken Malanje, and in the process captured twenty Soviet advisors and thirty-five Cubans. No such event ever took place. Another false story put out by the CIA in Lusaka, says Stockwell, was one that said that Cuban soldiers were committing atrocities, whereas in truth "Cuban soldiers had universally fallen in love with Angola and were singularly well behaved" (pp. 194–95).

While it is not necessary to go into all the details of how efforts— eventually unsuccessful—to crush the MPLA were brought about, it will suffice to note that this ignominious effort on the part of the United States and its allies (including apartheid South Africa) would tip the Angolan people over into a cauldron of a brutal and bloody civil war in which thousands upon thousands of innocent Angolans who had no interest in (or knowledge of) the superpower machinations of the Cold War would lose their lives and limbs and millions more would become refugees and from which only now, close to three decades following the 1974 Portuguese coup, the country is beginning to emerge.[11]

Following a gunfight with the Angolan government forces in February 2002 in which the UNITA leader, Jonas Savimbi, lost his life, the Angolan government and the UNITA rebels managed to declare a ceasefire a few months later and brought to an end the terrible and senseless conflict that had engulfed their country. The fact that it took the death of one man for this to come to pass is in itself telling: quite often in Africa it takes only the megalomaniacal ambitions of just one person—but almost always supported by external actors—to sustain or even precipitate a brutal conflict. The relative peace in Angola (the armed conflict in Cabinda led by Frente de Libertacao do Estado de Cabinda [FLEC] has not yet abated), as of this writing, continues to hold.[12]

Mozambique

Meanwhile, on the other side of the continent a similar conflagration would engulf Mozambique but for slightly different reasons, though the principal actors would still include the United States and the apartheid government (though not the USSR or Cuba).[13] There were four basic factors that made Mozambique a prime target for the Cold War machinations of the ultra-right wing in Washington and the racist machinations of apartheid Pretoria (subsumed under the former's policy of *constructive engagement* and the latter's policy of *total strategy*): (a) Ideologically the Mozambican government was perceived to be a "communist" government; therefore it was concluded (erroneously) that it was a pawn of the Soviet Union and hence an enemy of the United States and South Africa.[14] (b) Capitalists in the United States and South Africa were very unhappy with Mozambique's desires to pursue an economic development path that required not only maintaining contacts with both the communist countries and the Western countries (nonalignment), but one that also entailed extensive state participation in the economy. With regard to the latter aspect, Mozambique's former colonial ruler too, Portugal, was particularly incensed because it meant that the Portuguese were no longer free to exploit Mozambique as they pleased. (c) Mozambique, like other most other independent African countries in the region and in keeping with the spirit and requirements of the U.N. charter, was naturally friendly toward the African National Congress (ANC), sharing its goal of seeing a nonracist majority-ruled South Africa emerge someday; ergo it permitted ANC members to live in Mozambique (though until 1981 the ANC was not permitted to have an open diplomatic presence in the country). While it is not true that the ANC had any military training bases in Mozambique at any time, as the apartheid government would claim, it is probable that Mozambique would later, in the period 1981–1984, turn a blind eye to transit of ANC personnel through the territory. (d) Mozambique was a critical linchpin in an economic organization that South Africa (and to some extent the United States too) found particularly troublesome: the Southern African Development Coordination Conference (SADCC). The SADCC was formally founded on April 1, 1980, in Lusaka and would come to comprise the countries of Angola, Botswana, Lesotho, Malawi, Mozambique, Swaziland, Tanzania, Zambia, and Zimbabwe. To the apartheid government the founding of the SADCC was a major setback for its own efforts to form a rival regional economic organization that it called Constellation of Southern African States (CONSAS), which would have been made up of the South African homelands and most of the SADCC members. The formation and success of CONSAS was of vital importance to South Africa from the perspective of its policy of total strategy; this is because not only would it have permitted it to derive major economic benefits from an intensification of its historical domination of the economically weaker states in the southern African region, but it would have also reaped major political benefits, such as: (i) blunting the international call for sanctions against South Africa (since such sanctions would also, indirectly, make the CONSAS members unfair targets); (ii) giving it greater leverage over the member states to dissuade them from assisting liberation movements like the ANC; and (iii) providing a basis for a tacit accommodation by the member states of the apartheid system. However, with the birth of the SADCC, apartheid government hopes for CONSAS were dashed; for, the SADCC was specifically formed in order to, among other objectives, reduce and perhaps someday eliminate the historically rooted economic links with apartheid South Africa.

Initially, says Hanlon (1986: 135–36), South Africa's response to Mozambique's independence on September 7, 1974, was one of confusion: the defense minister (at that time P. W. Botha) ordered an invasion of Mozambique in support of an uprising by the Portuguese settlers (the principal white minority) in Mozambique who did not wish to see blacks, especially FRELIMO that had waged a successful guerrilla war against them, rule the country. However, the head of the apartheid government's bureau of state security (BOSS), H. J. Van den Berg, acting on orders from Prime Minister Vorster, intervened and prevented the invasion from taking place. Explanation for this extraordinary, but for Mozambique very fortunate, turn of events rests, it appears, on two factors according to Hanlon: first was that Vorster did not wish to jeopardize his efforts to continue his dialogue with independent African countries that was under way (e.g., in 1974 he would visit the Ivory Coast, in 1975 Liberia and also in the same year he would meet President Kaunda of Zambia); and second Van den Berg was under the mistaken impression that the Portuguese government would use its troops in Mozambique to defend it against the invasion. Thereafter, for five years (1975–1980), South Africa seems to have left Mozambique relatively in peace. It, however, did continue to provide military and other assistance to Ian Smith of Rhodesia in his efforts to destabilize Mozambique because FRELIMO was providing sanctuary and logistical support to the ZANU guerrillas fighting for Zimbabwean independence. In 1980, however, circumstances changed and Mozambique would henceforth become a victim of widespread persistent and savage aggression, targeted specifically at the defenseless Mozambican peasant population (and reminiscent in its awful brutality of the Nazi German treatment of Jews and other minorities) via surrogates masterminded by the apartheid government.

What had changed? One, the SADCC was formed. Two, Ronald Reagan came to power in Washington and launched his right-wing supported policy of constructive engagement. Three, Botha was now the prime minister and would begin implementing the total strategy plan with zeal. Four, Zimbabwe became independent with a government led by a group that Europeans in southern Africa had hated and despised: Robert Mugabe's ZANU-PF. This last event was of crucial importance in two ways: (a) the apartheid government considered Zimbabwe a hostile country and therefore any efforts by Zimbabwe to weaken the strong economic chains, inherited from the Smith regime, that linked it to South Africa (via which the apartheid government could exert pressure on it whenever the need arose) was going to be met with resistance from the apartheid government; and (b) it enabled the apartheid government to acquire a surrogate terrorist group—which it would eventually nurture to a level where it would become an uncontrollable monster—to use against Mozambique: the so-called Mozambique National Resistance (MNR or RENAMO).

Before going on to look at this terrorist group, it should be noted that the apartheid government's aggression against Mozambique took, as in Angola, both forms: aiding and abetting its surrogate, as well as through direct action of its own. Hence, for example, with reference to the latter, on January 31, 1981, as if to celebrate the coming to power of Reagan in Washington, apartheid government commandos (including mercenaries) attacked a number of ANC houses in a residential neighborhood of Maputo called Matola, killing thirteen ANC members and a Portuguese civilian. It turned out that the raid was carried out with the cooperation of not only the CIA, but some high-level Mozambican government officials too—including a member of FRELIMO's Central Committee—who presumably were in the pay of the CIA and apartheid government security agents (Hanlon 1986: 136). Thereafter, the apartheid government continued to carry out commando raids on a recurring basis against the ANC (including very specific targeted murders, such as in the case of Ruth First, a highly respected professor teaching at Eduardo Mondlane University, who was assassinated via a parcel bomb on August 17, 1982), and Mozambican infrastructural facilities: bridges, railroads, oil storage facilities, and ports. Even though these raids were in their own right destructive of both lives and property and psychologically highly debilitating (for, they pointed out Mozambique's inability to defend itself against this unprovoked flagrant, arrogant and illegal apartheid government aggression), compared to the devastation that Mozambique would be subjected to indirectly by the apartheid government via its terrorist surrogate the MNR in subsequent years, they were mere pin-pricks (or in Hanlon's words: "really a sideshow in South Africa's undeclared war on FRELIMO" (1986: 139).

Who or what then was the MNR? The MNR was initially a creature of the Rhodesian Central Intelligence Organization (CIO); though it would receive from time to time cooperation from the apartheid government in running the MNR. It was formed in 1974 by Ian Smith's European minority regime to harass both ZANU and FRELIMO guerrillas, and after independence in Mozambique, the FRELIMO government. The actual deal that led to the creation of the MNR took place between the CIO director-general, Ken Flower, and the head of the infamous Portuguese security police, PIDE (International Police for the Defense of the State), Silva Pais, in Lisbon in late April 1974. Thereafter, on June 2, the first contingent of the soon to be mercenaries from Mozambique arrived in Rhodesia led by Oscar Cardoso. However, most of them would leave for greener pastures within a year: they left to join the FNLA in ZAIRE where CIA largess promised better pay. It was not until June 1976, however, when an escapee from an open rural prison at Sacuze in Mozambique—a former FRELIMO officer by the name of Andre Matade Matsangaiza convicted of stealing a Mercedes Benz automobile—that the CIO was able to make headway in its efforts to create the MNR.[15]

Specifically, the purpose behind MNR's creation was to use it as a fifth column and to gather intelligence for the Rhodesian intelligence services in respect of ZANU guerrillas operating out of Mozambique—as well as act as a "cat's paw" (to borrow Hanlon's term) for the Rhodesian Army. Initially, the MNR comprised people who had been part of special commando units set up by the Portuguese to terrorize the civilian population in areas where FRELIMO operated, as well as to carry out specific actions against FRELIMO itself. These people had fled Mozambique to Rhodesia in 1974, either because they were unwilling to live under a FRELIMO government or because they feared retribution for their savagery from those of their victims who were still alive. The MNR would remain in Rhodesian hands only until 1980 when Rhodesia became independent. Thereafter the MNR was transferred into the hands of the apartheid government, with grave consequences for Mozambique. For, by the time the apartheid government took direct charge of the MNR, FRELIMO had, by and large, secured the safety of the country from MNR's activities. With the apartheid government in charge, however, this situation would not last for long.

The apartheid government changed the mission and character of the MNR with devastating results for Mozambique: whereas before its purpose had been limited, henceforth it would be used specifically to terrorize and destabilize Mozambique on an unimaginable scale. At the same time, given the much greater resources at its command, the apartheid government was able to expand the MNR into a potent terrorist machine. Hence as the group began to operate in Mozambique under the direction of the apartheid government after 1980, it was enlarged by additions of various types of recruits: (a) villagers forcibly press-ganged into the group; (b) recalcitrant inmates of FRELIMO re-education camps (open rural prisons); (c) corrupt FRELIMO petty officers, "many of whom," says Hanlon (1986: 139), "had been detained because they believed that after a decade in the bush, they had an automatic right to take cars, houses, and women"; (d) illegal Mozambican migrant workers in South Africa, given the choice of joining the MNR or face imprisonment; and (e) discontented villagers who had become victims of FRELIMO's state authoritarianism in the countryside (e.g., those who had been forcibly grouped to live in villages set up by FRELIMO as part of its villagization program—designed to accelerate rural development, at least that was the intent).

Right from its inception then, the MNR was primarily a group of disparate antisocial malcontents (leaving aside those forcibly recruited).[16] In other words, they were simply terrorists; they were not freedom fighters, as ultra-right-wing Reaganites, for example, would claim. This explained why they would fail to develop a coherent political program or resolve their endemic leadership crises—which have included unexplained murders of leaders, such as Christina, the Bomba brothers, and Fernandes—or why their targets, as years went by, became primarily civilians (many of them women and children).[17]

Sometime in late 1980, the MNR began to establish bases in central Mozambique, which the apartheid government supplied with tons of material (weapons, food, clothing, etc.) via air drops at night. Material was also supplied by sea; boats would come to isolated beaches and drop off supplies for the MNR to pick up. Reinforced with the support of the apartheid government (including military advice and technical assistance) the MNR would begin a series of campaigns at the apartheid government's behest to destroy not only the transportation infrastructure crucial to the SADCC, but also the economy of Mozambique. Hanson provides a glimpse of the kinds of activities that the apartheid government got the MNR to undertake in Mozambique:

In three years, ninety-three locomotives and 250 wagons were destroyed or damaged; 150 rail workers were killed. South Africa also wanted to paralyze the Mozambican economy by disrupting transport. Roads as well as railways were mined, and traffic attacked. In dozens of horrific massacres, MNR guerrillas derailed trains and wrecked buses, then shot at the passengers as they climbed from the wreckage and burned the vehicles with the wounded still inside. Hundreds of private cars, vans and lorries were also attacked... . The MNR burned peasant grain stores and mined roads. It destroyed 900 rural shops in 1982 and 1983. In 1982 alone the MNR burned 140 villages, destroyed 102 medical centers and rural health posts, and destroyed or forced the closure of 489 primary schools. Teachers were often a special target; many were killed or had their ears hacked off (1986: 141).

To make matters worse for Mozambique, it was hit by the most severe drought in living memory in the northern and central regions beginning in 1980 and extending all the way into 1984. The drought, which in 1984 in the south would be accompanied by devastating floods, coupled with the terrorist activities of the MNR that disrupted the means of distributing food meant that thousands upon thousands died of starvation, and thousands more became refugees pouring across the borders into Malawi, Zimbabwe, and even South Africa! By 1984 the situation Mozambique was facing was one of a desperate nationwide crisis. The 400 years of neglect by the Portuguese culminating in a guerrilla war extending over a decade, the fact that during the period 1975 to 1980 Mozambique was the target of incessant destabilizing activities of the Rhodesian forces (while using the MNR as a front), and the renewed MNR activities from 1980 onward within the context of a severe drought, would all combine to produce a situation of near total military and economic collapse. The following quotes that appear in Cammack (1987: 71–73) provide a glimpse of the horror that had befallen the rural civilian population.

[A survivor of an MNR atrocity recounted:] Ten [MNR] men came to our village and left with all our food. They returned that night, handcuffed our husbands and made them lie on the ground. They crushed their heads with mealie [corn] grinders. The women and children of the village were forced to watch the killings: 19 men were killed. We were not allowed to bury the dead, but were forced to carry the bundles of looted goods to the

[MNR] camp ....[A report in the British newspaper, the *Financial Times* of March 23, 1987, describing the condition of the MNR-ravaged Mozambique stated:] "The victims of the war... are malnourished, widowed, raped, mutilated, terrorized and shocked. The children are the worse. A Mozambican can survive on eating roots and berries, but at what level of existence? The people had lost dignity. They have lost land. They have no cloths, no cooking pots, no soap. They wear tree bark, they go nude, especially in the north. Children don't go to school because they have no cloths. Women hide in their homes because they have nothing to cover themselves."

The MNR objective was threefold: to cut Mozambique in half, facilitate a seaborne supply route to MNR forces, and provide a greater level of claims to international legitimacy by pointing to its holding of "liberated" territory. Access to any international legitimacy by the MNR would have greatly helped friends of the apartheid government and the MNR working on their behalf in Washington, such as the ultra-right-wing groups like the Heritage Foundation and the Conservative Action Foundation, to garner more support for the MNR. In fact such "upright, freedom and democracy loving" citizens as Gordon James (of the Heritage Foundation) and Bonner Cohen (of Conservative Action), their consciences untroubled in the least bit by the horribly evil and barbaric nature of the MNR monster that the apartheid beast had produced, had already begun to lobby Congress for direct U.S. aid to the MNR along the lines extended to UNITA in Angola. To make matters worse for Mozambique, in 1986 the MNR opened a lobbying office in Washington located in the Heritage Foundation building; in charge was not a Mozambican but a U.S. citizen by the name of Thomas Schaaf. His lobbying efforts would bear some fruit: for example the 1988 presidential candidate and Republican Senate leader, Bob Dole, would become an MNR supporter, as would nearly thirty or so other senators.[18]

Yet despite all the dastardly subversive efforts of the apartheid government and the United States, the situation in Mozambique by the end of the Reagan presidential term, from the perspective of the objectives of total strategy and constructive engagement, was clearly far less than satisfactory. If the objective of the Reaganites and the apartheid government had been to either replace FRELIMO with the MNR, or at the minimum to get it to share power with the MNR, then in this they had failed. The combined efforts of FRELIMO, the Zimbabweans, and the Tanzanians would roll back the gains made by the MNR in many parts of the country—albeit not completely. If, however, the objective had been to open Mozambique up to foreign (Western and South African) capitalist penetration then in this they succeeded—but at what cost! Thousands upon thousands of lives lost (not to mention the thousands more injured and thousands more rendered refugees) and the economy in such disarray that foreign capitalists would not find it worthwhile to invest on a scale they would have liked to. (In this sense, the destabilization policy had worked against the interests of both South African and Western capital—at least in the short term.)

In any case there is nothing to suggest that the Mozambicans would not have, on their own, without external interference, moved in the direction of developing an economy that was open to foreign capitalist investment after witnessing the pitfalls of the Soviet economic model. If the objective was to "pluck Mozambique out of the Soviet orbit" then, in truth, Mozambique was never in the Soviet orbit: in fact its relation with the Soviet Union had generally been a strained one. Right from the beginning FRELIMO had always had relations with many different countries: China, the USSR, and other eastern European countries and many Scandinavian and Western European countries. If the objective was to get Mozambique to expel the ANC then in this they had succeeded. If the objective was to destroy the SADCC then in this they failed, though of course they did manage to weaken it considerably; but again, given the level of infrastructural destruction, this had not been in the best interests of South African and foreign capital.

Peace would not come to Mozambique until 1994 when a combination of war weariness and the arrival of freedom in South Africa would propel the belligerents toward some form of compromise: the freedom fighter and the terrorist would hesitantly turn to the ballot box to settle disputes. A fragile peace continues to hold in Mozambique as of this writing.

Against the backdrop of the foregoing, then, as would be expected, educational development has not been where it ought to be, considering that the two countries have been self-governing for more than two decades—though Mozambique has fared a little better because armed conflict in that country ended, mercifully, in 1994. Still, universities now exist in both countries. In Angola, the original University of Luanda became the University of Augustinho Neto in 1985. It has campuses in Huango and Lubango as well. Similarly in Mozambique, the University of Laurenco Marques became in 1976, the Eduardo Mondlane University Maputo. Mozambique also boasts two other public higher education institutions: the Higher Institute for International Relations, and Pedagogical University (see Mario 2003, and Teferra and Altbach 2003).

As for Portugal's other two former colonies, tiny Guinea-Bissau, and even tinier Sao Tome and Principe, they do not have universities. Guinea-Bissau, however, does have a number of teacher training colleges.

THE BELGIAN COLONIES

The transformation in 1908 of the Congo Free State from a personal fiefdom of Belgian's King Leopold II, following an international outcry against the horrors perpetrated by his agents on the Congolese people, to a Belgian colony (renamed Belgian Congo) meant that a modicum of support for educational development in the Congo, in cooperation with the missionaries, was now assured. The educational policy that the Belgians pursued was based on the idea that all administrative posts were to be held by Belgians, therefore the primary purpose of education was to provide vocational training for the Congolese. The only ones who were to have access to literary education were the select few chosen for priesthood. Following the Second World War, a slight change in policy was made with the implementation of an academic oriented curricula at the secondary-level, and, of more relevance here, the establishment of the Lovanium University Center in 1949 in Kinshasha. The center, a few years later, was upgraded to become the overseas campus of the Catholic University of Louvain in Belgium in 1954.

The Protestant missionaries, who through out the missionary presence in Congo had taken on the role of rivals to the French missionaries, refused to be outdone and proceeded to establish their own higher education institution, the University of Kisangani, in 1955. Demands by the Congolese that higher education should not be the exclusive preserve of religious bodies led to the creation of a state-sponsored university in 1956: University of the Belgian Congo and Ruanda-Urundi (after independence to become the State University of Lumumbashi). As in the case of institutions in British and French colonial Africa, governance of all three universities was based in the metropole, involving Belgium universities.

The star of all the higher education institutions, by the time independence came to the Congo, was without doubt Lovanium. Lovanium, as (Ashby 1966: 359) observes, was designed by its founders to be a mini-clone of Louvain in almost all respects. One positive outcome of this approach was that Lovanium, like the Asquith colleges, took an uncompromising position on the matter of quality and standards, thereby vindicating the position of the Africans that they were just as intellectually capable as people in the metropole. In the early 1960s, the academic status of Lovanium could be described thus: "In quality of teaching, in standard of achievement demanded for graduation, in content and range of curriculum, in the amount and sophistication of its research work, Lovanium stands very high indeed among African universities. It combines the prime virtue of the Asquith colleges—insistence on a high standard of achievement—with the prime virtue of the American university—a broad-based education which incorporates indigenous material into the undergraduate curriculum" (Ashby 1966: 362). (It ought to be noted here in passing, that it is somewhat paradoxical, that whatever racist views the colonial countries had toward the African peoples in the their colonies, these views were not permitted to compromise by one iota the demand that the universities and colleges they had transplanted in their colonies live up to or even excel the academic quality and standards of the metropolitan universities. To their credit, the Africans willingly obliged.)

Independence came to Belgian Congo on June 30, 1960, quickly and unexpectedly in that the Belgians had neither planned for it nor were the Congolese ready for it. Perhaps, not surprisingly, the country would quickly fragment and descend into a civil war as different groups within this huge and ethnically highly diverse country jockeyed for power (aided and abetted by various external players, including foreign commercial interests, the Belgians themselves, the United States, the former Soviet Union, and so on).[19] Political instability would last for almost five years culminating in a military coup on November 25, 1965 that would bring to power a corrupt, kleptocratic, and blood-soaked dictatorship—led by the strongman Colonel Joseph Mobutu (who would later, in 1970, rename the country Zaire and himself as Mobutu Sese Seko) and externally supported by, among others, the United States. His despotic rule would last until 1997, when as a result of another civil war that would consume the lives of thousands upon thousands of civilians in demonic massacres, a new regime would come to power under the leadership of Laurent-Desire Kabila, while Zaire would be renamed Democratic Republic of the Congo. As of this writing the civil war has yet to end, and to make matters worse, at one point it had drawn into it armed forces from the neighboring countries of Angola, Namibia, Rwanda, Uganda, and Zimbabwe.[20]

Given this awful postindependence history, one needs hardly any imagination to realize that the development of higher education, like almost every other aspect of civil society, would suffer enormous setbacks. In fact, the spiral downwards began as early as April 1969 when students demonstrated against the government, resulting, a couple of years later, in the closure of Lovanium University in June 1971 for two years (following attempts by students to commemorate the 1969 demonstrations), and the conscription of the entire student body into the army! That year also saw the creation of a federated university system, National University of Zaire, incorporating the three existing universities and some seventeen institutes of technology, teacher training, and so on. This move enabled the infiltration of almost all aspects of university governance with elements of government bureaucracy and Mobutu's political party machine (Ngobassu 1973). Under the weight of overstretched logistics in a huge country with poorly developed communication and transport resources, the federated system did not last for long: for, ten years later in 1981, it fractured into its constituent units, with each reclaiming its university status. However, the National University was retained as a bureaucratic apparatus to coordinate higher education in the country.

Besides Belgian Congo, the Belgians had also ruled the small, but densely populated neighboring territory of Ruanda-Urundi that they had inherited from the Germans as trust territories. As in the Congo, educational provision in Ruanda-Urundi was left primarily in the hands of the Catholic missionaries. Local higher education opportunity for the very select few came only with the creation of the University of the Belgian Congo and Ruanda-Urundi. (Lovanium would also become available for students from Ruanda-Urundi.) In 1960, however, a truly local institution was established with the founding of the University of Ruandi-Urundi in Usumbura with all of two departments (agronomy and applied science) and an enrollment of thirty students.

In 1962 this territory became independent with the creation of two countries: Rwanda and Burundi. A year later, the National University of Rwanda was founded in Butare, while Burundi had already acquired its own university, the University of Burundi in Bujumbura in 1960. Given the presence of centuries old ethnic rivalry between the minority Nilo-Hamitic overlords, the Tutsi, and the majority Bantu peoples, the Hutu (upon whom the Tutsi had imposed a feudal system when they invaded the territory in the fifteenth-century), it is, perhaps, not surprising that both countries have experienced genocidal conflagrations of mind-numbing proportions. (Of course, colonialism did not help matters because it entrenched the ethnic divisions.) The latest to occur was in Rwanda beginning in 1994 when it is estimated that more than half a million Tutsi were either shot or more often butchered to death with pangas by the Hutu militias. Peace of some sort has been restored by the Tutsi rebel dominated government that came to power following military victory by the rebels—they had operated out of neighboring countries following the massacres.

In Burundi, one of the largest massacres occurred in 1963 against the Hutu by the Tutsi. A few years later, in 1972, yet another massacre was visited upon the Hutus when they tried to rebel against the Tutsi dominated government; an estimated 100,000 would be killed. In 1988, a much smaller number, but still in the thousands, would perish once more at the hands of the Tutsi-dominated military. (For more on the politics of the two countries see Gourevitch 1998, Huband 2001, Mamdani 2001, and Prunier 1995.)

Added to the barbaric genocidal carnage, there have been, as one would expect, accompanying movements of refugees in the millions. Yet many of them too would not escape death at the hands of various factions infiltrating their camps or ambushing them as they escaped—not to mention the fatal diseases and hunger that would also plague them. Given these endemic and horrific conflagrations, all forms of education, including higher education, would come to periodic standstill, in both countries. In sum: although meaningful progress had been achieved in building up the universities in the 1980s in both countries, it is only in the past few years that the situation in Rwanda has begun to improve once more, while in Burundi, it is only a little better.

THE ITALIAN COLONIES

Of all the post–World War II European colonial powers, the Italians, because of their relative weakness, as well as their gross error in placing themselves on the wrong side of history during the war, appear to have had the least influence in Africa (expressed, for instance, in their early exit from Ethiopia and Eritrea). There is one part of Africa, however, where the legacy of their presence was sufficiently strong enough to warrant their inclusion in this chapter; that place is Somalia. (Though it may be legitimate, perhaps, to also include Libya in this regard, but that country has already been discussed elsewhere—see Chapter 3.) In Somalia, it is the Italians who planted the first seeds of Western secular higher education that would lead, in time, to the development of that country's first and only national university. The rest of this chapter, therefore, will be devoted to Somalia (given especially its current circumstances).

Somalia is located on the northeast edge of the continent that faces Arabia, and which is commonly referred to as the Horn—for obvious reasons, as one look at a map of Africa will reveal. The country stretches first eastward from Djibouti (once part of Somali domain) along the perimeter of the Horn and then goes down south along the east coast of Africa to the Kenyan border, forming the shape of the Arabic numeral seven. In other words, it is located in a part of Africa that is steeped in ancient history. The Greeks, for instance, knew of its existence (Herodotus mentions it in Book 2 of his *Histories*, albeit in passing), for they traded along its coast, as did many others (Arabs, Indians, Chinese, and so on).[21] The ancient Egyptians referred to it as the "Land of Punt" (God's Land). After all, it is among the Mediterranean lands from whence came the aromatic arboreal gum resins, frankincense and myrrh (highly prized, to the perplexity of modern medical science, by the ancients throughout the Afro-Eurasian ecumene)—and still does to this day—not to mention such other much-sought-after commodities as ivory, ostrich feathers, and clarified butter *(ghee).*[22]

However, a rich past rooted in ancient history is no antidote to a chaotic and anarchic present that characterizes, to put it in mildest terms, present-day Somalia as of this writing (2005). Somalia fell apart in 1991; it has yet to become whole again. Here are two accounts, one written in 1992, and the other in 2005, that provide some idea of the tragedy that is Somalia today.

Nineteen ninety-one is the year Somalia died. Since the full-scale civil war broke out on November 17, at least 14,000 people have been killed and 27,000 wounded in the capital city of Mogadishu. Most of the casualties are civilians. Rivalry between the forces of two ruthless men—interim President Mohammed Ali Mahdi and General Mohammed Farrah Aidid, both of whom belong to the same clan and the same movement, the United Somali Congress (USC)—has made Mogadishu an exceptionally dangerous place. In addition to troops loyal to both men, hundreds of armed "freelance" soldiers and looters contribute to the violence....Mogadishu and south-central Somalia also face the worst famine in the country's history. Drought has played only a minor role in this crisis. The famine, which has already begun, is largely man-made, the result of warfare during the past two years (Omaar 1992: 230).

A blast has killed at least 14 people and injured 30 at a rally in a football stadium in Somalia's capital being addressed by the prime minister. The explosion went off as Ali Mohammed Ghedi began his speech. He later told the BBC that a security guard had accidentally set off a grenade. Mr Ghedi, on his first Mogadishu visit since being appointed, is negotiating his government's return from exile....The transitional government, which is based in Nairobi in neighboring Kenya, is under pressure from foreign donors to relocate to Somalia. But Somalia's political leaders and warlords are divided over where in Somalia the administration should be based. Somalia has been devastated by 14 years of war. While the interim constitution names Mogadishu as the capital, the city is considered the most dangerous place in Somalia....Most of the city's government buildings are in ruins, or are inhabited by refugees after 14 years of anarchy....As many as 10,000 regional peacekeepers are due to start arriving in the next few weeks to provide security for the government. But some local warlords, who have been named as ministers, remain opposed to their deployment (source: www.BBC.com—the news story, "Blast Strikes Somali PM's Rally," is dated May 3, 2005).

The relevant historical antecedents of this awful circumstance, therefore, where Somalia is considered today as an example par excellence of a failed state, must be considered here, but only in barest outline for reasons of space.[23] To begin with, a note on the Somali people—an Eastern Cushitic (Afro-Asiatic family) language speaking people. They are thought to have spread either from the south going north or from the north moving south (or both) over a period of hundreds of years, beginning perhaps in the first half of the last millennium, into a region that at one point by the early twentieth century had been forcibly carved up among the French (French Somaliland), the Ethiopians (the Ogaden), the British (British Somaliland in the north and the Northern Frontier District of Kenya in the south), and Italy (Italian Somaliland).

While the Somali are a *relatively* homogenous people, with the exception of the interriverine minority in the south between the Shabeelle and the Jubba Rivers, sharing the same language and culture, their interaction with a harsh desert environment with episodic rainfall that comprises most of their lands of habitation (with the exception of the interriverine area), led to the development of a segmentary society—as a logical outcome of a culture in which nomadic pastoral transhumance has been the central ecological response to this environment. This society was marked not only by the distinct absence of a central governing authority, *but also by an allegiance of the individual and his/her family to fiercely competitive territorially-based subclans, clans, and clan-families* with lineages going back centuries, as a means, at the minimum, of "negotiating" access to water and pasturage, and best captured by these two Somali proverbs (from Cassanelli 1982: 21): "If you love a person, love him moderately, for you do not know whether you will hate him one day; on the other hand, if you hate someone, hate him moderately also, for you do not know whether you will love him one day."

I and my clan against the world.
I and my brother against the clan.
I against my brother.

At the same time, the varied mode of transmission of the Islamic religion to the Somali people over the centuries, perhaps beginning as early as in the eighth century, if not even in the seventh, involving itinerant "saints" with their diverse and competitive Islamic Orders *(tariiqas)* considerably dampened the integrating influence of Islam at the political level. Ergo, even though almost all Somali people claim adherence to Sunni Islam and believe, perhaps mythically, that they are all descended from the Quraishi clan of Prophet Muhammed, their membership of the *ummah* has done little to encourage the Somalis to submerge their clannish divisions, except on those few occasions in history when faced with an external enemy—as at the time of their struggle with the Ethiopians in the sixteenth century under the leadership of Imam Ahmed ibn Ibrahim al-Ghazi (nicknamed by the Ethiopian Christians, Ahmed the Gran—see Chapter 2) when they almost wiped out the Ethiopian state, and in the early twentieth century while resisting British colonial rule under the leadership of Shaykh Muhammed ibn Abd'Allah Hassan (nicknamed by the British, the "Mad Mullah") of the Ogaadeen clan. (See Cassanelli 1982 for more on this issue.)

By the time of its colonization in the nineteenth century, quite unusually for Africa, Somalia was already a unified "nation" given its territorially-based ethnically and culturally homogenous population (excluding the Gosha living in the interriverine area who at one time had been enslaved by the Somali—see Besteman [1999]). However, colonization meant the forcible dismemberment, against the wishes of the Somali, of the lands of the Somali nation. Those involved were no less than five: the Ethiopians, specifically Menelik II, following his defeat of the Italians at the Battle of Adwa in 1896, who established claims over the Ogaden (the western part of Somalia); the French, beginning in 1862, who went on to establish French Somaliland by colonizing the northwestern portion of Somalia on the Red Sea (today the tiny independent country of Djibouti), the Italians who began their forays into Somalia in 1869, the Egyptians who arrived in 1870 to take over Bullaxaar and Berbera on the Red Sea; and finally the British who took over the area adjacent to Aden between 1884 and 1886 (by which time the Egyptians had vacated the ports following the Mahdist revolt in Sudan) to give rise to British Somaliland, and in the south they took control of a portion that they eventually incorporated into Kenya in 1895 (the Northern Frontier District).

The final outcome of the various maneuverings of these different rivals over the lands of the Somali over the course of nearly a century, extending into the post–World War II era (involving machinations at the United Nations of not only the old colonial rivals, but also the newly emergent superpowers, the United States and the Soviet Union), is that by the time Somalia gained independence in 1960 from the British and the Italians—the latter had been allowed to return to southern Somalia by the United Nations in 1950 to oversee Somali's U.N.-mandated decade-long passage to independence—it was beset with two major encumbrances. One was the fragmentation of the Somali people as a result of the permanent loss of some of their smaller territories to Kenya and Djibouti on one hand, and on the other, the much larger western territory of the

Ogaden to Ethiopia; and the other was the fusion of the remaining two halves of the country with radically different colonially-determined political, economic, linguistic, and administrative cultures in which the southern half under the control of the Italians was, interestingly (considering Italy's parlous economic circumstance relative to that of Britain's), much more advanced than the northern half administered by the British. Unlike the Italians, the British had never had much enthusiasm for their Somali colony, seeing it only as an adjunct to their main colonial interest in Egypt and Aden.[24]

Now, writing sympathetically in 1982, the consequences of a legacy of such a history for the Somali people was described by Cassanelli when he presciently raised a number of very pertinent dilemmas that faced the new Somali state and which help to throw light on the present terrible predicament of the Somali people—for it is the failure to resolve these dilemmas that explains, to a considerable degree, this predicament:

How...does a government create an agriculturally self-sufficient society from a nation of nomads whose long struggle against the environment has proven time and again the resiliency of a pastoral existence? How can it sedentarize a population for whom regional mobility is an ingrained way of life? How are the proud descendants of once-powerful clans to be incorporated into the political leadership of a state determined to abolish "tribalism" and equalize opportunity? How is the deeply rooted but regionally focused tradition of Somali Islam to be marshaled in the creation of a modern socialist society? And how is the great legacy of Somali oral tradition to be preserved for posterity when some of its best examples consist of poetic diatribes by one clan's poets against members of another clan or region? (p. 261).

We may add yet one more important dilemma: How is the irredentist nationalism of a culturally and ethnically homogenous nation to be assuaged when world powers refuse to recognize the deeply felt legitimate desire of the Somali nation to reconstitute itself into a whole by bringing back the territories they lost to the various colonial projects? The effort to resolve these dilemmas, as we now know, eventually coalesced into a massive failure expressed in the total collapse of the Somali state into one of mayhem and anarchy. The critical events of *agency*—in contrast to those of *structures* of history just outlined—marking this path of failure include, first, the collapse of representative democracy under the weight of nepotism and corruption when the government of Prime Minister Muhammed Haji Ibrahim Egal was overthrown by the military in a coup led by Major General Muhammed Siad Barre on October 21, 1969, following the assassination of President Abdirashid Ali Shermarke some days earlier on October 15.[25]

The new military government would remain in power for the next two decades in which while it made some meaningful progress in bringing economic and social development to Somalia—at birth a country with the lowest per capita income in the world—including the successful introduction of a Latin-based orthography (against the ideological backdrop of yet another variant of African "socialism"), it also simultaneously began to sink into a virulent form of praetorian despotism, most especially in later years, characterized by an ever increasingly corrupt and nepotistic personality-cult-oriented governance.

To shore up his regime that was facing ever-mounting opposition from various clan-based Somali factions, in 1977, Siad Barre undertook a project dear to the hearts of most Somalis: launching an attack on Ethiopia in a bid to liberate the Ogaden. The attack, however, in the process provoked/encouraged a major realignment of the Cold War superpowers in the region. The United States was replaced by the Soviet Union as the ally of Ethiopia and the Soviet Union was replaced by the United States as the ally of Somalia. This realignment proved to be the undoing of the initially successful Ogaden project; whereas the United States was a lukewarm ally, the Soviet Union (assisted by Cuban soldiers) was quite the opposite. By early 1978 the Somali forces, who had managed to capture the Ogaden a year earlier were on the retreat, leaving in their wake thousands dead; and the country would be plunged into a massive economic crisis against the backdrop of a deeply parasitic militarized state budget dominating the economy.

The defeat of the Somali in the sands of the Ogaden at the hands of their former Cold War ally, further deepened the resolve of the various Somali opposition groups to work toward the armed ouster of Siad Barre as his popularity plummeted even further, most especially after he signed a peace-accord in 1988 with Ethiopia under Western pressure. The latter event provoked a civil war, beginning in the northern part of the country, as Somali guerrillas fighting the Ethiopians now turned their sights on Siad Barre's forces in one of a number of other developments (e.g. conflicts between Ogaden refugees and the local population in which the locals, the Isaak clan, came to believe that the Siad Barre regime was on the side of the refugees since his wife was an Ogaden). Thereafter one catastrophic event led to another unified by the theme of clan– and sub-clan– based armed violence in a country awash with armaments (acquired over decades from the Soviet Union, the United States, and others during the period of the Cold War), as each group sought to establish claims of hegemony over different parts of Somalia and different sectors of the capital, Mogadishu. As the civil war spiraled out of control, especially in 1990-91 (against the backdrop of international disinterest now that the Cold War was over with the collapse of the Soviet Union in 1991), famine began to stalk the land as food production and distribution was disrupted. The sight of thousands of starving children on television (against the backdrop of clan-based thugs looting food-relief supplies) *as Christmas approached* in the West proved too much for Western publics to bear. They put pressure on their governments to intervene.

In December 1992, a fairly sizeable multinational U.N.-approved military task force of some 30,000 soldiers, led by the United States, arrived in Somalia with the aim of bringing a modicum of order to the business of food distribution—the project was code named "Operation Restore Hope." At first greeted warmly by most Somalis, within about six months the mission was in tatters and by March of the following year (1994) the last of Western troops were withdrawn. Emblematic of the disaster that the mission had become, which it is estimated cost a total of some four billion dollars (amounting to roughly two whole year's income for each and every Somali), was the shooting down of a U.S. "Black Hawk" helicopter that led to the death of some eighteen marine soldiers (with many more injured) at the hands of the Somali, and the alleged involvement of Canadian soldiers in the torture/murders of Somali civilians.[26]

While this is not the place to go into the whys and wherefores of how one of those rare, truly well-intentioned missions of mercy ended in a massive military debacle, it will suffice to simply say, on the basis of hindsight (which is always 20/20) that at the heart of it was the failure to see that security preceded all else in the violent chaos that was Somalia where access to food itself was also a weapon of war among the combatants. The planners of "Operation Restore Hope" did not realize that the various Somali factions (who had steadily degenerated into pure warlordism) would force the militarization of what was essentially planned as a humanitarian famine relief operation; the planners were caught unprepared for this eventuality with disastrous consequences.[27]

It is against the backdrop of the foregoing that one may delineate the history of higher education in Somalia, and it should be obvious that it is a history that lends itself to periodization along four main avenues: the pre-colonial period; the colonial period; the pre-1991 postindependence period; and the post-1991 period. During the pre-colonial period the chief agency for the development of higher education in Somalia was Islam with its mosque-madrasahs as well as other places of higher learning—such as those found in Harar (now in Ethiopia), an important Somali Islamic center of higher learning. Since madrasahs have already been discussed elsewhere at some length in this work (see Chapter 1 and Appendix I) nothing more need be said further about them here.

During the colonial period our main focus must be when Somalia was handed back to the Italians as a trust territory, for in the pre-World War II era Italian Somaliland did not have any secular institution of higher learning (the same was true for British Somaliland). The Italy that came back to Somalia in 1950 was not the same Italy of the pre-War period (that is fascist Italy). The new Italy, a democratic Italy, was committed to preparing Somalia for independence as mandated by the United Nations. In this task educational development was considered by the United Nations as an important item on Italy's trusteeship agenda. Italy obliged by launching an educational development program that included at the higher education level the establishment of the Teacher Training Institute (opened in 1953), the School of Islamic Studies (opened in 1952), the School of Politics and Administration (opened in 1950-51), and the Higher Institute of Economics and Law (opened in 1954, with Padua University providing curricular guidance and logistical support). In 1960, the institute would become the University Institute of Somalia (and it would be affiliated with University of Rome which provided curricular guidance and logistical support). It ought to be noted that the U.N. trusteeship agreement did not require Italy to build *higher* education institutions within Somalia, but rather it was required to provide places for qualified Somalis at its universities in Italy. In this regard too, the Italians were forthcoming and they provided higher education opportunities for hundreds of Somali students, in Italy.

In British Somaliland of the post–World War II era, in stark contrast, there was practically no higher education comparable to that being developed by the Italians, other than a teacher training institute and one or two vocational schools. The principal determinant of this parsimony in educational provision appears to have been the decision by the British to govern British Somaliland as cheaply as possible. The principle that underlay the British approach to educational provision for the Somalis was spelled out in one of the Education Department's Annual Reports (for 1953): "Quite apart from the very strict limitations imposed by financial considerations on the rate and extent of the expansion of educational facilities, it is not intended at present to attempt to provide formal education on a very wide scale nor to make an attempt at mass literacy" (from Kitchen 1962: 97).

When independence came to Somalia, and especially after the military coup in 1969, the Somalis (like others elsewhere in Africa) proceeded to put vigorous energy into the development of the entire education sector. One outcome of this effort was the upgrading of the University Institute of Somalia to the status of a national university—thus was born the National University of Somalia in 1969 with six constituent colleges. It should be noted that while the university provided tuition-free education, the main beneficiaries were (as in most countries in Africa) the emerging urban-based elites and not the children of the vast majority of the Somalis, the rural poor. By the time of the overthrow of the Siad Barre regime, the university had grown to the point where it had an enrollment of over 15,000 students, spread out among twelve faculties of learning (ranging from law to industrial chemistry).

Turning now to the post-1991 period where higher education (as in the case of other levels of the education system) has been, until very recently, in almost complete state of collapse. Even as late as 1998, an observer of the educational circumstances of Somalia would have come up with a chilling description, as this one, by Abdi (1998: 327):

Since the collapse of the Somali state in January 1991, Somalia has been a country without any level of organized systems of learning. This is obviously the result of the division of the country into clan-based fiefdoms....In this process of social disintegration, schools, technical training centers and university facilities and resources became among the first casualties of the senseless mass destruction of the country's total infrastructure. The physical destruction of the facilities was, at times, peculiarly coupled with the targeting of the educated cadre among the warring factions. As a result, under-developed Somalia seems to have embarked on the treacherous road of de-development, defined in this sense as reversing the limited trend of development by deliberately de-stroying everything that could function in, and sustain a civil society.

Today, there is clear evidence that some heart-warming positive change is afoot, but it is taking place mainly through the initiative of private individuals. For instance, although the National University of Somalia no longer exists, a private secular not-for-profit university (the first of its kind in the history of Somalia) has replaced it in the guise of Mogadishu University.[28] The university, the brainchild of a group of former professors from the old university, opened for business in 1997, even in the absence of a functioning government (which says a great deal for the resolve and perseverance of its founders). Its financial base rests on both money and in-kind donations from the Somali diaspora and other international well-wishers (NGOs, universities, some governments, etc.), a trust fund, and student tuition. There are at present six faculties of learning: Shari'ah and law, education, math and physics, social science, arts and human sciences, economics and management sciences, computer science and informa-tion technology, and nursing. The language of instruction is English in the sci-ence and technology faculties, and Arabic in others. The student population in 2000 was less than 500. The university also has a graduate program (up to doc-toral level) offered in conjunction with Sudan's Omdurman Islamic University. The role of Mogadishu University is to host the program, while Omdurman is in charge of everything else, from admissions to provision of teaching staff to thesis supervision and final conferral of degrees.

Turning to the internationally unrecognized, but thriving (in relative terms) breakaway regions of Puntland and Somaliland in the north, there too there are significant signs of progress: they have started their own independent universi-ties as well. While Puntland appears to have only one, East Africa University, located in the port city of Bosasso and which commenced operations in 2003 (offering courses in subjects ranging from the Shari'ah to business studies), Somaliland has four: Amoud University in Borama (founded in 1998), Univer-sity of Hargeisa (opened its doors in 2000), Berbera University (established in 2004), and Burao University (commenced operations in 2005 at the site once occupied by a German-funded technical institute). As would be expected, all these institutions are essentially small shoe-string operations based on finances derived from varied ephemeral-type sources such as donations from the Somali diaspora and contributions from NGOs and U.N. agencies. Support has also come through in-kind donations (such as books and computer equipment) from well-wishers from abroad. Government funding for these institutions is ex-tremely limited; however, when Somalia reunites (possibly as a federated state) this hopefully should change.[29]

By way of concluding this section, we ought to consider, even if only briefly, an important question that the violent and cataclysmic breakdown of the Somali state raises: Had Somalia possessed a well-developed educational system, going all the way to university level, capable of providing quality education to anyone who qualified without regard to ability to pay (and thereby creating a large population of highly educated citizens), would Somalia still have collapsed in the way it did? The answer is not a difficult one to surmise: the presence of an educated population *in itself* does not guarantee a *vibrant* civil society, which is the only insurance against total anarchy that Somalia became from 1991 onwards. Yes, education is a prerequisite for the emergence of such a civil society, but it is not a sufficient condition. The examples of Nazi Germany, the former Soviet Union, the present-day China, and the former apartheid South Africa provide ample testimony to this fact. No matter how much faith educators may place in the broader liberatory and civilizing powers of education (formal or otherwise), there are limits to what it can do in the absence of conducive circumstances at the political level. Moreover, history shows us that even among the educated, tyrants have not been missing.

NOTES

1. "Indirect rule" refers to the type of colonial administrative practice that meaningfully relied, albeit at a lower administrative level, on indigenous (often traditional hereditary) rulers who had been allowed to retain nominal power over their subjects; "direct rule" was the obverse of this approach to colonial government. One may note here that in the case of acephalous societies where traditional rulers did not exist, *indirect rule* led to the imposition of artificially created "traditional" rulers.

One should remind the reader of another type of comparative approach to the study of European colonialism in Africa: comparing the internal differences in colonial practices among the colonies ruled by a given single colonial power: an especially fruitful exercise in Africa in the case of the two major colonial powers, the French and the English. For instance, the most obvious contrasts emerge between colonies that were targets of sustained European colonial settlement (e.g., Algeria and South Africa, for instance), and those that were not (e.g., Nigeria and Mali). (See the Chapter 1 for more on this point.)

2. From the perspective of French colonialism, the evolue were those colonial subjects who had demonstrated the potential to evolve toward a "civilized" condition (and thereby merit French citizenship) by the acquisition of modern education and French cultural patterns of behavior. Within the context of colonially inspired racism they were both a much despised group and a potential ally in the colonial project. In the movement toward the devolution of governmental authority (albeit circumscribed) in the colonies in the waning days of European colonialism in the aftermath of the Second World War, it is the evolue that the French hoped to enlist in this exercise. In the British colonial empire their equivalents, to give two examples, were the *educated natives* of Africa and the *babus* of India; while in the Portuguese colonies they were referred to as the *assimilado*. (Note: in time they would come to constitute Fanon's campradorial elite.)

3. The federation of French Equatorial Africa (Afrique Equatorial Francaise) was

established in 1910 with a federal government located in Congo-Brazzaville and subordinate governments in the other three West African French colonial territories: Gabon, Ubanghi-Shari, and Chad. The federation was disbanded in 1958 when the constituent territories gained independence.

4. The conference (of mainly French government and top French colonial officials) was called by the provisional French government of Charles de Gaulle to discuss the future of the French colonies (and which de Gaulle attended), primarily as a publicity stunt for international consumption. The Conference, therefore, it should be emphasized, did not mark the beginning of the end of French colonialism in Africa. On the contrary, and even though it was organized by the Afro-Caribbean governor of Chad, Felix Eboue (that is, a member of the African diaspora, even if a dyed-in-the wool francophile) and chaired by him, the conference insisted that "The ends of the civilizing mission accomplished in the colonies exclude any idea of autonomy, all possibility of evolution outside the French bloc; also excluded is the eventual establishment of self-government in the colonies, even in a distant future" (emphasis added; from Shipway 1999: 131–32). What the conference did do, however, was to discuss ways of humanizing French colonialism by making recommendations for social reforms (in such areas health, education, administrative efficiency, and so on).

5. The current circumstances of higher education in Ivory Coast are not clear (other than to assume the worse) given the ethnic-religious based civil war that erupted in that country beginning in 2002 that has left the country divided into two: a rebel-held north and a government forces-controlled south (see International Crisis Group [2005b] for an overview of the conflict).

6. Awareness of this difference between the nature of Portuguese colonialism and say British colonialism among Africans has prompted sentiments such as that expressed by a person from a former British African colony to the effect that if the European colonization of his country had been decreed by fate to be absolutely inevitable, then he was glad that it was the British and not the other European powers (e.g., Portugal, Spain, and Belgium) who had colonized his country.

7. For more information see Africa Information Service (1973); Davidson (1969); Hanlon (1984); and Munslow (1983).

8. Shortly after Mozambique became independent, it was the turn of the European minority regime of Ian Smith in Zimbabwe to give in as pressure began to mount from the guerrilla forces of ZANU operating out of the east and southeast with the assistance of the Mozambicans—alongside whom they had also fought when FRELIMO was opening the southern front in Mozambique. Zimbabwe would become independent in 1980.

9. These acronyms recur in this section: FRELIMO (Front for the Liberation of Mozambique); PAIGC (African Party for the Independence of Guinea Bissau and Cape Verde); MPLA (Movement for the Liberation of Angola) FNLA (National Front for the Liberation of Angola); and UNITA (National Union for the Total Independence of Angola).

Besides the sources already mentioned, this and the note that follows on the history of the three movements is based on the following sources: Bender (1981); Bloomfield (1988) Burchett (1978); Danaher (1985); Holness (1988), Ignatyev (1977) Kempton (1989), Klinghoffer (1980), Legum and Hodges (1978), Marcum (1969, 1978), Pomeroy

(1986), Stockwell (1978), and Wolfers and Bergerol (1983). The reader should be fore-warned that on some issues the sources are conflicting.

10. At this point a short of history of the three movements is necessary to facilitate greater understanding of the events to be described below.

MPLA. Founded in Kinshasa in December 1956 out of fusion of two clandestine Angolan organiza-tions, Party for the United Struggle of Angolan Africans (founded in 1953) and the Angolan Communist Party (founded in 1956) MPLA launched its first (amateurish) attack against the Portuguese on February 4, 1961. The target was to free a number of MPLA leaders arrested by the Portuguese months earlier (and sentenced in December 1960) for political offenses. They were being held in a prison in Luanda. Using mainly axes, clubs, and the like they attacked the prison but failed to free any prisoners. Instead the Portuguese not only successfully repelled the attack but began a brutal wave of repression involving indiscriminate arrests, torture, and murder of Angolans. (Considering that Portugal was at that time ruled by a dictatorship with little regard for civil and human rights of its own citizens, the response of the Portuguese au-thorities to political protests—even if nonviolent—in its African colonies was, as is to be ex-pected, traditionally one of severe brutality.) With this beginning, MPLA launched its military struggle against the Portuguese having learned through bitter experience that the Portuguese dictatorship did not leave any room for nonviolent strategies of change. (This political situa-tion, incidentally, was prevalent not only in the colonies, but in Portugal itself—hence the need for the military coup in 1974.)

FNLA. Founded in Kinshasa on March 28, 1962, out of the merger of the Union of Angolan People (formed in 1958 as the successor to the Union of the Peoples of Northern Angola founded the previous year) and the smaller ethnic-based Peoples Democratic Party. The leader of FNLA would be one Holden Roberto (alias: Jose Guilmore). Roberto developed links with the CIA very early on, probably from around 1959 when he visited New York, via, reportedly, the me-diation of George Houser of the American Committee on Africa.

UNITA On March 13, 1966, a former FNLA member by the name of Jonas Savimbi announced the formation of UNITA to be based in the southern part of Angola where he came from. While the reasons for Savimbi's defection two years earlier are not entirely clear, it appears that one of them was certainly his own personal ambition for power coupled with a genuine disillusion-ment with the leadership of Holden Roberto. That Savimbi himself was to become a power-hungry opportunist, in many respects no different from Roberto, would be demonstrated soon enough: he would strike an alliance with the Portuguese forces (instead of fighting them) in order to fight the MPLA. Observe also that there does not seem to be any record of Savimbi ever being politically active in his younger days in Angola before he left for overseas studies in Portugal and Switzerland. In fact, some African student contemporaries of his have alleged that even in Lisbon he was an informer for the notorious Portuguese security police, PIDE (Wolfers and Bergerol 1983: 194). While a student, Savimbi would acquire a taste for the "good life" (sex, song and alcohol) and build a reputation for being a playboy. He would find it impossible to abandon this lifestyle even after he had formed UNITA—he would pursue it in Zambia dur-ing the period when he would claim he was in the Angolan bush organizing his mythical resis-tance against the Portuguese (Wolfers and Bergerol 1983: 194; see also Minter 1988). Such ig-nominious treachery to the cause of the Angolan liberation struggle would come to light fol-lowing the discovery of documents in Lisbon (after the 1974 coup) showing correspondence between Savimbi and the Portuguese Army. (See Burchett 1978 for a flavor of this correspon-dence.) While it is not clear when exactly UNITA began to cooperate with the Portuguese it appears that it began very soon after its formation, probably around 1968/69. Given this his-tory, Is it surprising that UNITA would eventually join forces with the apartheid government (and the United States) in their joint effort to crush the MPLA?

In describing this short history of the three Angolan organizations, four key points should be noted: (a) Of the three groups, MPLA was without any doubt the only authentic liberation movement with the sole aim of freeing Angola from Portuguese colonialism. The other two groups may have been formed with the same goal, initially, but along the way their narrow ethnic-based interests misled them into directing their energy against the wrong enemy. (b) While all the three movements drew support from specific ethnic groups, MPLA was the only movement that from the very beginning had sought to incorporate all ethnic groups and who tended to see society less in terms of race and ethnicity than in terms of exploiters and the exploited, that is, class. It is not surprising that among the urban working class, MPLA was by far the most popular movement. FNLA and UNITA, in contrast, were essentially narrowly ethnic-based groups seeking to impose their domination on other groups, if and when they took charge of Angola upon the exit of the Portuguese. In fact, as already mentioned, FNLA's original mission (when it existed as the Union of the People of North Angola) was to seek an independent secessionist state based on the ancient Kongo kingdom (northern portion of Angola). Fortunately, the United States quietly told UPNA's representative in the United States, Holden Roberto, to drop the idea when he raised it with the U.N. secretary-general in 1956 on grounds that there would be almost no support for it within the international community (see Burchett 1978: 10). (c) If UNITA had compromised itself by seeking an alliance with the Portuguese colonial authorities, FNLA had also compromised itself very early on (around 1962) when its leader, Holden Roberto, became involved with the CIA. This is somewhat ironic considering that the United States was supporting the Portuguese colonialists, sometimes covertly (e.g., during the Kennedy/Johnson administrations), and sometimes overtly (during the Nixon administration.) (d) Among the principal external backers of the three movements prior to 1974 were as follows: MPLA was supported by Congo-Brazzaville, the OAU, Cuba, Soviet Union, and other Eastern bloc countries; FNLA was supported by Zaire, the OAU, China and the United States; and UNITA was supported by Zambia, Portugal, and possibly China.

11. The unconscionable and dastardly U.S. involvement in fomenting and prolonging the postindependence Angolan conflict began even before the 1974 Portuguese coup! While the MPLA was undergoing a serious internal factional crisis toward the end of 1973, the CIA had already begun to fund a forced recruiting drive for the FNLA in Kinshasa, to ready it to make a bid for power if and when the opportunity arose (Wolfers and Bergerol 1983: 4). Starting in July 1974 it semi-secretly increased its funding of Holden Roberto's activities, but without the knowledge of the so-called 40 Committee, an NSC group entrusted with the supervision of CIA covert activities. ("[S]mall amounts at first," explains Stockwell (1978: 67), "but enough for word to get around that the CIA was dealing itself into the race.") In the months ahead, the CIA, in close cooperation with its long-term Zairean ally that it had helped to install in power in 1965, a corrupt, heavily blood-stained dictator by the name of Mobuto Sese-Soko, would slowly escalate funds, and later, arms shipments to the FNLA. According to Stockwell (1978: 55), President Gerald Ford would authorize the expenditure of $6 million on July 16, 1975, and an additional $8 million on July 27—prior to these expenditures, the CIA had been authorized by the 40 Committee to give the FNLA $300,000 on January 22, 1975. (By November the CIA budget for Angola operations would reach

$31.7 million before it would attempt, unsuccessfully, to secure more funds from Congress [Stockwell 1978: 21].) It may be noted that because of deliberate false accounting procedures (e.g., undervaluing armaments), on the ground the CIA budget would be amplified almost three-fold. The first planeload of arms destined directly for the FNLA would leave the United States on July 29.

Emboldened by support from the CIA (and the Chinese), and acting in concert with Zairean troops, the FNLA eventually struck in February 1975. They poured into northern Angola occupying a number of key towns such as Ambriz and Uije (Carmona). They then launched a concerted attack against MPLA in the Luanda suburbs of Gazenga and Vila Alice followed by the murder on March 25, of some fifty MPLA recruits at Kifangondo, a place some twenty kilometers to the north of Luanda. Once the conflagration had begun there was now no stopping it. The MPLA struck back, supported by regular arms from the Soviet Union and technical expertise provided by Cuban military advisors flown in from Congo-Brazzaville. On July 12, the MPLA forces drove both FNLA and UNITA forces out of Luanda. Repeated efforts in succeeding months by FNLA forces based in the north, later supported by CIA-funded mercenaries recruited in the West (Portugal, France, Britain, and the United States), failed to capture Luanda.

Meanwhile, in the south there was a new enemy, the apartheid government, preparing to intervene on the side of UNITA and the FNLA (a deal negotiated by FNLA's new ally, Daniel Chipenda). Beginning in early August the apartheid government forces entered Angola and occupied towns near the Angolan/Namibian border. On August 21, UNITA officially declared war on MPLA. It is not until October 23, however (by which date MPLA was in control of most of the country), when the apartheid government launched its infamous Angolan invasion (according to the apartheid government with the tacit support of the United States), involving combat troops and armaments, and assisted by UNITA forces, Western mercenaries and elements of the Portuguese Army and settlers. The objective of the invasion was to join forces with the FNLA/Zairean troops from the north in a north-south pincer action and capture Luanda from the MPLA before the November 11, 1975, independence date. The objective was never reached. With massive armaments support from the Soviet Union coupled with help provided by thousands of Cuban combat troops, brought in by sea and air beginning on November 7, and continuing throughout the month, the MPLA forces were able to decisively turn the tide against them: they triumphantly routed both the FNLA and the apartheid government invasion forces in January and February, 1976.

The defeat of FNLA and UNITA lead their respective leaders to announce in February that they would maintain their anti-MPLA struggle via guerrilla warfare. On February 11, 1976, the Organization of African Unity (OAU) admitted Angola under the MPLA government as a full member. Many other countries that had not recognized the MPLA government when it had declared itself as the legitimate government of Angola on November 11, when the Portuguese formally withdrew, would also grant it recognition shortly thereafter. (The United States, however, would remain adamant and refused to recognize the MPLA government for decades) Meanwhile, the apartheid government withdrew from Angola in March.

12. For more on the Angolan conflict, including an account of the role of the United States and others in that absolutely unnecessary conflict see: Barber and Barratt (1990), Bender (1981), Bloomfield (1988), Brittain, (1988a, 1988b), Burchett (1978), Campbell

(1989), Ciment (1997b), Danaher (1985), Hodges (2004), Holness (1988), Ignatyev (1977), Kempton (1989), Klinghoffer (1980), Legum and Hodges (1978), Maier (1996), Stockwell (1978), and Wolfers and Bergerol (1983). Note that on some issues, as would be expected, these sources have divergent positions. For an account of the denouement of the Angolan conflict see Anstee (1996), the International Crisis Group (2003a, 2003b), and the news archives at www.bbc.com website.

13. Among the sources used in preparing this section, the following were relied upon extensively: Barber and Barrett (1990), Bloomfield (1988), Brittain (1988b), Cammack (1987), Hanlon (1984), Hanlon (1986), Johnson and Martin (1988), Msabaha and Shaw (1987) and Seidman (1985). For a brief account of the denouement of the Mozambican conflict see Manning (2002).

14. To be sure Mozambique was no friend of South Africa, but this had nothing to do with communism; it was to do with the racism of South Africa, i.e., the apartheid system that denied the black majority the right to form a government, together with the apartheid government's long history of supporting Portuguese colonialism.

15. The actual name of MNR was concocted, it appears, at a meeting on May 1, 1977, at the suburban Salisbury home of a former PIDE agent, Orlando Cristina (who was working for the CIO-MNR radio station, Voz da Africa Livre which had been broadcasting—mainly anti-FRELIMO propaganda—since July 5, 1976). At this meeting, besides Cristina, were three others: Armando Khembo Dos Santos, once a member of FRELIMO at the time of its formation; Evo Fernandes, a Portuguese national who once worked for Jorge Jardim, the Portuguese tycoon with extensive business interests in Mozambique when it was still under the Portuguese (and godson of the Portuguese dictator Antonio Salazar) who would play an important role in the financing of the MNR; and Leo Aldrige Clinton, Jr., an African American from Texas, who had, while pretending to be a Mozambican and going by the pseudonym Leo Milas had at the time of the formation of FRELIMO, become an important official in the organization until his expulsion on August 25, 1964. For more information on the formation of the MNR see Martin and Johnson (1988: 3–5).

16. Even its leaders, such as Andre Matzangaissa (killed in 1979 by FRELIMO) and Alfonso Dhlakama, says Hanlon (1986: 139) were corrupt FRELIMO officers.

17. Mention may be made here of a similar type of organization developed in another part of the world in late 1981 by the CIA, under Reagan, to achieve similar objectives against a similar type of government that had emerged out of a similar type of struggle (guerrilla warfare): namely, the infamous *Contras* (or counterrevolutionaries for short, comprising mainly remnants of the brutal Somoza dictatorship's National Guard and ex-Sandanista malcontents and opportunists) who would be set upon the Sandanista government—which had emerged after fighting a successful guerrilla war against the U.S.-supported dictatorship of Anastasio Somoza Debayle—in Nicaragua by the Reagan administration. The objective was to overthrow the Sandanista government for having the audacity to attempt to develop an alternative society free of U.S. economic domination; though, of course this was not the official explanation offered by the United States. The Sandinastas were eventually overthrown, but indirectly via the ballot box. (For more information on the Contras and the U.S. role in their genesis and development, see *Congressional Quarterly* 1987.) It may be noted that in the case of both Nicaragua and Mozambique (and Grenada, and Chile at one time) the ultimate issue

was not that the United States and South Africa were unable to live, respectively, with the governments that came to power in these countries in the sense that they even remotely presented a military threat to the United States and South Africa, but rather the issue was, *against the backdrop of the Cold War*, the type of societies that these governments were trying to build: nonracist, noncapitalist and nonexploitative. In this regard they presented an alternative vision of the existing socioeconomic and political order; but it was one that these countries (rightly or wrongly) believed could only be constructed on the basis of a concerted and brave attempt—in the spirit of David versus Goliath—to expunge from their countries the politically, economically, socially, and culturally corrupting and debilitating activities and influence of the West (and its surrogates, such as South Africa) that grew out of the West's hegemonic quest for cheap labor, cheap raw materials, excessive profits, and markets for their goods in the PQD countries. Though this is not say by any means that they did not desire any relations with the West; it was rather that they wished to see relations that were free from hegemonic influence and exploitation.

18. See Brittain (1988b: 141–42) for more information on the despicable MNR Washington lobby.

Mention must also be made of the increasing support, in terms of military and financial assistance, that the MNR began to receive (even after the Nkomati Peace Accord had been ratified) from other right-wing groups in Europe. Even the CIA, allegedly, would begin providing assistance via West Germany, and such other traditional whores of imperialism as Saudi Arabia and Malawi. See Hanlon 1986: 147 about this allegation.

19. In Zaire (now called the Democratic Republic of the Congo) the United States, under the umbrella of the United Nations, which at the time was headed by a man who was largely sympathetic to U.S. Cold War interests, Dag Hammarskjold, had intervened on the side of the Belgians and one Moise Thsombe, who together were in the process of dismembering Zaire by organizing the secession of the mineral rich province of Katanga. The government of Patrice Lumumba, who the West (especially the United States) came to detest because it was perceived as anti-Western (and therefore ipso facto pro-Soviet), in order to save the country from this externally mediated fragmentation called upon the Soviets for assistance. The United States conveniently interpreted this action as a vindication that the Lumumba government was simply a communist front. It would mark the beginning of the end of the Lumumba government and Zairean independence.

In a CIA-supported coup, Joseph-Desire Mobuto (who would later rename himself as Mobuto Sese-Seko), the chief of staff of the Congolese National Army who had already shown his true sadistic colors via massacres of civilians in Katanga, deposed the Lumumba government on September 14, 1960. Five years later, in a second CIA supported coup, Mobuto, who by now had established his reputation as an ambitious pro-Western opportunist, would become the head of state. (The governments of Cyrille Adoula and later Moise Tshombe in the intervening period had failed to live up to U.S. expectations.) In the mean time, on January 17, 1961, Lumumba, now imprisoned, was murdered by his captors while being transferred to Elizabethville from Thysville—aided and abetted by the West, particularly the United States. In fact, President Eisenhower had already issued an order to assassinate him at a National Security Council meeting on August 18, 1960. The CIA's Sidney Gottlieb duly prepared a cobra venom for administration to Lumumba, but in the end it was not necessary to use it. Other means evolved in the course of events. (For more on the U.S. intervention in Zaire see Kalb 1982; and Weissman 1974, 1978.) Undoubtedly, for the West (and the apartheid government too), Mobuto was a godsend—but then, through out the history of Africa and other PQD regions, people like him, willing to sell their country into bondage for the price of Western trinkets and a few pieces of gold and silver, have always abounded. Thus since 1965 until Mobutu's eventual demise at the hands of rebels, U.S. policy "[had] consisted of an unswerving support for Mobuto, his corrupt, arbitrary, and dictatorial rule notwithstanding. The support was based on at least three premises: (1) that a vast and multiethnic country like Zaire need[ed] a strong man whose iron rule would help maintain stability and thereby safeguard Western interests; (2) that the United States ought to support its loyal friends, regardless of their behavior; and (3) that Zaire under a pro-Western government [could] play a gendarme role in the region as a whole" (Nzongola-Ntalaja 1985: 233).

It is this type of government capable of meeting these kinds of objectives that the United States and the apartheid government had wished to see installed in both Angola and Rhodesia (and one may add even Mozambique). It did not matter that such a government would consist virtually of a gang of thugs (armed and supported by the United States and its allies); inflicting terror on their people to keep them subservient, while systematically looting the national treasury. To take the example of Zaire itself, and here it is important to emphasize that Zaire was not alone in this, its human rights record was awfully abysmal. Arbitrary arrests, torture, murder, and mutilation of opponents or simply suspected opponents was rampant under Mobutu. As for corruption, the following example provided by Young (1985: 221) is graphically indicative. He describes: "Mobuto spent at least $2 million in 1982 taking an entourage of ninety-three, many of them close relatives in mourning for recently deceased senior kinsman (and vintage embezzler) Litho Maboti, to Disney World in Florida, aboard a chartered aircraft."

20. For more on the politics and history of Zaire see International Crisis Group (2005), Kelly (1993), Hochschild (1998), and Nzongola-Ntalaja (1988).

21. For a useful introduction to *The Histories* by Herodotus, a combined reading of the Waterfield translation (Herodotus 1998) and the excellent three-volume commentary on Book 2 of *The Histories* by Lloyd (1975-1988) is the best approach.

22. For more on the precolonial history of Somalia see Ahmed (1995), Cassanelli (1982), Lewis (1960), Lewis (1966), Taddesse (1977), and Turton (1975). For a general quick overview of the history of Somalia from the precolonial era to the present see Laitin and Samatar (1987), Lewis (2002), Metz (1992), and Mukhtar and Castagno (2003).

23. But what exactly does one mean by a "failed state"? The chilling description provided by Adam (2004) with respect to Somalia sums it up best:

Around January 1991 and during the ensuing months, Somalia experienced a cataclysmic event, virtually unseen since the Second World War. It was not simply a military coup, a revolutionary replacement of a decayed and ineffective dictatorship, or a new, radical regime coming to power through a partisan uprising. Somalia's collapsed state represented the literal implosion of state structures and of residual forms of authority and legitimacy, and the situation has lasted for over a full decade. In some respects, the country seems to have reverted to a nineteenth-century status: no internationally recognized polity; no recognized national administration exercising real authority; no formal countrywide legal and judiciary system; no national banking and insurance services; no national telephone and postal systems; no national public services; no national educational and health systems; no national police and public security services; and no reliable electricity or piped water services (p. 254).

There is, of course, from the perspective of the place of a failed state in the international arena, more to it than that hinted by Adam: it becomes available for the activities of all kinds of international carpetbaggers and organized crime. For instance, there are reports circulating that European organized crime has been dumping nuclear waste in Somalia, a country with the longest but unpatrolled coastline in Africa. It is not enough that the Somali poor must deal with the conditions of their abject poverty, but now they must also confront, in the cruelest of ironies, the garbage of the foreign rich (see news story titled "Waves 'Brought Waste to Somali'" dated March 2, 2005, at the www.bbc.com website, as a starting point).

24. The following sources on the colonial period of Somalia's history, when considered together, provide a useful survey: Ben-Ghiat and Fuller (2002), Fatoke (1982), Hess (1966), Jardine (1969 [1923]), Kelly (2000), Mohamed (1996), Palumbo (2000), and Tripodi (1999).

25. On the matter of historical structures and the collapse of the Somalian state, some, such as Tripodi (1999), have suggested that the economically weak colonialism of the Italians (what Tripodi describes as a "ragamuffin" colonialism) also played a part in setting the stage for the tragedy that befell Somalia by its failure to build in that country robust institutional political and economic structures—capable of withstanding the gale force winds of violent anarchy that were unleashed on the country upon the collapse of the Siad Barre regime. That may be so, but it has to be considered as only *one* among a number of factors—and possibly it is not among the most important ones. The past or current experiences of Algeria, Chad, Congo Democratic Republic, Ivory Coast, Nigeria, Rwanda, Sierra Leone, Sudan, Uganda, and so on, suggests to us that civil war and anarchy in Africa has, perhaps, little to do with *who* the colonizing power was and *what its relative economic strength was in Europe*.

26. The following quote from the section titled "The Somalia Affair" at the Canadian Broadcasting Corporation website (http://archives.cbc.ca) provides a brief overview of the Canadian dimension of the debacle (however, for a detailed examination of this topic see Brodeur [1997], Razack [2004], and the report of the Commission of Inquiry into the Deployment of Canadian Forces to Somalia [1997]).

Canadian peacemakers were lauded as heroes when they went into an untamed land ruled by rebels. Their mission, Operation Deliverance, charged them with restoring order in Somalia. But in fact, the Canadian Airborne regiment was splitting apart at the seams, lacking both leadership and accountability. Murder after murder, the troops came home disgraced. Tracks were covered and responsibility shifted up and down the chain of command during an investigation that would dismantle the army and implicate the government in a high-level cover-up.

For the "Black Hawk" debacle see Bowden (1991), DeLong and Tuckey (1994), and Center of Military History (2003).

27. As, perhaps, would be expected, there are scores upon scores of sources on the

collapse of the Somali state, its historical antecedents, and its aftermath, as well as on the subject of the "Operation Restore Hope" mission. As a starting point into this still-growing literature see: Besteman (1996, 1999), Bryden (1995), Center of Military History (2003), FitzGibbon (1982), Fox (2001), Gardner and El-Bushra (2004), International Crisis Group (2004), Issa-Salwe (2000), Little (2003), Maren (1996), Menkhaus (2002, 2003), Mukhtar and Castagno (2003), Peterson (2000), Prunier (1998), Razack (2004), Samatar (1993), Samatar (1994), Simmons (1995), and Tareke (2000).

28. Here is a description of what one journalist saw of what had remained of the old National University of Somalia, while on a visit to Somalia in 1995:

We arrived at Lafoole [LaFolle] College. A low-rise, modern-looking place, it had been the home of the college of education and the history faculty of the national university. Now it was a displaced-persons camp. The classrooms and dormitories were full of families; the walls were blackened by cooking fires. We pulled up to a row of small cinder-block houses standing apart in the scrub—faculty housing. A tall, middle-aged man [Professor Hussein]...came out to greet us.... The college had closed in December, 1990, two days before the final battle for Mogadishu began, Professor Hussein said. It had been closed ever since.... He offered to show us around the college.... We came to a large green building. It was the old main library.... It was a world of dust. Books were piled everywhere, on sagging shelves, on toppling heaps. Some were stained and disintegrating, but most were intact. Every title I saw seemed, under the circumstances, absurdly ironic: "The Psychology of Adolescence," "Adolescents Grow in Groups," "Primitive Government," "The Red Badge of Courage." Sunlight drifted through high windows on the west wall. A cow mooed somewhere. The dust was so deep it was as though the desert itself were creeping through the walls, burying the books in fine sand (Finnegan 1995).

29. For information on Somali higher education it will be necessary to mine the following: Abdi (1998), Adam (1980), Bennaars, Seif, and Mwangi (1996), Dawson (1964), Hoben (1988), Kitchen (1962), Mebrahtu (1992), Nur-Awaleh (2003), Perry, Schmutterer, and Pride (1964), Robinson (1971), and Samatar (2001). Of these, consult Nur-Awaleh first. Some of the sources on the Italian colonial period, such as Tripodi (1999), are also of relevance here too (see note above).

7

Thematic Perspective: The Role of Foreign Aid

For reasons that should be obvious from reading Appendix II, the autarkic development of African countries in the modern post–1492 period was completely ruled out. Regardless of the sector in question, African countries would be reduced to what has turned out to be, so far, as permanent supplicants for foreign development assistance, be it in the form of finance or technical assistance or both—and higher education has been especially dependent on such assistance. From the first education missions sent out abroad (by Egypt's Muhammed Ali) more than a 100 years ago, to the current World Bank loans and U.S. philanthropic donations, foreign assistance has been a vitally integral component of university development in Africa in the modern period. There is good reason for this circumstance: For any country, higher education is not only highly resource dependent by its very nature, but it is also a relatively complex sector of the economy and society. Higher education is a fusion of extremely heavy capital expenditures (physical plant) and highly labor-intensive saturated processes in which there is an exceptionally high dose of creativity and imagination (teaching, learning and research) that takes place within a context of fiscally burdensome and permanently recurrent budgetary allocations (salaries, stipends, utilities, etc.). As if this is not enough, the sector produces an output (graduates) that not only has an economically intangible component to it that is large, but has the ever-present potential to become an economic waste (under/unemployment).

Therefore, it is not surprising that one of the central themes that runs throughout the history of the development of modern higher education in Africa is that Africa has always depended upon external assistance in support of all these different aspects of higher education from not only governmental sources, but nongovernmental ones as well.[1] Besides colonial governments (and their proxies, the Christian missionaries—from the perspective of education) such assistance, during both the colonial period and throughout the post-independence period up to the present, also came from other overseas actors and agencies who have played (and continue to play) a highly critical support role. During the colonial period there were two that stand out for mention, overseas universities and private philanthropic organizations. In the postindependence period, in addition to the traditional latter two, critical foreign assistance has come not only from the former colonial powers, but from other foreign governments and multilateral development agencies as well.[2] The donors, in turn, for a variety of reasons (moral, altruistic, strategic, religious, etc.), have obliged, but as will be shown below, not always in a constructive way. Of all these various donors, it would not be an exaggeration to say, that the current circumstances of African higher education bears the biggest imprint of the multilateral development agencies (specifically, UNESCO and the World Bank); consequently the focus of this chapter is on them.[3] But first, however, a brief look at bilateral aid.

The postindependence development of higher education in Africa, especially in the early years, was greatly assisted by bilateral government support, without which African higher education would have not have seen as much progress as it did. This was the period, it must be remembered, when higher education had not yet fallen into disrepute in policy circles at the World Bank and at the United Nations agencies. The kinds of bilateral support received by higher education in countries throughout independent Africa echoed the complexity of that sector. That is, almost every aspect of higher education has been targeted for support, including: assistance with buildings construction; provision of student scholarships for staff development; payment of partial or whole salaries of both local and externally recruited staff; assistance with logistical purchases (library materials, computers, lab equipment, etc.); assistance with the establishment of programs of study; and so on.

Over the decades following independence, among the prominent country donors (and their relevant assistance agencies) have included the following: Belgium; Canada (Canadian International Development Agency); former Eastern bloc countries (USSR, etc.); France; Germany (German Academic Exchange Service); the Netherlands (Netherlands Universities Foundation for International Cooperation, International Training Center, Royal Tropical Institute, International Agricultural Center, Institute of Social Studies); Norway (Norwegian Agency for International Development); Sweden (Swedish International Development Authority); United Kingdom (the British Council, the Inter-University Council for Higher Education Overseas); and the United States (Agency for International Development).

Compared to the period immediately following independence, the role of bilateral aid has steadily diminished as multilateral aid (especially through the World Bank) has grown in importance. In this trend the termination of the Cold War (beginning around 1990) has also played a part. During the Cold War, bilateral aid from the United States and its allies on one hand and the former Soviet Union (together with China and Cuba) on the other was made available to allies (or potential allies) in Africa—usually in the form of scholarships for African students to study at institutions in donor countries, the loan of teaching staff, financing of some element of the infrastructure and so on. In one of the few studies of Soviet aid to Africa in the area of training and research programs, Weaver (1985), concludes that generally this aid was of greater relevance to African needs than Western aid (because of the ideologically driven Soviet effort to support not only the political but the economic independence of Africa).

One of the legendary channels for Soviet aid to Africa (and other pre/quasi/developing countries) was the establishment of the Lumumba Friendship University in 1960. Although the Soviet Union was already hosting thousands of students from Africa and elsewhere at its existing institutions, it felt it necessary to build a separate university targeted at the special needs of foreign students (e.g., providing them with Russian language skills).[4] More importantly, from the Soviet point of view, Lumumba was to provide training to the nonofficial students coming from abroad (that is those who were not part of the official bilateral relationship). The aim here was three-fold: provide access to higher education to students of working-class and peasant backgrounds; develop curricula that were better suited to societies that were in the early stages of industrialization, and create a pool of international graduate alumnus sympathetic to the Soviet Union and its allies. (See Weaver for the inner workings of the institution during the Soviet period.)

Incidentally, the university continues to function but with a new name, Russian University of People's Friendship, and it is no longer free; it charges fees. While most of the students who go there continue to come from outside, roughly a quarter of its enrollment is made up of Russian students. Fields of study remain roughly same as in the Soviet era: agriculture, engineering, history and philology, economics, and law, and so on. Lately the institution has been in the news because of the growing racial intolerance toward foreigners (especially people of color) in Russia today—some foreign students have even been murdered with the police looking the other way. Foremost among the perpetrators of hate crimes against foreign students is the thriving neo-Nazi skinhead movement, which gets semi-official encouragement because of its fierce and reactionary loyalty to the Russian state.[5]

UNESCO

There are two prominent multilateral assistance agencies that, historically, have been concerned with the development of higher education in Africa, and both are part of the United Nations system: the International Bank for Reconstruction and Development (IBRD) and its two associates: the International Finance Corporation and the International Development Association (often referred to collectively as the World Bank) and the United Nations Educational and Cultural Organization (UNESCO). (In practice, it ought to be mentioned, the former, unlike the latter, is virtually independent of the U.N. system.) Given their multilateral reach, coupled with their prestigious status in international development circles—born of both actual and verbal accomplishments—these agencies, taken together, have had a virtual monopoly lock on shaping policy on higher education among assistance donors throughout the postindependence period up to the present. Unfortunately, from the perspective of the development of higher education in the developing world generally, and in Africa specifically, the outcome of this stranglehold on policy directions has not been an unmitigated blessing; on the contrary, to some degree, it has been quite detrimental to the development of African higher education, as will be shown below.

Until very recently, UNESCO shared the same mistaken view of the World Bank that the priority subsectors of education were primary and secondary-level education, and not higher education. With its sponsorship of the World Conference on Higher Education in 1998 (Paris, October 5–9), there appears to be some indication that its views in this regard began to change (see the *Summary of the World Declaration on Higher Education* produced by the conference). UNESCO, in any case, is a financially poor agency in that its ability to provide financial assistance to countries that need it is extremely limited. While it does undertake, from time to time, what are referred to as *technical cooperation projects*, these are generally financed through sources outside its own budget (e.g., the World Bank, philanthropic foundations, other U.N. agencies, bilateral assistance agencies—such as Britain's Ministry of Overseas Development, etc.) African beneficiaries of these projects have included Ethiopia, Ghana, Kenya, Lesotho, Nigeria, and Zambia.

However, UNESCO's greatest contribution with regard to the education sector generally, and the higher education subsector specifically, has been in the area of ideas. That is, whatever support UNESCO has provided to the development of higher education in Africa to date has occurred primarily in the form of consultations, symposia, workshops, conferences, publications, and the collection of statistical data. Through these avenues, UNESCO has provided those involved with the development of higher education with benchmarks (against which progress can be evaluated), targets to aim for (as a means of motivating progress), and opportunities for interchange of ideas among planners, practitioners, and holders of purse strings.

With specific reference to Africa, one of the most important contributions UNESCO made in the realm of ideas was to sponsor, in 1962, the first Africawide higher education conference of its kind. It was held in Tananarive (September 3–12), and it was appropriately titled, "Development of Higher Education in Africa." The conference looked at such issues as the role of higher education in economic and social development; higher education planning; financing of higher education; staffing of higher education institutions; curricular choice and adaptation; inter-African cooperation; and the role of foreign assistance in the development of higher education in Africa (see the conference report: UNESCO 1963).

The next UNESCO conference dealing specifically with higher education in Africa did not come until the 1990s, when, in preparation for the UNESCO-sponsored World Conference on Higher Education (Paris, October 5–9, 1998), The Regional Conference on Higher Education for Africa was held in Dakar (April 1–4, 1997). This conference covered essentially the same issues as those dealt with by the 1962 conference (not surprisingly, since these issues have remained current up to the present), as well as concerns of more recent vintage, such as autonomy and academic freedom, sex equity, and information technology.

Of course, in between these two major conferences UNESCO has sponsored (and continues to sponsor) a number of symposia, workshops, and special projects dealing with specific higher education issues and usually executed through its regional offices in Dakar, Nairobi, and Harare. Examples of these include: Project on Strengthening the Social Sciences in Africa (included the formation of the African Council of the Social Sciences); Seminar on Institutional Development of Higher Education in Africa (held in Lagos from November 25–29, 1991 in alliance with the Association of African Universities and with funding from the United Nations Development Program); University Twinning—UNITWIN—(a project to promote networking between higher education institutions along a North-South and South-South global axis); Regional Project on Development of Learning/Training Materials in Engineering Education in Africa; project to develop capacity for collection of statistical data for educational planning by creating the National Education Statistical Information Systems (NESIS); infrastructural and curriculum projects to help increase the output of scientists and engineers; and so on. Mention must also be made here of the series of conferences of African ministers of education that UNESCO has sponsored over the years. (Officially titled "Conference of Ministers of Education and Those Responsible for Economic Planning in African Member States," it has been held six times so far: in 1961 in Addis Ababa, in 1964 in Abidjan, in 1968 in Nairobi, in 1976 in Lagos, in 1982 in Harare, and in 1991 in Dakar.)

THE ASSOCIATION OF AFRICAN UNIVERSITIES

One very important indirect outcome of the 1962 UNESCO conference was the birth of the Association of African Universities. The few heads of African universities present at the conference took the initiative to meet in Khartoum in 1963 to propose a draft constitution for an association of African universities that would promote cooperation among them and serve as a research clearinghouse for its members. Of course, they had already had an example before them when a year earlier, in 1961, the International Seminar on Inter-University Cooperation West Africa, meeting in Freetown, had proposed an Association of West African Universities (see recommendations of plenary session in Congress for Cultural Freedom [1962]). The Association of African Universities was officially inaugurated, after a few delays, in Rabat, Morocco, on November 12, 1967. The decision for the location of its headquarters (Accra), however, was not taken until three years later at the sixth meeting of its executive board in Lagos. In its early years it received help from the Africa-America Institute in the United States, and through the institute, the U.S. Agency for International Development.[6]

Among the notable achievements of the association over the years have been sponsorship of a scholarship program (the INTERAF Scholarship Program) to permit exchange students to study at member institutions, and a staff exchange program. Donors to these programs have included the United States, Britain, Canada, Germany, and others. Other significant activities have included a publishing program by its documentation center; sponsorship of workshops and seminars; publication of a *Handbook on Academic Freedom and University Autonomy* (reproduced as Appendix I of Ajayi, Goma, and Johnson 1996) and *Code of Conduct for Academics* (reproduced as Appendix II of Ajayi, Goma, and Johnson 1996); cooperation with the U.N. Economic Commission for Africa in the African Priority Program of Economic Recovery; and cooperation with external donors in instituting higher education support programs.

The association has also produced two major reports on the state of higher education in Africa: one in 1973 (Yesufu 1973) and the other in 1996 (Ajayi, Goma, and Johnson 1996). Among other things, both reports have reiterated the mission of the African university originally promulgated by the 1962 UNESCO conference: namely, that the African university must go beyond simply serving as a factory for the production of certified personnel to fulfill the personpower needs of a country. It must undertake an active role in the national development effort by helping to articulate the national development agenda and determining ways by which the university can help in implementing it. The 1996 report, however, is candid enough to conclude that this developmental role of the African university has yet to see any significant implementation by African universities, with the exception of a handful.

While on the subject of pan-African cooperation, it is necessary to be reminded of the fact that ultimately, the development of the African continent as a whole will always be hobbled by that elephant in the room that few wish to discuss: the colonial legacy of the fragmentation of the African continent into small countries with radically different ideological affiliations. Such a fragmentation has made it almost impossible to develop a single, Africa-wide, economic and political entity, without which for any one country in isolation, comprehensive and organically integrated but diversified economic development is impossible, because of limitations imposed by economies of scale problems, as well as lack of balanced natural resources. To further clarify this point: the assertion here is that the present political, economic, and social difficulties of individual African countries, for example, would be of a considerably lower magnitude and impact if these countries were simply provinces or states belonging to a single country called, perhaps, the U.S.A.—the *United States of Africa* (for a seminal contribution on this issue, see Green and Seidman [1968]).[7]

WORLD BANK

UNESCO, as already noted, is a financially poor agency, therefore its capacity to provide financial assistance to countries that need it is extremely limited; consequently, it is the World Bank that has been the principal architect of postindependence educational assistance policies in Africa (and elsewhere for that matter), given its control of the purse strings; coupled of course with its domination of the arena of development assistance generally, both financially and intellectually.[8] In other words: to state that from the perspective of educational planning in Africa, throughout the postindependence period, of all the international agencies (including nongovernmental organizations), it is the imprint of the World Bank that has proven to be the most enduring, would not be an exaggeration. In essence, this imprint has been characterized by the view that higher education generally, but most especially universities (in contrast to other postsecondary institutions, such as colleges, institutes, polytechnics, etc.), were, in its view, more of a hindrance than a help to the national development effort for three primary reasons: they sucked up a highly disproportionate amount of scarce educational resources; they were, primarily because of state involvement, inefficient (both internally and externally) even on their own terms; and they, at the same time, existed mainly for the benefit of elites, rather than the vast poverty-stricken masses burdened by, among other things, widespread illiteracy. How the bank came to adopt this view, and the impact it had on the development of higher education in Africa following independence, is a story that constitutes one of the major strands of the history of higher education in postindependence Africa.[9]

Now, up until the beginning of the 1960s, the World Bank did not provide loans for any purpose other than economic infrastructural development (roads, bridges, etc.); mainly because it felt that as a multilateral *governmental* institution it was in the business of precisely this type of non-entrepreneurial economic activity that was the legitimate province of the state; and at the same time it firmly believed that the success of all other economic development efforts depended on the presence of an adequate economic infrastructure. However, for reasons well described by Jones (1992), the bank soon thereafter began to provide loans to the education sector—slowly at first, but becoming in time the most prominent international provider of funds for educational development in Africa and elsewhere. It executed its first education loan in 1962; the recipient was Tunisia. That loan was a harbinger of the general approach the bank would adopt toward educational development in Africa: the loan was for the purpose of building secondary schools.

That is, initially and for many years to come, the bank was not overly keen on providing loans for university development, in part because the bank's leadership, specifically in the person of George Woods (became president of the World Bank in 1963), was distrustful of universities—especially with regard to their budgetary practices. Woods held the perception, to quote Jones, "that university presidents were crafty characters who could not be trusted to spend grant monies for purposes approved by donors" (p. 49). This view, in practice, was taken to mean that the bank was to be minimally involved in university funding—unless the loan was for an institution specializing exclusively in technical or professional education (e.g., an agricultural or medical or teacher training college). The first policy document of the bank on the subject of educational funding, in fact, stated this position (Jones 1992). Subsequent published documents, in the form of sector policy papers, would reiterate *in various guises* the same essential policy (see, for example, World Bank 1971, 1974, 1980, and 1999).

Now, although lending to the education sector would be greatly expanded during the presidency of the former U.S. Secretary of Defense, Robert McNamara (became World Bank president in 1968 and remained at the helm until 1981 and who over the course of this period transformed the bank from a comparatively nondescript institution with an annual loan disbursement portfolio of only $1 billion to about $100 billion by the time he left), university development remained, largely, a stepchild relative to other subsectors (e.g., primary, secondary, vocational) of the education sector. Justification for continuation of this approach was now freshly available in the form of McNamara's well intentioned insistence that development priorities be based on addressing the needs of the poorest segments of society—that is, the vast majority of the population who resided in the countryside—and not the small populations of urban elites. This view came to be called the *basic-needs approach* to development.[10]

The "Basic Needs Approach"

In terms of education, the basic-needs approach found its expression in a policy that it laid out thusly: "The bank considers first-level education the minimum foundation on which countries should gradually and systematically build higher levels of a comprehensive network of formal and nonformal education and training equally accessible to all segments of the population." The bank articulated its rationale for this approach in these terms: "Appropriate basic education enables the majority of the poor, in both rural and urban areas, to lead productive lives and to benefit from social and economic development of the community. Moreover, the effectiveness of higher levels of education depends on the completion of the basic level. Therefore, support for basic education should not be justified by considerations of needs for trained manpower" (from the 1980 *Education Sector Policy Paper*, p. 88, in which tellingly there was almost no mention of higher education).

From the perspective of practice, that is actual policy implementation, the basic-needs approach to economic development, according to Jones (1992), would remain for the most part in the rhetorical realm (see also Kapur, Lewis and Webb 1997). Why? Cooper (1993: 88–89) puts his finger on the problem:

The very people who benefited from inequality were politely asked to redistribute their gains. The state became a dues ex machine solution to the shortcomings of the growth model. Such a view fails to penetrate the connection of economic and political power, substituting a pious hope that considerations of long-term stability would triumph over self-interest....Thus the World Bank defined the problem as poverty, avoided asking if subordination and exploitation were intrinsic parts of certain forms of economic growth, and implied that the 'problem' could be solved without disturbing the power of capital.

Not surprisingly, a decade or so later, even this well intentioned rhetoric on basic-needs began to recede into the background (to be replaced by the policy of *structural adjustment*) in the face of a massive deterioration of the economic circumstances of most of Africa in the early 1980s. The reality, therefore, was that meeting basic-needs was a concept that could not be sustained even rhetorically, given that the policy of structural adjustment demanded the adoption of severe austerity measures by African governments—most especially with respect to social spending. Under these circumstances, the bank was even more adamant than before that the development of higher education be put on the back burner. Consequently, when in 1988 it published an important policy document, *Education in Sub-Saharan Africa: Adjustment, Revitalization, and Expansion* (World Bank 1988), not only there was no policy departure regarding the relative weighting of the different subsectors of education, but, instead, with respect specifically to higher education it called for retrenchment, arguing that in the face of budgetary constraints the first order of business was to institute reforms toward three simultaneous ends: transfer some of the burden of financing higher education on to parents and students, reduce unit costs, and at the same time shrink public sector participation in favor of the private sector. These set of reforms were termed by the report as *adjustment* because they facilitated "[a]djustment to current demographic and fiscal realities" (p. 2).

Seven years later, in 1995, the bank issued its *Priorities and Strategies for Education: A World Bank Review* (World Bank 1995) and it reiterated the 1988 policy recommendations with even greater emphasis: "Basic education will continue to receive the highest priority in the bank's education lending to countries that have not yet achieved universal literacy and adequate access, equity, and quality at that level." The report went on: "As the basic education system develops in coverage and effectiveness, more attention can be devoted to the upper-secondary and higher levels. Bank lending for higher education will support countries efforts to adopt policy reforms that will allow the subsector to operate more efficiently and at lower public cost. Countries prepared to adopt a higher education policy framework that stresses a differentiated institutional structure and diversified resource base, with greater emphasis on private providers and private funding, will continue to receive priority" (World Bank 1995).

What is especially instructive about the 1995 document is that from the perspective of higher education, it reflected in substance, a universities-specific report, *Higher Education: The Lessons of Experience* (World Bank 1994) that it had released the year before (and which in turn would spawn a substantive critique by experts allied with European assistance donors—see their report, Buchert and King 1995). This latter World Bank publication was an interesting document in that it was a policy document that masqueraded as just another "reference" document surveying what it called "best-practices" in higher education throughout the world (and from which, as its title indicates, one could extract policy lessons for the bank and others). Support for making this charge comes from considering Girdwood (in Buchert and King 1995) who, in the course of describing the genesis of the document and the internal World Bank politics behind it, astutely pointed out that in identifying the so-called best-practices, the bank was hardly in a position to avoid being guided by its own policy visions, developed over decades, on the role of higher education— compare, for instance, with World Bank (1988), mentioned a moment ago, in which one clearly detects the seeds of the major policy concerns (see below) of the best-practices document.[11]

It is telling that one area of the world from where the document gleaned a number of best-practices was Asia. The document blithely trotted out examples from such countries as China, Singapore, South Korea, and India, as if their unique (and recall, dirigiste) histories were of no significance in the matter of exporting their best-practices to some other parts of the world, such as Africa. King (in Buchert and King 1995), for example, reminded us that if we took the case of India we would have observed that during the colonial period, higher education in that country had developed along completely different lines than it had in British colonial Africa, where in the case of the latter, as will be recalled from Chapter 4, a major foundational principle of the British was not to replicate, in their view, the errors of India; namely, a proliferation of diverse low-quality higher education institutions (albeit with little state funding) producing a vast population of unemployable *babus*.[12] (See also Ashby 1966.) In other words, the very element that the World Bank considered laudatory (high capacity with relatively low government funding) was based on a history of higher education development that was widely denigrated by India's colonial masters.[13] The document was flawed in another very elementary way: coming up with one-size-fits-all blunderbuss-type policy proposals. For instance, it was all very well to propose a concerted and expanded role for the private sector in higher education for say a country such as China, but could one seriously consider the same strategy for many of the African countries whose levels of development boasted per capita incomes of around a dollar a day or less. (Even in the case of China, one had to be careful in not assuming that all of that vast country was undergoing the same level of economic development—see Cheng in Buchert and King 1995.)

However, leaving such methodological issues of relevance and ahistoricism aside, the significance of the 1994 document for Africa lay in the fact that in this one of the very few World Bank documents *that dealt exclusively with higher education policy*, it clearly reflected, to all intents and purposes, the bank's policy trend *as it had been evolving up to that point and would be pursued with even greater vigor from that point on*; which in a nutshell, as has already been noted above, was—with regard to Africa certainly—the marginalization of higher education relative to the other subsectors of education by means of first the basic-needs approach to education policy and now, what one may correctly describe here, the structural adjustment approach to higher education.[14] Of course, such a policy of marginalization has probably never been openly described as such; in fact, on the contrary, rhetorical nods to the importance of higher education in terms of national development were rarely wanting in World Bank policy documents. Even more to the point, the spirited pursuit of the central policy concerns of the 1994 publication, *on the surface*, appeared to seductively suggest quite an opposite perspective: the desire to make higher education "relevant" to the economic circumstances of countries such as those in Africa by encouraging the adoption of what it saw as capacity-building reform measures. [15]

However, if one were to unwrap the dry techno-diplomatic language characteristic of World Bank documents in which its policy prescriptions were delivered, the thrust of its general policy line was unmistakably clear. In the case of the 1994 document, for instance, if the bank had never played a critically positive role in the development of higher education in Africa up to that point, then at this critical juncture when that sector was in dire straits, it was not yet about to step up to the plate; instead, to put it bluntly, the bank was willing *at the level of practice* to allow the sector to wither on the vine. Consider the significance of the message behind the following statements that undergirded the document:

[T]he overwhelming fiscal reality in most developing countries is such that quality improvements and enrollment expansion in higher education will have to be achieved with little or no increase in public expenditures (p. 3).

Within the education sector…there is evidence that higher education investments have lower social rates-of-return than investments in primary and secondary education and that investments in basic education can also have a more direct impact on poverty reduction, because they tend to improve income equality (p. 85).

[Consequently,]…primary and secondary education will continue to be the highest-priority subsectors in the bank's education lending to countries that have not yet achieved universal literacy and adequate access, equity, and quality at the primary and secondary-levels. In these countries, the bank's involvement in higher education will continue to be mainly to make its financing more equitable and cost effective, so that primary and secondary education can receive increased attention at the margin (p. 85).

[Therefore, c]ountries prepared to adopt a higher education policy framework that stresses a differentiated institutional structure and diversified resource base, with greater emphasis on private providers and private funding, will continue to receive priority (pp. 85–86).

The truth, however, is that this approach rested on a singular disregard or (perhaps) ignorance of African circumstances, which meant that strategies in support of the structural adjustment approach to higher education development helped to merely reinforce the beleaguered status of higher education that characterized much of Africa by the 1980s. There was a time when African universities could hold their own in the international community of universities, but by the 1980s they were, with the few exceptions located at the extremities of the continent, in a parlous state. The grim fact was that the remarkable quantitative progress that African higher education had registered in the decades following independence, masked, sadly, a proportionate qualitative degeneration on a massive scale. It was symptomatic of the emergence (to varying degrees of course, depending on what part of Africa one was looking at) of an enduring pattern of woes: crippling budgetary constraints as institutions were starved of funds; large-scale deterioration of physical plant; overflowing classrooms; poorly equipped laboratories and other similar facilities set against a logistical background of intermittent supply of even such basics as water and electricity (not to mention consumables like chemicals); shrinking and outdated libraries as collection development came to a virtual standstill against a backdrop of widespread looting of holdings; overworked and underpaid faculty who often moonlighted to make ends meet; inefficient administrations as talented and able administrators left for greener pastures; teaching, learning, and research that was bereft of even the most basic logistical support (such as chalk, textbooks, photocopy machines, etc.); almost complete loss of autonomy as governments vilified and obliterated academic freedom; and the list went on. As for the quality of the teaching and learning enterprise specifically, given this awful state of affairs, one could only assume the worst. In fact, the bank itself, in its 1988 report (mentioned a moment ago), had observed on this matter: "The low (and possibly declining) standard in African higher education is now pervasively bemoaned by teacher, student, employer, and government official alike. Nor could the situation be otherwise, since indirect evidence of a crisis of quality in African education is overwhelming."[16] The report goes on to state:

The most immediate consequences of the drying up of nonsalary inputs to higher education are that research ceases and instruction is reduced to little more than rote learning of theory from professorial lectures and chalked notes on blackboards. Chemists who have not done a titration; biologists who have not done a dissection; physicists who have never measured an electrical current; ...engineers who have never disassembled the machinery they are called upon to operate; social scientists of all types who have never collected, or conducted an analysis, of their own empirical data; ...lawyers who do not have access to recent judicial opinions; medical doctors whose only knowledge of laboratory test procedures is from hearing them described in a lecture hall—qualitatively deprived graduates such as these are now appearing in countries that have been hardest hit by the scarcity of nonsalary inputs (World Bank 1988: 74–75).[17]

By 1990s the situation had become so critical that even the U.S. Congress was moved to hold a special hearing in May of 1993 on the subject (U.S. Congress 1994); as Senator Paul Simon, the chair of the Subcommittee on African Affairs of the U.S. Senate, explained after first drawing attention to the initial heartening progress in higher education achieved by African countries following independence: "We are holding a hearing on the question of higher education in Africa.... there has been a rapid deterioration in the higher education [subsector] as the economies in Africa decline." He went on: "Of the thirty African countries with higher education institutions, there are few institutions that really thrive today. Many of them are in very bad shape. And even among those that exist, opportunities, for example, for women and the number of women faculty members is not at a healthy level" (p. 1).

However, there is more to this matter on two scores: First, the bank, throughout its relations with Africa, appeared to be completely unconcerned with the problematic of developing a science and technology infrastructure in the absence of university development. The reason for this is of course obvious, and it has already been mentioned in passing: it did not see the necessity of advocating a meaningful development of a scientific and technological infrastructure for Africa in the first place—for reasons that will be evident shortly.[18] Now, while science and technology cannot solve all the problems of Africa, there is absolutely no question that in terms of the narrower focus of economic development, absolutely no success is possible without the massive (but appropriate) use of science and technology.

At the same time, in a context where there were almost no non-university research institutions, the university was the only viable institution that could create and sustain the necessary science and technology infrastructure.[19] Moreover, it was somewhat ironic that there was almost no report that surveyed the state of higher education in Africa that did not make its obligatory call for a greater emphasis on the development of a science and technology infrastructure. As a report written for the Association of African Universities (Ajayi, Goma, and Johnson 1996) observed: "The literature is replete with calls for the countries of Africa to strive determinedly to become active and significant contributors to scientific and technological advancement; to refuse to be mere recipients of or mere spectators to, the rapidly emerging sciences and technologies; and to struggle to promote a culture of science-inspired creativity and technology innovation linked to the entrepreneurial enterprise" (p. 213).

Second, the issue of World Bank policy on African higher education, it should be stressed, is not only one of simply inadequate funding of university development by the bank itself, but its policy influence as well on other foreign assistance donors: they too became reluctant to provide financial and technical assistance to the higher education sector. Consider the example of the United States; at the Congressional hearing mentioned above, the U.S. agency responsible for managing U.S. foreign aid, the U.S. Agency for International Development (A.I.D.), through its representative at the hearing, John Hicks, articulated its policy position on higher education that in essence was a reflection of World Bank thinking: Beginning with the question, "Why has A.I.D. focused on supporting African basic [primary-level] education?," he went on to explain "A.I.D. has chosen to support basic education for a variety of reasons. First we have chosen to focus in this area because the need was evident and the opportunity to work with the African and donor community was present. Second, the underlying economic rationale was provided several years ago in a number of studies, culminating in the 1988 World Bank study on Basic Education in Sub-Saharan Africa. These studies indicated that the rates-of-return to basic education were higher relative to other segments of the education sector and at least as favorable relative to investments in physical capital."[20] As for A.I.D.'s policy response to the predicament of the African universities that had led to the hearing: it was a vintage World Bank policy position:

Let me underline that until the Africans deal systematically with the current underlying problems concerning the African higher educational system, it is difficult to envision major across-the-board engagement and investments in the higher education sector on the part of the donor community. While we see indications that many Africans understand the depth of the fundamental issues confronting their universities, it will require tough decisions and commensurate action on their part to address the difficult issues of finance, governance and autonomy, quality and equity, before the donor community is likely to engage in any substantive assistance to higher education (p. 7; emphasis in the original).

The pervasive influence of the bank on policies of other educational assistance donors is further corroborated by Samoff and Assie-Lumumba (1996). In an extensive review of scores of educational sector policy papers (these are papers that outline educational assistance policies and provide theoretical justifications) produced by a variety of external donor agencies to guide educational assistance policy in Africa, they conclude, among other things, that higher education generally received short shrift in these documents (see also Banya and Elu 2001).[21]

The foregoing, of course, it is important to stress, does not imply by any means, that there was no lending whatsoever for the purposes of university development—after all, the bank was (and continues to remain to date) the single largest supplier of funds to the higher education subsector as a whole—rather, it was much less than should have been available had World Bank educational lending been informed by a different policy perspective: one that emphasized *balanced* development of the entire education sector.[22] After all, it is not as if the World Bank was unaware, *at least at the rhetorical level,* of the importance of universities in the overall national development effort. Even in one of its latest comprehensive publications on Africa, it reiterates a long held rhetorical position: "universities have a potentially greater role to play in Africa than in many other regions—they are often the only national institutions with the skills, equipment and mandate to generate new knowledge through research or to adapt global knowledge to help solve local problems" (2000b: 106). However, in spite of this position, it had always held the view that the level of this importance was not sufficiently high enough to merit *a concerted public-sector support.* As Jones (1992: 212), had observed: "Despite the retention of the bank view of the developmental potential of higher education, it is currently imposing through project covenants all manner of restrictions on public support for higher education, and not always in countries displaying an imbalance between publicly supported primary and higher education."

In the final analysis, the awful circumstances of higher education in much of Africa was a function of a combination of two factors: the massive contraction of educational budgets, which itself was a reflection of the severe economic predicament that most African countries were now grappling with (discussed below), and lack of competent guidance in the evolution of African higher education during the postindependence period that could have helped to nip in the bud the kinds of problems that would later arise and which the World Bank would legitimately (one can concede) complain about with increasing stridency, such as the inefficiencies and the high unit costs.[23] Regarding the latter, so long as the World Bank and other foreign assistance donors remained disinterested in university development in Africa, then it also meant that African universities were denied much needed policy *guidance.*

One can legitimately conjecture, for example, that had foreign assistance donors become intimately involved with university development in Africa *on a consistent basis* throughout the postindependence period, from the very beginning up to the present, then they could perhaps have played a positive role in coming up with policy strategies for increasing internal and external efficiencies; as well as reducing unit costs without at the same time undermining access for those on the margins—the poor, women, and so on. (The underlying suggestion here, in other words, is that the ability of African higher education to weather the financial downturn it would later experience was severely compromised by some of the policies it had adopted in the past.)

Yet, the best that the bank could come up with to address the rapidly deteriorating circumstances of African higher education was insistence on a structural adjustment approach: since, in its view, universities were not as critically important to Africa as lower levels of education, the budgetary difficulties were an opportune time, it felt, to rethink their financing and their role; hence the call for user fees, privatization, a moratorium on creating new universities, and so on, among other proposals.[24] Surely, the bank ought to have recognized that given that most African countries had arrived at independence with almost no experience with creating universities, thanks to colonialism, and given that they were, at the same time, burdened *by extremely low per capita income levels*, responsibility for the development of universities (the most expensive subsector of education) could only be entrusted to the state. The bank, however, had never let this "minor" fact get in the way of its educational policies. Now, the question that stridently emerges here is: Why? Why had the World Bank taken such a consistently jaundiced view of university development (relative to other sectors of education), *even long before African countries began to reel from budgetary crises in the early 1980s*?

There are several possible answers that one can postulate; but none are rooted in malevolence one must hasten to emphatically add—rather it's a question of good intentions resting on bad policy because of the inherent limitations of the bank as both a *Western* and a *capitalist* institution on one hand, and on the other the problem of faulty theories (which, of course, has been the bane of many development assistance programs in Africa). Some examples regarding the inherent limitations of the thinking that undergirds the work of the bank: it had never contemplated championing the idea that may be the budgetary difficulties facing governments in not only Africa, but all across the planet, could have been alleviated to a considerable degree by—preposterous this may sound to the typical Western mind—drastically reducing expenditures on the warmaking apparatus (euphemistically termed "defense"). Neither did it contemplate suggesting, for instance, to some of the African governments, that it was time to begin looking at the issue of good governance (something that it would only take up years later, around 2000 and after, and even then only because of external pressures) so as to eliminate waste (e.g., financing white elephant projects) and corruption (e.g., embezzlement of funds), and thereby save money.[25] On the contrary, the bank, preposterously, appeared to see no contradiction in enforcing repayment from borrowers for projects *that the bank itself had designed and funded but which had completely failed* (Surin 2003). Nor did it champion equitable economic relations between the West and Africa from the perspective of trade, investment, surplus extraction, and so on (contrast here the recommendations of the report of the British sponsored Commission for Africa [2005]).

It felt reluctant to ask (and act upon) such simple but highly pertinent questions as: Why was the West bent on lumbering the vast majority of Africa's peoples, the barefoot and illiterate poor, with the burden of heavy debts for generations to come by lending to their illegitimate and corrupt governments for illegitimate and white elephant projects from which they (Africa's poor) would derive no benefits whatsoever? How could genuine development occur in a continent that was so politically and economically fragmented when one of the abiding lessons of economic history is that without mass markets—first internal (and later, if necessary, external)—no real development is possible? Why was the West so keen to sell billions of dollars worth of armaments to a continent that neither needed them nor afford them? As for faulty theories there are at least three that quickly come to mind: one has to do with the place of Africa in the global economic schema, another concerns the role of the state in society, and the third has to do with higher education and educational planning.

The Bank and the Economic Place of Africa in the Global Arena

In the course of subjecting a report produced for the World Bank in 1991 titled *Education in a Declining Economy: The Case of Zambia, 1975–1985* (authored by one, Michael J. Kelly), to scathing criticism, Caffentzis (2000) writes: "This reduction [of higher education] is advocated in the name of higher efficiency and a more egalitarian distribution of educational resources. Yet, the evidence provided and the guidelines prescribed raise serious doubts about the actual motives behind this policy. More likely, the [World Bank's] attempt to cut higher education stems from its bleak view of Africa's economic future and its belief that African workers are destined for a long time to remain unskilled laborers. This would explain why the World Bank has made the shrinking of Africa's higher education institutions the centerpiece of its policy and has identified the improvement of academic life with this reduction" (p. 3–4). In other words, the allusion here is to the bank's perspective on where Africa's comparative advantage lay in the international economic system: as a producer of natural resources for the West, which in turn brings up the broader issue of the development strategies that had been historically (and continues to be) advocated for much of Africa.

Now, consider this sobering fact: Western countries and international institutions, together, had poured into Africa since independence in the early 1960s, billions of dollars of foreign aid; yet, by the late 1980s and certainly by the 1990s (and since then the situation has only worsened) much of Africa found itself poorer than it had been at the time of independence. On almost every measure of development, Africa lagged behind (with little sign of improvement) when compared to other PQD countries elsewhere: per capita food production, the lowest in the world and constantly declining (in the minus column for years); the ratio of external (public) debt to GNP, the highest; the frequency of famine-induced hunger, the highest; the rate of HIV infections, the highest; annual population growth, the highest; percentage of world trade, the lowest; intra-regional trade as a percentage of external trade, the lowest; average life expectancy, the lowest; the ratio of debt to export earnings, the highest; levels of industrialization, the lowest; export earnings, the lowest and frequently on the decline; the population of refugees, the highest; the number of violent conflagrations (wars), the highest; the rate of literacy, the lowest; the rate of school achievement, the lowest; and so on and so on.[26] Not surprisingly, symptomatic of this abysmal statistical picture is that, without any doubt, the vast majority of the African peoples have suffered massive declines in their standards of living over the past forty or so years despite all the aid the continent has received.[27]

There are, of course, many complex economic, geographic, political, and social factors that *taken together* explain this situation—not least among them the irresponsible governance and stewardship of the African leadership itself, coupled with the Western support of tyrants and dictators during the Cold War—a dark period in Western history marked by immense wastage of resources as a result of the arms buildup and massive violations of human rights in the PQD countries through proxy wars. However, among these complex factors must also be included this one: the strategies of economic development that Africa had been advised to pursue as a conditionality for accepting foreign aid. These strategies not only helped to drive African economies into their awful economic predicament, but also took away from it avenues for recovery, especially in circumstances of natural disasters and such external economic shocks as that brought about by the sudden and massive international oil price increases. What are these strategies then? There are two that specifically come to mind: the *import substitution* strategy and the *comparative advantage* strategy.

Throughout the past four decades of independence, the kind of economic development that Western countries have always pushed for in Africa has been one based on highly limited industrialization resting on manufacturing and/or assembly of consumer goods for domestic consumption in a context of a small limited market. This strategy is sometimes referred to as *import substitution industrialization* (ISI) and it stands in opposition to true industrialization because in reality (and ironically) it is *import-dependent* import substitution. Yet, even here, the import substitution that was pursued in practice was not one that truly addressed the needs of the mass market, but rather the elites (hence concentration on the production of luxury commodities, that not only can not be sustained for long in a market dominated by the poor, but also requires a large degree of importation of the necessary inputs—thereby consuming enormous amounts of scarce and highly precious foreign exchange).[28] Not surprisingly, this strategy had run its course very early on, with the result that most industries that were set up under this strategy fell apart in most of Africa (and are now gone) with disastrous socioeconomic consequences.

Coupled with the ISI strategy, under the influence of classical economics theory that the Bretton Woods institutions espouse—and to some degree the U.N. agencies as well (but mainly because of influences from the former), Western aid donors to Africa emphasized the importance of producing raw materials for export (e.g., cash crops like tobacco, cotton, coffee, and cocoa; and minerals like gold and copper) because therein lay a comparative advantage, it was so argued, for natural resource-rich Africa. In other words, from the very beginning up to the present, they have not seen independence as a reason for the Africans to deviate from the economic role (supplier of raw materials) that colonialism had delegated to it.[29] It will be remembered that economic development under colonialism was highly constricted given that the colonial economies where considered to be no more than mere appendages of the metropolitan economic system. This in effect meant that their principal function was to supply raw materials to the metropolitan industries on one hand, and on the other, provide a market for their output.

Without going further into the merits of the notion of comparative advantage and the ISI strategy (the proof of the pudding is in the eating: look at the abysmal economic circumstances of Africa over the past several decades up to the present, a hint of which was provided a moment ago), it will suffice to note two points. (1) Even on its own terms, the Africans were not told that a devastating hypocrisy underlay advocacy of the comparative advantage strategy: their commodity exports would be subject to unfair competition in the West through such measures as tariff barriers and domestic agricultural subsidies (with resultant economically crippling consequences for Africa). One should also mention here another consequence of such ill-conceived advice: the depression of world commodity prices (to the benefit of the industrialized economies) because of over-production—as countries were encouraged to undertake production of these commodities *in competition with each other.*

(2) An outcome of these strategies was a de-emphasis of the development of higher education in general and science and technology in particular.[30] Why would you need scientists and engineers if the economy was designed to remain agrarian (and not only that, but one that would not require industrialization), or if the economy was to rest on the production of minerals for export, or

if the only form of industrialization advocated was one that would be restricted to the manufacture of light consumer goods (soap, beverages, etc.) and assembly of a few industrial goods from imported parts for limited domestic consumption? In other words, the idea that Africa would require a viable research and development infrastructure never even entered the equation.[31] Note that this matter brings up the dialectical relationship between the development of higher education in general and the development of science and technology infrastructure on the other: downplay one and it negatively affects the other. The World Bank was never keen to encourage the development of the science and technology infrastructure in Africa either—as already stated.

The Bank, the State, and Structural Adjustment

Like all modern capitalist institutions, the bank has always had an anathema for direct state participation in the economic arena, for both economic reasons (judging it to be highly inefficient, not to mention the fear of unequal competition for capital) and political reasons (its revolutionary potential for distributive justice, which would undermine the dominant position of capital). The latter concern is usually unstated. This jaundiced view of the role of the state at the policy-level found its expression in the anti-*dirigisme* strategy of *structural adjustment*.

Structural adjustment strategy is a strategy that economists at the World Bank devised on the basis of neoliberal monetarism (devaluation of currencies, unrestrained convertibility of currencies, etc.) and neoclassical (elimination of trade barriers, privatization of state enterprises, free flow of investment capital, etc.) macroeconomic principles. In essence the strategy called for a drastic reduction of state participation in the economy and society, in consonance with the theme of the supremacy of market forces that underlay and unified these principles, and firmly eschewed any attention to the inequitable domestic and international social relations of production (see, for example, World Bank 1981). The strategy arose out of a misguided characterization of a number of African economies as, in so many words, "socialist"—and therefore perceived as not only inherently inefficient but viewed as an anathema in the context of the Cold War—because of the large economic role accorded to state and *parastatal* corporations.[32]

The practical policies that ensued from this strategy included a wholesale move toward privatization of as many government functions as possible; devaluation of national currencies; elimination of barriers to currency convertibility; implementation of packages of deep austerity measures in an effort to balance national budgets; removal of state subsidies and price controls; renewed emphasis on agricultural production for export (in consonance with the theory of comparative advantage); removal of controls on trade and payments; and a reduction and rationalization of bureaucracies (see Biersteker 1990). Most of these measures when taken together came to be referred to as the "Washington Consensus" (on the solution to the economic woes of PQD countries). In reality their net effect was to benefit the continued domination—as well as its further deepening—of the PQD countries by transnational monopolies (most of whom are domiciled in the West).[33] While it is true that advocacy of *some* of these measures was certainly a step in the right direction, when the package is taken as whole it has been a prescription for disaster. Why? A central component of the basis of the economic ills plaguing Africa was never addressed (and could not be addressed given the ideological underpinnings of the consensus): the web of Western-dominated international economic relations in which Africa has been enmeshed for centuries ever since it was forged in the wake of 1492 (see Appendix II)—ranging from unnecessary heavy debt burdens to inequitable terms of trade; from unfair trade policies to resource squandering and environment degrading investment projects; from economically crippling extraction of investable surpluses to import-dependent investment enterprises. In other words, in the absence of other much needed reforms—especially in the political realm domestically, and the economic realm, internationally—whatever benefits may have accrued to the structural adjustment strategy have, after more than twenty years, yet to materialize. As *The Economist* (a magazine that is *de rigueur* reading for Western capitalist classes) observed in its recent survey of Africa: "Sub-Saharan Africa...is the world's poorest continent: half of its 700m[illion] people subsist on 65 U.S. cents or less a day. Even more worryingly, it is the only continent to have grown poorer in the past 25 years, despite the explosion of technology and trade that has boosted incomes in other regions" (2004: 3–4).[34] The case of Zambia is classic: it is among the most structurally adjusted countries in Africa; yet, it has failed to halt its descent from a country with among the highest per capita income in Africa at the time of independence, to one with among the lowest today—in fact, in terms of development indices, it ranks among the poorest in the world.[35]

What is of interest here, however, is that among the consequences of the structural adjustment strategy that most of Africa has been forced to accept, in return for foreign assistance, has been both direct and indirect negative implications for the development of higher education. The direct implication arose out of massive cutbacks in state budgets that have left virtually no funds for even the most rudimentary of state functions—including education—let alone such "luxuries" as developing higher education. The indirect implication stems from the notion of comparative advantage and the relegation of Africa to a producer of raw materials, as explained above.

Higher Education from the Perspective of Educational Planning

Because the bank is fundamentally a capitalist economic institution, not surprisingly, economic theory (neoliberal/ neoclassical economic theory) undergirds all its major policy decisions. Consequently, when the bank first began its assistance foray into the education sector, it only did so under the aegis of the newly rediscovered economic theory of human capital (see below); most especially that part of the theory that spawned the rates-of-return techniques for the purposes of educational planning. A recent report co-sponsored, ironically, by the bank itself (together with UNESCO—see World Bank 2000), is critically candid about the influence of these techniques:

These techniques seemed to demonstrate that higher education offered lower private returns than primary education. They also showed that social returns were lower and, considering that higher education absorbs considerably higher investment, they demonstrated that the public interest in higher education was substantially lower than that in primary education. Taken together, these results provided a powerful justification—especially for international donors and lenders—for focusing public educational investment at the primary-level. This justification was further reinforced by the obvious gains in social equity associated with such a strategy, as highlighted and endorsed by the Jomtien Declaration in 1990. The World Bank drew the conclusion that its lending strategy should emphasize primary education, relegating higher education to a relatively minor place on its development agenda. The World Bank's stance has been influential, and many other donors have also emphasized primary and, to some extent, secondary education as instruments for promoting economic and social development (p. 39).

Given, then, the enormous influence that the theory of human capital has had on educational planning in PQD countries under the sponsorship of international assistance donors like the World Bank over the past forty years or so, it is necessary (at the risk of eyes glazing over), to provide an overview of it, *as well as* consider the merits of the theory as it has been applied in practice through the rates-of-return techniques.

Human Capital Theory

Now, it will be recalled that the emergence of new nations out of the chrysalis of colonialism in the 1950s and early 1960s, in Africa and Asia, was accompanied by an escalation of the Cold War, which in turn would set in motion powerful ideological winds that would blow through the corridors of social science departments in many universities in North America (and in the West generally). The result was the birth of a desire among those academics with interest in PQD countries to contribute through their work to international assistance policy decisions with the hope that the new nations could be nurtured on to a development path that would replicate that taken by the capitalist West (and not the communist East). Altruism, of course, was not the name of the game, one must hasten to add; rather, it was opportunism—given the preponderance of ideology and government funding opportunities in their calculations. Be that as it may, one such academic, among many, was W. W. Rostow, who published an unapologetic paean to economic growth, detailing the path Western nations had supposedly followed in achieving super abundant economic growth and which the developing nations would have to emulate if they wished to arrive at the same levels.

His book, titled *The Stages of Economic Growth: A Non-Communist Manifesto*, (Rostow 1990—third edition), identified five stages in this path: the traditional society, the preconditions for take-off, the take-off, the drive to maturity, and the age of high mass consumption. Even though the book proved to be very controversial, what is important to note here is that this emphasis on economic growth (as measured by increases in per capita GNP) as the engine of development found resonance among neoclassical economists concerned with the fate of the newly independent nations. The most important question in their minds, then, was how to promote economic growth because to them economic growth became synonymous with development.[36] In seeking to answer this question they had to, however, first resolve a puzzle that some of them had been grappling with on this very issue of economic growth, but with respect to the experiences of Western nations, such as the United States.

The puzzle was how to explain the "residual" that economists had discovered when charting economic growth in the United States. Specifically, economic output (measured in terms of the gross national product), had been growing at a relatively fast rate and yet this growth rate was not paralleled by increases in the conventional factors of production. Thus, whereas the average increases in the GNP in the United States between 1919 and 1957 had been 3.1% annually, the average increases in human-hours employed and capital equipment deployed during the same period was 0.8% and 1.8% respectively (Schultz 1961a). At first, explanation for this phenomenon was sought in terms of technical change. It is the improvement in machinery and technology that had given rise to large increments in output beyond the measured conventional inputs. This explanation however, begged the question, and in response Schultz (1961a) emerged with the theory that education was the missing variable in the explanation, and thereby overturned the long-held notion that education was a consumption rather than an investment item.

Schultz, in another article published during the same year (1961b), went even further and argued that expenditures on education constituted an investment in "human capital"—thus was the classical economics theory of human capital reincarnated. To many, the beauty of human capital theory in essence was that it appeared to render the intuitive factual: educational systems as a whole provided inputs (albeit unobserved by economists hitherto—or so it seemed) that were essential to economic growth, such as: skills and knowledge necessary for technological advancement; the proper workforce conditioning through the agency of the hidden curriculum of schools (discipline, punctuality, respect for authority, etc.); greater productivity, creativity and commitment to work; and so on. In other words, to invest in education was to invest in economic growth.[37]

With the reformulation of the human capital theory by Schultz, there emerged a new branch of economics, called the "economics of education," which its practitioners confidently assumed would allow them to quantify the complex linkages between education and the economy.[38] Two kinds of research emerged in this field as it developed: one concerning the economic analysis of the educational system (e.g., how to allocate resources to the different parts of the system); and the other concerning the interaction of the educational system with the economy (e.g., what portions of resources must be allocated to the educational sector). It is the latter kind of research, where the dominant underlying concept is that economic development is not only predicated by education, but education itself is also a factor of growth, that is of particular interest here. Economics of education gave birth to three basic types of studies that would soon become the basis for educational planning in PQD countries: correlational studies, manpower planning studies, and the rates-of-return studies.

Correlational studies involved international comparisons of the levels of GNP and levels of educational provision. The key work in this kind of research was undoubtedly that of Harbison and Myers (1964). They collected data from seventy-five countries and devised a so-called "composite index of human resource development." They then proceeded, via correlation techniques involving the index, national income and other socioeconomic indices to validate the thesis that a high-level of national income was a function of a high score on the index of human resource development. Other similar kinds of research that found a positive correlation between education and economic growth included the work of Anderson and Bowman (1965), who studied correlations between levels of literacy and per capita GNP; and Bennett (1967), who correlated general and vocational education to three economic indices, and found a positive correlation between growth in technological education and economic development.

Manpower planning studies were primarily concerned with calculating future manpower needs of a country. As already explained earlier, the basic technique involved was the calculation of the quantitative links between the occupational-educational structure of the labor force and the level of output (measured usually in terms of sectional value added). This then became the basis for forecasting manpower needs.

The rates-of-return studies (also sometimes known as cost-benefit analysis) grew out of disenchantment with the manpower forecasting approach to educational planning because of a number of serious weaknesses (see above), as well as dissatisfaction with the correlational studies.[39] Very briefly, the rates-of-return (to investment in education) approach involves calculation of social costs, which includes the true cost of providing the education and the cost of lost production while the student is absent from the world of work; and the social benefits (which in the first instance is the difference in pretax salaries between graduates of the educational level for which the analysis is being made and graduates from levels below this level). In a similar fashion, private rates-of-return can also be calculated. Thus for example Carnoy and Thias (1969) calculated that in Kenya the individual rate-of-return on higher education was 20% (while the social rate-of-return for the same type of education was only 9%).

Among the more well-known studies on rates-of-return to investment in education is undoubtedly the work of George Psacharopoulos (1973, 1981, and 1994). The principal conclusions of his work were: rates-of return are generally higher in PQD countries; primary-level education tends to yield the highest returns; (returns to human capital exceed those on physical capital—taking the 10% opportunity cost benchmark for physical capital); returns to general education exceed those for such other forms of education as technical, vocational and scientific training; and differences in per capita income can be explained better by differences in human than in physical capital.

As can be easily surmised, with such findings the stage was set for not only pouring large amounts of resources into educational development, but also for insisting that resources be directed away from higher education toward the lower levels of the educational system, especially primary-level schooling. Schultz (1974), for example, was adamant: "What are the implications of my guide for investors in education? Let me venture to suggest the following approaches in contribution to education in the developing countries. 1. Concentrate on the enlargement and improvement of elementary schooling; and thus give less attention to college and university instruction than has been true during recent years." (p. 56). Even at the basic intuitive level, this recommendation appeared to possess the hallmark of common sense: how could you plan for the development of higher education when large sections of the population did not even know how to read and write? However, as one looks in retrospect it is evident that not only did the massive infusion of resources in educational development not achieve the desired economic results, but the relative neglect of higher education did not have positive effects on the general development effort either (witness the current awful predicament of most countries in Africa). Leaving aside the many political, social, and economic variables that account for this outcome (not least among them the extremely problematical nature of the mode of insertion of the former colonies into the world economic system—see Appendix II—and the continued perpetuation up to the present of the basic parameters of that insertion, which neoclassical economists like Schultz, Psacharopoulos, and others appear to have never understood), there is also the very questionable issue of subjecting the highly complex relationship between education and the economy to quantitative reduction techniques (see, however, McMahon [2002] for a more promising approach in this regard).

The Pseudo-economics of Economics of Education

Painful as this may sound to economists, the simple fact is that even at the basic intuitive level, most educators know that education is too complex a phenomenon to approach with such quantitative techniques, and that more importantly, the "technical" relationship of education to the economy encapsulates but only a fragment of this relationship, and even then it is only a sliver of the entire educational system that is engaged thusly. To elaborate on the latter point, in almost all societies today, only a small portion of the entire educational system has a relationship with the economy that can be termed as *technical*, meaning that the educational system is a factor supplier—in this case skilled personpower. This is the portion that comprises vocational educational institutions that train welders, plumbers, bricklayers, and so on; departments and faculties of higher education institutions that train professionals such as doctors, lawyers, and engineers; and colleges for agricultural extension officers, teachers, secretarial workers, and so on. As for the rest of the educational system that is involved with producing persons with general education (or academic education) qualifications, the relationship with the economy *as posited by the human capital theorists* is a very tenuous one indeed. For, the basic function of general education is not economic but rather sociological; that is, it is a means for social differentiation (Hussain 1976). Educational qualifications enable society to differentiate between different classes of occupations (e.g., low-wage manual-labor occupations, and high-wage mental-labor occupations) not because of the technical content of the occupations themselves, but because of the demands of a social structure that is specific to societies with a dichotomous economic system, where not only the producers are not the owners of the means of production, but they have no control over why, how, and what is produced and how it is disposed of. Most occupations, when seen purely from the point of technical competence required in performing them, bear little or no relationship to the educational qualification required to enter them.

The fact that there is a *perception* of the presence of such a link between education and occupations has little to do with any present-day empirical facts. Rather, it seems that it is an outcome of what was generally true in preindustrial times. To explain: the dual process of the formalization of education, and the uncoupling of education from the world of work characteristic of present-day modern societies is, as Amin (1982) has observed, essentially a product of a particular form of division of labor intrinsic to modern industrial societies: a form involving on one end of the production spectrum (the technology/machinery inventing/manufacturing end) a continuous *accretion* of super-labor skills, and on the other end (the technology/machinery use/operating end) a continuous *attrition* of almost all labor skills that go beyond the rudimentary.

In preindustrial societies, however, no such comparable division of labor was present. Though that does not imply that there was no division of labor, but that the division was *between* and not also *within* the production processes of discrete occupations (farming, weaving, carpentry, pottery, metal working, etc.). In preindustrial societies therefore, the linkage between education (be it formal or informal) and work was extremely tight. In the interest of increasing productivity (achieved via rationalization of production techniques involving such measures as the introduction of mass assembly line production systems—which demand a labor force bereft of skills like those possessed by the black-smiths of preindustrial times), modern societies have broken this link. Yet in breaking this link, which has had to be preceded by the monopoly of the means of production within the hands of a small group of owners, without which large aggregated production units could not have emerged, it has been necessary to imbue education with its social differentiation function, as well as the ideological function of rendering this differentiation justifiable in the eyes of both those in the upper strata of the social structure (comprising in the main the owners of the means of production) and those in the lower strata (comprising in the main the workers). In this ideology, those who possess a larger share of educational credentials are deemed to be entitled to a greater share of social benefits (employment, income, status, etc.). Furthermore, intrinsic to this ideology has been the notion, albeit a false one, that attainment of educational credentials is a function of purely individual effort and attributes *(agency)* and no other factors come into play, such as socioeconomic background *(structure)*. Consider for a moment that if one were to extend the logic of the meritocratic reasoning by performing a thought experiment, this is the ridiculous conclusion one would arrive at: there is no reason why every one in society should not all be wealthy to the point where they are all members of a single class, the upper class. What is the thought experiment? By means of a miracle every one in society woke up tomorrow morning *possessing the best individual qualities necessary for the highest levels of academic achievement.* Clearly, the thought experiment reveals the supreme asininity of the meritocratic logic.

It follows from all this, that if the distribution of a particular qualification along a given educational axis, such as length of period of school attendance, or subject of specialization, or level of academic performance required for a given occupation were to increase dramatically in the labor force, thereby producing a glut of qualified persons far in excess of the numbers of vacancies in the occupation, then one should see a corresponding change in the qualification requirements for that occupation. That is, for example, if the differences within the labor force along the axis of the length of school attendance were to diminish through a measure such as compulsory schooling, then employers would turn to find another axis, such as type of curriculum pursued, to differentiate job applicants. For a detailed description of the educational consequences of this phenomenon, see Dore (1976) and Seidman (1982).

Clearly then, if the relationship between general-education qualifications and occupations in the economy is not a technical one—specific knowledge/skills required for a given occupation are not functionally correlated to a particular general-education qualification—then it is obvious that (1) personal income is not determined by the type of general education qualification, but rather it is determined by the type of occupation, (2) an increase in educational provision will not lead to disappearance of low-wage paying occupations, and (3) the number of vacancies in an occupation has no relationship to output of educational qualifications, but rather it is related to the general health of the economy (for more details on this see Hussain 1976).

In light of the foregoing, one can assert with absolute confidence that the numerous rates-of-return studies much beloved by people such as George Psacharopoulos and his colleagues at the World Bank (see, for example, Psacharopoulos 1973 and 1981) do not show what their proponents claim they show. Rather all that these studies demonstrate is that some occupations carry with them higher incomes than others. However the differences in income between different occupations is not a function of the levels of education demanded for entry into them, but rather it is social differentiation. Thus certain classes of jobs for example will almost always have low wages/status attached to them, regardless of the level of educational qualifications of those performing these jobs. To demonstrate positive correlation between income and lengths of education, as rates-of-return studies often do, cannot be taken to automatically imply that educational qualifications per se are sources of income. *If this were so then there would be no unemployment among the educated.* The basic function of education, especially *general* education is to serve as a selection mechanism for employers; and it is a mechanism that has little to do with the productivity merits of the employee.

This point becomes forcefully obvious the moment it is recognized that the triple underlying assumptions of rates-of-return studies are fallacious. These are: (1) the labor market in capitalist societies rest on competition for wages; (2) that the market itself exists to match supply and demand; and (3) all educational access is market determined (whereas only a small segment is). In other words, for all the econometric engineering human capital theorists may indulge in, at the end of the day they are left with this fundamental fact: there is absolutely no empirical basis to the assertion that wages are rooted in the marginal productivity of educated labor that investment in education supposedly increases. For further details see Hussain (1976) and Maglen (1990). In addition, see Klees (1986) and Eisemon (1987), both of whom delineate major methodological weaknesses of these types of studies. Paul Hurst's pithy review article (1987) is also relevant here. He subjects the whole number-crunching approach, which undergirds rates-of-return studies, to the study of educational phenomenon to severe criticism: "an ounce of insight is worth a mountain of multiple regression" (p. 69).[40]

This is not all, however. Even if these studies, like the other human capital studies, were on their own merits sound, that is that they captured the education–economy nexus beautifully, there still remains this fundamental weakness: the inordinate emphasis on characteristics of the individual in the effort to promote economic growth, with little regard to structural impediments. In other words, human capital theory, like all modernization theories, fail to take into account that it is not simply *subjective* factors (agency), but *objective* factors too (structure) that stand in the way of economic growth (and national development). Among the latter factors are three major *sets* of *dialectically* interrelated factors: One set are those bequeathed by colonialism, another set of factors are the distortions that have emerged in the postindependence period, and the third set are those connected with participation in an international economic system in which the rules of the game are determined primarily by those who first set up the system: the Western industrialized nations. To briefly elaborate on each set:

The colonially inherited set of factors include: a monoculture export-dependent economy, which facilitates a hand-to-mouth economic predicament where investable surpluses are almost nonexistent for purposes of economic diversification—a situation that has now caught up with many of the oil exporters too—which is so absolutely essential for long-term economic health and stability; lack of an indigenous capitalist class sufficiently developed to stem the hemorrhage of surplus and resources taking place via activities of foreign multinational corporations; and fragmentation of large geographical areas (e.g., the African continent) into small countries with radically different ideological affiliations, making it almost impossible to develop a single, large, economic and political entity, without which for any one country in isolation comprehensive and organically integrated but diversified economic development is impossible, because of limitations imposed by economies-of-scale problems, as well as lack of *balanced* natural resources.

The postindependence distortions include: planning and implementation of development projects aimed to benefit the minority urban elites rather than the rural masses; economic mismanagement on the part of governments of PQD countries via misuse of whatever little investable surplus that has been available in order to sustain economically parasitic middle-class standards of living enjoyed by their elites who model their lifestyles on those of the elites of the Western industrialized nations; outright economic corruption by elites where financial resources have simply been siphoned out of the country to build financial egg-nests abroad—usually in the West; political instability as rival elite factions have sought to gain control of political power upon which their very status as the elite has come to depend, given the lack of alternative viable modes of large-scale acquisition of wealth, such as ownership of the major means of production; and political corruption—often aided and abetted by Western multinationals and governments, as in the case of Chile in 1973—of which endemic military coups and dictatorships are simply but one manifestation, thus preventing the development of democratic institutions that can help to eradicate these politically induced economic ills.

The third set of factors include: the unequal terms of trade between the Western industrialized nations and the PQD countries, made possible in part by the monoculturally induced hand-to-mouth economic position of the PQD countries, as well as the extremely low demand-elasticity of many of their exports—clearly demonstrating the irrelevance of the theory of comparative advantage when applied to trading partners of unequal economic strength; usurious lending rates of foreign financial institutions; massive transfers of investable surpluses out of PQD countries via "legal" as well as such illegal activities of foreign multinationals as false pricing and invoicing; and concentration of investments by foreign multinationals in those branches of economic sectors that provide maximum returns to investments in the shortest possible time and with minimal capital and technological outlay—usually the light, elite-oriented, consumer industry or the resource extraction sectors. Among this third set of factors, one must not also forget the inappropriate planning advice and assistance from international organizations such as the International Monetary Fund, and the World Bank, of which the strategy of pursuing import-dependent import-substitution industrialization advocated in the sixties, or the human-capital strategy, or the trickle-down (crumbs from the table) theory, are excellent examples.

In light of the foregoing, then, it is little wonder that one of the early well-known practitioners of economics of education, Mark Blaug (see, for example, his *Economics of Education* published in 1970), would more or less recant and simply denounce the entire field of economics of education that human capital theory first helped to create by simply stating that, in his words, "[o]ne might also go so far as to say that the economics of education now lies dead in the mind of both professional economists and professional educators" (Blaug 1999: 101). He further explains:

The simple fact is that the field has failed to deliver the goods. We are certain that education contributes to economic growth but then so does health care, housing, roads, capital markets, et cetera, and in any case we cannot quantify the growth-enhancing effects of education under different circumstances and we cannot even describe these effects except in the most general terms. We can measure private and social returns to educational investment but since we cannot specify, much less measure, the externalities generated by educated individuals, not to mention the consumption benefits of education, the "social" rate of return to education is a bogus label. But even if the externalities of education were nil, it would still be true to say that we have been unable to separate the productivity from the screening functions of schooling and hence cannot even say what the social rate of return to education means.... A subject that after 25 years of study and investigation is unable convincingly to resolve at least some of these issues is not to be taken seriously. And, indeed, it is not taken seriously (p. 102).

Yet, the fact is that organizations such as the World Bank, the OECD, and USAID, are highly unlikely to pay heed to these criticisms any time soon—*at least at the level of policy formulation and implementation.* To be sure, under pressure from assistance recipients and the enlightened elsewhere, the bank has recently begun to make noises to the effect that it is reconsidering its view of the role of universities in development (see Bollag 1998 and World Bank 2002). However, a convincing program of funding support still appears to be absent. The reassessment remains in the rhetorical realm. Consider the 1999 education sector report. It states that bank staff, "now look more at education as an integrated system, one part of which cannot function well if another is ailing. The emphasis on basic education, for instance, does not mean that nothing should be done in tertiary education: the role of tertiary institutions as centers of excellence, research hubs and training grounds for tomorrow's teachers and leaders is critical" (World Bank 1999: 24).[41] But when the proposed policy implementation plan of the report is examined, one quickly notes that higher education is hardly even mentioned! It is only in an important 2002 publication that we see indications of some rethink within the Bank; but even here one has to be wary.[42]

The truth really is this: The international donor agencies are too heavily invested in the human capital theory as expressed by the rates-of-return techniques to give it up as the principle determinant of their educational assistance policies so easily. But not only that, as Marginson (1999) points out from a sociology of knowledge perspective, economics of education is too tied in to the existing power system given that its principle focus is also a major function of the state. Consequently, they will blithely continue to use human capital theory as a basis for educational planning and funding.

Three further points will conclude this chapter: First, as long as support for higher education by the bank and its allies in the development assistance business continue to insist on a structural adjustment approach to higher education, it does not bode well for Africa, especially for the marginalized. While one may, *perhaps*, accept the necessity to introduce some kind of "user fees," given the level of poverty in most of Africa, there has to be mechanisms instituted that will allow the needy to pursue further education (e.g., student loans).[43] Yet, the question here is, Do African countries have robust and relatively efficient bureaucracies that can manage such mechanisms? The answer is that most do not. (See Johnstone and Teferra [2004] for more on issues of finance in the African context.) Ultimately, a mix of private and public education institutions *may* be desirable; however, the bank's approach *in practice* has been to push for privatization or even marginalization of *existing* institutions rather than calling for expansion of higher education through addition of new but private institutions. However, even here one must be careful not to reproduce the U.S. model where private institutions become the means for the permanent reproduction of the capitalist class. Leaving the issue of morality and ethics aside, deep levels of inequality *may* be tolerable in societies such as the United States, but certainly not in PQD countries (for that is an invitation to instability).

Second, the description of sources and types of assistance to African higher education (see also endnote 3), it is necessary to point out, should not be taken to imply that such assistance has been an unmitigated blessing. Especially in the postindependence era, the benefits of assistance to African higher education is, at times, questionable in light of the fact that the assistance does not serve its intended purpose, or is much too limited to be effective, or is misused, or even "misplanned." In fact, in recent years, the dire economic straits of many African countries has helped to highlight another kind of problem: the uselessness of assistance given a context where no local funds exist (for reasons of severe budgetary constraints) to permit the continued functioning of the assistance project following its completion. For example, building expensive laboratories when maintenance of the laboratories—especially from the perspective of consumables—cannot be guaranteed. Under these circumstances, the motives of the donor become highly questionable: perhaps the assistance project was agreed to for primarily diplomatic/political reasons instead of altruistic ones.

There is without doubt a need for the development of a new assistance model: perhaps one that involves not only *capital* expenditure support for a given project, but also *recurrent* expenditure support on a diminishing shared-cost basis (e.g., 100% support in the first year, 90% in the second year, 80% in the third year, etc.), upon completion of the project. There is a clear need for imaginative approaches to the assistance relationship than the prevalent one. For example, consider tweaking the above suggested model in this way: the recurrent expenditure support does not necessarily have to come from a single or project-originating donor, it could come from a consortium of two, three or more donors. (An excellent book on the general issue of assistance to African education that is still very relevant today more than a decade and a half since its publication, sadly (suggesting unlearned lessons), is Hawes and Coombe 1986.)

Third, although some within and without the foreign assistance community have begun to advocate the elimination of foreign assistance altogether—other than humanitarian assistance—(see, for instance, Dichter 2003, and Theroux 2003)—foreign assistance, especially of the type provided by the World Bank (that is, publicly-funded assistance) is still necessary. What is required is a new and imaginative restructuring of the bank and its allied institutions, such that there is a genuine commitment to the poor (who—Westerners constantly need to be reminded about this—constitute a *majority* of the world's population). However, is such restructuring possible in the present international political climate, dominated as it is by the agendas of the transnational monopolies (effected through proxy by their inordinate influence on the governments of countries like the United States)? [44] Perhaps not. As Pincus and Winters have observed: "The need to reinvent the World Bank is urgent and will remain so for the foreseeable future. But the prospects for reinvention are as dim as they have been at any time in the institution's history" (2002: 4–5). The reason why this is so, can be best assessed from what Caufield's excellent but mind-numbing book (1996) states about the range of actors involved who have a deep interest in maintaining the status quo: the bank's bureaucracy (today about 11,000 strong—with their dependents they can easily constitute a small town); heads of governments, especially the illegitimate ones; "well-connected contractors, exporters, consultants, and middlemen" in the wealthy countries; and transnational monopolies and banks. The upshot of this circumstance is summarized by Caufield thusly: "The past half-century of development has not profited the poorest people, nor the poorest countries. Rather, they have paid dearly—and their descendants will continue to pay dearly—for the disproportionately small benefits they have received." On the other hand, she continues: "Their relatively small investment in fifty years of development has left the rich countries—and especially their richest citizens—richer than ever before. Given all this, and given the fact that development funds, including the World Bank's, are ultimately supplied by ordinary taxpayers in donor nations, there is much truth in the saying that development—at least in the monopolistic, formulaic, foreign-dominated, arrogant, and failed form that we have known—is largely a matter of poor people in rich countries giving money to rich people in poor countries" (Caufield 1996: 338). What is particularly chilling is that this assessment was already clear more than two decades ago when Payer (1982) came out with her devastating critique of the bank. Clearly, the World Bank, *as it is presently constituted (and given that its origins are rooted in a time period when roughly two-thirds of the planet was under some form of European colonial rule)* should be disbanded. However, the pseudointellectual representatives of the ignorantsia (let alone the politicians) who regularly feed at the bank's trough will hardly disagree more.

NOTES

1. One may want to acknowledge here that, in a sense, all university development throughout history, regardless of country, has depended on foreign assistance if one were to enlarge the scope of the term to include the interchange of scholars and researchers. As Appendix I demonstrates, for instance, the development of universities in the West owed a great deal to the Islamic ecumene. And even today, Western universities continue to receive assistance (though that is not how they probably would perceive it) in the form of subsidized intellectual labor (foreign teachers and teaching/graduate assistants, whose education in the early stages of their careers have been paid for by societies they come from).

2. Some may also add a third actor: foreign scholarly societies. Informal (and sometimes formal) support has also come to African higher education through membership by their staff, on an individual basis, of foreign scholarly societies, such as the African Studies Association (United States), the American Economic Association, the American Association for the Advancement of Science, and so on. This support is essential not only for the personal academic growth of the individual staff member, but also for the institution as a whole because it provides it with links to the international scholarly community. Of course, as African higher education develops its internet connections,

the importance of such international scholarly support will increase. (See McMurtie 2000, for more on this issue.)

3. While space does not permit an exploration of the roles of all the various donors in the history of the development of African higher education in the colonial and postindependence periods, a hint of their presence in that history can be had from considering the following brief descriptions of the two principal nongovernmental actors, categorized by period:

Overseas Universities—Colonial Period: During the colonial period, the role played by overseas higher education institutions in the development of higher education in Africa took three basic forms: first, was a passive role effected through overseas training of African students; the second was also a passive role played out by means of externally-run secondary school (and even university level) examinations; and the third was a direct role involving institutional affiliation and the granting of external degrees.

Overseas Universities—Postindependence Period: As in the colonial period, support for the development of higher education in Africa would take several forms: the passive one of providing overseas training for African students destined to become teachers in the their home universities (staff development); and such active ones as the following: sending staff to work in African universities for temporary periods to facilitate program, departmental, and institutional development; creating partnerships between themselves and their African counterparts in support of various institutional programs, sending staff to provide advice on institutional planning, and so on. Select higher education institutions in all countries throughout the world with well-developed higher education systems have played this postindependence role: The institutions range from those in the former Soviet Union and the Eastern bloc to those in the United States; from those in India to those in Canada; from those in China to those in Britain; from those in France to those in Australia.

Private Philanthropic Organizations—Colonial Period: When discussing the role of overseas private philanthropic foundations in the development of higher education in colonial Africa, there is in essence only one that really comes to mind: The Phelps-Stokes Foundation. The Foundation came to play, for a short time, an important role through the agency of the Phelps-Stokes African Education Commission (discussed earlier in this work).

Private Philanthropic Organizations—Postindependence Period: Mention has already been made of the prominent role played by one private philanthropic organization in the postindependence period: the Carnegie Corporation (founded by Andrew Carnegie, who had made his fortune in the U.S. steel industry, in 1911). The corporation, it may be noted here, had already begun to develop links with Africa much early on, in the 1920s. It played a part in the development of a public library system in South Africa. The corporation, as part of its effort to improve the quality of educational and cultural life in British colonial Africa, had dispatched Milton J. Ferguson (the well-known state librarian of California) to study libraries (the few that there were) in southern Africa in 1928. Upon his recommendation, and with some $63,500 in matching funds donated by the corporation, a program was launched to develop a nation-wide public library system in South Africa. (One may note in passing, that, unfortunately, the plan that emerged did not include a racially integrated approach to the library system [Hull 1990].) The corporation's role in the development of higher education in independent anglophone Africa began with the funding of the Nigerian Commission led by Sir Eric Ashby, discussed earlier.

The corporation also helped to finance the Lockwood Commission report on the establishment of the University of Zambia, also mentioned earlier. Now, the significance of this activity should not be underrated, it assisted in funding higher education planning initiatives that helped to continue the tradition of U.S. involvement in African education. If the early involvement, through the Phelps-Stokes Commission, was a mixed blessing for the Africans (encouraged the British government to be directly involved in expanding educational provisions, but at the same time considerably narrowed the type of educational provision), the postindependence involvement has been overwhelmingly positive. Why? Because it has led to a much needed modification of the British civic university model that the Asquith plan helped to export to colonial anglophone Africa. (For an extensive look at the role of the Carnegie Corporation in African higher education, see Murphy [1976].)

Other foundations that have been involved with higher education assistance in Africa include the Edward W. Hazen Foundation, W. K. Kellog Foundation, the Ford Foundation, the John D. and Catherine T. MacArthur Foundation and the Rockefeller Foundation. These foundations provide assistance directly, or is more often the case through contracts with either individual U.S. universities or through such U.S. organizations as the American Council on Education, the Institute of International Education (which also administers the Fulbright exchange pogram begun under the 1944 Fulbright Act sponsored by Senator William Fulbright that facilitates the exchange of scholars to lecture, study, research, etc.) and the Africa-America Institute.

More recently (in 2000), a consortium of four philanthropic foundations in the United States began an initial five-year partnership program (renewable depending upon outcomes for another five years) to assist select universities in a number of African countries (which include Kenya, Nigeria, Mozambique, Tanzania, Uganda, and South Africa). The four foundations are: the Carnegie Corporation of New York, the Ford Foundation, the John D. and Catherine T. MacArthur Foundation, and the Rockefeller Foundation. Their justification for this initiative, described in their press release (Carnegie Corporation 2000), was the recognition that any renewal process African nations undertook could not proceed without the involvement of higher education, given "the multifaceted contributions that universities can make in national development and poverty alleviation," and the fact that "(s)trong African universities can play a role in protecting basic freedoms, enhancing intellectual life, and informing policy making." The principal criteria for the selection of universities to receive assistance was explained thusly: "Being located in a country undergoing systemic public policy reform; Supporting innovation, particularly through use of new technologies, to better position the institutions to meet the specific needs of their countries; Engaging in a strategic planning process in which a key element is a commitment to helping build national capacity for social and economic development; Having creative, broad-based institutional leadership" (Carnegie Corporation 2000).

4. Hard data on international students, in general, studying in the then Soviet Union is hard to come by (see Kuraev-Maxah 2004 for a discussion of this problem). However, Weaver (1985: 109, 111) provides some data: for instance, between 1956–57 and 1963–64 the number of African students in the Soviet Union would jump from around 14 to 3,000! (In these figures students from some 37 African countries would be represented.)

5. For recent news stories on Russian hate crimes against foreign students go to the news archives of the www.bbc.com website.

6. The Africa-America Institute, a nonprofit organization founded in 1953, it may be noted, continues to be active in support of African higher education. The institute, which is funded by a variety of donors (private, corporate, the U.S. government, and so on), helps to provide opportunities for Africans to obtain short and long-term graduate education and professional training in the United States, among its many activities. The institute also ran, from 1963 to when it was dissolved in 1997, the well-known long-running African Graduate Fellowship Program (AFGRAD). Among its current ongoing programs is the African Technology for Education and Workforce Development Initiative (AFTECH), which aims to provide Africans with technological skills in order to enhance Africa's global competitiveness and growth.

7. A new USA—the United States of Africa—is a dream that has been articulated

by countless African intellectuals for more than a century. Yet, as the 21st century continues to unfold, its realization appears as remote as ever (witness the ongoing heart-wrenching civil wars). However, if one may take a page from the history of Europe—where a borderless Europe is, today, within the realms of possibility (clearly demonstrating that internal conflagrations, however longstanding, are not insurmountable)—the initial path to a borderless Africa may lie in the less romantic, but yet meaningful, sectorally diverse, cross-border institution-building that rests on the premise of exploiting economies of scale. One such institution that holds out the promise of cross-border cooperation for the mutual benefit of all participants is the university. Universities need not wait for a borderless Africa, they can help toward its realization by engaging in the creation of cross-border consortia where universities can share resources optimally, develop regional centers of research specialization, exploit the educational benefits of the flow of students and faculty across borders, and so on. Cross-border institution building is the quickest way to demonstrate the practical benefits of a borderless Africa as a precursor to its eventual creation.

8. The World Bank is made up of three closely knit institutions (hence it is sometimes referred to as the World Bank Group): The International Bank for Reconstruction and Development, The International Finance Corporation, and the International Development Association.

9. While Girdwood's point is well taken (Girdwood 1995) that in referring to the International Bank for Reconstruction and Development (IBRD) as "the World Bank" or "the Bank" one risks reifying it, from the perspective of the recipients of its attentions across the world, however, its alien and seemingly monolithic public face does take on a reified form (notwithstanding the very human differences, disagreements, etc., in the internal workings of the organization—a characteristic of all human organizations). Moreover, the bank's own publications are not averse to the use of the same terminology.

10. A word or two about this once much-vaunted World Bank policy approach: To the observer with perspicacity, the beginnings of the almost messianic zeal with which McNamara would take up this policy theme, to the chagrin of the rank and file at the bank—and recall that in irony of ironies this is the same man who had presided over an immoral war (as he himself would later come to describe it) in which tens upon tens of thousands of the poor had perished, that is the infamous Vietnam War—was already evident in McNamara's maiden address to the bank's Board of Governors (on September 30, 1968). In it he began with the observation that the "cheerful statistics" that appeared to show progress in the development of the poorer countries, concealed "a far less cheerful picture in many countries" in which "much of the growth is concentrated in the industrial areas, while the peasant remains stuck in his immemorial poverty, living on the bare margin of subsistence" and went on to insist that the richer countries, despite being afflicted with aid-fatigue had to do more by way of development assistance, especially considering that over the preceding decade they had "added to their annual real incomes a sum of about $400 billion, an addition itself far greater than the total annual incomes of the underdeveloped countries of Asia, Africa and Latin America" (McNamara 1981: 4).

A decade or so later, in another address to the governors (on September 26, 1977), he would be even more forthright and adamant, though ever mindful that the bank was not after all in the business of philanthropy: "Basic human needs are by definition critical. And for governments to assist the poor to satisfy them is not public philanthropy, but a wise investment in human capital formation." "It is the poverty itself," he argued, "that is a social liability. Not the people who happen to be poor. They represent immense human potential. Investing in their future productivity—if it is done effectively—is very sound economics. Certainly what is very unsound economics is to permit a culture of poverty to so expand and grow within a nation that it begins to infect and erode the entire social fabric" (p. 463).

However, even as McNamara continued to insist on targeting development efforts toward the masses, the poor, the *basic-needs* development policy would founder on the shoals of a number of negative realities, ranging from the global politics of the Cold War that intruded in bank operations, through bureaucratic inertia and resistance within the World Bank itself (an institution long nurtured on the milk of neoclassical economics in which the goal of economic growth reigned above all else, including issues of equity), on to sometimes insurmountable elite-resistance within the PQD countries themselves. As Caufield (1996: 106) has pointed out: "McNamara's passionate rhetoric created the impression that the bank was now concentrating on fighting poverty, but his statistics show otherwise. Most of the $77 billion worth of loans made during his reign supported industrialization through traditional infrastructure projects: highways, dams, gas pipelines, ports, cargo handling facilities, and the like. Less than 10% went to education, health, family planning, water supply, and other programs that might help the poor directly. In that category, too, most of the funds were spent on construction and the import of high-tech equipment, not on the provision of services." In fact, by the time he left, a new concern was beginning to become the overriding policy at the bank, especially with respect to Africa, that of structural adjustment. (For a sympathetic history of the rise and fall of the poor at the bank see Kapur, Lewis, and Webb 1997. For a critique of the supposed resurgence of the poor in World Bank thinking in recent years Bergeron 2003 provides a useful entry point. Wolff's critique (2003) of the absence of social structural considerations—specifically "class"—in World Bank thinking and in the thinking of its detractors is also relevant here.)

11. As Girdwood comments: "It must be acknowledged at the outset that the team responsible for *Higher Education: The Lessons of Experience* prepared a thorough analysis of the difficulties facing higher education in many countries." However, she continues, "[m]uch of the data was generated within the bank to meet its own institutional needs, and therefore implicitly prepared to reach certain conclusions. Many of these issues remain contentious; and yet throughout the commissioned literature the World Bank's overall concerns and orthodoxies are often referred to 'as conventional wisdom.'" (p. 66)

12. A *babu* was a derogatory term applied in colonial India by the British to an educated East Indian who they despised as an "uppity nigger" who did not know his proper place.

13. See also Cheng (in Buchert and King) who, in contextualizing the merits of some of the document's "best-practices" from the perspective of China, has this "health warning" label (to borrow an apt phrase from Buchert and King): "The Chinese reform was formally launched in 1985 with little input of international experience and with little adherence to theories developed elsewhere.... The reform in China agrees in form with many of the World Bank recommendations, but the causes and results of such reform measures may differ from those in the World Bank analysis.... Much of what is quoted in the World Bank paper about China's reform occurs only in some part of

China, or occurs more effectively in some part of China than in others. Decentralization and diversification have caused some institutions to prosper but have put others in deep crisis.... [T]he reality in China demonstrates that few reform policies bring about absolutely positive results" (pp. 206–207). What is more, as in the case of Chile as well to which the document refers approvingly, there is no mention of the political circumstances within which the reforms were accomplished: the absence, to put it politely, of a democratic government. Perhaps, brutal blood-soaked dictatorships (the horrors of Augusto Pinochet's Chile, are, as of this moment, at long last receiving official acknowledgement by way of a commission of inquiry, and one should not forget Tiananmen Square—to give just one example from China), do have their uses.

14. See also King's summary of the World Bank policies on higher education up to 1994 in Buchert and King (1995). Here Ilon (2003) is useful as well.

15. What, then, were these policy concerns that shaped the identification of the best-practices surveyed in the document? There were essentially four, very briefly: diversification of higher education provision (Chapter 2 of the document): that is, the arrest of traditional patterns of university development, and instead the transformation of higher education in two other (hitherto neglected) directions: nonuniversity-level institutions (e.g., technical colleges) and privately-funded universities and colleges; diversification of funding sources (Chapter 3): that is, development of alternative mechanisms for financing higher education ranging from fees from students to financial support from industry (but with due regard to issues of equity); the eclipse of the direct role of the state in higher education (Chapter 4): ranging from measures to support institutional autonomy to encouragement of privatization of higher education; and the enhancement of efficiency (Chapter 5); that is, the improvement of the quality of higher education—in terms of both internal matters (e.g., quality of teaching) and external matters (e.g., efficient matching of training with labor market needs). On the surface, and baldly stated thus, there wasn't much that one could quarrel with here. However, a closer look at them demonstrated three fundamental limitations: weaknesses at the conceptual level of some of the individual policy prescriptions; the inapplicability of many of the suggested directions of reform to the specific economic circumstances of much of Africa; and the marginalization of universities as engines of progress and development. While space does not permit exploration of these limitations in depth and here the reader is directed, instead, to consult Buchert and King, some examples illustrating these limitations will suffice:

The relationship between lower levels of education and higher education is a dialectical one: improving one, improves the other; at the same time, neglecting one effects the other negatively. To put the matter in another way: good primary schools strengthen secondary schools and good secondary schools strengthen higher education (for the simple reason that the student who enters higher education begins his/her educational journey at the primary school level); conversely, good primary schools and good secondary schools can only come about through good teacher training which is the province of higher education, especially universities. It is, in fact, interesting that the Asquith Commission had dealt with this very question decades back in its report; and had arrived at this exact same reasoning:

While admitting that the development of popular instruction is most urgent, we cannot agree with the inference that the development of university education should be postponed. On the contrary, we hold that the latter is all the more imperative on this account. For the situation does not present a simple issue between the claims of higher and lower education; progress at any level of education is dependent upon progress at other levels.... Indeed, the lesson to be drawn from history is quite clear even if at first sight quite paradoxical; it is that where education as a whole is backward, effort is most rewarding when it is directed at higher levels. It may be remembered that the development of universities in Europe preceded the systematic organization of popular education. (United Kingdom 1945a: 12)

In light of this commonsensical fact, how then could the World Bank have insisted (and continues to do so in practice, despite recent policy noises to the contrary) that countries such as those in Africa concentrate on the issue of universalizing primary-level education and pay less attention to the development of higher education—because, in its view, wiping out illiteracy came before all else (never mind the fact that historically universities in the West developed amidst a sea of illiteracy or never mind the fact that some of the very countries from whom it derived its best-practices examples, such as India and China, harbored huge numbers of people who were illiterate [a situation that still persists to the present and this in countries that can build atomic bombs!]). Although, to give another example, the World Bank was adamant on marginalizing the role of the state, if one stopped and thought for a moment—and as Watson (in Buchert and King) points out—the true lesson of the best-practices was that the state had to continue to play a central role in higher education for without it none of the best-practices could be implemented. Regarding the matter of the inapplicability to the economic circumstances of Africa: consider the issue of the development of science and technology educational infrastructure. As King (in Buchert and King) pointed out, World Bank lending to this sector of higher education was traditionally highly biased in favor of the Asia/Pacific region, with only a small fraction (less than 5% of the dollar amount) going to Africa. Now, as King further observed, the ability of the former region to absorb such lending was predicated on a prior, historically determined, presence of infrastructural capacity (in which indigenous ownership of capital—regardless of whether it was owned by the state or the individual—had been determinatively critical), however, the document in its characteristic air of unrealism waxed lyrical on the necessity of building industry–university relations as a basis for developing the science and technology educational infrastructure with minimal recourse to state funding.

Yet, anyone with even the slightest knowledge of Africa knew that historically, much of capital in Africa had been and continued to be foreign owned, and therefore the research and development wing of capital, with rare exceptions, had never been located in Africa, but abroad. Given this circumstance (which one should emphasize continues to be the case to the present day), On what, one may derisively ask, was the linkage between industry and higher education to be based? What is more, the bank had (and has) never seriously looked at Africa in terms of promoting genuine industrial development—viewing the continent, instead, as a supplier of raw materials to the world. To give another example: while the bank was correct on the necessity of some form of user-fees because tuition-free higher education is subsidized by the poor, it proposed dealing with the issue of equity through student loans. Now, when governments in the West have never really been able to efficiently operate student loan schemes, on what basis could it assume that such administratively weak governments as those that characterize much of Africa could operate student loan schemes?

On the marginalization of universities, symptomatic of which was, for instance, its vehement decrying of the traditional tendency of lower-level higher education institutions being eventually upgraded to university status (never mind the fact that the history of higher education tells us that almost throughout the world, including in the West, that is how most universities came into being), Court (in Buchert and King) captured the problem: beginning by noting that the general thrust of the best-practices document was to champion the vocationalization of higher education (including the universities) he goes on to counter: "While this might seem a particularly appropriate emphasis for the poorest continent in the world, Africa—perhaps more than other places—also needs institutions for *unapplied* teaching, learning, reflection and research. This is because of the powerful and continuing sense of technological, intellectual and cultural dependence upon the West and the consequent need to think out its own course and model of development." He further explains: "The point is hardly a novel one: universities, particularly in an era of pluralistic politics, represent the most likely places for the training of original thought and the conduct of basic research which in the last resort are the only means by which societies can take control of their own destiny." Moreover, he notes, "[s]uch a function…is not a luxury that can be dispensed with for a period, pending better economic times, but an integral part of the development process itself" (p. 111).

16. Tragically, the situation since then, as all who have visited a number of African countries in recent years know from first hand, has worsened considerably. Here, one may also wish to look at Theroux 2003 for a sympathetic but honest grass-roots level eyewitness account of the terribly depressing broader socioeconomic and political circumstances that characterizes much of Africa today, and of which the awful predicament of the education sector generally and the higher education subsector specifically is a reflection. See also the report of the British sponsored Commission for Africa (2005).

17. Or consider this chilling description of the circumstances of what used to be one of the most prestigious African universities in East Africa: University of Makerere: "By 1990, Makerere exhibited in extreme form the resource constraints facing universities throughout Africa. No new physical structures had been built and no maintenance carried out in twenty years. Journal subscriptions had declined to zero, as had chemicals for science laboratories…. A 'pillage' or survival culture prevailed which put at risk to private theft any saleable and removable item, from computers and telephones to electric wires and door fixtures—and sometimes the doors themselves! In a situation of limited transport, few if any working telephones, and the absence of needed equipment and stationery, it is remarkable that the university managed to remain open throughout this period" (Court 1999: 3).

18. The phrase "science and technology infrastructure" is meant to encapsulate all the software and hardware elements of training, research and development in the areas of both basic and applied science and technology: ranging from classroom courses and programs of study to laboratories to research and development centers.

19. It is characteristic of World Bank "experts" that they never saw a contradiction in suggesting that there were high rates-of-return to primary education, especially in agrarian Africa (comprising much of the continent), and therefore that is where all the effort was to be concentrated, but at the same time did not see the need to build a science and technology infrastructure that could provide the necessary research inputs for best agricultural practices that could allow the realization of the high rates-of-return!

20. See the discussion in this chapter on the issue of *rates-of-return* studies and their influence on educational policy in PQD countries.

21. This point raises a broader issue: Few appear to realize how powerful the intellectual influence of the World Bank, for good or ill, has been—and continues to be—on how the problem of economic development (of which educational planning is a part) in PQD countries has come to be perceived, from the perspective of knowledge, theories and ideas, over the years. The matter is well described by Stern and Ferreira (1997: 524). Given, they observe, the enormous research budget (relative to one that any university anywhere in the world can ever afford—in the 1990s averaging $25 million annually), the army of economist and researchers it employs, and of course the magnitude of the lending program itself (running into tens of billions of dollars annually), "the bank's potential influence is profound, and that the bank cannot be seen as just one of a number of fairly equal actors in the world of development economics" (emphasis added). This intellectual reach of the bank, they explain, is effected through a variety of mechanisms at its disposal that when considered in combination are almost unique to itself: generating ideas (e.g., by setting research agendas, conducting research for operational purposes, collating and disseminating raw data, extracting lessons from its field experiences); stimulating research activities and ideas in the external academic community (e.g., by commissioning research, organizing conferences, participating in conferences organized by others, etc.); disseminating and promoting internally and externally generated ideas, theories, research, etc. (e.g., by establishing research centers in target countries, providing training for external researchers, serially producing *must-read* influential documents—such as its country studies, world development reports, sector policy papers, and journals—moving personnel from its research wing to its operational wing); and most important of all the application of ideas and theories through its operations (project implementation) in the field (e.g., by means of its "lending leverage, policy dialogue, and technical assistance on projects").

What is particularly troubling about this influence (though not mentioned by Stern and Ferreira) is that anecdotal evidence suggests that those in the academic community concerned with education in PQD countries, regardless of where they are located, have often found it difficult to mount genuine critiques of World Bank policies once they have gotten used to drinking at the trough of World Bank largesse while in pursuit of research grants, research commissions, and so on. (On this matter contrast, for example, Court's trenchant critique of the bank's structural adjustment approach to higher education that he appears to have written in his capacity as an academic, Court 1995, with another paper he wrote, Court 1999, albeit some years later, in his capacity as a research consultant for the bank—in the latter he waxes lyrical on the relevance of the same approach.)

22. The method the bank uses to disburse loans is to select projects, rather than sectors (an approach that itself is highly problematic), that it finances jointly with the receiving country. Now, consider the following: taking the total expenditure on all projects that the bank helped finance for the education sector as a whole, throughout the world, during the period 1963 to 1990, then the allocation for higher education was only about 12% (calculation based on data in Jones (1992, p. 137, 182). If higher education is defined to include all forms of postsecondary education, including vocational training, then the percentage rises to about 30%. (See also Banya and Elu [2001], and Ilon [2003] for more on World Bank lending patterns for higher education.) However, the bulk of total lending for higher education sector as a whole, broadly defined, appears to have gone to Asia; certainly in the period 1980–1993, according to the best-practices

document, Asia received 54% compared to Africa's 10.7% (p. 81).

23. See Lulat (2003) on this issue; that is the genesis of the high unit costs of African higher education.

24. Mamdani (1993: 10) states that the bank was privately even more belligerent than it was in its public pronouncements (reports, etc.). He recalls: "At a meeting with African vice-chancellors in Harare in 1986, the World Bank argued that higher education in Africa was a luxury: that most African countries were better off closing universities at home and training graduates overseas. The thrust of the bank's logic ran as follows: that education is an investment like any other, foolish to make unless the returns are profitable." However, Mamdani further comments, "[r]ecognizing that its call for a closure of universities was politically unsustainable, the bank subsequently modified its agenda, calling for universities to be trimmed and restructured to produce only those skills which the market demands."

25. Good governance also has to do with the issue of democracy and human rights—and the latter in turn impinges on the matter of the war-making apparatus since governments in the developing world have tended to use this apparatus against their own people. One ought to point out here that the term *good governance* (like "civil society") is a relatively new buzzword in the lexicon of Western development experts and aid donors. It is as if all of a sudden they have woken up to discover that things like good governance (and a vibrant civil society) are necessary after all for national development to succeed. Consider, for example, the following statement which is almost laughable in its obviousness made by the African Development Bank, an affiliate of the World Bank, in one of its recent reports: "Governance is now one of the cornerstones of economic development. Good governance, in its political, social, and economic dimensions, underpins sustainable human development and the reduction of poverty in that it defines the processes and structures that guide political and socioeconomic relationships" (African Development Bank 2001). Of course, despite calls for good governance there is a palpable absence of accompanying analysis of why good governance has been absent in most of Africa all these years. Could it be that one factor (among many, it goes without saying) has been the role played by external agents: Cold War super powers, former colonial masters, foreign multinational corporations, and, yes, even multilateral agencies such as the Bretton Woods institutions (the World Bank and the International Monetary Fund)?

26. Information source: various data banks and publications available online through websites maintained by the World Bank and its affiliates; the various U.N. agencies; and bilateral donor agencies like the U.S. Agency for International Development. This data is also available by consulting the annual hard-copy statistical publications of these institutions and government agencies. Note that no single source of data exists for the information provided here; multiple sources must be consulted. However, if one were to insist on a single source, then the recent report from the World Bank (2000b) titled *Can Africa Claim the 21st Century* comes closest.

27. Consider the following simple, but awful statistic: for most of the past three decades, the annual average percentage growth rate of per capita GDP for the African continent as a whole has never made it into positive territory! Or contemplate this fact: in 1965 the per capita GDP for Sub-Saharan Africa was at $841 while that of East Asia and the Pacific stood at $632. Compare these figures thirty years later: in 1995, $933 for Sub-Saharan Africa and $2,253 for East Asia and the Pacific (World Bank 2000c: 131).

Not surprisingly, on the Human Development Index Sub-Saharan Africa is at the very bottom. Note also: data just presented for Sub-Saharan Africa also includes South Africa. If South Africa was not included the figures would be even more astounding and depressing. Of course such statistics in themselves tell us nothing, especially these particular variety, about the awful "tears of blood" inducing qualitative circumstances of the lives of ordinary people, as those who have visited Africa—specifically rural Africa—in recent years will attest to.

What is more: it is not simply that the economic circumstances of the majority of the African population have deteriorated terribly since independence, but as if to add insult to injury, the population has been simultaneously subjected to political thuggery of the worst kind on a relentless basis. As if the daily life struggles of simply putting bread on the table has not been challenging enough for the vast majority, they have been forced to endure widespread and relentless political oppression over the years involving massive violations of their basic human rights. Only the slightest hint—it can not be any more than that—of this circumstance can be elicited from considering these stark facts compiled by the African Development Bank in its latest report: Between 1963 and 2000 there were 180 leadership successions in Africa. Of these over 50% took place through coups, wars or invasions. The rest involved retirement, assassinations or impeachment. Only about 7% occurred because the incumbent lost an election. During this same period, to look at this matter from a different angle, the political life over 200 regimes was terminated by means of coups, civil wars or invasions. The report from which this data comes (African Development Bank 2001), further observes:

Africa is famous for leaders with long tenure. Fourteen present national heads in the region have been in office for between ten and 20 years; nine have served more than 20 years. The mean tenure for all former African leaders is 7.2 years, and about twice that for leaders who died in office or retired.... Of the 101 past leaders who left office due to a coup or similar unauthorized event, roughly two-thirds were killed, imprisoned, or banished to a foreign country. Twenty-seven former rulers died violently, counting five whose deaths appear to have been independent of a coup or coup attempt. The remaining 22 leaders in this category clearly perished as a direct result of coups. Of Africa's overthrown leaders who were not executed or assassinated, 37 were detained and held in jail or placed under house arrest. Twenty-nine other ex-leaders were forced into exile, at least temporarily. That figure does not include nine ex-leaders who experienced periods of both imprisonment and banishment.

A very strong word of caution is in order here: there will be the temptation among some, especially the Eurocentrists (and the like-minded), to immediately jump to the conclusion on the basis of the foregoing that all of Africa's problems are a matter of *agency* rather than the *structure* of the Western-dominated international political and economic order. In other words, the question that emerges here is this: Are the problems just mentioned a symptom or a cause of Africa's current awful predicament. The answer is that it is both; *it is not entirely one or the other*. That is, Africa's current circumstance is a product of *both* structure and agency, dialectically intertwined (see Appendix II on the matter of structure).

28. The issue of a mass market (for elite goods) could have been resolved to some degree if there had been a push for a borderless economic union of Africa; but neither the foreign powers nor most of Africa's leaders had any interest in the matter. On the contrary, the foreign powers—especially the former colonial powers—found it in their

interest to encourage Africa to remain divided (and continue to do so), initially for both Cold War reasons and for relative economic advantage (though today it is only the latter factor that is relevant).

29. It never occurred to the foreign aid donors that circumstances of comparative advantage could be created. The notion of comparative advantage is a false concept as has been amply demonstrated by countries such as Taiwan and South Korea. However, the more serious flaw in their thinking is, of course, the failure to be cognizant of the inherently unequal terms of trade between the PQD countries and the industrialized countries, coupled with the low demand-elasticity of many of the raw materials exports of the PQD countries. (See, for example, Dasgupta 1998.)

30. Of course, one can also argue that the West had taken this position (of advocating an elementary economic role for Africa) because it was hardly in a position to use its resources to assist Africa to become its economic competitor in the global market—at least that is how the Western politicians and public would have seen it. The fact that the United States and other Western countries, for example, continued (and continue) to refuse to lower their high tariff barriers against labor-intensive, low capital manufactured products (e.g., textiles, processed foods, etc.) from African countries—that is countries that are among the poorest in the world—lends support to this view. Yet, the economically astute would have recognized that, on the contrary, an economically thriving Africa could only have meant greater economic opportunities for the West as well, because of increased commerce and trade that would have ensued (much in the same way as would occur with respect to East Asia)—not to mention such other benefits as reduction or elimination of foreign aid to Africa, and so on. Imagine this scenario: an economically united Africa—that would include South Africa—with a well-developed industrial base capable of producing commodities for export to countries within Africa itself and globally as well. It could well have happened if the West had pushed for it from the very beginning, that is, at the time of independence.

31. The literature on economic development in Africa is now vast, diverse, complex, confusing and at times even highly contradictory. Given the depth and duration of the development malaise that afflicts the continent, this is, perhaps, not surprising. Anyhow, those wishing to delve further into the economic aspects of development briefly mentioned here may want to look at the following sources: Cooper (1993); Gereffi and Fonda (1992); Leys (1996); Logan and Mengisteab (1993); Lewis (1996); Lubeck (1992); Mbaku and Saxena (2004); McPherson and Goldsmith (1998); Mytelka (1989); Rieff (1998); Saul and Leys (1999); and various past and present issues of the journal, *Review of African Political Economy*, published in the United Kingdom.

32. There was a complete failure here to understand that in reality these were still capitalist economies, except that while the means of production was state-owned, the appropriation of surplus was at the individual level (politicians and bureaucrats). At the same time, there was little appreciation of the roots of the development of state capitalism in Africa: colonialism had left the state as the only indigenous player with access to reasonable amounts of capital. The obsession with market-driven economic growth strategies, one must add here, however, went beyond echoes of Cold War rhetoric. As Surin (2003) points out, even in circumstances where judicious state intervention in the economy had been the hallmark of capitalist economic success—as in East Asia—the World Bank did everything it could to downplay this fact even as it touted the so-called East Asian "economic miracle." (See also Wade [1996] for a critique of the "East Asia

Miracle paradigm," and the sources in endnote 21 in Chapter 8.) The fact is that no matter what the World Bank experts said, they were absolutely wrong on at least two counts if one examined the circumstances of such newly industrializing countries in Asia as Hong Kong, Singapore, South Korea, and Taiwan: state intervention in the economy was necessary, and higher education (though broadly defined) had an important role in their economic development. Now, to be sure, there were many other variables that accounted for the phenomenal success these countries had in registering average growth rates in the order of 7% per capita GNP, decade after decade, and in the process radically transforming their countries into relatively powerful economic players in the global market. However, it is also clear that the state had played a very crucial role in directing economic development by means of policies of judicious intervention in various economic sectors—in fact it would not be an exaggeration to say that in most of these countries dirigisme had been the order of the day; and it is also clear that the relationship between the development of higher education and economic growth had been a dialectical one (and here again, of course, the state was playing a very important role). Note: the emphasis here is on dialectical and not unidirectional causality. That is (taking the higher education side of the equation) these countries had expended a great deal of resources (both private and public) in providing education and training in two main areas: science and technology and the entrepreneurial/vocational arts (business, accounting, management, etc.). (For more on the experiences of these countries see, for example, Ashton, Green, James, and Sung [1999]; Dasgupta [1998]; and endnote 21 in Chapter 8. For a general discussion of universities and their role in economic growth see Gray [1999].) Notice also that an important difference, which somehow completely escapes the experts at the World Bank, is that in much of Africa, capital is foreign owned. In Asia, in relative terms, this has not been the case; there for a long time much of capital was locally owned and only later did they begin to allow foreign capital to come in and form partnerships with local capital. What the East Asian economic "miracle" appears to suggest is that in terms of successful economic growth (not necessarily development—for the jury is still out on whether all in those countries have benefited from the miracle) three conjunctural factors (the key word here is conjunctural) are essential: political stability (though not necessarily accompanied by democracy one must admit—how else can one account for the growth-friendly wage/productivity ratios ["slave labor"?]), local ownership of capital and judicious intervention by the state in the economy (which includes production of human capital, meaning development of the higher education sector—but beyond just the universities). With respect to all these three factors the World Bank has traditionally been out of tune with reality in terms of its policy prescriptions and practice. Two other points need to be noted here: as the recent financial crisis in East Asia has demonstrated there are limits to the economic miracle; however, what is even worse for them is that the policy prescriptions of the IMF and the World Bank are likely to place their economies in even greater jeopardy over the long-run if they pursue them (see, for example, the discussion by Medley and Caroll [2003]). Notice also that in the absence of this tri-partite conjuncture, a strategy of structural adjustment could only be a policy prescription for economic disaster, as country after country in Africa has found out over the past decade and a half.

33. The self-confessed father of the phrase "Washington Consensus" is one John Williamson, a senior fellow at the conservative (neoliberal) Washington-based think-tank, the Institute for International Economics. See his summary and discussion of the

term as he defined it, together with a critique by others in the work edited by Auty and Toye (1996). See also Stiglitz (2002), and Kuczynski and Williamson (2003).

34. Of course, in the typical Eurocentrist fashion it lays the blame for this circumstance squarely on Africa itself: "Why is Africa so poor?" it asks. "The short answer... is 'bad government'" (2004: 4). It conveniently forgets that good government while highly desirable for its own sake, in of itself it can do little in a structurally inequitable global economic environment dominated by Western corporate capitalist interests.

35. As can be gathered from the foregoing, the crux of the structural adjustment thinking is that those who are deemed to need it are responsible for their economic predicament. It is, in other words, a classic blame-the-victim strategy much beloved by the West whenever issues of global economic injustice are raised by PQD countries. Schultheis, writing two decades ago (1984) described this approach, which has been a central theme of the numerous World Bank reports and documents on Africa, well: "Scapegoating the victims seems to be a popular pastime in the drawing rooms of the wealthy. These World Bank reports, supported by country and sectoral studies, of many African nations, manifest this same tendency of 'blaming the victims.' They are classical expositions of 'horse and sparrow economics,' patronizingly instructing the sparrows to improve their techniques so that they might more completely pick out the oats in the horses droppings. But they are deadly serious, as the geography of hunger and hunger-related deaths again expands" (p. 9). One must also note that the structural adjustment approach smacked of a considerable degree of blatant hypocrisy: social expenditures were legitimate for Western countries in order to provide their citizenries with economic "safety-nets" (measures ranging from health insurance to unemployment insurance to food-stamps), but they were deemed illegitimate for the PQD countries. For more on the structural adjustment strategy in Africa see also Enos (1995), Mkandawire and Soludo (2003), Mosely, Subasat, and Weeks (1995); Schatz (1994); Sender (2002); and Van de Walle, Ball, and Ramachandran (2003). Biersteker (1990), Hutchful (1995); and Schatz (1996) are also relevant here because they demonstrate the weakness of the strategy on its own conceptual merits. For structural adjustment from a global comparative perspective see SAPRIN (2004)—a visit to their website, www.saprin.org, is also helpful. For a more sympathetic view of the bank's role in Africa see Kapur, Lewis, and Webb (1997). For structural adjustment and its consequences that focuses exclusively on higher education in Africa see Federici, Caffentzis, and Alidou (2000).

36. The fact that economic growth could occur without development never occurred to them (nor for that matter were they in a position, such were their theoretical premises, to contemplate the possibility that the very relations that they championed between the developed and the newly PQD countries could be the basis of the underdevelopment of the latter.) So, what is the difference between economic growth and economic development? The answer is that the former does not necessarily presuppose structural change, whereas the latter does. In other words, under an economic growth model the present configuration of factor inputs, existing institutions and the current social structure remain a constant; whereas under an economic development model all of these are to be transformed on the basis of innovation, new technologies, and so on. Economic development is both a quantitative and a qualitative phenomenon. Consider this fact as well: economic development also implies poverty reduction, but economic growth may or may not lead to poverty reduction (see also endnote 20 in Chapter 8).

37. Of course, as Vaizey (1972) reminds us, the theory of human capital was not an

original idea. The concept has a long pedigree in that it is implicitly threaded through some of the work of such classical and neoclassical economists as Sir William Petty (seventeenth-century political economist with interests in the economic role of the state and the labor theory of value); Adam Smith (eighteenth-century social philosopher and political economist who was a strong proponent of laissez-faire economics and free market competition); and Alfred Marshall (nineteenth-century political economist whose accomplishments included the introduction of such new economic concepts as the representative firm, consumer's surplus, and elasticity of demand). However, the difference is that Schultz's formulation was far more explicit in imputing economic growth to education, by likening it to physical capital. More important than that, however, was that this explicit formulation occurred at an opportune time, from the perspective of development planning. For, not only was the notion of catapulting the PQD countries on to the Rostowian "take-off" trajectory gaining currency, but just about the time that Schultz's formulation appeared, the United Nations had inaugurated (in 1960) the First Development Decade in the wake of a dramatic shift in the numerical balance in the General Assembly with the entry of a host of newly independent African countries. Thus the call was sounded for large and rapid increases in the growth rate of the per capita GNP of the developing nations. That education would do the trick, many development experts thought, was also given credence by the fact that previous experiences with development efforts among the Asian nations in the preceding decade had shown that large infusions of capital—along the lines of the Marshall Plan in the post-war years in Europe and Japan—had not had the same effect (of producing rapid economic growth). The view quickly took hold that it was the absence of adequate human capital that was to blame for this outcome. Thus in drawing the policy implications of his theory, Schultz (1961b) strongly advocated investment in human capital as the best means of achieving economic growth. Clearly then, if the missing variable in the development effort among the newly independent Asian nations in the 1950s had been deemed to be physical capital, then in the succeeding decade the missing variable was seen to be human capital.

38. For a comprehensive overview of the field see the reference work for Pergamon edited by Psacharopoulos (1987).

39. Consider this major flaw, well described by Rado (1966): "If the purpose [is] to test, however, crudely, whether education contributes to economic growth, then what had to be correlated with GNP per capita was the educational level of the employed labor force who produced the national income which was being measured. Current enrollment ratios of students are irrelevant to current GNP. For, their education, if it contributes to anything, will contribute to the income levels of future decades, and not at all to that of today." This is not all, there other equally serious weaknesses that afflict any attempt to economically quantify the role of education in promoting economic growth; they include:

(a) The issue of causality: positive correlation, however strong, does not ipso facto imply causation; one factor could very easily be the cause of the other. It is quite possible, theoretically, that increases in economic growth may lead to increases in educational development, and not necessarily vice versa. In practice, however, it is more likely the case that the relationship between educational development and economic growth is a *dialectical* one (see Chapter 1 for the definition of dialectical).

(b) The assumption that education is a homogenous input and yet, as Streeten (1972) points out, this is clearly not so. Thus, even if one were to accept that education predicated economic growth, it would be necessary to state what kinds of education would be appropriate. The teaching of Latin has different results from the teaching of agronomy.

(c) Education, in the final analysis, is a matter of personal choice. What this implies is that for many, education has a dual function: it is a means to an end and it is an end in itself (Rado 1966). Consider this thought experiment: If education was freely available, but there were no direct economic benefits attached to it, would education simply whither away altogether? History tells us that the answer is no; for, in many societies being a learned person carried benefits that were other than economic.

(d) The role of education in economic growth cannot be ascertained simply on the basis of a single statistic of aggregate growth. Structure, pattern, social distribution, etc., are all variables of economic growth that demand attention in any calculation that purports to examine the relationship between economic growth and education (Todaro 1977).

(e) Education in isolation may have very little use in promoting economic growth. In other words, it is erroneous to treat education in isolation from other factors, just as it was erroneous to do the same with respect to capital when considering its role in inducing economic growth in PQD countries in the 1950s (Streeten 1972).

(f) The quality of education is an important variable in the education-economy nexus and yet it is completely ignored in the calculations of economists (albeit not deliberately since no method yet exists of quantifying quality). (Georgescu-Roegen 1976) .

40. It goes without saying that even on its own methodological grounds, the rates-of-return approach to educational planning is ridden with serious fallacies and weaknesses. A few of the more critical ones may be spelled out here:

(a) Perhaps one of the chief weaknesses of rates-of-return studies is that they fail to take an adequate account of institutional traits that affect the system of remuneration. To assume that increases in remuneration are a sole or the main function of increases in productivity that ostensibly comes with increases in the level of education is highly erroneous. Thus, for example; Georgescu-Roegen (1976) draws attention to the fact that calculations made by John C. Hause and others indicate that as a consequence of the social bias toward academic diplomas and certifications, employers tend to more or less ignore ability altogether. Hence, whereas a very significant difference in ability (represented by as much as ten I.Q. points) will yield only a 1% increase in income, an increase in one-year of schooling will result in a 4.6% increase. Among the PQD nations this constitutes a very serious problem where high returns to education is not a function of, in the words of Balogh (1964), "the relative actual productivity, usefulness, experience or knowledge of the individual but the injustice of the system." In other words, in many of these countries the emerging elite has managed to retain the old colonial wage structures that were developed without regard to the national averages of wages and salaries (see also Dore 1976).

(b) The rates-of-return studies pay considerable attention to income foregone by students while engaged in studying, but they tend to ignore income foregone by other groups in society such as housewives, voluntary workers, and those who due to other benefits accept lower incomes (e.g., university teachers). Similarly, they also tend to ignore non-financial benefits that accrue to students while in school—especially those going to universities in developed countries. In PQD countries too, this point may be significant where government paid university education entails such benefits for the student as three full meals a day and an escape from the drudgery of back-breaking domestic chores (especially for girls).

(c) Rates-of-return have to be calculated over the lifetime of the individual, and therefore the present differentials in income (assuming that they can be attributed to different levels of education) must be seen in terms of the educational situation in the 1950s and 1960s. Yet, among many African countries educational provision was at a very low level of development at that time. Therefore, it is illegitimate to assume that the present levels of educational provision (which in many cases has expanded a hundred-fold since independence) will yield the same pattern of output in the future as in the past. In fact, within two decades or so of independence it had become clear to the observant that as more and more graduates poured out of the educational systems on to a super saturated labor market, the same job and income was demanding an ever-increasing level of education. (See Dore [1976] for more on this phenomenon of *qualification escalation*.)

(d) Rates-of-return to investment in education can serve as a very poor basis for policy decisions because too often there is the danger of falling into the trap of linear thinking. Thus because an X% of income spent on education will yield (for example) X times 5% income, then it is quickly assumed that X times 10% spent on education will result in X time 50% income. Yet, of course, this is not true because income does not grow exponentially as a result of ever-increasing expenditures on education (Reubens 1977).

(e) Dependence on consideration of formal schooling as a data base for the rates-of-return calculations implies another serious defect of such kinds of studies: they overlook the importance of nonformal education, such as on-the-job training, training in the armed forces, training through correspondence colleges, etc.; In other words, the rates-of-return calculations tend to ignore the benefits to the efficiency of schooling derived from concealed transfers of efficiency from nonformal sources of education and training (Georgescu-Roegen 1976).

(f) The input-output neoclassical economics modeling approach that undergird these studies is an inappropriate model since education for the most part constitutes a nonmarket sector. As Marginson (1999) explains: "unless educational services are sold in a market there can be no conclusive measure of output, or of value added in the course of production, or of efficiency and productivity. The economics of education literally cannot contemplate nonmarket production and has failed to develop analytical tools with which to deal with it" (p. 207).

41. Similarly, in a report published in 2000 by the bank and prepared by a task force (Task Force on Higher Education and Society) that the bank and UNESCO convened together, there is this enlightened passage:

We have not asked whether higher education matters more than other key sectors such as agriculture, health, transportation, and basic education. But we are absolutely confident that it is much more important to development than one would surmise from the comparative neglect it has received in most quarters of the international development community in recent decades. Higher education's benefits must now be recognized more widely so it can take its place in the mainstream of the international development agenda. The information revolution that is driving the new economy is dependent on educated and literate workers; and more than ever, the new ideas fueling this expansion have come from people with tertiary degrees (World Bank 2000c: 92).

42. The 2002 report, of course, is the much touted, Constructing Knowledge Societies (World Bank 2002). While there is much in the report to commend it, not least the fact that it expands on the sentiments expressed in World Bank 2000 (see preceding note), it is important not to get carried away by the report. Yes, there is now acknowledgement of the importance of higher education for the development of PQD countries—especially in an age of exploding information and communication technologies. However, note that the publication disingenuously observes that "reexamining the World Bank's policies and experiences in tertiary education has become a matter of urgency," because "there is a perception that the Bank has not been fully responsive to the growing demand by clients for tertiary education interventions and that, especially in

the poorest countries, lending for the subsector has not matched the importance of tertiary education systems for economic and social development" (p. xviii, emphasis added).
Years of relative neglect and policy denigration of the importance of higher education
for PQD countries is nonchalantly swept aside with a wave of the word "perception."
Be that as it may, one must strongly caution that the bank is not yet about to develop
policies in support of the developmental university (see chapter 8). It is still fundamentally driven by the logic of structural adjustment in which its support for higher education is only to the extent that the traditional universities remain peripheral; instead it is
championing the newer private forms that have emerged (largely under the globalization
imperative), such as the for-profit, the corporate-sponsored, the franchise, the virtual
and other similar institutions—that is, it wants the state to be marginally involved in
higher education. While the foolishness of such an approach has already been noted (see
the discussion on East Asia), for only the state has the capacity and the obligation to effectively harness higher education, whatever forms they take, in a rational manner for
purposes of development, there is another major flaw in the bank's thinking: its failure
to comprehend the critical importance of the traditional university in the task of building democratic societies. Authentic universities (possess academic freedom) are not just
factories for human capital, they do more than that. Obsessed with the commodification
of knowledge on a global scale—driven by the erroneous belief that capitalism ipso
facto equals democracy—there is a singular failure by the bank to comprehend that the
traditional university it denigrates, albeit not in so many words, is also the repository
par excellence of a society's democratic impulse (see Halvorsen [2005] and Halvorsen
and Skauge [2004], and endnote 110 in Chapter 3 for more on this issue).

43. For a useful overview of global trends in this aspect of university finance, see
Johnstone and Shroff-Mehta (2001), Johnstone (2004), and Woodhall (2003).

44. See Swedberg (1986), who challenges the notion much espoused by the Bretton
Woods institutions that their work rests entirely on economics, and politics has no part
to play in it. Labelling it as the "doctrine of economic neutrality" he shows how the
these institutions are used by countries such as the United States to impose their economic agendas on PQD countries (see also Bello [2001]).

8

Conclusion:
The Colonial Legacy
and Beyond

Historians live in the present, they do not live in the past (though some, perhaps tongue in cheek, may question that), even if the object of their labors has
very much to do with the past. Consequently, it is not unreasonable for those
whose work revolves entirely with grappling with the realities of the present—
such as, for instance, the educational planner or the policy analyst—to impa-
tiently enjoin the historian to charge history with a more practical task, not one
of comprehending the past, but one of shedding light on the present (and possibly even the future too). Ergo, as we turn our gaze away from the past to the
present and the future, our objective in this concluding chapter is to harness the
explicatory power of history in the service of an important task: to delineate the
central aspects of the legacy of the colonial imprint on the development of
modern higher education in Africa, so as to provide a basis for understanding
the current predicament of the African university across the length and breadth
of the continent;[1] and to hazard an opinion on the future of the African university, albeit in generic terms, from the perspective of its relevance to African societies.

THE LEGACY OF THE COLONIAL PAST

At the time when political independence came to most of Africa, it would
be a gross understatement to say that the colonial powers were not ready for it.
Now, it is true that leaving aside colonial settler Africa (as well as Portuguese
colonial Africa), the British certainly, and the French to some degree too, had

already begun to anticipate that some day in the distant future their African colonies would eventually gain independence—no longer a white man's burden. However, they did not believe on the morrow of the Second World War that independence for their colonies, especially their African colonies, was right around the corner. The Second World War, however, changed everything.[2] As a consequence, the colonial powers in Africa came to face the immediate prospect of decolonization (in the political sense) much sooner than they had ever anticipated; obviously, they were ill-prepared for it when it came upon them so soon within a decade and a half or two of the conclusion of the war in 1945. Faced with the absence of a credible indigenous bureaucratic elite capable of not only taking on the reigns of power, but one that would also ensure that the newly independent nations would continue to remain within the diplomatic, economic, and ideological embrace of the West—especially against the backdrop of a mounting Cold War—they belatedly turned to higher education as the mechanism for creating such an elite; but here their colonial education policies had left them with an almost barren landscape. Consequently, in their hurry to create higher education institutions in their former colonies, they turned to models for these institutions within their own countries—as one would logically expect.

Yet, however good their intentions (recall that in those heady days the unwritten principle was that only the best institutions would do for their colonies), they bequeathed to them institutions that many would come to feel were ill-suited to the task of national development in all its dimensions—economic, political, and social. They were ivory towers in the truest sense of the word. The problem has been articulated forcefully by Mamdani (1993: 11), for example: "Faced with popular pressures for democracy in education, universities and independent states were determined, not only to preserve intact those universities inherited from colonial mentors but also to reproduce replicas several times over to maintain standards." He continues: "The new postindependence African university was triumphantly universalistic and uncompromisingly foreign." In other words, as Ashby (1966) and Janus (1980) have argued, the stress on maintaining standards created a conflict between relevance and authenticity on one hand, and on the other, the desire for international standards of academic quality and excellence. Yet, they correctly state, conceptually there is no inherent conflict between the two. With judicious planning it would have been possible to satisfy both needs.

Specifically, then: In what ways did the "belated good intentions gone awry" manifest itself? There are several that immediately come to mind: the matter of high unit costs; the insufficient emphasis on science and technology; the problem of language of instruction; the matter of class-reproduction and equality of opportunity; and the problematic issue of community service in the context of the "ivory tower" syndrome.

The Problem of High Unit Costs

Without any doubt, one of the most crippling historically rooted factors that Sub-Saharan universities face today is the question of the extremely high unit costs. In a continent where private higher education is still a rarity, the burdens placed on the public purse of high unit costs have been severe. Moreover, it has lead to a gross imbalance in resource allocation across the different subsectors of the education sector with profound implications for both equity and efficient use of scarce resources. Of course, those familiar with the current deep predicament of universities in Africa will not miss the apparent irony here: amidst the very real crippling budgetary constraints that they face, there is the issue of excessive expenditures in the form of high unit costs. However, upon reflection one will conclude that the contradiction is only apparent: the renewal of the fortunes of universities in Africa from a financial point of view is a two-step process: lowering unit costs is the first step, *increasing* budgetary allocations *judiciously* is the second step. (Unfortunately, the latter step is almost never mentioned by most international aid agencies.)[3]

Why is the unit cost of universities in Africa so high? There are many factors that explain this circumstance and almost all have their origins in policies and practices established in the past, which while well-intentioned (for the most part) at that time have led today to the proverbial chickens coming home to roost. They include: (1) The wholesale transplantation of institutions from abroad requiring the creation of physical infrastructures (almost in the form of alien mini-cities) that were not organically linked to the local economy and society, and therefore requiring huge capital and recurrent expenditures. (2) The decision to insist on free on-campus residence of all students, thereby requiring the building and maintenance of expensive dormitories, as well as provision of tax-payer-funded board. Coupled with this approach was the decision to provide tuition-free education to all students—without even requiring a means test. (3) The decision to retain high salary levels (relative to salaries for similar positions in the rest of society) for teaching staff and administrators; even going to the extent of seeking foreign aid to maintain these levels, coupled with heavy subsidization of living expenses. (4) The use of universities by ruling political parties as sites of patronage-driven employment for their partisan supporters (symptomatic of which is the comparatively high teaching staff and nonteaching staff to student ratios). (5) The failure to maximize the impact of resources by not devising programs for nontraditional students (part-time students, evening students, intercession students, etc.) (6) The failure to engage in meaningful cross-border cooperation by developing regional university systems (rather than small, atomistic systems) and thereby foregoing savings that arise from economies of scale, not to mention such other benefits as permitting concentration of scholarly expertise—thereby facilitating research specialization and collaboration. (7) The existence of high student wastage rates in many African universities arising from both political causes as well as traditional educational practices within the universities. (8) The endemic unscheduled clo-sures of universities by governments arising out of conflicts with the univer-sity—principally with students.[4]

The Marginalization of Science and Technology

As already noted in Chapter 7, there is almost no report on the state of Afri-can higher education or national development generally that does not make its obligatory call for an emphasis on the development of a science and technol-ogy infrastructure. For instance, recently one of the latest World Bank reports on Africa (World Bank 2000b), titled *Can Africa Claim the 21st Century?*, ob-served: "At the university-level religious studies and civil service needs have resulted in the development of the humanities and the social sciences and the neglect of the natural sciences, applied technology, business-related skills, and research capabilities" (p. 106). Similarly, and even more recently, the report of the London- based Commission for Africa notes: "[S]pecific action for strengthening science, engineering and technology capacity is an imperative for Africa." The report then goes on to call for the establishment of centers of scientific excellence in Africa that can "act as springboards for developing sci-entific capacity" (Commission for Africa 2005: 138).

Now, while science and technology cannot solve all the problems of Africa (vide the lessons of Egypt), there is absolutely no question that in terms of the narrower focus of economic development, absolutely no success is possible without the massive (but appropriate) use of science and technology.[5] At the same time, in a context where there are almost no non-university research insti-tutions, the university is the only viable institution that can create and sustain the necessary science and technology infrastructure. So, Why then has the mat-ter remained more in the domain of rhetoric rather than actual policy imple-mentation? After all, one of the few claims to fame that African intellectuals concerned with higher education say they have is in giving birth to the concept of the "developmental university." [6] First articulated in Accra (at a workshop sponsored by the Association of African Universities on the emerging issues confronting African universities in the 1970s), in response to the criticism that the development of African universities in the preceding decade had rendered them to be "hardly more than white elephants and flashy symbols of moderni-zation: ivory towers occupied by a minority elite, expensively educated, and as expensively continuously maintained, at the expense of the vast majority of the population, with whom they have little in common" (Yesufu 1973: 39), the concept demanded relevance from the universities to the specifics of the Afri-can circumstance, in terms of curricula and function.

Relevance, in essence meant being immediately and directly responsive to the development needs of the African countries and therefore requiring a reori-entation of the function of the university to, among other things, emphasis on development-oriented research (which in essence meant the use of science and technology to solve problems of development): "A university must be dedicated to research—fundamental and applied. But again priority must be given to research into local problems that will contribute to the amelioration, in particular, of the life of the ordinary man and the rural poor. Emphasis must accordingly, be placed on such topics as: rural health; the problems of poverty in its varying contexts; the conflict of cultures in multiethnic societies and the basis for unity and agricultural and rural development" (p. 42).

Leaving aside the matter of costs (it is very expensive to train scientific and technological personnel) the surprising answer as to why African universities have not given science and technology the kind of emphasis demanded by the long tradition of rhetoric, as well as of course the practical realities of the African condition, is that, very simply, there has been a relative absence of domestic will and foreign support, coupled with misguided educational planning. That is, while African leaders and intellectuals have always been aware of the tight relationship between science and technology on one hand, and on the other, modernization and development, there has been no concerted effort expended to translate this awareness into practice—both, on their part as well as on the part of foreign aid donors. Why? There are, at least six factors that, *when considered together*, explain this circumstance: (a) The wholesale importation of the metropolitan university curricular model; (b) The narrow focus on growth versus structural change in the development of human resource capacity: the manpower planning approach; (c) the erroneous rates-of-return approach to educational planning that downgraded the importance of higher education (which in turn had obvious negative implications for the development of a science and technology infrastructure); (d) the poor development of math and science in the educational tributaries upstream; (e) the neglect of doctoral-level graduate education; and (f) the adherence to misguided strategies of economic development.[7]

Colonialism and Language

Although we have a tendency to view language in neutral terms as merely an instrument of communication; in reality language is never neutral; it is almost always bound up with existing power relations; this is nowhere more clearly so than in the case of those societies that were introduced to a foreign language by a colonizing power. For, in such societies the foreign language was invariably among the arsenals of domination and control in that access to any form of power, however rudimentary, almost always necessitated access to the foreign language. Yet, there was a contradiction that ensued from this circumstance: the struggle for independence usually entailed a nationalism that demanded the rejection of the foreign language in the name of cultural authenticity and egalitarianism. For those nations that were primarily artificial creations of the colonialist project (incorporating a multiplicity of diverse ethnicities with their own languages—often mutually unintelligible for good measure), such as those in most of Sub-Saharan Africa, such a perspective quickly foundered on the sands of reality: nation-building required a single language; and for the sake of convenience the colonizer's language would have to do.

However, in the case of Islamic Africa, given its relative precolonial linguistic homogeneity (with one or two exceptions), the call for authenticity could be answered by a language policy championing Arabization. Most countries did proceed to undertake this and in educational terms this meant the use of Arabic as a language of instruction even at the university level. However, these nations in their eternal wisdom appear to have never considered creating a single, region-wide language institute (similar to the Academy of Arabic Language established in the early 1920s in Egypt under Taha Hussein) that could undertake the task of reviving Arabic as a language of science and technology as it had once been (see Appendix I). The result is that almost all higher education institutions today (with the exception of those specializing only in the Islamic sciences) are bilingual: Arabic is reserved mainly for the arts, humanities, and some social sciences, while the sciences (including technology) are taught in a foreign colonial language, usually French or English. Yet, this in turn has created an unintended political fallout: those who are not bilingual have found that access to the most remunerative positions in the economy are not accessible to them because almost invariably these positions demand educational qualifications in the sciences.

Furthermore, under the relentless pressures of "globalization" it is the bilingual person who has the most opportunity to join the ranks of the global elite—even if migration is never on the agenda—for, it is the languages of the former colonizers that are the lingua franca of the business and diplomatic world.[8] The ruling elites in these countries long aware of this fact, while advocating Arabization for the children of the masses, have however chosen the bilingual route for their children by means of private secular schooling (either abroad or locally) or by ensuring that they specialize in the sciences. In other words, bilingualism is not only a means of access to power, but it is also a marker of elite status. In fact, in this regard the situation that is fast developing all across Islamic Africa, is that some sections of the elite are becoming unilingual in a perverse way: they no longer know how to speak Arabic (or refuse to speak Arabic at all) preferring the language of the former colonizers. (Even Algeria, according to Naylor [2000: 260], is the world's second most francophone country, despite decades of emphasis on Arabic in the education sector; see also Hawkins 2003.) Yet this development has not been greeted with equanimity by all: significant sections of the population, notably the Islamists, under the banner of authenticity (and recall that Arabic is the language of the *Qur'an*) have demanded a rollback of this trend.

The volatility of the language issue is demonstrated by two contradictory examples: Violent conflicts erupted at University of Constantine in 1974, 1975, 1976, and University of Algiers (1979–80). "In every instance such eruptions," explains Entelis (1986: 93–94), "reflected increased student dissatisfaction with the quality, purpose, and usability of an all-Arab education in Algeria when government decision makers regard bilingual training and other features of modern, secular education as integral to the overall development process." Arab-speaking students wanted greater use of Arabic in the country at the higher levels of the polity and economy. Now, on the other hand, in some countries where there are significant populations for whom Arabic is not their mother tongue (e.g., Algeria, Morocco, Sudan) and who therefore opt for the language of the former colonial power for participation in the economic and other public spheres, Arabization has become a highly charged issue. In Algeria, for instance, there have been violent clashes between the pro-French language Kabyles (a Berber group) and the pro-Arab language Algerian state, from time to time (vide those of March 1980 at the University of Tizi-Ouzou and their periodic recurrence in subsequent years in Kabylia). In fact, the teaching of Kabyle language and culture was reintroduced in universities after it had been abolished.

Today, the language issue is being further complicated because of the emerging competition between English and French as the foreign language of choice inadvertently being engendered by the ever-increasing presence of U.S. influence in Afro-Arab Islamic Africa, coupled with the realization among the elites that English and not French is the dominant language at the level of global relations, and the perception among some francophone countries (like Algeria) that English is a politically neutral language, unlike French with its colonial past.[9]

There is another dimension to the issue of language that we ought to mention: The problem of bridging the gap between the community and the university. As long as the language of instruction in a university differs from that spoken by the rest of the populace, it is to that extent emphasizing the institution's foreignness. Not only that, however, even in purely educational terms there are problems that ensue from conducting classes in a language that is foreign to the bulk of the student body.

In raising this issue of language and the colonial legacy, it is necessary to concede here that it is an exercise in futility if one has the problem of remedy in mind, as a corollary of the issue. For, the sad truth is that these problems are part of a colonial heritage that simply cannot be changed. So long as there are a multiplicity of linguistically diverse ethnicities sharing an artificially created common geographic space the need for a lingua franca will remain permanent; under such circumstances the language of the metropole will have to do. Yet, even in the case of ethnically homogenous societies, the problematic issue of language does not necessarily go away, given the colonial heritage. In support of this observation we may bring up the example of Somalia.

When that country became independent it had at least four principal languages in play: Somali, Arabic, Italian (in the South), and English (in the

North). Somali was the language of the masses, while Arabic was primarily spoken by the Somali ulama (though the masses also had access to it, but at very rudimentary level, for liturgical purposes). The other two languages were spoken by the educated elites, and therein lay the source of divisiveness because it created an intra-elite, regionally based (therefore clan based) competition for higher level jobs in government and business. The process that underlay this competition was the steady marginalization of Italian, as English began to replace it as the language of choice of the elites, brought about by, among other factors, Somalia's broadening of international relations (an arena where English is the lingua franca for all practical purposes) beyond those inherited at the time of independence.

Even though the introduction of Latin orthography in 1972, shortly after Siad Barre came to power, officially placed Somali at the top of the country's linguistic hierarchy, those who could speak English fluently (that is many of the northerners) continued to have a decided advantage in competition for jobs, access to higher education, and so on; thereby creating severe tension between educated northerners who flocked south to Mogadishu and the local elites. In fact, as Omaar (1992: 233) notes, the decision to adopt Somali as the official language by the Barre dictatorship was viewed by some northern elites as "partly—if not entirely—motivated by the determination to blunt the educational advantages enjoyed by the north as an English-speaking region."[10]

While it is not clear as of this moment (in 2005) what the future, from a linguistic point of view, holds for Somalia when it becomes a viable whole again, it would appear that even though Somali is (or was) an official language of the country, the language of one of the former colonizers (the British) will continue to flourish (certainly in the North, as it does now, and over time in the South as well), giving material and other advantages to those who can speak English over those who cannot—thereby continuing to serve as yet one more tension-causing layer of divisiveness in the country. Italian will have only marginal significance. While Somali will continue to be spoken by all, those who are bilingual or even trilingual will be at an advantage. To give an example: admission to the new Mogadishu University requires fluency in both English and Arabic (which means the average Somali student must be trilingual).[11]

Universities and Elites

There is, however, another kind of legacy of colonialism that has been even more pernicious: it does not concern higher education directly, *but indirectly*. Among the many roles of higher education in capitalist societies is its role as a reproducer of the elite (the ideology of meritocracy notwithstanding—see endnote 108 in Chapter 3). In this regard the African universities have fulfilled this role within the limits of their resources admirably. Equality of educational opportunity, regardless of class and other avenues of social structural differentiation, has not materialized in Africa, at least at the level of higher education (see the discussion Chapter 3).

The problem, however, is: What kind of elite has it been? The answer is that it has been an essentially parasitic compradorial elite such that even when it has been faced with that rare circumstance of a surfeit of investable surpluses (as in the case of Libya, and to varyingly lesser degrees in Algeria, Nigeria, etc.) it has been unable to move Africa toward sustained economic growth and development, even when judged against the limited standards of neoclassical capitalism—which, one should be reminded, has no patience for matters of social equity and distributive justice.[12] Similarly, the predicament of countries like Egypt also point to the fact that the development of a science and technology infrastructure in itself (as already indicated in Chapter 3) does not lead to growth and development, in the absence of an enlightened elite.

Is it accurate to suggest, then, that under these circumstances the role of the modern African university is totally inimical to the development of the continent? Therefore, it should be disbanded (as the structural adjustment theorists often argued, albeit sotto voce and for completely different reasons—see Chapter 7). This would be a simplistic view to take. Yes, the modern African university as it is presently constituted does help to *reproduce* an elite that appears, behaviorally at least, to be less concerned with development than self-aggrandizement. However, the university is not the source of a parasitic elite, the blame for that lies with the nature of Africa's integration into the Western dominated world political and economic order (see Appendix II). In other words, the problem of underdevelopment in Africa (and elsewhere for that matter) lies in the dialectic of both *agency* and *structure*.[13] That is, the African elite is just as much to blame as the historically-determined structural conditions it operates under. Given these circumstances the developmental role of the university (to be discussed in a moment) becomes considerably circumscribed.

Community Service and the Ivory Tower Syndrome

The issue of community service from the perspective of the mission of the university in a PQD country has already been discussed at some length elsewhere in this work (see Chapter 4, endnote 35); therefore, what follows is simply a reiteration, in the main, of the basic points of that discussion. In essence, from the very beginning of the founding of the post-independence African university, community service (understood broadly in the African context to mean engagement directly with the task of national development), has been integral to its mission—at least at the rhetorical level. For instance, at the two major conferences on higher education that sought to influence the establishment and growth of higher education in Africa, the 1962 Tananarive Conference (see the report UNESCO 1963) and the 1972 Accra Workshop (see the report Yesufu 1973), there were calls for the creation of the "developmental university" (a university intimately involved with the task of national development).

In fact, in recent years, even in countries where the dominant university model is that of the research university, such as the United States, there have been calls to rethink this model and transform it to include community service as a *key* part of the university mission. For example, the late Ernest Boyer (who, among the many important posts he had held during his career, was that of the president of the influential Carnegie Foundation for the Advancement of Teaching), had called for the elevation of community service within U.S. higher education to the point where one could talk about the "citizenship" role of higher education institutions (see, for example, Boyer 1996). Of course, there is probably no university anywhere that does not engage in some form of community service, or that does not include in its mission statement reference to community service.[14] The truth, however, is that in practice, the African universities, in general, have not lived up to the concept of the developmental university for a number of reasons, including the colonial legacy (as already indicated in Chapter 4). It will suffice to note here, then, that in a twist particularly characteristic of the PQD environment, the effort to indigenize the personnel of the university in the post-independence period was quickly and cynically reframed into the notion that this effort in itself constituted implementing the mission of a developmental university. At the same time, the desire to maintain some kind of parity, in terms of international status, with universities worldwide by African academics did not help matters. As Mamdani (1993), for instance, observed:

In our single-minded pursuit to create centers of learning and research of international standing, we had nurtured researchers and educators who had little capacity to work in surrounding communities but who could move to any institution in any industrialized country, and serve any privileged community around the globe with comparative ease. In our failure to contextualize standards and excellence to the needs of our own people, to ground the very process and agenda of learning and research in our conditions, we ended up creating an intelligentsia with little stamina for the process of development whose vanguard we claimed to be" (p. 15).

However, things are changing—a little, but perceptibly; that is, there is now an increasing involvement of the university in community service than has been the case in the past, even if it is still on an ad hoc basis—for reasons that have already been discussed.[15] The fact still, however, remains that at a broader level, the African university has a long way to go before it can be truly considered as a developmental university. One should be reminded here that a developmental university should not be understood to imply an institution with a narrowly defined "economistic" role in which the university's principal and only function becomes one of servicing capital's eternal quest for accumulation (see endnote 110 in Chapter 3). A developmental university is, in the final analysis, an institution that is guided in its overall work by the objective of supporting democracy—to be understood here in the broadest sense to mean not just political democracy, but economic democracy, social democracy, environmental democracy, cultural democracy, and so on. (In other words, the university in the truest sense, is a subversive institution.)

THE FUTURE OF THE UNIVERSITY IN AFRICA

We have, by now, traversed across a historical timeframe spanning thousands of years; moreover, along the way we have had occasion to visit almost every continent (see Appendix I and II). We have seen that the African university, from the perspective of its genealogy, is truly an embodiment of a host of civilizational influences, whether viewed in terms of a precolonial proto-university or a postindependence university. What can one say then about the modern African university as we look out into the future? To begin with, we should note that no society that aspires toward higher levels of economic, political and social development can, as we have seen, dispense with some type of an institution of higher learning (see endnote 110 in Chapter 3). Therefore, there is absolutely no question that no progress of any meaningful kind can be secured by Africa in the absence of higher education. Yet, on the other hand, this truism is rendered problematic because of the pre-modern/modern disjuncture (explored at length in Appendix II) that Africa's historical trajectory has been burdened with—a consequence of which is that we are presented with the problem of questioning whether the modern African university represents the form of higher education that can propel Africa toward a better future.

In other words, we face here the question of relevance: specifically, is the modern African university an institution *in* Africa rather than *of* Africa. Now, we have already seen at least two concrete instances where transformed historical circumstances of a society can render extant institutions of higher learning obsolete: in the case of the madrasahs in the Islamic empire, and in the case of the proto-universities during the colonial era in Africa. The key question, therefore, is: Is the African university as it is presently constituted relevant to the task of moving Africa out of the current awful predicament it faces (expressed by facts such as, of all the world's continents, Africa is host today to the largest number of civil wars and most of the world's poorest nations)?[16] The short answer is that perhaps not. The reason is that, as Van den Bor and Shute (1991) point out, the contribution of universities in PQD countries to development is hampered by the fact that they themselves need to be developed. Perhaps at more than any other time in history, Africa today must confront this potent fact: that the relation between the African university and African society is absolutely dialectical; that is, the fate of each rests in the hands of the other. Yet, the lords of structural adjustment appear to be unaware of this fact.[17] What is more, even as they sing the praises of "globalization" on one hand and the "information age" on the other, there is an insufficient understanding of not only the place of the African university in relation to these ongoing economic

and technological transformations, but that in so far as they are touted as panaceas, their relevance to the solution of the current African predicament must be
viewed with the deepest suspicion.[18]

If the present is any guide, then, we can foresee an accelerated march toward a privatized, narrowly utilitarian higher education sector in which the
publicly funded flagship university will be relegated to the margins. But what
does this mean for Africa's development prospects? It means that the idea of
the developmental university (that is a university *of* Africa) is, perhaps, dead in
the water, for a privatized higher education sector will march, as is already the
case in some PQD countries, to the beat of a different drummer: the imperatives of globalization, which its proponents disingenuously refuse to point out,
is nothing more, *at its fundamental core,* than an intensification at the global
level of capitalist accumulation—in principle, no different from the globalization of the post-1492 imperialist era (even if the form of capital has changed in
that the modern transnational corporation is a vertically and horizontally integrated *monopolistic* economic behemoth). (As a reminder, see Amin [2003]
and Foster [2002]. See also Baran and Sweezy [1966], which though dated, is
still relevant conceptually.)[19]

In other words, public universities in Africa will, of course, continue to exist, and perhaps even thrive, but as for their relevance to development, that is a
horse of a different color.[20] To end this work on such a note of pessimism may
be depressing, dear reader, but one must face the fact that if the current Western
capital-dominated civilization has a paradigmatic shelf-life of a thousand years,
then it still has some 500 years to go (barring a cataclysmic nuclear accident of
a planetary order, or an unforeseen sudden severely debilitating depletion of
world's natural resources). There is nothing in Africa's current secular historical trajectory that is even remotely suggestive of an "East Asian miracle"—
itself a highly questionable concept as it is.[21]

NOTES

1. Whenever this issue of the legacy of colonialism is brought up there is almost always an underlying assumption that despite all the current ills plaguing the continent
Africa is better off today for having experienced European colonialism (and in any case
it is not colonialism that accounts for these ills, it is added further). But was colonialism
a good thing for Africa? To a person, Westerners in general (regardless of their ideological orientations) are likely to answer in the affirmative; and here, perhaps, many African
elites will also concur. However, going on the basis of Appendix II the answer is definitely no. The hijacking by Europe of Africa's historical trajectory is the cause of the
present awful predicament of the African continent. To suggest on the other hand that
Africa's current circumstances are essentially an outcome of the inability of Africans to
make good use of the "gifts" of modernity European colonialism bequeathed them is to
simply engage in the usual racist "blame-the-victim" thinking that has been the stock in

trade of Westerners ever since they left Europe on their self-appointed missions of "civilizing" the world (the white man's burden—compare, for example, the latest survey of the African continent by that popular media's bastion of unrepentant capitalism, *The Economist* [2004]).

Consider this thought–experiment: suppose that one woke up tomorrow to find that all the ruling elites of Africa have been replaced by angels, would the continent's basic situation of dependency and underdevelopment change *in the absence of any accompanying transformation of the Western corporate-dominated global economic system?* The answer is self-evident: a little, yes, but not by much. For the Africans at the individual day-to-day level there would be some qualitative difference in their lives that cannot be sneezed at: their human and civil rights would be protected. In a few cases (as in Zimbabwe where that despot, Robert Mugabe, has virtually run the country into the ground) *some* economic development would again be in the cards. (See Gibbon [1992] on the difficulties external donors, such as the World Bank, have faced in moving African governments themselves to adopt pro-poor policies.) But as for the vast majority, would their abject poverty be alleviated? Sadly, the answer is no.

The problem here, in the final analysis, is the failure by most Westerners (and many Africans too) who consider this matter to understand the difference between *structure* and *agency* in accounting for the current awful predicament of most of the African continent. That is, their thinking is clouded by the perception that blame for this predicament must lie at the door of African *agency* (and here the influence of Eurocentrism in such thinking cannot be ruled out), and not at the door of global capitalist *structures* put in place by Western imperialism after 1492 (see Appendix II). *But agency is only one part of the equation, structure is the other; and the two are dialectically intertwined.* Until Westerners (and others) understand this basic fact, this debate will continue to be endless, generating much heat but little light—but with continued awful consequences for the people of Africa as they continue to labor under a Western-dominated international relations regime that subscribes to the fallacy of the primacy of agency over structure. (Of course, those on the left—such as the dependency theorists—also make a similar mistake in their analyses by tilting the balance completely to the other side—the structural side.)

An aside: yet, once again, we are witness to the same tired and embarrassing spectacle: the Africans lining up with begging bowls in hand at the latest summit of the so-called G8 (a self-selected club of eight of the world's most industrialized nations: Canada, France, Germany, Italy, Japan, Russia, Britain and United States) taking place at an $800-a-night Sea Island resort off the coast of the state of Georgia in the United States (June 8–10, 2004); and it is the same story: they came, they had a brief two-hours meeting in a four-day conference with the G8 leaders (with possibly a good lunch thrown in as a palliative), and they left—virtually empty handed. The full debt relief they had sought for Africa's twenty-seven poorest nations was not granted—mainly because of U.S. opposition. (Here is a tidbit of information to put things in perspective: the Africans represent a continent where average annual income is less than a dollar a day for the vast majority: the cost of a *single night* at the resort would cover over *two years* of their income.)

2. Consider the consequences of that event that would help propel the African countries to independence as rapidly as they had been colonized (on paper at least), some

three quarter of a century or so before:

- The war helped to further accelerate the development of nationalism among the colonial peoples, in at least three ways: many of them had participated in the war in behalf of the metropole (few in the West appear to realize that many nationalities from all across the European colonial empires, including those in Africa, fought in the war) which not only opened up their horizons as they traveled abroad, but also made them think about their own contradictory circumstances: fighting for the freedom of their colonial masters while they themselves were not free. At the same time, the war helped to make them realize that the propaganda of the invincibility of the European fed to them over the years in the aftermath of the defeats of their grandparents during the colonial wars of conquest (the Scramble for Africa was not a bloodless affair by any stretch of the imagination) was just that, propaganda—being asked to kill or assist in killing one group of whites in behalf of another was the ultimate irony. Third, the experience of meeting Africans from other parts of Africa helped to further galvanize their political consciousness as they exchanged views on the commonality of their experiences as a colonized people.
- The war helped to weaken the European powers because it was ultimately a highly destructive fratricidal affair. Under the circumstances, the problems of postwar reconstruction would take precedence over all else, including any desire to hang on to their colonies in the face of any credible nationalist resistance (moreover, the European populace was not in the mood for more sustained military adventures abroad). To some degree this explains why the French gave up their colonial wars as early as they did in both Algeria and in Vietnam.
- The war helped to create two superpowers, the United States and the Soviet Union, which in turn helped to inaugurate the Cold War as each side of Winston Churchill's Iron Curtain divide sought to firmly establish their grip on their respective spheres of influence. (Few appear to realize today that prior to the Second World War, the United States was, in relative terms, a small bit player on the global scene—the same was true of the Soviet Union.) Now, an offshoot of this struggle between the United States on one hand, and the Soviet Union on the other, was pressure by both on the European colonial powers to relinquish their colonies as both sought to gain allies among the emergent nationalist elites. There was, of course, an economic self-interest on the part of the United States, as well: independence among the European colonies would help advance the long-standing U.S. foreign policy of "open door" aimed at creating economic opportunities (trade, investment, markets, etc.) for its businesses in large parts of the world that had generally been closed off to them during the colonial era. (Later, however, toward the end of the 1960s and beyond, the United States would come to play a very retrogressive role in Africa as the Cold War heated up: it would side with the white minority ruled regimes against the nationalists in the Portuguese colonies, as well as in Zimbabwe and South Africa.)
- The war helped to weaken the legitimacy of the concept of colonies within the European countries as a whole, now that they themselves had witnessed what it meant to be a colony (having been colonized briefly by Nazi Germany).

For more on the political decolonization of Africa the following sources considered together will provide a good start: Betts (2004), Duara (2004), Gifford and Louis (1988), Hargreaves (1988), Mazrui (1981), and Newsom (2001).

3. The best measure available to gauge how high this unit cost is, is to look at the per student expenditure in higher education as a percentage of per capita GNP for Sub-

Saharan Africa and compare it with that for other parts of the world. The figures are startling and sobering: in 1995 (latest year for which such data is available) the percentage for the world as a whole was 77%, but for Sub-Saharan Africa it was 422%! Furthermore, compare the Sub-Saharan figure with that of low and middle-income countries taken together (91%), or South Asia (74%), or Latin America and the Caribbean (43%), or the high-income countries taken together (26%) (World Bank 2000c: 123). Now, it is of course true that per capita income for Sub-Saharan Africa is also relatively low compared to other parts of the world, but that alone does not explain the astronomical figure of 422% The fact is that quite clearly, the provision of university education in Africa is simply a very, very expensive undertaking—more so than anywhere else in the world. Not surprisingly, government after government is no longer willing or even able to fund it to the extent warranted by their needs.

4. See Lulat 2003 for more on these issues.

5. A similar argument as that for science and technology can be advanced for vocational/entrepreneurial education (accounting, business, management, etc.). For, it too is critically necessary and it too has been virtually neglected—in relative terms.

6. In reality, the concept was a rehash of the U.S. land-grant university concept, and therefore, was hardly original. It may be remembered from Chapter 4 that the concept of the land-grant university was one that rested on the issue of immediate practical relevance to the needs of the majority of the population. See also the discussion by Coleman (1984) regarding the concept of the developmental university.

7. See Lulat 2003 for more on these issues. See also Commission for Africa (2005).

8. Even those who may never join the ranks of the elite, find that being bilingual is the ticket to relative upward mobility; such as by means of migration—as in the case of rural Algerian Berbers migrating legally and illegally to France—or by working in the tourist industry, as in Tunisia or Morocco, for instance.

9. For more on the language issue see also de Mejia (2002) and Suleiman (2003).

10. Laitin and Samatar (1987: 83), who discuss the language issue, have a slightly different take on the matter by arguing that the adoption of Somali as an official language "helped to reduce the tensions that continued to exist between the northern and southern regions," this is because, they write, "northerners lost their advantage in the competition for jobs."

11. For sources on the Somali language issue see also Warsame (2001) and the sources on higher education in Somalia in Chapter 6.

12. For obvious reasons colonialism did not permit the development of an indigenous capitalist elite (the kind of elite that in Fanon's language would constitute "captains of industry"). The consequences of this have been disastrous for the continent.

13. Here the term "structure" refers to the historically-rooted institutionalized and seemingly "natural" relationships that systemically bind a whole together, but whose construction, while the prerogative of those with a monopoly over power and to which the powerless are in thrall, is often transparent to neither with the passage of time once it is completed. This definition draws on the *structuralism* of Louis Althusser *and* the concept of *structuration* first articulated by Anthony Giddens. The *Annales* approach to historiography as represented by Fernand Braudel's work, from the perspective of history, is also relevant here (see, for instance, Althusser [1972], Braudel [1982-1984], and Giddens [1986]).

14. For examples and discussion of some of the recent initiatives being taken by (or being forced upon) universities in the United States in the area of community outreach, see Pappas (1997).

15. For a current example of community-outreach activities by an African institution of higher education see Butare (2004).

16. An inkling—only an inkling, and it can be nothing more than that in the absence of an extended field-visit to the continent—of the gravity of the circumstances that Africa faces today can be best assessed by comparing what the author of this work wrote twenty years ago with what is happening today:

nations such as those in Africa are saddled with a legacy of, among other things, steeply spiraling mass poverty; deep ethnic/regional conflagratory cleavages that threaten to destroy national integrity, heavily debt-ridden stagflation economies; endemic military takeovers; and a spreading pattern of gross violations of the mass of the citizenry's basic human rights by states dominated by increasingly cynical and corrupt elites. Furthermore, as we approach the year 2000, whereas the majority of the people in the WINs [Western industrialized nations] will continue to enjoy a materially superabundant life (based on an immensely wasteful system that requires two-thirds of the world's key finite resources to keep it going) the people of the African nations (i.e., those who will have survived the present large-scale famine ravaging huge areas in Africa and estimated to threaten nearly one-quarter of the entire African population with starvation)...will face even greater levels of deterioration in their standards of living (Lulat 1985: 555).

If those were the circumstances of Africa twenty years ago, today the situation is even grimmer. Witness, for example: the mercilessly and horrifyingly savage, kleptocratic, ethnic-based armed conflicts of the recent past and the present in the Democratic Republic of Congo, Liberia, Sierra Leone, Somalia, and Sudan; the senseless and vicious blood-letting in the past and present civil wars of Algeria, Sudan, and Angola; the recent grisly genocidal murders of Burundi and Rwanda; and the equally senseless cross-border armed violence between Uganda and Congo or between Eritrea and Ethiopia; and so on. Even, however, in the absence of armed conflict, many African states are reeling from the ever-mounting and crushing debt burden; an epidemic of the disease AIDS (acquired immune deficiency syndrome) that has consumed thousands of people and cruelly wrenched from thousands of orphaned children their childhood (as they are forcibly thrust overnight into adult roles); and the continuation of widespread kleptocratic and political corruption, spiraling mass poverty in the context of disintegrating stagflation economies, massive and persistent gross violations of human rights of the citizenry; (and the list goes on and on). Tragically, as if the human-engineered disasters are not enough, nature has also persisted to conspire to add its part to the human misery: large parts of Africa continue to be engulfed by widespread famines and floods of cataclysmic proportions (the latest occurring as recently as in 1999/2000).

To put the matter differently then: in the twenty years that have elapsed, the state of the African continent—especially Sub-Saharan Africa—has not improved; on the contrary it has become worse. To be sure, there are some bright spots in Africa, but they are few, very few. In fact, even in their case, the watchword must remain ultra cautious optimism. As Rieff (1998) astutely observes: "Unfortunately, for all the promising signs that could lead an African or a sympathetic foreign observer to believe in the reality of an 'African renaissance,' it is far more likely that the new 'Afro-optimism' is, tragically, yet another false dawn, based on little more than some promising but unrepresentative social developments, a move toward formal democracy that has not and shows no real promise of being translated into grass-roots democracy, a brief and transient spike in Africa's economic fortunes, and a vast overestimation of the qualities and commitment to democracy of a new generation of African rulers who, however different stylistically they are from their predecessors, are cut from very much the same basic mold— the African 'Big Man'" (p. 11). Under these circumstances, as one can only imagine, the fate of the universities (as with the education sector as a whole) has been, in qualitative terms, one of a relentless downward spiral, with little or no relief in sight.

Blame for these circumstances, however, *does not lie entirely with the compradorial African elite*, it must also be laid at the door of European colonialism, and, of course, the continued Western corporate domination of the planet. About the latter, Caufield (1996: 331) reminds us that in 1948 the average annual per capital income was around U.S. $100 in PQD countries as against $1,600 in the United States. Today the ratio is in the order of $1,000 as against $23,000 (these averages, it may be noted, mask deep inequalities among the PQD countries themselves too). What is more, this inequality manifests itself at the global resource level in terms of one third of the world's population consuming two thirds of the world's resources to sustain a standard of living that the remaining two thirds can only dream of. Now, Can one legitimately argue that this enormous and ever-widening gap between these two different parts of the world has nothing to do whatsoever with the global policies of the rich (mainly Western countries) which have their roots in the colonial period—and further back (see Appendix II)? The truth is that by never considering these kinds of matters *in a historical context*, one can sink back into the comfort of a general amnesia that allows one to resort to theories that at their core are driven by the project of "blaming-the-victim." Hence, for instance, the common tendency of the DO (developed/overdeveloped) countries (including often even those directly involved in the development-aid business), is to "forget" that the global inequality between them and the PQD countries is neither divinely mandated nor genetically predetermined; it is a function of human engineered international economic, political and legal structures in which those who garnered initial economic advantages through accident of history have shaped the "rules of the game" to maintain and bolster these advantages. It must be remembered that the conditions of poverty or wealth are not a matter of choice for most people at the group level (and probably at the individual level too). The poor are not poor because they have *chosen* to be poor.

17. The appointment in 2005 of that neoconservative Pentagon hawk, Paul D. Wolfowitz, to the presidency of the World Bank at the behest of the United States, does not bode well for Africa in this regard. (See Mann [2004] for more on Wolfowitz.)

18. See, for example, World Bank (1998, 2000d, and 2002) on how these transformations are supposed to assist PQD countries in their development effort.

19. Given the dominance of U.S. capital in the global arena, some have even sug-

gested that globalization should be seen as nothing more than a project of a post–Cold War revived U.S. imperialism. This view has been articulated (though not in so many words), for instance, by no less a personage than that Cold War hawk, Henry Kissinger. (See his speech titled "Globalization and World Order" that he delivered at Trinity College in Dublin on October 12, 1999, and reproduced in its entirety in the *Irish Independent* in the following day's issue, in which in the course of criticizing the conventional wisdom on globalization he states: "The basic challenge is that what is called globalization is really another name for the dominant role of the United States." See also Amin [2004] and the sources in endnote 21 below.)

20. The term "development" has not been explicitly defined in this work, but it is not too late to remedy that. Although development implies some form of economic growth, it must be distinguished from it because the latter is a phenomenon of a much narrower compass. Development should be defined (in addition to the matter of personal security and the protection of basic human and civil rights), as economically and ecologically *sustainable* economic growth that leads to a convergence between the rich and the poor by means of a qualitatively authentic ascendancy in the standard of living of the *masses* such as to guarantee them a *basic minimum* in seven key areas: nutrition, health, housing, sanitation, environment, employment, and education (for a quick overview of the main issues regarding development see Seligson and Passé-Smith [2003]).

21. The literature on the key subtopics that undergird this final section is vast. However, these sources capture the central issues *when considered together: on privatization*: Alexander (2003), Altbach (1999, 2001), Atchoarena and Esquieu (2002), Deng (1997), Kruss (2004), Morey (2004), Sall (2004), Steier (2003), Teixeira and Amaral (2001), and Thaver (2003); *on globalization in general*: Allen (2001), Amin (2004), Appelbaum and Robinson (2005), Balakrishnan (2003), Bello (2001), Berberoglu (2004), Edelman and Haugerud (2005), Harrison (2005), Harvey (2003), Hopkins (2002), Magdoff (2004), and Stiglitz (2002); *on globalization and education; and on policy*: Altbach (2001, 2002, 2003), Brock-Utne (2003), Burbules and Torres (1999), CERI (2004), Cloete (2002), Coulby and Zambeta (2005), Currie and Newson (1998), Enders and Fulton (2002), Geo-Jaja (2003), Halvorsen (2005), Masschelein and Simons (2002), Mundy and Iga (2003), Prewitt (2004), Ramphele (2004), Stromquist and Monkman (2000), Salmi and Verspoor (1994), Savini (2005), Teichler (2004), Torres and Schugurensky (2002), and Yang (2003); and *on the East Asian miracle:* Burkett and Hart-Landsberg (2000), Hart-Landsberg and Burkett (2005), Ohnu and Ohnu (1998), Rao (2001), and that World Bank's mea culpa: Yusuf and Stiglitz (2000). On all these issues (except for the last), see also the sources mentioned in endnote 1 in the preface.

Appendix I

An Exploration into the Provenance of the Modern African University

It is a truism that regardless of where we are educated, we all carry a cartographic vision of the world that is essentially Eurocentric. One consequence of this has been our inability to see Africa as part of the Eurasian landmass, culturally and geographically. Be that as it may, for the present purposes it will suffice to accept that Islam is primarily an Afro-Asian civilization. Given this fact, it is not surprising then to find that Africa, as we have seen, was host to a number of very important Islamic centers of higher learning (Cairo, Al-Qayrawan, Timbuktu, etc.), which were tied together in a web-like manner by peripatetic scholars with other centers of Islamic learning elsewhere in the Islamic empire. Now, this knowledge presents us with an interesting challenge, which can be articulated in the following manner: The existence of Islamic higher education institutions in Africa (and elsewhere) in the Islamic empire as early as the eighth-century (even though in its most developed incarnation, the *madrasah*, it does not make its appearance until the arrival of the Ayyubids toward the end of the twelfth-century), raises the intriguing matter of the pedigree of the modern African university of today.

In Chapter 2 we had noted the assertion by Ashby (1966) that the modern African university is an import from the West, and as such it is an entirely Western creation for it is the West that first invented the university as we know it today. A similar sentiment about the latter point is expressed by Cobban (1975: 21–22): "The medieval university was essentially an indigenous product of Western Europe.... However much the universities may have owed to the impulse of Greek, Roman or Arabic intellectual life," he explains further, "their institutional crystallization was a new departure born of the need to enlarge the scope of professional education in an increasingly urbanized society." Similarly, Verger (1992: 35) states: "No one today would dispute the fact that universities, in the sense in which the term is generally understood, were a creation of the Middle Ages, appearing for the first time between the twelfth and thirteenth centuries." He continues: "It is no doubt true that other civilizations, prior to, or wholly alien to, the medieval West, such as the Roman Empire, Byzantium, Islam, or China, were familiar with forms of higher education, which a number of historians, for the sake of convenience, have sometimes described as universities." However, he asserts that these institutions were not really universities, they were a different kind of institutional animal; ergo, they have no link with Western universities. He then concludes: "Until there is definite proof to the contrary, these latter must be regarded as the sole source of the model which gradually spread through the whole of Europe and then to the whole world." Makdisi (1981: 292) is even more adamant: "Islam never developed the university; it simply borrowed it from Europe in the nineteenth-century along with many other borrowings, at a time when Western culture was far superior to that of the east." Presented this way, it would seem that the matter needs no further discussion. Yet, as Chapter 1 has tried to demonstrate, albeit subtextually, that historical truth is rarely simple truth (paradoxical though this may appear to the nonhistorian); especially the further one goes back in history.

The truth really is that historical truth is usually much, much more complex. Of course, no one can dispute the fact that the birth of an institution in any society of such ubiquity and long duration as the university, must in the first instance speak to the specific internal motivating circumstances of that society—the presence of external circumstances, if any, notwithstanding (see the discussion regarding this matter by Ruegg 1992). At the same time, one should be forewarned against the very serious threat of historiographical seduction presented by the "*propter hoc* and therefore *post hoc*" (that is, the fallacy of temporal sequence as causality) type of explanations. With these caveats in mind, here is the specific challenge that this chapter seeks to address: to demonstrate that even though the modern university readily found a fertile institutional soil in the specifics of European societies of the twelfth and thirteenth centuries, its genesis required the catalytic role of an external factor: specifically, an Afro-Asian civilization; that is, the Islamic civilization.

In responding to this challenge, the underlying motivating objective, to be discussed in the conclusion, is to go beyond simply the usual questions of the type that Ruegg, for example, poses ("How is the origin of the university to be explained? Is it a resultant of the society in which it exists or is it a factor in the formation of society?" p. 9) and consider the broader question of the relationship between historiography and historical truth. Of course, in the process, Ruegg's questions will also be dealt with: as the chapter will show, the answer is that it is both: it is a *resultant* and a *formative* factor. In other words, it is the thesis of this chapter that Islam had a decisive role to play in both the twin dialectical dimensions of the equation that Ruegg posits thusly: "Without the intellectual stimulus of the rationally controlled search for knowledge, there would be no university." Yet on the other hand, as he continues further, "the university, could have arisen only in the particular economic, political, and social circumstances obtaining in certain cities of Europe in the early Middle Ages." In other words, as Ruegg, quoting P. Classen, observes: "the spirit alone cannot create its body" (p. 11). In the first half of this chapter the spirit will be the focus of attention, to be followed by the body in the second half.

One can begin the discussion by first noting that the university is but just one form of a higher educational institution; there are other forms, the most common of which is the college. Now, if the college and the university were to be considered as institutionally related then one can easily challenge the claim of Western originality. For, as Makdisi (1981) clearly shows, the West borrowed from the Muslims the concept of the college. The college in its early beginnings, as an eleemosynary institution, was already common in Islam (the *madrasah*). It is not surprising, therefore, that the earliest college in the West, was most probably modeled on the Islamic college. This was the College des Dix-Huit, founded in Paris in 1180 by John of London; who, not coincidentally, as Makdisi (1981) observes, had just returned from pilgrimage to Jerusalem. It is through that endeavor (which entailed journeying through Muslim lands) that he most likely came to learn of the idea of the college. (This model would later also be the basis of the founding of the earliest of the three Oxford colleges, Balliol, according to Makdisi 1981.)

The question, however, is: Can one say that the two are related in that the one, the college, is the precursor of the other, the university? Makdisi suggests that this is not so. Unlike in the United States, he states, in Europe the university emerged as an entirely separate higher educational institution with its own identity; that is, it did not begin its life as a college, but as a *studium generale* (a prototype European university that in its creation embodied the critical concept of *incorporation*). He is not alone on this point. Cobban (1975), Huff (1993), Pedersen (1997), and Verger (1992), for example, all share his view.

However, the matter cannot be left to rest here. To be sure, if one were to take the *narrow* legalistic definition of the university—as a higher educational institution that is virtually independent of state and/ or religious *administrative control* through the mechanism of *incorporation* (and the key words here are *narrow* and *incorporation*)— then, yes, they are quite correct: the university in this *limited* sense is a Western invention. Islam did not and could not recognize incorporation as a basis for the organization of an institution of higher education (or any other institution for that matter)—and yet without it, the modern university could not have emerged in the form that it is today.[1] If, on the other hand, the issue of the origin of the modern Western university was looked at in broader terms then it becomes more complicated. Why?

Because from a broader historical perspective, the modern university that was brought to Africa by the colonial powers *is as much Western in origin as it is Islamic (that is Afro-Asiatic) in origin.* How? Nakosteen (1964: vii) explains it this way: "At a time when European monarchs were hiring tutors to teach them how to sign their names, Muslim educational institutions were preserving, modifying and improving upon the classical cultures in their progressive colleges and research centers under enlightened rulers. Then as the results of their cumulative and creative genius reached the Latin West through translations... they brought about that Western revival of learning which is our modern heritage." Making the same observation, James Burke (1995: 36) reminds us that at the point in time when the first European universities at Bologna and Charters were being created, their future as academic centers of learning was far from certain. The reason? He explains: "The medieval mind was still weighed down by centuries of superstition, still fearful of new thought, still totally obedient to the Church and its Augustinian rejection of the investigation of nature. They lacked a system for investigation, a tool with which to ask questions and, above all, they lacked the knowledge once possessed by the Greeks, of which medieval Europe had heard, but which had been lost." But then, he further explains: "In one electrifying moment it was rediscovered. In 1085 the [Muslim] citadel of Toledo in Spain fell, and the victorious Christian troops found a literary treasure beyond anything they could have dreamed of." Through the mediation of Spanish Jews, European Christians, and others, much of that learning would now be translated from Arabic, which for centuries had been *the* language of science, into Latin, Spanish, Hebrew, and other languages, to be disseminated all across Europe. (This translation activity, one would be remiss not to point out here parenthetically, was a replication of an earlier translation activity undertaken by the Muslims themselves over a 300-year period, eighth to tenth centuries, when they *systematically* organized the translation of Greek scientific works into Arabic—see Gutas 1998, and O'Leary 1949, for a detailed and fascinating account.)

Before proceeding further, however, there is a clarifying point of context that must be dispensed with concerning the presence of Arabic names in the historical literature dealing with the Islamic empire. An Arabic name does not in of itself guarantee that the person in question is an Arab Muslim; it is quite possible that the person is a Muslim of some other ethnicity. The reason is that for a considerable period of time not only was Arabic the lingua franca of such activities as learning and commerce in the Islamic empire, but then as today, for all Muslims throughout the world, Arabic is their liturgical language and this also often implies taking on Muslim (and hence Arabic) names. Therefore, the Islamic empire and civilization was not exclusively an Arabic empire and civilization, it was an *Islamic* empire and civilization in which all manner of nationalities and cultures had a hand, at indeterminable and varying degrees, in its evolution.[2] Consider, for example, this fact: over the centuries—from antiquity through the Islamic period—millions of Africans would go to Asia (as slaves, as soldiers, etc.) and yet the absence of a distinct group of people today in Asia who can be categorized as part of the African diaspora—akin to the situation in the Americas—is testament to the fact that in time they were genetically and culturally absorbed by the Asian societies. To be sure, in the early phases of the evolution of the Islamic empire, Arab Muslims were dominant; but note that domination does not translate into exclusivity.

Ultimately, then, one can assert that the Islamic civilization was and is primarily an *Afro-Asian* civilization—which boasted a web-like network of centers of learning as geographically dispersed as Al-Qarawiyyin (Tunisia), Baghdad (Iraq), Cairo (Egypt), Cordoba (Muslim Spain), Damascus (Syria), Jundishapur (Iran), Palermo (Muslim Sicily), Timbuktu (Mali), and Toledo (Muslim Spain)—and in which, furthermore, the Asian component ranges from Arabic to Persian to Indian to Chinese contributions and influences. As Pedersen (1997: 117) points out: "Many scholars of widely differing race and religion worked together...to create an Arab culture, which would have made the modest learning of the Romans seem pale and impoverished if a direct comparison had been possible." In other words, the presence of Arabic names in relation to the Islamic civilization can also indicate simply the Arabization of the person's name even though the person may not have been a Muslim at all! (Take the example of that brilliant Jewish savant of the medieval era, Moses Maimonides; he was also known by the Arabic name of *Abu Imran Musa ibn Maymun ibn Ubayd Allah.*) This fact is of great relevance whenever the issue of Islamic secular scholarship is considered. Secular knowledge and learning in the Islamic civilization (referred to by the Muslims as the "foreign sciences" to distinguish it from the Islamic religious sciences) had many diverse contemporary contributors; including savants who were from other faiths: Christianity, Hinduism, Judaism, Zoroastrianism, and so on. Consequently, when one talks about the Islamic contribution to knowledge and learning, one does not necessarily mean it is the contribution of Muslim scholars alone, but rather that it is the output of scholars who included non-Muslims (albeit a numerical minority in relative terms), *but who all worked under the aegis of the Islamic civilization in its centers of learning and whose lingua franca was primarily Arabic.* The use of the phrase *Islamic* scholars or *Arabic* scholars in this book, therefore, should not imply that the scholars were necessarily Muslim scholars (or even Arab scholars for that matter), though most were—that is, most were Muslim scholars, but here again they were not all necessarily Arabs; they could have been of any ethnicity or nationality. (See Iqbal 2002; Nakosteen 1964; and Lindberg 1992, for more on this point.)

To move on then, it ought to be noted that long periods of peaceful co-existence among Christians, Jews, Muslims and others in Spain, even after the fall of Toledo, was also highly instrumental in facilitating the work of translation and knowledge export into Western Europe. To a lesser extent, but important still, the fall of Muslim Sicily, beginning with the capture of Messina in 1061 by Count Roger (brother of Robert Guiscard), and ending with his complete takeover of the island from the Muslims in 1091, was yet another avenue by which Muslim learning entered, via translations, Western Europe (see Ahmed 1975, for more).[3] This export of Islamic and Islamic-mediated Greek science to the Latin West would continue well into the thirteenth-century (after all, Islam was not completely vanquished from the Iberian peninsula until the capture of the Muslim province of Granada, more than 400 years after the fall of Toledo, in 1492).

Among the more prominent of the translators who worked in either Spain or Sicily (or even both) included: Abraham of Toledo; Adelard of Barth; Alfonso X the El Sabio; Constantine the African (Constantinus Africanus); the Archdeacon of Segovia (Dominicus Gundissalinus); Eugenius of Palermo; Gerard of Cremona; Isaac ibn Sid; John of Seville; Leonardo Pisano; Michael Scott; Moses ibn Tibbon; Qalonymos ben Qalonymos; Robert of Chester; Stephanus Arnoldi, and so on. (See Nakosteen 1964 for more names—including variants of these names—and details on when and what they translated.) To really drive the point home, however, it is necessary to provide here (even if, due to space constraints, only most cursorily) a few examples of the kinds of contributions that the Muslim savants (and non-Muslim savants too, but all working under the aegis of the Islamic civilization)—many of whom, it may be further noted, were polymaths in the truest sense of the word—made to the intellectual and scientific development of Europe on the eve of the Renaissance; and without which the development of the modern Western university would have been greatly compromised. This task is accomplished by the following highly *select* chronological listing (based on sources mentioned in the note that continues this listing) of some of the most important names in the pantheon of Islamic savants of the Middle Ages, together with a briefest delineation of their work, some of which would eventually make its way to the Latin West:

Abu Musa Jabir ibn-Hayyan (c. 721–815, known in the Latin West as Geber), an alchemist who advocated the importance of experiments in advancing scientific knowledge: "It must be taken as an absolutely rigorous principle that any proposition which is not supported by proofs is nothing more than an assertion which may be true or may be false" (quoted in Artz 1980: 166). His work would be foundational to the development of the field of chemistry, even if the raison d'etre of his scientific work (alchemy) was, from the vantage point of today, misguided.

Musa al-Khwarazmi (d. c. 863), his seminal contributions in mathematics helped to develop that field enormously. In fact, through his mathematical treatise, *al-Jabr wa 'l-Muqabalah*, he not only gave the West the term "algebra" (Latinized shorthand of the title of his treatise), but far more significant than that, he was the conduit for the passage of arithmetic numerals from India to the West. For example, he would be responsible for the introduction to the Latin West of such key mathematical tools as the concept of "zero" (an independent Hindu/ Chinese invention in the sixth-century C.E.), and the decimal system. His other contributions included sine and cotangent tables, astronomical tables, and the cartographic concepts of latitude and longitude. Even the term algorithm comes from him, albeit unwittingly—it is the Latinized version of his name. He also produced a revised version of Ptolemy's geography, which he called *The Face of the Earth*.

Abu Yosuf Ya'qub Ibn Ishaq ibn al-Sabbah al-Kindi (died c. 870) a philosopher and mathematician, his contributions included works on Hindu numerals and geometry, and physiological optics.

Abu Bakr Muhammed bin Zakariyya' al-Razi (844–926, known as Rhazes in the Latin West), a physician whose work helped to further greatly the development of clinical medicine. His work on smallpox and measles would remain authoritative in the West for almost 400 years; and his work on the diseases of childhood would earn him the accolade of "Father of Pediatrics" in the West. It is no wonder that a large part of the medical curriculum at the Universities of Salerno and Paris comprised his work.

Muhammed Ibn Muhammed Ibn Tarkhan ubn Uzalagh al-Farabi (c. 878–c. 950, known in the Latin West as Alpharabius), author of the *Enumeration of the Sciences*, provided an integrated approach to the sciences and reiterated the distinction between divine knowledge and human knowledge.

Abu Al-Husayn Ali Ibn Al-Husayn Al-Masudi (d. 957), historian and explorer who is sometimes referred to as the "Herodotus of the Arabs." His works included the 132-chapter *The Meadows of Gold and Mines of Gems*, an abridgement of a multidisciplinary multivolume treatise on history and scientific geography of the world *Abd al-Rahman al-Sufi* (903–986), among the greatest Muslim astronomers (together with *Ibn Yunus* and *Ulegh Beg*), his contributions include a major treatise on observational astronomy titled *The Book of Fixed Stars*

Abu al-Qasim Khalaf ibn al-Abbas Al-Zahrawi (930–1013, known to the Latin West as Albucasis), a famous physician and surgeon, he wrote a treatise on medicine and medical practice that ran into thirty volumes. The last of these volumes was extremely important because in it he covered all aspects of surgery including providing illustrations of surgical instruments. This work is thought to have been the first work on surgery ever written anywhere and it would in time become a standard text in medical schools in the Latin West. Interestingly, some of the surgical procedures that he described in his work are still carried out to this day in like manner.

Abu Alimacr al-Hassan Ibn al-Haitham (c. 965–1039, known in the Latin West as Alhazen). Through his works in optics and related fields, he became a major contributor to the development of the physical sciences in the Latin West. By means of his experiments with light he discovered the laws of refraction as well as the various colors that make up light. He was the first scientist to conclude that sight involved the transmission of light from the seen object to the eye, which acted as a lens. He also introduced the method of using the *camera obscura* for the purposes of studying solar eclipses. It would not be an exaggeration to say that his scientific work would remain unchallenged for nearly 600 years until the arrival of Johannes Kepler. In fact, Crombie (1990: 189) observes that Ibn al Haitham "ranks with Ptolemy and Kepler as an architect of scientific optics." He further adds, "[I]n his explorations of the physics, physiology and psychology of vision he stands comparison intellectually with Descartes and Helmholtz."

Abu' Ali Al-Husain Ibn Abdallah Ibn Sina (980–1037, known in the Latin West as Avicenna), who was among the progenitors of Scholasticism in the West and whose intellectual influence would touch Western thinkers as diverse as Thomas Aquinas, Roger Bacon, Robert Grosseteste, Albertus Magnus, Duns Scotus, was a great philosopher and scientist with one of the most prolific pens of his day: among his many works, two that the West got to know well are *The Book of the Remedy* (Kitab al-Shifa)—which, according to Stanton (1990: 85) stands as the "longest encyclopedia of knowledge ever authored by a single person"—and *The Canon of Medicine*, which would remain the principal textbook par excellence on medicine in the West for many, many years. Going by Crombie (1990), Ibn Sina's contributions also included determinative influences on the beginnings of the scientific experimental method (without which no modern science would have been possible), as well as on a number of theories relating to blood circulation, fossils, vision, motion, music and the debunking of the alchemic theory of gold manufacture.

This super-abbreviated listing continues in endnote 4 at the end of this chapter.[4] Of course, it must be conceded, that the contributions by the Muslims to the intellectual and scientific development of Europe was made unwittingly; even so, it must be emphatically stressed, it was of no less significance. Moreover, that is how history, after all, really unfolds in practice; it is not made in the way it is usually presented in history textbooks: as a continuous chain of teleological developments. To explain: those who study history, especially comparative history, are burdened by the constant and sobering reminder that no matter how intelligently purposeful human beings (the Europeans in this particular instance) may consider themselves, at the end of the day, major social transformations are as much a product of chance and circumstance, as directed human endeavors (in the shape of "social movements"—a phrase that should be understood here broadly).[5] In other words, any grand purposive human design that may appear to exist in any history of major social transformations is in reality nothing more than an embodiment of the fallacy of historical teleology.

History (regardless of whether it is written or oral) is, ultimately, a selective chronicle of a series of conjunctures of fortuitously "propitious" historical factors where the role of purposive human agency, is, more often than not, absent from the social transformation in question. Stephen K. Sanderson, in his book, *Social Transformations: A General Theory of Historical Development* (1995: 13), makes this point with even greater clarity when he observes that "individuals acting in their own interests create social structures and systems that are the sum total and product of these socially oriented individual actions." However, he points out, "[t]hese social structures and systems are frequently constituted in ways that individuals never intended, and thus individually purposive human action leads to many unintended consequences." In other words, he concludes, "[s]ocial evolution is driven by purposive or intended human actions, but it is to a large extent not itself a purposive or intended phenomenon." Looking from the perspective of the West, the veracity of this fact was embodied at a particular point in time, on the eve of the Renaissance, in the retreat of the Muslims from Europe, under the aegis of the *Reconquista*—symbolized by the fall of Toledo in that fateful summer of 1085. The Europeans who entered Toledo under the leadership of Alfonso VI of Castille-Leon, could never have envisioned, much less planned, the centrality of Muslim intellectual and scientific contributions to the development of Europe, for centuries to come, that their actions would precipitate.[6]

The truth of the matter really, then, is this: during the medieval era, the Europeans acquired from the savants of the Islamic empire a number of essential elements that would be absolutely central to the foundation of the modern Western university: *First*, they acquired a huge corpus of knowledge that the Muslims had gathered together over the centuries in their various centers of learning (e.g., Baghdad, Cairo, and Cordoba) through a dialectical combination of their own investigations, as well as by gathering knowledge from across geographic space (from Afghanistan, China, India, the Levant, Persia, etc.) and from across time: through systematic translations of classical works of

Greek, Alexandrian, and other scholars.[7] Lest there is a misunderstanding here, it must be stressed that it is not that the Muslims were mere transmitters of Hellenic knowledge (or any other people's knowledge); far from it: they, as the French philosopher Alain de Libera (1997) points out, also greatly elaborated on it by the addition of their own scholarly findings. "Yet it would be wrong to think that the Arabs [sic] confined themselves to a slavish appropriation of Greek results. In practical and in theoretical matters Islam faced problems that gave rise to the development of an independent philosophy and science," states Pedersen (1997: 118) as he makes a similar observation—and as do Benoit and Micheau (1995), Huff (1993); King (2000); and Stanton (1990), among others).

What kinds of problems is Pedersen referring to here? Examples include: the problems of reconciling faith and scientific philosophy; the problems of ocean navigation (e.g., in the Indian Ocean); the problem of determining the direction to Mecca (*qibla*) from the different parts of the Islamic empire for purposes of daily prayers; the problem of resolving the complex calculations mandated by Islamic inheritance laws; the problems of constructing large congregational mosques (*jami al masjid*); the problems of determining the accuracy of the lunar calendar for purposes of fulfilling religious mandates, such as fasting (*ramadhan*); the problems of planning new cities; and so on. Commenting on the significance of this fact, Stanton (1990) reminds us that even if the West would have eventually had access to the Greek classical texts maintained by the Byzantines after the fall of Constantinople, it would have missed out on this very important Islamic contribution of commentaries, additions, revisions, interpretations, and so on, of the Greek classical texts.[8] A good example of the Muslim contribution to learning derived from Greek sources is Ibn Sina's *Canon Medicinae*, and from the perspective of medieval medical teaching, its importance, according to Pedersen (1997: 125) "can hardly be overrated, and to this day it is read with respect as the most superior work in this area that the past has ever produced."

Now, as Burke explains, this knowledge alone would have wrought an intellectual revolution by itself. However, the fact that it was accompanied by the Aristotelian concept of argument by syllogism that Muslim philosophers like Ibn Sina had incorporated into their scholarly work, which was now available to the Europeans for the first time, so to speak, that would prove to be an explosive "intellectual bombshell." In other words, they learned from the Muslims (and this is the *second* critical element) rationalism, combined with, in Burke's words "the secular, investigative approach typical of Arab natural science," that is, the scientific experimental method (1995: 42). Pedersen (1997: 116) makes the same point in his analysis of the factors that led to the development of the *studium generale* and from it the modern university: "To recreate Greek mathematics and science from the basic works was obviously out of the question, since even the knowledge of how to do research had passed into oblivion....That the study of the exact sciences did not end in a blind alley, was due to a completely different stream of culture now spilling out of [Islamic] civilization into the Latin world."

Until recently, the traditional Western view had been that the father of the scientific experimental method was the Englishman, Roger Bacon (born c. 1220 and died in 1292). However, as Qurashi and Rizvi (1996) demonstrate, even a cursory examination of the works of such Islamic savants as Abu Musa Jabir ibn-Hayyan, Abu Alimacr al-Hassan ibn al-Haitham, Abu Raihan al-Biruni, and Abu al-Walid Muhammed ibn Ahmad ibn Muhammed Ibn Rushd proves this view to be patently false.[9] What Bacon ought to be credited with is the fact that he was a fervent proselytizer of the experimental method, the knowledge of which he had acquired from the Muslims through their translated works while studying at Oxford University. Bacon, it should be remembered, was well acquainted with the work of the university's first chancellor, Robert Grosseteste, who was an indefatigable apostle of Greco-Islamic learning in the Latin West (see also Crombie [1990]).

The *third* critical element was an elaborate and intellectually sophisticated map of scientific knowledge. The Muslims provided the Europeans a body of knowledge that was already divided into a host of academic subjects in a way that was very unfamiliar to the medieval Europeans: "medicine, astrology, astronomy, pharmacology, psychology, physiology, zoology, biology, botany, mineralogy, optics, chemistry, physics, mathematics, algebra, geometry, trigonometry, music, meteorology, geography, mechanics, hydrostatics, navigation, and history" (Burke 1995: 42).[10] The significance of this map of knowledge is that the European university, as de Libera (1997) observes, became its institutional embodiment. As he states: "The Muslim learning that was translated and passed on to the West formed the basis and the scientific foundation of the university in its living reality—the reality of its syllabus, the content of its teaching."

In other words, the highly restrictive and shallow curriculum of Martianus Capella's Seven Liberal Arts (divided into the *trivium* and the *quadrivium*), which the Carthaginian had promulgated sometime in the middle of the fifth-century C.E. to become, in time, the foundation of Latin education in the cathedral schools—the forerunners of the *studium generale*—would now be replaced by the much broader curriculum of "Islamic" derived education. It ought to be noted here that the curriculum of the medieval universities was primarily based on the teaching of science; and it was even more so, paradoxically, than it is in the modern universities of today. The fact that this was the case, however, it would be no exaggeration to state, was entirely due to Islam! As Grant (1994), for example, shows, the growth of the medieval European universities was, in part, a direct response to the Greco-Islamic science that arrived in Europe after the fall of Toledo (see also Beaujouan [1982], Grant [1996], Nakosteen [1964], and Stanton [1990]).

But what of the traditional view that the medieval universities had little or nothing to do with the scientific advances of the seventeenth-century that are supposed to have occurred primarily in the scientific academies/societies that emerged during this period? Those who have advanced such a view (see Cohen [1994], Gascoigne [1990], and Porter [1996], for a summary of the key literature on the matter) appear to forget to ask one very elementary question, Where did these scientists obtain their education in the first place? The answer, of course, is that most of them received their education in the medieval universities. As Gascoigne puts it: "There is, after all, something anomalous about the fact that these institutions, which are generally accorded so negative a role in the scientific revolution, were also the places where the vast majority of those representative of the scientific revolution received their education" (p. 208). Another related question is, How did these scientists make their living? Again the answer is that a substantial portion made their living by teaching in the medieval universities.

In other words, as Gascoigne and Porter demonstrate, the medieval universities, depending to some extent on which part of Europe one is looking at, were not as irrelevant to the scientific progress achieved by the dramatis personae of the seventeenth-century as has been traditionally portrayed. In fact, by carefully examining the curricula of these universities they prove that many of the universities were flexible enough to permit innovation—at least to the point where the task could be taken over by the scientific academies/ societies when they emerged. As Porter observes, "[r]evisionist studies are... demonstrating beyond question that early modern universities were not benighted, hidebound, monolithic institutions which shut their doors and minds to all but a diet of dead science and medicine, washed down with stale scholastic commentators" (p. 534). What is more, Gascoigne points out that the traditional view that there was an antagonistic disjointure between the academies/societies and the universities is not entirely borne out by facts. With some exceptions, universities did not always see the academies as competition to be opposed; rather they were often (though not always) viewed as complementary institutions with a different but legitimate mission from theirs: to do research (whereas they saw their mission as primarily teaching).

The *fourth* was the extrication of the individual from the grip of what de Libera describes as the "medieval world of social hierarchies, obligations, and highly codified social roles," so as to permit the possibility of a civil society, without which no university was possible. A university could only come into being on the basis of a community of scholars who were individuals in their own right, intellectually unbeholden to no one but reason, but yet gathered together in pursuit of one ideal: "the scientific ideal, the ideal of shared knowledge, of a community of lives based on the communication of knowledge and on the joint discovery of the reality of things." In other words, universities "were laboratories in which the notion of the European individual was invented. The latter is always defined as someone who strikes a balance between culture, freedom, and enterprise, someone who has the capacity to show initiative and innovate. As it happens, and contrary to a widely held view, this new type of person came into being at the heart of the medieval university world, prompted by the notion—which is not Greek but [Muslim]—that [scientific] work liberates" (de Libera 1997).

A *fifth* was the arrival of Islamic inspired scholarship, such as that of Averroes (Ibn Rushd), that helped to extricate the curriculum from the theological oversight of the church. In the struggle over the teaching of "Averroeism" in the academy, for example, the academy triumphed and the church retreated behind the compromise that there would be two forms of knowledge: divine or revealed knowledge that could not be challenged, and temporal knowledge that could go its separate way. (See Iqbal [2002] and Lindberg [1992], for an accessible summary of this struggle.) Henceforth, academic freedom in terms of what was taught and learned became an ever-increasing reality, jealously guarded by the academy. The implications of this development cannot be overstated: it would unfetter the pursuit of scientific inquiry from the shackles of religious dogma and thereby permit the emergence of those intellectual forces that in time would bring about the scientific revolution in the seventeenth-century (see also Benoit [1995]).

The *sixth* critical element was the standardization of the university curricula across Europe that the arrival of Greco-Islamic learning made possible. Independent of where a university was located, Paris, Bologna, Oxford, and so on, the general pattern was that the curriculum rested on the same or similar texts addressing the same or similar problems in philosophy, science, theology, and so on, regardless of the curricular emphasis or specialty of the institution. What benefit did this standardization of the curricula confer on the development of universities in Europe? "For the first time in history," as Lindberg (1992: 212) explains, "there was an educational effort of international scope, undertaken by scholars conscious of their intellectual and professional unity." In other words, a standardized curricula helped to facilitate the development of a variety of attributes characteristic of modern-day universities; such as the professionalization of the professoriate, universalization of academic qualifications, cross-fertilization of ideas through teacher/student interchanges across geographically dispersed institutions, the relative uniformity of entrance qualifications among institutions, and so on.

On the basis of the foregoing, then, what has been established? That the modern university is an Islamic invention? Not at all. Rather, that it is an institutional expression of a confluence of originality and influences. Makdisi (1981: 293) sums it up best: "The great contribution of Islam is to be found in the college system it originated, in the level of higher learning it developed and transmitted to the West, in the fact that the West borrowed from Islam basic elements that went into its own system of education, elements that had to do with both substance and method." At the same time, "[t]he great contribution of the Latin West," Makdisi continues, "comes from its organization of knowledge and its further development—knowledge in which the Islamic-Arabic component is undeniably considerable—as well as the further development of the college system itself into a corporate system."

The matter, however, cannot end here; having dealt with the spirit there is the matter of the body in the line quoted from Ruegg (1992: 11) at the beginning of this chapter (to repeat: "the spirit alone cannot create its body"). That is, in laying out earlier some of the very specific intellectual avenues of Islamic contribution to the growth of the modern Western university, one risks being blinded to an even more fundamental Islamic contribution: its assistance in the development of the *civilizational context* that facilitated the emergence and development of the modern university in Europe in the first place, that is, European *modernity* itself! To elaborate: the modern Western university emerged as a corporate institution at precisely the time (in the latter half of the twelfth-century and in the first half of the thirteenth-century) when Western Europe was about to undergo the Renaissance. But a critical question emerges here: How had Europe managed to developmentally come this far? After all, when the Muslims made their appearance in Europe in the eighth-century C.E., Europe was in almost every way a Neolithic cultural, economic, intellectual, scientific, and technological backwater. What is more: the presence of a few isolated individuals such as Boethius, Isidore of Seville, Gregory of Tours, Bede the Venerable, merely served to emphasize this state of affairs.[11] The answer, in one word, is: Islam! The Islamic civilization—which one must be reminded is primarily an Afro-Asian civilization—was highly *instrumental* (no, not causational it must be cautioned, but instrumental) in the creation of the *civilizational context* in Europe that produced the *studium generale* and from there the modern university.[12]

Before proceeding, one must begin by noting that European modernity was a generalized expression of a dialectic between the development of science and technology on one hand, and on the other, socioeconomic transformations that led to that momentous event—when seen through the eyes of Europe—the Columbian project of 1492 (without which Europe would never have achieved modernity—see Appendix II). This dialectic was characterized by such developmental markers as the invention of gunnery, the birth of the Copernican revolution, the invention of the printing press, the undertaking of voyages of *exploitation* (to use Berman's, term [1989]), the emergence of mercantile capitalism and commercial law, and so on. Yet, one of the central factors that helped to facilitate this dialectic was Islam. That is, at both levels—modernity in general and the development of science and technology in particular—the hand of Islam was *catalytically* present. How so?

Through the Muslim invasions of Spain in the eighth-century and Italy in the nineth-century, and later through the Crusades against the Muslims unleashed by Europe at turn of the eleventh-century (that would last, if one includes the final stages of the Spanish *Reconquista*—the fall of Granada in 1492—well into the fifteenth-century), Europe would learn much (theories and methods) and take much (artifacts and products) from the Islamic civilization that would prove absolutely decisive in its eventual quest for a sea route to the East and all the consequences that would ensue for Europe's journey to modernity.[13] Evidentiary support for this claim about Islam's critical role in helping to sow the seeds of Europe's journey to modernity during the period eighth through fifteenth-century—which, not coincidentally, encompasses the classical period of Islamic higher learning—is of course necessary here. However, because of space limitation, this task must regrettably be, perforce, cursory. *First,* Islam enabled Europe to reacquaint itself with its Greek and Alexandrian classical roots—in terms of knowledge and learning. Since this has already been noted above, no more need be said here other than this: It is not that Europe had completely lost all the classical texts as a result of such factors as the depredations of the Germanic barbarians (fourth to fifth centuries C.E.); the destructions of ancient places of learning by Christian zealots (such as Justinian I who, for example, in sixth-century C.E. ordered the closure of the famous Academy of Athens founded by Plato in fourth-century B.C.E.—forcing many of the scholars to take refuge in Sassanid Persia. They would take up residence in its capital, Jundishapur, and thereby inadvertently facilitate the early flowering of a purposive multicultural international scholarship that would later achieve explosively extensive development under the banner of Islam); and the vandalism of the Viking predators (nineth- to eleventh- century C.E.). A few of the texts had survived in the monasteries, but that is where the rub is. The monasteries, enthralled by Augustinian neoplatonist teachings (knowledge based on the material was of no consequence compared to that derived from the spiritual), to all intents and purposes, simply sat on these texts; moreover, the fact that the *studium generale* was not linked to the monastic schools in lineage also meant that whatever classical knowledge the monks had preserved was, for the most part, unavailable to the emerging academy.[14]

Second, Europe experienced a scientific and technological advancement that involved a critical (though not necessarily exclusive) Islamic role—without which it is doubtful that the Europeans would have experienced this advancement at all, in terms of magnitude and significance. (As Dorn [1991: 109] puts it: "[t]he line of scientific development and transmission from ancient Greece to modern Europe was drawn through a series of Middle Eastern cities—Alexandria, Pergamum, Constantinople, Jundishapur, and Baghdad.") Before proceeding any further with this point it is necessary to pause here for a moment to note this irony: in a world that is so heavily dominated by science and technology, there is, to one's chagrin, so little interest (relatively speaking) in researching and writing about the *history* of science and technology among scientists—the people best qualified to undertake this work—mainly because of the feeling among them that it is work that belongs to humanists. Though going by Turner (1990: 23), however, it would appear that the problem goes even deeper: many working scientists regard the study of the history of science as "some kind of intellectual weakness, or as an occupation suitable for ageing members of the profession who have lost their flair and are being put out to grass, a phase of life for which one scientist coined the pejorative term 'philopause.'" On the other hand, among the humanists, too, interest in the subject is tardy, primarily because of a lack of confidence—not unjustified since few have the necessary science background. The outcome of this inadvertent academic stalemate is that adequate and thorough investigations of histories of science and technology remain to be written, most especially in circumstances where tracing the roots and origins of scientific and technological discoveries require simultaneous multicultural, transgeographic foci (e.g., China, India, Persia, etc.)[15] After all, when it comes to Islamic science, for example, it must be recognized that it was the first truly *international* science that the world had ever witnessed.

Nevertheless, there exists enough histories of science to give one at least a fair if not complete picture of the role of Islam in the genesis of Europe's scientific and technological developments. This role—which it must be reiterated was not always exclusively Muslim in origin (a point already hinted at above), but was most certainly mediated by the Islamic civilization—took the form of the introduction and reintroduction to the Latin West of essential scientific concepts, methods, and knowledge; a glimpse of which has already been provided at some length above. As Huff (1993: 13) succinctly puts it: "modern science is the product of intercivilizational encounters, including, but not limited to, the interaction between Arabs, Muslims, and Christians, but also other 'dialogues between the living and the dead' involving Greeks, Arabs, and Europeans."[16] Consider that if one were to insist on a clear marker for the beginning of scientific upsurgence in Europe than the prime candidate has to be the emergence of heliocentricism (*a la* Copernicus) in the middle of the sixteenth-century. Yet, everything, in terms of data, that the Copernican revolution was predicated on was acquired directly and indirectly from Islamic astronomers; they had already amassed this data centuries before.[17]

Of course, it is true that the Islamic scholars did not make the final leap, it is the Europeans who instead did.[18] However, that does not detract from the fact that without the import of Greco-Arabic science into Western Europe that was facilitated by the systematic translations of Islamic scientific scholarship (an exercise that, recall, was itself an echo of another systematic translation effort—Greek scholarship into Arabic—begun some 300 years earlier by the Muslims), the European scientific advancements may not have emerged at the time they did, if at all! "From the tenth to the thirteenth centuries, the [Muslims] acted as intermediaries between Greek science and the West," explain Benoit and Micheau (1995: 220–221). That is, "[t]hrough them came the first stirrings in the tenth and eleventh centuries, through them too the great mass of texts which in the twelfth-century provided the foundation for the intellectual renewal of the West." As to another related matter they are equally unequivocal: "This transfer affected all the disciplines: mathematics and physics, astronomy and medicine, chemistry and optics. *The role of direct transmission from Greek to Latin was minor, even if later the Latins found it convenient to turn to the original texts*" (emphasis added).

In fact, the science that the European scientific revolution was built upon is best described, as indeed Benoit and Micheau (1995: 221) do, as a Euro-Asiatic science. However, given the very nature of scientific progress, how else could it be? For, one should be reminded here of the fact that it is in the area of science, perhaps more than in any other area of human endeavor, that the following axiom is foundational: the present is always rooted in the past, just as the future is always rooted in the present. To put it another way, all scientific progress rests on the achievements and failures of existing science, which in turn rests on the achievements and failures of past science.[19] As Crombie (1990), Dorn (1991), Grant (1984), Huff (1993), Turner (1995) and others have correctly pointed out: "The translations of Greco-Arabic science, with Aristotle's natural books forming the core," to quote Grant, "laid the foundation for the continuous development of science to the present" This is because, to quote Grant again: "Without the translations, which furnished a well articulated body of theoretical science to Western Europe, the great scientists of the sixteenth and seventeenth centuries, such as Copernicus, Galileo, Descartes, and Newton, would have had little to reflect upon and reject, little that could focus their attention on significant physical problems." What is more, he notes: "The overthrow of one world system by another does not imply a lack of continuity" (pp. 91–92). Lindberg (1992: 364–365) also makes the same point when he observes: "If, as we know by hindsight, ancient thought supplied the foundation on which Western scientific tradition would be build, it follows that the reception, assimilation, and institutionalization of ancient thought was a prerequisite to the further construction of that particular edifice."

Whether or not the methodologies and the content of medieval science bore any resemblance to those of the seventeenth-century (the period of the supposed scientific revolution), the fact that the scientists of the seventeenth-century were not working from a scientific *tabula rasa*, but rather were heirs to a medieval science that they still had to digest in order to eventually reject its basic Aristotelian core, points to an organic continuity that is the basis of all scientific progress (remember, the apocryphal tale of Archimedian Eureka was just that and nothing more; for, "eurekas" are not born in bathtubs, but rather emerge as precipitates of historically rooted intellectual matrixes).

In other words, and this point cannot be overemphasized, the "discontinuity" that European historians have traditionally identified between "medieval" and "modern" science marked by the arrival of the plague in the mid-fourteenth century, is essentially fallacious. Why? Because, as Dorn (1991: 131), for example, argues: "[g]eographically, European science is a coherent entity on the same analytical level as the scientific cultures that preceded it—in Islam, Persia, Byzantium, the Hellenistic kingdoms, classical Greece, and the Asiatic societies of the east." Therefore, he concludes, "[t]he division of European science into intellectual movements and the designation of a modern achievement may stroke the European ego, but its historiography loses sight of the essential unity of the European scientific enterprise."

This "continuity" versus "discontinuity" debate is of course central to the question, specifically, of the origins of the scientific developments of the seventeenth-century and European modernity, generally. However, Dorn has put his finger on the basic problem that is at the heart of this seemingly irresoluble debate among Western historians of science: it is freighted with ideology: specifically, a chauvinism that pits, on one hand, the ancient and the medieval against the modern (within Europe) and, on the other hand, the Western European against "others" (outside Europe)—for example, Muslims, Chinese, Jews, and so on. [20] Moreover, it is a debate that rests on the prior construction of a mythology: the so-called scientific revolution (credit for the conceptualization, as presently understood, of this mythology undoubtedly must go, according to Cohen [1994], to the Russian scholar, Alexandre Koyre [1978 (1939)]).

To explain: the penchant of many European historians—especially since Koyre—to isolate a seventeenth-century phase in the history of scientific developments in Europe and calling it the scientific revolution for the purpose of demonstrating the supposed uniqueness of European science on one hand, and on the other, its supposed unique centrality to European modernity, is a misguided endeavor. Even someone such as Cohen (1994) who devotes a lengthy work to a history of the historiography of this phase and therefore appears to be much enamored by the concept, eventually concludes toward the end of his densely printed 600-page tome that the concept has less meaning than it was once thought to have. He even poses the question that is it not time perhaps to discard the concept altogether because "[t]he concept has by now fulfilled its once useful services." "After all," he further notes, "historical concepts are nothing but metaphors, which one should beware to reify; they may help focus the historical imagination for a while, but we should never forget that they are no more than lenses placed between our vision and the ultimately unknowable reality of a past irrevocably behind us" (p. 500). In the end Cohen, it may be noted, balks from taking the final logical step; but there others who do not. For example, Shapin (1996), and Frank (1996), are adamant that the isolation of a supposedly unique phase in the history of scientific and technological developments in Europe is a clear exercise in mythology. As Shapin observes: "Many historians are now no longer satisfied that there was any singular and discrete event, localized in time and space, that can be pointed to as 'the' scientific revolution." He continues: "And many historians do not now accept that the changes wrought on scientific beliefs and practices during the seventeenth-century were as 'revolutionary' as has been widely portrayed. The continuity of seventeenth-century natural philosophy with its medieval past is now routinely asserted" (pp. 3–4).

Third, through the agency of Islam—involving a variety of mechanisms of diffusion, such as direct residential contacts with immigrant Muslims (e.g., in Muslim Sicily and Muslim Spain), the Arabic to Latin translation movement during the *Reconquista,* the Crusades, and long-distance trade—Europe was introduced to a range of technological artifacts and methods derived from within the Islamic empire, as well as from without (from such places as China and India).[21] It is necessary, however, to briefly linger here on the concept of "technological diffusion." As Glick's study (1979) of Islamic Spain, for example, attests, one of the most important handmaidens of technological innovation is technological diffusion. However, one must be specific about what this concept means. It should be understood here to refer not only to the *direct* passage of artifacts and techniques from one culture to another (usually known as technology transfer), but also the *indirect* form of transmission that Pacey (1996) points to: the spread of information (actively or passively via travelers, traders, books, letters, etc.) about a given technology from one culture to another provoking an "independent" development of similar or even improved technology in the latter culture. Pacey refers to this technology as "responsive inventions."

Further, in the category of responsive inventions one may also throw in inventions arising out of direct imitation of technological artifacts acquired through trade (for commercial purposes), or acquired through some other means (including illegal means) for the explicit purpose of local manufacture. It follows then that the concept of technological diffusion also embodies (seemingly paradoxically) the possibility of independent inventions. A good example of this that immediately comes to mind is the windmill. It has been suggested (Hill 1993: 116), that whereas in all probability the European windmill—considering its design—was independently invented sometime toward the end of the twelfth-century, the concept of using wind as an energy source may, however, have arrived in Europe through the agency of Islam (windmills—of a different design—had long been in use in the Islamic empire). Another example is the effort by Europeans to imitate the manufacture of a high-quality steel common in the Islamic empire called Damascus steel (primarily used in sword making). Even though, observes Hill (1993: 219), in the end Europeans never learned to reproduce Damascus steel, their 150-year-long effort in this direction was not entirely in vain: it provided them with a better insight into the nature of this steel, thereby allowing them to devise other methods to manufacture steel of a similar quality.

Anyhow, whatever the mode of diffusion, the arrival of Islamic technology and Islamic mediated technology of non-Islamic (e.g., Chinese, Indian) and pre-Islamic (e.g., Egyptian, Persian, etc.) provenance—examples would include: the abacus; the astrolabe; the compass; paper-making; the ogival arch; gun powder; specialized dam building (e.g., the use of desilting sluices, the use of hydropower, etc.); sericulture; weight-driven clocks; the traction trebuchet; specialized glass-making; sugarcane production and sugar-making; the triangular lateen sail (allowed a ship to sail into wind more efficiently than a regular square sail common on European ships); and cartographic maps (upon which the European nautical charts called *portolans* were based)—had profound catalytic consequences for Europe.[22] It became the basis of European technological advancement in a number of key areas and which in turn would help to propel it on its journey toward the fateful year of 1492 and therefrom modernity (see Appendix II).

Consider this: four of the most important technological advancements that would be foundationally critical to the development of a modern Europe (navigation, warfare, communication and plantation agriculture) had their roots outside Europe, in the East! Reference here, is, of course, to the compass (plus other seafaring aids such as the lateen sail, etc.); gunpowder; paper-making and printing (that is, block printing and printing with movable type); and cane sugar production. All four technologies first originated in the East and then slowly found their way to the West through the mediation of the Muslims.[23] Along the way, of course, the Muslims improved on them. Now it is true that Europe's ability to absorb these technologies was a function of internal developments, some unique to itself. As Pacey (1996: 44) observes: "if we see the use of non-human energy as crucial to technological development, Europe in 1150 was the equal of Islamic and Chinese civilizations." But, as he continues, the key point here is this: "In terms of the sophistication of individual machines, however, notably for textile processing, and in terms of the broad scope of its knowledge, Europe was still a backward region, which stood to benefit much from its contacts with Islam." [24]

Fourth, Islam introduced Europe to international commerce on a scale it had never experienced before. The characterization by Watt (1972: 15) that "Islam was first and foremost a religion of traders, not a religion of the desert and not a religion of peasants," is very close to the truth. Not surprisingly, then, the twin factors of geographic breadth of the Islamic empire (which included regions with long traditions of commerce going back to antiquity, such as the Mediterranean Basin) and the acceptance of commerce as a legitimate occupational endeavor for Muslims—one that had been pursued by no less than Prophet Muhammed himself—had created a vast and truly global long-distance trade unmatched by any civilization hitherto. In fact, the reach of the Islamic dominated commercial network was such that it would embrace points as far apart as China and Italy on the east-west axis and Scandinavia and the deepest African hinterland on the north-south axis, with the result that the tonnage and variety of cargo carried by this network went far beyond that witnessed by even Greece and Rome in their heyday

(Turner 1995: 117). Al-Hassan and Hill (1986: 18) reminds us that the discovery of thousands upon thousands of Islamic coins dating from the seventh to thirteenth centuries in Scandinavia and the Volga basin region highlights the fact that for many centuries Europe relied on Islamic currency for its commercial activities, such was the domination of international trade by the Muslims (see also Watson 1995 for more on the East-West numismatic relations).

Recall also that the wealth of the Italian city-states like Venice and Genoa (the latter being the birthplace of Christopher Columbus, it may be noted) in medieval Europe rested to a considerable degree on trade in Eastern luxury and other commodities. Now, to be sure, it is mainly Italian and Jewish merchants, trading in places such as Alexandria, Aleppo, and Cairo, who were responsible for the final Mediterranean leg of the huge transoceanic trade that spanned the entire Indian Ocean (see the remarkable study by Goitein [1967] of the awesome treasure house of Jewish historical documents, known as the Cairo Geniza documents, that span a period of nearly three centuries, eleventh through thirteenth, and discovered in Old Cairo around 1890). However, as Chaudhuri (1985) shows us in his fascinating history of this trade, it is Muslim merchants who recreated and came to dominate this transoceanic trade—the same pattern held also for the transcontinental trade that was carried on in the hinterland of the Indian Ocean, behind the Himalayan range.[25]

Consider the list of luxury and other commodities that Europe received from the East (including Africa) through the agency of the Muslim merchants: coffee; cotton textiles (a luxury commodity in Europe prior to the industrial revolution); fruits and vegetables of the type that medieval Europe had never known (e.g., almonds, apricots, bananas, eggplants, figs, lemons, mangoes, oranges, peaches); gold; ivory, paper; tulips; porcelain; rice; silks; spices (these were especially important in long-distance trade and they included cardamom, cinnamon, cloves, coriander, cumin, ginger, nutmeg, pepper, saffron, and turmeric); alum; dyes and dye-making products; medicinal drugs; aromatics (e.g., frankincense, myrrh, musk); cane sugar and sugarcane; and so on. (The last is of special historical significance, sadly, considering the ignominious role it would play in the genesis of the Atlantic slave trade—see Appendix II.) What is more, with the exception of a few items such as gold, silk, some aromatics, and a few spices like cinnamon and saffron, medieval Europe had not even known of the existence of most of these products prior to the arrival of Islam.[26]

In other words, the Islamic civilization, through its commercial network, introduced Europe, often for the first time, to a wide range of Eastern consumer products (the variety and quantity of which was further magnified via the agency of the Crusades) that whet the appetite of the Europeans for more—not surprisingly, they felt compelled to undertake their *voyages of exploitation, a la* Bartolomeu Diaz, Vasco da Gama, Christopher Columbus, Fernao de Magalhaes (Ferdinand Magellan), and so on.[27] This quest for an alternative trade route to the East—one that would have to be seaborne—was also, of course, a function of the desire to bypass the very people who had introduced them to the Eastern luxury commodities they so eagerly sought: their hated enemies, the Muslim intermediaries, who straddled the land-bridge between the East and the West and who at the same time held a monopoly over this ever-increasingly important and obscenely profitable East/West trade. (Only a few decades earlier [on May 29, 1453], prior to the departure of Columbus [on August 3, 1492] on his historic sea quest, Constantinople had fallen before the victorious forces of the Muslim Turks under the leadership of Sultan Mehmed II, thus effectively and permanently placing the landbridge in the hands of the Muslims.)[28]

Yet, the European commercial debt to Islam goes even deeper. For, as Fernand Braudel (1982) reminds one in volume 2 of his three-volume *magnum opus* (grandly titled *Civilization and Capitalism*), a number of critical elements of European long-distance trade were of Islamic origin; such as the "bill of exchange," the *commenda* (a partnership of merchants), and even the art of executing complex calculations—without which no advanced commerce is possible.[29] In fact, as Braudel further points out (p. 559), the very practice of long-distance trade itself in medieval Europe was an Islamic borrowing. Now, without long-distance trade, it is quite unlikely that Europe would have experienced the rise of mercantile capitalism (and therefrom industrial capitalism following the colonization of the Americas); for, while such trade may not be a sufficient condition for its development, it is a necessary condition.

Of course, it is not, it must be stressed here, that Europe had never engaged in long-distance trade before—consider the long-distance trade of the Greeks and the Romans with the East—but, like so many other things, it was reintroduced to them by the Islamic civilization, since the Europeans had, for all intents and purposes, "lost" it over the centuries with their retrogressive descent into the post–Alaric world of the Germanic dominated European Early Middle Ages.[30] On the basis of these observations, Braudel, is compelled to remark: "To admit the existence of these borrowings means turning one's back on traditional accounts of the history of the West as pioneering genius, spontaneous inventor, journeying alone along the road toward scientific and technical rationality. It means denying the claim of the medieval Italian city-states to have invented the instruments of modern commercial life. And it logically culminates in denying the Roman empire its role as the cradle of progress" (p. 556).

Fifth, and this point cannot be overemphasized, without Islam—albeit in a perverse way—Europe would not have become Europe, psychologically, culturally, and geographically, but rather would have remained a fratricidally riven heterogeniety of perhaps little consequence for centuries to come. It is not without reason that some have even suggested, with a hint of ironic jest, that the founding father of Europe was Prophet Muhammed (see Cardini 2001). To elaborate: Islam created for Western Europe the feared and despised "other" as the basis of its eventual genesis, as the European center of gravity was forced to move, as a result of Muslim conquests, from the classical Mediterranean to *Francia* and the Rhineland. The process began with the Carolingian Renaissance that had its roots in the defeat of the Muslims at the hands of the grandfather of Charlemagne, Charles Martel (as mentioned earlier) and ended in the inauguration of *Europeanized* Christendom in the wake of the Schism of 1054 under Pope Leo IX and the unleashing of the Crusades against the Muslims at the behest of Pope Urban II (the call went out on November 27, 1095, in Clermont, France). About the last factor, while more will be said about the Crusades in Appendix II, though in a slightly different context, their importance in the creation of the Christian (and therefore European) identity cannot be over emphasized. As Mastnak (2002: 117) explains:

[T]he launching of the First Crusade was the historical moment in which the *respublica christiana* became conscious of its unity. An essential moment in the articulation of the self-awareness of the Christian commonwealth was the construction of the Muslim enemy. The antagonistic difference between themselves and the Muslims was a constitutive element of the Latin Christian's collective identity. The work of this collective identity or, rather, this collective identity at work was the new holy war against this fundamental enemy; for the Muslims represented infidelity as such. They were regarded as precisely the fundamental enemy of Christendom: the personification of the very religion of the Antichrist.

In fact, it is instructive to observe here, as Mastnak (2002) does, that the institutionalization of the malevolent, hierarchic us-versus-them duality effected through the Crusading project was of such depth that even the ongoing systematic effort at importing Greco-Arabic learning appeared, over the long run, to have earned the Muslims not an iota of gratitude from the luminaries of the Christian West (let alone, of course, the masses). On the contrary, the appreciation of the superiority of the Greco-Arabic learning by the Latins, in a seemingly bizarre way, seems to have been directly proportional to the vilification of Islam and the Muslims—such was the corrupting power of the Crusading project (see Appendix II), as well as the depth of Europe's perception of its own inferiority.[31] As Watt (1972: 84), for example, points out: "Not merely did Islam share with Western Europe many material products and technological discoveries; not merely did it stimulate Europe intellectually in the fields of science and philosophy; but it provoked Europe into forming a new image of itself. Because Europe was reacting against Islam," he continues, "it belittled the influence of the Saracens [Muslims] and exaggerated its dependence on its Greek and Roman heritage." [32] Blanks, in his introduction to the excellent collection of papers on the Western perceptions of Islam (Blanks and Frassetto 1999) also makes a similar observation:

During the Middle Ages, Islamic civilization was far ahead of its Christian rival, offering enticing advances in architecture, law, literature, philosophy, and, indeed, in most areas of cultural activity. It was therefore from a position of military and, perhaps more importantly, cultural weakness that Christian Europe developed negative images, some of which survive to the present day. In part, this hostility was the result of continued political and military conflict, but it likewise ensued from a Western sense of cultural inferiority.... By debasing the images of their rivals, Western Christians were enhancing their own self-images and trying to build self-confidence in the face of a more powerful and more culturally sophisticated enemy (Blanks 1999a: 3).

Clearly, then, it is because of the arrival of Islam on to the stage of human history that the East/ West continuum became a dichotomous geographic and cultural fragmentation.[33] That is, on one hand, through the Islamic mediated introduction to Europe of such intellectual and material artifacts ranging from the mathematical concept of zero and Arabic numerals to paper and paper making, from cane-sugar and cane-sugar production (which, via the Americas, would in time be foundational to the accumulation of capital necessary for the launching of the industrial revolution) to silk production, from navigation instruments like the astrolabe to the pointed vaulted arch in architecture, from paper money to the abacus; and on the other, the geographic and cultural containment of Europe beginning in the eighth-century, Islam came to play a critical role in the genesis of European science, modernity and identity. In other words, it was a role that was critical enough to permit Europe to emerge from the self-engendered, nearly 600-year, somnambulist interregnum of the Middle Ages (a period that, recall, historians of the past had often referred to as the Dark Ages—an exaggeration of course, but not entirely without reason.)

The Islamic civilization was a scientific, technological and cultural bridge in terms of both time (between the ancient and the modern) and geography (between the East and the West). Moreover, it was not a passive bridge but an active one, without which it is highly unlikely that Europe could have crossed over from barbarism into modernity, as early as it did—if at all! In other words, no matter how much one may struggle to erect the chimeral edifice of "Western European exceptionalism"—which at its fundamental core is nothing more than a racist inspired project (as scholars such as Blaut [1993], and Frank [1998], would probably point out)—the fundamental truth is that historical facts will force one to recognize that there is no single variable that one can isolate to explain Europe's journey toward scientific and technological progress in particular and modernity in general; for, such monumental intellectual and social transformations that they represent, can only be explained on the basis of a conjuncture of fortuitously propitious historical factors originating from within and without Europe—central among these factors was the Islamic civilization with its tendency toward a global transformative centripetality of transgeographic and transtemporal civilizational contributions.[34]

To the extent, then, that Islam is an *Afro-Asian* civilization, both the Western civilization in general and one of its progeny in specific, the modern university, have a significant part of their roots within Africa and Asia. This is not to deny, of course, the immense significance of the Latin contribution itself to the development of the modern university. The critical point here, however, is this: to say that the modern university is an *entirely* Western invention is to assert only partial truth; not the whole truth. The whole truth is that the modern "Western" university—like so many other things that Westerners have so stridently claimed as their very own unique inventions—is the product of the Islamic-mediated intersection of three major civilizations: the Greek, the Islamic, and the Latin. (Yet, even this cannot constitute the whole truth. Why? Because each of these civilizations, in turn, in their genesis, incorporated contributions from other civilizations as well: Sumerian, Assyrian, Babylonian, Egyptian, Persian, East Indian, Chinese, etc.) Any view to the contrary, is simply an echo—albeit a recurrent one—of the narrow-minded, super ethnocentric perspective of the early Western European Christians who in their tirades against Muslims, Jews, and others often forgot that even the religion that they thought was their very own did not originate from within Europe, but came from the East. They refused then, as even many of their descendents of today refuse, to observe, for example, this simple fact: that Christ was not a European at all! But, then, when has universal historical memory ever been secure from being hijacked by those with the power to do so, for iniquitous ends?

Yet, this is not all: Makdisi (1981: 285–86) in dismissing the obscurantist claims of such European scholars as G. E. von Grunebaum (1961) that except for Averroism, Western intellectual development owes nothing to Islam, reminds one that "It is inconceivable that two cultures could develop side by side for literally centuries without being aware of developments on either side."[35] The fact that "Islam cared little for what was going on in the West is proof of its indifference to a lesser developed culture," he continues. "On the other hand," he points out, "it is common knowledge that the West was not oblivious of the higher civilization of Islam: it learned its language and translated its works in order to bring itself up to the level of the higher culture, the better to defend itself against it." Moreover, after identifying many parallels in the development of higher education in the West and in Islam he concludes with justifiable degree of impatience at Western obscurantism on this matter by saying "It unduly taxes the imagination to conceive parallel developments devoid of influence (1) when the number of parallels is so high, (2) when their points of correspondence are so identical, and (3) when the course of development involves a time-lag of roughly a century."

Among these parallels he covers in his work, there is one that deserves special attention: the Islamic technique of consensus-disagreement—known as *ijma'-khilaf,* and in the Latin West known as *sic et non*—as the basis for establishing legitimacy for a given Islamic doctrine, practiced by Islamic jurisconsults (since Islam does not possess such ecclesiastical institutions as councils and synods). It is on the basis of this technique that requires, by means of disputation, the triumph of *ijma* over *khilaf* (the authoritative body of disagreements on a given question) that the scholastic method arose in Islamic legal education. Since khilaf, a very specific Islamic institution, is an essential component of the scholastic method (adopted by the Western medieval universities and which laid the foundation for the triumph of reason and rationality—the backbone of science), one can assert with utmost confidence that Islam had a significant hand in "influencing the fundamental structure of the West," to quote Makdisi (1981: 289).

However, however, notwithstanding everything that has been said so far in this appendix, one is compelled to conclude with this point: in the final analysis, the fundamental question really is, Does it really matter as to *who* created the first universities? (Or, for that matter, Who were the first astronomers? The first mathematicians? The first scientists? And so on.) It matters only if one refuses to abandon those socially constructed categories that the modern world, paradoxically, is so obscenely mesmerized by (such as race or ethnicity) in order to deny the commonality of all humanity in which every ethnic variation of humankind has made some contribution at some point (even if only at the most rudimentary level of domestication of plant and/or animal life) to the totality of the modern human cultural experience. (See the fascinating study by Weatherford [1988], with respect to the last point.) As Joseph Needham (1954: 9) sagely observed in volume 1 of his work: "Certain it is that no people or group of peoples has had a monopoly in contributing to the development of science." For all its proclamation of the virtues of "civilization" (to be understood here in its normative sense) the denial of this fact has been, sadly, as much a project of the West as its other, laudable, endeavors—for reasons that, of course, one does not have to be a rocket scientist to fathom: domination of the planet under the aegis of various forms of imperialism (an endeavor that, even now in the twenty-first century, most regrettably, has yet to see its demise).

Consequently, under these circumstances, the true historian is burdened by the need for constant vigilance against this Western intellectual tradition of *erasure* of universal historical memory for the purposes of rendering irrelevant the contributions of others.[36] Moreover, one must be cognizant of the fact that it is a tradition that relies on a number of techniques: the most direct of which is "scholarly silence"—where there is a complete (or almost complete) absence of any recognition of a contribution. However, given the obvious transparency of this technique, it has increasingly been replaced by one that is more subtle (hence of greater intractability): achieving erasure not by a total lack of acknowledgement, but by the method of *token* (and sometimes even derisory) acknowledgement where the object of the erasure is mentioned in passing and then promptly dismissed from further consideration despite continuing relevance to the subject at hand.

As an extension of this last point, and as a prelude to Appendix II: it is questionable to even talk about a Western civilization at all; so much of its inheritance is from outside Europe—a more fitting term perhaps would be Afro-Eurasian civilization. To the ignorantsia, who are heirs to a Western ethnocentric mind-set honed over a period of some 600 years, of seeing humankind in no other terms than a color-coded hierarchical cultural fragmentation, this new appellation may, at first blush, appear hysterically preposterous; yet, in actuality, there is a growing body of literature that cogently demonstrates that the so-called Western civilization is simply a developmental extension of Afro-Asian civilizations.[37] After all, if one were to take the entire 5,000-year period of recorded human history, commencing from say approximately thirtieth-century B.C.E. to the present twenty-first-century C.E., the European civilizational imprint, from a global perspective, becomes simply an *atomized* blip (the *notion* of an unbroken path going from the Greeks to the Renaissance to the Industrial Revolution, is just that, an illusory fabrication), and what is more, geographically, demographically, and culturally, a peripheral one at that when viewed against that of the neighboring Afro-Asian civilizations, taken together (ranging from the Sumerian to the Egyptian to the Chinese to the Islamic).[38]

It is only in the last 300 years or so that, civilizationally, Western Europe has taken center stage. The fact that many European and U.S. historians appear to be unaware of this simple fact is testimony to the enduring Western ethnocentric teleological tunnel vision that thoroughly imbues their work.[39] Note that Western ethnocentrism is to be understood here as an ideology that is shared by all classes of Western Europeans and their diasporic descendants, that is rooted in the assumption that, to quote Harding (1993: 2), "Europe functions autonomously from other parts of the world; that Europe is its own origin, final end, and agent; and that Europe and people of European descent in the Americas and elsewhere owe nothing to the rest of the world." See also Amin (1989) and Blaut (1993, 2000), for a brilliant, but scathing critique of the Western ethnocentric paradigm that undergirds much of Western historiography.

NOTES

1. A word or two about the concept of incorporation: to begin with, Islam does not recognize, in general, the legality of the "corporation"—"an abstraction endowed with legal rights and responsibilities"—because only a human being, not an organization, can have "juristic personality" (Makdisi 1981: 224—for an alternative, albeit unconvincing, view on this matter see Iqbal 2002). Moreover, within the Islamic world, the necessity for the incorporation of universities per se was absent. Why? Makdisi (1981) points out that because of the great difference in how citizenship was regarded between medieval Europe and the Islamic world (in the latter, as already noted, all Muslims, whatever their nationality, origin, ethnicity, and so on, had practically the same citizenship rights regardless of where they went in the Islamic world, whereas in the former, Europeans did not enjoy an equivalent privilege), there arose the need in medieval Europe to protect "foreign" students (students from out of town or out of region or out of country) in the inevitable town-and-gown conflicts that emerged wherever universities were beginning to be established (Bologna, Paris, etc.). This protection took the form of incorporation—a legal concept rooted in Roman law which permitted groups of persons bound together by a common purpose (as in guilds) to behave as individual persons in law (such an entity, interestingly, was referred to as *universitas*). Through papal or royal decrees, universities acquired, over time, protections and privileges that established their independ-

ence in virtually all matters: governance, curricula, instruction, finance, and so on. See Benoit (1995); Cobban (1975); Huff (1993), and Pedersen (1997), for an extensive account of how the process transpired; the last also proposes one more compelling factor: power struggles between the emperor and the pope.

2. The term civilization is used in this work in a very loose sense. Consider the problem: the Islamic civilization at one point encompassed a number of other civilizations, Byzantium, Persian, Hindu, and so on.

3. While it is true that evidence so far indicates that the bulk of Greco-Islamic learning arrived in Europe through the translation activity in Spain and Italy, Burnett (2003) shows that some of this learning also seeped into Europe by means of translations of works that were imported directly from the Islamic East, but executed by Latin scholars in other places (like Antioch and Pisa).

4. Continuation of a select listing of Islamic scholars:

Abu Raihan al-Biruni (c. 973–1051), a natural scientist whose work helped to lay the foundations of natural sciences in the Latin West. His work on astronomy would become the principal text for schools in the Latin West. In addition, he wrote extensively in almost every subfield of mathematics, astronomy, physics, and so on. He also wrote a treatise on drugs titled *The Book on Drugs,* in which he described numerous drugs and their effects, as well as providing their names in several other languages besides Arabic.

Ibn al-Zarqali (c. 1029–c.1080, known in Latin West as Arzachel). An astronomer who was responsible, among his accomplishments, for the invention of an improved astrolabe (named saphaea Arzachelis), the editing of the planetary tables produced by astronomers such as *Ibn Said* working in Muslim Toledo that came to be called the Toledan Tables, and authorship of an introductory work on trigonometry.

Ghiyath al-Din Abul Fateh Omar Ibn Ibrahim al-Nisaburi al-Khayyami (1044–1123) Omar Khayyam, as he is commonly known, achieved fame in the West primarily because of his poetry (following the English translation of the Rubaiyat by Edward Fitzgerald). Yet, he was also an accomplished mathematician and astronomer making significant contributions in the area of algebra (e.g., binomial theorem). In the area of astronomy one of his achievements is the creation of a solar calendar (named *Al-Tarikh-al-Jalali*) that is said to be even more accurate then the Gregorian calendar. Khayyam's influence on the development of mathematics and analytical geometry in the West should not be underestimated. Among his works in this regard is *Treatise on Demonstration of Problems of Algebra.*

Ibn Bajjah (c. 1095–c. 1138, known in the Latin West as Avempace). A philosopher, whose work on the theory of motion is among his many contributions.

Ash-Sharif al-Idrisi (1100–1165/66?), a geographer and advisor to the Norman king of Sicily, Roger II, was the author of one of the most important medieval texts on geography titled *The Pleasure Excursion of One Who Is Eager to Traverse the Regions of the World.* He spent most of the later part of his life in the service of the Norman king who provided him with the resources necessary to undertake his scholarly pursuits, which included a number of texts that combined descriptive and astronomical geography.

Abu al-Walid Muhammed ibn Ahmad ibn Muhammed Ibn Rushd (1126–1198, known in the West as Averroes), considered to be among the most important commentators on Aristotelian philosophy of his time (hence he was also known by the name of the Commentator—such was his scholarly authority), would have a far-reaching influence on Western thought; in fact, so much so that it would be symbolized by the intellectual crisis that it would precipitate between the church and the academy as the former attempted to battle what it thought was the theologically corrupting influence of "Averroism" (the belief that philosophy and religion were not only compatible but that philosophy was, in a sense, religion in its purest form). Significantly, he was a great advocate of syllogism, the Aristotlian method of logic.

Nasir al-Din al-Tusi (Muhammad ibn Muhammad ibn al-Hasan al-Tusi) (1201–1274), an astronomer par excellence, he would greatly influence the work of such Western astronomers as Nicolaus Copernicus, Johannes Kepler, and Tyco Brahe by means of his accurate astronomical tables that he and his colleagues produced at a famous observatory he helped establish at Maraghah (in modern-day Iran)—under the sponsorship of the Mongols no less.

It ought to be mentioned here, as Ullman (1978) for example points out, in some instances—especially where the author was unknown—the translations of the Islamic scholarship arrived in Europe masquerading as scholarship authored by the translators themselves or their benefactors (rather than as translations of Islamic scholarship). In fact there appears to be some evidence that even at that time Muslims were aware of this problem: d'Alverny (1982: 440) quotes a late eleventh-century Muslim scholar in Spain, Ibn Abdun, admonishing his fellow Muslims: "You must not sell books of science to Jews and Christians... because it happens that they translate these scientific books and attribute them to their own people and to their bishops, when they are indeed Muslim works." In other words, even if all the translated Islamic works were available today, the fullest extent of the Islamic scientific scholarly contribution to the Latin West will never be known because of such unashamed wholesale plagiarism.

For more on the Islamic and Islamic mediated scientific/philosophic contributions, the reader is directed to look at the following sources, among others: Alioto (1987); Authier (1995); Benoit and Micheau (1995); Crombie (1990); d'Alverny (1982); Grant (1974 and 1996); Gutas (1998); Hill (1993); Hodgson (1974); Hogendijk and Sabra (2003); Huff (1993); Kennedy (1966); King (2000); Leiser (1983); Lindberg (1978, and 1992); Mirza and Siddiqi (1986); Nakosteen (1964); Nasr (1968); Nasr and Leaman (1996); Peters (1968); Qurashi and Rizvi (1996); Rashed and Morelon (1996); Sabra (1994); Saliba (1994); Sarton 1962 (1927–1948); Schacht and Bosworth (1974); Selin (1997); Stock (1978); Turner (1975); Ullman (1978); Watt (1972). In addition to these specific sources, the reader should also mine the following three excellent multivolume encyclopedic sources for information on a range of issues covered in this chapter: *Dictionary of the Middle Ages* (1982–89); *Dictionary of Scientific Biography* (1970–80); and *Encyclopedia of Islam: New Edition* (1986). Note: in bludgeoning the reader with this list, the objective is to leave no doubt as to the significance of Islamic science for the development of the curricular knowledge base of European medieval universities specifically, and the advancement of science in Europe generally.

5. On this point about fortuity, see also Dorn [1991], whose exegesis on geography as among the factors of historical chance in the evolution of major scientific developments—to take one example—is brilliantly suggestive.

6. One more example: consider this mind-boggling "what ifs" of history: Would the European civilization have evolved to be the dominant civilization it has become had the Mongols possessed a succession mechanism different from the one that required the founder of the Golden Horde empire, Batu (the grandson of Genghis Khan), to return home just as he was poised to invade Western Europe in December of 1241? (The succession issue was precipitated by the death of the reigning head of the entire Mongol empire, Khagan (Great Khan) Ogadai, son of Genghis Khan.) Recall that by that point, the fate awaiting Western Europe at the hands of the Mongols had already befallen the Russians, the Poles, the Hungarians, and so on, which was: total and merciless slaughter and devastation, perhaps not even matched, in terms of ferocity, by that inflicted by Europe's own barbarians of an earlier period: the Vikings. Even the Muslims: they too, as already mentioned, would not be spared the barbarous Mongolian devastation beginning with the invasion of Northern Iran in 1218 by Genghis Khan. In the year 1238, to give just one example, close to a million would be slaughtered in a little over a month in the city of Baghdad alone. And all major artifactual expressions of cultural achievement (schools, libraries, bookstores, observatories, etc.), would be burned to the ground as the city was laid waste—it would mark the end of the 600-year classical period of Islam. In other words, the decision by Batu to return home, most likely, put Europe—and the

world—on to a very different historical trajectory than the one that would have emerged had he not withdrawn from Europe. (See Chambers [2001]; Holland [1999]; and Spuler [1972] for more on the Mongols. See also the rest of the work that contains Holland for more examples of *what ifs* of history.)

7. See, for example: Grant (1996); Gutas (1998); Huff (1993); Nakosteen (1964); O'Leary (1949); Schacht and Bosworth (1974); Stanton (1990); and Watt (1972).

8. It should be remembered that the Byzantines did almost nothing, in comparative terms, with the Greek intellectual heritage they had come to possess; though they had the good sense to at least preserve it (see Gutas 1998, for an account of the Byzantine role in the Muslim acquisition of Greek scientific knowledge).

9. It is interesting to note here that the suggestion by some, that "the failure of Arabic science to yield modern science was due to a failure to develop and use the experimental method are confronted with the fact that the Arabic scientific tradition was richer in experimental techniques than any other, whether European or Asian" (Huff 1993: 209). It also ought to be mentioned here, that in one of those unexplainable ironies of history, not even the Greeks (for the most part) were enamored with the scientific experimental method; rather their approach was predominantly one that may be described as (for want of a better phrase) "contemplative observation."

10. The European scientific debt to Islam is also attested to by etymology: Consider the following examples of words in the English language (culled from Watt 1972: 85–92) that have their origins in the Arabic language (either directly, or indirectly—that is, having originally come into Arabic from elsewhere): alchemy, alcohol, alembic, algebra, algorithm, alkali, amalgam, arsenal, average, azimuth, camphor, chemistry, cupola, drug, elixir, gypsum, natron, rocket, saccharin, sugar, zenith, zero.

11. Huff (1993: 48) reminds one, for example, that during the 700-year period marked by the eighth to almost the beginning of the fifteenth-century, "Arabic science was," in his words, "probably the most advanced science in the world, greatly surpassing the West and China." He continues: "In virtually every field of endeavor—in astronomy, alchemy, mathematics, medicine, optics and so forth—Arabic scientists (that is, Middle Eastern individuals primarily using the Arabic language but including Arabs, Iranians, Christians, Jews, and others) were in the forefront of scientific advance. The facts, theories, and scientific speculations contained in their treatises were the most advanced to be had anywhere in the world, including China." Making a similar point, Grant (1996) states: "Contrary to prevailing opinion, the roots of modern science were planted in the ancient and medieval worlds long before the scientific revolution of the seventeenth-century. Indeed, that revolution would have been inconceivable without the cumulative antecedent efforts of three great civilizations: Greek, Islamic, and Latin. With the scientific riches it derived by translation from Greco-Islamic sources in the twelfth and thirteenth centuries, the Christian Latin civilization of Western Europe began the last leg of the intellectual journey that culminated in a scientific revolution that transformed the world."

12. In drawing attention to this fact in the present political climate—where it is once again fashionable for Westerners of almost every stripe (except for an exemplary scholarly minority who will hew to the truth no matter what) to loudly and unabashedly proclaim themselves as bearers of a superior, self-made civilization in a style not seen since the heyday of eighteenth- and nineteenth-century Western imperialism—it runs the serious risk of being dismissed out of hand. This, of course, is one of the consequences of the anti-Islamic sentiment—reminiscent of the period of the Crusades (no historian writing about the Crusades today can escape experiencing the feeling of déjà vu)—that has once again enveloped the Western world in the wake of the terrorist attack that misguided "Muslim" zealots inflicted on the United States on September 11, 2001, and which has acted to serve as yet one more ideological layer to preserve the seemingly unassailable, granite-like ignorance about the Islamic civilization that characterized the vast bulk of the European peasantry during the Crusades. It is an ignorance that remains widespread to this day among both the elites and the masses in the West (and to some degree in the rest of the world as well) and which in turn

has rendered the West blind to how much the so-called "Western" civilization owes to Islam. Yet even where ignorance is not a factor, there is the problem of prejudice: "For our cultural indebtedness to Islam... we Europeans have a blind spot. We sometimes belittle the extent and importance of Islamic influence in our heritage, and sometimes overlook it altogether." This observation by Watt (1972: 2) is as relevant today as it was when he made it more than three decades ago (see also Cardini [2001]).

13. Even the very concept of the crusade as a "holy war," observes Watt (1965: 172), may have been another one of Western Christendom's borrowings from Islam (compare: the jihad of the Muslims) (See also Daniel [1989a], who has a dissenting view on this matter.)

14. This observation is also in order here: the traditional European view used to be, Crowthier (1967) reminds one, that it is with the fall of Constantinople to the Turkish Muslim Army on May 29, 1453, that Europe was reacquainted with the Greek intellectual heritage, which the Byzantines had preserved and which they now took with them to Europe as they fled the Muslims. This, however, is only partial truth, he notes, because Europe had already had access to much of the Greek knowledge through the Muslims. What the fleeing Byzantines brought with them that the Europeans did not yet have, was what the Muslims had had the least interest in: the arts and humanities of the Greeks (history, poetry, drama, etc). He further observes: "The Renaissance, insofar as it is regarded exclusively as a result of the fall of Constantinople, is of restricted interest for science. The cultural effects of the flight from Constantinople were at first narrowly literary, and on the whole may have been unfortunate" (p. 118). Moreover, one ought to also note here the point made by Gutas (1991) that the Muslims were also to some extent instrumental in the very preservation of the Greek texts within Byzantium because until the Muslims created a relatively lucrative market for these texts, the Byzantines may have been less inclined to preserve them. Recall that by this period (eighth-century) when the Greek to Arabic translation movement was underway in the Islamic empire, secular knowledge had fallen almost completely out of favor in Byzantium.

15. Iqbal (2002) reminds us that thousands of Arabic scholarly manuscripts from the past, scattered in libraries across the world, still await the scrutiny of the researcher. One can only surmise the tremendous consequences for the historiography of science in general if there were scholars willing to subject the sciences of Islam and India, for example, to what one may generically refer to as "The Joseph Needham Treatment." That is, a scholarly approach that is characterized by an awe-inspiring, multidisciplinary and relentless lifetime devotion to the historiographical study of science and technology—like the one undertaken by, needless to say, Joseph Needham with respect to Chinese science and technology and captured for posterity by his monumental multivolume magnum opus titled *Science and Civilization in China* (which the Cambridge University Press began publishing in 1954 as each volume was written [and which continues to be written, though others have now taken over authorship of the volumes published in recent years]). See also Serres (1995) on the challenges of producing a historiography of science.

16. Now, one can imagine here a small hand being raised hesitatingly, at the very back of the room, accompanied by the question, in a faltering voice: But, but... Sir/Madam, what about the Romans? Ah..., the Romans! For reasons that need not detract one here, one is on sure ground—pending of course research a la Pierre Duhem (whose monumental research effort rescued medieval European science from the dustbin of history) that may unearth findings to the contrary—when one boldly states that the Roman contribution to the development of modern science was about as much as that of the Byzantines: nothing to write home about. It is one of those ironies of history, that for all its brilliantly outstanding architectural and technological accomplishments, the Roman civilization was almost barren when it came to scientific achievements (Alioto 1987). No, the torch of science bypassed—for the most part—the Romans as it was transferred by the forces of history from the Greeks to the Muslims.

17. Benoit and Micheau (1995: 203) draw attention to this interesting and telling tidbit of history: there exists an annotated edition of Ptolemy's The Great Treatise (a work that came to be known by its Arabic derived name of Almagest—from al-Majisiti—in the Latin West); but the an-

notations are in the hand of none other than Nicolaus Copernicus himself; however, what is really fascinating is this: that the edition itself is a Latin translation of the Arabic translation of the Almagest! One, of course, will never know the magnitude of the influence of Islamic astronomy on Copernicus—for this was astronomy that did not just rest on the Greek and Alexandrian heritage alone, but was also based on the findings of astronomers from the East (India, Persia, etc.), as well as the observations of the Muslims themselves. (See Huff [1993], and Turner [1995].) While on the subject of astronomy, it should also be noted here that the computational basis of it, trigonometry, was an entirely Islamic invention. The Greeks did not appear to possess trigonometry. (See, for example, Kennedy [1983].)

18. See Iqbal (2002) for an analysis of the factors that led to the decline of scientific progress in the Islamic empire. For contrasting views, with which Iqubal is in strong disagreement, on this matter see Cohen (1994); Huff (1993); and Huff and Schluchter (1999).

19. One of the earliest proponents of this rule, which he termed "the law of continuity," is Pierre Duhem. Severely castigating those who appeared to be unaware of this law, writing in 1906, he would state: "It is commonly thought that progress in science is made by a succession of sudden and unexpected discoveries and thus, so one believes, is the work of men of genius who have no precursors at all. It is a useful effort, and one worth insisting on, to mark the point where these ideas are erroneous, the point where the history of scientific development is subject to the *law of continuity*. Great discoveries are almost always the fruit of slow and complex preparation, *which is pursued in the course of centuries*." (emphasis added; translated from the French by Cohen 1994: 48, and quoted in his book). An aside: it is ironic that Duhem dismissed the significance of Islamic science in the development European medieval science—is it possible that his strong Christian beliefs (he was an ardent Roman Catholic) greatly colored his views on this matter?

20. For a summary of this debate see Cohen (1994), as well as Lindberg (1992) whose verdict on it is an attempt to come down somewhere in the middle: there was continuity within discontinuity. However, contrary to his protestations, Lindberg appears to favor the continuity side of the debate if one goes by his exegesis on the matter. Moreover, his observation that a separation of macro-level (entire scientific enterprise) versus micro-level (individual scientific disciplines) analysis decisively tilts the debate toward continuity, is worth noting. What is Cohen's position? "There are no absolute discontinuities in history," he states. "Nothing," he continues, "happens entirely out of the blue; no event, however unexpected, is without prior preparation" (p. 147).

21. Regarding the Crusades, even though intuition alone would suggest otherwise (the Crusaders had colonized parts of the Islamic lands for considerable periods of time spanning almost two centuries), some Western scholars have tended to downplay the role of the Crusades in accelerating Eastern influences on the development of the West. However, there are at least three areas of Crusader activity that bore considerable fruit in this regard: namely, emulation of sumptuous lifestyles of the Muslims by wealthy resident Crusaders (yielding influences in art and architecture, for example); agricultural production (especially sugarcane); and trade and commerce. About the last: Hillenbrand's fascinating study clearly points to remarkable interchange between the Franks and the Muslims, even—unbelievable this may appear—during times of ongoing conflict. Consider this: while the robust siege of Karak by the forces under the command of Salah Ad-din Yusuf ibn Ayyub (Saladin) was underway in 1184, trading caravans from Egypt on their way to Damascus were allowed to pass through Crusader-held territories unhindered. This phenomenon would lead one Muslim chronicler of the period to remark: "One of the strangest things in the world is that Muslim caravans go forth to Frankish lands, while Frankish captives enter Muslims lands" (Hillenbrand 1999: 399). That the Muslims and the Franks refused to put aside the peaceful activity of trade and commerce between them on many an occasion (which it should be noted often required the conclusion of treaties and agreements), even as they fought each other, is indicative of how important such activity was for both sides. What is more, the Crusaders undertook these economic relations often in the face of strong strictures on the part of various popes condemning such activity. Note also that the importance of trade is also attested to, of course, by the currency in Crusader-held ter-

ritories: it was an imitation of Islamic currency—in terms of design. (See also Bates and Metcalf [1989]; Ballard [2003]; and Verlinden [1995]). In other words, then, through trade and commerce, regardless of whether it was local trade or international trade, Europe opened yet another door to Eastern influences. (For more on this topic, see Abulafia [1994], and Ashtor [1976], and the *Dictionary of the Middle Ages*. About the last item, as already pointed out, the reader will do well to mine it for a number of other issues too, covered in this chapter.)

22. A note on the *portolans*, given their critical importance to the European sea navigators, that should further give pose to those who continue to insist on European exceptionalism: while the immediate provenance of many of them was Islamic, the Muslims themselves were also indebted for some of their maps to the Chinese. Of singular importance are those that were of relevance to the European Atlantic voyages given that the Chinese had already preceded Columbus to the Americas—vide for example the voyage of Zhou Wen described by Menzies (2003). (Note: Menzies also discusses the Chinese contribution to the development of the portalans.)

23. There is some doubt as to exactly how the compass arrived in the West from the East in that, according to Watt (1972), it was probably invented jointly by the Muslims and Westerners (one reciprocally improving on the creation of the other) on the basis of the original Chinese discovery of the magnetic properties of the lodestone. Be that as it may, it is yet another instance pointing to the fact that the story of the diffusion to the West (via the Islamic intermediary) of the products of the Eastern technological genius *is one that has yet to be told in its entirety.*

24. For sources on the Eastern provenance of the technological artifacts mentioned and their Islamic mediated diffusion to the West, see also, besides Pacey (1991), al-Hassan and Hill (1986); Dold-Samplonius (2003); Dyson (2001); Jayyusi and Marin (1994); Kunitzsch (2003); Hill (1993); Pan (1996); Qurashi and Rizvi (1996); Williams (2000).

25. For more on the East/West trade see also Abulafia (1994); Abu-Lughod (1989); Ashtor (1976); Curtin (1984); Frank (1998); Hillenbrand (1999); Huzayyin (1942); Lach (1965); Lombard and Aubin (2000); and Lopez and Raymond (1967), Pomeranz (2000).

26. One can hardly imagine what would have been the fate of Europe if it had never found out about some of these commodities. Take, for instance, that absolutely wondrous plant fiber called cotton. Ahhh cotton… What would the world be like without cotton? Cotton was first domesticated, records so far indicate, in the Indus Valley civilization of India thousands of years ago. The cultivation of cotton and the technology of manufacturing cotton textiles (which in time would become the engine of European Industrial Revolution) eventually spread from India to the rest of the world, and Islam was highly instrumental in this diffusion. What did Europe export to the Islamic empire (specifically the Mediterranean region) in return for its imports, one may ask out of curiosity? According to Watt (1972), the principal exports comprised raw materials, such as timber and iron, and up to the eleventh-century, European slaves from the Slavic region. (About the latter export: following the conversion of the Slav peoples to Christianity in the eleventh-century, observes Watt, the enslavement of the Slavs soon petered out. Incidentally, this aspect of European history points to the etymology of the word *slave*.)

27. The use of the phrase "voyages of exploitation" instead of the more common "voyages of exploration," in this work should not be considered as an expression of gratuitous churlishness; rather it speaks to that popular misconception well described by Hallet (1995: 56): "It is commonly assumed that it was a passionate desire to expand the boundaries of knowledge or, more sharply defined, the rational curiosity of scientific research that formed the mainspring of the European movement of exploration. Undoubtedly such motives have inspired many individual explorers; but a review of the whole history of exploration reveals a process more complicated than is generally realized…. Three motives had led Europeans to venture into the unknown parts of the world: the search for wealth, the search for political advantage, the search for souls to save." An excellent example of how these factors were played out in practice is provided by Newitt's (1995) fascinating exegesis on the origins of the Portuguese voyages of exploitation down the coast of West Africa and finally on to the other side of the continent and therefrom into the Indian Ocean basin. Even the

long cherished myth of Henry the Navigator as the heroic architect of the mission to the East and as "scientist and scholar of the Renaissance, the founder of the School of Navigation at Sagres," is laid to rest and in its place we are presented with the real "Henry the consummate politician" as a shrewd, powerful and wealthy man in fifteenth-century Portugal whose preoccupations were primarily with matters much more closer to home; such as the colonization of Morocco, piracy, and rent (levying taxes and dues on others involved in maritime profiteering activities in places like the Canaries and off the coast of West Africa). See also the riveting account by Bergeen (2003) of the three-year harrowing odyssey (1519–22) of Magellan's fleet, Armada de Molucca (named, tellingly, after the Indonesian Spice Islands), as it circumnavigated the globe and the motivating forces behind it, including the powerful lure for the West of Eastern spices which, as in this case, literally propelled it to the "ends of the earth" despite unimaginable hardships. Moreover, as Appendix II will demonstrate, the veracity of his conclusion that "[I]n their lust for power, their fascination with sexuality, their religious fervor, and their often tragic ignorance and vulnerability, Magellan and his men," as with the other similar voyages, "epitomized a turning point in history," for, "[t]heir deeds and character, for better or worse, still resonate powerfully," is absolutely incontrovertible (p. 414). (Incidentally, Magellan was not the first to circumnavigate the planet—though perhaps he was the first European—the Chinese had already preceded him in that effort. See Menzies 2003.)

28. Taking Columbus's project specifically: that Islam is written all over it, directly and indirectly, is attested to, for instance, by the fact that only a few months prior to the departure of Columbus under the sponsorship of Spain, the Spanish crown, in what may be considered Europe's final crusade against the Muslims, had just defeated (on January 2) the last Muslim Spanish stronghold (the province of Granada). In bringing to an end the 700-year Muslim presence in Spain, the Spanish crown, after it had initially rejected Columbus's project on two different occasions as a hair brained scheme, now saw it in an entirely new light. The victory over the Muslims allowed the Spanish crown (specifically Queen Isabella) to dream of even grander possibilities of sidelining the Muslims (as well as Spain's other arch enemy, the Portuguese) in its quest for "Christian" glory, gold, spices, and perhaps even an empire that Columbus's project so coincidentally now promised. In fact, Columbus himself was present at the siege of Granada, and he was quick to bring to the queen's attention the larger import of the fall of Granada in the context of his project. As he would write in his log of the first voyage while addressing the Spanish monarchs (Ferdinand and Isabella): "Because, O most Christian, most elevated, most excellent, and most powerful princes, king and queen of the Spains and of the islands of the sea, our lords in this present year of 1492, after your highnesses had put an end to the war with the Muslims, who had been reigning in Europe, and finished the war in the great city of Granada, where on January 2 in this same year I saw the royal standards of your highnesses raised by force of arms atop the towers of the Alhambra, which is the fortress of that city, and I saw the Muslim king come out to the gates of the city.... your highnesses, as Catholic Christians and princes who love the holy Christian faith, exalters of it and enemies of the sect of Muhammad and of all idolatries and heresies, thought to send me, Christopher Columbus, to those aforementioned regions of India to see the princes, peoples, and lands, and their disposition and all the rest, and determine what method should be taken for their conversion to our holy faith.... So it was that, after having expelled all the Jews from your kingdoms and domains, in that same month of January, your highnesses commanded that I should go to the said regions of India with a suitable fleet" (from his journal—the *Repertorium Columbianum* edition, vol. 6 [ed. by Lardicci 1999], p. 37).

Then there is the matter of Columbus's monumental navigational blunder: Alioto (1987: 163) reminds one that even the chance "discovery" of the Americas by Columbus has its root in the mathematics of an Islamic scholar, Al-Farghani—albeit involving erroneous mathematical calculations on the part of this ninth-century astronomer. (In the Latin West, where his work, titled *The Elements*, on Ptolemaic astronomy had achieved considerable popularity, was known by the name of Alfraganus.) On the basis of these calculations, Columbus came to conclude that Cathay (China) lay only 2,500 miles due west of the Canary Islands! For good or ill, depending on whose interests one has in mind, how wrong he would turn out to be.

29. In a riveting exegesis, Benoit (1995) not only demonstrates the Islamic roots of Western mathematics, but also alerts one to a less well-known fact: it is primarily through the agency of commerce that Islamic mathematics in general was diffused to the West and it is in the environment of commerce that it first began to undergo innovation—greatly helped of course with the introduction of those seemingly mundane (as seen from the vantage point of today) artifacts of Eastern origin: Indo-Arabic numerals and paper! This process especially got underway in Europe in the fourteenth-century as parts of it, notably the Italian city states like Florence, evolved on to the path of mercantile capitalism.

30. The importance of the development of European long-distance trade (and Islam's role in it) cannot be overemphasized. For, long-distance trade had the indirect outcome of accelerating a number of internally rooted, but incipient transformations in Europe, that in time would be of great import, including: its urbanization, the emergence of mercantile capitalism, and the disintegration of European feudalism (the last precipitating, in turn, the massive European diasporic movement to the Americas, and elsewhere, with all the other attendant consequences, including the monumental Columbian Exchange).

31. For more on Islam and the birth of Europe, see Davies (1996), and Roberts (1997). On the Crusades, excellent sources include: Hillenbrand (1999); Mastnek (2002); Payne (1984); Richard (1999 (1996); and the monumental six-volume work edited by Setton (1962–1989)—though of immediate relevance here from that work is Daniel (1989b).

32. The obsession among some Spanish historians with advocacy of the broad-as-daylight myth of non-Islamic origins of many aspects of modern Spanish culture—recall that Islam had a foothold in Spain for more than 700 years—is a case in point; see the superb critique of this chauvinistic historiography by Glick (1979). See also Iqbal (2002) for a summary of the Western European jingoistic movement that began some time toward the end of the seventeenth-century to denigrate the Islamic heritage in Western scientific learning, the legacy of which still fundamentally colors much of Western European thought vis-à-vis Islam to this day.

33. Here is a thought–experiment: Would the *Ancient Greece*—which, remember, was primarily based, in terms of early intellectual accomplishments, in Ionia (the present-day Turkish side of the Mediterranean); see, for example, Dorn (1991: 77)—that Westerners are so keen to call their own (without much protest from modern Greece—understandably, of course, given the context of the current international geopolitics) be so claimed today if Islam had not emerged to give rise to an unrelenting European jingoism? Would Greece not have remained what it really is: a Mediterranean, and therefore Eastern (but most certainly not Western) geographic and cultural entity? In fact, it should also be pointed out, that the Ancient Greeks themselves saw Ionia as part of Asia. Herodotus, that great historian and traveler, for example, went even further in that he did not see Europe as independent of Asia, but as an extension of it.

34. In discussing origins, one is not even taking into consideration here that whole other matter: the Afro-Asian roots—a la Bernal—of the foundations of the premodern Western civilization: the Greek civilization itself, discussed earlier.

35. Von Grunebaum is a perfect example of that unadulterated Eurocentrism still rampant today through out the West which even in the face of awe-inspiring counter evidence is unable to forsake the racist desire to deny credit where its due simply because it is not of the Occident. Vide: in the very same breath as he states that except for Averroism Islam has made no long-lasting contribution to the development of the Occident, he goes on to say: "There is hardly an area of human experience where Islam has not enriched the Western tradition. Foods and drinks, drugs and medicaments, armor and heraldry, industrial, commercial and maritime techniques, and again artistic tastes and motives, not to speak of the many terms of astronomy or mathematics—a list indicative of the full measure of the Islamic contribution would take up many a page without being even remotely complete." His laudation doesn't stop here: "The very existence of the Muslim world has done much to mold European history and European civilization.... Muslim narrative and poetical

imagery, Muslim eschatology and the boldness of Muslim mysticism, all have left their traces on the medieval West. The greatest theologian[s] and the greatest poet[s] of the European Middle Ages are deeply indebted to Islam for inspiration as well as material" (p. 342). (He gives the examples of Thomas Aquinas and Dante.) Yet on the very same page, he has the temerity to insist that "never did original Muslim thought influence Western thought so as to remain a live force over a prolonged period of time completely integrated and indispensable to its further growth." (See also the discussion in Chapter 2 on the matter of civilizational influences.) Or consider his observation on the very next page: "Mastery of nature, public morality, and the condition of the common man have been suggested as measures of backwardness or the achievement of a civilization. It does not require elaborate demonstration that, by these standards, the Islamic world has but a small contribution to make."

36. Consider, for example, the long line of Western science historians who have grappled with the issue of the origins of Europe's scientific revolution and who feature in Cohen's overview of their work (1994) but yet almost none of them deigned to even nod at the precursory presence of Islamic science.

37. Of course, the adoption of *civilization* as a unit of analysis presents its own set of problems given that it is more a historian's imaginary construct than a construct of reality. This entire chapter, in a sense, stands in complete opposition to a historiography that relies on encapsulating human experiences into normatively hierarchical, discrete, time, and spatially bounded categories labeled civilizations. Hodgson (1974: 31) alludes to the difficulties when he questions the delimitations of boundaries in the "Afro-Eurasian Oikoumene." As he observes, "it has been effectively argued on the basis of cultural techniques and resources to be found there, that all the lands from Gaul to Iran, from at least ancient classical times onward, have formed a single cultural world." "But," he argues, "the same sort of arguments would lead us on to perceive a still wider Indo-Mediterranean unity, or even (in lesser degree) the unity of the whole Afro-Eurasian citied zone." To decisively drive home the point: the myth of civilization becomes readily apparent when one turns one's gaze to the present and pose the question—regardless of one's geographic place of abode in this age of "globalization"—What civilization are we living in today? A world civilization, perhaps? (See also Wigen and Martin 1997.)

38. Consider what Hodgson says in volume 1 of his work on the matter of the geographic peripherality of Western Europe: "[T]he artificial elevation of the European peninsula to the status of a continent, equal in dignity to the rest of Eurasia combined, serves to reinforce the natural notion shared by Europeans and their overseas descendents, that they have formed at least half of the main theater (Eurasia) of world history, and, of course, the more significant half. Only on the basis of such categorization has it been possible to maintain for so long among Westerners the illusion that the 'mainstream' of world history ran through Europe" (p. 49).

39. For an antidote to this shallow type of history and in support of the foregoing thesis, see also: Amin (1989); Abu-Lughod (1989); Berman (1989); Bernal (1987, 1991, and 2001); Blaut (1992, 1993, and 2000); de Libera (2001); Frank (1998); Hodgson (1993); Needham, et al. (1954–to present); Pomeranz (2000).

Appendix II

The Historical Antecedents of the Disjuncture Between Premodern and Modern African Higher Education

This appendix is sanctioned by the underlying logic of these facts: in 1798, Napoleon Bonaparte's Army would retrace the arrival in Egypt over 1,000 years before, in 639 C.E., of another army, that of the Muslims under the command of Amr ibn al-'As. Although Napoleon's stay in Egypt was brief, thanks to the British, in echoing 639 C.E., he would inaugurate, for good or ill, an entirely new historical trajectory for not only North Africa, but the entire African continent. Yet, however "natural" to Westerners 1798 may be from the perspective of today, the irony is that without 639 C.E. it would never ever have come about. How so? The seeds of 1798 were sown in 1492, but the seeds of 1492, in turn (as the preceding chapter has shown), were planted in 639 C.E.— since it is from North Africa that Islam would enter Europe. Now to elaborate by first drawing the relevance of these events to the subject matter of this work:

In surveying higher education institutions in Africa (in Chapter 2) that existed prior to the advent of the West precipitates this unavoidable question: Why were these institutions, in time, either completely replaced or eclipsed by those imported from the West? Leading Ashby (1966: 147) to observe about these new institutions that they, to quote him once more, "owe[d] nothing to [the] ancient tradition of scholarship" because, he states, "[t]he modern universities of Africa have their roots not in any indigenous system of education, but in a system brought from the West." A quick and simple answer is, obviously, the arrival of European colonialism. Yet, this response raises an even more fundamental question: Why did Africa (and many other parts of the world as well, of course) become prey to European colonialism in the first place? For many this question is tantamount to asking a vacuous question, in the order of "Why do birds fly?" However, the question is far from inane because its importance stems not only from the need to move away from the Eurocentric notion of the natural inevitability of European hegemonic dominance across the planet, which appears to pervade most Western histories of those they colonized, but from the perspective of a history of higher education in Africa specifically, it emerges out of consideration of the implications of the two dates just mentioned (639 C.E. and 1798 C.E.), which are of particular relevance to that part of Africa that boasted the largest number of precolonial higher education institutions: Islamic Africa.[1] For, these two dates are parenthetical points of African history that enclose an interregnum of about 1,000 years within which a powerful Afro-Asian civilization (Islamic) becomes eclipsed and is *effectively* marginalized by an even more powerful civilization (Western) in North Africa (and elsewhere too). To the astute, this historical development would serve as yet one more confirmation of that profoundly humbling fact: that all civilizations are impermanent; however, that is not the issue that is of immediate concern here.

The problem presented here is different; it has been raised by many of course, albeit in different contexts. Hodgson (1974), for example, raises it in volume 3 of his brilliant *magnum opus*. Phrasing the rise of Europe in the typical Hodgsonian vocabulary as the "Great Western Transmutation" (of which the renaissance was an antecedent), and the consequence of which was "that by about 1800 the Occidental peoples (together with the Russians) found themselves in a position to dominate the lands of Islamdom" (p. 177), the question he asks is, How did this transmutation come about in the first place? For, as he further explains, "[i]t was not merely, or perhaps even primarily, that the Europeans and their overseas settlers found themselves in a position to defeat militarily any powers they came in contact with," but it was far more profound than that because "both occupied ('colonial or settled') areas and unoccupied ('independent') areas were fairly rapidly caught up in a worldwide political and commercial system, the rules of which were made by, and for the advantage of, the Europeans and their overseas settlers." What is more, he explains, "[e]ven 'independent' areas could retain their local autonomy only to the extent that they provided European merchants, European missionaries, even European tourists, with a certain minimum of that type of international law and order to which they had become accustomed in Europe, so that the Europeans remained free to vaunt a privileged position and to display among all peoples the unexampled new physical and intellectual luxuries of Europe."

Hodgson's response to his own rhetorical question is that it was an outcome of what he calls the saturation of all levels of society (economic, technological, intellectual, scientific, artistic, administrative, agricultural, educational, etc.) with the spirit of what he terms as "technicalism," (defined by him as large-scale and permanent "improvement in technical methods of achieving concrete, material ends by way of multiple, interdependent specialization," p. 183)—symptomatic of which were such developments as the ubiquitous rise of capitalism and capital accumulation, the agricultural transformation, the industrial transformation, the replacement of monarchical dictatorships with democracies, modernization, and so on.[2] Given that there was a time when in the "Afro-Eurasian ecumene" (his term—though he uses the Greek etymological spelling: "oikoumene") when the Occident lagged far behind the East from almost all perspectives, Why is it that it is the Occident and not the East that experienced this rise of technicalism?

In this age of overspecialization there is a temptation to come up with a simplistic, single variable explanation—especially of such ethnocentric variety as: the genetically inherent genius of the Western European mind, or the rise of the Weberian Protestant

Ethic, or the inherent tendency toward decay and degeneracy in Afro-Asian civilizations, and so on.[3] As is being implied here, Eurocentrism is an excellent example of this
ethnocentrism. The Eurocentric mythology regarding the rise of Western global hegemony rests on two pillars. First, as was indicated in Chapter 2, that whatever contributions
arrived in Europe from elsewhere (be it in the form of scientific ideas, or technology or
capital accumulation, etc.) were irrelevant to the rise of Europe because they were of
inconsequential magnitude. Second, that the Europeans, being blessed by God (or nature), were always destined for great things because of their inherent intellectual and/or
environmental superiority. In other words: the Eurocentric version of history posits the
following scenario as valid: imagine that the planet had only comprised the European
peninsula populated only by Europeans; the Europe of today (in terms of modernity)
would still have emerged, because modernity is an entirely autarkic European invention.
This version of history is only possible by means of a mythic construction of a highly
distorted and abbreviated European history: "a progression," in the words of Amin
(1989: 90–91), "from Ancient Greece to Rome to feudal Christian Europe to capitalist
Europe."[4] Observe that it is a myth, as Blaut (1993: 59) reminds us, in both senses of
the word: a patent untruth and as a widely accepted false belief by a culture regarding
the history of its own genesis.[5]

While openly racist views such as those expressed by Western intellectual luminaries of the caliber of a Hegel or a Marx or a Weber or a Piaget are no longer as common
as they once were in the era when they were writing, one is still stunned by the fact that
these views continue to reappear from time to time, even today, in their unadorned
form—but yet all the while pretending to be serious scholarship.[6] Take the example of
the Australian academic Eric L. Jones, an unrepentant Eurocentrist if there ever was
one, who insists that Europe was always destined for civilizational greatness because,
on one hand, despotism, corruption, senseless breeding, irrationality, exploitation, and
so on, were not among its vices, while on the other it was endowed with a political and
economic-friendly ecological environment. Gushing about the latter, he states: "Europe
possessed such special features of site, location, and resource endowment that we are
bound to try to grasp the nettle of environmental explanation" (p. 226). In fact, the title
of the book itself is telling: *The European Miracle*. That is, it is nothing less than an unashamed celebration of the mythology of Western exceptionalism. If Jones's work deserves any attention at all then it is only because it has been published by no less than
Cambridge University Press (a fairly prestigious university press). Plus, it has gained
enough popularity among a sufficient number of Western academics as to have merited
a second and a third edition (2003)—with a number of reprints thrown in between—a
fact that in itself speaks volumes for the Eurocentric prejudices that continue to mes-
merize many Western scholars.

It ought to be noted too that those who may have detected a mea culpa (of sorts) in
his semi-apologetic book that came out after the first edition (Jones 1988), may be surprised (or perhaps not) to see that in this latest edition (which, except for the introduction and the afterword, remains completely unchanged), he blithely continues to reiterate his Eurocentric convictions by arguing that none of his critics have convincingly
challenged them. Under the circumstances, it is not surprising that this singularly pane-
gyric and inadequately referenced work, based in part on suspect pro-imperialist sources
(as one would expect)—written in the spirit of "I was born and brought up an Englishman," as he puts it in his 1988 book (p. 184)—makes a mockery of true scholarship.

Constructed on a shameless foundation of hubris, it is replete with such hoary and long discredited drivel as this:

- Europeans from ancient times have been "peculiarly inventive" because "ceaseless tinkering is a defining characteristic of [their] culture" (pp. 227, 62).
- "European society always contained a number of individuals whose creative talents were directed to improving the means of production. The supply of their talents was inelastic with respect to material reward: it was their hobby or obsession" (p. 228).
- Asian males, unlike their European counterparts, have historically preferred sex to material goods; as he puts it, "seemingly, copulation was preferred above commodities" (p. 15). In other words, "Europe did not spend the gifts of its environment 'as rapidly as it got them in a mere insensate multiplication of the common life.'" This, Jones argues, "sums up the quality of Europeanness" (p. 3).
- Unlike European rulers, Asian rulers were too despotic to allow political and economic progress: "Emperors were surrounded by sycophants. They possessed multiple wives, concubines, and harems of young women, a phenomenon that may have been less the perquisite of wealth and power than the assertion of dominance relationships, the propensity to use people as objects.... Great attention was paid to submission symbols, kneeling, prostration, the kowtow, in recognition of the emperor's personal dominance" (p. 109).
- "Despite great creative surges in times when Europe had still been primitive, despotic Asian institutions suppressed creativity or diverted it into producing voluptuous luxuries. Palace revolutions were all their internal politics seemed to offer" (p. 231).
- Africans were too technologically primitive to achieve anything civilizationally worthy as is attested by their animal-like closeness with nature. To quote him: "In Africa man adapted himself to nature. The hunter felt part of the ecosystem, not outside of it looking in with wonder, and definitely not above it and superior.... The most evocative symbol of this ecological oneness may be the honeyguides (*Indicator* spp), birds commensal with man. They fly, chattering loudly, ahead of bands of hunters, leading them a quarter of a mile or more to the tree hives of wild bees and feeding on the wax after the men have broken open the hives and taken the honey" (p. 154).
- The African environment was simply not conducive to progress: "The defects of the environment did indeed strike so close to the heart of economic life that it is not clear what indigenous developments were possible. All told, there was no development of the African economy to set alongside that of Europe in the Middle Ages and later" (p. 156).
- A common denominator of "oriental philosophies" has been "the emphasis on emotions, values, and cosmologies and the relative absence of the empirical enquiry and criticism of the Graeco-Judaeo-Christian tradition" (note, though, that he ends his sentence with one of the many contradictions that suffuses his entire work "though this Western tradition is in fact partly of Arab origin" (p. 161).

One could go on ad nauseam. Moreover, it is not just simply the crass and essentially racist value judgments that laces Jones's entire polemical work, but his patent disregard for historical facts that would put even a first-year undergraduate to shame that leaves one wondering how the manuscript made it past the editors in the first place. Take, for instance, his assertion that trade in Asia was primitive with no potential for economic growth because he thinks it comprised only "luxuries... [such as] "miscellaneous garnerings of the natural world from kingfisher feathers through precious stones to drugs no modern pharmacopoeia would own" "Many of these items," he further asserts, "were little more than biological junk and the growth potential of such a trade was slim." So, now, that explains why people like Columbus, Dias, Vasco da Gama, and other Europeans were rushing to the East (or tried to do so) the moment they learned how to cross the oceans—it was to get junk! The level of ignorance he betrays through such statements is indeed stupendous.[7]

Anyhow, to move on: while the economic and social transformations of the sixteenth, seventeenth, and eighteenth centuries that preceded the rise of European *technicalism* are familiar to even schoolchildren (such as: the bourgeois revolutions toward the end of the sixteenth-century—of which the 1688 Glorious Revolution in England is an epitome—that allowed the ascendant mercantile and protocapitalist classes to seize effective state power from the traditional monarchal-led landed aristocracies; the bourgeois engineered erosion of the feudal order; and toward the end of the eighteenth-century the industrial transformation itself), Eurocentric historians fail to explain *why* some of these developments occurred in Europe *decisively* and not elsewhere *in a like manner*, other than to fall back on that hoary Western canon of European exceptionalism.[8]

Yet, the fundamental truth is this: that if one were to cast one's historical gaze back to the eighth-century when the Muslims arrived in Europe one has no difficulty whatsoever in categorically stating that there was nothing that one could read in the entrails of Europe then—comparatively backward as it was in almost all ways—that pointed to anything that could predict its eventual rise to global hegemony. What is more, even after fast forwarding 700 years, to arrive in the fifteenth-century, a different reading would still not have been forthcoming. In other words, dear reader, after you have ploughed through Appendix I there should be no difficulty in accepting the fact that at the point in time when Columbus left Europe in what would eventually prove to be a portentous journey for the entire planet, the cultures of many developing *parts* of the Afro-Eurasian ecumene outside the European peninsula were *no less* rational, achievement-oriented, materialistic, predatory, belligerent, ambitious, scientific, capitalistic, technologically innovative, urbanized, capable of ocean navigation, and so on, than were the cultures of developing *parts* of Europe of the period (nor should it be difficult to accept that the opposites of these qualities, for that matter, existed at comparable levels of magnitude in both areas of the world).[9] In fact, on the contrary, in some respects they were more advanced than those of Europe.

Now, of course, it is true that when one considers where Europe was some 700 years earlier (at the time of the Islamic invasion), the rapidity of the European cultural advance is nothing short of miraculous! No, this is not in the least a hint, even remotely, of the much-vaunted "European miracle." Because, remember, this progress, as was shown in Appendix I, was not achieved by the Europeans independently; they did not do it alone (on the basis of their own intellectual uniqueness, inventiveness, rationality, etc.) that the Eurocentrists are so fond of arguing. Rather, it was an outcome of nothing less than a *dialectical* interplay between European cultures and the Islamic and other cultures of the Afro-Eurasian ecumene. Hodgson, for instance, is adamant that one must cast ones historiographical gaze across the history of the *entire* ecumene, for, as he explains, "most of the more immediately formative elements that led to the Transmutation, both material and moral, had come to the Occident, earlier or later, from other regions," (p. 197). In other words, as he puts it: "[w]ithout the cumulative history of the whole of Afro-Eurasian ecumene, of which the Occident had been an integral part, the Western Transmutation would be almost unthinkable" (p. 198). Or in the words of Frank (1998: 4): "Europe did not pull itself up by its own economic bootstraps, and certainly not thanks to any kind of European exceptionalism of rationality, institutions, entrepreneurship, technology, geniality, in a word—of race."

Yet, one is still not closer to an answer—other than to accept as axiomatic (unless one continues to insist on being a pseudo-historian) the fact that the elucidation of any such major transmutation of global import that took *centuries in the making in a small corner of the world that had never known isolation in most (if not all) of its entire history*, must rest on a multivariate transgeographic explanation. Ergo, taking the cue from Hodgson, and building on his work (recall that his work appeared three decades ago and much research has been done in this area since then), the tentative answer—and that, whether one likes it or not, is all that it can ever be, given the magnitude and complexity of the phenomenon at hand—is this: that it was a *conjuncture of fortuitously propitious historical factors* (see Chapter 1 for an explanation of this concept)—analogous in mechanism to that which accompanied, say, the demise of the Greek civilization and the ascendance of the Roman, or the demise of the Roman Empire and the ascendance of the Islamic. Now, a detailed exegesis of these factors will take one much too far from the subject at hand (higher education in Arabic Africa), therefore one must do with the briefest delineation of the broadest parameters: of which the inadvertent arrival by Columbus in the Americas will hold pride of place in the account that will now be unfolded.[10]

Before going further, however, it is necessary to confront a related problem that if not dealt with right away will threaten the cogency of what follows. It is a problem on which much ink has been expended by many scholars and it arises out of the history of science. It will be recalled from the discussion on the provenance of the modern university (in the preceding Appendix) that in the period immediately preceding the early modern era—namely, during the medieval era—the most advanced civilization in scientific (and other) terms was the Islamic civilization. Yet, by the seventeenth-century it is very clear that Europe had taken over, in unmistakably decisive terms, from Islam, the baton of scientific advancement. For the most part it would be true to say, without much exaggeration, that by this point Islam had no counterparts to such leading lights of Western scientific achievement as Copernicus, Brahe, Kepler, Galileo, and Newton (much in the same way that in the preceding centuries, going as far back as the eighth-century, Europe had no counterparts to such luminaries of Islamic scientific achievement as al-Khwarazmi, Ibn al-Haitham, Ibn Sina, al Biruni, Ibn Rushd, and Nasir al-Din al-Tusi). The question that appears to logically ensue in the minds of historians of science is this: Why? Why this reversal? What is more, the seeming profoundness of the question is highlighted by the fact that, as shown in that same discussion, not only was one dealing with "science in the real sense of the word," and not "protoscience" to quote the *Dictionary of the Middle Ages* (vol. 11, p. 88), but also because the Muslims and the Europeans were both albeit at different points in time, inheritors of the same Hellenic scientific tradition. Underlying this question, of course, which is why it is being raised here, is the corollary assumption (albeit a false one as will be shown by this appendix) that modernity—especially as symbolized by the industrial transformation—bypassed the Islamic world *because of the deceleration of its scientific achievement.*

The history of the historiographical treatment of this question is summarized by Cohen (1994), Huff (1993), and Iqbal (2002), among others (as a prelude to their own attempts to grapple with the same question. However, one need not be detained here by the specifics of the answers to this grand question *a la* Needham (recall that he had raised a similar question in respect to Chinese science [Needham 1954: 4])—they range widely, albeit almost all undergirded by Eurocentrism, depending upon who is providing the answer: from the tyrannical and corrupt nature of the Ottoman Empire to the knowledge ceilings imposed by Islamic theocracy; from the racial inferiority of the Arabs to the retrogressive character of Eastern feudalism; from lack of institutionalization of scientific research to obstacles placed by theological orthodoxy; from arrogance characteristic of a once advanced civilization to legalistic impediments; and so on—*nor should one be concerned with their validity.* Rather, what is necessary to point out is that the very question itself is illegitimate because it rests on two assumptions that are both patently false: one, that Western hegemonic domination of the world that commenced at the beginning of the nineteenth-century was rooted in science and technology; and two that scientific and/or technological progress exists independently of the social and material conditions of society. The veracity of the foregoing point will become obvious as one moves on with the discussion.

THE COLUMBIAN FACTOR

Writing a little over 200 years ago—specifically in the same year that the new nation of United States of America declared its independence from the British crown over the question of the status of Native Americans and their lands that had been precipitated by the Royal Proclamation of 1763—the Scottish economist, Adam Smith, would observe in his now classic manifesto of capitalism, *The Wealth of Nations*: "The discovery of America, and that of a passage to the East Indies by the Cape of Good Hope, are the two greatest and most important events recorded in the history of mankind. Their consequences have already been very great: but in the short period of between two and three centuries that has elapsed since these discoveries were made, it is impossible that the whole extent of their consequences can have been seen. What benefits, or what misfortunes to mankind may hereafter result from those great events, no human wisdom can foresee."

Yet, in the next breath Smith would further note: "To the natives, however, both of the East and West Indies, all the commercial benefits which can have resulted from those events have been sunk and lost in the dreadful misfortunes which they have occasioned.... At the particular time when these discoveries were made, the superiority of force happened to be so great on the side of the Europeans, that they were enabled to commit with impunity every sort of injustice in those remote countries." Smith, an eternal optimist, however, would further write: "Hereafter, perhaps, the natives of those countries may grow stronger, or those of Europe may grow weaker, and the inhabitants of all the different quarters of the world may arrive at that equality of courage and force which, by inspiring mutual fear, can alone overawe the injustice of independent nations into some sort of respect for the rights of one another" (1961 [1776], Vol. 2: 141).

As we look back over the past 200 years since he made these observations we now know what happened: the equality of nations never did materialize. On the contrary, those events, most specifically the first, that of 1492 (without which the second event would have been almost meaningless), set in motion forces that would lead to the decisive movement of the loci of capitalism from the eastern end of the Afro-Eurasian ecumene to the western end, the European peninsula, as a result of the simultaneous quickening of the pace of capitalist development within Western Europe, and the European undermining of capitalism elsewhere in the ecumene. We still continue to live today with the fallout from this development that 1492 brought about (and which for want of a better term may be labeled the *Columbian factor*. Lest, however, one may be accused here of a touch of melodrama in portraying the historical significance of 1492 thusly (and note that it is a significance that understandably receives scant attention from Eurocentrists), it is necessary to elaborate on this matter further.

"In 1492, Columbus sailed the ocean blue." While almost all Westerners learn this fact as schoolchildren, few of them today (that includes academics) are even remotely conscious of how significant that year is from the perspective of the historical trajectory followed by Europe vis-à-vis the rest of the world.[11] For, contrary to established Western historical canon on the subject, prior to this event there was nothing in the historical antecedents of Europe that spoke to the *certainty* of the emergence of Hodgson's technicalism and the consequent Western global hegemony that was to follow, especially in the centuries after 1800. After all, one need not be reminded here that the Columbian project (the quest for an Atlantic sea route to the East) was itself born in a crucible of historical events in which Islam and the East had no small part to play—as was indicated in the preceding appendix.[12]

Now, it is not the Columbian project *in of itself*, however, that is of importance in explaining the rise of Western global hegemony in the nineteenth-century, but rather it is that conjuncture of fortuitously propitious historical factors—both contingent factors (in the sense of being outside human agency) and conjunctural (of human agency, but not in itself purposive)—and of which the Columbian project was a part that is of signal importance. After all, recall that during the reign of emperor Yong-Le (see blow) the Chinese had already visited the America's decades before in what were truly "voyages of *exploration*" that included the circumnavigation of the planet years before even Magellan undertook his.[13] What are these factors, then, that together help to elevate the Columbian project to a special pride of place in any credible account of the rise of Europe? Going by Blaut (1993 and 2000), Frank (1998), and Pomeranz (2000), among others, the following are the most salient: [14]

First, was the bi-dimensional issue of geography. To explain, it is not uncommon for many among the Western media these days to refer to the Atlantic as "the pond" in that typical proprietary flourish so characteristic of Westerners (as if the Atlantic does not belong to Africans as well—compare also with the use of the term America [itself a misnomer since Columbia should have been the preferred name, if one insists on a European appellation] to refer only to the United States). Leaving aside the arrogance that belies such language, the use of the term pond is not entirely without basis in geography in that if one were to compare distances between the Americas and Asia (India, China, etc.) with those between Europe and the Americas the Atlantic does become a pond. To get to the point, it is the geographic proximity of the Americas to Europe that gave it a commercial advantage that would far surpass anything that others in the Afro-Eurasian ecumene had ever enjoyed hitherto in their thousands of years of commercial relations with each other—dating back to the time of the Egyptian (and perhaps even Babylonian) civilizations—and which, as mentioned in the preceding appendix, also included long-distance, cross-ocean voyaging (albeit restricted to the Mediterranean and Indian Ocean basins). Yes, of course, the Chinese were not unfamiliar with the Americas, having ventured upon it before Columbus, but regular relations with the Americas across the vast oceanic distances was a different proposition altogether!

The other dimension of geography has to do with the maritime technology of the period that everyone in the Afro-Eurasian ecumene shared: namely, its reliance on wind power. The winds were not favorable for any one attempting to sail to the Euro-American ecumene from the Indian Ocean region, whereas the chance arrival by Italian and Iberian sailors in the Atlantic archipelago (the Canaries, the Madeiras, and the Azores) in the thirteenth and fourteenth centuries—which they would later colonize—allowed Columbus to have access to knowledge of the existence of the circular Atlantic trade winds. Without these winds Columbus and other Europeans who followed him would never have made it to the Euro-American ecumene.[15] While it is true that Columbus was an "accident" (not only because he had originally not set out to look for the Americas, but also because of the mutiny on his ships—which if it had succeeded would have scuttled the project), the key point here is that it was an accident *waiting to happen*, given the geographic proximity of the Americas to Europe.[16] The lure of the East was of such duration and intensity, especially in the Western Mediterranean littoral, that if not Columbus, then some other maritime entrepreneur from Europe would have stumbled across the Americas sooner or later (recall John Cabot's project, for instance).[17]

But what about the Africans, specifically West Africans? After all, they also had access to the pond too, and therefore were also geographically close to the Americas (remember that Columbus's launching pad for his trip to the Americas were the Canary Islands off the coast of West Africa). The potential was never realized by them because any one with knowledge of even a modicum of African history knows that the commercial interests of the West Africans, as Blaut (1993) points out, had historically always flowed in the opposite direction, toward the hinterland and beyond, to the northeast, because their trade was tied in with the trade of the Mediterranean and Asia (traversing of course a different type of ocean, the ocean of sand).

The celebration of Columbus Day every year in the United States (and this brings us to the second contingent factor) is a Eurocentrist celebration par excellence. Why? Because for the original citizens of the Euro-American ecumene, the Native Americans, Columbus Day is in reality nothing more than a celebration of the subjection of their peoples to biological weapons of mass destruction (diseases) that were responsible for very quickly laying their people and their civilizations prostrate before the first European colonizers. It is true that the Europeans had superior military technology (though, initially, they only had a slight edge over the Native Americans given the state of medieval armament technology in Europe at that time) to assist them in their first steps of predation, but recall that the Native Americans were numerous enough and organized enough to resist this predation—had it not been for the diseases of the Afro-Eurasian ecumene (e.g., small pox, measles, cholera, typhoid, etc.), to which they had no immunity, that the Europeans brought with them (albeit inadvertently). One will never know exactly what the population numbers of the Native Americans were when the Europeans first arrived on their doorstep, but one horrible fact is incontrovertible: within a space of a mere 100 years, millions upon millions were wiped out by the diseases (as well as, a little later, enslavement)—so much so, that some ethnic groups were completely erased from the face of the earth. In other words, then, it was the lack of immunity among Native Americans to the diseases that the Europeans brought with them that allowed Europe to colonize the Americas *as rapidly and as completely* as it did.[18]

The third contingent factor was climate. Most of the Euro-American ecumene has tropical and subtropical climate. Imagine, however, if the climate of the entire ecumene had been identical to that of North America, north of the Canadian border. It is very doubtful that the commercial advantages that accrued to the Europeans (relative to others in the Afro-Asian ecumene) would have been sufficiently large to permit the Europeans to forge ahead of the rest. In other words, it is climate that allowed the establishment of plantation agriculture where commodities like sugar (and later tobacco and cotton) would have far-reaching economic implications for Europe.

The fourth contingent factor was the presence of critically important minerals, beginning with precious metals (and then, as European economic development progressed in subsequent centuries, to include oil, bauxite, etc.). Had the landmass of the Euro-American ecumene been bereft of these minerals—especially precious metals—it is unlikely that 1492 would have played as critical a role in the hegemonic development of Europe as it did, as will be shown in a moment.

In addition to these factors, there were also a number of highly significant *conjunctural* factors; those that are particularly worthy of mention are these five: One, was the decision by the Chinese some time early in the fourteenth-century to adopt silver as the basis for their currency. Two, was the defeat of the Muslims during the First Crusade that allowed the Latins access to the technology of sugar production.[19] Three, was the overarching predatory Christian worldview that Columbus, and others who came after him, carried with them from Europe as they set out on their oceanic voyages in the fifteenth-century, and onward. Given the immense political and economic importance of this Christian ideological worldview in shaping those initial encounters between the Europeans and the original citizens of the Euro-American ecumene in which not only the entire ecumene, lock, stock, and barrel was completely and permanently hijacked for the exclusive economic benefit of Europe, but that the magnitude of this benefit was directly proportional to the depth of the predation (the brutalization and extermination of the Native Americans, the enslavement of the Africans, the looting of their natural resources, the wholesale and permanent alienation of their lands by settlers, etc.), necessitates a somewhat lengthy exegesis into the genesis of this worldview.[20] The conclusion to this appendix has been assigned this task.

A fourth conjunctural factor was the arrival in Europe of gunpowder and guns from the East through the agency of either the Muslims or the Mongols or both.[21] While Blaut (1993) is correct in noting that one cannot ascribe too much historical importance to the relative superiority of any side's military technology among adversaries because it does not take long for one side to acquire it (by hook or by crook) from the other side as well, in the specific context of 1492, however, the superior military technology of the Europeans was decisive in their *first encounters* with the Native Americans. Why? Because it allowed the Europeans to establish the initial beachhead to permit other forces (such as diseases) to takeover. A similar example emerges from considering the earliest Portuguese forays into the Indian Ocean basin on the heels of the rounding of the Cape by Bartolomeu Diaz in 1488. Without their cannons they could not have established commercial dominance *so quickly* given that in those first ensuing commercial encounters they had little to offer to the Asians by way of commodities; the gold and silver would come some decades later.[22]

The matter of superior military technology becomes even more significant, of course, in the later periods of European colonization of the world. Take the example of

Africa in the nineteenth-century: by this time European military technology had advanced so greatly under the aegis of the industrial transformations, that it was clearly beyond anything that the Africans could have brought out into the battlefield—ergo, the fate of the Africans was sealed.[23] Obviously, it wasn't just the Africans who were made to taste the power of the rapidly evolving military technology in Europe, as Messrs Archer, Ferris, Herwig, and Travers (2002), for example, document in their chapter "The West Conquers the World." Taking a leaf from Blaut (1993), however, a cautionary note must be sounded before one is tempted to mindlessly run with this factor to the exclusion of all others (remember, it is a conjunctural factor—meaning it is required, but it is not sufficient by itself). Therefore, Archer and his colleagues' observation, while certainly true that "[b]etween 1757 and 1914 the West took over the world.... British conquered India, Russians campaigned to Istanbul, European armies dominated east Asia and seized southeast Asia, central Asia, and almost all of Africa, and the United States and Canada annexed North America" (pp. 440, 448), their account of how this happened must be taken with a large dose of salt.[24]

In 1368, a mendicant Buddhist monk of peasant origin, by the name of Hong-wu, would establish what historians now refer to as the Ming dynasty—and this brings us to the fifth conjunctural factor.[25] Of particular interest here is the third emperor in this dynasty, Yong-Le. He would undertake a number of major economic and political projects during his reign; among them a revival of the imperial tradition of Genghis Khan's famous grandson Kublai Khan (the ruler of the entire Mongol Empire, including China, whose unification was one of his major accomplishments) to project China's power beyond its borders, even into the Indian Ocean basin—recall, for instance, Kublai Khan's ill-fated attempts to invade Japan; and twice no less, in 1274 and 1281. The most well-known of these efforts to date with respect to the Indian Ocean region was the dispatch of huge Chinese fleets under the command of Cheng Ho, the Chinese Muslim general, to show the Chinese flag to the various potentates and in the process institute among them at least a nominal form of vassalage.

Given the might of the Chinese naval power that these expeditions placed on display (although outright military aggression was never on their agenda—since deference rather than territorial conquest appeared to be their chief goal—they were, as Finlay 1995 reminds us, "armed to the teeth"), almost all the territories and kingdoms that Cheng Ho visited (over a total of seven expeditions were undertaken: in 1405, 1407, 1408, 1413, 1416, 1421, and 1431) agreed to send envoys to China with tribute; even Japan fell into line for a while. At the same time, these expeditions also undertook to suppress piracy, which China viewed as an affront to the orderly business of securing and maintaining its overlordship. By the time of the penultimate Ming expedition to India in 1417 and the last to East Africa and the Persian Gulf in 1431 (see Chang 1995, for details of these expeditions), it was clear to everyone within the entire Indian Ocean region as to who indeed was the naval superpower. If there were any doubts in this regard, then a fleet on one's doorstep of about 300 ships (some equipped with bombards and the largest of the ships could boast 3000-tons capacity), with some 28,000 heavily armed men, had miraculous powers of concentrating the mind.[26] (See Finlay [1995] on details of how some recalcitrants were put in their place.)

Now, what is of capital significance for our purposes of all this is that with the death of Yong-Le in 1424, the Ming dynasty withdrew itself from the Indian Ocean (it would authorize only one more expedition, the one in 1431) for a number of reasons—but all internal to Chinese politics. The implications of this major historical turn of events from the perspective of the European foray into the Indian Ocean, inaugurated by the Portuguese more than three decades later, should be self-evident; however, if one is still uncertain it is well described by Finlay: "A precondition for da Gama's voyage marking an epochal turning-point was the prior retreat of the Chinese navy from the Indian Ocean, an unwitting withdrawal from a contest for world dominion." With some exaggeration he goes on to say: "[m]uch of world history may be said to revolve around this Chinese retreat; and Western advance" (p. 96). Still, to some extent he is correct; for, this fact is incontestable: that insofar as the eventual European domination of Indian Ocean commerce was *among* the critically instrumental factors in the rise of Europe, then surely the Chinese did a great service to the rise of global European imperialism; for, one cannot envisage the Portuguese maritime swagger (punctuated as it was with military aggression and gratuitous barbaric cruelty) in the Indian Ocean had the Chinese been around when they first arrived.[27]

Even while placing before you this set of contingent and conjunctural factors, it ought to be firmly stressed here that to say that without the colonization and settlement of the Euro-American ecumene, Europe would not have achieved the kind of economic progress that eventually underwrote its post–*1800* global hegemony is not in any sense whatsoever to belittle the significance of whatever major economic, political and social transformations that were going on in Europe prior to 1492. *One must be absolutely and resolutely emphatic about this point.* Rather, the argument here is that relative to other areas in the Afro-Eurasian ecumene, there was nothing going on in Europe (Western Europe, to be precise) prior to 1800, *that was so unique* that the triumph of European industrial capitalism was preordained as Eurocentrists are so fond of arguing. In fact, as Pomeranz (2000) and others have pointed out, in many sectors, other societies in the ecumene were ahead of Europe (e.g., in agronomy, land management, irrigation, textiles, ceramics, iron and steel, medicine, ship-building, etc.) even as late as the onset of the industrial transformation'.

As he explains regarding agriculture, for instance: "[t]ake away the enormous amounts of extra land that Europe gained across the Atlantic (through luck, smallpox, and violence, as well as navigational and commercial skills) and it is easy to imagine Europe's marked technological backwardness in the largest sector of eighteenth-century economies having a significance as great as whatever advantages it had in other sectors" (p. 45). He then concludes: "The point to emphasize... is that non-European societies retained significant technological advantages in many areas even in the late eighteenth-century, and it was not inevitable that they would turn out to seem relatively unimportant in the long-run.... Nor should we assume that these areas of non-European advantage were merely the lingering effects of once great, but now stagnant traditions" (p. 47). Yet, even *before* 1492, there was nothing extraordinary going on in Europe relative to the rest of the Afro-Eurasian ecumene as Janet Abu-Lughod's (1989) path-breaking work has shown; in fact the opposite was probably true: As Fernandez-Armesto (1995: xiv–xv) observes: "The most dynamic, the most powerful and, from the point of view of imperial potential, the most promising states on the eve of the 'age of expansion,' were all outside Latin Christendom. ...[T]he most conspicuous cases of expansion would have been those of Muscovy and the Ottoman Empire."[28]

To leave the matter here, however, would render the foregoing somewhat hollow; because one needs to explain precisely how Europe was economically advantaged *deci-*

sively (the key word here is decisive) by its brutal colonization and settlement of the Euro-American ecumene. While space precludes a thorough exegesis, two examples of the kinds of enterprises that proved of great determinative value to Europe should suffice: the production of cane sugar and the mining of precious metals (gold and silver).[29]

SUGAR AND PRECIOUS METALS

The present-day ubiquity of sugar is of such magnitude that very few in the West— even academics—are remotely aware that the source of this amazingly protean substance, the sugarcane (saccharum officinarum), is of Eastern provenance, having been brought to the Mediterranean region by the Muslims as part of that great Islamic East-West technology and knowledge transfer described in the preceding appendix.[30] Europe acquired the technology of sugar production through two avenues: first, through Latin contacts with Muslims during the various periods of Muslim rule in places such as Spain, Portugal, Sicily and Cyprus; and second, as a consequence of the Crusades. However, it appears that for much of Europe the latter avenue turned out to be of greater import. Verlinden (1995), in documenting the route of diffusion of this technology across the Atlantic, notes that the Latins inherited sugarcane plantations with their colonization of Palestine from the Muslims following the defeat of the latter during the First Crusade (1096–1102). Soon, the Latins (principally the Italians) were exporting sugar to the West in significantly increasing quantities.

Toward the end of the thirteenth-century, however, the Latins experienced a reversal of fortunes in Palestine that in time would prove to be permanent; consequently, sugar exports from Palestine to the West slowed down to a trickle as the exports were redirected by the Muslims to their traditional markets in the East. Given that by this point the Latin trade in sugar had become so highly lucrative for its participants, it was a matter of time as alternative export sources were established. Consequently, by the early fifteenth-century, the primary loci of sugar production for export to the West had been decisively moved toward the western end of the Mediterranean basin, becoming localized in places such as Cyprus, Crete, Sicily, Spain, and Portugal. At around the same time, with the Iberian colonization of the Atlantic archipelago, sugar production expanded geographically—through the agency of, as before, primarily Italian capital—to what came to be known as the *sugar islands* (the habited Canaries, colonized by the Spanish in about 1404 [leading to the eventual genocidal extermination of its inhabitants, the Guanches, a Berber people]; the uninhabited Madeiras, colonized by the Portuguese in 1421; and the uninhabited Azores, colonized by the Portuguese in 1432). The Portuguese also established sugarcane plantations on the island of Sao Tome off the coast of West Africa, which they colonized in the 1480s; it would eventually become the world's largest producer of sugar, until its eclipse by Brazilian sugar exports in the seventeenth-century.

As the century wore on, the movement of the sugar technology further westward into the Atlantic continued, this time thanks to Columbus (recall that not only he had married into a Madeiran family—his wife Felipa Perestrelo y Moniz was the daughter of the governor of one of the islands, Porto Santo—but had lived in the Madeiras for about three years, 1480–83). Shortly after Columbus had arrived in the Caribbean it had became clear to him that the spices he so desperately sought were not available, and neither was gold—at least in the quantities he desired (as a result of arrogance-inspired ignorance, he never made it to the mainland of South America). A different type of "gold," however, was promised by the wet tropical climate of the islands. Having spent some time in the service of the Iberians in the sugar islands earlier in his naval career, he was aware of the technology of sugar production and the climatic/agronomic requirements for growing the cane. Consequently, on his second voyage (1493) he brought with him the sugarcane cuttings and thereby introduced to the Euro-American ecumene for the first time the sugarcane (together with the technology of sugar production).

In tracing this highly abbreviated history of sugar production, what is of utmost relevance here is this: that given the agronomic specifics of this crop, it was very conducive to the plantation technique of production.[31] Two facts about this production need to be highlighted here: first, is that in the context of the medieval era, sugar production constituted among the earliest agro-industries (marrying both agriculture and industry, and therefore requiring large capital investments) and second, it was quickly determined by the plantation owners that the most ideal labor for this agro-industry was the use of unpaid labor, that is slave labor (it is telling that to this day, extremely low-paid, often highly exploited, manual labor remains the principal motor of sugarcane cultivation and harvest throughout the world—including in the United States).[32] It is not surprising, then, that the production of sugar would quickly become the principal factor in motivating the flow of enslaved Africans to the Americas and would remain in the early years of European colonization the biggest consumer of such labor.

That sugar and its related products (molasses and rum) would achieve enormous economic significance in what historians have dubbed as the "triangular" trade of the Atlantic should not be of any surprise; sugar had become ever-increasingly important to the European consumer as a result of two mutually reinforcing but seemingly contradictory factors: increasing demand, accompanied by increasing supply at falling prices.[33] The accelerating demand was the result of its use as a sweetener for such nonalcoholic, mildly addictive bitter beverages as tea, coffee, and cocoa. Consumption rose in ever-larger quantities within the European populace (these beverages were not only family and work safe, but especially for the poor, as Pomeranz 2000 points out, sugar provided much needed additional calories cheaply); while the falling prices was explained by the expanded use of the unpaid labor of the enslaved.[34]

Side by side with this "white gold" (that sugar had indeed become for the European mercantile capitalists), the Euro-American ecumene also became a major source of another equally important commodity: precious metals. Now, most school children in the West are familiar with the romanticized exploits of such sixteenth-century English swashbuckling buccaneers as Sir Francis Drake (c. 1540–96) and Sir John Hawkins (1532–95) subjecting Spanish ships, returning from the Americas leaden with treasure, to piracy on the high seas. But, of course, they are usually never told how these treasures, principally gold and silver, were obtained and what their significance was for Europe. They are not told that, in a sense, it was armed robbery that pitted one group of robbers against another: the English (and others) looting the Spanish and the Spanish robbing the Native Americans. However, what is of capital interest here is that regardless of how the precious metals arrived in Europe, and who took of possession of it, its impact on the overall European economy would prove to be profound, as will be indicated in a moment.

For a number of reasons (aesthetic, utilitarian, relative scarcity, availability in pure forms in nature, etc.) both gold and silver have been considered precious metals almost throughout the world from antiquity to the present. Gold and silver ornaments have been found, for example, in Egyptian royal tombs going as far back as 4000 B.C. For centuries, one of the major sources of gold for Europe had been Africa. However, the chief drawback there was that it passed through the intermediary hands of their hated enemies, the Muslims. It is not surprising, then, that the quest for gold was one of the chief motivations of Columbus's voyage. When Columbus arrived in Hispaniola he did find some gold (he saw the Tainos, a subgroup of the Arawak, wearing gold ornaments). However, had he managed to make it to the mainland of South America he would have realized that is where the relatively large deposits of gold and silver—most especially silver—were to be found. The Spanish soon established silver mines—using extremely brutalized Native American slave labor—in the sixteenth-century in Mexico, Bolivia, and Peru; thusly arose the annual precious metals (bullion and coin) galleon runs across the Atlantic to which European buccaneers were attracted like moths to a candle. (In any tallies of the quantity of precious metals imports into Europe from the Euro-American ecumene, one must also, therefore, consider not only the official figures, but estimates of contraband as well.) One is reminded here of the fact that, according to Barrett (1990), some 85% of the world's silver, and 70% of the gold supply, during the three centuries leading up to 1800 came from mines in the Euro-American ecumene. (There is the saying that "money does not grow on trees." Yet, in a sense, for the Europeans, it did after 1492.)

What did Europe do with its precious metals, most especially the unending supply of silver? One can turn to an economist best placed to provide us with an answer because he witnessed first hand what became of the metals: Adam Smith. This is what he observed: "the precious metals are a commodity which it always has been, and still continues to be, extremely advantageous to carry from Europe to India. There is scarce any commodity which brings a better price there; or which, in proportion to the quantity of labor and commodities which it costs in Europe, will purchase or command a greater quantity of labor and commodities in India." Notice also, however, what he says specifically about the importance of silver: "It is more advantageous too to carry silver thither than gold; because in China, and the greater part of the other markets of India, the proportion between fine silver and fine gold is but ten, or at most twelve, to one; whereas in Europe it is as fourteen of fifteen to one." Not surprisingly, then, he continues: "In the cargoes, therefore, of the greater part of European ships which sail to India, silver has generally been one of the most valuable articles. It is the most valuable article in the Acapulco ships which sail to Manilla [sic]. The silver of the new continent seems in this manner to be one of the principle commodities by which the commerce between the two extremities of the old one is carried on, and it is by means of it, in a great measure, that those distant parts of the world are connected with one another" (1961 [1776], vol. 1: 229–30).

In a nutshell, then, from the fifteenth-century onward, as enslaved Native Americans were worked to death (to be joined later, especially in Brazil, by enslaved Africans) in the mines of South America, Europe got into the lucrative business of re-exporting a substantial portion of the cheaply produced precious metals to the East in the form of bullion and coinage.[35] Why did the East import such large quantities of bullion and coinage? One answer has to do specifically with China. Beginning in the early fifteenth-century, China, which up to that point was arguably the largest economic entity in the world (and threatens to become so once again), had begun to transform its currency toward a silver standard and with a silver-based coinage—see Pomeranz 2000, for reasons. Under the circumstances, silver became more important in China than even gold itself, especially since China produced very little of its own silver.

It is thought that perhaps as much as half of the American silver was eventually absorbed by continental Asia during the period 1450 to 1800.[36] There was, in addition, another factor at work, well described by Pacey (1991: 68): "One other problem facing Europeans in Asia was that their trade was chronically out of balance, because there were very few goods manufactured in Europe which Asians wanted to buy. European products were of inferior quality, or irrelevant to Asian needs. Guns were certainly in demand, but muskets and cannons manufactured in the Islamic countries or Thailand were often of good quality. Thus almost everything which Europeans bought in India or China had to be paid for with gold or silver, often in the form of coin." In other words, given the primitive state of European manufacturing industry prior to the industrial transformation, there was in reality, little else of value that the Europeans could export to the Asian markets. On the other hand, the European ships came back laden with treasures of incredible profit-maximizing value: from gold to spices to silk to porcelain.

Having established these four commodities—sugar, slaves, gold, and silver—as *examples* (one could easily add other commodities to the mix: cotton, tobacco, timber, etc.) illustrating how critically important the Euro-American ecumene would become for the economies of Western Europe, it remains to briefly delineate precisely how Europe was economically and decisively advantaged relative to the rest of the Afro-Eurasian ecumene during the nearly 300 years (1492 to 1800) leading up to the Western European industrial transformation. Before proceeding to do so, it is important to emphasize that any explanation of the rise of Europe and the relative fall of the rest of the great economies of the Afro-Eurasian ecumene must be understood as occurring in a *global* world economy in which all were participants, including of course those of the Euro-American ecumene.

The first and most obvious economic benefit was, not surprisingly, the enormous profits that were generated directly from activities such as the following: the production and/or sale within Europe of the various American commodities of sugar, precious metals, molasses, rum, tobacco, cotton, furs, and so on (plus, remember, since most of these commodities were produced at rates far below the normal costs of production by using brutalized and unpaid forced labor, these profits were greatly magnified beyond the "usual" levels); the trade in enslaved Africans in the Euro-American ecumene, together with the manufacture of products necessary for the maintenance of this evil trade (from ships to armaments to commodities for barter in Africa—cloth, utensils, guns, rum, etc.); and the geographic expansion of European markets across the Atlantic occasioned by the need to produce armaments, ships, various manufactures that went into the direct upkeep of the plantation economy (from machinery to cloth for the enslaved), and products for the maintenance of the settler economies as a whole (recall that in the early years these economies were in essence producers of primary goods for export—in the tradition of the present-day PQD countries—and therefore most of their manufactures had to be imported).[37] To be sure, relative to the entire GDP of Western Europe these profits were not immense; however, such a comparison misses the point. *They were substantive enough to decisively accelerate the structural transformation of Western*

Europe necessary to underwrite its transition to industrial capitalism, as will be shown momentarily.

Second, although the comparatively marginal European economies had very little to offer the great economies of the Afro-Eurasian ecumene (such as those of the various empires in China and the Islamic world: Ch'ing (1644–1912), Ming (1368–1644), Mughal (1526–1748), Omani (1698–1856), Ottoman (1400s–1800s), Safavid (1502–1736), etc.) prior to the nineteenth-century, as just noted, the capital generated from the Euro-American ecumene allowed Europe to become a participant in these other economies where even greater profits and economic benefits were to be derived, through activities such as: the unending export of precious metals bullion and coinage *as a commodity* to Asia for arbitrage; the sale of Asian imports (spices, silk, etc.) within Europe made possible by stimulating Asian production for export to Europe through infusion of European precious metals (this meant that prices of imports remained relatively stable for the European importer); the re-export of Asian imports to the markets of the Americas and Africa; and the trade in Asian commodities within the Indian Ocean basin itself as the European ships plied from one country to another (here they began taking over the trading activities of the original Asian entrepreneurs through a combination of armed force and higher purchasing power facilitated by possession of precious metals currency).

Third, the infusion of precious metals from the Euro-American ecumene (as well as profits from overseas trade, of course) allowed a general investment-induced stimulation of the economies of Europe (the Keynesian multiplier effect) toward accelerated, internally oriented, economic growth based on such developments as expanding internal markets, increase in consumption, and so on. At the same time, the imports of Asian luxury commodities (silk, porcelain, arts and crafts, etc.) stimulated import-substitution industries within Europe, which in turn spawned industries based on attendant upstream economic inputs and downstream economic outputs.

The totality of these benefits garnered over the course of some 300 years after 1492 (and made possible by 1492) put Europe firmly on a path that the rest of the developed parts of the Afro-Eurasian ecumene eventually found impossible to follow, thereby guaranteeing their subordination to the imperialism of a part of the world that millennia before was a barbaric irrelevance in terms of world history. The precise mechanisms involved in this transformation of the global balance of power included the following:

First, the geographic extension of the European economy across the Atlantic allowed Europeans to escape an ecological bottleneck that their Asian counterparts faced *and could not escape*: the shortage of land (in the face of population expansion, increased per capita consumption, etc.) to provide for the four critical Malthusian necessities that, especially in the era of the preindustrial transformation, were so intimately tied in with terra firma: food, energy, clothing, and housing. The Euro-American ecumene provided Europe with not only such *land-dependent* products as sugar, cotton, tobacco, grain, timber, meat, wool, etc.), but also the potato (which generated far more calories per acre than did any other European food crop), and as Pomeranz (2000) points out, natural fertilizer (guano) to restore its lands. To give an example of the benefits of these imports from the perspective of land conservation in Europe, consider the role of sugar: in 1800, in the United Kingdom, according to calculations by Pomeranz (on the basis of data derived from Mintz 1985), the quantities of calories replaced by sugar consumption for that one-year would have required an output from English farms with an acreage that would have totaled 1,300,000 acres—assume the farms to have been of average productivity (p. 275).[38] Mention must also be made here of another very important food source: fish from the rich North Atlantic fisheries (first reported on in Europe in 1498 by John Cabot), which, in terms of quantities, was unmatched by any available in the Mediterranean and the Indian Ocean basin—given the relative virginity of these fisheries (as well as the specifics of that particular marine environment). Land-saving was also, of course, greatly enhanced by the simple device of the export of surplus populations for settlement in the colonies (the added benefit of which was that they assisted in the expansion of European markets, as just noted).

Second, as Chaudhuri (1995: 308–309) reminds us: "For nearly 800 years before Vasco da Gama landed in Calicut, Europe was connected with the ancient civilizations of the Indian Ocean through a great chain of transcontinental trade. It began in the ports of southern China, in Hangchow, Chuanchou, and Canton, passed through the Sunda and Malacca straits in Southeast Asia, touched on the Coromandel, Malabar, and Gujarat before finally reaching the commercial turn-tables of Aden, Hormuz, Cairo, Alexandria, Aleppo and Beirut."[39] However, the massive infusion of precious metals currency in the Indian Ocean basin, where money was principally in the form gold and silver coinage, allowed the European traders to commandeer this trade for their exclusive benefit by undercutting their Asian rivals in two significant ways: One, as the European merchants increased their commercial activities in the Afro-Eurasian ecumene in the sixteenth-century and onward, they soon discovered that they were now in a position to permanently outbid their local counterparts because they could offer much higher prices to producers.

Two, by connecting Europe directly with their long-distance voyaging caravels and galleons to East Africa and Asia, they disrupted the economic logic of the centuries old finely balanced "emporia trading" (where large urbanized commercial trading centers were chain linked through trade in both luxury commodities that changed many hands and bulk commodities that involved fewer intermediaries) that had governed the Indian Ocean basin for centuries, thereby, again, marginalizing their Asian rivals (see Chaudhuri [1985] for more on this). Moreover, even the Muslim merchants of the Middle East were not spared the slow-but-sure spiraling decay of their economic fortunes (though according to Issawi,1995, the decay was already underway as a result of processes brought about by the *Reconquista* and the Crusades), arising from the massive deflection of their centuries-old traditional trade between the East and the West that they had executed as part of their role as commercial intermediaries—as well as the loss of European markets for commodities that the Middle East itself had produced for centuries (such as sugar and coffee, for example).[40]

The net result was the relentless downward spiral of the economic power of the local Afro-Asian mercantile capitalists with the simultaneous upward spiral of the economic power of the European capitalists. Ergo, if there was any possibility of an emergent, economically powerful, *indigenous* mercantile and protocapitalist class usurping power from the traditional ruling dynasties, by the end of the nineteenth-century it was no longer in the cards. Instead, as economic power slipped into the hands of the Europeans by the end of the eighteenth-century, it was a matter of time before the full coercive force of the European state was eventually harnessed to ensure the complete monopoly of this economic power vis-à-vis not only the indigenous capitalists, but also other competing European capitalists.[41] (Consider this stark reality: by the end of the nineteenth-century, except for one or two areas, there was virtually no part of the entire planet left free of European suzerainty—even the Ottoman Empire was on its last legs.)

Third, on the other hand, the dramatic expansion in both numerical terms and in terms of economic prowess, of the emergent European mercantile and protocapitalist classes, facilitated by 1492, eventually allowed them (from around 1700 onward) to effectively depose the traditional landed aristocracies and takeover the reigns of state within Europe—especially Western Europe—which thereby greatly enhanced the conditions for the breakdown of the feudal order and the development of capitalist institutions.[42] Further, this also meant that, henceforth, the resources of the state (which, do not forget, included the constant and large infusion of precious metals from the Euro-American ecumene) were not only available for the purposes of internal pro-capitalist policies and programs, but, equally importantly, for the purposes of overseas colonization and the execution of the resultant European interstate competition (which sometimes took the form of internecine warfare). The latter was effected through both direct means (militarized and unmilitarized official state "diplomacy"), as well as indirectly through the various armed monopoly trading corporations, such as the Dutch East India Company and the British East India Company. This development, needless to say, did not occur in the rest of the Afro-Eurasian ecumene.

Fourth, even as Africa, the Caribbean, and South America were forcibly drawn into the Western European economic system, whatever economic development they would experience would propel them on to a path that would eventually culminate in *underdevelopment*. To take the example of Africa, while it is true that much research still awaits to be done by relevant specialists, the broad parameters of the subject are, as of this writing, sufficiently congealed, so that only a racist inspired myopia would permit the denial of the critical role played by the Atlantic slave trade in the *current* horrendous economic predicament of the continent; for not only was it instrumental in creating the conditions that produced the European imperialism of the nineteenth-century in the first place, as just shown, but in losing tens of millions of its inhabitants to that ignominious enterprise it experienced a permanent disruption of its historical progression to such an extent as to eternally encumber it with structures that would subserviently tie its economic fate to that of its former imperial masters—even long after the nominal political fetters had been dissolved.

The mechanisms that were involved were many; those that readily come to mind include (in no particular order): the demographic imbalance, created by the massive and systematic skimming off of the most productive component of the population, deprived African societies of reservoirs of creative and productive energy; armed predation through generalized warfare put a break on peaceful economic activities including legitimate long-distance trade; the negative population growth drastically eroded whatever forces that were underway of social differentiation, urbanization, the division of labor, agricultural development, and so on (without which economic progress is impossible); the flooding of cheap manufactures from Europe and elsewhere (in exchange for captives) undermined whatever indigenous industries that existed (e.g., textiles and metalware manufacture); the development of militarized elites distorted societal priorities in terms of social, political and economic development; and some African societies engaged in the external slave trade also began to institute internal slave-based production activities, which were of course inimical to the development of balanced economies.[43]

Fifth, with the end of the more than two-decade-long fratricidal Napoleonic Wars (Napoleon was defeated at Waterloo on June 18, 1815)—which had a salutary effect on industrialization as it moved apace with that dynamic "fusion" of coal, steam, and mechanization so familiar to every school child—Europe was strategically poised militarily and economically, relative to others in the Afro-Eurasian ecumene, to commence a massive worldwide project of colonization and settlement under the aegis of a permutation, at various levels of strength (depending upon time and place), of capitalist interests (who sought raw materials and markets), nationalist religious interests (nationalist Christian missionaries looking to widen the domains of a fragmented nationalist oriented Christendom) and nationalist secular interests (motivated by intra-European state competition for global influence and advantages).

As this project got underway, Europe was in a position to make use of even greater magnitudes of coerced *land and labor-dependent* natural resources (from minerals to agricultural outputs) from its new and old colonial empires (and which simultaneously continued to provide it with markets—often forcibly commandeered, as in the legendary case of British India—for its manufactures). At the same time, Europe's, by now, large handicraft industrial sector (the protocapitalist sector) began to undergo Dickensian proletarianization on a massive scale. Here, relative to others, Europe had a distinct advantage: for, not only was it spared the need to raid the agricultural sector for this new industrial workforce, but as Pomeranz (2000) points out, access to land and labor elsewhere outside Europe meant that Europe was exempted from the necessity of extensively encumbering its own labor force with the task of exploiting scarce land in an ecologically optimal (hence labor intensive) manner—as in Asia. Compare the circumstances of the Asians in this regard: to generate an industrial labor force of a proportionally equivalent magnitude, they would have had to go into the agricultural sector as well, but in the process lower agricultural production—and they could have ill afforded that.

Sixth, once large areas of the Afro-Eurasian ecumene outside the European peninsula had become entangled in the web of Western European colonialism as the 1800s progressed, with the dawn of the twentieth-century their fate was more or less permanently sealed, both economically and militarily. They would be coerced into that classic dead-end subordinate economic position that one is all too familiar with today: net importers of manufactures *(and food staples)* and exporters of primary commodities—thereby their economies being almost immutably tethered to those of a new expanded European ecumene (to be understood here to mean Europe proper and its former settler colonies in North America, Australia, etc.). In other words, *under*development would be their lot where genuine industrial transformation would bypass them—and in the process, of course, the standards of living between those of expanded Europe and the rest of the Afro-Eurasian ecumene would diverge permanently by leaps and bounds—only Japan (and China to some extent) would be spared this fate (having escaped European colonization at a critical moment in its history). In military terms, expanded Europe would use all of its resources toward the production of weapons of ever-increasing sophistication and lethality that could never be matched by the colonized. In other words, the processes of underdevelopment that were initiated after 1492, were now reinforced with even greater severity.

Clearly, then, the so-called European miracle was in reality not so much a miracle as a conjuncture of fortuitously propitious historical factors arising out of 1492, which allowed Europe to forge a path of "capital-intensive, energy-intensive, land-gobbling" economic development, instead of taking the other path that the rest of the Afro-Eurasian ecumene had been fated to pursue: one of a "'protoindustrial cul de sac, in which even with steadily increasing labor inputs, the spread of best known production practices, and a growing commercialization making possible an ever-more efficient division of labor, production was just barely staying ahead of population growth" (Pomeranz 2000: 207). Even Adam Smith was not unaware of the transformations taking place around him wrought by the fallout from 1492:

In the mean time one of the principal effects of those discoveries [1492, etc.] has been to raise the mercantile system to a degree of splendor and glory which it could never have otherwise attained to. *It is the object of that system to enrich a great nation rather by trade and manufactures than by the improvement and cultivation of land, rather by the industry of the towns than by that of the country.* But, in consequence of those discoveries, the commercial towns of Europe, instead of being the manufacturers and carriers for but a very small part of the world (that part of Europe which is washed by the Atlantic ocean, and the countries which lie around the Baltic and Mediterranean seas), have now become the manufacturers for the numerous and thriving cultivators of America, and the carriers, and in some respects the manufacturers too, for almost all the different nations of Asia, Africa and America. Two new worlds have been opened to their industry, each of them much greater and more extensive than the old one (1961 [1776], vol. 2: 141–142. Emphasis added).

Moreover, remember that even 1492 itself did not come about as a result of yet another European "miracle," but rather it was an outgrowth of developments in the Afro-Eurasian ecumene as a whole (which included Europe of course) during the preceding 800 years or so in which the hand of Islam looms large, as shown in the preceding appendix.

To hammer home the central thesis of the foregoing, consider this thought-experiment: interchange in 1492, but only in ethnic terms, the populations of Asia with those of Africa, and the populations of the Americas with those of Europe, leaving everything else, in terms of history, the same. The world we would be living in today would still be the same structurally, except the personnel (in ethnic terms) would be different. Ethnicity has nothing to do with civilization (however one seeks to define the word). Yet the entire edifice of Eurocentric ideology that the vast majority of Europeans and their descendants subscribe to, either openly or subconsciously, is built on a foundation that is the obverse of this truism.

CONCLUSION: TYING UP LOOSE ENDS

There are three loose ends that need to be tied up as we conclude this appendix: one has to do with the *Ethiopia/Japan anomaly*; the second concerns Islam, science, and industrial transformation; and the third is about the significance of the Western Christian ideological worldview relative to 1492.

To begin with, so far, this appendix has concentrated primarily on explicating the absolutely critical role of external forces in explaining the political and economic demise of the Afro-Asian ecumene in the wake of 1492, as a much needed corrective to explanations rooted in the ideology of Eurocentrist exceptionalism that generally holds sway (even today) among Western academics in explaining this demise. However, there is the danger of going too far in the other direction; that is, neglecting completely the role of internal factors. After all, common sense alone tells us that the rise and fall of civilizations, empires, nations, and so on, are a function of a *dialectical* interplay of both internal and external factors.

The Ethiopia/Japan Anomaly

Beyond common sense, however, the importance of also considering internal factors is forced upon us by a problem that we came across in Chapters 2 and 5 and which was referred to as the Ethiopia/Japan anomaly. Specifically, the problem arose in the course of explaining the divergent histories of Japan and Ethiopia (despite the significant similarities in some key aspects of their historical trajectories, chief among them being their escape from European colonization). In fact, to highlight the importance of this matter, we can go so far as to say that a cosmic observer in, say, the fourth-century C.E. (when the Aksumite Kingdom was at its apogee), comparing the sociopolitical and economic circumstances of the two countries, would have been forgiven if he/she was to have pronounced the Ethiopians as the ones most likely to achieve the kind of economic development that the Japanese have experienced to date; for in the fourth-century Japan was still in its formative stages as a coherent national political and economic entity.

One answer that emerges from the literature faults the Ethiopians, for not being politically astute; both Marcus (1975) and Kebede (1997), for example, are of this opinion. Concentrating on the reigns of Tewedros II and Menelik II in the later nineteenth-century (which roughly cover the same period in which the Meiji reforms were underway in Japan), they conclude that, in the words of Kebede, "the failure of Ethiopian modernization [was due] more to the lack of political determination than to the inadequacy of the objective reality." That is, he continues, "[d]ue to a subjective error, the failure was caused not so much by the inappropriateness of the objective conditions as by a faltering political will" (p. 639). Levine (1997), on the other hand, suggests that despite the historical similarities between the two countries, there were also profound differences and that is where one should find the answer; the differences he points to include factors stemming from geography, level of urbanization, ethnic homogeneity, domestic peace, monetary currency, political structures and so on. In sum, he argues that "in Japan, unlike Ethiopia, an extensive commercial class and a disciplined work force were securely in place when the two countries faced a need to modernize in the course of the nineteenth-century" (p. 667).

In comparing the two explanations, Levine's at first glance is more convincing; for those of the other two really boils down to suggesting that the Japanese were simply more intelligent than the Ethiopians (a variant of Orientalism where Asians are held to be superior to Africans and others, but not Europeans). Levine's, however, also has limitations, stemming primarily from his isolation of Ethiopia from the rest of the African continent. That is to say, that what ever explanation one comes up with regarding the fate of Ethiopia, it must also be recognized that it is one that has been shared by much of the rest of the continent. In other words, the issue really is whether or not Ethiopia was colonized or whether or not the Ethiopians possessed foresight, their historical trajectory was not going to be that much different from that of the rest of the continent (including Liberia—which also did not experience European colonialism in the classic sense). Moreover, the variables he points to in explaining Ethiopia's disadvantages are more of a Eurocentrist variety (Weberian), rooted in the subjective more so than in the objective—for example, religious values that emphasized (or deemphasized) individualism, the work ethic, entrepreneurship, and so on. In other words, Levine's explanation for the Ethiopia/Japan anomaly is merely a sophisticated variant of the other two.

To explain Ethiopia's divergent fate we must place it back into Africa, which then forces us to consider two sets of dialectically interrelated factors. One set is external and these we have now looked at length; they all hinge on the rise of Europe on the back of 1492 (the Columbian factor). The other is internal. Before going on to look at the internal factors it is important to stress that their significance lie only in relation to the Columbian factor; that is, without that external factor, the internal factors would have ceased, over time, to be obstacles to the development of the African ecumene. What then were these internal factors that placed Africa at a disadvantage in relation to a surgent post–1492 Europe—and in relation to Asia as well? (In bringing in Asia, the argument here is that while both Africa and Asia were victimized by the post–1492 phenomenon, Africa [compared to Asia] was less well placed to defend itself against this victimization over the long-term; thereby emerging more economically brutalized than Asia—hence the difference in the current circumstances of the two different poles of the Afro-Asian ecumene.)

To get at the answer to this question it will help to rephrase it in another way: Why is it that even the most advanced African kingdoms, possessing complex and advanced social and political systems involving a considerable degree of labor specialization, were not able to evolve further to a stage where significant surplus production and capital accumulation would have created the potential for the emergence of a modern capitalist economic system? The immediate answer that most will be tempted to reach for, forgetting that there is an issue of temporality behind the question, is this: when *close* and *direct* contact took place between Africans and Europeans, it occurred within the context of European imperialism (taking the form, at the formal level, of the infamous Scramble for Africa); the outcome of this was "the collision of two heterogenous modes of production: capitalist and African, and the overthrow of one by another" (Coquery-Vidrovitch 1985: 114). This answer misses the point. While one agrees that the appearance of colonialism halted and deflected the relatively logical economic evolution of African societies, the question remains: Why is it that in the long period, spanning thousands of years, intervening between the establishment of first trading contacts among Africans and those from the rest of the Afro-Eurasian ecumene, and the eventual destruction of the African structures by European imperialism, the more advanced African societies did not generate technological and other advances *on a meaningful scale*, nor take up and internalize elements of externally mediated technologies, economics, cultures, and so on (to which it had access through long-distance trade), and thereby evolve a socioeconomic system that would have been better able to weather the depredations of European imperialism (or in the specific case of Ethiopia allow it to have the potential to take the Meiji Japan route)?

The answer has to do with a particular economic configuration that characterized the precapitalist African economic system that developed in Africa over hundreds of years, long before the arrival of the first European on the continent. Moreover, it is a configuration that in broadest terms was particularly applicable, *in varying degrees* of course, to much of Africa (especially in the pre-Islamic era, and to a considerable degree even in the Islamic era, though perhaps to a lesser extent in Islamic North Africa) and it was marked by a uniquely distinctive feature: the relative (the key word here is relative) impermeability between the spheres of production and exchange—incredibly strange though that this may appear at first blush. In other words, even advanced African societies were characterized by an economic system that did not allow for surplus production in a manner that could facilitate substantive economic progress; for, whatever surplus production there was, it was one that: (1) took place outside the village-level economic system (sometimes referred as the *lineage mode of production* by the "articulationists"); and (2) was aimed at long-distance trade to obtain exotic goods (consumption goods as opposed to capital goods; hence involving parasitic exploitation of resources such as slave-raiding, gold-mining and elephant-hunting [ivory]). The nature of the trade contact between Africa and the rest of the world, therefore, for a long period of time—coming all the way to the colonial era—was one that involved, essentially, luxury goods (exotic or prestige goods).[44] To elaborate, let's begin by considering the village-level economy.

The local market where villagers exchanged goods (locally produced) did not represent an economic institution mediating the realization of surplus for those marketing the goods, but rather it was "a multifunctional institution—social, religious and political" (Coquery-Vidrovitch 1985). The market constituted, in the main, a congregation of villagers who were related to each other via social, economic, and political ties. Thus here, in other words, was a situation where although the village community possessed a marketplace, in their relations with each other they did not as a general rule subscribe to the rules of market-exchange. While the presence of a marketplace does point to the presence of some surplus in the village subsistence economy, this surplus was minimal in volume, relative to the volume of production. And given that there was little incentive to effect substantial increases in production for surplus, the level of sophistication of technology demanded by the village subsistence economy remained at a very low level, typified, for instance, by the absence of even such elementary forms of agricultural technology as the plough. This low level of technological sophistication further meant that the implements of production (that is, the means of production) were accessible to all who needed them; and thereby further ensuring that no one group could monopolize ownership of the implements at the expense of another.

Side by side with the local village subsistence economy, a broad economy existed based on *long-distance* trade (and war to further facilitate this trade).That is to say, this was an economy dominated by the sphere of *exchange* (and thereby lending specificity to the African economic system). This sphere of exchange had a number of unique characteristics; including:

(1) The commodities involved in the long-distance trade, and here consideration is being restricted to the trade originating from the coasts, and not derived from production in the village economy; for not only was the surplus not large enough to meet the requirements of the trade, but there was little demand for the products of the village economy. The commodities were "produced" in an economic system largely external to the village economy; and the "production" took the form of not so much as production in the usual (manufacturing) sense of the word, but as extraction—for example, mining (gold and copper); hunting (ivory); and warring (slaves).

(2) The growth in the long-distance trade was often accompanied by the development of large bureaucratic systems (with strong military content)—usually because of the need to provide security for the traders. As a result, there arose centralized kingdoms with a sovereign at the head to oversee the maintenance of stability and security. Hymer

(1970: 42–43), explaining this development, points to the dialectic that was operative between long-distance trade and the growth of the centralized bureaucratic systems:

> Without a strong state, long-distance trade is continuously in danger of predatory attacks by armed robbers. A military group, able to maintain peace and security in a given area, can ensure the safety of traders and then tax them accordingly. This symbiotic relationship between the military and the merchants has a dynamic which can lead to the formation of larger and larger trading empires. The more effective the political and military organization is, the wider an area it can encompass, the greater the trade it can stimulate, the greater the taxes it can collect, and hence the greater an area it can pacify.

This development of centralized kingdoms, however, was essentially a *political* development, rather than an *economic* one—signifying fundamental changes in the economic system. The economic basis of these kingdoms, in other words, was not the village-subsistence economy, but rather the *extractive and parasitic* economy of external trade, warfare, and hunting. Consequently, an important aspect of the structural position of the sovereign was that given the tenuous nature of the economic base of the kingdom, the power and position of the sovereign could suffer demise at any time that the long-distance trade passing through his kingdom was deflected away from the area under his jurisdiction to that of another sovereign or authority (for whatever reason: internal instability, competition from a neighboring group, and so on—compare the demise of the Axumite kingdom with the rise of Islam and the latter's domination of trade in the Red Sea region mentioned in Chapter 2).

(3) The surplus generated from the long-distance trading activities was largely destined for the chiefs and kings, who however, either hoarded or redistributed whatever surplus that could not be consumed. They did not and could not use the surplus for investment (and thereby stimulate production) because no mechanism existed that could allow this, given the absence of organic linkages between the two economic spheres (of production and exchange). As Coquery-Vidrovitch (1985: 101) explains: "the sovereign's power was closely tied up with a specific economic formula: absolute control over a large sector of trade not integrated into local trade and a massive exchange of products rather than true trade, since the king was not looking for profit so much as ways to obtain certain merchandise from far off lands—weapons (basic to his power and his supply of slaves), textiles, alcohol, and various trade merchandise (la pacotille)." It is precisely because of this accessibility to luxury commodities generated virtually entirely within the sphere of exchange that the sovereign never felt inclined to intervene in the sphere of production (that is in the village subsistence economy).

It follows from the foregoing that the most important factor at play in sustaining the long-distance trade was not *demand* but *effective supply* (which depended not so much on production, but in Wallerstein's words (1976: 32) on "the politico-technological ability of the long-distance traders to transport the material." In this circumstance, there were two consequences: first, that no incentives existed in modifying the production process since production was not linked directly to demand variations; and second, the trade was not so much a question of transfer of surplus, but simply "a mutual windfall" as Wallerstein puts it.

To sum up, then, on the eve of the establishment of European colonial rule in Africa, the political economy of most of the continent—could be described as one dominated by a unique feature: *the absence of a meaningful level of articulation between the sphere of production and the sphere of exchange (at the territorial level).* That is, it was characterized by, on one hand, village-based subsistence production involving limited exchange of goods at the local level, and on the other, the primacy of long-distance trade involving in many instances links with coastal trade on both the Atlantic and the Mediterranean/Indian Ocean seaboards. Ergo, despite the fact that Africa was firmly tied in into the international economic system, the economies of most of its societies were not based on capitalist relations of production that could have taken advantage of economic changes elsewhere in the global system—such as in Europe.

Why did Africa come to possess such an economic system? Any number of factors may be suggested for consideration, but the most plausible one may be that of a vast, natural, resource-rich environment with an abundance of products that others outside Africa hungered for (and of course continue to do so to this day) against the backdrop of a relatively low population-to-environment ratio. However, contrary to Eurocentrist perceptions, Africa was not mired in stasis; that is, in time, African societies could have evolved past this configuration, as some had already begun to do (for instance in parts of Islamic Africa) to acquire the more typical characteristics of societies dominated by the capitalist mode of production. The opportunity for such a development, however, did not arise in Africa (including in Ethiopia), thanks to the arrival, as a direct result of the Columbian factor, of the Atlantic slave trade and later colonialism (with its distorted forms of capitalism).

Those familiar with the literature will immediately spot the source of the line of reasoning pursued in the foregoing paragraphs: the so-called *articulated modes of production* theory that was first advanced in the late 1970s and the early 1980s in response to the work of the world systems and dependency theorists such as Immanuel Wallerstein and Andre Gunder Frank, by, primarily, French neo-Marxists (the articulationists).[45] As they will recall, the theory had provoked much commotion, mainly due to the failure on the part of the critics to see the theory as nothing more than a heuristic device (and also as a result, perhaps, of a knee-jerk reaction in the positivist circles against the theory because of its Marxist lineage).[46] Representative of the rancor was the debate, for example, in the pages of a special issue of the *Canadian Journal of African Studies*.[47] For our purposes it is not necessary to go into the arcane details of the controversy generated by the theory, constituting as it is the not so atypical controversies that have marked, over the decades, the effort to comprehend the extremely difficult circumstances of the Afro-Eurasian ecumene in the post–1492 era of world history (e.g., Afrocentrism, Eurocentrism, Orientalism, Asiatic mode of production theory, lineage mode of production theory, modernization theory, Hamitic theory, dependency theory, world systems theory, and so on).[48] It will suffice to simply state this: that until we have a better alternative explanation, *but one that does not impugn the intellect of the peoples of the African ecumene,* the one presented here that relies on a dyadic consideration of the external factor (the Columbian factor) and the internal factor (the unique precapitalist African economic system) will have to do to explain why whatever Mennelik II may have wished for his people, or however much a genius he may have been, the "Meiji option" was not in the cards. (Compare also the fate of Egypt under Muhammed Ali in this regard, discussed in Chapter 3.) By the middle of the nineteenth-century, the rulers of Ethiopia (and Liberia), whether astute or feckless, would not have been able to save their country from the economic fate that befell most of the rest of the continent: dependency and underdevelopment.

Islam, Science and the Industrial Transformation

It should be, by now, obvious that the "rise of Europe" did not take place on the back of its scientific achievement. European scientific progress, especially one that would assist it toward *solidifying* its global hegemony was a phenomenon primarily of the period that *followed* long after the onset of industrial transformation. Recall that almost all major advancements that one associates with European modernity today were breakthroughs of the nineteenth and twentieth centuries (and what is more, owed less directly to scientists *as inventors* than to entrepreneurs): the Bessemer converter, rail transportation, the internal combustion engine, the breech-loading magazine rifle, the machine gun, mechanical flight, the automobile, the light bulb, the phonograph, the telegraph and radio, cinema, and so on. However, more importantly (for present purposes), during the three centuries preceding the commencement of industrial transformation, European scientific achievement was of marginal importance in that it was not a harbinger of Europe's eventual global supremacy. The industrial transformation (in terms of the flying shuttle, the spinning jenny, the cotton gin, the steam engine, etc.), in other words, was not an outgrowth of scientific advancement (had that been the case it is Italy, the hearth of European renaissance, that would have experienced the industrial transformation first, not Britain).

In fact, it would not be an exaggeration to say that the period when industrial transformation was underway was when technology led science, rather than the other way around. What is more, in the absence of 1492, these advancements would have been meaningless—assuming that they had been forthcoming. Without the backdrop of 1492, it is unlikely that major industrial transformations would have emerged at all. Even though the following truism is obvious to the point of banality, it bears repeating for the benefit of technological determinists (like White 1964): "necessity is the mother of all inventions."[49] Or to put the matter differently: science and technology does not exist independently of the material conditions of society. The 1492 factor helped to create the socioeconomic matrix in Western Europe that demanded technological innovations (see Blaut [1993], Frank [1998], and Pomeranz [2000] for a discussion of this fact). What this also implies is that even if Islamic scientific achievements had kept pace with those in Europe or remained ahead, it would not have ipso facto translated into an Islamic industrial transformation.

Notwithstanding the foregoing, however, one may still ask why Islam experienced a dramatic deceleration in scientific achievement relative to Europe. The question surfaces time and again whenever the subject of Islam and science is discussed, and there is a good reason why. For, as Sabra (1988: 88) explains: "It is precisely the high quality and sophisticated content of Islamic science that give poignancy to the problem of decline. The question is not why," he continues, "the efforts of Islamic scientists did not produce the scientific revolution (probably a meaningless question), but why their work declined and eventually ceased to develop after the impressive flowering of the earlier centuries." This question, he further observes, is "forced upon us by the fact that what we have in the extant works of Arabic scientists is not protoscience but science in the proper sense of the word." There are two possible explanations one can offer in response: one was the arrival of the Mongol catastrophe (first mentioned in the preceding paragraph), and the other was the equally devastating scourge of the bubonic plague that

historians call the "black death" (and which itself, it has been suggested, was a consequence of the Mongol catastrophe).[50]

Of these two events, one in the thirteenth and the other in the fourteenth-century,
that in a sense, broke the back of the Islamic civilization and transformed it in a very
different direction from the one that had prevailed during the classical period, the Mongol catastrophe suggests itself as the most significant; for, the characterization of the
Mongol onslaught, by Roberts (1997: 364), in these terms is certainly apt: "they blew
up like a hurricane to terrify half a dozen civilizations, slaughtered and destroyed on a
scale the twentieth-century alone has emulated, and then disappeared almost as suddenly as they came." In other words: it is not simply that the scale of the devastation
wrought, or the depth of the barbarity (neither Atilla the Hun nor the Vikings could have
held up a candle to the Mongols), or the magnitude of the geographic terrain affected
(from the outskirts of Vienna in the West to Peking in the East, from Lake Baikal in the
North to the Indus and the Bramaputra in the South) was incomparable to anything that
had occurred up to that point, but their deep disdain for civilization and its accoutrements (characteristic of most nomadic people) ensured that both the Islamic and the
Chinese civilizations would suffer major setbacks, but most especially the former.[51]

It is true that in the end the conquerors not only became one with the conquered
when some of their descendants converted to Islam (especially those of the Golden
Horde) and even more remarkably the Turks too, who in time had become the majority
willing partners in the Mongol empire building—in the classic case of "if you can't beat
them, join them"—would also convert; eventually giving rise to three new Islamic empires, the Ottoman (Eastern Europe and the Middle East), the Safavid (Persia) and the
Mogul (India), the damage it appears had been done. Certainly, Islam would never be
able to regain its glory of the classical period and the torch of science would pass into
the hands of their enemies: the Christians of Europe.

The Christian Worldview and 1492

Before we proceed, it will be instructive to introduce at this point some quotes familiar to all who know the details of what we have already seen as one of the most important events in the annals of modern human history.

They do not bear arms nor do they know them, for I showed them swords, and out of ignorance
they took by the edge and cut themselves....They ought to make good and clever servants, for I see
that they very quickly say all that I have said to them.... Our lord being pleased, I will take six of
them from here to your highnesses at the time of my departure, so that they may learn to speak....
These people are very gentle (p. 48). [If] your highnesses should so command, all of them can be
brought to Castile or be kept captive on their own island, for with fifty men you will keep them all
in subjugation and make them do anything you wish (p. 50).

[We put up a large cross] as a sign that your highnesses consider the land your own, and, most
important, as the emblem of our Lord Jesus Christ and in honor of Christianity (p. 86).

Your highnesses should believe that these lands are good and fertile... And you should believe
that this island and all of the others are, thereby, as much yours as Castile is, for nothing is lacking
here but a foothold and to command the natives to do whatever you might wish for.... They have no
weapons, and they are all naked and have no aptitude for arms... and so they are good for being
given commands and being made to till, to plant, and to do everything else that may be necessary
(p. 91).

The point of these quotes, then? They speak to this: As one goes through the absolutely fascinating volume six of the remarkable *Repertorium Columbianum, A Synoptic Edition of the Log of Columbus's First Voyage* (edited by Francesca Lardicci and published in 1999), among the several themes that jump out at the reader (for example, the shamefully relentless maniacal quest for gold; the constant amazement at how peaceful and hospitable the Taino were; the fascination with the absence of much body clothing on the Taino; the obsessively forced reading by Columbus into everything he came across as an indication that they had arrived in the Far East [India, Japan and China]; and the wonderment at the lush and unusual vegetation), is one that is of much relevance here: the almost nonchalant assumption of ownership in the spirit of "I found it first, so it is mine!" As Adam Smith, writing more than 200 years ago, would observe: "In consequence of the representations of Columbus, the council of Castile determined to take possession of countries of which the inhabitants were plainly incapable of defending themselves. The pious purpose of converting them to Christianity sanctified the injustice of the project." ("But the hope of finding treasures of gold there," he further points out, "was the sole motive which prompted him to undertake it" [1961 (1776)], vol. 2: 72.)

It appeared to have mattered little to Columbus and his men that the ownership they were establishing was over other human beings and their rightful domain and neither it appears (with the exception of perhaps a few at a later time) were their Christian consciences troubled in the least bit by, to quote Smith again, "the injustice of coveting the possession of a country whose harmless natives, far from having ever injured the people of Europe, had received the first adventurers with every mark of kindness and respect."(p. 102)[52] In other words, they were with great impunity violating that "sacred" law, *the natural law of prior claim.*[53]

The project of ownership commenced almost as soon as Columbus set sail and the process of actualizing it with the moment he and his men stumbled upon the Tainos of the Bahama Islands in 1492 and set foot on dry land with the renaming of the islands that they visited (as if their residents didn't have their own names for their islands), and then proceeded to the promulgation of Spanish dominion over the islands under Spanish law in a language that the inhabitants did not understand, literally and figuratively; the capture and transportation to Spain of some of the inhabitants; and so on. In other words, the Columbus project was also a racist project in that the peoples he encountered were considered but just one more exotica in the Edenesque landscape of the mysterious and fascinating flora and fauna; ultimately to be possessed and exploited for the purposes of self-aggrandizement.

Now, the question that emerges here is this: Where did such unabashed European arrogance regarding other peoples and their territories come from? To the Europeans like Columbus, the Tainos were not human beings, they were property; but not only that, what is of critical importance to observe here, is that they had been dehumanized long before the actual encounter was forced on them. How? When the Europeans left Europe on their journeys of exploitation in the fifteenth-century (and thereafter) they were carrying with them not only weapons of mass destruction for the time period (to use a term currently in vogue)—guns, cannons and diseases—but also an ideological worldview that was thoroughly imbued with a virulent form of ethnocentrism. One that saw other human beings that they came across as a legitimate target for murder, enslavement and dispossession of their lands. Recall too, that unlike today, for Western Europeans of the fifteenth, sixteenth, seventeenth, and eighteenth centuries, religion was not just a very, but an extremely important part of their daily lives.

How then did this highly malevolent European worldview originate? One response would be to say that it was simply capitalist greed. However, that would be too simplistic an answer, even though that was the basic motive force behind that fateful voyage. To Columbus and his backers, his project was not an evil or an unholy undertaking (religiously or otherwise); on the contrary, it was also a "Christian" project (see, for example, Watts 1995). After all, like other people of his day, Christian piety was an integral part of his person. It is the contention here that it was born out of the development of a Western European ethnocentrification of Christianity (or more simply put, Westernization of Christianity); that is a Christianity that no matter its Eastern provenance, was now thoroughly laced with Western European ethnocentrism.[54] In essence, what this meant is that at the most basic experiential-level for most ordinary Western European Christians, Christ had been plucked out of the Middle East, shorn of his Semitic ethnic heritage, and reincarnated as a European-born savior—as is so well attested by Christian iconography to this day.

The Westernization of Christianity itself, however, in turn, rested on three principal factors: the development of the East-West schism (also referred to as the *Schism of 1054*), the mythologization of the Curse of Ham, and the launching of the Crusades against the Muslims. The second factor, the Biblical Curse of Ham, where the descendents of the three sons of Noah, (Japhet, Shem and Ham) were, through mythological trickery, imbued with a spiritually and materially corrupting racial hierarchy, has already been described at some length in Chapter 2—so it need not detain us here further. As for the first factor, it is not necessary to go into the whyfors and wherefores of the schism other than to note that it entailed political rivalry between the two major centers of Christianity: Rome and Constantinople. The rivalry itself was an outcome of an evolving papal monarchy in Western Europe seeking to define the realm of its domain, Christendom, and which found a doctrinal basis for it—leading eventually to the separation of the two geographic wings of the Church and mutual excommunications of their pontiffs in 1054—namely, whether the Holy Ghost issued just from the Father (Byzantine belief) or from both the Father and the Son (Roman Catholic belief). It may be noted in parenthesis that in historical terms, the year 1054 should be considered as nominal rather than strictly factual; that is, its a historiographical device of convenience; for, phenomenon of this kind tend to be part of a long-term process that cannot be pinned down to a single date. One is not surprised therefore, when Runciman (1955) convincingly shows that, in terms of permanence, the real cause of the East-West schism were the Crusades because they introduced a powerful political factor (control of the symbolically important Holy Land) into the rivalry that could not be as easily dealt with as would have been possible with respect to mere doctrinal difference over the nature of the Holy Ghost. As he pithily puts it: "The Crusaders brought not peace but a sword; and the sword was to sever Christendom" (p. 101).

What is of importance here is the consequence of this rift for others over the long-term: it rendered true Christianity in the eyes of Westerners as essentially the Christianity as promulgated by the Western Church for they came to view the eastern Orthodox Church, in time, as a church of heretics. That the eastern Christians were also ethnically and linguistically different (Greeks, Syrians, etc.) was not coincidental in the evolution and cementing of this perception. Under the circumstances, it is not surprising that the eastern Christians that the Crusaders encountered were sometimes victimized by them just as much as the Muslims were. Courbages and Fargues (1997: 47), point out that it was not unusual for the Crusaders to slaughter the eastern Christians as well because they appeared to them to look like Muslims in terms of their dress and appearance (and plus, of course, they spoke a different language). They further note that for both political and economic reasons the eastern Christians were quickly reduced to the same juridical inferior status as that of the remaining Muslims and Jews, and they suffered "the supreme humiliation," of having the Church of the Holy Sepulchre wrested from their stewardship; the Latin Christians would now be in charge of the church.

In fact, Daniel (1989a: 6), goes further by noting that: "As soon as the pilgrims left the Latin world, and long before they met a [Muslim], they came into conflict with cultures, different from their own, and an inflexible Latin cultural intolerance remained with most of them throughout the crusading period." He continues: "From the beginning, it was implicit in Urban's decision to preach the crusade at all, in his choice of Clermont, and in the way he was understood in the West, that the crusade in the East should be an expansion of Western European society." In fact, as the Crusading project matured, the culturally rooted mutual antagonism between the Easterners and the Westerners, where each thought that the other was guilty of un-Christian and perfidious behavior, reached such heights that some ecclesiastical leaders in the West even talked about launching a holy war against the Byzantines themselves! (especially after the failure of the Second Crusade). Runciman (1955: 128) describes the situation well: "It began to shock the West that the precious relics kept at Constantinople should be in the hands of such un-Christian owners. It was after the Second Crusade that the ordinary Westerner began to regard the East Christian as being something less than a fellow Christian."

However, it wasn't simply the matter of the disastrous failure of the Second Crusade (the blame for which, quite unfairly, was laid by the Franks at the door of the Byzantines), but the problem went even much deeper, as just noted; Runciman himself alludes to it: "They had set out to rescue Western Christendom, but when they came to the land of the East Christians they found it strange and unwelcoming. The language was incomprehensible, the great cities unfamiliar and alarming. The Churches looked different; the priests with their black beards and buns and black robes were quite unlike any Christian priests they had seen before.... [and so on]" (p. 80). The Byzantines, for their part, saw the Franks, perhaps justifiably, as nothing less than an uncultured, thieving, insolent and blood thirsty rabble that had arrogated to itself the Crusading project. Any notion of even nominally submitting to the authority of the papacy was unthinkable. "How could they possibly allow their great and holy Church to submit itself to the domination of a bishop belonging to such a people" (p. 128). Courbages and Fargues (1997: 53) go so far as to suggest that the degree of mutual animosity between the Easterners and the Westerners was such that the Eastern Christians (and Jews too, of course) may have collaborated with the Muslims when, under Saladin, the Muslims retook Jerusalem in 1187. In the end, the Latin Christians could not be held back; under papal approval (Pope Innocent III, to be recanted by him later), and instigated by the greed of the Venetians, the Fourth Crusader Army entered Constantinople, on April 13, 1204, to unleash a three-day orgy of bloodshed, looting and destruction of the Byzantine capital.[55] This event stands out as among the clearest examples of the depth of intolerance exhibited by the Christian ignorantsia from the West toward other ethnicities, even those who were fellow Christians!

Against the backdrop of such history, is it any wonder then that in centuries to come, Westerners would regard Christians of other races (blacks, Latinos, Native Americans, etc.) as not worthy of full equality—racially or spiritually—even though the missionary effort to seek their conversion was actively pursued. How else can one explain the collusion of the European clergy with the racial segregation of the peoples they converted, including their enslavement and exploitation? So blinded were the Westerners by their ethnocentrism that they saw no contradiction in this regard—and notwithstanding the fact that Christ himself was not a Western European, but an Easterner, a Semite of Palestinian Jewish descent. (One may legitimately conjecture here that had the Crusaders come across Christ himself, they would have probably killed him too in their disbelief at his appearance.) Like the second factor, the third factor, too, rested on yet another Western perversion of Biblical teachings: "thou shalt not kill," was now converted into "thou shalt kill so you may attain the Kingdom of Heaven." Thusly were the struggles of the emerging *papal monarchy* (this apt term is borrowed from Mastnak [2002: 130], implying "a universal Christian society under the supreme rule of the papacy") with the Muslims on one hand, and, this is important to emphasize, *with the temporal powers within Western Europe itself, on the other*, over the definition of the internal (political) and external (geographic) boundaries of Christendom, now acquire a violent expression: the launching of the Crusades.[56]

Before proceeding further, one is forced to preface what follows with this observation: centuries of derisory glance-backs at the medieval period by European historians in general (hence once upon a time the label the Dark Ages) have left their mark—the lack of full appreciation among them of the magnitude of the impact of the Crusades on the development of Western European institutions and psyche, even long after the last Crusader had put down his sword. Yet, as Brundage (1997: 251), for example, has pointed out, without the Crusades, Europe would not have evolved in the manner it did; for, "the incorporation of processes, systems and ideas that originated in medieval attempts to reconquer the Holy Land," he explains, "remained part of European life for centuries after crusading had ceased." Consequently, in establishing the importance of the Crusades for the development of Western European thinking regarding other peoples down the centuries, coming all the way to the present, one must be forewarned against the temptation to dismiss it from the historical calculus.[57]

To move on, by the time Pope Urban II had launched the First Crusade with his sermon on Thursday, November 27, 1095, the papacy had over the course of nearly three centuries following the arrival of the Muslims in Europe in the eighth-century, slowly developed the notion that the entire planet was potentially a Christian realm to be headed by a papal monarchy and that to bring this into fruition was the objective of a Christian *just war* to be waged against any one who stood in the way of this project, and in which violence, plunder, enslavement, and so on, was now deemed as morally permissible for Christians. The first step in the creation of this global Christian realm, which notice was a religious, political, and economic project intertwined together, was the eradication of Islam from Europe and the Middle East, and later from the Afro-Asian land mass as well, and the second was to simultaneously work toward ensuring the subservience of the European princes and monarchies to papal authority—the Crusades had the potential to achieve both. However, the latter objective was part of a dyadic goal: the Crusading project would not only be a papal controlled mechanism for temporal authorities to acquire legitimacy ("you are either with us or you are against us," to borrow the current phrase in vogue—and notice—involving essentially the same protagonists, Westerners and Muslims, even after almost 1,000 years), but it would also help to achieve at one and the same time peace among the warring factions within Europe itself, without which the authority of the papal monarchy would be greatly undermined. (Under the circumstances, it is not surprising then, as Mastnak [2002] points out, that the "liberation" of the Holy Land in the later stages of the Crusades became of secondary importance to the broader goal of expanding ad infinitum the borders of Christendom.)

To effect such a grandiose project there was the very "small" problem of how to convince a superstitious, highly parochial, illiterate, and ignorant peasantry (and the nobility was not too far behind either in these terms) to abandon their fields and villages and journey hundreds of miles to a foreign land—in an age where there were no trains, planes, cars or bicycles, to do battle with the infidel; and what is more, at one's own expense! As it turned out, in this regard, the papacy need not have been too overly concerned; the response from the European populace went beyond its wildest dreams. The question is, Why?[58] In a time when religion was of such great importance to people's daily lives, where piety was universal, that is it was as much the preserve of the laity as of the clergy, four factors appear to have been highly significant in underwriting the magnitude of this positive response: one, was the promise of religious deliverance through penance, martyrdom and the forgiveness of one's sins (see Maier [2000], and Riley-Smith [1997]); two, was the promise of adventure, booty, and so on; three, was the notion that the Crusades were an extension of the effort to bring universal peace to Christendom (*pax Dei* and *treuga Dei*, that is, the "Peace of God" and the "Truce of God")—itself a project undertaken by the papacy as a device to keep an increasingly upsurgent secular authority at bay (Mastnak 2002); and four, was the propaganda-driven systematic vilification of Islam and the demonization of the Muslims (without which of course the other three factors become irrelevant). It is the fourth factor that is of interest here. Initially, Mastnak suggests, the general view of Muslims held by Christians, at least until the eleventh-century, was that they were one among a number of other Christian enemies (Jews, Magyars, Norsemen, Slavs, etc.); with the launching of the Crusades however, their perceptions changed dramatically: the Muslims were now the chosen enemy. How was this change in attitudes effected? He explains:

In practical life, ignorance is often a powerful argument. The fact that Latin Christians knew nothing (or next to nothing) about Islam did not prevent them from making Muslims the enemy of Christianity and Christendom.... Urban II raised to new heights the hostility toward the Muslims that had hitherto been dormant in the Latin West. Without the elaboration of this enemy image, the new holy war, the crusade, was unimaginable. Whereas from the Carolingian times onward, holy wars had been fought against infidels in general, the crusade was at its inception the war of Christendom against the Muslims, "animated by a generalized hatred of Islam" (p. 115—see also Vitkus 1999).

It is instructive to note that even the fact that for centuries Christian pilgrims had been allowed to visit the Muslim-held Jerusalem (except for a brief atypical period under al-Hakim) and to travel through Muslim lands unmolested, or the fact of the ubiquitous Levantine trade involving Christian and Muslim (and Jewish) merchants, appeared to have had no mitigating effect on the anti-Muslim hysteria that would now be whipped up by the papacy.[59] The truth is that at the time when the First Crusade was launched, Mastnak (2002: 118) points out, the Muslims were at peace with Western Europe, and that the Eastern Christians who lived among them were, notwithstanding Urban II's propaganda, going about their business as they had always done under Muslim rule. "They continued to live as a subject minority population, protected by Islamic law, paying taxes, and having a measure of freedom of worship" (p. 118–119—see also Courbages and Fargues 1997). (After all, recall from Chapter 2 that the acceptance of the diversity of faiths, ethnicities and cultures was built into the genesis of the Islamic civilization.)

Moreover, given that the Crusades were a response to primarily internal Western European developments and not to anything that the Muslims were doing, to the Christian patriots it would have mattered little had they known that the Muslims on their side regarded them relatively benignly as the *People of the Book*—that is as adherents of a religion that was regarded as legitimate, so much so that even in the hereafter, the Muslim heaven was not barred to them. Neither would have their Christian patriotic fervor weakened in the least had they known that Muslims revered Christ as among a long line of prophets (Abraham, Moses, and so on—with Prophet Muhammed being the last); or that the God of the Christians (and the Jews) was the same God that the Muslims worshipped; or that Jerusalem was sacrosanct to the Muslims (and to the Jews) too, or that the Muslims, even when the Crusades were in full swing, did not see the invading hostile Christians as part of a global war of Christianity versus Islam (Hillenbrand 1999)—much to their own detriment as they would find out centuries later (for, as Daniel 1989a: 38, points out "there is a clear continuous line from the crusades to the aggressive imperialism of the Western European powers in the Levant and North Africa in the nineteenth-century"); and so on. Had they known all this it would not have mattered: for, the view that was now adopted in Western Europe under papal propaganda was not only that Islam should be eradicated from the face of the earth, but that its believers were beyond redemption; so much so that even an attempt at their conversion was considered futile.

Daniel (1989b: 77) in his exegesis on the character and mechanics of the ecclesiastical engineered and managed Crusade propaganda describes admirably the context from which such thinking arose: "To establish that a whole religion, society, lex, was in every respect the reverse or denial of European society was immensely helpful in creating a mental as well as a physical frontier. It was the best war propaganda in that it made the enemy the proper recipients of treatment unworthy of humanity in ordinary conditions." He continues: "The evil alleged of Islam made the rules of the crusade, or of the just war, emotionally acceptable. All war is more effective if it is fought with hatred and if the humanity of the enemy is minimized." Not surprisingly, throughout the Crusading project, but most especially in the early phases, missionary work among the Muslims was rarely part of the papal calculus.[60] On the contrary, there arose says Mastnak (2002: 126), a new kind of love: a Christian love that was exclusive to Western European Christians and therefore one that did not include those who were of other faiths (or even other Christians if they were of a different ethnicity). Consequently, "[t]he new exclusivity of Christian love—love that inspired the use of violence— opened the gate for the crusader's shocking brutality toward the Muslims" (p. 126). But it went even beyond this; as Mastnak explains:

A disciplinary force within the Christian family, love turned into the annihilation of those outside the family. The power of that love was expressed in the fullness of hatred.... The destruction of paganism, the eradication of infidel peoples, became logical and necessary. Ideally, Christian holy war was genocidal, the ultimate victory in that war was genocide, and the peace achieved was the peace of the cemetery: perpetual peace (pax perpetua)—"for the dead do not fight any longer." Integration of the infidel into Christian society, which perceived itself as a manifestation of the absolute, was inconceivable. "In Christendom, there is no place for non-Christians" (pp. 126–127).

Against this religious ideological background, is it any surprise at all that when both ordinary and elite Europeans first made contact with other peoples outside Western Europe on a global scale from the fifteenth-century onward, it occurred in the context of European greed, but underwritten by a hate and distrust developed over the centuries of peoples of other faiths and ethnicities?[61] It is from this perspective that one must view the behavior of the first Europeans who set out across the oceans in search of riches (and notice the coincidence of timing: it occurred on the heels of the Crusades, of which the last was when the province of Granada in Spain, the remaining Muslim stronghold, was overrun by the Spanish Christians). In making this point, it is not to detract in any way from the fact that the European seaborne ventures were primarily economic projects, but that the ecclesiastical imprimatur on these projects also rendered them religious exercises in which all Western Christians were enjoined to participate. The path to the kingdom of heaven, therefore, also lay through the plunder and murder of others in far off lands (and in one's backyard too—reference here is to the pogroms). As Mastnak (2002: 346) points out: "As an ideal and as a movement, the Crusades had a deep, crucial influence on the formation of Western civilization, shaping culture, ideas, and institutions."

Consequently, is it any surprise that when the first conquistadors arrived in the Americas (at whose hands, in an unimaginable, relentless orgy of bloodbath, entire civilizations and peoples would disappear within the short period of a lifetime or two) they did so accompanied by crusader iconography, as Brundage (1997: 260) observes. "Thus both the intellectual and institutional foundations of European expansion in the sixteenth-century," he further continues, "rested squarely on the medieval crusades, which provided their rationale and much of their structure." Imperialism, regardless of the forms it took, was not just an economic phenomenon, it was also an ideological phenomenon in which a Westernized Christianity played a prominent role. Yet, sadly, this is not all: the Westernization of Christianity laid the groundwork for the ecclesiastical acceptance of racism, slavery and exploitation, *even when the victims were Christians*, so long as the Christians were of a different ethnicity. This was most graphically demonstrated when Westernized Christianity was introduced in European colonies in Africa, in the Americas and in Australasia. This Christianity proved no barrier to the mass enslavement of Africans and Native Americans—their eventual conversion to Christianity notwithstanding; and a Western European God accepted, apparently without so much as a dissenting murmur, even racially segregated worship.

To return now to the discussion that opened this chapter: so it was that the descendants of those who had thwarted the westward European advance of Islam, in the eighth-century in France, arrived about 1,000 years later under the leadership of Napoleon Bonaparte, in 1798, in Egypt to inaugurate a different future for North Africa (and the rest of the African continent).[62] Yes, it is true that France was not the first European power to succeed in imposing its will on a North African country, even if only temporarily. Recall that Portugal had captured the Moroccan city of Ceuta in 1415. That, however, was a different time period because the relative political and economic strength of the North Africans had not yet diverged greatly from that of their enemies; the Portuguese would be decisively defeated at the Battle of the Three Kings by Moroccan forces in 1578.

Two hundred or so years later, however, times had changed, for Western Europe had had time to draw succor from 1492 and qualitatively transform itself. The era of modern Western imperialism underwritten by an emergent industrial capitalism had now begun. That this was a new era is most clearly highlighted by the fact that in the preceding 300 years or so, even as Africa had been buffeted by the winds of predation unleashed by the Atlantic slave trade, it had largely retained its political autonomy (with the exception of one or two European intrusions on the continent, such as at the southern tip); yet a mere 100 years or so after Napoleon, virtually the entire continent had been carved up by Western European powers.

NOTES

1. Lest there are doubts as to the relevance of this appendix—one can almost hear the words: It is all very interesting, but is it really relevant?—it should be further pointed out that the importance of explaining (in contrast to describing) the arrival of European imperialism in Africa also stems from consideration of two other kindred issues: one, the necessity to bring awareness of this subject to those in the West today who, motivated by good intentions, would like to assist in the revival of the sorry fortunes of higher education in Africa. The history of aid relations between Africa and the West is replete with examples of good intentions gone awry because of the subtle and sometimes not so subtle "we-know-better-than-you-what-is-good-for-you" arrogance that has often tainted these relations. It is an arrogance that is underwritten by a Eurocentric reading of world history, to which this appendix aims to provide a corrective. Two, to allow these same people to gain at least a modicum of understanding of the historical basis of the awful economic predicament that faces much of Africa today (in terms of national development) and from which the fate of African higher education cannot be separated. While it is true, of course, that to place the blame for this predicament entirely at the door of Western imperial history—specifically the post–Columbian portion of history that saw the eventual hijacking of the African historical trajectory by the West—and thereby absolve Africans of any complicity in this predicament would be a gross distortion of the truth; the fact still remains, however, that sentiments such as the following that continue to be espoused by many Westerners and articulated here by that doyen of unrepentant Western arrogance, the U.S. American economist P. T. Bauer, is nothing more than confabulation of the truth: Beginning with some lines from W. B. Yeats ("Come, fix upon me that accusing eye. I thirst for accusation."), he goes on to unfold such drivel as this: "Acceptance of emphatic routine allegations that the West is responsible for Third World poverty reflects and reinforces Western feelings of guilt.... Yet the allegations can be shown to be without foundation. They are readily accepted because the Western public has little first-hand knowledge of the Third World, and because of widespread feelings of guilt. The West has never had it so good, and has never felt so bad about it" (1981: 66). In other words, pseudointellectuals like Bauer ignorantly refuse to accept the fact that the same structuration of the post–Columbian Atlantic economic system that decisively propelled Western Europe to modernity also simultaneously placed Africa in the straitjacket of underdevelopment (not to be mistaken with undevelopment) and dependence.

2. The word *transformation* (e.g., "industrial transformation") is to be preferred to the more common usage of *revolution* (e.g., "agricultural revolution") when referring to the major changes in

agricultural and industrial technology that began to appear and cumulatively accelerate as the seventeenth-century wore on. A revolution is always suggestive of a quick, decisive, and wholesale break with the past; yet no such break can be clearly identified in the history of Western Europe where these revolutions are first said to have occurred. Adoption of new technologies is always a haphazard process and takes place over considerable lengths of time (and sometimes only transiently). Even more importantly, however, technological change does not occur in a vacuum; it is always part of not only wider socioeconomic and political historical processes, but it occurs on the back of existing technology. That is, even within the so-called industrial revolution there was historical continuity. In other words, the terms industrial revolution or agricultural revolution signify ahistorical categories; hence they are nothing more than a historian's figment of imagination. (See also Cameron [1994], for a review of the historiographical treatment of this issue.)

Note also that if the process of technological change that Europe experienced, as it moved toward the era of industrial capitalism, is viewed in this manner then it also takes care of one of the red herrings that Eurocentrists are often obsessed with and expressed in the question: Why did the industrial revolution take place in Europe? (Underlying this question, of course, are the usual myths associated with the notion that this was something very uniquely European that Europe experienced and which the rest of the world did not and could not.) Technological change is an ongoing process, but most importantly: manufacturers will adopt new technologies if and when it suits them. (This simple logic appears to escape Eurocentrists. There is, in truth, no evidence to support the bizarre Eurocentric notion of fortuitous autonomous technological change in Europe giving rise to production for the market; yet, as Inikori's work [2002], for example, reminds us, there is plenty of evidence proving the logical, that is the opposite.) This phenomenon was not unique to Europe; it existed throughout the Afro-Eurasian ecumene wherever products were manufactured for the market. After all, as was indicated in the preceding appendix, there was a time when the East was far ahead technologically than the West—the presence of such industries as sugar manufacture, paper making, high-quality steel manufacture, ceramics, sericulture, cotton textiles, and so on, long before Europe acquired them provides ample testimony. (How come then one does not talk about an industrial revolution in the East?)

In other words, if 1492 had not taken place then one can confidently assert that Europe (specifically Western Europe) would not have experienced the level of industrial transformation that it underwent. (Conversely, had the rest of the Afro-Eurasian ecumene experienced the same economic opportunities that 1492 created, then they too would have experienced the same kind of industrial transformation.) The need to produce for expanding internal and external markets which, note, included the pursuit of the economic strategy of import substitution on a very large-scale (the cotton textile industry in England being a classic case—and recall too that there was a time when Europeans did not even know what cotton was, a fact that in itself speaks volumes for the low level of economic development in Europe prior to 1492) led manufacturers to innovate when new technologies became available through their own efforts or those of others. However, this was always contingent upon their realization that it was in their economic interest to do so, meaning whether they saw the need to over come whatever bottlenecks they may have been facing—e.g., an inferior quality product, high wage labor, high energy costs, low production-runs, and so on—in outsmarting the domestic (within Europe), as well as international (outside Europe), competition. (See Pomeranz [2000]. For more on the role of the import substitution industrialization strategy in the industrial transformation of Europe see Inikori [2002].) *But this can hardly qualify as a uniquely European response that took place at a unique time in world history.* On the contrary, this is a response that is intrinsic to the logic of any manufacturing activity aimed at the market, without regard to time and place.

3. In fact on this point it is worth noting, albeit on the basis of anecdotal evidence, that no one from outside the West who has had the experience of interacting for a sufficient length of time with Westerners (regardless of who they are in terms of their multiple social locations: working class/middle class, male/female, liberal/conservative, student/teacher, Marxist/non-Marxist,

young/old,   clergy/laity,   progressive/nonprogressive,   academic/nonacademic,   politi-
cian/nonpolitician, and so on (including those who profess to be anti-racists) can avoid noticing an
ideological perspective—sometimes expressed blatantly, but more often, in the world of the twenty-
first century, expressed innocently and unselfconsciously in the subtlest of ways—shared by almost
all of them with few exceptions (of which there are, but remember: exceptions only prove the rule),
a self-confident arrogance characterized by a "we are more intelligent than you, better than you,
more civilized than you" superiority complex vis-à-vis those who are not Westerners by origin; that
is, those who are, from their perspective, not "whites" or Europeans. In part this attitude is a result
of growing up in a racist society, but in part it is also an outcome of being taught misguided, simplistic and plainly false histories (symbolized in the United States, for instance, by the institution of
the two public holidays, Columbus Day and Thanksgiving Day). This is not a new phenomenon by
any means given that it has roots that go back to the Crusades; it is its persistence in this day and
age that elicits notice. Under the circumstances, is it any wonder at all, then, that such arrogance
has also seeped into Western scholarship (with rare exception) on almost all matters relating to the
world outside the West, including explaining the genesis of the current Western hegemonic domination of the planet.

4. Writing more than three decades ago, Hodgson (1993: 86), would respond to this kind of
shallow history thusly: "All attempts that I have yet seen to invoke premodern seminal traits in the
Occident can be shown to fail under close historical analysis, once other societies begin to be
known as intimately as the Occident. This applies also to the great master, Max Weber, who tried to
show that the Occident inherited a unique combination of rationality and activism. [Yet] ...most of
the traits, rational or activist, by which he sought to set off the Occident either are found in strength
elsewhere also; or else, so far as they are unique (and all cultural traits are unique to a degree), they
do not bear the weight of being denominated as so uniquely 'rational' as he would make them." As
he goes on to specifically address Weber's views on Western law and theology, he points out that
that Weber "partly mistook certain sorts of formalism for rationality, and partly simply did not
know the extent among Muslims, for instance, of a probing rational drive."

5. Note that the concept of *Eurocentrism*, as Amin (1989) has pointed out, embodies two
senses: one signifies values (in the form of racism, bigotry, prejudices, etc.), while the other refers
to a presumed empirical reality (embodied in the notion of European exceptionalism or historical
priority as constituting a historical actuality). While it is possible that not all Eurocentrists are
guilty of subscribing to the concept in both senses in that theoretically one can believe in the em-
piricism of European exceptionalism without holding any racist prejudices, it is difficult to imagine
that the two can be separated in practice because subscription to the first is bound to seduce one
into subscription to the other. In other words, to believe in the myth of European exceptionalism
and simultaneously believe in the equality and dignity of all human beings does not appear to be a
viable project in practice; certainly those from outside the West who interact with Westerners generally, going by anecdotal evidence, see this to be the case. Additionally: it may also be pointed out
(as Blaut [1993] does) that Eurocentrism does not refer to a love of things European, but of believing that things European are inherently superior to things elsewhere; for example, to be a lover of
European cuisine does not in of itself make one a Eurocentric, but on the other hand the belief that
European cuisine is superior to that of others, does.

6. Like many of their contemporaries, these men were not immune from racist views of other
peoples outside the West, and depending on whose writing one is considering, they saw people outside the West as mentally inferior, civilizationally backward, irrational, in need of Western tutelage
and aid, and so on. See for example, Jung (1964), Piaget (1971) and Weber (1967, and 1998). Even
Marx, no matter how indisputably brilliant he was in his analysis of the development of capitalism
within Europe, when it came to considering the historical trajectories of societies outside Europe,
was unable to break out of the Eurocentric cocoon of ignorance that many scholars of his day had
fashioned for themselves. Here, for example, is how he portrayed the economies of Asia: "[I]n most
of the Asiatic landforms, the comprehensive unity standing above all these little communities [vil-

lages] appears as the higher proprietor or as the sole proprietor; the real communities hence only as hereditary possessors.... The surplus product—which is, incidentally, determined by law in consequence of the real appropriation through labor—thereby automatically belongs to this highest unity. Amidst oriental despotism and the propertylessness which seems legally to exist there, this clan or communal property exists in fact as the foundation, created mostly by a combination of manufactures and agriculture within the small commune.... A part of their surplus labor belongs to the higher community, which exists ultimately as a person, and this surplus labor takes the form of tribute, and so on, as well as of common labor for the exaltation of the unity, partly of the real despot, partly of the imagined clan-being, the god" (Marx 1973: 472–473). This exceedingly stereotyped and naive portrayal of the highly complex and diverse economies of Asia as essentially mired in stasis (unlike in the West) was characteristic of Marx's episodic writings generally about societies outside Europe; and the damage was done: generations of Marxist and Marxist-inspired scholars would labor under the yoke of Marxian Eurocentrism. As for Hegel (Marx's mentor in spirit), his views have already been mentioned in Appendix I. (See also Dalal [1988] on Jung; and Bailey and Llobera [1981], Chandra [1981], Hindess and Hirst [1975], and Avineri [1968] on Marx.)

Note: given their unquestioningly significant scholarly contributions to some areas of knowledge, in categorizing people like Marx, Weber, and so on, as racists, creates some discomfort among even those enlightened academics who would normally have no difficulty in calling a mango a mango when grappling with sensitive topics; so Blaut (1993: 65), for example, has sought to minimize their racism by referring to it as "moderate racism" (in contrast to what he calls "classical racism"). This is a specious distinction (in the order of moderately pregnant) because the so-called moderate racism is always pregnant with the potential to degenerate into classical racism under appropriate circumstances (classic examples of this phenomenon are to be found in the histories of Nazi Germany, apartheid South Africa, the Jim Crow South (in the United States) and in modern-day Serbia, Israel, and so on. (Here is a thought-experiment: Would these Western luminaries of the past—or even those of the present—ever have deigned to invite black scholars into their homes to break bread with them [and thereby acknowledge their humanity]?) Furthermore, today examples of this process in the West can be seen whenever issues such as immigration, affirmative action, terrorism, and so on, surface to the forefront of public discourse. In this regard see, for example, Bonilla-Silva's work (2003).

7. For an excellent rebuttal of Jones see Blaut (2000); other counter-Eurocentric sources mentioned in this chapter are also pertinent at a more general level (such as Frank 1998—interestingly, he makes no reference to Blaut's either work, 1993 or 2000.)

8. The core elements of the canon of Western exceptionalism (of which the work of people like Jones is emblematic) are generally familiar to almost all at some basic level, both to Westerners and the rest of the world alike, given that when woven together they emerge as that almost universally accepted Western ideology, the ideology of Western modernity—which asserts that the West is not only superior to the rest of the world in every way, *but it is entitled to exercise hegemony over the planet* since it alone is authentically modern because modernity is a trait that is part of the genetic makeup of the Westerner (though, of course, it is not, these days, always expressed thusly)—and they need only be recapped here briefly in their various permutations of (a) plain factual untruths, (b) factual distortions, (c) ahistoricism, (d) contradictions, (e) ideologically driven ignorance, (f) technological determinism, (g) hypocrisy, (h) erroneous mirror-projections of images of the present on to the past, (i) environmental determinism, (j) confusion between cause and symptom, and so on, to name some of the ethnocentrically driven acrobatic moves against empirical truth:

- Europeans (specifically the "white race") have superior biological qualities that sets them apart from other human beings: they are, compared to everybody else, more intelligent, courageous, creative, enterprising, freedom-loving, adventurous, and so on. (At one point in history, it may be noted, such a view was generally reserved for Western Europeans alone, not all Europeans).

This is why Europe was the first to achieve modernity (while the rest of the world could only be coaxed into imitation; or, if necessary, forced into imitation through the benevolent agency of colonialism and imperialism—the white man's burden.).

- It is only Europeans who possess the true religion, Christianity; consequently, not only are they the chosen recipient's of God's blessings (as expressed in the trappings of modernity), but they have a duty to provide guidance to the rest of the world—by force if necessary.
- Unlike everybody else, Europeans are inherently highly rational beings and that is why they were able to invent modernity.
- The superior inventiveness of the European mind led to critical autonomous technological advances in the Middle Ages that set the stage for Europe's passage to modernity and global dominance.
- The Asian ruling classes were too fond of luxuries; therefore they were unable to amass their surpluses for investment, instead consuming them in an orgy of sumptuous living.
- The nuclear family, with marriages based on romantic love, are uniquely European social inventions which helped to propel Europe toward modernity.
- The Chinese did come up with some important technological inventions, but they didn't have the requisite intelligence to exploit these inventions in the manner that the Europeans were able to do.
- The Asians, unlike Europeans, had an irrational love for precious metals, and so instead of using it for economic development they simply sat on it (the infamous "hoarding" thesis).
- Europeans, unlike the peoples of the Afro-Asian ecumene (for example), are less prone to sexual over-indulgence and therefore, historically, they were able to avoid "Malthusian disasters" that supposedly flow from over-population. (Paradoxically, massive population expansion within Europe is also cited as a positive aspect of European history that accounts for its rise.)
- Only Europe had a genuine aristocracy, others did not; therefore only Europe had a class of people capable of shepherding it to modernity.
- The Muslims may have possessed some science, but it was all borrowed science (they couldn't have had the intelligence to create any new science).
- In complete contrast to Europe, tropical areas (such as Africa or India) are inherently inimical to civilizational progress because their natural environments are highly disease prone, agriculturally infertile, endemically liable to natural disasters, mentally debilitating and lethargy inducing (because of the heat), unchallenging in terms of imagination and creativity (because of the abundant natural food supply available through hunting and gathering), transportationally handicapped (because of unnavigable rivers), and so on.
- Asians were inherently despotic, traditional, irrational, superstitious, and civilizationally stagnant in part because that is their character, and in part because of living in arid regions that required large oppressive state bureaucracies to manage water supply through irrigation (the infamous theory of the "hydraulic society" and its consequence: "Oriental despotism.")
- If other parts of the world are poorer and destitute relative to the West then it is entirely their fault, for their condition has nothing to do with the West (consequently no Westerner need really lose any sleep over the matter). On the contrary, they should be thankful that if it wasn't for the West who brought them all the benefits of modernity, their condition would be even worse than it is today.
- European colonialism and imperialism was (and is) a positive force on the planet because it brought democracy, freedom and economic progress (modernity) to the entire planet. (That imperialism by its very nature is undemocratic is an issue that is sidestepped here. The corollary of this view is that if any country seeks to advance and prosper today, then its only recourse is to imitate Western cultural and economic attributes; failure to do so is to court poverty and underdevelopment. The fact that the Western consumerist lifestyle rests on immense waste and the highly disproportionate, relative to population, unjust consumption of the world's re-

sources—not to mention such factors as environmental destruction, pollution, near slave-like exploitation of labor, and so on—is in terms of this view not a matter worthy of attention.)

It should be noted that those parts of this listing that relate specifically to Asian societies form a subconstruct of Eurocentrism called *Orientalism*. (Orientalists study, admire, and may even have a grudging respect for Asian civilizations, but it is always from the viewpoint that in the last analysis they are inferior to Western civilization.) This list is based on a number of sources, of which the following stand out for mention: Anderson (1979); Bauer (1981); Baechler, Hall, and Mann (1988); Blum (1978); Brenner (1997); Cipolla (1996); Diamond (1997); Hagen (1964); Hall (1985); Huntington (1924); Landes (1988); Levy-Bruhl (1985); Macfarlane (1978); Mann (1986, and 1993); Moore (1966); Wittfogel (1957); and White (1964). See also, of course, Jones (2003). For sources specifically dealing with Orientalism the classic is of course the 1978 work of the same title by the late Professor Edward Said. On this latter subject see also Halliday (1993); Hussain, Olson, and Qureshi (1984); Macfie (2000); Prakash (1995); Rahme (1999); Rodinson (2002); and Said and Paul (1988).

It must be emphasized here that the foregoing summary of the constitutive elements of the Western canon on Western exceptionalism is not always subscribed to by all in their entirety, of course. However, even in this day and age most (but not all) Westerners accept most of the elements—at the very minimum at the subterranean levels of the psyche, but which find tangible behavioral expression the moment they interact with people who are not Westerners. (Note: the interaction need not necessarily always be of a direct kind, that is in person; it can also be indirect, effected through such inert mechanisms as the media and the scholarly enterprise or simply conversational discourse among themselves.) What is more, even those scholars who appear to have a much greater sensitivity to the achievements of others outside the West and whose work is organically rooted in global comparative analyses are unable to resist the seduction of mirroring the present on to the past (meaning the current planetary domination by the West is simply a reflection of a historically determined destiny); two obvious representatives of such fallacious thinking are Braudel (1981–83) and Wallerstein (1974–89).

For works that critique the Eurocentric perspective on world history, then Blaut (1993, and 2000) is a good place to begin; his brilliant debunking project on Western exceptionalism, titled *The Colonizer's Model of the World*, brings together in one place the core elements of the Western exceptionalist canon for much-needed critical scrutiny. (It should be pointed out that, sadly, his project is incomplete and will remain so given his untimely death in the same year that the second of his projected three volumes was published.) Blaut of course is not alone among the debunkers, the reader may also wish to look at the work of such others as: Abu-Lughod (1989); Amin (1989); Bernal (1987 1991, and 2001); Frank (1998); Goody (1996); Hodgson (1993); Inikori (2002); Inikori and Engerman (1992); Needham, et al. (1954–to Present); Pohl (1990); Pomeranz (2000); and Wigen and Martin (1997). Mention must also be made here of a great resource edited by Russell-Wood (1995–2000) titled *An Expanding World: The European Impact on World History, 1450–1800*, published in 31 volumes. (Note: the title of the series is somewhat misleading; it may give the impression that it is a Eurocentric work, but it is not.)

The term "protocapitalism" refers to the capitalism that emerged in the Afro-Eurasian ecumene as an extension of mercantile capitalism, but as a precursor of industrial capitalism; the time period when this form of capitalism was dominant is very roughly fifteenth through eighteenth centuries (see Blaut 1993).

9. This issue, to drill home the point, can be presented in another way: all human progress, in the civilizational sense, ultimately rests either on structural factors (both contingent and conjunctural) or ideational factors. If one accepts the former then it becomes easy to explain, for example, the rise and fall of civilizations and empires throughout history (including the collapse of the British and the Russian empires not too long ago). Moreover, one can enlist the support of science here

in that it is now an incontrovertibly established scientific fact that there is no fraction of humanity (whatever the social structural criteria for the division: ethnicity, sex, age, class, etc.) that holds a monopoly over intelligence and talent. If, on the other hand, one privileges the latter, then one must be content with ethnocentrically driven historiography unsupported by evidence, other than fantastical conjectures. Yes, yes… of course, ideas do matter; but only when placed within the context of structures. (This applies even to religious ideas—at the end of the day the metaphysical and the transcendental are still rooted in the material; for, how else it can it be as long as human beings remain human, that is biological entities.)

10. In according considerable significance to Columbus to the account that follows should not in any way take away from the fact that he was not the first to arrive in the Americas from the Afro-Eurasian ecumene; others had preceded him; there were the Vikings, for instance, then there were the Chinese for another (see Menzies 2003 about the latter.) However, the difference is that Columbus was the first to arrive with a particular worldview (to be elaborated in the course of the pages to follow).

11. While it may be true, as Berman (1989) for example argues and amply demonstrates, that the desire by human beings to find out what lies on the other side is universal and therefore in this sense the Columbian voyage was not singular. However, the fact is that in dispensing to this voyage a pride of place in the annals of human history, one is recognizing that there was something unique about this and other similar Italian/Iberian voyages of the fifteenth-century: a concerted, deliberate and systematic effort involving the blessing of the church and the resources of the state to seek out new routes across the oceans to lands in the East—which for Western Europe (specifically the Italians and the Iberians) were not entirely terra incognita—for one basic and overriding purpose: capital accumulation. (In this regard, the fact that it was this specific group, is in itself telling: in terms of commercial relations with the East through the agency of the Muslims, no other group of Europeans up to that point could have boasted a comparable history.) In other words, these were not chance adventures, unlike most of the voyages of centuries past.

12. The number of books that have been published on the life of Columbus and his project can fill a small library. For a comprehensive overview the following sources considered together, however, should suffice: Bedini (1992); Blaut (1992); Stannard (1992); Viola and Margolis (1992); and Yewell, Dodge and DeSirey (1992). Mention of course should also be made here of the volume edited by Lardicci (1999), as well as others, in the multivolume series, *Repertorium Columbianum* (and whose general editor is Geoffrey Symcox).

13. See the fascinating account by Menzies (2003) of the voyages of Hong Bao, Zhou Man, Zho Wen, and others that led them to places as far away from China as the America's and eventually even leading to their circumnavigation of the world. Of these voyages, of course, the one's by Cheng Ho are the most well-known (in relative terms). (See also McNeil [2005])

14. It ought to be noted that given the nature of the subject—its complexity—it should not be surprising that there will be some disagreement among these three, for example, over the relative saliency of the different factors; that is, privileging this or that factor in explaining the importance of 1492. For our purposes, the key point of significance is that they all agree on the centrality of the Columbian project, at least, in explaining the global rise of Europe after 1800.

15. The term *Euro-American ecumene* is coined here, for want of a better term, to signify the historically specific Europeanized Americas that emerged after 1492 with the permanent colonization by Europe of, initially, the Caribbean basin islands, Central America, and South America, and a century and a half or so later, North America. Note that this term may still have relevance today, but it would have a slightly different connotation: that of an *expanded Europe* (in all senses: geographic, political, linguistic, cultural and economic—despite the existence within the ecumene of politically sovereign states) and involving the addition of Australia and New Zealand on one hand and the subtraction of the southern portion of the Americas on the other (leaving only North America). In labeling this revised version of the Euro-American ecumene as an expanded Europe, is to testify to its possession of a sufficient unity of political-economic and cultural identity as to mark it

out from the rest of the planet—plus at this present point in time it is further identified by the fact that it continues to enjoy hegemonic preeminence in global affairs relative to most of the world, except, perhaps, China.

16. That the project was an accident is of course attested to even to this day in the continued use of the delusional vocabulary of Columbus even by Native Americans who continue to call themselves "Indians."

17. Remember also the doomed voyage of the Vivaldi brothers some 200 years before Columbus. The two brothers, Ugolino and Vadino, who, like Columbus, were from Genoa and like him were driven by the same motivations, had set out in 1291 to seek a sea route to the East across the Atlantic. They never returned; it is presumed that they perished. Lopez (1995: 306) makes the intriguing suggestion that the voyage of the brothers achieved such legendary status in medieval Italy that it prompted no less a personage than Dante himself to immortalize it, by idealizing them through the character of Ulysses (the hero of Homer's Odyssey) in the first canticle, *The Inferno*, of his monumental Christian epic poem, *The Divine Comedy*. This suggestion is not as far-fetched as it may seem if one considers that not only was Dante unfamiliar with Homer (he neither knew Greek nor were translations of Homer available in Western Europe in his time), but there is no clear indication in classical literature of how Ulysses met his death. Ulysses makes his appearance in canto 26 of the *Inferno* by way of a monologue, the first part of which reads thusly:

Therefore, I set out on the open sea
with but one ship and that small company
of those who never had deserted me.

I saw as far as Spain, far as Morocco,
along both shores; I saw Sardinia
and saw the other islands that sea bathes.

And I and my companions were already
old and slow, when we approached the narrows
where Hercules set up his boundary stones

that men might heed and never reach beyond:
upon my right, I had gone past Seville,
and on the left, already passed Ceuta.

"Brothers," I said, "O you, who having crossed
a hundred thousand dangers, reach the west,
to this brief waking-time that still is left

unto your senses, you must not deny
experience of that which lies beyond
the sun, and of the world that is unpeopled."

Consider well the seed that gave you birth:
"you were not made to live your lives as brutes,
but to be followers of worth and knowledge."

(From the translation by Allen Mandelbaum and available on the internet as part of the Dante Digital project of the Institute of Learning Technologies of Columbia University. For more on the brothers' voyage see also the entry in Bedini 1992.)

18. For a discussion of the relationship between disease and demography following the critical

year of 1492 among Native Americans see the entry under *disease and demography*, by Douglas B. Ubelaker in Bedini (1992). McNeill (1977), Kiple and Beck (1997), and Stannard (1992) are also relevant on this subject.

19. Unless specified otherwise, all references to sugar in this chapter is to sugar produced from sugarcane.

20. Sources that examine the less romantic side of the European arrival in the Americas from the perspective of Native Americans include Gallay (2003); Gentry and Grinde (1994); Stannard (1992); Yewell, Dodge, and DeSirey (1992), and Wright (1992).

21. Gunpowder, also known as *black powder*, is not a naturally occurring substance; it is a human manufactured chemical product comprising roughly 75% potassium nitrate (saltpeter), 15% charcoal, and 10% sulfur. Although it is unlikely that we will ever know with a 100% exactitude to whom the ignominious honor of inventing this awful substance that would claim, over the centuries, the lives of thousands of millions of human beings should be assigned, it is quite likely that it was invented either by the Chinese or the Muslims (in Persia) or both—perhaps as a byproduct of their pursuit of alchemy—though the general consensus favors the Chinese. Moreover, the supposed reference by the Muslims themselves to an incendiary substance by the name of *Chinese Snow*, has also been taken to mean that gunpowder must have originated in China (where it was certainly known no later than C.E. 900). On the other hand, however, Chinese Snow was a reference not to gunpowder itself, but to the main ingredient, saltpeter, which is white in color and which, it appears, was relatively abundant in China (Saunders 1971: 199; however, his discussion of this topic in general from the vantage point of today is a little dated.)

If it was the Muslims who first invented gunpowder then one may conjecture here that gunpowder and weapons based on it may have first diffused to China and from there diffused to the West via the Mongols. (One may recall here the common Mongol practice of shanghaiing into their service the talented craftsmen of a defeated population while the rest, including women and children, were brutally put to the sword.) Whatever the case may be, we are on slightly more firmer ground when it comes to tracing the invention of lethal devices based on gunpowder, guns, and their precursors. According to Pacey (1991: 47), among the earliest instances of Europeans being subjected to weapons based on gunpowder, it appears, was during the Crusades when the Muslims spread considerable terror among the Latin forces with these weapons in 1249. However, Pacey states that these gunpowder-based weapons (incendiary devices, grenade like devices, fire-lances, etc.), most likely invented jointly—in the sense of one reciprocally improving on the invention of the other—by the Chinese and the Muslims, were not exactly a gun technology. A gun in the strictest sense of the word must not only have the three standard elements, a barrel, a projectile, and an incendiary substance, but they must be linked by a process that involves an explosion within the barrel. The Chinese and/or the Muslims were apparently the original inventors of such a device based on gunpowder; and Pacey suggests that these highly primitive guns (which were characteristically bottle shaped) diffused to the West sometime toward the end of the thirteenth-century, possibly via the Mongols when they were ruling southern Russia. By the early fourteenth-century, this primitive gun technology was now fairly widespread within the Islamic empire (including Spain and North Africa). However, by the time Columbus left Europe nearly two centuries later, it is clear that the Europeans had the edge in the technology of gunnery: they had moved the technology along in the direction of cannons and smooth bore muzzle-loading weapons: pistols and muskets. (See also Archer, Ferris, Herwig, and Travers [2002].)

22. The Portuguese, under Vasco da Gama, first made contact with India in 1498; yet just a decade or so later they had captured the Indian port of Goa (in 1510) and the equally important commercial port of Malacca on the Malayan peninsula (in 1511). Portuguese gunnery (together with, some might say, their barbaric cruelty) was decisive in these predatory exercises because viewed purely from the perspective of naval military power they had more or less stepped into a vacuum in light of the Chinese imperial withdrawal in 1435 with the death of Cheng Ho.

23. Even the celebrated Zulu victory over British forces at the Battle of Isandhlwana in 1879

(January 22–23) was based more on tactics than on Zulu weaponry (which included almost no guns). This fact clearly comes out when one remembers that the remaining British troops stationed at their military base at nearby Rorke's Drift, numbering a mere 120 men, were able to rebuff a Zulu attack that involved perhaps 2,000 warriors. In the end of course the British defeated the Zulu decisively two months later at the Battle of Kambula (March 28–29) with minimal casualties, whereas the Zulu forces suffered huge losses. (The colonization of the Zulu homeland by the British would be completed with the capture of the Zulu capital, Ulundi, a few months later in July.) For more on this particular historical event see Floca (1974), Furneaux (1963) and Knight (1995); for accounts of other post 1492 imperial military onslaughts by the West on the rest of the planet the following should suffice: Alavi (1995), Bayly (1989), De Moor and Wesseling (1989), Headrick (1982), Packenham (1991), Parker (1996), and Peers (1995, 1997).

24. They state: "This, the greatest conquest in history, had many sources, but one was the most fundamental of them all: Western armies crushed the others, making imperialism so cheap that minor causes sparked great conquests. Ultimately, the greatest cause of imperialism was not profound political and economic factors but simply the military ease with which it could be accomplished. European armies were superior in technology, tactics, and organization *because for centuries their states had regularly fought major wars against each other*" (p. 440; emphasis added). Leaving aside the fact that even the most cursory perusal of world history indicates that, sadly, very sadly, Europeans alone did not hold a monopoly over fratricidal aggression in the preimperialist era, to ascribe the eventual successful overlay of the European imperialist order upon the planet, as the industrial transformation got underway, to European bloodthirstiness is being somewhat overly simplistic; however, it is most certainly indicative of a succumbency to that ever-present temptation that is the bane of all military historians: technological determinism (and in this case Eurocentric technological determinism). Military technology alone—especially in the prenuclear era of European imperialism—cannot explain everything.

Yes, superior military technology was important, but political and economic opportunity was equally important (as a careful analysis of the evidence in their own text indicates). In fact, one cannot even discount such cultural factors as chivalry, where the use of the gun was considered cowardly because a true soldier fights at close quarters (p. 462). However, even more significant perhaps, was the economic factor on the battlefield: European wealth itself that allowed the European imperialists to recruit indigenous soldiers from competing sides, in a given territory, in the classic power-play of "divide, conquer and rule." Prior to 1800, as Marshall (1995: 43) explains: "The military resources of an industrialized Europe had not yet been directed against Asia. This was not to happen until iron-clad ships, rifles and new artillery made their appearance in the mid-nineteenth-century. Until then, European technological advantages were marginal ones, such as greater standardization of equipment. To a large extent Europeans were making war with the resources of Asia: Asian soldiers paid for by Asian taxation." To give one example: one cannot satisfactorily explain how a handful of British soldiers (numbering just a few thousand) could have conquered and held in subjection for about 200 years a continent as large, as heavily populated, and as technologically advanced (at the time when the British first made their appearance on the continent's doorstep) as India, unless one also takes into consideration such political and social factors as deep internal rivalries among kingdoms and states, profound religiously motivated enmities, and the presence of the caste system that rendered the Brahmin ruling caste a groveling "yes Sahib," feet-kissing puppet of the British (and who, as time wore on, achieved a deep sense of psychic inferiority complex vis-à-vis all Westerners and which to this day it has yet to dispose of).

25. Chinese name variations of prominent personages stem from the practice of acquiring new names, such as with the acquisition of new positions (e.g., on becoming an emperor); or with the establishment of new dynasties; and so on. Moreover, the existence of two forms of romanization of Chinese names, Wade-Giles and the newer Pinyin does not help matters. For the present account, the following name/spelling variations (based mainly but not only on *Encyclopedia Brittanica* 2004 edition) are relevant:

Genghis Khan (c. 1162–1227): also spelled Ching-gis, Chingis, Jenghiz, and so on. Also known as Temüjin (Temuchin). He established the dynasty that his grandson, Kublai Khan, later proclaimed as the Yuan dynasty (1206–1368—also known as the Mongol dynasty) and of which Kublai Khan would be the first emperor.

Kublai Khan (1215–94): also spelled Khubilai, or Kubla Hung-wu (1328–1398): also spelled Hongwu—also known as Kao-ti, T'ai Tsu, and Chu Yuan-chang (Zhu Yuanzhang).

Cheng Ho (1371–1435): also spelled Zheng He Also known as Ma San-pao, Ma Ho, San Bao. His family claimed that they were descendants of an early Mongol governor of Yunnan and a descendant of King Muhammed of Bukhara. The family name Ma came from the Chinese rendition of Muhammad.

Yung-lo (1360–1424; third emperor of the Ming dynasty from 1402–1424): also spelled Yonglo— also known as Ch'eng Tsu, T'ai Tsung, Wen Ti, and Chu Ti [Zhu Di].

26. To fully appreciate the might of the naval power these expeditions represented for the time period, consider this comparison by Finlay (1995): The Portuguese Army that attacked Morocco and captured Ceuta in 1415 numbered about 12,000; the fall of the Muslim province of Granada in 1492 had been achieved with 20,000 men, while the French invasion of Italy in 1494 under Charles VIII had involved about 28,000 soldiers. The usual number that made up a field army in the early sixteenth-century in Europe ranged roughly from 25,000 to 30,000 men—vide, Philip II's Spanish Armada, for example, that was sent to invade England in 1588, it had aboard a total of about 29,500 soldiers. As for the size of the European ships, they were absolutely no match for the Chinese ones: the largest of Vasco da Gama's ships, for example, could only displace 300 tons at the most and carry 170 men (versus 600 men for Cheng Ho's 3,000-ton ships). Even in the case of the Spanish Armada, the size of their ships were wanting: the largest had a capacity of only 1,294 tons. Clearly then, as Finlay, concludes, the Ming Indian Ocean expeditions "were the largest long-distance enterprises before the modern age, dwarfing anything that the most powerful European state could produce" (p. 95).

27. For more on the Cheng Ho expedition, besides Finlay, see Chang (1995) and Filesi (1972).

28. While his reference to Muscovy makes sense considering the rapidity and magnitude of its expansion to give rise to an enormous empire, his mention of the Ottoman Empire may cause some surprise given the Timurian (Tamerlane to Westerners) juggernaut it had suffered in early 1400s. However, as he explains, the empire did recover: "The Ottomans ruled the most powerful empire in a civilization which seemed coiled for long-range expansion. If the sudden and dramatic expansion of Christendom in the sixteenth-century had not intervened to grab historians attention, the late medieval out-thrust of Islam would be acknowledged for what it was: recovery of pace and power comparable to those of Islam's unprecedented success in the century after the death of Muhammad" (p. xv).

29. The ensuing discussion in the rest of this chapter, ideally, should be accompanied by quantitative data (e.g., on demographic changes, population flows, magnitude of the Atlantic slave trade, production levels, growth differentials, quantities of commodities traded, etc.)—notwithstanding its inherently tentative nature given the historical time period under discussion here—to illustrate some of the points made. However, since space does not permit inclusion of such data, especially in a chapter that is already overstretched in terms of relevance to the subject of this work, you are advised dear reader to, instead, consult the following sources: Abu-Lughod (1989); Acemoglu, Johnson, and Robinson (2002); Barrett (1990); Blaut (1993); Chaudhuri (1995); Dols (1977); Frank (1998); Inikori (2002); Inikori and Engerman (1992); McNeill (1977); Mintz (1985); Pomeranz (2000); and Richards (1983).

30. Hill and Hassan (1986) state that the sugarcane arrived in Islamic Persia from India and therefrom it spread into the rest of the Islamic empire, including North Africa and Palestine. Their

work further describes how the sugar was actually produced during the Islamic era. They tellingly note that given the agro-industrial character of sugar production it was always, from the very beginning, an enterprise beyond that of the individual farmer or artisan. Little wonder then that sugarcane was among the earliest plantation crops. For a general history of the importance of sugar to humankind and the role of the Muslims among others in this history see the fascinating study of confectionary by Richardson (2002).

31. Some basic facts about sugar, the import of which will become clear soon enough: For biological reasons not yet fully clear to science, all primates, humans and nonhumans, instinctually love the sweet taste; there are it appears no exceptions. For thousands of years the chief sources of this taste for all primates has been fruits, honey, some tubers, and sap from certain plant and tree species. However, somewhere along the way humans figured out other natural sources, but based on cultivation. The king of these cultivated sources is sugarcane, a grass—that is, a relative of both the bamboo, corn, and rice, for example. It has been suggested that the domestication of the sugarcane first took place in Oceania, specifically New Guinea around 8000 B.C.E. (Mintz 1985: 19). The cultivation of sugarcane would then spread over the course of thousands of years to Asia. However, while the consumption of sugarcane as a dessert "fruit" may have a long history behind it, the production of sugar from the cane is, it would appear, of relatively recent undertaking in human history. It is in India, perhaps as early as 800–700 B.C.E. (Mazumdar 1998: 13), where the technique of crystallizing sugar from the sap of the sugarcane, it is thought, would be first invented. From there the technique would spread to other parts of Asia, including China and Persia. From Persia, as already noted, the Muslims would move the technology westward; and it is only after they had arrived in Europe in the eighth-century, Mintz explains, that Europe came to know and consume sugar—albeit in very limited proportions on account of scarcity and price.

Sugarcane, like other such other grasses as rice, has very specific agriculturally onerous requirements: it must be grown in quantity to produce an appreciable amount of the end product; its cultivation requires rich soils, plentiful supply of water, high temperatures characteristic of the subtropics/tropics and back-breaking intensive manual labor at all stages: planting (propagation is through cuttings), weeding, harvesting (which must be accomplished on time and quickly once the cane is ripe), and processing (the window of opportunity to begin the processing of sugarcane into sugar is usually counted in hours once the cane has been harvested). Now although manufactured sugar is not a basic food requirement, unlike rice, for instance, and therefore it is a luxury commodity that humans can easily do without, given its great versatility (it can be used as a preservative too for example), societies that can afford sugar have found it impossible to do without it. For Europeans, for instance, the universalization of a number of other luxury commodities in the realm of confectionary and the bitter beverages (tea, coffee, and cocoa) would transform sugar almost into a staple. (Note: beet sugar, the other major form of commercial sugar, does not acquire importance in Europe until the twentieth-century—the technology for producing it was invented in the preceding century.)

32. Prior to the fifteenth-century, that is before sugar production spread to the *sugar islands*, the slaves came primarily from within Europe and the Mediterranean region itself: Slavs, Latins, Arabs, Spaniards, Italians, North Africans, and so on, appear to have all been represented as slave labor at one point or another in the preceding nearly 600–700-year history of cane-sugar production; for, who enslaved whom depended on who was in power at any given moment. Recall that all the three major religions of Europe and the Mediterranean region, Judaism, Christianity, and Islam, had historically sanctioned slavery—given the unfortunate omnipresence of this awful institution in almost all societies going all the way back to antiquity throughout the entire length and breadth of the Afro-Eurasian ecumene; from Ireland to China, from Scandinavia to southern Africa. (The association of race with slavery, needless to say, was of a later ideological manufacture.)

It should also be pointed out here that even though the Muslims had continued the thousands of years old practice of exporting the enslaved from Africa into the rest of the Afro-Eurasian ecumene, the commonly known fact of the association of African slave labor with sugar production in the Atlantic does not begin in earnest, however, until after the Portuguese had established a direct sea route to the West African coast in the mid–1400s.The Portuguese initially took enslaved Africans to meet labor needs in the Iberian and western Mediterranean regions and the Atlantic archipelago, and only later, especially after the Native American population had been decimated, did they (together with other European nations of course) began transshipping them across the Atlantic in ever-increasing numbers as sugar production expanded in the Euro-American ecumene—beginning first, in terms of significant exports to Europe, in Brazil and later expanding to the Antilles.

33. On the profitability of sugar, even Adam Smith was moved to write: "It is commonly said that a sugar planter expects that the rum and the molasses should defray the whole expense of his cultivation, and that his sugar should be all clear profit. If this be true... it is as if a corn farmer expected to defray the expense of his cultivation with the chaff and the straw, and that the grains should be all clear profit" (1961 [1776], vol. 1: 175).

34. The first triangle involved the export of manufactures from Europe to Africa, the shipment of enslaved Africans to the Caribbean and South America, and finally on the third side of the triangle the export of sugar, rum, precious metals, and other products to Europe. After the settlement of North America the first triangle was expanded to also include North America and an additional triangle emerged: enslaved Africans were taken to the Caribbean from Africa, from the Caribbean sugar and molasses were exported to the North American colonies. The colonies in turn exported rum and other barter commodities to Africa. Then of course there were the direct trade routes between Europe and the Americas (including the Caribbean) where European manufactures were exchanged for primary commodities from the Americas. Those European nations who came to dominate these various trade routes across the Atlantic became, of course, enormously wealthy; to say therefore that the initial accumulation of European investible surplus was achieved on the backs of generations of unpaid African labor (sometimes referred to as the *Williams thesis* because it was first advanced by Eric Williams in 1944) is not entirely farfetched; there is some validity to it. See the sympathetic discussion of the Williams (1944) thesis by Blaut (1993), Frank (1998), Inikori (2002) and Pomeranz (2000). Of course, as Inikori (2002) convincingly demonstrates, the contribution of the enslaved Africans to the development of Western Europe can be best appreciated if viewed from the perspective of the overall function of the slave trade as one of the principal motors of the entire post–1492 economic system of the Euro-American ecumene, and without which the economic system may never have arisen in its specific *1492* form. Besides Inikori, for a useful account of the genesis and import of the Atlantic slave trade generally, the following sources taken together are helpful: Inikori and Engerman (1992), Mariner's Museum (2002), Miller (1988), Northrup (2002b), Postma (2003), and Thornton (1992). For a general discussion of the specifics of cane-sugar production and its role in world history, the following are of singular relevance: Deerr (1949–50), Dunn (1973), Galloway (1989), MacInnis (2002), Mazumdar (1998), Mintz (1985), and Taylor (1978).

35. Interestingly, according to Davidson (1995: 211–12), some of the gold was also sent to Africa to purchase slaves.

36. See Barrett (1990), and Frank (1998), for various estimates of figures on the magnitude of precious metal flows around the world from the West to the East. See also Flynn and Giraldez (1997) and Richards (1983) for a general overview of the role of bullion and coinage in the post–1492 emerging global economy.

37. One ought to also mention here the transfer of the surplus of the Afro-Asian ecumene to Europe through the agency of ocean piracy. Christian piety of the period notwithstanding, accompanying the arrival of European trading ships in the Indian and Pacific oceans, were the freebooters and privateers; in other words, the thugs of the sea: the pirates. With no power able to throw an effective security blanket over the emerging sea lanes of the world, for many centuries both state and privately sponsored European ships of prey plied the oceans, raking in loot of Afro-Asian (as well as Euro-American) provenance. It appears that the Portuguese led the way, beginning with their ac-

tivities in the western end of the Mediterranean in the mid-fifteenth-century (see Newitt [1995]). However, it is in the Atlantic (ships from the newly emerging economies of the Euro-American ecumene were targets as already indicated) and in the Indian and Pacific ocean regions where rich pickings were to be had. The Portuguese would be not be alone in their dastardly activities (remember that piracy also usually entailed the wholesale murder of the looted ship's crew); others would quickly follow: Dutch, English, French, Spanish, Scandinavians, and so on, and as the centuries progressed Euro-Americans would join in too. (In fact, Scammell [1995] points out that the origins of the Indian Ocean to Atlantic trade is to be found in sea piracy.) Given the inherent nature of the activity, it is impossible to determine the quantity of surplus that was drained by Europeans from the Afro-Asian ecumene through this avenue, but Scammell (see also Perotin-Dumont,1991), clearly shows that it was of a sufficient magnitude as to make a perceptible difference to the local economies of a number of European countries, including the new eastern seaboard colonies of North America. (For more on piracy generally during the period under purview, see also Galvin [1999], Kris [1998], and Peterson [1975].)

38. Pomeranz also suggests that another very important benefit that the Europeans got from their tropical colonies in the Americas and elsewhere was critically important ecological knowledge; that is, by observing the rapidly changing interrelationships, often of a negative consequence, between climate and land use that only a tropical environment could facilitate, Europeans were able to apply lessons they derived from these observations to saving their own lands from further deterioration through deforestation, soil erosion, and so on. In other words, there is a dual benefit here: Europe not only benefited from experientially derived ecological knowledge, but it was also shielded from the negative consequences that the inadvertent acquisition of this knowledge entailed: the potential for massive land degradation that would have ensued within Europe itself in the absence of the demographic safety-valve that the forcible requisition from Native Americans of millions upon millions of acres of their land constituted. In support of this observation consider the comments of a Native American boy in a prize-winning essay for the *Wyoming-Farmer Stockman* (the editors of which had solicited from its readers submission of the best hundred-word essay on land erosion) in the early 1940s. "The picture," the boy wrote, referring to the photo of a desolate farmhouse on sand-swept barren land that the editors had published to go along with the essay competition, "show white man crazy." Writing in the same vein he continued: "Cut down trees. Make too big teepee. Plow land, water wash, wind blow soil. Grass gone, door [sic] gone, squaw gone. Whole place gone to hell. No pig, no corn, no pony." In contrast, he further writes: "Indian no plow land. Keep grass. Buffalo eat grass. Indian eat buffalo. Hide make plenty big teepee. Make moccasin. All time Indian eat. No work—no hitchhike. Ask no relief. No build dam. No give damn. White man heap crazy" (from Appendix H in Yewell, Dodge, and DeSirey 1992).

39. See also Sidebotham and Wendrich (2002), whose archeological work at Berenike (an abandoned but once, in antiquity, a well-known Egyptian port located on the Red Sea, close to the present day Sudanese border) has revealed an alternative and an equally important route to the famous Silk Road that allowed the Romans access to luxuries from the East. This was of course a sea route in which Berenike played a pivotal role, dating back at least as far as 1 C.E. until its demise (for as yet unknown reasons) around 500 C.E.They observe that the archeological artifacts found at the port indicate a three way trade between Roman Europe, Egypt and Sub-Saharan Africa, and India (the last was also a transit point for goods from further east). They have determined at least eleven different written languages in use at the port; hence speaking to its importance in both regional and international terms.

40. An interesting question that some historians have raised is why is it that the Portuguese were not challenged by the rulers of the Ottoman Empire when they (the Portuguese) first arrived in the Indian Ocean; for, after all, the Indian Ocean at that time was clearly a Muslim "pond." The underlying suggestion behind this question being that had they done so, then perhaps, the West would not have risen to eventually dominate even the House of Islam itself. Leaving aside the question of whether the emergence of the Euro-American ecumene would have been irrelevant to the historical

trajectory of Europe (and the world) if the Muslims had prevented the Europeans from entering the Indian Ocean, the truth is that as long as the Europeans stayed away from the eastern Mediterranean, the Red Sea, and the Persian Gulf regions, the Ottomans were content to expend their energies elsewhere: specifically the expansion of their empire into other domains, from Egypt to the Balkans. In other words, this question is irrelevant because its assumptions are false. (See Hess [1995] for a full discussion of this issue.)

41. This point also explains why it was that while Europe thirsted for commodities of the Afro-Asian ecumene for centuries, throughout the history of West-East commercial relations indigenous capitalists of the Afro-Asian ecumene did not send their ships to Europe. For, by the time the ecumene began to express interest in imports of European manufactures toward the beginning of the nineteenth-century (that is by the time the European industrial transformation was underway) the power of its capitalist classes had waned considerably under pressure from their European competitors. This in turn had a political consequence—to take the example of Asia: "European armed ships and European fighting men came to Asia, even if in small quantities before the later eighteenth-century; there was no corresponding movement of ships and men from Asia to Europe, once Turkish offensives had ceased. Thus Europe could export war to Asia, but Asia could not return the complement" (Marshall 1995: 51). The denouement of this circumstance is known to all: nearly 400 years after Columbus had stumbled upon the Taino, West-East ocean trade eventually transmuted into European imperial colonization of almost the entire ecumene in the nineteenth-century. (Note: a similar intriguing question of why it was that while the Africans controlled the Atlantic slave trade on their side [from the African interior to the coast], they were not part of the immensely lucrative triangular Atlantic trade, cannot be addressed here as it would widen an already extended focus of attention beyond the forbearance of the editors; however a hint has already been indicated with the discussion earlier of the Ethiopia/Japan anomaly.)

42. Interestingly, where the power of the landed aristocracy remained relatively intact (as a consequence initially of pre–1492 internal European factors), participation in the new economic opportunities opened up by 1492 proved not only to be ephemeral, but in the long-run inconsequential. The classic example here is that of Portugal and Spain (see Acemoglu, Johnson, and Robinson [2002], for more on this.)

43. For more on the impact of the Atlantic slave trade on Africa itself, see Curtin (1975), Davidson (1980); DeCorse (2001); Inikori (1982, 1992); Inikori and Engerman (1992); Law (1991); Rodney (1981, 1982); and Thornton (1999).

44. Here one ought to define precisely what is meant by *luxury goods*. Specifically, the definition must go beyond simply pointing to the trade-goods of beads, cloth, guns, ivory, and so on, as luxury commodities (merely because a minority within society, such as the kings and their courtiers, were involved in their consumption); it must link these goods directly to the production process within an economic system. Pierro Sraffa defines luxury products in the context of an economic system thus:

Luxury products have no part in the determination of the system. Their role is purely passive. If an invention were to reduce by half the quantity of each of the means of production which are required to produce a unit of a "luxury" commodity of this type, the commodity itself would be halved in price, but there would be no further consequences.

What has just been said of the passive role of luxury goods can be readily extended to such "luxuries" as are merely used in their own reproduction either directly (e.g., race horses) or indirectly (e.g., ostriches and ostrich-eggs) or merely for the production of other luxuries. The criterion is whether a commodity enters (no matter whether directly or indirectly) into the production of all commodities (from Wallerstein, 1976: 31).

45. To be more specific, while the theory can trace its intellectual heritage to the work of Marx

in his various writings (e.g., *Preface to the Critique of Political Economy; The Communist Manifesto*; and *Grundrisse*) as well as Lenin's early writings on Russian capitalism, and of course Trotsky's *History of the Russian Revolution* with its thesis, the *Law of Uneven and Combined Development*, in terms of its more immediate origins the theory come out of the work of French anthropologists working within the Althusserian structuralist tradition. They included Dupre and Rey, van Binsbergen, Coquery-Vidrovitch, and Geschiere.

Their formulation of the articulated modes of production theory it must be stressed was not a Marxist theory in its orthodox sense—given that it was a response to the inadequacy of Marx's treatment of precapitalist social formations specifically, and the situation of PQD countries generally. To be sure, Marx's work abounds with methodological pointers, but nowhere in his writings does the precapitalist mode receive anywhere near the kind of treatment that he gave the capitalist of mode of production. As Meillassoux, one of the more well-known precursors of the theory, emphatically states:

Marx's approach to the study of precapitalist formations is mainly centered around the demonstration of the historicity of capitalism. His foremost purpose is to show that capitalism is a product of history, that it was preceded by other types of economic formations and that it is bound to give way, in turn, to a different one. But while Capital is thorough investigation into the mechanisms and laws of capitalist development, Marx's approach to precapitalist formations is a relatively superficial one. Let us emphasize that this contribution is, among Marx's works, the least elaborated and probably the least "Marxist" (Meillassoux 1980: 192)

Marx's notion of the "Asiatic mode of production" mentioned in the preface to his *A Contribution to the Critique of Political Economy*, but not really described or analyzed, bears out Meillassoux's judgment. In other words, Marx, as Avineri (1969) also points out, fails to logically weave into his dialectical theory of history with its three principal modes of production (the ancient, feudal and capitalist), this "new" mode of production that he introduces for the first time—unlike the other three that he had already mentioned in the *Communist Manifesto*. The end result is that, in Avineri's words, "(d)espite the explicit dynamism of Marx's dialectical model, it seems to be an uneasy combination of two sets of disparate elements: a sophisticated, carefully worked out schema describing the historical dynamism of European societies, rather simple-mindedly grafted upon a dismissal of all non-European forms of society under the blanket designation of a mere geographic terminology of the 'Asiatic mode of production,' which appears static, unchanging, and totally non-dialectical" (pp. 5–6). Furthermore, as is well-known, Marx's study of the impact of capitalist countries on the development of PQD countries (in his period, via the agency of colonialism) is both sketchy and extremely weak. In fact his thoughts on the situation of PQD countries are generally to be found more among his newspaper articles—an excellent collection of these are to be found in Avineri (1969)—than in his major academic writings. Moreover, in a strange twist of irony, given the much fascination with Marxism among many intellectuals in PQD countries, many of these thoughts were very racist indeed.

Clearly Marx's materialist theory of economic development was relevant only to the experiences of the Western European nations, and in fact it appears that he himself was probably aware of this. He, for example, had warned readers of a Russian socialist journal, in a letter, not to "metamorphose my historical sketch of the genesis of capitalism in Western Europe into an historico-philosophic theory of the general path every people is fated to tread." Later in the same letter he hints at the geographical specificity of his major work, *Capital*: "The chapter on primitive accumulation does not pretend to do more than trace the path by which, in Western Europe, the capitalist order of economy emerged from the womb of the feudal order of society" (from Avineri 1969: 6). It is in response therefore, to this weakness in Marxist political economy, regarding the situation of PQD countries that the French neo-Marxist anthropologists emerged with their theory, the *Ar-*

ticulation of Modes of Production.

Note: A situation of articulated mode of production exists when there is an interpenetration of the different modes, but yet each retains at the same time a sufficient degree of autonomy to render its identification possible. The articulation of the modes of production therefore is more than simply the co-occurrence of different modes of production in a given society (or *social formation* to be exact).

46. As Raatgever (1985: 26) reminds us, a mode of production is a theoretical construct that does not emerge out of direct empirical observations. Instead it "brings out, rather than abstracts, the fundamental inter-relationships that constitute reality." The mode of production, therefore, is a complex that is forged by means of theoretical reconstruction. This conception of the mode of production, it may be noted, differs fundamentally from the Stalinist/Marxist conception that sees the mode of production as an empirical rather than a theoretical construct (in the sense of a Weberian ideal-type), deducible from direct empirical observations.

The following vignette by Dale Johnson, in which he describes the proceedings of a panel (of the Congress of Americanists) meeting in Vancouver, Canada (in July 1979), to discuss the theory, provides a hint of the commotion that it generated among scholars:

The well-attended feature panel of the congress was scheduled from 9: 00 a.m. to noon. At 1: 00 p.m. we broke for lunch. An even larger crowd appeared for the afternoon dialogue. Discussion raged among the panelists, between members of the audience and the panelists, and within the audience, becoming ever more heated. At about 4: 00 p.m. an indignant person jumped onto his chair, denounced Andre Gunder Frank, and led a walkout of some of the audience. At 5: 00 p.m. I put down my now useless gavel and left (Johnson in Chilcote and Johnson 1983: 7).

47. To provide a flavor of the commotion, two or three quotes from the journal should do the trick:

The concept of modes of production was originally hailed with excessive enthusiasm; having now failed, like structuralism, to lead us into the Promised Land of total human self-understanding, it is now being widely abandoned, often with a sigh of relief. It is paradoxical that anthropology, proclaiming itself a science, should apparently proceed by a series of religious movements. (Macgaffey 1985: 51)

The mode of production concept helps identify the questions that must be considered in interpreting gaps in data; but the concept should not seduce us into so stretching our evidence as to disguise or completely fill them. Neither a comprehensive theoretical approach, nor a complete empirical record can reproduce the historical experience of an earlier social formation. But just as we do not discard empirical data because it does not completely reconstruct reality, we should not totally reject theoretical tools such as the mode of production concept because they have limitations. (Cordell 1985: 63)

The fashion for modes of production swept through African studies like a bush fire, which seems now to have burnt itself out. One can only breathe a sigh of relief at the disappearance of much of the jargon of the 1970s.... (Clarence-Smith 1985: 19)

48. In addition to the sources already mentioned, for more on the relations of production versus dependency/world systems theories, see Chilcote and Johnson (1983); Seddon (1978); van Binsbergen and Geschiere (1985); and Wolpe (1980).

49. As my primary school teacher, by no means fondly remembered, would frequently proclaim to his befuddled charges in his history lessons.

50. In what appears to be the first recorded case of germ warfare, historians state that the bubonic plague originated from the Genoese-frequented trading city of Kaffa on the Black Sea in 1346. In the preceding year a Kipchak Army in the service of the Golden Horde Mongols had commenced a siege of the unfortunate city, and the army's Mongol commander, observing that its numbers were rapidly beginning to thin with the rise of a horrendous pestilence among its ranks, instructed that diseased corpses be catapulted across the walls of the city in order to bring the siege to a speedier end. It was a matter of time before the flea-borne virus did its gruesome work along the trade routes that lead all the way into Europe and the Middle East. For more on the Black Death and its consequences, see Abu-Lughod (1989); Dols (1977); and McNeill (1977).

51. As a contemporaneous chronicler of Mongol history, the Muslim Persian, Ala-ad-Din Ata-Malik Juvaini, would bitterly record (even as he served his new masters): "[T]o-day the surface of the earth in general and the land of Khorasan in particular (which was the rising-place of felicities and charities, the location of desirable things and good works, the fount of learned men, the rendezvous of the accomplished, the spring-abode of the talented, the meadow of the wise, the thoroughfare of the proficient and the drinking-place of the ingenious—the pearl-raining words of the Prophet have a tradition on this subject: 'Knowledge is a tree which hath its roots in Mecca and beareth its fruit in Khorasan')... to-day, I say, the earth hath been divested of the adornment of the presence of those clad in the gown of science and those decked in the jewels of learning and letters" (Juvaini 1997: 6). Besides Juvaini (specifically the 1997 edition), for more on the Mongols and their empires see Allsen (1987); Morgan (1986); Saunders (1971) and Paul Khan's adaptation of that official contemporaneous fact-plus-fantasy history of the Mongols titled *The Secret History of the Mongols* (Kahn 1984).

52. One may conjecture here that perhaps this very "kindness and respect" proved to be the undoing of many peoples in the end. In any case, it is certainly true that, to take the example of Africa (excluding Islamic Africa for obvious reasons), it was highly uncommon for Africans, as Stokes and Brown (1966: xxv) have observed, to approach the white man on their first meeting with "instinctual aggression." There are cases in African history, for instance, among the Nguni on the east coast of South Africa, where white survivors of shipwrecks were allowed to settle among the Africans to eventually become full members of the community. Survivors of Portuguese shipwrecks in 1554 (the *Sao Bento*) and 1635 (the *Nossa Senhora de Belem*) met some of these "Africanized whites," and were surprised to find that they would not join the Portuguese in their search for coastal settlements to the north to find ships to take them home (Wilson and Thompson 1969/1971 [Vol. 1]: 78–84, 233). In 1790, Jacob Van Reenen records meeting an old woman by the name of Bessie who was the daughter of a girl who had been shipwrecked with other whites many years earlier. The survivors settled among the Nguni to eventually give rise to a clan known to the present day as the Lungu. The girl herself had in time married the Mpondo chief Xwabiso (Wilson 1969: 233).

53. The *natural law of prior claim* (and *natural law),* which should be understood here in the Aristotelian sense, can be defined, thusly: those who are the first (original) residents of a territory, possess an inalienable right to that territory regardless of the claims of all others who come afterward. (It is a law that finds its echo in the modern concept of "citizenship by birth.") That is the reason why for, instance, no one would legitimately question the right of Africans to live in Africa, or the Chinese to live in China, or Indians in India, Europeans in Europe, and so on. Moreover, it is a law that can only be contravened on the basis of armed power and violence. The profound and sobering implications of this law can be deduced from the following thought-experiment: What if, tomorrow, Native Americans were to acquire the power sufficient to propel them to the headship (in all senses of the word, political, military, etc.) of the Americas? How would citizenship of the present descendents of all those who have migrated into the Americas over the centuries, literally at the point of the gun, be now defined? A taste of the answer—however repugnant it may be to all those who believe in the desirability of a multicultural democracy in that country, and anywhere else for that matter—is to be found today in the ongoing events in Zimbabwe (Will South Africa be next?)

where the moral claims to citizenship by its white residents have been proven to have rested all along on armed political power that slipped out of their hands with independence in the 1980s. In other words, regardless of how one wishes to prevaricate on this matter: citizenship in lands that were colonized by Europeans, where the original inhabitants are still present, ultimately resides in monopoly over power, and not moral claims.

54. Among the hallmarks of this new *Westernized* Christianity with its racialized "us-versus-them" approach was, of course, a religious intolerance of frightening proportions and a legacy that would include events ranging from the bloody massacre of the inhabitants of Jerusalem by the Crusaders to the Spanish Inquisition, and from the pogroms against the Jews (beginning with the massacres in Latin Christendom with the commencement of the First Crusade and culminating in the mind-numbing horrors of the Hitlerite Holocaust) to what many Muslims (judging by news reports) perceive as the current "crusade" against Islam: in Afghanistan, Chechnya, Iran, Iraq, Palestine, the Philippines, and so on, in Bosnia about a decade ago, and the U.S.-led fight against "Islamic terrorism." See also Mastnak (2002: 347), and Munjee (2001) on this point.

55. It may be noted here that the sacking of Constantinople inaugurated a period of Latin rule (1204 to 1261) that all modern historians agree was one of absolute disaster for that city—marked among other things by the barbarous looting of the city's vast art treasures of incalculable value; even the sacred Christian relics were not to be spared (the magnitude of the despoliation of the Christian churches could only have been matched by the barbarians of an earlier period, the Vikings.)

56. That the Crusades were aimed at a number of different perceived enemies of Christendom, and not just the Muslims alone, is indicated by the fact that by the time one arrives at the end of the thirteenth-century, crusades had been undertaken against "the Mongols, non-Christians peoples in the Baltic, heretics in Languedoc, Germany, Italy and the Balkans, Orthodox Christians in Greece, and the Hohenstaufen rulers and their supporters in Italy and Germany" (Maier 2000: 3). However, it would be true to say that war against the Muslims would remain the principal task of much of the Crusader project.

57. The importance of the Crusades in coloring perceptions, even today (after more than five centuries later), in the West—and in the East—cannot be underestimated. Many among both Christians and Muslims perceive the U.S.-led fight against "Islamic terrorism," for instance, as the modern replay of the Crusades. In the Islamic world especially, the conflagrations in Afghanistan, Chechnya, Iran, Iraq, Palestine, the Philippines, in Bosnia about a decade ago, and so on, are openly described as a global conflict between Christians and Muslims reminiscent of the Crusades. Consider, for example, the remarks of the Prime Minister of Malaysia in his address to the leaders of Islamic countries gathered for the tenth session of the Islamic Summit conference in Putrajaya, Malaysia, on October 16, 2003: "our detractors and enemies do not care whether we are true Muslims or not. To them we are all Muslims, followers of a religion and a Prophet whom they declare promotes terrorism, and we are all their sworn enemies....Today we, the whole Muslim ummah [global Muslim community] are treated with contempt and dishonor. Our religion is denigrated. Our holy places desecrated. Our countries are occupied. Our people starved and killed." He then goes on to invoke the memory of Muslim victories over the Crusaders, as a counter rallying point: "Remember Salah El Din [Saladin] and the way he fought against the so-called Crusaders, King Richard of England in particular." On the other side, consider the staunch defense by right-wing Christian zealots in the United States of a high-ranking U.S. military official when his remarks during a talk to a Christian prayer group, in June of 2003, sparked some public controversy because they appeared to suggest that the United States was engaged in a holy war against idol worshippers, the Islamic radicals. (The reference to idol worship by Muslims, it may be noted, is a very old Christian canard that was popular even in the time of the Crusades, and of course betrays a depth of ignorance of Islam—an uncompromisingly monotheistic religion—that is virtually bottomless.) Note too that recent allegations of the desecration of the Qur'an by U.S. soldiers have not helped matters (see news archives at www.bbc.com website). See also Mastnak (2002: 347), Munjee (2001) on this

issue of the current relevance of the Crusades.

58. Daniel (1989b: 40) posits the same question in an interesting way: "The Gibbonian—and, indeed medieval—disillusion with the crusader's greed for land and booty has created a picture of them as rogues cynically exploiting religious sentiment to their profit. For us the interesting question is the reverse. How did the rogues come to be imbued with either the appearance or the reality of religious motivation?"

59. Even some of the leading lights of Latin Europe would play their part in the anti-Islamic propaganda over the course of the Crusading project, in one form or another; they would include Peter the Vulnerable, St. Francis of Assisi, Roger Bacon, St. Thomas Aquinas, Ramon Lull, Dante Alighieri, and so on (see Mastnak [2002], and Tolan [2002] for more on this issue).

60. Kedar (1984), suggests that the general absence of mission as an objective of the Crusades, especially in the early years of the project, is to be explained by the perception that the Muslims were implacably intolerant of Christian missionary work (ergo only the Christian sword could pave the way for it). While this perception was probably quite true, in reading Kedar one is unable to find sufficient evidence to disprove the fact that the primary goal of the Crusading project was crusade and not mission for reasons internal to the rise of the papal "monarchy." In other words, what one finds in Kedar is evidence that there were mission exceptions to the rule of crusading (but then exceptions do not disprove the rule, they confirm it). The prime motive behind the Crusading project was never proselytism given its essential underlying political objectives. Consequently, given the need to dehumanize the Muslims by demonizing them, as a means of justifying the Crusading project and at the same time as a device to recruit the European peasantry and nobility to execute it, the objective of acquiring Christian converts among the Muslims would have hardly entered into the calculations of the papacy—regardless of whether it was feasible or not. How else can one explain, for example, the great rejoicing by the Crusaders at their handiwork when they finally breached the walls of Jerusalem on Friday, July 15, 1099: the almost total and merciless slaughter of thousands upon thousands of its inhabitants, including children. See France (1997) for a chilling account of the capture of Jerusalem. Consider this thought—experiment: supposing that the Muslims had permitted missionary work, Would the Crusading project then have become irrelevant to the papal objective of erecting a papal monarchy?

61. For a dissenting view, albeit an unconvincing one, on some of the points raised here regarding the Crusades, see the concluding chapter of Richard (1999) whose bias in favor of the Crusader project is betrayed by lines like: "a liturgical feast was instituted in the breviary of the Holy Sepulcher to commemorate the capture of Jerusalem. *And the whole historical literature born of the crusade, like the epic, ends with this wonderful event*" (p. 67; emphasis added).

62. Perhaps there is some thing to the notion of a 1,000-year life cycle of civilizations.

Appendix III

European Colonial Empires in Africa on the Eve of Political Independence

The following data provides a snapshot of the various European colonial domains in Africa at the time of independence—the years in parenthesis indicate the approximate period that the territory or parts of the territory were under colonial rule. (The dates of independence for countries such as Egypt, South Africa, and Zimbabwe may raise some eyebrows, but from the perspective of the majority of the populations in these countries these were the true dates of independence.) In relevant instances colonial names are indicated in parenthesis, and for further clarifications see notes that follow each entry (based on information culled from a variety of encyclopedias and almanacs and supplemented by Chamberlain (1998). (Note: even though Liberia was an unofficial U.S. colony—controlled primarily by the American Colonization Society that helped found it—from 1815 to 1847 when it declared itself a sovereign state with a constitution modeled on that of the U.S., as an English speaking country it is included in this chapter as part of Anglophone Africa). It should also be noted that the Africans, as would be expected of any people, rarely accepted colonization willingly consequently, in what exact year *full* colonial rule was established for a given territory is subject to fungibility some other year may do just as well depending upon the level and duration of African resistance to the colonial project.

BRITAIN

Botswana (Bechuanaland) (1890–1968)
Egypt (1882–1956)
Gambia (1816–1965)
Ghana (1874–1957)

Kenya (1886–1964)
Lesotho (Basutoland) (1868–1966)
Malawi (Nyasaland) (1891–1964)
Namibia (South West Africa) (1884–1989)
Nigeria (1861–1960)
Sierra Leone (1807–1961)
Somalia (British Somaliland) (1867–1960)
South Africa (1814–1993)
Sudan (1898–1956)
Swaziland (1890–1968)
Tanzania—comprising:
    Tanganyika (1886–1964) and
    Zanzibar (1890–1964)
Uganda (1888–1962)
Zambia (Northern Rhodesia) (1891–1964)
Zimbabwe (Southern Rhodesia) (1888–1980).

Clarifications

(a) Tanganyika was known as German East Africa and in 1920 it became a British trust territory under the League of Nations mandate.
(b) In 1964 Tanganyika was joined with Zanzibar to form Tanzania.
(c) From 1953 through 1963 the countries of Malawi, Zambia and Zimbabwe were constituent parts of the Central African Federation.
(d) From 1965 to 1980 Zimbabwe was known as Rhodesia and ruled unilaterally (that is without British government authorization) by the white minority government of Ian Smith.
(e) Zambia and Zimbabwe commenced their entry into colonial status as a country known as Charterland ruled under a charter from the British government by Cecil Rhodes' British South Africa Company from 1891 until 1924.
(f) South Africa's journey toward a British colony commenced with the establishment of what would in time become the Cape Colony by the Dutch in 1652 later it would pass into French hands and from them, with the culmination of the Napoleonic Wars (1799–1815), Britain would inherit the colony in 1814.
(g) Namibia was a German colony that became a League of Nations trust territory under South African rule in 1915.
(h) Egypt became nominally independent in 1922, but the British retained effective control through their military presence until 1956.
(i) Somalia was formed by fusing together British Somaliland (northern regions ruled by the British from around 1867) with Italian Somaliland (eastern region).

FRANCE

Algeria (1830–1962)
Djibouti (French Somaliland, also known after 1967 as French Territory of Afars and Issas) (1888–1977)
Madagascar (1885–1960)
Morocco (1912–1956)
Tunisia (1881–1956)
West Africa:

Cameroon (1884–1960)
Togo (Togoland) (1884–1960)
French Equatorial Africa—comprising:
    Central African Republic (Ubanghi–Shari) (1885–1960)
    Chad (1885–1960)
    Gabon (1885–1960)
    Republic of the Congo (Middle Congo) (1882–1960)
French West Africa—comprising:
    Benin (Dahomey) (1889–1960)
    Burkina Faso (Upper Volta) (1896–1960)
    Cote d'Ivoire (Ivory Coast) (1887–1960)
    Equatorial Guinea (1891–1958)
    Mali (French Soudan) (1893–1960)
    Mauritania (1905–1960)
    Niger Territory (1890–1960)
    Senegal (1848–1960).

Clarifications

(a) French Equatorial Africa was established as a federal administrative unit in 1910 similarly French West Africa constituted as a unit in 1895.
(b) In 1919 the League of Nations mandated the German colony of Kamerun as a trust territory to France and Britain forming French and British Cameroons respectively. The latter comprised Northern and Southern Cameroons and a year following independence in 1960 the Northern portion of British Cameroons fused with Nigeria while the Southern part joined Cameroon
(c) The eastern portion of Togo—also a German colony—became a French trust territory in 1922 and became independent in 1960 as Togo. The British ruled western portion, following a plebiscite, was fused with Ghana in 1956.

PORTUGAL

Angola (1665–1975)
Cape Verde (1495–1975)
Mozambique (1505–1975).
Portuguese–Guinea (Guinea–Bissau) (1879–1974)
Sao Tome e Principe (1522–1975)

BELGIUM

Burundi (Ruanda–Urundi) (1885/1920–1960)
Democratic Republic of the Congo (Congo) (1885/1908–1960)
Rwanda (Ruanda–Urundi) (1885/1920–1962).

Clarifications

(a) Originally the Democratic Republic of the Congo became (through the Berlin Conference) the personal fiefdom of King Leopold of Belgium however in 1908, after revelations of the horrendous atrocities committed by his agents (it is estimated that some 10 million people were murdered over a 20 year period), it officially became the colony of Belgium proper.

(b) The present Democratic Republic of the Congo had the same name at independence in 1960 however, in 1971 the then ruling military dictator Joseph Mobutu (Sese–Seko) changed its name to Zaire after he was overthrown by Lawrence Kabila in 1997, it reverted back to its old name.

(c) Ruanda–Urundi was mandated over to the Belgians as a trust territory in 1920 by the League of Nations it was formerly one of the German colonies. At independence in 1960 it was divided into its present components.

ITALY

Eritrea (1869–1941)
Ethiopia (Abyssinia) (1936–1941)
Libya (1912–1951).
Somalia (Italian Somaliland) (1889–1960)

Clarifications

(a) Eritrea was governed by the British from 1941 to 1952 thereafter it was federated with Ethiopia until Ethiopia terminated the federation and absorbed it as one of its provinces in 1962. However, the year before, the Ethiopian Liberation Front had launched its liberation struggle that would eventually lead to independence from Ethiopia in 1993.

(b) Somalia was formed by fusing together British Somaliland (northern regions ruled by the British from around 1867) with Italian Somaliland (eastern region) in 1960.

SPAIN

Ceuta (1580–?),
Equatorial Guinea (Spanish Guinea) (1778/1844–1968)
Ifini (1476–1969)
Melilla (1497–?),
Morocco—Northern portion (Spanish Morocco) (1904–1956)
Saharan Arab Democratic Republic (Spanish Sahara) (1884–1976).

Clarifications

(a) Originally Spanish Guinea comprised the Island of Fernando Po (ceded by Portugal to Spain in 1778) and the province of Rio Muni acquired by the Spanish in 1844. In 1904 the two territories became a single unit with the name West African Territories—later changed to Spanish Guinea.

(b) Until 1958, Spanish Sahara was two different territories, Rio de Oro (southern two thirds) and Saguia el Hamra (the northern third). After Spain vacated Spanish Sahara in 1976, Morocco and Mauritania took over the country against the wishes of its inhabitants (the Sahrawi), some of whom were now engaged in a liberation struggle under the name Polisario (Popular Front for the Liberation of Saguia el Hamra and Rio de Oro). In 1979 Morocco took over the Mauritanian portion as well when the latter reached a peace agreement with Polisario (who had by now renamed the country Saharan Arab Democratic Republic. Although the majority of the World's countries have recognized the Republic and its Polisario led government in exile, the Moroccans have refused to relinquish their colonial hold on it to date—the liberation struggle continues as of 2005.

(c) Ifni was ceded to Morocco in 1969.

(d) Although both Melilla and Ceuta are geographically part of Morocco the Spanish continue to rule over these small 'city–states' (they also rule three other small outposts: Alhucemas, Chafarinas Islands, and Penon de Velez de la Gomera on and off the coast of Morocco). These five areas together make up the *plazas* of Spanish North Africa.

Glossary

---

alim — religious scholar who has mastered a body of Islamic religious sciences. Note: the plural of alim is **ulama**.)

Al'lah — God (Islam's monotheistic deity—the same deity worshipped also by Jews and Christians).

awail — category of knowledge represented by the "foreign sciences," meaning secular subjects such as astronomy, biology, physics, mathematics, medicine, etc.

bid'aa — heretical innovation.

dhimma — contractual understanding between a Muslim state and the **dhimmi** in which the former undertakes to protect the latter in exchange for a poll tax called the **jizya**.

dhimmi — non-Muslim subjects of an Islamic state subject to the **dhimma**.

fatwa — binding legal opinion issued by a **mufti**.

fiqh — short for **usul-al-fiqh**.

hadith — one of the major sources of Islamic law comprising the tradition of Prophet Muhammed—which itself rests on precedent established by his *authenticated* public utterances and deeds.

hajj — annual pilgrimage to the Islamic holy city of Mecca mandatory on all Muslims who can afford it at least once in their lifetime.

halqahs — study circles in a **masjid** or **madrasah**.

hubus — Maghrebi word for **waqf**.

ijaza — certificate issued by a member of the **ulama** to a student attesting to mastery of a specific body of Islamic sciences; it authorizes the student to be a teacher of this body of Islamic knowledge.

ijma — consensus of opinion on issues pertaining to the **Shari'ah** among Islamic legal scholars.

imam — usually a congregational prayer leader who may or may not be educated in the Islamic sciences beyond the absolute minimum required to serve in this role. Among the Shi'a, however, the term has a much more specific meaning signifying a spiritual leader with lines of descent traceable to the fourth Caliph of Islam, Ali.

infitah — "Open Door." The policy that opened the door to the Egyptian economy through liberalization of the state capitalist polices of Jamal Abdel Nasser by his successor, Anwar Sadat (equivalent to the World Bank's structural adjustment policy). The **infitah** also had the effect, in turn, of liberalizing some of Nasser's other autocratic policies as well.

jami-al-masjid — the **masjid** where the mandatory congregational prayers on Islam's holiest day of the week, Friday, take place.

jihad — struggle for the sake of **Al'lah**. (There are two related meanings of struggle here: at the community level the struggle takes the form of a defensive war; at the individual level it takes the form of a personal quest for salvation.)

jizya — poll tax levied on the **dhimmi**.

kuttab — Qur'anic school (a form of primary school found through out the Islamic world where literacy and the basic elements of religious knowledge are taught).

madina — center of a city (not to be confused with the Islamic holy city of Medina in Saudi Arabia).

madrasah — this word has three related but different geographic-specific meanings: in most of the Islamic world it refers to a mosque-university/college; in the Maghrebi part of North Africa it refers to the student dormitory attached to the mosque-university/college; and in Islamic A sia it refers to both the mosque-university/college and the **kuttab**.

Maghreb — a geographic term referring to the part of North Africa west of Egypt. It is the shortened form of the Arabic term that the conquering Muslims applied to all of North Africa west of Egypt: Bilad-al-Maghreb (meaning "Lands of Sunset"). The Maghreb as a province of the Islamic empire was known as "Ifriqiyah." The Maghreb today constitutes Algeria, Libya, Mauritania, Morocco, Tunisia and Western Sahara. (Note: the geographical opposite of Maghreb is *Mashreq*, which refers to Egypt and other Arab countries in the East: Yemen, Saudi Arabia, etc.)

maktab — generally a **kuttab** (though it may have specific localized meaning differentiating it slightly from a kuttab-level education).

masjid — mosque, a place where religious worship and other community-centered religious and educational activities take place.

mufti — jurisconsult who can issue a **fatwa**.

qadi — Muslim judge who renders judgments according to the **Shari'ah**, in the employ of an Islamic state.

qira'at — trained recitation of the **Qur'an**.

Qur'an — the holy book of Muslims equivalent in importance to the Bible (in Christianity) and the Torah (in Judaism).

Shari'ah — religious Islamic laws, both civil and criminal, based on the **Qur'an**, **hadith**, and **ijma**.

shaykh — another term for an **alim**; but also used to mean a political leader or notable.

Shi'a — those who belong to the other (much smaller) part of the major division that arose in Islam over the question of the rightful heir to the Islamic caliphate. The Shi'a pressed the claims of Ali (the son in law of Prophet Muhammed) and his descendants, in opposition to the **Sun'ni** (who supported claims to the caliphate based not on blood lines but consensually determined elections—hence their recognition of the Ummayads). It should be noted that neither parts of this major schismatic division recognizes the legitimacy of the other as members of the **Um'mah**, that is, as authentic Muslims.

Sufi — practitioner of **Sufism**.

Sufism — ascetic ecstatic Islamic mysticism practiced and venerated in some parts of the Islamic world, while in other parts it is considered an embodiment of profanation; that is, a heretical innovation (referred to in Islam as **bid'a**).

sunnah — traditions of Prophet Muhammed, in this case his behavioral precedents as verified by the **hadith**.

Sun'ni — see **Shi'a**.

tafsir — exegesis of the **Qur'an**.

ulama — community of **alims**.

Um'mah — global community of Muslims (that *theologically*, though not in practice, brooks no boundaries: national, ethnic, race, class, and so on.)

usul-al-fiqh — Islamic jurisprudence.

waqf — a permanent endowed charitable trust established to finance any project of benefit to the public—ranging from **madrasahs** to roads to sewage systems. Note: there are, in practice, two types of waqfs, the public or charitable trust (referred to as *waqf qhayri*) and the private family trust (known as *waqf ahli*). It is the former and not the latter that is being referred to here.

zawiyah — monastic religious complex run by a Sufi order that usually has a shrine, a **madrasah**, a guesthouse, etc. as part of the complex.

Bibliography

Note: Some of the documents produced by multilateral agencies and nongovernmental organizations cited in this work and mentioned here, are available on the Internet. However, because of the inherently peripatetic nature of web documents, it is pointless to provide web addresses (URLs) for these documents. Instead, the reader is advised to locate the websites of the relevant organizations and proceed from there. Alternatively, select a global search engine like Google, Yahoo, or Altavista and do a search by entering the full document title.

Abdalla, Ahmed. 1985. *The Student Movement and National Politics in Egypt, 1923–1973*. London: Al Saqi (distributed by Zed).

Abd'allah Harir, Sharif; Tvedt, Terje; and Badal, Raphael K. 1994. *Short-Cut to Decay: The Case of the Sudan*. Uppsala: Nordiska Afrikainstitutet.

Abdel-Rahim, Muddathir. 1969. *Imperialism and Nationalism in the Sudan: A Study in Constitutional and Political Development, 1899–1956*. Oxford: Clarendon.

Abdi, Ali A. 1998. "Education in Somalia: History, Destruction, and Calls for Reconstruction." *Comparative Education* 34 (no. 3): 327–40.

Abdi, Ali A. 2002. *Culture, Education, and Development in South Africa*. Westport, CT: Bergin & Garvey.

Abraham, Kinfe. 1993. *Ethiopia: The Challenge of 20th Century Education and Modernization—and the Role of Swedish Aid*. Uppsala: Scandinavian Institute of African Studies (for the Swedish International Development Authority, Education Division).

Abu-Izzeddin, Nejla M. 1981. *Nasser of the Arabs: An Arab Assessment*. London: Third World Center for Research and Publishing.

Abu-Lughod, Janet L. 1989. *Before European Hegemony: The World System A. D. 1250–1350.* New York: Oxford University Press.

Abulafia, D. 1994. "The Role of Trade in Muslim-Christian Contact During the Middle Ages." In *The Arab Influence in Medieval Europe,* ed. by D. A. Agius, and R. Hitchcock, pp. 1–24. Reading, U. K.: Ithaca.

Abun-Nasr, Jamil M. 1987. *A History of the Maghreb in the Islamic Period.* New York: Cambridge University Press.

Acemoglu, Daron; Johnson, Simon; and Robinson, James A. 2002. *The Rise of Europe: Atlantic Trade, Institutional Change and Economic Growth.* Cambridge, MA: National Bureau of Economic Research.

Adam, H. 1980. "Somali Policies toward Education, Training and Manpower." In *Policy Developments in Overseas Training,* ed. by T.L. Maliyamkono. Dar es Salaam: Eastern African Universities Research Project.

Adam, Hussein M. 2004. "Somalia: International versus Local Attempts at Peacebuilding." In *Durable Peace: Challenges for Peacebuilding in Africa,* ed. by Taisier M. Ali and Robert O. Matthews, pp. 253–81. Buffalo, NY: University of Toronto Press.

Adams, William Y. 1977. *Nubia: Corridor to Africa.* Princeton, NJ: Princeton University Press.

Adebe Zegeye, and Pausewang, Siegfried. 1994. *Ethiopia in Change: Peasantry, Nationalism and Democracy.* London: British Academic.

Adi, Hakim. 1998. *West Africans in Britain, 1900–1960: Nationalism, Pan-Africanism and Communism.* London: Lawrence & Wishart.

African Development Bank. 2001. *African Development Report 2001.* Oxford: Oxford University Press.

Ahmad, Abdussamad H. 1997. "Trade and Islam: Relations of the Muslims with the Court in Gondar 1864–1941." In *Ethiopia in Broader Perspective: Papers of 13th International Conference of Ethiopian Studies,* vol. 1 (of 3), ed. by Katsuyoshi Fukui, Eisei Kurimoto, and Masayoshi Shigeta, pp. 128–37. Kyoto: Shokado.

Ahmad, Aziz. 1975. *A History of Islamic Sicily.* Edinburgh: Edinburgh University Press.

Ahmed, Ali Jimale (ed.) 1995. *The Invention of Somalia.* Lawrenceville, NJ: Red Sea.

Ahmed, E. 1992. "The Murder of History." *Covert Action Quarterly* (no. 41, summer): 4.

Ahmed, Hussein. 2001. *Islam in Nineteenth-Century Wallo, Ethiopia: Revival, Reform and Reaction.* Boston: Brill.

Ajayi, J. F. Ade; Goma, Lameck K. H.; and Johnson, G. Ampah. 1996. *The African Experience with Higher Education.* Athens: Ohio University Press.

Akapelwa, Emma. 1989. "Problems of Music Education: A Comparative Study [Zambia, Great Britain]." Ph.D. dissertation, Queen's University of Belfast.

Aklilu Habte. 1974. "Higher Education in Ethiopia in the 1970s and Beyond: A Survey of Some Issues and Responses." In *Education and Development Reconsidered: The Bellagio Conference Papers,* ed. by F. Champion Ward, pp. 214–40. New York: Praeger.

Alaka I. Kalewold. 1970. *Traditional Ethiopian Church Education.* New York: Teachers College Press.

Alavi, Seema. 1995. *The Sepoy and the Company, Tradition and Transition in Northern India, 1770–1830*. New York: Oxford University Press.

Alem Asres. 1990. "History of the Ethiopian Student Movement in Ethiopia and North America: Its Impact on Internal Social Change 1960–1974." Ph.D. dissertation, University of Maryland.

Alexander, K. 2003. "The Washington Consensus, Globalization, Equalization, and School Privatization." *Journal of Education Finance* 29 (no. 2): 185–90.

Alghailani, Said Ali. 2002. "Islam and the French Decolonization of Algeria: The Role of the Algerian Ulama, 1919–1940." Ph.D. dissertation, Indiana University.

Al-Hassan, Ahmad Y., and Hill, Donald R. 1986. *Islamic Technology: An Illustrated History.* Cambridge: Cambridge University Press.

Alioto, Anthony M. 1987. *A History of Western Science.* Englewood Cliffs, NJ: Prentice-Hall.

Allen, James; Als, Hilton; Lewis, John; and Litwack, Leon F. 2000. *Without Sanctuary: Lynching Photography in America.* Santa Fe, NM: Twin Palms.

Allen, Ricky Lee. 2001. "The Globalization of White Supremacy: Toward a Critical Discourse on the Racialization of the World." *Educational Theory* 51 (no. 4): 467–85.

Allen, Theodore W. 1994. *The Invention of the White Race.* (2 vols.) London: Verso.

Allsen, Thomas T. 1987. *Mongol Imperialism: The Policies of the Grand Qan Möngke in China, Russia and the Islamic Lands, 1251–1259.* Berkeley: University of California Press.

Altbach, Philip G. (ed.) 1989. *Student Political Activism: An International Reference Handbook.* Westport, CT: Greenwood.

Altbach, Philip G. 1998. *Comparative Higher Education: Knowledge, the University and Development.* Greenwich, CT: Ablex.

Altbach, Philip G. (ed.) 1999. *Private Prometheus: Private Higher Education and Development in the 21st Century.* Westport, CT: Greenwood.

Altbach, Philip G. 2001. "The Rise of the Pseudouniversities." *International Higher Education* (no. 25, fall): 2–3.

Altbach, Philip G. 2002. "Knowledge and Education as International Commodities: The Collapse of the Common Good." *International Higher Education* (no. 28, summer): 2–5.

Altbach, Philip G. 2003. "Globalization and the University: Myths and Realities in an Unequal World." *Current Issues in Catholic Higher Education* 23 (no. 1): 5–25.

Althusser, Louis. 1972. *Lenin and Philosophy, and Other Essays.* (Translated from the French by Ben Brewster.) New York: Monthly Review.

Amare Tekle. 1990. "Continuity and Change in Ethiopian Politics." In *The Political Economy of Ethiopia*, ed. by Marina Ottaway, pp. 31–52. New York: Praeger.

Amin, Samir. 1982. "The New International Economic Order and the Problems of Education." In *Higher Education and the New International Order: A Collection of Papers*, ed. by B. Sanyal, pp. 145–58. Paris: UNESCO.

Amin, Samir. 1989. *Eurocentrism.* New York: Monthly Review.

Amin, Samir. 2003. *Obsolescent Capitalism: Contemporary Politics and Global Disorder.* (Translated by Patrick Camiller.) London: Zed.

Amin, Samir. 2004. "U.S. Imperialism, Europe, and the Middle East." *Monthly Review* 56 (no. 6): 13–33.

Amnesty International. 2004 (a). *Sudan, Darfur: Too Many People Killed for No Reason.* London: International Secretariat.

Amnesty International. 2004 (b). *Sudan, Darfur: Rape as a Weapon, Sexual Violence and Its Consequences.* London: Amnesty International, International Secretariat.

Amoako, K. Y. 2000. *Claiming the 21st Century: Africa's Agenda.* Washington, DC: Center for Strategic and International Studies, Global Information Infrastructure Commission. (Paper presented at the National Summit on Africa, Washington, DC, February 17, 2000.)

Amonoo-Neizer, Eugene H. 1998. "Universities in Africa—The Need for Adaptation, Transformation, Reformation and Revitalization." *Higher Education Policy* 11 (no. 4, December): 301–09.

Amukugo, Elizabeth Magano. 1993. *Education and Politics in Namibia: Past Trends and Future Prospects.* Windhoek: Gamsberg Macmillan.

Andargachew Tiruneh. 1993. *The Ethiopian Revolution, 1974–1987: A Transformation from an Aristocratic to a Totalitarian Autocracy.* New York: Cambridge University Press.

Anderson, C. A., and Bowman M. J. 1965. *Education and Economic Development.* Chicago: Aldine.

Anderson, G. Norman. 1999. *Sudan in Crisis: The Failure of Democracy.* Gainesville: University Press of Florida.

Anderson, Gregory M. 2002. *Building a People's University in South Africa: Race, Compensatory Education and the Limits of Democratic Reform.* New York: Peter Lang.

Anderson, Perry. 1979 (1974). *Lineages of the Absolutist State.* London: Verso.

Andrew, C. M., and Kanya–Forstner, A. S. 1974. "Gabriel Hanotaux, the Colonial Party and the Fashoda Strategy." *Journal of Imperial and Commonwealth History* 3: 55–104.

Anstee, Margaret Joan. 1996. *Orphan of the Cold War: The Inside Story of the Collapse of the Angolan Peace Process, 1992–1993.* New York: St. Martin's.

Aoki, Sumio, and Kurimoto, Eisei. 1997. "Japanese Interest in Ethiopia (1868–1940): Chronology and Bibliography." In *Ethiopia in Broader Perspective: Papers of 13th International Conference of Ethiopian Studies,* vol. 1 (of 3), ed. by Katsuyoshi Fukui, Eisei Kurimoto, and Masayoshi Shigeta, pp. 713–28. Kyoto: Shokado.

Apel, Dora. 2004. *Imagery of Lynching: Black Men, White Women, and the Mob.* Piscataway, NJ: Rutgers University Press.

Appel, Stephen W. 1989. "Outstanding Individuals Do Not Arise from Ancestrally Poor Stock: Racial Science and the Education of Black South Africans." *Journal of Negro Education* 58 (no. 4): 544–57.

Appelbaum, Richard P., and Robinson, William I. (eds.) 2005. *Critical Globalization Studies.* London: Routledge.

Archer, Christon I.; Ferris, John R.; Herwig, Holger H.; and Travers, Timothy H. E. 2002. *World History of Warfare.* Lincoln: University of Nebraska Press.

Arkell, A. J. 1973. *A History of the Sudan from the Earliest Times to 1821.* Westport, CT: Greenwood.

Artz, Frederick B. 1980. *The Mind of the Middle Ages.* Chicago: University of Chicago Press.

Asante, Molefi K. 1992. *Kemet, Afrocentricity and Knowledge.* Trenton, NJ: Africa World.

Asante, Molefi K., and Mazama, Ama. (eds.) 2002. *Egypt vs. Greece and the American Academy.* Chicago: African American Images.

Ashby, Eric. 1964. *African Universities and Western Tradition: The Godkin Lectures at Harvard University.* Cambridge: Harvard University Press.

Ashby, Eric. 1966. *Universities: British, Indian, African: A Study in the Ecology of Higher Education.* Cambridge: Harvard University Press; London: Weidenfeld & Nicolson.

Ashton, David; Green, Francis; James, Donna; and Sung, Johnny. 1999. *Education and Training for Development in East Asia: The Political Economy of Skill Formation in East Asian Newly Industrialized Countries.* London: Routledge.

Ashtor, Eliyahu. 1976. *A Social and Economic History of the Near East in the Middle Ages.* Berkeley: University of California Press.

Asres, Alem. 1990. See Alem Asres. 1990.

Assie-Lumumba, N'Dri T. 1996. "The Role and Mission of African Higher Education: Preparing for the 21st Century and Beyond." *South African Journal of Higher Education* 10 (no. 2): 5–12.

Association of African Universities and the World Bank. 1997. *Revitalizing Universities in Africa: Strategies and Guidelines.* Washington, DC: The World Bank.

Atchoarena, David, and Esquieu, Paul. 2002. *Private Technical and Vocational Education in Sub–Saharan Africa: Provision Patterns and Policy Issues.* Paris: International Institute for Educational Planning.

Authier, Michel. 1995. "Refraction and Cartesian 'Forgetfulness'." In *A History of Scientific Thought: Elements of a History of Science,* ed. by Michel Serres, pp. 315–43. Oxford: Blackwell.

Auty, Richard M., and Toye, John. (eds.) 1996. *Challenging the Orthodoxies.* New York: St. Martin's.

Avineri, Shlomo. 1968. *Karl Marx on Colonialism and Modernization.* Garden City, NY: Doubleday.

Ayittey, George B. N. 1998. Africa in Chaos. New York: St. Martin's.

Azikiwe, Nnamdi. 1961. *Zik: A Selection from the Speeches of Nnamdi Azikiwe.* Cambridge: Cambridge University Press.

Azikiwe, Nnamdi. 1970. *My Odyssey: An Autobiography.* New York: Praeger.

Azvedo, Mario. 1970. "A Century of Colonial Education in Mozambique." In *Independence Without Freedom: The Political Economy of Colonial Education in Southern Africa,* ed. by Agrippah T. Mugomba, and Mougo Nyaggah, pp. 191–213. Santa Barbara, CA: ABC-Clio.

Badat, Saleem. 2002 (1999). *Black Student Politics: Higher Education and Apartheid: From SASO to SANSCO.* New York: RoutledgeFalmer.

Baechler, Jean; Hall, John A.; and Mann, Michael. (eds.) 1988. *Europe and the Rise of Capitalism.* New York: Blackwell.

Bahru Zewde. 2001. *A History of Modern Ethiopia: 1855–1991*. Athens: Ohio University Press.

Bailey, Anne M., and Llobera, Josep R. (eds.) 1981. *The Asiatic Mode of Production: Science and Politics*. Boston: Routledge & Kegan Paul.

Balakrishnan, Gopal. (ed.) 2003. *Debating Empire*. New York: Verso.

Balard, Michel. 2003. "Notes on the Economic Consequences of the Crusades." In *The Experience of Crusading* (vol. 2), ed. by Peter Edbury, and Jonathan Phillips, pp. 233–39. Cambridge: Cambridge University Press.

Ballantyne, Tony. 2002. "Empire, Knowledge and Culture: From Proto-Globalization to Modern Globalization." In *Globalization in World History*, ed. by A. G. Hopkins, pp. 116–40. New York: W. W. Norton.

Balogh, T. 1964. "The Economics of Educational Planning: Sense and Nonsense" *Comparative Education* 1 (no. 1): 5–17.

Balsvik, Randi R. 1985. *Haile Sellassie's Students: The Intellectual and Social Background to Revolution, 1952–1977*. East Lansing: African Studies Center, Michigan State University in cooperation with the Norwegian Council of Science and the Humanities.

Banya, K., and Elu, J. 2001. "The World Bank and Financing Higher Education in Sub-Saharan Africa." *Higher Education* 42 (1): 1–34.

Baran, Paul A., and Sweezy, Paul M. 1966. *Monopoly Capital: An Essay on the American Economic and Social Order*. Harmondsworth: Penguin.

Barber, James P., and Barratt, John. 1990. *South Africa's Foreign Policy: The Search for Status and Security, 1945–1988*. New York: Cambridge University Press.

Bard, Kathryn A., and Fattovich, Rodolfo. 2001. "Some Remarks on the Processes of State Formation in Egypt and Ethiopia." In *Africa and Africans in Antiquity*, ed. by Edwin M. Yamauchi, pp. 276–90. East Lansing: Michigan State University Press.

Barett, Ward. "World Bullion Flows, 1450–1800." In *The Rise of the Merchant Empires: Long Distance Trade in the Early Modern World, 1350–1750*, ed. by James D. Tracy, pp. 224–54. Cambridge: Cambridge University Press.

Bartels, Francis L. 2003. *The African University at the Threshold of the New Millennium: Potential, Process, Performance and Prospects*. Paris: UNESCO (Meeting of Higher Education Partners).

Bates, Darrell. 1984. *The Fashoda Incident of 1898: Encounter On the Nile*. Oxford: Oxford University Press.

Batou, Jean. 1991. "Muhammad Ali's Egypt, 1805–48: A Command Economy in the 19th Century?" In *Between Development and underdevelopment: The Precarious Attempts at Industrialization of the Periphery, 1800–70*, ed. by Jean Batou, pp. 181–217. Geneva: Droz.

Bauer, P. T. 1981. *Equality, the Third World and Economic Delusion*. Cambridge: Harvard University Press.

Bayart, Jean-Francois; Ellis, Stephen; and Hibou, Beatrice. 1999. *The Criminalization of the State in Africa*. Bloomington: Indiana University Press.

Bayly, C. A. 1989. *Imperial Meridian: The British Empire and the World, 1780–1830*. New York: Longman.

Beaujouan, Guy. 1982. "The Transformation of the Quadrivium." In *Renaissance and Renewal in the Twelfth Century*, ed. by Robert L. Benson and Giles Constable with Carol D. Lanham, pp. 463–87. Cambridge: Harvard University Press.

Bedini, Silvio A. (ed.) 1992. *The Christopher Columbus Encyclopedia*. New York: Simon & Schuster.

Behrens-Abouseif, Doris. 1994. *Egypt's Adjustment to Ottoman Rule: Institutions, Waqf and Architecture in Cairo (16th and 17th Centuries)*. Leiden: E. J. Brill.

Beinin, Joel, and Stork, Joe. (eds.) 1997. *Political Islam: Essays from the Middle East Report*. Berkeley: University of California Press.

Bell, Derrick A. 1988. "White Superiority in America: Its Legal Legacy, Its Economic Costs." *Villanova Law Review* 33 (September): 767–79.

Bell, Derrick A. 1990. "After We're Gone: Prudent Speculations on America in a Post–Racial Epoch." *Saint Louis University Law Journal* 34 (Spring): 393–405.

Bell, Terry, and Ntsebeza, Dumisa Buhle. 2001. *Unfinished Business: South Africa, Apartheid and Truth*. Cape Town: Redworks.

Bello, Walden. 2001. *The Future in the Balance: Essays on Globalization and Resistance*. Oakland, CA: Food First.

Ben-David, Joseph. 1992 (1977). *Centers of Learning: Britain, France, Germany, United States*. New Brunswick, NJ: Transaction.

Bender, Gerald J. 1981. "Kissinger in Angola: Anatomy of Failure." In *American Policy in Southern Africa: The Stakes and the Stance, Second Edition*, ed. by Rene Lemarchand, pp. 63–143. Washington, DC: University Press of America.

Ben-Ghiat, Ruth, and Fuller, Mia. 2002. *Italian Colonialism*. New York: Palgrave Macmillan.

Bennaars, Gerard A.; Seif, Huda A.; and Mwangi, Doris. 1996. *Mid-Decade Review of Progress towards Education for All: The Somalia Country Case Study*. Paris: UNESCO and the International Consultative Forum on Education for All.

Bennett, W. S. 1967. "Educational Change and Economic Development" *Sociology of Education* 40 (Spring): 101–14.

Bennoune, Mahfoud. 1988. *The Making of Contemporary Algeria, 1830–1987: Colonial Upheavals and Post-Independence Development*. New York: Cambridge University Press.

Benoit, Paul. 1995. "Theology in the Thirteenth Century: A Science Unlike the Others." In *A History of Scientific Thought: Elements of a History of Science*, ed. by Michel Serres, pp. 222–45. Oxford: Blackwell.

Benoit, Paul, and Micheau, Francoise. 1995. "The Arab Intermediary." In *A History of Scientific Thought: Elements of a History of Science*, ed. by Michel Serres, pp. 191–221. Oxford: Blackwell.

Berberoglu, Berch. (ed.) 2004. *Globalization and Change: The Transformation of Global Capitalism*. Lanham: Lexington.

Berger, Stefan; Feldner, Heiko; and Passmore, Kevin. (eds.) 2003. *Writing History: Theory and Practice*. London: Hodder Arnold.

Bergeron, Suzanne. 2003. "Challenging the World Bank's Narrative of Inclusion." In *World Bank Literature*, ed. by Amitava Kumar, pp. 157–71. Minneapolis: University of Minnesota Press.

Bergreen, Laurence. 2003. *Over the Edge of the World: Magellan's Terrifying Circumnavigation of the Globe*. New York: William Morrow.

Berkes, Niyazi. 1964. *The Development of Secularism in Turkey*. Montreal: McGill University Press.

Berlinerblau, Jacques. 1999. *Heresy in the University: The Black Athena Controversy and the Responsibilities of American Intellectuals*. New Brunswick, NJ: Rutgers University Press.

Berman, Edward. 1989. *The World Before Columbus, 1100–1492*. London: W. H. Allen.

Berman, Edward. (ed.) 1975. *African Reactions to Missionary Education*. New York: Teachers College Press.

Bernal, Martin. 1987. *The Afroasiatic Roots of Classical Civilization. Vol. 1. The Fabrication of Ancient Greece, 1785–1985*. New Brunswick, NJ: Rutgers University Press.

Bernal, Martin. 1991. *The Afroasiatic Roots of Classical Civilization. Vol. 2. The Archaeological and Documentary Evidence*. New Brunswick, NJ: Rutgers University Press.

Bernal, Martin. 2001. *Black Athena Writes Back: Martin Bernal Responds to His Critics*. Ed. by David Chioni Moore. Durham: Duke University Press.

Beshir, Mohamed Omer. 1969. *Educational Development in the Sudan, 1898–1956*. Oxford: Clarendon.

Besteman, Catherine. 1996. "Violent Politics and the Politics of Violence: The Dissolution of the Somali Nation-State." *American Ethnologist* 23 (no. 3): 579–96.

Besteman, Catherine. 1999. *Unraveling Somalia: Race, Violence, and the Legacy of Slavery*. Philadelphia: University of Pennsylvania Press.

Beswick, Stephanie. 2004. *Sudan's Blood Memory: the Legacy of War, Ethnicity, and Slavery in Early South Sudan*. Rochester: University of Rochester Press.

Betts, Raymond F. 2004. *Decolonization*. (2nd ed.) New York: Routledge.

Bieder, Robert E. 1986. *Science Encounters the Indian, 1820–1880: The Early Years of American Ethnology*. Norman: University of Oklahoma Press.

Biersteker, Thomas J. 1990. "Reducing the Role of the State in the Economy: A Conceptual Exploration of IMF and World Bank Prescriptions." *International Studies Quarterly* 34 (no. 4): 477–92.

Bizos, George. 1998. *No One to Blame? In Pursuit of Justice in South Africa*. Cape Town: David Philip.

Blanks, David R. 1999 (a). "Introduction." In *Western Views of Islam in Medieval and Early Modern Europe: Perceptions of Other*, ed. by David R. Blanks and Michael Frassetto, pp. 1–9. New York: St. Martin's Press.

Blanks, David R., and Frassetto, Michael. (eds.) 1999 (b). *Western Views of Islam in Medieval and Early Modern Europe: Perceptions of Other*. New York: St. Martin's Press.

Blaug, M. 1999. "Review of *Economics of Education: Research and Studies*." In *Education Policy*, ed. by J. Marshall and M. Peters, pp. 101–05. Cheltanham: Edward Elgar.

Blaut, J. M. 1992. *1492: The Debate on Colonialism, Eurocentrism and History*. Trenton, NJ: Africa World.

Blaut, J. M. 1993. *The Colonizer's Model of the World: Geographical Diffusionism and Eurocentric History*. New York: Guilford.

Blaut, J. M. 2000. *Eight Eurocentric Historians*. New York: Guilford.

Bloomfield, Richard J. 1988. "U. S. Policy: Doctrine vs. Interest." In *Regional Conflict and U. S. Foreign Policy: Angola and Mozambique*, ed. by Richard J. Bloomfield, pp. 207–28. Algonac, MI: Reference Publications.

Blum, Jeffrey M. 1978. *Pseudoscience and Mental Ability: The Origins and Fallacies of the IQ Controversy*. New York: Monthly Review.

Blurton, Craig. 1999. "[Information and Communication Technologies and Social Processes] New Directions in Education." In *World Communication and Information Report, 1999/2000*, pp. 46–61. Paris: UNESCO.

Blyden, Edward Wilmot. 1967. *Christianity, Islam and the Negro Race*. Edinburgh: Edinburgh University Press.

Boahen, A. Adu. (ed.) 1985. *General History of Africa, Volume VII: Africa under Colonial Domination, 1880–1935*. Berkeley: University of California Press.

Bollag, Burton. 1998. "International Aid Groups Shift Focus to Higher Education in Developing Nations." *Chronicle of Higher Education* (October 30): A51.

Bonilla-Silva, Eduardo. 2003. *Racism without Racists: Color-Blind Racism and the Persistence of Racial Inequality in the United States*. Blue Ridge Summit, PA: Rowman & Littlefield.

Booth, Alan R. 1976. *The United States Experience in South Africa, 1784–1870*. Cape Town: A. A. Balkema.

Boren, Mark Edelman. 2001. *Student Resistance: A History of the Unruly Subject*. New York: Routledge.

Bowden, Mark. 1999. *Black Hawk Down: A Story of Modern War*. New York: Atlantic Monthly.

Boyer, Ernest L. 1996. "The Scholarship of Engagement." *Journal of Public Service and Outreach* 1 (no. 1): 11–20.

Boyle, Patrick M. 1999. *Class Formation and Civil Society: The Politics of Education in Africa*. Aldershot: Ashgate.

Braathen, Einar; Bas, Morten; and Sther, Gjermund. 1999. *Ethnicity Kills: The Politics of War, Peace and Ethnicity in Sub-Saharan Africa*. New York: St. Martin's Press.

Braudel, Fernand. 1982–1984. *Civilization and Capitalism: 15th–18th Century*. (3 vols.) New York: Harper & Row.

Braukämper, Ulrich. 2003. *Islamic History and Culture in Southern Ethiopia: A Collection of Essays*. London: Lit.

Brenner, Robert. 1997. "The Origins of Capitalist Development: A Critique of Neo-Smithian Marxism." *New Left Review* (no. 104): 25–93.

Brett, Michael. 2001. The Rise of the Fatimids: The World of the Mediterranean and the Middle East in the Fourth Century of the Hijra, Tenth Century CE. Leiden: Brill.

Brittain, Victoria. 1988 (a). "Cuba and Southern Africa." *New Left Review* (no. 172, November/December): 117–24.

Brittain, Victoria. 1988 (b). *Hidden Lives, Hidden Deaths: South Africa's Crippling of a Continent*. London: Farber and Farber.

Brock-Utne, Birgit. 2003. "Formulating Higher Education Policies in Africa: The Pressure from External Forces and the Neoliberal Agenda." *Journal of Higher Education in Africa* 1 (no. 1): 24–56.

Brodeur, Jean–Paul. 1997. *Violence and Racial Prejudice in the Context of Peacekeeping: A Study Prepared for the Commission of Inquiry into the Deployment of Canadian Forces to Somalia.* Ottawa: Commission of Inquiry into the Deployment of Canadian Forces to Somalia.

Brown, Godfrey N. 1964. "British Educational Policy in West and Central Africa." *The Journal of Modern African Studies* 2 (no. 3): 365–77.

Brundage, James A. 1997. "Immortalizing the Crusades: Laws and Institutions." In *Montjoie: Studies in Crusader History in Honour of Hans Eberhard Mayer*, ed. by Benjamin Z. Kedar; Jonathan Riley-Smith; and Rudolf Hiestand, pp. 251–60. Brookfield, VT: Variorum/ Ashgate.

Bryden, Matthew. 1995. "Somalia: The Wages of Failure." *Current History* 94 (April): 145–51.

Buchert, Lene, and King, Kenneth (eds.) 1995. *Learning from Experience: Policy and Practice in Aid to Higher Education.* The Hague: Center for the Study of Education in Developing Countries.

Bullough, V. L. 1961. "Status and Medieval Medicine." *Journal of Health and Human Behavior* 2 (3): 204–10.

Bundy, Colin. 1979. *The Rise and Fall of the South African Peasantry.* Berkeley: University of California Press.

Bunting, Ian. 1994. *A Legacy of Inequality: Higher Education in South Africa.* Rondelbosch: UCT Press.

Burawoy, Michael. 1976. "Consciousness and Contradiction: A Study of Student Protest in Zambia." *British Journal of Sociology* 27 (no. 1): 78–97.

Burbules, Nicholas C., and Torres, Carlos Alberto. (eds.) 1999. *Globalization and Education: Critical Perspectives.* New York: Routledge.

Burchett, Wilfred. 1978. *Southern Africa Stands Up: The Revolutions In Angola, Mozambique, Zimbabwe, Namibia and South Africa.* New York: Urizen.

Burkett, Paul, and Hart–Landsberg, Martin. 2000. "Alternative Perspectives on Late Industrialization in East Asia: A Critical Survey." *Review of Radical Political Economics.* 32 (no. 2): 222–64.

Burger, John S. 1976 "Captain Harry Dean: Pan-Negro-Nationalist in South Africa." *International Journal of African Historical Studies* 9 (no. 1): 83–90.

Burke, James. 1995. *The Day the Universe Changed.* Boston: Little, Brown.

Burnett, Charles. 2003. "The Transmission of Arabic Astronomy via Antioch and Pisa in the Second Quarter of the Twelfth Century." In *The Enterprise of Science in Islam: New Perspectives*, ed. by Jan P. Hogendijk, and Abdelhamid I. Sabra, pp. 23–52. Cambridge, MA: The M.I.T. Press.

Burr, Millard, and Collins, Robert O. 2003. *Revolutionary Sudan: Hasan Al–Turabi and the Islamist State, 1989–2000.* Boston, MA: Brill.

Butare, Albert. 2004. "Income-Generating Activities in Higher Education: The Case of Kigali Institute of Science, Technology and Management (KIST)." *Journal of Higher Education in Africa* 2 (no. 3): 37–54.

Butler, Alfred Joshua. 1998 [1902]. *Arab Invasion of Egypt and the Last 30 years of the Roman Dominion.* Brooklyn, NY: A & B Publishing Group. (Originally published by Clarendon Press, Oxford, 1902.)

Caffentzis, G. 2000. "The World Bank and Education in Africa." In *A Thousand Flowers: Social Struggles against Structural Adjustment in African Universities*, ed. by S. Federici, G. Caffentzis, and O. Alidou. Trenton, NJ: Africa World Press.

Cain, P. J., and Hopkins, A. G. 1993. *British Imperialism: Innovation and Expansion, 1688–1914*. New York: Longman.

Cameron, Rondo. 1994. "The Industrial Revolution: Fact or Fiction?" *Contention* 4 (no. 1): 163–88.

Cammack, Diana. 1987. "Mozambique: The 'Human Face' of Destabilization." *Review of African Political Economy* (no. 40, December): 65–75.

Campbell, Horace. 1989. "The Military Defeat of the South Africans in Angola." *Monthly Review* 40 (no. 11, April): 1–15.

Campbell, James Tierney. 1989 (a). "Our Fathers, Our Children: The African Methodist Episcopal Church in the United States and South Africa." Ph.D. dissertation, Stanford University.

Canfora, Luciano. 1989. *The Vanished Library*. Berkeley : University of California Press.

Cardini, Franco. 2001. *Europe and Islam*. Oxford: Blackwell.

Carnegie Corporation. 2000. "Four Foundations Launch $100 Million Initiative in Support of Higher Education in African Countries (Press Release, New York, April 24, 2000)." New York: Carnegie Corporation.

Carnoy, M. 1974. *Education as Cultural Imperialism*. New York: David McKay.

Carnoy, M. 1994. "Universities, Technological Change, and Training in the Information Age." In *Revitalizing Higher Education*, ed. by Jamil Salmi and Adriaan M. Verspoor, pp. 41–98. New York: Pergamon (for the International Association of Universities).

Carnoy, M., and Thias, H. 1969. *Cost Benefit Analysis in Education: A Case-Study of Kenya*. Washington, DC: World Bank.

Carrington, Selwyn H. H. 1988. "The State of the Debate on the Role of Capitalism in the Ending of the Slave System." *Journal of Caribbean History* 22 (nos. 1–2): 20–41.

Carr-Saunders, A. M. 1961. *New Universities Overseas*. London: George Allen & Unwin.

Cassanelli, Lee V. 1982. *The Shaping of Somali Society: Reconstructing the History of a Pastoral People, 1600–1900*. Philadelphia: University of Pennsylvania Press.

Casson, Lionel. 2001. *Libraries in the Ancient World*. New Haven: Yale University Press.

Caufield, Catherine. 1996. *Masters of Illusion: The World Bank and the Poverty of Nations*. New York: Henry Holt.

Cell, John 1982. *The Highest Stage of White Supremacy: The Origins of Segregation in South Africa and the American South*. New York: Cambridge University Press.

Center of Military History. 2003. *United States Forces, Somalia: After Action Report and Historical Overview: the United States Army in Somalia, 1992–1994*. Washington, D.C.: Center of Military History, U.S. Army.

CERI (Centre for Educational Research and Innovation). 2004. *Internationalization and Trade in Higher Education: Opportunities and Challenges*. Paris: Organization for Economic Co-operation and Development.

Chabal, Patrick; and Daloz, Jean-Pascal. 1999. *Africa Works: Disorder as Political Instrument.* Bloomington: Indiana University Press.

Chamberlain, Muriel E. 1998. *The Longman Companion to European Decolonization in the Twentieth Century.* New York: Addison Wesley Longman.

Chambers, James. 2001. *The Devil's Horsemen: The Mongol Invasion of Europe.* London: Phoenix.

Chandra, B. 1981. "Karl Marx, His Theories of Asian Societies and Colonial Rule." *Review: A Journal of the Fernand Braudel Center* 5 (no. 1): 13–94.

Chang, Kuei-Sheng. 1995. "The Ming Maritime Enterprise and China's Knowledge of Africa prior to the Age of Great Discoveries." In *The Global Opportunity* (vol. 1 of "An Expanding World: The European Impact on World History, 1450–1800"), ed. by Felipe Fernandez-Armesto, pp. 121–32. Brookfield, VT: Variorum/Ashgate.

Chaudhuri, K. N. 1985. *Trade and Civilization in the Indian Ocean: An Economic History from the Rise of Islam to 1750.* Cambridge: Cambridge University Press.

Chaudhuri, K. N. 1995. In *The Global Opportunity* (vol. 1 of "An Expanding World: The European Impact on World History, 1450–1800"), ed. by Felipe Fernandez-Armesto, pp. 299–312. Brookfield, VT: Variorum/Ashgate.

Cheng, Kai-ming. 1995. "A Chinese Model of Higher Education? Lessons from Reality." In *Learning from Experience: Policy and Practice in Aid to Higher Education*, ed. by Lene Buchert, and Kenneth King, pp. 197–210. The Hague: Center for the Study of Education in Developing Countries.

Cherif, M. H. 1989. "New Trends in the Maghreb: Algeria, Tunisia and Libya." In *General History of Africa, Volume VI: Africa in the Nineteenth Century until the 1880s*, ed. by J. F. Ade Ajayi, pp. 448–96. Berkeley: University of California Press.

Chideya, Ngoni. 1991. "Zimbabwe." In *International Higher Education: An Encyclopedia*, ed. by Philip G. Altbach, pp. 437–50. New York: Garland.

Chilundo, Arlindo. 2003. "Mozambique." In *African Higher Education: An International Reference Handbook*, ed. by Damtew Teferra and Philip G. Altbach, pp. 462–75. Bloomington: Indiana University Press.

Chirenje, J. Mutero. 1976. "The Afro-American Factor in Southern African Ethiopianism, 1890–1906." In *Profiles of Self-Determination: African Responses to Colonialism in Southern Africa, 1652–Present*, ed. by David Chanaiwa, pp. 250–80. Northridge: California State University at Northridge.

Christie, Pam, and Collins, Colin. 1984. "Bantu Education: Apartheid Ideology and Labor Reproduction." In *Apartheid and Education: The Education of Black South Africans*, ed. by Peter Kallaway, pp. 160–83. Braamfontein: Ravan.

Ciment, James. 1997 (a). *Algeria: The Fundamentalist Challenge.* New York: Facts on File.

Ciment, James. 1997 (b). *Angola and Mozambique: Postcolonial Wars in Southern Africa.* New York: Facts on File.

Cipolla, Carlo M. 1996 (1965). *Guns, Sails and Empires: Technological Innovation and the Early Phases of European Expansion, 1400–1700.* New York: Barnes & Noble.

Clagett, Marshall. 1989. *Ancient Egyptian Science: A Source Book.* (Volume 1, Tome 1). Philadelphia, PA: American Philosophical Society.

Clancy-Smith, Julia A. 1994. *Rebel and Saint: Muslim Notables, Populist Protest, Colonial Encounters (Algeria and Tunisia, 1800–1904)*. Berkeley: University of California Press.

Clarence-Smith, Gervase. 1985. "Thou Shalt Not Articulate Modes of Production." *Canadian Journal of African Studies* 19 (no. 1): 19–22.

Clegg, Claude A., III. 2004. *The Price of Liberty: African Americans and the Making of Liberia*. Chapel Hill: University of North Carolina Press.

Cliffe, Lionel, and Davidson, Basil. 1987. *The Long Struggle of Eritrea for Independence and Constructive Peace*. Nottingham: Spokesman.

Cloete, Nico (ed.) 2002. *Transformation in Higher Education: Global Pressures and Local Realities in South Africa*. Lansdowne (South Africa): Juta.

Cloete, Nico; Pillay, Pundy; and Badat, Saleem. 2004. *National Policy and a Regional Response in South African Higher Education*. Oxford: James Currey (in association with Partnership for Higher Education in Africa, USA).

Cobban, A. B. 1975. *The Medieval Universities: Their Development and Organization*. London: Methuen.

Cochran, Judith. 1986. *Education in Egypt*. London: Croom Helm.

Cock, Jacklyn, and Nathan, Laurie. (eds.) 1989. *Society at War: The Militarization of South Africa*. New York: St. Martin's.

Cohen, H. Floris. 1994. *The Scientific Revolution: A Historiographical Inquiry*. Chicago: University of Chicago Press.

Cohen, Ralph, and Roth, Michael S. (eds.) 1995. *History and... Histories within the Human Sciences*. Charlottesville: University Press of Virginia.

Cohen, William B. 1980. *The French Encounter with Africans: White Response to Blacks, 1530–1880*. Bloomington: Indiana University Press.

Colclough, Christopher. 1995. "Diversifying the Funding of Tertiary Institutions: Is the Bank's Agenda the Right One?" In *Learning from Experience: Policy and Practice in Aid to Higher Education*, ed. by Lene Buchert, and Kenneth King, pp. 145–56. The Hague: Center for the Study of Education in Developing Countries.

Coleman, James S., and Court, David. 1993. *University Development in the Third World: The Rockefeller Foundation Experience*. New York: Pergamon.

Coleman, Max. 1998. *A Crime against Humanity: Analyzing The Repression of the Apartheid State*. Cape Town: Human Rights Committee and David Philip.

Collier, Paul. 2000. *Economic Causes of Civil Conflict and their Implications for Policy*. Washington, DC World Bank.

Collins, Robert O. 1983. *Shadows in the Grass: Britain in the Southern Sudan, 1918–1956*. New Haven: Yale University Press.

Collins, Robert O.; Burns, James McDonald; and Ching, Erik Kristofer. (eds.) 1994. *Historical Problems of Imperial Africa*. Princeton, NJ: Markus Wiener.

Commission for Africa. 2005. *Our Common Interest: Report of the Commission for Africa*. London: Commission for Africa Secretariat.

Commission of Inquiry into the Deployment of Canadian Forces to Somalia. 1997. *Dishonoured Legacy: The Lessons of the Somalia Affair: Report of the Commission of Inquiry into the Deployment of Canadian Forces to Somalia*. (5 vols.) Ottawa: The Commission of Inquiry into the Deployment of Canadian Forces to Somalia.

Congress for Cultural Freedom. 1962. *The West African Intellectual Community: Papers and Discussions of an International Seminar on Inter-University Co-operation in West Africa, held in Freetown, Sierra Leone, 11–16 December 1961*. Ibadan: Ibadan University Press.

Constantine, Stephen. 1984. *The Making of British Colonial Development Policy, 1914–1940*. Totowa, NJ: Frank Cass.

Cooksey, Brian; Levey, Lisbeth A.; and Mkude, Daniel J. 2003. *Higher Education in Tanzania: A Case Study*. Oxford: James Currey (in association with Partnership for Higher Education in Africa, USA).

Coombe, Trevor. 1993. 'The New System of Higher Education in Namibia: Turner Report on Higher Education in Namibia." *Journal of Southern African Studies* 19 (no 1): 60–79.

Cooper, Frederick. 1993. "Africa and the World Economy." In *Confronting Historical Paradigms: Peasants, Labor and the Capitalist Word System in Africa and Latin America*, ed. by Frederick Cooper; Allen F. Isaacman, Florencia E. Mallon, William Roseberry, and Steve J. Stern, pp. 84–204. Madison: University of Wisconsin Press.

Coquery-Vidrovitch, Catherine. 1972. "Research on an African Mode of Production." In *Perspectives on the African Past*, ed. by M. A. Klein, and G. W. Johnson. Boston: Little, Brown.

Coquery-Vidrovitch, Catherine. 1985. "The Political Economy of the African Peasantry and Modes of Production." In *The Political Economy of Contemporary Africa*, ed. by Peter C. W. Gutkind, and Immanuel Wallerstein, pp. 94–116. Beverly Hills, CA: Sage.

Cordell, Dennis D. 1985. "The Pursuit of the Real: Modes of Production and History." *Canadian Journal of African Studies* 19 (no. 1): 58–63.

Coulby, David, and Zambeta, Evie. (eds.) 2005. *World Yearbook of Education, 2005: Globalization and Nationalism in Education*. London: Routledgefalmer.

Courbage, Youssef, and Fargues, Phillipe. 1997. *Christians and Jews under Islam*. New York: I. B. Tauris.

Court, David. 1995. "The Challenge to the Liberal Vision of Universities in Africa." In *Learning from Experience: Policy and Practice in Aid to Higher Education*, ed. by Lene Buchert, and Kenneth King, pp. 109–24. The Hague: Center for the Study of Education in Developing Countries.

Court, David. 1999. *Financing Higher Education in Africa: Makerere, the Quiet Revolution*. Washington, DC: The World Bank, Tertiary Education Thematic Group and the Rockefeller Foundation.

Crawford, Osbert Guy Stanhope. 1951. *The Fung Kingdom of Sennar: With a Geographical Account of the Middle Nile Region*. Gloucester: J. Bellows.

Crecelius, Daniel. 1968. "The 'Ulama,' and the State in Modern Egypt." Ph.D. dissertation, University of Princeton.

Crombie, A. C. 1990. *Science, Optics and Music in Medieval and Early Modern Thought*. London: Hambledon.

Crowthier, J. G. 1967. *The Social Relations of Science*. London: Cresset.

Cuno, Kenneth M. 1992. *The Pasha's Peasants: Land, Society and Economy in Lower Egypt, 1740–1858*. Cambridge: Cambridge University Press.

Curle, A. 1962. "Nationalism and Higher Education in Ghana." *Universities Quarterly* 26 (no. 3): 229–42.

Currie, Jan, and Newson, Janice Angela. (eds.) 1998. *Universities and Globalization: Critical Perspectives.* Thousand Oaks, CA: Sage.

Curtin, Philip D. 1975. *Economic Change in Precolonial Africa: Senegambia in the Era of the Slave Trade.* Madison: University of Wisconsin Press.

Dakak, Fred. 1966. "Development of Higher Education after World War II in the Arab Near Eastern Countries." Ph.D. dissertation, Southern Illinois University.

Dalal, F. 1988. "The Racism of Jung." *Race and Class* 29 (no. 3): 1–22.

Daly, M. W. 1991. *Imperial Sudan: the Anglo–Egyptian Condominium, 1934–1956.* New York: Cambridge University Press.

Daly, M. W. 2002. *Empire On the Nile: The Anglo-Egyptian Sudan, 1898–1934.* Cambridge: Cambridge University Press.

d'Almaine, G. Frederick; Manhire, Brian; and Atteh, Samuel O. 1997. "Engineering Education at South Africa's Technikons." *Journal of Negro Education* 66 (no. 4): 434–42.

d'Alverny, Marie-Therese. 1982. "Translations and Translators." In *Renaissance and Renewal in the Twelfth Century,* ed. by Robert L. Benson, and Giles Constable with Carol D. Lanham, pp. 421–62. Cambridge: Harvard University Press.

Damtew Teferra, and Altbach, Philip G. (eds.) 2003. *African Higher Education: An International Reference Handbook.* Bloomington: Indiana University Press.

Danaher, Kevin. 1985. *The Political Economy of U. S. Policy toward South Africa.* Boulder, CO: Westview.

Daniel, M. L. 2000. "The Demographic Impact of HIV/AIDS in Sub-Saharan Africa." *Geography* 85 (Part 1, January): 46–55.

Daniel, Norman. 1989 (a). "The Legal and Political Theory of the Crusade." In *A History of the Crusades: Volume VI: The Impact of the Crusades on Europe,* edited by Harry W. Hazard, and Norman P. Zaccour, pp. 3–38. Madison: University of Wisconsin Press.

Daniel, Norman. 1989 (b). "Crusade Propaganda." In *A History of the Crusades: Volume VI: The Impact of the Crusades on Europe,* edited by Harry W. Hazard, and Norman P. Zaccour, pp. 39–97. Madison: University of Wisconsin Press.

Dasgupta, B. 1998. *Structural Adjustment, Global Trade and the New Political Economy of Development.* London: Zed.

Davenport, T. R. H., and Saunders, Christopher C. 2000. *South Africa: A Modern History.* New York: St. Martin's.

Davidson, Basil. 1980. *The African Slave Trade* (revised and expanded edition). Boston: Little, Brown.

Davidson, Basil. 1995. *Africa in History: Themes and Outlines* (revised and expanded edition). New York: Simon and Schuster.

Davies, Merryl Wyn; Nandy, Ashis, and Sardar, Ziauddin. 1993. *Barbaric Others: A Manifesto on Western Racism.* Boulder, CO: Pluto.

Davies, Norman. 1996. *Europe: A History.* New York: Oxford University Press.

Davis, David Brion. 2001. *In the Image of God: Religion, Moral Values and Our Heritage of Slavery.* New Haven: Yale University Press.

Davis, R. Hunt, Jr. 1978. "The Black American Education Component in African Responses to Colonialism in South Africa: (ca. 1890–1914)." *Journal of Southern African Affairs* 3 (no. 1): 65–84.

Davis, Stephen M. 1987. *Apartheid's Rebels: Inside South Africa's Hidden War*. New Haven: Yale University Press.

Dawson, George G. 1964. "Education in Somalia." *Comparative Education Review* 8 (no. 2): 199–214.

DeCorse, Christopher R. (ed.) 2001. *West Africa During the Atlantic Slave Trade: Archaeological Perspectives*. London: Leicester University Press.

Deerr, Noël. 1949–1950. *The History of Sugar*. (2 vols.) London: Chapman and Hall.

de Ketele, Jean-Marie. 1998. *[African] Higher Education in the 21st Century*. Paris: UNESCO. (Document prepared for the World Conference on Higher Education, October 5–9, 1998.)

de Libera, Alain. 1997. "The Muslim Forebears of the European Renaissance." *UNESCO Courier* (February): 4–9.

de Libera, Alain. 2003. "Medieval Philosophy and Exchanges Between the Two Shores of the Mediterranean." In *Civilizations: How We See Others, How Others See Us; Proceedings of the International Symposium, Paris, 13 and 14 December, 2001*. Paris: UNESCO (published on the world wide web at the UNESCO web site as part of its "Dialogue among Civilizations" project).

Delong, Kent, and Tuckey, Steven. 1994. *Mogadishu!: Heroism and Tragedy*. Westport, CT: Praeger.

Deng, Peng. 1997. *Private Education In Modern China*. Westport, CT: Greenwood/Praeger.

de Mejia, Anne Marie. 2002. *Power, Prestige and Bilingualism: International Perspectives on Elite Bilingual Education*. Clevedon: Multilingual Matters.

De Moor, J. A., and Wesseling, H. L. (eds.) 1989. *Imperialism and War: Essays on Colonial Wars in Asia and Africa*. Leiden: E. J. Brill.

De Waal, Alexander. 1991. *Evil Days: Thirty Years of War and Famine in Ethiopia*. New York: Human Rights Watch.

Diamond, Jared. 1997. *Guns, Germs and Steel: The Fates of Human Societies*. New York: Norton.

Dichter, Thomas W. 2003. *Despite Good Intentions: Why Development Assistance to the Third World has Failed*. Amherst: University of Massachusetts Press.

Dictionary of the Middle Ages. 1982–1989. New York: Scribner.

Dictionary of Scientific Biography. 1970–1980. New York: Scribner.

Diop, Cheikh Anta. 1983. *The African Origin of Civilization: Myth or Reality*. Arvada, CO: Lawrence Hill.

Diouf, Sylviane A. 1998. *Servants of Allah: African Muslims Enslaved in the Americas*. New York University Press.

Dodge, Bayard. 1961. *Al-Azhar: A Millennium of Muslim Learning*. Washington, DC: The Middle East Institute.

Dodge, Bayard. 1962. *Muslim Education in Medieval Times*. Washington, DC: The Middle East Institute.

Dold-Samplonius, Yvonne. 2003. "Calculating Surface Areas and Volumes in Islamic Architecture." In *The Enterprise of Science in Islam: New Perspectives*, ed.

by Jan P. Hogendijk, and Abdelhamid I. Sabra, pp. 235–66. Cambridge, MA: The M. I. T. Press.

Dols, Michael A. 1977. *The Black Death in the Middle East.* Princeton: Princeton University Press.

Dorn, H. 1991. *The Geography of Science.* Baltimore: Johns Hopkins University Press.

Dore, R. 1976. *The Diploma Disease: Education, Qualification. and Development.* London: George Allen and Unwin.

Doss, Cheryl; Evenson, Robert E.; and Ruther, Nancy L. (eds.) 2004. "Special Issue: African Higher Education: Implications for Development." *Journal of Higher Education in Africa* 2 (no. 1): 1–242.

Dray, Philip. 2002. *At the Hands of Persons Unknown: The Lynching of Black America.* New York: Random House.

Drescher, Seymour. 1992. "The Ending of the Slave Trade and the Evolution of European Scientific Racism." In *The Atlantic Slave Trade: Effects on Economies, Societies and Peoples in Africa, the Americas and Europe,* ed. by Joseph E. Inikori, and Stanley E. Engerman, pp. 361–96. Durham: Duke University Press.

Drescher, Seymour. 1999. *From Slavery to Freedom: Comparative Studies in the Rise and Fall of Atlantic Slavery.* New York: New York University Press.

Duara, Prasenjit. 2004. *Decolonization: Perspectives from Now and Then.* New York: Routledge.

Dubois, Felix. 1969 [1896]. *Timbuctoo: The Mysterious.* New York: Negro Universities Press.

Du Bois, W. E. B. 1996. *The Oxford W. E. B. Du Bois Reader,* ed. by Eric J. Sundquist. New York: Oxford University Press.

Dunbar, Roberta Ann. 2000. "Muslim Women in African History." In *The History of Islam in Africa,* ed. by Nehemia Levitzion, and Randall L. Pouwels, pp. 397–418. Athens: Ohio University Press.

Dunn, Richard S. 1973. *Sugar and Slaves: The Rise of the Planter Class in the English West Indies, 1624–1713.* London: Jonathan Cape.

Dupre, Georges, and Rey, Pierre-Philippe. 1973. "Reflections on the Pertinence of a Theory of the History of Exchange." *Economy and Society* 2 (May): 131–63.

Dyson, James. 2001. *A History of Great Inventions.* New York: Carroll & Graf.

Eccel, A. Chris. 1984. *Egypt, Islam and Social Change: Al-Azhar in Conflict and Accommodation.* Berlin: Klaus Schwarz Verlag.

Eckert, Andreas. 2003. "Fitting Africa into World History: A Historiographical Exploration." In *Writing World History, 1800–2000,* ed. by Benedikt Stuchtey and Eckhardt Fuchs, pp. 255–70. Oxford: Oxford University Press.

Economist. 2004. "How to Make Africa Smile: A Survey of Sub-Saharan Africa." *Economist* (January 17): 3–16.

Edelman, Marc, and Haugerud, Angelique. (eds.) 2005. *The Anthropology of Development and Globalization: From Classical Political Economy to Contemporary Neoliberalism.* Malden, MA: Blackwell.

Edwards, David N. 2004. *The Nubian Past: An Archaeology of the Sudan.* London: Routledge.

Ehret, Christopher. 2002. *The Civilizations of Africa: A History to 1800.* Charlottesville: University Press of Virginia.

Ehrlich, Haggai. 1989. *Students and University in 20th Century Egyptian Politics*. London: Frank Cass.

Ehrlich, Haggai. 1994. *Ethiopia and the Middle East*. Boulder, CO: Lynne Rienner.

Eicher, Jean-Claude, and Chevaillier, Thierry. 1996. "Rethinking the Financing of Post-Compulsory Education." In *Higher Education in an International Perspective: Critical Issues*, ed. by Zaghloul Morsy, and Philip G. Altbach, pp. 90–110. New York: Garland.

Eickelman, Dale F. 1985. *Knowledge and Power in Morocco: The Education of a Twentieth-Century Notable*. Princeton: Princeton University Press.

Eisemon, T. O. 1987. *Benefiting from Basic Education in Developing Countries: A Review of Research on the External Efficiency of Educational Investments*. Buffalo: Comparative Education Center, State University of New York at Buffalo.

El-Abbadi, Mostafa. 1992. *The Life and Fate of the Ancient Library of Alexandria*. Paris: UNESCO/UNDP.

El Gizouli, El Subki Mohamad. 1999. *Higher Education in the Sudan 1898–1966*. Khartoum: Khartoum University Press, 1999.

El-Tayeb, Salah El Din El Zein. 1971. *The Students' Movement in the Sudan: 1940–1970*. Khartoum: Khartoum University Press.

El Tom, M. E. A. 2003. "Sudan." In *African Higher Education: An International Reference Handbook*, ed. by Damtew Teferra and Philip G. Altbach, pp. 563–73. Bloomington: Indiana University Press.

Encyclopedia of Islam: New Edition. 1986. New York: Brill Academic.

Enders, Jürgen, and Fulton, Oliver. (eds.) 2002. *Higher Education in a Globalizing World: International Trends and Mutual Observations: A Festschrift in Honour of Ulrich Teichler*. Boston: Kluwer Academic.

Enos, John L. 1995. *In Pursuit of Science and Technology in Sub-Saharan Africa: The Impact of Structural Adjustment Programs*. New York: Routledge.

Entelis, John P. 1986. *Algeria: The Revolution Institutionalized*. Boulder, CO: Westview.

Entelis, John P. (ed.) 1997. *Islam, Democracy and the State in North Africa*. Bloomington: Indiana University Press.

Esposito, John L. (ed.) 2000. *The Oxford History of Islam*. New York: Oxford University Press.

Evans, Gareth J. 2002. *God, Oil and Country: Changing the Logic of War in Sudan*. Brussels: International Crisis Group.

Evans, Gill Cofer. 1970. "Politics and Higher Education: Relations between Governments and Institutions of Higher Education in Francophone Africa." Ph.D. Dissertation, Columbia University.

Fahmy, Khaled. 1997. *All the Pasha's Men: Mehmed Ali, His Army and the Making of Modern Egypt*. Cambridge: Cambridge University Press.

Fanon, Frantz. 1968 (1961) *The Wretched of the Earth*. New York: Grove.

Fatoke, Aderemi S. O. 1982. "British Colonial Administration of Somaliland Protectorate, 1920–1960." Ph. D. dissertation, University of Illinois at Chicago Circle.

Federici, Silvia, and Caffentzis, G. 2000. "Chronology of African University Students' Struggles: 1985–1998." In *A Thousand Flowers: Social Struggles against Structural Adjustment in African Universities*, ed. by S. Federici, G. Caffentzis, and O. Alidou, pp. 115–50. Trenton, NJ: Africa World Press.

Federici, Silvia; Caffentzis, George; and Alidou, Osseina. (eds.) 2000. *A Thousand Flowers: Social Struggles against Structural Adjustment in African Universities*. Trenton, NJ: Africa World Press.

Fernandez-Armesto, Felipe. 1995. "Introduction." In *The Global Opportunity* (vol. 1 of "An Expanding World: The European Impact on World History, 1450–1800"), ed. by Felipe Fernandez-Armesto, pp. xiii–xxiv. Brookfield, VT: Variorum/Ashgate.

Finlay, Robert. 1995. "The Treasure Ships of Zheng He: Chinese Maritime Imperialism in the Age of Discovery." In *The Global Opportunity* (vol. 1 of "An Expanding World: The European Impact on World History, 1450–1800"), ed. by Felipe Fernandez-Armesto, pp. 93–104. Brookfield, VT: Variorum/Ashgate.

Finnegan, William. 1995. "Letter from Mogadishu." *New Yorker* 71 (no. 4): 64, 77.

Fisher, Humphrey J. 2001. *Slavery in the History of Muslim Black Africa*. New York: New York University Press.

Fitzgibbon, Louis. 1982. *The Betrayal of the Somalis*. London: Rex Collings.

Fleisch, Brahm. 2002. "State Formation and the Origins of Bantu Education." In *The History of Education under Apartheid 1948–1994: The Doors of Learning and Culture Shall be Opened*, ed. by Peter Kallaway, pp. 39–52. New York: Peter Lang.

Floca, Samuel W., Jr. 1974. "A Study in Parallels: Isandhlwana and Little Big Horn." *Army* 24 (January): 31–36.

Flynn, Dennis O., and Giráldez, Arturo. (eds.) 1997. *Metals and Monies in an Emerging Global Economy* (vol. 14 of "An Expanding World: The European Impact on World History, 1450–1800") Brookfield, VT: Variorum/Ashgate.

Foster, John Bellamy. 2002. "Monopoly Capital and the New Globalization." *Monthly Review* 53 (no. 8): 1–16.

Fourie, M. 1999. "Institutional Transformation at South African Universities: Implications for Academic Staff." *Higher Education* 38 (no. 3, October): 275–90.

Fox, John G. 2001. "Approaching Humanitarian Intervention Strategically: The Case of Somalia." *SAIS Review* 21 (no. 1): 147–58.

France, John. 1997. "The Capture of Jerusalem." *History Today* 47 (April): 37–43.

Frank, Andre Gunder. 1998. *ReOrient: Global Economy in the Asian Age*. Berkeley: University of California Press.

Fraser, P. M. 1972. *Ptolemaic Alexandria*. Oxford: Clarendon.

Frederickson, George M. 1981. *White Supremacy: A Comparative Study in American and South African History*. New York: Oxford University Press.

Frederickson, George M. 1995. *Black Liberation: A Comparative History of Black Ideologies in the United States and South Africa*. Oxford University Press.

Frederickson, George M. 2002. *Racism: A Short History*. Princeton: Princeton University Press.

Fukui, Katsuyoshi; Kurimoto, Esei; and Shigeta, Masayoshi. (eds.) 1997. *Ethiopia in Broader Perspective: Papers of 13*th *International Conference of Ethiopian Studies* (3 vols.). Kyoto: Shokado.

Furley, O. W., and Watson, T. 1978. *A History of Education in East Africa*. New York: NOK Publishers.

Furneaux, Rupert. 1963. *The Zulu War: Isandhlwana and Rorke's Drift*. Philadelphia: Lippincott.

Gaillard, Anne Marie, and Gaillard, Jacques. 1998. *International Migration of the Highly Qualified: A Bibliographic and Conceptual Itinerary*. New York: Center for Migration Studies.

Galabawa, Justinian C. J. 1993. *Study on Cost Effectiveness and Efficiency in African Universities: A Case Study of the University of Zambia (UNZA)*. Accra: Association of African Universities.

Gallay, Alan. 2003. *The Indian Slave Trade: The Rise of the English Empire in the American South, 1670–1717*. New Haven: Yale University Press.

Galloway, J. H. 1989. *The Sugar Cane Industry: An Historical Geography from Its Origins to 1914*. New York: Cambridge University Press.

Galvin, Peter R. 1999. *Patterns of Pillage: A Geography of Caribbean-Based Piracy in Spanish America, 1536–1718*. New York: Peter Lang.

Garang, John, and Khalid, Mansur. 1987. *John Garang Speaks*. New York: KPI.

Gardner, Brian. 1968. *The Quest for Timbuctoo*. New York: Harcourt, Brace & World.

Gardner, Judith. ; El–Bushra, Judy. 2004. *Somalia—the Untold Story: The War Through the Eyes of Somali Women*. Sterling, VA: Pluto.

Gascoigne, John. 1990. "A Reappraisal of the Role of the Universities in the Scientific Revolution." In *Reappraisals of the Scientific Revolution*, ed. by David C. Lindberg, and Robert S. Westman, pp. 207–60. Cambridge: Cambridge University Press.

Gebru Tareke. 2000. "The Ethiopia-Somalia War of 1977 Revisited." *International Journal of African Historical Studies* 33 (no. 3): 635–67.

Gelfand, Michael. 1978. *A Non-Racial Island of Learning: A History of the University College of Rhodesia from Its Inception to 1966*. Gwelo (Zimbabwe): Mambo.

Gentry, Carole M., and Grinde, Donald A. (eds.) 1994. *The Unheard Voices: American Indian Responses to the Columbian Quincentenary, 1492–1992*. Los Angeles: American Indian Studies Center, University of California.

Geo-Jaja, M. A. (ed.) 2003. "Symposium: Globalization and Internationalization: Education, Human Development and Nation–Building." *World Studies in Education* 4 (no. 2): 3–107.

Georgescu-Roegen, N. 1976. "Economics and Educational Development." *Journal of Education Finance* 2 (summer).

Gereffi, G., and Fonda, S. 1992. "Regional Paths of Development." *Annual Review of Sociology* 18: 419–48.

Ghalioungui, Paul. 1973. *The House of Life, Per Ankh: Magic and Medical Science in Ancient Egypt*. Amsterdam: B. M. Israel.

Gibb, Camilla. 1997. "Constructing Past and Present in Harar." In *Ethiopia in Broader Perspective: Papers of 13th International Conference of Ethiopian Studies*, vol. 2 (of 3), ed. by Katsuyoshi Fukui, Eisei Kurimoto, and Masayoshi Shigeta, pp. 378–90. Kyoto: Shokado.

Gibbon, Edward. 1910 (1776–1778) *Gibbon's Decline and Fall of the Roman Empire: In Six Volumes*. Volume 5. London: J. M. Dent/Everyman's Library edition.

Gibbon, Peter. 1992. "The World Bank and African Poverty, 1973–91." *Journal of Modern African Studies* 30 (no. 2): 193–220.

Giddens, Anthony. 1986. *The Constitution of Society: Outline of the Theory of Structuration*. Berkeley: University of California Press.

Gifford, Prosser, and Louis, Wm. George. 1988. *Decolonization and African Independence: The Transfer of Power, 1960–1980.* New Haven: Yale University Press.

Gifford, Prosser, and Weiskel, Timothy C. 1971. "African Education in a Colonial Context: French and British Styles." In *France and Britain in Africa: Imperial Rivalry and Colonial Rule,* ed. by Prosser Gifford, and W. M. Roger Louis, pp. 663–712. New Haven: Yale University Press.

Ginzburg, Ralph. (ed.) 1988. *100 Years of Lynchings.* Baltimore: Black Classic Press.

Girdwood, Alison. 1995. "Shaping the World Bank's Higher Education Paper: Dialogue, Consultation and Conditionality." In *Learning from Experience: Policy and Practice in Aid to Higher Education,* ed. by Lene Buchert, and Kenneth King, pp. 41–76. The Hague: Center for the Study of Education in Developing Countries.

Glazer, Sarah. 2004. "Stopping Genocide: Should the U.S. and U.N. Take Action in Sudan?" *CQ Researcher* 14 (no. 29): 686–707.

Glick, Thomas F. 1979. *Islamic and Christian Spain in the Early Middle Ages.* Princeton: Princeton University Press.

Glubb, Sir John. 1973. *Soldiers of Fortune: The Story of the Mamlukes.* New York: Stein and Day.

Goitein, S. D. 1967. *A Mediterranean Society: The Jewish Communities of the Arab World as Portrayed in the Documents of the Cairo Geniza.* (Vol. 1: Economic Foundations) Berkeley: University of California Press.

Goldenberg, David M. 2003. *The Curse of Ham: Race and Slavery in Early Judaism, Christianity and Islam.* Princeton: Princeton University Press.

Goody, Jack. 1996. *East in the West.* Cambridge: Cambridge University Press.

Gordon, Murray. 1989. *Slavery in the Arab World.* New York: New Amsterdam.

Gorman, Anthony. 2003. Historians, State and Politics in Twentieth Century Egypt: Contesting the Nation. London: RoutledgeCurzon.

Gosnell, Jonathan K. 2002. *The Politics of Frenchness in Colonial Algeria, 1930–1954.* Rochester, NY: University of Rochester Press.

Gould, Stephen Jay. 1996. *The Mismeasure of Man.* New York: Norton.

Gourevitch, Philip. 1998. *We Wish to Inform You That Tomorrow We Will be Killed With Our Families: Stories from Rwanda.* New York: Farrar, Straus & Giroux.

Grant, Edward. 1974. *A Source Book in Medieval Science.* Cambridge: Harvard University Press.

Grant, Edward. 1984. "Science and the Medieval University." In *Rebirth, Reform and Resilience: Universities in Transition, 1300–1700,* ed. by James M. Kittleson, and Pamela J. Transue. Columbus: Ohio State University Press.

Grant, Edward. 1996. *The Foundations of Modern Science in the Middle Ages: Their Religious, Institutional and Intellectual Contexts.* Cambridge: Cambridge University Press.

Graves, Robert, and Patai, Raphael. 1966. *Hebrew Myths: The Book of Genesis.* New York: McGraw-Hill.

Gray, Harry. (ed.) 1999. *Universities and the Creation of Wealth.* Buckingham: Open University Press.

Green, Anna, and Troup, Kathleen. (eds.) 1999. *The Houses of History: A Critical Reader in Twentieth-Century History and Theory.* New York: New York University Press.

Green, Arnold H. 1978. *The Tunisian Ulama, 1873–1915: Social Structure and Response to Ideological Currents*. Leiden: E. J. Brill.

Green, R. H., and Seidman, A. 1968. *Unity or Poverty? The Economics of Pan-Africanism*. Harmondsworth: Penguin.

Greenberg, Stanley. 1980. *Race and State in Capitalist Development: Comparative Perspectives*. New Haven: Yale University Press.

Guidice, Barbara. 1999. "New Government in Nigeria Offers Little Hope to Academics: Universities Are Short on Funds and Overcrowded; Brain Drain Depletes Institutions of Top Scholars." *Chronicle of Higher Education* (May 21): A51.

Gumbel, Peter; Nystrom, Kjell; and Samuelsson, Rolf. 1983. *Education in Ethiopia 1974–82*. Uppsala: Scandinavian Institute of African Studies (for the Swedish International Development Authority, Education Division).

Gutas, Dimitri. 1998. *Greek Thought, Arabic Culture: The Graeco-Arabic Translation Movement in Baghdad and Early 'Abbasid Society (2nd–4th/8th–10th Centuries)*. New York: Routledge.

Haberland, E. 1992. "The Horn of Africa." In *General History of Africa, Volume V: Africa from the Sixteenth to the Eighteenth Century*, ed. by B. A. Ogot, pp. 703–49. Berkeley: University of California Press.

Habte, Aklilu. 1974. See Aklilu Habte. 1974.

Hagen, Everett Einar. 1964. *On the Theory of Social Change: How Economic Growth Begins*. London: Tavistock.

Haile-Selassie, Teferra. 1997. See Teferra Haile-Selassie. 1997.

Hall, John A. 1985. *Powers and Liberties: The Causes and Consequences of the Rise of the West*. Oxford: Blackwell.

Haller, John S. 1971. *Outcasts from Evolution: Scientific Attitudes of Racial Inferiority, 1859–1900*. Urbana: University of Illinois Press.

Hallett, Robin. 1995. "The European Approach to the Interior of Africa in the Eighteenth Century." In *Historiography of Europeans in Africa and Asia, 1450–1800* (vol. 4 of "An Expanding World: The European Impact on World History, 1450–1800"), ed. by Anthony Disney, pp. 53–68. Brookfield, VT: Variorum/Ashgate.

Halliday, Fred. 1993. "'Orientalism' and Its Critics." *British Journal of Middle Eastern Studies* 20 (no. 2): 145–63.

Halm, Heinz. 1997. *The Fatimids and Their Traditions of Learning*. London: I. B. Tauris.

Halvorsen, Tor. 2005. "Knowledge Shopping or Identity Formation in Times of Globalization." Paper presented at the Third Conference on Knowledge and Politics, May 18–20, University of Bergen.

Halvorsen, Tor, and Skauge, Tom. 2004. "Constructing Knowledge Societies? The World Bank and the New Lending Policy for Tertiary Education." *Journal of Higher Education in Africa* 2 (no. 3): 139–51.

Hamilton, Charles V.; Huntley, Lynn; Alexander, Neville; Guimaraes, Antonio Sergio Alfredo; and Wilmot, James. (eds.) 2001. *Beyond Racism: Race and Inequality in Brazil, South Africa and the United States*. Boulder, CO: Lynne Rienner.

Hanlon, Joseph. 1984. *Mozambique: The Revolution under Fire*. London: Zed.

Hanlon, Joseph. 1986. *Beggar Your Neighbours: Apartheid Power and Southern Africa*. London: James Currey.

Hanna, William John. 1975. *University Students and African Politics.* New York: Africana.

Hannaford, Ivan. 1996. *Race: The History of an Idea in the West.* Washington, DC: Woodrow Wilson Center Press.

Harbisorn, F., and Myers, C. A. 1964). *Education, Manpower and Economic Growth.* New York: McGraw-Hill.

Hardacre, Helen, and Kern, Adam L. (eds.) 1997. *New Directions in the Study of Meiji Japan.* New York: Brill.

Harding, Sandra. "Introduction: Eurocentric Scientific Illiteracy—A Challenge for the World Community." In *The 'Racial' Economy of Science: Toward a Democratic Future*, ed. by Sandra Harding, pp. 1–29. Bloomington: Indiana University Press.

Hargreaves, John D. 1988. *Decolonization in Africa.* New York: Longman.

Harlow, Barbara, and Carter, Mia. (eds.) 1999. *Imperialism & Orientalism: A Documentary Sourcebook.* Oxford: Blackwell.

Harrison, Graham. (ed.) 2005. *Global Encounters: International Political Economy, Development, and Globalization.* New York: Palgrave Macmillan.

Hart-Landsberg, Martin, and Burkett, Paul. 2005. *China and Socialism: Market Reforms and Class Struggle.* New York: Monthly Review.

Harvey, David. 2003. *The New Imperialism.* New York: Oxford University Press.

Hassan, Yusuf F. 1967. *The Arabs and the Sudan: From the Seventh to the Early Sixteenth Century.* Chicago, Aldine.

Hassen, Mohammed. 1990. *The Oromo of Ethiopia: A History (1570–1850).* New York: Cambridge University Press.

Hawes, Hugh, and Coombe, Trevor. (eds.) 1986. *Education Priorities and Aid Responses in Sub-Saharan Africa.* London: Her Majesty's Stationary Office (for the Overseas Development Administration).

Hawkins, Simon. 2003. "Globalization vs. Civilization: The Ideologies of Foreign Language Learning in Tunisia." Ph.D. dissertation, University of Chicago.

Hayman, John. 1993. "Bridging Higher Education's Technology Gap in Africa." *THE Journal (Technological Horizons in Education)* 20 (no. 6, January): 63–69.

Haywood, Carl Norman. 1967. "American Whalers and Africa." Ph.D. dissertation, Boston University.

Headrick, Mathew. 1981. *The Tools of Empire: Technology and European Imperialism in the Nineteenth Century.* Oxford: Oxford University Press.

Hedon, J. Christopher. 1963. *Bonaparte in Egypt.* London: Hamish Hamilton.

Hegel, George W. F. 1971 [1845]. *Philosophy of Mind (Part III of the Encyclopedia of the Philosophical Sciences).* Translated by William Wallace. Oxford: Oxford University Press.

Henry, Keith S. 1976. *The Formative Influences in Earlier Twentieth Century African Responses to America.* Buffalo: Council on International Studies, State University of New York at Buffalo.

Henze, Paul B. 2000. *Layers of Time: A History of Ethiopia.* New York : St. Martin's.

Herodotus. 1998. *The Histories.* (Translated by Robin Waterfield, with an introduction and notes by Carolyn Dewald.) New York: Oxford University Press.

Herrnstein, Richard J., and Murray, Charles. 1994. *The Bell Curve: Intelligence and Class Structure in American Life.* New York: Free Press.

Hershberg, Eric, and Moore, Kevin W. (eds.) 2002. *Critical Views of September 11: Analyses from Around the World*. New York: The New Press.

Hess, Andrew C. 1995. "The Evolution of the Ottoman Seaborne Empire in the Age of the Oceanic Discoveries, 1453–1525." In *The Global Opportunity* (vol. 1 of "An Expanding World: The European Impact on World History, 1450–1800"), ed. by Felipe Fernandez-Armesto, pp. 196–223. Brookfield, VT: Variorum/Ashgate.

Hess, Robert L. 1966. *Italian Colonialism in Somalia*. Chicago: University of Chicago Press.

Heyworth-Dunne, J. 1939. *An Introduction to the History of Education in Modern Egypt*. London: Luzac.

Hill, Donald R. 1993. *Islamic Science and Engineering*. Edinburgh: Edinburgh University Press.

Hill, Robert A., and Pirio, Gregory A. 1987. "'Africa for the Africans': The Garvey Movement in South Africa, 1920–1940." In *The Politics of Race, Class and Nationalism in Twentieth-Century South Africa*, ed. by Shula Marks, and Stanley Trapido, pp. 209–53. New York: Longman.

Hillenbrand, Carole. 1999. *The Crusades: Islamic Perspectives*. Edinburgh: Edinburgh University Press.

Hindess, Barry, and Hirst, Paul Q. 1975. *Pre-capitalist Modes of Production*. Boston: Routledge and Kegan Paul.

Hirschmeier, Johannes. 1964. *The Origins of Entrepreneurship in Meiji Japan*. Cambridge: Harvard University Press.

Hirson, Baruch. 1979. *Year of Fire, Year of Ash: The Soweto Revolt, Roots of a Revolution?* London: Zed.

Hiskett, Mervyn. 1984. *The Development of Islam in West Africa*. New York: Longman.

Hoben, Susan. 1988. "Language Issues and Education in Somalia." in *Proceedings of the Third International Congress of Somali Studies*, ed. by Annarita Puglielli. Roma: Pensiero Scientifico Editore.

Hodges, Tony. 2004. *Angola: Anatomy of an Oil State*. Bloomington: Indiana University Press.

Hodgson, Marshall G. S. 1974. *The Venture of Islam: Conscience and History in a World Civilization*. (3 vols.) Chicago: University of Chicago Press.

Hodgson, Marshall G. S. 1993. *Rethinking World History: Essays on Europe, Islam and World History*. (Edited, with an Introduction and Conclusion by Edmund Burke III.) Cambridge: Cambridge University Press.

Hoff, Advertus A. 1962. *A Short History of Liberia College and the University of Liberia*. Monrovia: Consolidated Publications.

Hoff, William Stateman. 1987. "The Role of the University of Liberia in National Development, 1960–1980." Ph.D. dissertation, University of Illinois at Urbana-Champaign.

Hoffman, Adonis. 1995–1996. "The Destruction of Higher Education in Sub-Saharan Africa." *Journal of Blacks in Higher Education* (no. 10): 83–87.

Hofmeyr, J. H. 1938. "The Education of the South African Native." *Journal of the Royal African Society* 37 (no. 147): 147–55.

Hogendijk, Jan P., and Sabra, Abdelhamid I. 2003. *The Enterprise of Science in Islam: New Perspectives*. Cambridge, MA: The M. I. T. Press.

Holland, Cecelia. 1999. "The Death That Saved Europe: The Mongols Turn Back." In *What If? The World's Foremost Military Historians Imagine What Might Have Been?*, ed. by Robert Cowley and Stephen Ambrose, pp. 93–106. New York: Putnam.

Holness, Marga. 1988. "Angola: The Struggle Continues." In *Frontline Southern Africa: Destructive Engagement*, ed. by Phyllis Johnson, and David Martin, pp. 101–51. New York: Four Walls Eight Windows.

Holt, P. M. 1975. "Egypt, the Funj, and Darfur." In *The Cambridge History of Africa*, vol. 4, ed. by J. D. Fage, pp. 14–57. Cambridge: Cambridge University Press.

Holt, P. M., and Daly, M. W. 2000. *A History of the Sudan: From the Coming of Islam to the Present Day* (5th edition). New York: Longman.

Hopkins, A. G. 1986. "The Victorians and Africa: A Reconsideration of the Occupation of Egypt, 1882." *Journal of African History* 27 (no. 2): 360–91.

Hopkins, A. G. 2002 (ed.) *Globalization in World History*. New York: W. W. Norton.

Hourani, Albert. 2002. *A History of the Arab Peoples*. Cambridge: Belknap Press of Harvard University Press.

Howard, Thomas C. 1982. "Black American Missionary Influence on the Origins of University Education in West Africa." In *Black Americans and the Missionary Movement in Africa*, ed. by Sylvia M. Jacobs, pp. 95–127. Westport, CT: Greenwood.

Howe, Stephen. 1998. *Afrocentrism: Mythical Pasts and Imagined Homes*. New York: Verso.

Huband, Mark. 2001. *The Skull Beneath the Skin: Africa After the Cold War*. Boulder, CO: Westview.

Huemer, A. A. 1998. *The Invention of 'Race': The Columbian Turn in Modern Consciousness*. Lander, WY: Agathon.

Huff, Tobby E. 1993. *The Rise of Early Modern Science: Islam, China and the West*. New York: Cambridge University Press.

Huff, Tobby E., and Schluchter, Wolfgang. (eds.) 1999. *Max Weber and Islam*. New Brunswick, NJ: Transaction.

Hugo, Pierre. 1998. "Transformation: the Changing Context of Academia in Post-apartheid South Africa." *African Affairs* 97 (no. 386, January): 5–27.

Hull, Richard W. 1990. *American Enterprise in South Africa: Historical Dimensions of Engagement and Disengagement*. New York: New York University Press.

Human Rights Watch. 2003. *Algeria, Time for Reckoning: Enforced Disappearances and Abductions in Algeria*. New York, NY: Human Rights Watch.

Hunter, F. Robert. 1984. *Egypt under the Khedives, 1805–1879*. Pittsburgh: University of Pittsburgh Press.

Huntington, Ellsworth. 1924. *Civilization and Climate*. New Haven: Yale University Press.

Huntington, Samuel P. 1998. *The Clash of Civilizations and the Remaking of World Order*. New York: Simon & Schuster.

Hunwick, John O., and Powell, Eve Troutt. (eds.) 2002. *The African Diaspora in the Mediterranean Lands of Islam*. Princeton, NJ: Markus Wiener Publishers.

Hurst, P. 1987. "Review Article: The Methodology of Qualitative Research." *International Journal of Educational Development* 7: 69–72.

Hussain, A. 1976. "The Economy and the Educational System in Capitalist Societies." *Economy and Society* 5: 413–34.

Hussain, Asaf; Olson, Robert; and Qureshi, Jamil. (eds.) 1984. *Orientalism, Islam and Islamists.* Brattleboro, VT: Amana.

Hutchful, Eboe. 1995. "Why Regimes Adjust: The World Bank Ponders Its 'Star Pupil.'" *Canadian Journal of African Studies* 29 (no. 2): 303–17.

Huzayyin, S. A. 1942. *Arabia and the Far East: Their Commercial and Cultural Relations in Graeco-Roman and Irano-Arabian Times.* Cairo: Geographical Society of Egypt.

Hyde, Georgie D. M. 1978. *Education in Modern Egypt: Ideals and Realities.* London: Routledge & Kegan Paul.

Hymer, Stephen. 1970. "Economic Forms in Pre-colonial Ghana." *Journal of Economic History* 30 (March): 33–50.

Ignatyev, Oleg. 1977. *Secret Weapon in Africa.* Moscow: Progress.

Ilon, Lynn. 2003. "Foreign Aid Financing of Higher Education in Africa." In *African Higher Education: An International Reference Handbook*, ed. by Damtew Teferra and Philip G. Altbach, pp. 61–72. Bloomington: Indiana University Press.

Inikori, Joseph E. 1982. *Forced Migration: The Impact of the Export Slave Trade on African Societies.* London: Hutchinson.

Inikori, Joseph E. 1992. "Africa in World History: The Export Slave Trade from Africa and the Emergence of the Atlantic Economic Order." In *General History of Africa, Volume V: Africa from the Sixteenth to the Eighteenth Century*, ed. by B. A. Ogot, pp. 74–112. Berkeley: University of California Press.

Inikori, Joseph E. 2002. *Africans and the Industrial Revolution in England: A Study in International Trade and Economic Development.* New York: Cambridge University Press.

Inikori, Joseph E., and Engerman, Stanley E. (eds.) 1992. The Atlantic Slave Trade: Effects on Economies, Societies and Peoples in Africa, the Americas and Europe. Durham: Duke University Press.

International Crisis Group. 2002. *Ending Starvation as a Weapon of War in Sudan.* Brussels: International Crisis Group.

International Crisis Group. 2003 (a). *Angola's Choice: Reform or Regress.* Brussels: International Crisis Group.

International Crisis Group. 2003 (b). *Dealing with Savimbi's Ghost: The Security and Humanitarian Challenges in Angola.* Brussels: International Crisis Group.

International Crisis Group. 2004. *Somalia: Continuation of War by other Means?* (Africa Report No. 88). Brussels: International Crisis Group.

International Crisis Group. 2005 (a). *Côte d'Ivoire: The Worst May Be Yet to Come* (Africa Report No. 90). Brussels: International Crisis Group.

International Crisis Group. 2005 (b). *The Congo's Transition Is Failing: Crisis in the Kivus* (Africa Report No. 91) Brussels: International Crisis Group.

Iqbal, Muzaffar. 2002. *Islam and Science.* Burlington, VT: Ashgate.

Irwin, Robert. 1986. *The Middle East in the Middle Ages: The Early Mamluk Sultanate, 1250–1382.* London: Croom Helm.

Isaak, Robert A. 2005. *The Globalization Gap: How the Rich Get Richer and the Poor Get Left Further Behind.* Upper Saddle River, NJ: Prentice Hall.

Issa-Salwe, Abdisalam M. 2000. *Cold War Fallout: Boundary Politics and Conflict in the Horn of Africa.* London: HAAN.

Issawi, Charles. 1995. "The Decline of Middle Eastern Trade, 1100–1850." In *The Global Opportunity* (vol. 1 of "An Expanding World: The European Impact on World History, 1450–1800"), ed. by Felipe Fernandez-Armesto, pp. 133–54. Brookfield, VT: Variorum/Ashgate.

Jackson, John P., and Weidman, Nadine M. 2004. *Race, Racism, and Science: Social Impact and Interaction.* Santa Barbara, CA: ABC–CLIO.

Jacobs, Sylvia M. (ed.) 1982. *Black Americans and the Missionary Movement in Africa.* Westport, CT: Greenwood Press, 1982.

James, George G. M. 1992 (1954). *Stolen Legacy: Greek Philosophy Is Stolen Egyptian Philosophy.* Trenton, NJ: Africa World.

Janus, Christopher G. 1980. "The Establishment and Adaptation of Primarily British Influenced Universities in West and North Africa." Ph.D. dissertation, University of Oxford.

Jardine, Douglas James. 1969. *The Mad Mullah of Somaliland.* New York: Negro Universities Press.

Jayyusi, Salma Khadra, and Marin, Manuela. 1994. *The Legacy of Muslim Spain* (Second Edition). New York: E. J. Brill.

Jenkins, Janet. 1989. "Some Trends in Distance Education in Africa: An Examination of the Past and Future Role of Distance Education as a Tool for National Development." *Distance Education* 10 (no. 1): 41–44, 46–48.

Jensen, Mike. 1999. "[Information and Communication Technologies Throughout the World] Sub-Saharan Africa." In *World Communication and Information Report, 1999/2000*, pp. 180–96. Paris: UNESCO.

Johnson, Phyllis, and Martin, David. 1988. *Frontline Southern Africa: Destructive Engagement.* New York: Four Walls Eight Windows.

Johnson, Shaun. (ed.) 1988. *South Africa: No Turning Back.* London: Macmillan.

Johnstone, D. Bruce. The Economics and Politics of Cost Sharing in Higher Education: Comparative Perspectives. *Economics of Education Review* 23 (no. 4): 403–10.

Johnstone, D. Bruce, and Shroff-Mehta, P. 2001. "Higher Education Finance and Accessibility: An International Comparative Examination of Tuition and Finance Assistance Policies." In *Higher Education Reform*, ed. by H. Eggins, London: Society for Research into Higher Education.

Johnstone, D. Bruce, and Teferra, Damtew. (eds.) 2004. "Special Issue: Cost Sharing and Other Forms of Revenue Supplementation in African Higher Education." *Journal of Higher Education in Africa* 2 (no. 2): 1–158.

Johnstone, Frederick A. 1976. *Class, Race and Gold: A Study of Class Relations and Racial Discrimination in South Africa.* London: Routledge and Kegan Paul.

Jok, Jok Madut. 2001. *War and Slavery in Sudan.* Philadelphia: University of Pennsylvania Press.

Jones, E. L. 1988. *Growth Recurring: Economic Change in World History.* New York: Oxford University Press.

Jones, E. L. 2003. *The European Miracle: Environments, Economies and Geopolitics in the History of Europe and Asia.* Cambridge: Cambridge University Press.

Jones, Phillip W. 1992. *World Bank Financing of Education: Lending, Learning and Development*. London: Routledge.

Jones, Thomas Jesse. 1922. *Education in East Africa: A Study of West, South and Equatorial Africa, by the African Education Commission*. New York: Phelps-Stokes Fund.

Jones, Thomas Jesse. 1925. *Education in East Africa: A Study of East, Central and South Africa, by the Second African Education Commission under the Auspices of the Phelps-Stokes Fund, in Cooperation with the International Education Board*. New York: Phelps-Stokes Fund.

Jordan, Winthrop D. 1968. *White Over Black: American Attitudes Toward the Negro, 1550–1812*. Chapel Hill: University of North Carolina Press.

Jung, C. G. 1964. *Civilization in Transition*. New York: Pantheon.

Juvaini, 'Ala'al-Din 'Aṭa Malik. 1997. *Genghis Khan: The History of the World Conqueror: Translated from the Text of Mizra Muhammad Qazvini by J. A. Boyle, With a New Introduction and Bibliography by David O. Morgan*. Seattle: University of Washington Press.

Kahn, Paul. 1984. *The Secret History of the Mongols: The Origin of Chinghis Khan: An Adaptation of the Yuan ch'ao pi shih, Based Primarily on the English Translation by Francis Woodman Cleaves*. San Francisco: North Point.

Kalewold, Alaka I. 1970. See Alaka I. Kalewold. 1970.

Kallaway, Peter. 2002 (a). "Introduction." In *The History of Education under Apartheid 1948–1994: The Doors of Learning and Culture Shall be Opened*, ed. by Peter Kallaway, pp. 1–38. New York: Peter Lang.

Kallaway, Peter. (ed.) 2002 (b). *The History of Education under Apartheid 1948–1994: The Doors of Learning and Culture Shall be Opened*. New York: Peter Lang.

Kallaway, Peter. (ed.) 1984. *Apartheid and Education: The Education of Black South Africans*. Johannesburg: Ravan.

Kelly, Saul. 2000. *Cold War in the Desert: Britain, the United States, and the Italian Colonies, 1945–52*. New York: St. Martin's.

Kamil, 'Abd al-'Aziz. 1970. *Islam and the Race Question*. Paris: UNESCO.

Kapteijns, Lidwein. 2000. "Ethiopia and the Horn of Africa." In *The History of Islam in Africa*, ed. by Nehemia Levitzion, and Randall L. Pouwels, pp. 227–50. Athens: Ohio University Press.

Kapur, Devesh; Lewis, John P.; and Webb, Richard. (eds.) 1997. *The World Bank: Its First Half Century*. (2 vols.) Washington, DC: Brookings Institution Press.

Karenga, Maulana, and Carruthers, Jacob H. 1986. *Kemet and the African Worldview: Research, Rescue and Restoration*. Los Angeles: University of Sankore Press.

Kashoki, Mubanga E. 1994. "The African University: Towards Innovative Management Strategies for the 21st Century. In *Higher Education Staff Development: Directions for the Twenty-First Century*, by Jennifer Barnes, et. al., pp. 149-62. Paris: UNESCO.

Katjavivi, Peter H. 1988. *A History of Resistance in Namibia*. London: James Currey.

Kebede, Massay. 1997. "Japan and Ethiopians: An Appraisal of Similarities and Divergent Courses." In *Ethiopia in Broader Perspective: Papers of 13th International Conference of Ethiopian Studies*, vol. 1 (of 3), ed. by Katsuyoshi Fukui, Eisei Kurimoto, and Masayoshi Shigeta, pp. 639–51. Kyoto: Shokado.

Kedar, Benjamin S. 1984. *Crusade and Mission: European Approaches toward the Muslims.* Princeton: Princeton University Press.

Keene, Donald. 2002. *Emperor of Japan: Meiji and His World, 1852–1912.* New York: Columbia University Press.

Kehoe, Monika. 1962. "Higher Education in Ethiopia: A Report on Haile Selassie I University." *Journal of Higher Education* 33 (no. 9): 475–78.

Keita, S. O. Y. 1993. "*Black Athena:* 'Race,' Bernal and Snowden." *Arethusa* 26 (no. 3): 295–314.

Kelly, Gail P. 1984. "Colonialism, Indigenous Society and School Practices: French West Africa and Indochina, 1918–1938." In *Education and the Colonial Experience (Second Revised Edition),* ed. by Philip G. Altbach, and Gail P. Kelly, pp. 9–32. New Brunswick, NJ: Transaction.

Kelly, Gail P. (ed.). 1989. *International Handbook of Women's Education.* Westport, CT: Greenwood.

Kelly, Gail P., and Elliott, Carolyn M. (eds.) 1982. *Women's Education in the Third World: Comparative Perspectives.* Albany: State University of New York Press.

Kelly, Gail P., and Slaughter, Sheila. (eds.) 1991. *Women's Higher Education in Comparative Perspective.* Boston: Kluwer Academic.

Kelly, Sean. 1993. *America's Tyrant: The CIA and Mobutu of Zaire.* Washington, DC: American University Press.

Kempton, Daniel R. 1989. *Soviet Strategy toward Southern Africa: The National Liberation Movement Connection.* New York: Praeger.

Kennedy, E. S. 1966. "Late Medieval Planetary Theory." *Isis* 57 (no. 3): 365–78.

Kennedy, E. S. 1983. "The History of Trigonometry: An Overview." In *Studies in the Islamic Exact Sciences,* ed. by E. S. Kennedy et al., pp. 3–29. Beirut: American University of Beirut Press.

Kent, John. 1992. *The Internationalization of Colonialism: Britain, France and Black Africa, 1939–1956.* Oxford: Clarendon.

Kerr, Alexander. 1968. *Fort Hare, 1915–1948: The Evolution of an African College.* New York: Humanities.

Kerr, C. 1966. *The Uses of the University.* New York: Harper and Row.

Khaldun, Ibn. 1967. *The Muqaddimah: An Introduction to History* (Translated from the Arabic by Franz Rosenthal). (3 vols.) Princeton: Princeton University Press.

Khalid, Mansur. 2003. *War and Prospects of Peace in the Sudan: A Tale of Two Countries.* London: Kegan Paul.

King, David A. 2000. "Mathematical Astronomy in Islamic Civilization." In *Astronomy across Cultures: The History of Non-Western Astronomy,* ed. by Helaine Selin, pp. 585–614. Norwell, MA: Kluwer Academic.

King, Elizabeth M., and Hill, M. Anne. (eds.) 1993. *Women's Education in Developing Countries: Barriers, Benefits and Policies.* Baltimore: Johns Hopkins University Press (for the World Bank).

King, Kenneth. 1971. *Pan-Africanism and Education: A Study of Race Philanthropy and Education in the Southern States of America and East Africa.* Oxford: Clarendon.

King, Kenneth. 1995. "World Bank Traditions of Support to Higher Education and Capacity-Building: Reflections on 'Higher Education: The Lessons of Experience'." In *Learning from Experience: Policy and Practice in Aid to Higher Education*, ed. by Lene Buchert, and Kenneth King, pp. 19–40. The Hague: Center for the Study of Education in Developing Countries.

King, Kimberly Lynease. 2001. 'Stumbling toward Racial Inclusion: The Story of Transformation at the University of Witwatersrand." In *Apartheid No More: Case Studies of Southern African Universities in the Process of Transformation*, ed. by Reitsumetse Obakeng Mabokela, and Kimberly Lynease King, pp. 73–90. Westport, CT: Bergin and Garvey.

Kiple, Kenneth F., and Beck, Stephen V. (eds.) 1997. *Biological Consequences of the European Expansion, 1450–1800*. (vol. 27 of "An Expanding World: The European Impact on World History, 1450–1800"). Brookfield, VT: Ashgate/Variorum.

Kiros, Fassil R. 1990. *Implementing Educational Policies in Ethiopia.* Washington, DC: The World Bank.

Kitchen, Helen. (ed.) 1962. *The Educated African: A Country by Country Survey of Educational Development in Africa*. (Compiled by Ruth Sloan Associates, Washington, DC). New York: Praeger.

Klees, S. 1986. "Planning and Policy Analysis in Education: What Can Economics Tell Us?" *Comparative Education Review* 30: 574–607.

Klees, S. 2002. "World Bank Education Policy: New Rhetoric, Old Ideology." *International Journal of Educational Development* 22: 451–74.

Klinghoffer, Arthur J. 1980. *The Angolan War: A Study in Soviet Policy in the Third World*. Boulder, CO: Westview.

Knight, Ian. 1995. *The Anatomy of the Zulu Army: From Shaka to Cetshwayo, 1818–1879*. Mechanicsburg, PA: Stackpole Books.

Kobishchanov, Yuri M. 1979 (1966). *Axum*. University Park: Pennsylvania State University Press.

Kornicki, Peter F. (ed.) 1998. *Meiji Japan: Political, Economic and Social History, 1868–1912*. (4 vols.) New York: Routledge.

Kovel, Joel. 1988. *White Racism: A Psychohistory (with a New Introduction by Ivan Ward)*. London: Free Association.

Koyre, Alexandre. 1978 (1939). *Galileo Studies*. Atlantic Highlands, NJ: Humanities Press.

Kramer, Samuel Noah. 1981. *History Begins at Sumer: Thirty Nine Firsts in Man's Recorded History*. Philadelphia: University of Pennsylvania Press.

Krige, Sue. 1997. "Segregation, Science and Commissions of Enquiry: The Contestation Over Native Education Policy in South Africa, 1930–36." *Journal of Southern African Studies* 23 (no. 3): 491–506.

Kros, Cynthia. 2002. "W. W. M. Eiselen: Architect of Apartheid Education." In *The History of Education under Apartheid 1948–1994: The Doors of Learning and Culture Shall Be Opened*, ed. by Peter Kallaway, pp. 53–73. New York: Peter Lang.

Kruss, Glenda. 2004. *Chasing Credentials and Mobility: Private Higher Education in South Africa*. Cape Town: HSRC Press.

Kucklick, Henrika. 1991. "Contested Monuments: The Politics of Archeology in Southern Africa." In *Colonial Situations: Essays on the Contextualization of Ethno-

graphic Knowledge, ed. by George W. Stocking, Jr., pp. 135–69. Madison: University of Wisconsin Press.

Kuczynski, Pedro-Pablo, and Williamson, John. (eds.) 2003. *After the Washington Consensus: Restarting Growth and Reform in Latin America*. Washington, DC: Institute for International Economics.

Kunitzsch, Paul. 2003. "The Transmission of Hindu-Arabic Numerals Reconsidered." In *The Enterprise of Science in Islam: New Perspectives*, ed. by Jan P. Hogendijk, and Abdelhamid I. Sabra, pp. 3–22. Cambridge, MA: The M. I. T. Press.

Kuraev-Maxah. 2004. "Missing Data in Russian International Higher Education." *International Higher Education* (no. 36): 20–21.

Küster, Sybille. 1999. *African Education in Colonial Zimbabwe, Zambia and Malawi: Government Control, Settler Antagonism and African Agency, 1890–1964*. Hamburg: Lit.

Lach, Donald F. 1965. *Asia in the Making of Europe*. (Volume 1, Book 1). Chicago: University of Chicago Press.

Laitin, David D., and Samatar, Said S. 1987. *Somalia: Nation in Search of a State*. Boulder, CO: Westview.

Lancaster, Carol. 1997. "The World Bank in Africa Since 1980: The Politics of Structural Adjustment." In *The World Bank: Its First Half Century* (vol. 2), ed. by Davesh Kapur, John P. Lewis, and Richard Webb, pp. 161–94. Washington, DC: Brookings Institution Press.

Landes, David S. 1988. *The Wealth and Poverty of Nations: Why Some are So Rich and Some So Poor*. New York: Norton.

Lane, Kris E. 1998. *Pillaging the Empire: Piracy in the Americas, 1500–1750*. Armonk, NY: M. E. Sharpe

Langley, J. A. 1973. *Pan Africanism and Nationalism in West Africa: 1900–1945*. Oxford: Clarendon.

Lanning, Greg, and Mueller, Marti. 1979. *Africa undermined: Mining Companies and the Underdevelopment of Africa*. Harmondsworth: Penguin, 1979.

Lardicci, Francesca. (ed.) 1999. *A Synoptic Edition of the Log of Columbus's First Voyage*. (vol. 6 of "Repertorium Columbianum") Turnhout: Brepols.

Law, Robin. 1991. *The Slave Coast of West Africa, 1550–1750: The Impact of the Atlantic Slave Trade on an African Society*. Oxford: Oxford University Press.

Layish, Aharon, and Warburg, Gabriel. 2002. *The Reinstatement of Islamic Law in Sudan Under Numayri: An Evaluation of a Legal Experiment in the Light of Its Historical Context, Methodology, and Repercussions*. Boston: Brill.

Lazarus-Yafeh, Hava. "Continuity and Innovation in Egyptian Islam: The Ulama vis-à-vis the Militants." In *Egypt from Monarchy to Republic: A Reassessment of Revolution and Change*, ed. by Shimon Shamir, pp. 173–80. Boulder, CO: Westview.

Lefkow, Leslie. 2004. *Darfur in Flames: Atrocities in Western Sudan*. New York: Human Rights Watch.

Lefkowitz, Mary. 1997. *Not Out of Africa: How Afrocentrism Became an Excuse to Teach Myth as History*. New York: New Republic Books.

Lefkowitz, Mary, and Rogers, Guy MacLean. (eds.) 1996. *Black Athena Revisited*. Chapel Hill: University of North Carolina Press.

Legum, Colin. 1971. "The Year of the Students: A Survey of the African University Scene." In *Africa Contemporary Record: Annual Survey and Documents 1971–1972.*, ed. by Colin Legum, and Anthony Hughes, pp. A3–A30. London: Rex Collings.

Legum, Colin. 1988. *The Battlefronts of Southern Africa*. New York: Africana.

Legum, Colin, and Hodges, Tony. 1978. *After Angola: The War Over Southern Africa*. New York: Africana.

Leiser, Gary. 1983. "Medical Education in Islamic Lands from the Seventh to the Fourteenth Century." *Journal of the History of Medicine and Allied Sciences* 38 (no. 1): 48–75.

Leiser, Gary La Viere. 1976. "The Restoration of Sunnism in Egypt: Madrasas and Mudarrisun, 495–647/1101–1249." Ph.D. dissertation, University of Pennsylvania.

Lemarchand, Rene. 1996. *Burundi: Ethnic Conflict and Genocide*. Cambridge: Cambridge University Press.

Lemarchand, Rene. (ed.) 1981. *American Policy in Southern Africa: The Stakes and the Stance* (Second Edition). Washington, DC: University Press of America.

Lesch, Ann Mosely. 1998. *The Sudan—Contested National Identities*. Bloomington: Indiana University Press.

Levine, Donald N. 1997. "Ethiopia and Japan in Comparative Civilizational Perspective." In *Ethiopia in Broader Perspective: Papers of 13th International Conference of Ethiopian Studies,* Vol. 1 (of 3), ed. by Katsuyoshi Fukui, Eisei Kurimoto, and Masayoshi Shigeta, pp. 652–75. Kyoto: Shokado.

Levtzion, Nehemia, and Pouwels, Randall L. (eds.) 2000. *The History of Islam in Africa*. Athens: Ohio University Press.

Lévy-Bruhl, Lucien. 1985 (1926). *How Natives Think*. Princeton, NJ: Princeton University Press.

Lewis, Bernard. 1971. *Race and Color in Islam*. New York: Harper & Row.

Lewis, Bernard. 1990. *Race and Slavery in the Middle East: An Historical Enquiry*. New York: Oxford University Press.

Lewis, Bernard. 1993. *Islam and the West*. New York: Oxford University Press.

Lewis, David L. 1987. *The Race to Fashoda: European Colonialism and African Resistance in the Scramble for Africa*. New York: Weidenfeld & Nicolson.

Lewis, Herbert S. 1966. "The Origins of the Galla and the Somali." *Journal of African History* 7 (no. 1): 27–46.

Lewis, I. M. 1960. "The Somali Conquest of the Horn of Africa." *Journal of African History* 1 (no. 2): 213–29.

Lewis, I. M. 2002. *A Modern History of the Somali: Nation and State in the Horn of Africa* (4th edition). Athens: Ohio University Press.

Lewis, P. M. 1996. "Economic Reform and Political Transition in Africa: The Quest for a Politics of Development." *World Politics* 49 (no. 1): 92–129.

Leys, Colin. 1971. "The Role of the University in an underdeveloped Country." *Journal of Eastern African Research and Development* 1 (no. 1): 29–40.

Leys, Colin. 1996. *The Rise and Fall of Development Theory*. Bloomington: Indiana University Press.

Leys, Colin, and Brown, Susan. 2001. *Histories of Namibia: Living through the Liberation Struggle*. London: Merlin.

Libby, David J.; Spickard, Paul; and Ditto, Susan. (eds.) 2005. *Affect and Power: Essays on Sex, Slavery, Race, and Religion in Appreciation of Winthrop D. Jordan.* Jackson: University Press of Mississippi.

Liebenow, J. Gus. 1969. *Liberia: The Evolution of a Privilege.* Ithaca, NY: Cornell University Press.

Lincicome, Mark Elwood. 1995. *Principle, Praxis and the Politics of Educational Reform in Meiji Japan.* Honolulu: University of Hawaii Press.

Lindberg, David C. 1978. "The Transmission of Greek and Arabic Learning to the West." In *Science in the Middle Ages,* ed. by David C. Lindberg, pp. 52–90. Chicago: University of Chicago Press.

Lindberg, David C. 1992. *The Beginnings of Western Science.* Chicago: University of Chicago Press.

Little, Peter D. 2003. *Somalia: Economy Without State.* Bloomington: Indiana University Press.

Livingstone, Thomas W. 1976. "The Exportation of American Higher Education to West Africa: Liberia College, 1850–1900." *Journal of Negro Education* 45 (no. 3): 246–62.

Lloyd, Alan B. 1975–1988. *Herodotus, Book II.* (3 vols.) Leiden: E.J. Brill.

Loban, Richard A.; Kramer, Robert S.; and Fluehr–Lobban, Carolyn. 2002. *Historical Dictionary of the Sudan* (third edition). Lanham, MD: Scarecrow.

Lockwood Commitee. 1964. *Report on the Development of a University in Northern Rhodesia.* Lusaka: Government Printer.

Logan, I. B., and Mengisteab, K. 1993. "IMF-World Bank Adjustment and Structural Transformation in Sub-Saharan Africa." *Economic Geography* 69 (1): 1–25.

Lombard, Denys, and Aubin, Jean. 2000. *Asian Merchants and Businessmen in the Indian Ocean and the China Sea.* New Delhi: Oxford University Press.

Lopez, Robert S. 1995. "European Merchants in the Medieval Indies: The Evidence of Commercial Documents." In *The European Opportunity* (vol. 2 of "An Expanding World: The European Impact on World History, 1450–1800"), ed. by Felipe Fernandez-Armesto, pp. 301–21. Brookfield, VT: Variorum/Ashgate.

Lopez, Robert S., and Raymond, Irving W. 1967. *Medieval Trade in the Mediterranean World.* New York: Norton.

Loram, Charles T. 1969 (1917). *The Education of the South African Native.* New York: Negro Universities Press.

Lubeck, P. M. 1992. "The Crisis of African Development: Conflicting Interpretations and Resolutions." *Annual Review of Sociology* 18: 519–40.

Lucas, Gerard. 1964. *Education as an Instrument of National Policy in Selected Newly Developing Nations.* (Cooperative Research Project no. 1032—Phase 3: Formal Education in the Congo-Brazzaville: A Study of Educational Policy and Practice.) Stanford, CA: Stanford University, School of Education, Comparative Education Center.

Lulat, Y. G-M. 1981. "Determinants of Third World Student Activism in the Seventies: The Case of Zambia." In *Student Politics: Perspectives for the Eighties,* edited by Philip G. Altbach, pp. 234-66. Metuchen, NJ: Scarecrow.

Lulat, Y. G-M. 1982. "Political Constraints on Educational Reform for Development: Lessons from an African Experience." *Comparative Education Review* 26 (June): 235–53.

Lulat, Y. G-M. 1985. "Zachariah's 'Plants' and 'Clay': A Rejoinder." *Comparative Education Review* 29 (no. 4): 549–56.

Lulat, Y. G-M. 1988. "Education and National Development: The Continuing Problem of Misdiagnosis and Irrelevant Prescriptions." *International Journal of Educational Development* 8 (no. 4): 315–28.

Lulat, Y. G-M. 1989. "Zambia." In *Student Political Activism: An International Reference Handbook*, ed. by Philip G. Altbach, pp. 37-56. Westport, CT: Greenwood.

Lulat, Y. G-M. 2003. "Confronting the Burden of the Past: The Historical Antecedents of the Present Predicament of African Universities." In *Higher Education: Handbook of Theory and Research* (vol. XVIII), ed. by John C. Smart, pp. 595–668. London: Kluwer Academic.

Lungu, Gatian F. 1980. "The Land-grant Model in Africa: A Study in Higher Education Transfer." Thesis (Ed.D.), Harvard University.

Lungu, Gatian F. 1993. "Educational Policy-Making in Colonial Zambia: The Case of Higher Education for Africans from 1924 to 1964. *Journal of Negro History* 78 (no. 4, Autumn): 207–32.

Lyons, Charles H. 1970. "The Educable African: British Thought and Action, 1835–1865." In *Essays in the History of African Education*, ed. by Vincent M. Battle, and Charles H. Lyons, pp. 1–32. New York: Teachers College Press.

Mabokela, Reitumetse Obakeng. 2000. *Voices of Conflict: Desegregating South African Universities*. New York: Routledge Farmer.

Mabokela, Reitumetse Obakeng. 2001. "Selective Inclusion: Transformation and Language Policy at the University of Stellenbosch." In *Apartheid No More: Case Studies of Southern African Universities in the Process of Transformation*, ed. by Reitsumetse Obakeng Mabokela, and Kimberly Linease King, pp. 59–72. Westport, CT: Bergin and Garvey.

Mabokela, Reitumetse Obakeng, and King, Kimberly Linease. (eds.) 2001. *Apartheid No More: Case Studies of Southern African Universities in the Process of Transformation*. Westport, CT: Bergin and Garvey.

Macaulay, Thomas B. 1935 (1835). *Speeches by Lord Macaulay with his Minute on Indian Education*. London: Oxford University Press.

Macfarlane, Alan. 1978. *The Origins of English Individualism: The Family, Property and Social Transition*. New York: Cambridge University Press.

Macfie, A. L. 1994. *Ataturk*. London: Longman.

Macfie, A. L. (ed.) 2000. *Orientalism: A Reader*. New York: New York University Press.

Macgaffey, Wyatt. 1985. On the Moderate Usefulness of Modes of Production. *Canadian Journal of African Studies* 19 (no. 1): 51–57.

MacInnis, Peter. 2002. *Bittersweet: The Story of Sugar*. London: Allen & Unwin.

MacLeod, Roy. 2000 (a). "Introduction: Alexandria in History and Myth." In *The Library of Alexandria: Center of Learning in the Ancient World*, ed. by Roy MacLeod, pp. 1–15. London: I. B. Tauris.

MacLeod, Roy. (ed.) 2000 (b). *The Library of Alexandria: Center of Learning in the Ancient World*. London: I. B. Tauris.

Macpherson, Margaret. 1964. *They Built for the Future: A Chronicle of Makerere University College 1922–1962*. Cambridge: Cambridge University Press.

Magdoff, Fred. 2004. "A Precarious Existence: The Fate of Billions?" *Monthly Review* 55 (no. 9): 1–14.

Magubane, Bernard Makhosezwe. 1996. *The Making of a Racist State: British Imperialism and the Union of South Africa, 1875–1910.* Trenton, NJ: Africa World.

Maier, Christoph T. 2000. *Crusade Propaganda and Ideology: Model Sermons for the Preaching of the Cross.* Cambridge: Cambridge University Press.

Maier, Karl. 1996. *Angola, Promises and Lies.* Rivonia (South Africa): W. Waterman.

Makdisi, George. 1981. *The Rise of Colleges: Institutions of Learning in Islam and the West.* Edinburgh: Edinburgh University Press.

Malherbe, E. G. 1925/1977. *Education in South Africa.* (2 vols.) Cape Town: Juta.

Mamdani, Mahmood. 1993. "University Crisis and Reform: A Reflection on the African Experience." *Review of African Political Economy* (no. 58): 7–19.

Mamdani, Mahmood. 2001. *When Victims Become Killers: Colonialism, Nativism, and the Genocide in Rwanda.* Princeton, NJ: Princeton University Press.

Mangan, J. A. (ed.) 1993. *The Imperial Curriculum: Racial Images and Education in the British Colonial Experience.* London: Routledge.

Mann, Jim. 2004. *Rise of the Vulcans: The History of Bush's War Cabinet.* New York: Penguin.

Mann, Michael. 1986. *The Sources of Social Power: Vol. 1: A History of Power from the Beginning to A.D. 1760.* Cambridge: Cambridge University Press.

Mann, Michael. 1993. *The Sources of Social Power: Vol. 2: The Rise of Classes and Nation-States 1760–1914.* Cambridge: Cambridge University Press.

Manning, Carrie L. 2002. *The Politics of Peace in Mozambique: Post-Conflict Democratization, 1992–2000.* Westport, CT: Praeger.

Marable, Manning. 1976. "John Langalibalele Dube, Booker T. Washington and the Ideology of Conservative Black Nationalism." In *Profiles of Self-Determination: African Responses to Colonialism in Southern Africa, 1652–Present,* ed. by David Chanaiwa, pp. 320–45. Northridge: California State University at Northridge.

Marcum, John A. 1982. *Education, Race and Social Change in South Africa.* Berkeley: University of California Press.

Marcus, Harold G. 1975. *The Life and Times of Mennelik II: Ethiopia 1844–1913.* Oxford: Clarendon Press.

Marcus, Harold G. 1994. *A History of Ethiopia.* Berkeley: University of California Press.

Marcus, Harold G. 1995. *The Politics of Empire: Ethiopia, Great Britain and the United States, 1941–1974.* Lawrenceville, NJ: Red Sea.

Maren, Michael. 1996. "Somalia: Whose Failure?" *Current History* 95 (May): 201–05.

Marginson, S. 1999. "Subjects and Subjugation: The Economics of Education as Power Knowledge." In *Education Policy,* ed. by J. Marshall, and M. Peters, pp. 206–18. Cheltenham: Edward Elgar.

Mariners' Museum. 2002. *Captive Passage: The Transatlantic Slave Trade and the Making of the Americas.* Washington, DC: Smithsonian Institution Press.

Mario, Mouzinho. 2003. *Higher Education in Mozambique: A Case Study.* Oxford: James Currey (in association with Partnership for Higher Education in Africa, USA).

Markakis, John. 1987. *National and Class Conflict in the Horn of Africa*. New York: Cambridge University Press.

Marmon, Shaun Elizabeth. 1999. *Slavery in the Islamic Middle East*. Princeton, NJ: Marcus Wiener.

Marshall, D. Bruce. 1971. "Free France in Africa: Gaullism and Colonialism." In *France and Britain in Africa: Imperial Rivalry and Colonial Rule*, ed. by Prosser Gifford, and W. M. Roger Louis, pp. 713–48. New Haven: Yale University Press.

Marshall, P. J. 1995. "Retrospect on J. C. van Leur's Essay on the Eighteenth Century as a Category in Asian History." In *The Historiography of Europeans in Africa and Asia, 1450–1800* (vol. 4 of "An Expanding World: The European Impact on World History, 1450–1800."), ed. by Anthony Disney, pp. 39–52. Brookfield, VT: Variorum/Ashgate.

Marsot, Afaf Lutfi al-Sayyid. 1984. *Egypt in the Reign of Muhammed Ali*. Cambridge: Cambridge University Press.

Martin, William G., and West, Michael O. (eds.) 1999. *Out of One, Many Africas: Restructuring the Study and Meaning of Africa*. Urbana: University of Illinois Press.

Martinez, Luis. 2000. *The Algerian Civil War, 1990–1998*. New York: Columbia University Press.

Marx, Karl. 1973. *Grundrisse: Foundations of the Critique of Political Economy (Rough Draft)*. Harmondworth: Penguin.

Maslen, Geoffrey. 2000. "South Africa Approves Branch Campuses for 2 Foreign Colleges." *Chronicle of Higher Education* (February 11): A53.

Masschelein, Jan, and Simons, Maarten. 2002. "An Adequate Education in a Globalized World? A Note on Immunization Against Being–Together." *Journal of Philosophy of Education* 36 (no. 4): 589–608.

Massey, Douglas S., and Denton, Nancy A. 1993. *American Apartheid: Segregation and the Making of the Underclass*. Cambridge: Harvard University Press.

Massialas, Byron G., and Jarrar, Samid Ahmed. 1983. *Education in the Arab World*. New York: Praeger.

Mastnak, Tomaz. 2002. *Crusading Peace: Christendom, the Muslim World and Western Political Order*. Berkeley: University of California Press.

Matos, Narciso. 1998. "Speech of Professor Narciso Matos, Secretary General of the Association of African Universities." In *Volume V—Plenary: World Conference on Higher Education, UNESCO, Paris, 5–9 October, 1998*. Paris: UNESCO (Document no. ED-99/HEP/WCHE/Vol. V-NGO-2).

Maunde, Raymund. 2000. "The Evolution of Higher Education in Zimbabwe." Ph. D. Dissertation, University of Alaska Fairbanks.

Maxwell, I. C. M. 1980. *Universities in Partnership: The Inter-University Council and the Growth of Higher Education in Developing Countries 1946–1970*. Edinburgh: Scottish Academic Press.

Mazrui, Ali A. (ed). 1986. *The Africans*. Westport, CT: Greenwood.

Mazrui, Ali A. (ed.) 1993. *General History of Africa, Volume VIII: Africa since 1935*. Berkeley: University of California Press.

Mazumdar, Sucheta. 1998. *Sugar and Society in China: Peasants, Technology and the World Market*. Cambridge: Harvard University Press.

Mbaku, John Mukum, and Saxena, Suresh Chandra. (eds.) 2004. *Africa at the Cross-roads: Between Regionalism and Globalization.* Westport, CT: Praeger.

McBride, Stephen, and John Wiseman, John. (eds.) 2000. *Globalization and Its Discontents.* New York: St. Martin's.

McClellan, James E., III, and Dorn, Harold. 1999. *Science and Technology in World History: An Introduction.* Baltimore: Johns Hopkins University Press.

McFadden, P. 1990. "Youth Transform Education: Observations at the Solomon Mahlangu Freedom College." In *Pedagogy of Domination: Toward a Democratic Education in South Africa*, ed. by Makobung O. Nkomo, pp. 217–29. Trenton, NJ: Africa World.

McMahon, Walter W. 2002. *Education and Development: Measuring the Social Benefits.* Oxford: Oxford University Press.

McMurtie, Beth. 2000. "America's Scholarly Societies Raise Their Flags Abroad: U.S. Associations Recruit Foreign Members and Start Efforts to Help Them." *Chronicle of Higher Education* (January 28): A53.

McNamara, Robert S. 1981. *The McNamara Years at the World Bank: Major Policy Addresses of Robert S. McNamara 1968–1981.* Baltimore: Johns Hopkins University Press.

McNeil, William F. 2005. *Visitors to Ancient America: The Evidence for European and Asian Presence in America Prior to Columbus.* Jefferson, NC: Mcfarland.

McNeill, William H. 1977. *Plagues and People: The Impact of Disease on History.* Oxford: Blackwell.

McPherson, M. F., and Goldsmith, A. A. 1998. "Africa: On the Move?" *SAIS Review* 18 (no. 2): 153–67.

Mebrahtu, T. 1992. "Somalia: National Systems of Higher Education." In *The Encyclopedia of Higher Education*, ed. by Burton R. Clark, and Guy R. Neave, pp. 630–35. New York: Pergamon.

Medley, Joseph, and Caroll, Lorrayne. 2003. "'Whooping it Up for Rationality' Narratives of the East Asian Financial Crisis." In *World Bank Literature*, ed. by Amitava Kumar, pp. 140–56. Minneapolis: University of Minnesota Press.

Meillassoux, Claude. 1972. "From Reproduction to Production: A Marxist Approach to Economic Anthropology." *Economy and Society* 1 (no. 1): 93–105.

Meillassoux, Claude. 1991. *The Anthropology of Slavery: The Womb of Iron and Gold.* Chicago: University of Chicago Press.

Mekouria, Tekle Tsadik. 1981. "Christian Aksum." In *General History of Africa, Volume II: Ancient Civilizations of Africa*, ed. by G. Mokhtar, pp. 401–422. Berkeley: University of California Press.

Menkhaus, Ken. 2002. "Somalia: In the Crosshairs of the War on Terrorism." *Current History* 101 (May): 210–18.

Menkhaus, Ken. 2003 "State Collapse in Somalia: Second Thoughts." *Review of African Political Economy* (no. 97): 405–22.

Menzies, Gavin. 2003. *1421 the Year China Discovered America.* New York: William Morrow.

Mermelstein, David. (ed.) 1987. *The Anti-Apartheid Reader: The Struggle against White Racist Rule in South Africa.* New York: Grove.

Metz, Helen Chapin. (ed.) 1993. *Somalia: A Country Study.* Washington, DC: Federal Research Division, Library of Congress.

Metzler, John David. 1988. "The State, Settlers, Missionaries and Rural Dwellers: A Comparative Historical Analysis of the Politics, Economics and Sociology of Education Policy: Its Formation, Its Implementation and Its Consequences: In Colonial Northern Rhodesia and Southern Rhodesia." Ph.D. dissertation, University of Wisconsin-Madison.

Miers, Suzanne. 1975. *Britain and the Ending of the Slave Trade.* New York: Africana.

Milkias, Paulos. 1976. "Traditional Institutions and Traditional Elites: The Role of Education in the Ethiopian Body-Politic." *African Studies Review* 19 (no. 3): 79–93.

Milkias, Paulos. 1982. *Political Linkage: The Relationship between Education, Western Educated Elites and the Fall of Haile Selassie's Feudal Regime.* Ph.D. dissertation, McGill University.

Miller, Joseph Calder. 1988. *Way of Death: Merchant Capitalism and the Angolan Slave Trade, 1730–1830.* Madison: University of Wisconsin Press.

Mintz, Sidney. 1985. *Sweetness and Power: The Place of Sugar in Modern History.* New York: Viking Penguin.

Mirza, Mohammad R., and Siddiqi, Muhammed Iqbal. (eds.) 1986. *Muslim Contribution to Science.* Lahore: Kazi.

Mkandawire, P. Thandika, and Soludo, Charles Chukwuma. (eds.) 2003. *African Voices on Structural Adjustment: A Companion to Our Continent, Our Future.* Trenton, NJ: Africa World.

Mohamed, Jama. 1996. "Constructing Colonial Hegemony in the Somaliland Protectorate, 1941–1960." Ph.D. dissertation, University of Toronto.

Moore, Barrington, Jr. 1966. *Social Origins of Dictatorship and Democracy: Lord and Peasant in the Making of the Modern World.* Boston: Beacon.

Moore, C. H. 1994. *Images of Development. Egyptian Engineers in Search of Industry.* (2nd ed.) Cairo: American University in Cairo Press.

Morey, A. I. 2004. "Globalization and the Emergence of For-Profit Higher Education." *Higher Education* 48 (no. 1): 131–50.

Morgan, D. J. 1980. *The Official History of Colonial Development, Vol. 1: The Origins of British Aid Policy, 1924–1945.* Atlantic Highlands, NJ: Humanities.

Morgan, David. 1986. *The Mongols.* New York: Blackwell.

Morrow, Sean. 1998. "Dakawa Development Centre: An African National Congress Settlement in Tanzania, 1982–1992." *African Affairs* 97 (no. 389): 497–521.

Morrow, Sean; Brown, Maaba; and Pulumani, Loyiso. 2002. "Education in Exile: The African National Congress's Solomon Mahlangu Freedom College (SOMAFCO) and Dakawa Development Center in Tanzania: 1978 to 1992." In *The History of Education under Apartheid, 1948–1994: The Doors of Learning and Culture Shall be Opened,* ed. by Peter Kallaway, pp. 154–73. New York: Peter Lang.

Morrow, Sean, and Gxabalashe, Khayalethu. 2000. "The Records of the University of Fort Hare." *History in Africa* 27: 481–97.

Mosely, Paul; Subasat, Turan; and Weeks, John. 1995. "Assessing Adjustment in Africa." *World Development* 23 (no. 9): 1459–73.

Msabaha, Ibrahim S. R., and Shaw, Timothy M. 1987. *Confrontation and Liberation In Southern Africa: Regional Directions after the Nkomati Accord.* Boulder, CO: Westview.

Mukhtar, Mohamed Haji, and Castagno, Margaret. 2003. *Historical Dictionary of Somalia*. Lanham, MD: Scarecrow.

Mumford, W. Bryant. 1970. *Africans Learn to be French*. New York: Negro Universities Press.

Mundy, Karen, and Iga, Mika. 2003. "Hegemonic Exceptionalism and Legitimating Bet-Hedging: Paradoxes and Lessons from the US and Japanese Approaches to Education Services under the GATS." *Globalisation, Societies and Education* 1 (no. 3): 281–319.

Munene, Irungu. 2003. "Student Activism in African Higher Education." In *African Higher Education: An International Reference Handbook*, ed. by Damtew Teferra and Philip G. Altbach, pp. 117–27. Bloomington: Indiana University Press.

Mungazi, Dickson A. 1990. *Education and Government Control in Zimbabwe: A Study of the Commissions of Inquiry, 1908–1974*. New York: Praeger.

Munjee, Aslam. 2001. *The Crusades: Then and Now.* Binghamton, NY: New Dialogue.

Munro-Hay, Stuart. 1991. *Aksum: An African Civilisation of Late Antiquity*. Edinburgh: Edinburgh University Press.

Murden, Simon W. 2002. *Islam, the Middle East and the New Global Hegemony*. Boulder, CO: Lynne Rienner.

Murphree, Marshall W. 1977. "Universalism, Particularism and Academic Freedom: The Rhodesian Case." In *The Future of the University in Southern Africa*, ed. by H. W. van der Merwe, and David Welsh, pp. 102–24. Claremont, Cape Town: David Philip.

Murphy, E. Jefferson. 1976. *Creative Philanthropy: Carnegie Corporation and Africa*. New York: Teachers College Press.

Murphy, Lawrence R. 1987. *The American University in Cairo: 1919–1987*. Cairo: The American University in Cairo Press.

Murray, Bruce K. 1997. *Wits, the 'Open' Years: A History of the University of the Witwatersrand, Johannesburg 1939–1959*. Johannesburg: Witwatersrand University Press, 1997.

Murray, Martin. 1987. *South Africa: Time of Agony, Time of Destiny*. London: Verso.

Mysliwiec, Karol. 2000. *The Twilight of Ancient Egypt: First Millennium B.C.E.* Ithaca, NY: Cornell University Press.

Mytelka, L. K. 1989. "The Unfulfilled Promise of African Industrialization." *African Studies Review* 32 (no. 3): 77–137.

Nakosteen, Mehdi. 1964. *History of Islamic Origins of Western Education: A. D. 800–1350*. Boulder, CO: University of Colorado Press.

Nasr, Seyyed Hossein. 1968. *Science and Civilization in Islam.* Cambridge: Harvard University Press.

Nasr, Seyyed Hossein, and Oliver, Leaman. 1996. *History of Islamic Philosophy.* (2 volumes) London: Routledge.

Naylor, Phillip C. 2000. *France and Algeria: A History of Decolonization and Transformation*. Gainesville: University Press of Florida.

Needham, Joseph, et al. 1954 to Present. *Science and Civilization in China.* (in various volumes and parts). Cambridge: Cambridge University Press.

Newbury, C. W., and Kanya-Foster, A. S. 1969. "The French Policy and the Origins of the Scramble for West Africa." *Journal of African History* 10 (no. 2): 170–75.

Newitt, Malyn. 1995. "Prince Henry and the Origins of European Expansion." In *The Historiography of Europeans in Africa and Asia, 1450–1800* (vol. 4 of "An Expanding World: The European Impact on World History, 1450–1800"), ed. by Anthony Disney, pp. 85–112. Brookfield, VT: Variorum/Ashgate.

Newsom, David D. 2001. *The Imperial Mantle: The United States, Decolonization and the Third World.* Bloomington: Indiana University Press.

Ngobassu, Akwesi. 1973. "The National University of Zaire (Unaza)." In *Creating the African University: Emerging Issues in the 1970's,* ed. by. T. M. Yesufu, pp. 164–73. Ibadan: Oxford University Press.

Ngubo, Anthony. 1981. "Contributions of the Black American Church to the Development of African Independence Movements in South Africa." In *For Better or Worse: The American Influence in the World,* ed. by Allen F. Davis, pp. 145–56. Westport, CT: Greenwood.

Niblock, Tim. 1987. *Class and Power in Sudan: the Dynamics of Sudanese Politics, 1898–1985.* London: Macmillan.

Nicoll, Fergus. 2004. *Sword of the Prophet: The Mahdi of Sudan and the Death of General Gordon.* Stroud: Sutton.

Nieman, Donald G. 1991. *Promises to Keep: African-Americans and the Constitutional Order, 1776 to the Present.* New York: Oxford University Press.

Niro, Brian. 2003. *Race.* New York: Palgrave Macmillan.

Nkomo, Mokubung O. 1984. *Student Culture and Activism in Black South African Universities: The Roots of Resistance.* Westport, CT: Greenwood.

Nkomo, Mokubung O. 1990. *Pedagogy of Domination: Toward a Democratic Education in South Africa.* Trenton, NJ: Africa World.

Noer, Thomas J. 1978. *Briton, Boer and Yankee: The United States and South Africa, 1870–1914.* Kent, OH: Kent State University Press.

Noer, Thomas J. 1985. *Black Liberation: The United States and White Rule in Africa, 1948–1968.* Columbia: University of Missouri Press.

Norberg, Viveca Halldin. 1977. *Swedes in Haile Selassie's Ethiopia, 1924–1952: A Study in Early Development Co-operation.* Stockholm: Almqvist & Wiksell.

Northrup, David. (ed.) 2002 (a). *Africa's Discovery of Europe: 1450–1850.* New York: Oxford University Press.

Northrup, David. (ed.) 2002 (b). *The Atlantic Slave Trade.* Boston: Houghton Mifflin.

Nur-Awaleh, Mohamed. 2003. "Somalia and Somaliland." In *African Higher Education: An International Reference Handbook,* ed. by Damtew Teferra and Philip G. Altbach, pp. 536–44. Bloomington: Indiana University Press.

Nwauwa, Apollos O. 1996. *Imperialism, Academe and Nationalism: Britain and University Education for Africans 1860–1960.* London: Frank Cass.

Nyang, Sulayman S., and Abed-Rabbo, Samir. 1984. "Bernard Lewis and Islamic Studies: An Assessment." In *Orientalism, Islam and Islamists,* ed. by Asaf Hussein; Robert Olson; and Jamil Qureshi, pp. 259–86. Brattleboro, VT: Amana.

Nzongola-Ntalaja. (ed.) 1988. *The Crisis in Zaire: Myths and Realities.* Trenton, NJ: Africa World.

Odendaal, Andre. 1984. *Black Protest Politics in South Africa to 1912.* Totowa, NJ: Barnes and Noble.

Odin, Jaishree Kak, and Manicas, Peter T. (eds.) 2004. *Globalization and Higher Education.* Honolulu: University of Hawaii Press.

Oduho, Joseph, and Deng, William. 1963. *The Problem of the Southern Sudan*. Oxford: Oxford University Press.

Ohno, Kenichi, and Ohno, Izumi. (eds.) 1998. *Japanese Views on Economic Development: Diverse Paths to the Market*. New York: Routledge.

Oilo, Didier. *From Traditional to Virtual: The New Information Technologies*. Paris: UNESCO. (Document no. ED-98/CONF. 202/CLD. 18, thematic debate prepared for the World Conference on Higher Education, October 5–9, 1998.)

Okafor, Nduka. 1973. "The University of Nigeria, Nsukka." In *Creating the African University: Emerging Issues in the 1970's*, ed. by. T. M. Yesufu, pp. 185–95. Ibadan: Oxford University Press.

O'Leary, De Lacy. 1949. *How Greek Science Passed to the Arabs*. London: Routledge & Kegan Paul.

Omi, Michael, and Winant, Howard. 1994. *Racial Formation in the United States: From the 1960s to the 1990s*. New York: Routledge.

Ommar, Rakiya. 1992. "Somalia: At War with Itself." *Current History* 91 (May): 230–34.

Omond, Roger. 1985. *The Apartheid Handbook: A Guide to South Africa's Everyday Racial Policies*. New York: Penguin Books.

Orfield, Gary, and Eaton, Susan E. 1996. *Dismantling Desegregation: The Quiet Reversal of Brown v. Board of Education*. New York: New Press.

Ottaway, Marina. (ed.) 1990. *The Political Economy of Ethiopia*. Westport, CT: Praeger.

Pacey, Arnold. 1996. *Technology in World Civilization: A Thousand Year History*. Cambridge, MA: The M.I.T. Press.

Packenham, Thomas. 1991. *The Scramble for Africa: 1876–1912*. New York: Random House.

Page, Carol A. 1982. "Colonial Reaction to AME Missionaries in South Africa, 1898–1910." In *Black Americans and the Missionary Movement in Africa*, ed. by Sylvia M. Jacobs, pp. 177–96. Westport, CT: Greenwood.

Palmer, Mabel. 1951. "Higher Education in Natal." *African Affairs* 50 (no. 199): 134–39.

Palumbo, Patrizia. 2003. *A Place in the Sun: Africa in Italian Colonial Culture from Post-Unification to the Present*. Berkeley: University of California Press.

Pan, Jixing. 1996. "The Origin of Rockets in China." In *Gunpowder: The History of an International Technology*, ed. by Brenda J. Buchanan, pp. 25–32. Bath: Bath University Press.

Panter-Brick, Keith. 1988. "Independence, French Style." In *Decolonization and African Independence: The Transfer of Power, 1960–1980*, ed. by Prosser Gifford, and Wm. Roger Louis, pp. 73–104. New Haven: Yale University Press.

Pappas, James P. (ed.) 1997. *The University's Role in Economic Development: From Research to Outreach*. San Francisco: Jossey–Bass.

Parker, Geoffrey. 1996. *The Military Revolution: Military Innovation and the Rise of the West, 1500–1800* . Cambridge: Cambridge University Press.

Parsons, Edward A. 1952. *The Alexandrian Library: Glory of the Hellenic World*. New York: American Elsevier.

Patterson, James T. 2001. *Brown v. Board of Education: A Civil Rights Milestone and Its Troubled Legacy* (New York: Oxford University Press.

Pausewang, Siegfried; Tronvoll, Kjetil; and Aalen, Lovise. (eds.) 2002. *Ethiopia since the Derg: A Decade of Democratic Pretension and Performance.* London: Zed.

Payer, Cheryl. 1982. *The World Bank: A Critical Analysis.* New York: Monthly Review.

Payne, Robert. 1984. *The Dream and the Tomb: A History of the Crusades.* New York: Dorset.

Pedersen, Olaf. 1997. *The First Universities: Studium Generale and the Origins of University Education in Europe.* Cambridge: Cambridge University Press.

Peers, Douglas M. 1995. *Between Mars and Mammon, Colonial Armies and the Garrison State in India, 1819–1835.* London: Tauris Academic Studies.

Peers, Douglas M. (ed.) 1997. *Warfare and Empires, Contact and Conflict Between European and Non-European Military and Maritime Forces and Cultures* (vol. 24 of "An Expanding World: The European Impact on World History, 1450–1800"). Brookfield, VT: Ashgate/ Variorum.

Perham, Margery. 1948. *The Government of Ethiopia.* New York: Oxford University Press.

Perotin-Dumont, Anne. 1991. "The Pirate and the Emperor: Power and the Law on the Seas, 1450–1850." In *The Political Economy of Merchant Empires,* ed. by James D. Tracy, pp. 196–227. New York: Cambridge University Press.

Perry, William G.; Schmutterer, H.; Pride, J. B. 1964. *Report of the UNESCO Advisory Mission On Higher Education to the Somali Republic.* Mogadishu: UNESCO.

Peters, F. E. 1968. *Aristotle and the Arabs: The Aristotelian Tradition in Islam.* New York: New York University Press.

Peterson, Mendel. 1975. *The Funnel of Gold.* Boston: Little, Brown.

Peterson, Scott. 2000. *Me Against My Brother: At War in Somalia, Sudan, and Rwanda: A Journalist Reports from the Battlefields of Africa.* New York: Routledge.

Petry, Carl. F. 1994. *Protectors or Praetorians? The Last Mamluk Sultans and Egypt's Waning as a Great Power.* Albany: State University of New York Press.

Petterson, Donald. 2003. *Inside Sudan: Political Islam, Conflict, and Catastrophe.* Boulder, CO: Westview.

Pfeifer, Michael J. 2004. *Rough Justice: Lynching and American Society, 1874–1947.* Urbana: University of Illinois Press.

Piaget, Jean. 1971. *Psychology and Epistemology.* New York: Grossman.

Pieterse, Jan Nederveen. 1992. *White on Black: Images of Africa and Blacks in Western Popular Culture.* New Haven: Yale University Press.

Pincus, Jonathan R., and Winters, Jeffrey A. 2002. "Reinventing the World Bank." In *Reinventing the World Bank,* ed. by Jonathan R. Pincus, and Jeffrey A. Winters, pp. 1–25. Ithaca, NY: Cornell University Press.

Pipes, Daniel. 1981. *Slave Soldiers and Islam: The Genesis of a Military System.* New Haven: Yale University Press.

Plaatje, Sol. T. 1969 (1916). *Native Life in South Africa, Before and Since the European War and the Boer Rebellion.* New York: Negro Universities Press.

Poel, Jean van der. 1935. "Native Education in South Africa." *Journal of the Royal African Society* 34 (no. 136): 313–31.

Pohl, Hans. (ed.) 1990. *The European Discovery of the World and Its Economic Effects on Pre-Industrial Europe, 1500–1800: Papers of the Tenth International Economic History Congress.* Stuttgart: Franz Steiner.

Pomeranz, Kenneth. 2000. *The Great Divergence: China, Europe and the Making of the Modern World Economy.* Princeton: Princeton University Press.

Porter, Geoffrey David. 2002. "At the Pillar's Base: Islam, Morocco and Education in the Qarawiyin Mosque, 1912–2000." Ph.D. dissertation, New York University.

Porter, Roy. 1996. "The Scientific Revolution and Universities." In *A History of the University in Europe* (volume II), ed. by Hilde de Ridder-Symoens, pp. 531–64. Cambridge: Cambridge University Press.

Postma, Johannes. 2003. *The Atlantic Slave Trade.* Westport, CT: Greenwood.

Powell, Eve Troutt. 2003. *A Different Shade of Colonialism: Egypt, Great Britain, and the Mastery of the Sudan.* Berkeley: University of California Press.

Prakash, Gyan. 1995. "Orientalism Now." *History and Theory* 34 (no. 3): 199–212.

Prewitt, Kenneth. 2004. "Higher Education, Society, and Government: Changing Dynamics." *Journal of Higher Education in Africa* 2 (no. 1): 35–56.

Prunier, Girard. 1995. *The Rwanda Crisis: History of a Genocide.* New York: Columbia University Press.

Prunier, Gerard. 1998. "Somaliland Goes it Alone." *Current History* 97 (May): 225–28.

Psacharapoulos, G. 1973. *Returns to Education: An International Comparison.* Amsterdam: Elsevier.

Psacharopoulos, G. 1981. "Returns to Education: An Updated International Comparison." *Comparative Education* 17: 321–41.

Psacharopoulos, G. 1994. "Return to Investment in Education: A Global Update." *World Development* 22.

Psacharopoulos, G. (ed.) 1987. *Economics of Education: Research and Studies.* Oxford: Pergamon.

Qurashi, M. M., and Rizvi, S. S. H. 1996. *History and Philosophy of Muslim Contributions to Science and Technology.* Islamabad: Pakistan Academy of Sciences.

Rabinow, Paul. 1989. *French Modern: Norms and Forms of the Social Environment.* Cambridge, MA: The MIT Press.

Rado, E. R. 1966. "Manpower, Education and Economic Growth." *Journal of Modern African Studies* 4 (no. 1): 83–93.

Radwan, Abu al-Futouh Ahmad. 1951. *Old and New Forces in Egyptian Education: Proposals for the Reconstruction of the Program of Egyptian Education in the Light of Recent Cultural Trends.* New York: Columbia University, Teachers College Press.

Ragsdale, John Paul. 1986. *Protestant Mission Education in Zambia, 1880 to 1954.* Toronto: Associated University Presses.

Rahme, Joseph G. 1999. "Ethnocentric and Stereotypical Concepts in the Study of Islamic and World History." *History Teacher* 32 (no. 4): 473–94.

Ralston, Richard. 1973. "Colonial African Leadership: American and Afro-American Influences," *Ufahamu* 4 (no. 2):

Ramphele, Mamphela. 2004. "The University as an Actor in Development: New Perspectives and Demands." *Journal of Higher Education in Africa* 2 (no. 1): 15–34.

Rao, Bhanoji. 2001. *East Asian Economies: The Miracle, a Crisis and the Future.* New York: Mcgraw–Hill.

Rashed, Roshdi, and Morelon, Regis. (eds.) 1996. *Encyclopedia of the History of Arabic Science.* London: Routledge.

Razack, Sherene. 2004. *Dark Threats and White Knights: The Somalia Affair, Peacekeeping, and the New Imperialism.* Buffalo, NY: University of Toronto Press.

Redkey, Edwin S. 1969. *The Meaning of Africa to Afro-Americans, 1890–1914.* Buffalo: Council on International Studies, State University of New York at Buffalo.

Reichmuth, Stefan. 2000. "Islamic Education and Scholarship in Sub-Saharan Africa." In *The History of Islam in Africa,* ed. by Nehemia Levitzion, and Randall L. Pouwels, pp. 419–40. Athens: Ohio University Press.

Reid, Donald Malcolm. 1990. *Cairo University and the Making of Modern Egypt.* Cambridge: Cambridge University Press.

Reilly, Joseph Daniel. 1995. "Teaching the 'Native': Anthropology in South African Education. A Study of the History of Ideas that were the Foundation of 'Native' Education Policy in South Africa, 1900–1936." Ph.D. dissertation, University of Connecticut.

Reilly, Kevin; Kaufman, Stephen; Bodino, Angela. (eds.) 2003. *Racism: A Global Reader.* Armonk, NY: M. E. Sharpe.

Reubens, Jean R. 1977. "College Jobs: International Problems." In *Relating Work and Education,* ed. by Dyckman Vermilye. San Francisco: Jossey-Bass.

Reynolds, Sonjai Amar. 2001. "Historically Disadvantaged Technikons in an Era of Transformation: Answering the Call, Confronting the Challenges." In *Apartheid No More: Case Studies of Southern African Universities in the Process of Transformation,* ed. by Reitsumetse Obakeng Mabokela, and Kimberly Linease King, pp. 139–56. Westport, CT: Bergin and Garvey.

Richard, Jean. 1999 (1996). *The Crusades, c. 1071–c. 1291.* Cambridge: Cambridge University Press.

Richards, John F. 1983. *Precious Metals in the Later Medieval and Early Modern Worlds.* Durham, NC: Carolina Academic Press.

Richardson, Tim. 2002. *Sweets: A History of Candy.* New York: Bloomsbury.

Rieff, D. 1998. "In Defense of Afro-Pessimism." *World Policy Journal* 15 (no. 4): 10–22.

Riley-Smith, Jonathan. 1997. *The First Crusaders, 1095–1131.* Cambridge: Cambridge University Press.

Rivlin, Helen Anne B. 1961. *The Agricultural Policy of Muhammed Ali in Egypt.* Cambridge: Harvard University Press.

Roberts, Andrew. (ed.) 1990. *The Colonial Moment in Africa. Essays on the Movement of Minds and Materials, 1900–1940.* Cambridge: Cambridge University Press.

Roberts, Hugh. 2003. *The Battlefield Algeria: 1988–2002.* London: Verso.

Roberts, J. M. 1997. *The Penguin History of Europe.* New York: Penguin Books.

Robertshaw, Peter. (ed.) 1990. *A History of African Archaeology.* Portsmouth, NH: Heinemann.

Robinson, Robert Smarlley. 1971. "Educational Integration in Somalia, 1960–1969." Ph.D. dissertation, University of Michigan.

Robinson, Ronald; Gallagher, John; and Denny, Alice. 1981. *Africa and the Victorians: The Official Mind of Imperialism.* (2nd ed.) London: Macmillan.

Rodinson, Maxime. 2002. *Europe and the Mystique of Islam.* London: I. B. Tauris.

Rodney, Walter. 1981. *How Europe Underdeveloped Africa.* Washington, DC: Howard University Press.

Rodney, Walter. 1982. (1970). *A History of the Upper Guinea Coast, 1545–1800.* New York: Monthly Review.

Rosenthal, Eric. 1968. *Stars and Stripes in Africa.* Cape Town: National Books.

Rosenthal, Franz. 1970. *Knowledge Triumphant: The Concept of Knowledge in Medieval Islam.* Leiden: E. J. Brill.

Rosenthal, Franz. 1990. *Science and Medicine in Islam: A Collection of Essays.* Brookfield, VT: Variorum.

Rostow, W. W. 1990. *The Stages of Economic Growth: A Non-Communist Manifesto* (3rd Edition). Cambridge: Cambridge University Press.

Rothenberg, Paula S. (ed.) 2002. *White Privilege: Essential Readings On the Other Side of Racism.* New York: Worth Publishers.

Rude, Darlene. 1999. "Reasonable Men and Provocative Women: An Analysis of Gendered Domestic Homicide in Zambia." *Journal of Southern African Studies* 25 (no. 1): 7–28.

Ruedy, John. 1992. *Modern Algeria: The Origins and Development of a Nation.* Bloomington: Indiana University Press.

Ruegg, Walter. 1992. "Themes." In *A History of the University in Europe (Vol. 1: Universities in the Middle Ages),* ed. by Hilde de Ridder-Symoens, pp. 3–34. Cambridge: Cambridge University Press.

Runciman, Steven. 1955. *The Eastern Schism: A Study of the Papacy and the Eastern Churches During the XIth and XIIth Centuries.* Oxford: Oxford University Press.

Russell, Terence M. (ed.) 2001. *The Napoleonic Survey of Egypt: Description de L'Egypte: The Monuments and Customs of Egypt, Selected Engravings and Texts.* (2 vols.) Burlington, VT: Ashgate.

Rusell-Wood, A. J. R. 1995–2000. (ed.) *An Expanding World: The European Impact on World History, 1450–1800.* (31 vols.) Brookfield, VT: Ashgate/ Variorum.

Saad, Elias N. 1983. *Social History of Timbuktu: The Role of Muslim Scholars and Notables, 1400–1900.* Cambridge: Cambridge University Press.

Sabatier, Peggy Roark. 1977. "Educating a Colonial Elite: The William Ponty School and Its Graduates." Ph.D. Dissertation, University of Michigan.

Sabra, A. I. 1988. "Science—Islamic." In *Dictionary of the Middle Ages* (vol. 11), ed. by Joseph Strayer, pp. 81–89. New York: Charles Scribner.

Sabra, A. I. 1994. *Optics, Astronomy and Logic: Studies in Arabic Science and Philosophy.* Brookfield, VT: Variorum.

Said, Edward. 1978. *Orientalism.* New York: Vintage.

Said, Edward. 1993. *Culture and Imperialism.* New York: Alfred A. Knopf.

Said, Edward M., and Paul, James. 1988. "Orientalism Revisited: An Interview with Edward M. Said." *MERIP Middle East Report* no. 150 (January–February): 32–36.

Saint, William. 1992. *Universities in Africa: Strategies for Stabilization and Revitalization.* Washington, DC: World Bank (World Bank Technical Paper no. 24).

Saint, William. 2004. "Higher Education in Ethiopia: The Vision and Its Challenges." *Journal of Higher Education in Africa* 2 (no. 3): 83–114.

Salahi, Adil. 2004. "First Thing First: Better Oppressed than Oppressor." *Impact International* 34 (August–September): 5.

Saliba, George. 1994. *A History of Arabic Astronomy: Planetary Theories During the Golden Age of Islam*. New York: New York University Press.

Sall, Ebrima. 2004. "Alternative Models to Traditional Higher Education: Market Demand, Networks, and Private Sector Challenges." *Journal of Higher Education in Africa* 2 (no. 1): 177–212.

Salmi, Jamil, and Verspoor, Adriaan M. (eds.) 1994. *Revitalizing Higher Education*. New York: Pergamon (for the International Association of Universities).

Samatar, Abdi Ismail. 1992. "Destruction of State and Society in Somalia: Beyond the Tribal Convention." *Journal of Modern African Studies* 30 (no. 4): 625–41.

Samatar, Abdi Ismail. 1993 "Structural Adjustment as Development Strategy? Bananas, Boom, and Poverty in Somalia." *Economic Geography* 69 (no. 1): 25–43.

Samatar, Abdi Ismail. 2001. "Somali Reconstruction and Local Initiative: Amoud University." *World Development* 29 (no. 4): 641–56.

Samatar, Ahmed I. (ed.) 1994. *The Somali Challenge: From Catastrophe to Renewal?* Boulder: L. Rienner.

Samoff, Joel, and Assie-Lumumba, N'Dri Therese. 1996. *Analyses, Agendas and Priorities in African Education: A Review of Externally Initiated, Commissioned and Supported Studies of Education in Africa, 1990–1994*. Paris: UNESCO (Working Group on Education Sector Analysis).

Samoff, Joel, and Carrol, Bidemi. 2003. *From Manpower Planning to the Knowledge Era: World Bank Policies on Higher Education in Africa*. Paris: UNESCO (UNESCO Forum Secretariat).

Samuels, Michael Anthony. 1970. *Education in Angola, 1878–1914: A History of Culture Transfer and Administration*. New York: Teachers College Press.

Sanders, Edith. 1969. "The Hamitic Hypothesis: Its Origins and Functions in Time Perspective." *Journal of African History* 10 (no. 4): 521–32.

Sanderson, G. N. 1965. *England, Europe and the Upper Nile, 1882–1899*. Edinburgh: Edinburgh University Press, 1965.

Sanderson, Lilian Passmore, and Sanderson, Neville. 1981. *Education, Religion & Politics in Southern Sudan, 1899–1964*. London: Ithaca.

Sanderson, Stephen K. 1995. *Social Transformations: A General Theory of Historical Development*. New York: Blackwell.

SAPRIN (Structural Adjustment Participatory Review International Network). 2004. *Structural Adjustment: The SAPRI Report: The Policy Roots of Economic Crisis, Poverty, and Inequality*. London: Zed.

Sarton, George. 1962 (1927–1948). *Introduction to the History of Science*. (3 volumes in 5 parts) Baltimore: Williams and Wilkins (published for the Carnegie Institution of Washington).

Saul, John S., and Gelb, Stephen. 1986. *The Crisis in South Africa* (revised edition). New York: Monthly Review.

Saul, John S., and Leys, Colin. 1999. "Sub-Saharan Africa in Global Capitalism." *Monthly Review* 51 (no. 3): 13–30.

Savini, Antonio. 2005. "Editorial: Global Challenges for our Universities." *Coimbra Group Newsletter* no. 23 (winter): 1–2.

Savory, R. M. (ed.) 1976. *Introduction to Islamic Civilization*. Cambridge: Cambridge University Press.

Sbacchi, Alberto. 1985. *Ethiopia under Mussolini: Fascism and the Colonial Experience*. London: Zed.

Scammell, G. V. 1995. "European Exiles, Renegades and Outlaws and the Maritime Economy of Asia, c. 1500–1750." In *Historiography of Europeans in Africa and Asia, 1450–1800* (vol. 4 of "An Expanding World: The European Impact on World History, 1450–1800"), ed. by Anthony Disney, pp. 289–309. Brookfield, VT: Variorum/Ashgate.

Schacht, Joseph, and Bosworth, C. E. 1974. *The Legacy of Islam* (2nd edition). Oxford: Oxford University Press.

Schatz, Sayre P. 1994. "Structural Adjustment in Africa: A Failing Grade So Far." *Journal of Modern African Studies* 32 (no. 4): 679–92.

Schatz, Sayre P. 1996. "The World Bank's Fundamental Misconception in Africa." *Journal of Modern African Studies* 34 (no. 2): 239–47.

Schlesinger, Arthur M., Jr. 1992. *The Disuniting of America*. New York: W. W. Norton.

Schofield, Alan. 1996. *Private Post-Secondary Education in Four Commonwealth Countries*. Paris: UNESCO (Document no. ED-96/WS-33).

Schultheis, Michael J. 1984. The World Bank and Accelerated Development: The Internationalization of Supply-Side Economics." *African Studies Review* 27 (no. 4): 9–16.

Schultz, Theodore. 1961 (a). "Education and Economic Growth." In *Sixtieth Yearbook of the National Society of Education*, Part II. Chicago: National Society of Education.

Schultz, Theodore. 1961 (b). "Investment in Human Capital." *American Economic Review* 51 .

Schultz, Theodore. 1974. "A 'Guide' to Investors in Education with Special Reference to Developing Countries." In *Education and Development Reconsidered: The Bellagio Conference Papers*, ed. by F. Champion Ward, pp. 48–57. New York: Praeger.

Scott, P. 1985. "The Sudan People's Liberation Movement (SPLM) and Liberation Army (SPLA)." *Review of African Political Economy* (no. 33): 69–82.

Segal, Ronald. 2001. *Islam's Black Slaves: The Other Black Diaspora*. New York: Farrar, Straus and Giroux.

Segalla, Spencer David. 2003. "Teaching Colonialism, Learning Nationalism: French Education and Ethnology in Morocco, 1912–1956." Ph.D. dissertation, State University of New York at Stony Brook.

Seidman, Ann. 1985. *The Roots of Crisis in Southern Africa*. Trenton, NJ: Africa World.

Seidman, R. H. 1982. "The Logic and Behavioral Principles of Educational Systems: Social Independence or Dependence?" In *The Sociology of Educational Expansion*, ed. by M. Archer. Beverly Hills, CA: Sage.

Seligson, Mitchell A., and Passé-Smith, John T. (eds.) 2004. *Development and Underdevelopment: The Political Economy of Global Inequality* (third edition). Boulder, CO: Lynne Rienner.

Selin, Helaine. (ed.) 1997. *Encyclopaedia of the History of Science, Technology and Medicine in Non-Western Cultures*. Boston: Kluwer Academic.

Sender, John. 2002. "Reassessing the Role of the World Bank in Sub-Saharan Africa." In *Reinventing the World Bank*, ed. by Jonathan R. Pincus, and Jeffrey A. Winters, pp. 185–202. Ithaca, NY: Cornell University Press.

Serres, Michel. 1995. "Introduction." In *A History of Scientific Thought: Elements of a History of Science*, ed. by Michel Serres, pp. 1–16. Oxford: Blackwell.

Setton, Kenneth M. (ed.) 1962–1989. *A History of the Crusades* (in six volumes). Madison: University of Wisconsin Press.

Seyon, Patrick L. N. 1973. "The University of Liberia." In *Creating the African University: Emerging Issues in the 1970's*, ed. by. T. M. Yesufu, pp. 208–17. Ibadan: Oxford University Press.

Seyon, Patrick L. N. 1977. "Education, National Integration and Nation-building in Liberia." Ph.D. dissertation, Stanford University.

Seyon, Patrick L. N. 1997. "Rebuilding the University of Liberia in the Midst of War." *International Higher Education* 8 (summer): 2.

Shabani, Juma. 1995. "Higher Education in Sub-Saharan Africa: Strategies for the Improvement of the Quality of Training." *Quality in Higher Education* 1 (no. 2): 173–78.

Shabani, Juma. (ed.) 1998. *Higher Education in Africa: Achievements, Challenges and Prospects*. Dakar: UNESCO Regional Office for Africa.

Shaeffer, Sheldon. 1994. *The Impact of HIV/AIDS on Education: A Review of Literature and Experience*. Paris, UNESCO.

Sharkey, Heather J. 2003. *Living With Colonialism: Nationalism and Culture in the Anglo-Egyptian Sudan*. Berkeley: University of California Press.

Shaw, Ian. (ed.) 2000. *The Oxford History of Ancient Egypt*. New York: Oxford University Press.

Shear, Mervyn. 1996. *Wits: A University in the Apartheid Era*. Johannesburg: Witwatersrand University Press.

Shepherd, R. H. W. 1955. "The South African Bantu Education Act." *African Affairs* 54 (no. 215): 138–42.

Shepperson, George. 1960. "Notes on Negro American Influences on the Emergence of African Nationalism." *Journal of African History* 1 (no. 2): 299–312.

Shick, Tom W. 1982. "Rhetoric and Reality: Colonization and Afro-American Missionaries in Early Nineteenth Century Liberia." In *Black Americans and the Missionary Movement in Africa*, ed. by Sylvia M. Jacobs, pp. 45–62. Westport, CT: Greenwood.

Shinnie, P. L. 1967. *Meroe: A Civilization of the Sudan*. New York: F. A. Praeger.

Shinnie, P. L. 1978. "Christian Nubia." In *The Cambridge History of Africa*, vol. 2, ed. by J. D. Fage, pp. 556–88. Cambridge: Cambridge University Press.

Shipman, Pat. 1994. *The Evolution of Racism: Human Differences and the Use and Abuse of Science*. New York: Simon & Schuster.

Shipway, Martin. 1999. "Reformism and the French 'Official Mind': The 1944 Brazzaville Conference and the Legacy of the Popular Front." In *French Colonial Empire and the Popular Front: Hope and Disillusion*, ed. by Tony Chafer, and Amanda Sackur, pp. 131–51. New York: St. Martin's Press.

Siaciwena, Richard. 1997. "Organizational Changes at the University of Zambia." *Open Learning* 12 (No. 3): 57-61.

Sibley, James L. 1926. *Education and Missions in Liberia: A Preliminary Survey of the Field for the American Advisory Committee on Education.* London: American Advisory Committee on Education in Liberia.

Sicherman, Carol. 2005. *Becoming an African University: Makerere, 1922–2000.* Trenton, NJ: Africa World.

Sidahmed, Abdel Salam. 1996. *Politics and Islam in Contemporary Sudan.* New York: St. Martin's.

Sidebotham, Steven E., and Wendrich, Willemina Z. 2002. "Berenike: Archaeological Fieldwork at a Ptolemaic-Roman Port on the Red Sea Coast of Egypt 1999–2001." *Sahara* 13 (July): 31–44.

Sikwibele, Anne Lungowe. 1989. "International Education Assistance to Higher Education Development in Zambia: Problems, Policy Implications, and Future Prospects." Ph.D. dissertation, University of Illinois at Urbana-Champaign.

Silvester, Jeremy, and Gewald, Jan-Bart. 2003. *Words Cannot Be Found German Colonial Rule in Namibia: An Annotated Reprint of the 1918 Blue Book.* Boston: Brill.

Simons, Anna. 1995. *Networks of Dissolution: Somalia Undone.* Boulder, CO: Westview.

Sivonen, Seppo. 1995. *White-Collar or Hoe Handle: African Education under British Colonial Policy, 1920–1945.* Helsinki: Suomen Historiallinen Seura.

Smedley, Audrey. 1993. *Race in North America: Origin and Evolution of a Worldview.* Boulder, CO: Westview.

Smith, Adam. 1961 (1776). *An Inquiry into the Nature and Causes of the Wealth of Nations.* (2 vols.) London: Methuen.

Smith, Edwin W. 1971 (1929). *Aggrey of Africa: A Study in Black and White.* Freeport, NY: Books for Libraries Press.

Snelson, P. D. 1970. *Educational Development in Northern Rhodesia 1883–1945.* Lusaka: National Educational Company of Zambia.

Soggott, David. 1986. *Namibia: The Violent Heritage.* London: Rex Collings.

Solow, Barbara L. (ed.) 1991. *Slavery and the Rise of the Atlantic System.* New York: Cambridge University Press.

Solow, Barbara L., and Engerman, Stanley L. (eds.) 1987. *British Capitalism and Caribbean Slavery: The Legacy of Eric Williams.* New York: Cambridge University Press.

Sonbol, Amira El-Azhary. 2000. *The New Mamluks: Egyptian Society and Modern Feudalism.* Syracuse, NY: Syracuse University Press.

Song, Ha-Joong. 1991. "Who Stays? Who Returns? The Choices of Korean Scientists and Engineers." Ph.D. dissertation, Harvard University.

Spínola, António de. 1974. *Portugal and the Future.* Johannesburg: Perskor.

Spuler, Bertold. 1972. *A History of the Mongols, Based on Eastern and Western Accounts of the Thirteenth and Fourteenth Centuries.* Berkeley: University of California Press.

Stabler, John B. 1968. "The University of Zambia: Its Origin and First Year." *Journal of Higher Education* 39 (January): 32-38.

Stannard, David E. 1992. *American Holocaust: Columbus and the Conquest of the New World.* New York: Oxford University Press

Stanton, Charles Michael. 1990. *Higher Learning in Islam: The Classical Period, A.D. 700–1300.* Savage: Rowman & Littlefield.

Stanton, William Ragan. 1960. *The Leopard's Spots: Scientific Attitudes toward Race in America, 1815–59.* Chicago: University of Chicago Press.

Steier, Francis A. 2003. "The Changing Nexus: Tertiary Education Institutions, the Marketplace and the State." *Higher Education Quarterly* 57 (no. 2): 158–80.

Stern, Nicholas, and Ferreira, Francisco. 1997. "The World Bank as Intellectual Actor." In *The World Bank: Its First Half Century* (vol. 2), ed. by Davesh Kapur; John P. Lewis; and Richard Webb, pp. 523–610. Washington, DC: Brookings Institution Press.

Stiglitz, Joseph E. 2002. *Globalization and Its Discontents.* New York: W. W. Norton.

Stock, Brian. 1978. "Science, Technology and Economic Progress in the Early Middle Ages." In *Science in the Middle Ages*, ed. by David C. Lindberg, pp. 52–90. Chicago: University of Chicago Press.

Stocking, George W., Jr. 1982. *Race, Culture and Evolution: Essays in the History of Anthropology.* Chicago: University of Chicago Press.

Stocking, George W., Jr. (ed.) 1988. *Bones, Bodies, Behavior: Essays on Biological Anthropology.* Madison: University of Wisconsin Press.

Stockwell, John. 1978. *In Search of Enemies: A CIA Story.* New York: W. W. Norton.

Stokes, Eric, and Brown, Richard. (eds.) 1966. *The Zambesian Past: Studies in Central African History.* Manchester: Manchester University Press (for the Institute of Social Research, University of Zambia).

Streeten, Paul. 1972. *The Frontiers of Development Studies.* New York: John Wiley.

Stromquist, Nelly P., and Monkman, Karen. (eds.) 2000. *Globalization and Education: Integration and Contestation Across Cultures.* Lanham, MD: Rowman & Littlefield.

Stuchtey, Benedikt, and Fuchs, Eckhardt. (eds.) 2003. *Writing World History 1800–2000.* New York: Oxford University Press.

Suleiman, Yasir. 2003. *The Arabic Language and National Identity: A Study in Ideology.* Washington, DC: Georgetown University Press.

Sundiata, Ibrahim. 2003. *Brothers and Strangers: Black Zion, Black Slavery, 1914–1940.* Durham: Duke University Press.

Surin, Kenneth. 2003. "Hostage to an Unaccountable Planetary Executive: The Flawed 'Washington Consensus' and Two World Bank Reports." In *World Bank Literature*, ed. by Amitava Kumar, pp. 128–39. Minneapolis: University of Minnesota Press.

Swedberg, Richard. 1986. "The Doctrine of Economic Neutrality of the IMF and the World Bank." *Journal of Peace Research* 23 (no. 4): 377–90.

Taddesse Tamrat. 1977. "Ethiopia, the Red Sea, and the Horn." In *The Cambridge History of Africa*, vol. 3, ed. by Richard Oliver, pp. 99–182. Cambridge: Cambridge University Press.

Taddesse Tamrat. 1984. "The Horn of Africa: The Solomonids in Ethiopia and the States of the Horn of Africa." In *UNESCO General History of Africa, Volume IV: Africa from the Twelfth to the Sixteenth Century*, ed. by D. T. Niane, pp. 423–54. Berkeley: University of California Press.

Talib, Y. (based on a contribution by F. Samir). 1988. "The African Diaspora in Asia." In *UNESCO General History of Africa, Volume III: Africa from the Seventh to the Eleventh Century*, ed. by M. Elfasi, and I. Hrbek, pp. 704–33. Berkeley: University of California Press.

Tamrat, Taddesse. See Taddesse Tamrat.

Tanner, R. G. 2000. "Aristotle's Works: The Possible Origins of the Alexandria Collection." In *The Library of Alexandria: Center of Learning in the Ancient World*, ed. by Roy MacLeod, pp. 79–91. London: I. B. Tauris.

Tareke, Gebru. See Gebru Tareke.

Taylor, A. J. P. 1967. *Germany's First Bid for Colonies*. Hamden, CT: Archon.

Taylor, Kit Sims. 1978. *Sugar and the Underdevelopment of Northeastern Brazil, 1500–1970*. Gainesville, FL: University Presses of Florida.

Teferra Haile-Selassie. 1997. *The Ethiopian Revolution, 1974–91: From a Monarchical Autocracy to a Military Oligarchy*. London: Kegan Paul International.

Teferra, Damtew, and Altbach, Philip G. (eds.) 2003. See Damtew Teferra, and Altbach, Philip G. (eds.) 2003.

Teichler, Ulrich. 2004. "The Changing Debate on Internationalization of Higher Education." *Higher Education* 48 (no. 1): 5–26.

Teixeira, Pedro, and Amaral, Alberto. 2001. "Private Higher Education and Diversity: An Exploratory Survey." *Higher Education Quarterly* 55 (no. 4): 359–95.

Tekle, Amare. 1990. See Amare Tekle. 1990.

Tembo, Lyson P. 1973. "University of Zambia." In *Creating the African University: Emerging Issues in the 1970's*, edited by. T. M. Yesufu, pp. 226-43. Ibadan and London: Oxford University Press.

Terreblanche, Sampie. 2002. *A History of Inequality in South Africa, 1652–2002*. Pietermaritzberg: University of Natal Press, and KMM Review Publishing.

Teshome G. Wagaw. 1979. *Education in Ethiopia: Prospect and Retrospect*. Ann Arbor: University of Michigan Press.

Teshome G. Wagaw. 1990. *The Development of Higher Education and Social Change: An Ethiopian Experience*. East Lansing: Michigan State University Press.

Tessler, Mark. 1997. "The Origins of Popular Support for Islamist Movements: A Political Economy Analysis." In *Islam, Democracy and the State in North Africa*, ed. by John P. Entelis, pp. 93–126. Bloomington: Indiana University Press.

Thaver, Bev. 2003. "Private Higher Education in Africa: Six Country Case Studies." In *African Higher Education: An International Reference Handbook*, ed. by Damtew Teferra and Philip G. Altbach, pp. 53–60. Bloomington: Indiana University Press.

Theroux, Paul. 2003. *Dark Star Safari: Overland from Cairo to Cape Town*. New York: Houghton Mifflin.

Thomas, Nicholas. 1994. *Colonialism's Culture: Anthropology, Travel and Government*. Princeton: Princeton University Press.

Thompson, Leonard 2001. *A History of South Africa* (3rd edition). New Haven, CT: Yale University Press.

Thornton, John Kelly. 1992. *Africa and Africans in the Making of the Atlantic World, 1400–1680*. New York: Cambridge University Press.

Thornton, John Kelly. 1999. *Warfare in Atlantic Africa, 1500–1800*. London: UCL.

Tibawi, A. L. 1972. *Islamic Education: Its Traditions and Modernization into the Arab National Systems*. London: Luzac.

Tilak, Jandhyala B. G. 1996. "The Privatization of Higher Education." In *Higher Education in an International Perspective: Critical Issues*, ed. by Zaghloul Morsy, and Philip G. Altbach, pp. 59–71. New York: Garland.

Tiruneh, Andargachew. 1993. See Andargachew Tiruneh. 1993.

Tocqueville, Alexis de. 2001. *Writings on Empire and Slavery* (edited and translated by Jennifer Pitts). Baltimore: Johns Hopkins University Press.

Todaro, Michael P. 1977. *Economic Development in the Third World*. London: Longman.

Todaro, Michael P., et al. 1974. "Education for National Development: The University." In *Education and Development Reconsidered: The Bellagio Conference Papers*, ed. by F. Champion Ward, pp. 204–13. New York: Praeger.

Tolan, John V. 2002. *Saracens: Islam in the Medieval European Imagination*. New York: Columbia University Press.

Tolnay, Stewart Emory, and Beck, E. M. 1995. *A Festival of Violence: An Analysis of Southern Lynchings, 1882–1930*. Urbana: University of Illinois Press.

Torres, Carlos A., and Schugurensky, Daniel. 2002. "The Political Economy of Higher Education in the Era of Neoliberal Globalization: Latin America in Comparative Perspective." *Higher Education* 43 (no. 4): 429–55.

Totah, Khalil A. 1926. *The Contribution of the Arabs to Education*. New York: Bureau of Publications, Teachers College, Columbia University.

Trevor-Roper, Hugh. 1965. *The Rise of Christian Europe*. London: Thames and Hudson.

Trimingham, J. Spencer. 1965. *Islam in Ethiopia*. London: Frank Cass.

Tripodi, Paolo. 1999. *The Colonial Legacy in Somalia: Rome and Mogadishu: From Colonial Administration to Operation Restore Hope*. New York: St. Martin's Press.

Tsehaie Yohannes. 2002. "Factors That Promoted or Limited the Development of Education in Ethiopia: A Historical Perspective." Ed.D. dissertation, Alliant International University.

Turner, Howard R. 1995. *Science in Medieval Islam: An Illustrated Introduction*. Austin: University of Texas Press.

Turner, John. 1990. *Education in Namibia*. Windhoek: Ministry for Education, Culture and Sport.

Turton, E. R. 1975. "Bantu, Galla, and Somali Migrations in the Horn of Africa: A Reassessment of the Juba-Tana Area." *Journal of African History* 16 (no. 4): 519–37.

Ullman, Manfred. 1978. *Islamic Medicine*. Edinburgh: Edinburgh University Press.

UNESCO. 1963. *The Development of Higher Education in Africa: Report of the Conference on the Development of Higher Education in Africa, Tananarive, 3–12 September 1962*. Paris: United Nations Educational, Scientific and Cultural Organization.

UNESCO. 1981–1993. International Scientific Committee for the Drafting of a General History of Africa. *General History of Africa*. (8 volumes). Berkeley: University of California Press.

UNESCO. 1992. *Higher Education in Africa: Trends and Challenges for the 21st Century*. Dakar: UNESCO Regional Office for Education in Africa (BREDA).

UNESCO. 1994. *The Role of African Student Movements in the Political and Social Evolution of Africa from 1900–1975*. Paris: UNESCO.

UNESCO. 1995. *Women in Higher Education in Africa*. Dakar: UNESCO Regional Office for Education in Africa (BREDA).

UNESCO. 1996. *Analyses, Agenda and Priorities for Education in Africa: Review of Externally Initiated, Commissioned and Supported Studies of Education in Africa, 1990–1994*. Paris: UNESCO.

UNESCO. 1998. *World Declaration on Higher Education for the Twenty-First Century: Vision and Action*. Paris: UNESCO.

United Kingdom. Colonial Office. 1945 (a). *Report of the Commission on Higher Education in the Colonies*. London: His Majesty's Stationary Office.

United Kingdom. Colonial Office. 1945 (b). *Report of the Commission on Higher Education in West Africa*. London: His Majesty's Stationary Office.

United States. Congress. Senate. Committee on Foreign Relations. Subcommittee on African Affairs. 1994. *Higher Education in Africa*. Hearing Before the Subcommittee on African Affairs of the Committee on Foreign Relations, United States Senate, One Hundred Third Congress, First Session, May 17, 1993. Washington, DC: United States Government Printing Office.

United States. Department of Interior. Bureau of Education. 1969 (1917). *Negro Education: A Study of the Private and Higher Schools for Colored People in the United States*. (2 vols.) New York: Negro Universities Press.

University of Zambia. 1977. *Report on the Long-term Development of the University of Zambia*. Lusaka: The University Printer.

Useem, Andrea. 1999 (a). "In East Africa, New Private Colleges Fill a Growing Gap between Supply and Demand." *Chronicle of Higher Education* (September 10): A65.

Useem, Andrea. 1999 (b). "Wiring African Universities Proves a Formidable Challenge." *Chronicle of Higher Education* (April 2): A51.

Useem, Andrea. 1999 (c). "Muslims in East Africa Develop Their Own Higher-Education Options." *Chronicle of Higher Education* (November 19): A69.

Useem, Andrea. 1999 (d). "University of Zimbabwe Suffers as Economic and Political Turmoil Envelop the Country." *Chronicle of Higher Education* (August 13): A46.

Vaizey, J. 1972. *The Political Economy of Education*. London: Duckworth.

Van Binsbergen, Wim M. J. 1997 (a) "Black Athena Ten Years After: Towards a Constructive Re-Assessment." In *Black Athena: Ten Years After*, edited by Wim M. J. van Binsbergen, pp. 11–64. Hoofddorp, The Netherlands: Dutch Archaeological and Historical Society.

Van Binsbergen, Wim M. J. (ed.) 1997 (b). *Black Athena: Ten Years After*. Hoofddorp, The Netherlands: Dutch Archaeological and Historical Society.

Van de Walle, Nicolas; Ball, Nicole; and Ramachandran, Vijaya. (eds). 2004. *Beyond Structural Adjustment: The Institutional Context of African Development*. New York: Palgrave Macmillan.

Van den Berghe, Pierre L. 1967. *Race and Racism: A Comparative Perspective*. New York: John Wiley. Van Den Bor, W., and Shute, J. C. M. 1991. "Higher Education in the Third World: Status Symbol or Instrument for Development." *Higher Education* 22: 1–15.

Vatikiotis, P. J. 1991. *The History of Modern Egypt: From Muhammed Ali to Mubarak*. London: Weidenfeld and Nicolson.

Verger, Jacques. 1992. "Patterns." In *A History of the University in Europe: Volume 1: Universities in the Middle Ages*, ed. by Hilde de Ridder-Symoens, pp. 35–75. Cambridge: Cambridge University Press.

Vergnani, Linda. 1998. "South African Universities Move to Cast Aside Legacy of Apartheid: Historically White and Black Institutions Face New Era of Recruiting Goals and 'Redress.'" *Chronicle of Higher Education* (September 4): A73.

Vergnani, Linda. 1999 (a). "Future of South Africa's Oldest Black University Is Imperiled, Report Warns." *Chronicle of Higher Education* (April 9): A52.

Vergnani, Linda. 1999 (b). "South Africa's Black Universities Struggle to Survive in a New Era: They Face a Declining Interest from Students Who Have More Options than under Apartheid." *Chronicle of Higher Education* (March 12): A45.

Vergnani, Linda. 1999 (c). "South Africa's New Education Minister Combines Bluntness and Charisma: Kader Asmal Says Some Colleges May Need to Merge and Others May Have to Change Their Missions." *Chronicle of Higher Education* (October 1): A59.

Vergnani, Linda. 2000. "South African Universities Grapple with the Growth of Distance Learning: Key Issues Include Quality Control, Language and Centralization." *Chronicle of Higher Education* (June 23): A45.

Verlinden, Charles. 1995. "The Transfer of Colonial Techniques from the Mediterranean to the Atlantic." In *The European Opportunity* (vol. 2 of "An Expanding World: The European Impact on World History, 1450–1800"), ed. by Felipe Fernandez-Armesto, pp. 225–54. Brookfield, VT: Variorum/Ashgate.

Viola, Herman J., and Margolis, Carolyn. (eds.) 1992. *Seeds of Change: A Quincentennial Commemoration*. Washington, DC: Smithsonian Institution Press.

Vitkus, Daniel J. 1999. "Early Modern Orientalism: Representations of Islam in Sixteenth– and Seventeenth– Century Europe." In *Western Views of Islam in Medieval and Early Modern Europe: Perceptions of Other*, ed. by David R. Blanks and Michael Frassetto, pp. 207–30. New York: St. Martins.

Von Grunebaum, Gustave E. 1961. *Medieval Islam: A Study in Cultural Orientation*. Chicago: University of Chicago Press.

Wade, Robert. 1996. "Japan, the World Bank and the Art of Paradigm Maintenance: The East Asian Miracle in Political Perspective." *New Left Review* (no. 217): 3–36

Wagaw, Teshome G. 1979. See Teshome G. Wagaw. 1979.

Wagaw, Teshome G. 1990. See Teshome G. Wagaw. 1990.

Wallerstein, Immanuel. 1974–1989. *The Modern World-System* (3 vols.) New York: Academic Press.

Wallerstein, Immanuel. 1976. "The Three Stages of African Involvement in the World Economy." In *The Political Economy of Contemporary Africa*, ed. by Peter C. W. Gutkind, and Immanuel Wallerstein, pp. 35–63. Beverly Hills, CA: Sage.

Walshe, A. P. 1969. "The Origins of African Political Consciousness in South Africa" *Journal of Modern African Studies* 7 (December): 583–610.

Walshe, A. P. 1970. "Black American Thought and African Political Attitudes in South Africa." *Review of Politics* 32 (January): 51–77.

Wandira, Asavia. 1977. *The African University in Development*. Johannesburg: Ravan.

Warburg, Gabriel. 2003. *Islam, Sectarianism and Politics in Sudan Since the Mahdiya*. London: C. Hurst.

Warsam, A. A. 2001. "How A Strong Government Backed an African Language: The Lessons of Somalia." *International Review of Education* 47 (no. 3–4): 341–360.

Wartenberg, Dieter, and Mayrhofer, Wolfgang. (eds.) 2001. *Education in Ethiopia.* Hamburg: Kovac.

Washington, Booker T. 1985 (1895). "Speech at the Atlanta Exposition." In *Afro-American Writing: An Anthology of Prose and Poetry,* ed. by Richard A. Long, and Eugenia W. Collier, pp. 150–53. University Park: Pennsylvania State University.

Watkins, Mel. 1994. *On the Real Side: Laughing, Lying and Signifying—The underground Tradition of African-American Humor That Transformed American Culture, from Slavery to Richard Pryor.* New York: Simon & Schuster.

Watkins, William H. 1994. "Pan-Africanism and the Politics of Education: Towards a New Understanding." In *Imagining Home: Class, Culture and Nationalism in the African Diaspora,* ed. by Sidney J. Lemelle and Robin D. G. Kelley, pp. 222–42. New York: Verso.

Watson, Andrew M. 1995. "Back to Gold—and Silver." In *The European Opportunity* (vol. 2 of "An Expanding World: The European Impact on World History, 1450–1800"), ed. by Felipe Fernandez-Armesto, pp. 141–74. Brookfield, VT: Variorum/Ashgate.

Watson, Keith. 1995. "Redefining the Role of Government in Higher Education: How Realistic Is the World Bank's Prescription?" In *Learning from Experience: Policy and Practice in Aid to Higher Education,* ed. by Lene Buchert and Kenneth King, pp. 125–44. The Hague: Center for the Study of Education in Developing Countries.

Watt, W. Montgomery. 1965. *A History of Islamic Spain.* Edinburgh: Edinburgh University Press.

Watt, W. Montgomery. 1972. *The Influence of Islam on Medieval Europe.* Edinburgh: Edinburgh University Press.

Watts, Pauline Moffitt. "Prophecy and Discovery: On the Spiritual Origins of Christopher Columbus's 'Enterprise of the Indies'." In *The European Opportunity* (vol. 2 of "An Expanding World: The European Impact on World History, 1450–1800"), ed. by Felipe Fernandez-Armesto, pp. 195–224. Brookfield, VT: Variorum/Ashgate.

Weatherford, J. McIver. 1988. *Indian Givers: How the Indians of the Americas Transformed the World.* New York: Crown.

Weaver, Harold Dodson. 1985. "Soviet Training and Research Programs for Africa." Ph.D. dissertation, University of Massachusetts.

Weber, Max. 1967 (1958) *The Religion of India: The Sociology of Hinduism and Buddhism.* New York: Free Press.

Weber, Max. 1998 (1909). *The Agrarian Sociology of Ancient Civilizations.* New York: Verso.

Wells-Barnett, Ida B. 1997. *Southern Horrors and Other Writings: The Anti-Lynching Campaign of Ida B. Wells, 1892–1900.* Boston: Bedford.

Welsh, David. 1971. *The Roots of Segregation: Native Policy in Colonial Natal, 1845–1910.* New York: Oxford University Press.

Welsh, David. 1979. "The Values of English Medium Universities." In *UCT at 150: Re-flections*, ed. by Alan Lennox-Short, and David Welsh, pp. 22–27. Cape Town: David Philip.

Welsh, Frank. 1999. *South Africa: A Narrative History*. New York: Kodansha International.

Wesseling, H. L. 1996. *Divide and Rule: The Partition of Africa, 1880–1914*. Westport, CT: Praeger.

White, Lynn Townsend. 1964. *Medieval Technology and Social Change*. New York: Oxford University Press.

Wigen, Karen, and Martin, Lewis W. 1997. *The Myth of Continents: A Critique of Metageography*. Berkeley: University of California Press.

Wilkin, Paul David. 1983. "To the Bottom of the Heap: Educational Deprivation and Its Social Implications in the Northwestern Province of Zambia, 1906–1945." Ph.D. dissertation, Syracuse University.

Wilkinson, Richard H. 2000. *The Complete Temples of Ancient Egypt*. New York: Thames & Hudson.

Williams, Eric. 1994 (1944). *Capitalism and Slavery* (with a new introduction by Colin A. Palmer). Chapel Hill: University of North Carolina Press.

Williams, Trevor I. (Updated and revised by William E. Schaaf, Jr., with Arianne E. Burnette.) 2000. *A History of Invention: From Stone Axes to Silicon Chips*. New York: Checkmark.

Williams, Walter L. 1982. *Black Americans and the Evangelization of Africa, 1877–1900*. Madison: University of Wisconsin Press, 1982.

Williamson, Bill. 1987. *Education and Social Change in Egypt and Turkey: A Study in Historical Sociology*. London: Macmillan.

Willis, John Ralph. (ed.) 1985. *Slaves and Slavery in Muslim Africa. Volume I: Islam and the Ideology of Enslavement*. London: Frank Cass.

Wilson, George M. 1992. *Patriots and Redeemers in Japan: Motives in the Meiji Restoration*. Chicago: University of Chicago Press.

Wilson, Monica, and Thompson, Leonard. (eds.) 1969/1971. *The Oxford History of South Africa*. (2 vols.) New York: Oxford University Press.

Wittfogel, Karl August. 1957. *Oriental Despotism: A Comparative Study of Total Power*. New Haven: Yale University Press.

Wolfers, Michael, and Bergerol, Jane. 1983. *Angola in The Frontline*. London: Zed.

Wolff, Richard. 2003. "World Bank/ Class Blindness." In *World Bank Literature*, ed. by Amitava Kumar, pp. 172–83. Minneapolis: University of Minnesota Press.

Wolpe, Harold. 1995. "The Debate on University Transformation in South Africa: The Case of the University of the Western Cape." *Comparative Education* 31 (no. 2): 275–92.

Wolpoff, Milford H., and Caspari, Rachel. 1997. *Race and Human Evolution*. New York : Simon & Schuster.

Woodhall, Maureen. 1988. "Designing a Student Loan Program for a Developing Country: The Relevance of International Experience." *Economics of Education Review* 7 (no. 1): 153–161.

Woodhall, Maureen. 2003. "Financing Higher Education: Old Challenges and New Messages." *Journal of Higher Education in Africa* 1 (no. 1): 78–100.

Woods, Rochelle L. 2001. "'Oh Sorry, I'm a Racist': Black Student Experiences at the University of Witwatersrand." In *Apartheid No More: Case Studies of Southern African Universities in the Process of Transformation*, ed. by Reitsumetse Obakeng Mabokela, and Kimberly Linease King, pp. 91–110. Westport, CT: Bergin and Garvey.

Woodward, Peter. 1990. *Sudan, 1898–1989: The Unstable State*. Boulder: Lynne Rienner.

World Bank. 1971. *Education Sector Working Paper*. Washington, DC: World Bank.

World Bank. 1974. *Education Sector Working Paper*. Washington, DC: World Bank.

World Bank. 1980. *Education Sector Paper*. Washington, DC: World Bank.

World Bank. 1981. *Accelerated Development in Sub-Saharan Africa: An Agenda for Action*. Washington, DC: World Bank.

World Bank. 1988. *Education in Sub-Saharan Africa: Policies for Adjustment, Revitalization and Expansion*. Washington, DC: World Bank.

World Bank. 1994. *Higher Education: The Lessons of Experience*. Washington, DC: World Bank.

World Bank. 1995. *Priorities and Strategies for Education. A World Bank Review*. Washington, DC: World Bank.

World Bank. 1998. *World Development Report, 1998/99: Knowledge For Development*. New York: Oxford University Press (published for the World Bank).

World Bank. 1999. *Education Sector Strategy*. Washington, DC: World Bank.

World Bank. 2000 (a). *African Development Indicators*. Washington, DC: World Bank.

World Bank. 2000 (b). *Can Africa Claim the 21st Century?* Washington, DC: World Bank. (Published in association with African Development Bank, African Economic Research Consortium, Global Coalition for Africa and United Nations Economic Commission for Africa.)

World Bank. 2000 (c). *Higher Education in Developing Countries: Peril and Promise*. Washington, DC: World Bank.

World Bank. 2000 (d). *World Development Report, 1999/2000: Entering the 21st Century*. New York: Oxford University Press (published for the World Bank).

World Bank. 2002. *Constructing Knowledge Societies: New Challenges for Tertiary Education*. Washington, DC: World Bank.

World Bank. 2002 (a). *Tertiary Education: Lessons from a Decade of Lending, FY1990–2000*. Washington, DC: World Bank.

World Bank. 2004 (a). *Building State Capacity in Africa—New Approaches, Emerging Lessons*. Washington, DC: World Bank.

World Bank. 2004 (b). *Crafting Institutional Responses to HIV/AIDS: Guidelines and Resources for Tertiary Institutions in Sub-Saharan Africa*. Washington, DC: World Bank.

World Bank. 2005. *Governance Matters IV: Governance Indicators for 1996–2004*. Washington, DC: World Bank.

Wright, Ronald. 1992. *Stolen Continents: The Americas Through Indian Eyes since 1492*. Boston: Houghton Mifflin.

Wylie, Diana. 1989. "The Changing Face of Hunger in Southern Africa, 1880–1980." *Past and Present* (no. 122, February): 159–99.

Wylie, Diana. 2001. *Starving on a Full Stomach: Hunger and the Triumph of Cultural Racism in Modern South Africa*. Charlottesville: University Press of Virginia.

Yang, Rui. 2003. "Globalization and Higher Education Development: A Critical Analysis." *International Review of Education* 49 (nos. 3–4): 269–91.

Yesufu, T. M. (ed). *Creating the African University: Emerging Issues in the 1970s.* Ibadan: Oxford University Press.

Yewell, John; Dodge, Chris; and DeSirey, Jan. (eds.) 1992. *Confronting Columbus: An Anthology.* Jefferson: McFarland.

Yohannes, Tsehaie. 2002. See Tsehaie Yohannes. 2002.

Young, John. 1997. *Peasant Revolution in Ethiopia: The Tigray People's Liberation Front, 1975–1991.* New York: Cambridge University Press.

Yusuf, Shahid, and Stiglitz, Joseph E. (eds.) 2000. *Rethinking the East Asian Miracle.* New York: Oxford University Press (published for the World Bank).

Zambia. Government. 1998. *Report of the Commission of Inquiry Appointed to Inquire into Operations at the University of Zambia and the Copperbelt University.* Lusaka: Government Printer.

Zegeye, Adebe, and Pausewang, Siegfried. 1994. See Adebe Zegeye, and Pausewang, Siegfried. 1994.

Zewde, Bahru. 2001. See Bahru Zewde. 2001.

Zeydan, Gergy. 1952. "The Burning of the Books at the Library of Alexandria and Elsewhere." In *The Alexandrian Library: Glory of the Hellenic World,* ed. by Edward A. Parsons, pp. 413–21. New York: American Elsevier.

Ziderman, Adrian, and Albrecht, Douglas. 1995. *Financing Universities in Developing Countries.* Washington, DC: The Falmer Press.

Index

AAU: *See* Association of African Universities

Abd al-Hamid Ibn Badis, 147, 191*n*.71

Abd al-Qadir ibn Muhyi al-Din, 189*n*.64

Abduh, Muhammed, 189*n*.62

Abu Al-Husayn Ali Ibn Al-Husayn Al-Masudi, 452

Abu' Ali Al-Husain Ibn Abdallah Ibn Sina, 452, 454

Abu Alimacr al-Hassan Ibn al-Haitham, 452

Abu al-Qasim Khalaf ibn al-Abbas Al-Zahrawi, 452

Abu al-Walid Muhammed ibn Ahmad ibn Muhammed Ibn Rushd, 456, 466, 469*n*.4, 476*n*.35

Abu Bakr, Syeddina, 93*n*.26

Abu Bakr Muhammed bin Zakariyya' al-Razi, 452

Abu Imran Musa ibn Maymun ibn Ubayd Allah: *See* Maimonides, Moses

Abu-Lughod, Janet L., 490, 531*n*.50

Abu Musa Jabir ibn-Hayyan, 451

Abu Raihan al-Biruni, 469*n*.4

Abu Yosuf Ya'qub Ibn Ishaq ibn al-Sabbah al-Kindi, 452

Academic freedom: and African universities, 132, 233–34, 249*n*.31, 256–57*n*.35, 274, 307, 456

Academic standards: and African universities, 225, 227, 229, 230

Access to education: *See* Equality of educational opportunity

Achimota College, 219–20

Accra Declaration on GATS and the Internationalization of Higher Education in Africa, 204*n*.110

ad-Din al-Afghani, Jamal, 189*n*.62

Acquired Immunodeficiency Syndrome/ Human Immunodeficiency Virus, 396, 443*n*.13, 444*n*.16

Addis Ababa University, 268–69, 274. *See also* Haile Selassie I University

Advisory Committee on Colonial Colleges of Arts, Science and Technology, 245*n*.21

Advisory Committee on Education in the Colonies, 214–15

Adwa, Battle of, 57, 266, 362

Africa: Anglophone, 207–329; division of, 86–87*n*.1, 107; and economic unity, 252*n*.32; europhone, 331–77; fragmentation of, 385, 407; future of the university in, 439; GDP of, 421*n*.27; leaders of, 421–22*n*.27; postindependence distortions of, 407; premodern, 41–105; and raw material production, 397; Scramble for, 20, 22, 207–8, 239–40*n*.3; size of, 28*n*.2; state of, 443–44*n*.13; subordinate economic position of, 498; "United States of," 252*n*32, 385, 413–14*n*.7; and the World Bank, 395–98

Africa-America Institute, 384, 413*nn*.3,6

African Americans, 14, 33–36*n*.22, 246*n*.25, 312*n*.22; in South Africa, 290–95, 320*n*.52, 324*nn*.55–56, 324*n*.59, 325–26*n*.62. *See also* Liberia; African Methodist Episcopal Church.

African Development Bank, 248*n*.30, 420*n*.25, 421*n*.27

African historicity, 81–86. *See also* Afrocentrism

African history, 19–20, 27–28*n*.2. *See also* African historicity

African Methodist Episcopal (AME) Church, 279, 290–95, 324–26*nn*.60–62

African National Congress: and education, 323–24*n*.54; formation, 325*n*.62; and Mozambique, 350; victory of, 288, 302, 320–22*n*.52

Afrikaners, 284

Afro-Arab Islamic Africa, 8, 12, 26, 27, 38*n*.38, 107–205; and Africa, 86*n*.1; categories of knowledge in, 176; East and West Africa and, 177–78*n*.2; and elites, 109–110; higher education in precolonial, 60–81

Afrocentrists, 47, 88*n*.6–8

Afro-Eurasian civilization, 467–68

Agency versus structure, concepts of: *See* Structure versus agency

Aggrey, James E. Kwegyir, 33–36*n*.22, 314*n*.30

Ahmed the Gran: *See* al-Ghazi, Imam Ahmed ibn Ibrahim

AID: *See* U.S. Agency for International Development

AIDS: *See* Acquired Immunodeficiency Syndrome/ Human Immunodeficiency Virus

Ajayi, J. F. Ade, 229, 233, 248, 298, 384, 392

Aklilu Habte, 269

Aksum, 52–54; 91*n*.14

Alawi dynasty (Morocco), 153, 196*n*.83

al-Azhar, 73, 76–81, 138–45; and the British, 141; and the constitutional government, 142; finances of, 79–80; and the French conquest, 139; and the Khedives, 141; and Muhammed Ali, 139; nationalization of, 144; and the praetorian oligarchic dynasty, 142; origins of, 76, 100*n*.54; reform of, 126, 142–44, 188–90*nn*.57, 59, 62, 63; relevance of, 145; secularization of, 80; student life at, 103*nn*.60, 61, 140–41; ulama of, 78–80, 140

al-Din Husayn, Kamal, 132

A-levels: *See* General Certificate in Education

Alexander the Conqueror (the Great), 48

Algeria: civil war, 191–95*nn*.71, 72; decolonization of, 191*n*.67; FLN uprising, 146; French takeover of, 145; higher education in, 145–49; Indigenous Code of, 190; Islamist tendency in, 148, 193*n*.72

al-Ghazi, Imam Ahmed ibn Ibrahim, 59, 362

Alhazen: *See* Abu Alimacr al-Hassan Ibn al-Haitham

Alighieri, Dante, 477*n*.35, 521*n*.17

Ali, Muhammed: *See* Muhammed Ali

al-Madrasah al Badisiyya: *See* Abd al-Hamid Ibn Badis

Alpharabius: *See* Muhammed Ibn Muhammed Ibn Tarkhan ubn Uzalagh al-Farabi

al-Qarawiyyin, 70–72, 153–56

Altbach, Philip G., x, 255*n*.34, 446*n*.21

Albucasis: *See* Abu al-Qasim Khalaf ibn al-Abbas Al-Zahrawi

Althusser, Louis, 443*n*.13

al-Zaitouna, 69–70, 168–170

A. M. Dogliotti College of Medicine, 280

AME: *See* African Methodist Episcopal Church

A.M.E. University, 279

American Colonization Society: *See* American Society for the Colonization of Free People of Color

American Mission: *See* United Presbyterian mission

American Society for the Colonization of Free People of Color, 277, 313*n*.23. *See also* Liberia

American University in Cairo (AUC), 128–30, 184–86*nn*.36–42

Amin, Samir, 481, 446*n*.21

Amir Abdel Qadir: *See* Abd al-Qadir ibn Muhyi al-Din

Amr ibn al-'As, 51, 159, 479

ANC: *See* African National Congress

Anglo-Egyptian Condominium, 162

Anglophone Africa, 207–329

Angola: conflict in, 347–49; universities in, 356

Anthropology, 12, 32–33*n*.21

Antiapartheid movement: *See* Apartheid

Apartheid, 287–88, 297, 318*n*.46; antiapartheid movement, 288, 304; collapse of apartheid, causes of, 320–22*n*.52; divide-and-rule strategy, 319*n*.48; and higher education institutions, 298–301; legislation, 287–288; in Namibia, 306;

and resource allocation, 303. *See also* South Africa

Arabic, 87*n*.1, 97*n*.30; 107–8, 278, 313*n*.25; and English word origins, 471*n*.10; language policy favoring, 434–35; role of, 64–65; and science, 450–51

Arabic names, 450–51

Arabs: and Muslims, 63; and racism, 93–96*n*.27

Arab Socialism, 131, 132, 186*n*.44

Archimedes, 89*n*.10

Aristarchus of Samos, 90*n*.10

Armstrong, Samuel Chapman, 33–36*n*.22, 313–314*n*.30

Arnett, Benjamin, 291

Articulated modes of production, 504, 529–30*n*.45

Arzachel: *See* Ibn al-Zarqali

Asante, Molefe, 47, 88*n*.6–8

Ashby Commission: *See* Commission on Post-School-Certificate and Higher Education in Nigeria

Ashby, Eric, ix–x, 42, 211, 213, 221, 226, 229, 230, 248*n*.27, 357, 447 *See also* Commission on Post-School-Certificate and Higher Education in Nigeria

Ash-Sharif al-Idrisi, 469*n*.4

Asiatic mode of production, 504, 529*n*.45

Asquith Commission: *See* Asquith colleges

Asquith colleges, 165, 208, 227–29, 243*n*.15, 248*n*.27, 416*n*.15. *See also* University of London

Asquith, Cyril: *See* Asquith colleges

Assie-Lumumba, N'Dri Therese, 393

Assimilation/association, 9, 16, 331, 333–34, 336; and World War II, 338

Association of African Universities, x, 384–85, 392, 432.

Ataturk, Mustafa Kemal, 187*n*.54

Atlantic Charter, 14, 36*n*.25

Atlantic slave trade: abolition of, 22–23, 207; role played by, 497, 504,

514, 524n.29, 526n.34, 528nn.41,43. *See also* Slavery
Avempace: *See* Ibn Bajjah
Averroes: *See* Abu al-Walid Muhammed ibn Ahmad ibn Muhammed Ibn Rushd
Avicenna: *See* Abu' Ali Al-Husain Ibn Abdallah Ibn Sina
Axum, see Aksum
Ayyubids, 77, 447
Azikiwe, Nnamdi, 231, 246nn.25, 26

Bacon, Roger, 454–55
Balliol college (Oxford), 449
Balogh, T., 426n.40
Baring, Sir Evelyn: *See* Cromer, Lord
"Basic Needs Approach": *See* World Bank
Battle of Adwa: *See* Adwa, Battle of
Battle of Dien Bien Phu: *See* Dien Bien Phu, Battle of
Battle of Isandhlwana: *See* Isandhlwana, Battle of
Battle of Poitiers: *See* Poitiers, Battle of
Battle of Tours: *See* Poitiers, Battle of
Bauer, P. T., 514n.1
Behrens-Abouseif, 78, 102n.55
Belgian colonies: higher education in, 356–59; independence of, 357–59; Lovanium University Center, 356–57
Ben Badis: *See* Ibn Badis
Benoit, Paul, 456, 459, 469n.1, 476n.29
Bennoune, Mahfoud, 147–48, 173
Bently, Harold, 269
Berbers, 114, 152
Berlin Conference: *See* Berlin West Africa Conference
Berlin West Africa Conference (of 1885), 198n.93
Bernal, Martin, 47, 88n.6–8
Bibliotheca Alexandrina, 47–52, 89–90nn.9–11, 203–06n.110, 204n.110
Bilateral aid: *See* Foreign aid

Black Athena: See Bernal, Martin
Black Consciousness Movement: in South Africa, 320n.52
Blanks, David R., 465
Blaug, Mark, 408
Blaut, J. M., 481, 486, 487, 488, 489, 505, 516n.5, 517nn.6–7, 519n.8, 526n.34
Blyden, Edward, 210–11, 277–78, 313n.25
Board of Public Examinations in Literature and Science: *See* University of South Africa
Boers: *See* Afrikaners
Booker T. Washington Institute, 280, 314
Borguiba, Habib irn Ali, 167
Boston College Center for International Higher Education, xin.1
Botha, P. W., 321n.52, 351
Boyer, Ernest, 438
Brain drain, 174, 187n.52, 261n.35, 274
Braudel, Fernand, 443n.13, 464
Brazzaville Conference, 331, 338, 341, 369n.4
British colonial policy, 208–28; Achimota College, 219–20; the Currie Report, 221–22; and development, 245n.22; Fourah Bay College, 209–13; Higher College at Yaba, 217–18; in India, 5, 226–27; indirect rule, 9, 16, 208, 241–42nn.7, 8, 331, 368n.1; and research, 223, 225, 226; self–rule, 208, 244n.15; and Somalia, 362, 365–66; in South Africa, 284; trusteeship, 215, 216; and university-level education, 216, 221–22; and vocational training, 215–16
British imperialism, 22, 241n.5; and al-Azhar, 141; and Cairo University, 127; expulsion from Egypt, 129; protectorate rule of Egypt, 124–27; in Sudan, 161–65
British university model, 229, 237–38

British West Africa, self-government
of, 211,
Brundage, James A., 513
Bubonic plague, 506, 530–31n.50
Burawoy, Michael, 251–52n.31
Burke, James, 449–50, 454
Burundi, genocide in, 359
Butler, Alfred J., 51–52
Byzantines, 93n.26; 448, 460, 469n.2,
472n.14, 510

Cabral, Amilcar, 346
Caetano, Marcello, 347
Cain, P. J., 21–22
Cairo, 76–77
Cairo University: *See* University of
Cairo
Camboni Sisters Missionary Congre-
gation, 268
Cammack, Diana, 354
Campbell, James Tierney, 289–90, 292
Camp David Accords, 134
Can Africa Claim the 21st Century
(World Bank), 420n.26, 432
Canaanites, 104n.66
Capitalism: imperialism and, 6, 7,
116–17; rise of, 464, 490, 496–97
Capitalist class, 407; reproduction of,
409
Capitalist institutions, 497
Carnegie Corporation, 230, 412n.3
Carnegie Foundation for the Ad-
vancement of Teaching, 438
Carnoy, M., 6, 205n.110
Cassanelli, Lee V., 361, 362, 363
Caufield, Catherine, 410–11, 415n.10
Central Intelligence Agency (United
States): and the contras, 373n.17;
and Liberia, 281; and the Portu-
guese colonies, 348–49, 351–52,
371–72nn.10–11
Channon, H. J., 222, 223, 226
Channon Report, 222–23
Chaudhuri, K. N., 496
Cheng Ho, 489, 520n.13, 522n.22,
524nn.25–27
Cherif, M. H., 29–30n.9

China, 138, 416–17n.13; names, 523–
24n.25; and commerce, 493–94,
496; voyages of, 486–87, 489–90,
524n.26. *See also* "East Asian
Miracle"
Christianity: in Ethiopia, 52–57; and
the Hamitic hypothesis, 82–85;
and slavery, 513; Westernization
of, 508–10, 532n.54; world view,
506–14. *See also* Crusades
Church Missionary Society, 209, 211
CIA: *See* Central Intelligence Agency
(United States)
Civil rights movement (U.S.), 23
Civil war, 315n.34; in the Democratic
Republic of the Congo, 357–58; in
Ethiopia, 272–74; in Somalia,
364–65
Civilization, problem of definition,
477n.37
Clarke, Fred, 229
*Clash of Civilizations and the Remak-
ing of World Order* (Huntington),
104n.64
Class, and higher education, 404–06.
See also Equality of educational
opportunity
Classical works, translation of, 453–54
Cobban, A. B., 447
Cochran, Judith, 135, 187–88n.52
Cohen, H. Floris, 52, 460–61
Cold War, 2, 10, 133, 272, 373–
74n.17, 441n.2; and bilateral aid,
381; and colonial possessions, 14–
15; and Somalia, 363–64; and the
"white man's burden," 11
College, concept of, 449, 313n.28
College of Fort Hare, 295–98, 303
College of West Africa (Liberia), 279
Colonial Development and Welfare
Act (1940 and 1950), 227–28
Colonial education, 2–3, 5–17; after
direct colonial rule, 170–71;
French versus British policy, 333–
337, 341; and independence, 430;
strategies of, 112–13

Colonialism, 1–2, 440n.1; and expansion, 10; different approaches, 331–333, internal, 282, 300, 302; protectorates, 9–10

Colonial legacy, 429–45; and community service, 437–38; and elites, 436–37; and high unit costs, 431–32; and language, 433–36; and science and technology, 432–33; structure and agency, 440n.1

Colonial settlers, 8, 10, 16; in Algeria, 145–46; and education, 111–12; and independence, 332; in Libya, 150; Portuguese, 350; in South Africa, 283–84; and Zimbabwe, 236, 254–55n.33

Columbian factor, 485–90, 501, 506–7, 520n.11. See also Columbus

Columbus, 475n.28, 491–92, 506–7, 520n.10

Commission for Africa (London), 395, 418n.16, 432, 443n.7

Commission of Enquiry into Native Education (1949–1951), 319n.49

Commission of Inquiry into the Deployment of Canadian Forces to Somalia (1997), 376n.26

Commission of Enquiry on Separate Training Facilities for Non-Europeans at Universities (1953–1954), 319n.49

Commission on Post-School-Certificate and Higher Education in Nigeria, 230–32. See also Ashby, Eric

Community service, and universities, 262–63n.35, 270–71; and the ivory tower syndrome, 437–38. See also "Developmental university"

Comparative advantage, strategy of, 397, 407–8, 422n.29

Conference on the Development of Higher Education in Africa (UNESCO), 255n.35

Conjuncture of fortuitously propitious historical factors, concept of, 23, 241n.5, 484

CONSAS: Constellation of Southern African States

Constantinople, 472n.14, 510, 532n.55

Constellation of Southern African States, 350

Constructing Knowledge Societies (World Bank), 427n.42

Constructive engagement, policy of (United States), 321n.52, 350, 351

Coppin, L. J., 294

Coquery-Vidrovitch, Catherine, 503

Correlational studies: See Human capital theory

Cotton, 463, 474n.26

Court, David, 418nn.15,17, 419n.21

Couvreur, A, 184

Craniometry: See Racism, and social Darwinism

Cromer, Lord, 127; 183n.31

Crusades, 464–65, 471–72nn.12, 13, 473n.21, 488; absence of mission in, 533n.60; and the conquistadors, 513; and the East-West schism, 508–10; impact on Western institutions, 510, 532n.57; and Islam, 511–13, 533n.59; perceived enemies of, 532n.56

Cuba: and Angola, 349; and Ethiopia, 310–311n.15, 364

Cultural diversity, 89n.8

Cultural imperialism, 5–6, 10, 17; and social Darwinism, 12–13

Curse of Ham: See Hamitic hypothesis

Currie report, 221–22

Currie, Sir James, 221, 222

Cuttington University College and Divinity School, 278–79

Dakawa Development Center, 323–24n.54

Damtew Teferra, x, xin.1

Daniel, Norman, 509, 512, 532n.58

Dante: See Alighieri, Dante

Dakar Medical School: See University of Dakar

Darfur, 160, 197n.89

Davidson, Basil, 61

de Magalhaes, Fernao: *See* Magellan, Ferdinand
de Gaulle, Charles, 369*n*.4
De Klerk, F. W., 302, 321*n*.52
De La Warr Commission, 165, 222
De La Warr, Lord: *See* De La Warr Commission
Demetrius Phalereus, 49
Democracy, 7, 248*n*.30; democratization of access, 174, 302; and the "developmental university," 445*n*.16; and "good governance," 394–95, 420*n*.25; "modern," 234, 248–49*n*.30
Democratic Republic of the Congo, 348. *See also* Mobutu, Joseph
Dergue (Ethiopia), 272–274, 308*n*.8, 311*nn*.16–17
de Tocqueville, Alexis, 190*n*.68
Development: definition, 446*n*.20; and higher education, 4. *See also* "Developmental university"
"Developmental university," 432, 438, 445*n*.16. *See also* Community service; Land-grant model
The Divine Comedy (Dante), 521*n*.17
Dien Bien Phu, Battle of, 146, 346, 189–190*n*.66
Doe, Samuel K., 281
Dorn, H., 458, 460, 476*n*.33
Drescher, Seymour, 22
Dube, John Langalibalele, 325–26*n*.62
Dubois, Felix, 72–73
DuBois, W. E. B., 35n22
Duhem, Pierre, 472*n*.16, 473*n*.19
Durham University, 209, 212
Dutch East India Company. *See* United East India Company

East African Community, 234–35, 251–53*n*.32
"East Asian Miracle," 205*n*.110, 422–23*n*.32, 440, 446*n*.21
East-West Schism: *See* Schism of 1054
Eccel, A. Chris, 96–97*n*.28

Ecole des Cadres Superieurs de Brazzaville, 339
Ecole Normal Ponty, 337
Economic development: economic growth and, 425*n*.36; strategies of, 395–97. *See also* Economic growth
Economic growth, 400–401; education and, 426*n*.39. *See also* Economic development; Economics of education
Economics of Education (Blaug), 408
Economics of education, 203–06*n*.110, 402–9. *See also* Human capital theory
The Economist, 399
Eduardo Mondlane University, 356
Education: balanced development of, 393; basic needs approach to, 387–95; and civil society, 367–68; and colonialism, 2–3, 5–17; Hampton/Tuskeegee model of, 13, 32–35*n*.22, 216, 292, 313–14*n*.30; and occupations, 404–6; and social differentiation, 405. *See also* Equality of educational opportunity; Higher education; Missionaries; Universities
Education in Sub-Saharan Africa: Adjustment, Revitalization, and Expansion (World Bank), 387–88
Egal, Muhammed Haji Ibrahim, 363
Egypt, 4, 114–45; al Azhar, 73, 76–81, 138–45; American University in Cairo (AUC), 128–30, 184–86*nn*.36–42; Arab socialism, 131, 132, 186*n*.44; Bibliotheca Alexandrina, 47–52; British protectorate rule of, 124–27; Cairo University, 126–28, 131–32, 133; and engineers, 136–37; expatriate instructors, 122–23; foreign student missions of, 118–22, 125; "Free Officers" military coup (1952), 130–31; French conquest of, 80, 114–17, 139; and the Hamitic hypothesis, 86; and industrialization, 118;

military schools of, 121–22; modernization of, 117–18, 182n.24; Ottoman rule of, 78–80; *per ankh*, 43–47; and the Soviet Union, 133; Suez Canal, 133, 181n.21; temples of, 87–88n.3; and the United States, 134–35

Egyptian University: *See* University of Cairo

Egyptians (Ancient), skin color of, 88n.6

Ehret, Christopher, 27–28n.2

Elites, 109–10; African *evolues*, 333, 337, 368n.2; capitalist, 443n.13; and the Cold War, 10; compradorial character of, 178n.3, 445n.16; and decadence, 6; fusion of, 178n.4–5; 180n.7; global, 434; and import substitution, 397; indigenous bureaucratic, 430; and indirect rule, 208, 241–42.nn.7, 8; intergenerational continuity of, 174, 204n.109; and secularism, 182n.24; transformation of, 176; universities and, 436–37. *See also* Equality of educational opportunity

Elliot Commission, 212, 214, 217–220, 223; and the West African university college, 224–27

Elliott, Walter: *See* Elliot Commission

Equality of educational opportunity, 132–33, 170, 175–76, 186n.48, 203n.109, 308n.8; and meritocracy, 202–03n.108, 269. *See also* South Africa

Erasistratus of Ceos, 90n.10

Eratosthenes of Cyrene, 90n.10

Ethiopia, 4, 265–76; access to education in, 268–69; civil war in, 272–74; community service in, 270–71; the Dergue, 272–74, 308n.8, 310–11n.16; famine in, 271–73; Haile Selassie I University, 269–72; Islamic education in, 57–59; Italian occupation of, 266–67; Jesuits in, 267–68; and modernization, 267,

275–76, 308–9n.9; monastic educational system, 54–56; premodern, 52–60; revolutionary student movement in, 272, 310n.14; and Sweden, 270; University College of Addis Ababa, 268–69, 274; war with Eritrea, 275, 311n.17

Ethiopia/Japan anomaly, 57, 275–76, 500–505; and the Columbian factor, 501; and long-distance trade, 502–3

Ethiopian Church/churches (South Africa), 290–91, 294, 324nn. 57–58; 326–27nn.63–64

Ethiopianism. *See* Ethiopian Church/churches (South Africa)

Ethnicity, manipulated for political ends, 161

Euclid, 90n.10

Euro-American ecumene, 494, 520–21n.15

Eurocentrism, 20, 47, 81, 476n.35, 481–85, 499, 514n.1; Marxian, 516–17n.6; and racism, 516n.5

Europe: breakdown of feudal order in, 497; economic advantage of, 490–95; exceptionalism, 498–99; extension of the economy of 495–96; Napoleonic Wars, 498; and proletarianization, 498; and transcontinental trade, 496–97. *See also* Eurocentrism

The European Miracle (Jones), 481–82

Europhone Africa, 331–77

Ezzitouna: *See* al-Zaitouna

Faculty: and brain drain, 187–88n.52, 261n.35, 274; female, 184n.34; of Fourah Bay College, 212; and languages of instruction, 123, 127; lecture notes of, 135; recruitment and retention of, 260–62n.35; salary levels of, 431

"Failed state": *See* Somalia

Fanon, Frantz, 6, 179

Faruq I University, 130

Fatimah al-Azhar-Zahra, 76
Fatimids, 76; 99*n*.53; 114
Federation of Rhodesias and
    Nyasaland, 236, 253–55*n*.33
Fernandez-Armesto, Felipe, 490
Fez, 70–72
Finance, and universities, 79–80,
    98*n*.39, 218, 219, 257–58*n*.35,
    308*n*.7, 390; and autonomy, 234;
    of Cairo University, 126–27; em-
    bezzlement and mismanagement
    of, 303; and francophone colonies,
    342–43; and high unit costs, 431,
    442–43*n*.3; looting of, 118; and oil
    price hikes, 151; World University
    Service, 236–37. *See also* Equality
    of educational opportunity
Firestone Plantation Corporation: in
    Liberia, 282
First, Ruth, 352
FLEC: *See* Frente da Libertacao do
    Estado de Cabinda
FLN (Algeria): *See* Front de Libera-
    tion Nationale
FNLA: *See* Frente Nacional para a Li-
    bertacao de Angola
Ford Foundation, 278, 306, 412*n*.3
Foreign aid, 270–71, 379–428,
    309*nn*.9–10, 411*n*.1; basic needs
    approach, 387–95; bilateral aid,
    380–81; elimination of, 410; for-
    eign scholarly societies, 411*n*.2;
    new assistance model, 410; over-
    seas universities, 412*n*.3; private
    philanthropic organizations, 412–
    13*n*.3; uselessness of, 409–10. *See
    also* Carnegie Corporation; Ford
    Foundation; United Nations Edu-
    cational, Scientific, and Cultural
    Organization; World Bank
Foreign students: *See* Study abroad
Fort Hare: *See* College of Fort Hare
Fourah Bay College, 209–13, 224,
    246*n*.23
France: assimilationist/associationist
    policies of, 9, 331, 333–34, 336;
    conquest of Egypt by, 80, 114–17,

139; and Egyptian students, 119;
    Franco-Vietnamese War, 190*n*.66;
    protectorate rule of Morocco, 152–
    53; protectorate rule of Tunisia,
    166–69; takeover of Algeria, 145.
    See also Afro-Arab Islamic Africa;
    Francophone colonies outside
    North Africa
Francophone colonies outside North
    Africa, 333–43; civil service in,
    335; Ecole Normal Ponty, 337;
    and French Universities, 337–39,
    341, 343; indigenization, 343; and
    Missionaries, 334–35; and racism,
    336
Frank, Andre Gunder, 483–84
Frente da Libertacao de Mocambique
    (Front for the Liberation of Mo-
    zambique), 346–47, 350–53, 355
Frente de Libertacao do Estado de
    Cabinda (Front for the Liberation
    of State of Cabinda), 349
Frente Nacional para a Libertacao de
    Angola (National Front for the Li-
    beration of Angola), 348, 370*n*.10
FRELIMO: *See* Frente da Libertacao
    de Mocambique
French colonial project, 30–31*n*.15
Front de Liberation Nationale, 146,
    191*n*.72

Garvey, Marcus: *See* Garveyism
Garveyism, 313*n*.22, 320*n*.52, 326*n*.62
Gascoigne, John, 455–56
GATS (General Agreement on Trades
    in Service): *See* World Trade Or-
    ganization
GCE: *See* General Certificate in Edu-
    cation
Geber: *See* Abu Musa Jabir ibn-
    Hayyan
General Certificate in Education, 231,
    238, 248*n*.28, 255–56*n*.35
Genghis Khan, 489, 524*n*.25. *See also*
    Mongols
Genocide: in Burundi, 359; and the
    Crusades, 513; in Rwanda, 358–59

Ghalioungui, Paul, 45–46
Ghiyath al-Din Abul Fateh Omar Ibn
    Ibrahim al-Nisaburi al-Khayyami,
    469n.4
Ghana, 233–34
Ghedi, Ali Mohammed, 360
Gibbon, Edward, 51–52
Giddens, Anthony, 443n.13
Girdwood, Alison, 415n.11
Globalization, 303, 434, 439, 440,
    446nn.19, 21
Glorious Revolution (1688), 483
Gold: and European commerce, 491,
    492, 493, 494, 496, 526n.35
Goldenberg, David M., 83–84
Goma, Lameck K. H., 229, 233, 248,
    298, 384, 392
"Good governance": See Democracy
Gordon, Charles George, 162
Gordon Memorial College, 164–65
Gosnell, Jonathan K., 11
Grant, Edward, 460
Greece/Greeks: and Egypt, 45, 47,
    158, 476n.34; and knowledge, 447,
    450, 451, 454, 456, 458, 459, 465,
    466, 471n.8, 471n.11, 473n.17,
    476n.33
Guinea, independence from France,
    342–43
Gunpowder, 488, 522n.21

Habte, Aklilu: See Aklilu Habte
Haile Selassie, 268; deposition of, 271,
    309n.12
Haile Selassie I University, 269–72.
    See also Addis Ababa University
Hajj (pilgrimage to Mecca), 63, 65, 68
Ham, Curse of: See Hamitic hypothe-
    sis
Hamites: See Hamitic hypothesis
Hamitic hypothesis, 82–86
Hampton/Tuskegee model of educa-
    tion, 13, 33–35n.22, 216, 292,
    313–14n.30, 327n.70. See also
    Aggrey, James E. Kwegyir; Jones,
    Thomas Jesse; Loram, Charles T.;
    Washington, Booker T.

Handbook on Academic Freedom and
    University Autonomy, 384
Hanlon, Joseph, 352–54
Harar, 58, 269, 274, 365
Hassan, Shaykh Muhammed ibn
    Abd'Allah, 362
Hawass, Zahi, 90n.10
Hayford, J. E. Casely, 215, 242n.9
Hedon, J. Christopher, 52
Hegel, Georg, 81–82
Hennessy, John Pope, 210–11
Heritage Foundation, 355
Herodotus, 360, 375n.21, 476n.33
Herophilus, 90n.10
Heyworth-Dunne, J., 119–24, 182n.27
Higher College at Yaba, 217–18, 227
Higher education: in Algeria, 145–49;
    in ancient Egypt, 43–52; and
    apartheid laws, 287–88; and au-
    thoritarianism, 175; best-practices
    document, 388–89, 416–18n.15;
    British colonial policy, 208–28;
    colonial legacy, 429–39; class-
    reproduction function of, 175; cost
    of, 379; disjuncture between pre-
    modern and modern, 479–514; and
    educational planning, 399–411; in
    Egypt, 118–45; founding of insti-
    tutions of, 21; in francophone
    colonies outside North Africa,
    333–43; historical antecedents of,
    20; history of, 23–24; and inde-
    pendence, 10–11, 15; land-grant
    model, 230–33, 248n.27; in Libya,
    150–52; and literacy, 5, 183n.31,
    226; marginalization of, 389–95,
    418n.15; in modern Ethiopia, 267–
    75; monastic system of, 54–56; na-
    tional universities, 228–39; and
    politics, 3–4; in the Portuguese
    colonies, 344, 356; in precolonial
    Islamic Africa, 60–81; in premod-
    ern Ethiopia, 52–60; in Sudan,
    161–66; UNESCO conferences on,
    383. See also Academic freedom;
    Academic standards; Equality of

educational opportunity; Science and technology; World Bank
Higher Education: The Lessons of Experience (World Bank), 388–90
Hill, Donald R., 461, 462
Hiskett, Mervyn, 73–75
Historiography, 1–27, 206*n*.111; method, 17–27; parameters, 1–17. *See also* Eurocentrism
History: as myth, 17; nation-state approach to, 18; perspective of, 23. *See also* Historiography
History of science, 458–62, 484–85
HIV: *See* Acquired Immunodeficiency Syndrome/Human Immunodeficiency Virus
Hodgson, Marshall G. S., 477*nn*.37–38, 480, 483, 484, 486, 516*n*.4
Hofmeyr, J. H., 297
Homelands (apartheid South Africa), 287, 298, 299, 300, 303
Hopkins, A. G., 21–22
Horton, James Africanus Beale, 210–11, 221, 239
Huff, Tobby E., 449, 459, 460, 469, 471*nn*.7,9,11, 473*nn*.17–18
Human capital theory, 134, 136–38, 307, 399–409, 426–28*n*.40; pedigree of, 425*n*.37
Husaynid dynasty, 167, 198*n*.95
Hussein, Taha, 189*n*.62, 434
Hypatia, 90*n*.10

Ibn al-Zarqali, 469*n*.4
Ibn Badis: *See* Abd al-Hamid Ibn Badis
Ibn Bajjah, 469*n*.4
Ibn Khaldun, 70; on black Africans, 94*n*.27; *Muqaddimah*, 18
Ibn Rushd: *See* Abu al-Walid Muhammed ibn Ahmad ibn Muhammed Ibn Rushd
Ibn Sina: *See* Abu' Ali Al-Husain Ibn Abdallah Ibn Sina
Ibrahim Pasha University in Cairo, 130

Ideology, 41–42; Arab-Socialism, 131–32; of assimilation, 9, 16, 331, 333–34; and educational credentials, 405; and the Hamitic hypothesis, 82–86; and Islamism, 202*n*.104; Marxist-Leninist, 272–73; and subjection, 15–16; of Western modernity, 517–19*n*.8; "white man's burden," 8–9, 11, 25; white supremacist, 283
Illiteracy, 5, 56, 123; and magic, 92*n*.19; in the Portuguese colonies, 344; and universities, 183*n*.31, 226
Imperialism: and capitalism, 6–7, 116–17; cultural, 5–6, 10, 12–13, 17; and fratricidal aggression, 523*n*.24; ideology of, 8–9
Import substitution industrialization, strategy of, 396–97, 408, 495
Independence, 14; and colonial settlement, 332; French idea of, 341; and higher education, 10–11, 15; Libyan, 150–51; and nationalism, 15, 16; and national universities, 228–39; and the Portuguese colonies, 345–56; readiness for, 429–30
India, 5, 91*n*.12; 181*n*.16; 226–27, 270, 388–89, 417*n*.15
Indirect rule, 9, 16, 208, 241–42*nn*.7, 8, 331, 368*n*.1. *See also* British colonial policy
Industrial revolution: *See* Industrial transformation
Industrial transformation, 118, 173, 505–6, 515*n*.2. *See also* Science and technology
Infitah (Egypt), 134, 137
Inikori, Joseph E., 515*n*.2, 526*n*.34
International Bank for Reconstruction and Development: *See* World Bank
International Development Association: *See* World Bank
International Finance Corporation: *See* World Bank

International Higher Education (news-
letter), xi*n*.1
International Network for Higher Edu-
cation in Africa, xi*n*.1
Inter-University Council for Higher
Education in the Colonies: *See* In-
ter-University Council for Higher
Education Overseas
Inter-University Council for Higher
Education Overseas, 228, 245*n*.22,
255*n*.35
Inventions, 461–62, 474*n*.23
Iqbal, Muzaffar, 451, 456, 468*n*.1,
472*n*.15,473*n*.18, 476*n*.32
Iraq, looting and burning of museums
in, 91*n*.12
Isandhlwana, Battle of, 522–523*n*.23
ISI: *See* Import substitution industrialization
Islam: astronomy, 472*n*.17; and bubonic plague, 506, 530–31*n*.50;
and commerce, 462–64, 475–
76*nn*.29, 30; consensus-
disagreement, 467; and the Crusades, 464–65, 511–13; and Ethiopia, 57–59; and government, 55,
199–201*n*.104; emergence of, 60–
63; and the industrial transformation, 505–6; and knowledge, 65;
mathematics, 475*n*.29; and the
Mongols, 506; piety in, 96–
97*n*.28; and racism, 93–96*n*.27,
178*n*.1; rejection of the West, 116;
savants of the Middle Ages, 451–
53, 469*n*.4; science and technology, 455, 457–62, 465, 470*n*.4,
471*n*.11, 505–6; transformative
contributions of, 466; and the university, 448–68. *See also* Afro-
Arab Islamic Africa; Madrasahs
Islamic Africa: *See* Afro-Arab Islamic
Africa
Islamic education, 64–69; co-opted by
government, 171; in Ethiopia, 58–
60; finances of, 67, 79–80; foreign
sciences, 69. *See also* Islam; Madrasahs

Islamism, 199–201*n*.104; in Algeria,
148, 193*n*.72; in Egypt, 187*n*.53;
rise of, 172; roots of, 201*n*.106
Israel, 133, 134, 135, 172, 201*n*.105
Italy: colonization of Libya, 149–50;
colonization of Somalia, 362, 365–
66; occupation of Ethiopia, 266–
67. *See also* Somalia

Jabavu, Davidson Don Tengo, 295
Janus, Christopher G., 227, 243*n*.10,
244*n*.19
Japan: *See* Ethiopia/Japan anomaly
Jefferson, Thomas, 312*n*.22
Jerusalem, 172, 202–3*n*.105, 509, 511,
512, 532*n*.54, 533*nn*.60–61
Jesuits, in Ethiopia, 267–68
Jewish oral traditions and the Hamitic
hypothesis, 84–85
"Jim Crow," 14, 35–36*n*.24
John D. and Catherine T. MacArthur
Foundation, 412*n*.3
Johnson, Dale, 530*n*.46
Johnson, G. Ampah, 229, 233, 248,
298, 384, 392
Johnson, James, 210
Johnstone, D. Bruce, 409, 428*n*.43
Jomtien Declaration (1990), 400
Jones African Education Commission,
344
Jones, Eric L., 481–83
Jones, Phillip W., 386–87, 393
Jones, Thomas Jesse, 13–14, 33–
36*n*.22, 215, 313–314*n*.30. *See
also* Phelps-Stokes Education
Commission
Journal of Higher Education in Africa,
xi*n*.1
Juvaini, Ala-ad-Din Ata Malik,
531*n*.51

Kabila, Laurent-Desire, 358
Kabyles, 190*n*.66
Kallaway, Peter, 23–24
Kassa Wolde-Marriam, 269
Kaunda, Kenneth, 351
Kebede, Massay, 500

Kedar, Benjamin S., 533n.60
Kehoe, Monika, 271, 310n.13
Kelly, Gail P., 336
Kerr, Alexander, 295–96, 327n.70
Khayr al-Din (Tunisia), 168, 169
Khedive dynasty, 118, 124–25; and al-Azhar, 141
King, Kenneth, 13, 388–89, 415n.13, 416–18nn.14–15
Kipling, Rudyard, 29n.7, 241n.5
Kissinger, Henry, 446n.19
Kitchener, Horatio Herbert, 162–63
Klees, S., 406
Kublai Khan, 489, 524n.25. See also Mongols
Kumasi University of Science and Technology, 234

Land-grant model (U.S.), 231, 232, 237–38, 246nn.24–27, 443n.6
Language: arabization, 434–35; at Cairo University, 127; and the colonial legacy, 433–36; and the community, 435; at Haile Selassie I University, 269; interpreters, 123, 182n.27; in Liberia, 278, 313n.25; in Somalia, 367; in South Africa, 300
Lazarus-Yafeh, Hava, 188n.56, 201n.104
League of Nations: and Liberia, 281; and Namibia, 305
Lefkowitz, Mary, 47, 88n.6–8
Legum, Colin, 250n.31
Lesch, Ann Mosely, 160
Levine, Donald N., 275–276, 500
Lewis, Bernard, 93–96n.27, 116
Libera, Alain de, 454, 456
Liberia, 4, 276–82, 311–12n.21; A.M.E. University, 279; atrocities in, 281, 315–16n.35; internal colonialism of, 282; missionaries in, 278–79; "racial" conflict in, 278, 315n.33; resettlement, 277, 312n.22; See also American Society for the Colonization of Free People of Color

Liberia College: See University of Liberia
Libya, 4; higher education in, 150–52; independence of, 150–51; Italian invasion of, 149–50
Lindberg, David C., 456, 460
Literacy: and magic, 92n.19
Lockwood Committee, 234, 236–38, 255–56n.35
Lockwood, Sir John: See Lockwood Committee
Long-distance trade, 476n.30, 502
Loram, Charles T., 13, 35n.22, 292, 296, 313–314n.30
Lovanium University Center, 356–57
Lovedale Mission, 289–90, 295, 323–24n.54
Lumumba Friendship University, 381
Lumumba, Patrice, 374n.19
Lungu, Gatian F., 253–54n.33
Luxury goods, 528n.44

Mabokela, Reitumetse Obakeng, 300
Macaulay, Thomas Babington, 5, 31n.16, 241n.5
Machuel, Louis, 168
"Mad Mullah": See Hassan, Shaykh Muhammed ibn Abd'Allah
Madden, Richard R., 214
Madrasahs, 8–9, 12, 30n.10, 65–66, 108–9, 182–83n.28, 200n.100; in Algeria, 146–47; al-madrasah al-Nizamiyah, 97n.33; al-Qarawiyyin mosque, 70–72; al-Zaitouna mosque, 69–70; and the college, 449; decline of, 68–69, 191n.68, 439; educational trusts of, 118; in Ethiopia, 59–60; looting of resources of, 118; marginalization of, 170–71; in Morocco, 153–55; peer learning in 67–68; in Somalia, 365; in Sudan, 165; support of, 98n.39; and terrorism, 103–5n.64; of Timbuktu, 72–75; of Tunisia, 167–68; and Western education, 111; and worship, 68. See also al-Azhar

Magellan, Ferdinand, 463, 475*n*.27
Maghreb, the, history of, 113–14
Magubane, Bernard Makhosezwe, 322*n*.53
Mahdi: *See* Muhammad Ahmad ibn Abd Allah
Maimonides (Moses Ben Maimon), 72, 450
Majderek, Grzegory, 90*n*.11
Makdisi, George, 448–49, 466
Makerere University, 222, 234, 243–44*n*.16, 418*n*.17
Malan, Daniel, 287
Mamdani, Mahmood, 420*n*.24, 430, 438
Mamluks, 77–78, 180*n*.15; 181*n*.18; origins of, 100–102*n*.55
Mandela, Nelson, 288, 298, 302
Manetho, 90*n*.10
Manpower planning studies: *See* Human capital theory
Manye, Charlotte. *See* Maxeke, Charlotte Manye
Marable, Manning, 314*n*.30
Marchand, Jean-Baptiste, 162
Marginson, S., 428*n*.40
Mariam, Mengistu Haile: *See* Mengistu Haile Mariam
Martel, Charles: *See* Battle of Poitiers
Marx, Karl, 516–17*n*.6, 529*n*.45
Mastnak, Tomaz, 464–65, 511–13
Matsangaiza, Andre Matade, 352
Matthews, Z. K., 296, 327*n*.69
Matte, Lucien, 268
Maulana Karenga, 47
Maxeke, Charlotte Manye, 291–92, 324*n*.56, 325*n*.61
Maxwell, I. C. M., 269
McNamara, Robert, 386, 414–15*n*.10
Mecca, pilgrimage to, 63, 65, 68
Meiji restoration. *See* Japan/Ethiopia anomaly
Menelik II, 266–267, 311*n*.16
Mengistu Haile Mariam, 272–73
Menzies, Gavin, 474*n*.22, 475*n*.27, 520*nn*.10,13

Meritocracy, 204*n*.108. *See also* Equality of educational opportunity
Middle East, and Africa, 107–8
Military schools, 121–22
Military slavery, 100–102*n*.55
Military technology, 488–89
Milkias, Paulos, 56–57
Ming dynasty, 489, 495, 524*nn*.25,26
Missionaries, 16, 328*n*.71; in the Belgian colonies, 356; and the Crusades, 533*n*.60; educational enterprise in Egypt, 184–85*n*.36; in Ethiopia, 270; and Fourah Bay College, 209–11; and francophone colonies, 334–35; in Liberia, 278–79; and the Phelps-Stokes Commission, 214–16; in South Africa, 288–94, 328*n*.71
MNR: *See* Mozambique National Resistance
Mobutu, Joseph-Desire (Sese Seko), 357, 371*n*.11, 374–75*n*.19
Modernization, 26, 433; of Egypt, 117–18, 182*n*.24; Ethiopia/Japan anomaly, 275–76
Modes of production, 529–30*nn*.45–47. *See also* Articulated modes of production
Mogadishu University, 366–67, 436
Mokone, Mangena, 290–91, 324*n*.58
Monastic educational system, 54–56
Mondlane, Eduardo, 346
Mongols, 470*n*.4, 470*n*.6, 506, 522*n*.21, 524*n*.25, 531*nn*.50, 51
Monrovia College: *See* A.M.E. University
Moore, C. H., 136–37
Morocco: French protectorate, 152–53; higher education in, 153–57; independence of, 154; Spanish enclaves, 153, 198*n*.84
Morrill, Justin Smith, 237
Moton, Robert Russa, 313–314*n*.30
Movimento para a Libertacao de Angola (Movement for the Liberation of Angola), 347–49, 370–71*n*.10

Mozambique: conflict in, 349–56; drought in, 354; universities in, 356

Mozambique National Resistance, 351–55, 373n.15

MPLA: *See* Movimento para a Libertacao de Angola

Mubarak, Muhammed Hosni Said, 134

Mugabe, Robert, 273, 298, 351

Muhammed: *See* Prophet Muhammed

Muhammad Ahmad ibn Abd Allah (Mahdi), 162–163

Muhammed Ali: and al-Azhar, 139-40; attitude toward Egyptians, 181n.18–20; higher education policy of, 118–24; legacy of, 124; and madrasahs, 118, 124, 183n.28; modernization program of, 117–18, 267, 379

Muhammad ibn Muhammad ibn al-Hasan al-Tusi, 470n.4

Muhammed ibn Muhammed ibn Tarkhan ubn Uzalagh al-Farabi, 452

Muqaddimah (Khaldun), 18

Musa al-Khwarazmi, 451

Muslims: and Arabs, 63; and the Hamitic hypothesis, 84; and racism, 94–96n.27. *See also* Islam

Myth of Continents (Lewis and Wigen), 25

Nakosteen, Mehdi, 449, 451

Namibia, 305–7; apartheid in, 306; higher education in, 306–7; Presidential Commission on Higher Education, 306–07; South African occupation of, 305–6

Napoleon, 8, 115–17, 139, 180n.11, 188n.58, 479, 497, 513

Nasir al-Din al-Tusi: *See* Muhammad ibn Muhammad ibn al-Hasan al-Tusi

Nasser, Jamal Abdel, 131–34

National borders, 252n.32

Nationalism: Algerian, 146, 191–95nn.71, 72; and elites, 178–79nn.3, 5; Free Madrasah system,

147; and independence, 15, 16; in India, 226; and Islamism, 202n.104; and language, 433–34; and populism, 174; in the Portuguese colonies, 345–56; and student activism, 250n.31; Sudanese, 163; and symbols of sovereignty, 228, 340

National universities, 228–39; autonomy of, 233–34, 256–57n.35; British university model, 229, 237–38; and community service, 262–63n.35; curricula of, 229–32, 238, 258–60n.35; governance of, 256–57n.35; land-grant motel, 230–33, 237, 248n.27; structure of, 234–39

National University of Somalia, 366, 377n.28

National University of Zaire, 358

Native Americans, 487, 488, 493, 506–7, 527n.38

Native Land Act (of 1913), 286, 318n.45

Natural law of prior claim, 146, 507, 531–32n.53

Ncwana, E., 296

Needham, Joseph, 467, 472n.15

Neocolonialism, 11; French, 200n.102

Neolithic peoples, 44

Nigeria: education needs of, 230–33; Yaba college, 217–18, 227

9/11: *See* September, 11, 2001

Nkrumah, Kwame, 233–34

Noah, and the Biblical curse of Ham, 83

Noer, Thomas J., 292, 294

Northern Rhodesia: *See* Zambia

Nubia, 158–159

Nwauwa, Apollos O., 229

Oil, 151, 159, 396

Oldham, J. H., 13

O-levels: *See* General Certificate in Education

Omar ibn Khattab, 51

Omar Khayyam: *See* Ghiyath al-Din Abul Fateh Omar Ibn Ibrahim al-Nisaburi al-Khayyami
Omdurman Islamic University, 367
"Operation Restore Hope": *See* Somalia
Ottoman Empire, 62; Egypt a province of, 78–80; and Muhammed Ali, 117
Ottoman Mamluks: *See* Mamluks

Pacey, Arnold, 462
PAIGC: *See* Partido Africano da Independencia de Cabo Verde
Palestinian conflict: *See* Israel
Pan-Africanism, 216
Panter-Brick, Keith, 341
Parsons, Edward A., 43
Partido Africano da Independencia de Cabo Verde (African Party for the Independence of Guinea Bissau and Cape Verde), 346–47
Patronage, 233, 431
Payer, Cheryl, 411
Pedersen, Olaf, 454
Per ankh (House of Life), 43–47
Perham, Margery, 309*n*.9
Phelps-Stokes Education Commission, 33–36*n*.22, 214–16, 221, 344. *See also* Aggrey, James E. Kwegyir; Phelps-Stokes Fund; Jones, Thomas Jesse
Phelps-Stokes Fund, 13–14, 36*nn*.22–23, 279–80. *See also* Phelps-Stokes Education Commission
Philitas of Cos, 90*n*.10
Phrenology. *See* Racism, and social Darwinism
Piracy (in the seas), 492, 526–27*n*.37
Poitiers, Battle of, 61; 93*n*.25
Politics: and higher education, 3–4, 176; of knowledge, 205*n*.110; patronage, 233, 431. *See also* Equality of educational opportunity; Higher education; World Bank
Pomeranz, Kenneth, 490, 495, 498

Portuguese colonies, 332, 344–56; higher education in, 344, 356; and Portuguese military coup, 320*n*.52, 347; revolutionary struggle in, 345–56
Precious metals, 492–95
Precolonial higher education, 42–43
Premodern Africa, 41–105
Priorities and Strategies for Education: A World Bank Review (World Bank), 388
Primary and secondary education, 390, 392, 400, 416–17*n*.15
Privatization, 394, 398, 409, 446*n*.21
Professional classes, and wasted talent, 136–38
Prophet Muhammed, 61
Psacharopoulos, George, 403, 406
Ptolemy I Soter, 48–49

Qhaddafi, Muammar al, 151, 196*n*.79, *Green Book* of, 195–96*n*.80
Qur'an, 62, 64, 66, 67, 77, 79, 94, 156, 199*n*.104, 434

Racism, 12–14, 17, 81, 229, 253*n*.33, 336, 481; and the Columbus project, 507; Eurocentrism and, 516*n*.5; functions of, 32*n*.20; Hamitic hypothesis, 82–86; hierarchies of, 177*n*.1; "moderate," 517*n*.6; and Muslim Arabs, 94–96*n*.27; race-class nexus, 322–23*n*.53; social Darwinism, 33*n*.21; in South Africa, 282–89, 322–23*n*.53; in Zimbabwe, 236. *See also* Islam; Anthropology; Apartheid
Rates-of-return studies: *See* Human capital theory
Reagan, Ronald, 351, 355, 373*n*.17. *See also* Constructive engagement
Red Terror Campaign (Ethiopia), 273, 274
Reilly, Joseph Daniel, 13
Renaissance, 472*n*.14

RENAMO: *See* Mozambique National Resistance

Report of the Parliamentary Committee (of 1865), 211

Research, 223, 225, 226, 260*n*.35, 398; into local problems, 433

Review of African Political Economy (journal), 422*n*.31

Rhazes: *See* Abu Bakr Muhammed bin Zakariyya' al-Razi

Rhodes, Cecil, 240*n*.3, 241*n*.5, 284–85

Rhodesia: *See* Zimbabwe

Rieff, D., 443–44*n*.13

Roberts, Andrew, 242*n*.8

Roberts, Hugh, 194*n*.72, 201*n*.104

Roberts, J. M., 506

Roberts, Joseph Jenkins, 277

Rockefeller Foundation, 412*n*.3

Rodinson, Maxine, 17–18, 21

Roman Empire/Romans, 51, 53, 60, 84, 90*n*.10, 100*n*.55, 448, 464, 465, 468*n*.1, 472*n*.16, 484, 508, 527

Roosevelt, Theodore, 183–84*n*.33, 295

Rosetta Stone, 180

Rostow, W. W., 400–401

Ruegg, Walter, 448, 457

Rules of engagement, 93–94*n*.26

Runciman, Steven, 508–9

Russian Revolution, 320*n*.52

Russian University of People's Friendship: *See* Lumumba Friendship University

Rwanda, genocide in, 358–59

Saad, Elias N., 73–75

Sabra, A. I., 505–6

Sadat, Muhammed Anwar, 134

SADCC: *See* Southern African Development Coordination Conference

Sadiki College, 169–170, 199*n*.101

Said, Edward, 5

Saladin (Salah Ad-din Yusuf ibn Ayyub), 72, 76

Salazar, Antonio, 347, 373*n*.15

Sallers, Raphael, 29*n*.7

Samatar, Abdi Ismail, 377*nn*.27, 29

Samatar, Ahmed I., 377*n*.27

Samoff, Joel, 393

Sanders, Edith, 82

Sanderson, Stephen K., 453

Sanussiya, 150, 151, 194*n*.75

Sastri College, 296

Savimbi, Jonas, 349

Schism of 1054, 508–509. *See also* Christianity

Scholastic method, 67

Schultz, Theodore, 401–3, 425*n*.37

Science and technology, 148, 165, 174, 218; applied, 246–48*n*.27; de-emphasis of, 397–98, 432–33; development of, 467; and European modernity, 457; Greco-Arabic, 455, 458–62, 465; human capital, 133; and the industrial transformation (industrial revolution), 505–6, 515*n*.2; infrastructure, 391–92, 418*n*.18, 437; inventions, 461–62; and language, 434; law of continuity, 473*n*.19; military, 488–89, 523*n*.24; technological diffusion, 461

Scientific revolution, 460–61. *See also* Science and technology

Scramble for Africa, 20–22, 207–8, 239–40*nn*.3–4. *See also* Berlin West Africa Conference

September 11, 2001 (United States), 193–94*n*.72

Shaykh Rifa'ah, 182*n*.22

Shermarke, Abdirashid Ali, 363

Shuttleworth Report (of 1847), 243*n*.13

Siad Barre, Muhammed, 363–64, 436

Sibley, James, 279

Sidi Muhammed ibn Ali-as-Sannusi: *See* Sanussiya

Sierra Leone, 210, 213

Silver: and European commerce, 488, 491, 492, 493, 494, 496

Simon, Paul, 391

Slavery: and Christianity, 513; and Columbus, 507–8; and Ethiopia, 502–3; and the Hamitic hypothe-

sis, 83–86; military, 100–102n.55; of the mind, 210–11; and Muslims, 94–95n.27; and precious metals, 493; in South Africa, 284; in Sudan, 159, 161; and sugar, 492. *See also* Atlantic slave trade
Smith, Adam, 485, 493, 499, 507, 526n.33
Smith, Ian, 236, 351–52, 369n.8
Smuts, Jan Christiaan, 287
Social Darwinism, 12–13
Socialism: African, 131, 132, 186n.44, 272–73, 310n.13; 363; and state capitalism, 201–02n.107
Social Transformations: A General Theory of Historical Development (Sanderson), 453
Society of Friends (Quakers), 312n.22
Solomon Mahlangu Freedom College, 323–24n.54
Solomonid dynasty, 54, 59, 266
Somalia, 359–68; attack on Ethiopia, 363–64; civil war in, 364–65; clan divisions of, 361–62; colonization of, 362; as failed state, 360, 375–76n.23, 376n.25; higher education in, 365–67; history of, 359–62; independence of, 362–63, 366; languages of, 436; Mogadishu University, 366–67; National University of Somalia, 366, 377n.28; Operation Restore Hope, 364–65; socialism in, 363
Somaliland: universities in, 367
South Africa, 4–5, 282–305; affirmative action in, 303; and Angola, 344–45, 348, 349, 372n.11; Bantu Education Act (of 1953), 288; Bantu Universities Amendment Act, 320n.51; Boer War, 284–5; destruction of African peasantry, 318n.44; Education Act No. 25 (of 1907), 287; equal-but-separate doctrine, 297, 299; Euro-South African institutions, 300–301; Extension of University Education Act (1959, 1971), 288, 319–20n.50,

320n.51; higher education for blacks, 289–300; history of, 283–88; the Khoikhoi, 283, 317n.41; languages of instruction in, 300; Lovedale Mission, 289–90, 323–24n.54; missionaries in, 288–94; and Mozambique, 350–56; postapartheid, 302–5; racial categories, 316–17n.38; racism in, 282–89; racist laws of, 285–86, 318n.45; role of African Americans, 290–95; unification of, 284–85; Universities Amendment Act (of 1983), 288, 300; vocational colleges of, 304; colonial wars of conquest, 317n.42; Wilberforce Institute, 292. *See also* Apartheid; College of Fort Hare; Ethiopian churches; University of South Africa
South African Native Affairs Commission, 293–94, 295
South African Native College: *See* College of Fort Hare
South West Africa People's Organization, 305
Southern African Development Coordination Conference, 350–51, 355
Soviet Union, 15, 320n.52, 356, 413n.4; and Egypt, 133; and Ethiopia, 363–64; and Guinea, 342–43; Lumumba Friendship University, 381. *See also* Cold War; Russia
Spain, North African enclaves of, 153, 197n.84
Spinola, Antonio de, 347
Sraffa, Pierro, 528n.44
Stages of Economic Growth: A Non-Communist Manifesto (Rostow), 401
State-capitalism, 172, 203–4n.107, 423–24n.32
Stevens, Philips, Jr., 92n.19
Stewart, James, 290
Stiglitz, Joseph E., 423–24n.33
Stockwell, John, 348–49

Southern Rhodesia: *See* Zimbabwe
Strabo, 90*n*.10
Streeten, Paul, 425–26*n*.39
Structure versus agency, concepts of,
    437, 441*n*.2, 443*n*.13
Structural adjustment, 203*n*.107,
    250*n*.31, 394, 398–99, 409,
    424*nn*.32, 35. *See also* World
    Bank
Students: at al-Azhar, 140–41; in Al-
    geria, 147; at al-Qarawiyyin Uni-
    versity, 156; at Cairo University,
    128; female, 127; life of,
    103*nn*.60, 61; recruitment of, 122–
    24, 230, 232; self-worth of, 229; at
    University of Zambia, 257*n*.35.
    See also Student political activism;
    Study abroad
Student political activism, 19, 176; ex-
    plaining, 249–52*n*.31; in Algeria,
    249*n*.31, in Egypt, 135, 249*n*.31;
    endemic, 233; in Ethiopia, 272,
    309*n*.12; 310*nn*.13–14; in French
    Universities, 339, 343; in precolo-
    nial institutions, 249*n*.31; in Sene-
    gal, 340, 343; in South Africa,
    249*n*.31, 320*n*.52; and structural
    adjustment, 250*n*.31; in Tunisia,
    167–68, 198*n*.97; in Zambia, 263–
    64*n*.35
Studium generale, 449, 454, 455, 457,
    458
Study abroad, 68, 173, 213, 216,
    242*n*.8, 243*n*.10, 384; Egyptians,
    119–21, 125; Ethiopians, 267,
    307*n*.2; French colonies, 339; Li-
    berians, 278; South Africans, 294,
    295. *See also* Soviet Union
Sudan, 157–66; British colonial rule
    in, 161–65; civil war in, 150–61,
    166; geography of, 157; Gordon
    Memorial College, 163–64; higher
    education in, 161–66; history of,
    157–59; ma'had al-ilmi, 165; Uni-
    versity of Khartoum, 165–66
Suez Canal, 87*n*.1, 181*n*.21; nationali-
    zation of, 133

Sugar, 488, 491–92, 495–96, 525–
    26*nn*.30–33
Sumeria, 43, 88*n*.4–5
Sundiata, Ibrahim, 281, 313*n*.22,
    313*n*.33, 316*nn*.35–36
SWAPO: *See* South West Africa Peo-
    ple's Organization
Sweden, and Ethiopia, 270
Swedish Evangelical Mission: *See*
Sweden, and Ethiopia

Taylor, Charles, 281–82, 316*n*.36
Technikons: *See* South Africa, voca-
    tional colleges
Teferra, Damtew: *See* Damtew Teferra
Terms of trade, 399, 407, 422*nn*.29, 30
Terreblanche, Sampie, 283, 304–5
Terrorism, 103–5*n*.64. *See also* Sep-
    tember 11, 2001
Teshome G. Wagaw, 269–72, 308*n*.8
Tewodros II, 266, 311*n*.16
Thaele, James S., 35*n*.22
Theophratus, 90*n*.10
Thomas, Nicholas, 10
Thompson, Leonard, 286
Timbuktu, madrasahs of, 72–75
Tomlinson Commission (1950–1954),
    319*n*.49
Tours, Battle of: *See* Poitiers, Battle of
Transcontinental trade, 496
Transnational monopolies, 137, 399
Trevor-Roper, Hugh, 2
Triangular trade, 492, 526*n*.34,
    528*n*.41
Trusteeship, 215, 216
Tuition, 212, 218, 219; free, 122, 131,
    132, 172, 175, 269, 307, 308*n*.7
Tunisia: al-Zaitouna, 69–70, 167–68,
    170; Bardo Military Academy,
    168; French protectorate, 166–69;
    independence of, 169–70; Sadiki
    College, 169
Turkey, 188*n*.54
Turner, Henry McNeal, 291, 293, 295,
    312*n*.22, 327*n*.65
Turner, John, 458

Tuskegee Institute: *See* Washington, Booker T.

Ulama (scholarly class), 64, 110; of al-Azhar, 78–79, 140; on government payroll, 179*n*.6; role in education, 68; security of, 188*n*.56; and the state, 199–201*n*.104

Unemployment and underemployment, 136, 173

UNESCO: *See* United Nations Educational, Scientific, and Cultural Organization

Uniao Nacional para a Independencia Total de Angola (National Union for the Total Independence of Angola), 348–49, 355, 370–71*n*.10

UNISA: *See* University of South Africa

UNITA: *See* Uniao Nacional para a Independencia Total de Angola

United East India Company, 283

United Free Church of Scotland Mission, 290. *See also* Lovedale Mission

United Nations: famine relief in Somalia, 364–65; and Somali independence, 365

United Nations Educational, Scientific, and Cultural Organization, 204*n*.110, 255*n*.35, 382–83, 385, 400

United Nations Institute for Namibia, 306

United Presbyterian mission, 129, 184*n*.36

United States: African higher education, 391–92; American Colonization Society, 277; civil rights movement in, 23; and colonial possessions, 14–15, 241*n*.4; and Egyptian education, 134–35; and Ethiopia, 269–70; and Libyan independence, 150–51; and Namibia, 306; and the Portuguese colonies, 345, 347–49, 351–52, 355, 371–72*n*.11; and the Scram-ble for Africa, 240–41*n*.4; and Somalia, 363–64; and the University of Nigeria, 231; world view of, 187*n*.49. *See also* Land-grant model; Cold War

United States Agency for International Development, 384, 392–93

"United States of Africa": *See* Africa

Universities, 20; access to, 132–33, 170, 174, 187*n*.48; in Angola, 356; civilizational context of, 457; closure of, 432; and cross-border consortia, 252–53*n*.32, 414*n*.7, 431; and curriculum, 246–47*n*.27; demand for West African, 210–12, 224–28, 239; and democracy, 203–06*n*.110; and elites, 436; federated, 234–35, 238–39; and foreign assistance, 411*n*.1; functions of, 176–77, 203–06*n*.110; the future of, 439–40; and Greco–Islamic science, 455; and the *hajj*, 68; high unit costs, 431–32, 442*n*.3; and individuals, 456; Islam and, 448–68; legal definition of, 449; and nonliterate societies, 183*n*.31, 226; provenance of, 447–77; and research, 223, 225, 226, 433; standardization of curricula, 456–57; as symbols of sovereignty, 228, 340; World Bank's view of, 385–86. *See also* Academic freedom, Academic standards; Finances; Globalization; Higher education; National universities; Privatization; and various universities under their individual names.

University of Algiers, 146

University of Asmara, 308*n*.6

University of Augustinho Neto, 356

University of Botswana, Lesotho, and Swaziland, 239

University of Cairo, 126–28, 131–32, 133

University College of Addis Ababa: *See* Addis Ababa University

University College of Fort Hare Transfer Act (1959), 288
University College of Ghana, 233
University College of Rhodesia and Nyasaland, 253–54n.33. *See also* University of Zimbabwe
University of Dakar, 340
University of Dar Es Salaam, 234–35
University of East Africa, 234–35, 252–53n.32
University of Ezzitouna: *See* al-Zaitouna
University of Khartoum, 165–66
University-level education, 216, 221–22
University of Liberia, 277–78, 280–81, 316n.37
University of Libya, 151
University of London, 219, 220, 222, 228, 229, 230, 234, 235, 244n.16, 255n.35, 268. *See also* Asquith colleges.
University of Nairobi, 234–35
University of Nigeria, 231–32, 248n.28
University of South Africa, 289, 296, 298–299, 328n.73
University of Tunis, 170
University of Zambia, 237, 253–54n.33, 255–64n.35
University of Zimbabwe, 236–37
USAID: *See* United States Agency for International Development
"User fees": *See* Finance, and universities

Vaizey, J., 424n.37
Van Riebeeck, Jan Anthoniszoon, 283
Verger, Jacques, 447–48
Verwoerd, Henrik, 288
Vietnam War: *See* Dien Bien Phu
Vischer, Hanns, 214
Vocational education, 13, 215–16, 221, 238, 246n.26, 292, 304; and the economy, 404; and the multiversity model, 231
Von Grunebaum, G. E., 466, 476n.35

Vorster, John, 351
Voyages of exploitation (exploration), 474–75n.27

Wagaw, Teshome G.: *See* Teshome G. Wagaw
Washington, Booker T., 33–34n.22, 243n.13, 292, 294, 295, 313–314n.30, 325–26n.62
Washington Consensus, 399, 424n.33
The Wealth of Nations (Smith), 485
Weber, Max, 516n.4
West Africa: development of, 210; self-government of, 211; Timbuktu, 72–75; tropical diseases of, 213; university colleges, 210–12, 224–28
Westerners, 516n.3
Western ethnocentrism, 467–68, 480–81, 517–19n.8
Western higher education, 110–12; ambivalence toward, 179n.7
Westernization of Christianity: *See* Schism of 1054
"White man's burden," 8–9, 11, 25, 29n.7, 267
Wilberforce Institute, 292
Wilberforce University, 290, 294
Wilkinson, Richard, 87–88n.3
Williams, Eric, 22
Williamson, John, 423–24n.33
Wilson, Monica, 286
Wolde-Marriam, Kassa: *See* Kassa Wolde-Marriam
Wolfowitz, Paul D., 445n.17
Women: acquisition of knowledge by, 98n.38; opportunities for, 391; professors, 184n.34; students, 127
Woods, George, 386
World Bank, 203–06n.110, 382, 385–411; basic needs approach of, 387–95, 414–15n.10; disbandment of, 411; and the economic place of Africa, 395–98; and human capital theory, 399–409; inappropriate advice from, 408; intellectual influence of, 419n.21; reinvention of,

410; and the state, 398–99; scape-
  goating by, 424n.35; view of universities, 385–86, 394, 420n.24
World Conference on Higher Educa-
  tion (1998), 383. *See also* United
  Nations Educational, Scientific,
  and Cultural Organization
"World Declaration on Higher Educa-
  tion for the Twenty First Century:
  Vision and Action," 204n.110
World Heritage sites: al-Qarawiyyin,
  71, 72; Timbuktu, 75–76
World Trade Organization, 174, 203–
  06n.110. *See also* Globalization
World University Service, 236
World War II, 14, 216, 223, 338, 430;
  consequences of, 441–42n.2
Writing, 43; in Ethiopia, 53–54
WTO: *See* World Trade Organization

Yesufu, T. M., x, 315, 384, 432, 437

Zaghlul, Ahmad, 126
Zaghlul Pasha ibn Ibrahim, Sa'ad, 126,
  189n.62
Zagwe dynasty, 54, 266
Zaire: *See* Democratic Republic of
  Congo
Zambia, 236, 253–64nn.33, 35, 399
ZANU: *See* Zimbabwe African Na-
  tional Union
Zaytuna(h): *See* al-Zaitouna
Zenodotus of Ephesus, 90n.10
Zheng He: *See* Cheng Ho
Zimbabwe, 236–37
Zimbabwe African National Union,
  352
Zimbabwe Ruins, 82, 105n.65
Zulus, victory of: *See* Isandhlwana,
  Battle of, 522–523n.23

About the Author

Y. G-M. LULAT is Assistant Professor of African American Studies at the State University of New York, Buffalo. He is the coauthor of *Research on Foreign Students and International Study: An Overview and Bibliography* (Praeger, 1985).